Instructor's Solutions Manual

to accompany

Intermediate Algebra

Third Edition

Mark Dugopolski
Southeastern Louisiana University

Boston   Burr Ridge, IL   Dubuque, IA   Madison, WI   New York   San Francisco   St. Louis
Bangkok   Bogotá   Caracas   Lisbon   London   Madrid
Mexico City   Milan   New Delhi   Seoul   Singapore   Sydney   Taipei   Toronto

McGraw-Hill Higher Education

A Division of The McGraw-Hill Companies

Instructor's Solutions Manual to accompany
INTERMEDIATE ALGEBRA, THIRD EDITION

This book is printed on acid-free paper.

2 3 4 5 6 7 8 9 0 QSR QSR 9 0 3 2 1 0

ISBN 0-07-229478-7

www.mhhe.com

Instructor's Solutions Manual
Intermediate Algebra

Third Edition

Table of Contents

1.1 WARM-UPS

1. False, since 5 is a counting number and $5 \notin A$.

2. False, since B has only 3 elements.

3. False, because the set has a specific number of members.

4. False, since $1 \notin B$.

5. True, since $3 \in A$.

6. True, because 3 and 4 are the only numbers that belong to both A and B.

7. True, because every member of C is also a member of B.

8. False, since $1 \in A$ but $1 \notin B$.

9. True, since $\emptyset$ is a subset of every set.

10. True, since $1 \in A$ and $1 \notin C$.

1.1 EXERCISES

1. A set is a collection of objects.

2. A finite set has a fixed number of elements and an infinite set does not.

3. A Venn diagram is used to illustrate relationships between sets.

4. The intersection of two sets consists of elements that are in both sets, while the union of two sets consists of elements that are in one, the other, or both sets.

5. A is a subset of B if every member of set A is also a member of set B.

6. The empty set is a subset of every set.

7. False, 6 is not odd.

8. False, because 8 is not odd.

9. True, because $1 \in A$ but $1 \notin B$.

10. False, A is a finite set.

11. True.

12. False, because 4 is a member of B.

13. False, because $5 \in A$.

14. True, since $6 \in B$ but $6 \notin C$.

15. False, because 0 is not a natural number.

16. False, because 2.5 is not a natural number.

17. False, because N is infinite and C is finite.

18. False, because N is infinite and A is finite.

19. $A = \{1, 3, 5, 7, 9\}$ and $B = \{2, 4, 6, 8\}$ so $A \cap B = \emptyset$.

20. $A = \{1, 3, 5, 7, 9\}$ and $B = \{2, 4, 6, 8\}$ so $A \cup B = \{1, 2, 3, 4, 5, 6, 7, 8, 9\}$.

21. $A = \{1, 3, 5, 7, 9\}$ and $C = \{1, 2, 3, 4, 5\}$ so $A \cap C = \{1, 3, 5\}$.

22. $A = \{1, 3, 5, 7, 9\}$ and $C = \{1, 2, 3, 4, 5\}$ so $A \cup C = \{1, 2, 3, 4, 5, 7, 9\}$.

23. The elements of B together with those of C give us $B \cup C = \{1, 2, 3, 4, 5, 6, 8\}$.

24. The only elements that belong to both B and C are 2 and 4. So $B \cap C = \{2, 4\}$.

25. Since the empty set has no members, $A \cup \emptyset = A$.

26. Since the empty set has no members, $B \cup \emptyset = B$.

27. Since $\emptyset$ has no members in common with A, $A \cap \emptyset = \emptyset$.

28. Since the empty set has no members in common with B, $B \cap \emptyset = \emptyset$.

29. Since every member of A is also a member of N, $A \cap N = A = \{1, 3, 5, 7, 9\}$.

30. Since every member of A is a member of N, $A \cup N = N = \{1, 2, 3, \ldots\}$.

31. Since the members of A are odd and the members of B are even, they have no members in common. So $A \cap B = \emptyset$.

32. Since 1 is a member of both A and C, $A \cap C \neq \emptyset$.

33. $A \cup B = \{1, 2, 3, 4, 5, 6, 7, 8, 9\}$ from problem 20.

34. Since A and B have no members in common, $A \cap B = \emptyset$.

35. Take the elements that B has in common with C to get $B \cap C = \{2, 4\}$.

36. Since the numbers 1, 2, 3, 4, 5, 6, and 8 are either members of B or C, we have $B \cup C = \{1, 2, 3, 4, 5, 6, 8\}$.

37. $3 \notin A \cap B$ since $3 \notin B$.

38. Since 3 is a member of A and 3 is a member of C, we have $3 \in A \cap C$.

39. Since 4 is in both sets, $4 \in B \cap C$.

40. Since 8 is a member of B, we have $8 \in B \cup C$.

41. True, since each member of A is a counting number.

42. True, since 2, 4, 6, and 8 are counting numbers.

43. True, since both 2 and 3 are members of C.

44. False, since 2 is a member of C, but 2 is not a member of A.

45. True, since $6 \in B$ but $6 \notin C$.

46. True, since 2 is a member of C, but 2 is not a member of A.

47. True, since $\emptyset$ is a subset of every set.

48. True, since the empty set is a subset of every set.

49. False, since $1 \in A$ but $1 \notin \emptyset$.

50. False, since $2 \in B$ but $2 \notin \emptyset$.

51. True, since $A \cap B = \emptyset$ and $\emptyset$ is a subset of any set.

52. True, since $B \cap C = \{2, 4\}$.

53. Using all numbers that belong to D or to E yields $D \cup E = \{2, 3, 4, 5, 6, 7, 8\}$.

54. D and E have no members in common. So $D \cap E = \emptyset$.

55. Using only numbers that belong to both D and F gives $D \cap F = \{3, 5\}$.

56. $D \cup F$ consists of numbers that are either in D or in F. So $D \cup F = \{1, 2, 3, 4, 5, 7\}$.

57. Using all numbers that belong to E or to F gives $E \cup F = \{1, 2, 3, 4, 5, 6, 8\}$.

58. The only numbers that belong to both E and F are 2 and 4. So $E \cap F = \{2, 4\}$.

59. Intersect $D \cup E$ from Exercise 53 with F to get $(D \cup E) \cap F = \{2, 3, 4, 5\}$.

60. $D \cup F = \{1, 2, 3, 4, 5, 7\}$ and $E = \{2, 4, 6, 8\}$. The only elements that these sets have in common are 2 and 4. So $(D \cup F) \cap E = \{2, 4\}$.

61. Take $E \cap F = \{2, 4\}$ together with D to get $D \cup (E \cap F) = \{2, 3, 4, 5, 7\}$.

62. $D = \{3, 5, 7\}$ and $F \cap E = \{2, 4\}$. Put all of the elements together in one set to form the union. $D \cup (F \cap E) = \{2, 3, 4, 5, 7\}$

63. Take the union of $D \cap F = \{3, 5\}$ with $E \cap F = \{2, 4\}$ to get $\{2, 3, 4, 5\}$.

64. $D \cap E = \emptyset$ and $F \cap E = \{2, 4\}$. So $(D \cap E) \cup (F \cap E) = \{2, 4\}$.

65. Intersect $D \cup E = \{2, 3, 4, 5, 6, 7, 8\}$ with $D \cup F = \{1, 2, 3, 4, 5, 7\}$ to get $\{2, 3, 4, 5, 7\}$.

66. $D \cup F = \{1, 2, 3, 4, 5, 7\}$ and $D \cup E = \{2, 3, 4, 5, 6, 7, 8\}$. So $(D \cup F) \cap (D \cup E) = \{2, 3, 4, 5, 7\}$.

67. Use $\subseteq$, since every element of D is an odd natural number.

68. The even natural numbers smaller than 9 are 2, 4, 6, and 8. So $E = \{x \mid x$ is an even natural number smaller than 9$\}$.

69. Use $\in$, since 3 is a member of D.

70. Since 3 is a member of D, $\{3\} \subseteq D$.

71. Use $\cap$, since D and E have no elements in common.

72. Any member of both D and E is a member of D. So $D \cap E \subseteq D$.

73. Use $\subseteq$, since every member of $D \cap F$ is a member of F.

74. Since 3 is a member of E but not a member of F, $3 \notin E \cap F$.

75. Use $\cap$, since $8 \in E$ but not in $E \cap F$.

76. Since every member of E is a member of $E \cup F$, $E \subseteq E \cup F$.

77. Use $\cup$, since $D \cup F$ and $F \cup F$ have exactly the same members.

78. Since the members of E and F are the same as the members of F and E, we have $E \cap F = F \cap E$.

79. The set of even natural number less than 20 is $\{2, 4, 6, \ldots, 18\}$.

80. The set of natural numbers greater than 6 is $\{7, 8, 9, \ldots\}$.

81. The set of odd natural numbers greater than 11 is $\{13, 15, 17, \ldots\}$.

82. The set of odd natural numbers less than 14 is $\{1, 3, 5, \ldots, 13\}$.

83. The set of even natural numbers between 4 and 79 is $\{6, 8, 10, \ldots, 78\}$.

84. The set of odd natural numbers between 12 and 57 is $\{13, 15, 17, \ldots, 55\}$.

85. $\{x \mid x$ is a natural number between 2 and 7$\}$

86. $\{x \mid x$ is an odd natural number less than 8$\}$

87. $\{x \mid x$ is an odd natural number greater than 4$\}$

88. $\{x \mid x$ is a natural number greater than 3$\}$

89. $\{x \mid x$ is an even natural number between 5 and 83$\}$

90. $\{x \mid x$ is an odd natural number between 8 and 52$\}$

91. If A has n elements and B has m elements, then the union of the two sets cannot have more members than $n + m$. So the union is also finite.

92. If all elements of A are in B, and all elements of B are in A, then $A = B$. If the union is contained in the intersection, then $A = B$.

93. a) $3 \in \{1, 2, 3\}$ b) $\{3\} \subseteq \{1, 2, 3\}$
c) $\emptyset \neq \{\emptyset\}$

94. a) $\emptyset, \{1\}, \{2\}, \{1, 2\}$
b) $\emptyset, \{1\}, \{2\}, \{3\}, \{1, 2\}, \{1, 3\}, \{2, 3\}, \{1, 2, 3\}$
c) There are 16 subsets of $\{1, 2, 3, 4\}$.
d) Every time we add an element we double the number of subsets. So the number of subsets for a set of n elements is 2^n.

1.2 WARM-UPS

1. False, π is irrational.

2. True, the reals are made up of the rationals and the irrationals.

3. False, 0 is not irrational, it is rational.

4. False, the set of irrational numbers is a subset of the set of real numbers.

5. True, since it is a repeating decimal.

6. False, it is not repeating.

7. True, because the points on the number line correspond to the real numbers.

8. True, there is no intersection between the rationals and the irrationals.

9. False, it is a finite set.

10. True, the counting numbers are infinite and they are in the set of rational numbers.

1.2 EXERCISES

1. The integers consist of the positive and negative counting numbers and zero.

2. The rational numbers consist of all numbers that can be expressed as a ratio of integers.

3. The repeating or terminating decimal numbers are rational numbers.

4. Decimals that neither repeat nor terminate are irrational numbers.

5. The set of real numbers is the union of the rational and irrational numbers.

6. The ratio of the circumference and diameter of any circle is π.

7. True, since -6 is rational.

8. True, since 2/7 is a rational number.

9. False, since 0 is rational.

10. True, since the smallest natural number is 1.

11. True, since a repeating decimal is rational.

12. False, since 0.00976 is a terminating decimal number and every terminating decimal number is a rational number.

13. True, since every natural number is rational.

14. False, since 1/2 is a rational number but it is not an integer.

15. $\{0, 1, 2, 3, 4, 5\}$

16. The natural numbers less than 7 are 1, 2, 3, 4, 5, and 6. $\{1, 2, 3, 4, 5, 6\}$

17. $\{-4, -3, -2, -1, 0, 1, \ldots\}$

18. List the integers between 2 and 12 in set notation. $\{3, 4, 5, 6, 7, 8, 9, 10, 11\}$

19. $\{1, 2, 3, 4\}$

20. $\{1, 2, 3, 4, 5, \ldots\}$

0 1 2 3 4...

21. $\{-2, -1, 0, 1, 2, 3, 4\}$

−3 −2 −1 0 1 2 3 4 5

22. $\{-3, -2, -1, 0, 1, 2, 3, 4, 5, 6\}$

−4 −3 −2 −1 0 1 2 3 4 5 6 7

23. All of the numbers are real numbers.
24. Since $8/2 = 4$, $8/2$ is the only natural number in the set. $\{8/2\}$
25. The whole numbers include 0. $\{0, 8/2\}$
26. The integers in the set are $-3, 0$, and $8/2$. $\{-3, 0, 8/2\}$
27. $\{-3, -5/2, -0.025, 0, 3\frac{1}{2}, 8/2\}$
28. The irrational numbers in the set are $-\sqrt{10}$ and $\sqrt{2}$. $\{-\sqrt{10}, \sqrt{2}\}$
29. True, since every rational number is also a real number.
30. False, since the set of irrational numbers and the set of rational numbers have no numbers in common.
31. False, since 0 is not irrational.
32. True, since every integer is a rational number. Every integer can be expressed as a ratio of two integers.
33. True, because the rational numbers together with the irrational numbers make up the set of real numbers.
34. False, since the set of integers is a subset of the set of rational numbers.
35. False, since nonrepeating decimals are irrational.
36. True, since repeating decimals are rational numbers.
37. False, since repeating decimals are rational.
38. True, since nonrepeating decimals are irrational.
39. False, since repeating decimals are rational.

40. True, since repeating decimals are rational.
41. True, since π is irrational.
42. False, because π is irrational.
43. $N \subseteq W$, since every natural number is a whole number.
44. Since every integer is a rational number, $J \subseteq Q$.
45. $J \nsubseteq N$, since $-9 \in J$ but $-9 \notin N$.
46. Since rational numbers such as $1/2$ are not whole numbers, $Q \nsubseteq W$.
47. $Q \subseteq R$, since every rational number is a real number.
48. Since every irrational number is a real number, $I \subseteq R$.
49. $\emptyset \subseteq I$, since $\emptyset$ is a subset of every set.
50. Since $\emptyset$ is a subset of every set, $\emptyset \subseteq Q$.
51. $N \subseteq R$, since every natural number is a real number.
52. Since every whole number is a real number, $W \subseteq R$.
53. $5 \in J$, since 5 is an integer.
54. Since -6 is an integer, $-6 \in J$.
55. $7 \in Q$, since 7 is a rational number.
56. Since 8 is a rational number, $8 \in Q$.
57. $\sqrt{2} \in R$, since $\sqrt{2}$ is a real number.
58. Since $\sqrt{2}$ is an irrational number, $\sqrt{2} \in I$.
59. $0 \notin I$, since 0 is rational.
60. Since 0 is a rational number, $0 \in Q$.
61. $\{2, 3\} \subseteq Q$, since both 2 and 3 are rational.
62. Since 0 is not a natural number, $\{0, 1\} \nsubseteq N$.
63. $\{3, \sqrt{2}\} \subseteq R$, since both numbers are real.
64. Since $\sqrt{2}$ is not rational, $\{3, \sqrt{2}\} \nsubseteq Q$.
65. A rational number is a repeating or terminating decimal and an irrational number never repeats or terminates as a decimal number. Since $\sqrt{9} = 3$ it is rational. Since $\sqrt{3}$ is a nonterminating nonrepeating decimal number, it is irrational.
66. The only rational numbers of the form $\sqrt{n}$ for n from 1 through 100 are $\sqrt{1}, \sqrt{4},$

$\sqrt{9}, \sqrt{16}, \sqrt{25}, \sqrt{36}, \sqrt{49}, \sqrt{64}, \sqrt{81}$, and $\sqrt{100}$.

67. a) Find the decimal representations with a calculator. Note that each decimal is repeating.
b) The number of digits that repeats is the same as the number of nines in the denominator.

1.3 WARM-UPS

1. True, since $-6 + 6 = 0$.
2. True, -5 and 5 are opposites of each other.
3. False, $|6| = 6$.
4. True, since $b - a = b + (-a)$.
5. True, because the product of two numbers with opposite signs is negative.
6. False, since $6 + (-4) = 2$.
7. False, since $-3 - (-6) = -3 + 6 = 3$.
8. False, since $6 \div (-1/2) = 6(-2) = -12$.
9. False, since division by zero is undefined.
10. True, because 0 divided by any nonzero number is 0.

1.3 EXERCISES

1. The absolute value of a number is the number's distance from 0 on the number line.
2. Add their absolute values, then affix the sign of the original numbers.
3. Subtract their absolute values and use the sign of the number with the larger absolute value.
4. The difference $a - b$ is defined as $a + (-b)$.
5. Multiply their absolute values, then affix a positive sign if the original numbers have the same sign and a negative sign if the original numbers have opposite signs.
6. The quotient $a \div b$ is defined as $a \cdot \frac{1}{b}$.
7. $|-34| = -(-34) = 34$
8. $|17| = 17$, because 17 is positive.
9. $|0| = 0$
10. $|-15| = -(-15) = 15$
11. $|-6| - |-6| = 6 - 6 = 0$
12. $|8| - |-8| = 8 - 8 = 0$
13. $-|-9| = -9$
14. $-|-3| = -[-(-3)] = -[3] = -3$
15. $-(-9) = 9$

16. $-(-(8)) = -(-8) = 8$
17. $-(-(-3)) = -(3) = -3$
18. $-(-(-2)) = -(2) = -2$
19. $(-5) + 9 = 9 - 5 = 4$
20. $(-3) + 10 = 10 - 3 = 7$
21. $(-4) + (-3) = -(4 + 3) = -7$
22. $(-15) + (-11) = -(15 + 11) = -26$
23. $-6 + 4 = -(6 - 4) = -2$
24. $5 + (-15) = -(15 - 5) = -10$
25. $7 + (-17) = -(17 - 7) = -10$
26. $-8 + 13 = 13 - 8 = 5$
27. $(-11) + (-15) = -(11 + 15) = -26$
28. $-18 + 18 = 0$
29. $18 + (-20) = -(20 - 18) = -2$
30. $7 + (-19) = -(19 - 7) = -12$
31. $-14 + 9 = -(14 - 9) = -5$
32. $-6 + (-7) = -(6 + 7) = -13$
33. $-4 + 4 = 0$
34. $-7 + 9 = 9 - 7 = 2$
35. $-\frac{1}{10} + \frac{1}{5} = \frac{1}{5} - \frac{1}{10} = \frac{2}{10} - \frac{1}{10} = \frac{1}{10}$

36. $-\frac{1}{8} + \left(-\frac{1}{8}\right) = -\left(\frac{1}{8} + \frac{1}{8}\right) = -\frac{2}{8}$
$$= -\frac{1}{4}$$

37. $\frac{1}{2} + \left(-\frac{2}{3}\right) = \frac{3}{6} + \left(-\frac{4}{6}\right) = -\frac{1}{6}$

38. $\frac{3}{4} + \frac{1}{2} = \frac{3}{4} + \frac{1}{2} = \frac{3}{4} + \frac{2}{4} = \frac{5}{4}$

39. $-15 + 0.02 = -(15.00 - 0.02)$
$$= -14.98$$
40. $0.45 + (-1.3) = -(1.30 - 0.45) = -0.85$
41. $-2.7 + (-0.01) = -(2.70 + 0.01)$
$$= -2.71$$
42. $0.8 + (-1) = -(1.0 - 0.8) = -0.2$
43. $47.39 + (-44.587) = 2.803$
44. $0.65357 + (-2.375) = -1.72143$
45. $0.2351 + (-0.5) = -0.2649$
46. $-1.234 + (-4.756) = -5.99$
47. $7 - 10 = -(10 - 7) = -3$
48. $8 - 19 = -(19 - 8) = -11$
49. $-4 - 7 = -4 + (-7) = -11$
50. $-5 - 12 = -(5 + 12) = -17$

51. $7 - (-6) = 7 + 6 = 13$

52. $3 - (-9) = 3 + 9 = 12$

53. $-1 - 5 = -1 + (-5) = -6$

54. $-4 - 6 = -4 + (-6) = -(4 + 6) = -10$

55. $-12 - (-3) = -12 + 3 = -9$

56. $-15 - (-6) = -15 + 6 = -(15 - 6)$
$$= -9$$

57. $20 - (-3) = 20 + 3 = 23$

58. $50 - (-70) = 50 + 70 = 120$

59. $\frac{9}{10} - \left(-\frac{1}{10}\right) = \frac{9}{10} + \frac{1}{10} = 1$

60. $\frac{1}{8} - \frac{1}{3} = -\left(\frac{1}{3} - \frac{1}{8}\right) = -\left(\frac{2}{8} - \frac{1}{8}\right)$
$$= -\frac{1}{8}$$

61. $1 - \frac{3}{2} = \frac{2}{2} - \frac{3}{2} = -\frac{1}{2}$

62. $-\frac{1}{2} - \left(-\frac{1}{3}\right) = -\frac{1}{2} + \frac{1}{3} = -\left(\frac{3}{6} - \frac{2}{6}\right)$
$$= -\frac{1}{6}$$

63. $2.00 - 0.03 = 1.97$

64. $-0.02 - 3 = -(3.00 + 0.02) = -3.02$

65. $5.3 - (-2) = 5.3 + 2 = 7.3$

66. $-4.1 - 0.13 = -(4.10 + 0.13) = -4.23$

67. $-2.44 - 48.29 = -50.73$

68. $-8.8 - 9.164 = -17.964$

69. $-3.89 - (-5.16) = 1.27$

70. $0 - (-3.5) = 3.5$

71. $(25)(-3) = -(25 \cdot 3) = -75$

72. $(5)(-7) = -(5 \cdot 7) = -35$

73. $\left(-\frac{1}{3}\right)\left(-\frac{1}{2}\right) = \frac{1}{6}$

74. $\left(-\frac{1}{2}\right)\left(-\frac{6}{7}\right) = \frac{6}{14} = \frac{3}{7}$

75. $(0.3)(-0.3) = -0.09$

76. $(-0.1)(-0.5) = (0.1)(0.5) = 0.05$

77. $(-0.02)(-10) = 0.02(10) = 0.2$

78. $(0.05)(-2.5) = -0.125$

79. The reciprocal of 20 is $\frac{1}{20}$ or 0.05.

80. The reciprocal of -5 is $-\frac{1}{5}$ or -0.2

81. The reciprocal of $-\frac{6}{5}$ is $-\frac{5}{6}$.

82. The reciprocal of $-\frac{1}{8}$ is -8.

83. The reciprocal of -0.3 is $-\frac{1}{0.3}$ or $-\frac{10}{3}$.

84. The reciprocal of 0.125 is $\frac{1}{0.125}$, $\frac{1}{1/8}$, or 8.

85. $-6 \div 3 = -2$

86. $84 \div (-2) = -42$

87. $30 \div (-0.8) = -37.5$

88. $(-9)(-6) = 54$

89. $(-0.8)(0.1) = -0.08$

90. $7 \div (-0.5) = -(7 \div 0.5) = -14$

91. $(-0.1) \div (-0.4) = 0.25$

92. $(-18) \div (-0.9) = 18 \div 0.9 = 20$

93. $9 \div \left(-\frac{3}{4}\right) = 9\left(-\frac{4}{3}\right) = -\frac{36}{3} = -12$

94. $-\frac{1}{3} \div \left(-\frac{5}{8}\right) = -\frac{1}{3}\left(-\frac{8}{5}\right) = \frac{8}{15}$

95. $-\frac{2}{3}\left(-\frac{9}{10}\right) = \frac{2}{3} \cdot \frac{9}{10} = \frac{18}{30} = \frac{3}{5}$

96. $\frac{1}{2}\left(-\frac{2}{5}\right) = -\left(\frac{1}{2} \cdot \frac{2}{5}\right) = -\frac{1}{5}$

97. $(0.25)(-365) = -91.25$

98. $7.5 \div (-0.15) = -50$

99. $(-51) \div (-0.003) = 17,000$

100. $(-2.8)(5.9) = -16.52$

101. $-62 + 13 = -(62 - 13) = -49$

102. $-88 + 39 = -(88 - 39) = -49$

103. $-32 - (-25) = -32 + 25 = -7$

104. $-71 - (-19) = -71 + 19 = -52$

105. $|-15| = -(-15) = 15$

106. $-|-75| = -(75) = -75$

107. $\frac{1}{2}(-684) = -342$

108. $\frac{1}{3}(-123) = -41$

109. $\frac{1}{2} - \left(-\frac{1}{4}\right) = \frac{2}{4} + \frac{1}{4} = \frac{3}{4}$

110. $\frac{1}{8} - \left(-\frac{1}{4}\right) = \frac{1}{8} + \frac{2}{8} = \frac{3}{8}$

111. $-57 \div 19 = -3$

112. $0 \div (-36) = 0$

113. $|-17| + |-3| = 17 + 3 = 20$

114. $64 - |-12| = 64 - 12 = 52$

115. $0 \div (-0.15) = 0$

116. $-20 \div \left(-\frac{8}{3}\right) = 20 \cdot \frac{3}{8} = \frac{60}{8} = \frac{15}{2}$

117. $27 \div (-0.15) = -180$

118. $33 \div (-0.2) = -165$

119. $-\frac{1}{3} + \frac{1}{6} = -\frac{2}{6} + \frac{1}{6} = -\frac{1}{6}$

120. $-\frac{2}{3} + \frac{1}{6} = -\left(\frac{2}{3} - \frac{1}{6}\right) = -\left(\frac{4}{6} - \frac{1}{6}\right)$
$$= -\frac{3}{6} = -\frac{1}{2}$$

121. $-63 + |8| = -63 + 8 = -55$

122. $|-34| - 27 = 34 - 27 = 7$

123. $-\frac{1}{2} + \left(-\frac{1}{2}\right) = -\frac{2}{2} = -1$

6

124. $-\frac{2}{3} + \left(-\frac{2}{3}\right) = -\frac{4}{3}$

125. $-\frac{1}{2} - 19 = -\frac{1}{2} - \frac{38}{2} = -\frac{39}{2}$

126. $-\frac{1}{3} - 22 = -\frac{1}{3} - \frac{66}{3} = -\frac{67}{3}$

127. $28 - 0.01 = 27.99$

128. $55 - 0.1 = 54.9$

129. $-29 - 0.3 = -29.3$

130. $-0.241 - 0.3 = -0.541$

131. $(-2)(0.35) = -0.7$

132. $(-3)(0.19) = -0.57$

133. $(-10)(-0.2) = 2$

134. $\left(-\frac{1}{2}\right)(-50) = 25$

135. $85{,}000 + (-45{,}000) + (-2300)$
$+ (-1500) + 1200 + 2(3{,}500) = 44{,}400$
Net worth is \$44,400.

136. Before recession: $15.6 + (-23.3) + 8.5$
$= 0.8$ million, or \$800,000 net worth. After recession: $15.6 + -23.3 + 4.8 = -2.9$, or $-\$2.9$ million net worth.

137. $14° - (-6°) = 20°$

138. $-20° - (-31°) = 11°$ C

139. $-282 - (-1296) = 1014$ ft

140. $29{,}028 - (-36{,}201) = 65{,}229$ ft

141. We learn addition first, because subtraction is defined in terms of addition.

142. The multiplicative inverse of a is $1/a$. Zero is the only number for which $1/a$ is undefined.

1.4 WARM-UPS

1. False, $2^3 = 8$.

2. True, because $2^2 = 4$ and $-1 \cdot 2^2 = -4$.

3. True, since $-2^2 = -(2^2) = -4$.

4. False, since $6 + 3 \cdot 2 = 6 + 6 = 12$.

5. False, since $(6 + 3) \cdot 2 = 9 \cdot 2 = 18$.

6. False, since $(6 + 3)^2 = 9^2 = 81$.

7. True, since $6 + 3^2 = 6 + 9 = 15$.

8. True, since $(-3)^3 = -27$ and $-3^3 = -27$.

9. False, since $|-3 - (-2)| = |-1| = 1$.

10. False, since $|7 - 8| = 1$ and $|7| - |8| = 7 - 8 = -1$.

1.4 EXERCISES

1. An arithmetic expression is the result of writing numbers in a meaningful combination with the ordinary operations of arithmetic.

2. An expression is called a sum, difference, product, or quotient if the last operation to be performed is addition, subtraction, multiplication, or division, respectively.

3. Grouping symbols are used to indicate the order in which operations are to be performed.

4. An exponential expression is an expression of the form a^n.

5. The order of operations tells us the order in which to perform operations when grouping symbols are omitted.

6. The value of -3^2 is -9 and the value of $(-3)^2$ is 9.

7. $(-3 \cdot 4) - (2 \cdot 5) = -12 - 10 = -22$

8. $|-3 - 2| - |2 - 6| = 5 - 4 = 1$

9. $4[5 - |3 - (2 \cdot 5)|] = 4[5 - 7] = -8$

10. $-2|(-3 \cdot 4) - 6| = -2|-18| = -36$

11. $(6 - 8)(|2 - 3| + 6) = (-2)(7) = -14$

12. $-5(6 + [(5 - 7) - 4]) = -5(6 + [-6])$
$\qquad\qquad\qquad\qquad\qquad = 0$

13. $2^5 = 2 \cdot 2 \cdot 2 \cdot 2 \cdot 2 = 32$

14. $3^4 = 3 \cdot 3 \cdot 3 \cdot 3 = 81$

15. $(-1)^4 = (-1)(-1)(-1)(-1) = 1$

16. $(-1)^5 = (-1)(-1)(-1)(-1)(-1) = -1$

17. $\left(-\frac{1}{3}\right)^2 = \left(-\frac{1}{3}\right)\left(-\frac{1}{3}\right) = \frac{1}{9}$

18. $\left(-\frac{1}{2}\right)^6$
$= \left(-\frac{1}{2}\right)\left(-\frac{1}{2}\right)\left(-\frac{1}{2}\right)\left(-\frac{1}{2}\right)\left(-\frac{1}{2}\right)\left(-\frac{1}{2}\right) = \frac{1}{64}$

19. $\sqrt{49} = 7$

20. $\sqrt{100} = 10$

21. $\sqrt{36 + 64} = \sqrt{100} = 10$

22. $\sqrt{25 - 9} = \sqrt{16} = 4$

23. $\sqrt{4(7 + 9)} = \sqrt{64} = 8$

24. $\sqrt{(11 + 2)(18 - 5)} = \sqrt{169} = 13$

25. $4 - 6 \cdot 2 = 4 - 12 = -8$

26. $8 - 3 \cdot 9 = 8 - 27 = -(27 - 8) = -19$

27. $5 - 6(3 - 5) = 5 - 6(-2)$
$\qquad\qquad\qquad = 5 + 12 = 17$

28. $8 - 3(4 - 6) = 8 - 3(-2) = 8 - (-6)$
$\qquad\qquad\qquad\qquad = 8 + 6 = 14$

29. $\left(\frac{1}{3}-\frac{1}{2}\right)\left(\frac{1}{4}-\frac{1}{2}\right)=\left(-\frac{1}{6}\right)\left(-\frac{1}{4}\right)$
$$=\frac{1}{24}$$

30. $\left(\frac{1}{2}-\frac{1}{4}\right)\left(\frac{1}{2}-\frac{3}{4}\right)=\left(\frac{1}{4}\right)\left(-\frac{1}{4}\right)$
$$=-\frac{1}{16}$$

31. $-3^2+(-8)^2+3=-9+64+3=58$

32. $-6^2+(-3)^3=-36-27=-63$

33. $-(2-7)^2=-(-5)^2=-25$

34. $-(1-3\cdot 2)^3=-(1-6)^3=-(-5)^3$
$$=-(-125)=125$$

35. $-5^2\cdot 2^3=-25\cdot 8=-200$

36. $2^4-4^2=16-16=0$

37. $(-5)(-2)^3=-5(-8)=40$

38. $(-1)(2-8)^3=(-1)(-6)^3=-1(-216)$
$$=216$$

39. $-(3^2-4)^2=-(9-4)^2=-5^2=-25$

40. $-(6-2^3)^4=-(6-8)^4=-(-2)^4$
$$=-16$$

41. $-60\div 10\cdot 3\div 2\cdot 5\div 6$
$$=-6\cdot 3\div 2\cdot 5\div 6$$
$$=-18\div 2\cdot 5\div 6$$
$$=-9\cdot 5\div 6$$
$$=-45\div 6=-7.5$$

42. $75\div(-5)(-3)\div\frac{1}{2}\cdot 6$
$$=-15(-3)\div\frac{1}{2}\cdot 6$$
$$=45\div\frac{1}{2}\cdot 6$$
$$=90\cdot 6=540$$

43. $5.5-2.3^4=-22.4841$

44. $5.3^2-4\cdot 6.1=3.69$

45. $(1.3-0.31)(2.9-4.88)=-1.9602$

46. $(6.7-9.88)^3=-32.157432$

47. $-388.8\div(13.5)(9.6)=-276.48$

48. $(-4.3)(5.5)\div(3.2)(-1.2)=8.86875$

49. $\frac{2-6}{9-7}=\frac{-4}{2}=-2$

50. $\frac{9-12}{4-5}=\frac{-3}{-1}=3$

51. $\frac{-3-5}{6-(-2)}=\frac{-8}{8}=-1$

52. $\frac{-14-(-2)}{-3-3}=\frac{-14+2}{-6}=\frac{-12}{-6}=2$

53. $\frac{4+2\cdot 7}{3\cdot 2-9}=\frac{18}{-3}=-6$

54. $\frac{-6-2(-3)}{8-3(-3)}=\frac{-6+6}{8+9}=\frac{0}{17}=0$

55. $\frac{-3^2-(-9)}{2-3^2}=\frac{-9+9}{2-9}=\frac{0}{-7}=0$

56. $\frac{-2^4-5}{3^2-2^4}=\frac{-16-5}{9-16}=\frac{-21}{-7}=3$

57. $3^2-4(-1)(-4)=9-16=-7$

58. $\sqrt{(-1)^2-4(3)(-4)}=\sqrt{1-4(-12)}$
$$=\sqrt{1+48}=7$$

59. $\frac{-1-3}{-1-(-4)}=\frac{-4}{-1+4}=-\frac{4}{3}$

60. $\frac{3-(-4)}{3-(-1)}=\frac{7}{4}$

61. $(-1-3)(-1+3)=(-4)(2)=-8$

62. $(-1-(-4))(-1+(-4))$
$$=(-1+4)(-5)$$
$$=(3)(-5)=-15$$

63. $\sqrt{(-4)^2-2(-4)+1}=\sqrt{16+8+1}$
$$=5$$

64. $(3)^2-2(3)-3=9-6-3=0$

65. $\frac{2}{-1}+\frac{3}{-4}-\frac{1}{-4}=-\frac{4}{2}-\frac{1}{2}=-\frac{5}{2}$

66. $\frac{-4}{-1}+\frac{-4}{3}-\frac{-1}{3}=4-\frac{4}{3}+\frac{1}{3}$
$$=4-\frac{3}{3}=4-1=3$$

67. $|-1-3|=|-4|=4$

68. $|3+(-4)|=|-1|=1$

69. $\frac{-6-4}{-7-2}=\frac{-10}{-9}=\frac{10}{9}$

70. $\frac{-3-(-3)}{-5-4}=\frac{0}{-9}=0$

71. $\frac{2-(-1)}{1-(-3)}=\frac{3}{4}$

72. $\frac{5-(-2)}{6-2}=\frac{7}{4}$

73. $\frac{5.6-2.4}{4.7-5.9}=-2.67$

74. $\frac{6.9-(-5.7)}{4.2-3.5}=18$

75. $-2^2+5(3)^2=-4+45=41$

76. $-3^2+3(6)^2=-9+108=99$

77. $(-2+5)3^2=3\cdot 9=27$

78. $(-3+3)6^2=0\cdot 36=0$

79. $\sqrt{5^2-4(1)(6)}=\sqrt{25-24}=1$

80. $\sqrt{6^2-4(2)(4)}=\sqrt{36-32}=2$

81. $[13 + 2(-5)]^2 = 3^2 = 9$

82. $[6 + 2(-4)]^2 = [-2]^2 = 4$

83. $\dfrac{4 - (-1)}{-3 - 2} = \dfrac{5}{-5} = -1$

84. $\dfrac{2 - (-3)}{3 - 5} = \dfrac{5}{-2} = -\dfrac{5}{2}$

85. $3(-2)^2 - 5(-2) + 4 = 12 + 10 + 4 = 26$

86. $3(-1)^2 + 5(-1) - 6 = 3 - 5 - 6 = -8$

87. $-4\left(\dfrac{1}{2}\right)^2 + 3\left(\dfrac{1}{2}\right) - 2$
$$= -4\left(\dfrac{1}{4}\right) + \dfrac{3}{2} - 2$$
$$= -\dfrac{2}{2} + \dfrac{3}{2} - \dfrac{4}{2} = -\dfrac{3}{2}$$

88. $8\left(\dfrac{1}{2}\right)^2 - 6\left(\dfrac{1}{2}\right) + 1 = 8 \cdot \dfrac{1}{4} - 3 + 1$
$$= 2 - 3 + 1 = 0$$

89. $-\dfrac{1}{2}\,|\,6 - 2\,| = -\dfrac{1}{2}(4) = -2$

90. $-\dfrac{1}{3}\,|\,9 - 6\,| = -\dfrac{1}{3}\,|\,3\,|$
$$= -\dfrac{1}{3} \cdot 3 = -1$$

91. $\dfrac{1}{2} - \dfrac{1}{3}\,|\,\dfrac{1}{4} - \dfrac{1}{2}\,| = \dfrac{1}{2} - \dfrac{1}{3} \cdot \dfrac{1}{4}$
$$= \dfrac{1}{2} - \dfrac{1}{12} = \dfrac{5}{12}$$

92. $\dfrac{1}{3} - \dfrac{1}{2}\,|\,\dfrac{1}{3} - \dfrac{1}{2}\,| = \dfrac{1}{3} - \dfrac{1}{2} \cdot \dfrac{1}{6}$
$$= \dfrac{1}{3} - \dfrac{1}{12} = \dfrac{1}{4}$$

93. $|\,6 - 3 \cdot 7\,| + |\,7 - 5\,|$
$$- |\,-15\,| + |\,2\,|$$
$$= 17$$

94. $|\,12 - 4\,| - |\,3 - 4 \cdot 5\,|$
$$= |\,8\,| - |\,3 - 20\,|$$
$$= 8 - |\,-17\,| = 8 - 17 = -9$$

95. $3 - 7[4 - (2 - 5)] = 3 - 7[4 + 3]$
$$= 3 - 49 = -46$$

96. $9 - 2[3 - (4 + 6)] = 9 - 2[-7] = 9 + 14$
$$= 23$$

97. $3 - 4(2 - |\,4 - 6\,|) = 3 - 4(2 - 2) = 3$

98. $3 - (|\,-4\,| - |\,-5\,|) = 3 - (-1)$
$$= 3 + 1 = 4$$

99. $4[2 - (5 - |\,-3\,|)^2] = 4[2 - (2^2)]$
$$= 4[-2] = -8$$

100. $[5 - (-3)]^2 + [4 - (-2)]^2 = 8^2 + 6^2$
$$= 100$$

101. $0.65(220 - 25) - 0.65(220 - 65) = 26$
The target heart rate for a 25-yr old woman is 26 beats per minute larger than the target heart rate for a 65 yr-old woman. A woman's target heart rate is 115 at about 43 years of age.

102. Target heart rate for 20-yr old man is $0.75(220 - 20) = 150$. Target heart rate for 50-yr old man is $0.75(220 - 50) = 127.5$. A man's target heart rate is 115 at about 67 years of age.

103. The perimeter is $2(34) + 2(18)$ or 104 feet.

104. The area of the property is $0.5 \cdot 150(260 + 220)$ or 36,000 ft^2.

105. a) Using the graph, the investment amounts to approximately \$60,000.
b) The investment amounts to $10,000(1 + 0.062)^{30}$ or \$60,776.47.

106. The amount invested in 1987 was $\dfrac{252,000}{(1 + 0.07)^{18}}$ or \$74,557.71.

107. a) According to the graph she owes approximately \$5,500.
b) The actual amount owed when the payments start is $4000(1 + 0.08)^4$ or \$5441.96.

108. In 15 years after 1990, the average cost of a one-year stay in nursing home will be $29,930(1.05)^{15}$ or \$62,222.

109. $29,930(1.08)^{15} - 62,222 = 32,721$
Using the formula in this exercise, a one-year stay costs \$32,721 more.

110. $5(5(5 \cdot 3 + 6) + 4) + 7$
$$= 5(5(21) + 4) + 7$$
$$= 5(105 + 4) + 7$$
$$= 5 \cdot 109 + 7$$
$$= 552$$
$$3 \cdot 5^3 + 6 \cdot 5^2 + 4 \cdot 5 + 7$$
$$= 375 + 150 + 20 + 7$$
$$= 552$$

These expressions are the same, because you can factor the second to make it appear the same as the first:

$$3 \cdot 5^3 + 6 \cdot 5^2 + 4 \cdot 5 + 7$$
$$= 5(3 \cdot 5^2 + 6 \cdot 5 + 4) + 7$$
$$= 5(5(3 \cdot 5 + 6) + 4) + 7$$

1.5 WARM-UPS

1. True, because of the commutative properties.

2. False, since $8 \div (4 \div 2) = 4$ and $(8 \div 4) \div 2 = 2$.

3. False, since $10 \div 2 = 5$ and $2 \div 10 = 0.2$.

4. False, since $5 - 3 = 2$ and $3 - 5 = -2$.

5. False, since $10 - (7 - 3) = 6$ and $(10 - 7) - 3 = 0$.

6. False, since $4(6 \div 2) = 12$ and $(4 \cdot 6) \div (4 \cdot 2) = 3$.

7. True, since $(0.02)(50) = 1$.

8. True, because of Warm-up number 2.

9. False, because if $x = 0$ we get $3 = 0$.

10. True, because $\dfrac{1 \text{ car}}{0.04 \text{ hours}} = \dfrac{25 \text{ cars}}{1 \text{ hour}}$.

1.5 EXERCISES

1. The commutative property of addition says that $a + b = b + a$ and the commutative property of multiplication says that $a \cdot b = b \cdot a$.

2. The associative property of addition says that $(a + b) + c = a + (b + c)$.

3. The commutative property of addition says that you get the same result when you add two numbers in either order. The associative property of addition has to do with which two numbers are added first when adding three numbers.

4. The distributive property says that $a(b + c) = ab + ac$.

5. Zero is the additive identity because adding zero to a number does not change the number.

6. One is the multiplicative identity because multiplying a number by 1 does not change the number.

7. $9 - 4 + 6 - 10 = 15 - 14 = 1$

8. $-3 + 4 - 12 + 9 = -15 + 13 = -2$

9. $6 - 10 + 5 - 8 - 7 = 11 - 25 = -14$

10. $5 - 11 + 6 - 9 + 12 - 2 = -22 + 23$
$$= 1$$

11. $-4 - 11 + 6 - 8 + 13 - 20 = -43 + 19$
$$= -24$$

12. $-8 + 12 - 9 - 15 + 6 - 22 + 3$
$$= -54 + 21 = -33$$

13. $-3.2 + 1.4 - 2.8 + 4.5 - 1.6$
$$= -7.6 + 5.9 = -1.7$$

14. $4.4 - 5.1 + 3.6 - 2.3 + 8.1$
$$= -7.4 + 16.1 = 8.7$$

15. $3.27 - 11.41 + 5.7 - 12.36 - 5$
$$= 8.97 - 28.77 = -19.8$$

16. $4.89 - 2.1 + 7.58 - 9.06 - 5.34$
$$= 12.47 - 16.5 = -4.03$$

17. $4(x - 6) = 4 \cdot x - 4 \cdot 6 = 4x - 24$

18. $5(a - 1) = 5 \cdot a - 5 \cdot 1 = 5a - 5$

19. $2m + 10 = 2 \cdot m + 2 \cdot 5 = 2(m + 5)$

20. $3y + 9 = 3 \cdot y + 3 \cdot 3 = 3(y + 3)$

21. $a(3 + t) = 3a + at$

22. $b(y + w) = by + bw$

23. $-2(w - 5) = -2w - (-10) = -2w + 10$

24. $-4(m - 7) = -4 \cdot m - (-4)(7)$
$$= -4m + 28$$

25. $-2(3 - y) = -6 - (-2y) = -6 + 2y$

26. $-5(4 - p) = -5 \cdot 4 - (-5)p = -20 + 5p$

27. $5x - 5 = 5 \cdot x - 5 \cdot 1 = 5(x - 1)$

28. $3y + 3 = 3y + 3 \cdot 1 = 3(y + 1)$

29. $-1(-2x - y) = (-1)(-2x) - (-1)y$
$$= 2x + y$$

30. $-1(-4y - w) = -1(-4y) - (-1)w$
$$= 4y + w$$

31. $-3(-2w - 3y) = -3(-2w) - (-3)3y$
$$= 6w + 9y$$

32. $-4(-x - 6) = -4(-x) - (-4)6$
$$= 4x + 24$$

33. $3y - 15 = 3 \cdot y - 3 \cdot 5 = 3(y - 5)$

34. $5x + 10 = 5 \cdot x + 5 \cdot 2 = 5(x + 2)$

35. $3a + 9 = 3 \cdot a + 3 \cdot 3 = 3(a + 3)$

36. $7b - 49 = 7b - 7 \cdot 7 = 7(b - 7)$

37. $\frac{1}{2}(4x + 8) = \frac{4}{2}x + \frac{8}{2} = 2x + 4$

38. $\frac{1}{3}(3x + 6) = \frac{1}{3} \cdot 3x + \frac{1}{3} \cdot 6 = x + 2$

39. $-\frac{1}{2}(2x - 4) = -\frac{2}{2}x + \frac{4}{2} = -x + 2$

40. $-\frac{1}{3}(9x - 3) = -\frac{1}{3} \cdot 9x - \left(-\frac{1}{3}\right)(3)$
$$= -3x + 1$$

41. The reciprocal of $\frac{1}{2}$ is 2 because $2 \cdot \frac{1}{2} = 1$.

42. The multiplicative inverse of $\frac{1}{3}$ is 3, because $3 \cdot \frac{1}{3} = 1$.

43. The reciprocal of 1 is 1 because $1 \cdot 1 = 1$.

44. The reciprocal of -1 is -1 because $-1(-1) = 1$.

45. The reciprocal of 6 is $\frac{1}{6}$, because $6 \cdot \frac{1}{6} = 1$.

46. The reciprocal of 8 is $\frac{1}{8}$, because $8 \cdot \frac{1}{8} = 1$.

47. Since $0.25 = \frac{1}{4}$, its reciprocal is 4.

48. Since $0.75 = \frac{3}{4}$, the reciprocal of 0.75 is $\frac{4}{3}$.

49. Since $-0.7 = -\frac{7}{10}$, its reciprocal is $-\frac{10}{7}$.

50. Since $-0.9 = -\frac{9}{10}$, its reciprocal is $-\frac{10}{9}$.

51. Since $-1.8 = -\frac{18}{10}$ or $-\frac{9}{5}$, the reciprocal of -1.8 is $-\frac{5}{9}$.

52. Since $-2.6 = -\frac{26}{10}$ or $-\frac{13}{5}$ the reciprocal of -2.6 is $-\frac{5}{13}$.

53. $\frac{1}{2.3} + \frac{1}{5.4} \approx 0.6200$

54. $\frac{1}{13.5} - \frac{1}{4.6} \approx -0.1433$

55. $\dfrac{\frac{1}{4.3}}{\frac{1}{5.6} + \frac{1}{7.2}} \approx 0.7326$

56. $\dfrac{\frac{1}{4.5} - \frac{1}{5.6}}{\frac{1}{3.2} + \frac{1}{2.7}} \approx 0.0639$

57. $\dfrac{1 \text{ mile}}{0.0006897 \text{ hours}} \approx 1450$ mph

58. $\dfrac{1 \text{ mile}}{0.000456 \text{ hours}} \approx 2193$ mph

59. $\frac{1}{0.01}$ bt/hr $+ \frac{1}{0.02}$ bt/hr $+ \frac{1}{0.015}$ bt/hr ≈ 217 buttons per hour

60. $\frac{1}{36.5}$ house/hr $+ \frac{1}{30}$ house/hour ≈ 0.06 house per hour

61. Commutative property of addition

62. The commutative property justifies the equation $x \cdot 5 = 5x$.

63. Distributive property

64. The associative property justifies the equation $a(3b) = (a \cdot 3)b$.

65. Associative property of multiplication

66. The distributive property justifies the equation $3(x - 1) = 3x - 3$.

67. Multiplicative inverse property

68. The commutative property of addition justifies the equation $0.3 + 9 = 9 + 0.3$.

69. Commutative property of multiplication

70. The multiplication property of 0 justifies the equation $0 \cdot 52 = 0$.

71. Multiplicative identity

72. The numbers 0.1 and 10 are reciprocals of each other. So the multiplicative inverse property justifies the equation $(0.1)(10) = 1$.

73. Distributive property

74. Zero is the additive identity. The additive identity property justifies the equation $8 + 0 = 8$.

75. Additive inverse property

76. One is the multiplicative identity. So the identity property justifies the equation $1 \cdot y = y$.

77. Multiplication property of zero

78. The distributive property justifies the equation $5x + 5 = 5(x + 1)$.

79. Distributive property

80. The distributive property justifies the equation $ab + 3ac = a(b + 3c)$.

81. $5 + w = w + 5$

82. $2x + 2 = 2 \cdot x + 2 \cdot 1 = 2(x + 1)$

83. $5(xy) = (5x)y$

84. $x + \frac{1}{2} = \frac{1}{2} + x$

85. $\frac{1}{2}x - \frac{1}{2} = \frac{1}{2}x - \frac{1}{2} \cdot 1 = \frac{1}{2}(x - 1)$

86. $3(x - 7) = 3x - 21$

87. $6x + 9 = 3 \cdot 2x + 3 \cdot 3 = 3(2x + 3)$

88. $(x + 7) + 3 = x + (7 + 3)$

89. Since 8 and 0.125 are reciprocals, $8(0.125) = 1$.

90. $-1(a - 3) = -1 \cdot a - (-1)3$
$$= -a + 3$$

91. $0 = 5(0)$

92. $8 \cdot (1) = 8$

93. $0.25(4) = 1$

94. $45(1) = 45$

95. Fortunately, the order in which the groceries are placed does not affect the total bill, because of the commutative and associative properties of addition.

96. Six percent of the total should be the same amount of tax as finding 6% of each item and then adding the results, because of the distributive property. Actually, there might be a slight difference due to rounding.

1.6 WARM-UPS

1. True by the distributive property.
2. False, because $-4x + 8 = -4(x - 2)$.
3. True, because multiplying by -1 is equivalent to finding the opposite.
4. True, by the distributive property.
5. False, $(2x)(5x) = 10x^2$
6. True because of the distributive property.
7. False, $a + a = 2a$.
8. False, $b \cdot b = b^2$.
9. False, because 1 and $7x$ are not like terms.
10. True, because the like terms are combined correctly.

1.6 EXERCISES

1. A term is a single number or a product of a number and one or more variables.
2. Like terms contain the same variables with the same powers.
3. The coefficient of a term is the number preceding the variables.
4. The distributive property is used to combine like terms.
5. You can multiply and divide unlike terms.
6. You can remove parentheses preceded by a negative sign by taking the opposite of every term in the parentheses.
7. $(45 \cdot 2) \cdot 100 = 90 \cdot 100 = 9000$
8. $25(300) = (25 \cdot 3)100 = 75 \cdot 100 = 7500$
9. $\frac{4}{3}(0.75) = \frac{4}{3} \cdot \frac{3}{4} = 1$
10. $5(0.2) = 5 \cdot \frac{2}{10} = 5 \cdot \frac{1}{5} = 1$
11. $427 + (68 + 32) = 427 + 100 = 527$
12. $(194 + 78) + 22 = 194 + (78 + 22)$
$$= 194 + 100 = 294$$

13. $47 \cdot 4 + 47 \cdot 6 = 47(4 + 6) = 470$
14. $53 \cdot 3 + 53 \cdot 7 = 53(3 + 7) = 53 \cdot 10$
$$= 530$$
15. $19 \cdot 2 \cdot 5 \cdot \frac{1}{5} = 19 \cdot 2 \cdot 1 = 19 \cdot 2 = 38$
16. $17 \cdot 4 \cdot 2 \cdot \frac{1}{4} = 17 \cdot 2 \cdot 4 \cdot \frac{1}{4} = 17 \cdot 2 \cdot 1$
$$= 34$$
17. $120 \cdot 4 \cdot 100 = 480 \cdot 100 = 48,000$
18. $150 \cdot 300 = 150 \cdot 3 \cdot 100 = 45,000$
19. $13 \cdot 377 \cdot 0 = 0$
20. $(456 \cdot 8)\frac{1}{8} = 456\left(8 \cdot \frac{1}{8}\right) = 456 \cdot 1 = 456$
21. $348 + (5 + 45) = 348 + 50 = 398$
22. $(135 + 38) + 12) = 135 + (38 + 12)$
$$= 135 + 50 = 185$$
23. $\frac{2}{3} \cdot 1.5 = \frac{2}{3} \cdot \frac{3}{2} = 1$
24. $(1.25)(0.8) = \frac{5}{4} \cdot \frac{4}{5} = 1$
25. $17 \cdot 101 - 17 \cdot 1 = 17(101 - 1) = 1700$
26. $33 \cdot 2 - 12 \cdot 33 = 33(2 - 12) = -330$
27. $354 + (7 + 3) + (8 + 2)$
$$= 354 + 10 + 10 = 374$$
28. $564 + 35 + 65 + 72 + 28$
$$= 564 + 100 + 100$$
$$= 764$$
29. $(567 + 874)(0) = 0$
30. $(567^2 + 48)[3(-5) + 15]$
$$= (567^2 + 48)[0] = 0$$
31. $-4n + 6n = (-4 + 6)n = 2n$
32. $-3a + 15a = 15a - 3a = 12a$
33. $3w - (-4w) = 3w + 4w = 7w$
34. $3b - (-7b) = 3b + 7b = 10b$
35. $4mw^2 - 15mw^2 = (4 - 15)mw^2$
$$= -11mw^2$$
36. $2b^2x - 16b^2x = (2 - 16)b^2x = -14b^2x$
37. $-5x - (-2x) = -5x + 2x = -3x$
38. Not like terms: $-11 - 7t$
39. Not like terms: $-4 - 7z$
40. $-19m - (-3m) = -19m + 3m$
$$= -16m$$
41. $4t^2 + 5t^2 = (4 + 5)t^2 = 9t^2$
42. Not like terms: $5a + 4a^2$
43. Not like terms: $-4ab + 3a^2b$
44. $-7x^2y + 5x^2y = (-7 + 5)x^2y = -2x^2y$
45. $9mn - mn = (9 - 1)mn = 8mn$
46. $3cm - cm = 3cm - 1cm = 2cm$

47. $x^3y - 3x^3y = 1x^3y - 3x^3y = -2x^3y$

48. $s^4t - 5s^4t = 1s^4t - 5s^4t = -4s^4t$

49. $-kz^6 - kz^6 = -1kz^6 + (-1kz^6)$
$\quad\quad = -2kz^6$

50. $m^7w - m^7w = 0$

51. $4(7t) = (4 \cdot 7)t = 28t$

52. $-3(4r) = (-3 \cdot 4)r = -12r$

53. $(-2x)(-5x) = (-2)(-5)x \cdot x = 10x^2$

54. $(-3h)(-7h) = (-3)(-7)h \cdot h = 21h^2$

55. $(-h)(-h) = (-1)(-1)h \cdot h = h^2$

56. $x(-x) = x(-1x) = -1 \cdot x \cdot x = -1x^2$
$\quad\quad = -x^2$

57. $7w(-4) = -4 \cdot 7w = -28w$

58. $-5t(-1) = (-5)(-1)t = 5t$

59. $-x(1 - x) = -x \cdot 1 - (-x)(x)$
$\quad\quad = -x + x^2$

60. $-p(p - 1) = -p \cdot p - (-p)1 = -p^2 + p$

61. $5k \cdot 5k = 5 \cdot 5 \cdot k \cdot k = 25k^2$

62. $(-4y)(-4y) = (-4)(-4)y \cdot y = 16y^2$

63. $3 \cdot \dfrac{y}{3} = 3 \cdot \dfrac{1}{3} \cdot y = 1 \cdot y = y$

64. $5z\left(\dfrac{z}{5}\right) = 5z \cdot \dfrac{1}{5}z = 5 \cdot \dfrac{1}{5} \cdot z \cdot z = z^2$

65. $9 \cdot \dfrac{2y}{9} = 9 \cdot \dfrac{1}{9} \cdot 2y = 1 \cdot 2y = 2y$

66. $8\left(\dfrac{y}{8}\right) = 8 \cdot \dfrac{1}{8} \cdot y = y$

67. $\dfrac{6x^3}{2} = \dfrac{6}{2}x^3 = 3x^3$

68. $\dfrac{-8x^2}{4} = \dfrac{-8}{4} \cdot x^2 = -2x^2$

69. $\dfrac{3x^2y + 15x}{3} = \dfrac{3x^2y}{3} + \dfrac{15x}{3} = x^2y + 5x$

70. $\dfrac{6xy^2 - 8w}{2} = \dfrac{6xy^2}{2} - \dfrac{8w}{2} = 3xy^2 - 4w$

71. $\dfrac{2x - 4}{-2} = \dfrac{2x}{-2} - \dfrac{4}{-2} = -x + 2$

72. $\dfrac{-6x - 9}{-3} = \dfrac{-6x}{-3} - \dfrac{9}{-3} = 2x - (-3)$
$\quad\quad = 2x + 3$

73. $\dfrac{-xt + 10}{-2} = \dfrac{-xt}{-2} + \dfrac{10}{-2} = \dfrac{1}{2}xt - 5$

74. $\dfrac{-2xt^2 + 8}{-4} = \dfrac{-2xt^2}{-4} + \dfrac{8}{-4} = \dfrac{1}{2}xt^2 - 2$

75. $a - (4a - 1) = a - 4a + 1 = -3a + 1$

76. $5x - (2x - 7) = 5x - 2x + 7 = 3x + 7$

77. $6 - (x - 4) = 6 - x + 4 = 10 - x$

78. $9 - (w - 5) = 9 - w + 5 = 14 - w$

79. $4m + 6 - m - 5 = 3m + 1$

80. $5 - 6t - (3t + 4) = 5 - 6t - 3t - 4$
$\quad\quad = 1 - 9t$

81. $-5b + at - 7b = -12b + at$

82. $-4x^2 - (-7x^2 + 2y) = -4x^2 + 7x^2 - 2y$
$\quad\quad = 3x^2 - 2y$

83. $t^2 - 5w + 2w + t^2 = 2t^2 - 3w$

84. $n^2 - 6m - (-n^2 - 2m)$
$\quad\quad = n^2 - 6m + n^2 + 2m$
$\quad\quad = 2n^2 - 4m$

85. $x^2 - x^2 + y^2 + z = y^2 + z$

86. $5w - (6w - 3xy - zy)$
$\quad\quad = 5w - 6w + 3xy + zy$
$\quad\quad = 3xy + zy - w$

87. $(2x + 7x) + (3 + 5) = 9x + 8$

88. $(3x + 4x) + (5 + 12) = 7x + 17$

89. $(-3x + 4) + (5x - 6) = 2x - 2$

90. $(-4x + 11) + (6x - 8) = 2x + 3$

91. $4a^2 - 5c - 6a^2 + 7c = -2a^2 + 2c$

92. $3x^2 - 4 - (x^2 - 5) = 3x^2 - 4 - x^2 + 5$
$\quad\quad = 2x^2 + 1$

93. $5t^2 - 15w + 6w + 2t^2 = 7t^2 - 9w$

94. $6(xy^2 + 2) - 5(-xy^2 - 1)$
$\quad\quad = 6xy^2 + 12 + 5xy^2 + 5$
$\quad\quad = 11xy^2 + 17$

95. $-7m + 3m - 12 + 5m = m - 12$

96. $-6m + 4(m - 3) + 7m$
$\quad\quad = -6m + 4m - 12 + 7m$
$\quad\quad = 5m - 12$

97. $8 - 7k^3 - 21 - 4 = -7k^3 - 17$

98. $6 + 5(k^3 - 2) - k^3 + 5$
$= 6 + 5k^3 - 10 - k^3 + 5 = 4k^3 + 1$

99. $x - 0.04x - 0.04(50) = 0.96x - 2$

100. $x - 0.03(x + 500)$
$\quad\quad = 1.00x - 0.03x - 15$
$\quad\quad = 0.97x - 15$

101. $0.10x + 0.5 - 0.04x - 2 = 0.06x - 1.5$

102. $0.06x + 0.14(x + 200)$
$\quad\quad = 0.06x + 0.14x + 28$
$\quad\quad = 0.20x + 28 = 0.2x + 28$

103. $3k + 5 - 6k + 8 - k + 3 = -4k + 16$

104. $5w - 2 + 4(w - 3) - 6(w - 1)$
$\quad\quad = 5w - 2 + 4w - 12 - 6w + 6$
$\quad\quad = 3w - 8$

105. $5.7 - 4.5x + (4.5)(3.9) - 5.42$
$\quad\quad = -4.5x + 17.83$

106. $0.04(5.6x - 4.9) + 0.07(7.3x - 34)$
$\quad\quad = 0.224x - 0.196 + 0.511x - 2.38$
$\quad\quad = 0.735x - 2.576$

107. $3 - 3xy - 2xy + 10 - 35 + xy$
$= -4xy - 22$

108. $2x^2 - 6 - 6x^2 + 2 - 14x^2 - 8$
$= -18x^2 - 12$

109. $3w^2 - 30w^2 - 2w^2 = -29w^2$

110. $3w^3 + 5w^3 - 4w^3 + 12w^3 - 2w^2$
$= 16w^3 - 2w^2$

111. $3a^2w^2 - 5a^2w^2 - 4a^2w^2 = -6a^2w^2$

112. $-3aw^2 - 15a^2w + 2a^2w + 2a^2w$
$= -11a^2w - 3aw^2$

113. $\frac{1}{6} - \frac{1}{3}\left(-6x^2y - \frac{1}{2}\right) = \frac{1}{6} + 2x^2y + \frac{1}{6}$
$= 2x^2y + \frac{1}{3}$

114. $-\frac{1}{2}bc - \frac{1}{2}bc(3 - a)$
$= -\frac{1}{2}bc - \frac{3}{2}bc + \frac{1}{2}abc$
$= \frac{1}{2}abc - 2bc$

115. $-\frac{1}{2}m\left(-\frac{1}{2}m\right) - \frac{1}{2}m - \frac{1}{2}m$
$= \frac{1}{4}m^2 - m$

116. $\frac{4wyt}{4} + \frac{-8wyt}{2} - \frac{-2wy}{2}$
$= wyt - 4wyt + wy$
$= -3wyt + wy$

117. $\frac{-8t^3}{-2} - \frac{6t^2}{-2} + \frac{2}{-2} = 4t^3 + 3t^2 - 1$

118. $\frac{2x^3 - 4}{-2} = \frac{2x^3}{-2} - \frac{4}{-2} = -x^3 + 2$

119. $\frac{-6xyz}{-3} - \frac{3xy}{-3} + \frac{9z}{-3}$
$= 2xyz + xy - 3z$

120.
$\frac{10a^2b^4 + 5}{-5} = \frac{10a^2b^4}{-5} + \frac{5}{-5} = -2a^2b^4 - 1$

121. Perimeter is $s + s + 2 + s + 4$ or $3s + 6$ ft.

122. Perimeter is $2(w) + 2(w + 50)$ or $4w + 100$ ft. No, it is not possible to find the area, because the height is needed to find the area of a parallelogram.

123. Perimeter is $2x + 2\left(x + \frac{1}{6}x\right)$ or $\frac{13}{3}x$ meters. Area is $x\left(x + \frac{1}{6}x\right) = \frac{7}{6}x^2$ square meters.

124. Perimeter is $4x$ in. and area is x^2 in^2.

Enriching Your Mathematical Word Power
1. a   2. c   3. a   4. d   5. a
6. c   7. a   8. d   9. b   10. a
11. b   12. a   13. b   14. c

CHAPTER 1 REVIEW

1. True, because 3 is the only number common to A and B.

2. False, because the only element that A and B have in common is 3. So $A \cap B = \{3\}$.

3. False, because $A \cup B = \{1, 2, 3, 4, 5\}$.

4. True, because every element of C is either in A or in B.

5. True, because $B \subseteq C$.

6. False, because only 1, 2, and 3 are in both A and C. So $A \cap C = \{1, 2, 3\}$.

7. False, $A \cap \emptyset = \emptyset$.

8. False, because $A \cup \emptyset = A$.

9. True, because $A \cap B = \{3\}$.

10. True, since $C \cap B = \{3, 4, 5\}$, $A = \{1, 2, 3\}$, and $(C \cap B) \cap A = \{3\}$.

11. True, because every member of B is also a member of C.

12. False, because 3 is a member of A, but not a member of E.

13. False, because $1 \in A$ and $1 \notin B$.

14. False, because $1 \in C$, but $1 \notin B$.

15. True, because 3 is a member of D.

16. True, because 5 is not a member of A.

17. False, because $0 \notin E$.

18. False because $3 \in D$, but $3 \notin \emptyset$.

19. True, because $\emptyset$ is a subset of every set.

20. True, because 1 is a member of A.

21. $\{0, 1, 31\}$

22. The only natural numbers in the set are 1 and 31.

23. $\{-1, 0, 1, 31\}$

24. The rational numbers in the set are -1, 0, 1, 1.732, 22/7, and 31.

25. $\{-\sqrt{2}, \sqrt{3}, \pi\}$

26. All of the numbers in the set are real numbers.

27. False, because 0 is a whole number but not a natural number.

28. False, because 0 is a rational number and a real number.

29. False, because -2, -1 and 0 are not natural numbers.

30. False, the set of rational numbers is infinite.

31. False, because 3.14 is not exactly π.

32. False, because 0.25 is a terminating decimal and it is not an integer.

33. True, because any decimal number that repeats or terminates is a rational number.

34. False, because $\sqrt{9}$ is the same as 3 and 3 is a rational number.

35. False, 0 is rational only.

36. False, because the irrational numbers are those decimal numbers that neither repeat nor terminate.

37. $9 - 4 = 5$

38. $-3 + (-5) = -8$

39. $25 - 37 = -12$

40. $-6 - 10 = -6 + (-10) = -16$

41. $(-4)(6) = -24$

42. $(-7)(-6) = 7 \cdot 6 = 42$

43. $(-8) \div (-4) = 2$

44. $40 \div (-8) = -5$

45. $-\frac{3}{12} + \frac{1}{12} = -\frac{2}{12} = -\frac{1}{6}$

46. $\frac{1}{3} - \left(-\frac{1}{12}\right) = \frac{4}{12} + \frac{1}{12} = \frac{5}{12}$

47. $\frac{-20}{-2} = 10$

48. $\frac{30}{-6} = -5$

49. $10.00 - 0.04 = 9.96$

50. $-0.05 + (-3) = -(0.05 + 3.00)$
$= -3.05$

51. $-6 - (-2) = -6 + 2 = -4$

52. $-0.2 - (-0.04) = -0.20 + 0.04$
$= -(0.20 - 0.04) = -0.16$

53. $-0.5 + 0.5 = 0$

54. $-0.04 \div 0.2 = -0.2$

55. $3.2 \div (-0.8) = -4$

56. $(0.2)(-0.9) = -0.18$

57. $0 \div (-0.3545) = 0$

58. $(-6)(-0.5) = 3$

59. $\frac{1}{4}(-12) = -\frac{12}{4} = -3$

60. $-7 - (-9) = -7 + 9 = 9 - 7 = 2$

61. $4 + 7 \cdot 5 = 4 + 35 = 39$

62. $(4 + 7)5 = 11 \cdot 5 = 55$

63. $(4 + 7)^2 = 11^2 = 121$

64. $4 + 7^2 = 4 + 49 = 53$

65. $5 + 3 \cdot |6 - 12| = 5 + 3 \cdot 6 = 5 + 18$
$= 23$

66. $6 - (7 - 8) = 6 - (-1) = 6 + 1 = 7$

67. $(-2) - (-4) = -2 + 4 = 2$

68. $5 - 6 - 8 - 10 = 5 - 24 = -19$

69. $3 - 5(6 - 10) = 3 - 5(-4) = 23$

70. $4^2 - 9 + 3^2 = 16 - 9 + 9 = 16$

71. $25 - (11)^2 = 25 - 121 = -96$

72. $|3 - 4 \cdot 2| - |5 - 8|$
$= |3 - 8| - |-3|$
$= |-5| - |-3| = 5 - 3 = 2$

73. $\sqrt{3^2 + 4^2} = \sqrt{9 + 16} = \sqrt{25} = 5$

74. $\sqrt{13^2 - 5^2} = \sqrt{169 - 25} = \sqrt{144}$
$= 12$

75. $\frac{-9}{7 + 2} = \frac{-9}{9} = -1$

76. $\frac{5 - 9}{2 - 4} = \frac{-4}{-2} = 2$

77. $1.00 - 0.24 = 0.76$

78. $5 - (0.2)(0.1) = 5.00 - 0.02 = 4.98$

79. $9 - 8 = 1$

80. $3^2 - 4(1)(-3) = 9 - (-12) = 9 + 12$
$= 21$

81. $3 - 2|-3| = 3 - 2 \cdot 3 = 3 - 6 = -3$

82. $3|4 - 6| + 1 = 3|-2| + 1$
$= 3 \cdot 2 + 1 = 7$

83. $\frac{-8}{-2} = 4$

84. $\frac{-6 + 3}{3 - 9} = \frac{-3}{-6} = \frac{1}{2}$

85. $\sqrt{3^2 - 4(-2)(-1)} = \sqrt{9 - 8}$
$= \sqrt{1} = 1$

86. $\sqrt{(-2)^2 + 4(3)} = \sqrt{4 + 12} = \sqrt{16} = 4$

87. $(-1 - 3)(-1 + 3) = -4 \cdot 2 = -8$

88. $(-2 + 3)(-2 - 3) = (1)(-5) = -5$

89. $(-2)^2 + 2(-2)(3) + 3^2 = 4 - 12 + 9 = 1$

90. $(-2)^2 - 2(-2)(3) + 3^2 = 4 + 12 + 9$
$= 25$

91. $(-2)^3 - 3^3 = -8 - 27 = -35$

92. $(-2)^3 + 3^3 = -8 + 27 = 19$

93. $\frac{3 + (-1)}{-2 + 3} = \frac{2}{1} = 2$

94. $\frac{3 - (-1)}{2(3) - (-2)} = \frac{4}{6 + 2} = \frac{4}{8} = \frac{1}{2}$

95. $|-2 - 3| = |-5| = 5$

96. $|3 - (-2)| = |3 + 2| = |5| = 5$

97. $(-2 + 3)(-1) = (1)(-1) = -1$

98. $(-2)(-1) + (3)(-1) = 2 + (-3) = -1$

99. Commutative property of addition

100. Multiplication property of zero

101. Distributive property

102. Additive inverse property

103. Associative property of multiplication

104. Commutative property of addition

105. Multiplicative identity

106. Multiplicative inverse

107. Multiplicative inverse

108. Multiplicative identity

109. Multiplication property of zero

110. Commutative property of addition

111. Additive identity

112. Distributive property

113. Additive inverse

114. Associative property of addition

115. $3x - 3a = 3(x - a)$

116. $5x - 5y = 5(x - y)$

117. $3 \cdot w + 3 \cdot 1 = 3w + 3$

118. $2(m + 14) = 2m + 2 \cdot 14 = 2m + 28$

119. $7x + 7 \cdot 1 = 7(x + 1)$

120. $3w + 3 = 3w + 3 \cdot 1 = 3(w + 1)$

121. $5(x - 5) = 5x - 5 \cdot 5 = 5x - 25$

122. $13(b - 3) = 13b - 13 \cdot 3 = 13b - 39$

123. $-3 \cdot 2x - (-3)(5) = -6x + 15$

124. $-2(5 - 4x) = -2 \cdot 5 - (-2)(4x)$
$$= -10 + 8x$$

125. $p \cdot 1 - pt = p(1 - t)$

126. $ab + b = ab + b \cdot 1 = b(a + 1)$

127. $3a + 7 + 4a - 5 = 7a + 2$

128. $2m + 6 + m - 2 = 3m + 4$

129. $5t - 20 - 6t + 18 = -t - 2$

130. $2(x - 3) + 2(3 - x) = 2x - 6 + 6 - 2x$
$$= 0$$

131. $-a + 2 + 2 - a = -2a + 4$

132. $-(w - y) + 3(y - w)$
$$= -w + y + 3y - 3w$$
$$= -4w + 4y$$

133. $5 - 3x + 6 + 7x + 28 - 6 = 4x + 33$

134. $7 - 2(x - 7) + 7 - x$
$$= 7 - 2x + 14 + 7 - x$$
$$= -3x + 28$$

135. $0.2x + 0.02 - x - 0.50 = -0.8x - 0.48$

136. $0.1(x - 0.2) - (x + 0.1)$
$$= 0.1x - 0.02 - x - 0.1$$
$$= 0.1x - 1.0x - 0.02 - 0.10$$
$$= -0.9x - 0.12$$

137. $0.05x + 0.15 - 0.10x - 2$
$$= -0.05x - 1.85$$

138. $0.02(x + 100) - 0.2(x + 50)$
$$= 0.02x + 2 - 0.20x - 10$$
$$= -0.18x - 8$$

139. $\frac{1}{2}x + 2 - \frac{1}{4}x + 2 = \frac{1}{4}x + 4$

140. $\frac{1}{2}(2x - 1) + \frac{1}{4}(x + 1)$
$$= x - \frac{1}{2} + \frac{1}{4}x + \frac{1}{4}$$
$$= \frac{4}{4}x + \frac{1}{4}x - \frac{2}{4} + \frac{1}{4} = \frac{5}{4}x - \frac{1}{4}$$

141. $\frac{-9x^2}{3} - \frac{6x}{3} + \frac{3}{3} = -3x^2 - 2x + 1$

142. $\frac{4x}{-2} - \frac{2}{-2} + \frac{4x}{2} + \frac{2}{2}$
$$= -2x + 1 + 2x + 1 = 2$$

143. $32(4)(-6 + 6) = 32(4)(0) = 0$,
additive inverse, multiplication property of 0

144. $(24 \cdot 4)\frac{1}{24} = 4\left(24 \cdot \frac{1}{24}\right) = 4 \cdot 1 = 4$,
multiplicative inverse, multiplicative identity

145. $768(4) + 768(6) = 768(10) = 7680$,
distributive property

146. $28(4) + 28(6) = 28(4 + 6) = 28 \cdot 10$
$= 280$, distributive property

147. $12 \cdot 4 + (-6 + 6) = 48 + 0 = 48$,
associative property of addition, additive
inverse

148. $(42 + (-6)) + 6 = 42 + (-6 + 6)$
$= 42 + 0 = 42$, associative property of
addition, additive inverse, additive identity

149. $752(-6) + 752(6) = 752(0) = 0$,
distributive property, additive inverse

150. $37(6) + 37(-6) = 37(6 + (-6)) = 37 \cdot 0$
$= 0$, distributive property, additive inverse,
multiplication property of 0

151. $(47 \cdot 6)\frac{4}{24} = 47 \cdot 1 = 47$, associative
property of multiplication, multiplicative
inverse

152. $3(24) + 3(6) = 3(24 + 6) = 3 \cdot 30 = 90$,
distributive property

153. $(-6 \cdot 24)\frac{1}{6} = 24(-6 \cdot \frac{1}{6}) = -24$,
commutative property of multiplication,
associative property of multiplication

154. $(-6 \cdot 4)\frac{1}{-6} = 4 \cdot (-6) \cdot \frac{1}{-6} = 4 \cdot 1 = 4$
commutative property of multiplication,
associative property of multiplication,
multiplicative inverse
155. $5(-6 + 6)(4 + 24) = 5 \cdot 0 \cdot 28 = 0$,
additive inverse, multiplication property of 0
156. $[4(-6) + 7 \cdot 6][24 + (-6)(4)]$
$= [-24 + 42][0] = 0$, multiplication property
of zero
157. $\frac{1}{0.2} + \frac{1}{0.5} = 7$ shingles per minute
158. Cost is the product of the area in square
yards and the price per square yard. So the cost
is $20x(x + 2)$ or $20x^2 + 4x$ dollars
159. $20{,}470(1.05)^{12} \approx 36{,}761$
The car will cost \$36,761 in the year 2000.
The first year in which the car is over \$30,000
will be 2006.
160. Volume is $7.5\pi(12)^2 \cdot 3$ or 10,179 gallons

CHAPTER 1 TEST

1. List the elements in A or in B:
$A \cup B = \{2, 3, 4, 5, 6, 7, 8, 10\}$
2. Only 6 and 7 are in both B and C. So
$B \cap C = \{6, 7\}$.
3. The intersection of $A = \{2, 4, 6, 8, 10\}$
with $B \cup C = \{3, 4, 5, 6, 7, 8, 9, 10\}$ is
$\{4, 6, 8, 10\}$.
4. $\{0, 8\}$
5. $\{-4, 0, 8\}$
6. $\{-4, -\frac{1}{2}, 0, 1.65, 8\}$
7. $\{-\sqrt{3}, \sqrt{5}, \pi\}$
8. $6 + (-15) = -9$
9. $\sqrt{(-2)^2 - 4(3)(-5)} = \sqrt{4 - (-60)}$
$\qquad\qquad\qquad = \sqrt{64} = 8$
10. $-5 + 6 - 12 = -17 + 6 = -11$
11. $0.02 - 2 = -1.98$
12. $\frac{-3 - (-7)}{3 - 5} = \frac{-3 + 7}{-2} = \frac{4}{-2} = -2$
13. $\frac{-8}{2} = -4$
14. $\left(\frac{2}{3} - 1\right)\left(\frac{1}{3} - \frac{1}{2}\right) = \left(-\frac{1}{3}\right)\left(-\frac{1}{6}\right)$
$\qquad\qquad = \frac{1}{18}$

15. $-\frac{4}{7} - \frac{1}{2}\left(24 - \frac{8}{7}\right) = -\frac{4}{7} - 12 + \frac{4}{7}$
$\qquad\qquad\qquad\qquad = -12$
16. $|\,3 - 10\,| = |-7| = 7$
17. $5 - 2\,|-4\,| = 5 - 2 \cdot 4 = 5 - 8 = -3$
18. $(452 + 695)[-8 + 8] = (452 + 695)[0]$
$\qquad\qquad\qquad\qquad = 0$
19. $478(8 + 2) = 478(10) = 4780$
20. $-24 - 4(6 - 9 \cdot 8) = -24 - 4(-66)$
$\qquad\qquad\qquad\qquad = 240$
21. $-3 + 5 - 18 - 4 + 8 - 18 = -43 + 13$
$\qquad\qquad\qquad\qquad\qquad = -30$
22. $(-4)^2 - 4(-3)(2) = 16 + 24 = 40$
23. $\frac{(-3)^2 - (-4)^2}{-4 - (-3)} = \frac{9 - 16}{-1} = 7$
24. $\frac{(-3)(-4) - 6(2)}{(-4)^2 - 2^2} = \frac{12 - 12}{16 - 4} = \frac{0}{12} = 0$
25. Distributive property
26. Commutative property of multiplication
27. Associative property of addition
28. Additive inverse property
29. Commutative property of multiplication
30. Multiplication property of 0
31. $3m - 15 + 8m + 12 = 11m - 3$
32. $x + 3 - 0.05x - 0.1 = 0.95x + 2.9$
33. $\frac{1}{2}x - \frac{4}{2} + \frac{1}{4}x + \frac{3}{4} = \frac{2}{4}x + \frac{1}{4}x - \frac{8}{4} + \frac{3}{4}$
$\qquad\qquad\qquad = \frac{3}{4}x - \frac{5}{4}$
34. $-3x^2 + 6y - 6y + 8x^2 = 5x^2$
35. $\frac{-6x^2}{-2} - \frac{4x}{-2} + \frac{2}{-2} = 3x^2 + 2x - 1$
36. $\frac{-8xy}{2} - \frac{6xy}{2} = -4xy - 3xy = -7xy$
37. $5x - 40 = 5x - 5 \cdot 8 = 5(x - 8)$
38. $7t - 7 = 7t - 7 \cdot 1 = 7(t - 1)$
39. $\frac{1 \text{ tree}}{0.0625 \text{ hours}} = 16$ trees/hour
40. The perimeter is $2x + 2(x - 4)$ or
$4x - 8$ feet. If $x = 9$, the perimeter is
$4 \cdot 9 - 8$ or 28 feet. The area is $x^2 - 4x$. If
$x = 9$, then the area is $9^2 - 4 \cdot 9$, or 45 ft^2.
41. $6(1.03)^{25} \approx 12.6$ billion

2.1 WARM-UPS

1. False, it is equivalent to $-2x = 5$.

2. True, because
$x - (x - 3) = x - x + 3 = 3$.

3. False, multiply each side by $\frac{4}{3}$.

4. True, because we can multiply each side by -1.

5. True, because all of the denominators divide into the LCD.

6. True, subtract 5 from each side and then divide each side by 3.

7. True, because it simplifies to $8 = 12$.

8. True, it is equivalent to $x = -3$.

9. True, it is equivalent to $0.8x = 0.8x$.

10. True, since it is equivalent to $3x - 12 = 0$.

2.1 EXERCISES

1. An equation is a sentence that expresses the equality of two algebraic expressions.

2. A number satisfies the equation if the equation is true when the variable is replaced by the number.

3. Equivalent equation are equations that have the same solution set.

4. A linear equation in one variable is an equation of the form $ax + b = 0$.

5. If the equation involves fractions then multiply each side by the LCD.

6. An identity is an equation that is satisfied by all values of the variable for which both sides are defined.

7. A conditional equation is an equation that has at least one solution but is not an identity.

8. An inconsistent equation is an equation that has no solution.

9. Yes, because $3 \cdot (-4) + 7 = -5$ is correct.

10. Yes, because $-3(-6) - 5 = 13$ is correct.

11. Yes, because $\frac{1}{2} \cdot 12 - 4 = \frac{1}{3} \cdot 12 - 2$.

12. Yes, because $\frac{9 - 7}{2} - \frac{1}{3} = \frac{9 - 7}{3}$.

13. No, because $0.2(200 - 50) = 30$ and $20 - 0.05 \cdot 200 = 10$.

14. Yes, because $0.12 \cdot 50 - (4 - 50) = 52$ and $1.02 \cdot 50 + 1 = 52$.

15. No because $0.1 \cdot 80 - 30 = -22$ and

$16 - 0.06 \cdot 80 = 11.2$.

16. Yes, because $0.08 \cdot 20 + 3.2 = 4.8$ and $0.1 \cdot 20 + 2.8 = 4.8$.

17.
$$-72 - x + 72 = 15 + 72$$
$$-x = 87$$
$$(-1)(-x) = -1 \cdot 87$$
$$x = -87$$

The solution set is $\{-87\}$.

18.
$$51 - x = -9$$
$$-x = -9 - 51$$
$$-x = -60$$
$$x = 60$$

The solution set is $\{60\}$.

19.
$$-3x - 19 = 5 - 2x$$
$$-3x = 24 - 2x$$
$$-3x + 2x = 24$$
$$-x = 24$$
$$x = -24$$

The solution set is $\{-24\}$.

20.
$$-5x + 4 = -9 - 4x$$
$$-5x = -13 - 4x$$
$$-x = -13$$
$$x = 13$$

The solution set is $\{13\}$.

21.
$$2x - 3 + 3 = 0 + 3$$
$$2x = 3$$
$$\frac{2x}{2} = \frac{3}{2}$$
$$x = \frac{3}{2}$$

The solution set is $\left\{ \frac{3}{2} \right\}$.

22.
$$5x + 7 = 0$$
$$5x + 7 - 7 = 0 - 7$$
$$5x = -7$$
$$x = -\frac{7}{5}$$

The solution set is $\left\{ -\frac{7}{5} \right\}$.

23.
$$-2x + 5 - 5 = 7 - 5$$
$$-2x = 2$$
$$\frac{-2x}{-2} = \frac{2}{-2}$$
$$x = -1$$

The solution set is $\{-1\}$.

24. $-3x - 4 = 11$

$$-3x = 15$$
$$x = -5$$

The solution set is $\{-5\}$.

25. $-12x - 15 + 15 = 21 + 15$

$$-12x = 36$$
$$\frac{-12x}{-12} = \frac{36}{-12}$$
$$x = -3$$

The solution set is $\{-3\}$.

26. $-13x + 7 = -19$

$$-13x = -26$$
$$x = 2$$

The solution set is $\{2\}$.

27. $26 - 16 = 4x + 16 - 16$

$$10 = 4x$$
$$\frac{10}{4} = \frac{4x}{4}$$
$$\frac{5}{2} = x$$

The solution set is $\left\{\frac{5}{2}\right\}$.

28. $14 = -5x - 21$

$$35 = -5x$$
$$-7 = x$$

The solution set is $\{-7\}$.

29. $-3(x - 16) = 12 - x$

$$-3x + 48 = 12 - x$$
$$-3x = -36 - x$$
$$-2x = -36$$
$$x = 18$$

The solution set is $\{18\}$.

30. $-2(x + 17) = 13 - x$

$$-2x - 34 = 13 - x$$
$$-2x = 47 - x$$
$$-x = 47$$
$$x = -47$$

The solution set is $\{-47\}$.

31. $2x + 18 - x = 36$

$$x + 18 = 36$$
$$x + 18 - 18 = 36 - 18$$
$$x = 18$$

The solution set is $\{18\}$.

32. $3(x - 13) - x = 9$

$$3x - 39 - x = 9$$
$$2x - 39 = 9$$
$$2x = 48$$
$$x = 24$$

The solution set is $\{24\}$.

33. $2 + 3x - 3 = x - 1$

$$3x - 1 = x - 1$$
$$3x - x = -1 + 1$$
$$2x = 0$$
$$x = 0$$

The solution set is $\{0\}$.

34. $x + 9 = 1 - 4x + 8$

$$x + 9 = 9 - 4x$$
$$5x = 0$$
$$x = 0$$

The solution set is $\{0\}$.

35. $-\frac{7}{3}\left(-\frac{3}{7}x\right) = -\frac{7}{3}(4)$

$$x = -\frac{28}{3}$$

The solution set is $\left\{-\frac{28}{3}\right\}$.

36. $\frac{5}{6}x = -2$

$$\frac{6}{5}\left(\frac{5}{6}x\right) = \frac{6}{5}(-2)$$
$$x = -\frac{12}{5}$$

The solution set is $\left\{-\frac{12}{5}\right\}$.

37. $-\frac{5}{7}x - 1 = 3$

$$-\frac{5}{7}x = 4$$
$$-\frac{7}{5}\left(-\frac{5}{7}x\right) = -\frac{7}{5}(4)$$

$$x = -\frac{28}{5}$$

The solution set is $\left\{-\frac{28}{5}\right\}$.

38. $4 - \frac{3}{5}x = -6$

$$5\left(4 - \frac{3}{5}x\right) = 5(-6)$$
$$20 - 3x = -30$$
$$-3x = -50$$
$$x = \frac{50}{3}$$

The solution set is $\left\{\frac{50}{3}\right\}$.

39. $6\left(\frac{x}{3} + \frac{1}{2}\right) = 6 \cdot \frac{7}{6}$

$$2x + 3 = 7$$

$$2x = 4$$
$$x = 2$$
The solution set is $\{2\}$.

40. $\frac{1}{4} + \frac{1}{5} = \frac{x}{2}$
$$20\left(\frac{1}{4} + \frac{1}{5}\right) = 20 \cdot \frac{x}{2}$$
$$5 + 4 = 10x$$
$$9 = 10x$$
$$\frac{9}{10} = x$$
The solution set is $\left\{\frac{9}{10}\right\}$.

41. $3\left(\frac{2}{3}x + 5\right) = 3\left(-\frac{1}{3}x + 17\right)$
$$2x + 15 = -x + 51$$
$$3x + 15 = 51$$
$$3x = 36$$
$$x = 12$$
The solution set is $\{12\}$.

42. $\frac{1}{4}x - 6 = -\frac{3}{4}x + 14$
$$4\left(\frac{1}{4}x - 6\right) = 4\left(-\frac{3}{4}x + 14\right)$$
$$x - 24 = -3x + 56$$
$$4x - 24 = 56$$
$$4x = 80$$
$$x = 20$$
The solution set is $\{20\}$.

43. $4\left(\frac{1}{2}x + \frac{1}{4}\right) = 4 \cdot \frac{1}{4}\left(x - 6\right)$
$$2x + 1 = x - 6$$
$$x + 1 = -6$$
$$x = -7$$
The solution set is $\{-7\}$.

44. $\frac{1}{3}(x - 2) = \frac{2}{3}x - \frac{13}{3}$
$$3 \cdot \frac{1}{3}(x - 2) = 3 \cdot \frac{2}{3}x - 3 \cdot \frac{13}{3}$$
$$x - 2 = 2x - 13$$
$$x = 2x - 11$$
$$-x = -11$$
$$x = 11$$
The solution set is $\{11\}$.

45. $4\left(8 - \frac{x-2}{2}\right) = 4\left(\frac{x}{4}\right)$
$$32 - 2(x - 2) = x$$
$$32 - 2x + 4 = x$$
$$-3x = -36$$

$$x = 12$$
The solution set is $\{12\}$.

46. $\frac{x}{3} - \frac{x-5}{5} = 3$
$$15 \cdot \frac{x}{3} - 15 \cdot \frac{x-5}{5} = 15 \cdot 3$$
$$5x - 3(x - 5) = 45$$
$$5x - 3x + 15 = 45$$
$$2x + 15 = 45$$
$$2x = 30$$
$$x = 15$$
The solution set is $\{15\}$.

47. $6\left(\frac{y-3}{3}\right) - 6\left(\frac{y-2}{2}\right) = 6(-1)$
$$2y - 6 - 3y + 6 = -6$$
$$-y = -6$$
$$y = 6$$
The solution set is $\{6\}$.

48. $\frac{x-2}{2} - \frac{x-3}{4} = \frac{7}{4}$
$$4 \cdot \frac{x-2}{2} - 4 \cdot \frac{x-3}{4} = 4 \cdot \frac{7}{4}$$
$$2(x - 2) - (x - 3) = 7$$
$$2x - 4 - x + 3 = 7$$
$$x - 1 = 7$$
$$x = 8$$
The solution set is $\{8\}$.

49. $10(x - 0.2x) = 10(72)$
$$10x - 2x = 720$$
$$8x = 720$$
$$x = 90$$
The solution set is $\{90\}$.

50. $x - 0.1x = 63$
$$0.9x = 63$$
$$x = \frac{63}{0.9} = 70$$

The solution set is $\{70\}$.

51. $0.03x + 0.03(200) + 0.05x = 86$
$$0.08x + 6 = 86$$
$$0.08x = 80$$
$$x = 1000$$
The solution set is $\{1000\}$.

52. $0.02(x - 100) + 0.06x = 62$
$$0.02x - 2 + 0.06x = 62$$
$$0.08x = 64$$
$$x = 800$$
The solution set is $\{800\}$.

53. $0.1x + 0.05x - 0.05(300) = 105$
$$0.15x - 15 = 105$$
$$0.15x = 120$$
$$x = 800$$
The solution set is $\{800\}$.

54. $0.2x - 0.05(x - 100) = 35$
$$0.20x - 0.05x + 5 = 35$$
$$0.15x + 5 = 35$$
$$0.15x = 30$$
$$x = 200$$
The solution set is $\{200\}$.

55. $2(x + 1) = 2(x + 3)$
$$2x + 2 = 2x + 6$$
$$2 = 6$$
The solution set is $\emptyset$. The equation is inconsistent.

56. $2x + 3x = 6x$
$$5x = 6x$$
$$0 = x$$
The solution set is $\{0\}$. The equation is conditional.

57. $2x = 2x$ The solution set is R. The equation is an identity.

58. $4x - 3x = x$
$$x = x$$
The solution set is the set of all real numbers. The equation is an identity.

59. $x + x = 2$
$$2x = 2$$
$$x = 1$$
Solution set: $\{1\}$ Equation is conditional.

60. $4x - 3x = 5$
$$x = 5$$
The solution set is $\{5\}$. The equation is conditional.

61. $x = x$
Solution set: R Equation is an identity.

62. $5x \div 5 = x$
$$x = x$$
The solution set is R. The equation is an identity.

63. $x \cdot x = x^2$
$$x^2 = x^2$$
Solution set: R Equation is an identity.

64. $\frac{2x}{2x} = 1$

$\frac{x}{x} = 1$
This equation is satisfied by any nonzero real number. The solution set is $\{x \mid x \neq 0\}$. The equation is an identity.

65. $2(x + 3) - 7 = 5(5 - x) + 7(x + 1)$
$$2x + 6 - 7 = 25 - 5x + 7x + 7$$
$$2x - 1 = 32 + 2x$$
$$-1 = 32$$
The solution set is $\emptyset$. The equation is inconsistent.

66. $2(x + 4) - 8 = 2x + 1$
$$2x + 8 - 8 = 2x + 1$$
$$2x = 2x + 1$$
$$0 = 1$$
The solution set is $\emptyset$. The equation is inconsistent.

67. $x + 3 - \frac{7}{2} = \frac{3}{2}x + \frac{3}{2} - \frac{1}{2}x - 2$
$$2x + 6 - 7 = 3x + 3 - x - 4$$
$$2x - 1 = 2x - 1$$
Solution set: R Equation is an identity.

68. $\frac{1}{2}x + 2 - 2 = \frac{1}{2}x$

$$\frac{1}{2}x = \frac{1}{2}x$$

Solution set: R Equation is an identity.

69. $x + 3 - 3.5 = 1.5x + 1.5$
$$x - 0.5 = 1.5x + 1.5$$
$$10x - 5 = 15x + 15$$
$$-20 = 5x$$
$$-4 = x$$
The solution set is $\{-4\}$. Conditional

70. $0.5x + 2 - 2 = 0.75x - 1.75$
$$0.5x = 0.75x - 1.75$$
$$50x = 75x - 175$$
$$-25x = -175$$
$$x = 7$$
The solution set is $\{7\}$. Conditional

71. $4 - 12x + 18 + 1 = 3 + 10 - 2x$
$$-12x + 23 = 13 - 2x$$
$$-10x = -10$$
$$x = 1$$
The solution set is $\{1\}$.

72. $3x - 30 + 10x = 4x - 32 + 3$
$$13x - 30 = 4x - 29$$
$$9x = 1$$

$$x = \tfrac{1}{9}$$

The solution set is $\left\{ \tfrac{1}{9} \right\}$.

73. $\tfrac{1}{2}y - \tfrac{1}{12} + \tfrac{2}{3} = \tfrac{5}{6} + \tfrac{1}{6} - y$

$$6y - 1 + 8 = 10 + 2 - 12y$$
$$6y + 7 = 12 - 12y$$
$$18y = 5$$
$$y = \tfrac{5}{18}$$

The solution set is $\left\{ \tfrac{5}{18} \right\}$.

74. $\tfrac{3}{4} - \tfrac{1}{6}y + \tfrac{2}{3} = 3y - \tfrac{3}{4}$
$$9 - 2y + 8 = 36y - 9$$
$$-2y + 17 = 36y - 9$$
$$-38y = -26$$
$$y = \tfrac{13}{19}$$

The solution set is $\left\{ \tfrac{13}{19} \right\}$.

75. $8 - 40x + 600 = 200x + 3$
$$-40x + 608 = 200x + 3$$
$$-240x = -605$$
$$x = \tfrac{605}{240} = \tfrac{121}{48}$$

The solution set is $\left\{ \tfrac{121}{48} \right\}$.

76. $20x - \tfrac{5}{2} + \tfrac{5}{2} = 11 - \tfrac{2}{3}x - 11$

$$20x = -\tfrac{2}{3}x$$
$$60x = -2x$$
$$62x = 0$$
$$x = 0$$

The solution set is $\{0\}$.

77. $12 \cdot \dfrac{a-3}{4} - 12 \cdot \dfrac{2a-5}{2}$
$$= 12 \cdot \dfrac{a+1}{3} - 12 \cdot \dfrac{1}{6}$$

$$3a - 9 - 12a + 30 = 4a + 4 - 2$$
$$-9a + 21 = 4a + 2$$
$$-13a = -19$$

$$a = \tfrac{19}{13}$$

The solution set is $\left\{ \tfrac{19}{13} \right\}$.

78. $\tfrac{b}{6} - \tfrac{2b}{5} + \tfrac{1}{6} = \tfrac{1}{3} - \tfrac{b}{2} + \tfrac{1}{2}$

$$30\left(\tfrac{b}{6} - \tfrac{2b}{5} + \tfrac{1}{6}\right) = 30\left(\tfrac{1}{3} - \tfrac{b}{2} + \tfrac{1}{2}\right)$$
$$5b - 12b + 5 = 10 - 15b + 15$$
$$-7b + 5 = -15b + 25$$
$$8b = 20$$
$$b = \tfrac{20}{8} = \tfrac{5}{2}$$

The solution set is $\left\{ \tfrac{5}{2} \right\}$.

79. $1.3 - 1.2 + 0.6x = 0.02x + 0.3$
$$130 - 120 + 60x = 2x + 30$$
$$10 + 60x = 2x + 30$$
$$58x = 20$$
$$x = \tfrac{20}{58} = \tfrac{10}{29}$$

The solution set is $\left\{ \tfrac{10}{29} \right\}$.

80. $5 - 0.3x = 5.4x + 200$
$$50 - 3x = 54x + 2000$$
$$-57x = 1950$$
$$x = -\tfrac{1950}{57} = -\tfrac{650}{19}$$

The solution set is $\left\{ -\tfrac{650}{19} \right\}$.

81. $3x = 9$
$$x = 3$$
Solution set: $\{3\}$

82. $5x + 1 = 0$
$$5x = -1$$
$$x = -\tfrac{1}{5}$$
The solution set is $\left\{ -\tfrac{1}{5} \right\}$.

83. $7 - z = -9$
$$16 = z$$
Solution set: $\{16\}$

84. $-3 - z = 3$
$$-z = 6$$
$$z = -6$$
The solution set is $\{-6\}$.

22

85. $\frac{2}{3}x = \frac{1}{2}$

$$x = \frac{3}{2} \cdot \frac{1}{2} = \frac{3}{4}$$

Solution set: $\left\{\frac{3}{4}\right\}$

86. $\frac{3}{2}x = -\frac{9}{5}$

$$x = \frac{2}{3} \cdot \left(-\frac{9}{5}\right) = -\frac{18}{15}$$

Solution set: $\left\{-\frac{6}{5}\right\}$

87. $-\frac{3}{5}y = 9$

$$y = -\frac{5}{3} \cdot 9 = -15$$

Solution set: $\{-15\}$

88. $-\frac{2}{7}w = 4$

$$w = -\frac{7}{2} \cdot 4 = -14$$

Solution set: $\{-14\}$

89. $3y + 5 = 4y - 1$

$$6 = y$$

The solution set is $\{6\}$.

90. $2y - 7 = 3y + 1$

$$-8 = y$$

The solution set is $\{-8\}$.

91. $5x + 10x + 20 = 110$

$$15x = 90$$
$$x = 6$$

Solution set: $\{6\}$

92. $1 - 3(x - 2) = 4(x - 1) - 3$

$$1 - 3x + 6 = 4x - 4 - 3$$
$$7 - 3x = 4x - 7$$
$$-7x = -14$$
$$x = 2$$

The solution set is $\{2\}$.

93. $15\left(\frac{p+7}{3}\right) - 15\left(\frac{p-2}{5}\right)$

$$= 15\left(\frac{7}{3}\right) - 15\left(\frac{p}{15}\right)$$

$$5p + 35 - 3p + 6 = 35 - p$$
$$2p + 41 = 35 - p$$
$$3p = -6$$
$$p = -2$$

Solution set: $\{-2\}$

94. $8 \cdot \frac{w-3}{8} - 8 \cdot \frac{5-w}{4}$

$$= 8 \cdot \frac{4w-1}{8} - 8 \cdot 1$$

$w - 3 - 2(5 - w) = 4w - 1 - 8$

$$w - 3 - 10 + 2w = 4w - 9$$
$$3w - 13 = 4w - 9$$
$$-w - 13 = -9$$
$$-w = 4$$
$$w = -4$$

The solution set is $\{-4\}$.

95. $x - 0.06x = 50,000$

$$0.94x = 50,000$$
$$x = \frac{50,000}{0.94}$$

Solution set: $\{53,191.49\}$

96. $x - 0.05x = 800$

$$0.95x = 800$$
$$x = \frac{800}{0.95} = 842.11$$

The solution set is $\{842.11\}$.

97. $2.365x = 14.8095 - 3.694$

$$2.365x = 11.1155$$
$$x = \frac{11.1155}{2.365}$$
$$x = 4.7$$

Solution set: $\{4.7\}$

98. $-3.48x + 6.981 = 4.329x - 6.851$

$$-7.809x = -13.832$$
$$x = \frac{-13.832}{-7.809} = 1.7713$$

The solution set is $\{1.7713\}$.

99. a) For 1992, $x = 7$.

$$0.45(7) + 39.05 = 42.2$$

Public school enrollment in 1992 was 42.2 million.

b) $\quad 0.45x + 39.05 = 50$

$$0.45x = 10.95$$
$$x \approx 24.3$$

So in 24.3 years (or during the 25th year) public school enrollment will reach 50 million. $1985 + 25 = 2010$.

c) Judging from the graph, enrollment is increasing.

100. a) $553.7(8) + 27,966 \approx 32,396$

Average teacher salary in 1993 was $32,396.

b) $\quad 553.7x + 27,966 = 40,000$

$$553.7x = 12034$$
$$x \approx 22$$

Average teacher salary will reach $40,000 in the year $1985 + 22$, or 2007.

101. a) The year in which the U.S. generated over 100 million tons of solid waste was 1964.

b)
$0.576n + 3.78 = 0.13(3.14n + 87.1)$
$0.576n + 3.78 = 0.13 \cdot 3.14n + 0.13 \cdot 87.1$
$(0.576 - 0.13 \cdot 3.14)n = 0.13 \cdot 87.1 - 3.78$
$$n = \frac{0.13 \cdot 87.1 - 3.78}{0.576 - 0.13 \cdot 3.14}$$
$n = 44.95$

U.S. recovered 13% in 1960 + 45, or 2005.

102. $0.576n + 3.78 = 0.14(3.14n + 87.1)$
$$0.576n + 3.78 = 0.4396n + 12.194$$
$$0.1364n = 8.414$$
$$n \approx 61.7$$

The year in which 14% of the solid waste will be recovered is 1960 + 62, or approximately 2022.

2.2 WARM-UPS

1. False, P is on both sides of the equation.
2. False, because we use the distributive property to factor out P on the right side.
3. False, because we divide each side by Pr to get $t = \frac{I}{Pr}$.
4. True, $\frac{5 \cdot 6}{2} = 15$.
5. False, $P = 2L + 2W$.
6. True, $V = LWH$.
7. False, $A = \frac{1}{2}h(b_1 + b_2)$.
8. True, $x - y = 5$ is equivalent to $x = 5 + y$, or $y = x - 5$.
9. True, because $-2(-3) - 4 = 6 - 4 = 2$.
10. False, perimeter is the distance around the outside edge.

2.2 EXERCISES

1. A formula is an equation involving two or more variables.
2. A formula is used to express a relationship between variables.
3. Solving for a variable means to rewrite the formula with the indicated variable isolated.
4. If a variable occurs twice, then we usually use the distributive property to isolate it.
5. To find the value a variable, solve for that variable, then replace all other variables with given numbers.

6. The formula for the volume of a rectangular solid is $V = LWH$.

7. $\dfrac{I}{Pr} = \dfrac{Prt}{Pr}$
$\dfrac{I}{Pr} = t$
$t = \dfrac{I}{Pr}$

8. $d = rt$
$\dfrac{d}{t} = \dfrac{rt}{t}$
$r = \dfrac{d}{t}$

9. $F - 32 = \frac{9}{5}C$
$\frac{5}{9}(F - 32) = \frac{5}{9} \cdot \frac{9}{5}C$
$C = \frac{5}{9}(F - 32)$

10. $A = \frac{1}{2}bh$
$2A = bh$
$\dfrac{2A}{b} = \dfrac{bh}{b}$
$h = \dfrac{2A}{b}$

11. $\dfrac{A}{L} = \dfrac{LW}{L}$
$\dfrac{A}{L} = W$
$W = \dfrac{A}{L}$

12. $C = 2\pi r$
$\dfrac{C}{2\pi} = \dfrac{2\pi r}{2\pi}$
$r = \dfrac{C}{2\pi}$

13. $2A = 2 \cdot \frac{1}{2}(b_1 + b_2)$
$2A = b_1 + b_2$
$2A - b_2 = b_1$
$b_1 = 2A - b_2$

14. $A = \frac{1}{2}(b_1 + b_2)$
$2A = b_1 + b_2$
$2A - b_1 = b_2$
$b_2 = 2A - b_1$

15. $3y = -2x + 9$
$\dfrac{3y}{3} = \dfrac{-2x}{3} + \dfrac{9}{3}$
$y = -\frac{2}{3}x + 3$

16. $4y + 5x = 8$
$4y = -5x + 8$
$y = -\frac{5}{4}x + 2$

17. $x - y = 4$
$$-y = -x + 4$$
$$\frac{-y}{-1} = \frac{-x}{-1} + \frac{4}{-1}$$
$$y = x - 4$$

18. $y - x = 6$
$$y = x + 6$$

19. $-\frac{1}{3}y = -\frac{1}{2}x + 2$
$$-3\left(-\frac{1}{3}y\right) = -3\left(-\frac{1}{2}x + 2\right)$$
$$y = \frac{3}{2}x - 6$$

20. $\frac{1}{3}x - \frac{1}{4}y = 1$
$$-\frac{1}{4}y = -\frac{1}{3}x + 1$$
$$-4\left(-\frac{1}{4}y\right) = -4\left(-\frac{1}{3}x + 1\right)$$
$$y = \frac{4}{3}x - 4$$

21. $y - 2 = \frac{1}{2}x - \frac{3}{2}$
$$y = \frac{1}{2}x + \frac{1}{2}$$

22. $y - 3 = \frac{1}{3}(x - 4)$
$$y - 3 = \frac{1}{3}x - \frac{4}{3}$$
$$y = \frac{1}{3}x - \frac{4}{3} + \frac{9}{3}$$
$$y = \frac{1}{3}x + \frac{5}{3}$$

23. $A - P = Prt$
$$\frac{A - P}{Pr} = \frac{Prt}{Pr}$$
$$\frac{A - P}{Pr} = t$$
$$t = \frac{A - P}{Pr}$$

24. $A = P + Prt$
$$A - P = Prt$$
$$\frac{A - P}{Pt} = \frac{Prt}{Pt}$$
$$r = \frac{A - P}{Pt}$$

25. $a(b + 1) = 1$
$$\frac{a(b + 1)}{b + 1} = \frac{1}{b + 1}$$
$$a = \frac{1}{b + 1}$$

26. $y - wy = m$
$$y(1 - w) = m$$
$$y = \frac{m}{1 - w}$$

27. $xy - y = -5 - 7$
$$y(x - 1) = -12$$
$$y = \frac{-12(-1)}{(x - 1)(-1)}$$
$$y = \frac{12}{1 - x}$$

28. $xy + 5 = x + 7$
$$xy - x + 5 = 7$$
$$xy - x = 2$$
$$x(y - 1) = 2$$
$$x = \frac{2}{y - 1}$$

29. $xy^2 + xz^2 - xw^2 = -6$
$$x(y^2 + z^2 - w^2) = -6$$
$$x = \frac{-6}{y^2 + z^2 - w^2}$$
$$x = \frac{6}{w^2 - y^2 - z^2}$$

30. $xz^2 + xw^2 = xy^2 + 5$
$$xz^2 + xw^2 - xy^2 = 5$$
$$x(z^2 + w^2 - y^2) = 5$$
$$x = \frac{5}{z^2 + w^2 - y^2}$$

31. $RR_1R_2\left(\frac{1}{R}\right)$
$$= RR_1R_2\left(\frac{1}{R_1}\right) + RR_1R_2\left(\frac{1}{R_2}\right)$$
$$R_1R_2 = RR_2 + RR_1$$
$$R_1R_2 - RR_1 = RR_2$$
$$R_1(R_2 - R) = RR_2$$
$$R_1 = \frac{RR_2}{R_2 - R}$$

32. $\frac{1}{a} + \frac{1}{b} = \frac{1}{2}$
$$2ab \cdot \frac{1}{a} + 2ab \cdot \frac{1}{b} = 2ab \cdot \frac{1}{2}$$
$$2b + 2a = ab$$
$$2b = ab - 2a$$
$$2b = a(b - 2)$$
$$\frac{2b}{b - 2} = a$$
$$a = \frac{2b}{b - 2}$$

33. $3.35x + 4.58x = 44.3 + 54.6$
$$x(3.35 + 4.58) = 44.3 + 54.6$$
$$x = \frac{44.3 + 54.6}{3.35 + 4.58}$$
$$x \approx 12.472$$

34. $-4.487 + 22.49x = 55.83 + 33.41$
$x(-4.487 + 22.49) = 55.83 + 33.41$
$$x = \frac{55.83 + 33.41}{-4.487 + 22.49}$$
$x \approx 4.957$

35. $4.59x - 66.7 = 3.2x - 3.2(5.67)$
$x(4.59 - 3.2) = 66.7 - 3.2(5.67)$
$$x = \frac{66.7 - 3.2(5.67)}{4.59 - 3.2}$$
$x \approx 34.932$

36. $457 \cdot 36x - 457 \cdot 99 = 34 \cdot 28x - 34 \cdot 239$
$457 \cdot 36x - 34 \cdot 28x = 457 \cdot 99 - 34 \cdot 239$
$x(457 \cdot 36 - 34 \cdot 28) = 457 \cdot 99 - 34 \cdot 239$
$$x = \frac{457 \cdot 99 - 34 \cdot 239}{457 \cdot 36 - 34 \cdot 28}$$
$x \approx 2.395$

37. $\dfrac{x}{19} + \dfrac{3x}{7} = \dfrac{4}{31} + \dfrac{3}{23}$
$x\left(\dfrac{1}{19} + \dfrac{3}{7}\right) = \dfrac{4}{31} + \dfrac{3}{23}$
$$x = \frac{\frac{4}{31} + \frac{3}{23}}{\frac{1}{19} + \frac{3}{7}} \approx 0.539$$

38. $\dfrac{1}{8} - \dfrac{5x}{7} + \dfrac{25}{154} = \dfrac{4x}{9} + \dfrac{1}{12}$
$-\dfrac{5x}{7} - \dfrac{4x}{9} = \dfrac{1}{12} - \dfrac{1}{8} - \dfrac{25}{154}$
$x\left(-\dfrac{5}{7} - \dfrac{4}{9}\right) = \dfrac{1}{12} - \dfrac{1}{8} - \dfrac{25}{154}$
$$x = \frac{\frac{1}{12} - \frac{1}{8} - \frac{25}{154}}{-\frac{5}{7} - \frac{4}{9}} \approx 0.176$$

39. $2(3) - 3y = 5$
$-3y = -1$
$y = \dfrac{1}{3}$

40. $-3x - 4y = 4$
$-4y = 3x + 4$
$y = -\dfrac{3}{4}x - 1$
If $x = 3$, then $y = -\dfrac{3}{4}(3) - 1 = -\dfrac{9}{4} - \dfrac{4}{4}$
$\qquad\qquad = -\dfrac{13}{4}.$

41. $-4(3) + 2y = 1$
$2y = 13$
$y = \dfrac{13}{2}$

42. $x - y = 7$
$-y = -x + 7$
$y = x - 7$
If $x = 3$, then $y = 3 - 7 = -4$.

43. $y = -2(3) + 5$

$y = -6 + 5$
$y = -1$

44. If $x = 3$, then $y = -3(3) - 6 = -15$.

45. $-3 + 2y = 5$
$2y = 8$
$y = 4$

46. $-x - 3y = 6$
$-3y = x + 6$
$y = \dfrac{x + 6}{-3}$

If $x = 3$, then $y = \dfrac{3 + 6}{-3} = \dfrac{9}{-3} = -3$.

47. $y - 1.046 = 2.63(3 - 5.09)$
$y - 1.046 = -5.4967$
$y = -4.4507$

48. Use $x = 3$ in the equation.
$y - 2.895 = -1.07(3 - 2.89)$
$y - 2.895 = -0.1177$
$y = 2.7773$

49. $4(2)x = 5$
$8x = 5$
$x = \dfrac{5}{8}$

50. Use $w = 4$ and $z = -3$ in $wxz = 4$.
$4x(-3) = 4$
$-12x = 4$
$x = -\dfrac{4}{12} = -\dfrac{1}{3}$

51. $x + (-3)x = 7$
$-2x = 7$
$x = -\dfrac{7}{2}$

52. Use $w = 4$ in $xw - x = 3$.
$4x - x = 3$
$3x = 3$
$x = 1$

53. $4[x - (-3)] = 2(x - 4)$
$4x + 12 = 2x - 8$
$2x = -20$
$x = -10$

54. Use $z = -3$ and $y = 2$ in
$z(x - y) = y(x + 5)$.
$-3(x - 2) = 2(x + 5)$
$-3x + 6 = 2x + 10$
$-5x = 4$
$x = -\dfrac{4}{5}$

55. $4 = \frac{1}{2}x(-3)$

$$4 = -\frac{3}{2}x$$

$$-\frac{2}{3}(4) = -\frac{2}{3}\left(-\frac{3}{2}x\right)$$

$$-\frac{8}{3} = x$$

56. Use $y = 2$ and $w = 4$ in $y = \frac{1}{2}wx$.

$$2 = \frac{1}{2} \cdot 4x$$

$$2 = 2x$$

$$1 = x$$

57. $\frac{1}{4} + \frac{1}{x} = \frac{1}{2}$

$$4x \cdot \frac{1}{4} + 4x \cdot \frac{1}{x} = 4x \cdot \frac{1}{2}$$

$$x + 4 = 2x$$

$$4 = x$$

58. Use $w = 4$ and $y = 2$ in $\frac{1}{w} + \frac{1}{y} = \frac{1}{x}$.

$$\frac{1}{4} + \frac{1}{2} = \frac{1}{x}$$

$$\frac{3}{4} = \frac{1}{x}$$

$$4x \cdot \frac{3}{4} = 4x \cdot \frac{1}{x}$$

$$3x = 4$$

$$x = \frac{4}{3}$$

59. $A = \pi r^2$

60. $C = \pi d$

61. Since $C = 2\pi r$, we can divide each side by 2π to get $r = \frac{C}{2\pi}$.

62. Because $C = \pi d$, we can divide each side by π to get $d = \frac{C}{\pi}$.

63. Because $P = 2L + 2W$, we can subtract $2L$ from each side to get $2W = P - 2L$, and then divide each side by 2 to get $W = \frac{P - 2L}{2}$.

64. Because $A = LW$, we can divide each side by W to get $L = \frac{A}{W}$.

65. $I = Prt$

$$300 = 1000 \cdot 2 \cdot r$$

$$r = \frac{300}{2000} = 15\%$$

66. Use $P = 2000$, $r = 0.18$, and $I = 180$ in the formula for simple interest $I = Prt$.

$$180 = 2000(0.18)t$$

$$180 = 360t$$

$$0.5 = t$$

The time is one-half year.

67. $A = LW$

$$23 = L(4)$$

$$L = \frac{23}{4} = 5.75 \text{ yards}$$

68. Use $L = 7$ and $A = 55$ in the formula for the area of a rectangle, $A = LW$.

$$55 = 7W$$

$$\frac{55}{7} = W$$

The width is $\frac{55}{7}$ meters.

69. $V = LWH$

$$36 = 2(2.5)H$$

$$36 = 5H$$

$$H = 7.2 \text{ feet}$$

70. Use $V = 2.5$, $H = 1$, and $W = 1.25$ in the formula for the volume of a rectangular solid $V = LWH$.

$$2.5 = L(1.25)(1)$$

$$2.5 = 1.25L$$

$$2 = L$$

The length is 2 meters.

71. $V - 900 \text{ gal.}\left(\frac{1\,\text{ft}^3}{7.5\,\text{gal}}\right) = 120 \text{ ft}^3$

$$V = LWH$$

$$120 = 4 \cdot 6 \cdot H$$

$$H = \frac{120}{24} = 5 \text{ feet}$$

72. First convert 60,000 gallons to cubic feet.

$$60{,}000 \text{ gallons} \cdot \frac{1 \text{ cubic foot}}{7.5 \text{ gallons}} = 8000 \text{ cubic feet}$$

Use $V = 8000$, $W = 40$, and $L = 100$ in the formula for the volume of a rectangular solid $V = LWH$.

$$8000 = 100 \cdot 40 \cdot H$$

$$8000 = 4000H$$

$$2 = H$$

The pool is 2 feet deep.

73. $A = \frac{1}{2}bh$

$$30 = \frac{1}{2}4h$$

$$30 = 2h$$

$$h = 15 \text{ feet}$$

74. Use $A = 40$ and $h = 10$ in the formula for the area of a triangle $A = \frac{1}{2}bh$.
$$40 = \frac{1}{2}b(10)$$
$$40 = 5b$$
$$8 = b$$
The base is 8 meters.

75. $\quad A = \frac{1}{2}h(b_1 + b_2)$
$$300 = \frac{1}{2}(20)(16 + b_2)$$
$$300 = 10(16 + b_2)$$
$$30 = 16 + b_2$$
$$b_2 = 14 \text{ inches}$$

76. Use $A = 200$, $b_1 = 16$, and $b_2 = 24$ in the formula for the area of a trapezoid $A = \frac{1}{2}h(b_1 + b_2)$.
$$200 = \frac{1}{2}h(16 + 24)$$
$$200 = 20h$$
$$10 = h$$
The height is 10 centimeters.

77. $\quad P = 2L + 2W$
$$600 = 2L + 2(132)$$
$$336 = 2L$$
$$L = 168 \text{ feet}$$

78. Use $P = 306\frac{2}{3} = \frac{920}{3}$ and $L = 100$ in the formula for the perimeter of a rectangle $P = 2L + 2W$.
$$\frac{920}{3} = 2(100) + 2W$$
$$\frac{920}{3} = 200 + 2W$$
$$920 = 600 + 6W$$
$$320 = 6W$$
$$\frac{320}{6} = W$$
The width is $\frac{160}{3}$ or $53\frac{1}{3}$ yards or 160 feet.

79. $\quad C = 2\pi r$
$$3\pi = 2\pi r$$
$$r = \frac{3\pi}{2\pi}$$
$$r = 1.5 \text{ meters}$$

80. Use $C = 12\pi$ in the formula $C = 2\pi r$.
$$12\pi = 2\pi r$$
$$6 = r$$

Since the radius is 6 inches, the diameter is 12 inches.

81. $\quad C = 2\pi r$
$$r = \frac{C}{2\pi}$$

$$r = \frac{25000}{2\pi}$$
$$r \approx 3,979 \text{ miles}$$

82. Use $C = 26,000$ in the formula $C = 2\pi r$.
$$26000 = 2\pi r$$
$$r = \frac{26000}{2\pi} \approx 4138$$

Since the radius of the earth is 3978.87 (from the previous exercise), the satellite is $4138 - 3979$, or approximately 159 miles above the earth.

83. $\quad V = \pi r^2 h$
$$30 = \pi(1)^2 h$$
$$30 = \pi h$$
$$h = \frac{30}{\pi} = 9.55 \text{ inches}$$

84. Use $V = 6.3$ and $r = 0.6$ in the formula for the volume of a cylinder $V = \pi r^2 h$.
$$6.3 = \pi(0.6)^2 h$$
$$6.3 = 0.36\pi h$$
$$h = \frac{6.3}{0.36\pi} \approx 5.57$$
The height is approximately 5.57 meters.

85. Let $W = 62$ lb/ft^3, $D = 32$ ft, and $A = 48$ ft^2 in $F = WDA$:
$$F = 62 \text{ lb/ft}^3 \cdot 32 \text{ ft} \cdot 48 \text{ ft}^2 = 95{,}232 \text{ lb}$$

86. Let $s = 38$ lb/in.^{2} and $r = 30$ in. in $F = s\pi r^2$:
$$F = 38 \text{ lb/in.}^2 \cdot \pi \cdot 30^2 \text{ in.}^2 \approx 107{,}442 \text{ lb}$$
The shear strength of the concrete shaft is larger than the force of the water.

87. a) $N = B + S - 1$
$$N = 2003 + 455 - 1 = 2457$$
b) $\quad 1452 = 1033 + S - 1$
$$420 = S$$

88. $P = 0.479 - 0.00949(24) \approx 0.251$
$$= 25.1\%$$
b) According to the graph it looks like smoking in this group will be eliminated in about 2024.
c) $\quad 0.479 - 0.00949n = 0$
$$-0.00949n = -0.479$$
$$n \approx 50$$

28

So smoking will be eliminated from this age group in the year $1974 + 50$, or 2024.

89. $\$1000 \div \$2 = 500$ feet

$$b_1 + b_2 = 500$$
$$A = \frac{1}{2}h(b_1 + b_2)$$
$$50{,}000 = \frac{1}{2}h \cdot 500$$
$$h = 200 \text{ feet}$$

90. Use $A = 25{,}000$ and $h = 200$ (from Exercise 89) in the formula for the area of a triangle $A = \frac{1}{2}bh$.

$$25{,}000 = \frac{1}{2}b(200)$$
$$25{,}000 = 100b$$
$$250 = b$$

Since she has 250 feet of frontage, her assessment will be $500.

91. $\quad A = bh$

$$60{,}000 = b \cdot 200$$
$$b = 300 \text{ feet}$$

There is 300 ft on each street. So 600 ft at $2 each is a $1200 assessment.

92. Let $L =$ the length of the driveway. The driveway is a rectangular solid with a volume of 12 cubic yards. The driveway is 12 ft or 4 yd wide. It is 4 in. or $\frac{4}{36} = \frac{1}{9}$ yard thick. Use the formula $V = LWH$.

$$12 = L(4)\tfrac{1}{9}$$
$$12 = \tfrac{4}{9}L$$
$$108 = 4L$$
$$27 = L$$

It is 27 yards or 81 feet from the street to her house.

2.3 WARM-UPS

1. False, first identify what the variable stands for.

2. True, we must know what the letters represent.

3. False, you may have the wrong equation.

4. False, odd integers differ by 2.

5. True, $x + 6 - x = 6$.

6. True, $x + 7 - x = 7$.

7. False, $5x - 2 = 3(x + 20)$ since $5x$ is larger than $3(x + 20)$.

8. True, because 8% of x is $0.08x$.

9. False, because 10% of $88,000 is $8,800 and you will not get $80,000.

10. False, because the acid in the mixture must be between 10% and 14%.

2.3 EXERCISES

1. Three unknown consecutive integers are represented by x, $x + 1$, and $x + 2$.

2. In either case we use x, $x + 2$, and $x + 4$, but for odd integers x represents an odd integer and for even integers x represents an even integer.

3. The formula $P = 2L + 2W$ expresses the perimeter in terms of the length and width.

4. Addition can be indicated by the words, sum, more than, or plus.

5. The commission is a percentage of the selling price.

6. Uniform motion is motion at a constant rate.

7. Since two consecutive even integers differ by 2, we can use x and $x + 2$ to represent them.

8. Since consecutive odd integers differ by 2, we can use x and $x + 2$ to represent two consecutive odd integers.

9. The expressions x and $10 - x$ have a sum of 10, since $x + 10 - x = 10$.

10. Two numbers with a difference of 3 can be represented as x and $x + 3$.

11. If x is the selling price, then eighty-five percent of the selling price is $0.85x$.

12. The product of an unknown number and 3 can be represented as $3x$.

13. Since $D = RT$, the distance is $3x$ miles.

14. Since $D = RT$, the time it takes to travel 100 miles at $x + 5$ miles per hour is represented as $\frac{100}{x + 5}$ hours.

15. Since the perimeter is twice the length plus twice the width, we can represent the perimeter by $2(x + 5) + 2(x)$ or $4x + 10$.

16. The sum of the length and width is one-half the perimeter, or 10 meters. If the length is x meters, then the width is $10 - x$ meters.

17. Let $x =$ the first integer, $x + 1 =$ the second integer, and $x + 2 =$ the third integer. Their sum is 84:

$$x + x + 1 + x + 2 = 84$$
$$3x + 3 = 84$$
$$x = 27$$

If $x = 27$, then $x + 1 = 28$, and $x + 2 = 29$. The integers are 27, 28, and 29.

18. Let $x =$ the first integer, $x + 1 =$ the second integer, and $x + 2 =$ the third integer. Since their sum is 171, we can write the following equation.

$$x + x + 1 + x + 2 = 171$$
$$3x + 3 = 171$$
$$3x = 168$$
$$x = 56$$
$$x + 1 = 57$$
$$x + 2 = 58$$

The three consecutive integers are 56, 57, and 58.

19. Let $x =$ the first even integer, $x + 2 =$ the second, and $x + 4 =$ the third. Their sum is 252:

$$x + x + 2 + x + 4 = 252$$
$$3x + 6 = 252$$
$$3x = 246$$
$$x = 82$$

If $x = 82$, then $x + 2 = 84$ and $x + 4 = 86$. The integers are 82, 84, and 86.

20. Let $x =$ the first even integer, $x + 2 =$ the second, and $x + 4 =$ the third. Since their sum is 84, we can write the following equation.

$$x + x + 2 + x + 4 = 84$$
$$3x + 6 = 84$$
$$3x = 78$$
$$x = 26$$
$$x + 2 = 28$$
$$x + 4 = 30$$

The three consecutive even integers are 26, 28, and 30.

21. Let $x =$ the first odd integer and $x + 2 =$ the second. Their sum is 128:

$$x + x + 2 = 128$$
$$2x = 126$$
$$x = 63$$

If $x = 63$, then $x + 2 = 65$. The integers are 63 and 65.

22. Let $x =$ the first odd integer, $x + 2 =$ the second, $x + 4 =$ the third, and $x + 6 =$ the

fourth. Since their sum is 56, we can write the following equation.

$$x + x + 2 + x + 4 + x + 6 = 56$$
$$4x + 12 = 56$$
$$4x = 44$$
$$x = 11$$
$$x + 2 = 13$$
$$x + 4 = 15$$
$$x + 6 = 17$$

The four consecutive odd integers are 11, 13, 15, and 17.

23. Let $x =$ the width, and $2x + 1 =$ the length. Since $P = 2L + 2W$ we can write the following equation.

$$2(x) + 2(2x + 1) = 278$$
$$6x + 2 = 278$$
$$6x = 276$$
$$x = 46$$

If $x = 46$, then $2x + 1 = 93$. The width is 46 meters and the length is 93 meters.

24. Let $x =$ the width of the frame and $x + 2 =$ the length of the frame. Since the perimeter of the frame is 10 feet, we can write the following equation.

$$2x + 2(x + 2) = 10$$
$$2x + 2x + 4 = 10$$
$$4x = 6$$
$$x = 1.5$$
$$x + 2 = 3.5$$

The width of the frame is 1.5 feet and the length of the frame is 3.5 feet.

25. Let $x =$ the length of the first side, $2x - 10 =$ the length of the second side, and $x + 50 =$ the length of the third side. Since the perimeter is 684, we have the following equation.

$$x + 2x - 10 + x + 50 = 684$$
$$4x + 40 = 684$$
$$4x = 644$$
$$x = 161$$

If $x = 161$ feet, then $2x - 10 = 312$ feet, and $x + 50 = 211$ feet.

26. Let $x =$ the length of each of the equal sides and $x - 3.5 =$ the length of the base. Since the perimeter of the triangle is 49 inches, we can write the following equation.

$$x + x + x - 3.5 = 49$$
$$3x - 3.5 = 49$$
$$3x = 52.5$$
$$x = 17.5$$

The length of each of the equal sides is 17.5 inches.

27. Let $x =$ the width, and $2x + 5 =$ the length. To fence the 3 sides, we use 2 widths and 1 length:

$$2(x) + (2x + 5) = 50$$
$$4x = 45$$
$$x = 11.25$$
$$2x + 5 = 27.5$$

Width is 11.25 feet and the length is 27.5 feet.

28. Let $x =$ the width and $2x + 1 =$ the height of the doorway. The equation expresses the fact that the total length of the 3 pieces is 17 feet.

$$x + 2(2x + 1) = 17$$
$$x + 4x + 2 = 17$$
$$5x = 15$$
$$x = 3$$
$$2x + 1 = 7$$

The doorway is 3 feet wide and 7 feet high.

29. Let $x =$ the amount invested at 6% and $x + 1000 =$ the amount invested at 10%. Since the interest on the investments is $0.06x$ and $0.10(x + 1000)$ we can write the equation

$$0.06x + 0.10(x + 1000) = 340$$
$$0.16x + 100 = 340$$
$$0.16x = 240$$
$$x = 1500$$
$$x + 1000 = 2500$$

He invested $1,500 at 6% and $2,500 at 10%.

30. Let $x =$ the amount lent to her brother at 9% and $\frac{1}{2}x =$ the amount lent to her sister at 16%. The equation expresses the fact that the total interest is 34 cents.

$$0.09x + 0.16 \cdot \tfrac{1}{2}x = 0.34$$
$$0.09x + 0.08x = 0.34$$
$$0.17x = 0.34$$
$$x = 2$$
$$\tfrac{1}{2}x = 1$$

She lent her brother $2 and her sister $1.

31. Let $x =$ the amount of his inheritance. He invests $\frac{1}{2}x$ at 10% and $\frac{1}{4}x$ at 12%. His total income of $6400 can be expressed as

$$0.10\left(\tfrac{1}{2}x\right) + 0.12\left(\tfrac{1}{4}x\right) = 6400$$
$$0.05x + 0.03x = 6400$$
$$0.08x = 6400$$
$$x = 80,000$$

His inheritance was $80,000.

32. Let $x =$ the amount of Gary's insurance settlement, $\frac{1}{3}x =$ the amount he invested at 12%, and $\frac{1}{3}x =$ the amount invested at 15%. The equation expresses the fact that the total income from these two investments was $10,800.

$$0.12 \cdot \tfrac{1}{3}x + 0.15 \cdot \tfrac{1}{3}x = 10800$$
$$0.04x + 0.05x = 10800$$
$$0.09x = 10800$$
$$x = 120,000$$

His insurance settlement was $120,000.

33. Let $x =$ the number of gallons of 5% solution. In the 5% solution there are $0.05x$ gallons of acid, and in the 20 gallons of 10% solution there are $0.10(20)$ gallons of acid. The final mixture consists of $x + 20$ gallons of which 8% is acid. The total acid in the mixture is the sum of the acid from each solution mixed together:

$$0.05x + 0.10(20) = 0.08(x + 20)$$
$$0.05x + 2 = 0.08x + 1.6$$
$$0.4 = 0.03x$$
$$x = \frac{0.4}{0.03} = \frac{40}{3}$$

Use $\frac{40}{3}$ gallons of 5% solution.

34. Let $x =$ the number of liters of 10% solution. In the 10% solution there are $0.10x$ liters of alcohol. In the 12 liters of 20% solution there are $0.20(12)$ liters of alcohol. In the $x + 12$ liters in the final 14% solution there are $0.14(x + 12)$ liters of alcohol.

$$0.10x + 0.20(12) = 0.14(x + 12)$$
$$0.10x + 2.4 = 0.14x + 1.68$$
$$2.40 - 1.68 = 0.04x$$
$$0.72 = 0.04x$$
$$18 = x$$

Use 18 liters of 10% solution.

35. Let $x =$ the number of gallons of pure acid. After mixing we will have $1 + x$ gallons of 6% solution. The original gallon has $0.05(1)$ gallons of acid in it. The equation totals up the acid:

$$0.05(1) + x = 0.06(1 + x)$$
$$0.05 + x = 0.06 + 0.06x$$
$$0.94x = 0.01$$
$$x = 0.010638 \text{ gallons}$$

Use 1 gallon $= 128$ ounces, to get 1.36 ounces of pure acid.

36. Let $x =$ the number of ounces of sodium hypochlorite to be added. Multiply 8.3 pounds by 16 to get 132.8 ounces. In the original 5.25% gallon there are $0.0525(132.8)$ ounces of sodium hypochlorite. In the final mixture there are $0.06(132.8 + x)$ ounces of sodium hypochlorite. We can write the following equation.

$$0.0525(132.8) + x = 0.06(132.8 + x)$$
$$6.972 + x = 7.968 + 0.06x$$
$$1.00x - 0.06x = 7.968 - 6.972$$
$$0.94x = 0.996$$
$$x = 1.0596$$

Add 1.0596 ounces of sodium hypochlorite.

37. Let $x =$ his speed in the fog and $x + 30 =$ his increased speed. Since $D = RT$, his distance in the fog was $3x$ and his distance later was $6(x + 30)$. The equation gives the total distance:

$$3x + 6(x + 30) = 540$$
$$9x + 180 = 540$$
$$9x = 360$$
$$x = 40$$

His speed in the fog was 40 mph.

38. Let $x =$ her walking speed and $2x =$ her running speed. The distance that she walked is $2x$ miles and the distance that she ran is $2x(1.5) = 3x$ miles. Since her total distance was 20 miles, we can write the following equation.

$$2x + 3x = 20$$
$$5x = 20$$
$$x = 4$$
$$2x = 8$$

She walks 4 miles per hour and runs 8 miles per hour.

39. Let $x =$ the speed of the commuter bus and $x + 25 =$ the speed of the express bus. Use $D = RT$ to get the distance traveled by each as $2x$ and $\frac{3}{4}(x + 25)$. The equation expresses the fact that they travel the same distance:

$$2x = \frac{3}{4}(x + 25)$$
$$4 \cdot 2x = 4 \cdot \frac{3}{4}(x + 25)$$
$$8x = 3x + 75$$
$$5x = 75$$
$$x = 15$$

The speed of the commuter bus was 15 mph.

40. Let $x =$ the speed of the freight train and $x + 40 =$ the speed of the passenger train in miles per hour. Since the time for the freight train is 1.25 hours, the distance for the freight is $1.25x$ miles. Since the time for the passenger train is 0.75 hours, the distance for the passenger train is $0.75(x + 40)$ miles. Since the distance traveled for each train is the same, we can write the following equation.

$$1.25x = 0.75(x + 40)$$
$$1.25x = 0.75x + 30$$
$$0.50x = 30$$
$$x = 60$$
$$x + 40 = 100$$

The speed of the passenger train is 100 miles per hour.

41. If $x =$ the selling price, then the commission is $0.08x$. The owner gets the selling price minus the commission:

$$x - 0.08x = 80,000$$
$$0.92x = 80,000$$
$$x = \$86,957$$

42. Let $x =$ the amount of her sales and $0.05x =$ the amount of sales tax. Since her total was 915.60, we can write the following equation.

$$x + 0.05x = 915.60$$
$$1.05x = 915.60$$
$$x = \frac{915.60}{1.05} = 872$$
$$0.05x = 43.60$$

The sales tax that she collected was \$43.60.

43. If $x =$ the selling price, then $0.07x =$ the amount of sales tax. The selling price plus the sales tax is the total amount paid:

$$x + 0.07x = 9041.50$$
$$1.07x = 9041.50$$
$$x = \$8450$$

44. Let $x =$ the selling price and $0.10x =$ the broker's commission. Since Roy wants to get $3000, we can write the following equation.
$$x - 0.10x = 3000$$
$$0.90x = 3000$$
$$x = \frac{3000}{0.9} = 3,333.33$$
The selling price should be $3,333.33.

45. Let $x =$ the distance from the base line to the service line and $x - 3 =$ the distance from the service line to the net. The total is 39 feet:
$$x + x - 3 = 39$$
$$2x = 42$$
$$x = 21$$
The distance from service line to the net is 18 ft.

46. Let $x =$ the width of the doubles court and $x + \frac{1}{3}x =$ the width of the singles court.
$$x + \frac{1}{3}x = 36$$
$$\frac{4}{3}x = 36$$
$$x = 27$$
The width of the singles court is 27 ft.

47. Let $x =$ the number of points scored by the Packers and $x - 25 =$ the number of points scored by the Chiefs.
$$x + x - 25 = 45$$
$$2x = 70$$
$$x = 35$$
The score was Packers 35, Chiefs 10.

48. Let $x =$ the market share for Wal-Mart and $x + 4 =$ the market share for Toys R Us.
$$x + x + 4 = 36$$
$$2x = 32$$
$$x = 16$$
$$x + 4 = 20$$
Wal-Mart had 16% of the toy market and Toys R Us had 20%.

49. Let $x =$ the price per pound for the blended coffee. The price of 0.75 lb of Brazilian coffee at $10 per lb is $7.50, and the price of 1.5 lb of Colombian coffee at $8 per lb is $12. The total price for 2.25 lb of blended coffee at x dollars per kg is $2.25x$ dollars. We write an equation expressing the total cost:

$$7.50 + 12 = 2.25x$$
$$19.50 = 2.25x$$
$$x = 8.67$$
The blended coffee should sell for $8.67 per lb.

50. Let $x =$ the price per ounce of the mixture. The total cost of 200 ounces of cinnamon at $1.80 per ounce is 200(1.80). The total cost of 100 ounces of nutmeg at $1.60 per ounce is 100(1.60). The total cost of 100 ounces of cloves at $1.40 per ounce is 100(1.40). Since there will be 400 ounces altogether, the total cost of the mix should be $400x$ dollars.
$$200(1.80) + 100(1.60) + 100(1.40) = 400x$$
$$660 = 400x$$
$$x = \frac{660}{400} = 1.65$$
The mixture should sell for $1.65/ounce.

51. Let $x =$ the number of pounds of apricots. The total cost of 10 pounds of bananas at $3.20 per pound is $32, the total cost of x pounds of apricots at $4 per pound is $4x$, and the total cost $x + 10$ pounds of mix at $3.80 per pound is $3.80(x + 10)$. Write an equation expressing the total cost:
$$32 + 4x = 3.80(x + 10)$$
$$32 + 4x = 3.80x + 38$$
$$0.20x = 6$$
$$x = 30$$
The mix should contain 30 pounds of apricots.

52. Let $x =$ the number of pounds of cashews. Note that x pounds of cashews at $4.80 per pound cost $4.80x$ and 20 pounds of Brazil nuts at $6.00 per pound cost 6.00(20). Since the final mixture of $x + 20$ pounds should cost $5.20 per pound, we can write the following equation.
$$4.80x + 6.00(20) = 5.20(x + 20)$$
$$4.80x + 120 = 5.20x + 104$$
$$16 = 0.40x$$
$$40 = x$$
Use 40 pounds of cashews.

53. Let $x =$ the number of quarts to be drained out. In the original 20 qt radiator there are 0.30(20) qts of antifreeze. In the x qts that are drained there are $0.30x$ qts of antifreeze, but in the x qts put back in there are x qts of antifreeze. The equation accounts for all of the antifreeze:

$$0.30(20) - 0.30x + x = 0.50(20)$$
$$6 + 0.70x = 10$$
$$0.7x = 4$$
$$x = \frac{4}{0.7} = \frac{40}{7}$$

The amount drained should be $\frac{40}{7}$ qts.

54. Let $x =$ the amount of the 40% solution that is to be replaced with a 70% solution. The amount of antifreeze in the original 16 quarts is $0.40(16)$. The amount of antifreeze in the x quarts that are removed is $0.40x$. The amount of antifreeze in the x quarts when they are put back in is $0.70x$. The amount of antifreeze in the radiator when the process is complete is $0.50(16)$.

$$0.40(16) - 0.40x + 0.70x = 0.50(16)$$
$$6.4 + 0.30x = 8$$
$$0.30x = 1.6$$
$$x = \frac{1.6}{0.3} = \frac{16}{3}$$

Replace $\frac{16}{3}$ quarts with 70% solution.

55. If $x =$ the profit in 1996. Since the profit in 1997 was 7.8% greater and the profit in 1997 was $324 billion, we have the following.

$$x + 0.078x = 324$$
$$1.078x = 324$$
$$x = \frac{324}{1.078} \approx 300.6$$

The total profit in 1996 was $300.6 billion.

56. If $x =$ the fertility rate in 1960. Since fertility rate in 1998 was 48% smaller, and the rate in 1998 was 3.1 children per woman, we have the following.

$$x - 0.48x = 3.1$$
$$0.52x = 3.1$$
$$x \approx 5.96$$

The fertility rate in 1960 was 5.96 children per woman.

57. Let $x =$ Brian's inheritance, $\frac{1}{2}x =$ Daniel's inheritance, and $\frac{1}{3}x - 1000 =$ Raymond's inheritance. The sum of the three amounts is $25,400:

$$x + \frac{1}{2}x + \frac{1}{3}x - 1000 = 25400$$

$$\frac{11}{6}x = 26400$$
$$x = \frac{6}{11} \cdot 26400$$
$$= 14400$$
$$\frac{1}{2}x = 7{,}200$$
$$\frac{1}{3}x - 1000 = 3{,}800$$

Brian gets $14,400, Daniel $7,200, and Raymond $3,800.

58. Let $x =$ Lauren's share, $\frac{1}{2}x =$ Lisa's share, and $\frac{1}{4}x =$ Lena's share. Since the lawyer gets $0.10x$, we can write the following equation.

$$x + 0.50x + 0.25x + 0.10x = 164{,}428$$
$$1.85x = 164{,}428$$
$$x = 88{,}880$$
$$0.5x = 44{,}440$$
$$0.25x = 22{,}220$$
$$0.10x = 8{,}888$$

Lauren gets $88,880, Lisa gets $44,440, Lena gets $22,220, and the lawyer gets $8,888.

59. Let $x =$ the first integer and $x + 1 =$ the second. Subtract the larger from twice the smaller to get 21:

$$2x - (x + 1) = 21$$
$$x - 1 = 21$$
$$x = 22$$
$$x + 1 = 23$$

The integers are 22 and 23.

60. Let $x =$ the first consecutive odd integer and $x + 2 =$ the second. If the smaller is subtracted from twice the larger, the result is 13.

$$2(x + 2) - x = 13$$
$$2x + 4 - x = 13$$
$$x + 4 = 13$$
$$x = 9$$
$$x + 2 = 11$$

The integers are 9 and 11.

61. Let $x =$ Berenice's time and $x - 2 =$ Jarrett's time. Berenice's distance is $50x$ and Jarrett's distance is $56(x - 2)$.

$$50x + 56(x - 2) = 683$$
$$106x - 112 = 683$$
$$106x = 795$$
$$x = 7.5$$

Berenice drove for 7.5 hours.

62. Let x = Fernell's time and
$x - 3$ = Dabney's time. Fernell's distance is
$50x$ and Dabney's distance is $64(x - 3)$

$$50x + 18 = 64(x - 3)$$
$$50x + 18 = 64x - 192$$
$$-14x = -210$$
$$x = 15$$

Fernell drove for 15 hours.

63. Let x = the length of a side of the square.
She will use x meters of fencing for each of 3
sides, but only $\frac{1}{2}x$ meters for the side with the
opening.

$$3x + \frac{1}{2}x = 70$$
$$\frac{7}{2}x = 70$$
$$x = \frac{2}{7} \cdot 70 = 20$$

The square will by 20 meters by 20 meters.

64. Let x = the length of the side of the square.
He will use x linear feet of siding on each of the
3 sides. On the side with the door he will use
$x - 4$ linear feet of siding. Since the total
number of linear feet should be 32, we can write
the following equation.

$$3x + x - 4 = 32$$
$$4x = 36$$
$$x = 9$$

The foundation should be 9 feet by 9 feet.

65. Let x = the amount invested at 8% and
$3000 - x$ = the amount invested at 10%.
Income on the first investment is $0.08x$ and
income on the second is $0.10(3000 - x)$. The
total income is $290:

$$0.08x + 0.10(3000 - x) = 290$$
$$0.08x + 300 - 0.10x = 290$$
$$-0.02x = -10$$
$$x = \frac{-10}{-0.02} = 500$$
$$3000 - x = 2500$$

She invested $500 at 8% and $2,500 at 10%.

66. Let x = the amount invested at 6% and
$8000 - x$ = the amount invested at 9%. Write
an equation expressing the fact that the total
income from the investments was $690.

$$0.06x + 0.09(8000 - x) = 690$$
$$0.06x + 720 - 0.09x = 690$$
$$-0.03x = -30$$
$$x = 1000$$

$$8000 - x = 7000$$

She invested $1000 at 6% and $7000 at 9%.

67. Let x = the number of gallons of 5%
alcohol and $5 - x$ = the number of gallons of
10% alcohol. The alcohol in the final 5 gallons
is the sum of the alcohol in the two separate
quantities that are mixed together:

$$0.05x + 0.10(5 - x) = 0.08(5)$$
$$0.05x + 0.5 - 0.10x = 0.4$$
$$-0.05x = -0.1$$
$$x = \frac{-0.1}{-0.05} = 2$$
$$5 - x = 3$$

Use 2 gallons of 5% solution and 3 gallons of
10% solution.

68. Let x = the number of liters of 12%
alcohol and $6 - x$ = the number of liters of
water. In the x liters there are $0.12x$ liters of
alcohol. In the water there is no alcohol. In the
6 liters there are $0.10(6)$ liters of alcohol.

$$0.12x + 0 = 0.10(6)$$
$$0.12x = 0.6$$
$$x = 5$$

She should use 5 liters of 12% alcohol and 1
liter of water to obtain 6 liters of 10% alcohol.

69. Let x = Darla's age now and
$78 - x$ = Todd's age now. In 6 years Todd
will be $78 - x + 6$ or $84 - x$, and 6 years ago
Darla was $x - 6$. Todd's age in 6 years is twice
what Darla's age was 6 years ago:

$$84 - x = 2(x - 6)$$
$$84 - x = 2x - 12$$
$$-3x = -96$$
$$x = 32$$
$$78 - x = 46$$

Todd is 46 now and Darla is 32 now.

70. Let x = the number of years of experience
for Al and $2x$ = the number of years of
experience for Bart. Since altogether they have
100 years of experience, Carl has $100 - 3x$
years of experience. In 3 years Carl will have
$100 - 3x + 3$ years of experience. A year ago
Al had $x - 1$ years of experience. In 3 years
Carl will have twice the experience that Al had
a year ago.

$$100 - 3x + 3 = 2(x - 1)$$
$$103 - 3x = 2x - 2$$

$$-5x = -105$$
$$x = 21$$
$$2x = 42$$
$$100 - 3x = 37$$

Al has 21 years of experience, Bart has 42 years, and Carl has 37 years of experience.

2.4 WARM-UPS

1. False, $0 = 0$.
2. False, $-300 < -2$.
3. True, because $-60 = -60$.
4. False, since $6 < x$ is equivalent to $x > 6$.
5. False, $-2x < 10$ is equivalent to $x > -5$.
6. False, $3x \geq -12$ is equivalent to $x \geq -4$.
7. True, multiply each side by -1.
8. True, because of the trichotomy property.
9. True, because of the trichotomy property.
10. True, because $3 - 4(-2) \leq 11$ is correct.

2.4 EXERCISES

1. An inequality is a sentence that expresses inequality between two algebraic expressions.
2. To express inequality we use the symbols $<$, $\leq$, $>$, and $\geq$.
3. If a is less than b, then a lies to the left of b on the number line.
4. A linear inequality is an inequality of the form $ax + b > 0$ or with any of the other inequality symbols used in place of $>$.
5. When you multiply or divide by a negative number, the inequality symbol is reversed.
6. We can verbally indicate inequality with words like less than, at least, greater than, and at most.
7. False, $-3 > -9$.
8. False, because -8 is to the left of -7 on the number line ($-8 < -7$).
9. True, because $0 < 8$.
10. True, because -6 is to the right of -8 on the number line ($-6 > -8$).
11. True, because $-60 > -120$.
12. False, because $3 < -5$ is incorrect.
13. True, because $9 - (-3) = 12$.
14. True, because the left side is 22 and $22 \geq 21$ is correct.

15. Yes, because $2(-3) - 4 < 8$ simplifies to $-10 < 8$.
16. No, because $5 - 3(6) > -1$ simplifies to $-13 > -1$.
17. No, because $2(5) - 3 \leq 3(5) - 9$ simplifies to $7 \leq 6$.
18. Yes, because $6 - 3(-4) \geq 10 - 2(-4)$ simplifies to $18 \geq 18$.
19. No, because $5 - (-1) < 4 - 2(-1)$ simplifies to $6 < 6$.
20. Yes, because $3(9) - 7 \geq 3(9) - 10$ simplifies to $20 \geq 17$.
21. Shade the numbers to the left of -1, including -1.

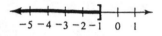

22. Shade the numbers to the right of -7, including -7.

23. Shade numbers to the right of 20.

24. Shade the numbers to the left of 30.

25. Since $3 \leq x$ is equivalent to $x \geq 3$, we shade the numbers to the right of 3, including 3.

26. The inequality $-2 > x$ is equivalent to $x < -2$. Shade the numbers to the left of -2.

27. Shade to the left of 2.3.

28. Shade the numbers to the left of 4.5, including 4.5.

4.5

0 1 2 3 4 5 6

29. The set of all real numbers greater than 1 is expressed as $(1, \infty)$.

30. The set of all real numbers less than 3 is expressed as $(-\infty, 3)$.

31. The set of all real numbers less than or equal to -3 is expressed as $(-\infty, -3]$.

32. The set of all real numbers greater than or equal to -2 is expressed as $[-2, \infty)$.

33. The set of all real numbers less than 5 is expressed as $(-\infty, 5)$.

34. The set of all real numbers greater than -7 is expressed as $(-7, \infty)$.

35. The set of all real numbers greater than or equal to -4 is expressed as $[-4, \infty)$.

36. The set of all real numbers less than or equal to -9 is expressed as $(-\infty, -9]$.

37. $x + 5 > 12$ is equivalent to $x > 7$.

38. $2x - 3 \leq -4$ is equivalent to $2x \leq -1$.

39. $-x < 6$ is equivalent to $x > -6$.

40. $-5 \geq -x$ is equivalent to $5 \leq x$.

41. $-2x \geq 8$ is equivalent to $x \leq -4$.

42. $-5x > -10$ is equivalent to $x < 2$.

43. $4 < x$ is equivalent to $x > 4$.

44. $-9 \leq -x$ is equivalent to $x \leq 9$.

45. $7x > -14$
$x > -2$
Solution set is $(-2, \infty)$.

−4 −3 −2 −1 0 1 2

46. $4x \leq -8$
$x \leq -2$
Solution set is $(-\infty, -2]$.

−6 −5 −4 −3 −2 −1 0

47. $-3x \leq 12$
$x \geq -4$
Solution set is $[-4, \infty)$.

−6 −5 −4 −3 −2 −1 0

48. $-2x > -6$
$x < 3$
Solution set is $(-\infty, 3)$.

−1 0 1 2 3 4 5

49. $2x - 3 > 7$
$2x > 10$
$x > 5$
Solution set is $(5, \infty)$.

3 4 5 6 7 8 9

50. $3x - 2 < 6$
$3x < 8$
$x < \dfrac{8}{3}$
Solution set is $(-\infty, 8/3)$.

$\frac{8}{3}$

−1 0 1 2 3 4

51. $3 - 5x \leq 18$
$-5x \leq 15$
$x \geq -3$
Solution set is $[-3, \infty)$.

−5 −4 −3 −2 −1 0 1

52. $5 - 4x \geq 19$
$-4x \geq 14$
$x \leq -\dfrac{7}{2}$
Solution set is $(-\infty, -7/2]$.

$-\frac{7}{2}$

−6 −5 −4 −3 −2 −1

53. $\dfrac{x-3}{-5} < -2$
$x - 3 > 10$
$x > 13$
Solution set is $(13, \infty)$.

11 12 13 14 15 16 17

54. $\dfrac{2x-3}{4} > 6$
$2x - 3 > 24$

$$2x > 27$$
$$x > \frac{27}{2}$$
Solution set is $(27/2, \infty)$.

55. $\frac{5 - 3x}{4} \leq 2$

$$5 - 3x \leq 8$$
$$-3x \leq 3$$
$$x \geq -1$$
Solution set is $[-1, \infty)$.

56. $\frac{7 - 5x}{-2} \geq -1$

$$7 - 5x \leq 2$$
$$-5x \leq -5$$
$$x \geq 1$$
Solution set is $[1, \infty)$.

57. $4\left(3 - \frac{1}{4}x\right) \geq 4(2)$

$$12 - x \geq 8$$
$$-x \geq -4$$
$$x \leq 4$$
Solution set is $(-\infty, 4]$.

58. $5 - \frac{1}{3}x > 2$

$$15 - x > 6$$
$$-x > -9$$
$$x < 9$$
Solution set is $(-\infty, 9)$.

59. $12\left(\frac{1}{4}x - \frac{1}{2}\right) < 12\left(\frac{1}{2}x - \frac{2}{3}\right)$

$$3x - 6 < 6x - 8$$
$$-3x < -2$$
$$x > \frac{2}{3}$$
Solution set is $(2/3, \infty)$.

60. $\frac{1}{3}x - \frac{1}{6} < \frac{1}{6}x - \frac{1}{2}$

$$6\left(\frac{1}{3}x - \frac{1}{6}\right) < 6\left(\frac{1}{6}x - \frac{1}{2}\right)$$
$$2x - 1 < x - 3$$
$$x < -2$$
Solution set is $(-\infty, -2)$.

61. $4 \cdot \frac{y - 3}{2} > 4 \cdot \frac{1}{2} - 4 \cdot \frac{y - 5}{4}$

$$2y - 6 > 2 - y + 5$$
$$3y > 13$$
$$y > \frac{13}{3}$$
Solution set is $(13/3, \infty)$.

62. $15 \cdot \frac{y - 1}{3} - 15 \cdot \frac{y + 1}{5} > 15 \cdot 1$

$$5y - 5 - 3y - 3 > 15$$
$$2y > 23$$
$$y > \frac{23}{2}$$
Solution set is $(23/2, \infty)$.

63. $2x + 3 > 2x - 8$

$$3 > -8$$
Solution set is $(-\infty, \infty)$.

64. $-10x + 2 \leq -25 - 10x$

$$2 \leq -25$$
Solution set is $\emptyset$.

65. $-8x + 20 \leq 12 - 8x$

$$20 \leq 12$$
Solution set is $\emptyset$.

66. $-6x + 3 \leq 10 - 6x$

$$3 \leq 10$$
Solution set is $(-\infty, \infty)$.

67. $-\frac{1}{2}x + 3 < \frac{1}{2}x + 2$
$$-x < -1$$
$$x > 1$$
Solution set is $(1, \infty)$.

68. $-\frac{3}{2}x + \frac{3}{4} > \frac{x}{2} - \frac{1}{4}$
$$-2x > -1$$
$$x < \frac{1}{2}$$
Solution set is $(-\infty, 1/2)$.

69. $-x + \frac{3}{2} + \frac{4}{3} - 2x \geq \frac{7}{4} - \frac{1}{2}x - 3$
$$-3x + \frac{17}{6} \geq -\frac{1}{2}x - \frac{5}{4}$$
$$12\left(-3x + \frac{17}{6}\right) \geq 12\left(-\frac{1}{2}x - \frac{5}{4}\right)$$
$$-36x + 34 \geq -6x - 15$$
$$-30x \geq -49$$
$$x \leq \frac{49}{30}$$
Solution set is $(-\infty, 49/30]$.

70. $\frac{3}{5}(x - 3) - \frac{1}{4}(7 - 5x) < \frac{2}{3}(3 - x) - 5$

$$\frac{3x}{5} - \frac{9}{5} - \frac{7}{4} + \frac{5x}{4} < 2 - \frac{2x}{3} - 5$$
$$60\left(\frac{3x}{5} - \frac{9}{5} - \frac{7}{4} + \frac{5x}{4}\right) < 60\left(2 - \frac{2x}{3} - 5\right)$$
$$36x - 108 - 105 + 75x < 120 - 40x - 300$$
$$111x - 213 < -180 - 40x$$
$$151x < 33$$
$$x < \frac{33}{151}$$
Solution set is $(-\infty, \frac{33}{151})$.

71. $4.273 + 2.8x \leq 10.985$
$$2.8x \leq 6.712$$
$$x \leq 2.397$$
Solution set is $(-\infty, 2.397]$.

72. $1.064 < 5.94 - 3.2x$
$$-4.876 < -3.2x$$
$$1.52375 > x$$
Solution set is $(-\infty, 1.52375)$.

73. $3.25x - 27.39 > 4.06 + 5.1x$
$$-1.85x > 31.45$$
$$x < -17$$
Solution set is $(-\infty, -17)$.

74. $4.86(3.2x - 1.7) > 5.19 - x$
$$15.552x - 8.262 > 5.19 - x$$
$$16.552x > 13.452$$
$$x > 0.8127$$
Solution set $(0.8127, \infty)$.

75. If $x =$ Tony's height, then $x > 6$.

76. If $a =$ Glenda's age, then $a < 60$.

77. If $s =$ Wilma's salary, then $s < 80,000$.

78. If $w =$ Bubba's weight, then $w > 80$.

79. If $v =$ speed of the Concorde, then $v \leq 1450$.

80. If $s =$ minimum speed, then $s \geq 45$.

81. If $a =$ amount Julie can afford, then $a \leq 400$.

82. If $a =$ Fred's grade point average, then $a \geq 3.2$.

83. If $b =$ Burt's height, then $b \leq 5$.

84. If $r =$ Ernie's speed, then $r \leq 10$ mph.

85. If $t =$ Tina's hourly wage, then $t \leq 8.20$.

86. If $s =$ selling price, then $s \geq 12,000$.

87. Let $x =$ the price of the car and $0.08x =$ the amount of tax. To spend less than $10,000 we must satisfy the inequality
$$x + 0.08x + 172 < 10,000$$
$$1.08x < 9828$$
$$x < 9100$$
The price range for the car is $x < \$9,100$.

88. Let $x =$ the price of the sewing machine and $0.10x =$ the amount of sales tax. His total must be less than or equal to $700.
$$x + 0.10x \leq 700$$
$$1.1x \leq 700$$
$$x \leq 636.36$$
The price of the sewing machine must be less than or equal to $636.36.

89. Let $x =$ the price of the truck and $0.09x =$ the amount of sales tax. The total cost of at least $10,000 is expressed as
$$x + .09x + 80 \geq 10,000$$
$$1.09x \geq 9920$$
$$x \geq 9100.9174$$
The price range for the truck is $x \geq \$9,100.92$.

90. Let $x =$ the amount of Curly's contribution and $2x =$ the amount of Larry's contribution. Since Moe will contribute exactly $50, we can write the following inequality.
$$x + 2x + 50 \geq 600$$
$$3x \geq 550$$
$$x \geq 183.33$$
Curly will contribute at least $183.33.

91. a) Increasing
b) $16.45n + 980.20 > 1,300$
$$16.45n > 319.8$$
$$n > 19.44$$
Since n is a whole number, the first value of n greater than 19.44 is 20. Bachelor's degrees will exceed 1.3 million in the year $1985 + 20$, or 2005.

92. $7.79n + 287.87 > 0.20(30.95n + 1808.22)$
$$7.79n + 287.87 > 6.19n + 361.644$$
$$1.6n > 73.774$$
$$n > 46.10875$$
Master's degrees will be more than 20% of all degrees in the year $1985 + 46.1$, or approximately 2031, or you could round to the next whole number and say 2032.

93. Let $x =$ the final exam score. One-third of the midterm plus two-thirds of the final must be at least 70:
$$\tfrac{1}{3}(56) + \tfrac{2}{3}x \geq 70$$
$$3\left(\tfrac{1}{3}(56) + \tfrac{2}{3}x\right) \geq 3(70)$$
$$56 + 2x \geq 210$$
$$2x \geq 154$$

$$x \geq 77$$
The final exam score must satisfy $x \geq 77$.

94. Let $x =$ his final exam score. We can write the following inequality.
$$\tfrac{2}{3}(56) + \tfrac{1}{3}x \geq 70$$
$$112 + x \geq 210$$
$$x \geq 98$$
Wilburt must score at least 98 to get an average at least 70.

95. Let $x =$ the price of a pair of A-Mart jeans and $x + 50 =$ the price of a pair of designer jeans. Four pairs of A-Mart jeans cost less than one pair of designer jeans is written as follows.
$$4x < x + 50$$
$$3x < 50$$
$$x < 16.6666$$
The price range for A-Mart jeans is $x < \$16.67$.

96. Let $x =$ Al's rate and $x + 20 =$ Rita's rate. In 5 hours Al drove $5x$ miles and in 3 hours Rita drove $3(x + 20)$ miles. Since his distance is less than Rita's, we can write the following inequality.
$$5x < 3(x + 20)$$
$$5x < 3x + 60$$
$$2x < 60$$
$$x < 30$$
Al's rate is less than 30 miles per hour.

97. a) Write the inequality $x \geq 2$ and subtract -6 from each side to get $x - (-6) \geq 2 - (-6)$, or $x + 6 \geq 8$. So the results are all greater than or equal to 8, which is the interval $[8, \infty)$.
b) Write the inequality $x < -3$ and multiply each side by 2 to get $2x < -6$. So the results are all less than -6, which is the interval $(-\infty, -6)$.
c) $(2, \infty)$ d) $(-\infty, -12)$ e) $(2, \infty)$

2.5 WARM-UPS

1. True, because both inequalities are true.
2. True, because both inequalities are correct.
3. False, because $3 > 5$ is incorrect.
4. True, because $3 \leq 10$ is correct.
5. True, because both inequalities are correct.

6. True, because both are correct.

7. False, because $0 < -2$ is incorrect.

8. True, because only numbers larger than 8 are larger than 3 and larger than 8.

9. False, because $(3, \infty) \cup [8, \infty) = (3, \infty)$.

10. True, because the numbers greater than -2 and less than 9 are between -2 and 9.

2.5 EXERCISES

1. A compound inequality consists of two inequalities joined with the words "and" or "or."

2. A compound inequality using and is true only when both simple inequalities are true.

3. A compound inequality using or is true when either one or the other or both inequalities is true.

4. Solve each simple inequality and then either union or intersect the solution sets.

5. The inequality $a < b < c$ means that $a < b$ and $b < c$.

6. The inequality $5 < x > 7$ has no meaning. All inequality symbols must point in the same direction in this notation.

7. No, because $-6 > -3$ is incorrect.

8. Yes, because $3 < 5$ is correct.

9. Yes, because both inequalities are correct.

10. Yes, because both inequalities are correct.

11. No, because both inequalities are incorrect.

12. Yes, because $0 \leq 0$ is correct.

13. No, because $-4 > -3$ is incorrect.

14. Yes, because even though $-4 > -3$ is incorrect, $-4 < 5$ is correct.

15. Yes, because $-4 - 3 \geq -7$ is correct.

16. Yes, because $2(-4) \leq -8$ and $5(-4) \leq 0$ are both correct.

17. Yes, because $2(-4) - 1 < -7$ is correct.

18. Yes, because $-3(-4) > 0$ and $3(-4) - 4 < 11$ are both correct.

19. The set of numbers between -1 and 4:

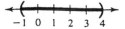

20. Graph the intersection of the two solution sets.

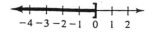

21. Graph the union of the two solution sets:

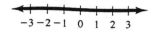

22. Graph the union of the two solution sets.

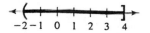

23. The union of the two solution sets consists of all real numbers:

24. The intersection of the two solution sets consists of the numbers greater than -2 and less than or equal to 4.

25. The solution set is $\emptyset$, because no number is greater than 9 and less than or equal to 6. There is no graph.

26. Graph the union of the two solution sets. Every real number is either less than 7 or greater than 0.

27. The union of the two solution sets is graphed as follows:

28. The intersection of the two solution sets is the empty set $\emptyset$. There is no real number that is greater than or equal to 4 and less than or equal to -4. There is no graph.

29. The solution set is $\emptyset$, there is no intersection to the two solution sets. There is no graph

30. Graph the union of the two solution sets.

41

31. $x - 3 > 7$ or $3 - x > 2$
$\qquad x > 10$ or $\quad -x > -1$
$\qquad x > 10$ or $\qquad x < 1$
$(-\infty, 1) \cup (10, \infty)$

32. $x - 5 > 6$ or $2 - x > 4$
$\qquad x > 11$ or $\quad -x > 2$
$\qquad x > 11$ or $\qquad x < -2$
$(-\infty, -2) \cup (11, \infty)$

33. $\quad 3 < x$ and $1 + x > 10$
$\qquad x > 3$ and $\qquad x > 9$
$(9, \infty)$

34. $-0.3x < 9$ and $0.2x > 2$
$\qquad x > -30$ and $x > 10$
$(10, \infty)$

35. $\quad \frac{1}{2}x > 5$ or $-\frac{1}{3}x < 2$
$\qquad x > 10$ or $\quad x > -6$
$(-6, \infty)$

36. $5 < x$ or $3 - \frac{1}{2}x < 7$
$\qquad 5 < x$ or $\quad -\frac{1}{2}x < 4$
$\qquad x > 5$ or $\qquad x > -8$
$(-8, \infty)$

37. $\quad 2x - 3 \leq 5$ and $x - 1 > 0$
$\qquad 2x \leq 8$ and $\qquad x > 1$
$\qquad x \leq 4$ and $\qquad x > 1$
$(1, 4]$

38. $\frac{3}{4}x < 9$ and $-\frac{1}{3}x \leq -15$
$\qquad x < 12$ and $\quad x \geq 45$
The solution set is $\emptyset$, because there are no real numbers less than 12 and greater than or equal to 45.

39. $\frac{1}{2}x - \frac{1}{3} \geq -\frac{1}{6}$ or $\frac{2}{7}x \leq \frac{1}{10}$
$\qquad 3x - 2 \geq -1$ or $\quad x \leq \frac{7}{2} \cdot \frac{1}{10}$
$\qquad x \geq \frac{1}{3}$ or $\quad x \leq \frac{7}{20}$
$(-\infty, \infty)$

40. $\frac{1}{4}x - \frac{1}{3} > -\frac{1}{5}$ and $\frac{1}{2}x < 2$
$60\left(\frac{1}{4}x - \frac{1}{3}\right) > 60\left(-\frac{1}{5}\right)$ and $2 \cdot \frac{1}{2}x < 2 \cdot 2$
$\quad 15x - 20 > -12$ and $\qquad x < 4$
$\qquad 15x > 8$ and $\qquad x < 4$
$\qquad x > \frac{8}{15}$ and $\qquad x < 4$
$(8/15, 4)$

41. $\quad 0.5x < 2$ and $-0.6x < -3$
$\qquad x < 4$ and $\qquad x > 5$
The solution set is $\emptyset$, because there are no numbers that are less than 4 and greater than 5. There is no graph.

42. $\quad 0.3x < 0.6$ or $0.05x > -4$
$\qquad x < 2$ or $\qquad x > -80$
$(-\infty, \infty)$

43. $\quad 5 < 2x - 3 < 11$
$\quad 5 + 3 < 2x - 3 + 3 < 11 + 3$
$\qquad 8 < 2x < 14$
$\qquad 4 < x < 7$
$(4, 7)$

44. $-2 < 3x + 1 < 10$
$\quad -3 < 3x < 9$
$\quad -1 < x < 3 \qquad\qquad (-1, 3)$

42

45.
$$-1 < 5 - 3x \le 14$$
$$-6 < -3x \le 9$$
$$\frac{-6}{-3} > \frac{-3x}{-3} \ge \frac{9}{-3}$$
$$2 > x \ge -3$$
$$-3 \le x < 2$$
$[-3, 2)$

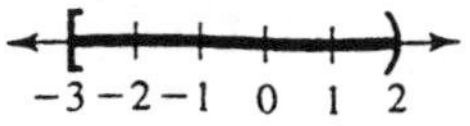

46.
$$-1 \le 3 - 2x < 11$$
$$-4 \le -2x < 8$$
$$2 \ge x > -4$$
$$-4 < x \le 2$$
$(-4, 2]$

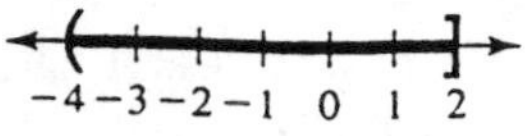

47.
$$2(-3) < 2 \cdot \frac{3m+1}{2} \le 2 \cdot 5$$
$$-6 < 3m + 1 \le 10$$
$$-7 < 3m \le 9$$
$$-\tfrac{7}{3} < m \le 3$$
$(-7/3, 3]$

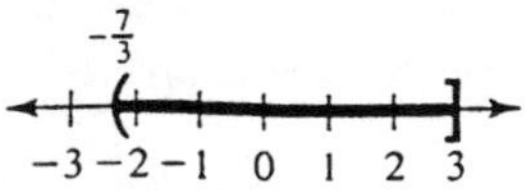

48.
$$0 \le \frac{3 - 2x}{2} < 5$$
$$0 \le 3 - 2x < 10$$
$$-3 \le -2x < 7$$
$$\tfrac{3}{2} \ge x > -\tfrac{7}{2}$$
$$-\tfrac{7}{2} < x \le \tfrac{3}{2}$$
$(-7/2, 3/2]$

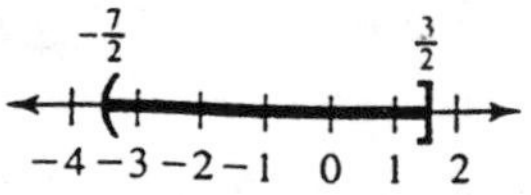

49.
$$-2(-2) > -2 \cdot \frac{1 - 3x}{-2} > -2(7)$$
$$4 > 1 - 3x > -14$$
$$3 > -3x > -15$$
$$-1 < x < 5$$
$(-1, 5)$

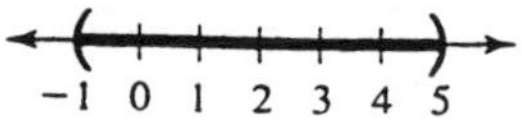

50.
$$-3 < \frac{2x - 1}{3} < 7$$
$$-9 < 2x - 1 < 21$$
$$-8 < 2x < 22$$

$$-4 < x < 11$$
$(-4, 11)$

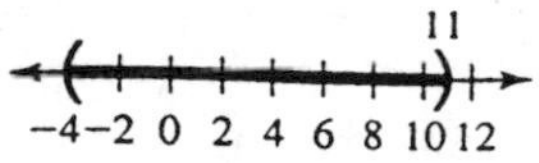

51.
$$3 \le 3 - 5x + 15 \le 8$$
$$3 \le 18 - 5x \le 8$$
$$-15 \le -5x \le -10$$
$$3 \ge x \ge 2$$
$$2 \le x \le 3$$
$[2, 3]$

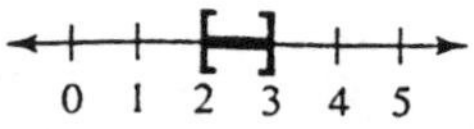

52.
$$2 \le 4 - \tfrac{1}{2}(x - 8) \le 10$$
$$2 \le 4 - \tfrac{1}{2}x + 4 \le 10$$
$$2 \le 8 - \tfrac{1}{2}x \le 10$$
$$-6 \le -\tfrac{1}{2}x \le 2$$
$$12 \ge x \ge -4$$
$$-4 \le x \le 12$$
$[-4, 12]$

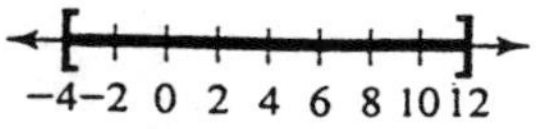

53. $(2, \infty) \cup (4, \infty) = (2, \infty)$
54. $(-3, \infty) \cup (-6, \infty) = (-6, \infty)$
55. $(-\infty, 5) \cap (-\infty, 9) = (-\infty, 5)$
56. $(-\infty, -2) \cap (-\infty, 1) = (-\infty, -2)$
57. $(-\infty, 4] \cap [2, \infty) = [2, 4]$
58. $(-\infty, 8) \cap [3, \infty) = [3, 8)$
59. $(-\infty, 5) \cup [-3, \infty) = (-\infty, \infty)$
60. $(-\infty, -2] \cup (2, \infty)$
61. $(3, \infty) \cap (-\infty, 3] = \emptyset$
62. $[-4, \infty) \cap (-\infty, -6] = \emptyset$
63. $(3, 5) \cap [4, 8) = [4, 5)$
64. $[-2, 4] \cap (0, 9) = (0, 4]$
65. $[1, 4) \cup (2, 6] = [1, 6]$
66. $[1, 3) \cup (0, 5) = (0, 5)$
67. The graph shows real numbers to the right of 2: $x > 2$
68. The graph shows the real numbers to the left of and including 5. The inequality is $x \le 5$.
69. The graph shows the real numbers to the left of 3: $x < 3$

43

70. The graph shows the real numbers less than -4 together with the real numbers to the right of 3. The inequality is $x < -4$ or $x > 3$.

71. This graph is the union of the numbers greater than 2 with the numbers less than or equal to -1: $x > 2$ or $x \le -1$

72. The graph shows the real numbers greater than -1 and less than 2. The inequality is $-1 < x < 2$.

73. This graph shows real numbers between -2 and 3: $-2 \le x < 3$

74. The graph shows the real numbers less than 2. The inequality is $x < 2$.

75. The graph shows real numbers greater than or equal to -3: $x \ge -3$

76. The graph shows the real numbers less than or equal to 0 together with the real numbers greater than 1: $x \le 0$ or $x > 1$.

77. $2 < x < 7$ and $x > 5$
The solution set consists of the numbers between 2 and 7 that are also greater than 5: $(5, 7)$

78.
$$3 < 5 - x < 8 \quad \text{or} \quad -3x < 0$$
$$-2 < -x < 3 \quad \text{or} \quad x > 0$$
$$2 > x > -3 \quad \text{or} \quad x > 0$$
$$-3 < x < 2 \quad \text{or} \quad x > 0$$
The union of the two solution sets is $(-3, \infty)$.

79. $-1 < 3x + 2 \le 5$ or $\frac{3}{2}x - 6 > 9$
$$-3 < 3x \le 3 \quad \text{or} \quad 3x - 12 > 18$$
$$-1 < x \le 1 \quad \text{or} \quad x > 10$$
Solution set is $(-1, 1] \cup (10, \infty)$.

80. $0 < 5 - 2x \le 10$ and $-6 < 4 - x < 0$
$$-5 < -2x \le 5 \quad \text{and} -10 < -x < -4$$
$$\tfrac{5}{2} > x \ge -\tfrac{5}{2} \quad \text{and} \quad 10 > x > 4$$
$$-2.5 \le x \le 2.5 \quad \text{and} \quad 4 < x < 10$$
No real number satisfies both of these compound inequalities. The solution set is $\emptyset$.

81. $-6 < x - 1 < 10$ and $-2 < 1 - x < 4$
$$-5 < x < 11 \quad \text{and} -3 < -x < 3$$
$$-5 < x < 11 \quad \text{and} \quad 3 > x > -3$$
The solution set is $(-3, 3)$.

82. $-15 < 3x - 1 < 2.5$ and
$$2 < 3 - 2x < 27$$
$$-14 < 3x < 3.5 \quad \text{and} -1 < -2x < 24$$
$$-\tfrac{14}{3} < x < \tfrac{7}{6} \quad \text{and} \quad \tfrac{1}{2} > x > -12$$
Solution set is $(-14/3, 1/2)$

83. Let x = the final exam score. We write an inequality expressing the fact that $1/3$ of the midterm plus $2/3$ of the final must be between 70 and 79 inclusive.
$$70 \le \tfrac{1}{3} \cdot 64 + \tfrac{2}{3}x \le 79$$
$$210 \le 64 + 2x \le 237$$
$$146 \le 2x \le 173$$
$$73 \le x \le 86.5$$

84. Let x = the final exam score. His average is calculated as $\frac{2}{3}(64) + \frac{1}{3}x$.
$$70 \le \tfrac{2}{3}(64) + \tfrac{1}{3}x \le 79$$
$$210 \le 2(64) + x \le 237$$
$$210 \le 128 + x \le 237$$
$$82 \le x \le 109$$

85. Let x = the price of the truck. The total spent will be $x + 0.08x + 84$.
$$12,000 \le x + 0.08x + 84 \le 15,000$$
$$12,000 \le 1.08x + 84 \le 15,000$$
$$11,916 \le 1.08x \le 14,916$$
$$\$11,033 \le x \le \$13,811$$

86. Let x = the selling price and $0.10x$ = the broker's commission. Renee gets the selling price minus the commission. Renee must get at least $13,104.
$$x - 0.10x \ge 13104$$
$$0.90x \ge 13104$$
$$x \ge 14560$$
Renee needs at least $14,560 to pay off the loan, but the car also will not sell for more than $14,900. So we can write the inequality $\$14,560 \le x \le \$14,900$.

87. Let x = the number of cigarettes smoked on the run, giving the equivalent of $\frac{1}{2}x$ cigarettes smoked. Thus, she smokes $3 + \frac{1}{2}x$ whole cigarettes per day and this number is between 5 and 12:
$$5 \le 3 + \tfrac{1}{2}x \le 12$$
$$10 \le 6 + x \le 24$$
$$4 \le x \le 18$$
She smokes from 4 to 18 cigarettes on the run.

88. Let w = the width and $w + 20$ = the length. Since $P = 2L + 2W$ for a rectangle, we can write the following inequality.
$$80 < 2w + 2(w + 20) < 100$$
$$80 < 2w + 2w + 40 < 100$$
$$80 < 4w + 40 < 100$$

44

$$40 < 4w < 60$$
$$10 < w < 15$$

89. a) In 1995, we have $n = 10$.
$16.45(10) + 980.20 = 1144.7$
In 1995, there were 1,444,700 bachelors degrees awarded.

b)
$$16.45n + 980.20 = 1,260$$
$$16.45n = 279.8$$
$$n = 17.0$$
$1985 + 17 = 2002$

c)
$$16.45n + 980.20 > 1,300$$
$$16.45n > 319.8$$
$$n > 19.44$$

$$7.79n + 287.87 > 500$$
$$7.79n > 212.13$$
$$n > 27.23$$

Both happen in the year $1985 + 28$, or 2013.
d) Either happens in the year $1985 + 20$, or 2005.

90. a) For 1998, $n = 28$.
$S = 0.48(28) + 19.71 = 33.15$
In 1998 there were 33.15 million seniors.

b)
$$-0.72n + 24.2 = 2.6$$
$$0.72n = -21.6$$
$$n = 30$$
$1970 + 30 = 2000$

c)
$$0.48n + 19.71 > 36$$
$$0.48n > 16.29$$
$$n > 33.94$$
$1970 + 34 = 2004$

Both (b) and (c) will be achieved in 2004.

91. If $a < b$ and $a < -x < b$, we can multiply each part of this inequality by -1 to get $-a > x > -b$ or $-b < x < -a$. In words, x is between $-b$ and $-a$.

92. Notation is used correctly in (a) and (e). The notation is incorrect in (c) and (b) because the inequality symbols point in different directions. The notation is incorrect in (d) because 6 is not less than -8.

93. a) If $3 < x < 8$, then $12 < 4x < 32$. $(12, 32)$
b) If $-2 \leq x < 4$, then
$(-5)(-2) \geq -5x > (-5)(4)$ or
$-20 \leq x < 10$.

$(-20, 10]$
c) $(0, 9)$
d) $[-3, -1]$

94. a) If $x > s$ and $x < t$, then the solution is (s, t) provided $s < t$. There is no solution if $t < s$.
b) If $x > s$ and $x > t$, then the solution is (s, ∞) if $s > t$, or (t, ∞) if $t > s$.

2.6 WARM-UPS

1. True, because both 2 and -2 have absolute value 2.

2. False, because $x = 0$ has only one solution.

3. False, because it is equivalent to $2x - 3 = 7$ or $2x - 3 = -7$.

4. True, because $|x| > 5$ means that x is more than 5 units away from 0.

5. False, because this equation has no solution.

6. True, because only 3 satisfies the equation.

7. False, because only inequalities that express x between two numbers are written this way.

8. False, because $|x| < 7$ is equivalent to $-7 < x < 7$.

9. True, subtract 2 from each side.

10. False, because $|x| < -2$ has no solution.

2.6 EXERCISES

1. Absolute value of a number is the number's distance from 0 on the number line.

2. Only 0 is 0 units from 0 on the number line.

3. Since both 4 and -4 are four units from 0, $|x| = 4$ has two solution.

4. Since $|x| \geq 0$ for every real number x, $|x| = -3$ is impossible.

5. Since the distance from 0 for every number on the number line is greater than or equal to 0, $|x| \geq 0$.

6. Since $|x| \geq 0$ for all x, $|x| < -3$ is impossible.

7. $a = 5$ or $a = -5$
Solution set: $\{-5, 5\}$

8. $|x| = 2$
$x = 2$ or $x = -2$
The solution set is $\{-2, 2\}$.

9. $x - 3 = 1$ or $x - 3 = -1$
$\quad\quad x = 4$ or $\quad\quad x = 2$
Solution set: $\{2, 4\}$

10. $|x - 5| = 2$
$\quad x - 5 = 2$ or $x - 5 = -2$
$\quad\quad x = 7$ or $\quad\quad x = 3$
The solution set is $\{3, 7\}$.

11. $3 - x = 6$ or $3 - x = -6$
$\quad -x = 3$ or $\quad -x = -9$
$\quad\quad x = -3$ or $\quad\quad x = 9$
Solution set: $\{-3, 9\}$

12. $\quad |7 - x| = 6$
$\quad 7 - x = 6$ or $7 - x = -6$
$\quad -x = -1$ or $\quad -x = -13$
$\quad\quad x = 1$ or $\quad\quad x = 13$
The solution set is $\{1, 13\}$.

13. $3x - 4 = 12$ or $3x - 4 = -12$
$\quad\quad 3x = 16$ or $\quad\quad 3x = -8$
$\quad\quad x = \frac{16}{3}$ or $\quad\quad x = -\frac{8}{3}$
Solution set: $\left\{-\frac{8}{3}, \frac{16}{3}\right\}$

14. $|5x + 2| = -3$
The solution set is $\emptyset$, because the absolute value of any quantity is nonnegative.

15. $\quad \frac{2}{3}x - 8 = 0$
$\quad\quad \frac{2}{3}x = 8$
$\quad\quad x = 12$
Solution set: $\{12\}$

16. $|3 - \frac{3}{4}x| = \frac{1}{4}$
$3 - \frac{3}{4}x = \frac{1}{4}$ or $3 - \frac{3}{4}x = -\frac{1}{4}$
$12 - 3x = 1$ or $12 - 3x = -1$
$\quad -3x = -11$ or $\quad -3x = -13$
$\quad\quad x = \frac{11}{3}$ or $\quad\quad x = \frac{13}{3}$
The solution set is $\left\{\frac{11}{3}, \frac{13}{3}\right\}$.

17. $6 - 0.2x = 10$ or $6 - 0.2x = -10$
$\quad -0.2x = 4$ or $\quad -0.2x = -16$
$\quad\quad x = -20$ or $\quad\quad x = 80$
Solution set: $\{-20, 80\}$

18. $|5 - 0.1x| = 0$
$\quad 5 - 0.1x = 0$
$\quad -0.1x = -5$
$\quad\quad x = 50$
The solution set is $\{50\}$.

19. Since absolute value is nonnegative, the solution set is $\emptyset$.

20. $|2(a + 3)| = 15$
$2a + 6 = 15$ or $2a + 6 = -15$

$2a = 9$ or $\quad 2a = -21$
$a = 4.5$ or $\quad a = -10.5$
The solution set is $\{-10.5, 4.5\}$.

21. $2(x - 4) + 3 = 5$ or $2(x - 4) + 3 = -5$
$\quad 2x - 5 = 5$ or $\quad 2x - 5 = -5$
$\quad\quad 2x = 10$ or $\quad\quad 2x = 0$
$\quad\quad x = 5$ or $\quad\quad x = 0$
Solution set: $\{0, 5\}$

22. $|3(x - 2) + 7| = 6$
$\quad |3x - 6 + 7| = 6$
$\quad\quad |3x + 1| = 6$
$3x + 1 = 6$ or $3x + 1 = -6$
$\quad 3x = 5$ or $\quad\quad 3x = -7$
$\quad x = \frac{5}{3}$ or $\quad\quad x = -\frac{7}{3}$
The solution set is $\left\{\frac{5}{3}, -\frac{7}{3}\right\}$.

23. $\quad 7.3x - 5.26 = 4.215$
$\quad\quad 7.3x = 9.475$
$\quad\quad x = 1.298$
or $\quad 7.3x - 5.26 = -4.215$
$\quad\quad 7.3x = 1.045$
$\quad\quad x = 0.143$
Solution set: $\{0.143, 1.298\}$

24. $|5.74 - 2.17x| = 10.28$
$5.74 - 2.17x = 10.28$ or
$\quad\quad\quad 5.74 - 2.17x = -10.28$
$-2.17x = 4.54$ or $-2.17x = -16.02$
$\quad x = -2.092$ or $\quad x = 7.382$
The solution set is $\{-2.092, 7.382\}$.

25. $3 + |x| = 5$
$\quad |x| = 2$
$x = 2$ or $x = -2$
Solution set: $\{-2, 2\}$

26. $|x| - 10 = -3$
$\quad |x| = 7$
$x = 7$ or $x = -7$
The solution set is $\{-7, 7\}$.

27. $2 - x + 3 = -6$
$\quad -x + 3 = -8$
$\quad\quad x + 3 = 8$
$x + 3 = 8$ or $x + 3 = -8$
$\quad x = 5$ or $\quad x = -11$
Solution set: $\{-11, 5\}$

28. $4 - 3|x - 2| = -8$
$\quad -3|x - 2| = -12$
$\quad\quad |x - 2| = 4$
$x - 2 = 4$ or $x - 2 = -4$

$$x = 6 \quad \text{or} \quad x = -2$$
The solution set is $\{-2, 6\}$.

29. $15 - |3 - 2x| = 12$
$$-|3 - 2x| = -3$$
$$|3 - 2x| = 3$$
$$3 - 2x = 3 \quad \text{or} \quad 3 - 2x = -3$$
$$-2x = 0 \quad \text{or} \quad -2x = -6$$
$$x = 0 \quad \text{or} \quad x = 3$$
The solution set is $\{0, 3\}$.

30. $6 - |\frac{1}{2}x - 4| = 4$
$$-|\tfrac{1}{2}x - 4| = -2$$
$$|\tfrac{1}{2}x - 4| = 2$$
$$\tfrac{1}{2}x - 4 = 2 \quad \text{or} \quad \tfrac{1}{2}x - 4 = -2$$
$$\tfrac{1}{2}x = 6 \quad \text{or} \quad \tfrac{1}{2}x = 2$$
$$x = 12 \quad \text{or} \quad x = 4$$
The solution set is $\{4, 12\}$.

31. $x - 5 = 2x + 1 \quad$ or $\quad x - 5 = -(2x + 1)$
$$-6 = x \qquad \quad \text{or} \quad x - 5 = -2x - 1$$
$$3x = 4$$
$$x = 4/3$$
Solution set: $\left\{-6, \frac{4}{3}\right\}$

32. $|w - 6| = |3 - 2w|$
$$w - 6 = 3 - 2w \quad \text{or} \quad w - 6 = -(3 - 2w)$$
$$3w = 9 \qquad \quad \text{or} \quad w - 6 = -3 + 2w$$
$$w = 3 \qquad \quad \text{or} \quad -3 = w$$
The solution set is $\{-3, 3\}$.

33. $\frac{5}{2} - x = 2 - \frac{x}{2} \quad$ or $\quad \frac{5}{2} - x = -\left(2 - \frac{x}{2}\right)$
$$5 - 2x = 4 - x \quad \text{or} \quad \tfrac{5}{2} - x = -2 + \tfrac{x}{2}$$
$$1 = x \qquad \quad \text{or} \quad 5 - 2x = -4 + x$$
$$-3x = -9$$
$$x = 3$$
Solution set: $\{1, 3\}$

34. $|x - \frac{1}{4}| = |\frac{1}{2}x - \frac{3}{4}|$
$$x - \tfrac{1}{4} = \tfrac{1}{2}x - \tfrac{3}{4} \quad \text{or} \quad x - \tfrac{1}{4} = -\left(\tfrac{1}{2}x - \tfrac{3}{4}\right)$$
$$4x - 1 = 2x - 3 \quad \text{or} \quad 4x - 1 = -2x + 3$$
$$2x = -2 \qquad \quad \text{or} \qquad 6x = 4$$
$$x = -1 \qquad \quad \text{or} \qquad x = 2/3$$
The solution set is $\left\{-1, \frac{2}{3}\right\}$.

35. $x - 3 = 3 - x \quad$ or $\quad x - 3 = -(3 - x)$
$$2x = 6 \qquad \quad \text{or} \quad x - 3 = -3 + x$$
$$x = 3 \qquad \quad \text{or} \quad x - 3 = x - 3$$

The second equation is an identity. So the solution set is the set of real numbers, $(-\infty, \infty)$.

36. $|a - 6| = |6 - a|$
$$a - 6 = 6 - a \qquad \text{or} \quad a - 6 = -(6 - a)$$
$$2a = 12 \qquad \quad \text{or} \quad a - 6 = -6 + a$$
$$a = 6 \qquad \quad \text{or} \quad a - 6 = a - 6$$
Since the second equation is an identity, the solution set is R, or $(-\infty, \infty)$.

37. The graph shows the real numbers between -2 and 2: $|x| < 2$

38. The graph shows the real numbers between -5 and 5. The inequality is $|x| \leq 5$.

39. The graph shows numbers greater than 3 or less than -3: $|x| > 3$

40. The graph shows the real numbers greater than or equal to 6 together with the real numbers less than or equal to -6. The inequality is $|x| \geq 6$.

41. The graph shows numbers between -1 and 1 inclusive: $|x| \leq 1$

42. The graph shows the real numbers between -1 and 1. The inequality is $|x| < 1$.

43. The graph shows numbers two or more units away from 0: $|x| \geq 2$

44. The graph shows the real numbers larger than 4 or smaller than -4. The inequality is $|x| > 4$.

45. No, because $|x| < 3$ is equivalent to $-3 < x < 3$.

46. No, because $|x| > 3$ is equivalent to $x > 3$ or $x < -3$.

47. Yes.

48. Yes.

49. No, because $|x - 3| \geq 1$ is equivalent to $x - 3 \geq 1$ or $x - 3 \leq -1$.

50. No, because $|x - 3| > 0$ is equivalent to $x - 3 > 0$ or $x - 3 < 0$.

51. Yes, because the following compound inequalities are equivalent.
$$|4 - x| < 1$$
$$4 - x < 1 \quad \text{and} \quad 4 - x > -1$$
$$4 - x < 1 \quad \text{and} \quad -(4 - x) < 1$$

52. Yes, because $|4 - x| > 1$ is equivalent to $4 - x > 1$ or $4 - x < -1$, which is equivalent to $4 - x > 1$ or $-(4 - x) > 1$.

47

53. $|x| > 6$

$\quad x > 6$ or $x < -6$

$(-\infty, -6) \cup (6, \infty)$

54. $|w| > 3$

$\quad w > 3$ or $w < -3$

$(-\infty, -3) \cup (3, \infty)$

55. $|2a| < 6$

$\quad -6 < 2a < 6$

$\quad -3 < a < 3$

$(-3, 3)$

56. $|3x| < 21$

$\quad -21 < 3x < 21$

$\quad -7 < x < 7$

$(-7, 7)$

57. $x - 2 \geq 3 \qquad$ or $x - 2 \leq -3$

$\qquad x \geq 5 \qquad$ or $\qquad x \leq -1$

$(-\infty, -1] \cup [5, \infty)$

58. $|x - 5| \geq 1$

$\quad x - 5 \geq 1 \quad$ or $x - 5 \leq -1$

$\qquad x \geq 6 \quad$ or $\qquad x \leq 4$

$(-\infty, 4] \cup [6, \infty)$

59. $|2x - 4| < 5$

$\quad -5 < 2x - 4 < 5$

$\quad -1 < 2x < 9$

$\quad -\frac{1}{2} < x < \frac{9}{2} \qquad\qquad \left(-\frac{1}{2}, \frac{9}{2}\right)$

60. $|2x - 1| < 3$

$\quad -3 < 2x - 1 < 3$

$\quad -2 < 2x < 4$

$\quad -1 < x < 2$

$(-1, 2)$

61. $|5 - x| \leq 7$

$\quad -7 \leq 5 - x \leq 7$

$\quad -12 \leq -x \leq 2$

$\quad 12 \geq x \geq -2 \qquad\qquad [-2, 12]$

62. $|6 - x| \leq 1$

$\quad -1 \leq 6 - x \leq 1$

$\quad -7 \leq -x \leq -5$

$\quad 7 \geq x \geq 5$

$\quad 5 \leq x \leq 7 \qquad\qquad [5, 7]$

63. $2|3 - 2x| \geq 24$

$\qquad |3 - 2x| \geq 12$

$\quad 3 - 2x \geq 12 \quad$ or $3 - 2x \leq -12$

$\quad -2x \geq 9 \qquad$ or $\quad -2x \leq -15$

$\quad x \leq -\frac{9}{2} \quad$ or $\qquad x \geq \frac{15}{2}$

$(-\infty, -\frac{9}{2}] \cup [\frac{15}{2}, \infty)$

64. $2|5 - 2x| \geq 20$

$\qquad |5 - 2x| \geq 10$

$\quad 5 - 2x \geq 10 \qquad$ or $5 - 2x \leq -10$

$\quad -2x \geq 5 \qquad$ or $\quad -2x \leq -15$

$\quad x \leq -\frac{5}{2} \qquad$ or $\qquad x \geq \frac{15}{2}$

$(-\infty, -\frac{5}{2}] \cup [\frac{15}{2}, \infty)$

65. $|x - 2| > 0$, except when $x = 2$.

$(-\infty, 2) \cup (2, \infty)$

48

66. The inequality $|6 - x| \geq 0$ is satisfied by every real number because the absolute value of any real number is nonnegative. The solution set is R.
$(-\infty, \infty)$

67. Since the absolute value of any quantity is greater than or equal to zero, the solution set is R. $(-\infty, \infty)$

68. The inequality $|3x - 7| \geq -3$ is satisfied by every real number because the absolute value of any real number is nonnegative. The solution set is R or $(-\infty, \infty)$.

69. $-2|3x - 7| > 6$ is equivalent to
$$|3x - 7| < -3.$$
Absolute value of an expression cannot be less than a negative number. Solution set is $\emptyset$.

70. $-3|7x - 42| > 18$ is equivalent to
$$|x - 42| < -6.$$
Absolute value of an expression cannot be less than a negative number because absolute value of any real number is nonnegative. The solution set is $\emptyset$.

71. $|2x + 3| > -6$
Since the absolute value of any expression is greater than or equal to zero, it is greater than any negative number. The solution set is R.

72. $|5 - x| > 0$
Since the absolute value of any real number is greater than or equal to 0, the only value of x that does not satisfy this inequality is one for which $|5 - x| = 0$. This inequality is satisfied by every real number except 5. The solution set is $(-\infty, 5) \cup (5, \infty)$.

73. $|x + 2| > 1$
$$x + 2 > 1 \quad \text{or} \quad x + 2 < -1$$
$$x > -1 \quad \text{or} \quad x < -3$$
$(-\infty, -3) \cup (-1, \infty)$

74. $5 \geq |x - 4|$
$$|x - 4| \leq 5$$
$$-5 \leq x - 4 \leq 5$$
$$-1 \leq x \leq 9$$
$[-1, 9]$

75. $|x| + 1 < 5$

$$|x| < 4$$
$$-4 < x < 4$$
$(-4, 4)$

76. $4 \leq |x| - 6$
$$10 \leq |x|$$
$$|x| \geq 10$$
$$x \geq 10 \text{ or } x \leq -10$$
$(-\infty, -10] \cup [10, \infty)$

77. $3 - 5|x| > -2$
$$-5|x| > -5$$
$$|x| < 1$$
$$-1 < x < 1$$
$(-1, 1)$

78. $1 - 2|x| < -7$
$$-2|x| < -8$$
$$|x| > 4$$
$$x > 4 \text{ or } x < -4$$
$(-\infty, -4) \cup (4, \infty)$

79. $-1.68 < 5.67x - 3.124 < 1.68$
$$1.444 < 5.67x < 4.804$$
$$0.255 < x < 0.847$$
$(0.255, 0.847)$

80. $|4.67 - 3.2x| \geq 1.43$
$$4.67 - 3.2x \geq 1.43 \quad \text{or} \quad 4.67 - 3.2x \leq -1.43$$
$$-3.2x \geq -3.24 \quad \text{or} \quad -3.2x \leq -6.1$$
$$x \leq 1.0125 \quad \text{or} \quad x \geq 1.90625$$
$(-\infty, 1.0125] \cup [1.90625, \infty)$

81. $-3 < 2x - 1 < 3 \text{ and } 2x - 3 > 2$
$$-2 < 2x < 4 \quad \text{and} \quad 2x > 5$$
$$-1 < x < 2 \quad \text{and} \quad x > 2.5$$
$\emptyset$

82. $|5 - 3x| \geq 3 \text{ and } 5 - 2x > 3$
$[5 - 3x \geq 3 \text{ or } 5 - 3x \leq -3] \text{ and } -2x > -2$
$[-3x \geq -2 \text{ or } -3x \leq -8] \text{ and } x < 1$
$[x \leq \frac{2}{3} \text{ or } x \geq \frac{8}{3}] \text{ and } x < 1$
The intersection of the solution set to the first compound inequality with the solution set to $x < 1$ is the set of real numbers less than or equal to 2/3. $(-\infty, 2/3]$

83. $-3 < x - 2 < 3 \quad \text{and} -3 < x - 7 < 3$
$$-1 < x < 5 \quad \text{and} \quad 4 < x < 10$$
$(4, 5)$

84. $|x - 5| < 4 \text{ and } |x - 6| > 2$
$-4 < x - 5 < 4 \text{ and}$
$$[x - 6 > 2 \text{ or } x - 6 < -2]$$
$1 < x < 9 \text{ and } [x > 8 \text{ or } x < 4]$

The intersection of the set of numbers between 1 and 9 with the numbers greater than 8 or less than 4 consists of the numbers between 1 and 4 together with the numbers between 8 and 9.
$(1, 4) \cup (8, 9)$

85. Let $x =$ the year of the battle of Orleans. Since the difference between x and 1415 is 14 years, we have $|x - 1415| = 14$.

$$x - 1415 = 14 \qquad \text{or } x - 1415 = -14$$
$$x = 1429 \qquad \text{or} \qquad x = 1401$$

The battle Agincourt was either in 1401 or 1429.

86. Let $x =$ the number of the day in July on which Cram set the record in the 1 mile race. We have $|x - 16| = 11$.

$$x - 16 = 11 \qquad \text{or } x - 16 = -11$$
$$x = 27 \qquad \text{or} \qquad x = 5$$

So the 1 mile record was set July 5 or July 27.

87. Let $x =$ the weight of Kathy. The difference between their weights is less than 6 pounds is expressed by the absolute value inequality

$$|x - 127| < 6$$
$$-6 < x - 127 < 6$$
$$121 < x < 133$$

Kathy weighs between 121 and 133 pounds.

88. Let $x =$ Jude's IQ score. Since Jude's score is more than 15 points away from Sherry's, we can write the following inequality.

$$|x - 110| > 15$$
$$x - 110 > 15 \qquad \text{or } x - 110 < -15$$
$$x > 125 \qquad \text{or} \qquad x < 95$$

Jude's IQ score is either greater than 125 or less than 95.

89. a) From the graph it appears that the balls are at the same height when $t = 1$ second.

b) Height of first ball is $S = -16t^2 + 50t$ and height of second ball is $S = -16t^2 + 40t + 10$. When the balls are at the same height we have

$$-16t^2 + 50t = -16t^2 + 40t + 10$$
$$50t = 40t + 10$$
$$10t = 10$$
$$t = 1$$

The balls are at the same height when $t = 1$ sec.

c) The difference between the heights is less than 5 feet when

$$|-16t^2 + 50t - (-16t^2 + 40t + 10)| < 5$$
$$|10t - 10| < 5$$
$$-5 < 10t - 10 < 5$$
$$5 < 10t < 15$$
$$0.5 < t < 1.5$$

90. The height of the dropped ball is $S = -16t^2 + 60$ and the height of the ball tossed upward is $S = -16t^2 + 80t$. The difference between the heights is less than or equal to 10 when

$$|-16t^2 + 60 - (-16t^2 + 80t)| \le 10$$
$$|60 - 80t| \le 10$$
$$-10 \le 60 - 80t \le 10$$
$$-70 \le -80t \le -50$$
$$0.875 \ge t \ge 0.625$$

Now $0.875 - 0.625 = 0.25$. So the balls are less than 10 feet apart for 0.25 sec.

91. a) The equation $|m - n| = |n - m|$ is satisfied for all real numbers, because $m - n$ and $n - m$ are opposites of each other and opposites always have the same absolute value. So both m and n can be in the interval $(-\infty, \infty)$.

b) $|mn| = |m| \cdot |n|$ is satisfied for all real numbers, because of the rules for multiplying real numbers. So both m and n can be in the interval $(-\infty, \infty)$.

c) Since you cannot have 0 in a denominator, the equation is satisfied by all real numbers except if $n = 0$.

92. $|m + n| \le |m| + |n|$

Enriching Your Mathematical Word Power
1. c   2. b   3. d   4. c
5. c   6. d   7. d   8. a
9. d   10. d   11. d   12. c
13. d

CHAPTER 2 REVIEW

1. $$\begin{aligned} 2x - 7 &= 9 \\ 2x &= 16 \\ x &= 8 \end{aligned}$$
Solution set: $\{8\}$

2. $$\begin{aligned} 5x - 7 &= 38 \\ 5x &= 45 \end{aligned}$$

$$x = 9$$

The solution set is {9}.

3. $5 - 4x = 11$
   $-4x = 6$
   $x = \frac{6}{-4} = -\frac{3}{2}$

Solution set: $\{-\frac{3}{2}\}$

4. $7 - 3x = -8$
   $-3x = -15$
   $x = 5$

The solution set is {5}.

5. $x - 6 - x + 6 = 0$
   $0 = 0$

Solution set: R

6. $x - 6 - 2x + 6 = 0$
   $-x = 0$
   $x = 0$

The solution set is {0}.

7. $2x - 6 - 5 = 5 - 3 + 2x$
   $2x - 11 = 2 + 2x$
   $-11 = 2$

Solution set: $\emptyset$

8. $2(x - 4) + 5 = -(3 - 2x)$
   $2x - 8 + 5 = -3 + 2x$
   $2x - 3 = 2x - 3$

The equation is an identity, the solution set is R

9. $\frac{3}{17}x = 0$
   $x = 0$

Solution set: {0}

10. $-\frac{3}{8}x = \frac{1}{2}$
   $x = -\frac{8}{3} \cdot \frac{1}{2} = -\frac{4}{3}$

Solution set: {−4/3}

11. $20\left(\frac{1}{4}x - \frac{1}{5}\right) = 20\left(\frac{1}{5}x + \frac{4}{5}\right)$
   $5x - 4 = 4x + 16$
   $x = 20$

Solution set: {20}

12. $\frac{1}{2}x - 1 = \frac{1}{3}x$
   $6\left(\frac{1}{2}x - 1\right) = 6 \cdot \frac{1}{3}x$
   $3x - 6 = 2x$
   $x = 6$

The solution set is {6}.

13. $6\left(\frac{t}{2}\right) - 6\left(\frac{t-2}{3}\right) = 6\left(\frac{3}{2}\right)$
   $3t - 2t + 4 = 9$
   $t + 4 = 9$
   $t = 5$

Solution set: {5}

14. $\frac{y+1}{4} - \frac{y-1}{6} = y + 5$

$12 \cdot \frac{y+1}{4} - 12 \cdot \frac{y-1}{6} = 12(y + 5)$
$3y + 3 - 2(y - 1) = 12y + 60$
$3y + 3 - 2y + 2 = 12y + 60$
$y + 5 = 12y + 60$
$-11y = 55$
$y = -5$

The solution set is {−5}.

15. $1 - 0.4x + 1.6 + 0.6x - 4.2 = -0.6$
$0.2x - 1.6 = -0.6$
$0.2x = 1$
$x = 5$

The solution set is {5}.

16. $0.04x - 0.06x + 0.48 = 0.1x$
$-0.12x = -0.48$
$x = 4$

The solution set is {4}.

17. $ax + b = 0$
   $ax = -b$
   $x = -\frac{b}{a}$

18. $mx + c = d$
   $mx = d - c$
   $x = \frac{d - c}{m}$

19. $ax + 2 = cx$
   $ax - cx = -2$
   $x(a - c) = -2$
   $\frac{x(a - c)}{a - c} = \frac{-2}{a - c}$
   $x = \frac{2}{c - a}$

20. $mx = 3 - x$
   $mx + x = 3$
   $x(m + 1) = 3$
   $x = \frac{3}{m + 1}$

21. $\frac{mwx}{mw} = \frac{P}{mw}$

   $x = \frac{P}{mw}$

22. $xyz = 2$
   $x = \frac{2}{yz}$

51

23.
$$2x\left(\tfrac{1}{x}\right) + 2x\left(\tfrac{1}{2}\right) = 2x(w)$$
$$2 + x = 2xw$$
$$x - 2xw = -2$$
$$x(1 - 2w) = -2$$
$$x = \frac{-2}{1 - 2w}$$
$$x = \frac{2}{2w - 1}$$

24.
$$\tfrac{1}{x} + \tfrac{1}{a} = 2$$
$$ax\left(\tfrac{1}{x} + \tfrac{1}{a}\right) = ax \cdot 2$$
$$a + x = 2ax$$
$$a = 2ax - x$$
$$a = x(2a - 1)$$
$$\frac{a}{2a - 1} = x$$
$$x = \frac{a}{2a - 1}$$

25.
$$3x - 2y = -6$$
$$-2y = -3x - 6$$
$$y = \frac{-3x - 6}{-2}$$
$$y = \tfrac{3}{2}x + 3$$

26.
$$4x - 3y + 9 = 0$$
$$-3y = -4x - 9$$
$$y = \tfrac{4}{3}x + 3$$

27.
$$y - 2 = -\tfrac{1}{3}x + 2$$
$$y = -\tfrac{1}{3}x + 4$$

28.
$$y + 6 = \tfrac{1}{2}(x - 4)$$
$$y + 6 = \tfrac{1}{2}x - 2$$
$$y = \tfrac{1}{2}x - 8$$

29.
$$4\left(\tfrac{1}{2}x - \tfrac{1}{4}y\right) = 4(5)$$
$$2x - y = 20$$
$$-y = -2x + 20$$
$$y = 2x - 20$$

30.
$$-\tfrac{x}{3} + \tfrac{y}{2} = \tfrac{5}{8}$$
$$\tfrac{y}{2} = \tfrac{x}{3} + \tfrac{5}{8}$$
$$2 \cdot \tfrac{y}{2} = 2 \cdot \tfrac{x}{3} + 2 \cdot \tfrac{5}{8}$$

$$y = \tfrac{2}{3}x + \tfrac{5}{4}$$

31. Let W = the width and $W + 5.5$ = the length. Since $2L + 2W = P$, we have
$$2(W + 5.5) + 2W = 45$$
$$2W + 11 + 2W = 45$$
$$4W = 34$$
$$W = 8.5$$
Length is 14 inches and width is 8.5 inches.

32. Let x = the length of the lower base and $x - 2$ = the length of the upper base. Use the formula for the area of a trapezoid to write the following equation.

$$\tfrac{1}{2} \cdot 5(x + x - 2) = 45$$
$$5(2x - 2) = 90$$
$$10x - 10 = 90$$
$$10x = 100$$
$$x = 10$$
The length of the lower base is 10 feet.

33. Let x = the wife's income and $x + 8000$ = Roy's income. Roy saves $0.10(x + 8000)$ and his wife saves $0.08x$. Since the total saved is \$5,660, we can write
$$0.10(x + 8000) + 0.08x = 5660$$
$$0.10x + 800 + 0.08x = 5660$$
$$0.18x = 4860$$
$$x = 27000$$
Roy's wife earns \$27,000 and Roy earns \$35,000.

34. Let x = Duane's income and $x + 1,000$ = his wife's income. Write an equation about the amount that each one gives to charity.
$$0.05x + 0.10(x + 1000) = 2500$$
$$0.05x + 0.10x + 100 = 2500$$
$$0.15x = 2400$$
$$x = 16,000$$
$$x + 1000 = 17,000$$
Duane makes \$16,000 per year and his wife makes \$17,000 per year.

35. Let x = the list price and $0.20x$ = the discount. The list price minus the discount is equal to \$7,600.
$$x - 0.20x = 7600$$

$$0.80x = 7600$$
$$x = 9500$$

The list price was $9,500.

36. Let $x =$ the list price and $0.25x =$ the amount of the discount. Since the selling price is the list price minus the discount, we can write the following equation.

$$x - 0.25x = 465$$
$$0.75x = 465$$
$$x = 620$$

The list price was $620.

37. Let $x =$ the number of nickels and $15 - x =$ the number of dimes. The value of x nickels is $5x$ cents and the value of $15 - x$ dimes is $10(15 - x)$ cents. Since she has a total of 95 cents, we can write the equation

$$5x + 10(15 - x) = 95$$
$$5x + 150 - 10x = 95$$
$$-5x = -55$$
$$x = 11$$
$$15 - x = 4$$

She has 11 nickels and 4 dimes.

38. Let $x =$ the number of quarters, $6x =$ the number of nickels, and $19 - x - 6x =$ the number of dimes. Write an equation expressing the total value of the coins.

$$0.25x + 0.05(6x) + 0.10(19 - 7x) = 1.60$$
$$25x + 5(6x) + 10(19 - 7x) = 160$$
$$25x + 30x + 190 - 70x = 160$$
$$-15x = -30$$
$$x = 2$$
$$6x = 12$$
$$19 - 7x = 5$$

She has 2 quarters, 12 nickels, and 5 dimes.

39. Let $x =$ her walking speed and $x + 9 =$ her riding speed. Since she walked for 3 hours, $3x$ is the number of miles that she walked. Since she rode for 5 hours, $5(x + 9)$ is the number of miles that she rode. Her total distance was 85 miles.

$$3x + 5(x + 9) = 85$$
$$3x + 5x + 45 = 85$$
$$8x = 40$$
$$x = 5$$

She walked 5 miles per hour for 3 hours, so she walked 15 miles.

40. Let $x =$ his flying speed and $x - 150 =$ his driving speed. His time flying was 90 minutes or 1.5 hours. His distance flying was $1.5x$ and his distance driving was $6(x - 150)$. Since the distance is the same for either driving or flying, we can write the following equation.

$$1.5x = 6(x - 150)$$
$$1.5x = 6x - 900$$
$$-4.5x = -900$$
$$x = 200$$

His flying speed was 200 miles per hour.

41.
$$3 - 4x < 15$$
$$-4x < 12$$
$$x > -3$$
$$(-3, \infty)$$

42.
$$5 - 6x > 35$$
$$-6x > 30$$
$$x < -5$$
$$(-\infty, -5)$$

43.
$$2x - 6 > -6$$
$$2x > 0$$
$$x > 0$$
$$(0, \infty)$$

44.
$$4(5 - x) < 20$$
$$5 - x < 5$$
$$-x < 0$$
$$x > 0$$
$$(0, \infty)$$

45.
$$-\tfrac{3}{4}x \geq 6$$
$$-3x \geq 24$$
$$x \leq -8$$
$$(-\infty, -8]$$

46. $-\frac{2}{3}x \leq 4$

$-2x \leq 12$

$x \geq -6$

$[-6, \infty)$

47. $3x + 6 > 5x - 5$

$-2x > -11$

$x < \frac{11}{2}$

$(-\infty, 11/2)$

48. $4 - 2(x - 3) < 0$

$4 - 2x + 6 < 0$

$-2x + 10 < 0$

$-2x < -10$

$x > 5$

$(5, \infty)$

49. $4\left(\frac{1}{2}x + 7\right) \leq 4\left(\frac{3}{4}x - 5\right)$

$2x + 28 \leq 3x - 20$

$48 \leq x$

$[48, \infty)$

50. $\frac{5}{6}x - 3 \geq \frac{2}{3}x + 7$

$6 \cdot \frac{5}{6}x - 6 \cdot 3 \geq 6 \cdot \frac{2}{3}x + 6 \cdot 7$

$5x - 18 \geq 4x + 42$

$x \geq 60$

$[60, \infty)$

51. $x + 2 > 3 \qquad$ or $x - 6 < -10$

$x > 1 \qquad$ or $\qquad x < -4$

$(-\infty, -4) \cup (1, \infty)$

52. $x - 2 > 5 \qquad$ or $\quad x - 2 < -1$

$x > 7 \qquad$ or $\qquad x < 1$

$(-\infty, 1) \cup (7, \infty)$

53. $x > 0$ and $x < 9$

$(0, 9)$

54. $x \leq 0$ and $x + 6 > 3$

$x \leq 0$ and $\qquad x > -3$

$(-3, 0]$

55. $-x < -3$ or $-x < 0$

$x > 3 \qquad$ or $\quad x > 0$

$(0, \infty)$

56. $-x > 0 \qquad$ or $x + 2 < 7$

$x < 0 \quad$ or $\qquad x < 5$

$(-\infty, 5)$

57. $2x < 8 \quad$ and $2x - 6 < 6$

$x < 4 \quad$ and $\qquad 2x < 12$

$x < 4 \quad$ and $\qquad x < 6$

$(-\infty, 4)$

58. $\frac{1}{3}x > 2 \quad$ and $\frac{1}{4}x > 2$

$x > 6 \quad$ and $\quad x > 8$

$(8, \infty)$

59. $x - 6 > 2$ and $6 - x > 0$

$x > 8 \qquad$ and $\qquad -x > -6$

$x > 8 \qquad$ and $\qquad x < 6$

No number is greater than 8 and less than 6.

$\emptyset$

54

60. $-\frac{1}{2}x < 6$ or $\frac{2}{3}x < 4$

$\qquad x > -12 \qquad$ or $\quad x < 6$

Every real number is either greater than -12 or less than 6. The solution set is R or $(-\infty, \infty)$.

61. $0.5x > 10 \qquad$ or $0.1x < 3$

$\qquad x > 20 \qquad$ or $\quad x < 30$

Every number is either greater than 20 or less than 30. Solution set is R or $(-\infty, \infty)$

62. $0.02x > 4 \qquad$ and $0.2x < 3$

$\qquad x > 200 \qquad$ and $\quad x < 15$

No real number is greater than 200 and less than 15. The solution set is $\emptyset$.

63. $10(-2) \le 10 \cdot \frac{2x-3}{10} \le 10(1)$

$\qquad -20 \le 2x - 3 \le 10$

$\qquad -17 \le 2x \le 13$

$\qquad -\frac{17}{2} \le x \le \frac{13}{2}$

$\left[-\frac{17}{2}, \frac{13}{2}\right]$

64. $\quad -3 < \frac{4-3x}{5} < 2$

$\qquad -15 < 4 - 3x < 10$

$\qquad -19 < -3x < 6$

$\qquad \frac{19}{3} > x > -2$

$\left(-2, \frac{19}{3}\right)$

65. $[1, 4) \cup (2, \infty) = [1, \infty)$

66. $(2, 5) \cup (-1, \infty) = (-1, \infty)$

67. $(3, 6) \cap [2, 8] = (3, 6)$

68. $[-1, 3] \cap [0, 8] = [0, 3]$

69. $(-\infty, 5) \cup [5, \infty) = (-\infty, \infty)$

70. $(-\infty, 1) \cup (0, \infty) = (-\infty, \infty)$

71. $(-3, -1] \cap [-2, 5] = [-2, -1]$

72. $[-2, 4] \cap (4, 7] = \emptyset$

73. $\quad 2x \ge 8$ or $2x \le -8$

$\qquad x \ge 4$ or $\quad x \le -4$

74. $\quad |5x - 1| \le 14$

$\qquad -14 \le 5x - 1 \le 14$

$\qquad -13 \le 5x \le 15$

$\qquad -\frac{13}{5} \le x \le 3$

75. Since $|x| \ge 0$ for any real number, the solution set is $\emptyset$.

76. $|x| + 2 = 16$

$\quad |x| = 14$

$x = 14$ or $x = -14$

77. $1 - \frac{x}{5} > \frac{9}{5} \qquad$ or $1 - \frac{x}{5} < -\frac{9}{5}$

$\quad 5 - x > 9$ or $5 - x < -9$

$\qquad -x > 4 \qquad$ or $\quad -x < -14$

$\qquad x < -4 \qquad$ or $\quad x > 14$

78. $|1 - \frac{1}{6}x| < \frac{1}{2}$

$\quad -\frac{1}{2} < 1 - \frac{1}{6}x < \frac{1}{2}$

$\quad -3 < 6 - x < 3$

$\quad -9 < -x < -3$

$\quad 9 > x > 3$

79. Since $|x - 3| \ge 0$ for any value of x, the solution set is $\emptyset$.

80. Since the absolute value of any real number is nonnegative, there is no value for x that will make $|x - 7| \le -4$ true. The solution set is $\emptyset$.

81. $\quad |\frac{x}{2}| - 5 = -1$

$\qquad |\frac{x}{2}| = 4$

$\qquad \frac{x}{2} = 4$ or $\frac{x}{2} = -4$

$\qquad x = 8 \qquad$ or $\quad x = -8$

82. Since the absolute value of any real number is nonnegative, no value of x will make $|\frac{x}{2} - 5| = -1$ correct. The solution set is $\emptyset$.

83. Since $|x + 4| \ge 0$ for any value of x, $|x + 4| \ge -1$ for any x. Solution set: R

84. Since the absolute value of any real number is nonnegative, $|6x - 1| \geq 0$ is correct for any number x. The solution set is R.

85.
$$2 - 3|x - 2| < -1$$
$$-3|x - 2| < -3$$
$$|x - 2| > 1$$
$$x - 2 > 1 \quad \text{or} \quad x - 2 < -1$$
$$x > 3 \quad \text{or} \qquad x < 1$$

86.
$$4 > 2|6 - x| - 3$$
$$7 > 2|6 - x|$$
$$\tfrac{7}{2} > |6 - x|$$
$$-\tfrac{7}{2} < 6 - x < \tfrac{7}{2}$$
$$-7 < 12 - 2x < 7$$
$$-19 < -2x < -5$$
$$\tfrac{19}{2} > x > \tfrac{5}{2}$$

87. Let x = the rental price, $0.45x$ = the overhead per tape, and $x - 0.45x$ or $0.55x$ = the profit per tape. The rental price must be less than or equal to $5 and satisfy the inequality
$$0.55x \geq 1.65$$
$$x \geq 3$$
The range of the rental price is $3 \leq x \leq \$5$.

88. Let x = the number of hours that she works per week. Since her pay is $6.80 per hour, she makes $6.80x$ dollars for x hours of work. Since she may not make more than $51, we can write the following equation.
$$0 \leq 6.80x \leq 51$$
$$0 \leq x \leq 7.5$$
The number of hours must be in [0, 7.5].

89. Since $150 < h < 180$, we have
$$150 < 60.089 + 2.238F < 180$$
$$89.911 < 2.238F < 119.911$$
$$40.2 < F < 53.6$$
The length of the femur is in (40.2, 53.6).

90. a) From the graph the approximate femur length is 43 cm.

b) If height is over 170 cm, then we have
$$61.412 + 2.317F > 170$$

$$2.317F > 108.588$$
$$F > 47.0$$
Femur is greater than 47.0 cm, or $F > 47.0$.

91. Let x = the number on the mile marker where Dane was picked up. We can write the absolute value equation
$$|x - 86| = 5$$
$$x - 86 = 5 \qquad \text{or} \quad x - 86 = -5$$
$$x = 91 \qquad \text{or} \qquad x = 81$$
He was either at 81 or 91.

92. Let x = Katie's score. Since Katie's score was more than 16 points away from Scott's, we can write the following inequality.
$$|x - 72| > 16$$
$$x - 72 > 16 \qquad \text{or} \quad x - 72 < -16$$
$$x > 88 \qquad \text{or} \qquad x < 56$$
Katie's score was either greater than 88 or less than 56.

93.
$$b = 0.20(300,000 - b)$$
$$b = 60,000 - 0.20b$$
$$1.2b = 60,000$$
$$b = 50,000$$
Bonus is $50,000 according to the accountant, and $60,000 according the employees.

94. If the bonus is $60,000, then the profit is $240,000 and the bonus is 25% of the profit.

95. Let x = the number of cows in Washington County and $3600 - x$ = the number of cows in Cade County. We have the equation
$$0.30x + 0.60(3600 - x) = 0.50(3600)$$
$$-0.30x + 2160 = 1800$$
$$-0.30x = -360$$
$$x = 1200$$
$$3600 - x = 2400$$
There are 1200 cows in Washington County and 2400 in Cade County.

96. If x = the amount of sales of best vinyl siding, then $90,000 + x$ = total sales. Profit on the good and better siding is $0.2(40,000) + 0.3(50,000)$ or $23,000. Total profit is at least 50% of total sales:
$$23,000 + 0.6x \geq 0.5(x + 90,000)$$
$$0.1x \geq 22,000$$
$$x \geq 220,000$$
UHI should sell at least $220,000 in best siding.

97. The numbers to the right of 1 are described by the inequality $x > 1$.

98. The numbers to left of and including 2 are described by the inequality $x \leq 2$.

99. The number 2 satisfies the equation $x = 2$.

100. The graph shows the numbers greater than or equal to 3 and less than 5. These numbers are the solution set to $3 \leq x < 5$.

101. The numbers 3 and -3 both satisfy the equation $|x| = 3$.

102. The graph shows the number 1. So $x = 1$.

103. The numbers to the left of and including -1 satisfy $x \leq -1$.

104. The numbers greater than 2 or less than -2 are described by $|x| > 2$.

105. The numbers between -2 and 2 including the endpoints satisfy $|x| \leq 2$.

106. The numbers 5 and -5 form the solution set to the absolute value equation $|x| = 5$.

107. $x \leq 2$ or $x \geq 7$

108. The numbers between -1 and 1 inclusive satisfy the absolute value inequality $|x| \leq 1$.

109. The numbers greater than 3 or less than -3 satisfy $|x| > 3$.

110. The numbers greater than 3 or less than -1 satisfy $x > 3$ or $x < -1$.

111. $5 < x < 7$

112. The numbers greater than 4 or less than -4 satisfy $|x| > 4$.

113. Every number except 0 has a positive absolute value and satisfies $|x| > 0$.

114. The numbers greater than or equal to -6 and less than 6 satisfy $-6 \leq x < 6$.

CHAPTER 2   TEST

1. $-6x - 5 = -4x + 3$
$$-2x = 8$$
$$x = -4$$
Solution set: $\{-4\}$

2. $6\left(\frac{y}{2}\right) - 6\left(\frac{y-3}{3}\right) = 6\left(\frac{y+6}{6}\right)$
$$3y - 2y + 6 = y + 6$$
$$y + 6 = y + 6$$
The equation is an identity.   Solution set: R

3. $|w| + 3 = 9$
$$|w| = 6$$
$$w = 6 \text{ or } w = -6$$
Solution set: $\{-6, 6\}$

4. $|3 - 2(5 - x)| = 3$
$$|-7 + 2x| = 3$$
$-7 + 2x = 3$ or $-7 + 2x = -3$
$2x = 10$ or $2x = 4$
$x = 5$ or $x = 2$
Solution set: $\{2, 5\}$

5. $2x - 5y = 20$
$$-5y = -2x + 20$$
$$y = \tfrac{2}{5}x - 4$$

6. $y = 3xy + 5$
$$y - 3xy = 5$$
$$y(1 - 3x) = 5$$
$$y = \frac{5}{1 - 3x}$$

7. $-2 \leq m - 6 \leq 2$
$$4 \leq m \leq 8$$
$[4, 8]$

8. $2|x - 3| > 20$
$$|x - 3| > 10$$
$x - 3 > 10$ or $x - 3 < -10$
$x > 13$ or $x < -7$
$(-\infty, -7) \cup (13, \infty)$

9. $2 - 3(w - 1) < -2w$
$$2 - 3w + 3 < -2w$$
$$-w < -5$$
$$w > 5$$
$(5, \infty)$

10. $3(2) < 3\left(\dfrac{5 - 2x}{3}\right) < 3(7)$
$$6 < 5 - 2x < 21$$
$$1 < -2x < 16$$
$$-\tfrac{1}{2} > x > -8$$
$\left(-8, -\tfrac{1}{2}\right)$

57

$-8{-}7{-}6{-}5{-}4{-}3{-}2{-}1\ 0$

11. $3x - 2 < 7$ and $-3x \le 15$
$\qquad 3x < 9$ and $\qquad x \ge -5$
$\qquad x < 3$ and $\qquad x \ge -5$
$[-5, 3)$

$-5{-}4{-}3{-}2{-}1\ 0\ 1\ 2\ 3$

12. $\frac{3}{2}\left(\frac{2}{3}y\right) < \frac{3}{2}(4)$ or $y - 3 < 12$
$\qquad\qquad y < 6$ or $\qquad y < 15$
$(-\infty, 15)$

$11\ 12\ 13\ 14\ 15\ 16\ 17$

13. $|\,2x - 7\,| = 3$
$\quad 2x - 7 = 3$ or $2x - 7 = -3$
$\qquad\quad 2x = 10$ or $\qquad 2x = 4$
$\qquad\qquad x = 5$ or $\qquad\quad x = 2$
$\{2, 5\}$

14. $x > 5$ or $x < 12$
$(-\infty, \infty)$

15. $x < 0$ and $x > 7$
No real number is both less than 0 and greater than 7. Solution set: $\emptyset$

16. Since no real number satisfies $|2x - 5| < 0$, we need only solve $|2x - 5| = 0$, which is equivalent to $2x - 5 = 0$, or $x = 2.5$.
Solution set: $\{\,2.5\}$

17. Since no real number satisfies $|x - 3| < 0$, the solution set is $\emptyset$.

18. Since $x + 3x = 4x$ is equivalent to $4x = 4x$, the solution set is R.

19. $2x + 14 = 2x + 9$
$\qquad\quad 14 = 9$
Solution set is $\emptyset$.

20. Since $|x - 6| \ge 0$ for any real number x, $|x - 6| \ge -6$ for any real number x. The solution set is R.

21. $x - 0.04x + 0.4 = 96.4$
$\qquad\qquad 0.96x = 96$
$\qquad\qquad\qquad x = 100$
$\{100\}$

22. Let $W =$ the width and $W + 16 =$ the length. Use $2W + 2L = P$ to write the equation
$$2W + 2(W + 16) = 84$$
$$4W + 32 = 84$$
$$4W = 52$$
$$W = 13$$
The width is 13 meters.

23. Let $h =$ the height. Use the formula $A = \frac{1}{2}bh$ to write the following equation.
$$\tfrac{1}{2} \cdot 3h = 21$$
$$3h = 42$$
$$h = 14$$
The height is 14 inches.

24. Let $x =$ the original price and $0.30x =$ the amount of discount. The original price minus the discount is equal to the price she paid.
$$x - 0.30x = 210$$
$$0.70x = 210$$
$$x = 300$$
The original price was $300.

25. Let $x =$ the number of liters of 11% alcohol. The mixture will be $x + 60$ liters of 7% alcohol. There are $0.11x$ liters of alcohol in the 11% solution, $0.05(60)$ liters of alcohol in the 5% solution, and $0.07(x + 60)$ liters of alcohol in the 7% solution.
$$0.11x + 0.05(60) = 0.07(x + 60)$$
$$0.11x + 3 = 0.07x + 4.2$$
$$0.04x = 1.2$$
$$x = 30$$
Use 30 liters of 11% alcohol solution.

26. Let $b =$ Brenda's salary.
$$|\,b - 28{,}000\,| > 3000$$
$b - 28{,}000 > 3000$ or $b - 28{,}000 < -3000$
$\qquad b > 31{,}000$ or $\qquad\quad b < 25{,}000$
Brenda's salary is either greater than $31,000 or less than $25,000.

Making Connections
Chapters 1-2
1. $5x + 6x = 11x$
2. $5x \cdot 6x = 30x^2$
3. $\frac{6x + 2}{2} = \frac{6x}{2} + \frac{2}{2} = 3x + 1$
4. $5 - 4(2 - x) = 5 - 8 + 4x = 4x - 3$

5. $(30 - 1)(30 + 1) = 29 \cdot 31 = 899$
6. $(30 + 1)^2 = 31^2 = 961$
7. $(30 - 1)^2 = 29^2 = 841$
8. $(2 + 3)^2 = 5^2 = 25$
9. $2^2 + 3^2 = 4 + 9 = 13$
10. $(8 - 3)(3 - 8) = 5(-5) = -25$
11. $(-1)(3 - 8) = -1(-5) = 5$
12. $-2^2 = -(2^2) = -4$
13. $3x + 8 - 5(x - 1) = 3x + 8 - 5x + 5$
   $= -2x + 13$
14. $(-6)^2 - 4(-3)2 = 36 + 24 = 60$
15. $3^2 \cdot 2^3 = 9 \cdot 8 = 72$
16. $4(-6) - (-5)(3) = -24 + 14 = -9$
17. $-3x \cdot x \cdot x = -3x^3$
18. $(-1)^6 = 1$
19. $\quad\quad 5x + 6x = 8x$
   $\quad\quad\quad 11x = 8x$
   $\quad\quad\quad\quad 3x = 0$
   $\quad\quad\quad\quad\quad x = 0$
Solution set: $\{0\}$

20. $\quad\quad 5x + 6x = 11x$
   $\quad\quad\quad 11x = 11x$
This equation is an identity. Solution set: R

21. $\quad\quad 5x + 6x = 0$
   $\quad\quad\quad 11x = 0$
   $\quad\quad\quad\quad x = 0$
Solution set: $\{0\}$

22. $\quad\quad 5x + 6 = 11x$
   $\quad\quad\quad -6x = -6$
   $\quad\quad\quad\quad x = 1$
Solution set: $\{1\}$

23. $\quad\quad 3x + 1 = 0$
   $\quad\quad\quad 3x = -1$
   $\quad\quad\quad\quad x = -\frac{1}{3}$
Solution set: $\left\{-\frac{1}{3}\right\}$

24. $\quad 5 - 4(2 - x) = 1$
   $\quad\quad 5 - 8 + 4x = 1$
   $\quad\quad\quad\quad 4x = 4$
   $\quad\quad\quad\quad\quad x = 1$
Solution set: $\{1\}$

25. $\quad\quad 3x + 6 = 3(x + 2)$
   $\quad\quad 3x + 6 = 3x + 6$
This equation is an identity. Solution set: R

26. $\quad\quad x - 0.01x = 990$
   $\quad\quad\quad 0.99x = 990$
   $\quad\quad\quad\quad x = 1000$
Solution set: $\{1000\}$

27. $\quad |5x + 6| = 11$
   $5x + 6 = 11 \quad\quad$ or $5x + 6 = -11$
   $\quad 5x = 5 \quad\quad$ or $\quad\quad 5x = -17$
   $\quad\quad x = 1 \quad\quad$ or $\quad\quad\quad x = -17/5$
Solution set: $\{-17/5, 1\}$

28. a) From the graph it appears that the cost of renting and buying are equal at 87,500 copies.

b) If $x =$ the number of copies made in 5 years, then the cost for renting is
$R = 60(75) + 0.06x$ dollars
or $R = 4500 + 0.06x$ dollars.
The cost if the copier is purchased is
$P = 8000 + 0.02x$ dollars.

c) $\quad 60(75) + 0.06x = 8000 + 0.02x$
   $\quad\quad\quad\quad 0.04x = 3500$
   $\quad\quad\quad\quad\quad\quad x = 87,500$
Five-year cost is same for 87,500 copies.

d) If 120,000 copies are made, then renting cost is \$11,700 and buying cost is \$10,400. So buying is \$1300 cheaper.

e) $|60(75) + 0.06x - (8000 + 0.02x)| < 500$
   $\quad\quad |-3500 + 0.04x| < 500$
   $\quad -500 < -3500 + 0.04x < 500$
   $\quad\quad 3000 < 0.04x < 4000$
   $\quad 75,000 < x < 100,000$
If the number of copies is between 75,000 and 100,000, then the plans differ by less than \$500.

3.1 WARM-UPS

1. False, because $3(5) - 2(2) = -4$ is not correct.

2. False, the vertical axis is called the y-axis.

3. False, because the point $(0, 0)$ is not in any quadrant.

4. True, because its first coordinate is 0.

5. True, because the graph of $x = k$ for any real number k is a vertical line.

6. True, because the graph of $y = k$ for any real number k is a horizontal line.

7. True, because if $x = 0$, then $y = -3$.

8. True, because if $n = 2$, then $C = 3(2) + 4 = 10$.

9. False, because if $P = 12$, then $3x = 12$ and $x = 4$.

10. True, because we usually put the dependent variable on the vertical axis.

3.1 EXERCISES

1. The origin is the point where the x-axis and y-axis intersect.

2. An ordered pair is a pair of real numbers in which there is a first number and a second.

3. Intercepts are points where a graph crosses the axes.

4. The graph of an equation of the type $y = k$ where k is a fixed number is a horizontal line.

5. The graph of an equation of the type $x = k$ where k is a fixed number is a vertical line.

6. The dependent variable usually goes on the vertical axis.

7. If $x = 2$, then $y = -3(2) + 6 = 0$.
If $y = -3$, then $-3 = -3x + 6$, or $x = 3$.
The points are $(2, 0)$ and $(3, -3)$.

8. If $x = -1$, then $y = \frac{1}{2}(-1) + 2 = \frac{3}{2}$.
If $y = 4$, then $4 = \frac{1}{2}x + 2$, or $x = 4$.
The points are $(-1, \frac{3}{2})$ and $(4, 4)$.

9. If $x = -4$, then $\frac{1}{2}(-4) - \frac{1}{3}y = 9$, or $y = -33$. If $y = 6$, then $\frac{1}{2}x - \frac{1}{3} \cdot 6 = 9$, or $x = 22$.
The points are $(-4, -33)$ and $(22, 6)$.

10. If $x = 3$, then $2(3) - 3y = 5$, or $y = 1/3$.
If $y = -1$, then $2x - 3(-1) = 5$, or $x = 1$.
The points are $(3, \frac{1}{3})$ and $(1, -1)$.

11. To plot $(2, 5)$, start at the origin and go 2 units to the right and up 5. The point is in quadrant I.

12. To plot $(-5, 1)$, start at the origin and go 5 units to the left and up 1. The point is in quadrant II.

13. To plot $(-3, -1/2)$, start at the origin and go 3 units to the left and down 1/2 unit. The point is in quadrant III.

14. To plot $(-2, -6)$, start at the origin and go 2 units to the left and 6 units down. The point is in quadrant III.

15. To plot $(0, 4)$, start at the origin and go 4 units upward. The point is on the y-axis.

16. To plot $(0, 2)$, start at the origin and go up 2 units. The point is on the y-axis.

17. To plot $(\pi, -1)$, start at the origin and go approximately 3.14 units to the right and 1 unit downward. The point is in quadrant IV.

18. To plot $(4/3, 0)$, start at the origin and go approximately 4/3 units to the right. The point is on the x-axis.

19. To plot $(-4, 3)$, start at the origin and go 4 units to the left and 3 units upward. The point is in quadrant II.

20. To plot $(0, -3)$, start at the origin and go 3 units downward. The point is on the y-axis.

21. To plot $(3/2, 0)$, start at the origin and go approximately 3/2 units to the right. The point is on the x-axis.

22. To plot $(3, 2)$, start at the origin and go 3 units to the right and 2 units upward. The point is in quadrant I.

23. To plot $(0, -1)$, start at the origin and go 1 unit downward. The point is on the y-axis.

24. To plot $(4, -3)$, start at the origin and go 4 units to the right and 3 units downward. The point is in quadrant IV.

25. $y = x + 1$
If $x = 0$, $y = 0 + 1 = 1$.
If $x = 1$, $y = 1 + 1 = 2$.
If $x = 2$, $y = 2 + 1 = 3$.
If $x = -1$, $y = -1 + 1 = 0$.
Plot $(0, 1)$, $(1, 2)$, $(2, 3)$, $(-1, 0)$, and draw a line through the points.

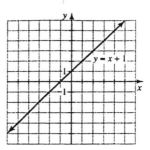

26. $y = x - 1$
If $x = 0, y = 0 - 1 = -1$.
If $x = 1, y = 1 - 1 = 0$.
If $x = 2, y = 2 - 1 = 1$.
If $x = -1, y = -1 - 1 = -2$.
Plot $(0, -1)$, $(1, 0)$, $(2, 1)$, $(-1, -2)$, and draw a line through the points.

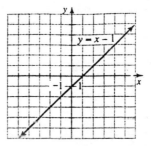

27. $y = -2x + 3$
If $x = 0, y = -2(0) + 3 = 3$.
If $x = 1, y = -2(1) + 3 = 1$.
If $x = 2, y = -2(2) + 3 = -1$.
If $x = -1, y = -2(-1) + 3 = 5$.
Plot $(0, 3)$, $(1, 1)$, $(2, -1)$, and $(-1, 5)$ and draw a line through the points.

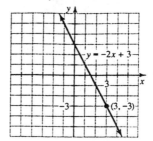

28. $y = 2x - 3$
If $x = 0, y = 2(0) - 3 = -3$.
If $x = 1, y = 2(1) - 3 = -1$.
If $x = 2, y = 2(2) - 3 = 1$.
If $x = -1, y = 2(-1) - 3 = -5$.
Plot $(0, -3)$, $(1, -1)$, $(2, 1)$, $(-1, -5)$, and draw a line through the points.

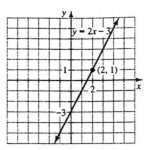

29. $y = x$ Since the x and y-coordinates are equal, plot $(0, 0)$, $(1, 1)$, $(2, 2)$, $(-1, -1)$ and draw a line through the points.

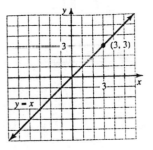

30. For the equation $y = -x$, the y-coordinate is the opposite of the x-coordinate. So plot $(0, 0)$, $(1, -1)$, $(2, -2)$, and $(-2, 2)$. Draw a line through the points.

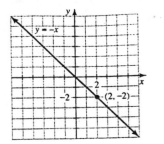

31. $y = 3$ The x-coordinate can be any number and the y-coordinate is 3. Plot $(0, 3)$, $(1, 3)$, $(2, 3)$, $(-1, 3)$, and draw a horizontal line through the points.

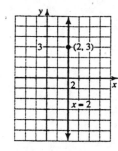

32. For the equation $y = -2$, the x-coordinate can be any number as long as the y-coordinate is -2. So plot the points $(0, -2)$, $(1, -2)$, $(2, -2)$, and $(-2, -2)$. Draw a line through the points.

33. For the equation $y = 1 - x$, plot the points $(0, 1)$, $(1, 0)$, $(2, -1)$, and $(-2, 3)$. Draw a line through the points.

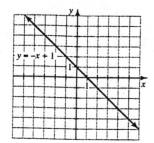

34. For the equation $y = 2 - x$, plot the points $(0, 2)$, $(1, 1)$, $(2, 0)$, and $(-2, 4)$. Draw a line through the points.

35. For $x = 2$, the y-coordinate can be any number, but the x-coordinate is 2. Plot $(2, 0)$, $(2, 1)$, $(2, 3)$, $(2, -1)$, and draw a vertical line through the points.

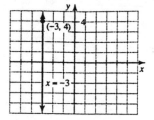

36. For the equation $x = -3$, the y-coordinate can be any number as long as the x-coordinate is -3. So plot the points $(-3, 0)$, $(-3, 1)$, $(-3, 2)$, and $(-3, -2)$. Draw a line through the points.

37. For the equation $y = \frac{1}{2}x - 1$, plot the points $(0, -1)$, $(2, 0)$, $(4, 1)$, and $(-4, -3)$. Draw a line through the points.

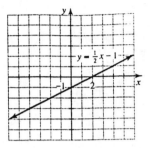

38. $y = \frac{1}{3}x - 2$
Plot $(0, -2)$, $(3, -1)$, $(6, 0)$, $(-3, -3)$, and draw a line through the points.

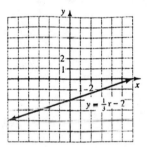

39. $x - 4 = 0$
$$x = 4$$
Plot $(4, 5)$, $(4, 2)$, $(4, -1)$, $(4, 1)$, and draw a line through the points.

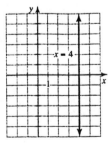

40. $y + 3 = 0$
$$y = -3$$
Plot $(-2, -3)$, $(0, -3)$, $(1, -3)$, and $(3, -3)$ and draw a line through the points.

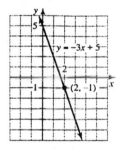

41. $3x + y = 5$
$$y = -3x + 5$$
Plot $(0, 5)$, $(1, 2)$, $(2, -1)$, $(-1, 8)$, and draw a line through the points.

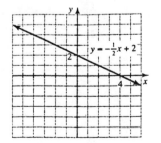

42. $x + 2y = 4$
$$y = -\frac{1}{2}x + 2$$
Plot the points $(0, 2)$, $(2, 1)$, $(4, 0)$, $(-2, 3)$. Draw a line through the points.

43. For the equation $y = -0.26x + 3.86$, plot the points $(0, 3.86)$, $(1, 3.60)$, $(2, 3.34)$, $(-1, 4.12)$, $(-2, 4.38)$. Draw a line through the points.

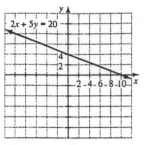

44. $y = 1.35x - 4.27$
If $x = -1$, $y = 1.35(-1) - 4.27 = -5.62$
If $x = 0$, $y = -4.27$
If $x = 2$, $y = 1.35(2) - 4.27 = -1.57$
Plot $(-1, -5.62)$, $(0, -4.27)$, $(2, -1.57)$, and draw a line through the points.

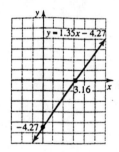

45. If $x = 0$, $4(0) - 3y = 12$,
$-3y = 12$, $y = -4$
If $y = 0$, $4x - 3(0) = 12$,
$4x = 12$, $x = 3$
Plot $(0, -4)$ and $(3, 0)$.

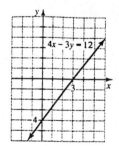

46. If $x = 0$ in $2x + 5y = 20$, then $2(0) + 5y = 20$, or $y = 4$.
If $y = 0$, then $2x + 5(0) = 20$, or $x = 10$. The intercepts are $(0, 4)$ and $(10, 0)$.

47. If $x = 0$, $0 - y + 5 = 0$
$$5 = y$$
If $y = 0$, $\quad x - 0 + 5 = 0$
$$x = -5$$
Plot $(0, 5)$ and $(-5, 0)$, and draw a line through the points.

48. If $x = 0$ in $x + y + 7 = 0$, then $y + 7 = 0$ or $y = -7$. If $y = 0$, then $x + 7 = 0$, or $x = -7$. Draw a line through the intercepts $(0, -7)$ and $(-7, 0)$.

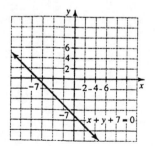

49. If $x = 0$, $2(0) + 3y = 5$
$$y = 5/3$$
If $y = 0$, $2x + 3(0) = 5$
$$x = 5/2$$
Plot $(0, 5/3)$ and $(5/2, 0)$, and draw a line through the points.

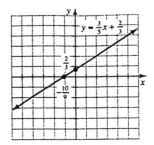

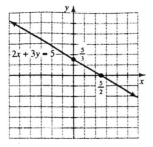

50. If $x = 0$ in $3x - 4y = 7$, then $-4y = 7$, or $y = -\frac{7}{4}$. If $y = 0$ then $3x = 7$, or $x = \frac{7}{3}$.
Draw a line through the intercepts $(0, -7/4)$ and $(7/3, 0)$.

52. If $x = 0$ in $y = -\frac{2}{3}x - \frac{5}{4}$, then $y = -\frac{5}{4}$.
If $y = 0$, then $-\frac{2}{3}x - \frac{5}{4} = 0$, or $x = -\frac{15}{8}$.
Draw a line through the intercepts $(0, -5/4)$ and $(-15/8, 0)$.

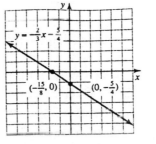

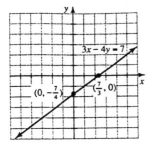

53. a) $P = 19,663 + 269n$
If $n = 10$, $P = 19,663 + 269(10) = 22,353$
In 2005 the car will cost $22,353.
b) If $n = 11$, the price is $22,622.
Every year the price goes up by $269.
c)

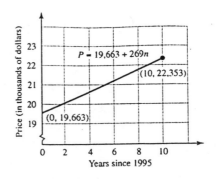

51. If $x = 0$, $y = \frac{3}{5}(0) + \frac{2}{3}$
$$y = \frac{2}{3}$$
If $y = 0$, $0 = \frac{3}{5}x + \frac{2}{3}$
$$-\frac{3}{5}x = \frac{2}{3}$$
$$x = -\frac{10}{9}$$
Plot $(0, 2/3)$ and $(-10/9, 0)$, and draw a line through the points.

65

54. $P = 18,675 - 1960n$

In $n = 4$, $P = 18,675 - 1960(4) = \$10,835$.

b) The car depreciate $1960 each year.

c) The graph is a line segment from (1, 16,715) to (4, 10,835).

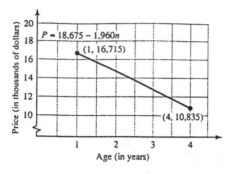

55. $C = 0.26m + 42$

If $m = 400$, $C = 0.26(400) + 42 = 146$.

The charge for a car driven 400 miles is $146.

If $m = 0$, $C = 0.26(0) + 42 = 42$.

If $m = 1000$, $C = 0.26(1000) + 42 = 302$.

Plot (0, 42) and (1000, 302), and draw a line segment with those endpoints.

(graph of $C = 0.26m + 42$ with points (0, 42) and (1000, 302))

56. To find the interest rate for a person with a rating of 8, use $t = 8$ in the formula

$r = 0.02t + 0.15$.

$r = 0.02(8) + 0.15 = 0.31$

The rate would be 31% for a rating of 8. The graph of the equation contains the points (0, 0.15), (8, 0.31), and (10, 0.35).

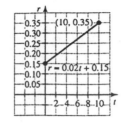

57. a) $C = 0.50(5) + 8.95 = \$11.45$.

b) $0.50t + 8.95 = 14.45$

$\qquad 0.50t = 5.50$

$\qquad\quad t = 11$

A pizza that sells for $14.45 has 11 toppings.

58. a) $L = 0.10(120) + 4.95 = \$16.95$

b) $0.10n + 4.95 = 23.45$

$\qquad 0.10n = 18.5$

$\qquad\quad n = 185$

c) The L-intercept has $n = 0$. If $n = 0$, then $L = 4.95$. So the L-intercept is (0, 4.95).

d) To find the n-intercept use $L = 0$.

$\qquad 0.10n + 4.95 = 0$

$\qquad\qquad 0.10n = -4.95$

$\qquad\qquad\quad n = -49.5$

The n-intercept is $(-49.5, 0)$.

59. a) If $x = 850$, then

$C = 0.55(850) + 50 = \$517.50$

$R = 1.50(850) = \$1275$

$P = 0.95(850) - 50 = \$757.50$.

b) If $P = 995$, then

$\qquad 0.95x - 50 = 995$

$\qquad\qquad\quad x = 1100$

Here profit was $950 when she sold 1100 roses.

c) If $x = 1100$, then $R = \$1650$ and $C = \$655$. So $R - C = \$995$. The difference between revenue and cost is $995, which is her profit.

60. a) If $t = 2$, then $v = -32(2) + 88 = 24$ ft/sec.

If $t = 3$, then $v = -32(3) + 88 = -8$ ft/sec. The velocity is negative when the ball is going downward.

b) The velocity is zero when

$\qquad -32t + 88 = 0$

$$t = 2.75$$

The velocity is zero when $t = 2.75$ sec and the ball is at its maximum height at this time.

c) The intercept $(0, 88)$ indicates that at $t = 0$ sec the velocity was 88 ft/sec and $(2.75, 0)$ indicates that at $t = 2.75$ sec the velocity was 0 ft/sec.

d) It takes 2.75 seconds for the ball to reach its maximum height and 2.75 seconds for the ball to fall back to the earth. So it $t = 2(2.75) = 5.5$ sec, we get $v = -32(5.5) + 88 = -88$ ft/sec, which is the velocity of the ball when it hits the ground.

61. a) $M = \left(\frac{1+5}{2}, \frac{2+6}{2}\right) = (3, 4)$

b) $M = \left(\frac{6+(-2)}{2}, \frac{-5+(-1)}{2}\right) = (2, -3)$

c) $M = \left(\frac{\frac{1}{2}+\frac{1}{3}}{2}, \frac{\frac{1}{4}+\frac{1}{2}}{2}\right) = \left(\frac{5}{12}, \frac{3}{8}\right)$

62. a) $M = \left(\frac{0+6}{2}, \frac{6+2}{2}\right) = (3, 4)$

$M = \left(\frac{6+2}{2}, \frac{2+(-2)}{2}\right) = (4, 0)$

$M = \left(\frac{0+2}{2}, \frac{6+(-2)}{2}\right) = (1, 2)$

c) The three medians intersect at $\left(\frac{8}{3}, 2\right)$.

63.

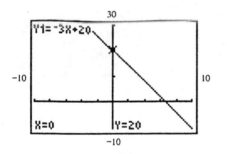

64.

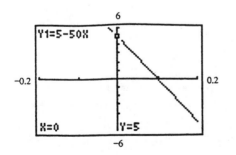

65.

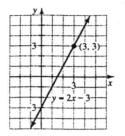

66.

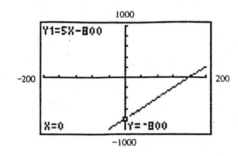

67.

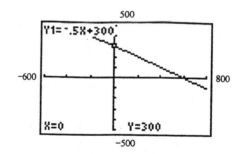

68.

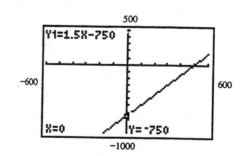

67

3.2 WARM-UPS

1. True.
2. False, slope is rise divided by run.
3. False, because it is horizontal line with 0 slope.
4. True, because it is a vertical line.
5. False, slope of a line can be any real number.
6. False, the slope is 2/5.
7. False, it has slope 1.
8. True.
9. False, lines with slope 2/3 and −3/2 are perpendicular.
10. False, because two vertical parallel lines do not have equal slopes.

3.2 EXERCISES

1. Slope measures the steepness of a line.
2. The rise is the change in y-coordinates and run is the change in x-coordinates.
3. A horizontal line has zero slope because it has no rise.
4. Slope is undefined for vertical lines because the run is zero and division by zero is undefined.
5. If m_1 and m_2 are the slopes of perpendicular lines, then $m_1 = -1/m_2$.
6. If m_1 and m_2 are the slopes of parallel lines, the $m_1 = m_2$.
7. In going from $(-3, 0)$ to $(0, 2)$ we rise 2 and run 3. The slope is 2/3.
8. In going from $(-3, 0)$ to $(0, -2)$ we rise −2 and run 3. The slope is −2/3.
9. The slope for this line is undefined because it is a vertical line.
10. The slope of any horizontal line is 0.
11. In going from $(0, 0)$ to $(1, -1)$, we rise −1 and run 1. The slope is −1.
12. In going from $(0, 0)$ to $(1, 1)$, we rise 1 and run 1. The slope is 1.
13. In going from $(0, -3)$ to $(2, 0)$ we rise 3 and run 2. The slope is 3/2.
14. In going from $(-1, 0)$ to $(0, 3)$, we rise 3 and run 1. The slope is 3.

15. In going from $(0, 2)$ to $(2, 0)$ we rise −2 and run 2. The slope is −1.
16. In going from $(0, 2)$ to $(4, 0)$ we rise −2 and run 4. The slope is −1/2.
17. $m = \frac{6-1}{2-5} = -\frac{5}{3}$
18. $m = \frac{10-4}{6-3} = \frac{6}{3} = 2$
19. $m = \frac{-1-3}{-3-4} = \frac{-4}{-7} = \frac{4}{7}$
20. $m = \frac{3-(-3)}{1-(-2)} = \frac{6}{3} = 2$
21. $m = \frac{2-7}{-2-(-1)} = \frac{-5}{-1} = 5$
22. $m = \frac{-6-5}{1-(-3)} = \frac{-11}{4} = -\frac{11}{4}$
23. $m = \frac{-5-0}{3-0} = \frac{-5}{3} = -\frac{5}{3}$
24. $m = \frac{-1-0}{-2-0} = \frac{-1}{-2} = \frac{1}{2}$
25. $m = \frac{3-0}{0-5} = -\frac{3}{5}$
26. $m = \frac{10-0}{0-3} = -\frac{10}{3}$
27. $m = \frac{-1-\left(-\frac{1}{2}\right)}{\frac{3}{4}-\left(-\frac{1}{2}\right)} = \frac{-\frac{1}{2}}{\frac{5}{4}} = -\frac{1}{2}\cdot\frac{4}{5} = -\frac{2}{5}$
28. $m = \frac{2-\frac{1}{2}}{\frac{1}{2}-\frac{1}{4}} = \frac{\frac{3}{2}}{\frac{1}{4}} = \frac{3}{2}\cdot\frac{4}{1} = 6$
29. $m = \frac{212-209}{6-7} = \frac{3}{-1} = -3$
30. $m = \frac{315-306}{1990-1988} = \frac{9}{2}$
31. $m = \frac{7-7}{4-(-12)} = \frac{0}{16} = 0$
32. $m = \frac{-3-(-3)}{9-5} = \frac{0}{4} = 0$
33. $\frac{6-(-6)}{2-2} = \frac{12}{0}$ The slope is undefined because 0 is in the denominator.
34. $m = \frac{2-0}{-3-(-3)} = \frac{2}{0}$ The slope is undefined because 0 is in the denominator.
35. $m = \frac{11.9-8.4}{24.3-3.57} = \frac{3.5}{20.73} = 0.169$
36. $m = \frac{19.3-(-3.28)}{-2.7-5.46} = \frac{22.58}{-8.16}$
$= -2.767$
37. $m = \frac{1-0}{\frac{\pi}{4}-\frac{\pi}{2}} = \frac{1}{-0.7854} = -1.273$
38. $m = \frac{-1-0}{\frac{\pi}{3}-\frac{\pi}{6}} = -1.910$
39. The line through $(-5, 1)$ and $(3, -2)$ has slope
$$m = \frac{1-(-2)}{-5-3} = \frac{3}{-8} = -\frac{3}{8}.$$
Any line perpendicular to this line has slope 8/3 because 8/3 is the opposite of the reciprocal of −3/8. Line l has slope 8/3.
40. The slope of the line through $(-2, 6)$ and $(5, 3)$ is

$$m = \frac{6-3}{-2-5} = -\frac{3}{7}.$$
A line perpendicular to a line with slope $-3/7$ has slope $7/3$.

41. The slope of the line through $(-3, -2)$ and $(4, 1)$ is
$$m = \frac{-2-1}{-3-4} = \frac{3}{7}.$$
Any line parallel to this line also has slope $3/7$. So line l has slope $3/7$.

42. The slope of the line through $(-3, -5)$ and $(4, -1)$ is
$$m = \frac{-5-(-1)}{-3-4} = \frac{-4}{-7} = \frac{4}{7}.$$
The slope of any line parallel to a line with slope $4/7$ also has slope $4/7$. Line l has slope $4/7$.

43. The opposite of the reciprocal of $4/5$ is $-5/4$. Line l has slope $-5/4$.

44. Any line perpendicular to a line with slope -5 has slope $1/5$. So line l has slope $1/5$.

45. Draw a quadrilateral with the four given points as vertices. Find the slope of each side.
$$m_1 = \frac{3-1}{0-(-6)} = \frac{1}{3} \qquad m_2 = \frac{3-1}{0-4} = -\frac{1}{2}$$

$$m_3 = \frac{1-(-1)}{4-(-2)} = \frac{1}{3} \qquad m_4 = \frac{-1-1}{-2-(-6)} = -\frac{1}{2}$$

Since opposite sides of the quadrilateral have equal slopes, the quadrilateral is a parallelogram.

46. Draw a quadrilateral with the four given points as vertices. Find the slope of each side.
$$m_1 = \frac{6-0}{-1-(-7)} = 1 \qquad m_2 = \frac{5-6}{6-(-1)} = -\frac{1}{7}$$

$$m_3 = \frac{5-(-2)}{6-(-1)} = 1 \qquad m_4 = \frac{-2-0}{-1-(-7)} = -\frac{1}{3}$$

Since opposite sides of the quadrilateral do not have equal slopes, the quadrilateral is not a parallelogram.

47. Draw a quadrilateral with the four given points as vertices. Find the slope of each side.
$$m_1 = \frac{6-2}{3-(-3)} = \frac{2}{3} \qquad m_2 = \frac{6-4}{3-6} = -\frac{2}{3}$$

$$m_3 = \frac{4-(-1)}{6-(-1)} = \frac{5}{7} \qquad m_4 = \frac{-1-2}{-1-(-3)} = -\frac{3}{2}$$

Since there are no parallel sides, this quadrilateral is not a trapezoid.

48. Draw a quadrilateral with the four given points as vertices. Find the slope of each side.
$$m_1 = \frac{6-4}{0-(-4)} = \frac{1}{2} \qquad m_2 = \frac{6-0}{0-3} = -2$$

$$m_3 = \frac{0-(-2)}{3-(-1)} = \frac{1}{2} \qquad m_4 = \frac{-2-4}{-1-(-4)} = -2$$

From the slopes, we see that opposite sides are parallel and adjacent sides are perpendicular. The quadrilateral is a rectangle.

49. Draw a triangle with the three given points as vertices. Find the slope of each side.
$$m_1 = \frac{6-3}{-1-(-3)} = \frac{3}{2} \qquad m_2 = \frac{6-0}{-1-0} = -6$$

$$m_3 = \frac{3-0}{-3-0} = -1$$

From the slopes we see that none of the line segments are perpendicular. The triangle is not a right triangle.

50. Draw a triangle with the three given points as vertices. Find the slope of each side.
$$m_1 = \frac{5-(-1)}{2-0} = 3 \qquad m_2 = \frac{5-4}{2-5} = -\frac{1}{3}$$

$$m_3 = \frac{4-(-1)}{5-0} = 1$$
From the slopes we see that the line with slope 3 is perpendicular to the line with slope $-1/3$. The triangle is a right triangle.

51. a) $m = \frac{20,115-21135}{1993-1998} = 204$
b) Using the graph we might guess that the price in 2005 will be \$22,500.
c) The slope is the average yearly increase in price. So from 1998 to 2005 there will be 7 increases of \$204 each time, for an increase of \$1428. So the price in 2005 should be \$21,135 + \$1428, or \$22,563.

52. a) From the graph we can estimate that the average price of a two year old car in 1998 was \$12,000.
b) $m = \frac{13,595 - 11095}{1-3} = -1250$
c) The slope is the average yearly depreciation. A two-year old Lumina Coupe in 1998 should cost $13,595 - 1250 = \$12,345$.

53. Use graph paper to solve this problem. The slope 4 means that we can rise 4 and run 1 to get additional points on this line. From $(2, 1)$ rise 4 and run 1 to get to $(3, 5)$. From $(2, 1)$ we

69

can rise -4 and run -1 to get to $(1, -3)$. From $(1, -3)$ we can rise -4 and run -1 to get to $(0, -7)$.

54. The slope $2/3$ indicates a ratio of rise to run of 2 to 3. When x changes from 5 to 8 we have a run of 3 so $\frac{2}{3} = \frac{\text{rise}}{3}$ and the rise is 2. So the point is $(8, 4)$. If we go 3 to the right and up 2 from $(8, 4)$ we get to $(11, 6)$. From $(11, 6)$ to $(12, \ )$ the run is 1 and the rise must be $2/3$. So the point is $(12, 6\frac{2}{3})$.

55. Find the slope:
$$\frac{k - (-5)}{2 - (-3)} = \frac{1}{2}$$
$$\frac{k + 5}{5} = \frac{1}{2}$$
$$2k + 10 = 5$$
$$k = -\frac{5}{2}$$

56. Find the slope:
$$\frac{3 - 0}{k - (-2)} = k$$
$$\frac{3}{k + 2} = k$$
$$k^2 + 2k = 3$$
$$k^2 + 2k - 3 = 0$$
$$(k + 3)(k - 1) = 0$$
$$k = -3 \text{ or } k = 1$$

57. The slope of the line perpendicular to the line with slope 0.247 is the opposite of the reciprocal of 0.247:
$$-\frac{1}{0.247} = -4.049$$

58. The line through $(3.27, -1.46)$ and $(-5.48, 3.61)$ has slope
$$m = \frac{3.61 - (-1.46)}{-5.48 - 3.27} = -0.57943$$
The slope of a line perpendicular to a line with slope -0.57943 has slope
$$m = -\frac{1}{-0.57943} = 1.726.$$

59. A horizontal line has zero slope and a vertical line has undefined slope.

60. Every line goes through at least two quadrants. A nonhorizontal nonvertical line that misses quadrant II or IV or both has positive slope. A nonhorizontal nonvertical line that misses quadrant I or III or both has negative slope.

61. Draw a quadrilateral with the four given vertices. The slope of the diagonal joining $(-3, -1)$ and $(5, 3)$ is $m_1 = \frac{3 - (-1)}{5 - (-3)} = \frac{1}{2}$.
The slope of the diagonal joining $(0, 3)$ and $(2, -1)$ is $m_2 = \frac{3 - (-1)}{0 - 2} = -2$.
Since the opposite of the reciprocal of $1/2$ is -2, the diagonals are perpendicular.

62. Plot the four points $(-5, 3)$, $(-3, -3)$, $(1, 5)$, and $(3, -1)$. Find the slope of each diagonal. The slope of the diagonal joining $(-5, 3)$ and $(3, -1)$ is
$$m = \frac{3 - (-1)}{-5 - 3} = \frac{4}{-8} = -\frac{1}{2}.$$
The slope of the diagonal joining $(1, 5)$ and $(-3, -3)$ is $m = \frac{5 - (-3)}{1 - (-3)} = \frac{8}{4} = 2$.
Since lines with slopes of 2 and $-1/2$ are perpendicular, the diagonals of the square are perpendicular.

63. Increasing m makes the graph increase faster. The slopes of these lines are 1, 2, 3, and 4.

64. Decreasing m makes the graph decrease faster. The slopes of these lines are -1, -2, -3, and -4.

3.3 WARM-UPS

1. True.

2. False, the line through (a, b) with slope m has equation $y - b = m(x - a)$.

3. False, $y = mx + b$ goes through $(0, b)$ and has slope m.

4. True, because the y-intercept has x-coordinate 0.

5. True, because the x-intercept has y-coordinate 0.

6. False, because vertical lines do not have equations in slope intercept form.

7. True, because if we solve the equation for y, we get $y = (-3/2)x + (7/2)$.

8. False, because a line perpendicular to a line with slope 3 has slope $-1/3$.

9. False, because if $x = 0$ in this equation, we get $y = 5/2$.

10. True, because even the vertical lines can be expressed in standard form.

3.3 EXERCISES

1. Point-slope form is $y - y_1 = m(x - x_1)$ where m is the slope and (x_1, y_1) is a point on the line.

2. Slope-intercept form is $y = mx + b$ where m is the slope and $(0, b)$ is the y-intercept.

3. To write an equation of a line we need the slope and a point on the line.

4. Standard form is $Ax + By = C$ where A, B, and C are real numbers with A and B not both zero.

5. To find the slope from standard form solve the equation for y to get the form $y = mx + b$ where m is the slope.

6. To graph a line knowing the slope and y-intercept, start at the y-intercept and count off the rise and run to locate a second point. Then draw a line through the y-intercept and your second point.

7. Use the given point and the given slope in the point-slope formula:
$$y - (-3) = 2(x - 2)$$
$$y + 3 = 2x - 4$$
$$y = 2x - 7$$

8. Use the point $(-2, 5)$ and slope 6 in the point-slope formula.
$$y - 5 = 6(x - (-2))$$
$$y - 5 = 6x + 12$$
$$y = 6x + 17$$

9. Use the point $(-2, 3)$ and the slope $-1/2$ in the point-slope formula:
$$y - 3 = -\tfrac{1}{2}(x - (-2))$$
$$y - 3 = -\tfrac{1}{2}x - 1$$
$$y = -\tfrac{1}{2}x + 2$$

10. Use the point $(3, 5)$ and slope $2/3$ in the point-slope formula.
$$y - 5 = \tfrac{2}{3}(x - 3)$$
$$y - 5 = \tfrac{2}{3}x - 2$$
$$y = \tfrac{2}{3}x + 3$$

11. The slope of the line through $(2, 3)$ and $(-5, 6)$ is
$$m = \frac{3 - 6}{2 - (-5)} = -\tfrac{3}{7}.$$
Use $(2, 3)$ and slope $-3/7$ in the point- slope formula:
$$y - 3 = -\tfrac{3}{7}(x - 2)$$

$$y - 3 = -\tfrac{3}{7}x + \tfrac{6}{7}$$
$$y = -\tfrac{3}{7}x + \tfrac{6}{7} + 3$$
$$y = -\tfrac{3}{7}x + \tfrac{27}{7}$$

12. First find the slope of the line through $(-2, 1)$ and $(3, -4)$.
$$m = \frac{1 - (-4)}{-2 - 3} = \frac{5}{-5} = -1$$
Use the point $(-2, 1)$ and slope -1 in the point-slope formula.
$$y - 1 = -1(x - (-2))$$
$$y - 1 = -x - 2$$
$$y = -x - 1$$

13. The slope of the line through $(-3, 1)$ and $(5, -1)$ is
$$m = \frac{1 - (-1)}{-3 - 5} = -\tfrac{1}{4}.$$
So the line we want has slope 4 and goes through $(3, 4)$:
$$y - 4 = 4(x - 3)$$
$$y - 4 = 4x - 12$$
$$y = 4x - 8$$

14. First find slope of the line through $(0, 6)$ and $(-5, 0)$.
$$m = \frac{6 - 0}{0 - (-5)} = \tfrac{6}{5}$$
Any line perpendicular to a line with slope 6/5 has slope $-5/6$. Use the point $(0, 0)$ and slope $-5/6$ in the point-slope formula.
$$y - 0 = -\tfrac{5}{6}(x - 0)$$
$$y = -\tfrac{5}{6}x$$

15. The line through $(9, -3)$ and $(-3, 6)$ has slope
$$m = \frac{6 - (-3)}{-3 - 9} = -\tfrac{3}{4}$$
Use the same slope $-3/4$ and $(0, 0)$ in the point-slope formula:
$$y - 0 = -\tfrac{3}{4}(x - 0)$$
$$y = -\tfrac{3}{4}x$$

16. First find the slope of the line through $(6, 2)$ and $(-2, 6)$.
$$m = \frac{2 - 6}{6 - (-2)} = \frac{-4}{8} = -\tfrac{1}{2}$$
Any line parallel to a line with slope $-1/2$ also has slope $-1/2$. Use the point $(2, -4)$ and slope $-1/2$ in the point-slope formula.
$$y - (-4) = -\tfrac{1}{2}(x - 2)$$
$$y + 4 = -\tfrac{1}{2}x + 1$$
$$y = -\tfrac{1}{2}x - 3$$

17. The line goes through $(0, 2)$ and $(2, 3)$.
The slope is $\frac{1}{2}$ and the y-intercept is $(0, 2)$.
Using slope-intercept form, we can write
$y = \frac{1}{2}x + 2$.

18. This line goes through $(-3, 0)$ and
$(0, -2)$. Its slope is $-2/3$ and its y-intercept is
$(0, -2)$.
So its equation is $y = -\frac{2}{3}x - 2$.

19. This is a vertical line with an x-intercept of
$(1, 0)$ and so its equation is $x = 1$.

20. This line has 0 slope and y-intercept
$(0, -2)$. So its equation in slope-intercept form
is $y = 0 \cdot x - 2$, or $y = -2$.

21. This line has a y-intercept of $(0, 0)$ and
also goes through $(3, -3)$. Its slope is -1. Its
equation in slope-intercept form is $y = -x$.

22. This line has y-intercept $(0, 0)$ and slope 1.
So its equation in slope-intercept form is $y = x$.

23. This line goes through $(2, 0)$ and $(0, -3)$.
Its slope is $3/2$ and its equation is $y = \frac{3}{2}x - 3$.

24. This line goes through $(-1, 0)$ and $(0, 3)$.
Its slope is 3 and its y-intercept is $(0, 3)$. Its
equation in slope-intercept form is $y = 3x + 3$.

25. This line goes through $(0, 2)$ and $(2, 0)$.
Since its slope is -1, its equation is
$y = -x + 2$.

26. This line goes through $(0, 2)$ and $(4, 0)$.
Its slope is $-1/2$ and its y-intercept is $(0, 2)$.
Its equation in slope-intercept form is
$y = -\frac{1}{2}x + 2$.

27.
$$3(y) = 3(\tfrac{1}{3}x - 2)$$
$$3y = x - 6$$
$$-x + 3y = -6$$
$$x - 3y = 6$$

28.
$$y = \tfrac{1}{2}x + 7$$
$$2y = x + 14$$
$$-x + 2y = 14$$
$$x - 2y = -14$$

29.
$$2(y - 5) = 2 \cdot \tfrac{1}{2}(x + 3)$$
$$2y - 10 = x + 3$$
$$-x + 2y = 13$$
$$x - 2y = -13$$

30.
$$y - 1 = \tfrac{1}{4}(x - 6)$$
$$4y - 4 = x - 6$$
$$-x + 4y = -2$$

31.
$$x - 4y = 2$$
$$6\left(y + \tfrac{1}{2}\right) = 6 \cdot \tfrac{1}{3}(x - 4)$$
$$6y + 3 = 2(x - 4)$$
$$-2x + 6y = -11$$
$$2x - 6y = 11$$

32.
$$y + \tfrac{1}{3} = \tfrac{1}{4}(x - 3)$$
$$y + \tfrac{1}{3} = \tfrac{1}{4}x - \tfrac{3}{4}$$
$$12\left(y + \tfrac{1}{3}\right) = 12\left(\tfrac{1}{4}x - \tfrac{3}{4}\right)$$
$$12y + 4 = 3x - 9$$
$$-3x + 12y = -13$$
$$3x - 12y = 13$$

33.
$$100(0.05x + 0.06y - 8.9) = 100(0)$$
$$5x + 6y - 890 = 0$$
$$5x + 6y = 890$$

34.
$$0.03x - 0.07y = 2$$
$$100(0.03x - 0.07y) = 100(2)$$
$$3x - 7y = 200$$

35.
$$2x + 5y = 1$$
$$5y = -2x + 1$$
$$y = -\tfrac{2}{5}x + \tfrac{1}{5}$$
The slope is $-\frac{2}{5}$ and the y-intercept is $(0, \frac{1}{5})$.

36.
$$3x - 3y = 2$$
$$-3y = -3x + 2$$
$$y = x - \tfrac{2}{3}$$
The slope is 1 and the y-intercept is $\left(0, -\frac{2}{3}\right)$.

37.
$$3x - y - 2 = 0$$
$$3x - 2 = y$$
The slope is 3 and the y-intercept is $(0, -2)$.

38.
$$5 - x - 2y = 0$$
$$-2y = x - 5$$
$$y = -\tfrac{1}{2}x + \tfrac{5}{2}$$
The slope is $-\frac{1}{2}$ and the y-intercept is $\left(0, \frac{5}{2}\right)$.

39.
$$y + 3 = 5$$
$$y = 2$$
The slope is 0 and the y-intercept is $(0, 2)$.

40. $y - 9 = 0$
$$y = 9$$
The slope is 0 and the y-intercept is $(0, 9)$.

41.
$$y - 2 = 3(x - 1)$$
$$y - 2 = 3x - 3$$
$$y = 3x - 1$$
The slope is 3 and the y-intercept is $(0, -1)$.

42.
$$y + 4 = -2(x - 5)$$
$$y + 4 = -2x + 10$$
$$y = -2x + 6$$

The slope is -2 and the y-intercept is $(0, 6)$.

43.
$$\frac{y-5}{x+4} = \frac{3}{2}$$
$$2(y-5) = 3(x+4)$$
$$2y - 10 = 3x + 12$$
$$2y = 3x + 22$$
$$y = \tfrac{3}{2}x + 11$$

The slope is $\frac{3}{2}$ and the y-intercept is $(0, 11)$.

44.
$$\frac{y-6}{x-2} = -\frac{3}{5}$$
$$y - 6 = -\tfrac{3}{5}(x-2)$$
$$y - 6 = -\tfrac{3}{5}x + \tfrac{6}{5}$$
$$y = -\tfrac{3}{5}x + \tfrac{36}{5}$$

The slope is $-\frac{3}{5}$ and the y-intercept is $\left(0, \frac{36}{5}\right)$.

45.
$$y - \tfrac{1}{2} = \tfrac{1}{3}\left(x + \tfrac{1}{4}\right)$$
$$y - \tfrac{1}{2} = \tfrac{1}{3}x + \tfrac{1}{12}$$
$$y = \tfrac{1}{3}x + \tfrac{1}{12} + \tfrac{1}{2}$$
$$y = \tfrac{1}{3}x + \tfrac{7}{12}$$

The slope is $\frac{1}{3}$ and the y-intercept is $\left(0, \frac{7}{12}\right)$.

46.
$$y - \tfrac{1}{3} = -\tfrac{1}{2}\left(x - \tfrac{1}{4}\right)$$
$$y - \tfrac{1}{3} = -\tfrac{1}{2}x + \tfrac{1}{8}$$
$$y = -\tfrac{1}{2}x + \tfrac{1}{8} + \tfrac{1}{3}$$
$$y = -\tfrac{1}{2}x + \tfrac{11}{24}$$

The slope is $-\frac{1}{2}$ and the y-intercept is $\left(0, \frac{11}{24}\right)$.

47.
$$y - 6000 = 0.01(x + 5700)$$
$$y - 6000 = 0.01x + 57$$
$$y = 0.01x + 6057$$

The slope is 0.01 and the y-intercept is $(0, 6057)$.

48.
$$y - 5000 = 0.05(x - 1990)$$
$$y - 5000 = 0.05x - 99.5$$
$$y = 0.05x + 4900.5$$

The slope is 0.05 and the intercept is $(0, 4900.5)$.

49. Since the y-intercept is $(0, 5)$ and the slope is $1/2$, we can use slope-intercept form to write the equation.
$$y = \tfrac{1}{2}x + 5$$
To get integral coefficients multiply by 2.
$$2y = x + 10$$
$$-x + 2y = 10$$
$$x - 2y = -10 \quad \text{(Standard form)}$$

50. Use slope-intercept form with slope 5 and y-intercept $(0, 1/2)$.
$$y = 5x + \tfrac{1}{2}$$

$$2y = 10x + 1$$
$$-10x + 2y = 1$$
$$10x - 2y = -1$$

51. The slope of the line through $(2, 0)$ and $(0, 4)$ is
$$m = \frac{4 - 0}{0 - 2} = -2.$$
Use slope-intercept form to write the equation of the line with slope -2 and y-intercept $(0, 4)$:
$$y = -2x + 4$$
$$2x + y = 4 \quad \text{(Standard form)}$$

52. Find the slope of the line through $(0, 5)$ and $(4, 0)$.
$$m = \frac{5 - 0}{0 - 4} = -\frac{5}{4}$$
Use the slope $-5/4$ and y-intercept $(0, 5)$ to write the equation.
$$y = -\tfrac{5}{4}x + 5$$
$$4y = -5x + 20$$
$$5x + 4y = 20$$

53. Any line parallel to $y = 2x + 6$ has slope 2. Use point-slope formula to find the equation of a line with slope 2 and going through $(-2, 1)$:
$$y - 1 = 2(x - (-2))$$
$$y - 1 = 2x + 4$$
$$-2x + y = 5$$
$$2x - y = -5 \quad \text{(Standard form)}$$

54. Any line parallel to $y = -3x - 5$ has slope -3. Use the point-slope formula with slope -3 and point $(1, -3)$.
$$y - (-3) = -3(x - 1)$$
$$y + 3 = -3x + 3$$
$$3x + y = 0$$

55. Write $2x + 4y = 1$ in slope-intercept form to identify the slope:
$$4y = -2x + 1$$
$$y = -\tfrac{1}{2}x + \tfrac{1}{4}$$
Any line parallel to $2x + 4y = 1$ has slope $-1/2$. Use the point-slope formula to find the equation of the line with slope $-1/2$ through $(-3, 5)$:
$$y - 5 = -\tfrac{1}{2}(x - (-3))$$
$$y - 5 = -\tfrac{1}{2}x - \tfrac{3}{2}$$
$$2y - 10 = -x - 3$$
$$x + 2y = 7 \quad \text{(Standard form)}$$

56. First find the slope of $3x - 5y = -7$.
$$-5y = -3x - 7$$
$$y = \tfrac{3}{5}x + \tfrac{7}{5}$$
Use slope 3/5 and the point $(2, 4)$ in the point slope formula.
$$y - 4 = \tfrac{3}{5}(x - 2)$$
$$y - 4 = \tfrac{3}{5}x - \tfrac{6}{5}$$
$$5y - 20 = 3x - 6$$
$$-3x + 5y = 14$$
$$3x - 5y = -14$$

57. A line perpendicular to $y = (1/2)x - 3$ has slope -2. Use the point-slope formula to find the equation of a line with slope -2 going through $(1, 1)$:
$$y - 1 = -2(x - 1)$$
$$y - 1 = -2x + 2$$
$$2x + y = 3 \quad \text{(Standard form)}$$

58. Any line perpendicular to $y = -3x + 7$ has slope 1/3. Use slope 1/3 and the point $(-1, -2)$ in the point-slope formula.
$$y - (-2) = \tfrac{1}{3}(x - (-1))$$
$$y + 2 = \tfrac{1}{3}x + \tfrac{1}{3}$$
$$3y + 6 = x + 1$$
$$-x + 3y = -5$$
$$x - 3y = 5$$

59. Write $x + 3y = 4$ in slope-intercept form to determine its slope:
$$3y = -x + 4$$
$$y = -\tfrac{1}{3}x + \tfrac{4}{3}$$

The slope of $x + 3y = 4$ is $-1/3$. Any line perpendicular to $x + 3y = 4$ has slope 3. Use the point-slope formula to find the equation of the line with slope 3 through $(-2, 3)$.
$$y - 3 = 3(x - (-2))$$
$$y - 3 = 3x + 6$$
$$-3x + y = 9$$
$$3x - y = -9 \quad \text{(Standard form)}$$

60. First find the slope of $2y + 5 - 3x = 0$.
$$2y = 3x - 5$$
$$y = \tfrac{3}{2}x - \tfrac{5}{2}$$
Any line perpendicular to this line has slope $-2/3$. Use slope $-2/3$ and the point $(2, 7)$ in the point-slope formula.
$$y - 7 = -\tfrac{2}{3}(x - 2)$$
$$y - 7 = -\tfrac{2}{3}x + \tfrac{4}{3}$$

$$3y - 21 = -2x + 4$$
$$2x + 3y = 25$$

61. Any line parallel to the x-axis has slope 0. If it goes through $(2, 5)$, it has y-intercept $(0, 5)$. Using slope-intercept form we get
$$y = 0 \cdot x + 5$$
$$y = 5$$

62. Any line parallel to the y-axis has undefined slope. A vertical line through $(-1, 6)$ has equation $x = -1$.

63. The slope of $y = (1/2)x$ is 1/2 and the y-intercept is $(0, 0)$. To graph the line start at $(0, 0)$ and go up 1 unit and 2 units to the right to find another point on the line, $(2, 1)$. Draw the line through $(0, 0)$ and $(2, 1)$.

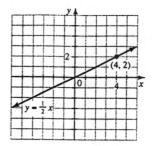

64. The graph of $y = -\tfrac{2}{3}x$ has a y-intercept of $(0, 0)$ and slope $-2/3$. Start at $(0, 0)$, rise -2, and then run 3 to the right.

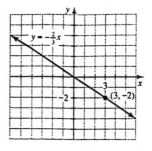

65. The slope of $y = 2x - 3$ is 2 and the y-intercept is $(0, -3)$. The slope of 2 is obtained from 2/1. To graph the line start at $(0, -3)$ and rise 2 units and go 1 unit to the right to get

74

to the point $(1, -1)$. Draw a line through the points $(0, -3)$ and $(1, -1)$.

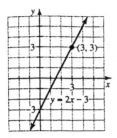

66. The graph of $y = -x + 1$ has slope -1 and y-intercept $(0, 1)$. To graph the line, start at $(0, 1)$, rise -1 unit, then run 1 unit to the right.

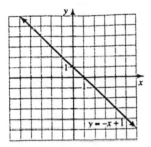

67. The slope of $y = (-2/3)x + 2$ is $-2/3$ and the y-intercept is $(0, 2)$. To graph the line start at $(0, 2)$ and go down 2 units and then 3 units to the right to locate the point $(3, 0)$. Draw a line through $(0, 2)$ and $(3, 0)$.

68. The line $y = 3x - 4$ has slope 3 and y-intercept $(0, -4)$. To graph the line start at $(0, -4)$, go up 3 units, and then 1 unit to the right. Draw a line through the two points.

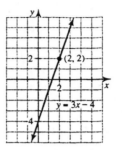

69. The equation $3y + x = 0$ can be written as $y = (-1/3)x$. Its slope is $-1/3$ and its y-intercept is $(0, 0)$. To graph the line start at $(0, 0)$ and go 1 unit down and 3 units to the right to locate the point $(3, -1)$. Draw a line through $(0, 0)$ and $(3, -1)$.

70. The equation $4y - x = 0$ is equivalent to $y = (1/4)x$. The slope is $1/4$ and the y-intercept is $(0, 0)$. To graph the line start at $(0, 0)$, go up 1 unit, and then go 4 units to the right. Draw a line through the two points.

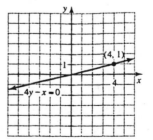

71. Write the equation as $y = x - 3$ to see that the slope is 1 and the y-intercept is $(0, -3)$. Since $1 = 1/1$, we start at $(0, -3)$ and go up 1 unit and 1 unit to the right to locate the point $(1, -2)$. Draw a line through $(0, -3)$ and $(1, -2)$.

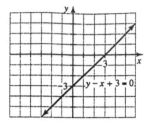

72. The equation $x - y = 4$ is equivalent to $y = x - 4$. The slope is 1 and the y-intercept is $(0, -4)$. To graph the line start at $(0, -4)$, go up 1 unit, and 1 unit to the right. Draw a line through the two points.

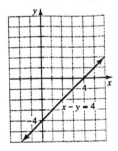

73. Solve the equation for y:
$$3x - 2y = 6$$
$$-2y = -3x + 6$$
$$y = \tfrac{3}{2}x - 3$$
The slope is 3/2 and the y-intercept is $(0, -3)$. Start at $(0, -3)$ and go 3 units upward and then 2 units to the right to locate the point $(2, 0)$. Draw a line through $(0, -3)$ and $(2, 0)$.

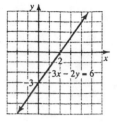

74. The equation $3x + 5y = 10$ is equivalent to $y = -\tfrac{3}{5}x + 2$. The line has slope $-3/5$ and y-intercept $(0, 2)$. Start at $(0, 2)$, move down 3 units, and move 5 units to the right. Draw a line through the two points.

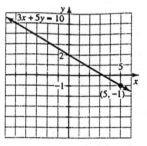

75. Solve the equation for y:
$$y + 2 = 0$$
$$y = -2$$
The slope is 0 and the y-intercept is $(0, -2)$. Draw a horizontal line through $(0, -2)$.

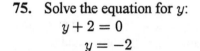

76. The equation $y - 3 = 0$ is equivalent to $y = 3$. The line has slope 0 and y-intercept $(0, 3)$. Draw a horizontal line through $(0, 3)$.

76

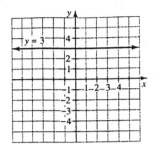

77. Solve the equation for x:
$$x + 3 = 0$$
$$x = -3$$
There is no slope-intercept form for this line because it is a vertical line. The x-intercept is $(-3, 0)$. Draw a vertical line through $(-3, 0)$.

78. The equation $x - 5 = 0$ is equivalent to $x = 5$. The line has no y-intercept and undefined slope. Draw a vertical line through $(5, 0)$.

79. Solve $x + 3y = 7$ for y to get $y = -\frac{1}{3}x + \frac{7}{3}$. The lines are perpendicular because there slopes are 3 and $-1/3$.

80. Solve $\frac{1}{2}x + \frac{1}{4}y = 1$ for y to get $y = -2x + 4$. The lines are perpendicular because their slopes are $1/2$ and -2.

81. Solve $2x - 4y = 9$ for y to get $y = \frac{1}{2}x - \frac{9}{4}$. Solve $\frac{1}{3}x = \frac{2}{3}y - 8$ for y to get $y = \frac{1}{2}x + 12$. The lines are parallel because there slopes are equal.

82. Solve $\frac{1}{4}x - \frac{1}{6}y = \frac{1}{3}$ for y to get $y = \frac{3}{2}x - 2$. Solve $\frac{1}{3}y = \frac{1}{2}x - 2$ for y to get $y = \frac{3}{2}x - 6$. The lines are parallel because there slopes are equal.

83. Solve $x - 6 = 9$ for x to get $x = 15$. Solve $y - 4 = 12$ for y to get $y = 16$. The lines are perpendicular, because one is horizontal and the other is vertical.

84. The lines are $x = 6$ and $x = 16$. The lines are parallel because any two vertical lines are parallel.

85. The slope of the line through $(0, 60)$ and $(120, 200)$ is
$$m = \frac{200 - 60}{120 - 0} = \frac{140}{120} = \frac{7}{6}.$$
Using slope-intercept form with a t-intercept of $(0, 60)$ we get $t = \frac{7}{6}s + 60$.
After 30 seconds the temperature will be
$$t = \frac{7}{6}(30) + 60 = 35 + 60 = 95°F.$$

86. The slope of the line through the two points $(1000, 1500)$ and $(2000, 2000)$ is
$$m = \frac{2000 - 1500}{2000 - 1000} = \frac{1}{2}.$$
Use slope $\frac{1}{2}$ and the point $(1000, 1500)$ in the point-slope formula of the line.
$$C - 1500 = \frac{1}{2}(n - 1000)$$
$$C - 1500 = \frac{1}{2}n - 500$$
$$C = \frac{1}{2}n + 1000$$
To find the cost for 1 circuit board, use $n = 1$ in the formula: $C = \frac{1}{2}(1) + 1000 = 1000.50$
To produce only one circuit board it would cost $1000.50.

87. a) $m = \dfrac{24 - 14}{1995 - 1970} = \dfrac{10}{25} = \dfrac{2}{5} = 0.4$

$$y - 14 = \frac{2}{5}(x - 1970)$$
$$y - 14 = \frac{2}{5}x - 788$$

$$y = \tfrac{2}{5}x - 774$$
b) If $x = 2005$, then
$$y = \tfrac{2}{5}(2005) - 774 = 28.$$
So in 2005 worldwide emission of CO_2 will be 28 billion tons

88. a) $m = \dfrac{6 - 3.5}{95 - 70} = \dfrac{2.5}{25} = 0.1$

$$y - 6 = 0.1(x - 95)$$
$$y - 6 = 0.1x - 9.5$$
$$y = 0.1x - 3.5$$

b) If $x = 2005$, then $y = 0.1(105) - 3.5 = 7$
So in 2005 worldwide energy use will be the equivalent of 7 billion tons of oil.

89. The slope of the line through $(8.24, 1015.5)$ and $(7.26, 717.1)$ is
$$m = \dfrac{717.1 - 1015.5}{7.26 - 8.24} \approx 304.49$$
Use the point-slope formula for the equation of a line with slope 304.49 and the point $(8.24, 1015.5)$.
$$w - 1015.5 = 304.49(d - 8.24)$$
$$w - 1015.5 = 304.49d - 2508.9976$$
$$w = 304.5d - 1493.5$$
b) Use $d = 7.81$ in the formula to find w.
$$w = 304.5(7.81) - 1493.5 \approx 892.5$$
When depth is 7.81 ft, the flow is 884.6 ft^3/sec.
c) As the depth increases, we can see from the graph that the flow increases.

90. a) If x shares of Ford were bought and y shares of GM were bought, then
$$58.25x + 47.50y = 5,031,250$$
b) If 35,000 shares of Ford were purchased, then
$$58.25(35,000) + 47.50y = 5,031,250$$
$$47.50y = 2992500$$
$$y = 63,000$$
c) The intercepts are $(0, 105,921.1)$ and $(86,373.4, 0)$. The intercepts give the number of shares if all money was spent on only one type of stock.
d) As one type increases, the other decreases.

93. The x-intercept is $(3000, 0)$ and the y-intercept is $(0, -3000)$.

94. The lines are perpendicular and will appear perpendicular in a window in which the length of one unit is the same on each axis.

95. The lines intersect at $(50, 97)$.

3.4 WARM-UPS

1. True, because $-3 > -3(2) + 2$.
2. False, because $3x - y > 2$ is equivalent to $y < 3x - 2$, which is below the line $3x - y = 2$.
3. True, because $3x + y < 5$ is equivalent to $y < -3x + 5$.
4. False, the region $x < -3$ is to the left of the vertical line $x = -3$.
5. True, because the word "and" is used.
6. True, because the word "or" is used.
7. False, because $(2, -5)$ does not satisfy the inequality $y > -3x + 5$.
Note that $-5 > -3(2) + 5$ is incorrect.
8. True, because $(-3, 2)$ satisfies $y \leq x + 5$.
9. False, it is equivalent to the compound inequality $2x - y \leq 4$ and $2x - y \geq -4$.
10. True, because in general $|x| > k$ (for a positive k) is equivalent to $x > k$ or $x < -k$.

3.4 EXERCISES

1. A linear inequality is an inequality of the form $Ax + By \leq C$ (or using $<$, $>$, or $\geq$) where A, B, and C are real numbers and A and B are not both zero.
2. The solution set to a linear inequality in two variables is usually illustrated with a graph.
3. If the inequality includes equality then the line should be solid.
4. We shade the side on which the inequality is satisfied.

5. The test point method is used to determine which side of the boundary line to shade.

6. To graph a compound inequality we find either the union or intersection of the regions determined by each simple inequality.

7. Graph the equation $y = x + 2$. Use its slope of 1 and y-intercept of $(0, 2)$.

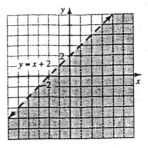

The graph of the inequality $y \leq -2x + 1$ is the region below the line and including the line. For this reason the line is drawn solid.

10. First graph the line $y = -3x + 4$, which has slope -3 and y-intercept $(0, 4)$. Because of the inequality symbol, the line is drawn solid. Shade the region above the line to indicate the points that satisfy $y \geq -3x + 4$.

The graph of $y < x + 2$ is the region below the line $y = x + 2$. The line is dashed because of the inequality symbol. Points on the line satisfy the equation but not the inequality.

8. Graph the equation $y = x - 1$. Use its slope of 1 and y-intercept of $(0, -1)$. The graph of $y < x - 1$ is the region below the line. The line is dashed because of the inequality symbol.

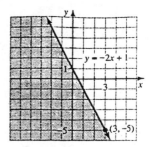

9. First graph the line $y = -2x + 1$. Start at its y-intercept $(0, 1)$ and use a slope of -2. Go down 2 units and 1 to the right to locate a second point on the line.

11. The inequality $x + y > 3$ is equivalent to $y > -x + 3$. First use slope of -1 and a y-intercept of $(0, 3)$ to graph $y = -x + 3$.

The graph of $y > -x + 3$ is the region above the line. The line is drawn dashed because of the inequality symbol.

12. Write the inequality as $y \leq -x - 1$. First draw a solid line for $y = -x - 1$, which has slope -1 and y-intercept $(0, -1)$. The graph of $y \leq -x - 1$ is the region below the line.

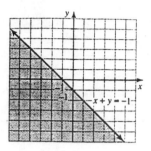

15. Solve the inequality for y:
$$3x - 4y \leq 8$$
$$-4y \leq -3x + 8$$
$$y \geq \tfrac{3}{4}x - 2$$
To graph the equation $y = \tfrac{3}{4}x - 2$, draw a solid line with y-intercept $(0, -2)$ and slope $3/4$. Since the inequality symbol is $\geq$, shade the region above the line.

13. The inequality $2x + 3y < 9$ is equivalent to $y < -\tfrac{2}{3}x + 3$. Use a slope of $-2/3$ and a y-intercept of 3 to graph the line $y = -\tfrac{2}{3}x + 3$. The graph of the inequality is the region below the line. The line is not included in the graph and so it is drawn dashed.

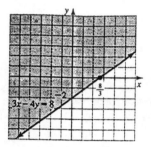

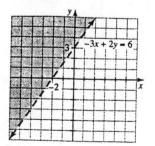

16. Rewrite $4x - 5y > 10$ as $y < \tfrac{4}{5}x - 2$. Draw a dashed line for $y = \tfrac{4}{5}x - 2$, which has slope $\tfrac{4}{5}$ and y-intercept $(0, -2)$. Shade the region below the line to indicate the points that satisfy $y < \tfrac{4}{5}x - 2$.

14. Rewrite the inequality $-3x + 2y > 6$ as $y > \tfrac{3}{2}x + 3$. Draw a dashed line for $y = \tfrac{3}{2}x + 3$, which has slope $\tfrac{3}{2}$ and y-intercept $(0, 3)$. Shade the region above the line to indicate the points that satisfy $y > \tfrac{3}{2}x + 3$.

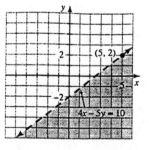

17. If we solve $x - y > 0$ for y we get $y < x$. To graph $y = x$, use a y-intercept of $(0, 0)$ and a slope of 1. Draw a dashed line and shade below the line for the graph of $y < x$.

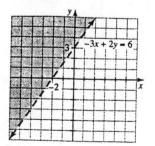

80

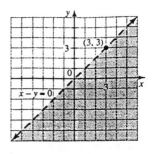

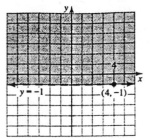

18. Rewrite $2x - y < 0$ as $y > 2x$. Draw a dashed line for $y = 2x$, using a slope of 2 and a y-intercept of $(0, 0)$. Shade the region above the line to indicate the points that satisfy $y > 2x$.

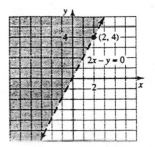

21. The graph of $y < 3$ is the region below the horizontal line $y = 3$. Draw a dashed horizontal line through $(0, 3)$ and shade the region below.

19. The graph of $x \geq 1$ consists of the vertical line $x = 1$ together with the region to the right of the line. Draw a solid vertical line through $(1, 0)$ and shade the region to the right.

22. To graph the inequality $y > -1$, first draw a dashed line for the equation $y = -1$. The line $y = -1$ is a horizontal line with a y-intercept of $(0, -1)$.

20. To graph the inequality $x < 0$, first graph the line $x = 0$. The line $x = 0$ is a vertical line that coincides with the y-axis. Draw a dashed

81

23. To graph $2x - 3y < 5$ using a test point, we can use the x and y-intercepts to determine the graph of the line $2x - 3y = 5$.
If $x = 0$, $2(0) - 3y = 5$ or $y = -5/3$.
If $y = 0$, $2x - 3(0) = 5$ or $x = 5/2$.
Locate the points $(0, -5/3)$ and $(5/2, 0)$ and draw a dashed line through them. Test the point $(0, 0)$ in the inequality:
$$2(0) - 3(0) < 5$$
Since $(0, 0)$ satisfies the inequality, we shade the side of the line that includes $(0, 0)$.

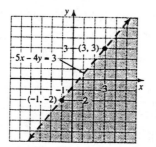

24. First graph the line $5x - 4y = 3$. Its y-intercept is $\left(0, -\frac{3}{4}\right)$ and its x-intercept is $\left(\frac{3}{5}, 0\right)$. Draw the line dashed. Select $(0, 0)$ as a test point. Since $5(0) - 4(0) > 3$ is incorrect, points in the region not containing $(0, 0)$ satisfy the inequality $5x - 4y > 3$.

25. Graph $x + y + 3 = 0$ by using the x and y-intercepts, $(0, -3)$ and $(-3, 0)$. Draw a solid line through these two points. Test $(0, 0)$ in the inequality: $\quad 0 + 0 + 3 \geq 0$

Since $(0, 0)$ satisfies the inequality, we shade the side of the line that includes $(0, 0)$.

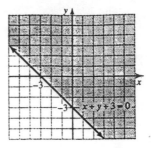

26. To graph $x - y - 6 \leq 0$, we first graph the line $x - y - 6 = 0$. Its y-intercept is $(0, -6)$ and its x-intercept is $(6, 0)$.

Draw the line solid because of the inequality symbol. Select $(0, 0)$ as a test point. Since $0 - 0 - 6 \leq 0$ is correct, all points in the region containing $(0, 0)$ satisfy the inequality.

27. Find x and y-intercepts for $\frac{1}{2}x + \frac{1}{3}y = 1$:
If $x = 0$, we get $\frac{1}{3}y = 1$ or $y = 3$.
If $y = 0$, we get $\frac{1}{2}x = 1$ or $x = 2$.
Draw a dashed line through the intercepts $(0, 3)$ and $(2, 0)$. Test the point $(0, 0)$ in the inequality:
$$\tfrac{1}{2}(0) + \tfrac{1}{3}(0) < 1$$
Since $(0, 0)$ satisfies the inequality, we shade the region that includes $(0, 0)$.

82

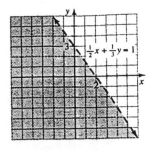

30. To graph the compound inequality $y < x$ and $y < -3x + 2$, first draw dashed lines for $y = x$ and $y = -3x + 2$. Test one point in each of the 4 regions to see if it satisfies the compound inequality. Test $(-3, 0)$, $(0, -3)$, $(0, 4)$, and $(4, 0)$. Only $(0, -3)$ satisfies both inequalities of the system. So shade the region containing $(0, -3)$.

28. First graph the line $2 - \frac{2}{5}y = \frac{1}{2}x$ by using its intercepts. If $x = 0$, then $2 - \frac{2}{5}y = 0$, or $y = 5$. If $y = 0$, then $2 = \frac{1}{2}x$, or $x = 4$. Draw a dashed line through the intercepts $(0, 5)$ and $(4, 0)$.

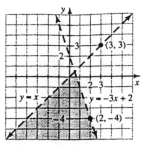

31. First graph the equations $y = x + 3$ and $y = -x + 2$. Test the points $(0, 5)$, $(5, 0)$, $(0, -5)$, and $(-5, 0)$ in the compound inequality. Only $(-5, 0)$ fails to satisfy the compound inequality. So shade all regions except the one containing $(-5, 0)$.

Select $(0, 0)$ as a test point. Since $2 - \frac{2}{5}(0) > \frac{1}{2}(0)$ is correct, we shade the region containing $(0, 0)$. All points in this region satisfy the inequality.

29. To graph $y > x$ and $y > -2x + 3$, we first draw dashed lines for $y = x$ and for $y = -2x + 3$. Test one point in each of the four regions to see if it satisfies the compound inequality. Test $(5, 0)$, $(0, 5)$, $(-5, 0)$ and $(0, -5)$. Only $(0, 5)$ satisfies both inequalities. So shade the region containing $(0, 5)$.

32. First graph the lines $y = x - 5$ and $y = -2x + 1$. Use solid lines because of the inequality symbols. Select a point in each region as a test point. Use $(0, 3)$, $(0, 0)$, $(0, -6)$, and $(6, 0)$. Only $(6, 0)$ fails to satisfy the compound sentence $y \geq x - 5$ or $y \leq -2x + 1$. So shade the three regions that do not contain $(6, 0)$.

83

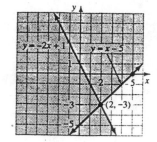

35. Graph the equations $x - 2y = 4$ and $2x - 3y = 6$. Only the region containing the point $(0, -5)$ fails to satisfy the compound inequality. Shade that region including the boundary lines.

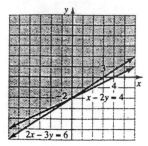

33. First graph the equations $x + y = 5$ and $x - y = 3$. Test one point in each of the 4 regions. Only points in the region containing $(0, 0)$ satisfy both inequalities. Shade that region including the boundary lines.

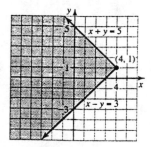

36. First graph the lines $4x - 3y = 3$ and $2x + y = 2$. Use solid lines as shown. Select a test point in each of the 4 regions. Use $(0, 4)$, $(0, 0)$, $(0, -4)$, and $(4, 0)$. Only $(0, -4)$ fails to satisfy the compound sentence $4x - 3y \leq 3$ or $2x + y \geq 2$. So we shade all regions except the one containing $(0, -4)$.

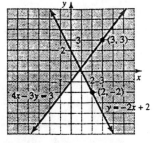

34. First graph the lines $2x - y = 3$ and $3x - y = 0$. Use dashed lines as shown. The points that satisfy $2x - y < 3$ $(y > 2x - 3)$ are above the line $y = 2x - 3$. Points that satisfy $3x - y > 0$ $(y < 3x)$ are below the line $y = 3x$. Points that lie above the first line and below the second line are shaded in the following graph.

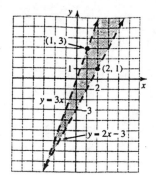

37. Graph the horizontal line $y = 2$ and the vertical line $x = 3$. Only points in the region containing $(0, 5)$ satisfy both inequalities. Shade that region with dashed boundary lines.

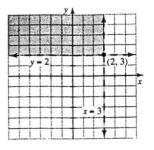

Only points in the region containing $(3, 1)$ satisfy both $y < x$ and $y > 0$. Shade that region.

38. First graph the lines $x = 5$ and $y = -1$. Only points in the region containing $(0, 4)$ satisfy the compound sentence $x \leq 5$ and $y \geq -1$. Shade that region and include the boundary lines.

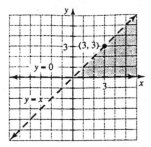

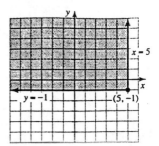

41. Graph $2x = y + 3$ and $y = 2 - x$. Only points in the region containing $(0, -5)$ fail to satisfy the compound inequality. Shade all regions except the one containing $(0, -5)$. Use dashed lines for the boundaries because of the inequality symbols.

39. Graph $y = x$ and $x = 2$. Only points in the region containing $(0, 5)$ satisfy both inequalities. Shade that region and include the boundary lines.

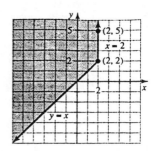

40. First draw dashed lines for $y = x$ and $y = 0$. Test one point in each of the 4 regions.

42. Rewrite the compound inequality as $y > -x + 1$ or $y < x - 5$. Draw dashed lines for the equations $y = -x + 1$ and $y = x - 5$. Test a point in each of the 4 regions. Only points in the region containing $(0, 0)$ fail to satisfy both inequalities. Points in the other 3 regions satisfy at least one of the inequalities. So shade the other 3 regions.

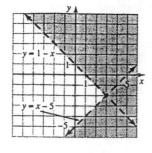

43. Graph the lines $y = x - 1$ and $y = x + 3$. Only points in the region containing $(0, 0)$ satisfy the compound inequality. Shade that region and use dashed boundary lines.

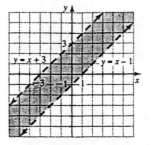

44. First graph the lines $y = x - 1$ and $y = 2x + 5$. Use dashed lines. Points that satisfy the compound inequality are above the line $y = x - 1$ and below the line $y = 2x + 5$ as shown below.

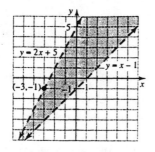

45. Graph the lines $y = 0$, $y = x$, and $x = 1$. Only points inside the triangular region bounded

by the lines satisfy the compound inequality. Shade that region and use solid boundary lines.

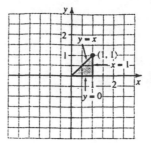

46. First graph the lines $y = x$, $y = 1$, and $x = 0$. Points that satisfy $x \leq y \leq 1$ and $x \geq 0$ are above $y = x$, below $y = 1$, and to the right of $x = 0$, as shown in the following graph.

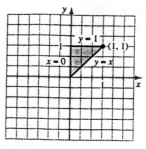

47. Graph $x = 1$, $x = 3$, $y = 2$, and $y = 5$.

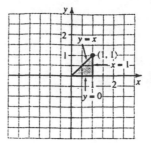

Only points inside the rectangular region satisfy the compound inequality. Shade that region and include the boundary lines.

48. Graph the lines $x = 1$, $x = -1$, $y = 1$, and $y = -1$. Points that satisfy $-1 < x < 1$ and $-1 < y < 1$ are between $x = 1$ and $x = -1$, and also between $y = 1$ and $y = -1$.

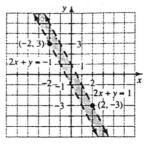

49. Graph the equations $x + y = 2$ and $x + y = -2$. Only points between these two parallel lines satisfy the absolute value inequality.

50. The absolute value inequality $|\, 2x + y\, | < 1$ is equivalent to the compound inequality $-1 < 2x + y < 1$. Graph the lines $2x + y = 1$ ($y = -2x + 1$) and $2x + y = -1$ ($y = -2x - 1$). Test one point in each of the 3 regions. Only points in the region containing $(0, 0)$ satisfy the original inequality. So shade the region containing $(0, 0)$.

51. Graph the parallel lines $2x + y = 1$ and $2x + y = -1$. Points between the lines do not satisfy the absolute value inequality. So shade the other two regions.

52. The inequality $|\, x + 2y\, | \geq 6$ is equivalent to the compound inequality $x + 2y \geq 6$ or $x + 2y \leq -6$. Graph the lines $x + 2y = 6$ and $x + 2y = -6$. Test one point in each of the 3 regions. Only points in the region containing $(0, 0)$ fail to satisfy the original inequality. So shade the other 2 regions.

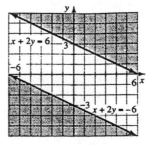

87

53. Rewrite the inequality:

$x - y - 3 > 5 \qquad$ or $x - y - 3 < -5$
$\qquad -y > -x + 8$ or $\qquad -y < -x - 2$
$\qquad y < x - 8 \qquad$ or $\qquad y > x + 2$

Graph the lines $y = x - 8$ and $y = x + 2$.
Points above $y = x + 2$ together with points
below $y = x - 8$ satisfy the absolute value
inequality.

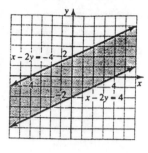

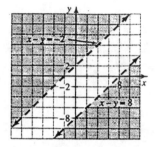

54. The inequality $|x - 2y + 4| > 2$ is
equivalent to $x - 2y + 4 > 2$ or
$x - 2y + 4 < -2$.
Graph the lines $x - 2y + 4 = 2$ $(y = \frac{1}{2}x + 1)$
and $x - 2y + 4 = -2$ $(y = \frac{1}{2}x + 3)$.

56. The inequality $|x - 3y| \le 6$ is
equivalent to the compound inequality
$-6 \le x - 3y \le 6$. Graph the lines $x - 3y = 6$
and $x - 3y = -6$. Test one point in each of the
3 regions in the original inequality. Only points
in the region containing $(0, 0)$ satisfy the
original inequality. So shade the region
containing $(0, 0)$.

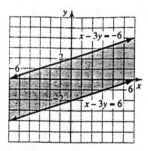

57. Graph the vertical lines $x = 2$ and $x = -2$.
Points in the region between the lines do not
satisfy the inequality but points in the other two
regions do.

Test one point in each of the 3 regions. Only
points in the region containing $(0, 2)$ fail to
satisfy the original inequality. So shade the
other 2 regions.

55. Graph the parallel lines $x - 2y = 4$ and
$x - 2y = -4$. Points in the region between the
lines satisfy the inequality.

88

58. The inequality $|x| \leq 3$ is equivalent to $-3 \leq x \leq 3$. Graph the two vertical lines $x = 3$ and $x = -3$. Test one point in each of the 3 regions. Only points in the region containing $(0, 0)$ satisfy the original inequality.

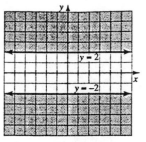

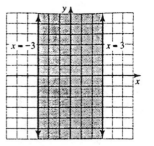

59. Graph the horizontal lines $y = 1$ and $y = -1$. Only points in the region between the lines satisfy $|y| < 1$.

61. Graph the equation $y = |x|$. Only points in the region below that graph satisfy $y < |x|$.

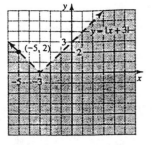

62. To find the graph of $y < |x + 3|$, we first draw the v-shaped graph of $y = |x + 3|$. The graph of $y < |x + 3|$ is the region below the graph of $y = |x + 3|$.

60. The inequality $|y| \geq 2$ is equivalent to the compound inequality $y \geq 2$ or $y \leq -2$. Graph the horizontal lines $y = 2$ and $y = -2$. Test one point in each of the 3 regions. Only points in the region containing $(0, 0)$ fail to satisfy the original inequality. Shade the other two regions.

63. Graph the lines $x = 2$, $x = -2$, $y = 3$, and $y = -3$. Only points inside the rectangular region bounded by the lines satisfy the

89

compound inequality $|x| < 2$ and $|y| < 3$.

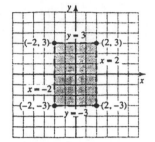

64. The compound sentence $|x| \geq 3$ or $|y| \geq 1$ is equivalent to $(x \geq 3$ or $x \leq -3)$ or $(y \geq 1$ or $y \leq -1)$. First graph the lines $x = 3$, $x = -3$, $y = 1$, and $y = -1$. Test one point in each of the regions determined by the lines. Only points in the region containing $(0,0)$ fail to satisfy the original sentence. Shade all regions except the one containing $(0,0)$.

65. The inequality $|x - 3| < 1$ is equivalent to $2 < x < 4$. The inequality $|y - 2| < 1$ is equivalent to $1 < y < 3$. Graph the lines $x = 2$, $x = 4$, $y = 1$, and $y = 3$. Only points inside the square region bounded by these lines satisfy the inequalities $|x - 3| < 1$ and $|y - 2| < 1$.

66. The sentence $|x - 2| \geq 3$ or $|y - 5| \geq 2$ is equivalent to the sentence $(x - 2 \geq 3$ or $x - 2 \leq -3)$ or $(y - 5 \geq 2$ or $y - 5 \leq -2)$. This last sentence is equivalent to $(x \geq 5$ or $x \leq -1)$ or $(y \geq 7$ or $y \leq 3)$. Graph the lines $x = 5$, $x = -1$, $y = 7$, and $y = 3$. Test one point in each of the regions. Only points in the region containing $(2, 4)$ fail to satisfy the original sentence. Shade all other regions.

67. Let $x =$ the number of compact cars and $y =$ the number of full-size cars. We have
$$15,000x + 20,000y \leq 120,000$$
$$3x + 4y \leq 24$$
We also have $x \geq 0$ and $y \geq 0$ because they cannot purchase a negative number of cars. Graph $3x + 4y \leq 24$, $x \geq 0$, and $y \geq 0$.

90

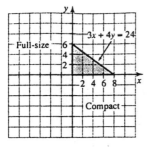

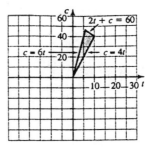

71. Graph $h \leq 187 - 0.85a$ and $h \geq 154 - 0.70a$ for $20 \leq a \leq 75$.

68. Let $x =$ the number of tables and $y =$ the number of chairs. We have
$$16x + 8y \leq 12(40)$$
$$16x + 8y \leq 480$$
$$2x + y \leq 60$$
Graph $2x + y \leq 60$, $x \geq 0$, and $y \geq 0$.

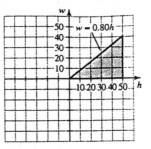

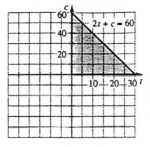

72. Graph $w \leq 0.80h$, $h \leq 50$, $w \geq 0$, and $h \geq 0$:

69. Graph $3x + 4y \leq 24$, $x \geq 0$, $y \geq 0$, and $y > x$:

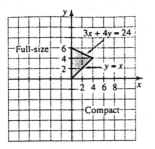

73. Let $x =$ the number of days of newspaper advertising and $y =$ the number times an ad is aired on TV.
$$300x + 1000y \leq 9000$$
$$3x + 10y \leq 90$$
Graph $3x + 10y \leq 90$, $x \geq 0$, and $y \geq 0$:

70. Graph $2x + y \leq 60$, $x \geq 0$, $y \geq 0$, $y \geq 4x$, and $y \leq 6x$

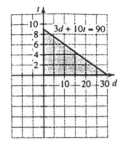

74. a) The slope of the line through $(0, 330)$ and $(110, 0)$ is -3. Using slope intercept form the equation of the line is $y = -3x + 330$ or $t = -3r + 330$. The region on or below the line is $t \leq -3r + 330$, or $t + 3r \leq 330$.

b) Because $118 + 3(71) \leq 330$ is incorrect, the truck will not hold 71 TVs and 118 refrigerators.

c) Because $176 + 3(51) \leq 330$ is correct, the truck will hold 176 TVs and 51 refrigerators.

3.5 WARM-UPS

1. False, $\{(1, 2), (1, 3)\}$ is not a function.

2. True, because $C = \pi D$.

3. True, because no two ordered pairs have the same first coordinate and different second coordinates.

4. False, because $\{(1, 2), (1, 3)\}$ is a relation but not a function.

5. False, because $(1, 5)$ and $(1, 7)$ have the same first coordinate and different second coordinates.

6. False, because 0 is also in the domain of the function.

7. True, because the absolute value of any number is greater than or equal to zero.

8. True, because $y = (1/4)x$ guarantees that no two ordered pairs can have the same first coordinate and different second coordinates.

9. False, because both $(16, 2)$ and $(16, -2)$ are in the function.

10. True, because $h(-2) = (-2)^2 - 3 = 4 - 3 = 1$.

3.5 EXERCISES

1. A function is a set of ordered pairs in which no two have the same first coordinate and different second coordinates.

2. A relation is any set of ordered pairs.

3. The domain of a relation is the set of all possible first coordinates.

4. The range of relation is the set of all possible second coordinates.

5. The f-notation is the notation in which we use $f(x)$ rather than y as the dependent variable.

6. The average rate of change of the function $f(x)$ on the interval $[a, b]$ is $(f(b) - f(a))/(b - a)$.

7. A set of ordered pairs is a function unless there are two pairs with the same first coordinate and different second coordinates. So this set is a function.

8. This set of ordered pairs is not a function because $(2, -5)$ and $(2, 5)$ have the same x-coordinate and different y-coordinates.

9. This set of ordered pairs is not a function because $(-2, 4)$ and $(-2, 6)$ have the same x-coordinate and different y-coordinates.

10. This set of ordered pairs is a function because no two ordered pairs have the same first coordinate and different second coordinates.

11. This set of ordered pairs is not a function because $(\pi, -1)$ and $(\pi, 1)$ have the same x-coordinate and different y-coordinates.

12. This set is not a function because $(-0.3, -0.3)$ and $(-0.3, 1)$ have the same first coordinate and different second coordinates.

13. This set is a function because no two ordered pairs have the same first coordinate and different second coordinates.

14. This set is a function because no two ordered pairs have the same first coordinate and different second coordinates.

15. This set is a function because for each value of x, $y = (x - 1)^2$ determines only one value of y.

16. This set is a function because for each value of x, $y = x^2 - 12x + 1$ determines only one value of y.

17. This set is not a function because $(2, 2)$ and $(2, -2)$ both belong to this set.

18. This set is not a function because $(3, -1)$ and $(3, 1)$ both belong to this set.

19. The set is a function because each value of s determines only one value of t by the formula $t = s$.

20. This set is a function because for each value of u, $v = 1/u$ determines only one value for v.

21. If we solve $x = 5y + 2$ for y, we get $y = \frac{x-2}{5}$. So the relation is a function because each value of x determines only one y value.

22. The equation $x = 3y$ is equivalent to $y = \frac{1}{3}x$. This set is a function because for each value of x, $y = \frac{1}{3}x$ determines only one y value.

23. Ordered pairs $(2, 1)$ and $(2, -1)$ both satisfy $x = 2y^2$. So $x = 2y^2$ does not define y as a function of x.

24. The equation $y = 3x^4$ defines y as a function of x because each value of x determines only one value of y.

25. The equation $y = 3x - 4$ defines y as a function of x because each value of x determines only one value of y.

26. The equation $y = 2x + 9$ defines y as a function of x because each value of x determines only one value of y.

27. This equation does not define a function because ordered pairs such as $(0, 1)$ and $(0, -1)$ satisfy $x^2 + y^2 = 1$.

28. This equation does not define a function because ordered pairs such as $(1, 1)$ and $(1, -1)$ satisfy $x^4 - y^4 = 0$.

29. The equation $y = \sqrt{x}$ is a function because to each value of x there corresponds only one value of y.

30. The relation $x = \sqrt{y}$ is a function because for each nonnegative value of x, there is only one y value that satisfies $x = \sqrt{y}$.

31. This relation is not a function because both $(2, -1)$ and $(2, 1)$ satisfy $x = 2\,|\,y\,|$.

32. The relation is a function because for each value of x, the equation $y = \,|\,x - 1\,|$ determines a unique value for y.

33. The domain is the set of first coordinates, $\{2\}$, and the range is the set of second coordinates, $\{3, 5, 7\}$.

34. The domain is the set of first coordinates, $\{3, 4, 5\}$. The range is the set of second coordinates, $\{1\}$.

35. Since we can find the absolute value of any number, the domain is R. Since the absolute values of real numbers are always greater than or equal to 0, the range is $[0, \infty)$.

36. Since any number can be use in place of x in $y = 2x + 1$, the domain is the set of all real numbers, R. Since any number can result as a y-coordinate, the range is R.

37. Since x is equal to the positive square root of y, the values of x must be greater than or equal to 0. The domain is $[0, \infty)$. Since square root is only defined on nonnegative numbers, the values of y must be nonnegative. The range is $[0, \infty)$.

38. Since $\sqrt{x}$ is not a real number for negative values of x, x must be nonnegative. The domain is $[0, \infty)$. Since $\sqrt{x}$ can be any nonnegative real number, $\sqrt{x} + 1$ must be greater than or equal to 1. So the range is $[1, \infty)$.

39. $f(4) = 3(4) - 2 = 12 - 2 = 10$

40. $f(100) = 3(100) - 2 = 298$

41. $g(-2) = (-2)^2 - 3(-2) + 2$
$$= 4 + 6 + 2 = 12$$

42. $g(6) = 6^2 - 3(6) + 2 = 20$

43. $h(-3) = \,|-3 + 2\,| = \,|-1\,| = 1$

44. $h(-19) = \,|-19 + 2\,| = \,|-17\,| = 17$

45. Since $f(x) = 3x - 2$ and $f(x) = 5$, we have
$$5 = 3x - 2.$$
$$7 = 3x$$
$$\tfrac{7}{3} = x$$

46. Replace $f(x)$ by 49 in $f(x) = 3x - 2$.
$$49 = 3x - 2$$

93

$$51 = 3x$$
$$17 = x$$

47. If $h(x) = |x+2|$ and $h(x) = 3$, then
$$|x+2| = 3$$
$$x+2 = 3 \text{ or } x+2 = -3$$
$$x = 1 \text{ or } \qquad x = -5$$

48. Replace $h(x)$ by 7 in the
$h(x) = |x+2|$.
$$7 = |x+2|$$
$$x+2 = 7 \text{ or } x+2 = -7$$
$$x = 5 \text{ or } \qquad x = -9$$

49. Since $f(x) = 4x - 1$, $f(a) = 4a - 1$.

50. Since $f(x) = 4x - 1$,
$f(a+1) = 4(a+1) - 1 = 4a + 3$.

51. Since $f(x) = 4x - 1$,
$f(x+2) = 4(x+2) - 1 = 4x + 7$.

52. Since $f(x) = 4x - 1$,
$f(x+h) = 4(x+h) - 1 = 4x + 4h - 1$.

53. Since $g(x) = \dfrac{1}{x+2}$,
$$g(x+3) = \frac{1}{x+3+2}$$
$$= \frac{1}{x+5}$$

54. Since $g(x) = \dfrac{1}{x+2}$,
$$g(x-2) = \frac{1}{x-2+2} = \frac{1}{x}.$$

55. $g(x+h) = \dfrac{1}{x+h+2}$

56. $g(a-2) = \dfrac{1}{a-2+2} = \dfrac{1}{a}$

57. $\dfrac{f(3) - f(1)}{3-1} = \dfrac{3^2 - 1^2}{2} = \dfrac{8}{2} = 4$

58. $\dfrac{g(9) - g(3)}{9-3} = \dfrac{13-1}{6} = \dfrac{12}{6} = 2$

59. $\dfrac{h(8) - h(4)}{8-4} = \dfrac{104-20}{4} = \dfrac{84}{4} = 21$

60. $\dfrac{f(9) - f(4)}{9-4} = \dfrac{\sqrt{9} - \sqrt{4}}{5} = \dfrac{3-2}{5} = \dfrac{1}{5}$

61. $\dfrac{g(4) - g(2)}{4-2} = \dfrac{\frac{1}{4} - \frac{1}{2}}{2} = \dfrac{-\frac{1}{4}}{2} = -\dfrac{1}{8}$

62. $\dfrac{h(2) - h(1)}{2-1} = \dfrac{\frac{2}{2^2} - \frac{2}{1^2}}{1} = -\dfrac{3}{2}$

63. $f(3.46) = \sqrt{3.46 + 2} = 2.337$

64. $g(-1.37) = 3(-1.37)^2 - 8(-1.37) + 2$
$$= 18.591$$

65. $g(-3.5) = 3(-3.5)^2 - 8(-3.5) + 2$
$$= 66.75$$

66. $f(-1.2) = \sqrt{-1.2 + 2} = 0.894$

67. $f(a-5) - f(a)$
$$= 3(a-5) - 2 - (3a-2)$$
$$= 3a - 17 - 3a + 2 = -15$$

68. $f(x+h) - f(x)$
$$= 3(x+h) - 2 - (3x-2)$$
$$= 3x + 3h - 2 - 3x + 2 = 3h$$

69. $g(a+2) - g(a)$
$$= 3 - 5(a+2) - (3-5a)$$
$$= 3 - 5a - 10 - 3 + 5a$$
$$= -10$$

70. $g(x+h) - g(x)$
$$= 3 - 5(x+h) - (3-5x)$$
$$= 3 - 5x - 5h - 3 + 5x$$
$$= -5h$$

71. The numerator was found in Exercise 68.
$$\frac{f(x+h) - f(x)}{h} = \frac{3h}{h} = 3$$

72. $\dfrac{f(n+3) - f(n)}{3}$
$$= \frac{3(n+3) - 2 - (3n-2)}{3}$$
$$= \frac{9}{3} = 3$$

73. The area of a square is found by squaring the length of a side: $A = s^2$.

74. Since a square has 4 equal sides, the perimeter is 4 times the length of a side, $P = 4s$.

75. The cost of the purchase, C, is the price per yard times the number of yards purchased: $C = 3.98y$.

76. Since her total pay is the product of her pay per hour and the number of hours worked, we can write $P = 14.5h$.

77. The total cost, C, is found by multiplying the number of toppings, n, by the cost for each topping, $0.50, and adding on the $14.95 base charge: $C = 0.50n + 14.95$

78. The total cost is $120 plus $10 for each yard over 9. So $C = 120 + 10(n-9)$, or $C = 10n + 30$ for $n \geq 9$.

79. We must find the linear equation through the points $(2, 78)$ and $(4, 86)$. First find the slope:
$$m = \frac{86 - 78}{4 - 2} = 4.$$
Now use point slope form:
$$h - 78 = 4(t-2)$$
$$h - 78 = 4t - 8$$

94

$$h = 4t + 70 \quad \text{for } 0 \le t \le 8$$

80. We must find the equation of the line through the points (400, 8.60) and (580, 12.20). First find the slope.

$$m = \frac{12.20 - 8.60}{580 - 400} = \frac{3.60}{180} = 0.02$$

Use the point (400, 8.60) and slope 0.02 in the point-slope formula.

$$C - 8.60 = 0.02(p - 400)$$
$$C - 8.60 = 0.02p - 8$$
$$C = 0.02p + 0.60$$

81. $\dfrac{11,640 - 3590}{1990 - 1998} = -\$1006.25$ per year

82. $\dfrac{69,680 - 16550}{1988 - 1998} = -\$5313$ per year

83. $\dfrac{60 - 0}{8 - 0} \approx 7.5$ mph per second

84. $\dfrac{580 - 634}{0 - 24} \approx \$2.25$ billion/year per month

85. $\dfrac{-16(2.8)^2 + 144 - (-16(3)^2 + 144)}{2.8 - 3}$
$$= -92.8 \text{ ft/sec,}$$

Repeat to get -94.4 ft/sec and -95.84 ft/sec

86. -95.984 ft/sec, -95.9984, -96 ft/sec

3.6 WARM-UPS

1. True, because the graph of a function consists of all ordered pairs that are in the function.

2. True, that is why they are called linear functions.

3. True, because absolute value functions are generally v-shaped.

4. False, because 0 is not in the domain of the function $f(x) = 1/x$.

5. True, because the graph of $y = ax^2 + bx + c$ for $a \ne 0$ is a parabola.

6. False, the domain of a quadratic function is $(-\infty, \infty)$ or R.

7. True, because $f(x)$ is just another name for the dependent variable y.

8. True, because if a vertical line crosses a graph more than once, the graph is not the graph of function.

9. False, because 1 is also in the domain of the function.

10. True, because any real number can be used in a quadratic function.

3.6 EXERCISES

1. A linear function is a function of the form $f(x) = mx + b$ where m and b are real numbers with $m \ne 0$.

2. A constant function is a function of the form $f(x) = k$ where k is a real number.

3. The graph of a constant function is a horizontal line.

4. The absolute-value function has v-shaped graph.

5. The graph of a quadratic function is a parabola.

6. If there is a vertical line that crosses a graph more than once, the graph is not the graph of a function.

7. The graph of $h(x) = -2$ is the same as the graph of the horizontal line $y = -2$.

The domain of the function is R. The only y-coordinate used is -2, and so the range is $\{-2\}$.

8. The graph of $f(x) = 4$ is the same as the graph of the line $y = 4$, a horizontal line. The domain is $(-\infty, \infty)$ and the range is $\{4\}$.

95

9. The graph of $F(x) = 2x - 1$ is the same as the graph of the linear equation $y = 2x - 1$. To draw the graph, start at the y-intercept $(0, -1)$, and use the slope of $2 = 2/1$. Rise 2 and run 1 to locate a second point on the line.

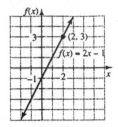

From the graph, we can see that the domain is $(-\infty, \infty)$ and the range is also $(-\infty, \infty)$.

10. The graph of $g(x) = x + 2$ is the same as the graph of $y = x + 2$. Use the y-intercept $(0, 2)$ and a slope of 1 to draw the graph of the line.

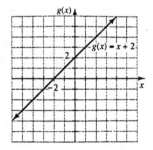

From the graph we can see that the domain is $(-\infty, \infty)$ and the range is also $(-\infty, \infty)$.

11. Graph the line $y = (1/2)x + 2$ by locating the y-intercept $(0, 2)$ and using a slope of $1/2$. The domain is $(-\infty, \infty)$ and the range is $(-\infty, \infty)$.

12. The graph of $h(x) = \frac{2}{3}x - 4$ is the same as the graph $y = \frac{2}{3}x - 4$. Graph the line with y-intercept $(0, -4)$ and slope $2/3$. The domain is $(-\infty, \infty)$ and the range is $(-\infty, \infty)$.

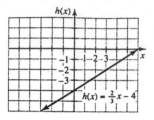

13. The graph of $y = -\frac{2}{3}x + 3$ is a straight line with y-intercept $(0, 3)$ and slope $-2/3$.

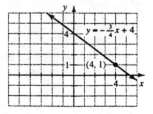

The domain is $(-\infty, \infty)$ and range is $(-\infty, \infty)$.

14. The graph of $y = -\frac{3}{4}x + 4$ is a straight line with y-intercept $(0, 4)$ and slope $-3/4$. From the graph we see that the domain is $(-\infty, \infty)$ and the range is $(-\infty, \infty)$.

15. The graph of $y = -0.3x + 6.5$ is a straight line with y-intercept $(0, 6.5)$ and slope $-3/10$.

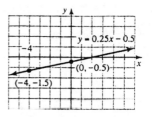

The domain is $(-\infty, \infty)$ and range is $(-\infty, \infty)$.

16. The graph of $y = 0.25x - 0.5$ is a straight line with y-intercept $(0, -0.5)$ and slope $0.25 = 1/4$. From the graph we can see that the domain is $(-\infty, \infty)$ and the range is $(-\infty, \infty)$.

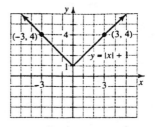

17. The graph of $y = |x| + 1$ contains the points $(0, 1)$, $(2, 3)$, and $(-2, 3)$. Plot these points and draw the v-shaped graph.

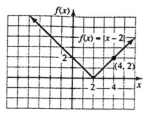

The domain is $(-\infty, \infty)$, and from the graph we can see that the range is $[1, \infty)$.

18. The graph of $g(x) = |x| - 3$ includes the points $(0, -3)$, $(1, -2)$, $(2, -1)$, $(-2, -1)$, and $(-3, 0)$. Plot these points and draw a v-shaped graph. From the graph we can see that the domain is $(-\infty, \infty)$. Since all y-

coordinates on the graph are greater than or equal to -3, the range is $[-3, \infty)$.

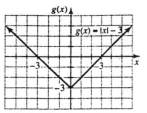

19. The graph of $h(x) = |x + 1|$ includes the points $(0, 1)$, $(1, 2)$, $(-1, 0)$, and $(-2, 1)$.

From the graph we can see that the domain is $(-\infty, \infty)$. In the vertical direction the graph is on or above the x-axis. Since all y-coordinates on the graph are greater than or equal to 0, the range is $[0, \infty)$.

20. The graph of $f(x) = |x - 2|$ includes the points $(0, 2)$, $(2, 0)$, $(4, 2)$, and $(-3, 5)$. From the graph we see that the domain is $(-\infty, \infty)$. Since all y-coordinates are nonnegative, the range is $[0, \infty)$.

21. The graph of $g(x) = |3x|$ includes the points $(0, 0)$, $(1, 3)$, and $(-1, 3)$. Plot these points and draw the graph.

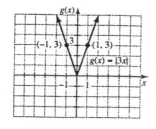

From the graph we can see that the domain is $(-\infty, \infty)$. Since all of the y-coordinates on the graph are greater than or equal to zero, the range is $[0, \infty)$.

22. The graph of $h(x) = |-2x|$ includes the points $(0, 0)$, $(1, 2)$, $(2, 4)$, and $(-2, 4)$. Plot these points and draw the v-shaped graph. From the graph we can see that the domain is $(-\infty, \infty)$. Since all y-coordinates are nonnegative, the range is $[0, \infty)$.

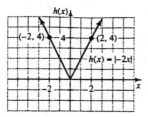

23. The graph of $f(x) = |2x - 1|$ includes the points $(0, 1)$, $(1/2, 0)$, $(1, 1)$, and $(2, 3)$. Plot these points and draw a v-shaped graph.

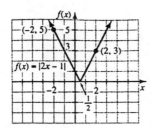

From the graph we can see that the domain is $(-\infty, \infty)$, and the range is $[0, \infty)$.

24. The graph of $y = |2x - 3|$ includes the points $(0, 3)$, $(1.5, 0)$, $(2, 1)$, $(3, 3)$, and $(-1, 5)$.

Plot these points and draw a v-shaped graph. The domain is $(-\infty, \infty)$. Since all y-coordinates are nonnegative, the range is $[0, \infty)$.

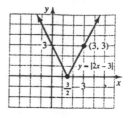

25. The graph of $f(x) = |x - 2| + 1$ includes the points $(2, 1)$, $(3, 2)$, $(4, 3)$, $(1, 2)$, and $(0, 3)$. Plot these points and draw a v-shaped graph. Form the graph we can see that the domain is $(-\infty, \infty)$. Since all y-coordinates are greater than or equal to 1, the range is $[1, \infty)$.

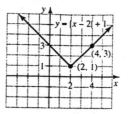

26. The graph of $y = |x - 1| + 2$ includes the points $(-1, 4)$, $(0, 3)$, $(1, 2)$, $(2, 3)$, and $(3, 4)$. Plot these points and draw a v-shaped graph.

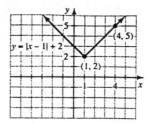

Since any number can be used for x, the domain is $(-\infty, \infty)$. From the graph we see that no y-coordinate is below 2, so the range is $[2, \infty)$.

27. The graph of $g(x) = x^2 + 2$ includes the points $(-2, 6)$, $(-1, 3)$, $(0, 2)$, $(1, 3)$, and $(2, 6)$. Plot these points and draw the parabola through them.

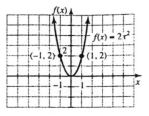

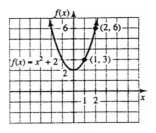

The domain is $(-\infty, \infty)$. Since no y-coordinate on the graph is below 2, the range is $[2, \infty)$.

28. The graph of $f(x) = x^2 - 4$ includes the points $(-2, 0)$, $(-1, -3)$, $(0, -4)$, $(1, -3)$, and $(2, 0)$. Plot these points and draw the parabola through them.

The domain is $(-\infty, \infty)$ and the range is $[0, \infty)$.

30. The graph of $f(x) = -3x^2$ includes the points $(0, 0)$, $(1, -3)$, $(-1, -3)$, $(2, -12)$, and $(-2, -12)$. Plot these points and draw a parabola through them.

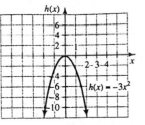

The domain is $(-\infty, \infty)$ and range is $(-\infty, 0]$.

31. The graph of $y = 6 - x^2$ includes the points $(-3, -3)$, $(0, 6)$, $(3, -3)$, $(-2, 2)$, and $(2, 2)$. Plot these points and draw a parabola through them.

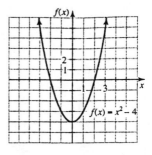

The domain is $(-\infty, \infty)$. Since no y-coordinate on the graph is below -4, the range is $[-4, \infty)$.

29. The graph of $f(x) = 2x^2$ includes the points $(0, 0)$, $(1, 2)$, $(-1, 2)$, $(2, 8)$, and $(-2, 8)$. Plot these points and draw a parabola through them.

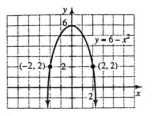

The domain is $(-\infty, \infty)$ and range is $(-\infty, 6]$.

32. The graph of $g(x) = -2x^2 + 3$ includes the points $(-2, -5)$, $(0, 3)$, $(1, 1)$, $(2, -5)$, and $(-1, 1)$. Plot these points and draw a parabola through them.

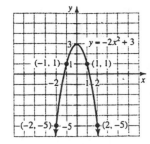

The domain is $(-\infty, \infty)$. From the graph we see that the range is $(-\infty, 3]$.

33. The graph of $y = -x^2 + 2x + 1$ includes the points $(-1, -2)$, $(0, 1)$, $(1, 2)$, $(2, 1)$, and $(3, -2)$. Plot these points and draw a parabola through them.

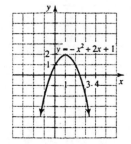

The domain is $(-\infty, \infty)$. From the graph we see that the range is $(-\infty, 3]$.

34. The graph of $g(x) = x^2 + 4x + 1$ includes the points $(-4, 1)$, $(-3, -2)$, $(-2, -3)$, $(-1, -2)$, and $(0, 1)$. Plot these points and draw a parabola through them.

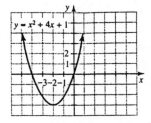

The domain is $(-\infty, \infty)$. From the graph we see that the range is $[-3, \infty)$.

35. The graph of $f(x) = x^2 + 4x + 3$ includes the points $(-4, 3)$, $(-3, 0)$, $(-2, -1)$, $(-1, 0)$, and $(0, 3)$. Plot these points and draw a parabola through them.

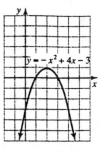

The domain is $(-\infty, \infty)$. From the graph we see that the range is $[-1, \infty)$.

36. The graph of $g(x) = -x^2 + 4x - 3$ includes the points $(0, -3)$, $(1, 0)$, $(2, 1)$, $(3, 0)$, and $(4, -3)$. Plot these points and draw a parabola through them.

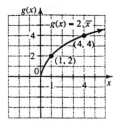

The domain is $(-\infty, \infty)$. From the graph we see that the range is $(-\infty, 1]$.

37. The graph of $g(x) = 2\sqrt{x}$ includes the points $(0, 0)$, $(1, 2)$, and $(4, 4)$. Plot these points and draw a curve through them.

Since we must have $x \geq 0$ in $\sqrt{x}$, the domain is $[0, \infty)$. The range is $[0, \infty)$

38. The graph of $g(x) = \sqrt{x} - 1$ includes the points $(0, -1)$, $(1, 0)$, and $(4, 1)$. Plot these points and draw a curve through them.

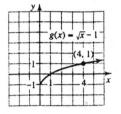

Since we must have $x \geq 0$ in $\sqrt{x}$, the domain is $[0, \infty)$. The range is $[-1, \infty)$.

39. The graph of $f(x) = \sqrt{x - 1}$ includes the points $(1, 0)$, $(2, 1)$, and $(5, 2)$. Plot these points and draw a smooth curve through them. The curve is half of a parabola, positioned on its side.

Since we must have $x - 1 \geq 0$, the domain is $[1, \infty)$. The range is $[0, \infty)$.

40. The graph of $f(x) = \sqrt{x + 1}$ includes the points $(-1, 0)$, $(0, 1)$, $(3, 2)$, and $(8, 3)$. Plot these points and draw a smooth curve through them.

The domain is $[-1, \infty)$ and the range is $[0, \infty)$.

41. The graph of $h(x) = -\sqrt{x}$ includes the points $(0, 0)$, $(1, -1)$, and $(4, -2)$. Plot these points and draw a curve through them.

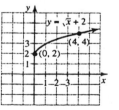

Since we must have $x \geq 0$ in $\sqrt{x}$, the domain is $[0, \infty)$. The range is $(-\infty, 0]$.

42. The graph of $h(x) = -\sqrt{x - 1}$ includes the points $(1, 0)$, $(2, -1)$, and $(5, -2)$. Plot these points and draw a curve through them.

Since we must have $x - 1 \geq 0$ in $\sqrt{x - 1}$, the domain is $[1, \infty)$. The range is $(-\infty, 0]$.

43. The graph of $y = \sqrt{x} + 2$ includes the points $(0, 2)$, $(1, 3)$, and $(4, 4)$. Graph these points and draw a curve through them.

Because $\sqrt{x}$ is a real number only for nonnegative values of x, the domain is $[0, \infty)$. From the graph we see that y-coordinates go no lower than 2, so the range is $[2, \infty)$.

44. The graph of $y = 2\sqrt{x} + 1$ includes the points $(0, 1)$, $(1, 3)$, and $(4, 5)$. Plot these points and draw a curve through them.

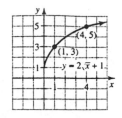

Since we must have $x \geq 0$ in $\sqrt{x}$, the domain is $[0, \infty)$. From the graph we can see that the range is $[1, \infty)$.

45. The graph of $x = |y|$ includes the points $(0, 0)$, $(1, -1)$, $(1, 1)$, $(2, -2)$, and $(2, 2)$. Note that in this case it is easier to pick the y-coordinate and then find the appropriate x-coordinate using $x = |y|$. Draw the v-shaped graph through these points.

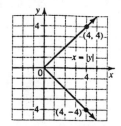

Since the x-coordinates are nonnegative, the domain is $[0, \infty)$. Since we are allowed to select any number for y, the range is $(-\infty, \infty)$.

46. The graph of $x = -|y|$ includes the points $(0, 0)$, $(-1, 1)$, $(-1, -1)$, $(-4, 4)$, and $(-4, -4)$. Plot these points and draw a v-shaped graph.

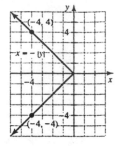

From the graph we see that all x-coordinates are nonpositive. So the domain is $(-\infty, 0]$. From the graph we can see that the y-coordinates can be any real number. So the range is $(-\infty, \infty)$.

47. To find pairs that satisfy $x = -y^2$, pick the y-coordinate first and then find the x-coordinate. The points $(0, 0)$, $(-1, 1)$, $(1, 1)$, $(-4, 2)$, and $(-4, -2)$ are on the graph.

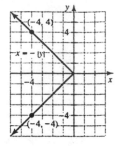

From the graph we see that only nonpositive x-coordinates are used, so the domain is $(-\infty, 0]$. Since any real number is allowable for y, the range is $(-\infty, \infty)$.

48. The graph of $x = 1 - y^2$ includes the points $(0, 1)$, $(0, -1)$, $(1, 0)$, $(-3, 2)$, and $(-3, -2)$. Plot these points and draw a curve through them. From the graph we see that the domain is $(-\infty, 1]$ and the range is $(-\infty, \infty)$.

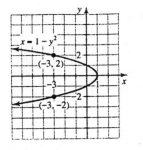

49. The equation $x = 5$ is the equation of a vertical line with an x-intercept of (5, 0).

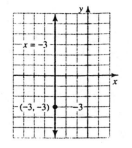

All points on this line have x-coordinate 5, so the domain is $\{5\}$. Every real number occurs as a y-coordinate, so the range is $(-\infty, \infty)$.

50. The graph of $x = -3$ is a vertical line through $(-3, 0)$. The domain is $\{-3\}$ and the range is $(-\infty, \infty)$.

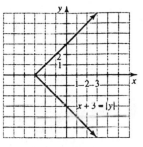

51. Rewrite $x + 9 = y^2$ as $x = y^2 - 9$. Select some y-coordinates and calculate the appropriate x-coordinates. The points $(-9, 0)$, $(0, 3)$, and $(0, -3)$ are on the parabola.

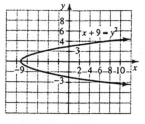

Since no x-coordinate is below -9, the domain is $[-9, \infty)$. Since we could select any value for y, the range is $(-\infty, \infty)$.

52. Write $x + 3 = |y|$ as $x = |y| - 3$. Plot the points $(-2, -1)$, $(-3, 0)$, $(-1, -2)$, $(0, -3)$, and $(-2, 1)$. Plot the points and draw a v-shaped graph. The domain is $[-3, \infty)$ and the range is $(-\infty, \infty)$.

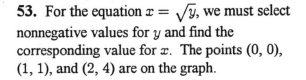

53. For the equation $x = \sqrt{y}$, we must select nonnegative values for y and find the corresponding value for x. The points $(0, 0)$, $(1, 1)$, and $(2, 4)$ are on the graph.

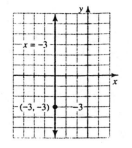

Since the x-coordinates are also nonnegative, the domain is $[0, \infty)$. Since we could only use nonnegative values for y, the range is $[0, \infty)$.

54. The graph of $x = -\sqrt{y}$ contains the points $(0, 0)$, $(-1, 1)$, and $(-2, 4)$. Draw a curve through these points. The domain is $(-\infty, 0]$ and the range is $[0, \infty)$.

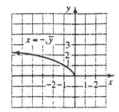

55. The graph of $x = (y - 1)^2$ includes the points $(0, 1)$, $(1, 0)$, $(1, 2)$, $(4, 3)$, and $(4, -1)$. Plot the points and draw a curve through them. From the graph we see that the domain is $[0, \infty)$ and the range is $(-\infty, \infty)$.

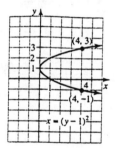

56. For the equation $x = (y + 2)^2$, we can select any value for y and find the corresponding value for x. The points $(0, -2)$, $(1, -1)$, $(1, -3)$, and $(4, 0)$ are on the graph. From the graph we see that x is nonnegative, so the domain is $[0, \infty)$. Since we could use any value for y in the equation, the range is $(-\infty, \infty)$.

57. It is easy to find a vertical line that crosses this graph more than once, so this graph is not the graph of a function.

58. It is easy to find a vertical line that crosses this graph more than once, so this graph is not the graph of a function.

59. No vertical line crosses this graph more than once, so this graph is the graph of a function.

60. No vertical line crosses this graph more than once, so this graph is the graph of a function.

61. It is easy to find a vertical line that crosses this graph more than once, so this graph is not the graph of a function.

62. No vertical line crosses this graph more than once, so this graph is the graph of a function.

63. To graph $f(x) = 1 - |x|$, we arbitrarily select a value for x and find the corresponding value for y. The points $(-2, -1)$, $(-1, 0)$, $(0, 1)$, $(1, 0)$, and $(2, -1)$ are on the graph.

Since any real number could be used for x, the domain is $(-\infty, \infty)$. From the graph we see that the y-coordinates are not higher than 1, so the range is $(-\infty, 1]$.

64. The graph of $h(x) = \sqrt{x - 3}$ includes the points $(3, 0)$, $(4, 1)$, and $(7, 2)$. Draw a smooth curve through those points. The domain of the function is $[3, \infty)$ and the range is $[0, \infty)$.

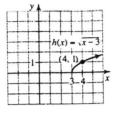

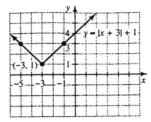

65. The graph of $y = (x - 3)^2 - 1$ includes the points $(1, 3)$, $(2, 0)$, $(3, -1)$, $(4, 0)$, and $(5, 3)$.

The domain is $(-\infty, \infty)$ and range is $[1, \infty)$.
68. The graph of $f(x) = -2x + 4$ is a straight line with y-intercept $(0, 4)$ and slope -2. The domain is $(-\infty, \infty)$ and the range is $(-\infty, \infty)$.

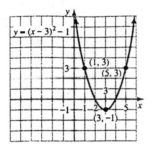

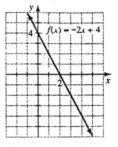

The domain is $(-\infty, \infty)$. Since the y-coordinates are greater than or equal to -1, the range is $[-1, \infty)$.
66. The graph of $y = x^2 - 2x - 3$: includes the points $(1, -4)$, $(2, -3)$, $(0, -3)$.

69. Graph of $y = \sqrt{x} - 3$ goes through $(0, -3)$, $(1, -2)$, and $(4, -1)$. Domain is $[0, \infty)$ and range is $[-3, \infty)$.

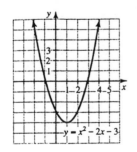

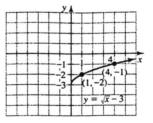

Domain is $(-\infty, \infty)$ and range is $[-4, \infty)$.
67. Graph of $y = |x + 3| + 1$ goes through $(-4, 2)$, $(-3, 1)$, $(-2, 2)$, $(-1, 3)$, $(0, 4)$.

70. The graph of $y = 2 |x|$ contains the points $(0, 0)$, $(1, 2)$, $(-1, 2)$, $(2, 4)$, and $(-2, 4)$. Draw a v-shaped graph through these points. The domain is $(-\infty, \infty)$ and the range is $[0, \infty)$.

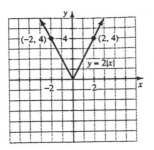

71. The graph of $y = 3x - 5$ is a straight line with y-intercept $(0, -5)$, and a slope of 3.

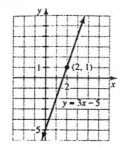

The domain is $(-\infty, \infty)$. From the graph we see that any real number could occur as a y-coordinate, so the range is $(-\infty, \infty)$.
72. The graph of $g(x) = (x + 2)^2$ includes the points $(0, 4)$, $(1, 9)$, $(-1, 1)$, $(-2, 0)$, and $(-3, 1)$. Draw a parabola through these points. The domain is $(-\infty, \infty)$ and the range is $[0, \infty)$.

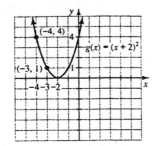

73. The graph of $y = -x^2 + 4x - 4$ goes through $(0, -4)$, $(1, -1)$, $(2, 0)$, $(3, -1)$, and $(4, -4)$.

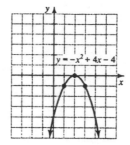

Domain is $(-\infty, \infty)$ and range is $(-\infty, 0]$.
74. Graph of $y = -2\,|\,x - 1\,| + 4$ goes through $(-1, 0)$, $(0, 2)$, $(1, 4)$, $(2, 2)$, $(3, 0)$. Domain is $(-\infty, \infty)$ and range is $(-\infty, 4]$.

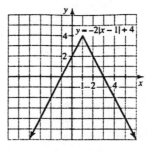

75. The points $(0, 0)$, $(1, 48)$, $(2, 64)$, $(3, 48)$, and $(4, 0)$ are on the graph of $h(t) = -16t^2 + 64t$.

From the graph, it appears that the maximum height reached by the ball is 64 feet.
76. The graph of $h(t) = -16t^2 + 32t$ includes

the points $(0, 0)$, $(1, 16)$, and $(2, 0)$. From the graph it appears that the maximum height reached by the ball is 16 feet.

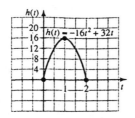

77. a) The nitrogen dioxide was at its maximum when $t = 8$, which is 8 hours after 6 A.M. or 2 P.M.

b) We can find the amount of nitrogen dioxide at the time by using $t = 8$ in the formula:

$A(8) = -2(8)^2 + 32(8) + 42 = 170.$

At 2 P.M. the level was 170 parts per million.

78. The graph of
$C(n) = 0.015n^2 - 4.5n + 400$ includes the points $(0, 400)$, $(150, 62.5)$, $(200, 100)$, and $(300, 400)$.

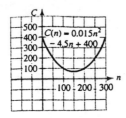

b) From the graph it appears that the minimum cost occurs when the number of prisoners is 150.

c) $C(150) = \$62.50$.

79. a) In 2050, $t = 200$.
$S(200) = -0.000133(200) + 0.24$
$= 0.2134 \text{ mg/mm}^2$

b) $-0.000133t + 0.24 = 0.23$
$-0.000133t = -0.01$
$t \approx 75$

The thickness was 0.23 mg/mm^2 in $1850 + 75$ or 1925.

80. $r(500) = \sqrt{\frac{500}{\pi}} = 12.6 \text{ cm}$

If $r = 30$, then $\sqrt{\frac{A}{\pi}} = 30$, $\frac{A}{\pi} = 30^2$,

or $A = \pi 30^2 = 2827.4 \text{ ft}^2$

81. Graph of $f(x) = \sqrt{x^2}$ is same as graph of $y = |x|$.

82. Domain $(-\infty, 0) \cup (0, \infty)$,
range $(-\infty, 0) \cup (0, \infty)$.

83. For large values of k the graph gets narrower and for smaller values of k the graph gets broader.

84. The graph of $y = x^2 + k$ moves upward for $k > 0$ and downward for $k < 0$.

85. The graph of $y = (x - k)^2$ moves to the right for $k > 0$ and to the left for $k < 0$.

86. The equation $x = y^2$ is equivalent to $y = \sqrt{x}$ or $y = -\sqrt{x}$.

87. The graph of $y = f(x - k)$ lies to the right of the graph of $y = f(x)$ when $k > 0$.

Enriching Your Mathematical Word Power
1. d   2. a   3. a   4. b   5. c
6. a   7. b   8. b   9. a   10. c
11. b   12. c   13. b   14. a   15. d
16. b   17. d

Chapter 3 Review

1. The point $(-3, -2)$ lies in quadrant III.
2. The point $(0, \pi)$ lies on the y-axis.
3. The point $(\pi, 0)$ lies on the x-axis. The quadrants do not include points on any axis.
4. The point $(-5, 4)$ is located by going 5 units to the left of the origin and then 4 units upward. The point is in quadrant II.
5. The point $(0, -1)$ is on the y-axis.
6. Since both coordinates of $(\pi/2, 1)$ are positive, the point is in quadrant I.
7. The point $(\sqrt{2}, -3)$ is in quadrant IV.
8. To locate $(6, -3)$, go 6 units to the right of the origin and then 3 units down. The point is in quadrant IV.
9. If $x = 0$, $y = -3(0) + 2 = 2$. The ordered pair is $(0, 2)$.
If $y = 0$, then $0 = -3x + 2$.

$$3x = 2$$
$$x = \tfrac{2}{3}$$

The ordered pair is $\left(\tfrac{2}{3}, 0\right)$.
If $x = 4$, $y = -3(4) + 2 = -10$.
The ordered pair is $(4, -10)$.
If $y = -3$, then $-3 = -3x + 2$.
$$3x = 5$$
$$x = \tfrac{5}{3}$$

The ordered pair is $\left(\tfrac{5}{3}, -3\right)$.

10. If $x = 0$, then $2(0) + 3y = 5$, or $y = \tfrac{5}{3}$.
The ordered pair is $\left(0, \tfrac{5}{3}\right)$.
If $y = 0$, then $2x + 3(0) = 5$, or $x = \tfrac{5}{2}$. The
ordered pair is $\left(\tfrac{5}{2}, 0\right)$.
If $x = -6$, then $2(-6) + 3y = 5$, or $3y = 17$,
or $y = \tfrac{17}{3}$. The ordered pair is $\left(-6, \tfrac{17}{3}\right)$.
If $y = 5$, then $2x + 3(5) = 5$, or $2x = -10$, or
$x = -5$. The ordered pair is $(-5, 5)$.

11. $m = \dfrac{9 - 6}{-2 - (-5)} = \dfrac{3}{3} = 1$

12. $m = \dfrac{-4 - 7}{3 - (-2)} = \dfrac{-11}{5} = -\dfrac{11}{5}$

13. $m = \dfrac{-2 - 1}{-3 - 4} = \dfrac{-3}{-7} = \dfrac{3}{7}$

14. $m = \dfrac{-3 - 0}{0 - 6} = \dfrac{-3}{-6} = \dfrac{1}{2}$

15. $m = \dfrac{-1 - (-4)}{5 - (-3)} = \dfrac{3}{8}$

The slope of any line parallel to one with slope
3/8 is also 3/8.

16. $m = \dfrac{1 - 1}{7 - (-2)} = 0$

The slope of a line through $(4, 6)$ parallel to a
line with slope 0 also has slope 0.

17. $m = \dfrac{-6 - 5}{4 - (-3)} = \dfrac{-11}{7} = -\dfrac{11}{7}$

The slope of any line perpendicular to one with
slope $-11/7$ is $7/11$.

18. $m = \dfrac{-2 - 4}{5 - 5} = \dfrac{-6}{0}$

Since slope is undefined the line is vertical.
any line perpendicular to a vertical line has
slope 0.

19. The slope for $y = -3x + 4$ is -3, and the
y-intercept is $(0, 4)$.

20. Write the equation in slope-intercept form.
$$2y - 3x + 1 = 0$$
$$2y = 3x - 1$$
$$y = \tfrac{3}{2}x - \tfrac{1}{2}$$

The slope is $\tfrac{3}{2}$ and the y-intercept is $\left(0, -\tfrac{1}{2}\right)$.

21. Write the equation in slope-intercept form.

$$y - 3 = \tfrac{2}{3}(x - 1)$$
$$y - 3 = \tfrac{2}{3}x - \tfrac{2}{3}$$
$$y = \tfrac{2}{3}x + \tfrac{7}{3}$$

The slope is $\tfrac{2}{3}$ and the y-intercept is $\left(0, \tfrac{7}{3}\right)$.

22. Write $y - 3 = 5$ as $y = 8$. The slope is 0
and the y-intercept is $(0, 8)$.

23.
$$3(y) = 3(\tfrac{2}{3}x - 4)$$
$$3y = 2x - 12$$
$$-2x + 3y = -12$$
$$2x - 3y = 12 \quad \text{(Standard form)}$$

24.
$$y = -0.05x + 0.26$$
$$100y = -5x + 26$$
$$5x + 100y = 26$$

25.
$$2(y - 1) = 2 \cdot \tfrac{1}{2}(x + 3)$$
$$2y - 2 = x + 3$$
$$-x + 2y = 5$$
$$x - 2y = -5 \quad \text{(Standard form)}$$

26.
$$\tfrac{1}{2}x - \tfrac{1}{3}y = \tfrac{1}{4}$$
$$12\left(\tfrac{1}{2}x - \tfrac{1}{3}y\right) = 12 \cdot \tfrac{1}{4}$$
$$6x - 4y = 3$$

27. Start with point-slope form:
$$y - (-3) = \tfrac{1}{2}(x - 1)$$
$$y + 3 = \tfrac{1}{2}x - \tfrac{1}{2}$$
$$2y + 6 = x - 1$$
$$-x + 2y = -7$$
$$x - 2y = 7$$

28. Start with slope-intercept form.
$$y = 3x + 2$$
$$-3x + y = 2$$
$$3x - y = -2$$

29. Start with point-slope form:
$$y - 6 = -\tfrac{3}{4}(x - (-2))$$
$$y - 6 = -\tfrac{3}{4}x - \tfrac{3}{2}$$
$$4(y - 6) = 4(-\tfrac{3}{4}x - \tfrac{3}{2})$$
$$4y - 24 = -3x - 6$$
$$3x + 4y = 18$$

30. Start with point-slope form.
$$y - \tfrac{1}{2} = \tfrac{1}{4}(x - 2)$$
$$y - \tfrac{1}{2} = \tfrac{1}{4}x - \tfrac{1}{2}$$
$$4\left(y - \tfrac{1}{2}\right) = 4\left(\tfrac{1}{4}x - \tfrac{1}{2}\right)$$
$$4y - 2 = x - 2$$
$$-x + 4y = 0$$
$$x - 4y = 0$$

31. Any line with slope 0 is a horizontal line.
Since it contains $(3, 5)$ its equation is $y = 5$.

32. Use slope-intercept form to write the equation of the line through $(0, 0)$ with slope -1.

$$y = -1x + 0$$
$$x + y = 0$$

33. To graph $y = 2x - 3$ note that the y-intercept is $(0, -3)$ the slope is $2 = 2/1$. Start at $(0, -3)$ and go up 2 units and 1 unit to the right to locate the second point $(1, -1)$. Draw a line through the two points.

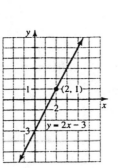

34. To graph $y = \frac{2}{3}x + 1$, start at the y-intercept $(0, 1)$. Use a slope of $2/3$ to locate a second point on the line. Go up 2 units and 3 units to the right. Draw a line through the two points.

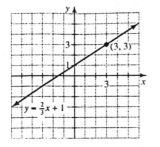

35. If $x = 0$, $3(0) - 2y = -6$, or $y = 3$
If $y = 0$, then $3x - 2(0) = -6$, $x = -2$.
Draw a line through the intercepts $(0, 3)$ and $(-2, 0)$.

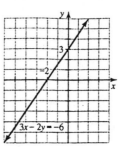

36. The equation $4x + 5y = 10$ is equivalent to $y = -\frac{4}{5}x + 2$. To graph the line, start at the y-intercept $(0, 2)$, go down 4 units and then 5 units to the right to locate a second point on the line. Draw a line through $(0, 2)$ and $(5, -2)$.

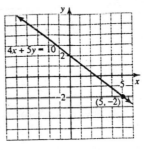

37. The equation $y - 3 = 10$ is equivalent to $y = 13$. Its graph is a horizontal line with a y-intercept of $(0, 13)$.

38. The equation $2x = 8$ is equivalent to $x = 4$, which is a vertical line with x-intercept $(4, 0)$. Draw a vertical line through $(4, 0)$

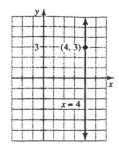

39. If $x = 0$, then $5(0) - 3y = 7$, or $y = -7/3$. If $y = 0$, then $5x - 3(0) = 7$, or $x = 7/5$. Draw a line through the intercepts $(0, -7/3)$ and $(7/5, 0)$.

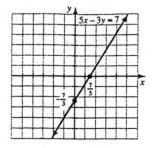

40. If $x = 0$, then $3(0) + 4y = -1$, or $y = -1/4$. If $y = 0$, then $3x + 4(0) = -1$, or $x = -1/3$. Draw a line through the intercepts $(0, -1/4)$ and $(-1/3, 0)$. The points $(-3, 2)$ and $(1, -1)$ also satisfy the equation $3x + 4y = -1$.

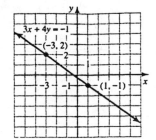

41. For $5x + 4y = 100$, the intercepts are $(0, 25)$ and $(20, 0)$.

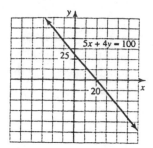

42. For $2x - y = 120$, the intercepts are $(0, -120)$ and $(60, 0)$.

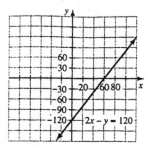

43. For $x - 80y = 400$ the intercepts are $(0, -5)$ and $(400, 0)$.

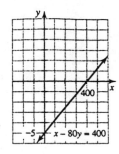

44. For $75x + y = 300$, the intercepts are $(0, 300)$ and $(4, 0)$.

110

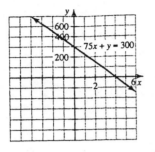

45. Use the slope $3 = 3/1$ and y-intercept $(0, -2)$ to graph the equation $y = 3x - 2$. Start at $(0, -2)$ and go up 3 units and 1 to the right. Draw a dashed line through the two points $(0, -2)$ and $(1, 1)$. Shade the region above the line to indicate the graph of $y > 3x - 2$.

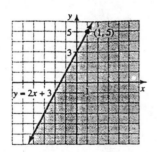

46. First graph the equation $y = 2x + 3$, using a slope of 2 and a y-intercept of $(0, 3)$. Draw the line solid. The line and the region below the line satisfy $y \leq 2x + 3$.

47. First graph $x - y = 5$ using the intercepts $(0, -5)$ and $(5, 0)$. The line should be solid because of the inequality symbol $\leq$. Test the point $(0, 0)$ in the inequality $x - y \leq 5$:
$$0 - 0 \leq 5$$
Since $(0, 0)$ satisfies the inequality, shade the region containing $(0, 0)$.

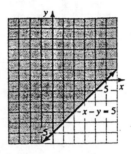

48. The inequality $2x + y > 1$ is equivalent to $y > -2x + 1$. First graph the line $y = -2x + 1$, using a slope of -2 and a y-intercept of $(0, 1)$. Draw the line dashed because of the inequality symbol. Shade the region above the line to indicate the points that satisfy $y > -2x + 1$.

49. The inequality $3x > 2$ is equivalent to $x > \frac{2}{3}$. First graph the vertical line $x = \frac{2}{3}$ as a dashed line through $(\frac{2}{3}, 0)$. The graph of $x > \frac{2}{3}$ is the region to the right of this line.

111

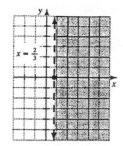

50. The inequality $x + 2 \le 0$ is equivalent to $x \le -2$. Graph the vertical line $x = -2$ and shade the region to the left.

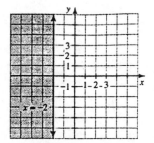

51. The inequality $4y \le 0$ is equivalent to $y \le 0$. Graph the line $y = 0$. The line $y = 0$ coincides with the x-axis. Draw the line solid. Points on the line and in the region below the line satisfy the inequality $y \le 0$.

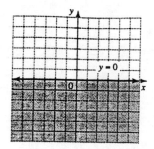

52. The inequality $4y - 4 > 0$ is equivalent to $y > 1$. Graph the horizontal line $y = 1$ (dashed) and shade the region above it.

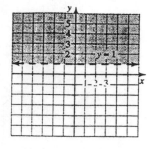

53. Solve $4x - 2y \ge 6$ for y:
$$-2y \ge -4x + 6$$
$$y \le 2x - 3$$
All points on the line $y = 2x - 3$ together with the points below the line satisfy the inequality. Use y-intercept $(0, -3)$ and slope 2 to graph the solid line.

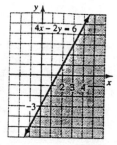

54. First graph the line $-5x - 3y = 6$. If $x = 0$, then $-3y = 6$, or $y = -2$. If $y = 0$, then $-5x = 6$, or $x = -6/5$. Draw a dashed line through the intercepts $(0, -2)$ and $(-6/5, 0)$. Since the point $(0, 0)$ does not satisfy $-5x - 3y > 6$, we shade the region not containing $(0, 0)$ to indicate the solution to the inequality.

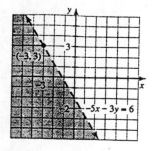

112

55. The x and y-intercepts for the line $5x - 2y = 9$ are $(0, -\frac{9}{2})$ and $(\frac{9}{5}, 0)$. Draw a dashed line through the intercepts. Check $(0, 0)$ in the inequality $5x - 2y < 9$:

$$5(0) - 2(0) < 9 \text{ is correct.}$$

Shade the region containing $(0, 0)$.

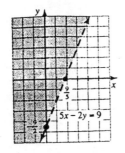

56. First graph the line $3x + 4y = -1$. If $x = 0$, then $4y = -1$, or $y = -1/4$. If $y = 0$, then $3x = -1$, or $x = -1/3$. Draw a solid line through the intercepts $(0, -1/4)$ and $(-1/3, 0)$. The line also goes through $(-3, 2)$ and $(1, -1)$. Use $(0, 0)$ as a test point. Since $(0, 0)$ does not satisfy $3x + 4y \leq -1$, we shade the region not containing $(0, 0)$.

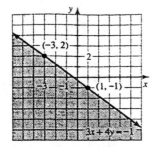

57. First graph the lines $y = 3$ and $y - x = 5$.

Test the points $(0, 0)$, $(0, 4)$, $(0, 6)$, and $(-6, 0)$. Only $(0, 4)$ satisfies $y > 3$ and $y - x < 5$. Shade the region containing $(0, 4)$.

58. First graph the lines $x + y = 1$ $(y = -x + 1)$ and $y = 4$. Select a test point in each of the 4 regions. Only points in the region containing $(0, 5)$ fail to satisfy the compound sentence $x + y \leq 1$ or $y \leq 4$. So shade the 3 other regions.

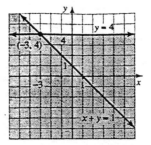

59. First graph the lines $3x + 2y = 8$ and $3x - 2y = 6$. Test the points $(0, 0)$, $(0, 5)$, $(0, -6)$, and $(5, 0)$. The points $(0, 0)$, $(0, 5)$, and $(5, 0)$ satisfy the compound inequality $3x + 2y \geq 8$ or $3x - 2y \leq 6$. Shade the regions containing those points.

60. First graph the lines $x + 8y = 8$ $(y = -\frac{1}{8}x + 1)$ and $x - 2y = 10$ $(y = \frac{1}{2}x - 5)$. Test one point in each of the 4 regions. Only points in the region containing $(0, 3)$ satisfy both of the inequalities. Shade the region containing $(0, 3)$.

113

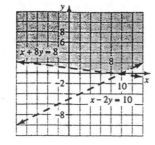

63. First graph the two vertical lines $x = 5$ and $x = -5$.

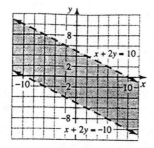

61. First graph the equations $x + 2y = 10$ and $x + 2y = -10$. Test the points $(0, 0)$, $(0, 8)$, and $(0, -8)$ in the inequality $|x + 2y| < 10$. Only $(0, 0)$ satisfies the inequality. So shade the region containing $(0, 0)$.

Test the points $(0, 0)$, $(0, 8)$, $(-8, 0)$ in the inequality $|x| \leq 5$. Only $(0, 0)$ satisfies the inequality. So shade the region containing $(0, 0)$, the region between the parallel lines.

64. The inequality $|y| > 6$ is equivalent to $y > 6$ or $y < -6$. Graph the horizontal lines $y = 6$ and $y = -6$. Use dashed lines. Points between the lines do not satisfy $|y| > 6$, but points in the other 2 regions satisfy the inequality. Shade those regions.

62. The inequality $|x - 3y| \geq 9$ is equivalent to $x - 3y \geq 9$ or $x - 3y \leq -9$. First graph the lines $x - 3y = 9$ $(y = \frac{1}{3}x - 3)$ or $x - 3y = -9$ $(y = \frac{1}{3}x + 3)$. Test one point in each of the 3 regions. Only points in the region containing $(0, 0)$ fail to satisfy the original inequality. So shade the other 2 regions.

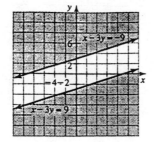

65. First graph the lines $y - x = 2$ and $y - x = -2$. Test the points $(0, 0)$, $(0, 4)$, and $(0, -4)$ in the inequality $|y - x| > 2$. The points $(0, 4)$ and $(0, -4)$ satisfy the inequality. Shade the regions containing those points.

114

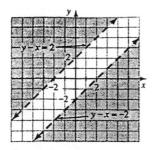

66. The inequality $|x - y| \le 1$ is equivalent to $-1 \le x - y \le 1$. Graph the lines $x - y = 1$ ($y = x - 1$) and $x - y = -1$ ($y = x + 1$). Use solid lines. Test one point from each region in the original inequality. Only points in the region containing $(0, 0)$ satisfy $|x - y| \le 1$. Shade the region containing $(0, 0)$.

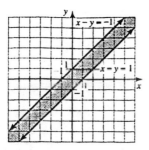

67. The relation is not a function because two ordered pairs have the same first coordinate and different second coordinates.

68. The relation is a function because no two ordered pairs have the same x-coordinate and different y-coordinates.

69. The relation is a function because the condition that $y = x^2$ guarantees that no two ordered pairs will have the same x-coordinate and different y-coordinates.

70. The relation $x^2 = 1 + y^2$ is not a function because the ordered pairs $(\sqrt{2}, 1)$ and $(\sqrt{2}, -1)$ both satisfy the equation.

71. This relation is not a function because the ordered pairs $(16, 2)$ and $(16, -2)$ are both in the relation.

72. The relation $y = \sqrt{x - 1}$ is a function because for each x-coordinate there is only one y-coordinate determined by the equation.

73. The domain is the set of x-coordinates $\{1, 2\}$, and the range is the set of y-coordinates $\{3\}$.

74. Since we can use any number for u in the equation $v = -u^2$, the domain is $(-\infty, \infty)$. Since $v = -u^2$, the value of v must by nonpositive. So the range is $(-\infty, 0]$.

75. Since any number can be used for t, the domain is the set of all real numbers, $(-\infty, \infty)$. Since any real number can occur as $f(t)$, the range is the set of all real numbers, $(-\infty, \infty)$.

76. In the equation $x = \sqrt{y}$, the value of y must be nonnegative. Since x is equal to the principal square root of y, the value of x is also nonnegative. The domain is $[0, \infty)$ and the range is $[0, \infty)$.

77. Since any number can be used for x, the domain is $(-\infty, \infty)$. Since $y = |x|$, the values of y will be nonnegative and so the range is $[0, \infty)$.

78. In the equation $y = \sqrt{x} - 1$ the value of x must be nonnegative. Since y is equal to the principal square root of x minus 1, the smallest that y can be is -1. So the domain is $[0, \infty)$ and the range is $[-1, \infty)$.

79. $f(0) = 2(0) - 5 = -5$

80. $f(-3) = 2(-3) - 5 = -11$

81. $g(0) = 0^2 + 0 - 6 = -6$

82. $g(-2) = (-2)^2 + (-2) - 6 = -4$

83. $g\left(\frac{1}{2}\right) = \left(\frac{1}{2}\right)^2 + \frac{1}{2} - 6$
$$= \frac{1}{4} + \frac{2}{4} - \frac{24}{4} = -\frac{21}{4}$$

84. $g(-1/2) = \left(-\frac{1}{2}\right)^2 + \left(-\frac{1}{2}\right) - 6$
$$= \frac{1}{4} - \frac{2}{4} - \frac{24}{4} = -\frac{25}{4}$$

85. $f(a) = 2a - 5$

86. $f(x + 3) = 2(x + 3) - 5 = 2x + 1$

87. $f(a - 1) = 2(a - 1) - 5$
$$= 2a - 7$$

88. $f(x + h) = 2(x + h) - 5$
$$= 2x + 2h - 5$$

89. If $f(a) = 1$, then $2a - 5 = 1$.
$$2a = 6$$
$$a = 3$$

90. If $f(x) = 0$, then $2x - 5 = 0$.
$$2x = 5$$
$$x = \frac{5}{2}$$

91. Average rate of change is
$$\frac{f(8) - f(2)}{8 - 2} = \frac{20 \cdot 8^2 - 20 \cdot 2^2}{6} = 200$$

92. Average rate of change is
$$\frac{g(89) - g(9)}{89 - 9} = \frac{\sqrt{89 - 8} - \sqrt{9 - 8}}{80} = \frac{1}{10}$$

93. Average rate of change is
$$\frac{h(4) - h(2)}{4 - 2} = \frac{\frac{1}{6} - \frac{1}{4}}{2} = -\frac{1}{24}$$

94. Average rate of change is
$$\frac{j(3) - j(1)}{3 - 1} = \frac{6 - 0}{2} = 3$$

95. The graph of $f(x) = 3x - 4$ is a straight line with y-intercept $(0, -4)$ and slope 3. Since any number can be used for x, the domain is $(-\infty, \infty)$. From the graph we see that any real number can occur as a y-coordinate, so the range is $(-\infty, \infty)$.

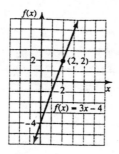

96. The graph of $y = 0.3x$ is a line with y-intercept $(0, 0)$ and slope 0.3. The domain is $(-\infty, \infty)$ and the range is $(-\infty, \infty)$.

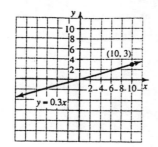

97. The graph of $h(x) = |x| - 2$ includes the points $(0, -2)$, $(1, -1)$, $(2, 0)$, $(-1, -1)$, and $(-2, 0)$. Draw a v-shaped graph through these points.

98. The graph of $y = |x - 2|$ includes the points $(0, 2)$, $(1, 1)$, $(2, 0)$, $(3, 1)$, and $(4, 2)$. Draw a v-shaped graph through these points.

Since any real number can be used for x, the domain is $(-\infty, \infty)$. From the graph we see that all y-coordinates are greater than or equal to -2, and so the range is $[-2, \infty)$.

The domain is $(-\infty, \infty)$. From the graph we can see that all y-coordinates are nonnegative. So the range is $[0, \infty)$.

99. The graph of $y = x^2 - 2x + 1$ includes the points $(0, 1)$, $(1, 0)$, $(2, 1)$, $(3, 4)$, and $(-1, 4)$. Draw a parabola through these points.

Since any number can be used for x, the domain is $(-\infty, \infty)$. From the graph we see that the y-coordinates are nonnegative, and so the range is $[0, \infty)$.

100. The graph of $g(x) = x^2 - 2x - 15$ is a parabola including the points $(-3, 0)$, $(0, -15)$, $(1, -16)$, and $(5, 0)$.

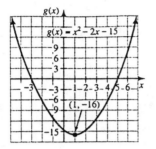

The domain is $(-\infty, \infty)$. From the graph we can see that no y-coordinate is smaller than -16. The range is $[-16, \infty)$

101. The graph of $k(x) = \sqrt{x} + 2$ includes the points $(0, 2)$, $(1, 3)$, and $(4, 4)$.

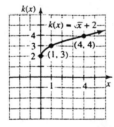

Since we can use only nonnegative numbers for x, the domain is $[0, \infty)$. From the graph we see that no y-coordinate is less than 2, and so the range is $[2, \infty)$.

102. The graph of $y = \sqrt{x - 2}$ includes the points $(2, 0)$, $(3, 1)$, and $(6, 2)$.

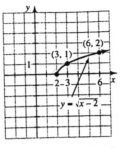

Since we must have $x - 2 \geq 0$, we have $x \geq 2$. The domain is $[2, \infty)$. From the graph we can see that the y-coordinates are nonnegative. The range is $[0, \infty)$.

103. The graph of $y = 30 - x^2$ includes the points $(-5, 5)$, $(0, 30)$, and $(5, 5)$.

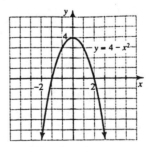

Since x can be any real number, the domain is $(-\infty, \infty)$. From the graph we see that y is at most 30. So the range is $(-\infty, 30]$.

104. The graph of $y = 4 - x^2$ includes the points $(-2, 0)$, $(0, 4)$, $(1, 3)$, and $(2, 0)$.

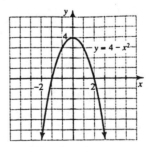

117

The domain is $(-\infty, \infty)$. Since no y-coordinate is larger than 4, the range is $(-\infty, 4]$.

105. The graph of $x = 2$ is the vertical line with x-intercept $(2, 0)$.

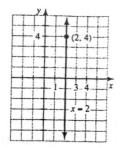

Since the only x-coordinate used on this graph is 2, the domain is $\{2\}$. Since all real numbers occur as y-coordinates, the range is $(-\infty, \infty)$.

106. The graph of $x = y^2 - 1$ includes the points $(-1, 0)$, $(0, 1)$, $(0, -1)$, $(3, 2)$, and $(3, -2)$.

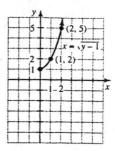

The x-coordinates on the graph are greater than or equal to -1. The domain is $[-1, \infty)$. From the graph we can see that a y-coordinate could be any real number. The range is $(-\infty, \infty)$.

107. The graph of $x = |y| + 1$ includes the points $(1, 0)$, $(2, 1)$, $(2, -1)$, $(3, 2)$, and $(3, -2)$. Draw a v-shaped graph through these points.

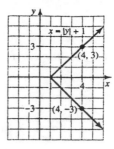

From the graph we see that the x-coordinates are not less than 1, and so the domain is $[1, \infty)$. Any number can be used for y, and so the range is $(-\infty, \infty)$.

108. The graph of $x = \sqrt{y - 1}$ includes $(0, 1)$, $(1, 2)$, and $(2, 5)$. Since the values for x are nonnegative, the domain is $[0, \infty)$. From the graph we can see that the range is $[1, \infty)$.

The x-coordinates on the graph are greater than or equal to -1. The domain is $[-1, \infty)$. From the graph we can see that a y-coordinate could be any real number. The range is $(-\infty, \infty)$.

109. This line contains the points $(2, 0)$ and $(0, -6)$. The line has slope
$$m = \frac{-6 - 0}{0 - 2} = 3.$$
In slope-intercept form its equation is
$$y = 3x - 6,$$
and in standard form $3x - y = 6$.

110. Use the point-slope formula with the point $(4, 0)$ and slope $-1/2$.
$$y - 0 = -\tfrac{1}{2}(x - 4)$$
$$y = -\tfrac{1}{2}x + 2$$
$$2y = -x + 4$$
$$x + 2y = 4$$

111. Use the point-slope formula.
$$y - 4 = -\tfrac{1}{2}(x - (-1))$$

118

$$y - 4 = -\tfrac{1}{2}x - \tfrac{1}{2}$$
$$2y - 8 = -x - 1$$
$$x + 2y = 7$$

112. The line through $(2, -3)$ with slope 0 is $y = -3$.

113. The line through $(2, -6)$ and $(2, 5)$ is a vertical line. All vertical lines are of the form $x = k$. So the equation is $x = 2$.

114. First find the slope of the line through $(-3, 6)$ and $(4, 2)$.
$$m = \frac{6 - 2}{-3 - 4} = \frac{4}{-7} = -\frac{4}{7}$$
Now use point-slope form with the point $(4, 2)$ and slope $-4/7$.
$$y - 2 = -\tfrac{4}{7}(x - 4)$$
$$y - 2 = -\tfrac{4}{7}x + \tfrac{16}{7}$$
$$7y - 14 = -4x + 16$$
$$4x + 7y = 30$$

115. Since $x = 5$ is a vertical line, a line perpendicular to it is horizontal. The equation of a horizontal line through $(0, 0)$ is $y = 0$.

116. Any line perpendicular to $y = -3x + 5$ has slope $1/3$. Use slope $1/3$ and the point $(2, -3)$ in the point-slope formula.
$$y - (-3) = \tfrac{1}{3}(x - 2)$$
$$y + 3 = \tfrac{1}{3}x - \tfrac{2}{3}$$
$$3y + 9 = x - 2$$
$$-x + 3y = -11$$
$$x - 3y = 11$$

117. Any line parallel to $y = 2x + 1$ has slope 2. Use the point-slope formula with the point $(-1, 4)$ and slope 2:
$$y - 4 = 2(x - (-1))$$
$$y - 4 = 2x + 2$$
$$-2x + y = 6$$
$$2x - y = -6$$

118. Any line perpendicular to $y = 10$ is a vertical line. The equation of a vertical line through $(2, 1)$ is $x = 2$.

119. The line with y-intercept $(0, 6)$ and slope 3 has equation $y = 3x + 6$. Written in standard form it is $3x - y = -6$.

120. Use the slope-intercept formula with slope -1 and y-intercept $(0, 0)$.
$$y = -1x + 0$$
$$y = -x$$
$$x + y = 0$$

121. A horizontal line has slope 0. If it goes through $(2, 5)$, its y-intercept is $(0, 5)$. Its equation is $y = 0 \cdot x + 5$ or simply $y = 5$.

122. The vertical line through $(-3, -2)$ has equation $x = -3$.

123. Draw a quadrilateral with the 4 points as vertices. Find the slope of each side:
$$m_1 = \frac{-5 - (-1)}{-5 - (-3)} = \frac{-4}{-2} = 2$$
$$m_2 = \frac{-1 - 2}{-3 - 6} = \frac{-3}{-9} = \frac{1}{3}$$
$$m_3 = \frac{2 - (-2)}{6 - 4} = \frac{4}{2} = 2$$
$$m_4 = \frac{-2 - (-5)}{4 - (-5)} = \frac{3}{9} = \frac{1}{3}$$
Since the slopes of the opposite sides are equal, it is a parallelogram.

124. Plot the points $(-5, -5)$, $(4, -2)$, and $(3, 1)$. Find the slope of each line segment.
$$m_1 = \frac{-5 - (-2)}{-5 - 4} = \frac{-3}{-9} = \frac{1}{3}$$
$$m_2 = \frac{-2 - 1}{4 - 3} = \frac{-3}{1} = -3$$
Since a line with slope $1/3$ is perpendicular to a line with slope -3, the triangle is a right triangle.

125. Plot the four points and find the slope of each side of the quadrilateral.
$$m_1 = \frac{2 - 6}{-2 - 2} = 1 \qquad m_2 = \frac{6 - 4}{2 - 4} = -1$$
$$m_3 = \frac{4 - 0}{4 - 0} = 1 \qquad m_4 = \frac{2 - 0}{-2 - 0} = -1$$
Since opposite sides have the same slope, the quadrilateral is a parallelogram. Since the slopes of the adjacent sides are 1 and -1, the adjacent sides are perpendicular. Therefore, the quadrilateral is a rectangle.

126. Plot the three points.
Find the slope of the line segment from $(-3, -14)$ to $(2, 1)$:
$$m_1 = \frac{-14 - 1}{-3 - 2} = 3$$

Find the slope of the line segment from $(2, 1)$ to $(4, 7)$:
$$m_2 = \frac{7-1}{4-2} = 3$$
Because these slopes are the same, the three points are in line.

127. a) Find the slope of the line through $(20, 200)$ and $(70, 150)$.
$$m = \frac{200-150}{20-70} = \frac{50}{-50} = -1$$
Use the point-slope formula with $m = -1$ and the point $(20, 200)$:
$$h - h_1 = m(a - a_1)$$
$$h - 200 = -1(a - 20)$$
$$h - 200 = -a + 20$$
$$h = 220 - a$$
b) If $a = 40$, then $h = 220 - 40 = 180$.
c) The maximum heart rate decreases as you get older.

128. Find the slope of the line through $(3, 82)$ and $(5, 89)$.
$$m = \frac{89-82}{5-3} = \frac{7}{2} = 3.5$$
Use the point-slope formula with $m = 3.5$ and the point $(3, 82)$:
$$h - h_1 = m(d - d_1)$$
$$h - 82 = 3.5(d - 3)$$
$$h - 82 = 3.5d - 10.5$$
$$h = 3.5d + 71.5$$
If $d = 10$, then $h = 3.5(10) + 71.5 = 106.5$.

129. To determine the number of days it would take for the rental charge to equal $1080, we solve the equation

$$1080 = 26 + 17d.$$
$$1054 = 17d$$
$$62 = d$$

It will take 62 days for the rental charge to equal the cost of the air hammer.
If $d = 1$, then $C = 26 + 17(1) = 43$.
If $d = 30$, then $C = 26 + 17(30) = 536$.
The graph of this function for d ranging from 1 to 30 is a straight line segment joining the two points $(1, 43)$ and $(30, 536)$.

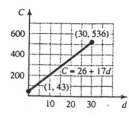

130. a) $w \leq 0.95h$
b) If $h = 37$, then $0.95(37) = 35.15$. Because the waist is 36, the waist is not less than or equal to 95% of the hip size. So the man is not in good health.
c) If $w = 38$, then $38 \leq 0.95h$, $h \geq 38/0.95$, or $h \geq 40$. His hip size must be at least 40 for him to be in good health.

CHAPTER 3 TEST

1. If $x = 0$, then $2(0) + y = 5$.
$$y = 5$$
If $y = 0$, then $2x + 0 = 5$.
$$x = 5/2$$
If $x = 4$, then $2(4) + y = 5$.
$$y = -3$$
If $y = -8$, then $2x + (-8) = 5$.
$$2x = 13$$
$$x = 13/2$$
The pairs are $(0, 5)$, $\left(\frac{5}{2}, 0\right)$, and $\left(\frac{13}{2}, -8\right)$.

2. $m = \frac{7-1}{-3-2} = \frac{6}{-5} = -\frac{6}{5}$

3. Solve the equation $8x - 5y = -10$ for y:
$$-5y = -8x - 10$$
$$y = \frac{8}{5}x + 2$$
The slope is $\frac{8}{5}$ and the y-intercept is $(0, 2)$.

4. Plot the four points and find the slopes of the sides of the quadrilateral.
$$m_1 = \frac{2-0}{6-0} = \frac{1}{3} \qquad m_2 = \frac{2-0}{6-5} = 2$$

$$m_3 = \frac{-2-0}{-1-5} = \frac{1}{3} \qquad m_4 = \frac{-2-0}{-1-0} = 2$$

Since the opposite sides have equal slopes, the quadrilateral is a parallelogram.

120

5. The first coordinate is a and the second coordinate is V. We want the equation of the line containing the two points $(0, 22{,}000)$ and $(3, 16{,}000)$. The slope of the line is
$$m = \frac{22{,}000 - 16{,}000}{0 - 3} = -2{,}000.$$
Using the slope and y-intercept, we can write the equation $V = -2000a + 22{,}000$.

6. The equation of the line with y-intercept $(0, 3)$ and slope $-1/2$ is
$$y = -\tfrac{1}{2}x + 3$$
$$2y = -x + 6$$
$$x + 2y = 6$$

7. Use the point-slope form to write the equation of the line through $(-3, 5)$ with slope -4:
$$y - 5 = -4(x - (-3))$$
$$y - 5 = -4(x + 3)$$
$$y - 5 = -4x - 12$$
$$4x + y = -7$$

8. Solve $3x - 5y = 7$ for y:
$$-5y = -3x + 7$$
$$y = \tfrac{3}{5}x - \tfrac{7}{5}$$
Since this line has slope $3/5$, any line perpendicular to it has slope $-5/3$. The line through $(2, 3)$ with slope $-5/3$ has equation
$$y - 3 = -\tfrac{5}{3}(x - 2)$$
$$y - 3 = -\tfrac{5}{3}x + \tfrac{10}{3}$$
$$3y - 9 = -5x + 10$$
$$5x + 3y = 19$$

9. The line shown goes through the points $(0, 2)$ and $(-4, 0)$. We can see from the graph that its slope is $2/4$ or $1/2$ and its y-intercept is $(0, 2)$. In slope-intercept form its equation is
$$y = \tfrac{1}{2}x + 2.$$
$$2y = x + 4$$
$$-x + 2y = 4$$
$$x - 2y = -4$$

10. First graph the equation $y = (-1/2)x + 3$, using y-intercept of $(0, 3)$, a slope of $-1/2$, and a dashed line. The graph of $y > (-1/2)x + 3$ is the region above this line.

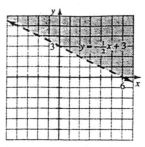

11. Graph the vertical line $x = 2$ using a dashed line. Graph $x + y = 0$ using a dashed line. Test the points $(-2, 0)$, $(1, 0)$, $(5, 0)$, and $(3, -5)$. Only $(5, 0)$ satisfies $x > 2$ and $x + y > 0$. So shade the region containing $(5, 0)$.

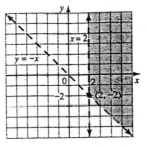

12. First graph the parallel lines $2x + y = 3$ and $2x + y = -3$, using solid lines. Test the points $(-5, 0)$, $(0, 0)$ and $(5, 0)$ in $|2x + y| \geq 3$. Both $(-5, 0)$ and $(5, 0)$ satisfy the inequality, so shade the regions containing those points.

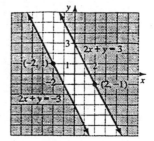

121

13. The line $f(x) = -\frac{2}{3}x + 1$ has a y-intercept of $(0, 1)$ and a slope of $-2/3$. Start at $(0, 1)$ and rise -2 and go 3 units to the right to locate a second point on the line.

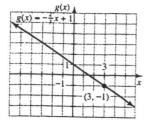

14. The graph of $y = |x| - 4$ contains the points $(-2, -2)$, $(-1, -3)$, $(0, -4)$, $(1, -3)$, and $(2, -2)$. Draw a v-shaped graph through these points.

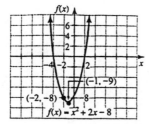

15. The graph of $g(x) = x^2 + 2x - 8$ contains the points $(-2, -8)$, $(-1, -9)$, $(0, -8)$, $(1, -5)$, and $(2, 0)$. Draw a parabola through these points.

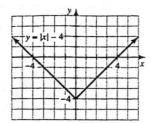

16. The graph of $x = y^2$ contains the points $(0, 0)$, $(1, -1)$, $(1, -1)$, $(4, -2)$, and $(4, -2)$. Draw a parabola through these points.

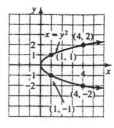

17. The graph of $h(x) = 2\sqrt{x} - 1$ contains the points $(0, -1)$, $(1, 1)$, $(4, 3)$, and $(9, 5)$. Draw a curve through these points. The curve is half of a parabola.

18. This set of ordered pairs is a function because no two of the ordered pairs have the same first coordinate and different second coordinates.

19. If $f(x) = -2x + 5$, then $f(-3) = -2(-3) + 5 = 11$ and $f(a + 1) = -2(a + 1) + 5 = -2a + 3$.

20. $\frac{f(4) - f(1)}{4 - 1} = \frac{48 - 3}{3} = 15$

21. In $f(x) = |x|$ we can use any real number for x. So the domain is $(-\infty, \infty)$. Because the absolute value of a real number is always greater than or equal to zero, the range is $[0, \infty)$.

22. The shipping and handling fee S is a linear function of the weight of the order n, $S = 0.50n + 3$.

23. Some ordered pairs for $A(t) = -16t^2 + 32t + 6$ are $(0, 6)$, $(1, 22)$, $(2, 6)$, $(3, -42)$. Draw a parabola through these points. The ball is at its highest when $t = 1$ sec.

122

Making Connections

Chapters 1 - 3

1. $2^3 \cdot 4^2 = 8 \cdot 16 = 128$

2. $2^7 - 2^6 = 128 - 64 = 64$

3. $3^2 - 4(5)(-2) = 9 + 40 = 49$

4. $3 - 2|5 - 7 \cdot 3| = 3 - 2 \cdot 16 = -29$

5. $\dfrac{2 - (-3)}{5 - 6} = \dfrac{5}{-1} = -5$

6. $\dfrac{-3 - 7}{-1 - (-3)} = \dfrac{-10}{2} = -5$

7. $3t \cdot 4t = 12t^2$

8. $3t + 4t = 7t$

9. $\dfrac{4x + 8}{4} = x + 2$

10. $\dfrac{-8y}{-4} - \dfrac{10y}{-2} = 2y - (-5y) = 7y$

11. $3(x - 4) - 4(5 - x)$
$= 3x - 12 - 20 + 4x = 7x - 32$

12. $-2(3x^2 - x) + 3(2x - 5x^2)$
$= -6x^2 + 2x + 6x - 15x^2$
$= -21x^2 + 8x$

13. $\quad 15(b - 27) = 0$
$\quad 15b - 405 = 0$
$\qquad\qquad 15b = 405$
$\qquad\qquad\quad b = 27$

The solution set is $\{27\}$.

14. $0.05a - 0.04(a - 50) = 4$
$\qquad\qquad 0.01a + 2 = 4$
$\qquad\qquad\quad 0.01a = 2$
$\qquad\qquad\qquad\quad a = 200$

The solution set is $\{200\}$.

15. $\quad |3v - 7| = 0$
$\qquad\quad 3v - 7 = 0$
$\qquad\qquad\quad 3v = 7$
$\qquad\qquad\quad v = \frac{7}{3}$

The solution set is $\left\{\frac{7}{3}\right\}$.

16. $\quad |3u - 7| = 3$
$3u - 7 = 3$ or $3u - 7 = -3$
$\quad 3u = 10$ or $\quad 3u = 4$
$\quad u = \frac{10}{3}$ or $\quad u = \frac{4}{3}$

The solution set is $\{4/3, 10/3\}$.

17. $\quad |3x - 7| = -77$

The absolute value of any quantity is nonnegative. So the equation has no solution. The solution set is $\emptyset$.

18. $\quad |3x - 7| + 1 = 8$
$\qquad\quad |3x - 7| = 7$
$3x - 7 = 7$ or $3x - 7 = -7$

$3x = 14$ $\qquad$ or $\qquad$ $3x = 0$
$x = \frac{14}{3}$ $\qquad$ or $\qquad$ $x = 0$

The solution set is $\{0, 14/3\}$.

19. $2x - 1 > 7$
$\qquad 2x > 8$
$\qquad\quad x > 4$

20. $\qquad 5 - 3x \le -1$
$\qquad\qquad -3x \le -6$
$\qquad\qquad\quad x \ge 2$

21. $\quad x - 5 \le 4$ and $3x - 1 < 8$
$\qquad x \le 9$ and $\qquad 3x < 9$
$\qquad x \le 9$ and $\qquad\quad x < 3$

The last compound inequality is equivalent to the simple inequality $x < 3$.

22. $\quad 2x \le -6$ or $5 - 2x < -7$
$\qquad x \le -3$ $\qquad$ or $\qquad -2x < -12$
$\qquad x \le -3$ $\qquad$ or $\qquad\quad x > 6$

23. $\qquad |x - 3| < 2$
$\quad -2 < x - 3 < 2$
$\qquad 1 < x < 5$

24. $\quad |1 - 2x| \ge 7$
$1 - 2x \ge 7$ $\qquad$ or $1 - 2x \le -7$
$\quad -2x \ge 6$ $\qquad$ or $\quad -2x \le -8$
$\qquad x \le -3$ $\qquad$ or $\qquad x \ge 4$

25. First graph the dashed line $y = 2x - 1$ through $(0, -1)$ with slope 2. Now shade below the line for $y < 2x - 1$.

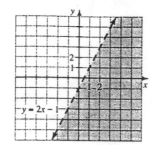

28. The graph of $y < 2$ consists of the points below the horizontal line $y = 2$. The graph of $x > -3$ consists of the points to the right of the vertical line $x = -3$. The region that lies below $y = 2$ and to the right of $x = -3$ is shaded on the graph. The boundary lines are drawn solid because of the $\leq$ and $\geq$ symbols.

26. First graph the solid line $3x - y = 2$ or $y = 3x - 2$ through $(0, -2)$ with slope 3. Now test $(0, 0)$ in $3x - y \leq 2$. Since $(0, 0)$ satisfies $3x - y \leq 2$, we shade the side of the line containing $(0, 0)$.

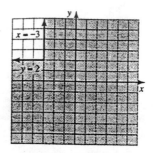

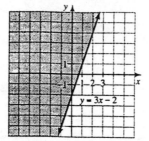

27. Graph the dashed line $y = x$ through $(0, 0)$ and $(1, 1)$. Next graph the dashed lin $y = -3x + 5$ through $(0, 5)$ with slope -3. Now test a point in each of the four regions. Only points that lie above $y = x$ and below $y = -3x + 5$ satisfy both inequalities. So shade that region.

29. a) For ages 62 through 64
$b = 500a - 24{,}000$.
For ages 65 through 67
$b = 667a - 34{,}689$.
For ages 68 through 70
$b = 800a - 43{,}600$.
b) At age 64 $b = 500(64) - 24{,}000 = \$8000$
c) If a person get $11,600 then
$$11{,}600 = 800a - 43{,}600$$
$$55{,}200 = 800a$$
$$69 = a$$
d) The slopes 500, 667, and 800 indicate the additional amount per year received beyond the basic amount in each category.

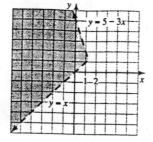

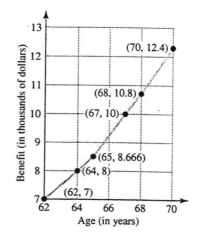

4.1 WARM-UPS

1. True, because if $x = 1$ and $y = 2$, then $2(1) + 2 = 4$ is correct.

2. False, because if $x = 1$ and $y = 2$, then $3(1) - 2 = 6$ is incorrect.

3. False, because $(2, 3)$ does not satisfy $4x - y = -5$.

4. True.

5. True, because when we substitute, one of the variables is eliminated.

6. True, because each of these lines has slope 3 and they are parallel.

7. True, because the lines are not parallel and they have different y-intercepts.

8. True, because the lines are parallel and have different y-intercepts.

9. True, because dependent equations have the same solution sets.

10. True, because a system of independent equations has one point in its solution set.

4.1 EXERCISES

1. The intersection point of the graphs is the solution to an independent system.

2. The lines do not intersect if the system has no solution.

3. The graphing method can be very inaccurate.

4. For substitution we eliminate a variable by substituting one equation into the other.

5. If the equation you get after substituting turns out to be incorrect, like $0 = 9$, then the system has no solution.

6. If substitution results in an identity, then the system is dependent.

7. The graph of $y = 2x$ is a straight line with y-intercept $(0, 0)$ and slope 2. The graph of $y = -x + 3$ is a straight line with y-intercept $(0, 3)$ and slope -1. The graphs appear to intersect at $(1, 2)$. Check that $(1, 2)$ satisfies both equations. The solution set is $\{(1, 2)\}$.

8. The graph of $y = x - 3$ is a line with y-intercept $(0, -3)$ and slope 1. The graph of $y = -x + 1$ is a line with y-intercept $(0, 1)$ and slope -1. The lines appear to intersect at $(2, -1)$. Check that $(2, -1)$ satisfies both equations. The solution set is $\{(2, -1)\}$.

9. The graph of $y = 2x - 1$ is a straight line with y-intercept $(0, -1)$ and slope 2. The graph of $y = \frac{1}{2}x - 1$ is a straight line with y-intercept $(0, -1)$ and slope $\frac{1}{2}$. The graphs intersect at $(0, -1)$. The solution set to the system of equations is $\{(0, -1)\}$.

10. The graph of $y = 2x + 1$ is a line with slope 2 and y-intercept $(0, 1)$. The graph of $x + y = -2$ (or $y = -x - 2$) is a line with slope -1 and y-intercept $(0, -2)$. The lines appear to intersect at $(-1, -1)$. Check that $(-1, -1)$ satisfies both equations. The solution set is $\{(-1, -1)\}$.

11. The graph of $y = x - 3$ is a straight line with y-intercept $(0, -3)$ and slope 1. The graph of $y = \frac{1}{2}x - 2$ is a straight line with y-intercept $(0, -2)$ and slope $\frac{1}{2}$. The lines appear to intersect at $(2, -1)$. To be sure, we check that $(2, -1)$ satisfies both of the original equations. The solution set is $\{(2, -1)\}$.

12. The graph of $y = -3x$ is a line with slope -3 and y-intercept $(0, 0)$. The graph of $x + y = 2$ (or $y = -x + 2$) is a line with slope -1 and y-intercept $(0, 2)$. The lines appear to intersect at $(-1, 3)$. Check that $(-1, 3)$ satisfies both equations. The solution set is $\{(-1, 3)\}$

13. If we rewrite these equations in slope-intercept form, we get $y = x + 1$ and $y = x + 3$. The graphs are parallel lines with slopes of 1 and y-intercepts of $(0, 1)$ and $(0, 3)$. Since the lines do not intersect, the solution set is the empty set, $\emptyset$.

14. The graph of $3y - 3x = 9$ (or $y = x + 3$) is a line with slope 1 and y-intercept $(0, 3)$. The graph of $x - y = 1$ (or $y = x - 1$) is a line with slope 1 and y-intercept $(0, -1)$. Since the lines are parallel, the solution set to the system is the empty set, $\emptyset$.

15. Solving $x + 2y = 8$ for y yields $y = -\frac{1}{2}x + 4$, which is the same equation as the first. So the equations have the same graph. The solution set is $\{(x, y) \mid x + 2y = 8\}$.

16. Solving $2x - 3y = 6$ for y yields $y = \frac{2}{3}x - 2$, which is the same as the second equation. So the equations have the same graph. The solution set is $\{(x, y) \mid 2x - 3y = 6\}$.

17. The lines in graph (c) intersect at $(3, -2)$ and $(3, -2)$ satisfies both equations.

18. The lines in graph (d) intersect at $(2, 3)$ and $(2, 3)$ satisfies both equations of the system.

19. The lines in graph (b) intersect at $(-3, -2)$ and $(-3, -2)$ satisfies both equations.

20. The lines in graph (a) intersect at $(-3, 2)$ and $(-3, 2)$ satisfies both equations.

21. Substitute $y = x - 5$ into $2x - 5y = 1$.
$$2x - 5(x - 5) = 1$$
$$2x - 5x + 25 = 1$$
$$-3x = -24$$
$$x = 8$$
Use $x = 8$ in $y = x - 5$ to find y.
$$y = 8 - 5$$
$$y = 3$$
The solution set is $\{(8, 3)\}$. The equations are independent.

22. Substitute $y = x + 4$ into $3y - 5x = 6$.
$$3(x + 4) - 5x = 6$$
$$3x + 12 - 5x = 6$$
$$-2x + 12 = 6$$
$$-2x = -6$$
$$x = 3$$
If $x = 3$, then $y = 3 + 4 = 7$. The solution set is $\{(3, 7)\}$. The equations are independent.

23. Substitute $x = 2y - 7$ into $3x + 2y = -5$.
$$3(2y - 7) + 2y = -5$$
$$6y - 21 + 2y = -5$$
$$8y = 16$$
$$y = 2$$
Use $y = 2$ in $x = 2y - 7$ to find x.
$$x = 2(2) - 7 = -3$$
The solution set is $\{(-3, 2)\}$. The equations are independent.

24. Substitute $x = y + 3$ into $3x - 2y = 4$.
$$3(y + 3) - 2y = 4$$
$$3y + 9 - 2y = 4$$
$$y = -5$$

If $y = -5$ then $x = -5 + 3 = -2$. The solution set is $\{(-2, -5)\}$. The equations are independent.

25. Write $x - y = 5$ as $x = y + 5$ and substitute into $2x = 2y + 14$.
$$2(y + 5) = 2y + 14$$
$$2y + 10 = 2y + 14$$
$$10 = 14$$
Since this last equation is incorrect no matter what values are used for x and y, the equations are inconsistent and the solution set is $\emptyset$.

26. Write $2x - y = 3$ as $y = 2x - 3$.
Substitute $y = 2x - 3$ into $2y = 4x - 6$.
$$2(2x - 3) = 4x - 6$$
$$4x - 6 = 4x - 6$$
Since the last equation is an identity, the solution set is $\{(x, y) \mid 2x - y = 3\}$. The system is dependent.

27. Substitute $y = 2x - 5$ into $y + 1 = 2(x - 2)$.
$$2x - 5 + 1 = 2(x - 2)$$
$$2x - 4 = 2x - 4$$
Since the last equation is an identity, the equations are dependent. Any ordered pair that satisfies one equation will also satisfy the other. So the solution set is $\{(x, y) \mid y = 2x - 5\}$.

28. Write $2y = 4x - 6$ as $y = 2x - 3$.
Substitute $y = 2x - 3$ into $3x - 6y = 5$.
$$3x - 6(2x - 3) = 5$$
$$3x - 12x + 18 = 5$$
$$-9x = -13$$
$$x = \frac{13}{9}$$
$$y = 2x - 3$$
$$y = 2\left(\frac{13}{9}\right) - 3 = \frac{26}{9} - \frac{27}{9} = -\frac{1}{9}$$
The solution set is $\left\{\left(\frac{13}{9}, -\frac{1}{9}\right)\right\}$. The system is independent.

29. Write $2x + y = 9$ as $y = -2x + 9$ and substitute into $2x - 5y = 15$.
$$2x - 5(-2x + 9) = 15$$
$$2x + 10x - 45 = 15$$
$$12x - 45 = 15$$
$$12x = 60$$
$$x = 5$$
Use $x = 5$ in $y = -2x + 9$ to find y.
$$y = -2(5) + 9 = -1$$

The solution set is $\{(5, -1)\}$. The equations are independent.

30. Write $3y - x = 0$ as $x = 3y$. Substitute $x = 3y$ into $x - 4y = -2$.
$$3y - 4y = -2$$
$$-y = -2$$
$$y = 2$$
If $y = 2$, then $x = 3(2) = 6$. The solution set is $\{(6, 2)\}$. The system is independent.

31. Write $x - y = 0$ as $y = x$ and substitute into $2x + 3y = 35$.
$$2x + 3x = 35$$
$$5x = 35$$
$$x = 7$$
Since $y = x$, $y = 7$ also. The solution set is $\{(7, 7)\}$ and the equations are independent.

32. Write $2y = x + 6$ as $x = 2y - 6$. Substitute $x = 2y - 6$ into $-3x + 2y = -2$.
$$-3(2y - 6) + 2y = -2$$
$$-6y + 18 + 2y = -2$$
$$-4y + 18 = -2$$
$$-4y = -20$$
$$y = 5$$
$$x = 2y - 6$$
$$x = 2(5) - 6 = 4$$
The solution set is $\{(4, 5)\}$. The system is independent.

33. Write $x + y = 40$ as $x = 40 - y$ and substitute into $0.1x + 0.08y = 3.5$.
$$0.1(40 - y) + 0.08y = 3.5$$
$$4 - 0.1y + 0.08y = 3.5$$
$$-0.02y = -0.5$$
$$y = 25$$
Since $x = 40 - y$, we get $x = 40 - 25 = 15$. The solution set is $\{(15, 25)\}$ and the equations are independent.

34. Write $x - y = 10$ as $y = x - 10$. Substitute $y = x - 10$ into $0.2x + 0.05y = 7$.
$$0.2x + 0.05(x - 10) = 7$$
$$0.2x + 0.05x - 0.5 = 7$$
$$0.25x = 7.5$$
$$x = 30$$
$$y = x - 10$$
$$y = 30 - 10 = 20$$
The solution set is $\{(30, 20)\}$. The system is independent.

35. Substitute $y = 2x - 30$ into the other equation.
$$\tfrac{1}{5}x - \tfrac{1}{2}(2x - 30) = -1$$
$$\tfrac{1}{5}x - x + 15 = -1$$
$$5\left(\tfrac{1}{5}x - x + 15\right) = 5(-1)$$
$$x - 5x + 75 = -5$$
$$-4x = -80$$
$$x = 20$$
If $x = 20$, then
$$y = 2x - 30 = 2(20) - 30 = 10.$$
The solution set is $\{(20, 10)\}$ and the equations are independent.

36. Substitute $y = \tfrac{3}{4}x - 2$ into $3x - 5y = 4$.
$$3x - 5\left(\tfrac{3}{4}x - 2\right) = 4$$
$$3x - \tfrac{15}{4}x + 10 = 4$$
$$12x - 15x + 40 = 16$$
$$-3x = -24$$
$$x = 8$$
If $x = 8$, then $y = \tfrac{3}{4}(8) - 2 = 4$. The solution set is $\{(8, 4)\}$. The equations are independent.

37. Write $x - y = 5$ as $x = y + 5$ and substitute into $x + y = 4$.
$$y + 5 + y = 4$$
$$2y = -1$$
$$y = -1/2$$
If $y = -1/2$, then
$$x = y + 5 = -1/2 + 5 = 9/2.$$
The solution set is $\left\{\left(\tfrac{9}{2}, -\tfrac{1}{2}\right)\right\}$ and the equations are independent.

38. Substitute $y = 2x - 3$ into $y = 3x - 3$.
$$2x - 3 = 3x - 3$$
$$-3 = x - 3$$
$$0 = x$$
If $x = 0$, then $y = 2(0) - 3 = -3$. The solution set is $\{(0, -3)\}$.

39. Write $2x - y = 4$ as $y = 2x - 4$ and substitute into $2x - y = 3$.
$$2x - (2x - 4) = 3$$
$$4 = 3$$
The equations are inconsistent and the solution set is $\emptyset$.

40. Substitute $y = 3(x - 4)$ into $3x - y = 12$.
$$3x - 3(x - 4) = 12$$
$$3x - 3x + 12 = 12$$
$$12 = 12$$

Since the last equation is an identity the equations are dependent. The solution set is $\{(x, y) \mid 3x - y = 12\}$.

41. First simplify.
$$3(y - 1) = 2(x - 3)$$
$$3y - 3 = 2x - 6$$
$$3y - 2x = -3$$
By simplifying the first equation we see that it is the same as the second equation. There is no need to substitute now. The equations are dependent and the solution set is $\{(x, y) \mid 3y - 2x = -3\}$.

42. Substitute $y = 3x$ into $y = 3x + 1$.
$$3x = 3x + 1$$
$$0 = 1$$
Since the last equation is false, the equations are inconsistent. The solution set to the system is the empty set, $\emptyset$.

43. Write $x - y = -0.375$ as $x = y - 0.375$ and substitute into $1.5x - 3y = -2.25$.
$$1.5(y - 0.375) - 3y = -2.25$$
$$1.5y - 0.5625 - 3y = -2.25$$
$$-1.5y = -1.6875$$
$$y = 1.125$$
If $y = 1.125$, then $x = 1.125 - 0.375 = 0.75$. The solution set is $\{(0.75, 1.125)\}$ and the equations are independent.

44. Write $y - 2x = 1.875$ as $y = 2x + 1.875$. Substitute $y = 2x + 1.875$ into
$$2.5y - 3.5x = 11.8125$$
$$2.5(2x + 1.875) - 3.5x = 11.8125$$
$$5x + 4.6875 - 3.5x = 11.8125$$
$$1.5x = 7.125$$
$$x = 4.75$$
If $x = 4.75$, then
$y = 2(4.75) + 1.875 = 11.375$. The solution set is $\{(4.75, 11.375)\}$.

45. Let x represent the width and y represent the length, then $2x + 2y = 82$ and $y = x + 15$.
$$2x + 2(x + 15) = 82$$
$$4x + 30 = 82$$
$$4x = 52$$
$$x = 13$$
$$y = 13 + 15 = 28$$
The length is 28 feet and the width is 13 feet.

46. Let x represent Alkena's salary and y represent Hsu's salary, then $x + y = 84326$ and $x = y + 12468$.
$$y + 12468 + y = 84326$$
$$2y = 71858$$
$$y = 35929$$
$$x = 35929 + 12468 = 48397$$
So Alkena earns \$48,397 and Hsu earns \$35,929.

47. Let $x =$ the amount invested at 5% and $y =$ the amount invested at 10%. The interest earned on the investments is $0.05x$ and $0.10y$ respectively. We can write two equations, one expressing the total amount invested, and the other expressing the total of the interest earned.
$$x + y = 30,000$$
$$0.05x + 0.10y = 2,300$$
Write the first equation as $y = 30,000 - x$ and substitute into the second.
$$0.05x + 0.10(30,000 - x) = 2,300$$
$$0.05x + 3,000 - 0.10x = 2,300$$
$$-0.05x = -700$$
$$x = 14,000$$
If $x = 14,000$, then
$y = 30,000 - 14,000 = 16,000$. She invested \$14,000 at 5% and \$16,000 at 10%.

48. Let $x =$ the population of Marysville and $y =$ the population of Springfield in 1990. One equation expresses the fact that the total population in 1990 was 25,000 and the other expresses the fact that the total increase in population in 1995 was 2380.
$$x + y = 25,000$$
$$0.10x + 0.09y = 2,380$$
Write the first equation as $y = 25,000 - x$ and substitute into the second equation.
$$0.10x + 0.09(25,000 - x) = 2,380$$
$$0.10x + 2250 - 0.09x = 2,380$$
$$0.01x + 2250 = 2,380$$
$$0.01x = 130$$
$$x = 13,000$$
$$y = 25,000 - x$$
$$y = 25,000 - 13,000 = 12,000$$
Population of Marysville was 13,000 and population of Springfield was 12,000.

49. Let x and y be the numbers. The fact that their sum is 2 and their difference is 26 gives us a system of equations:

$$x + y = 2$$
$$x - y = 26$$

Write $x + y = 2$ as $x = 2 - y$ and substitute.

$$2 - y - y = 26$$
$$-2y = 24$$
$$y = -12$$

If $y = -12$, then

$x = 2 - y = 2 - (-12) = 14$. The numbers are -12 and 14.

50. Let $x =$ one number and $y =$ the other number. One equation expresses the fact that their sum is -16 and the other expresses the fact that their difference is 8.

$$x + y = -16$$
$$x - y = 8$$

Write $x - y = 8$ as $x = 8 + y$ and substitute into $x + y = -16$.

$$8 + y + y = -16$$
$$8 + 2y = -16$$
$$2y = -24$$
$$y = -12$$
$$x = 8 + y$$
$$x = 8 + (-12) = -4$$

The numbers are -4 and -12.

51. Let $x =$ the number of toasters and $y =$ the number of vacation coupons. We write one equation expressing the fact that the total number of prizes is 100 and the other expressing the total bill of $708.

$$x + y = 100$$
$$6x + 24y = 708$$

Write $x + y = 100$ as $x = 100 - y$ and substitute.

$$6(100 - y) + 24y = 708$$
$$600 - 6y + 24y = 708$$
$$18y = 108$$
$$y = 6$$

If $y = 6$, then $x = 100 - y = 100 - 6 = 94$. He gave away 94 toasters and 6 vacation coupons.

52. Let $x =$ the number of adult tickets sold and $y =$ the number of student tickets sold. Since there were twice as many adult tickets sold, $x = 2y$. The other equation expresses the fact that the total receipts were $824,

$3x + 2y = 824$. Substitute $x = 2y$ into the other equation.

$$3(2y) + 2y = 824$$
$$8y = 824$$
$$y = 103$$
$$x = 2y$$
$$x = 2(103) = 206$$

There were 103 student tickets sold and 206 adult tickets sold.

53. $s = 0.05(100,000 - f)$
$f = 0.30(100,000 - s)$

$s = 5,000 - 0.05f$
$f = 30,000 - 0.30s$

$$f = 30,000 - 0.30(5000 - 0.05f)$$
$$f = 30,000 - 1500 + 0.015f$$
$$0.985f = 28,500$$
$$f = 28,934$$
$$s = 5,000 - 0.05(28,934)$$
$$= 3553$$

State tax is $3,553 and federal tax is $28,934.

54. $s = 0.06(300,000 - f)$
$f = 0.40(300,000 - s)$

$s = 18,000 - 0.06f$
$f = 120,000 - 0.40s$

$$f = 120,000 - 0.40(18,000 - 0.06f)$$
$$f = 120,000 - 7200 + 0.024f$$
$$0.976f = 112,800$$
$$f = 115,574$$
$$s = 18,000 - 0.06(115,574)$$
$$= 11,066$$

State tax is $11,066 and federal tax is $115,574.

55. $B = 0.20N$
$N = 120,000 - B$

$$N = 120,000 - 0.20N$$
$$1.2N = 120,000$$
$$N = 100,000$$
$$B = 0.20 \cdot 100,000 = 20,000$$

The bonus is $20,000.

56. a) From the graph it appears that the tax is about $35,000 and the bonus is about $15,000.

b) $B = 0.2(100,000 - T)$
$T = 0.4(100,000 - B)$

$B = 20,000 - 0.2T$
$T = 40,000 - 0.4B$

$T = 40,000 - 0.4(20,000 - 0.2T)$
$T = 40,000 - 8000 + 0.08T$
$0.92T = 32,000$
$T = 34,783$
$B = 20,000 - 0.2(34,783) = 13,043$

So the bonus is $13,043 and the taxes are $34,783.

57. a) The cost of 10,000 textbooks is $500,000.

b) The revenue for 10,000 textbooks is $300,000.

c) The cost is equal to the revenue for 20,000 textbooks.

d) The fixed cost is $400,000.

58. a) The graph of $S = 5000 + 200x$ goes through (0, 5000) and (20, 9000). The graph of $D = 9500 - 100x$ goes through (0, 9500) and (20, 7500).

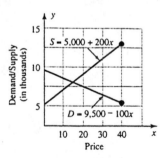

b) As the price increases, the supply increases.
c) As the price increases, the demand decreases.
d) Solve the system to find the equilibrium price.

$5000 + 200x = 9500 - 100x$
$300x = 4500$
$x = 15$

The equilibrium price is $15.

59. Solve each equation for y to get $y = \frac{2}{3}x - 2$ in every case except (a), which is $y = \frac{2}{3}x + 2$.

60. Solve $3x + 4y = 8$ for y to get $y = -\frac{3}{4}x + 2$. This is inconsistent with equation (c) which has the same slope and a different y-intercept.

61. a) $(2.8, 2.6)$ **b)** $(1.0, -0.2)$

4.2 WARM-UPS

1. True, because when we add the equations, the y-terms add up to 0 and one variable is eliminated.
2. False, multiply the first by -2 and the second by 3 to eliminate x.
3. True, multiplying the second by 2 and adding will eliminate both x and y.
4. True, because both ordered pairs satisfy both equations.
5. False, solution set is $\{(x, y) \mid 4x - 2y = 20\}$.
6. True, because the equations are inconsistent.
7. True.
8. False, as long as we add the left sides and the right sides, the form does not matter.
9. True.
10. True.

4.2 EXERCISES

1. In this section we learned the addition method.
2. We try to eliminate a variable by adding the equations.
3. In some cases we multiply one or both of the equations on each side to change the coefficients of the variable we are trying to eliminate.
4. If a false equation (such as $3 = 4$) results from addition of the equations, then the equations are inconsistent.
5. If an identity (such as $0 = 0$) results form addition of the equations, then the equations are dependent.

6. Addition is usually easier to use when the equations are in the same form.

7.
$$x + y = 7$$
$$\underline{x - y = 9}$$
$$2x \quad = 16$$
$$x = 8$$
Use $x = 8$ in $x + y = 7$ to find y.
$$8 + y = 7$$
$$y = -1$$
The solution set is $\{(8, -1)\}$.

8.
$$3x - 4y = 11$$
$$\underline{-3x + 2y = -7}$$
$$-2y = 4$$
$$y = -2$$
Use $y = -2$ in $3x - 4y = 11$.
$$3x - 4(-2) = 11$$
$$3x + 8 = 11$$
$$3x = 3$$
$$x = 1$$
The solution set is $\{(1, -2)\}$.

9.
$$x - y = 12$$
$$\underline{2x + y = 3}$$
$$3x \quad = 15$$
$$x = 5$$
Use $x = 5$ in $x - y = 12$.
$$5 - y = 12$$
$$-7 = y$$
The solution set is $\{(5, -7)\}$.

10.
$$x - 2y = -1$$
$$\underline{-x + 5y = 4}$$
$$3y = 3$$
$$y = 1$$
Use $y = 1$ in $x - 2y = -1$.
$$x - 2(1) = -1$$
$$x = 1$$
The solution set is $\{(1, 1)\}$.

11. If we multiply $2x - y = -5$ by 2, we get $4x - 2y = -10$. Add this equation to the second equation.
$$4x - 2y = -10$$
$$\underline{3x + 2y = 3}$$
$$7x \quad = -7$$
$$x = -1$$
Use $x = -1$ in $2x - y = -5$.
$$2(-1) - y = -5$$
$$-2 - y = -5$$

$$3 = y$$
The solution set is $\{(-1, 3)\}$.

12. If we multiply the second equation $x - 2y = 11$ by -3, we get $-3x + 6y = -33$. Add this equation to the first equation.
$$3x + 5y = -11$$
$$\underline{-3x + 6y = -33}$$
$$11y = -44$$
$$y = -4$$
Use $y = -4$ in $3x + 5y = -11$.
$$3x + 5(-4) = -11$$
$$3x - 20 = -11$$
$$3x = 9$$
$$x = 3$$
The solution set is $\{(3, -4)\}$.

13. Multiply the first equation by 4 and the second by 5.
$$4(2x - 5y) = 4(13)$$
$$5(3x + 4y) = 5(-15)$$

$$8x - 20y = 52$$
$$\underline{15x + 20y = -75}$$
$$23x \quad = -23$$
$$x = -1$$
Use $x = -1$ in $2x - 5y = 13$.
$$2(-1) - 5y = 13$$
$$-2 - 5y = 13$$
$$-5y = 15$$
$$y = -3$$
The solution set is $\{(-1, -3)\}$.

14. Multiply the first equation by -5 and the second equation by 3.
$$-5(3x + 4y) = -5(-5)$$
$$3(5x + 6y) = 3(-7)$$

$$-15x - 20y = 25$$
$$\underline{15x + 18y = -21}$$
$$-2y = 4$$
$$y = -2$$
Use $y = -2$ in $3x + 4y = -5$.
$$3x + 4(-2) = -5$$
$$3x - 8 = -5$$
$$3x = 3$$
$$x = 1$$
The solution set is $\{(1, -2)\}$.

15. Rewrite the first equation to match the form of the second. $\quad 2x - 3y = 11$
$$7x - 4y = 6$$
Multiply the first equation by -7 and the second by 2.
$$-7(2x - 3y) = -7(11)$$
$$2(7x - 4y) = 2(6)$$

$$\begin{aligned}-14x + 21y &= -77 \\ \underline{14x - 8y} &= \underline{12} \\ 13y &= -65 \\ y &= -5\end{aligned}$$
Use $y = -5$ in $2x = 3y + 11$.
$$2x = 3(-5) + 11$$
$$2x = -4$$
$$x = -2$$
The solution set is $\{(-2, -5)\}$.

16. Rewrite the first equation to match the form of the second.
$$2x + y = 2$$
$$3x + y = -1$$
Multiply the first equation by -1 to get $-2x - y = -2$. Add this equation to the second equation.
$$\begin{aligned}-2x - y &= -2 \\ \underline{3x + y} &= \underline{-1} \\ x \quad\;\; &= -3\end{aligned}$$
Use $x = -3$ in $2x + y = 2$ to find y.
$$2(-3) + y = 2$$
$$-6 + y = 2$$
$$y = 8$$
The solution set is $\{(-3, 8)\}$.

17. $\quad -12(x + y) = -12(48)$
$$12x + 14y = 628$$

$$\begin{aligned}-12x - 12y &= -576 \\ \underline{12x + 14y} &= \underline{628} \\ 2y &= 52 \\ y &= 26\end{aligned}$$
$$x + 26 = 48$$
$$x = 22$$
The solution set is $\{(22, 26)\}$.

18. $\quad -22(x + y) = -22(13)$
$$22x + 36y = 356$$

$$\begin{aligned}-22x - 22y &= -286 \\ \underline{22x + 36y} &= \underline{356} \\ 14y &= 70 \\ y &= 5\end{aligned}$$
$$x + 5 = 13$$
$$x = 8$$
The solution set is $\{(8, 5)\}$.

19. $\quad 3x - 4y = 9$
$$\begin{aligned}\underline{-3x + 4y} &= \underline{12} \\ 0 &= 21\end{aligned}$$
Since we obtained an incorrect equation by addition, the equations are inconsistent and the solution set is $\emptyset$.

20. Multiply $x - y = 3$ by 6 to get $6x - 6y = 18$. Add this result to the other equation.
$$\begin{aligned}6x - 6y &= 18 \\ \underline{-6x + 6y} &= \underline{17} \\ 0 &= 35\end{aligned}$$
The equations are inconsistent and the solution set is $\emptyset$.

21. Multiply $5x - y = 1$ by -2, to get $-10x + 2y = -2$. Add this equation to the second equation.
$$\begin{aligned}-10x + 2y &= -2 \\ \underline{10x - 2y} &= \underline{2} \\ 0 &= 0\end{aligned}$$
Since we obtained an identity by adding the equations, the equations are dependent and the solution set is $\{(x, y) \mid 5x - y = 1\}$.

22. Multiply $4x + 3y = 2$ by 3 to get $12x + 9y = 6$. Add this result to the other equation.
$$\begin{aligned}12x + 9y &= 6 \\ \underline{-12x - 9y} &= \underline{-6} \\ 0 &= 0\end{aligned}$$
Since we obtained an identity by adding the equations, the equations are dependent and the solution set is $\{(x, y) \mid 4x + 3y = 2\}$.

23. $\quad 2x - y = 5$
$$\begin{aligned}\underline{2x + y} &= \underline{5} \\ 4x \quad\;\; &= 10 \\ x &= 10/4 = 5/2\end{aligned}$$
Use $x = 5/2$ in $2x + y = 5$ to find y.
$$2(5/2) + y = 5$$
$$5 + y = 5$$

$$y = 0$$

The solution set is $\{(5/2, 0)\}$ and the equations are independent.

24. Add the equations.
$$-3x + 2y = 8$$
$$\underline{3x + 2y = 8}$$
$$4y = 16$$
$$y = 4$$

Use $y = 4$ in $-3x + 2y = 8$ to find x.
$$-3x + 2(4) = 8$$
$$-3x = 0$$
$$x = 0$$

The solution set is $\{(0, 4)\}$.

25. Multiplying the first equation by 12 to eliminate the fractions gives us the following system.
$$3x + 4y = 60$$
$$x - y = 6$$

Multiply the second equation by 4 and then add.
$$3x + 4y = 60$$
$$\underline{4x - 4y = 24}$$
$$7x = 84$$
$$x = 12$$

Use $x = 12$ in $x - y = 6$ to find y.
$$12 - y = 6$$
$$6 = y$$

The solution set is $\{(12, 6)\}$.

26. Multiply the first equation by 6 and the second by 2 to eliminate the fractions. We get the following system.
$$9x - 4y = 60$$
$$x + y = -2$$

Multiply $x + y = -2$ by 4 to get $4x + 4y = -8$. Add this result to the first equation.
$$9x - 4y = 60$$
$$\underline{4x + 4y = -8}$$
$$13x = 52$$
$$x = 4$$

Use $x = 4$ in $x + y = -2$ to find y.
$$4 + y = -2$$
$$y = -6$$

The solution set is $\{(4, -6)\}$.

27. If we multiply the first equation by 12 and the second by 24 to eliminate fractions, we get the following system.

$$3x - 4y = -48$$
$$\underline{3x + 4y = 0}$$
$$6x = -48$$
$$x = -8$$

Use $x = -8$ in $3x + 4y = 0$ to find y.
$$3(-8) + 4y = 0$$
$$4y = 24$$
$$y = 6$$

The solution set is $\{(-8, 6)\}$.

28. Multiply the first equation by 6 and the second by 15 to get the following system.
$$2x - 3y = -5$$
$$3x - 5y = -9$$

Multiply the first equation by -3 and the second by 2 to get the following system.
$$-6x + 9y = 15$$
$$\underline{6x - 10y = -18}$$
$$-y = -3$$
$$y = 3$$

Use $y = 3$ in $2x - 3y = -5$ to find x.
$$2x - 3(3) = -5$$
$$2x - 9 = -5$$
$$2x = 4$$
$$x = 2$$

The solution set is $\{(2, 3)\}$.

29. Multiply the first equation by 8 and the second by -16 to get the following system.
$$x + 2y = 40$$
$$\underline{-x - 8y = -112}$$
$$-6y = -72$$
$$y = 12$$
$$x + 2(12) = 40$$
$$x = 16$$

The solution set is $\{(16, 12)\}$.

30. Multiply both equations by 63.
$$27x + 35y = 1701$$
$$7x + 18y = 441$$

Multiply first by -7 and second by 27:
$$-189x - 245y = -11907$$
$$\underline{189x + 486y = 11907}$$
$$241y = 0$$
$$y = 0$$
$$7x + 18(0) = 441$$
$$x = 63$$

The solution set is $\{(63, 0)\}$.

31. Multiply the first equation by 100 and the second by -10 to get the following system.

$$5x + 10y = 130$$
$$\underline{-10x - 10y = -190}$$
$$-5x \qquad\quad = -60$$
$$x = 12$$

Use $x = 12$ in $x + y = 19$ to get $y = 7$. The solution set is $\{(12, 7)\}$.

32. Multiply each equation by 100 to eliminate the decimal numbers.

$$10x + 6y = 900$$
$$9x + 50y = 5270$$

Multiply the first equation by -9 and the second by 10, to get the following system.

$$-90x - 54y = -8100$$
$$\underline{90x + 500y = 52700}$$
$$446y = 44600$$
$$y = 100$$

Use $y = 100$ in $10x + 6y = 900$ to find x.

$$10x + 6(100) = 900$$
$$10x + 600 = 900$$
$$10x = 300$$
$$x = 30$$

The solution set is $\{(30, 100)\}$.

33. Multiply the first equation by -9 and the second by 100 to get the following system.

$$-9x - 9y = -10800$$
$$\underline{12x + 9y = 12000}$$
$$3x \qquad\quad = 1200$$
$$x = 400$$

Use $x = 400$ in $x + y = 1200$ to get $y = 800$. The solution set is $\{(400, 800)\}$.

34. Multiply the first equation by 6 and the second equation by 100 to get the following system.

$$6x - 6y = 600$$
$$\underline{20x + 6y = 15000}$$
$$26x \qquad\quad = 15600$$
$$x = 600$$

Use $x = 600$ in $x - y = 100$ to find y.

$$600 - y = 100$$
$$-y = -500$$
$$y = 500$$

The solution set is $\{(600, 500)\}$.

35. Multiply the first equation by -2 to get the following system.

$$-3x + 4y = 0.5$$
$$\underline{3x + 1.5y = 6.375}$$
$$5.5y = 6.875$$
$$y = 1.25$$

Use $y = 1.25$ in $3x + 1.5y = 6.375$ to find x.

$$3x + 1.5(1.25) = 6.375$$
$$3x + 1.875 = 6.375$$
$$3x = 4.5$$
$$x = 1.5$$

The solution set is $\{(1.5, 1.25)\}$.

36. Multiply the first equation by 10 and the second by -12 to get the following system.

$$10(3x - 2.5y) = 10(7.125)$$
$$-12(2.5x - 3y) = -12(7.3125)$$

$$30x - 25y = 71.25$$
$$\underline{-30x + 36y = -87.75}$$
$$11y = -16.5$$
$$y = -1.5$$

Use $y = -1.5$ in $3x - 2.5y = 7.125$ to find x.

$$3x - 2.5(-1.5) = 7.125$$
$$3x + 3.75 = 7.125$$
$$3x = 3.375$$
$$x = 1.125$$

The solution set is $\{(1.125, -1.5)\}$.

37. Let $x =$ the price of one doughnut and $y =$ the price of one cup of coffee. His bills for Monday and Tuesday give us the following system of equations.

$$3x + 2y = 2.54$$
$$2x + 3y = 2.46$$

Multiply the first equation by -2 and the second by 3.

$$-6x - 4y = -5.08$$
$$\underline{6x + 9y = 7.38}$$
$$5y = 2.30$$
$$y = 0.46$$

Use $y = 0.46$ in $3x + 2y = 2.54$ to find x.

$$3x + 2(0.46) = 2.54$$
$$3x + 0.92 = 2.54$$
$$3x = 1.62$$
$$x = 0.54$$

Doughnuts are $0.54 each and a cup of coffee is $0.46. So his total bill on Wednesday was $1.00.

38. Let x = the price of a book and y = the price of a magazine. We can write two equations.

$$4x + 3y = 1.45$$
$$2x + 5y = 1.25$$

Multiply the second equation by -2 to get $-4x - 10y = -2.50$. Add this result to the first equation.

$$\begin{array}{r} 4x + 3y = 1.45 \\ -4x - 10y = -2.50 \\ \hline -7y = -1.05 \\ y = 0.15 \end{array}$$

Use $y = 0.15$ in $4x + 3y = 1.45$ to find x.

$$4x + 3(0.15) = 1.45$$
$$4x + 0.45 = 1.45$$
$$4x = 1.00$$
$$x = 0.25$$

The books were $0.25 each and the magazines were $0.15 each.

39. Let x = the number of boys and y = the number of girls at Freemont High. We get a system of equations from the number of boys and girls who attended the dance and game.

$$\tfrac{1}{2}x + \tfrac{1}{3}y = 570$$
$$\tfrac{1}{3}x + \tfrac{1}{2}y = 580$$

Multiply the first equation by 12 and the second equation by -18.

$$\begin{array}{r} 6x + 4y = 6840 \\ -6x - 9y = -10440 \\ \hline -5y = -3600 \\ y = 720 \end{array}$$

Use $y = 720$ in $6x + 4y = 6840$ to find x.

$$6x + 4(720) = 6840$$
$$6x + 2880 = 6840$$
$$6x = 3960$$
$$x = 660$$

There are 660 boys and 720 girls at Freemont High, or 1380 students.

40. Let x = the number of boys and y = the number of girls. Since there are 2 girls for every boy, we have $y = 2x$. Since two-thirds of the boys are surfers and one-twelfth of the girls are surfers, we can write the following system.

$$\tfrac{2}{3}x + \tfrac{1}{12}y = 385$$
$$y = 2x$$

Substitute $y = 2x$ into the first equation.

$$\tfrac{2}{3}x + \tfrac{1}{12}(2x) = 385$$
$$\tfrac{2}{3}x + \tfrac{1}{6}x = 385$$
$$6\left(\tfrac{2}{3}x + \tfrac{1}{6}x\right) = 6(385)$$
$$4x + x = 2310$$
$$5x = 2310$$
$$x = 462$$

$$y = 2x$$
$$y = 2(462) = 924$$

There are 462 boys and 924 girls in Surf City.

41. Let x = the number of dimes and y = the number of nickels. We write one equation about the total number of the coins and the other about the value of the coins (in cents).

$$x + y = 35$$
$$10x + 5y = 330$$

Multiply the first equation by -5.

$$\begin{array}{r} -5x - 5y = -175 \\ 10x + 5y = 330 \\ \hline 5x = 155 \\ x = 31 \end{array}$$

Use $x = 31$ in $x + y = 35$ to find that $y = 4$. He has 31 dimes and 4 nickels.

42. Let x = the number of nickels and y = the number of pennies. Since she has 52 coins, we can write $x + y = 52$. Since the coins are worth $1.20, we can express the total value in cents as $5x + y = 120$.

$$x + y = 52$$
$$5x + y = 120$$

Multiply the first equation by -1 and add the result to the second equation.

$$\begin{array}{r} -x - y = -52 \\ 5x + y = 120 \\ \hline 4x = 68 \\ x = 17 \end{array}$$

Use $x = 17$ in the equation $x + y = 52$ to find y.

$$17 + y = 52$$
$$y = 35$$

She has 17 nickels and 35 pennies.

43. a) From the graph it appears that there should be about 20 pounds of Chocolate fudge and 30 pounds of Peanut Butter fudge.

b) Let x = the number of pounds of Chocolate fudge and y = the number of pounds of Peanut Butter fudge.

$$x + y = 50$$
$$0.35x + 0.25y = 0.29(50)$$

$$y = 50 - x$$
$$0.35x + 0.25(50 - x) = 14.5$$
$$0.10x = 2$$
$$x = 20$$
$$20 + y = 50$$
$$y = 30$$

Use 20 pounds of Chocolate fudge and 30 pounds of Peanut Butter fudge.

44. Let r = the number of pounds of regular yogurt and n = the number of pounds of no-fat yogurt.
$$r + n = 60$$
$$0.03r + 0 \cdot n = 0.01(60)$$
Simplify the second equation as follows:
$$0.03r = 0.6$$
$$r = 20$$
Now find n:
$$n = 60 - r$$
$$n = 60 - 20 = 40$$
Use 20 pounds of regular yogurt and 40 pounds of no-fat yogurt.

45. Let a = the time from Allentown to Harrisburg and h = the time from Harrisburg to Pittsburgh.
$$a + h = 6$$
$$42a + 51h = 288$$

$$-51a - 51h = -306$$
$$\underline{42a + 51h = \ 288}$$
$$-9a \qquad\ = -18$$
$$a = 2$$
$$h = 6 - 2 = 4$$

It took 4 hours to go from Harrisburg to Pittsburgh.

46. Let r = the time from Rochester to Syracuse and s = the time from Syracuse to Albany.
$$r + s = 5$$
$$45r + 49s = 237$$

$$-45r - 45s = -225$$
$$\underline{45r + 49s = 237}$$
$$4s = 12$$
$$s = 3$$

Driving for 3 hours at 49 mph he drove 147 miles from Syracuse to Albany.

47. Let p = the probability of rain and q = the probability that it doesn't rain:
$$p + q = 1$$
$$p = 4q$$

$$4q + q = 1$$
$$5q = 1$$
$$q = 0.20 = 20\%$$
$$p = 80\%$$
The probability of rain is 80%.

48. Let p = the probability the S.F plays in the Super Bowl and q = the probability that S.F. does not play.
$$p = 9q$$
$$p + q = 1$$

$$9q + q = 1$$
$$10q = 1$$
$$q = 0.10 = 10\%$$
$$p = 90\%$$
The probability that S.F. plays the S.B. is 90%.

49. Let W = the width and L = the length.
$$W = 0.75L$$
$$2W + 2L = 700$$

$$2(0.75L) + 2L = 700$$
$$1.5L + 2L = 700$$
$$3.5L = 700$$
$$L = 200$$
$$W = 0.75(200) = 150$$
The width is 150 m and the length is 200 m.

50. Let a = the amount painted by Darren and b = the amount painted by Douglas.
$$a = 1.20b$$
$$a + b = 792$$

$$1.20b + b = 792$$
$$2.2b = 792$$
$$b = 360$$
$$a = 1.2 \cdot 360 = 432$$
Darren paints 432 feet and Douglas paints 360 feet.

4.3 WARM-UPS

1. False, because $1 + (-2) - 3 = 4$ is incorrect.

2. False, because there are infinitely many ordered triples that satisfy $x + y - z = 4$.

3. True, because if $x = 1$, $y = -1$, and $z = 2$ then each of the equations is satisfied.

4. False, we can use substitution and addition to eliminate variables.

5. False, because two planes never intersect in a single point.

6. True, because if we multiply the second one by -1 and add, then we get $0 = 2$.

7. True, because -2 times the first equation is the same as the second equation.

8. False, because the graph is a plane.

9. False, because the value of x nickels, y dimes, and z quarters is $5x + 10y + 25z$ cents.

10. False, because $x = -2$, $z = 3$, and $-2 + y + 3 = 6$ implies that $y = 5$.

4.3 EXERCISES

1. A linear equation in three variables is an equation of the form $Ax + By + Cz = D$ where A, B, and C cannot all be zero.

2. An order triple is a collection of three numbers (written as (a, b, c)) in which the order of the numbers is important.

3. A solution to a system of linear equations in three variable is an ordered triple that satisfies all of the equations in the system.

4. We solve systems in three variables by using addition or substitution to eliminate variables.

5. The graph of a linear equation in three variables is a plane in a three dimensional coordinate system.

6. For an inconsistent system, at least two of the planes are parallel.

7. Add the first two equations.

$$x + y + z = 2$$
$$\underline{x + 2y - z = 6}$$
$$2x + 3y \quad\;\; = 8 \quad \text{A}$$

Add the first and third equations.

$$x + y + z = 2$$
$$\underline{2x + y - z = 5}$$
$$3x + 2y \quad\;\; = 7 \quad \text{B}$$

Multiply equation A by 3 and equation B by -2.

$$6x + 9y = 24 \qquad 3 \times \text{A}$$
$$\underline{-6x - 4y = -14} \quad -2 \times \text{B}$$
$$5y = 10$$
$$y = 2$$

Use $y = 2$ in the equation $3x + 2y = 7$.

$$3x + 2(2) = 7$$
$$3x = 3$$
$$x = 1$$

Use $x = 1$ and $y = 2$ in $x + y + z = 2$.

$$1 + 2 + z = 2$$
$$z = -1$$

The solution set is $\{(1, 2, -1)\}$.

8. Add the first and second equation, and add the first and third equation.

$$2x - y + 3z = 14 \qquad 2x - y + 3z = 14$$
$$\underline{x + y - 2z = -5} \qquad \underline{3x + y - z = 2}$$
$$3x \quad\;\; + z = 9 \qquad 5x \quad\;\; + 2z = 16$$

Multiply $3x + z = 9$ by -2 and add the result to $5x + 2z = 16$.

$$-6x - 2z = -18$$
$$\underline{5x + 2z = 16}$$
$$-x \quad\;\; = -2$$
$$x = 2$$

Use $x = 2$ in $3x + z = 9$ to find z.

$$3(2) + z = 9$$
$$6 + z = 9$$
$$z = 3$$

Use $x = 2$ and $z = 3$ in $x + y - 2z = -5$ to find y.

$$2 + y - 2(3) = -5$$
$$y - 4 = -5$$
$$y = -1$$

The solution set is $\{(2, -1, 3)\}$.

9. Multiply the first equation by -1 to get $-x + 2y - 4z = -3$. Now add this equation and the second, and this equation and the third.

$$-x + 2y - 4z = -3 \qquad -x + 2y - 4z = -3$$
$$\underline{x + 3y - 2z = 6} \qquad \underline{x - 4y + 3z = -5}$$
$$5y - 6z = 3 \qquad -2y - z = -8$$

Multiply $-2y - z = -8$ by -6 and add the result to $5y - 6z = 3$.

$$12y + 6z = 48$$
$$\underline{5y - 6z = 3}$$
$$17y \quad\quad = 51$$
$$y = 3$$

Use $y = 3$ in $5y - 6z = 3$.
$$5(3) - 6z = 3$$
$$-6z = -12$$
$$z = 2$$

Use $y = 3$ and $z = 2$ in $x + 3y - 2z = 6$.
$$x + 3(3) - 2(2) = 6$$
$$x = 1$$

The solution set is $\{(1, 3, 2)\}$.

10. Multiply the first equation $2x + 3y + z = 13$ by -1 to get $-2x - 3y - z = -13$. Add this result to the second equation and the third equation.

$$-2x - 3y - z = -13 \quad\quad -2x - 3y - z = -13$$
$$\underline{-3x + 2y + z = -4} \quad\quad \underline{4x - 4y + z = 5}$$
$$-5x - y \quad\quad = -17 \quad\quad 2x - 7y \quad\quad = -8$$

Multiply $-5x - y = -17$ by -7 to get $35x + 7y = 119$. Add this equation to $2x - 7y = -8$.

$$35x + 7y = 119$$
$$\underline{2x - 7y = -8}$$
$$37x \quad\quad = 111$$
$$x = 3$$

Use $x = 3$ in $2x - 7y = -8$ to find y.
$$2(3) - 7y = -8$$
$$-7y = -14$$
$$y = 2$$

Use $x = 3$ and $y = 2$ in $4x - 4y + z = 5$ to find z.
$$4(3) - 4(2) + z = 5$$
$$12 - 8 + z = 5$$
$$z = 1$$

The solution set is $\{(3, 2, 1)\}$.

11. Multiply $2x - y + z = 10$ by 2 to get $4x - 2y + 2z = 20$. Add this equation and the second and this equation and the third.

$$4x - 2y + 2z = 20 \quad\quad 4x - 2y + 2z = 20$$
$$\underline{3x - 2y - 2z = 7} \quad\quad \underline{x - 3y - 2z = 10}$$
$$7x - 4y \quad\quad = 27 \quad\quad 5x - 5y \quad\quad = 30$$
$$\quad\quad\quad\quad\quad\quad\quad\quad\quad x - y \quad\quad = 6$$

Multiply $x - y = 6$ by -4 to get $-4x + 4y = -24$. Add this to $7x - 4y = 27$.

$$-4x + 4y = -24$$
$$\underline{7x - 4y = 27}$$
$$3x \quad\quad = 3$$
$$x = 1$$

Use $x = 1$ in $7x - 4y = 27$ to find y.
$$7(1) - 4y = 27$$
$$-4y = 20$$
$$y = -5$$

Use $x = 1$ and $y = -5$ in $2x - y + z = 10$.
$$2(1) - (-5) + z = 10$$
$$z = 3$$

The solution set is $\{(1, -5, 3)\}$.

12. Multiply the first equation by -2 and add the result to the second equation. Multiply the first equation by -3 and add the result to the third equation.

$$-2x + 6y - 4z = 22 \quad\quad -3x + 9y - 6z = 33$$
$$\underline{2x - 4y + 3z = -15} \quad\quad \underline{3x - 5y - 4z = 5}$$
$$2y - z = 7 \quad\quad\quad\quad 4y - 10z = 38$$

Multiply $2y - z = 7$ by -2 to get $-4y + 2z = -14$. Add this result to $4y - 10z = 38$.

$$-4y + 2z = -14$$
$$\underline{4y - 10z = 38}$$
$$-8z = 24$$
$$z = -3$$

Use $z = -3$ in $2y - z = 7$ to find y.
$$2y - (-3) = 7$$
$$2y + 3 = 7$$
$$2y = 4$$
$$y = 2$$

Use $y = 2$ and $z = -3$ in $x - 3y + 2z = -11$ to find x.
$$x - 3(2) + 2(-3) = -11$$
$$x - 12 = -11$$
$$x = 1$$

The solution set is $\{(1, 2, -3)\}$.

13. Multiply $x - y + 2z = -5$ by 2 to get $2x - 2y + 4z = -10$. Add this equation and the second equation, and add the first and second equations.

$$2x - 2y + 4z = -10 \quad\quad 2x - 3y + z = -9$$
$$\underline{-2x + y - 3z = 7} \quad\quad \underline{-2x + y - 3z = 7}$$
$$-y + z = -3 \quad\quad\quad -2y - 2z = -2$$
$$\quad\quad\quad\quad\quad\quad\quad\quad\quad y + z = 1$$

Add the last two equations to eliminate y.

$$-y + z = -3$$
$$y + z = 1$$
$$2z = -2$$
$$z = -1$$

Use $z = -1$ in $y + z = 1$ to get $y = 2$. Now use $z = -1$ and $y = 2$ in $x - y + 2z = -5$.

$$x - 2 + 2(-1) = -5$$
$$x = -1$$

The solution set is $\{(-1, 2, -1)\}$.

14. Add the first two equations. Multiply $x - 2y + 5z = 17$ by 2 to get $2x - 4y + 10z = 34$. Add the result to the second equation.

$$
\begin{array}{ll}
3x - 4y + z = 19 & 2x - 4y + 10z = 34 \\
2x + 4y + z = 0 & 2x + 4y + z = 0 \\
\hline
5x \quad + 2z = 19 & 4x \quad + 11z = 34
\end{array}
$$

Multiply $5x + 2z = 19$ by -4 and multiply $4x + 11z = 34$ by 5. Add the results.

$$-4(5x + 2z) = -4(19)$$
$$5(4x + 11z) = 5(34)$$

$$-20x - 8z = -76$$
$$20x + 55z = 170$$
$$47z = 94$$
$$z = 2$$

Use $z = 2$ in $5x + 2z = 19$ to find x.

$$5x + 2(2) = 19$$
$$5x = 15$$
$$x = 3$$

Use $x = 3$ and $z = 2$ in $x - 2y + 5z = 17$ to find y.

$$3 - 2y + 5(2) = 17$$
$$-2y + 13 = 17$$
$$-2y = 4$$
$$y = -2$$

The solution set is $\{(3, -2, 2)\}$.

15. Multiply the first equation by -2 and add the result to the last equation.

$$-4x + 10y - 4z = -32$$
$$4x - 3y + 4z = 18$$
$$7y = -14$$
$$y = -2$$

Multiply the first equation by 3 and the second by 2 and add the results.

$$6x - 15y + 6z = 48$$
$$6x + 4y - 6z = -38$$
$$12x - 11y = 10$$

Use $y = -2$ in the last equation to find x.

$$12x - 11(-2) = 10$$
$$12x = -12$$
$$x = -1$$

Use $x = -1$ and $y = -2$ in $2x - 5y + 2z = 16$.

$$2(-1) - 5(-2) + 2z = 16$$
$$2z = 8$$
$$z = 4$$

The solution set is $\{(-1, -2, 4)\}$.

16. Multiply the second equation by 2 and add the result to the first equation.

$$-2x + 3y - 4z = 3$$
$$6x - 10y + 4z = 8$$
$$4x - 7y = 11$$

Multiply the second equation by 3 and the third equation by 2 and add the results.

$$9x - 15y + 6z = 12$$
$$-8x + 4y - 6z = 0$$
$$x - 11y = 12$$

Multiply $x - 11y = 12$ by -4 to get $-4x + 44y = -48$. Add this result to $4x - 7y = 11$.

$$-4x + 44y = -48$$
$$4x - 7y = 11$$
$$37y = -37$$
$$y = -1$$

Use $y = -1$ in $4x - 7y = 11$ to find x.

$$4x - 7(-1) = 11$$
$$4x + 7 = 11$$
$$4x = 4$$
$$x = 1$$

Use $x = 1$ and $y = -1$ in $-2x + 3y - 4z = 3$ to find z.

$$-2(1) + 3(-1) - 4z = 3$$
$$-5 - 4z = 3$$
$$-4z = 8$$
$$z = -2$$

The solution set is $\{(1, -1, -2)\}$.

17. If we add the last two equations we get $x + 2y = 7$. Multiply the first equation by -1 to get $-x - y = -4$. Add these two equations.

$$x + 2y = 7$$
$$\underline{-x - y = -4}$$
$$y = 3$$

Use $y = 3$ in $x + y = 4$ to get $x = 1$. Use $y = 3$ in $y - z = -2$.

$$3 - z = -2$$
$$5 = z$$

The solution set is $\{(1, 3, 5)\}$.

18. Add the first and second equation to eliminate y. Add the second and third equation to eliminate y.

$$\begin{array}{ll} x + y - z = 0 & x - y \quad= -2 \\ \underline{x - y \quad= -2} & \underline{\quad\ y + z = 10} \\ 2x \quad - z = -2 & x \quad\ + z = 8 \end{array}$$

Add these two results to eliminate z.

$$2x - z = -2$$
$$\underline{x + z = 8}$$
$$3x \quad= 6$$
$$x = 2$$

Use $x = 2$ in $x - y = -2$ to find y.

$$2 - y = -2$$
$$-y = -4$$
$$y = 4$$

Use $y = 4$ in $y + z = 10$ to get $z = 6$. The solution set is $\{(2, 4, 6)\}$.

19. Multiply the first equation by -1 and add the result to the second equation.

$$-x - y \quad= -7$$
$$\underline{\quad\ y - z = -1}$$
$$-x \quad - z = -8$$

Add this result to the last equation.

$$-x - \ z = -8$$
$$\underline{x + 3z = 18}$$
$$2z = 10$$
$$z = 5$$

Use $z = 5$ in $x + 3z = 18$ to get $x + 15 = 18$ or $x = 3$. Use $x = 3$ in $x + y = 7$ to get $3 + y = 7$ or $y = 4$. The solution set is $\{(3, 4, 5)\}$.

20. Add the first and second equation to eliminate y.

$$2x - y \quad= -8$$
$$\underline{\quad\ y + 3z = 22}$$
$$2x \quad + 3z = 14$$

Multiply $x - z = -8$ by 3 to get $3x - 3z = -24$. Add this result to $2x + 3z = 14$.

$$3x - 3z = -24$$
$$\underline{2x + 3z = 14}$$
$$5x \quad= -10$$
$$x = -2$$

Use $x = -2$ in $x - z = -8$ to find z.

$$-2 - z = -8$$
$$-z = -6$$
$$z = 6$$

Use $x = -2$ in $2x - y = -8$ to find y.

$$2(-2) - y = -8$$
$$-4 - y = -8$$
$$-y = -4$$
$$y = 4$$

The solution set is $\{(-2, 4, 6)\}$.

21. Add the first two equations.

$$x - y + 2z = 3$$
$$\underline{2x + y - z = 5}$$
$$3x \quad + z = 8 \quad \text{A}$$

Multiply the second equation by 3 and add the result to the last equation.

$$6x + 3y - 3z = 15$$
$$\underline{3x - 3y + 6z = 4}$$
$$9x \quad + 3z = 19 \quad \text{B}$$

Multiply A by -3 and add the result to B.

$$-9x - 3z = -24$$
$$\underline{9x + 3z = 19}$$
$$0 = -5$$

Since the last equation is false no matter what values the variables have, the solution set is $\emptyset$.

22. Multiply the last equation $-x + 2y - 3z = -6$ by -2 to get $2x - 4y + 6z = 12$, the first equation. Multiply the last equation $-x + 2y - 3z = -6$ by -6 to get $6x - 12y + 18z = 36$, the second equation. Since the first and second equations are multiples of the last equation, the system is dependent. The solution set is $\{(x, y, z) \mid -x + 2y - 3z = -6\}$.

23. The second equation is the same as 3 times the first equation, and the third equation is the same as -4 times the first equation. So the system is a dependent system. All three equations are equivalent. The solution set is

$\{(x, y, z) \mid 3x - y + z = 5\}$.

24. Add the first and last equations.
$$\begin{array}{r} 4x - 2y - 2z = 5 \\ -4x + 2y + 2z = 6 \\ \hline 0 = 11 \end{array}$$
Since a false statement is the result of the addition, there is no solution to the system. The solution set is $\emptyset$.

25. Add the first and second equation to get $x + z = 11$. Multiply this equation by -2 and then add the result to the last equation.
$$\begin{array}{r} -2x - 2z = -22 \\ 2x + 2z = 7 \\ \hline 0 = -15 \end{array}$$
Since the last result is false, the solution set is $\emptyset$.

26. Multiply the first equation by 2 to get $4x - 2y = 12$. Add this result to the second equation.
$$\begin{array}{r} 4x - 2y \quad = 12 \\ 2y + z = -4 \\ \hline 4x \quad + z = 8 \end{array}$$
Multiply $4x + z = 8$ by -2 to get $-8x - 2z = -16$. Add the result to $8x + 2z = 3$.
$$\begin{array}{r} -8x - 2z = -16 \\ 8x + 2z = 3 \\ \hline 0 = -13 \end{array}$$
Since a false statement is the result of the addition, there is no solution to the system. The solution set is $\emptyset$.

27. Multiply the first equation by 300 to get $30x + 24y - 12z = 900$. Multiply the second equation by 6 to get $30x + 24y - 12z = 900$. Multiply the third equation by 100 to get $30x + 24y - 12z = 900$. Since all three of these equations are different forms of the same equation, the system is dependent. The solution set is
$\{(x, y, z) \mid 5x + 4y - 2z = 150\}$.

28. If we multiply the first equation by 50, we get $3x - 2y + 50z = 300$, which is the second equation. If we multiply the last equation by 100, we also get the second equation. So the three equations are equivalent. The solution set is $\{(x, y, z) \mid 3x - 2y + 50z = 300\}$.

29. Multiply the second equation by 10 and add the result to the first equation.
$$\begin{array}{r} 37x - 2y + 0.5z = 4.1 \\ 3x + 2y - 0.4z = 0.1 \\ \hline 40x \quad + 0.1z = 4.2 \quad \text{A} \end{array}$$
Multiply the second equation by 19 and add the result to the last equation.
$$\begin{array}{r} 70.3x - 3.8y + 0.95z = 7.79 \\ -2x + 3.8y - 2.1z = -3.26 \\ \hline 68.3x \quad - 1.15z = 4.53 \quad \text{B} \end{array}$$
Multiply equation A by 11.5 and add the result to equation B.
$$\begin{array}{r} 460x + 1.15z = 48.3 \\ 68.3x - 1.15z = 4.53 \\ \hline 528.3x \quad = 52.83 \\ x = 0.1 \end{array}$$
Use $x = 0.1$ in $40x + 0.1z = 4.2$.
$$\begin{array}{r} 40(0.1) + 0.1z = 4.2 \\ 0.1z = 0.2 \\ z = 2 \end{array}$$
Use $x = 0.1$ and $z = 2$ in $3x + 2y - 0.4z = 0.1$.
$$\begin{array}{r} 3(0.1) + 2y - 0.4(2) = 0.1 \\ 0.3 + 2y - 0.8 = 0.1 \\ 2y = 0.6 \\ y = 0.3 \end{array}$$
The solution set is $\{(0.1, 0.3, 2)\}$.

30. Multiply the second equation by -10 to get $-3x - 50y + 80z = 9.72$. Add this result to the first equation.
$$\begin{array}{r} 3x - 0.4y + 9z = 1.668 \\ -3x - 50y + 80z = 9.72 \\ \hline -50.4y + 89z = 11.388 \quad \text{A} \end{array}$$
Multiply the first equation by -5 and the last by 3 and add the results.
$$-5(3x - 0.4y + 9z) = -5(1.668)$$
$$3(5x - 4y - 8z) = 3(1.8)$$
$$\begin{array}{r} -15x + 2y - 45z = -8.34 \\ 15x - 12y - 24z = 5.4 \\ \hline -10y - 69z = -2.94 \quad \text{B} \end{array}$$
Multiply A by 10 and B by -50.4.
$$\begin{array}{r} -504y + 890z = 113.88 \\ 504y + 3477.6z = 148.176 \\ \hline 4367.6z = 262.056 \\ z = 0.06 \end{array}$$

Use $z = 0.06$ in $-10y - 69z = -2.94$ to find y.

$$-10y - 69(0.06) = -2.94$$
$$-10y - 4.14 = -2.94$$
$$-10y = 1.2$$
$$y = -0.12$$

Use $y = -0.12$ and $z = 0.06$ in $5x - 4y - 8z = 1.8$ to find x.

$$5x - 4(-0.12) - 8(0.06) = 1.8$$
$$5x = 1.8$$
$$x = 0.36$$

The solution set is $\{(0.36, -0.12, 0.06)\}$.

31. Let $x =$ her investment in stocks, $y =$ her investment in bonds, and $z =$ her investment in mutual funds. We can write 3 equations concerning x, y, and z.

$$x + y + z = 12000$$
$$0.10x + 0.08y + 0.12z = 1230$$
$$x + y = z$$

Substitute $z = x + y$ into the first equation.

$$x + y + x + y = 12000$$
$$2x + 2y = 12000$$
$$x + y = 6000 \quad \text{A}$$

Substitute $z = x + y$ into the second equation.

$$0.10x + 0.08y + 0.12(x + y) = 1230$$
$$0.22x + 0.20y = 1230$$
$$-5(0.22x + 0.20y) = -5(1230)$$
$$-1.1x - y = -6150 \quad \text{B}$$

Add equations A and B.

$$x + y = 6000$$
$$\underline{-1.1x - y = -6150}$$
$$-0.1x = -150$$
$$x = 1500$$

Use $x = 1500$ in $x + y = 6000$ to get $y = 4500$. Since $z = x + y$, we must have $z = 6000$. So Ann invested \$1500 in stocks, \$4500 in bonds, and \$6000 in a mutual fund.

32. Let $x =$ the amount invested at 5%, $y =$ the amount invested at 6%, and $z =$ the amount invested at 7%. Write three equations concerning x, y, and z.

$$x + y + z = 60{,}000$$
$$0.05x + 0.06y + 0.07z = 3760$$
$$z = 2x$$

Substitute $z = 2x$ into each of the first two equations to eliminate z.

$$x + y + 2x = 60{,}000$$
$$0.05x + 0.06y + 0.07(2x) = 3760$$

$$3x + y = 60{,}000$$
$$0.19x + 0.06y = 3760$$

Multiply $3x + y = 60{,}000$ by -0.06 and add the result to $0.19x + 0.06y = 3760$.

$$-0.18x - 0.06y = -3600$$
$$\underline{0.19x + 0.06y = 3760}$$
$$0.01x = 160$$
$$x = 16{,}000$$

Since $z = 2x$, we have $z = 32{,}000$. Since $x + y + z = 60{,}000$, we get

$$16{,}000 + y + 32{,}000 = 60{,}000$$

or $y = 12{,}000$. He invested \$16,000 at 5%, \$12,000 at 6%, and \$32,000 at 7%.

33. Let $x =$ the price of one cup of coffee, $y =$ the price of one doughnut, and $z =$ the amount of the tip. We can write an equation for each day.

$$2x + y + z = 170$$
$$x + 2y + z = 165$$
$$x + y + z = 130$$

Multiply the first equation by -1 and add the result to the second and the third equation.

$$\begin{array}{ll} -2x - y - z = -170 & -2x - y - z = -170 \\ \underline{x + 2y + z = 165} & \underline{x + y + z = 130} \\ -x + y = -5 & -x = -40 \\ & x = 40 \end{array}$$

Use $x = 40$ in the $-x + y = -5$.

$$-40 + y = -5$$
$$y = 35$$

Use $x = 40$ and $y = 35$ in $x + y + z = 130$.

$$40 + 35 + z = 130$$
$$z = 55$$

The price of coffee is \$0.40, the price of a doughnut is \$0.35, and the tip is always \$0.55.

34. Let $x =$ Anna's weight, $y =$ Bob's weight, and $z =$ Chris's weight. We are given three equations.

$$x + y = 226$$
$$y + z = 210$$
$$x + z = 200$$

From the first equation we get $y = 226 - x$. Substitute this equation into the second equation to eliminate y.

$$226 - x + z = 210$$
$$-x + z = -16$$
Add this last equation to $x + z = 200$ to eliminate x.
$$-x + z = -16$$
$$\underline{x + z = 200}$$
$$2z = 184$$
$$z = 92$$
If $z = 92$ and $x + z = 200$, we get $x = 108$. If $z = 92$ and $y + z = 210$, we get $y = 118$. So Anna weighs 108 pounds, Bob weighs 118 pounds, and Chris weighs 92 pounds.

35. Let $x =$ the price of a banana, $y =$ the price of an apple, and $z =$ the price of an orange. We can write 3 equations.
$$3x + 2y + z = 180$$
$$4x + 3y + 3z = 305$$
$$6x + 5y + 4z = 465$$
Multiply the first equation by -3 and add the result to the second equation.
$$-9x - 6y - 3z = -540$$
$$\underline{4x + 3y + 3z = 305}$$
$$-5x - 3y \quad = -235 \quad \text{A}$$
Multiply the first equation by -4 and add the result to the third equation.
$$-12x - 8y - 4z = -720$$
$$\underline{6x + 5y + 4z = 465}$$
$$-6x - 3y \quad = -255$$
$$6x + 3y \quad = 255 \quad \text{B}$$
Add equation B and equation A.
$$6x + 3y = 255$$
$$\underline{-5x - 3y = -235}$$
$$x \quad = 20$$
Use $x = 20$ in $6x + 3y = 255$ to find y.
$$6(20) + 3y = 255$$
$$3y = 135$$
$$y = 45$$
Use $x = 20$ and $y = 45$ in $3x + 2y + z = 180$.
$$3(20) + 2(45) + z = 180$$
$$z = 30$$
The price of one banana is \$0.20, one apple is \$0.45, and one orange is \$0.30. So the lunch-box -special should sell for \$0.95.

36. Let $x =$ Edwin's age, $y =$ his father's age and $z =$ his grandfather's age. Since their average age is 53, we can write

$$\frac{x + y + z}{3} = 53$$
or $\qquad x + y + z = 159.$
We can also write
$$\tfrac{1}{2}z + \tfrac{1}{3}y + \tfrac{1}{4}x = 65$$
or $\quad 12\left(\tfrac{1}{2}z + \tfrac{1}{3}y + \tfrac{1}{4}x\right) = 12(65)$
or $\quad 6z + 4y + 3x = 780.$
Four years ago Edwin was $x - 4$ years old and his grandfather was $z - 4$ years old. Since 4 years ago the grandfather was 4 times as old as Edwin, we can write
$$z - 4 = 4(x - 4)$$
$$z - 4 = 4x - 16$$
$$z = 4x - 12.$$
Substitute $z = 4x - 12$ into the two equations above.
$$x + y + 4x - 12 = 159$$
$$6(4x - 12) + 4y + 3x = 780$$

$$5x + y = 171$$
$$27x + 4y = 852$$
Substitute $y = 171 - 5x$ into $27x + 4y = 852$.
$$27x + 4(171 - 5x) = 852$$
$$7x + 684 = 852$$
$$7x = 168$$
$$x = 24$$
Since $z = 4x - 12$ we have $z = 84$. Since $x + y + z = 159$, we have $24 + y + 84 = 159$, or $y = 51$. So Edwin is 24, his father is 51, and his grandfather is 84 years old.

37. Let $x =$ the weight of a can of soup, $y =$ the weight of a can of tuna, and $z =$ the constant error. We can write three equations.
$$x + y + z = 24$$
$$4x + 3y = 80$$
$$2y + z = 18$$
Multiply the third equation by -1 and add the result to the first equation.
$$-2y - z = -18$$
$$\underline{x + y + z = 24}$$
$$x - y \quad = 6$$
Multiply $x - y = 6$ by 3 and add the result to the second equation.
$$3x - 3y = 18$$
$$\underline{4x + 3y = 80}$$
$$7x \quad = 98$$
$$x = 14$$

Use $x = 14$ in $x - y = 6$ to get $y = 8$. Use $x = 14$ and $y = 8$ in $x + y + z = 24$ to get $z = 2$. So a can of soup weighs 14 ounces, a can of tuna weighs 8 ounces, and the scale has a constant error of 2 ounces.

38. Let $x =$ the one's digit, $y =$ the ten's digit, and $z =$ the hundred's digit. Since the sum of the digits is 11, $x + y + z = 11$. Since the hundreds digit plus twice the tens digit is equal to the units digit, $z + 2y = x$. The value of the number is $100z + 10y + x$. If the digits are reversed, then the one's digit and the hundreds digit change places. So the new value is $z + 10y + 100x$. Since the new number is 46 more than 5 times the old number, we can write the following equation.
$$z + 10y + 100x = 5(100z + 10y + x) + 46$$
$$z + 10y + 100x = 500z + 50y + 5x + 46$$
$$95x - 40y - 499z = 46$$

The system of 3 equations is written as follows.
$$95x - 40y - 499z = 46$$
$$x + y + z = 11$$
$$x = z + 2y$$
Substitute $x = z + 2y$ into the first two equations to eliminate x.
$$95(z + 2y) - 40y - 499 = 46$$
$$z + 2y + y + z = 11$$

$$95z + 150y = 545$$
$$2z + 3y = 11$$
Multiply the second equation by -50.
$$95z + 150y = 545$$
$$\underline{-100z - 150y = -550}$$
$$-5z \qquad = -5$$
$$z = 1$$
Use $z = 1$ in $2z + 3y = 11$ to get $2 + 3y = 11$, or $y = 3$. Use $z = 1$ and $y = 3$ in $x = z + 2y$ to get $x = 1 + 2(3) = 7$. So the one's digit is 7, the ten's digit is 3, and the hundred's digit is 1. The number is 137.

39. Let $x =$ her income from teaching, $y =$ her income from house painting, and $z =$ her royalties.
$$x + y + z = 48000$$
$$x - y = 6000$$

$$z = \tfrac{1}{7}(x + y)$$
The last equation can be written as $x + y = 7z$. Replacing $x + y$ in the first equation by $7z$ gives us $7z + z = 48000$, or $z = 6000$. If $z = 6000$, then $x + y = 42000$. Add $x + y = 42000$ and the second equation.
$$x + y = 42000$$
$$\underline{x - y = 6000}$$
$$2x \qquad = 48000$$
$$x = 24000$$
Use $x = 24000$ in $x - y = 6000$ to get $y = 18000$. So she made \$24,000 teaching, \$18,000 house painting, and \$6,000 from royalties.

40. Let $x =$ the number of nickels, $y =$ the number of dimes, and $z =$ the number of quarters. Since he has 27 coins altogether, $x + y + z = 27$. Since the value of the coins in cents is 225, we have $5x + 10y + 25z = 225$. Since twice as many nickels with half as many dimes and the same number of quarters is worth \$2.50, we can write the final equation.
$$5(2x) + 10\left(\tfrac{y}{2}\right) + 25z = 250$$
$$10x + 5y + 25z = 250$$
The system of equations follows.
$$x + y + z = 27$$
$$5x + 10y + 25z = 225$$
$$10x + 5y + 25z = 250$$
Multiply the first equation by -5 and add the result to the second equation.
$$-5x - 5y - 5z = -135$$
$$\underline{5x + 10y + 25z = 225}$$
$$5y + 20z = 90 \quad \text{A}$$
Multiply the first equation by -10 and add the result to the third equation.
$$-10x - 10y - 10z = -270$$
$$\underline{10x + 5y + 25z = 250}$$
$$-5y + 15z = -20 \quad \text{B}$$

Add equations A and B.
$$5y + 20z = 90$$
$$\underline{-5y + 15z = -20}$$
$$35z = 70$$
$$z = 2$$
Use $z = 2$ in $5y + 20z = 90$.

144

$$5y + 20(2) = 90$$
$$5y = 50$$
$$y = 10$$

Use $z = 2$ and $y = 10$ in $x + y + z = 27$ to find that $x = 15$. So Harry has 15 nickels, 10 dimes, and 2 quarters.

4.4 WARM-UPS

1. True
2. True.
3. True, replace R_2 of (a) by $R_1 + R_2$ to get matrix (b).
4. False, because matrix (c) corresponds to an inconsistent system and (d) corresponds to a dependent system.
5. True, because the last row represents the equation $0 = 7$.
6. False, replace R_2 by $2R_1 + R_2$ to get $0 = -3$ which is inconsistent.
7. False, the system corresponding to (d) consists of two equations equivalent to $x + 3y = 5$.
8. False, the augmented matrix is a 2×3 matrix.
9. True.
10. False, it means to interchange R_1 and R_2.

4.4 EXERCISES

1. A matrix is a rectangular array of numbers.
2. A row runs horizontally and a column runs vertically.
3. The order of a matrix is the number of rows and columns.
4. An element of a matrix is a number that occupies a position in the matrix.
5. An augmented matrix is a matrix where the entries in the first column are the coefficients of x, the entries in the second column are the coefficients of y, and the entries in the third column are the constants from a system of two linear equations in two unknowns.
6. The goal of Gaussian elimination is to get ones on the diagonal.
7. 2×2
8. 2×3

9. 3×2
10. 3×3
11. 3×1
12. 1×3
13. Use the coefficients 2 and -3, and the constant 9 as the first row. Use the coefficients -3 and 1, and the constant -1 as the second row.
$$\begin{bmatrix} 2 & -3 & 9 \\ -3 & 1 & -1 \end{bmatrix}$$

14. $\begin{bmatrix} 1 & -1 & 4 \\ 2 & 1 & 3 \end{bmatrix}$

15. Use the coefficients 1, -1, and 1, and the constant 1 as the first row. Use the coefficients 1, 1, and -2, and the constant 3 as the second row. Use the coefficients 0, 1, and -3, and the constant 4 as the third row.
$$\begin{bmatrix} 1 & -1 & 1 & 1 \\ 1 & 1 & -2 & 3 \\ 0 & 1 & -3 & 4 \end{bmatrix}$$

16. $\begin{bmatrix} 1 & 1 & 0 & 2 \\ 0 & 1 & -3 & 5 \\ -3 & 0 & 2 & 8 \end{bmatrix}$

17. The entries in the first row $(5, 1, -1)$ represent the equation $5x + y = -1$. The entries in the second row $(2, -3, 0)$ represent the equation $2x - 3y = 0$. So the matrix represents the following system.
$$5x + y = -1$$
$$2x - 3y = 0$$

18. The entries in the first row $(1, 0, 4)$ represent the equation $x = 4$. The entries in the second row $(0, 1, -3)$ represent the equation $y = -3$. So the matrix corresponds to the following system.
$$x = 4$$
$$y = -3$$

19. The entries in the first row $(1, 0, 0, 6)$ represent the equation $x = 6$. The entries in the second row $(-1, 0, 1, -3)$ represent the equation $-x + z = -3$. The entries in the third row $(1, 1, 0, 1)$ represent the equation

$x + y = 1$. So the matrix represents the following system.

$$x = 6$$
$$-x + z = -3$$
$$x + y = 1$$

20. The entries in the first row $(1, 0, 4, 3)$ represent the equation $x + 4z = 3$. The entries in the second row $(0, 2, 1, -1)$ represent the equation $2y + z = -1$. The entries in the third row $(1, 1, 1, 1)$ represent the equation $x + y + z = 1$. So the matrix represents the following system.

$$x + 4z = 3$$
$$2y + z = -1$$
$$x + y + z = 1$$

21. $R_1 \leftrightarrow R_2$

22. $-3R_1 + R_2 \to R_2$

23. $\frac{1}{5}R_2 \to R_2$

24. $R_2 + R_1 \to R_1$

25. $\begin{bmatrix} 1 & 1 & 3 \\ -3 & 1 & -1 \end{bmatrix}$

$\begin{bmatrix} 1 & 1 & 3 \\ 0 & 4 & 8 \end{bmatrix}$ $3R_1 + R_2 \to R_2$

$\begin{bmatrix} 1 & 1 & 3 \\ 0 & 1 & 2 \end{bmatrix}$ $R_2 \div 4 \to R_2$

$\begin{bmatrix} 1 & 0 & 1 \\ 0 & 1 & 2 \end{bmatrix}$ $-R_2 + R_1 \to R_1$

The solution set is $\{(1, 2)\}$.

26. $\begin{bmatrix} 1 & -1 & -1 \\ 2 & -1 & 2 \end{bmatrix}$

$\begin{bmatrix} 1 & -1 & -1 \\ 0 & 1 & 4 \end{bmatrix}$ $-2R_1 + R_2 \to R_2$

$\begin{bmatrix} 1 & 0 & 3 \\ 0 & 1 & 4 \end{bmatrix}$ $R_2 + R_1 \to R_1$

The solution set is $\{(3, 4)\}$

27. $\begin{bmatrix} 2 & -1 & 3 \\ 1 & 1 & 9 \end{bmatrix}$

$\begin{bmatrix} 1 & 1 & 9 \\ 2 & -1 & 3 \end{bmatrix}$ $R_2 \to R_1$ and $R_1 \to R_2$

$\begin{bmatrix} 1 & 1 & 9 \\ 0 & -3 & -15 \end{bmatrix}$ $-2R_1 + R_2 \to R_2$

$\begin{bmatrix} 1 & 1 & 9 \\ 0 & 1 & 5 \end{bmatrix}$ $R_2 \div (-3) \to R_2$

$\begin{bmatrix} 1 & 0 & 4 \\ 0 & 1 & 5 \end{bmatrix}$ $-R_2 + R_1 \to R_1$

The solution set is $\{(4, 5)\}$.

28. $\begin{bmatrix} 3 & -4 & -1 \\ 1 & -1 & 0 \end{bmatrix}$

$\begin{bmatrix} 1 & -1 & 0 \\ 3 & -4 & -1 \end{bmatrix}$ $R_2 \to R_1$ and $R_1 \to R_2$

$\begin{bmatrix} 1 & -1 & 0 \\ 0 & -1 & -1 \end{bmatrix}$ $-3R_1 + R_2 \to R_2$

$\begin{bmatrix} 1 & -1 & 0 \\ 0 & 1 & 1 \end{bmatrix}$ $R_2 \div (-1) \to R_2$

$\begin{bmatrix} 1 & 0 & 1 \\ 0 & 1 & 1 \end{bmatrix}$ $R_2 + R_1 \to R_1$

The solution set is $\{(1, 1)\}$.

29. $\begin{bmatrix} 3 & -1 & 4 \\ 2 & 1 & 1 \end{bmatrix}$

$\begin{bmatrix} 1 & -2 & 3 \\ 2 & 1 & 1 \end{bmatrix}$ $-R_2 + R_1 \to R_1$

$\begin{bmatrix} 1 & -2 & 3 \\ 0 & 5 & -5 \end{bmatrix}$ $-2R_1 + R_2 \to R_2$

$\begin{bmatrix} 1 & -2 & 3 \\ 0 & 1 & -1 \end{bmatrix}$ $R_2 \div 5 \to R_2$

$\begin{bmatrix} 1 & 0 & 1 \\ 0 & 1 & -1 \end{bmatrix}$ $2R_2 + R_1 \to R_1$

The solution set is $\{(1, -1)\}$

30. $\begin{bmatrix} 2 & -1 & -3 \\ 3 & 1 & -2 \end{bmatrix}$

$\begin{bmatrix} 2 & -1 & -3 \\ 1 & 2 & 1 \end{bmatrix}$ $\quad -R_1 + R_2 \rightarrow R_2$

$\begin{bmatrix} 1 & 2 & 1 \\ 2 & -1 & -3 \end{bmatrix}$ $\quad R_1 \leftrightarrow R_2$

$\begin{bmatrix} 1 & 2 & 1 \\ 0 & -5 & -5 \end{bmatrix}$ $\quad -2R_1 + R_2 \rightarrow R_2$

$\begin{bmatrix} 1 & 2 & 1 \\ 0 & 1 & 1 \end{bmatrix}$ $\quad R_2 \div (-5) \rightarrow R_2$

$\begin{bmatrix} 1 & 0 & -1 \\ 0 & 1 & 1 \end{bmatrix}$ $\quad -2R_2 + R_1 \rightarrow R_1$

The solution set is $\{(-1, 1)\}$.

31. $\begin{bmatrix} 6 & -7 & 0 \\ 2 & 1 & 20 \end{bmatrix}$

$\begin{bmatrix} 0 & -10 & -60 \\ 2 & 1 & 20 \end{bmatrix}$ $\quad -3R_2 + R_1 \rightarrow R_1$

$\begin{bmatrix} 0 & 1 & 6 \\ 2 & 1 & 20 \end{bmatrix}$ $\quad R_1 \div (-10) \rightarrow R_1$

$\begin{bmatrix} 2 & 1 & 20 \\ 0 & 1 & 6 \end{bmatrix}$ $\quad R_1 \leftrightarrow R_2$

$\begin{bmatrix} 2 & 0 & 14 \\ 0 & 1 & 6 \end{bmatrix}$ $\quad -R_2 + R_1 \rightarrow R_1$

$\begin{bmatrix} 1 & 0 & 7 \\ 0 & 1 & 6 \end{bmatrix}$ $\quad R_1 \div 2 \rightarrow R_1$

The solution set is $\{(7, 6)\}$.

32. $\begin{bmatrix} 2 & 1 & 11 \\ 2 & -1 & 1 \end{bmatrix}$

$\begin{bmatrix} 2 & 1 & 11 \\ 0 & -2 & -10 \end{bmatrix}$ $\quad -R_1 + R_2 \rightarrow R_2$

$\begin{bmatrix} 2 & 1 & 11 \\ 0 & 1 & 5 \end{bmatrix}$ $\quad R_2 \div (-2) \rightarrow R_2$

$\begin{bmatrix} 2 & 0 & 6 \\ 0 & 1 & 5 \end{bmatrix}$ $\quad -R_2 + R_1 \rightarrow R_1$

$\begin{bmatrix} 1 & 0 & 3 \\ 0 & 1 & 5 \end{bmatrix}$ $\quad R_1 \div 2 \rightarrow R_1$

The solution set is $\{(3, 5)\}$.

33. $\begin{bmatrix} 2 & -3 & 4 \\ -2 & 3 & 5 \end{bmatrix}$

$\begin{bmatrix} 2 & -3 & 4 \\ 0 & 0 & 9 \end{bmatrix}$ $\quad R_1 + R_2 \rightarrow R_2$

Since the second row represents the equation $0 = 9$, there is no solution to the system.

34. $\begin{bmatrix} 1 & -3 & 8 \\ 2 & -6 & 1 \end{bmatrix}$

$\begin{bmatrix} 1 & -3 & 8 \\ 0 & 0 & -15 \end{bmatrix}$ $\quad -2R_1 + R_2 \rightarrow R_2$

Since the second row represents the equation $0 = -15$, there is no solution to the system.

35. $\begin{bmatrix} 1 & 2 & 1 \\ 3 & 6 & 3 \end{bmatrix}$

$\begin{bmatrix} 1 & 2 & 1 \\ 0 & 0 & 0 \end{bmatrix}$ $\quad -3R_1 + R_2 \rightarrow R_2$

Since the system is equivalent to the single equation $x + 2y = 1$, the equations are dependent and the solution set is $\{(x, y) \mid x + 2y = 1\}$.

36. $\begin{bmatrix} 2 & -3 & 1 \\ -6 & 9 & -3 \end{bmatrix}$

$\begin{bmatrix} 2 & -3 & 1 \\ 0 & 0 & 0 \end{bmatrix}$ $\quad 3R_1 + R_2 \rightarrow R_2$

Since the system is equivalent to the single equation $2x - 3y = 1$, the equations are dependent and the solution set is $\{(x, y) \mid 2x - 3y = 1\}$.

37.
$$\begin{bmatrix} 1 & 1 & 1 & 6 \\ 1 & -1 & 1 & 2 \\ 0 & 2 & -1 & 1 \end{bmatrix}$$

$$\begin{bmatrix} 1 & 1 & 1 & 6 \\ 0 & -2 & 0 & -4 \\ 0 & 2 & -1 & 1 \end{bmatrix} \quad -R_1 + R_2 \to R_2$$

$$\begin{bmatrix} 1 & 1 & 1 & 6 \\ 0 & 1 & 0 & 2 \\ 0 & 2 & -1 & 1 \end{bmatrix} \quad R_2 \div (-2) \to R_2$$

$$-R_2 + R_1 \to R_1$$

$$\begin{bmatrix} 1 & 0 & 1 & 4 \\ 0 & 1 & 0 & 2 \\ 0 & 0 & -1 & -3 \end{bmatrix}$$

$$-2R_2 + R_3 \to R_3$$

$$\begin{bmatrix} 1 & 0 & 1 & 4 \\ 0 & 1 & 0 & 2 \\ 0 & 0 & 1 & 3 \end{bmatrix}$$

$$R_3 \div (-1) \to R_3$$

$$\begin{bmatrix} 1 & 0 & 0 & 1 \\ 0 & 1 & 0 & 2 \\ 0 & 0 & 1 & 3 \end{bmatrix} \quad -R_3 + R_1 \to R_1$$

The solution set is $\{(1, 2, 3)\}$.

38.
$$\begin{bmatrix} 1 & -1 & -1 & 0 \\ -1 & -1 & 1 & -4 \\ -1 & 1 & -1 & -2 \end{bmatrix}$$

$$\begin{bmatrix} 1 & -1 & -1 & 0 \\ 0 & -2 & 0 & -4 \\ 0 & 0 & -2 & -2 \end{bmatrix} \quad \begin{array}{l} R_1 + R_2 \to R_2 \\[6pt] R_1 + R_3 \to R_3 \end{array}$$

$$\begin{bmatrix} 1 & -1 & -1 & 0 \\ 0 & 1 & 0 & 2 \\ 0 & 0 & 1 & 1 \end{bmatrix} \quad \begin{array}{l} R_2 \div (-2) \to R_2 \\[6pt] R_3 \div (-2) \to R_3 \end{array}$$

$$\begin{bmatrix} 1 & 0 & -1 & 2 \\ 0 & 1 & 0 & 2 \\ 0 & 0 & 1 & 1 \end{bmatrix} \quad R_2 + R_1 \to R_1$$

$$\begin{bmatrix} 1 & 0 & 0 & 3 \\ 0 & 1 & 0 & 2 \\ 0 & 0 & 1 & 1 \end{bmatrix} \quad R_3 + R_1 \to R_1$$

The solution set is $\{(3, 2, 1)\}$.

39.
$$\begin{bmatrix} 2 & 1 & 1 & 4 \\ 1 & 1 & -1 & 1 \\ 1 & -1 & 2 & 2 \end{bmatrix}$$

$$\begin{bmatrix} 1 & 1 & -1 & 1 \\ 2 & 1 & 1 & 4 \\ 1 & -1 & 2 & 2 \end{bmatrix} \quad R_1 \leftrightarrow R_2$$

$$\begin{bmatrix} 1 & 1 & -1 & 1 \\ 0 & -1 & 3 & 2 \\ 0 & -2 & 3 & 1 \end{bmatrix} \quad \begin{array}{l} -2R_1 + R_2 \to R_2 \\[6pt] -R_1 + R_3 \to R_3 \end{array}$$

$$\begin{bmatrix} 1 & 1 & -1 & 1 \\ 0 & 1 & -3 & -2 \\ 0 & -2 & 3 & 1 \end{bmatrix} \quad -1 \cdot R_2 \to R_2$$

$$\begin{bmatrix} 1 & 0 & 2 & 3 \\ 0 & 1 & -3 & -2 \\ 0 & 0 & -3 & -3 \end{bmatrix} \quad \begin{array}{l} -1 \cdot R_2 + R_1 \to R_1 \\[6pt] 2R_2 + R_3 \to R_3 \end{array}$$

$$\begin{bmatrix} 1 & 0 & 2 & 3 \\ 0 & 1 & -3 & -2 \\ 0 & 0 & 1 & 1 \end{bmatrix} \quad -1 \cdot R_3 \to R_3$$

$$\begin{array}{l} -2R_3 + R_1 \to R_1 \\[6pt] 3R_3 + R_2 \to R_2 \end{array}$$

$$\begin{bmatrix} 1 & 0 & 0 & 1 \\ 0 & 1 & 0 & 1 \\ 0 & 0 & 1 & 1 \end{bmatrix}$$

The solution set is $\{(1, 1, 1)\}$.

40. Write the second equation first.

$$\begin{bmatrix} 1 & 1 & 1 & 4 \\ 3 & -1 & 0 & 1 \\ 1 & 0 & 2 & 3 \end{bmatrix}$$

$$\begin{bmatrix} 1 & 1 & 1 & 4 \\ 0 & -4 & -3 & -11 \\ 0 & -1 & 1 & -1 \end{bmatrix} \quad \begin{array}{l} -3R_1 + R_2 \rightarrow R_2 \\[1em] -R_1 + R_3 \rightarrow R_3 \end{array}$$

$$\begin{bmatrix} 1 & 1 & 1 & 4 \\ 0 & -1 & 1 & -1 \\ 0 & -4 & -3 & -11 \end{bmatrix} \quad R_3 \leftrightarrow R_2$$

$$\begin{bmatrix} 1 & 1 & 1 & 4 \\ 0 & 1 & -1 & 1 \\ 0 & -4 & -3 & -11 \end{bmatrix} \quad -R_2 \rightarrow R_2$$

$$\begin{bmatrix} 1 & 0 & 2 & 3 \\ 0 & 1 & -1 & 1 \\ 0 & 0 & -7 & -7 \end{bmatrix} \quad \begin{array}{l} -R_2 + R_1 \rightarrow R_1 \\[1em] 4R_2 + R_3 \rightarrow R_3 \end{array}$$

$$\begin{bmatrix} 1 & 0 & 2 & 3 \\ 0 & 1 & -1 & 1 \\ 0 & 0 & 1 & 1 \end{bmatrix} \quad R_3 \div (-7) \rightarrow R_3$$

$$\begin{bmatrix} 1 & 0 & 0 & 1 \\ 0 & 1 & 0 & 2 \\ 0 & 0 & 1 & 1 \end{bmatrix} \quad \begin{array}{l} -2R_3 + R_1 \rightarrow R_1 \\[1em] R_3 + R_2 \rightarrow R_2 \end{array}$$

The solution set is $\{(1, 2, 1)\}$.

41.
$$\begin{bmatrix} 1 & 1 & -3 & 3 \\ 2 & -1 & 1 & 0 \\ 1 & -1 & 1 & -1 \end{bmatrix}$$

$$\begin{bmatrix} 1 & 1 & -3 & 3 \\ 0 & -3 & 7 & -6 \\ 0 & -2 & 4 & -4 \end{bmatrix} \quad \begin{array}{l} -2R_1 + R_2 \rightarrow R_2 \\[1em] -R_1 + R_3 \rightarrow R_3 \end{array}$$

$$\begin{bmatrix} 1 & 1 & -3 & 3 \\ 0 & 1 & -1 & 2 \\ 0 & -2 & 4 & -4 \end{bmatrix} \quad -2R_3 + R_2 \rightarrow R_2$$

$$\begin{bmatrix} 1 & 0 & -2 & 1 \\ 0 & 1 & -1 & 2 \\ 0 & 0 & 2 & 0 \end{bmatrix} \quad \begin{array}{l} -R_2 + R_1 \rightarrow R_1 \\[1em] 2R_2 + R_3 \rightarrow R_3 \end{array}$$

$$\begin{bmatrix} 1 & 0 & -2 & 1 \\ 0 & 1 & -1 & 2 \\ 0 & 0 & 1 & 0 \end{bmatrix} \quad R_3 \div 2 \rightarrow R_3$$

$$\begin{bmatrix} 1 & 0 & 0 & 1 \\ 0 & 1 & 0 & 2 \\ 0 & 0 & 1 & 0 \end{bmatrix} \quad \begin{array}{l} 2R_2 + R_1 \rightarrow R_1 \\[1em] R_3 + R_2 \rightarrow R_2 \end{array}$$

The solution set is $\{(1, 2, 0)\}$.

42.
$$\begin{bmatrix} 1 & -1 & -1 & 0 \\ -1 & -1 & 2 & -1 \\ -1 & 1 & -2 & -3 \end{bmatrix}$$

$$\begin{bmatrix} 1 & -1 & -1 & 0 \\ 0 & -2 & 1 & -1 \\ 0 & 0 & -3 & -3 \end{bmatrix} \quad \begin{array}{l} R_1 + R_2 \rightarrow R_2 \\[1em] R_1 + R_3 \rightarrow R_3 \end{array}$$

$$\begin{bmatrix} 1 & -1 & -1 & 0 \\ 0 & -2 & 1 & -1 \\ 0 & 0 & 1 & 1 \end{bmatrix} \quad R_3 \div (-3) \rightarrow R_3$$

$$\begin{bmatrix} 1 & -1 & 0 & 1 \\ 0 & -2 & 0 & -2 \\ 0 & 0 & 1 & 1 \end{bmatrix} \quad \begin{array}{l} R_3 + R_1 \rightarrow R_1 \\[1em] -R_3 + R_2 \rightarrow R_2 \end{array}$$

$$\begin{bmatrix} 1 & -1 & 0 & 1 \\ 0 & 1 & 0 & 1 \\ 0 & 0 & 1 & 1 \end{bmatrix} \quad R_2 \div (-2) \rightarrow R_2$$

$$\begin{bmatrix} 1 & 0 & 0 & 2 \\ 0 & 1 & 0 & 1 \\ 0 & 0 & 1 & 1 \end{bmatrix} \quad R_2 + R_1 \rightarrow R_1$$

The solution set is $\{(2, 1, 1)\}$.

43. $\begin{bmatrix} 1 & -1 & -4 & -3 \\ -1 & 3 & 1 & 0 \\ 1 & 1 & 2 & 3 \end{bmatrix}$

$\begin{bmatrix} 1 & -1 & -4 & -3 \\ 0 & 2 & -3 & -3 \\ 0 & 2 & 6 & 6 \end{bmatrix}$ $R_1 + R_2 \rightarrow R_2$

$-R_1 + R_3 \rightarrow R_3$

$\begin{bmatrix} 1 & -1 & -4 & -3 \\ 0 & 2 & -3 & -3 \\ 0 & 0 & 9 & 9 \end{bmatrix}$ $-R_2 + R_3 \rightarrow R_3$

$\begin{bmatrix} 1 & -1 & -4 & -3 \\ 0 & 2 & -3 & -3 \\ 0 & 0 & 1 & 1 \end{bmatrix}$ $R_3 \div 9 \rightarrow R_3$

$4R_3 + R_1 \rightarrow R_1$

$\begin{bmatrix} 1 & -1 & 0 & 1 \\ 0 & 2 & 0 & 0 \\ 0 & 0 & 1 & 1 \end{bmatrix}$ $3R_3 + R_2 \rightarrow R_2$

$\begin{bmatrix} 1 & -1 & 0 & 1 \\ 0 & 1 & 0 & 0 \\ 0 & 0 & 1 & 1 \end{bmatrix}$ $R_2 \div 2 \rightarrow R_2$

$\begin{bmatrix} 1 & 0 & 0 & 1 \\ 0 & 1 & 0 & 0 \\ 0 & 0 & 1 & 1 \end{bmatrix}$ $R_2 + R_1 \rightarrow R_1$

The solution set is $\{(1, 0, 1)\}$.

44. $\begin{bmatrix} -1 & 0 & 1 & -2 \\ 2 & -1 & 0 & 5 \\ 0 & 1 & 3 & 9 \end{bmatrix}$

$-R_1 \rightarrow R_1$

$\begin{bmatrix} 1 & 0 & -1 & 2 \\ 2 & -1 & 0 & 5 \\ 0 & 1 & 3 & 9 \end{bmatrix}$

$-2R_1 + R_2 \rightarrow R_2$

$\begin{bmatrix} 1 & 0 & -1 & 2 \\ 0 & -1 & 2 & 1 \\ 0 & 1 & 3 & 9 \end{bmatrix}$

$\begin{bmatrix} 1 & 0 & -1 & 2 \\ 0 & 1 & -2 & -1 \\ 0 & 1 & 3 & 9 \end{bmatrix}$ $-R_2 \rightarrow R_2$

$\begin{bmatrix} 1 & 0 & -1 & 2 \\ 0 & 1 & -2 & -1 \\ 0 & 0 & 5 & 10 \end{bmatrix}$ $-R_2 + R_3 \rightarrow R_3$

$\begin{bmatrix} 1 & 0 & -1 & 2 \\ 0 & 1 & -2 & -1 \\ 0 & 0 & 1 & 2 \end{bmatrix}$ $R_3 \div 5 \rightarrow R_3$

$R_3 + R_1 \rightarrow R_1$

$\begin{bmatrix} 1 & 0 & 0 & 4 \\ 0 & 1 & 0 & 3 \\ 0 & 0 & 1 & 2 \end{bmatrix}$ $2R_3 + R_2 \rightarrow R_2$

The solution set is $\{(4, 3, 2)\}$.

45. $\begin{bmatrix} 1 & -1 & 1 & 1 \\ 2 & -2 & 2 & 2 \\ -3 & 3 & -3 & -3 \end{bmatrix}$

$\begin{bmatrix} 1 & -1 & 1 & 1 \\ 0 & 0 & 0 & 0 \\ 0 & 0 & 0 & 0 \end{bmatrix}$ $-2R_1 + R_2 \rightarrow R_2$

$3R_1 + R_3 \rightarrow R_3$

Since the system of equations is equivalent to the first equation, the solution set is $\{(x, y, z) \mid x - y + z = 1\}$.

46. $\begin{bmatrix} 2 & -1 & 1 & 1 \\ 4 & -2 & 2 & 2 \\ -2 & 1 & -1 & -1 \end{bmatrix}$

$\begin{bmatrix} 2 & -1 & 1 & 1 \\ 0 & 0 & 0 & 0 \\ 0 & 0 & 0 & 0 \end{bmatrix}$ $-2R_1 + R_2 \rightarrow R_2$

$R_1 + R_3 \rightarrow R_3$

Since the system of equations is equivalent to the first equation, the solution set is $\{(x, y, z) \mid 2x - y + z = 1\}$

47.
$$\begin{bmatrix} 1 & 1 & -1 & 2 \\ 2 & -1 & 1 & 1 \\ 3 & 3 & -3 & 8 \end{bmatrix}$$

$$\begin{bmatrix} 1 & 1 & -1 & 2 \\ 0 & -3 & 3 & -3 \\ 0 & 0 & 0 & 2 \end{bmatrix} \quad -2R_1 + R_2 \rightarrow R_2$$

$$-3R_1 + R_3 \rightarrow R_3$$

Since the third equation is $0 = 2$, there is no solution to the system.

48.
$$\begin{bmatrix} 1 & 1 & 1 & 5 \\ 1 & -1 & -1 & 8 \\ -1 & 1 & 1 & 2 \end{bmatrix}$$

$$\begin{bmatrix} 1 & 1 & 1 & 5 \\ 0 & -2 & -2 & 3 \\ 0 & 2 & 2 & 7 \end{bmatrix} \quad -R_1 + R_2 \rightarrow R_2$$

$$-R_1 + R_3 \rightarrow R_3$$

$$\begin{bmatrix} 1 & 1 & 1 & 5 \\ 0 & -2 & -2 & 3 \\ 0 & 0 & 0 & 10 \end{bmatrix} \quad R_2 + R_3 \rightarrow R_3$$

Since the third equation is $0 = 10$, there is no solution to the system.

4.5 WARM-UPS

1. True. because the determinant is $(-1)(-5) - (2)(3) = -1$.

2. False, because the determinant is $2 \cdot 8 - (-4)(4) = 32$.

3. False, because if $D = 0$, then Cramer's rule fails to give us the solution.

4. True, the determinant is the value of $ad - bc$.

5. True, this is the case where Cramer's rule fails to give the precise solution.

6. True.

7. True, this is precisely when Cramer's rule works.

8. True, because if x is the tens digit then the value is $10x + y$, and if y is the tens digit then the value is $10y + x$.

9. False, because the total of the perimeters is $4x + 3y$.

10. False, because if the digits are reversed then b is the tens digit and the value of the number is $10b + a$.

4.5 EXERCISES

1. A determinant is a real number associated with a square matrix.

2. Cramer's rule can be use to solve systems of linear equations.

3. Cramer's rule works on systems that have exactly one solution.

4. For inconsistent and dependent systems the determinant of the matrix of coefficients is 0.

5. $\begin{vmatrix} 2 & 5 \\ 3 & 7 \end{vmatrix} = 2 \cdot 7 - 3 \cdot 5 = -1$

6. $\begin{vmatrix} -1 & 0 \\ 1 & 1 \end{vmatrix} = -1 \cdot 1 - 1 \cdot 0 = -1$

7. $\begin{vmatrix} 0 & 3 \\ 1 & 5 \end{vmatrix} = 0 \cdot 5 - 1 \cdot 3 = -3$

8. $\begin{vmatrix} 2 & 4 \\ 6 & 12 \end{vmatrix} = 2 \cdot 12 - 6 \cdot 4 = 0$

9. $\begin{vmatrix} -3 & -2 \\ -4 & 2 \end{vmatrix} = -3 \cdot 2 - (-4)(-2) = -14$

10. $\begin{vmatrix} -2 & 2 \\ -3 & -5 \end{vmatrix} = -2 \cdot (-5) - (-3)(2) = 16$

11. $\begin{vmatrix} 0.05 & 0.06 \\ 10 & 20 \end{vmatrix} = 0.05(20) - 0.06(10)$
$$= 0.4$$

12. $\begin{vmatrix} 0.02 & -0.5 \\ 30 & 50 \end{vmatrix} = 0.02(50) - (-0.5)(30)$
$$= 16$$

13. $D = \begin{vmatrix} 2 & -1 \\ 3 & 2 \end{vmatrix} = 7$

$$D_x = \begin{vmatrix} 5 & -1 \\ -3 & 2 \end{vmatrix} = 7$$

$$D_y = \begin{vmatrix} 2 & 5 \\ 3 & -3 \end{vmatrix} = -21$$

$$x = \frac{D_x}{D} = \frac{7}{7} = 1 \qquad y = \frac{D_y}{D} = \frac{-21}{7} = -3$$

The solution set is $\{(1, -3)\}$.

14.
$$D = \begin{vmatrix} 3 & 1 \\ 1 & 2 \end{vmatrix} = 5$$
$$D_x = \begin{vmatrix} -1 & 1 \\ 8 & 2 \end{vmatrix} = -10$$
$$D_y = \begin{vmatrix} 3 & -1 \\ 1 & 8 \end{vmatrix} = 25$$
$$x = \frac{D_x}{D} = \frac{-10}{5} = -2 \qquad y = \frac{D_y}{D} = \frac{25}{5} = 5$$
The solution set is $\{(-2, 5)\}$.

15.
$$D = \begin{vmatrix} 3 & -5 \\ 2 & 3 \end{vmatrix} = 19$$
$$D_x = \begin{vmatrix} -2 & -5 \\ 5 & 3 \end{vmatrix} = 19$$
$$D_y = \begin{vmatrix} 3 & -2 \\ 2 & 5 \end{vmatrix} = 19$$
$$x = \frac{D_x}{D} = \frac{19}{19} = 1 \qquad y = \frac{D_y}{D} = \frac{19}{19} = 1$$
The solution set is $\{(1, 1)\}$.

16.
$$D = \begin{vmatrix} 1 & -1 \\ 3 & -2 \end{vmatrix} = 1$$
$$D_x = \begin{vmatrix} 1 & -1 \\ 0 & -2 \end{vmatrix} = -2 \quad D_y = \begin{vmatrix} 1 & 1 \\ 3 & 0 \end{vmatrix} = -3$$
$$x = \frac{D_x}{D} = \frac{-2}{1} = -2 \qquad y = \frac{D_y}{D} = \frac{-3}{1} = -3$$

The solution set is $\{(-2, -3)\}$.

17.
$$D = \begin{vmatrix} 4 & -3 \\ 2 & 5 \end{vmatrix} = 26$$
$$D_x = \begin{vmatrix} 5 & -3 \\ 7 & 5 \end{vmatrix} = 46 \quad D_y = \begin{vmatrix} 4 & 5 \\ 2 & 7 \end{vmatrix} = 18$$
$$x = \frac{D_x}{D} = \frac{46}{26} = \frac{23}{13} \qquad y = \frac{D_y}{D} = \frac{18}{26} = \frac{9}{13}$$

The solution set is $\left\{ \left(\frac{23}{13}, \frac{9}{13} \right) \right\}$.

18.
$$D = \begin{vmatrix} 2 & -1 \\ 3 & -2 \end{vmatrix} = -1$$
$$D_x = \begin{vmatrix} 2 & -1 \\ 1 & -2 \end{vmatrix} = -3 \quad D_y = \begin{vmatrix} 2 & 2 \\ 3 & 1 \end{vmatrix} = -4$$
$$x = \frac{D_x}{D} = \frac{-3}{-1} = 3, y = \frac{D_y}{D} = \frac{-4}{-1} = 4$$

The solution set is $\{(3, 4)\}$.

19.
$$D = \begin{vmatrix} 0.5 & 0.2 \\ 0.4 & -0.6 \end{vmatrix} = -0.38$$

$$D_x = \begin{vmatrix} 8 & 0.2 \\ -5 & -0.6 \end{vmatrix} = -3.8$$
$$D_y = \begin{vmatrix} 0.5 & 8 \\ 0.4 & -5 \end{vmatrix} = -5.7$$
$$x = \frac{D_x}{D} = \frac{-3.8}{-0.38} = 10, y = \frac{D_y}{D} = \frac{-5.7}{-0.38} = 15$$

The solution set is $\{(10, 15)\}$.

20.
$$D = \begin{vmatrix} 0.6 & 0.5 \\ 0.5 & -0.25 \end{vmatrix} = -0.4$$
$$D_x = \begin{vmatrix} 18 & 0.5 \\ 7 & -0.25 \end{vmatrix} = -8$$
$$D_y = \begin{vmatrix} 0.6 & 18 \\ 0.5 & 7 \end{vmatrix} = -4.8$$
$$x = \frac{D_x}{D} = \frac{-8}{-0.4} = 20, y = \frac{D_y}{D} = \frac{-4.8}{-0.4} = 12$$

The solution set is $\{(20, 12)\}$.

21. Multiply the first equation by 4 an$D$ the second by 6 to eliminate the fractions.
$$2x + y = 20$$
$$2x - 3y = -6$$
$$D = \begin{vmatrix} 2 & 1 \\ 2 & -3 \end{vmatrix} = -8$$
$$D_x = \begin{vmatrix} 20 & 1 \\ -6 & -3 \end{vmatrix} = -54$$
$$D_y = \begin{vmatrix} 2 & 20 \\ 2 & -6 \end{vmatrix} = -52$$
$$x = \frac{D_x}{D} = \frac{-54}{-8} = \frac{27}{4} \qquad y = \frac{D_y}{D} = \frac{-52}{-8} = \frac{13}{2}$$
The solution set is $\left\{ \left(\frac{27}{4}, \frac{13}{2} \right) \right\}$.

22. Multiply the first equation by 6 and the second by 12 to eliminate the fractions.
$$3x + 4y = 24$$
$$9x + 4y = -24$$
$$D = \begin{vmatrix} 3 & 4 \\ 9 & 4 \end{vmatrix} = 12 - 36 = -24$$
$$D_x = \begin{vmatrix} 24 & 4 \\ -24 & 4 \end{vmatrix} = 192$$

$$D_y = \begin{vmatrix} 3 & 24 \\ 9 & -24 \end{vmatrix} = -288$$

$$x = \frac{D_x}{D} = \frac{192}{-24} = -8, \quad y = \frac{D_y}{D} = \frac{-288}{-24} = 12$$

The solution set is $\{(-8, 12)\}$.

23. $D = \begin{vmatrix} 2 & -3 \\ 4 & -6 \end{vmatrix} = 0$

Since Cramer's rule does not apply, multiply the first equation by -2 and add the result to the second equation.

$$-4x + 6y = -10$$
$$\underline{\quad 4x - 6y = 8 \quad}$$
$$0 = -2$$

The solution set is $\emptyset$.

24. $D = \begin{vmatrix} -1 & 3 \\ 3 & -9 \end{vmatrix} = 0$

Since Cramer's rule does not apply, multiply the first equation by 3 and add the result to the second equation.

$$-3x + 9y = 18$$
$$\underline{\quad 3x - 9y = -18 \quad}$$
$$0 = 0$$

The equations are dependent. The solution set is $\{(x, y) \mid -x + 3y = 6\}$.

25. $D = \begin{vmatrix} 1 & -1 \\ 1 & 2 \end{vmatrix} = 3$

$$D_x = \begin{vmatrix} 4 & -1 \\ 6 & 2 \end{vmatrix} = 14 \quad D_y = \begin{vmatrix} 1 & 4 \\ 1 & 6 \end{vmatrix} = 2$$

$$x = \frac{D_x}{D} = \frac{14}{3} \quad\quad y = \frac{D_y}{D} = \frac{2}{3}$$

The solution set is $\left\{ \left(\frac{14}{3}, \frac{2}{3} \right) \right\}$.

26. $D = \begin{vmatrix} 2 & -1 \\ 3 & 2 \end{vmatrix} = 7$

$$D_x = \begin{vmatrix} 7 & -1 \\ -7 & 2 \end{vmatrix} = 7 \quad D_y = \begin{vmatrix} 2 & 7 \\ 3 & -7 \end{vmatrix} = -35$$

$$x = \frac{D_x}{D} = \frac{7}{7} = 1 \quad\quad y = \frac{D_y}{D} = \frac{-35}{7} = -5$$

The solution set is $\{(1, -5)\}$.

27. $D = \begin{vmatrix} 4 & -1 \\ -8 & 2 \end{vmatrix} = 0$

Since Cramer's rule does not apply, multiply the first equation by 2 and add the result to the second equation.

$$8x - 2y = 12$$
$$\underline{\quad -8x + 2y = -12 \quad}$$
$$0 = 0$$

The solution set is $\{(x, y) \mid 4x - y = 6\}$.

28. $D = \begin{vmatrix} -1 & 2 \\ 3 & -6 \end{vmatrix} = 0$

Since Cramer's rule does not apply, multiply the first equation by 3 and add the result to the second equation.

$$-3x + 6y = 9$$
$$\underline{\quad 3x - 6y = 10 \quad}$$
$$0 = 19$$

The solution set is the empty set $\emptyset$.

29. To use Cramer's rule, we must rewrite each equation.

$$y = 3x - 12 \quad\quad 3(x + 1) - 11 = y + 4$$
$$-3x + y = -12 \quad\quad 3x - 8 = y + 4$$
$$3x - y = 12 \quad\quad 3x - y = 12$$

After rewriting the equations, we see that the equations are equivalent. If we calculate D for Cramer's rule we get $D = \begin{vmatrix} 3 & -1 \\ 3 & -1 \end{vmatrix} = 0$.

The solution set is $\{(x, y) \mid y = 3x - 12\}$.

30. To use Cramer's rule we must rewrite each equation as follows.

$$x - y = 7$$
$$2x + y = 5$$

$$D = \begin{vmatrix} 1 & -1 \\ 2 & 1 \end{vmatrix} = 3$$

$$D_x = \begin{vmatrix} 7 & -1 \\ 5 & 1 \end{vmatrix} = 12 \quad D_y = \begin{vmatrix} 1 & 7 \\ 2 & 5 \end{vmatrix} = -9$$

$x = \dfrac{D_x}{D} = \dfrac{12}{3} = 4 \qquad y = \dfrac{D_y}{D} = \dfrac{-9}{3} = -3$

The solution set is $\{(4, -3)\}$.

31. Rewrite each equation.

$\begin{array}{ll} x - 6 = y + 1 & y = -3x + 1 \\ x - y = 7 & 3x + y = 1 \end{array}$

Apply Cramer's rule to the following system.

$\begin{array}{l} x - y = 7 \\ 3x + y = 1 \end{array}$

$D = \begin{vmatrix} 1 & -1 \\ 3 & 1 \end{vmatrix} = 4$

$D_x = \begin{vmatrix} 7 & -1 \\ 1 & 1 \end{vmatrix} = 8 \qquad D_y = \begin{vmatrix} 1 & 7 \\ 3 & 1 \end{vmatrix} = -20$

$x = \dfrac{D_x}{D} = \dfrac{8}{4} = 2 \qquad y = \dfrac{D_y}{D} = \dfrac{-20}{4} = -5$

The solution set is $\{(2, -5)\}$.

32. Rewrite the system as follows.

$\begin{array}{l} x + y = -5 \\ -2x + y = 1 \end{array}$

$D = \begin{vmatrix} 1 & 1 \\ -2 & 1 \end{vmatrix} = 3$

$D_x = \begin{vmatrix} -5 & 1 \\ 1 & 1 \end{vmatrix} = -6 \quad D_y = \begin{vmatrix} 1 & -5 \\ -2 & 1 \end{vmatrix} = -9$

$x = \dfrac{D_x}{D} = \dfrac{-6}{3} = -2 \qquad y = \dfrac{D_y}{D} = \dfrac{-9}{3} = -3$

The solution set is $\{(-2, -3)\}$.

33. Rewrite the system.

$\begin{array}{l} -0.05x + y = 0 \\ x + y = 504 \end{array}$

$D = \begin{vmatrix} -0.05 & 1 \\ 1 & 1 \end{vmatrix} = -1.05$

$D_x = \begin{vmatrix} 0 & 1 \\ 504 & 1 \end{vmatrix} = -504$

$D_y = \begin{vmatrix} -0.05 & 0 \\ 1 & 504 \end{vmatrix} = -25.2$

$x = \dfrac{D_x}{D} = \dfrac{-504}{-1.05} = 480$

$y = \dfrac{D_y}{D} = \dfrac{-25.2}{-1.05} = 24$

The solution set is $\{(480, 24)\}$.

34. Rewrite the system as follows.

$\begin{array}{l} 5x + 10y = 600 \\ x + y = 98 \end{array}$

$D = \begin{vmatrix} 5 & 10 \\ 1 & 1 \end{vmatrix} = -5$

$D_x = \begin{vmatrix} 600 & 10 \\ 98 & 1 \end{vmatrix} = -380$

$D_y = \begin{vmatrix} 5 & 600 \\ 1 & 98 \end{vmatrix} = -110$

$x = \dfrac{D_x}{D} = \dfrac{-380}{-5} = 76 \quad y = \dfrac{D_y}{D} = \dfrac{-110}{-5} = 22$

The solution set is $\{(76, 22)\}$.

35. **a)** From the graph it appears that there should be approximately 9 servings of peas and 11 servings of beets.

b) Let $x =$ the number of servings of canned peas and $y =$ the number of servings of canned beets. In the first equation we find the total grams of protein and in the second the total grams of carbohydrates.

$\begin{array}{l} 3x + y = 38 \\ 11x + 8y = 187 \end{array}$

$D = \begin{vmatrix} 3 & 1 \\ 11 & 8 \end{vmatrix} = 13 \quad D_x = \begin{vmatrix} 38 & 1 \\ 187 & 8 \end{vmatrix} = 117$

$D_y = \begin{vmatrix} 3 & 38 \\ 11 & 187 \end{vmatrix} = 143$

$x = \dfrac{D_x}{D} = \dfrac{117}{13} = 9 \quad y = \dfrac{D_y}{D} = \dfrac{143}{13} = 11$

To get the required grams of protein and carbohydrates we need 9 servings of peas and 11 servings of beets.

36. Let x = the number of servings of Cornies and y = the number of servings of Oaties. We can write one equation for the total protein and a second equation for the total carbohydrates.

$$2x + 4y = 24$$
$$25x + 20y = 210$$

Simplify the equations by dividing the first one by 2 and the second by 5.

$$x + 2y = 12$$
$$5x + 4y = 42$$

$$D = \begin{vmatrix} 1 & 2 \\ 5 & 4 \end{vmatrix} = -6 \quad D_x = \begin{vmatrix} 12 & 2 \\ 42 & 4 \end{vmatrix} = -36$$

$$D_y = \begin{vmatrix} 1 & 12 \\ 5 & 42 \end{vmatrix} = -18$$

$$x = \frac{D_x}{D} = \frac{-36}{-6} = 6 \quad y = \frac{D_y}{D} = \frac{-18}{-6} = 3$$

To get the required grams of protein and carbohydrates we need 6 servings of Cornies and 3 servings of Oaties.

37. Let x = the tens digit and y = the ones digit. The value of the number is $10x + y$, and if the digits are reversed the value is $10y + x$.

$$x + y = 10$$
$$2(10x + y) = 10y + x + 1$$

After rewriting the second equation we get the following system.

$$x + y = 10$$
$$19x - 8y = 1$$

$$D = \begin{vmatrix} 1 & 1 \\ 19 & -8 \end{vmatrix} = -27$$

$$D_x = \begin{vmatrix} 10 & 1 \\ 1 & -8 \end{vmatrix} = -81$$

$$D_y = \begin{vmatrix} 1 & 10 \\ 19 & 1 \end{vmatrix} = -189$$

$$x = \frac{D_x}{D} = \frac{-81}{-27} = 3 \quad y = \frac{D_y}{D} = \frac{-189}{-27} = 7$$

The number is 37.

38. Let x = the units digit and y = the tens digit. Since the units digit is twice the tens digit, $x = 2y$. The value of the number is $x + 10y$. The value of the number obtained by reversing the digits is $10x + y$. Since this new number is 36 more than the original number we can write $10x + y = x + 10y + 36$. Rewrite the equations as follows.

$$x - 2y = 0$$
$$9x - 9y = 36$$

$$x - 2y = 0$$
$$x - y = 4$$

$$D = \begin{vmatrix} 1 & -2 \\ 1 & -1 \end{vmatrix} = 1 \quad D_x = \begin{vmatrix} 0 & -2 \\ 4 & -1 \end{vmatrix} = 8$$

$$D_y = \begin{vmatrix} 1 & 0 \\ 1 & 4 \end{vmatrix} = 4$$

$$x = \frac{D_x}{D} = \frac{8}{1} = 8 \quad y = \frac{D_y}{D} = \frac{4}{1} = 4$$

The original number is 48.

39. Let x = the price of a gallon of milk and y = the price of the magazine. Note that she paid $0.30 tax. The first equation expresses the total price of the goods and the second expresses the total tax.

$$x + y = 4.65$$
$$0.05x + 0.08y = 0.30$$

$$D = \begin{vmatrix} 1 & 1 \\ 0.05 & 0.08 \end{vmatrix} = 0.03$$

$$D_x = \begin{vmatrix} 4.65 & 1 \\ 0.3 & 0.08 \end{vmatrix} = 0.072$$

$$D_y = \begin{vmatrix} 1 & 4.65 \\ 0.05 & 0.3 \end{vmatrix} = 0.0675$$

$$x = \frac{D_x}{D} = \frac{0.072}{0.03} = 2.4$$

$$y = \frac{D_y}{D} = \frac{0.0675}{0.03} = 2.25$$

The price of the milk was \$2.40 and the price of the magazine was \$2.25.

40. Let $x =$ the number of washing machines and $y =$ the number of refrigerators. Write one equation about the total value of the appliances and the other about the total volume occupied by the appliances.
$$300x + 900y = 51,000$$
$$36x + 45y = 3600$$
Rewrite the equations as follows.
$$x + 3y = 170$$
$$4x + 5y = 400$$

$$D = \begin{vmatrix} 1 & 3 \\ 4 & 5 \end{vmatrix} = -7$$

$$D_x = \begin{vmatrix} 170 & 3 \\ 400 & 5 \end{vmatrix} = -350$$

$$D_y = \begin{vmatrix} 1 & 170 \\ 4 & 400 \end{vmatrix} = -280$$

$$x = \frac{D_x}{D} = \frac{-350}{-7} = 50$$

$$y = \frac{D_y}{D} = \frac{-280}{-7} = 40$$

There were 50 washing machines and 40 refrigerators on the truck.

41. Let $x =$ the number of singles and $y =$ the number of doubles. Write one equation for the patties and one equation for the tomato slices.
$$x + 2y = 32$$
$$2x + y = 34$$

$$D = \begin{vmatrix} 1 & 2 \\ 2 & 1 \end{vmatrix} = -3 \quad D_x = \begin{vmatrix} 32 & 2 \\ 34 & 1 \end{vmatrix} = -36$$

$$D_y = \begin{vmatrix} 1 & 32 \\ 2 & 34 \end{vmatrix} = -30$$

$$x = \frac{D_x}{D} = \frac{-36}{-3} = 12 \quad y = \frac{D_y}{D} = \frac{-30}{-3} = 10$$

He must sell 12 singles and 10 doubles.

42. Let $x =$ the number of box wrenches and $y =$ the number of open-end wrenches. Write one equation about the total number of wrenches and the other about the total value of the wrenches.
$$x + y = 28$$
$$3x + 2.5y = 78$$

$$D = \begin{vmatrix} 1 & 1 \\ 3 & 2.5 \end{vmatrix} = -0.5$$

$$D_x = \begin{vmatrix} 28 & 1 \\ 78 & 2.5 \end{vmatrix} = -8$$

$$D_y = \begin{vmatrix} 1 & 28 \\ 3 & 78 \end{vmatrix} = -6$$

$$x = \frac{D_x}{D} = \frac{-8}{-0.5} = 16 \quad y = \frac{D_y}{D} = \frac{-6}{-0.5} = 12$$

He has 16 box and 12 open-end wrenches.

43. Let $x =$ Gary's age and $y =$ Harry's age. Since Gary is 5 years older than Harry, $x = y + 5$. Twenty-nine years ago Gary was $x - 29$ and Harry was $y - 29$. Gary was twice as old as Harry (29 years ago) is expressed as $x - 29 = 2(y - 29)$. These equations can be rewritten as follows.
$$x - y = 5$$
$$x - 2y = -29$$

$$D = \begin{vmatrix} 1 & -1 \\ 1 & -2 \end{vmatrix} = -1$$

$$D_x = \begin{vmatrix} 5 & -1 \\ -29 & -2 \end{vmatrix} = -39$$

$$D_y = \begin{vmatrix} 1 & 5 \\ 1 & -29 \end{vmatrix} = -34$$

$$x = \frac{D_x}{D} = \frac{-39}{-1} = 39 \quad y = \frac{D_y}{D} = \frac{-34}{-1} = 34$$

So Gary is 39 and Harry is 34.

44. Let $x =$ the number of degrees in the smaller acute angle and $2x + 3 =$ the number of degrees in the other acute angle. Since the total number of degrees in the 3 angles of this

right triangle is 180, we can write the following equation.
$$x + 2x + 3 + 90 = 180$$
$$3x = 87$$
$$x = 29$$
$$2x + 3 = 61$$
The measures of the acute angles are 29° and 61°.

45. Let $x =$ the length of a side of the square and $y =$ the length of a side of the equilateral triangle. Since the perimeters are to be equal, $4x = 3y$. Since the total of the two perimeters is 80, $4x + 3y = 80$. Rewrite the equations as follows.
$$4x - 3y = 0$$
$$4x + 3y = 80$$

$$D = \begin{vmatrix} 4 & -3 \\ 4 & 3 \end{vmatrix} = 24$$

$$D_x = \begin{vmatrix} 0 & -3 \\ 80 & 3 \end{vmatrix} = 240$$

$$D_y = \begin{vmatrix} 4 & 0 \\ 4 & 80 \end{vmatrix} = 320$$

$$x = \frac{D_x}{D} = \frac{240}{24} = 10 \qquad y = \frac{D_y}{D} = \frac{320}{24} = \frac{40}{3}$$

The length of the side of the square should be 10 feet and the length of the side of the triangle should be 40/3 feet.

46. Let $x =$ the price of a cup of coffee and $y =$ the price of a doughnut. Since a cup of coffee, a doughnut, and the tip total $2.25, we can write $x + y = 1.25$. Since 2 coffees, 3 doughnuts, and the tip total $4.00, we can write $2x + 3y = 3.00$.
$$x + y = 1.25$$
$$2x + 3y = 3$$

$$D = \begin{vmatrix} 1 & 1 \\ 2 & 3 \end{vmatrix} = 1 \qquad D_x = \begin{vmatrix} 1.25 & 1 \\ 3 & 3 \end{vmatrix} = 0.75$$

$$D_y = \begin{vmatrix} 1 & 1.25 \\ 2 & 3 \end{vmatrix} = 0.50$$

$$x = \frac{D_x}{D} = \frac{0.75}{1} = 0.75$$

$$y = \frac{D_y}{D} = \frac{0.50}{1} = 0.50$$

The price of a cup of coffee is $0.75.

47. Let $x =$ the number of gallons of 10% solution and $y =$ the number of gallons of 25% solution. Since the total mixture is to be 30 gallons, $x + y = 30$. The next equation comes from the fact that the chlorine in the two parts is equal to the chlorine in the 30 gallons, $0.10x + 0.25y = 0.20(30)$. Rewrite the equations as follows.
$$x + y = 30$$
$$0.10x + 0.25y = 6$$

$$D = \begin{vmatrix} 1 & 1 \\ 0.10 & 0.25 \end{vmatrix} = 0.15$$

$$D_x = \begin{vmatrix} 30 & 1 \\ 6 & 0.25 \end{vmatrix} = 1.5$$

$$D_y = \begin{vmatrix} 1 & 30 \\ 0.10 & 6 \end{vmatrix} = 3$$

$$x = \frac{D_x}{D} = \frac{1.5}{0.15} = 10 \qquad y = \frac{D_y}{D} = \frac{3}{0.15} = 20$$

Use 10 gallons of 10% solution and 20 gallons of 25% solution.

48. Let $x =$ Emily's rate and $y =$ Camille's rate. Since they each drove for 3 hours, Emily drove $3x$ miles and Camille drove $3y$ miles.
$$3x + 3y = 354$$
$$3x - 3y = 18$$
Simplify the equations as follows.
$$x + y = 118$$
$$x - y = 6$$

$$D = \begin{vmatrix} 1 & 1 \\ 1 & -1 \end{vmatrix} = -2$$

$$D_x = \begin{vmatrix} 118 & 1 \\ 6 & -1 \end{vmatrix} = -124$$

$$D_y = \begin{vmatrix} 1 & 118 \\ 1 & 6 \end{vmatrix} = -112$$

$$x = \frac{D_x}{D} = \frac{-124}{-2} = 62$$

$$y = \frac{D_y}{D} = \frac{-112}{-2} = 56$$

Emily drives 62 mph and Camille drives 56 mph.

4.6 WARM-UPS

1. True, because of the definition of minor.
2. False, the row and column of the element are deleted from the matrix.
3. True, because of the definition of determinant of a 3×3 matrix.
4. False, because expansion by minors is used to find the determinant.
5. False, because $x = D_x/D$ by Cramer's rule.
6. True.
7. True.
8. True, because we can choose to expand about a row or column that has a zero in it.
9. False, because if $D = 0$ there is either no solution or infinitely many solutions.
10. False, because Cramer's rule does not work on nonlinear equations.

4.6 EXERCISES

1. A minor for an element in a 3×3 matrix is the determinant of a 2×2 matrix.
2. A minor for an element is obtained by deleting the row and column of the element and then finding the determinant of the 2×2 matrix that remains.
3. The sign array tells what signs to use in the expansion by minors.
4. Cramer's rule solves only those systems that have a unique solution.
5. The minor for 3 is the determinant of the matrix obtained by deleting the row and column containing 3, the first row and first column.
$$\begin{vmatrix} -3 & 7 \\ 1 & -6 \end{vmatrix} = 11$$

6. The minor for -2 is the determinant of the matrix obtained by deleting the row and column containing -2, the first row and second column.
$$\begin{vmatrix} 4 & 7 \\ 0 & -6 \end{vmatrix} = -24$$
7. The minor for 5 is the determinant of the matrix obtained by deleting the first row and third column.
$$\begin{vmatrix} 4 & -3 \\ 0 & 1 \end{vmatrix} = 4$$
8. The minor for -3 is the determinant of the matrix obtained by deleting the second row and second column.
$$\begin{vmatrix} 3 & 5 \\ 0 & -6 \end{vmatrix} = -18$$
9. The minor for 7 is the determinant of the matrix obtained by deleting the second row and third column.
$$\begin{vmatrix} 3 & -2 \\ 0 & 1 \end{vmatrix} = 3$$
10. The minor for 0 is the determinant of the matrix obtained by deleting the third row and first column.
$$\begin{vmatrix} -2 & 5 \\ -3 & 7 \end{vmatrix} = 1$$
11. The minor for 1 is the determinant of the matrix obtained by deleting the third row and second column.
$$\begin{vmatrix} 3 & 5 \\ 4 & 7 \end{vmatrix} = 1$$
12. The minor for -6 is the determinant of the matrix obtained by deleting the third row and third column.
$$\begin{vmatrix} 3 & -2 \\ 4 & -3 \end{vmatrix} = -1$$

13. $1 \begin{vmatrix} 3 & 1 \\ 1 & 5 \end{vmatrix} - 2 \begin{vmatrix} 1 & 2 \\ 1 & 5 \end{vmatrix} + 3 \begin{vmatrix} 1 & 2 \\ 3 & 1 \end{vmatrix}$

$$= 1(14) - 2(3) + 3(-5) = -7$$

14. $2 \begin{vmatrix} 1 & 2 \\ 4 & 6 \end{vmatrix} - 1 \begin{vmatrix} 1 & 3 \\ 4 & 6 \end{vmatrix} + 3 \begin{vmatrix} 1 & 3 \\ 1 & 2 \end{vmatrix}$

$$= 2(-2) - 1(-6) + 3(-1)$$
$$= -4 + 6 - 3 = -1$$

15. $2\begin{vmatrix} 0 & 1 \\ 1 & 2 \end{vmatrix} - 1\begin{vmatrix} 1 & 0 \\ 1 & 2 \end{vmatrix} + 3\begin{vmatrix} 1 & 0 \\ 0 & 1 \end{vmatrix}$

$$= 2(-1) - 1(2) + 3(1) = -1$$

16. $1\begin{vmatrix} 1 & 3 \\ 3 & 0 \end{vmatrix} - 2\begin{vmatrix} 0 & 2 \\ 3 & 0 \end{vmatrix} + 4\begin{vmatrix} 0 & 2 \\ 1 & 3 \end{vmatrix}$

$$= 1(-9) - 2(-6) + 4(-2) = -5$$

17. $-2\begin{vmatrix} 3 & 1 \\ 4 & 0 \end{vmatrix} + 3\begin{vmatrix} 1 & 2 \\ 4 & 0 \end{vmatrix} - 5\begin{vmatrix} 1 & 2 \\ 3 & 1 \end{vmatrix}$
$$= -2(-4) + 3(-8) - 5(-5) = 9$$

18. $-2\begin{vmatrix} 4 & 2 \\ 1 & 1 \end{vmatrix} - (-1)\begin{vmatrix} 1 & 3 \\ 1 & 1 \end{vmatrix} + 2\begin{vmatrix} 1 & 3 \\ 4 & 2 \end{vmatrix}$
$$= -2(2) + 1(-2) + 2(-10) = -26$$

19. $1\begin{vmatrix} 3 & 2 \\ 2 & 3 \end{vmatrix} - 0\begin{vmatrix} 1 & 5 \\ 2 & 3 \end{vmatrix} + 0\begin{vmatrix} 1 & 5 \\ 3 & 2 \end{vmatrix}$
$$= 1(5) - 0(-7) + 0(-13) = 5$$

20. $1\begin{vmatrix} 1 & 4 \\ 0 & 9 \end{vmatrix} - 0\begin{vmatrix} 0 & 6 \\ 0 & 9 \end{vmatrix} + 0\begin{vmatrix} 0 & 6 \\ 1 & 4 \end{vmatrix}$
$$= 1(9) - 0(0) + 0(-6) = 9$$

21. Expand by minors about the second column because it has two zeros in it.

$$-1\begin{vmatrix} 2 & 6 \\ 4 & 1 \end{vmatrix} + 0\begin{vmatrix} 3 & 5 \\ 4 & 1 \end{vmatrix} - 0\begin{vmatrix} 3 & 5 \\ 2 & 6 \end{vmatrix}$$
$$= -1(-22) = 22$$

22. Expand by minors about the third row because it has two zeros in it.
$$3\begin{vmatrix} 1 & 2 \\ 2 & 5 \end{vmatrix} + 0\begin{vmatrix} 2 & 2 \\ 1 & 5 \end{vmatrix} - 0\begin{vmatrix} 2 & 1 \\ 1 & 2 \end{vmatrix}$$
$$= 3(1) = 3$$

23. Expand by minors about the first column because it has one zero in it.
$$-2\begin{vmatrix} 1 & -1 \\ -4 & -3 \end{vmatrix} - 0\begin{vmatrix} 1 & 3 \\ -4 & -3 \end{vmatrix} + 2\begin{vmatrix} 1 & 3 \\ 1 & -1 \end{vmatrix}$$
$$= -2(-7) + 2(-4) = 6$$

24. Expand by minors about the first row because it has one zero in it.
$$-2\begin{vmatrix} 2 & -5 \\ -2 & 6 \end{vmatrix} - 0\begin{vmatrix} -3 & -5 \\ 4 & 6 \end{vmatrix}$$
$$+ 1\begin{vmatrix} -3 & 2 \\ 4 & -2 \end{vmatrix}$$

$$= -2(2) + 1(-2) = -6$$

25. Expand by minors about the third column because it has two zeros in it.
$$0\begin{vmatrix} 4 & -1 \\ 0 & 3 \end{vmatrix} - 0\begin{vmatrix} -2 & -3 \\ 0 & 3 \end{vmatrix} + 5\begin{vmatrix} -2 & -3 \\ 4 & -1 \end{vmatrix}$$
$$= 5(14) = 70$$

26. Expand by minors about the second row because it has two zeros in it.
$$0\begin{vmatrix} 6 & 3 \\ -4 & 5 \end{vmatrix} + 4\begin{vmatrix} -2 & 3 \\ -1 & 5 \end{vmatrix} + 0\begin{vmatrix} -2 & 6 \\ -1 & -4 \end{vmatrix}$$
$$= 4(-7) = -28$$

27. Expand by minors about the second column.
$$-1\begin{vmatrix} 0 & 5 \\ 5 & 4 \end{vmatrix} + 0\begin{vmatrix} 2 & 1 \\ 5 & 4 \end{vmatrix} - 0\begin{vmatrix} 2 & 1 \\ 0 & 5 \end{vmatrix}$$
$$= -1(-25) = 25$$

28. Expand by minors about the third column.
$$0\begin{vmatrix} 6 & 4 \\ 1 & 2 \end{vmatrix} - 1\begin{vmatrix} 2 & 3 \\ 1 & 2 \end{vmatrix} + 0\begin{vmatrix} 2 & 3 \\ 6 & 4 \end{vmatrix}$$
$$= -1(1) = -1$$

29. $D = \begin{vmatrix} 1 & 1 & 1 \\ 1 & -1 & 1 \\ 2 & 1 & 1 \end{vmatrix} = 2$

$$D_x = \begin{vmatrix} 6 & 1 & 1 \\ 2 & -1 & 1 \\ 7 & 1 & 1 \end{vmatrix} = 2$$

$$D_y = \begin{vmatrix} 1 & 6 & 1 \\ 1 & 2 & 1 \\ 2 & 7 & 1 \end{vmatrix} = 4$$

$$D_z = \begin{vmatrix} 1 & 1 & 6 \\ 1 & -1 & 2 \\ 2 & 1 & 7 \end{vmatrix} = 6$$

$$x = \frac{D_x}{D} = \frac{2}{2} = 1, y = \frac{D_y}{D} = \frac{4}{2} = 2,$$

$$z = \frac{D_z}{D} = \frac{6}{2} = 3$$

The solution set is $\{(1, 2, 3)\}$.

30. $D = \begin{vmatrix} 1 & 1 & 1 \\ 1 & -1 & -2 \\ 2 & -1 & 1 \end{vmatrix} = -7$

$D_x = \begin{vmatrix} 2 & 1 & 1 \\ -3 & -1 & -2 \\ 7 & -1 & 1 \end{vmatrix} = -7$

$D_y = \begin{vmatrix} 1 & 2 & 1 \\ 1 & -3 & -2 \\ 2 & 7 & 1 \end{vmatrix} = 14$

$D_z = \begin{vmatrix} 1 & 1 & 2 \\ 1 & -1 & -3 \\ 2 & -1 & 7 \end{vmatrix} = -21$

$x = \dfrac{D_x}{D} = \dfrac{-7}{-7} = 1, \quad y = \dfrac{D_y}{D} = \dfrac{14}{-7} = -2,$

$z = \dfrac{D_z}{D} = \dfrac{-21}{-7} = 3$

The solution set is $\{(1, -2, 3)\}$.

31. $D = \begin{vmatrix} 1 & -3 & 2 \\ 1 & 1 & 1 \\ 1 & -1 & 1 \end{vmatrix} = -2$

$D_x = \begin{vmatrix} 0 & -3 & 2 \\ 2 & 1 & 1 \\ 0 & -1 & 1 \end{vmatrix} = 2$

$D_y = \begin{vmatrix} 1 & 0 & 2 \\ 1 & 2 & 1 \\ 1 & 0 & 1 \end{vmatrix} = -2$

$D_z = \begin{vmatrix} 1 & -3 & 0 \\ 1 & 1 & 2 \\ 1 & -1 & 0 \end{vmatrix} = -4$

$x = \dfrac{D_x}{D} = \dfrac{2}{-2} = -1, \quad y = \dfrac{D_y}{D} = \dfrac{-2}{-2} = 1,$

$z = \dfrac{D_z}{D} = \dfrac{-4}{-2} = 2$

The solution set is $\{(-1, 1, 2)\}$.

32. $D = \begin{vmatrix} 3 & 2 & 2 \\ 1 & -1 & 1 \\ 1 & 1 & -1 \end{vmatrix} = 8$

$D_x = \begin{vmatrix} 0 & 2 & 2 \\ 1 & -1 & 1 \\ 3 & 1 & -1 \end{vmatrix} = 16$

$D_y = \begin{vmatrix} 3 & 0 & 2 \\ 1 & 1 & 1 \\ 1 & 3 & -1 \end{vmatrix} = -8$

$D_z = \begin{vmatrix} 3 & 2 & 0 \\ 1 & -1 & 1 \\ 1 & 1 & 3 \end{vmatrix} = -16$

$x = \dfrac{D_x}{D} = \dfrac{16}{8} = 2, \quad y = \dfrac{D_y}{D} = \dfrac{-8}{8} = -1,$

$z = \dfrac{D_z}{D} = \dfrac{-16}{8} = -2$

The solution set is $\{(2, -1, -2)\}$.

33. $D = \begin{vmatrix} 1 & 1 & 0 \\ 0 & 2 & -1 \\ 1 & 1 & 1 \end{vmatrix} = 2$

$D_x = \begin{vmatrix} -1 & 1 & 0 \\ 3 & 2 & -1 \\ 0 & 1 & 1 \end{vmatrix} = -6$

$D_y = \begin{vmatrix} 1 & -1 & 0 \\ 0 & 3 & -1 \\ 1 & 0 & 1 \end{vmatrix} = 4$

$D_z = \begin{vmatrix} 1 & 1 & -1 \\ 0 & 2 & 3 \\ 1 & 1 & 0 \end{vmatrix} = 2$

$x = \dfrac{D_x}{D} = \dfrac{-6}{2} = -3, \quad y = \dfrac{D_y}{D} = \dfrac{4}{2} = 2,$

$z = \dfrac{D_z}{D} = \dfrac{2}{2} = 1$

The solution set is $\{(-3, 2, 1)\}$.

34. $D = \begin{vmatrix} 1 & -1 & 0 \\ 1 & 0 & -2 \\ 1 & 1 & -1 \end{vmatrix} = 3$

$D_x = \begin{vmatrix} 8 & -1 & 0 \\ 0 & 0 & -2 \\ 1 & 1 & -1 \end{vmatrix} = 18$

$D_y = \begin{vmatrix} 1 & 8 & 0 \\ 1 & 0 & -2 \\ 1 & 1 & -1 \end{vmatrix} = -6$

$D_z = \begin{vmatrix} 1 & -1 & 8 \\ 1 & 0 & 0 \\ 1 & 1 & 1 \end{vmatrix} = 9$

$x = \dfrac{D_x}{D} = \dfrac{18}{3} = 6, \quad y = \dfrac{D_y}{D} = \dfrac{-6}{3} = -2,$

$z = \dfrac{D_z}{D} = \dfrac{9}{3} = 3$

The solution set is $\{(6, -2, 3)\}$.

35. $D = \begin{vmatrix} 1 & 1 & -1 \\ 2 & 2 & 1 \\ 1 & -3 & 0 \end{vmatrix} = 12$

$D_x = \begin{vmatrix} 0 & 1 & -1 \\ 6 & 2 & 1 \\ 0 & -3 & 0 \end{vmatrix} = 18$

$D_y = \begin{vmatrix} 1 & 0 & -1 \\ 2 & 6 & 1 \\ 1 & 0 & 0 \end{vmatrix} = 6$

$D_z = \begin{vmatrix} 1 & 1 & 0 \\ 2 & 2 & 6 \\ 1 & -3 & 0 \end{vmatrix} = 24$

$x = \dfrac{D_x}{D} = \dfrac{18}{12} = \dfrac{3}{2}, \quad y = \dfrac{D_y}{D} = \dfrac{6}{12} = \dfrac{1}{2},$

$z = \dfrac{D_z}{D} = \dfrac{24}{12} = 2$

The solution set is $\{(\tfrac{3}{2}, \tfrac{1}{2}, 2)\}$.

36. $D = \begin{vmatrix} 1 & 1 & 1 \\ 5 & -1 & 0 \\ 3 & 1 & 2 \end{vmatrix} = -4$

$D_x = \begin{vmatrix} 1 & 1 & 1 \\ 0 & -1 & 0 \\ 0 & 1 & 2 \end{vmatrix} = -2$

$D_y = \begin{vmatrix} 1 & 1 & 1 \\ 5 & 0 & 0 \\ 3 & 0 & 2 \end{vmatrix} = -10$

$D_z = \begin{vmatrix} 1 & 1 & 1 \\ 5 & -1 & 0 \\ 3 & 1 & 0 \end{vmatrix} = 8$

$x = \dfrac{D_x}{D} = \dfrac{-2}{-2} = \dfrac{1}{2}, \quad y = \dfrac{D_y}{D} = \dfrac{-10}{-4} = \dfrac{5}{2},$

$z = \dfrac{D_z}{D} = \dfrac{8}{-4} = -2$

The solution set is $\{(\tfrac{1}{2}, \tfrac{5}{2}, -2)\}$.

37. $D = \begin{vmatrix} 1 & 1 & 1 \\ 0 & 2 & 2 \\ 3 & -1 & 0 \end{vmatrix} = 2$

$D_x = \begin{vmatrix} 0 & 1 & 1 \\ 0 & 2 & 2 \\ -1 & -1 & 0 \end{vmatrix} = 0$

$D_y = \begin{vmatrix} 1 & 0 & 1 \\ 0 & 0 & 2 \\ 3 & -1 & 0 \end{vmatrix} = 2$

$D_z = \begin{vmatrix} 1 & 1 & 0 \\ 0 & 2 & 0 \\ 3 & -1 & -1 \end{vmatrix} = -2$

$x = \dfrac{D_x}{D} = \dfrac{0}{2} = 0, \quad y = \dfrac{D_y}{D} = \dfrac{2}{2} = 1,$

$z = \dfrac{D_z}{D} = \dfrac{-2}{2} = -1$

The solution set is $\{(0, 1, -1)\}$.

38. $D = \begin{vmatrix} 1 & 0 & 1 \\ 1 & -3 & 0 \\ 0 & 4 & -3 \end{vmatrix} = 13$

$D_x = \begin{vmatrix} 0 & 0 & 1 \\ 1 & -3 & 0 \\ 3 & 4 & -3 \end{vmatrix} = 13$

$D_y = \begin{vmatrix} 1 & 0 & 1 \\ 1 & 1 & 0 \\ 0 & 3 & -3 \end{vmatrix} = 0$

$$D_z = \begin{vmatrix} 1 & 0 & 0 \\ 1 & -3 & 1 \\ 0 & 4 & 3 \end{vmatrix} = -13$$

$$x = \frac{D_x}{D} = \frac{13}{13} = 1, \qquad y = \frac{D_y}{D} = \frac{0}{13} = 0,$$

$$z = \frac{D_z}{D} = \frac{-13}{13} = -1$$

The solution set is $\{(1, 0, -1)\}$.

39. $D = \begin{vmatrix} 2 & -1 & 1 \\ -6 & 3 & -3 \\ 4 & -2 & 2 \end{vmatrix} = 0$

Since $D = 0$, we must use elimination of variables to solve the system. Note that if we multiply the first equation by -3, the result is the same as the second equation. If we multiply the first equation by 2, the result is the same as the third equation. So the system is dependent and the solution set is
$\{(x, y, z) \mid 2x - y + z = 1\}$.

40. $D = \begin{vmatrix} 1 & -1 & 1 \\ 2 & -2 & 2 \\ 4 & -1 & -1 \end{vmatrix} = 0$

Since $D = 0$, we must use elimination of variables to solve the system. Multiply the first equation by -2 and add the result to the second equation as follows.
$$\begin{aligned} -2x + 2y - 2z &= -8 \\ 2x - 2y + 2z &= 3 \\ \hline 0 &= -5 \end{aligned}$$
Since the result of the addition is a false statement, there is no solution to the system. The solution set is $\emptyset$.

41. $D = \begin{vmatrix} 1 & 1 & 0 \\ 0 & 1 & 2 \\ 1 & 2 & 2 \end{vmatrix} = 0$

Since $D = 0$, we must solve the system by elimination of variables. Multiply the second equation by -1 and add the result to the third equation to get $x + y = 2$. Multiply $x + y = 2$ by -1 and add the result to the first equation.
$$\begin{aligned} -x - y &= -2 \\ x + y &= 1 \\ \hline 0 &= -1 \end{aligned}$$

The last equation is false no matter what values the variables have. The solution set is $\emptyset$.

42. $D = \begin{vmatrix} 1 & -1 & 1 \\ 2 & -2 & 2 \\ 3 & -3 & 3 \end{vmatrix} = 0$

Since $D = 0$, we must solve the system by elimination of variables. Note that if we multiply the first equation by 2, we get the second equation. If we multiply the first equation by 3, we get the third equation. Since all three equations are equivalent, the solution set to the system is the set of points that satisfies one of them,
$\{(x, y, z) \mid x - y + z = 5\}$.

43. $D = \begin{vmatrix} 1 & 1 & 0 \\ 0 & 1 & 1 \\ 1 & 0 & 1 \end{vmatrix} = 2$

$$D_x = \begin{vmatrix} 4 & 1 & 0 \\ -3 & 1 & 1 \\ -5 & 0 & 1 \end{vmatrix} = 2$$

$$D_y = \begin{vmatrix} 1 & 4 & 0 \\ 0 & -3 & 1 \\ 1 & -5 & 1 \end{vmatrix} = 6$$

$$D_z = \begin{vmatrix} 1 & 1 & 4 \\ 0 & 1 & -3 \\ 1 & 0 & -5 \end{vmatrix} = -12$$

$$x = \frac{D_x}{D} = \frac{2}{2} = 1, \qquad y = \frac{D_y}{D} = \frac{6}{2} = 3,$$

$$z = \frac{D_z}{D} = \frac{-12}{2} = -6$$
The solution set is $\{(1, 3, -6)\}$.

44. $D = \begin{vmatrix} 1 & 1 & 0 \\ 1 & 0 & -1 \\ 0 & 1 & 1 \end{vmatrix} = 0$

Since $D = 0$, we must solve the system by elimination of variables. Add the second and third equations to eliminate z.
$$\begin{aligned} x \quad\;\; - z &= -1 \\ y + z &= 3 \\ \hline x + y \quad\;\; &= 2 \end{aligned}$$

162

Since the first equation is $x + y = 0$, there is no solution to the system. The solution set is $\emptyset$.

45. Let $x =$ Mimi's weight, $y =$ Mitzi's weight, and $z =$ Cassandra's weight. We can write 3 equations.

$$x + y + z = 175$$
$$x \quad\;\; + z = 143$$
$$y + z = 139$$

$$D = \begin{vmatrix} 1 & 1 & 1 \\ 1 & 0 & 1 \\ 0 & 1 & 1 \end{vmatrix} = -1$$

$$D_x = \begin{vmatrix} 175 & 1 & 1 \\ 143 & 0 & 1 \\ 139 & 1 & 1 \end{vmatrix} = -36$$

$$D_y = \begin{vmatrix} 1 & 175 & 1 \\ 1 & 143 & 1 \\ 0 & 139 & 1 \end{vmatrix} = -32$$

$$D_z = \begin{vmatrix} 1 & 1 & 175 \\ 1 & 0 & 143 \\ 0 & 1 & 139 \end{vmatrix} = -107$$

$$x = \frac{D_x}{D} = \frac{-36}{-1} = 36,$$

$$y = \frac{D_y}{D} = \frac{-32}{-1} = 32,$$

$$z = \frac{D_z}{D} = \frac{-107}{-1} = 107$$

So Mimi weights 36 pounds, Mitzi weighs 32 pounds, and Cassandra weighs 107 pounds.

46. Let $x =$ the number of nickels, $y =$ the number of dimes, and $z =$ the number of quarters. We can write three equations.

$$x + y + z = 41$$
$$5x + 10y + 25z = 400$$
$$y + z = x + 1$$

Rewrite the system and apply Cramer's Rule.

$$x + y + z = 41$$
$$x + 2y + 5z = 80$$
$$-x + y + z = 1$$

$$D = \begin{vmatrix} 1 & 1 & 1 \\ 1 & 2 & 5 \\ -1 & 1 & 1 \end{vmatrix} = -6$$

$$D_x = \begin{vmatrix} 41 & 1 & 1 \\ 80 & 2 & 5 \\ 1 & 1 & 1 \end{vmatrix} = -120$$

$$D_y = \begin{vmatrix} 1 & 41 & 1 \\ 1 & 80 & 5 \\ -1 & 1 & 1 \end{vmatrix} = -90$$

$$D_z = \begin{vmatrix} 1 & 1 & 41 \\ 1 & 2 & 80 \\ -1 & 1 & 1 \end{vmatrix} = -36$$

$$x = \frac{D_x}{D} = \frac{-120}{-6} = 20,$$

$$y = \frac{D_y}{D} = \frac{-90}{-6} = 15,$$

$$z = \frac{D_z}{D} = \frac{-36}{-6} = 6$$

Bernard has 20 nickels, 15 dimes, and 6 quarters.

47. Let $x =$ the number of degrees in the larger of the two acute angles, $y =$ the number of degrees in the smaller acute angle, and $z =$ the number of degrees in the right angle. We can write 3 equations about the sizes of the angles.

$$x + y + z = 180$$
$$x - y \quad\;\; = 12$$
$$z = 90$$

$$D = \begin{vmatrix} 1 & 1 & 1 \\ 1 & -1 & 0 \\ 0 & 0 & 1 \end{vmatrix} = -2$$

$$D_x = \begin{vmatrix} 180 & 1 & 1 \\ 12 & -1 & 0 \\ 90 & 0 & 1 \end{vmatrix} = -102$$

$$D_y = \begin{vmatrix} 1 & 180 & 1 \\ 1 & 12 & 0 \\ 0 & 90 & 1 \end{vmatrix} = -78$$

$$D_z = \begin{vmatrix} 1 & 1 & 180 \\ 1 & -1 & 12 \\ 0 & 0 & 90 \end{vmatrix} = -180$$

$$x = \frac{D_x}{D} = \frac{-102}{-2} = 51,$$

$$y = \frac{D_y}{D} = \frac{-78}{-2} = 39,$$

$$z = \frac{D_z}{D} = \frac{-180}{-2} = 90$$

The measures of the three angles of the triangle are 39°, 51°, and 90°.

48. Let x = the number of degrees in the smallest angle, y = the number of degrees in the next larger angle, and z = the number of degrees in the largest angle. We can write the following three equations.

$$x + y + z = 180$$
$$z = 2(x + y)$$
$$x = \tfrac{1}{8}(y + z)$$

Rewrite the equations to get the following system.

$$x + y + z = 180$$
$$2x + 2y - z = 0$$
$$8x - y - z = 0$$

$$D = \begin{vmatrix} 1 & 1 & 1 \\ 2 & 2 & -1 \\ 8 & -1 & -1 \end{vmatrix} = -27$$

$$D_x = \begin{vmatrix} 180 & 1 & 1 \\ 0 & 2 & -1 \\ 0 & -1 & -1 \end{vmatrix} = -540$$

$$D_y = \begin{vmatrix} 1 & 180 & 1 \\ 2 & 0 & -1 \\ 8 & 0 & -1 \end{vmatrix} = -1080$$

$$D_z = \begin{vmatrix} 1 & 1 & 180 \\ 2 & 2 & 0 \\ 8 & -1 & 0 \end{vmatrix} = -3240$$

$$x = \frac{D_x}{D} = \frac{-540}{-27} = 20,$$

$$y = \frac{D_y}{D} = \frac{-1080}{-27} = 40,$$

$$z = \frac{D_z}{D} = \frac{-3240}{-27} = 120$$

The angles have measures of 20°, 40°, and 120°.

4.7 WARM-UPS

1. False, because $x \geq 0$ consists of the points on or to the right of the y-axis.
2. False, because $y \geq 0$ consists of the points on or above the x-axis.
3. False, because $x + y \leq 6$ consists of the points on or below the line $x + y = 6$.
4. False, because the x-intercept is (15, 0) and the y-intercept is (0, 10).
5. False, because the solution set to a system is the intersection of the solution sets.
6. True, because that is the definition of constraint.
7. False, because a linear function does not have an x^2 in it.
8. True, because $R(2, 4) = 3(2) + 5(4) = 26$.
9. False, because
$C(0, 5) = 12(0) + 10(5) = 50$.
10. True, because the maximum or minimum of a linear function occurs at a vertex.

4.7 EXERCISES

1. A constraint is an inequality that restricts the values of the variables.
2. Linear programming is the process used to maximize or minimize a linear function subject to linear constraints.
3. Constraints may be limitations on the amount of available supplies, money, or other resources.
4. A linear function of two variables is a function of the form $f(x, y) = Ax + By + C$.
5. The maximum or minimum of a linear function subject to linear constraints occurs at a vertex of the region determined by the constraints.
6. Write the constraints, graph the region that they determine, locate each vertex, then evaluate

the function at each vertex, and identify the maximum or minimum.

7. The graph of $x \geq 0$ is the region on or to the right of the y-axis. The graph of $y \geq 0$ is the region on or above the x-axis. The graph of $x + y \leq 5$ is the region on or below the line $x + y = 5$. The intersection of these 3 regions is shaded here.

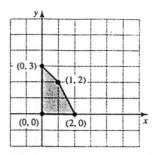

10. The graph of $x \geq 0$ is the region on or to the right of the y-axis. The graph of $y \geq 0$ is the region on or above the x-axis. The graph of $x + y \leq 4$ is the region on or below the line $x + y = 4$. The graph of $x + 2y \leq 6$ is the region on or below the line $x + 2y = 6$. The intersection of these regions is shaded below.

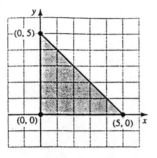

8. The graph of $x \geq 0$ is the region on or to the right of the y-axis. The graph of $y \geq 0$ is the region on or above the x-axis. The graph of $y \leq 5$ is the region on or below the horizontal line $y = 5$. The graph of $y \geq x$ is the region on or above the line $y = x$. The intersection of these regions is shaded below.

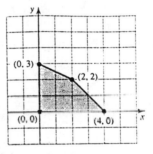

11. The graph of $x \geq 0$ is the region on or to the right of the y-axis. The graph of $y \geq 0$ is the region on or above the x-axis. The graph of $2x + y \geq 3$ is the region on or above the line $2x + y = 3$. The graph of $x + y \geq 2$ is the region on or above the line $x + y = 2$. The intersection of these regions is shaded below.

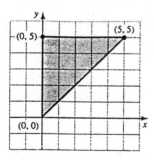

9. The graph of $x \geq 0$ is the region on or to the right of the y-axis. The graph of $y \geq 0$ is the region on or above the x-axis. The graph of $2x + y \leq 4$ is the region on or below the line $2x + y = 4$. The graph of $x + y \leq 3$ is the region on or below the line $x + y = 3$. The intersection of these regions is shaded below.

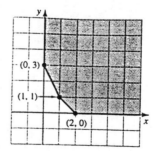

12. The graph of $x \geq 0$ is the region on or to the right of the y-axis. The graph of $y \geq 0$ is the region on or above the x-axis. The graph of $3x + 2y \geq 12$ is the region on or above the line $3x + 2y = 12$. The graph of $2x + y \geq 7$ is the region on or above the line $2x + y = 7$. The intersection of these regions is shaded below.

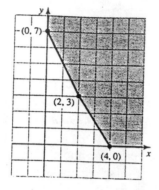

13. The graph of $x \geq 0$ is the region on or to the right of the y-axis. The graph of $y \geq 0$ is the region on or above the x-axis. The graph of $x + 3y \leq 15$ is the region on or below the line $x + 3y = 15$. The graph of $2x + y \leq 10$ is the region on or below the line $2x + y = 10$. The intersection of these regions is shaded below.

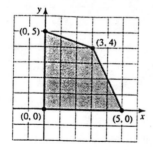

14. The graph of $x \geq 0$ is the region on or to the right of the y-axis. The graph of $y \geq 0$ is the region on or above the x-axis. The graph of $2x + 3y \leq 15$ is the region on or below the line $2x + 3y = 15$. The graph of $x + y \leq 7$ is the region on or below the line $x + y = 7$. The intersection of these regions is shaded below.

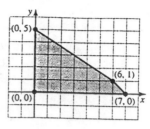

15. The graph of $x \geq 0$ is the region on or to the right of the y-axis. The graph of $y \geq 0$ is the region on or above the x-axis. The graph of $x + y \geq 4$ is the region on or above the line $x + y = 4$. The graph of $3x + y \geq 6$ is the region on or above the line $3x + y = 6$. The intersection of these regions is shaded below.

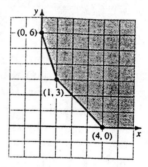

16. The graph of $x \geq 0$ is the region on or to the right of the y-axis. The graph of $y \geq 0$ is the region on or above the x-axis. The graph of $x + 3y \geq 6$ is the region on or above the line $x + 3y = 6$. The graph of $2x + y \geq 7$ is the region on or above the line $2x + y = 7$. The intersection of these regions is shaded below.

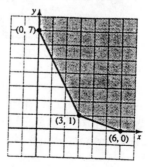

166

17. a) $A(0,0) = 0$

$A(0,80) = 9000(0) + 4000(80) = 320,000$

$A(50,0) = 9000(50) + 4000(0) = 450,000$

$A(30,60) = 9000(30) + 4000(60) = 510,000$

b) To maximize the audience they should use 30 TV ads and 60 radio ads.

18. a) $A(0,0) = 0$

$A(0,80) = 9000(0) + 2000(80) = 160,000$

$A(50,0) = 9000(50) + 2000(0) = 450,000$

$A(30,60) = 9000(30) + 2000(60) = 390,000$

b) To maximize the audience they should use 50 TV ads and 0 radio ads.

19. Let $x =$ the number of doubles and $y =$ the number of triples. We can write four inequalities.

$x \geq 0$

$y \geq 0$

$2x + 3y \leq 24$

$6x + 3y \leq 48$

Graph the system of inequalities. The vertices of the region are (0, 8), (6, 4), (8, 0), and (0, 0). Since Doubles are $1.20 each and Triples are $1.50 each, the revenue in dollars from x Doubles and y Triples is given by $R(x, y) = 1.2x + 1.5y$.

Find the revenue at each vertex.

$R(0, 0) = 0$

$R(0, 8) = 1.2(0) + 1.5(8) = \$12.00$

$R(6, 4) = 1.2(6) + 1.5(4) = \$13.20$

$R(8, 0) = 1.2(8) + 1.5(0) = \$9.60$

The maximum revenue occurs at (6, 4). So they should make 6 Doubles and 4 Triples to maximize their revenue.

20. Let $x =$ the number of chairs and $y =$ the number of swings. We can write four inequalities concerning x and y.

$x \geq 0$

$y \geq 0$

$3x + 2y \leq 48$

$2x + 2y \leq 40$

Graph the system of inequalities. The vertices of the region are (0, 0), (0, 20), (16, 0), and (8, 12). Since the chairs sell for $160 each and the swings sell for $100 each, the total revenue in dollars from x chairs and y swings is given by the function

$R(x, y) = 160x + 100y$.

Find the revenue at each vertex.

$R(0, 0) = 0$

$R(0, 20) = 160(0) + 100(20) = \$2,000$

$R(16, 0) = 160(16) + 100(0) = \$2,560$

$R(8, 12) = 160(8) + 100(12) = \$2,480$

The maximum revenue subject to the constraints occurs at (16, 0). So they should make 16 rocking chairs and no porch swings.

21. Let $x =$ the number of Doubles and $y =$ the number of Triples. The constraints and the graph are the same as in Exercise 19. Since the Doubles now sell for $1.00 each and the Triples now sell for $2.00 each, the revenue in dollars is given by the function is $R(x, y) = x + 2y$. Find the revenue at each vertex.

$R(0, 0) = 0$

$R(0, 8) = 0 + 2(8) = \$16.00$

$R(6, 4) = 6 + 2(4) = \$14.00$

$R(8, 0) = 8 + 2(0) = \$8.00$

The maximum revenue occurs at (0, 8). So to maximize the revenue they should make no Doubles and 8 Triples.

22. Let $x =$ the number of rocking chairs and $y =$ the number of porch swings. The constraints and the region are the same as in Exercise 20. Since the chairs now sell for $120 each and the swings sell for $100 each, the revenue in dollars is given by $R(x, y) = 120x + 100y$. Find the revenue at each vertex.

$R(0, 0) = 0$

$R(0, 20) = 120(0) + 100(20) = \$2,000$

$R(16, 0) = 120(16) + 100(0) = \$1,920$

$R(8, 12) = 120(8) + 100(12) = \$2,160$

The maximum revenue occurs at (8, 12). So they should make 8 rocking chairs and 12 swings to maximize their revenue.

23. Let $x =$ the number of cups of Doggie Dinner, and $y =$ the number of cups of Puppie Power. We can write four inequalities.

$x \geq 0$

$y \geq 0$

$20x + 30y \geq 200$

$40x + 20y \geq 180$

Graph the region that satisfies the constraints. Since one cup of Doggie Dinner costs 16 cents

167

and one cup of Puppie Power costs 20 cents, the total cost in dollars for x cups of DD and y cups of PP is $C(x, y) = 0.16x + 0.20y$.

Find the cost at each vertex.
$C(0, 9) = 0.16(0) + 0.20(9) = \$1.80$
$C(1.75, 5.5) = 0.16(1.75) + 0.20(5.5) = \$1.38$
$C(10, 0) = 0.16(10) + 0.20(0) = \$1.60$

The minimum cost occurs at $(1.75, 5.5)$. To minimize the cost and satisfy the constraints she should use 1.75 cups of DD and 5.5 cups of PP.

24. Let $x =$ the number of supervisors and $y =$ the number of helpers. We can write 4 inequalities.
$x \geq 0$
$y \geq 0$
$2x + 6y \geq 24$
$3x + 3y \geq 18$

Graph the system of inequalities. Since a supervisor makes \$90 per day and a helper makes \$100 per day, the total daily cost in dollars is given by the function
$C(x, y) = 90x + 100y$.

Find the cost at each vertex.
$C(0, 6) = 90(0) + 100(6) = \$600$
$C(3, 3) = 90(3) + 100(3) = \$570$
$C(12, 0) = 90(12) + 100(0) = \$1080$

The minimum cost occurs at $(3, 3)$. So they should employ 3 supervisors and 3 helpers per day to get a minimum cost for labor subject to the given constraints.

25. If the cost of one cup of DD is 4 cents and one cup of PP is 10 cents then the total cost in dollars of x cups of DD and y cups of PP is $C(x, y) = 0.04x + 0.10y$. The inequalities and the region are the same as in Exercise 23. Find the cost at each vertex of the region.

$C(0, 9) = 0.04(0) + 0.10(9) = \$0.90$
$C(1.75, 5.5) = 0.04(1.75) + 0.10(5.5) = \$0.62$
$C(10, 0) = 0.04(10) + 0.10(0) = \$0.40$

The minimum cost occurs at $(10, 0)$. She should use 10 cups of DD and 0 cups of PP to satisfy the constraints and minimize the cost.

26. If the supervisor makes \$110 per day and the helper makes \$100 per day, then the cost in dollars is given by the function
$C(x, y) = 110x + 100y$. The constraints and the region are the same as in Exercise 24. Find the cost at each vertex.
$C(0, 6) = 110(0) + 100(6) = \$600$
$C(3, 3) = 110(3) + 100(3) = \$630$
$C(12, 0) = 110(12) + 100(0) = \$1320$
The minimum cost occurs at $(0, 6)$. So they should use no supervisors and 6 helpers to minimize the cost subject to the given constraints.

27. Let $x =$ the amount invested in the laundromat and $y =$ the amount invested in the car wash. We can write four inequalities.
$x \geq 0$
$y \geq 0$
$x + y \leq 24{,}000$
$2x \leq y \leq 3x$

Graph the region that satisfies the system of inequalities. Since she makes 18% on the money invested in the laundry and 12% on the money invested in the car wash, the income in dollars is given by the function
$I(x, y) = 0.18x + 0.12y$.
Find the income at each vertex.

$I(0, 0) = 0$
$I(8000, 16000) = 0.18(8000) + 0.12(16000)$
$\qquad\qquad\qquad = \$3{,}360$
$I(6000, 18000) = 0.18(6000) + 0.12(18000)$
$\qquad\qquad\qquad = \$3{,}240$

The maximum income occurs at $(8000, 16000)$. So she should invest \$8,000 in the laundromat and \$16,000 in the car wash.

28. Let $x =$ the number of economy models and $y =$ the number of deluxe models. We can write four inequalities.

$x \geq 0$

$y \geq 0$

$2x + 3y \leq 180$

$4x + 4y \leq 280$

Graph the region that satisfies the system of inequalities. Since the profit on an economy model is \$60 and the profit on a deluxe model is \$100, the total profit in dollars is given by the function $P(x, y) = 60x + 100y$. Find the profit at each vertex of the region.

$P(0, 0) = 0$

$P(0, 60) = 60(0) + 100(60) = \$6{,}000$

$P(30, 40) = 60(30) + 100(40) = \$5{,}800$

$P(70, 0) = 60(70) + 100(0) = \$4{,}200$

The maximum profit occurs at $(0, 60)$. So he should order no economy models and 60 deluxe models to maximize his profit subject to the given constraints.

Enriching Your Mathematical Word Power

1. c   2. a   3. a   4. d
5. b   6. c   7. a   8. c
9. d   10. b   11. a   12. d

CHAPTER 4 REVIEW

1. The graph of $y = 2x - 1$ has y-intercept $(0, -1)$ and slope 2. the graph of $y = -x + 2$ has y-intercept $(0, 2)$ and slope -1. The graphs appear to intersect at $(1, 1)$. Check that $(1, 1)$ satisfies both equations. The solution set is $\{(1, 1)\}$ and the system is independent.

2. The graph of $y = -x$ is a line with y-intercept $(0, 0)$ and slope -1. The graph of $y = -x + 3$ is a line with slope -1 and y-intercept $(0, 3)$. The lines are parallel and the equations are inconsistent. The solution set is $\emptyset$.

3. The graph of $y = 3x - 4$ has y-intercept $(0, -4)$ and slope 3. The graph of $y = -2x + 1$ has y-intercept $(0, 1)$ and slope -2. The lines appear to intersect at $(1, -1)$. After checking that $(1, -1)$ satisfies both

equations, we can be certain that the solution set is $\{(1, -1)\}$ and the system is independent.

4. The graph of $x + y = 5$ (or $y = -x + 5$) is a line with y-intercept $(0, 5)$ and slope -1. The graph of $x - y = -1$ (or $y = x + 1$) is a line with slope 1 and y-intercept $(0, 1)$. The lines appear to intersect at $(2, 3)$. Check that $(2, 3)$ satisfies both equations of the system. The system is independent. The solution set is $\{(2, 3)\}$.

5. Substitute $y = 3x + 11$ into $2x + 3y = 0$.

$2x + 3(3x + 11) = 0$

$11x + 33 = 0$

$11x = -33$

$x = -3$

$y = 3(-3) + 11 = 2$

The solution set is $\{(-3, 2)\}$ and the system is independent.

6. Write $x - y = 3$ as $y = x - 3$ and substitute into $3x - 2y = 3$.

$3x - 2(x - 3) = 3$

$3x - 2x + 6 = 3$

$x = -3$

$y = x - 3$

$= -3 - 3 = -6$

The solution set is $\{(-3, -6)\}$. The system is independent.

7. Substitute $x = y + 5$ into $2x - 2y = 12$.

$2(y + 5) - 2y = 12$

$2y + 10 - 2y = 12$

$10 = 12$

The solution set is $\emptyset$ and the system is inconsistent.

8. Write $2x - y = 3$ as $y = 2x - 3$. Substitute into $6x - 9 = 3y$.

$6x - 9 = 3(2x - 3)$

$6x - 9 = 6x - 9$

Since the last equation is an identity, the solution set is $\{(x, y) \mid 2x - y = 3\}$. The system is dependent.

9. Multiply the first equation by 2 and the second by 3, and then add the resulting equations.

$0x - 6y = -40$

$9x + 6y = 21$

$\overline{19x \qquad = -19}$

$$x = -1$$

Use $x = -1$ in $3x + 2y = 7$.
$$3(-1) + 2y = 7$$
$$2y = 10$$
$$y = 5$$

The solution set is $\{(-1, 5)\}$ and the system is independent.

10. Multiply the first equation by 3 and add the result to the second equation.
$$\begin{array}{r} -9x + 3y = 9 \\ \underline{2x - 3y = 5} \\ -7x \quad\quad = 14 \\ x = -2 \end{array}$$

Use $x = -2$ in $-3x + y = 3$ to find y.
$$-3(-2) + y = 3$$
$$6 + y = 3$$
$$y = -3$$

The solution set is $\{(-2, -3)\}$. The system is independent.

11. Rewrite the first equation.
$$2(y - 5) + 4 = 3(x - 6)$$
$$2y - 10 + 4 = 3x - 18$$
$$-3x + 2y = -12$$

Add this last equation to the original second equation.
$$\begin{array}{r} -3x + 2y = -12 \\ \underline{3x - 2y = 12} \\ 0 = 0 \end{array}$$

The two equations are just different forms of an equation for the same straight line. The solution set is $\{(x, y) \mid 3x - 2y = 12\}$ and the system is dependent.

12. Rewrite the first equation in the same form as the last so that they can be added.
$$3x - 4(y - 5) = x + 2$$
$$3x - 4y + 20 = x + 2$$
$$2x - 4y = -18$$
$$x - 2y = -9$$
$$-2y + x = -9$$

Add this last equation with the second equation.
$$\begin{array}{r} -2y + x = -9 \\ \underline{2y - x = 7} \\ 0 = -2 \end{array}$$

Since the result of the addition is a false statement, the system is inconsistent. The solution set is $\emptyset$.

13. Add the first and second equations.
$$\begin{array}{r} 2x - y - z = 3 \\ \underline{3x + y + 2z = 4} \\ 5x \quad\quad + z = 7 \quad \text{A} \end{array}$$

Multiply the first equation by 2 and add the result to the last equation.
$$\begin{array}{r} 4x - 2y - 2z = 6 \\ \underline{4x + 2y - z = -4} \\ 8x \quad\quad - 3z = 2 \quad \text{B} \end{array}$$

Multiply equation A by 3 and add the result to equation B.
$$\begin{array}{r} 15x + 3z = 21 \\ \underline{8x - 3z = 2} \\ 23x \quad\quad = 23 \\ x = 1 \end{array}$$

Use $x = 1$ in $8x - 3z = 2$.
$$8(1) - 3z = 2$$
$$-3z = -6$$
$$z = 2$$

Use $x = 1$ and $z = 2$ in $3x + y + 2z = 4$.
$$3(1) + y + 2(2) = 4$$
$$y = -3$$

The solution set is $\{(1, -3, 2)\}$.

14. Multiply the last equation by -2 and add the result to the first equation.
$$\begin{array}{r} 2x + 3y - 2z = -11 \\ \underline{-2x + 8y - 8z = -28} \\ 11y - 10z = -39 \quad \text{A} \end{array}$$

Multiply the last equation by -3 and add the result to the second equation.
$$\begin{array}{r} 3x - 2y + 3z = 7 \\ \underline{-3x + 12y - 12z = -42} \\ 10y - 9z = -35 \quad \text{B} \end{array}$$

Multiply A by -10 and B by 11, and add the resulting equations.
$$\begin{array}{r} -110y + 100z = 390 \\ \underline{110y - 99z = -385} \\ z = 5 \end{array}$$

Use $z = 5$ in $10y - 9z = -35$ to find y.
$$10y - 9(5) = -35$$
$$10y = 10$$
$$y = 1$$

Use $z = 5$ and $y = 1$ in $x - 4y + 4z = 14$ to find x.
$$x - 4(1) + 4(5) = 14$$
$$x + 16 = 14$$

$$x = -2$$

The solution set is $\{(-2, 1, 5)\}$.

15. Add the first two equations.
$$x - 3y + z = 5$$
$$2x - 4y - z = 7$$
$$\overline{\hspace{1em} 3x - 7y \hspace{1.5em} = 12 \hspace{1em}} \quad \text{A}$$
Multiply the second equation by 2 and add the result to the last equation.
$$4x - 8y - 2z = 14$$
$$2x - 6y + 2z = 6$$
$$\overline{\hspace{1em} 6x - 14y \hspace{1.5em} = 20 \hspace{1em}} \quad \text{B}$$
Multiply equation A by -2 and add the result to equation B.
$$-6x + 14y = -24$$
$$6x - 14y = 20$$
$$\overline{\hspace{4em} 0 = -4 \hspace{1em}}$$
The solution set is $\emptyset$.

16. Multiply the first equation by -2 and add the result to the second equation.
$$-2x + 2y - 2z = -2$$
$$2x - 2y + 2z = 2$$
$$\overline{\hspace{4em} 0 = 0 \hspace{1em}}$$
Multiply the first equation by 3 and add the result to the third equation.
$$3x - 3y + 3z = 3$$
$$-3x + 3y - 3z = -3$$
$$\overline{\hspace{4em} 0 = 0 \hspace{1em}}$$
Since each of the equations is a multiple of the first equation, the system is dependent. The solution set is $\{(x, y, z) \mid x - y + z = 1\}$.

17. $\begin{bmatrix} 1 & -3 & 14 \\ 2 & 1 & 0 \end{bmatrix}$

$\begin{bmatrix} 1 & -3 & 14 \\ 0 & 7 & -28 \end{bmatrix}$ $-2R_1 + R_2 \to R_2$

$\begin{bmatrix} 1 & -3 & 14 \\ 0 & 1 & -4 \end{bmatrix}$ $R_2 \div 7 \to R_2$

$\begin{bmatrix} 1 & 0 & 2 \\ 0 & 1 & -4 \end{bmatrix}$ $3R_2 + R_1 \to R_1$

The solution set is $\{(2, -4)\}$.

18. $\begin{bmatrix} 2 & -1 & 8 \\ 3 & 2 & -2 \end{bmatrix}$

$\begin{bmatrix} 2 & -1 & 8 \\ 1 & 3 & -10 \end{bmatrix}$ $-R_1 + R_2 \to R_2$

$\begin{bmatrix} 1 & 3 & -10 \\ 2 & -1 & 8 \end{bmatrix}$ $R_1 \leftrightarrow R_2$

$\begin{bmatrix} 1 & 3 & -10 \\ 0 & -7 & 28 \end{bmatrix}$ $-2R_1 + R_2 \to R_2$

$\begin{bmatrix} 1 & 3 & -10 \\ 0 & 1 & -4 \end{bmatrix}$ $R_2 \div (-7) \to R_2$

$\begin{bmatrix} 1 & 0 & 2 \\ 0 & 1 & -4 \end{bmatrix}$ $-3R_2 + R_1 \to R_1$

The solution set is $\{(2, -4)\}$.

19. $\begin{bmatrix} 1 & 1 & -1 & 0 \\ 1 & -1 & 2 & 4 \\ 2 & 1 & -1 & 1 \end{bmatrix}$

$\begin{bmatrix} 1 & 1 & -1 & 0 \\ 0 & -2 & 3 & 4 \\ 0 & -1 & 1 & 1 \end{bmatrix}$ $-R_1 + R_2 \to R_2$

$-2R_1 + R_3 \to R_3$

$\begin{bmatrix} 1 & 1 & -1 & 0 \\ 0 & -1 & 1 & 1 \\ 0 & -2 & 3 & 4 \end{bmatrix}$ $R_2 \leftrightarrow R_3$

$\begin{bmatrix} 1 & 1 & -1 & 0 \\ 0 & 1 & -1 & -1 \\ 0 & -2 & 3 & 4 \end{bmatrix}$ $-R_2 \to R_2$

$\begin{bmatrix} 1 & 0 & 0 & 1 \\ 0 & 1 & -1 & -1 \\ 0 & 0 & 1 & 2 \end{bmatrix}$ $-R_2 + R_1 \to R_1$

$2R_2 + R_3 \to R_3$

$\begin{bmatrix} 1 & 0 & 0 & 1 \\ 0 & 1 & 0 & 1 \\ 0 & 0 & 1 & 2 \end{bmatrix}$ $R_3 + R_2 \to R_2$

The solution set is $\{(1, 1, 2)\}$.

20.
$$\begin{bmatrix} 2 & -1 & 2 & 9 \\ 1 & 3 & 0 & 5 \\ 3 & 0 & 1 & 9 \end{bmatrix}$$

$$\begin{bmatrix} 1 & 3 & 0 & 5 \\ 2 & -1 & 2 & 9 \\ 3 & 0 & 1 & 9 \end{bmatrix} \quad R_1 \leftrightarrow R_2$$

$$\begin{bmatrix} 1 & 3 & 0 & 5 \\ 0 & -7 & 2 & -1 \\ 0 & -9 & 1 & -6 \end{bmatrix} \quad -2R_1 + R_2 \to R_2$$
$$-3R_1 + R_3 \to R_3$$

$$\begin{bmatrix} 1 & 3 & 0 & 5 \\ 0 & 1 & -2/7 & 1/7 \\ 0 & -9 & 1 & -6 \end{bmatrix} \quad R_2 \div (-7) \to R_2$$

$$\begin{bmatrix} 1 & 0 & 6/7 & 32/7 \\ 0 & 1 & -2/7 & 1/7 \\ 0 & 0 & -11/7 & -33/7 \end{bmatrix} \quad -3R_2 + R_1 \to R_1$$
$$9R_2 + R_3 \to R_3$$

$$\begin{bmatrix} 1 & 0 & 6/7 & 32/7 \\ 0 & 1 & -2/7 & 1/7 \\ 0 & 0 & 1 & 3 \end{bmatrix}$$

$$-\tfrac{6}{7}R_3 + R_1 \to R_1$$
$$\begin{bmatrix} 1 & 0 & 0 & 2 \\ 0 & 1 & 0 & 1 \\ 0 & 0 & 1 & 3 \end{bmatrix} \quad \tfrac{2}{7}R_3 + R_2 \to R_2$$

The solution set is $\{(2, 1, 3)\}$.

21. $\begin{vmatrix} 1 & 3 \\ 0 & 2 \end{vmatrix} = 1 \cdot 2 - 0 \cdot 3 = 2$

22. $\begin{vmatrix} -1 & 2 \\ -3 & 5 \end{vmatrix} = -1 \cdot 5 - (-3) \cdot 2 = 1$

23. $\begin{vmatrix} 0.01 & 0.02 \\ 50 & 80 \end{vmatrix} = 0.01(80) - 0.02(50)$
$$= 0.8 - 1 = -0.2$$

24. $\begin{vmatrix} 1/2 & 1/3 \\ 1/4 & 1/5 \end{vmatrix} = \tfrac{1}{2} \cdot \tfrac{1}{5} - \tfrac{1}{4} \cdot \tfrac{1}{3}$
$$= \tfrac{1}{10} - \tfrac{1}{12} = \tfrac{1}{60}$$

25. $D = \begin{vmatrix} 2 & -1 \\ 3 & 1 \end{vmatrix} = 5$

$D_x = \begin{vmatrix} 0 & -1 \\ -5 & 1 \end{vmatrix} = -5$

$D_y = \begin{vmatrix} 2 & 0 \\ 3 & -5 \end{vmatrix} = -10$

$x = \frac{D_x}{D} = \frac{-5}{5} = -1 \qquad y = \frac{D_y}{D} = \frac{-10}{5} = -2$
The solution set is $\{(-1, -2)\}$.

26. $D = \begin{vmatrix} 3 & -2 \\ 2 & 3 \end{vmatrix} = 13$

$D_x = \begin{vmatrix} 14 & -2 \\ -8 & 3 \end{vmatrix} = 26$

$D_y = \begin{vmatrix} 3 & 14 \\ 2 & -8 \end{vmatrix} = -52$

$x = \frac{D_x}{D} = \frac{26}{13} = 2 \qquad y = \frac{D_y}{D} = \frac{-52}{13} = -4$
The solution set is $\{(2, -4)\}$.

27. Write the system in standard form.
$$-2x + y = -3$$
$$3x - 2y = 4$$

$D = \begin{vmatrix} -2 & 1 \\ 3 & -2 \end{vmatrix} = 1$

$D_x = \begin{vmatrix} -3 & 1 \\ 4 & -2 \end{vmatrix} = 2$

$D_y = \begin{vmatrix} -2 & -3 \\ 3 & 4 \end{vmatrix} = 1$

$x = \frac{D_x}{D} = \frac{2}{1} = 2 \qquad y = \frac{D_y}{D} = \frac{1}{1} = 1$

The solution set is $\{(2, 1)\}$.

28. $2x - 5y = -1$
$$-4x + 10y = 2$$

$D = \begin{vmatrix} 2 & -5 \\ -4 & 10 \end{vmatrix} = 0$

Since $D = 0$, Cramer's Rule does not apply. If we multiply the first equation by -2, we get the second equation. So the equations are equivalent and the system is dependent. The solution set is $\{(x, y) \mid 2x - 5y = -1\}$.

29. Rewrite the system in standard form.
$$3x - y = -1$$
$$-6x + 2y = 5$$

$$D = \begin{vmatrix} 3 & -1 \\ -6 & 2 \end{vmatrix} = 0$$

Since $D = 0$, we cannot use Cramer's rule. Multiply the first equation by 2 and add the result to the second equation.
$$6x - 2y = -2$$
$$\underline{-6x + 2y = 5}$$
$$0 = 3$$
The solution set is $\emptyset$.

30. Rewrite the system as follows.
$$2x - y = 5$$
$$3x - 4y = 0$$

$$D = \begin{vmatrix} 2 & -1 \\ 3 & -4 \end{vmatrix} = -5$$

$$D_x = \begin{vmatrix} 5 & -1 \\ 0 & -4 \end{vmatrix} = -20$$

$$D_y = \begin{vmatrix} 2 & 5 \\ 3 & 0 \end{vmatrix} = -15$$

$$x = \frac{D_x}{D} = \frac{-20}{-5} = 4 \qquad y = \frac{D_y}{D} = \frac{-15}{-5} = 3$$

The solution set is $\{(4, 3)\}$.

31. Expand by minors using the first column.

$$2 \begin{vmatrix} 2 & 4 \\ 1 & 1 \end{vmatrix} - (-1) \begin{vmatrix} 3 & 1 \\ 1 & 1 \end{vmatrix} + 6 \begin{vmatrix} 3 & 1 \\ 2 & 4 \end{vmatrix}$$

$$= 2(-2) + 2 + 6(10) = 58$$

32. Expand by minors using the last column.

$$0 \begin{vmatrix} -2 & 0 \\ 3 & 1 \end{vmatrix} - (0) \begin{vmatrix} 1 & -1 \\ 3 & 1 \end{vmatrix} + 5 \begin{vmatrix} 1 & -1 \\ -2 & 0 \end{vmatrix}$$
$$= 0(-2) - 0(4) + 5(-2) = -10$$

33. Expand by minors using the second column.

$$-3 \begin{vmatrix} 2 & 4 \\ -1 & 3 \end{vmatrix} + 0 \begin{vmatrix} 2 & -2 \\ -1 & 3 \end{vmatrix} - 0 \begin{vmatrix} 2 & -2 \\ 2 & 4 \end{vmatrix}$$
$$= -3(10) = -30$$

34. Expand by minors using the third row.

$$-2 \begin{vmatrix} -1 & 4 \\ -1 & 1 \end{vmatrix} - 0 \begin{vmatrix} 3 & 4 \\ 2 & 1 \end{vmatrix} + 1 \begin{vmatrix} 3 & -1 \\ 2 & -1 \end{vmatrix}$$
$$= -2(3) - 0(-5) + 1(-1) = -7$$

35. $D = \begin{vmatrix} 1 & 1 & 0 \\ 1 & 1 & 1 \\ 1 & -1 & -1 \end{vmatrix} = 2$

$$D_x = \begin{vmatrix} 3 & 1 & 0 \\ 0 & 1 & 1 \\ 2 & -1 & -1 \end{vmatrix} = 2$$

$$D_y = \begin{vmatrix} 1 & 3 & 0 \\ 1 & 0 & 1 \\ 1 & 2 & -1 \end{vmatrix} = 4$$

$$D_z = \begin{vmatrix} 1 & 1 & 3 \\ 1 & 1 & 0 \\ 1 & -1 & 2 \end{vmatrix} = -6$$

$$x = \frac{D_x}{D} = \frac{2}{2} = 1, \qquad y = \frac{D_y}{D} = \frac{4}{2} = 2,$$

$$z = \frac{D_z}{D} = \frac{-6}{2} = -3$$

The solution set is $\{(1, 2, -3)\}$.

36. $D = \begin{vmatrix} 2 & -4 & 2 \\ 1 & -1 & -1 \\ 1 & -2 & 1 \end{vmatrix} = 0$

Since $D = 0$, Cramer's rule does not apply. Multiply the second equation by 2 and add the result to the first equation.
$$2x - 4y + 2z = 6$$
$$\underline{2x - 2y - 2z = 2}$$
$$4x - 6y \qquad = 8 \qquad \text{A}$$
Add the second and third equations.
$$x - y - z = 1$$
$$\underline{x - 2y + z = 4}$$
$$2x - 3y \qquad = 5 \qquad \text{B}$$
Multiply B by -2 and add the result to A.

$$4x - 6y = 8$$
$$\underline{-4x + 6y = -10}$$
$$0 = -2$$

Since the last equation is false, there is no solution to the system. The solution set is $\emptyset$.

37. $D = \begin{vmatrix} 2 & -1 & 1 \\ 4 & 6 & -2 \\ 1 & -2 & -1 \end{vmatrix} = -36$

$D_x = \begin{vmatrix} 0 & -1 & 1 \\ 0 & 6 & -2 \\ -9 & -2 & -1 \end{vmatrix} = 36$

$D_y = \begin{vmatrix} 2 & 0 & 1 \\ 4 & 0 & -2 \\ 1 & -9 & -1 \end{vmatrix} = -72$

$D_z = \begin{vmatrix} 2 & -1 & 0 \\ 4 & 6 & 0 \\ 1 & -2 & -9 \end{vmatrix} = -144$

$x = \dfrac{D_x}{D} = \dfrac{36}{-36} = -1,$

$y = \dfrac{D_y}{D} = \dfrac{-72}{-36} = 2,$

$z = \dfrac{D_z}{D} = \dfrac{-144}{-36} = 4$

The solution set is $\{(-1, 2, 4)\}$.

38. $D = \begin{vmatrix} 3 & -3 & -3 \\ 2 & -2 & -2 \\ 1 & -1 & -1 \end{vmatrix} = 0$

Since $D = 0$, Cramer's rule does not apply. Note that if we multiply the last equation by 2, we get the second equation. If we multiply the last equation by 3, we get the first equation. So all three equations are equivalent. The solution set is $\{(x, y, z) \mid x - y - z = 1\}$.

39. The graph of $x \geq 0$ consists of points on and to the right of the y-axis. The graph of $y \geq 0$ consists of points on and above the x-axis. The graph of $x + 2y \leq 6$ consists of points on and below the line $x + 2y = 6$. The graph of $x + y \leq 5$ consists of points on and below the line $x + y = 5$. Points that satisfy all 4 inequalities are shown in the following graph.

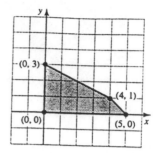

The vertices of the region are $(0, 3)$, $(4, 1)$, $(5, 0)$, and $(0, 0)$.

40. The graph of $x \geq 0$ consists of points on and to the right of the y-axis. The graph of $y \geq 0$ consists of points on and above the x-axis. The graph of $3x + 2y \geq 12$ consists of points on and above the line $3x + 2y = 12$. The graph of $x + 2y \geq 8$ consists of points on and above the line $x + 2y = 8$. Points that satisfy all 4 inequalities are shown in the following graph.

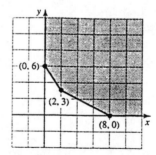

The vertices of the region are $(0, 6)$, $(2, 3)$, and $(8, 0)$.

41. First graph the region that satisfies the four inequalities. The vertices of the region are $(0, 0)$, $(0, 3)$, $(2, 2)$, and $(3, 0)$.
Evaluate $R(x, y) = 6x + 9y$ at each vertex.
$R(0, 0) = 0$

$R(0, 3) = 6(0) + 9(3) = 27$
$R(2, 2) = 6(2) + 9(2) = 30$

174

$R(3, 0) = 6(3) + 9(0) = 18$

The maximum value of $R(x, y)$ is 30.

42. First graph the region that satisfies all four inequalities. The vertices of the region are $(0, 6)$, $(1, 3)$, and $(4, 0)$. Evaluate $C(x, y) = 9x + 10y$ at each vertex of the region.

$C(0, 6) = 9(0) + 10(6) = 60$
$C(1, 3) = 9(1) + 10(3) = 39$
$C(4, 0) = 9(4) + 10(0) = 36$

The minimum value of $C(x, y)$ is 36.

43. Let $x =$ the tens digit and $y =$ the ones digit. The value of the number is $10x + y$. If the digits are reversed the value will be $10y + x$.
We can write the following two equations.

$x + y = 15$
$10x + y = 10y + x - 9$

$x + y = 15$
$9x - 9y = -9$

$\begin{array}{r} x + y = 15 \\ x - y = -1 \\ \hline 2x = 14 \\ x = 7 \end{array}$

$y = 8$ Since $x + y = 15$

The number is 78.

44. Let $x =$ the tens digit and $y =$ the ones digit. The value of the original number is $10x + y$ and the value of the number after the digits are reversed is $x + 10y$. We can write two equations.

$x + y = 8$
$x + 10y = 10x + y - 18$

$x + y = 8$
$-9x + 9y = -18$

$\begin{array}{r} x + y = 8 \\ -x + y = -2 \\ \hline 2y = 6 \end{array}$

$y = 3$
Since $x + y = 8$ and $y = 3$, we have $x = 5$. So the original number is 53.

45. Let $b =$ his boat's speed in still water and $c =$ the speed of the current. Let $t =$ his time to go the same distance in the lake.

	Distance	Rate	Time
Down	$\frac{1}{2}(b + c)$	$b + c$	$\frac{1}{2}$
Back	$\frac{3}{4}(b - c)$	$b - c$	$\frac{3}{4}$
Lake	bt	b	t

Since the distance down the stream is the same as the distance going back, we can write the following equation.

$\frac{1}{2}(b + c) = \frac{3}{4}(b - c)$
$\frac{1}{2}b + \frac{1}{2}c = \frac{3}{4}b - \frac{3}{4}c$
$2b + 2c = 3b - 3c$
$5c = b$

Since $bt = \frac{1}{2}(b + c)$, we can substitute $b = 5c$ into this equation.

$(5c)t = \frac{1}{2}(5c + c)$
$5ct = 3c$
$t = \frac{3c}{5c} = \frac{3}{5}$

So the time in the lake is 3/5 of an hour or 36 minutes.

46. Let $x =$ Gasper's age now and $y =$ Gasper's age when he is old enough to drive.

$x + 4 = y$
$x - 3 = \frac{1}{2}(y + 2)$

Use substitution.

$x - 3 = \frac{1}{2}(x + 4 + 2)$
$2x - 6 = x + 6$
$x = 12$
$y = 12 + 4 = 16$

Gasper is now 12 years old and he must be 16 years old to drive.

47. Let $x =$ the number of liters of solution A, $y =$ the number of liters of solution B, and $z =$ the number of liters of solution C. We can write 3 equations.

$x + y + z = 20$
$0.30x + 0.20y + 0.60z = 0.38(20)$
$z = 2x$

Substitute $z = 2x$ into the other two equations.

$$x + y + 2x = 20$$
$$0.3x + 0.2y + 0.6(2x) = 7.6$$

$$3x + y = 20$$
$$1.5x + 0.2y = 7.6$$

Substitute $y = 20 - 3x$ into the second equation.
$$1.5x + 0.2(20 - 3x) = 7.6$$
$$0.9x + 4 = 7.6$$
$$0.9x = 3.6$$
$$x = 4$$

If $x = 4$, then $y = 30 - 3(4) = 8$ and $z = 2(4) = 8$. She should use 4 liters of 30% solution, 8 liters of 20% solution, and 8 liters of 60% solution.

48. a) From the graph, it appears that she invested about \$13,000 in Dell and \$7000 in bonds.

b) Let $x =$ the amount invested at 70% and $y =$ the amount invested at 5%. We can write two equations.
$$x + y = 20{,}000$$
$$0.70x + 0.05y = 9580$$

Substitute $y = 20{,}000 - x$ into the second equation.
$$0.70x + 0.05(20{,}000 - x) = 9580$$
$$0.70x + 1000 - 0.05x = 9580$$
$$0.65x = 8580$$
$$x = 13{,}200$$

If $x = 13{,}200$ and $x + y = 20{,}000$, then $y = 6{,}800$. She invested \$13,200 at 70% and \$6,800 at 5%.

49. Let $x =$ the number of servings of beets and $y =$ the number of servings of beans. We can write two equations.
$$x + 6y = 21$$
$$6x + 20y = 78$$

Substitute $x = 21 - 6y$ into $6x + 20y = 78$.
$$6(21 - 6y) + 20y = 78$$
$$126 - 36y + 20y = 78$$
$$-16y = -48$$
$$y = 3$$

If $y = 3$, then $x = 21 - 6(3) = 3$. It would take 3 servings of each.

Chapter 4 TEST

1. The graph of $y = -x + 4$ is a straight line with y-intercept $(0, 4)$ and slope -1. The graph of $y = 2x + 1$ is a straight line with y-intercept $(0, 1)$ and slope 2. The graphs appear to intersect at $(1, 3)$. After checking that $(1, 3)$ satisfies both equations, we can be sure that the solution set is $\{(1, 3)\}$.

2. Substitute $y = 2x - 8$ into $4x + 3y = 1$.
$$4x + 3(2x - 8) = 1$$
$$10x = 25$$
$$x = \tfrac{5}{2}$$

If $x = 5/2$, then $y = 2(5/2) - 8 = -3$. The solution set is $\left\{ \left(\tfrac{5}{2}, -3 \right) \right\}$.

3. Substitute $y = x - 5$ into the second equation $3x - 4(y - 2) = 28 - x$.
$$3x - 4(x - 5 - 2) = 28 - x$$
$$3x - 4(x - 7) = 28 - x$$
$$28 - x = 28 - x$$

Since the last equation is an identity, the solution set is $\{(x, y) \mid y = x - 5\}$.

4. Multiply the first equation by 3 and the second by 2 and add the results.
$$9x + 6y = 9$$
$$\underline{8x - 6y = -26}$$
$$17x \quad\quad = -17$$
$$x = -1$$

Use $x = -1$ in $3x + 2y = 3$ to find y.
$$3(-1) + 2y = 3$$
$$2y = 6$$
$$y = 3$$

The solution set is $\{(-1, 3)\}$.

5. Multiply the first equation by 2 and then add the result to the second equation.
$$6x - 2y = 10$$
$$\underline{-6x + 2y = 1}$$
$$0 = 11$$

The solution set to the system is $\emptyset$.

6. The lines both have slope 3 and different y-intercepts, so they are parallel. There is no solution to the system. The system is inconsistent.

7. If we multiply the second equation by 2, the result is the same as the first equation. These are two equations for the same straight line. The system is dependent.

8. The lines have different slopes and different y-intercepts. They will intersect in exactly one point. The system is independent.

9. Add the first two equations.

$$x + y - z = 2$$
$$\underline{2x - y + 3z = -5}$$
$$3x \quad\ + 2z = -3 \quad \text{A}$$

Multiply the first equation by 3 and add the result to the last equation.

$$3x + 3y - 3z = 6$$
$$\underline{x - 3y + z = 4}$$
$$4x \quad\ - 2z = 10 \quad \text{B}$$

Add equations A and B.

$$3x + 2z = -3$$
$$\underline{4x - 2z = 10}$$
$$7x \qquad = 7$$
$$x = 1$$

Use $x = 1$ in $3x + 2z = -3$.

$$3(1) + 2z = -3$$
$$2z = -6$$
$$z = -3$$

Use $x = 1$ and $z = -3$ in $x + y - z = 2$.

$$1 + y - (-3) = 2$$
$$y = -2$$

The solution set is $\{(1, -2, -3)\}$.

10.
$$\begin{bmatrix} 1 & 2 & 12 \\ 3 & -1 & 1 \end{bmatrix}$$

$$\begin{bmatrix} 1 & 2 & 12 \\ 0 & -7 & -35 \end{bmatrix} \quad -3R_1 + R_2 \to R_2$$

$$\begin{bmatrix} 1 & 2 & 12 \\ 0 & 1 & 5 \end{bmatrix} \quad R_2 \div (-7) \to R_2$$

$$\begin{bmatrix} 1 & 0 & 2 \\ 0 & 1 & 5 \end{bmatrix} \quad -2R_2 + R_1 \to R_1$$

The solution set is $\{(2, 5)\}$.

11.
$$\begin{bmatrix} 1 & -1 & -1 & 1 \\ -1 & -1 & 2 & -2 \\ -1 & -3 & 1 & -5 \end{bmatrix}$$

$$\begin{bmatrix} 1 & -1 & -1 & 1 \\ 0 & -2 & 1 & -1 \\ 0 & -4 & 0 & -4 \end{bmatrix} \quad \begin{array}{l} R_1 + R_2 \to R_2 \\[4pt] R_1 + R_3 \to R_3 \end{array}$$

$$\begin{bmatrix} 1 & -1 & -1 & 1 \\ 0 & -4 & 0 & -4 \\ 0 & -2 & 1 & -1 \end{bmatrix} \quad R_2 \leftrightarrow R_3$$

$$\begin{bmatrix} 1 & -1 & -1 & 1 \\ 0 & 1 & 0 & 1 \\ 0 & -2 & 1 & -1 \end{bmatrix} \quad R_2 \div (-4) \to R_2$$

$$\begin{bmatrix} 1 & 0 & -1 & 2 \\ 0 & 1 & 0 & 1 \\ 0 & 0 & 1 & 1 \end{bmatrix} \quad \begin{array}{l} R_2 + R_1 \to R_1 \\[4pt] 2R_2 + R_3 \to R_3 \end{array}$$

$$\begin{bmatrix} 1 & 0 & 0 & 3 \\ 0 & 1 & 0 & 1 \\ 0 & 0 & 1 & 1 \end{bmatrix} \quad R_3 + R_1 \to R_1$$

The solution set is $\{(3, 1, 1)\}$.

12. $\begin{vmatrix} 2 & 3 \\ 4 & -3 \end{vmatrix} = 2(-3) - 4(3) = -18$

13. Expand by minors using the third column.

$$-1 \begin{vmatrix} 2 & 3 \\ 1 & 1 \end{vmatrix} - 1 \begin{vmatrix} 1 & -2 \\ 1 & 1 \end{vmatrix} + 0 \begin{vmatrix} 1 & -2 \\ 2 & 3 \end{vmatrix}$$
$$= -1(-1) - 1(3) + 0(7) = -2$$

14. $D = \begin{vmatrix} 2 & -1 \\ 3 & 1 \end{vmatrix} = 5$

$$D_x = \begin{vmatrix} -4 & -1 \\ -1 & 1 \end{vmatrix} = -5$$

$$D_y = \begin{vmatrix} 2 & -4 \\ 3 & -1 \end{vmatrix} = 10$$

$$x = \frac{D_x}{D} = \frac{-5}{5} = -1 \qquad y = \frac{D_y}{D} = \frac{10}{5} = 2$$

The solution set is $\{(-1, 2)\}$.

15. $D = \begin{vmatrix} 1 & 1 & 0 \\ 1 & -1 & 2 \\ 2 & 1 & -1 \end{vmatrix} = 4$

$D_x = \begin{vmatrix} 0 & 1 & 0 \\ 6 & -1 & 2 \\ 1 & 1 & -1 \end{vmatrix} = 8$

$D_y = \begin{vmatrix} 1 & 0 & 0 \\ 1 & 6 & 2 \\ 2 & 1 & -1 \end{vmatrix} = -8$

$D_z = \begin{vmatrix} 1 & 1 & 0 \\ 1 & -1 & 6 \\ 2 & 1 & 1 \end{vmatrix} = 4$

$x = \frac{D_x}{D} = \frac{8}{4} = 2, \qquad y = \frac{D_y}{D} = \frac{-8}{4} = -2,$
$z = \frac{D_z}{D} = \frac{4}{4} = 1$ The solution set is
$\{(2, -2, 1)\}$.

16. Let $x =$ the price of a single and $y =$ the price of a double. We can write an equation for each night.

$5x + 12y = 390$
$9x + 10y = 412$

Multiply the first equation by -9 and the second by 5, then add the results.

$\begin{array}{r} -45x - 108y = -3510 \\ \underline{45x + 50y = 2060} \\ -58y = -1450 \\ y = 25 \end{array}$

Use $y = 25$ in $5x + 12y = 390$ to find x.

$5x + 12(25) = 390$
$5x + 300 = 390$
$5x = 90$
$x = 18$

So singles rent for $18 per night and doubles rent for $25 per night.

17. Let $x =$ Jill's study time, $y =$ Karen's study time, and $z =$ Betsy's study time. We can write three equations.

$x + y + z = 93$
$x + y = \frac{1}{2}z$
$x = y + 3$

Rewrite the equations as follows.

$x + y + z = 93$
$2x + 2y - z = 0$
$x - y = 3$

Adding the first two equations to eliminate z gives us $3x + 3y = 93$, or $x + y = 31$. Add this result to the third equation.

$\begin{array}{r} x + y = 31 \\ \underline{x - y = 3} \\ 2x = 34 \\ x = 17 \end{array}$

Since $x + y = 31$, we get $y = 14$. Use $x = 17$ and $y = 14$ in the first equation.

$17 + 14 + z = 93$
$z = 62$

So Jill studied 17 hours, Karen studied 14 hours, and Betsy studied 62 hours.

18. First graph the system of inequalities. The vertices of the region are $(0, 0)$, $(0, 4)$, $(3, 2)$, and $(5, 0)$. Evaluate the function $P(x, y) = 8x + 10y$ at each vertex.

$P(0, 0) = 0$
$P(0, 4) = 8(0) + 10(4) = 40$
$P(3, 2) = 8(3) + 10(2) = 44$
$P(5, 0) = 8(5) + 10(0) = 40$

The maximum value of the function $P(x, y)$ is 44.

Making Connections

Chapters 1 - 4

1. $-3^4 = -(3^4) = -81$

2. $\frac{1}{3}(3) + 6 = 1 + 6 = 7$

3. $(-5)^2 - 4(-2)(6) = 25 - (-48) = 73$

4. $6 - (0.2)(0.3) = 6 - 0.06 = 5.94$

5. $5(t - 3) - 6(t - 2) = 5t - 15 - 6t + 12$
$ = -t - 3$

6. $0.1(x - 1) - (x - 1) = 0.1x - 0.1 - x + 1$
$ = -0.9x + 0.9$

7. $\frac{-9x^2 - 6x + 3}{-3} = 3x^2 + 2x - 1$

8. $\frac{4y - 6}{2} - \frac{3y - 9}{3} = 2y - 3 - (y - 3)$
$\phantom{\frac{4y-6}{2}-\frac{3y-9}{3}} = y$

9. $3x - 5y = 7$
$-5y = -3x + 7$
$y = \frac{3}{5}x - \frac{7}{5}$

10. $Cx - Dy = W$

$$-Dy = -Cx + W$$
$$y = \frac{C}{D}x - \frac{W}{D}$$

11. $Cy = Wy - K$

$$K = Wy - Cy$$
$$K = y(W - C)$$
$$y = \frac{K}{W - C}$$

12. $A = \frac{1}{2}b(w - y)$

$$2A = bw - by$$
$$by = bw - 2A$$
$$y = \frac{bw - 2A}{b}$$

13. $2x + 3(x - 5) = 5$

$$5x - 15 = 5$$
$$5x = 20$$
$$x = 4$$
$$y = x - 5 = 4 - 5 = -1$$

The solution set is $\{(4, -1)\}$.

14. $y = 1200 - x$

$$0.05x + 0.06(1200 - x) = 67$$
$$-0.01x + 72 = 67$$
$$-0.01x = -5$$
$$x = 500$$
$$y = 1200 - x = 1200 - 500 = 700$$

The solution set is $\{(500, 700)\}$.

15. $x = 5y - 17$

$$3(5y - 17) - 15y = -51$$
$$15y - 51 - 15y = -51$$
$$-51 = -51$$

The equations are equivalent and the solution set is $\{(x, y) \mid x + 17 = 5y\}$.

16. Multiply the first equation by 100 to get $7a + 30b = 670$. This equation is inconsistent with the equation $7a + 30b = 67$. So the solution set is the empty set $\emptyset$.

17. The slope of the line is 55/99 or 5/9. Since the y-intercept is $(0, 55)$, the equation is $y = \frac{5}{9}x + 55$.

18. The slope of the line through $(2, -3)$ and $(-4, 8)$ is $11/-6$ or $-11/6$. Use the point-slope formula:

$$y - 8 = -\frac{11}{6}(x - (-4))$$
$$y - 8 = -\frac{11}{6}x - \frac{44}{6}$$
$$y = -\frac{11}{6}x - \frac{22}{3} + \frac{24}{3}$$
$$y = -\frac{11}{6}x + \frac{2}{3}$$

19. Any line parallel to $y = 5x$ has slope 5.

$$y - 6 = 5(x - (-4))$$
$$y - 6 = 5x + 20$$
$$y = 5x + 26$$

20. Any line perpendicular to $y = -2x + 1$ has slope $1/2$.

$$y - 7 = \frac{1}{2}(x - 4)$$
$$y - 7 = \frac{1}{2}x - 2$$
$$y = \frac{1}{2}x + 5$$

21. Any line parallel to the x-axis has slope 0 and is of the form $y = k$. Since it must go through $(3, 5)$ it is $y = 5$.

22. Any line perpendicular to the x-axis is of the form $x = k$. So the equation is $x = -7$.

23. a) From the y-intercept we see that the purchase price for A is \$4000 and for B is \$2000. So A has the larger purchase price.

b) Machine B makes 300,000 copies for \$12,000, or \$0.04 per copy. Machine A makes 300,000 copies for \$9,000 or \$0.03 per copy.

c) The slope of the line for machine B is 0.04 and the slope of the line for machine A is 0.03, which is the per copy cost for each machine.

d) Machine B: $y = 0.04x + 2000$
Machine A: $y = 0.03x + 4000$

e) $0.04x + 2000 = 0.03x + 4000$

$$0.01x = 2000$$
$$x = 200,000$$

The total costs are equal at 200,000 copies.

5.1 WARM-UPS

1. True, because $3^5 \cdot 3^4 = 3^{5+4} = 3^9$.
2. False, because $3 \cdot 3 \cdot 3^{-1} = 9 \cdot \frac{1}{3} = 3$.
3. False, because $10^{-3} = \frac{1}{1000} = 0.001$.
4. True, because the reciprocal of 1 is 1.
5. True, because $\frac{2^5}{2^{-2}} = 2^{5-(-2)} = 2^7$.
6. False, because $2^3 \cdot 5^2 = 8 \cdot 25 = 200$.
7. True, because $-2^{-2} = -\frac{1}{2^2} = -\frac{1}{4}$.
8. True, $46.7 \times 10^5 = 4.67 \times 10^1 \times 10^5$.
9. True, $0.512 \times 10^{-3} = 5.12 \times 10^{-1} \times 10^{-3}$.
10. False, because $\frac{8 \times 10^{30}}{2 \times 10^{-5}} = 4 \times 10^{35}$.

5.1 EXERCISES

1. An exponential expression is an expression of the form a^n.
2. The expression $a^{-n} = 1/a^n$ for any positive integer n and $a \neq 0$.
3. The product rule says that $a^m a^n = a^{m+n}$.
4. The quotient rule says that $a^m / a^n = a^{m-n}$.
5. To convert a number in scientific notation to standard notation move the decimal point n places to the left if the exponent on 10 is $-n$ or move the decimal point n places to the right if the exponent on 10 is n, assuming that n is a positive integer.
6. To convert from standard notation to scientific notation, count the number of decimal places, n, required to move the decimal point so that there is one nonzero digit to the left of the decimal point. Use 10^n if you moved the decimal point to the left and use 10^{-n} if you moved the decimal point to the right.
7. $4^2 = 4 \cdot 4 = 16$
8. $3^3 = 3 \cdot 3 \cdot 3 = 27$
9. $4^{-2} = \frac{1}{4^2} = \frac{1}{16}$
10. $3^{-3} = \frac{1}{3^3} = \frac{1}{27}$
11. $\left(\frac{1}{4}\right)^{-2} = 4^2 = 16$
12. $\left(\frac{3}{5}\right)^{-1} = \frac{5}{3}$
13. $\left(-\frac{3}{4}\right)^{-2} = \left(-\frac{4}{3}\right)^2 = \frac{16}{9}$
14. $10^2 \cdot \left(-\frac{1}{10}\right)^{-2} = 10^2 \cdot 10^2 = 10^4$
    $= 10,000$
15. $-2^{-1}(-6)^2 = -\frac{1}{2} \cdot 36 = -18$
16. $-2^{-3}(-4)^2 = -\frac{1}{8} \cdot 16 = -2$

17. $3 \cdot 10^{-3} = 3 \cdot \frac{1}{1000} = 0.003$
18. $5 \cdot 10^4 = 5 \cdot 10,000 = 50,000$
19. $\frac{1}{2^{-4}} = 2^4 = 16$
20. $\frac{2}{2^{-3}} = 2 \cdot 2^3 = 2 \cdot 8 = 16$
21. $2^5 \cdot 2^{12} = 2^{5+12} = 2^{17}$
22. $2x^2 \cdot 3x^3 = 6x^{2+3} = 6x^5$
23. $2y^{3+2-7} = 2y^{-2} = \frac{2}{y^2}$
24. $2 \cdot 10^6 \cdot 5 \cdot 10^{-7} = 10 \cdot 10^{-1} = 1$
25. $5 \cdot 6 \cdot x^{-3}x^{-4} = 30x^{-7} = \frac{30}{x^7}$
26. $4a^{-13}a^{-4} = 4a^{-17} = \frac{4}{a^{17}}$
27. $-8^0 - 8^0 = -1 - 1 = -2$
28. $(-8 - 8)^0 = (-16)^0 = 1$
29. $(x - y)^0 = 1$
30. $(x^2 - y^2)^0 = 1$
31. $2w^{-3+7-4} = 2w^0 = 2 \cdot 1 = 2$
32. $5y^2 zy^{-3}z^{-1} = 5y^{-1}z^0 = \frac{5}{y}$
33. $\frac{2}{4^{-2}} = 2 \cdot 4^2 = 2 \cdot 16 = 32$
34. $\frac{5}{10^{-3}} = 5 \cdot 10^3 = 5 \cdot 1000 = 5000$
35. $\frac{3^{-1}}{10^{-2}} = \frac{10^2}{3^1} = \frac{100}{3}$
36. $\frac{2y^{-2}}{3^{-1}} = \frac{2 \cdot 3^1}{y^2} = \frac{6}{y^2}$
37. $\frac{2x^{-3}(4x)}{5y^{-2}} = \frac{8x^{-2}}{5y^{-2}} = \frac{8y^2}{5x^2}$
38. $\frac{5^{-2}xy^{-3}}{3x^{-2}} = \frac{x^3}{25 \cdot 3y^3} = \frac{x^3}{75y^3}$
39. $\frac{4^{-2}x^3 x^{-6}}{3x^{-3}x^2} = \frac{x^{-3}}{16 \cdot 3x^{-1}} = \frac{x^{-2}}{48} = \frac{1}{48x^2}$
40. $\frac{3y^{-4}y^{-6}}{2^{-3}y^2 y^{-7}} = \frac{3 \cdot 2^3 y^{-10}}{y^{-5}} = 24y^{-5} = \frac{24}{y^5}$
41. $x^{5-3} = x^2$
42. $\frac{a^8}{a^3} = a^{8-3} = a^5$
43. $3^{6-(-2)} = 3^8$
44. $\frac{6^2}{6^{-5}} = 6^{2-(-5)} = 6^7$
45. $\frac{4a^{-5-(-2)}}{12} = \frac{a^{-3}}{3} = \frac{1}{3a^3}$
46. $\frac{-3a^{-3}}{-21a^{-4}} = \frac{a^{-3-(-4)}}{7} = \frac{a}{7}$
47. $-3w^{-5-3} = -3w^{-8} = \frac{-3}{w^8}$
48. $\frac{10x^{-6}}{-2x^2} = -5x^{-6-2} = -5x^{-8} = \frac{-5}{x^8}$
49. $\frac{3^3 w^3}{3^{-5}w^{-3}} = 3^8 w^6$
50. $\frac{2^{-3}w^5}{2^5 w^3 w^{-7}} = \frac{2^{-3-5}w^{12}}{w^3} = 2^{-8}w^9 = \frac{w^9}{2^8}$

51. $\dfrac{3x^{-4}y}{6x^{-5}} = \dfrac{x^{-4-(-5)}y}{2} = \dfrac{xy}{2}$

52. $\dfrac{2r^{-3}t^{-1}}{10r^5t^{-1}} = \dfrac{1}{5r^8}$

53. $3^{-1} \cdot \left(\frac{1}{3}\right)^{-3} = \frac{1}{3} \cdot 3^3 = 9$

54. $2^{-2} \cdot \left(\frac{1}{4}\right)^{-3} = \frac{1}{4} \cdot 4^3 = 4^2 = 16$

55. $-2^4 + \left(\frac{1}{2}\right)^{-1} = -16 + 2 = -14$

56. $-3^4 - (-3)^4 = -81 - 81 = -162$

57. $-(-2)^{-3} \cdot 2^{-1} = -\left(-\frac{1}{8}\right)\frac{1}{2} = \frac{1}{16}$

58. $-(-3)^{-1} \cdot 9^{-1} = -\left(-\frac{1}{3}\right)\frac{1}{9} = \frac{1}{27}$

59. $\left(1 + \frac{1}{2}\right)^{-2} = \left(\frac{3}{2}\right)^{-2} = \left(\frac{2}{3}\right)^{2} = \frac{4}{9}$

60. $(2^{-1} + 2^{-1})^{-2} = \left(\frac{1}{2} + \frac{1}{2}\right)^{-2} = 1^{-2} = 1$

61. $-5a^2 \cdot 3a^2 = -15a^4$

62. $2x^2 \cdot 5x^{-5} = 10x^{-3} = \dfrac{10}{x^3}$

63. $5a \cdot a^2 + 3a^{-2} \cdot a^5 = 5a^3 + 3a^3 = 8a^3$

64. $2x^2 \cdot 5y^{-5} = 10x^2y^{-5} = \dfrac{10x^2}{y^5}$

65. $\dfrac{-3a^5(-2a^{-1})}{6a^3} = \dfrac{6a^4}{6a^3} = a$

66. $\dfrac{6a(-ab^{-2})}{-2a^2b^{-3}} = \dfrac{-6a^2b^{-2}}{-2a^2b^{-3}} = 3b$

67. $\dfrac{(-3x^3y^2)(-2xy^{-3})}{-9x^2y^{-5}} = \dfrac{6x^4y^{-1}}{-9x^2y^{-5}}$

$\qquad = \dfrac{-2x^2y^4}{3}$

68. $\dfrac{(-2x^{-5}y)(-3xy^6)}{-6x^{-6}y^2} = \dfrac{6x^{-4}y^7}{-6x^{-6}y^2} = -x^2y^5$

69. $\dfrac{2^{-1} + 3^{-1}}{2^{-1}} = \left(\frac{1}{2} + \frac{1}{3}\right) \cdot \frac{2}{1} = \frac{5}{6} \cdot \frac{2}{1} = \frac{5}{3}$

70. $\dfrac{3^{-1} + 4^{-1}}{12^{-1}} = \left(\frac{1}{3} + \frac{1}{4}\right)\frac{12}{1} = \frac{7}{12} \cdot \frac{12}{1} = 7$

71. $\dfrac{(2+3)^{-1}}{2^{-1} + 3^{-1}} = \dfrac{5^{-1}}{\frac{1}{2} + \frac{1}{3}} = \frac{1}{5} \div \frac{5}{6} = \frac{6}{25}$

72. $\dfrac{(3-4)^{-1}}{3 \cdot 2^{-1}} = \dfrac{(-1)^{-1}}{\frac{3}{2}} = -1 \cdot \frac{2}{3} = -\frac{2}{3}$

73. $8 = 2^3$

74. $27 = 3^3$

75. $\frac{1}{4} = 2^{-2}$

76. $\frac{1}{125} = 5^{-3}$

77. $16 = \left(\frac{1}{2}\right)^{-4}$

78. $81 = \left(\frac{1}{3}\right)^{-4}$

79. $10^{-3} = 0.001$

80. $10^4 = 10,000$

81. Since the exponent in 4.86×10^8 is positive, we move the decimal point 8 places to the right: 486,000,000

82. Since the exponent in 3.80×10^2 is positive, move the decimal point 2 places to the right: 380

83. Since the exponent in 2.37×10^{-6} is negative, we move the decimal point 6 places to the left:
0.00000237

84. Since the exponent in 1.62×10^{-3} is negative, we move the decimal point 3 places to the left: 0.00162

85. Since the exponent in 4×10^6 is positive, we move the decimal point 6 places to the right:
4,000,000

86. Since the exponent in 496×10^3 is positive, we move the decimal point 3 places to the right: 496,000

87. Since the exponent in 5×10^{-6} is negative, we move the decimal point 6 places to the left:
0.000005

88. Since the exponent in 48×10^{-3} is negative, we move the decimal point 3 places to the left: 0.048

89. The decimal point in 320,000 must be moved 5 places to the left for scientific notation. Since the original number is larger than 10 the exponent is positive: 3.2×10^5

90. The decimal point in 43,298,000 must be moved 7 places to the left for scientific notation. Since the original number is larger than 10 the exponent is positive: 4.3298×10^7

91. The decimal point in 0.00000071 must be moved 7 places to the right to get scientific notation. Since the original number is smaller than 1, the exponent is negative: 7.1×10^{-7}

92. The decimal point in 0.00000894 must be moved 6 places to the right to get scientific notation. Since the original number is smaller than 1, the exponent is negative: 8.94×10^{-6}

93. Move the decimal point 5 places to the right: 7×10^{-5}

94. Move the decimal point 6 places to the left: 8.2951×10^6

95. $235 \times 10^5 = 2.35 \times 10^2 \times 10^5$
$\qquad = 2.35 \times 10^7$

96. $0.43 \times 10^{-9} = 4.3 \times 10^{-1} \times 10^{-9}$
$\qquad = 4.3 \times 10^{-10}$

97. $\dfrac{5 \times 10^6 \cdot 3 \times 10^{-4}}{2 \times 10^3} = \dfrac{7.5 \times 10^2}{10^3}$

$\qquad = 7.5 \times 10^{-1}$

98. $\dfrac{(6000)(0.00004)}{(30,000)(0.002)} = \dfrac{6 \times 10^3 \cdot 4 \times 10^{-5}}{3 \times 10^4 \cdot 2 \times 10^{-3}}$

$= 4 \times 10^{3+(-5)-4-(-3)} = 4 \times 10^{-3}$

99. By the quotient rule, we subtract exponents when we divide exponential expressions:
3×10^{22}

100. $\dfrac{4.6 \times 10^{12}}{2.3 \times 10^5} = 2 \times 10^7$

101. $\dfrac{(-4 \times 10^5)(6 \times 10^{-9})}{2 \times 10^{-16}}$

$\qquad = -12 \times 10^{5+(-9)-(-16)}$

$\qquad = -12 \times 10^{12}$

$\qquad = -1.2 \times 10^1 \times 10^{12} = -1.2 \times 10^{13}$

102. $\dfrac{(4.8 \times 10^{-3})(5 \times 10^{-8})}{(1.2 \times 10^{-6})(2 \times 10^{12})}$

$= 4 \times 10^{-3-(-6)} \cdot 2.5 \times 10^{-8-12}$

$= 4 \times 10^3 \cdot 2.5 \times 10^{-20}$

$= 10 \times 10^{-17} = 1 \times 10^{-16}$

103. Enter the numbers into a calculator using scientific notation. The calculator will give answers to the computations in scientific notation. 1.578×10^5

104. Use a calculator to get
$(2.34 \times 10^6)(8.7 \times 10^5) = 2.036 \times 10^{12}$.

105. 9.187×10^{-5}

106. $(6.72 \times 10^5) + (8.98 \times 10^6)$

$\qquad = 9.652 \times 10^6$

107. Multiply 9.27 and 6.43 on a calculator to get 59.606. Since most calculators do not handle scientific notation with exponents higher than 99, we must add the exponents without entering the numbers as scientific notation. We get $59.606 \times 10^{156} = 5.961 \times 10^1 \times 10^{156}$
$= 5.961 \times 10^{157}$

108. $(1.35 \times 10^{66})(2.7 \times 10^{74})$
$= (1.35)(2.7) \times 10^{140} = 3.645 \times 10^{140}$

109. 3.828×10^{30}

110. $\dfrac{(3.51 \times 10^{-6})^3(4000)^5}{2\pi} = 7.048$

111. $9.3 \times 10^7 \text{miles} \times \dfrac{5280 \text{ feet}}{1 \text{ mile}}$

$\qquad = 4.910 \times 10^{11}$ ft

112. Use 93 million miles or 4.910×10^{11} ft from Exercise 111 as the distance from the sun to the earth and the fact that $T = D/R$.

$T = \dfrac{4.910 \times 10^{11} \text{ ft}}{9.83569 \times 10^8 \text{ ft/sec}} = 499.2$ seconds

$= 499.2 \text{ seconds} \cdot \tfrac{1 \text{ minute}}{60 \text{ seconds}} = 8.3$ minutes

113. Since $T = \dfrac{D}{R}$, $T = \dfrac{4.6 \times 10^{12} \text{ km}}{1.2 \times 10^5 \text{ kps}}$

$\qquad = 3.83 \times 10^7$ seconds

114. Since $C = \pi D$, we have $D = C/\pi$.

$D = \dfrac{2.35 \times 10^{-8}}{\pi} = 7.480 \times 10^{-9}$ meters

115. $\dfrac{8.71 \times 10^7 \text{ ton} \times \frac{2000 \text{ lb}}{1 \text{ ton}}}{1.80863 \times 10^8 \text{ people}} \div 365 \text{ day} =$

2.6 lb/person/day

116. a) $\dfrac{4.324 \times 10^{11} \text{ lb}}{2.70058 \times 10^8 \text{ people}} \div 365 \text{ day}$

$\qquad = 4.4$ lb/person/day in 1998

b) 5.0 lb/person/day in 2010

5.2 WARM-UPS

1. False, because $(2^2)^3 = 2^6$.

2. True, because $(2^{-3})^{-1} = 2^3 = 8$.

3. True, because we $3(-3) = -9$.

4. False, because $(2^3)^3 = 2^9$.

5. False, because $(2x)^3 = 2^3 x^3 = 8x^3$.

6. False, because $(-3y^3)^2 = 9y^6$.

7. True, the reciprocal of $\frac{2}{3}$ is $\frac{3}{2}$.

8. True, because $\left(\frac{2}{3}\right)^3 = \frac{2^3}{3^3} = \frac{8}{27}$.

9. True, because $\left(\frac{x^2}{2}\right)^3 = \frac{x^6}{2^3} = \frac{x^6}{8}$.

10. True, because $\left(\frac{2}{x}\right)^{-2} = \left(\frac{x}{2}\right)^2 = \frac{x^2}{4}$.

5.2 EXERCISES

1. The power of a power rule says that $(a^m)^n = a^{mn}$.

2. The power of a product rule says that $(ab)^m = a^m b^m$.

3. The power of a quotient rule says that $(a/b)^m = a^m/b^m$.

4. Principal is the amount of money invested initially.

5. To compute the amount A when interest is compounded annually use $A = P(1 + i)^n$

where P is the principal, i is the annual interest rate, and n is the number of years.

6. To compute the present value P for the amount A in n years at annual interest rate i, use $P = A(1+i)^{-n}$.

7. $2^6 = 64$

8. $(3^2)^2 = 3^4 = 81$

9. $y^{2\cdot 5} = y^{10}$

10. $(x^6)^2 = x^{6\cdot 2} = x^{12}$

11. $(x^2)^{-4} = x^{(2)(-4)} = x^{-8} = \dfrac{1}{x^8}$

12. $x^{-14} = \dfrac{1}{x^{14}}$

13. $(m^{-3})^{-6} = m^{(-3)(-6)} = m^{18}$

14. $(a^{-3})^{-3} = a^{(-3)(-3)} = a^9$

15. $x^6 x^{-6} = x^0 = 1$

16. $(m^{-3})^{-1}(m^2)^{-4} = m^3 \cdot m^{-8} = m^{-5}$
$$= \dfrac{1}{m^5}$$

17. $\dfrac{x^{-12}}{x^{-10}} = x^{-2} = \dfrac{1}{x^2}$

18. $\dfrac{(a^2)^{-3}}{(a^{-2})^4} = \dfrac{a^{-6}}{a^{-8}} = a^{-6-(-8)} = a^2$

19. $9^2 y^2 = 81 y^2$

20. $(-2a)^3 = -2^3 a^3 = -8a^3$

21. $(-5w^3)^2 = (-5)^2 w^6 = 25w^6$

22. $(-2w^{-5})^3 = (-2)^3(w^{-5})^3 = -8w^{-15}$
$$= \dfrac{-8}{w^{15}}$$

23. $x^9 y^{-6} = \dfrac{x^9}{y^6}$

24. $(a^2 b^{-3})^2 = (a^2)^2 (b^{-3})^2 = a^4 b^{-6} = \dfrac{a^4}{b^6}$

25. $3^{-2} a^{-2} b^2 = \dfrac{b^2}{9a^2}$

26. $(2x^{-1} y^2)^{-3} = 2^{-3} \cdot x^3 \cdot y^{-6} = \dfrac{x^3}{8y^6}$

27. $\dfrac{2xy^{-2}}{3^{-1} x^{-2} y^{-1}} = 2 \cdot 3 x^3 y^{-1} = \dfrac{6x^3}{y}$

28. $\dfrac{3ab^{-1}}{(5ab^2)^{-1}} = \dfrac{3ab^{-1}}{5^{-1} a^{-1} b^{-2}}$
$$= 3 \cdot 5 a^{1-(-1)} b^{-1-(-2)} = 15 a^2 b$$

29. $\dfrac{2^{-2} a^{-2} b^{-2}}{2ab^2} = 2^{-3} a^{-3} b^{-4} = \dfrac{1}{8a^3 b^4}$

30. $\dfrac{(3xy)^{-3}}{3xy^3} = \dfrac{3^{-3} x^{-3} y^{-3}}{3xy^3}$
$$= 3^{-4} x^{-3-1} y^{-3-3}$$
$$= 3^{-4} x^{-4} y^{-6} = \dfrac{1}{81 x^4 y^6}$$

31. $\dfrac{w^3}{2^3} = \dfrac{w^3}{8}$

32. $\left(\dfrac{m}{5}\right)^2 = \dfrac{m^2}{5^2} = \dfrac{m^2}{25}$

33. $\dfrac{(-3)^3 a^3}{4^3} = -\dfrac{27a^3}{64}$

34. $\left(-\dfrac{2}{3b}\right)^4 = \dfrac{(-2)^4}{3^4 b^4} = \dfrac{16}{81 b^4}$

35. $\dfrac{2^{-2} x^2}{y^{-2}} = \dfrac{x^2 y^2}{4}$

36. $\left(\dfrac{2a^2 b}{3}\right)^{-3} = \dfrac{2^{-3} a^{-6} b^{-3}}{3^{-3}} = \dfrac{27}{8 a^6 b^3}$

37. $\left(\dfrac{-3x^3}{y}\right)^{-2} = \dfrac{(-3)^{-2}(x^3)^{-2}}{y^{-2}} = \dfrac{x^{-6} y^2}{(-3)^2}$
$$= \dfrac{y^2}{9x^6}$$

38. $\dfrac{(-2)^{-3} y^{-6}}{x^{-3}} = -\dfrac{x^3}{8y^6}$

39. $\left(\dfrac{2}{5}\right)^{-2} = \left(\dfrac{5}{2}\right)^2 = \dfrac{25}{4}$

40. $\left(\dfrac{3}{4}\right)^{-2} = \left(\dfrac{4}{3}\right)^2 = \dfrac{4^2}{3^2} = \dfrac{16}{9}$

41. $\left(-\dfrac{1}{2}\right)^{-2} = (-2)^2 = 4$

42. $\left(-\dfrac{2}{3}\right)^{-2} = \left(-\dfrac{3}{2}\right)^2 = \dfrac{3^2}{2^2} = \dfrac{9}{4}$

43. $\left(-\dfrac{3}{2x}\right)^3 = -\dfrac{3^3}{2^3 x^3} = -\dfrac{27}{8x^3}$

44. $\left(-\dfrac{ab}{c}\right)^{-1} = -\dfrac{c}{ab}$

45. $\left(\dfrac{3y}{2x^2}\right)^3 = \dfrac{3^3 y^3}{2^3 (x^2)^3} = \dfrac{27 y^3}{8x^6}$

46. $\left(\dfrac{ab^{-3}}{a^2 b}\right)^2 = \dfrac{a^{-2} b^6}{a^{-4} b^{-2}} = a^{-2-(-4)} b^{6-(-2)}$
$$= a^2 b^8$$

47. $5^{2t} \cdot 5^{4t} = 5^{6t}$

48. $3^{2n-3} \cdot 3^{4-2n} = 3^1 = 3$

49. $\left(2^{-3w}\right)^{-2w} = 2^{6w^2}$

50. $6^{8x}\left(6^{2x}\right)^{-3} = 6^{8x} \cdot 6^{-6x} = 6^{2x}$

51. $\dfrac{7^{2m+6}}{7^{m+3}} = 7^{2m+6-m-3} = 7^{m+3}$

52. $\dfrac{4^{-3p}}{4^{-4p}} = 4^{-3p+4p} = 4^p$

53. $8^{2a-1}\left(8^{a+4}\right)^3 = 8^{2a-1} \cdot 8^{3a+12}$
$$= 8^{5a+11}$$

54. $\left(5^{4-3y}\right)^3 \left(5^{y-2}\right)^2 = 5^{12-9y} \cdot 5^{2y-4}$
$$= 5^{8-7y}$$

55. Add the exponents: $6x^9$

56. $(3x^4)^2 = 3^2(x^4)^2 = 9x^8$

57. Multiply the exponents: $-8x^6$

58. $3x^2 \cdot 2x^{-4} = 6x^{2+(-4)} = 6x^{-2} = \dfrac{6}{x^2}$

183

59. Eliminate negative exponents: $\dfrac{3z}{x^2y}$

60. $\dfrac{2^{-1}x^2}{y^{-2}} = \dfrac{x^2y^2}{2}$

61. The reciprocal of $-\frac{2}{3}$ is $-\frac{3}{2}$.

62. $\left(\frac{-1}{5}\right)^{-1} = (-5)^1 = -5$

63. Multiply the exponents: $\dfrac{4x^6}{9}$

64. $\left(\dfrac{-2y^4}{x}\right)^3 = \dfrac{(-2)^3(y^4)^3}{x^3} = -\dfrac{8y^{12}}{x^3}$

65. $(-2x^{-2})^{-1} = (-2)^{-1}x^2 = -\dfrac{x^2}{2}$

66. $(-3x^{-2})^3 = (-3)^3x^{-6} = -\dfrac{27}{x^6}$

67. $\left(\dfrac{2x^2y}{xy^2}\right)^{-3} = \left(\dfrac{xy^2}{2x^2y}\right)^3 = \dfrac{x^3y^6}{8x^6y^3} = \dfrac{y^3}{8x^3}$

68. $\left(\dfrac{2x^3y^2}{3xy^3}\right)^{-1} = \dfrac{3xy^3}{2x^3y^2} = \dfrac{3y}{2x^2}$

69. $\dfrac{5^3a^{-3}b^6}{5^4a^4b^{-8}} = 5^{-1}a^{-7}b^{14} = \dfrac{b^{14}}{5a^7}$

70. $\dfrac{(2m^2n^{-3})^4}{mn^5} = \dfrac{2^4(m^2)^4(n^{-3})^4}{mn^5}$

$= \dfrac{16m^8n^{-12}}{mn^5} = \dfrac{16m^7}{n^{17}}$

71. $\dfrac{2^{-3}x^6y^{-3}}{2^2x^2y^{-2}} \cdot 2x^2y^{-7} = 2^{-4}x^6y^{-8} = \dfrac{x^6}{16y^8}$

72. $\dfrac{(3x^{-1}y^3)^{-2}}{(3xy^{-1})^3} \cdot 9x^{-9}y^5 = \dfrac{3^{-2}x^2y^{-6} \cdot 9x^{-9}y^5}{3^3 \cdot x^3y^{-3}}$

$= 3^{-5} \cdot 9 \cdot x^{-10}y^2 = \dfrac{y^2}{27x^{10}}$

73. $\dfrac{6^{-2}a^4b^{-6}}{2^{-2}c^{-8}} \cdot 3^3a^{-3}b^6 = 3a^1b^0c^8 = 3ac^8$

74. $(7xz^2)^{-4}\left(\dfrac{7xy^{-1}}{z}\right)^3$

$= 7^{-4}x^{-4}z^{-8} \cdot \dfrac{7^3x^3y^{-3}}{z^3}$

$= \dfrac{7^{-1}x^{-1}z^{-8}y^{-3}}{z^3} = \dfrac{1}{7xy^3z^{11}}$

75. $32 \cdot 64 = 2^5 \cdot 2^6 = 2^{11}$

76. $8^{20} = (2^3)^{20} = 2^{60}$

77. $81 \cdot 6^{-4} = 3^4(2 \cdot 3)^{-4} = 3^4 2^{-4} 3^{-4} = 2^{-4}$

78. $(10)^{-6} \cdot (2 \cdot 10)^6 = 2^6$

79. $4^{3n} = (2^2)^{3n} = 2^{6n}$

80. $(2 \cdot 3)^{n-5} \cdot 3^{5-n} = 2^{n-5}3^{n-5}3^{5-n}$

$= 2^{n-5}$

81. $\left(\dfrac{1}{(2^4)^{-m}}\right)^m = \left(\dfrac{1}{2^{-4m}}\right)^m = (2^{4m})^m$

$= 2^{4m^2}$

82. $\dfrac{(2^5)^n}{(2^7)^{3n}} = \dfrac{2^{5n}}{2^{21n}} = 2^{-16n}$

83. $\dfrac{1}{5^{-2}} = 25$

84. $\dfrac{(2.5)^{-3}}{(2.5)^{-5}} = 6.25$

85. $2^{-1} + 2^{-2} = 0.75$

86. $\left(\frac{2}{3}\right)^{-1} + 2^{-1} = 2$

87. $(0.036)^{-2} + (4.29)^3 \approx 850.559$

88. $3(4.71)^2 - 5(0.471)^{-3} \approx 18.700$

89. $\dfrac{(5.73)^{-1} + (4.29)^{-1}}{(3.762)^{-1}} \approx 1.533$

90. $[5.29 + (0.374)^{-1}]^3 \approx 505.080$

91. $40{,}000(1 + 0.12)^3 = 40{,}000(1.12)^3$
$= \$56{,}197.12$

92. a) $10{,}000(1 + 0.09)^{10} = \$23{,}673.64$
b) $10{,}000(1 + 0.19)^{10} = \$56{,}946.84$
Stock investment worth \$33,273.20 more than bond investment.

93. $10{,}000(1 + 0.07)^{-18} = \$2{,}958.64$

94. $2{,}000{,}000(1 + 0.045)^{-45} = \$275{,}928.73$

95. a) $L = 72.2(1.002)^{20} \approx 75.1$ yr
b) $L = 72.2(1.002)^{60} \approx 81.4$ yr

96. a) $L = 78.5(1.001)^{20} \approx 80.1$
b) $78.5(1.001)^{26} = 80.6$ years
$72.2(1.002)^{30} = 76.7$ years.
When Bob dies at 76.7, Ashley will be 72.7 years old and will live until 80.6, or 7.9 years as a widow.
c) At 80 both males and females have about 5 years of life expectancy.

99. All expressions have value -1 except (d) which has value 1.

100. a) True, because $(ab)^2 = a^2b^2$.
b) False, because $(a + b)^2 = a^2 + 2ab + b^2$.

101. b) $(6.116, 20{,}000)$ c) 6.116 years

102. b) $(87.54, 86)$ c) At 87.54 years of age you can expect to live until 86. The model fails here.

5.3 WARM-UPS

1. False, because it has a negative exponent.
2. False, because the coefficient of x is -5.
3. False, because the highest power of x is 3.
4. True, because $5^2 - 3 = 22$.
5. False, because $P(0) = 30(0) + 10 = 10$.

6. True, because the two trinomials are added correctly.

7. False, because
$$(x^2 - 5x) - (x^2 - 3x) = -2x$$
for any value of x.

8. True, because the monomial and binomial are correctly multiplied.

9. True, because $-(a - b) = b - a$ for any values of a and b.

10. False, because $-(y + 5) = -y - 5$ for any value of y.

5.3 EXERCISES

1. A term of a polynomial is a single number or the product of a number and one or more variables raised to whole number powers.

2. The number preceding the variable in each term is the coefficient of that variable.

3. A constant is simply a number.

4. A polynomial is a single term or a finite sum of terms.

5. The degree of a polynomial in one variable is the highest power of the variable in the polynomial.

6. To multiply a binomial and a trinomial, we use the distributive property.

7. Yes, it is a monomial.

8. Yes, it is a monomial.

9. No, because polynomials do not have negative exponents.

10. No, because polynomials do not have negative exponents.

11. Yes, it is a trinomial.

12. Yes, it is a trinomial.

13. No, because $\frac{1}{x}$ is not allowed in a polynomial.

14. No, $x^{50} - 9y^{-2}$ has a negative exponent.

15. The degree is 4 because 4 is the highest power. The coefficient of x^3 is -8. It is a binomial because it has two terms.

16. The degree is 3 and the coefficient of x^3 is -1. It is a binomial because it has 2 terms.

17. The degree of -8 is 0 and the coefficient of x^3 is 0. It is a monomial.

18. The degree of 17 is 0 and the coefficient of x^3 is 0. It is a monomial.

19. The degree is 7 because 7 is the highest power. The coefficient of x^3 is 0, because x^3 is missing. It is a monomial because it has one term.

20. Its degree is 4 and the coefficient of x^3 is 0. It is a monomial because it has one term.

21. The degree is 6 because 6 is the highest power. The coefficient of x^3 is 1. It is a trinomial because it has three terms.

22. Its degree is 3 and the coefficient of x^3 is $\frac{1}{2}$. It is a trinomial because it has 3 terms.

23. Replace x by 3 in $P(x) = x^4 - 1$.
$$P(3) = 3^4 - 1 = 81 - 1 = 80$$

24. Replace x by -1 in $P(x) = x^2 - x - 2$.
$$P(-1) = (-1)^2 - (-1) - 2 = 1 + 1 - 2$$
$$= 0$$

25. Replace x by -2:
$$M(-2) = -3(-2)^2 + 4(-2) - 9 = -29$$

26. Replace w by 0, in $C(w) = 3w^2 - w$.
$$C(0) = 3(0)^2 - 0 = 0$$

27. Replace x by 1:
$$R(1) = 1^5 - 1^4 + 1^3 - 1^2 + 1 - 1 = 0$$

28. Replace a by -1 in $T(a) = a^7 + a^6$.
$$T(-1) = (-1)^7 + (-1)^6 = -1 + 1 = 0$$

29. $2a + a - 3 + 5 = 3a + 2$

30. $2w + w - 6 + 5 = 3w - 1$

31. $7xy + 30 - 2xy - 5 = 5xy + 25$

32. $5ab + 7 - 3ab - 6 = 2ab + 1$

33. $x^2 - x^2 - 3x + 5x - 9 = 2x - 9$

34. $2y^2 + y^2 - 3y + 4y - 8 - 1$
$$= 3y^2 + y - 9$$

35. $2x^3 - x^2 - 4x + 2x - 3 - 5$
$$= 2x^3 - x^2 - 2x - 8$$

36. $2x - 5 - x^2 + 3x - 2 = -x^2 + 5x - 7$

37. Add the like terms to get $11x^2 - 2x - 9$.

38. Add like terms to get $-x^2 - 8x + 9$.

39. $5x - 4x + 2 - (-3) = x + 5$.

40. $4x - 2x + 3 - (-6) = 2x + 9$

41. Change the sign of every term on the bottom and add it to the appropriate like term on the top to get $-6x^2 + 5x + 2$.

42. Change the sign of each term on the bottom and add it to the appropriate term on top to get $-4x^2 + 10x + 4$.

43. Add the like terms to get $2x$.

44. Add the like terms to get $w + 1$.

45. Add exponents to get $-15x^6$.

46. $(-ab^5)(-2a^2b) = 2a^3b^6$

47. $-1(3x - 2) = -3x + 2$

48. $-1(-x^2 + 3x - 9) = x^2 - 3x + 9$

49. $5x^2y^3(3x^2y - 4x) = 15x^4y^4 - 20x^3y^3$

50. $3y^4z(8y^2z^2 - 3yz + 2y)$
$= 24y^6z^3 - 9y^5z^2 + 6y^5z$

51. $(x - 2)(x + 2) = (x - 2)x + (x - 2)2$
$= x^2 - 2x + 2x - 4 = x^2 - 4$

52. $(x - 1)(x + 1) = (x - 1)x + (x - 1)1$
$= x^2 - x + x - 1 = x^2 - 1$

53. $(x^2 + x + 2)2x + (x^2 + x + 2)(-3)$
$= 2x^3 + 2x^2 + 4x - 3x^2 - 3x - 6$
$= 2x^3 - x^2 + x - 6$

54. $(x^2 - 3x + 2)(x - 4)$
$= (x^2 - 3x + 2)x + (x^2 - 3x + 2)(-4)$
$= x^3 - 3x^2 + 2x - 4x^2 + 12x - 8$
$= x^3 - 7x^2 + 14x - 8$

55. Multiply $-5x$ by $2x - 3$ to get
$-10x^2 + 15x$.

56. Multiply each term on the top line by $-2a$
to get $-6a^4 + 10a^3 - 14a$.

57.
$$x + 5$$
$$\underline{x + 5}$$
$$5x + 25$$
$$\underline{x^2 + 5x}$$
$$x^2 + 10x + 25$$

58.
$$a + b$$
$$\underline{a - b}$$
$$-ab - b^2$$
$$\underline{a^2 + ab}$$
$$a^2 \qquad - b^2$$

59.
$$x + 6$$
$$\underline{2x - 3}$$
$$-3x - 18$$
$$\underline{2x^2 + 12x}$$
$$2x^2 + 9x - 18$$

60.
$$3x^2 + 2$$
$$\underline{2x^2 - 5}$$
$$-15x^2 - 10$$
$$\underline{6x^4 + 4x^2}$$
$$6x^4 - 11x^2 - 10$$

61.
$$x^2 + xy + y^2$$
$$\underline{x - y}$$
$$-x^2y - xy^2 - y^3$$
$$\underline{x^3 + x^2y + xy^2}$$
$$x^3 \qquad\qquad - y^3$$

62.
$$a^2 - ab + b^2$$
$$\underline{a + b}$$
$$a^2b - ab^2 + b^3$$
$$\underline{a^3 - a^2b + ab^2}$$
$$a^3 \qquad\qquad + b^3$$

63. Add like terms to get $2x - 5$.

64. Add like terms to get $x^3 + 6x - 8$.

65. Add like terms: $4a^2 - 11a - 4$

66. $(w^2 - 3w + 2) + (2w - 3 + w^2)$
$= w^2 + w^2 - 3w + 2w + 2 - 3$
$= 2w^2 - w - 1$

67. $w^2 - 7w - 2 - w + 3w^2 - 5$
$= 4w^2 - 8w - 7$

68. $(a^3 - 3a) - (1 - a - 2a^2)$
$= a^3 - 3a - 1 + a + 2a^2$
$= a^3 + 2a^2 - 2a - 1$

69. $(x - 2)x^2 + (x - 2)2x + (x - 2)4$
$= x^3 - 2x^2 + 2x^2 - 4x + 4x - 8$
$= x^3 - 8$

70. $(a - 3)(a^2 + 3a + 9)$
$= (a - 3)(a^2) + (a - 3)(3a) + (a - 3)(9)$
$= a^3 - 3a^2 + 3a^2 - 9a + 9a - 27$
$= a^3 - 27$

71. $(x - w)z + (x - w)2w$
$= xz - wz + 2xw - 2w^2$

72. $(w^2 - a)(t^2 + 3)$
$= (w^2 - a)t^2 + (w^2 - a)3$
$= w^2t^2 - at^2 + 3w^2 - 3a$

73. $(2xy - 1)3xy + (2xy - 1)5$
$= 6x^2y^2 - 3xy + 10xy - 5$
$= 6x^2y^2 + 7xy - 5$

74. $(3abb - 4)(ab + 8)$
$= (3ab - 4)ab + (3ab - 4)8$
$= 3a^2b^2 - 4ab + 24ab - 32$
$= 3a^2b^2 + 20ab - 32$

75. $(2.31x - 5.4)6.25x + (2.31x - 5.4)1.8$
$= 14.4375x^2 - 29.592x - 9.72$

76. $(x - 0.28)(x^2 - 34.6x + 21.2)$
$= (x - 0.28)x^2 + (x - 0.28)(-34.6x)$
$\qquad + (x - 0.28)(21.2)$
$= x^3 - 34.88x^2 + 30.888x - 5.936$

186

77. $(3.759 + 11.61)x^2 - 4.71x + 6.59x$
$\qquad + 2.85 - 3.716$
$= 15.369x^2 + 1.88x - 0.866$

78. $(43.19x^3 - 3.7x^2 - 5.42x + 3.1)$
$\qquad - (62.7x^3 - 7.36x - 12.3)$
$= 43.19x^3 - 3.7x^2 - 5.42x + 3.1 - 62.7x^3$
$\qquad + 7.36x + 12.3$
$= -19.51x^3 - 3.7x^2 + 1.94x + 15.4$

79. $\frac{2}{4}x + \frac{4}{2} + \frac{1}{4}x - \frac{1}{2} = \frac{3}{4}x + \frac{3}{2}$

80. $\left(\frac{1}{3}x + 1\right) + \left(\frac{1}{3}x - \frac{3}{2}\right) = \frac{2}{3}x + \frac{2}{2} - \frac{3}{2}$
$\qquad\qquad\qquad\qquad = \frac{2}{3}x - \frac{1}{2}$

81. $\frac{1}{2}x^2 + \frac{1}{3}x - \frac{1}{5} - \frac{2}{2}x^2 + \frac{2}{3}x + \frac{1}{5}$
$\qquad = -\frac{1}{2}x^2 + x$

82. $\left(\frac{2}{3}x^2 - \frac{1}{3}x + \frac{1}{6}\right) - \left(-\frac{1}{3}x^2 + x + 1\right)$
$= \frac{2}{3}x^2 - \frac{1}{3}x + \frac{1}{6} + \frac{1}{3}x^2 - x - 1$
$= x^2 - \frac{4}{3}x - \frac{5}{6}$

83. Combine like terms within the first set of brackets:
$x^2 - 3 - x^2 - 5x + 4 = -5x + 1$
Combine like terms within the second set of brackets:
$x - 3x^2 + 15x = -3x^2 + 16x$
Now subtract these results:
$[-5x + 1] - [-3x^2 + 16x]$
$\qquad = -5x + 1 + 3x^2 - 16x$
$\qquad = 3x^2 - 21x + 1$

84. $[x^3 - 4x(x^2 - 3x + 2) - 5x]$
$\qquad\qquad\qquad + [x^2 - 5(4 - x^2) + 3]$
$= [x^3 - 4x^3 + 12x^2 - 8x - 5x]$
$\qquad\qquad\qquad + [x^2 - 20 + 5x^2 + 3]$
$= [-3x^3 + 12x^2 - 13x] + [6x^2 - 17]$
$= -3x^3 + 18x^2 - 13x - 17$

85. $[x + 12][-4x - 14]$
$\qquad = [x + 12](-4x) + [x + 12](-14)$
$\qquad = -4x^2 - 48x - 14x - 168$
$\qquad = -4x^2 - 62x - 168$

86. $[x^2 - (5x - 2)][x^2 + (5x - 2)]$
$= [x^2 - 5x + 2][x^2 + 5x - 2]$
$= [x^2 - 5x + 2]x^2 + [x^2 - 5x + 2]5x$
$\qquad\qquad\qquad + [x^2 - 5x + 2](-2)$
$= x^4 - 5x^3 + 2x^2 + 5x^3 - 25x^2 + 10x - 2x^2$
$\qquad\qquad\qquad\qquad + 10x - 4$
$= x^4 - 25x^2 + 20x - 4$

87. $[x^2 - m - 2][x^2 + m + 2]$
$= x^4 - mx^2 - 2x^2 + mx^2 - m^2 - 2m$
$\qquad\qquad\qquad + 2x^2 - 2m - 4$
$= x^4 - m^2 - 4m - 4$

88. $[3x^2 - (x - 2)][3x^2 + (x + 2)]$
$\qquad = [3x^2 - x + 2][3x^2 + x + 2]$
$\qquad = [3x^2 - x + 2]3x^2 + [3x^2 - x + 2]x$
$\qquad\qquad\qquad\qquad + [3x^2 - x + 2]2$
$\qquad = 9x^4 - 3x^3 + 6x^2 + 3x^3 - x^2 + 2x$
$\qquad\qquad\qquad\qquad + 6x^2 - 2x + 4$
$\qquad = 9x^4 + 11x^2 + 4$

89. $10x^2 - 8x - 3x[2x^2 + 21x]$
$\qquad = 10x^2 - 8x - 6x^3 - 63x^2$
$\qquad = -6x^3 - 53x^2 - 8x$

90. $-3x(x - 2) - 5[2x - 4(x + 6)]$
$\qquad = -3x^2 + 6x - 5[2x - 4x - 24]$
$\qquad = -3x^2 + 6x - 10x + 20x + 120$
$\qquad = -3x^2 + 16x + 120$

91. $(a^{2m} + 3a^m - 3) + (-5a^{2m} - 7a^m + 8)$
$\qquad = -4a^{2m} - 4a^m + 5$

92. $(b^{3z} - 6) - (4b^{3z} - b^{2z} - 7)$
$\qquad = -3b^{3z} + b^{2z} + 1$

93. $(x^n - 1)(x^n + 3)$
$\qquad\qquad = (x^n - 1)x^n + (x^n - 1)3$
$\qquad\qquad = x^{2n} - x^n + 3x^n - 3$
$\qquad\qquad = x^{2n} + 2x^n - 3$

94. $(2y^t - 3)(4y^t + 7)$
$\qquad\qquad = (2y^t - 3)4y^t + (2y^t - 3)7$
$\qquad\qquad = 8y^{2t} - 12y^t + 14y^t - 21$
$\qquad\qquad = 8y^{2t} + 2y^t - 21$

95. $z^{3w} - z^{2w}(z^{1-w} - 4z^w)$
$\qquad = z^{3w} - z^{1+w} + 4z^{3w} = 5z^{3w} - z^{1+w}$

96. $(w^p - 1)(w^{2p} + w^p + 1)$
$\qquad = (w^p - 1)w^{2p} + (w^p - 1)w^p + (w^p - 1)1$
$\qquad = w^{3p} - w^{2p} + w^{2p} - w^p + w^p - 1$
$\qquad = w^{3p} - 1$

97. $(x^{2r} + y)x^{4r} + (x^{2r} + y)(-x^{2r}y)$
$\qquad\qquad\qquad + (x^{2r} + y)y^2$
$\qquad = x^{6r} + x^{4r}y - x^{4r}y - x^{2r}y^2 + x^{2r}y^2 + y^3$
$\qquad = x^{6r} + y^3$

98. $(2x^a - z)2x^a + (2x^a - z)z$
$\qquad = 4x^{2a} - 2x^a z + 2x^a z - z^2 = 4x^{2a} - z^2$

99. $C(3) = 20(3) + 15 = \$75$

100. $B(20) = 0.1(20)^2 + 3(20) + 50$
$\qquad\qquad = 0.1(400) + 60 + 50$
$\qquad\qquad = 40 + 60 + 50 = 150$
Her bonus is $150.

101. $C(3) = 50 \cdot 3 - 0.01(3)^4 = 149.19$
$C(2) = 50 \cdot 2 - 0.01(2)^4 = 99.84$
$C(3) - C(2) = 49.35$
Marginal cost of 3rd window is $49.35.
$C(10) - C(9) = 400 - 384.39$
Marginal cost of 10th window is $15.61.
102. $P(4) = 4 \cdot 4 + 0.9(4)^3 = 73.6$
$P(3) = 4 \cdot 3 + 0.9(3)^3 = 36.3$
$P(4) - P(3) = 73.6 - 36.3 = 37.3$
Marginal cost for 4th opener is $37.30.
$P(10) - P(9) = 940 - 692.10 = 247.90$
Marginal cost for 10th opener is $247.90.
There is a greater difference in height between adjacent bars as the number of openers increases.
103. a) $F(1950) - M(1950) = 6.2$ years
b) The lines are not parallel because the slopes are different.
c) $0.18268y - 284.98$
$= 0.16252y - 251.91 + 8$
$0.02016y = 41.07$
$y = 2037$
104. $M(1975) = 0.16252(1975) - 251.91$
$= 69.067$
The year of death for the male should equal the year of death for the female:
$F(y) + y = 1975 + 69.067$
$0.18268y - 284.98 + y = 1975 + 69.067$
$1.18268y = 2329.047$
$y = 1969$
b) $\dfrac{M(y) + F(y)}{2}$
$= \dfrac{0.16252y - 251.91 + 0.18268y - 284.98}{2}$
$= 0.1726y - 268.445$

5.4 WARM-UPS

1. True, because the binomials are multiplied correctly.
2. True, because the binomials are multiplied correctly.
3. False, $(2 + 3)^2 = 5^2 = 25$ and $2^2 + 3^2 = 4 + 9 = 13$.
4. True, because the binomial is squared correctly.
5. False, $(8 - 3)^2 = 5^2 = 25$ and $64 - 9 = 55$.

6. True.
7. True, $(60 - 1)(60 + 1) = 60^2 - 1^2$
$= 3600 - 1$.
8. True, because the binomial is squared correctly.
9. False, $(x - 3)^2 = x^2 - 6x + 9$ for any value of x.
10. False, it is a product of two monomials.

5.4 EXERCISES

1. The distributive property is used in multiplying binomials.
2. FOIL stands for first, outer, inner, last.
3. The purpose of FOIL is to provide a fast way to find the product of two binomials.
4. The square of a sum is the square of the first term plus twice the product of the two terms plus the square of the last term.
5. The square of a difference is the square of the first term minus twice the product of the two terms plus the square of the last term.
6. The product of a sum and a difference of the same two terms is the square of the first term minus the square of the second term.
7. $x^2 - 2x + 4x - 8 = x^2 + 2x - 8$
8. $(x - 3)(x + 5) = x^2 - 3x + 5x - 15$
$= x^2 + 2x - 15$
9. $2x^2 + x + 6x + 3 = 2x^2 + 7x + 3$
10. $(2y + 3)(y + 2) = 2y^2 + 3y + 4y + 6$
$= 2y^2 + 7y + 6$
11. $2a^2 + 3a - 10a - 15 = 2a^2 - 7a - 15$
12. $(-3x - 5)(-x + 6)$
$= 3x^2 + 5x - 18x - 30$
$= 3x^2 - 13x - 30$
13. $(2x^2 - 7)(2x^2 + 7)$
$= 4x^2 - 14x^2 + 14x^2 - 49$
$= 4x^4 - 49$
14. $(3y^3 + 8)(3y^3 - 8)$
$= 9y^6 + 24y^3 - 24y^3 - 64$
$= 9y^6 - 64$
15. $(2x^3 - 1)(x^3 + 4) = 2x^6 - x^3 + 8x^3 - 4$
$= 2x^6 + 7x^3 - 4$
16. $(3t^2 - 4)(2t^2 + 3) = 6t^4 - 8t^2 + 9t^2 - 12$
$= 6t^4 + t^2 - 12$
17. $6zw + w^2 - 6z^2 - wz = w^2 + 5wz - 6z^2$

18. $(4y + w)(w - 2y)$
$$= 4wy + w^2 - 2wy - 8y^2$$
$$= w^2 + 2wy - 8y^2$$

19. $(3k - 2t)(4t + 3k)$
$$= 12kt - 8t^2 + 9k^2 - 6tk$$
$$= 9k^2 + 6kt - 8t^2$$

20. $(7a - 2x)(x + a)$
$$= 7ax - 2x^2 + 7a^2 - 2ax$$
$$= 7a^2 + 5ax - 2x^2$$

21. $xy - 3y + xw - 3w$

22. $(z - 1)(y + 2) = yz - y + 2z - 2$

23. $m^2 + 2(3)(m) + 3^2 = m^2 + 6m + 9$

24. $(a + 2)^2 = a^2 + 2(a)(2) + 2^2$
$$= a^2 + 4a + 4$$

25. $a^2 - 2(4)(a) + 4^2 = a^2 - 8a + 16$

26. $(b - 3)^2 = b^2 - 2(b)(3) + 3^2$
$$= b^2 - 6b + 9$$

27. $(2w)^2 + 2(2w)(1) + 1^2 = 4w^2 + 4w + 1$

28. $(3m + 4)^2 = (3m)^2 + 2(3m)(4) + 4^2$
$$= 9m^2 + 24m + 16$$

29. $(3t)^2 - 2(3t)(5u) + (5u)^2$
$$= 9t^2 - 30tu + 25u^2$$

30. $(3w - 2x)^2 = (3w)^2 - 2(3w)(2x) + (2x)^2$
$$= 9w^2 - 12wx + 4x^2$$

31. $x^2 - 2(-x)(1) + 1^2 = x^2 + 2x + 1$

32. $(-d - 5)^2 = d^2 - 2(-d)(5) + 5^2$
$$= d^2 + 10d + 25$$

33. $a^2 - 2(a)(3y^3) + (3y^3)^2$
$$= a^2 - 6ay^3 + 9y^6$$

34. $(3m - 5n^3)^2$
$$= (3m)^2 - 2 \cdot 3m \cdot 5n^3 + (5n^3)^2$$
$$= 9m^2 - 30mn^3 + 25n^6$$

35. $\left(\frac{1}{2}x - 1\right)^2 = \frac{1}{4}x^2 - 2 \cdot \frac{1}{2}x \cdot 1 + 1$
$$= \frac{1}{4}x^2 - x + 1$$

36. $\left(\frac{2}{3}x - \frac{1}{2}\right)^2 = \frac{4}{9}x^2 - 2 \cdot \frac{2}{3}x \cdot \frac{1}{2} + \frac{1}{4}$
$$= \frac{4}{9}x^2 - \frac{2}{3}x + \frac{1}{4}$$

37. $w^2 - 9^2 = w^2 - 81$

38. $(m - 4)(m + 4) = m^2 - 16$

39. $(w^3)^2 - y^2 = w^6 - y^2$

40. $(a^3 - x)(a^3 + x) = a^6 - x^2$

41. $(2x)^2 - 7^2 = 4x^2 - 49$

42. $(5x + 3)(5x - 3) = 25x^2 - 9$

43. $(3x^2)^2 - 2^2 = 9x^4 - 4$

44. $(4y^2 + 1)(4y^2 - 1) = (4y^2)^2 - 1^2$
$$= 16y^4 - 1$$

45. $[(m + t) + 5][(m + t) - 5]$
$$= (m + t)^2 - 25$$
$$= m^2 + 2mt + t^2 - 25$$

46. $[(2x + 3) - y][(2x + 3) + y]$
$$= (2x + 3)^2 - y^2$$
$$= 4x^2 + 12x + 9 - y^2$$

47. $[y - (r + 5)][y + (r + 5)] = y^2 - (r + 5)^2$
$$= y^2 - r^2 - 10r - 25$$

48. $[x + (3 - k)][x - (3 - k)]$
$$= x^2 - (3 - k)^2$$
$$= x^2 - 9 + 6k - k^2$$

49. $[(2y - t) + 3]^2$
$$= (2y - t)^2 + 6(2y - t) + 9$$
$$= 4y^2 - 4yt + t^2 + 12y - 6t + 9$$

50. $[(u - 3v) - 4]^2$
$$= (u - 3v)^2 - 8(u - 3v) + 16$$
$$= u^2 - 6uv + 9v^2 - 8u + 24v + 16$$

51. $[3h + (k - 1)]^2$
$$= 9h^2 + 6h(k - 1) + (k - 1)^2$$
$$= 9h^2 + 6hk - 6h + k^2 - 2k + 1$$

52. $[2p - (3q + 6)]^2$
$$= 4p^2 - 4p(3q + 6) + (3q + 6)^2$$
$$= 4p^2 - 12pq - 24p + 9q^2 + 36q + 36$$

53. $x^2 - 6x + 9x - 54 = x^2 + 3x - 54$

54. $(2x^2 - 3)(3x^2 + 4)$
$$= 6x^4 - 9x^2 + 8x^2 - 12$$
$$= 6x^4 - x^2 - 12$$

55. $5^2 - x^2 = 25 - x^2$

56. $(4 - ab)(4 + ab) = 4^2 - (ab)^2$
$$= 16 - a^2b^2$$

57. $6x^2 - 8ax + 15ax - 20a^2$
$$= 6x^2 + 7ax - 20a^2$$

58. $(x^5 + 2)(x^5 - 2) = (x^5)^2 - 2^2 = x^{10} - 4$

59. $2t^2 + 2tw - 3t - 3w$

60. $(5x - 9)(ax + b)$
$$= 5ax^2 - 9ax + 5bx - 9b$$

61. $(3x^2)^2 + 2(3x^2)(2y^3) + (2y^3)^2$
$$= 9x^4 + 12x^2y^3 + 4y^6$$

62. $(5a^4 - 2b)^2 = (5a^4)^2 - 2 \cdot 5a^4 \cdot 2b + (2b)^2$
$$= 25a^8 - 20a^4b + 4b^2$$

63. $6y^2 + 6y - 10y - 10 = 6y^2 - 4y - 10$

64. $(3b - 3)(2b + 3) = 6b^2 - 6b + 9b - 9$
$$= 6b^2 + 3b - 9$$

65. $50^2 - 2^2 = 2500 - 4 = 2496$

66. $(100 - 1)(100 + 1) = 100^2 - 1^2$
$$= 10,000 - 1 = 9,999$$

189

67. $3^2 + 2(3)(7x) + (7x)^2 = 49x^2 + 42x + 9$

68. $(1 - pq)^2 = 1^2 - 2 \cdot 1 \cdot pq + (pq)^2$
$$= 1 - 2pq + p^2 q^2$$

69. $4y\left(3y + \frac{1}{2}\right)^2$
$$= 4y\left((3y)^2 + 2(3y)\frac{1}{2} + \left(\frac{1}{2}\right)^2\right)$$
$$= 4y\left(9y^2 + 3y + \frac{1}{4}\right)$$
$$= 36y^3 + 12y^2 + y$$

70. $25y\left(2y - \frac{1}{5}\right)^2$
$$= 25y\left((2y)^2 - 2 \cdot 2y \cdot \frac{1}{5} + \frac{1}{25}\right)$$
$$= 25y\left(4y^2 - \frac{4}{5}y + \frac{1}{25}\right)$$
$$= 100y^3 - 20y^2 + y$$

71. $(a + h)^2 - a^2 = a^2 + 2ah + h^2 - a^2$
$$= 2ah + h^2$$

72. $\dfrac{(x + h)^2 - x^2}{h} = \dfrac{x^2 + 2xh + h^2 - x^2}{h}$
$$= \frac{2xh + h^2}{h} = \frac{2xh}{h} + \frac{h^2}{h} = 2x + h$$

73. $(x + 2)(x + 2)^2 = (x + 2)(x^2 + 4x + 4)$
$$= x(x^2 + 4x + 4) + 2(x^2 + 4x + 4)$$
$$= x^3 + 6x^2 + 12x + 8$$

74. $(a + 1)^2 (a + 1)^2$
$$= (a^2 + 2a + 1)(a^2 + 2a + 1)$$
$$= a^2(a^2 + 2a + 1) + 2a(a^2 + 2a + 1)$$
$$+ 1(a^2 + 2a + 1)$$
$$= a^4 + 4a^3 + 6a^2 + 4a + 1$$

75. $(y - 3)^3 = (y - 3)(y^2 - 6y + 9)$
$$= y(y^2 - 6y + 9) - 3(y^2 - 6y + 9)$$
$$= y^3 - 9y^2 + 27y - 27$$

76. $(2b + 1)^4 = (4b^2 + 4b + 1)(4b^2 + 4b + 1)$
$$= 4b^2(4b^2 + 4b + 1) + 4b(4b^2 + 4b + 1)$$
$$+ 1(4b^2 + 4b + 1)$$
$$= 16b^4 + 32b^3 + 24b^2 + 8b + 1$$

77. $(3.2)(5.1)x^2 - (4.5)(5.1)x + (3.9)(3.2)x$
$$- (4.5)(3.9)$$
$$= 16.32x^2 - 10.47x - 17.55$$

78. $(5.3x - 9.2)^2$
$$= (5.3x)^2 - 2 \cdot 5.3x \cdot 9.2 + (9.2)^2$$
$$= 28.09x^2 - 97.52x + 84.64$$

79. $(3.6y)^2 + 2(3.6)(4.4)y + (4.4)^2$
$$= 12.96y^2 + 31.68y + 19.36$$

80. $(3.3a - 7.9b)(3.3a + 7.9b)$
$$= (3.3a)^2 - (7.9b)^2$$
$$= 10.89a^2 - 62.41b^2$$

81. $x^m x^{2m} + 2x^{2m} + 3x^m + 6$
$$= x^{3m} + 2x^{2m} + 3x^m + 6$$

82. $(a^n - b)(a^n + b) = (a^n)^2 - b^2 = a^{2n} - b^2$

83. $a^{n+1+2n} + a^{n+1+n} - 3a^{n+1}$
$$= a^{3n+1} + a^{2n+1} - 3a^{n+1}$$

84. $x^{3b}(x^{-3b} + 3x^{-b} + 5) = x^0 + 3x^{2b} + 5x^{3b}$
$$= 1 + 3x^{2b} + 5x^{3b}$$

85. $(a^m)^2 + 2a^m a^n + (a^n)^2$
$$= a^{2m} + 2a^{m+n} + a^{2n}$$

86. $(x^w - x^t)^2 = x^{2w} - 2 \cdot x^w x^t + x^{2t}$
$$= x^{2w} - 2x^{w+t} + x^{2t}$$

87. $5y^m 3y^{2m} + 3 \cdot 8y^{2m} z^k + 4 \cdot 5y^m z^{3-k}$
$$+ 32z^{k+3-k}$$
$$= 15y^{3m} + 24y^{2m}z^k + 20\,y^m z^{3-k} + 32z^3$$

88. $(4x^{a-1} + 3y^{b+5})(x^{2a-3} - 2y^{4-b})$
$$= 4x^{a-1+2a-3} + 3y^{b+5}x^{2a-3}$$
$$- 8x^{a-1}y^{4-b} - 6y^{b+5+4-b}$$
$$= 4x^{3a-4} + 3y^{b+5}x^{2a-3} - 8x^{a-1}y^{4-b} - 6y^9$$

89. Use $L = x + 3$ and $W = x + 1$ in the formula for the area of a rectangle, $A = LW$.
$A = (x + 3)(x + 1) = x^2 + 4x + 3$

90. If the square has an area of x^2 square feet, then each side has length x feet. The new plans call for a house $x + 20$ feet by $x - 6$ feet. Since the area is the length times the width, the area is $(x + 20)(x - 6) = x^2 + 14x - 120$ square feet.

91. $A = (8 - 2x)(10 - 2x) = 4x^2 - 36x + 80$
If $x = 0.4$, then $A = 4(0.4)^2 - 36(0.4) + 80$
$$= 66.24 \text{ km}^2$$

92. $(x + 4)^3 = (x + 4)(x^2 + 8x + 16)$
$$= x(x^2 + 8x + 16) + 4(x^2 + 8x + 16)$$
$$= x^3 + 12x^2 + 48x + 64 \text{ in.}^3$$

93. $V = x(4 - 2x)(6 - 2x)$
$$= x(4x^2 - 20x + 24)$$
$$= 4x^3 - 20x^2 + 24x$$
If $x = 4$ in. $= \frac{1}{3}$ ft, then
$V = 4\left(\frac{1}{3}\right)^3 - 20\left(\frac{1}{3}\right)^2 + 24\left(\frac{1}{3}\right)$
$$= 5\frac{25}{27} \text{ ft}^3 \approx 5.9 \text{ ft}^3$$

94. Insulation in floor: $V = 12x(0.5) = 6x$ ft^3.
Insulation in ceiling: $V = 12x(2/3) = 8x$ ft^3.
Total square feet of walls:
$96 + 96 + 8x + 8x - 80 = 112 + 16x$ ft^2
Wall insulation: $V = (112 + 16x)\frac{1}{4} = 28 + 4x$ ft^3

Total cost:
$0.25(6x + 8x + 28 + 4x) = 4.5x + 7$ dollars

In this solution the regions on the edges that are common to the walls and ceiling or the walls and floor are ignored.

5.5 WARM-UPS

1. False, c is the quotient.

2. False,
(quotient)(divisor) + remainder = dividend.

3. True, because
$(x + 2)(x + 3) = x^2 + 5x + 6$ and
$(x + 2)(x + 3) + 1 = x^2 + 5x + 7$.

4. True. From warm-up number 3 we can see that if $x + 3$ is the divisor then $x + 2$ is the quotient.

5. True. From warm-up number 2 we can see that if $x + 2$ is the divisor then $x + 3$ is the quotient and 1 is the remainder.

6. False, to divide by $x - c$ with synthetic division we use c.

7. False, synthetic division is used only for dividing by $x - c$.

8. True, when dividing by $x - c$ the degree of the quotient is 1 less than the degree of the dividend.

9. True, because if remainder is zero, then (quotient)(divisor) = dividend.

10. True, because if remainder is zero, then (quotient)(divisor) = dividend.

5.5 EXERCISES

1. If $a \div b = c$, then the divisor is b, the dividend is a, and the quotient is c.

2. For long division, polynomials should be written with the exponents in descending order.

3. If the term x^n is missing in the dividend, insert the term $0 \cdot x^n$ for the missing term.

4. Stop the long division process when the remainder has smaller degree than the divisor.

5. Synthetic division is used only for dividing by a binomial of the form $x - c$.

6. The remainder is zero if and only if the dividend is a factor of the divisor.

7. $\dfrac{36x^7}{3x^3} = 12x^4$

8. $-30x^3 \div (-5x) = \dfrac{-30x^3}{-5x} = 6x^{3-1} = 6x^2$

9. $\dfrac{16x^2}{-8x^2} = -2$

10. $-22a^3 \div (11a^2) = \dfrac{-22a^3}{11a^2} = -2a^{3-2}$
$$= -2a$$

11. $\dfrac{6b - 9}{3} = \dfrac{6b}{3} - \dfrac{9}{3} = 2b - 3$

12. $(8x^2 - 6x) \div 2 = \dfrac{8x^2 - 6x}{2}$
$$= \dfrac{2(4x^2 - 3x)}{2} = 4x^2 - 3x$$

13. $\dfrac{3x^2 + 6x}{3x} = \dfrac{3x^2}{3x} + \dfrac{6x}{3x} = x + 2$

14. $(5x^3 - 10x^2 + 20x) \div (5x)$
$$= \dfrac{5x^3 - 10x^2 + 20x}{5x}$$
$$= \dfrac{5x^3}{5x} - \dfrac{10x^2}{5x} + \dfrac{20x}{5x} = x^2 - 2x + 4$$

15. $\dfrac{10x^4 - 8x^3 + 6x^2}{-2x^2}$
$$= \dfrac{10x^4}{-2x^2} - \dfrac{8x^3}{-2x^2} + \dfrac{6x^2}{-2x^2}$$
$$= -5x^2 + 4x - 3$$

16. $(-9x^3 + 6x^2 - 12x) \div (-3x)$
$$= \dfrac{-9x^3}{-3x} + \dfrac{6x^2}{-3x} - \dfrac{12x}{-3x}$$
$$= 3x^2 - 2x + 4$$

17. $\dfrac{7x^3 - 4x^2}{2x} = \dfrac{7x^3}{2x} - \dfrac{4x^2}{2x} = \dfrac{7}{2}x^2 - 2x$

18. $(6x^3 - 5x^2) \div (4x^2) = \dfrac{6x^3}{4x^2} - \dfrac{5x^2}{4x^2}$
$$= \dfrac{3}{2}x - \dfrac{5}{4}$$

19.
$$
\begin{array}{r}
x + 5 \\
x + 3 \overline{)\, x^2 + 8x + 13} \\
\underline{x^2 + 3x} \\
5x + 13 \\
\underline{5x + 15} \\
-2
\end{array}
$$

Quotient: $x + 5$ Remainder: -2

20.
$$
\begin{array}{r}
x + 2 \\
x + 3 \overline{)\, x^2 + 5x + 7} \\
\underline{x^2 + 3x} \\
2x + 7 \\
\underline{2x + 6} \\
1
\end{array}
$$

Quotient: $x + 2$ Remainder: 1

21.
$$x+2 \overline{\smash{\big)}\, x^2 - 2x} \quad \overset{x-4}{}$$
$$\underline{x^2 + 2x}$$
$$-4x$$
$$\underline{-4x - 8}$$
$$8$$
Quotient: $x - 4$ Remainder: 8

22.
$$x-1 \overline{\smash{\big)}\, 3x + 0} \quad \overset{3}{}$$
$$\underline{3x - 3}$$
$$3$$
Quotient: 3   Remainder: 3

23.
$$x+2 \overline{\smash{\big)}\, x^3 + 0x^2 + 0x + 8} \quad \overset{x^2 - 2x + 4}{}$$
$$\underline{x^3 + 2x^2}$$
$$-2x^2 + 0x$$
$$\underline{-2x^2 - 4x}$$
$$4x + 8$$
$$\underline{4x + 8}$$
$$0$$
Quotient: $x^2 - 2x + 4$ Remainder: 0

24.
$$y-1 \overline{\smash{\big)}\, y^3 + 0y^2 + 0y - 1} \quad \overset{y^2 + y + 1}{}$$
$$\underline{y^3 - y^2}$$
$$y^2 + 0y$$
$$\underline{y^2 - y}$$
$$y - 1$$
$$\underline{y - 1}$$
$$0$$
Quotient: $y^2 + y + 1$ Remainder: 0

25.
$$a-2 \overline{\smash{\big)}\, a^3 + 0a^2 + 4a - 5} \quad \overset{a^2 + 2a + 8}{}$$
$$\underline{a^3 - 2a^2}$$
$$2a^2 + 4a$$
$$\underline{2a^2 - 4a}$$
$$8a - 5$$
$$\underline{8a - 16}$$
$$11$$
Quotient: $a^2 + 2a + 8$ Remainder: 11

26.
$$w-2 \overline{\smash{\big)}\, w^3 + w^2 + 0w - 3} \quad \overset{w^2 + 3w + 6}{}$$
$$\underline{w^3 - 2w^2}$$
$$3w^2 + 0w$$
$$\underline{3w^2 - 6w}$$
$$6w - 3$$
$$\underline{6w - 12}$$
$$9$$
Quotient: $w^2 + 3w + 6$ Remainder: 9

27.
$$x+1 \overline{\smash{\big)}\, x^3 - x^2 + x - 3} \quad \overset{x^2 - 2x + 3}{}$$
$$\underline{x^3 + x^2}$$
$$-2x^2 + x$$
$$\underline{-2x^2 - 2x}$$
$$3x - 3$$
$$\underline{3x + 3}$$
$$-6$$
Quotient: $x^2 - 2x + 3$ Remainder: -6

28.
$$a+2 \overline{\smash{\big)}\, a^3 - a^2 + a - 4} \quad \overset{a^2 - 3a + 7}{}$$
$$\underline{a^3 + 2a^2}$$
$$-3a^2 + a$$
$$\underline{-3a^2 - 6a}$$
$$7a - 4$$
$$\underline{7a + 14}$$
$$-18$$
Quotient: $a^2 - 3a + 7$ Remainder: -18

29.
$$x-2 \overline{\smash{\big)}\, x^4 + x^3 + 0x^2 - x - 1} \quad \overset{x^3 + 3x^2 + 6x + 11}{}$$
$$\underline{x^4 - 2x^3}$$
$$3x^3 + 0x^2$$
$$\underline{3x^3 - 6x^2}$$
$$6x^2 - x$$
$$\underline{6x^2 - 12x}$$
$$11x - 1$$
$$\underline{11x - 22}$$
$$21$$
Quotient: $x^3 + 3x^2 + 6x + 11$ Remainder: 21

30.

$$x + 2 \overline{\smash{\big)}\ 3x^4 + 0x^3 - x^2 + 3x + 6}$$

quotient line: $3x^3 - 6x^2 + 11x - 19$

$$\underline{3x^4 + 6x^3}$$
$$-6x^3 - x^2$$
$$\underline{-6x^3 - 12x^2}$$
$$11x^2 + 3x$$
$$\underline{11x^2 + 22x}$$
$$-19x + 6$$
$$\underline{-19x - 38}$$
$$44$$

Quotient: $3x^3 - 6x^2 + 11x - 19$
Remainder: 44

31.

$$x^2 - 2 \overline{\smash{\big)}\ -3x^4 + 0x^3 + 5x^2 + x - 2}$$

quotient line: $-3x^2 \qquad -1$

$$\underline{-3x^4 \qquad + 6x^2}$$
$$-x^2 + x - 2$$
$$\underline{-x^2 \qquad + 2}$$
$$x - 4$$

Quotient: $-3x^2 - 1$ \qquad Remainder: $x - 4$

32.

$$x^2 + 3 \overline{\smash{\big)}\ x^4 + x^3 + 0x^2 + 0x - 2}$$

quotient line: $x^2 + x - 3$

$$\underline{x^4 \qquad + 3x^2}$$
$$x^3 - 3x^2 + 0x - 2$$
$$\underline{x^3 \qquad + 3x}$$
$$-3x^2 - 3x - 2$$
$$\underline{-3x^2 \qquad - 9}$$
$$-3x + 7$$

Quotient: $x^2 + x - 3$ \quad Remainder: $-3x + 7$

33.

$$2x - 3 \overline{\smash{\big)}\ x^2 - 4x + 2}$$

quotient line: $\frac{1}{2}x - \frac{5}{4}$

$$\underline{x^2 - \frac{3}{2}x}$$
$$-\frac{5}{2}x + 2$$
$$\underline{-\frac{5}{2}x + \frac{15}{4}}$$
$$-\frac{7}{4}$$

Quotient: $\frac{1}{2}x - \frac{5}{4}$ \quad Remainder: $-\frac{7}{4}$

34.

$$3x + 6 \overline{\smash{\big)}\ x^2 - 5x + 1}$$

quotient line: $\frac{1}{3}x - \frac{7}{3}$

$$\underline{x^2 + 2x}$$
$$-7x + 1$$
$$\underline{-7x - 14}$$
$$15$$

Quotient: $\frac{1}{3}x - \frac{7}{3}$ \quad Remainder: 15

35.

$$3x - 2 \overline{\smash{\big)}\ 2x^2 - x + 6}$$

quotient line: $\frac{2}{3}x + \frac{1}{9}$

$$\underline{2x^2 - \frac{4}{3}x}$$
$$\frac{1}{3}x + 6$$
$$\underline{\frac{1}{3}x - \frac{2}{9}}$$
$$\frac{56}{9}$$

Quotient: $\frac{2}{3}x + \frac{1}{9}$ \quad Remainder: $\frac{56}{9}$

36.

$$2x + 1 \overline{\smash{\big)}\ 3x^2 + 4x - 1}$$

quotient line: $\frac{3}{2}x + \frac{5}{4}$

$$\underline{3x^2 + \frac{3}{2}x}$$
$$\frac{5}{2}x - 1$$
$$\underline{\frac{5}{2}x + \frac{5}{4}}$$
$$-\frac{9}{4}$$

Quotient: $\frac{3}{2}x + \frac{5}{4}$ \quad Remainder: $-\frac{9}{4}$

37.

$$x - 5 \overline{\smash{\big)}\ 2x + 0}$$

quotient line: 2

$$\underline{2x - 10}$$
$$10$$

$$\frac{2x}{x - 5} = 2 + \frac{10}{x - 5}$$

38.

$$x - 1 \overline{\smash{\big)}\ x + 0}$$

quotient line: 1

$$\underline{x - 1}$$
$$1$$

$$\frac{x}{x - 1} = 1 + \frac{1}{x - 1}$$

39.

$$x + 1 \overline{\smash{\big)}\ x^2 + 0x + 0}$$

quotient line: $x - 1$

$$\underline{x^2 + x}$$
$$-x + 0$$
$$\underline{-x - 1}$$
$$1$$

$$\frac{x^2}{x + 1} = x - 1 + \frac{1}{x + 1}$$

40.

$$x + 3 \overline{\smash{\big)}\ x^2 + 0x + 9}$$

quotient line: $x - 3$

$$\underline{x^2 + 3x}$$
$$-3x + 9$$
$$\underline{-3x - 9}$$
$$18$$

$$\frac{x^2+9}{x+3} = x-3+\frac{18}{x+3}$$

41.
$$x+2 \overline{\smash{\big)}\ x^3 + 0x^2 + 0x + 0}$$
$$\underline{x^3 + 2x^2}$$
$$-2x^2 + 0x$$
$$\underline{-2x^2 - 4x}$$
$$4x + 0$$
$$\underline{4x + 8}$$
$$-8$$

Quotient: $x^2 - 2x + 4$

$$\frac{x^3}{x+2} = x^2 - 2x + 4 + \frac{-8}{x+2}$$

42.
$$x-2 \overline{\smash{\big)}\ x^3 + 0x^2 + 0x - 1}$$
$$\underline{x^3 - 2x^2}$$
$$2x^2 + 0x$$
$$\underline{2x^2 - 4x}$$
$$4x - 1$$
$$\underline{4x - 8}$$
$$7$$

Quotient: $x^2 + 2x + 4$

$$\frac{x^3 - 1}{x-2} = x^2 + 2x + 4 + \frac{7}{x-2}$$

43. $\dfrac{x^3 + 2x}{x^2} = \dfrac{x^3}{x^2} + \dfrac{2x}{x^2} = x + \dfrac{2}{x}$

44. $\dfrac{2x^2 + 3}{2x} = \dfrac{2x^2}{2x} + \dfrac{3}{2x} = x + \dfrac{3}{2x}$

45.
$$x+2 \overline{\smash{\big)}\ x^2 - 4x + 9}$$
$$\underline{x^2 + 2x}$$
$$-6x + 9$$
$$\underline{-6x - 12}$$
$$21$$

Quotient: $x - 6$

$$\frac{x^2 - 4x + 9}{x+2} = x - 6 + \frac{21}{x+2}$$

46.
$$x-3 \overline{\smash{\big)}\ x^2 - 5x - 10}$$
$$\underline{x^2 - 3x}$$
$$-2x - 10$$
$$\underline{-2x + 6}$$
$$-16$$

Quotient: $x - 2$

$$\frac{x^2 - 5x - 10}{x-3} = x - 2 + \frac{-16}{x-3}$$

47.
$$x-1 \overline{\smash{\big)}\ 3x^3 - 4x^2 + 0x + 7}$$
$$\underline{3x^3 - 3x^2}$$
$$-x^2 + 0x$$
$$\underline{-x^2 + x}$$
$$-x + 7$$
$$\underline{-x + 1}$$
$$6$$

Quotient: $3x^2 - x - 1$

$$\frac{3x^3 - 4x^2 + 7}{x-1} = 3x^2 - x - 1 + \frac{6}{x-1}$$

48.
$$x+2 \overline{\smash{\big)}\ -2x^3 + x^2 + 0x - 3}$$
$$\underline{-2x^3 - 4x^2}$$
$$5x^2 + 0x$$
$$\underline{5x^2 + 10x}$$
$$-10x - 3$$
$$\underline{-10x - 20}$$
$$17$$

Quotient: $-2x^2 + 5x - 10$

$$\frac{-2x^3 + x^2 - 3}{x+2} = -x^2 + 5x - 10 + \frac{17}{x+2}$$

49.
$$
\begin{array}{r|rrrr}
2 & 1 & -5 & 6 & -3 \\
  &   & 2 & -6 & 0 \\
\hline
  & 1 & -3 & 0 & -3
\end{array}
$$

The quotient is $x^2 - 3x$ and the remainder is -3.

50.
$$
\begin{array}{r|rrrr}
3 & 1 & 6 & -3 & -5 \\
  &   & 3 & 27 & 72 \\
\hline
  & 1 & 9 & 24 & 67
\end{array}
$$

The quotient is $x^2 + 9x + 24$ and the remainder is 67.

51.
$$
\begin{array}{r|rrr}
-1 & 2 & -4 & 5 \\
   &   & -2 & 6 \\
\hline
   & 2 & -6 & 11
\end{array}
$$

The quotient is $2x - 6$ and the remainder is 11.

52.
$$
\begin{array}{r|rrr}
-2 & 3 & -7 & 4 \\
   &   & -6 & 26 \\
\hline
   & 3 & -13 & 30
\end{array}
$$

194

The quotient is $3x - 13$ and the remainder is 30.

53.
$$3 \quad \begin{array}{rrrrr} 3 & 0 & -15 & 7 & -9 \\ & 9 & 27 & 36 & 129 \\ \hline 3 & 9 & 12 & 43 & 120 \end{array}$$

The quotient is $3x^3 + 9x^2 + 12x + 43$ and the remainder is 120.

54.
$$2 \quad \begin{array}{rrrrr} -2 & 0 & 3 & 0 & -5 \\ & -4 & -8 & -10 & -20 \\ \hline -2 & -4 & -5 & -10 & -25 \end{array}$$

The quotient is $-2x^3 - 4x^2 - 5x - 10$ and the remainder is -25.

55.
$$1 \quad \begin{array}{rrrrrr} 1 & 0 & 0 & 0 & 0 & -1 \\ & 1 & 1 & 1 & 1 & 1 \\ \hline 1 & 1 & 1 & 1 & 1 & 0 \end{array}$$

The quotient is $x^4 + x^3 + x^2 + x + 1$ and the remainder is 0.

56.
$$-1 \quad \begin{array}{rrrrrrr} 1 & 0 & 0 & 0 & 0 & 0 & -1 \\ & -1 & 1 & -1 & 1 & -1 & 1 \\ \hline 1 & -1 & 1 & -1 & 1 & -1 & 0 \end{array}$$

The quotient is $x^5 - x^4 + x^3 - x^2 + x - 1$ and the remainder is 0.

57.
$$-2 \quad \begin{array}{rrrr} 1 & 0 & -5 & 6 \\ & -2 & 4 & 2 \\ \hline 1 & -2 & -1 & 8 \end{array}$$

The quotient is $x^2 - 2x - 1$ and the remainder is 8.

58.
$$4 \quad \begin{array}{rrrr} 1 & 0 & -3 & -7 \\ & 4 & 16 & 52 \\ \hline 1 & 4 & 13 & 45 \end{array}$$

The quotient is $x^2 + 4x + 13$ and the remainder is 45.

59.
$$0.32 \quad \begin{array}{rrr} 2.3 & -0.14 & 0.6 \\ & 0.736 & 0.19072 \\ \hline 2.3 & 0.596 & 0.79072 \end{array}$$

The quotient is $2.3x + 0.596$ and the remainder is 0.79072.

60.
$$-1.8 \quad \begin{array}{rrr} 1.6 & -3.5 & 4.7 \\ & -2.88 & 11.484 \\ \hline 1.6 & -6.38 & 16.184 \end{array}$$

The quotient is $1.6x - 6.38$ and the remainder is 16.184.

61. If we divide the polynomials we get a quotient of $x^2 - 3x + 1$ and remainder 4. So the first polynomial is not a factor of the second.

62. If we divide the polynomials we get a quotient of $x^2 - 3x + 13$ and remainder -4. So the first polynomial is not a factor of the second.

63. If we divide the polynomials we get a quotient of $x^2 + 4x + 3$ and remainder 0. So the first polynomial is a factor of the second.

64. If we divide the polynomials we get a quotient of $x^2 + 4x - 1$ and remainder -1. So the first polynomial is not a factor of the second.

65. If we divide the polynomials we get a quotient of $x^2 - 2$ and remainder 0. So the first polynomial is a factor of the second.

66. If we divide the polynomials we get a quotient of $2x + 1$ and remainder -1. So the first polynomial is not a factor of the second.

67. Divide the polynomials to get a quotient of $9w^2 - 3w + 1$ and remainder 0. So the first polynomial is a factor of the second.

68. Divide the polynomials to get a quotient of $4w^2 - 6w + 9$ and a remainder of 0. So the first polynomial is a factor of the second.

69. If we divide the polynomials we get a quotient of $a^2 + 5a + 25$ and remainder 0. So the first polynomial is a factor of the second.

70. If we divide the polynomials we get a quotient of $a^5 + 2a^4 + 4a^3 + 8a^2 + 16a + 32$ and remainder 0. So the first polynomial is a factor of the second.

71. If we divide the polynomials we get a quotient of $x^2 + 3x + 2$ and remainder 0. So the first polynomial is a factor of the second.

72. If we divide the polynomials we get a quotient of $x^2 + 2x - 1$ and remainder 0. So the first polynomial is a factor of the second.

73. Divide $x^2 - 6x + 8$ by $x - 4$:

```
4   1  -6   8
          4  -8
    1  -2   0
```

So $x^2 - 6x + 8 = (x - 4)(x - 2)$.

74. Divide $x^2 + 3x - 40$ by $x + 8$:

```
-8   1   3  -40
         -8   40
     1  -5   0
```

So $x^2 + 3x - 40 = (x + 8)(x - 5)$.

75. Divide $w^3 - 27$ by $w - 3$:

```
3   1   0   0  -27
        3   9   27
    1   3   9   0
```

So $w^3 - 27 = (w - 3)(w^2 + 3w + 9)$.

76. Divide $w^3 + 125$ by $w + 5$:

```
-5   1   0    0   125
    -5   25  -125
     1  -5   25    0
```

So $w^3 + 125 = (w + 5)(w^2 - 5w + 25)$.

77. Divide $x^3 - 4x^2 + 6x - 4$ by $x - 2$:

```
2   1  -4   6  -4
        2  -4   4
    1  -2   2   0
```

So $x^3 - 4x^2 + 6x - 4 = (x^2 - 2x + 2)(x - 2)$.

78. Divide $2x^3 + 0x^2 + 5x + 7$ by $x + 1$:

```
-1    2   0   5   7
         -2   2  -7
      2  -2   7   0
```

So $2x^3 + 5x + 7 = (2x^2 - 2x + 7)(x + 1)$.

79. Divide $z^2 + 6z + 9$ by $z + 3$:

```
-3    1   6   9
         -3  -9
      1   3   0
```

So $z^2 + 6z + 9 = (z + 3)(z + 3)$.

80. Divide $4a^2 - 20a + 25$ by $2a - 5$:

$$
\begin{array}{r}
2a - 5 \\
2a - 5 \overline{)\ 4a^2 - 20a + 25} \\
\underline{4a^2 - 10a} \\
-10a + 25 \\
\underline{-10a + 25} \\
0
\end{array}
$$

So $4a^2 - 20a + 25 = (2a - 5)(2a - 5)$.

81. Divide $6y^2 + 5y + 1$ by $2y + 1$:

$$
\begin{array}{r}
3y + 1 \\
2y + 1 \overline{)\ 6y^2 + 5y + 1} \\
\underline{6y^2 + 3y} \\
2y + 1 \\
\underline{2y + 1} \\
0
\end{array}
$$

So $6y^2 + 5y + 1 = (2y + 1)(3y + 1)$.

82. Divide $12y^2 - y - 6$ by $4y - 3$:

$$
\begin{array}{r}
3y + 2 \\
4y - 3 \overline{)\ 12y^2 - y - 6} \\
\underline{12y^2 - 9y} \\
8y - 6 \\
\underline{8y - 6} \\
0
\end{array}
$$

So $12y^2 - y - 6 = (4y - 3)(3y + 2)$.

83. a) Divide $0.03x^2 + 300x$ by x to get $AC(x) = 0.03x + 300$.
b) $AC(x)$ is not constant, it is a linear function.
c) Because $AC(x)$ is very close to 300 for x less than 15, the graph looks horizontal.

84. Divide $100x + 2x^2$ by x to get $AP(x) = 100 + 2x$.
$AP(12) = 100 + 2 \cdot 12 = \$124$.

85. Divide $x^2 - 1$ by $x + 1$ to get $x - 1$. The width is $x - 1$ ft.

86. Since $V = LWH$,
$h^3 + 5h^2 + 6h = W(h + 2)h$.
So $W = (h^3 + 5h^2 + 6h) \div (h^2 + 2h)$ or $W = h + 3$.

87. $V = \dfrac{10(30^3 - 20^3)}{3(30 - 20)} \approx 6{,}333.3 \text{ m}^3$

88. Divide $a^3 - b^3$ by $a - b$ to get the quotient

$a^2 + ab + b^2$. So $V = \dfrac{H(a^2 + ab + b^2)}{3}$.

5.6 WARM-UPS

1. True, $3xy(x - 2y) = -3xy(-x + 2y)$.
2. True.
3. True, because $-2(2 - x)$
$= -4 + 2x = 2x - 4$ for any value of x.
4. True, $a^2 - b^2 = (a + b)(a - b)$.
5. False, because $x^2 + 12x + 36$ is a perfect square trinomial.
6. False, because $y^2 + 8y + 16$ is a perfect square trinomial.
7. False, because $(3x + 7)^2 = 9x^2 + 42x + 49$.
8. True, $x^3 + 1 = (x + 1)(x^2 - x + 1)$.
9. False, $x^3 - 27 = (x - 3)(x^2 + 3x + 9)$.
10. False, $x^3 - 8 = (x - 2)(x^2 + 2x + 4)$.

5.6 EXERCISES

1. A prime number is a natural number greater than 1 that has no factors other than itself and 1.
2. A natural number is factored completely when it is expressed as a product of prime numbers.
3. The greatest common factor for the terms of a polynomial is a monomial that includes every number or variable that is a factor of all terms of the polynomial.
4. The greatest common factor can be factored out with a positive coefficient or a negative coefficient.
5. A linear polynomial is a polynomial of the form $ax + b$ with $a \neq 0$.
6. A quadratic polynomial is a polynomial of the form $ax^2 + bx + c$ with $a \neq 0$.
7. A prime polynomial is a polynomial that cannot be factored. Any monomial is also called a prime polynomial.
8. A polynomial is factored completely when it is expressed as a product of prime polynomials.

9. Since $48 = 2 \cdot 2 \cdot 2 \cdot 2 \cdot 3$ and $36x = 2 \cdot 2 \cdot 3 \cdot 3x$, the greatest common factor is $2 \cdot 2 \cdot 3 = 12$.
10. Since $42a = 2 \cdot 3 \cdot 7a$ and $28a^2 = 2^2 \cdot 7a^2$, the greatest common factor is $2 \cdot 7a = 14a$.
11. The gcf for 9, 21, and 15 is 3. Since there are no variables in common to all three terms, the gcf is 3.
12. Since $70x^2 = 2 \cdot 5 \cdot 7x^2$, $84x = 2^2 \cdot 3 \cdot 7x$, and $42x^3 = 2 \cdot 3 \cdot 7x^3$, the greatest common factor is $2 \cdot 7x = 14x$.
13. Since $24 = 2 \cdot 2 \cdot 2 \cdot 3$, $42 = 2 \cdot 3 \cdot 7$, and $66 = 2 \cdot 3 \cdot 11$, the GCF of 24, 42, and 66 is $2 \cdot 3$ or 6. Using each common variable with the lowest power, we get the GCF $6xy$.
14. $60a^2b^5 = 2^2 \cdot 3 \cdot 5 \cdot a^2b^5$,
$140a^9b^2 = 2^2 \cdot 5 \cdot 7 \cdot a^9b^2$,
$40a^3b^6 = 2^3 \cdot 5a^3b^6$
The GCF is $2^2 \cdot 5 \cdot a^2b^2$, or $20a^2b^2$.
15. $x^3 - 5x = x \cdot x^2 - x \cdot 5 = x(x^2 - 5)$
16. $10x^2 - 20y^3 = 10(x^2 - 2y^3)$
17. $48wx + 36wy = 12w \cdot 4x + 12w \cdot 3y$
$= 12w(4x + 3y)$
18. $42wz + 28wa = 14w(3z + 2a)$
19. $2x \cdot x^2 - 2x \cdot 2x + 2x \cdot 3$
$= 2x(x^2 - 2x + 3)$
20. $6x^3 - 12x^2 + 18x = 6x(x^2 - 2x + 3)$
21. $36a^3b^6 - 24a^4b^2 + 60a^5b^3$
$= 12a^3b^2(3b^4 - 2a + 5a^2b)$
22. $44x^8y^6z - 110x^6y^9z^2$
$= 22x^6y^6z(2x^2 - 5y^3z)$
23. Factor out the quantity $x - 6$:
$(x - 6)a + (x - 6)b = (x - 6)(a + b)$
24. $(y - 4)3 + (y - 4)b = (y - 4)(3 + b)$
25. Factor out $(y - 1)^2$:
$(y - 1)^2y + (y - 1)^2z = (y - 1)^2(y + z)$
26. $(w - 2)^2 \cdot w + (w - 2)^2 \cdot 3$
$= (w - 2)^2(w + 3)$
27. $2 \cdot x - 2 \cdot y = 2(x - y)$
$-2(-x) - 2 \cdot y = -2(-x + y)$
28. $-3x + 6 = 3(-x + 2)$
$= -3(x - 2)$
29. $6x^2 - 3x = 3x(2x - 1)$
$= -3x(-2x + 1)$

30. $10x^2 + 5x = 5x(2x + 1)$
$$= -5x(-2x - 1)$$

31. $w^2 \cdot (-w) + w^2(3) = w^2(-w + 3)$
$-w^2 \cdot w - (-w^2) \cdot 3 = -w^2(w - 3)$

32. $-2w^4 + 6w^3 = 2w^3(-w + 3)$
$$= -2w^3(w - 3)$$

33. $-a^3 + a^2 - 7a = a(-a^2 + a - 7)$
$$= -a(a^2 - a + 7)$$

34. $-2a^4 - 4a^3 + 6a^2 = 2a^2(-a^2 - 2a + 3)$
$$= -2a^2(a^2 + 2a - 3)$$

35. The polynomial is a difference of two squares and so it factors as the product of a sum and a difference: $(x - 10)(x + 10)$

36. $81 - y^2 = 9^2 - y^2 = (9 - y)(9 + y)$

37. $4y^2 - 49 = (2y)^2 - 7^2$
$$= (2y - 7)(2y + 7)$$

38. $16b^2 - 1 = (4b)^2 - 1^2 = (4b - 1)(4b + 1)$

39. $9x^2 - 25a^2 = (3x)^2 - (5a)^2$
$$= (3x - 5a)(3x + 5a)$$

40. $121a^2 - b^2 = (11a)^2 - b^2$
$$= (11a - b)(11a + b)$$

41. $(12wz)^2 - 1^2 = (12wz - 1)(12wz + 1)$

42. $x^2y^2 - 9c^2 = (xy)^2 - (3c)^2$
$$= (xy - 3c)(xy + 3c)$$

43. This polynomial is a perfect square trinomial. The middle term is twice the product of the square roots of the first term and last term. $x^2 - 2(x)(10) + 10^2 = (x - 10)^2$

44. $y^2 + 10y + 25 = y^2 + 2 \cdot 5y + 5^2$
$$= (y + 5)^2$$

45. $4m^2 - 4m + 1 = (2m)^2 - 2 \cdot 2m + 1^2$
$$= (2m - 1)^2$$

46. $(3t)^2 + 2(3t)(5) + 5^2 = (3t + 5)^2$

47. $w^2 - 2wt + t^2 = (w - t)^2$

48. $4r^2 + 20rt + 25t^2$
$$= (2r)^2 + 2 \cdot 2r \cdot 5t + (5t)^2$$
$$= (2r + 5t)^2$$

49. $a^3 - 1^3 = (a - 1)(a^2 + a + 1)$

50. $w^3 + 1 = w^3 + 1^3 = (w + 1)(w^2 - w + 1)$

51. $w^3 + 3^3 = (w + 3)(w^2 - 3w + 9)$

52. $x^3 - 64 = x^3 - 4^3$
$$= (x - 4)(x^2 + 4x + 16)$$

53. $(2x)^3 - 1^3 = (2x - 1)(4x^2 + 2x + 1)$

54. $27x^3 + 1 = (3x)^3 + 1^3$
$$= (3x + 1)(9x^2 - 3x + 1)$$

55. $a^3 + 2^3 = (a + 2)(a^2 - 2a + 4)$

56. $m^3 - 2^3 = (m - 2)(m^2 + 2m + 4)$

57. $2(x^2 - 4) = 2(x + 2)(x - 2)$

58. $3x^3 - 27x = 3x(x^2 - 9)$
$$= 3x(x - 3)(x + 3)$$

59. $x(x^2 + 10x + 25) = x(x + 5)^2$

60. $5a^4m - 45a^2m = 5a^2m(a^2 - 9)$
$$= 5a^2m(a - 3)(a + 3)$$

61. $(2x)^2 + 2(2x)(1) + 1^2 = (2x + 1)^2$

62. $ax^2 - 8ax + 16a = a(x^2 - 8x + 16)$
$$= a(x - 4)^2$$

63. $(x + 3)(x + 7)$

64. $(x - 2)x - (x - 2)5 = (x - 2)(x - 5)$

65. $3y \cdot 2y + 3y \cdot 1 = 3y(2y + 1)$

66. $4y^2 - y = y(4y - 1)$

67. $(2x)^2 - 2(2x)(5) + 5^2 = (2x - 5)^2$

68. $a^3x^3 - 6a^2x^2 + 9ax$
$$= ax(a^2x^2 - 6ax + 9)$$
$$= ax(ax - 3)^2$$

69. $2m^4 - 2mn^3 = 2m(m^3 - n^3)$
$$= 2m(m - n)(m^2 + mn + n^2)$$

70. $5x^3y^2 - y^5 = y^2(5x^3 - y^3)$

71. $(2x - 3)(x - 2)$

72. $(2x + 1)x + (2x + 1)3 = (2x + 1)(x + 3)$

73. $a(9a^2 - w^2) = a(3a + w)(3a - w)$

74. $2bn^2 - 4b^2n + 2b^3 = 2b(n^2 - 2bn + b^2)$
$$= 2b(n - b)^2$$

75. $-5(a^2 - 6a + 9) = -5(a - 3)^2$

76. $-2x^2 + 50 = -2(x^2 - 25)$
$$= -2(x - 5)(x + 5)$$

77. $16 - 54x^3 = 2(8 - 27x^3)$
$$= 2(2 - 3x)(4 + 6x + 9x^2)$$

78. $27x^2y - 64x^2y^4 = x^2y(27 - 64y^3)$
$$= x^2y(3 - 4y)(9 + 12y + 16y^2)$$

79. $-3y(y^2 + 6y + 9) = -3y(y + 3)^2$

80. $-2m^2n - 8mn - 8n$
$$= -2n(m^2 + 4m + 4)$$
$$= -2n(m + 2)^2$$

81. $-7(a^2b^2 - 1) = -7(ab + 1)(ab - 1)$

82. $-17a^2 - 17a = -17a(a + 1)$

83. If $a = x^5$ then
$x^{10} - 9 = (x^5)^2 - 3^2 = a^2 - 3^2$
$$= (a - 3)(a + 3) = (x^5 - 3)(x^5 + 3)$$

84. If $a = y^4$, then
$y^8 - 4 = (y^4)^2 - 2^2 = a^2 - 2^2$
$$= (a - 2)(a + 2) = (y^4 - 2)(y^4 + 2)$$

85. $z^{12} - 6z^6 + 9 = (z^6 - 3)^2$

86. $a^6 + 10a^3 + 25 = (a^3 + 5)^2$

87. $2x^7 + 8x^4 + 8x = 2x(x^6 + 4x^3 + 4)$
$$= 2x(x^3 + 2)^2$$

88. $x^{13} - 6x^7 + 9x = x(x^{12} - 6x^6 + 9)$
$$= x(x^6 - 3)^2$$

89. $4x^5 + 4x^3 + x = x(4x^4 + 4x^2 + 1)$
$$= x(2x^2 + 1)^2$$

90. $18x^6 + 24x^3 + 8 = 2(9x^6 + 12x^3 + 4)$
$$= 2(3x^3 + 2)^2$$

91. $x^6 - 8 = (x^2)^3 - 2^3$
$$= (x^2 - 2)(x^4 + 2x^2 + 4)$$

92. $y^6 - 27 = (y^2)^3 - 3^3$
$$= (y^2 - 3)(y^4 + 3y^2 + 9)$$

93. $2x^9 + 16 = 2(x^9 + 8) = 2((x^3)^3 + 2^3)$
$$= 2(x^3 + 2)(x^6 - 2x^3 + 4)$$

94. $x^{13} + x = x(x^{12} + 1) = x((x^4)^3 + 1^3)$
$$= x(x^4 + 1)(x^8 - x^4 + 1)$$

95. $a^{2n} - 1 = (a^n)^2 - 1^2 = (a^n - 1)(a^n + 1)$

96. $b^{4n} - 9 = (b^{2n})^2 - 3^2$
$$= (b^{2n} - 3)(b^{2n} + 3)$$

97. $a^{2r} + 6a^r + 9 = (a^r)^2 + 6a^r + 3^2$
$$= (a^r + 3)^2$$

98. $u^{6n} - 4u^{3n} + 4 = (u^{3n} - 2)^2$

99. $x^{3m} - 8 = (x^m)^3 - 2^3$
$$= (x^m - 2)(x^{2m} + 2x^m + 4)$$

100. $y^{3n} + 1 = (y^n)^3 + 1^3$
$$= (y^n + 1)(y^{2n} - y^n + 1)$$

101. $a^{3m} - b^3 = (a^m)^3 - b^3$
$$= (a^m - b)(a^{2m} + a^m b + b^2)$$

102. $r^{3m} + 8t^3 = (r^m)^3 + (2t)^3$
$$= (r^m + 2t)(r^{2m} - 2r^m t + 4t^2)$$

103. $k^{2w+1} - 10k^{w+1} + 25k$
$$= k(k^{2w} - 10k^w + 25) = k(k^w - 5)^2$$

104. $4a^{2t+1} + 4a^{t+1} + a$
$$= a(4a^{2t} + 4a^t + 1) = a(2a^t + 1)^2$$

105. $uv^{6k} - 2u^2 v^{4k} + u^3 v^{2k}$
$$= uv^{2k}(v^{4k} - 2uv^{2k} + u^2)$$
$$= uv^{2k}(v^{2k} - u)^2$$

106. $u^{3m}v^n + 2u^{2m}v^{2n} + u^m v^{3n}$
$$= u^m v^n(u^{2m} + 2u^m v^n + v^{2n})$$
$$= u^m v^n(u^m + v^n)^2$$

107. If we choose $k = 9$, then $x^2 + 6x + k$ will be the perfect square $x^2 + 6x + 9$.

108. If we choose $k = 16$, then $y^2 - 8y + k$ will be the perfect square $y^2 - 8y + 16$.

109. If we choose $k = 20$, then $4a^2 - ka + 25$ will be the perfect square $4a^2 - 20a + 25$.

110. If we choose $k = 42$, then $9u^2 + kuv + 49v^2$ will be the perfect square $9u^2 + 42uv + 49v^2$

111. If we choose $k = 16$, then $km^2 - 24m + 9$ will be the perfect square $16m^2 - 24m + 9$.

112. If we choose $k = 25$, then $kz^2 + 40z + 16$ will be the perfect square $25z^2 + 40z + 16$.

113. Choose $k = 100$ so that $81y^2 - 180y + k$ is the perfect square $81y^2 - 180y + 100$.

114. Choose $k = 25$ so that $36a^2 + 60a + k$ is the perfect square $36a^2 + 60a + 25$.

115. a) $b^3 - 6b^2 + 9b$
$$= b(b^2 - 6b + 9)$$
$$= b(b - 3)^2$$
Since $V = LWH$ and the height is b, the sides of the square bottom are each $b - 3$ cm.
b) $V = 18(4 \cdot 18 + 3)^2 = 18 \cdot 25^2 = 4050$ in.^{3}
c) From the graph it appears that the height of a cage with a volume of 20,000 in.^{3} is 30 in.

116. $3y^3 + 12y^2 + 12y = 3y(y^2 + 4y + 4)$
$$= 3y(y + 2)^2$$
Use $V = ha^2/3$. Since the height is y,
$$\frac{a^2}{3} = 3(y + 2)^2$$
$$a^2 = 9(y + 2)^2$$
$$a = 3(y + 2)$$
So the length of a side of the square base is $3y + 6$ cm.

5.7 WARM-UPS

1. True. Check by multiplying $(x + 3)(x + 6)$.

2. False, $y^2 + 2y - 35 = (y + 7)(y - 5)$.

3. False, $x^2 + 4$ cannot be factored. It is a sum of two squares.

4. False, $x^2 - 5x - 6 = (x - 6)(x + 1)$.

5. True. Check by multiplying $(x - 6)(x + 2)$.

6. False, $x^2 + 15x + 36 = (x + 12)(x + 3)$.

7. False, $3x^2 + 4x - 15 = (3x - 5)(x + 3)$.

8. False, $4x^2 + 4x - 3 = (2x + 3)(2x - 1)$.

9. True. Check by multiplying.

10. True. Check by multiplying.

5.7 EXERCISES

1. To factor $x^2 + bx + c$, find two integers whose sum is b and whose product is c.

2. To factor $ax^2 + bx + c$, find two numbers whose sum is ac and whose product is b and then use grouping.

3. Trial and error means to simply write down possible factors and then use FOIL to check until you get the correct factors.

4. When factoring a polynomial, first factor out the greatest common factor.

5. Two numbers that have a product of 3 and a sum of 4 are 1 and 3: $(x + 1)(x + 3)$

6. Two numbers with a product of 6 and a sum of 5 are 2 and 3: $y^2 + 5y + 6 = (y + 2)(y + 3)$

7. Two numbers that have a product of 50 and a sum of 15 are 5 and 10: $(a + 10)(a + 5)$

8. Two numbers with product 24 and sum 11 are 8 and 3: $t^2 + 11t + 24 = (t + 8)(t + 3)$

9. Two numbers that have a product of -14 and a sum of -5 are -7 and 2: $(y - 7)(y + 2)$

10. Two numbers that have a product of -18 and a sum of -3 are -6 and 3: $(x - 6)(x + 3)$

11. Two numbers that have a product of 8 and a sum of -6 are -2 and -4: $(x - 2)(x - 4)$

12. Two numbers with product 30 and sum -13 are -10 and -3:
$y^2 - 13y + 30 = (y - 10)(y - 3)$

13. Two numbers with product 27 and sum -12 are -9 and -3:
$a^2 - 12a + 27 = (a - 9)(a - 3)$

14. Two numbers with product -30 and sum -1 are -6 and 5:
$x^2 - x - 30 = (x - 6)(x + 5)$

15. Two numbers that have a product of -30 and a sum of 7 are -3 and 10: $(a + 10)(a - 3)$

16. Two numbers with product -30 and sum 29 are 30 and -1:
$$w^2 + 29w - 30 = (w + 30)(w - 1)$$

17. Two numbers with a product of $6 \cdot 1 = 6$ and a sum of 5 are 2 and 3:
$$\begin{aligned} 6w^2 + 5w + 1 &= 6w^2 + 3w + 2w + 1 \\ &= 3w(2w + 1) + 1(2w + 1) \\ &= (3w + 1)(2w + 1) \end{aligned}$$

18. Two numbers with a product of $4 \cdot 6 = 24$ and a sum of 11 are 8 and 3:

$$\begin{aligned} 4x^2 + 11x + 6 &= 4x^2 + 8x + 3x + 6 \\ &= 4x(x + 2) + 3(x + 2) \\ &= (4x + 3)(x + 2) \end{aligned}$$

19. Using the ac method we find two numbers that have a product of $2(-3) = -6$ and a sum of -5. These numbers are -6 and 1:
$$\begin{aligned} 2x^2 - 5x - 3 &= 2x^2 - 6x + 1x - 3 \\ &= 2x(x - 3) + 1(x - 3) \\ &= (2x + 1)(x - 3) \end{aligned}$$

20. Using the ac method we find two numbers that have a product of $2(-2) = -4$ and a sum of 3. These numbers are -1 and 4:
$$\begin{aligned} 2a^2 + 3a - 2 &= 2a^2 + 4a - a - 2 \\ &= 2a(a + 2) - 1(a + 2) \\ &= (2a - 1)(a + 2) \end{aligned}$$

21. Two numbers with a product of $4(15) = 60$ and a sum of 16 are 6 and 10:
$$\begin{aligned} 4x^2 + 16x + 15 &= 4x^2 + 6x + 10x + 15 \\ &= 2x(2x + 3) + 5(2x + 3) \\ &= (2x + 5)(2x + 3) \end{aligned}$$

22. Two numbers with a product of $6 \cdot 12 = 72$ and a sum of 17 are 9 and 8:
$$\begin{aligned} 6y^2 + 17y + 12 &= 6y^2 + 8y + 9y + 12 \\ &= 2y(3y + 4) + 3(3y + 4) \\ &= (2y + 3)(3y + 4) \end{aligned}$$

23. Two numbers with a product of $6 \cdot 1 = 6$ and a sum of -5 are -2 and -3:
$$\begin{aligned} 6x^2 - 5x + 1 &= 6x^2 - 2x - 3x + 1 \\ &= 2x(3x - 1) - 1(3x - 1) \\ &= (2x - 1)(3x - 1) \end{aligned}$$

24. Two numbers with a product of $6 \cdot 12 = 72$ and a sum of -1 are -9 and 8:
$$\begin{aligned} 6m^2 - m - 12 &= 6m^2 - 9m + 8m - 12 \\ &= 3m(2m - 3) + 4(2m - 3) \\ &= (3m + 4)(2m - 3) \end{aligned}$$

25. Two numbers with a product of $12(-1) = -12$ and a sum of 1 are 4 and -3:
$$\begin{aligned} 12y^2 + y - 1 &= 12y^2 - 3y + 4y - 1 \\ &= 3y(4y - 1) + 1(4y - 1) \\ &= (3y + 1)(4y - 1) \end{aligned}$$

26. Two numbers with a product of $12(-2) = -24$ and a sum of 5 are 8 and -3:
$$\begin{aligned} 12x^2 + 5x - 2 &= 12x^2 + 8x - 3x - 2 \\ &= 4x(3x + 2) - 1(3x + 2) \\ &= (4x - 1)(3x + 2) \end{aligned}$$

27. Two numbers with a product of $-5(6) = -30$ and a sum of 1 are 6 and -5:
$$6a^2 + a - 5 = 6a^2 + 6a - 5a - 5$$
$$= 6a(a + 1) - 5(a + 1)$$
$$= (6a - 5)(a + 1)$$

28. Two numbers with a product of $30(-3) = -90$ and a sum of -1 are -10 and 9:
$$30b^2 - b - 3 = 30b^2 - 10b + 9b - 3$$
$$= 10b(3b - 1) + 3(3b - 1)$$
$$= (10b + 3)(3b - 1)$$

29. $2x^2 + 15x - 8 = (2x - 1)(x + 8)$

30. $3a^2 + 20a + 12 = (3a + 2)(a + 6)$

31. $3b^2 - 16b - 35 = (3b + 5)(b - 7)$

32. $2y^2 - 17y + 21 = (2y - 3)(y - 7)$

33. $6w^2 - 35w + 36 = (3w - 4)(2w - 9)$

34. $15x^2 - x - 6 = (3x - 2)(5x + 3)$

35. $4x^2 - 5x + 1 = (4x - 1)(x - 1)$

36. $4x^2 + 7x + 3 = (4x + 3)(x + 1)$

37. $5m^2 + 13m - 6 = (5m - 2)(m + 3)$

38. $5t^2 - 9t - 2 = (5t + 1)(t - 2)$

39. $6y^2 - 7y - 20 = (3y + 4)(2y - 5)$

40. $7u^2 + 11u - 6 = (7u - 3)(u + 2)$

41. $x^6 - 2x^3 - 35 = (x^3 + 5)(x^3 - 7)$

42. $x^4 + 7x^2 - 30 = (x^2 + 10)(x^2 - 3)$

43. $a^{20} - 20a^{10} + 100 = (a^{10} - 10)^2$

44. $b^{16} + 22b^8 + 121 = (b^8 + 11)^2$

45. $-12a^5 - 10a^3 - 2a$
$$= -2a(6a^4 + 5a^2 + 1)$$
$$= -2a(3a^2 + 1)(2a^2 + 1)$$

46. $-4b^7 + 4b^4 + 3b = -b(4b^6 - 4b^3 - 3)$
$$= -b(2b^3 - 3)(2b^3 + 1)$$

47. Two numbers with a product of -15 and a sum of 2 are 5 and -3:
$$x^{2a} + 2x^a - 15 = (x^a + 5)(x^a - 3)$$

48. Two numbers with a product of -20 and a sum of 1 are 5 and -4:
$$y^{2b} + y^b - 20 = (y^b + 5)(y^b - 4)$$

49. $x^{2a} - y^{2b} = (x^a)^2 - (y^b)^2$
$$= (x^a - y^b)(x^a + y^b)$$

50. $w^{4m} - a^2 = (w^{2m})^2 - a^2$
$$= (w^{2m} - a)(w^{2m} + a)$$

51. $x^8 - x^4 - 6 = (x^4 - 3)(x^4 + 2)$

52. $m^{10} - 5m^5 - 6 = (m^5 - 6)(m^5 + 1)$

53. $x^a(x^2 - 1) = x^a(x - 1)(x + 1)$

54. $y^{2a+1} - y = y(y^{2a} - 1)$

$$= y(y^a - 1)(y^a + 1)$$

55. $(x^a)^2 + 2 \cdot x^a \cdot 3 + 3^2 = (x^a + 3)^2$

56. $x^{2a} - 2x^a y^b + y^{2b} = (x^a)^2 - 2x^a y^b + (y^b)^2$
$$= (x^a - y^b)^2$$

57. $4y^3 z^6 + 5z^3 y^2 - 6y$
$$= y(4y^2 z^6 + 5z^3 y - 6)$$
$$= y(4yz^3 - 3)(yz^3 + 2)$$

58. $2u^6 v^6 + 5u^4 v^3 - 12u^2$
$$= u^2(2u^4 v^6 + 5u^2 v^3 - 12)$$
$$= u^2(2u^2 v^3 - 3)(u^2 v^3 + 4)$$

59. $2x^2 + 20x + 50 = 2(x^2 + 10x + 25)$
$$= 2(x + 5)^2$$

60. $3a^2 + 6a + 3 = 3(a^2 + 2a + 1)$
$$= 3(a + 1)^2$$

61. $a^3 - 36a = a(a^2 - 36)$
$$= a(a - 6)(a + 6)$$

62. $x^3 - 5x^2 - 6x = x(x^2 - 5x - 6)$
$$= x(x - 6)(x + 1)$$

63. $5(a^2 + 5a - 6) = 5(a + 6)(a - 1)$

64. $2a^2 - 2a - 84 = 2(a^2 - a - 42)$
$$= 2(a - 7)(a + 6)$$

65. $2(x^2 - 64y^2) = 2(x + 8y)(x - 8y)$

66. $a^3 - 6a^2 + 9a = a(a^2 - 6a + 9)$
$$= a(a - 3)^2$$

67. $-3(x^2 - x - 12) = -3(x + 3)(x - 4)$

68. $xy^2 - 3xy - 70x = x(y^2 - 3y - 70)$
$$= x(y - 10)(y + 7)$$

69. $m^3(m^2 + 20m + 100) = m^3(m + 10)^2$

70. $4a^2 - 16a + 16 = 4(a^2 - 4a + 4)$
$$= 4(a - 2)^2$$

71. Two numbers with a product of $6 \cdot 20 = 120$ and a sum of 23 are 8 and 15:
$$6x^2 + 23x + 20 = 6x^2 + 15x + 8x + 20$$
$$= 3x(2x + 5) + 4(2x + 5)$$
$$= (3x + 4)(2x + 5)$$

72. $2y^2 - 13y + 6 = 2y^2 - 12y - y + 6$
$$= 2y(y - 6) - 1(y - 6)$$
$$= (2y - 1)(y - 6)$$

73. $y^2 - 2 \cdot 6y + 6^2 = (y - 6)^2$

74. $m^2 - 2m + 1 = m^2 - 2 \cdot m \cdot 1 + 1^2$
$$= (m - 1)^2$$

75. $(3m)^2 - (5n)^2 = (3m - 5n)(3m + 5n)$

76. $m^2 n^2 - 2mn^3 + n^4$
$$= n^2(m^2 - 2mn + n^2)$$
$$= n^2(m - n)^2$$

77. $5(a^2 + 4a - 12) = 5(a + 6)(a - 2)$

78. $-3y^2 + 9y + 30 = -3(y^2 - 3y - 10)$
$$= -3(y - 5)(y + 2)$$
79. $-2(w^2 - 9w - 10) = -2(w - 10)(w + 1)$
80. $x^2z + 2xyz + y^2z = z(x^2 + 2xy + y^2)$
$$= z(x + y)^2$$
81. $x^2(w^2 - 100) = x^2(w + 10)(w - 10)$
82. $9x^2 + 30x + 25 = (3x)^2 + 2 \cdot 3x \cdot 5 + 5^2$
$$= (3x + 5)^2$$
83. $(3x)^2 - 1^2 = (3x + 1)(3x - 1)$
84. $6w^2 - 19w - 36 = 6w^2 - 27w + 8w - 36$
$$= 3w(2w - 9) + 4(2w - 9)$$
$$= (3w + 4)(2w - 9)$$
85. Two numbers with a product of $-15 \cdot 8 = -120$ and a sum of -2 are -12 and 10:
$$8x^2 - 2x - 15 = 8x^2 - 12x + 10x - 15$$
$$= 4x(2x - 3) + 5(2x - 3)$$
$$= (4x + 5)(2x - 3)$$
86. $4w^2 + 12w + 9 = (2w)^2 + 2 \cdot 2w \cdot 3 + 3^2$
$$= (2w + 3)^2$$
87. $(2x)^2 - 2 \cdot 10x + 5^2 = (2x - 5)^2$
88. $9m^2 - 121 = (3m - 11)(3m + 11)$
89. $(3a)^2 + 2 \cdot 3a \cdot 10 + 10^2 = (3a + 10)^2$
90. $10w^2 + 20w - 80 = 10(w^2 + 2w - 8)$
$$= 10(w + 4)(w - 2)$$
91. $4(a^2 + 6a + 8) = 4(a + 2)(a + 4)$
92. $20x^2 - 23x + 6 = 20x^2 - 15x - 8x + 6$
$$= 5x(4x - 3) - 2(4x - 3)$$
$$= (5x - 2)(4x - 3)$$
93. $3m^4 - 24m = 3m(m^3 - 8)$
$$= 3m(m - 2)(m^2 + 2m + 4)$$
94. $6w^3z + 6z = 6z(w^3 + 1)$
$$= 6z(w + 1)(w^2 - w + 1)$$
95. The polynomials in (a) and (b) are not perfect square trinomials.
96. Only (b) is not a difference of two squares.

5.8 WARM-UPS

1. False, $x^2 - 9 = (x - 3)(x + 3)$ for any value of x.
2. True, because $4x^2 + 12x + 9 = (2x + 3)^2$.
3. True.
4. False, because $x^2 - 4$ is not a prime polynomial.
5. False, because
$$y^3 - 27 = (y - 3)(y^2 + 3y + 9)$$

for any value of y.
6. True, because $y^6 - 1 = (y^3)^2 - 1^2$.
7. False, because $2x - 4$ is not prime.
8. True, because it cannot be factored.
9. True, because $a^6 - 1 = (a^2)^3 - 1^3$.
10. False, because if we factor x out of the first two terms and a out of the last two terms we get $x^2 + 3x - ax + 3a = x(x + 3) + a(-x + 3)$ and we cannot finish. If we factor x out of the first two terms and $-a$ out of the last two terms we get $x(x + 3) - a(x - 3)$ and again we cannot finish the factoring.

5.8 EXERCISES

1. Always factor out the greatest common factor first.
2. In factoring a binomial look for a difference of two squares, and a sum or difference of two cubes.
3. In factoring a trinomial look for the perfect square trinomials.
4. In factoring a four-term polynomial try factoring by grouping.
5. Prime, because it is a sum of two squares.
6. Not prime, because $3x^2 + 27 = 3(x^2 + 9)$.
7. Not prime, because
$-9w^2 - 9 = -9(w^2 + 1)$.
8. Prime, because it is sum of two squares.
9. Not prime, $x^2 - 2x - 3 = (x - 3)(x + 1)$.
10. To factor $x^2 - 2x + 3$, we would need two integers with a product of 3 and a sum of -2. Since there are no such integers, the polynomial is prime.
11. Prime, because no two integers have a product of 3 and a sum of 2.
12. To factor $x^2 + 4x + 3$, we need two integers with a product of 3 and a sum of 4. The integers are 3 and 1, and $x^2 + 4x + 3 = (x + 1)(x + 3)$. So the polynomial is not prime.
13. Prime, because no two numbers have a product of -3 and a sum of -4.
14. To factor $x^2 + 4x - 3$ we need two integers with a product of -3 and a sum of 4. Since there are no such integers, the polynomial is prime.

15. Prime, because no two numbers have a product of $6 \cdot (-4) = -24$ and a sum of 3.

16. To factor $4x^2 - 5x - 3$ we need two integers with a product of $4(-3) = -12$ and a sum of -5. Since there are no such integers, the polynomial is prime.

17. Let $y = a^2$ in the polynomial:
$a^4 - 10a^2 + 25 = y^2 - 10y + 25$
$\quad = (y - 5)^2 = (a^2 - 5)^2$

18. Let $x = y^2$ in the polynomial:
$9y^4 + 12y^2 + 4 = 9x^2 + 12x + 4$
$\quad = (3x + 2)^2 = (3y^2 + 2)^2$

19. Let $y = x^2$ in the polynomial:
$x^4 - 6x^2 + 8 = y^2 - 6y + 8 = (y - 2)(y - 4)$
$= (x^2 - 2)(x^2 - 4) = (x^2 - 2)(x - 2)(x + 2)$

20. If we let $a = x^3$, then $a^2 = (x^3)^2 = x^6$.
$x^6 + 2x^3 - 3 = a^2 + 2a - 3 = (a + 3)(a - 1)$
$\quad = (x^3 + 3)(x^3 - 1)$
$\quad = (x^3 + 3)(x - 1)(x^2 + x + 1)$

21. Let $y = 3x - 5$ in the polynomial:
$(3x - 5)^2 - 1 = y^2 - 1 = (y - 1)(y + 1)$
$\quad = (3x - 5 - 1)(3x - 5 + 1)$
$\quad = (3x - 6)(3x - 4)$
$\quad = 3(x - 2)(3x - 4)$

22. Let $y = 2x + 1$.
$(2x + 1)^2 - 4 = y^2 - 4 = (y - 2)(y + 2)$
$\quad = (2x + 1 - 2)(2x + 1 + 2)$
$\quad = (2x - 1)(2x + 3)$

23. If we let $a = y^3$, then $a^2 = (y^3)^2 = y^6$.
$2y^6 - 128 = 2(y^6 - 64) = 2(a^2 - 64)$
$= 2(a - 8)(a + 8) = 2(y^3 - 8)(y^3 + 8)$
$= 2(y - 2)(y^2 + 2y + 4)(y + 2)(y^2 - 2y + 4)$

24. If we let $a = y^3$, the $a^2 = y^6$.
$6 - 6y^6 = 6 - 6a^2 = 6(1 - a^2)$
$= 6(1 - a)(1 + a) = 6(1 - y^3)(1 + y^3)$
$= 6(1 - y)(1 + y + y^2)(1 + y)(1 - y + y^2)$

25. $32a^4 - 18 = 2(16a^4 - 9)$
$\quad = 2(4a^2 + 3)(4a^2 - 3)$

26. $2a^4 - 32 = 2(a^4 - 16)$
$\quad = 2(a^2 - 4)(a^2 + 4)$
$\quad = 2(a - 2)(a + 2)(a^2 + 4)$

27. Let $a = x^2$ and $b = x - 6$:
$x^4 - (x - 6)^2 = a^2 - b^2 = (a + b)(a - b)$
$\quad = (x^2 + x - 6)(x^2 - [x - 6])$
$\quad = (x + 3)(x - 2)(x^2 - x + 6)$

28. Let $a = 2y + 1$.

$y^4 - (2y + 1)^2 = y^4 - a^2 = (y^2 - a)(y^2 + a)$
$\quad = (y^2 - (2y + 1))(y^2 + 2y + 1)$
$\quad = (y^2 - 2y - 1)(y^2 + 2y + 1)$
$\quad = (y^2 - 2y - 1)(y + 1)^2$

29. Let $y = m + 2$ in the polynomial:
$(m + 2)^2 + 2(m + 2) - 3 = y^2 + 2y - 3$
$= (y + 3)(y - 1) = (m + 2 + 3)(m + 2 - 1)$
$= (m + 5)(m + 1)$

30. Let $y = 2w - 3$ in the polynomial:
$(2w - 3)^2 - 2(2w - 3) - 15 = y^2 - 2y - 15$
$\quad = (y + 3)(y - 5)$
$\quad = (2w - 3 + 3)(2w - 3 - 5)$
$\quad = (2w)(2w - 8)$
$\quad = 2w \cdot 2(w - 4) = 4w(w - 4)$

31. Let $w = y - 1$ in the polynomial:
$3(y - 1)^2 + 11(y - 1) - 20$
$\quad = 3w^2 + 11w - 20$
$\quad = (3w - 4)(w + 5)$
$\quad = [3(y - 1) - 4][y - 1 + 5]$
$\quad = (3y - 7)(y + 4)$

32. Let $a = w + 2$.
$2(w + 2)^2 + 5(w + 2) - 3 = 2a^2 + 5a - 3$
$\quad = (2a - 1)(a + 3)$
$\quad = (2(w + 2) - 1)(w + 2 + 3)$
$\quad = (2w + 3)(w + 5)$

33. Let $a = y^2 - 3$:
$(y^2 - 3)^2 - 4(y^2 - 3) \quad 12 = a^2 - 4a - 12$
$\quad = (a - 6)(a + 2)$
$\quad = (y^2 - 3 - 6)(y^2 - 3 + 2)$
$\quad = (y^2 - 9)(y^2 - 1)$
$\quad = (y - 3)(y + 3)(y - 1)(y + 1)$

34. Let $a = m^2 - 8$:
$(m^2 - 8)^2 - 4(m^2 - 8) - 32 = a^2 - 4a - 32$
$\quad = (a - 8)(a + 4)$
$\quad = (m^2 - 8 - 8)(m^2 - 8 + 4)$
$\quad = (m^2 - 16)(m^2 - 4)$
$\quad = (m - 4)(m + 4)(m - 2)(m + 2)$

35. $ax + ay + bx + by = a(x + y) + b(x + y)$
$\quad = (a + b)(x + y)$

36. $7x + 7z + kx + kz$
$\quad = 7(x + z) + k(x + z)$
$\quad = (7 + k)(x + z)$

37. $x^3 + x^2 - 9x - 9 = x^2(x + 1) - 9(x + 1)$
$\quad = (x^2 - 9)(x + 1)$
$\quad = (x - 3)(x + 3)(x + 1)$

203

38. $x^3 + x^2 - 25x - 25$
$= x^2(x+1) - 25(x+1)$
$= (x^2 - 25)(x+1)$
$= (x-5)(x+5)(x+1)$

39. $aw - bw - 3a + 3b$
$= w(a-b) - 3(a-b)$
$= (w-3)(a-b)$

40. $wx - wy + 2x - 2y$
$= w(x-y) + 2(x-y)$
$= (w+2)(x-y)$

41. $a^4 + 3a^3 + 27a + 81$
$= a^3(a+3) + 27(a+3)$
$= (a^3 + 27)(a+3)$
$= (a+3)(a^2 - 3a + 9)(a+3)$
$= (a+3)^2(a^2 - 3a + 9)$

42. $ac - bc - 5a + 5b = c(a-b) - 5(a-b)$
$= (c-5)(a-b)$

43. $y^4 - 5y^3 + 8y - 40$
$= y^3(y-5) + 8(y-5)$
$= (y-5)(y^3 + 8)$
$= (y-5)(y+2)(y^2 - 2y + 4)$

44. $x^3 + ax - 3a - 3x^2$
$= x(x^2 + a) - 3(x^2 + a)$
$= (x-3)(x^2 + a)$

45. $ady + d - w - awy$
$= d(ay+1) - w(ay+1)$
$= (d-w)(ay+1)$

46. $xy + by + ax + ab = y(x+b) + a(x+b)$
$= (y+a)(x+b)$

47. $x^2 y - y + ax^2 - a$
$= y(x^2 - 1) + a(x^2 - 1)$
$= (a+y)(x^2 - 1)$
$= (a+y)(x-1)(x+1)$

48. $a^2 c - b^2 c + a^2 d - b^2 d$
$= c(a^2 - b^2) + d(a^2 - b^2)$
$= (c+d)(a^2 - b^2)$
$= (c+d)(a-b)(a+b)$

49. $y^4 + y + by^3 + b = y(y^3 + 1) + b(y^3 + 1)$
$= (y+b)(y^3 + 1)$
$= (y+b)(y+1)(y^2 - y + 1)$

50. $ab + bm + aw^2 + mw^2$
$= b(a+m) + w^2(a+m)$
$= (b+w^2)(a+m)$

51. This is a perfect square trinomial.
$9x^2 - 24x + 16 = (3x-4)^2$

52. $-3x^2 + 18x + 48 = -3(x^2 - 6x - 16)$

$= -3(x-8)(x+2)$

53. Two numbers whose product is 36 and whose sum is -13 are -4 and -9.
$12x^2 - 13x + 3 = 12x^2 - 4x - 9x + 3$
$= 4x(3x-1) - 3(3x-1)$
$= (3x-1)(4x-3)$

54. To factor $2x^2 - 3x - 6$ we must find two integers with a product of $2(-6) = -12$ and a sum of -3. Since there are no such integers, the polynomial is prime.

55. $3a^4 + 81a = 3a(a^3 + 27)$
$= 3a(a+3)(a^2 - 3a + 9)$

56. $-a^3 + 25a = -a(a^2 - 25)$
$= -a(a-5)(a+5)$

57. $32 + 2x^2 = 2(x^2 + 16)$

58. $x^3 + 4x^2 + 4x = x(x^2 + 4x + 4)$
$= x(x+2)^2$

59. Prime, because there are no two numbers that have a product of 72 and a sum of -5.

60. $x^4 + 2x^3 - x - 2 = x^3(x+2) - 1(x+2)$
$= (x^3 - 1)(x+2)$
$= (x-1)(x^2 + x + 1)(x+2)$

61. Let $a = x + y$: $(x+y)^2 - 1 = a^2 - 1$
$= (a-1)(a+1) = (x+y-1)(x+y+1)$

62. $x^3 + 9x = x(x^2 + 9)$

63. $a^3 b - ab^3 = ab(a^2 - b^2)$
$= ab(a-b)(a+b)$

64. $2m^3 - 250 = 2(m^3 - 125)$
$= 2(m-5)(m^2 + 5m + 25)$

65. $x^4 + 2x^3 - 8x - 16$
$= x^3(x+2) - 8(x+2)$
$= (x+2)(x^3 - 8)$
$= (x+2)(x-2)(x^2 + 2x + 4)$

66. Let $a = x + 5$: $(x+5)^2 - 4 = a^2 - 4$
$= (a-2)(a+2) = (x+5-2)(x+5+2)$
$= (x+3)(x+7)$

67. $m^2 n + 2mn^2 + n^3 = n(m^2 + 2mn + n^2)$
$= n(m+n)^2$

68. $a^2 b - 6ab + 9b = b(a^2 - 6a + 9)$
$= b(a-3)^2$

69. $2m + 2n + wm + wn$
$= 2(m+n) + w(m+n)$
$= (2+w)(m+n)$

70. $aw + bw - 5a - 5b$
$= w(a+b) - 5(a+b)$
$= (w-5)(a+b)$

204

71. Two numbers with a product of -12 and a sum of 4 are 6 and -2:

$4w^2 + 4w - 3 = 4w^2 - 2w + 6w - 3$
$\qquad = 2w(2w - 1) + 3(2w - 1)$
$\qquad = (2w + 3)(2w - 1)$

72. To factor $4w^2 + 8w - 63$ we need two integers with a product of $4(-63) = -252$, and a sum of 8. The only ways to factor 252 are $2 \cdot 126$, $4 \cdot 63$, $7 \cdot 36$, $6 \cdot 42$, $9 \cdot 28$, $12 \cdot 21$, and $14 \cdot 18$. We cannot get a sum of 8 for any of these possibilities. So the polynomial is prime.

73. Let $a = t^2$:

$t^4 + 4t^2 - 21 = a^2 + 4a - 21$
$\qquad = (a + 7)(a - 3)$
$\qquad = (t^2 + 7)(t^2 - 3)$

74. $m^4 + 5m^2 + 4 = (m^2 + 1)(m^2 + 4)$

75. $-a^3 - 7a^2 + 30a = -a(a^2 + 7a - 30)$
$\qquad = -a(a + 10)(a - 3)$

76. $2y^4 + 3y^3 - 20y^2 = y^2(2y^2 + 3y - 20)$
$\qquad = y^2(2y - 5)(y + 4)$

77. Let $a = y + 5$: $(y + 5)^2 - 2(y + 5) - 3$
$\qquad = a^2 - 2a - 3 = (a - 3)(a + 1)$
$\qquad = (y + 5 - 3)(y + 5 + 1)$
$\qquad = (y + 2)(y + 6)$

78. Let $a = 2t - 1$:

$(2t - 1)^2 + 7(2t - 1) + 10$
$\qquad = a^2 + 7a + 10 = (a + 2)(a + 5)$
$\qquad = (2t - 1 + 2)(2t - 1 + 5)$
$\qquad = (2t + 1)(2t + 4)$
$\qquad = 2(2t + 1)(t + 2)$

79. $-2w^4 + 1250 = -2(w^4 - 625)$
$\qquad = -2(w^2 - 25)(w^2 + 25)$
$\qquad = -2(w - 5)(w + 5)(w^2 + 25)$

80. $5a^5 - 5a = 5a(a^4 - 1)$
$\qquad = 5a(a^2 - 1)(a^2 + 1)$
$\qquad = 5a(a - 1)(a + 1)(a^2 + 1)$

81. $8a^3 + 8a = 8a(a^2 + 1)$

82. $awx + ax = ax(w + 1)$

83. Let $y = w + 5$:

$(w + 5)^2 - 9 = y^2 - 9$
$\qquad = (y - 3)(y + 3)$
$\qquad = (w + 5 - 3)(w + 5 + 3)$
$\qquad = (w + 2)(w + 8)$

84. Let $y = a - 6$:

$(a - 6)^2 - 1 = y^2 - 1$
$\qquad = (y - 1)(y + 1)$

$\qquad = (a - 6 - 1)(a - 6 + 1)$
$\qquad = (a - 7)(a - 5)$

85. $4aw^2 - 12aw + 9a = a(4w^2 - 12w + 9)$
$\qquad = a(2w - 3)^2$

86. $9an^3 + 15an^2 - 14an$
$\qquad = an(9n^2 + 15n - 14)$
$\qquad = an(3n - 2)(3n + 7)$

87. $x^2 - 6x + 9 = (x - 3)^2$

88. $x^3 + 12x^2 + 36x = x(x^2 + 12x + 36)$
$\qquad = x(x + 6)^2$

89. $3x^4 - 75x^2 = 3x^2(x^2 - 25)$
$\qquad = 3x^2(x - 5)(x + 5)$

90. $3x^2 + 9x + 12 = 3(x^2 + 3x + 4)$

Note that $x^2 + 3x + 4$ is prime.

91. $m^3n - n = n(m^3 - 1)$
$\qquad = n(m - 1)(m^2 + m + 1)$

92. $m^4 + 16m^2 = m^2(m^2 + 16)$

Note that $m^2 + 16$ is prime.

93. $12x^2 + 2x - 30 = 2(6x^2 + x - 15)$
$\qquad = 2[6x^2 - 9x + 10x - 15]$
$\qquad = 2[3x(2x - 3) + 5(2x - 3)]$
$\qquad = 2(3x + 5)(2x - 3)$

94. $90x^2 + 3x - 60 = 3(30x^2 + x - 20)$
$\qquad = 3(5x - 4)(6x + 5)$

95. $2a^3 - 32 = 2(a^3 - 16)$

96. Find two integers with a product of $12(15) = 180$ and a sum of -28. The integers are -18 and -10.

$12x^2 - 28x + 15 = 12x^2 - 18x - 10x + 15$
$\qquad = 6x(2x - 3) - 5(2x - 3)$
$\qquad = (2x - 3)(6x - 5)$

97. $a^{3m} - 1 = (a^m)^3 - 1^3$
$\qquad = (a^m - 1)(a^{2m} + a^m + 1)$

98. $x^{6a} + 8 = (x^{2a})^3 + 2^3$
$\qquad = (x^{2a} + 2)(x^{4a} - 2x^{2a} + 4)$

99. $a^{3w} - b^{6n} = (a^w)^3 - (b^{2n})^3$
$\qquad = (a^w - b^{2n})(a^{2w} + a^w b^{2n} + b^{4n})$

100. $x^{2n} - 9 = (x^n)^2 - 3^2$
$\qquad = (x^n - 3)(x^n + 3)$

101. $t^{4n} - 16 = (t^{2n})^2 - 4^2$
$\qquad = (t^{2n} - 4)(t^{2n} + 4)$
$\qquad = (t^n - 2)(t^n + 2)(t^{2n} + 4)$

102. $a^{3n+2} + a^2 = a^2(a^{3n} + 1)$
$\qquad = a^2[(a^n)^3 + 1^3]$
$\qquad = a^2(a^n + 1)(a^{2n} - a^n + 1)$

103. $a^{2n+1} - 2a^{n+1} - 15a$
$$= a(a^{2n} - 2a^n - 15)$$
$$= a(a^n - 5)(a^n + 3)$$

104. $x^{3m} + x^{2m} - 6x^m = x^m(x^{2m} + x^m - 6)$
$$= x^m(x^m + 3)(x^m - 2)$$

105. $a^{2n} - 3a^n + a^n b - 3b$
$$= a^n(a^n - 3) + b(a^n - 3)$$
$$= (a^n - 3)(a^n + b)$$

106. $x^m z + 5z + x^{m+1} + 5x$
$$= z(x^m + 5) + x(x^m + 5)$$
$$= (z + x)(x^m + 5)$$

5.9 WARM-UPS

1. False, because 4 is a solution to $x - 1 = 3$, but $(4 - 1)(4 + 3) \neq 12$.

2. True, both 2 and 3 satisfy $(x - 2)(x - 3) = 0$.

3. True, because of the zero factor property.

4. False, $|x^2 + 4| = 5$ is equivalent to $x^2 + 4 = 5$ or $x^2 + 4 = -5$.

5. True, because of the zero factor property.

6. False, the Pythagorean theorem applies only to right triangles.

7. True, because the sum of the length and width of a rectangle is one-half of the perimeter.

8. True, $x + (8 - x) = 8$ for any number x.

9. False, the solution set also includes 0 because of the factor x.

10. False, because 3 is not a solution.

5.9 EXERCISES

1. The zero factor property says that if $a \cdot b = 0$ then either $a = 0$ or $b = 0$.

2. A quadratic equation is an equation of the form $ax^2 + bx + c = 0$ with $a \neq 0$.

3. The hypotenuse of a right triangle is the side opposite the right angle.

4. The legs of a right triangle are the sides that form the right angle.

5. The Pythagorean theorem says that a triangle is a right triangle if and only if the sum of the squares of the legs is equal to the square of the hypotenuse.

6. The diagonal of a rectangle is the line segment that joins two opposite vertices.

7. $(x - 5)(x + 4) = 0$
$$x - 5 = 0 \quad \text{or} \quad x + 4 = 0$$
$$x = 5 \text{ or} \qquad x = -4$$
Solution set: $\{-4, 5\}$

8. $(a - 6)(a + 5) = 0$
$$a - 6 = 0 \quad \text{or} \quad a + 5 = 0$$
$$a = 6 \text{ or} \qquad a = -5$$
The solution set is $\{-5, 6\}$.

9. $(2x - 5)(3x + 4) = 0$
$$2x - 5 = 0 \qquad \text{or } 3x + 4 = 0$$
$$2x = 5 \qquad \text{or} \qquad 3x = -4$$
$$x = \tfrac{5}{2} \qquad \text{or} \qquad x = -\tfrac{4}{3}$$
Solution set: $\left\{ \tfrac{5}{2}, -\tfrac{4}{3} \right\}$

10. $(3k + 8)(4k - 3) = 0$
$$3k + 8 = 0 \qquad \text{or } 4k - 3 = 0$$
$$3k = -8 \qquad \text{or} \qquad 4k = 3$$
$$k = -\tfrac{8}{3} \qquad \text{or} \qquad k = \tfrac{3}{4}$$
Solution set: $\left\{-\tfrac{8}{3}, \tfrac{3}{4}\right\}$

11. $w^2 + 5w - 14 = 0$
$$(w + 7)(w - 2) = 0$$
$$w + 7 = 0 \qquad \text{or } w - 2 = 0$$
$$w = -7 \qquad \text{or} \qquad w = 2$$
Solution set: $\{-7, 2\}$

12. $t^2 - 6t - 27 = 0$
$$(t - 9)(t + 3) = 0$$
$$t - 9 = 0 \quad \text{or} \qquad t + 3 = 0$$
$$t = 9 \quad \text{or} \qquad\quad t = -3$$
The solution set is $\{-3, 9\}$.

13. $m^2 - 7m = 0$
$$m(m - 7) = 0$$
$$m = 0 \qquad \text{or } m - 7 = 0$$
$$m = 0 \qquad \text{or} \qquad m = 7$$
Solution set: $\{0, 7\}$

14. $h^2 - 5h = 0$
$$h(h - 5) = 0$$
$$h = 0 \qquad \text{or } h - 5 = 0$$
$$h = 5$$
The solution set is $\{0, 5\}$.

15. $a^2 - a = 20$
$$a^2 - a - 20 = 0$$
$$(a - 5)(a + 4) = 0$$
$$a - 5 = 0 \text{ or } a + 4 = 0$$

$$a = 5 \quad \text{or} \quad a = -4$$

Solution set: $\{-4, 5\}$

16. $\quad p^2 - p = 42$

$$p^2 - p - 42 = 0$$
$$(p - 7)(p + 6) = 0$$
$$p - 7 = 0 \quad \text{or} \quad p + 6 = 0$$
$$p = 7 \quad \text{or} \quad p = -6$$

The solution set is $\{-6, 7\}$.

17. $\quad 3(x^2 - x - 12) = 0$

$$3(x - 4)(x + 3) = 0$$
$$x - 4 = 0 \quad \text{or} \quad x + 3 = 0$$
$$x = 4 \quad \text{or} \quad x = -3$$

Solution set: $\{-3, 4\}$

18. $-2x^2 - 16x - 24 = 0$

$$-2(x^2 + 8x + 12) = 0$$
$$-2(x + 2)(x + 6) = 0$$
$$x + 2 = 0 \quad \text{or} \quad x + 6 = 0$$
$$x = -2 \quad \text{or} \quad x = -6$$

The solution set is $\{-6, -2\}$.

19. $\quad 2\left(z^2 + \frac{3}{2}z\right) = 2(10)$

$$2z^2 + 3z = 20$$
$$2z^2 + 3z - 20 = 0$$
$$(2z - 5)(z + 4) = 0$$
$$2z - 5 = 0 \quad \text{or} \quad z + 4 = 0$$
$$2z = 5 \quad \text{or} \quad z = -4$$
$$z = \frac{5}{2}$$

Solution set: $\left\{-4, \frac{5}{2}\right\}$

20. $\quad m^2 + \frac{11}{3}m = -2$

$$3m^2 + 11m = -6$$
$$3m^2 + 11m + 6 = 0$$
$$(3m + 2)(m + 3) = 0$$
$$3m + 2 = 0 \quad \text{or} \quad m + 3 = 0$$
$$3m = -2 \quad \text{or} \quad m = -3$$
$$m = -\frac{2}{3}$$

The solution set is $\left\{-3, -\frac{2}{3}\right\}$.

21. $\quad x^3 - 4x = 0$

$$x(x^2 - 4) = 0$$
$$x(x - 2)(x + 2) = 0$$
$$x = 0 \quad \text{or} \quad x - 2 = 0 \quad \text{or} \quad x + 2 = 0$$
$$x = 0 \quad \text{or} \quad x = 2 \quad \text{or} \quad x = -2$$

Solution set: $\{-2, 0, 2\}$

22. $\quad 16x - x^3 = 0$

$$x(16 - x^2) = 0$$
$$x(4 - x)(4 + x) = 0$$
$$x = 0 \quad \text{or} \quad 4 - x = 0 \quad \text{or} \quad 4 + x = 0$$

$$4 = x \quad \text{or} \quad x = -4$$

The solution set is $\{-4, 0, 4\}$.

23. $\quad w^3 + 4w^2 - 25w - 100 = 0$

$$w^2(w + 4) - 25(w + 4) = 0$$
$$(w^2 - 25)(w + 4) = 0$$
$$(w - 5)(w + 5)(w + 4) = 0$$
$$w - 5 = 0 \quad \text{or} \quad w + 5 = 0 \quad \text{or} \quad w + 4 = 0$$
$$w = 5 \quad \text{or} \quad w = -5 \quad \text{or} \quad w = -4$$

Solution set: $\{-5, -4, 5\}$

24. $\quad a^3 + 2a^2 - 16a - 32 = 0$

$$a^2(a + 2) - 16(a + 2) = 0$$
$$(a^2 - 16)(a + 2) = 0$$
$$(a - 4)(a + 4)(a + 2) = 0$$
$$a - 4 = 0 \quad \text{or} \quad a + 4 = 0 \quad \text{or} \quad a + 2 = 0$$
$$a = 4 \quad \text{or} \quad a = -4 \quad \text{or} \quad a = -2$$

The solution set is $\{-4, -2, 4\}$.

25. $\quad n^3 - 2n^2 - n + 2 = 0$

$$n^2(n - 2) - 1(n - 2) = 0$$
$$(n^2 - 1)(n - 2) = 0$$
$$(n - 1)(n + 1)(n - 2) = 0$$
$$n - 1 = 0 \quad \text{or} \quad n + 1 = 0 \quad \text{or} \quad n - 2 = 0$$
$$n = 1 \quad \text{or} \quad n = -1 \quad \text{or} \quad n = 2$$

Solution set: $\{-1, 1, 2\}$

26. $\quad w^3 - w^2 - 25w + 25 = 0$

$$w^2(w - 1) - 25(w - 1) = 0$$
$$(w^2 - 25)(w - 1) = 0$$
$$(w - 5)(w + 5)(w - 1) = 0$$
$$w - 5 = 0 \quad \text{or} \quad w + 5 = 0 \quad \text{or} \quad w - 1 = 0$$
$$w = 5 \quad \text{or} \quad w = -5 \quad \text{or} \quad w = 1$$

The solution set is $\{-5, 1, 5\}$.

27. $\quad |x^2 - 5| = 4$

$$x^2 - 5 = 4 \quad \text{or} \quad x^2 - 5 = -4$$
$$x^2 - 9 = 0 \quad \text{or} \quad x^2 - 1 = 0$$
$$(x - 3)(x + 3) = 0 \quad \text{or} \quad (x - 1)(x + 1) = 0$$
$$x - 3 = 0 \quad \text{or} \quad x + 3 = 0 \quad \text{or} \quad x - 1 = 0$$
$$\text{or} \quad x + 1 = 0$$
$$x = 3 \quad \text{or} \quad x = -3 \quad \text{or} \quad x = 1 \quad \text{or} \quad x = -1$$

Solution set: $\{-3, -1, 1, 3\}$

28. $\quad |x^2 - 17| = 8$

$$x^2 - 17 = 8 \quad \text{or} \quad x^2 - 17 = -8$$
$$x^2 - 25 = 0 \quad \text{or} \quad x^2 - 9 = 0$$
$$(x - 5)(x + 5) = 0 \quad \text{or} \quad (x - 3)(x + 3) = 0$$
$$x - 5 = 0 \quad \text{or} \quad x + 5 = 0 \quad \text{or} \quad x - 3 = 0$$
$$\text{or} \quad x + 3 = 0$$
$$x = 5 \quad \text{or} \quad x = -5 \quad \text{or} \quad x = 3 \quad \text{or} \quad x = -3$$

The solution set is $\{-5, -3, 3, 5\}$.

29. $|x^2 + 2x - 36| = 12$
$x^2 + 2x - 36 = 12$ or $x^2 + 2x - 36 = -12$
$x^2 + 2x - 48 = 0$ or $x^2 + 2x - 24 = 0$
$(x + 8)(x - 6) = 0$ or $(x + 6)(x - 4) = 0$
$x = -8$ or $x = 6$ or $x = -6$ or $x = 4$
Solution set: $\{-8, -6, 4, 6\}$

30. $|x^2 + 2x - 19| = 16$
$x^2 + 2x - 19 = 16$ or $x^2 + 2x - 19 = -16$
$x^2 + 2x - 35 = 0$ or $x^2 + 2x - 3 = 0$
$(x + 7)(x - 5) = 0$ or $(x + 3)(x - 1) = 0$
$x + 7 = 0$ or $x - 5 = 0$ or $x + 3 = 0$
$\qquad\qquad\qquad\qquad$ or $x - 1 = 0$
$x = -7$ or $x = 5$ or $x = -3$ or $x = 1$
The solution set is $\{-7, -3, 1, 5\}$.

31. $|x^2 + 4x + 2| = 2$
$x^2 + 4x + 2 = 2$ or $x^2 + 4x + 2 = -2$
$x^2 + 4x = 0$ or $x^2 + 4x + 4 = 0$
$x(x + 4) = 0$ or $(x + 2)^2 = 0$
$x = 0$ or $x + 4 = 0$ or $x + 2 = 0$
$x = 0$ or $\qquad x = -4$ or $\qquad x = -2$
Solution set: $\{-4, 0, -2\}$

32. $|x^2 + 8x + 4| = 8$
$x^2 + 8x + 8 = 8$ or $x^2 + 8x + 8 = -8$
$x^2 + 8x = 0$ or $x^2 + 8x + 16 = 0$
$x(x + 8) = 0$ or $(x + 4)^2 = 0$
$x = 0$ or $x + 8 = 0$ or $x + 4 = 0$
$x = 0$ or $\qquad x = -8$ or $\qquad x = -4$
The solution set is $\{-8, -4, 0\}$

33. $|x^2 + 6x + 1| = 8$
$x^2 + 6x + 1 = 8$ or $x^2 + 6x + 1 = -8$
$x^2 + 6x - 7 = 0$ or $x^2 + 6x + 9 = 0$
$(x + 7)(x - 1) = 0$ or $(x + 3)^2 = 0$
$x + 7 = 0$ or $x - 1 = 0$ or $x + 3 = 0$
$\qquad x = -7$ or $\qquad x = 1$ or $\qquad x = -3$
Solution set: $\{-7, -3, 1\}$

34. $|x^2 - x - 21| = 9$
$x^2 - x - 21 = 9$ or $x^2 - x - 21 = -9$
$x^2 - x - 30 = 0$ or $x^2 - x - 12 = 0$
$(x - 6)(x + 5) = 0$ or $(x - 4)(x + 3) = 0$
$x - 6 = 0$ or $x + 5 = 0$ or $x - 4 = 0$
$\qquad\qquad\qquad\qquad$ or $x + 3 = 0$
$x = 6$ or $x = -5$ or $x = 4$ or $x = -3$
The solution set is $\{-5, -3, 4, 6\}$.

35. $2x^2 - x = 6$
$2x^2 - x - 6 = 0$
$(2x + 3)(x - 2) = 0$

36. $3x^2 + 14x = 5$
$3x^2 + 14x - 5 = 0$
$(3x - 1)(x + 5) = 0$
$3x - 1 = 0$ or $x + 5 = 0$
$3x = 1$ or $\qquad x = -5$
$x = \frac{1}{3}$ or $\qquad x = -5$
The solution set is $\left\{-5, \frac{1}{3}\right\}$.

37. $|x^2 + 5x| = 6$
$x^2 + 5x = 6$ or $\qquad x^2 + 5x = -6$
$x^2 + 5x - 6 = 0$ or $x^2 + 5x + 6 = 0$
$(x + 6)(x - 1) = 0$ or $(x + 2)(x + 3) = 0$
$x + 6 = 0$ or $x - 1 = 0$ or $x + 2 = 0$
$\qquad\qquad\qquad\qquad$ or $x + 3 = 0$
$x = -6$ or $x = 1$ or $x = -2$ or $x = -3$
Solution set: $\{-6, -3, -2, 1\}$

38. $|x^2 + 6x - 4| = 12$
$x^2 + 6x - 4 = 12$ or $x^2 + 6x - 4 = -12$
$x^2 + 6x - 16 = 0$ or $x^2 + 6x + 8 = 0$
$(x + 8)(x - 2) = 0$ or $(x + 4)(x + 2) = 0$
$x + 8 = 0$ or $x - 2 = 0$ or $x + 4 = 0$
$\qquad\qquad\qquad\qquad$ or $x + 2 = 0$
$x = -8$ or $x = 2$ or $x = -4$ or $x = -2$
The solution set is $\{-8, -4, -2, 2\}$.

39. $x^2 + 5x = 6$
$x^2 + 5x - 6 = 0$
$(x + 6)(x - 1) = 0$
$x + 6 = 0$ or $x - 1 = 0$
$x = -6$ or $\qquad x = 1$
Solution set: $\{-6, 1\}$

40. $x + 5x = 6$
$6x = 6$
$x = 1$
Solution set: $\{1\}$

41. $(x + 2)(x + 1) = 12$
$x^2 + 3x + 2 = 12$
$x^2 + 3x - 10 = 0$
$(x + 5)(x - 2) = 0$
$x + 5 = 0$ or $x - 2 = 0$
$x = -5$ or $\qquad x = 2$
The solution set is $\{-5, 2\}$.

42. $(x + 2)(x + 3) = 20$
$x^2 + 5x + 6 = 20$
$x^2 + 5x - 14 = 0$

$$(x+7)(x-2)=0$$
$$x+7=0 \text{ or } x-2=0$$
$$x=-7 \text{ or } \quad x=2$$
The solution set is $\{-7, 2\}$.

43. $\quad y^3 + 9y^2 + 20y = 0$
$$y(y^2 + 9y + 20) = 0$$
$$y(y+4)(y+5) = 0$$
$$y = 0 \text{ or } y+4 = 0 \text{ or } y+5 = 0$$
$$y = 0 \text{ or } \quad y = -4 \text{ or } \quad y = -5$$
Solution set: $\{-5, -4, 0\}$

44. $\quad m^3 - 2m^2 - 3m = 0$
$$m(m^2 - 2m - 3) = 0$$
$$m(m-3)(m+1) = 0$$
$$m = 0 \text{ or } m-3 = 0 \text{ or } m+1 = 0$$
$$m = 0 \text{ or } \quad m = 3 \text{ or } \quad m = -1$$
The solution set is $\{-1, 0, 3\}$.

45. $\qquad 5a^3 = 45a$
$$5a^3 - 45a = 0$$
$$5a(a^2 - 9) = 0$$
$$5a(a-3)(a+3) = 0$$
$$a = 0 \text{ or } a-3 = 0 \text{ or } a+3 = 0$$
$$a = 0 \text{ or } \quad a = 3 \text{ or } \quad a = -3$$
Solution set: $\{-3, 0, 3\}$

46. $\qquad 5x^3 = 125x$
$$5x^3 - 125x = 0$$
$$5x(x^2 - 25) = 0$$
$$5x(x-5)(x+5) = 0$$
$$x = 0 \text{ or } x-5 = 0 \text{ or } x+5 = 0$$
$$x = 0 \text{ or } \quad x = 5 \text{ or } \quad x = -5$$
The solution set is $\{-5, 0, 5\}$.

47. $(2x-1)(x^2-9) = 0$
$$(2x-1)(x-3)(x+3) = 0$$
$$2x-1 = 0 \text{ or } x-3 = 0 \text{ or } x+3 = 0$$
$$x = \tfrac{1}{2} \text{ or } \quad x = 3 \text{ or } \quad x = -3$$
The solution set is $\{-3, \tfrac{1}{2}, 3\}$.

48. $(x-1)(x+3)(x-9) = 0$
$$x-1 = 0 \text{ or } x+3 = 0 \text{ or } x-9 = 0$$
$$x = 1 \text{ or } \quad x = -3 \text{ or } x = 9$$
The solution set is $\{-3, 1, 9\}$.

49. $\quad 4x^2 - 12x + 9 = 0$
$$(2x-3)^2 = 0$$
$$2x-3 = 0$$
$$x = \tfrac{3}{2}$$
The solution set is $\{\tfrac{3}{2}\}$.

50. $\quad 16x^2 + 8x + 1 = 0$
$$(4x+1)^2 = 0$$

$$4x+1 = 0$$
$$x = -\tfrac{1}{4}$$
The solution set is $\{-\tfrac{1}{4}\}$.

51. $\qquad y^2 + by = 0$
$$y(y+b) = 0$$
$$y = 0 \text{ or } y+b = 0$$
$$y = 0 \text{ or } \qquad y = -b$$
Solution set: $\{0, -b\}$

52. $\quad y^2 + ay + by + ab = 0$
$$y(y+a) + b(y+a) = 0$$
$$(y+b)(y+a) = 0$$
$$y+b = 0 \text{ or } y+a = 0$$
$$y = -b \text{ or } \quad y = -a$$
The solution set is $\{-a, -b\}$.

53. $\qquad a^2y^2 - b^2 = 0$
$$(ay-b)(ay+b) = 0$$
$$ay-b = 0 \text{ or } ay+b = 0$$
$$ay = b \text{ or } \qquad ay = -b$$
$$y = \frac{b}{a} \text{ or } \qquad y = -\frac{b}{a}$$
Solution set: $\{-\frac{b}{a}, \frac{b}{a}\}$

54. $9y^2 + 6ay + a^2 = 0$
$$(3y+a)^2 = 0$$
$$3y+a = 0$$
$$3y = -a$$
$$y = -\frac{a}{3}$$
The solution set is $\left\{-\frac{a}{3}\right\}$.

55. $\quad 4y^2 + 4by + b^2 = 0$
$$(2y+b)^2 = 0$$
$$2y+b = 0$$
$$2y = -b$$
$$y = -\frac{b}{2}$$
Solution set: $\{-\frac{b}{2}\}$

56. $\qquad y^2 - b^2 = 0$
$$(y-b)(y+b) = 0$$
$$y-b = 0 \text{ or } y+b = 0$$
$$y = b \text{ or } \qquad y = -b$$
The solution set is $\{-b, b\}$.

57. $\qquad ay^2 + 3y - ay = 3$
$$ay^2 + 3y - ay - 3 = 0$$
$$y(ay+3) - 1(ay+3) = 0$$
$$(y-1)(ay+3) = 0$$
$$y-1 = 0 \text{ or } ay+3 = 0$$
$$y = 1 \text{ or } \qquad y = -\frac{3}{a}$$
Solution set: $\{-\frac{3}{a}, 1\}$

209

58.
$$a^2y^2 + 2aby + b^2 = 0$$
$$(ay + b)^2 = 0$$
$$ay + b = 0$$
$$ay = -b$$
$$y = -\frac{b}{a}$$

The solution set is $\left\{-\frac{b}{a}\right\}$.

59. Let $x =$ the width and $x + 2 =$ the length.
Since $A = LW$, we can write the equation
$$x(x + 2) = 24$$
$$x^2 + 2x = 24$$
$$x^2 + 2x - 24 = 0$$
$$(x + 6)(x - 4) = 0$$
$$x + 6 = 0 \quad \text{or} \quad x - 4 = 0$$
$$x = -6 \quad \text{or} \quad x = 4$$
$$x + 2 = 6$$
Since the width cannot be -6, we have a width of 4 inches and a length of 6 inches.

60. Let $x =$ the length and $x - 4 =$ the width.
Since the area is 117 yd^2 we can write
$$x(x - 4) = 117$$
$$x^2 - 4x - 117 = 0$$
$$(x - 13)(x + 9) = 0$$
$$x - 13 = 0 \text{ or } x + 9 = 0$$
$$x = 13 \text{ or } \quad x = -9$$
$$x - 4 = 9$$
The length is 13 yards and the width is 9 yards.

61. Let $x =$ one number and $13 - x =$ the other. Their product is 36:
$$x(13 - x) = 36$$
$$-x^2 + 13x - 36 = 0$$
$$x^2 - 13x + 36 = 0$$
$$(x - 4)(x - 9) = 0$$
$$x - 4 = 0 \quad \text{or} \quad x - 9 = 0$$
$$x = 4 \quad \text{or} \quad x = 9$$
$$13 - x = 9 \quad \text{or} \quad 13 - x = 4$$
The numbers are 4 and 9.

62. Let $x =$ one number and $6.5 - x =$ the other. Since their product is 9, we can write the following equation.
$$x(6.5 - x) = 9$$
$$6.5x - x^2 = 9$$
$$-x^2 + 6.5x - 9 = 0$$
$$-2x^2 + 13x - 18 = 0$$
$$2x^2 - 13x + 18 = 0$$
$$(2x - 9)(x - 2) = 0$$
$$2x - 9 = 0 \quad \text{or} \quad x - 2 = 0$$

$$2x = 9 \quad \text{or} \qquad x = 2$$
$$x = 4.5 \text{ or} \qquad x = 2$$
$$6.5 - x = 2 \quad \text{or} \quad 6.5 - x = 4.5$$
The numbers are 2 and 4.5.

63. Let $x =$ the width and $x + 21 =$ the length.
$$x(x + 21) = 946$$
$$x^2 + 21x - 946 = 0$$
$$(x + 43)(x - 22) = 0$$
$$x + 43 = 0 \text{ or } x - 22 = 0$$
$$x = -43 \quad \text{or} \quad x = 22$$
$$x + 21 = 43$$
The length is 43 in. and the width is 22 in.

64. If $x =$ the amount of the increase, then $x + 4 =$ the new width and $x + 6 =$ the new length. Since the new area is to be 48 square feet, we can write the equation
$$(x + 4)(x + 6) = 48$$
$$x^2 + 10x + 24 = 48$$
$$x^2 + 10x - 24 = 0$$
$$(x + 12)(x - 2) = 0$$
$$x + 12 = 0 \quad \text{or} \quad x - 2 = 0$$
$$x = -12 \quad \text{or} \quad x = 2$$
An increase of 2 feet on each dimension will make the new flower bed 6 feet by 8 feet.

65. a) From the graph it appears the ball is in the air for 4 seconds.

b) To find the time the ball is in the air we need the values of t that gives $h(t)$ a value of 0. We must solve the equation
$$-16t^2 + 64t = 0$$
$$-16t(t - 4) = 0$$
$$t = 0 \quad \text{or} \quad t - 4 = 0$$
$$t = 0 \quad \text{or} \qquad t = 4$$
The ball is in the air for 4 seconds.

c) From the graph it appears that the maximum height is 64 feet.

d) The arrow reaches its maximum height at time $t = 2$ seconds.

66. Use $s_0 = 1600$ and $S = 0$ in the formula.
$$-16t^2 + 1600 = 0$$
$$-16(t^2 - 100) = 0$$
$$-16(t - 10)(t + 10) = 0$$
$$t - 10 = 0 \text{ or } t + 10 = 0$$
$$t = 10 \text{ or} \qquad t = -10$$
It takes 10 seconds to reach the ground.

67. Let x = the width and $2x + 2$ = the length. Using the Pythagorean theorem we can write

$$x^2 + (2x + 2)^2 = 13^2$$
$$x^2 + 4x^2 + 8x + 4 = 169$$
$$5x^2 + 8x - 165 = 0$$
$$(5x + 33)(x - 5) = 0$$
$$5x + 33 = 0 \quad \text{or} \quad x - 5 = 0$$
$$x = -\frac{33}{5} \quad \text{or} \quad x = 5$$
$$2x + 2 = 12$$

Since the dimensions must be positive numbers, the width is 5 feet and the length is 12 feet.

68. Let x = the length of one leg and $x + 2$ = the length of the other leg. Since the hypotenuse is 10, we can write the following equation.

$$x^2 + (x + 2)^2 = 10^2$$
$$x^2 + x^2 + 4x + 4 = 100$$
$$2x^2 + 4x - 96 = 0$$
$$x^2 + 2x - 48 = 0$$
$$(x + 8)(x - 6) = 0$$
$$x + 8 = 0 \quad \text{or} \quad x - 6 = 0$$
$$x = -8 \quad \text{or} \quad x = 6$$
$$x + 2 = 8$$

The legs are 6 feet and 8 feet long.

69. Since the perimeter is 34 feet the sum of the length and width is 17 feet. Let x = the width and $17 - x$ = the length. Using the Pythagorean theorem we can write

$$x^2 + (17 - x)^2 = 13^2$$
$$x^2 + 289 - 34x + x^2 = 169$$
$$2x^2 - 34x + 120 = 0$$
$$x^2 - 17x + 60 = 0$$
$$(x - 5)(x - 12) = 0$$
$$x - 5 = 0 \quad \text{or} \quad x - 12 = 0$$
$$x = 5 \quad \text{or} \quad x = 12$$
$$17 - x = 12 \quad \text{or} \quad 17 - x = 5$$

The width is 5 feet and the length is 12 feet.

70. If the perimeter of a rectangle is 28 inches, then the sum of the length and width is 14 inches. Let x = the length and $14 - x$ = the width. Since the diagonal is 10 inches, we can write the following equation.

$$x^2 + (14 - x)^2 = 10^2$$
$$x^2 + 196 - 28x + x^2 = 100$$
$$2x^2 - 28x + 96 = 0$$

$$x^2 - 14x + 48 = 0$$
$$(x - 6)(x - 8) = 0$$
$$x - 6 = 0 \quad \text{or} \quad x - 8 = 0$$
$$x = 6 \quad \text{or} \quad x = 8$$
$$14 - x = 8 \quad \text{or} \quad 14 - x = 6$$

The length is 8 inches and the width is 6 inches.

71. Let x = the first integer and $x + 1$ = the second integer. The sum of their squares is 25:

$$x^2 + (x + 1)^2 = 25$$
$$x^2 + x^2 + 2x + 1 = 25$$
$$2x^2 + 2x - 24 = 0$$
$$x^2 + x - 12 = 0$$
$$(x + 4)(x - 3) = 0$$
$$x + 4 = 0 \quad \text{or} \quad x - 3 = 0$$
$$x = -4 \quad \text{or} \quad x = 3$$
$$x + 1 = -3 \quad \text{or} \quad x + 1 = 4$$

The integers are 3 and 4, or -4 and -3.

72. Since one dimension can accommodate 2 more rows, it must be 6 feet larger than the other dimension. Let x = the width and $x + 6$ = the length. Since the area of the rectangle is 135 square feet, we can write the following equation.

$$x(x + 6) = 135$$
$$x^2 + 6x = 135$$
$$x^2 + 6x - 135 = 0$$
$$(x + 15)(x - 9) = 0$$
$$x + 15 = 0 \quad \text{or} \quad x - 9 = 0$$
$$x = -15 \quad \text{or} \quad x = 9$$
$$x + 6 = 15$$

The width is 9 feet and the length is 15 feet.

73. Let x = the original length. Since the length times the width is 240 square feet, the width is $240/x$. The new length is $x - 4$ and the new width is $(240/x) + 3$. Since the area is still 240 square feet, we can write the following equation.

$$(x - 4)\left(\frac{240}{x} + 3\right) = 240$$
$$x \cdot \frac{240}{x} - 4 \cdot \frac{240}{x} + 3x - 12 = 240$$
$$240 - \frac{960}{x} + 3x - 252 = 0$$
$$-\frac{960}{x} + 3x - 12 = 0$$
$$x\left(-\frac{960}{x} + 3x - 12\right) = x \cdot 0$$
$$-960 + 3x^2 - 12x = 0$$
$$3x^2 - 12x - 960 = 0$$
$$x^2 - 4x - 320 = 0$$

211

$$(x - 20)(x + 16) = 0$$
$$x - 20 = 0 \text{ or } x + 16 = 0$$
$$x = 20 \text{ or } \quad x = -16$$
$$\frac{240}{x} = 12$$

The length is 20 feet and the width is 12 feet.

74. Let x = the original number of rows and $x - 1$ = the new number of rows. Since he has 112 students in x rows, he has $\frac{112}{x}$ students in each row. After rearranging he has 2 more students in each row, so he has $x - 1$ rows with $\frac{112}{x} + 2$ students in each row. Since the number of rows times the number of students in each row gives 112, we can write the following equation.

$$(x - 1)\left(\frac{112}{x} + 2\right) = 112$$
$$x \cdot \frac{112}{x} - 1 \cdot \frac{112}{x} + 2x - 2 = 112$$
$$112 - \frac{112}{x} + 2x - 114 = 0$$
$$x\left(-2 - \frac{112}{x} + 2x\right) = x \cdot 0$$
$$-2x - 112 + 2x^2 = 0$$
$$2x^2 - 2x - 112 = 0$$
$$x^2 - x - 56 = 0$$
$$(x - 8)(x + 7) = 0$$
$$x - 8 = 0 \text{ or } x + 7 = 0$$
$$x = 8 \text{ or } \quad x = -7$$

He originally had 8 rows.

Enriching Your Mathematical Word Power

1. d   2. b   3. c   4. d   5. b   6. a
7. c   8. a   9. d   10. a   11. d   12. c
13. a   14. c   15. b   16. c   17. a   18. c

CHAPTER 5 REVIEW

1. $2 \cdot 2 \cdot 2^{-1} = 4 \cdot \frac{1}{2} = 2$

2. $5^{-1} \cdot 5 = \frac{1}{5} \cdot 5 = 1$

3. $2^2 \cdot 3^2 = 4 \cdot 9 = 36$

4. $3^2 \cdot 5^2 = 9 \cdot 25 = 225$

5. $(-3)^{-3} = -\frac{1}{3^3} = -\frac{1}{27}$

6. $(-2)^{-2} = \frac{1}{(-2)^2} = \frac{1}{4}$

7. $-(-1)^{-3} = -\frac{1}{(-1)^3} = -\frac{1}{-1} = 1$

8. $3^4 \cdot 3^7 = 3^{11}$

9. $2x^3 \cdot 4x^{-6} = 8x^{-3} = \frac{8}{x^3}$

10. $-3a^{-3} \cdot 4a^{-4} = -12a^{-7} = -\frac{12}{a^7}$

11. $\frac{y^{-5}}{y^{-3}} = y^{-2} = \frac{1}{y^2}$

12. $\frac{w^3}{w^{-3}} = w^{3-(-3)} = w^6$

13. $\frac{a^5 a^{-2}}{a^{-4}} = \frac{a^3}{a^{-4}} = a^7$

14. $\frac{2m^3 \cdot m^6}{2m^{-2}} = \frac{m^9}{m^{-2}} = m^{9-(-2)} = m^{11}$

15. $\frac{6x^{-2}}{3x^2} = 2x^{-4} = \frac{2}{x^4}$

16. $\frac{-5y^2 x^{-3}}{5y^{-2}x^7} = -\frac{y^{2-(-2)}}{x^7 x^3} = -\frac{y^4}{x^{10}}$

17. Move the decimal 6 places to the right: $8.36 \times 10^6 = 8{,}360{,}000$

18. Move the decimal point 7 places to the right: $3.4 \times 10^7 = 34{,}000{,}000$

19. Move the decimal point 4 places to the left: $5.7 \times 10^{-4} = 0.00057$

20. Move the decimal point 3 places to the left: $4 \times 10^{-3} = 0.004$

21. Move the decimal point 6 places to the left: $8{,}070{,}000 = 8.07 \times 10^6$

22. Move the decimal point 4 places to the left: $90{,}000 = 9 \times 10^4$

23. Move the decimal point 4 places to the right: $0.000709 = 7.09 \times 10^{-4}$

24. Move the decimal point 7 places to the right: $0.0000005 = 5 \times 10^{-7}$

25. $\frac{(4 \times 10^9)(6 \times 10^{-7})}{(1.2 \times 10^{-5})(2 \times 10^6)} = \frac{24 \times 10^2}{2.4 \times 10^1}$
$$= 10 \times 10^1 = 1 \times 10^2$$

26. $\frac{(1.2 \times 10^{32})(2 \times 10^{-5})}{4 \times 10^{-7}} = \frac{2.4 \times 20^{27}}{4 \times 10^{-7}}$
$$= 0.6 \times 10^{34} = 6 \times 10^{-1} \times 10^{34} = 6 \times 10^{33}$$

27. $(a^{-3})^{-2} \cdot a^{-7} = a^6 \cdot a^{-7} = a^{-1} = \frac{1}{a}$

28. $(-3x^{-2}y)^{-4} = (-3)^{-4}x^8 y^{-4} = \frac{x^8}{81y^4}$

29. $(m^2 n^3)^{-2}(m^{-3}n^2)^4 = m^{-4}n^{-6}m^{-12}n^8$
$$= m^{-16}n^2 = \frac{n^2}{m^{16}}$$

30. $(w^{-3}xy)^{-1}(wx^{-3}y)^2 = w^3 x^{-1} y^{-1} w^2 x^{-6} y^2$
$$= w^5 x^{-7} y = \frac{w^5 y}{x^7}$$

31. $\left(\frac{2}{3}\right)^{-4} = \left(\frac{3}{2}\right)^4 = \frac{3^4}{2^4} = \frac{81}{16}$

32. $\left(\frac{a^4}{3}\right)^{-2} = \frac{a^{-8}}{3^{-2}} = \frac{3^2}{a^8} = \frac{9}{a^8}$

33. $\left(\frac{1}{2} + \frac{1}{3}\right)^2 = \left(\frac{5}{6}\right)^2 = \frac{25}{36}$

34. $\left(\frac{1}{2} - \frac{1}{3}\right)^{-2} = \left(\frac{3}{6} - \frac{2}{6}\right)^{-2} = \left(\frac{1}{6}\right)^{-2} = 36$

35. $\left(-\frac{3a}{4b^{-1}}\right)^{-1} = -\frac{4b^{-1}}{3a} = -\frac{4}{3ab}$

36. $\left(-\frac{4x^5}{5y^{-3}}\right)^{-1} = -\frac{5y^{-3}}{4x^5} = -\frac{5}{4x^5y^3}$

37. $\frac{(a^{-3}b)^4}{(ab^2)^{-5}} = \frac{a^{-12}b^4}{a^{-5}b^{-10}} = \frac{b^{14}}{a^7}$

38. $\frac{(2x^3)^3}{(3x^2)^{-2}} = \frac{8x^9}{3^{-2}x^{-4}} = 8x^9 \cdot 3^2 x^4 = 72x^{13}$

39. $5^{2w} \cdot 5^{4w} \cdot 5^{-1} = 5^{6w-1}$

40. $3^y(3^{2y})^3 = 3^y \cdot 3^{6y} = 3^{7y}$

41. $\left(\frac{7^{3a}}{7^8}\right)^5 = \frac{7^{15a}}{7^{40}} = 7^{15a-40}$

42. $\left(\frac{2^{6-k}}{2^{2-3k}}\right)^3 = \frac{2^{18-3k}}{2^{6-9k}} = 2^{12+6k}$

43. $(2w - 3) + (6w + 5) = 8w + 2$

44. $(3a - 2xy) + (5xy - 7a) = 3xy - 4a$

45. $(x^2 - 3x - 4) - (x^2 + 3x - 7)$
$= x^2 - 3x - 4 - x^2 - 3x + 7 = -6x + 3$

46. $(7 - 2x - x^2) - (x^2 - 5x + 6)$
$\qquad = 7 - 2x - x^2 - x^2 + 5x - 6$
$\qquad = -2x^2 + 3x + 1$

47. $(x^2 - 2x + 4)(x) - (x^2 - 2x + 4)(2)$
$\qquad = x^3 - 2x^2 + 4x - 2x^2 + 4x - 8$
$\qquad = x^3 - 4x^2 + 8x - 8$

48. $(x + 5)(x^2 - 2x + 10)$
$\qquad = (x + 5)x^2 - (x + 5)2x + (x + 5)10$
$\qquad = x^3 + 5x^2 - 2x^2 - 10x + 10x + 50$
$\qquad = x^3 + 3x^2 + 50$

49. $xy + 7z - 5(xy - 3z)$
$= xy + 7z - 5xy + 15z = -4xy + 22z$

50. $7 - 4(x - 3) = 7 - 4x + 12 = -4x + 19$

51. $m^2(5m^3 - m + 2) = 5m^5 - m^3 + 2m^2$

52. $(a + 2)^3 = (a + 2)(a + 2)^2$
$\qquad = (a + 2)(a^2 + 4a + 4)$
$\qquad = a(a^2 + 4a + 4) + 2(a^2 + 4a + 4)$
$\qquad = a^3 + 4a^2 + 4a + 2a^2 + 8a + 8$
$\qquad = a^3 + 6a^2 + 12a + 8$

53. $(x - 3)(x + 7) = x^2 - 3x + 7x - 21$
$\qquad = x^2 + 4x - 21$

54. $(k - 5)(k + 4) = k^2 - 5k + 4k - 20$
$\qquad = k^2 - k - 20$

55. $(z - 5y)(z + 5y) = z^2 - (5y)^2$
$\qquad = z^2 - 25y^2$

56. $(m - 3)(m + 3) = m^2 - 9$

57. $(m + 8)^2 = m^2 + 2 \cdot 8m + 8^2$

$\qquad = m^2 + 16m + 64$

58. $(b + 2a)^2 = b^2 + 2 \cdot 2a \cdot b + 4a^2$
$\qquad = b^2 + 4ab + 4a^2$

59. $(w - 6x)(w - 4x)$
$\qquad = w^2 - 6xw - 4xw + 24x^2$
$\qquad = w^2 - 10xw + 24x^2$

60. $(2w - 3)(w + 6) = 2w^2 + 9w - 18$

61. $(k - 3)^2 = k^2 - 2 \cdot 3 \cdot k + 9$
$\qquad = k^2 - 6k + 9$

62. $(n - 5)^2 = n^2 - 2 \cdot 5n + 5^2$
$\qquad = n^2 - 10n + 25$

63. $(m^2 - 5)(m^2 + 5)$
$\qquad = m^4 - 5m^2 + 5m^2 - 25$
$\qquad = m^4 - 25$

64. $(3k^2 - 5t)(2k^2 + 6t)$
$\qquad = 6k^4 - 10k^2t + 18k^2t - 30t^2$
$\qquad = 6k^4 + 8k^2t - 30t^2$

65.
$$\begin{array}{r}
x^2 + 3x - 5 \\
x - 2 \overline{)\, x^3 + x^2 - 11x + 10} \\
\underline{x^3 - 2x^2} \\
3x^2 - 11x \\
\underline{3x^2 - 6x} \\
-5x + 10 \\
\underline{-5x + 10} \\
0
\end{array}$$

Quotient: $x^2 + 3x - 5$ Remainder: 0

66.
$$\begin{array}{r}
2x^2 - x + 3 \\
x + 3 \overline{)\, 2x^3 + 5x^2 + 0x + 9} \\
\underline{2x^3 + 6x^2} \\
-x^2 + 0x \\
\underline{-x^2 - 3x} \\
3x + 9 \\
\underline{3x + 9} \\
0
\end{array}$$

Quotient: $2x^2 - x + 3$ Remainder: 0

67.
$$\begin{array}{r}
m^3 - m^2 + m - 1 \\
m + 1 \overline{)\, m^4 + 0m^3 + 0m^2 + 0m - 1} \\
\underline{m^4 + m^3} \\
-m^3 + 0m^2 \\
\underline{-m^3 - m^2} \\
m^2 + 0m \\
\underline{m^2 + m} \\
-m - 1 \\
\underline{-m - 1} \\
0
\end{array}$$

Quotient: $m^3 - m^2 + m - 1$ Remainder: 0

68.
$$x - 1 \overline{\smash{\big)}\ x^4 + 0x^3 + 0x^2 + 0x - 1}$$
with work above showing $x^3 + x^2 + x + 1$

$$\begin{array}{r}
x^3 + x^2 + x + 1 \\
x - 1 \overline{\smash{\big)}\ x^4 + 0x^3 + 0x^2 + 0x - 1} \\
\underline{x^4 - x^3} \\
x^3 + 0x^2 \\
\underline{x^3 - x^2} \\
x^2 + 0x \\
\underline{x^2 - x} \\
x - 1 \\
\underline{x - 1} \\
0
\end{array}$$

Quotient: $x^3 + x^2 + x + 1$ Remainder: 0

69.
$$\begin{array}{r}
a^6 + 2a^3 + 4 \\
a^3 - 2 \overline{\smash{\big)}\ a^9 + 0a^6 + 0a^3 - 8} \\
\underline{a^9 - 2a^6} \\
2a^6 + 0a^3 \\
\underline{2a^6 - 4a^3} \\
4a^3 - 8 \\
\underline{4a^3 - 8} \\
0
\end{array}$$

Quotient: $a^6 + 2a^3 + 4$ Remainder: 0

70.
$$\begin{array}{r}
a + b \\
a - b \overline{\smash{\big)}\ a^2 + 0ab - b^2} \\
\underline{a^2 - ab} \\
ab - b^2 \\
\underline{ab - b^2} \\
0
\end{array}$$

Quotient: $a + b$ Remainder: 0

71. $\dfrac{3m^3 + 6m^2 - 18m}{3m}$

$= \dfrac{3m^3}{3m} + \dfrac{6m^2}{3m} - \dfrac{18m}{3m}$

$= m^2 + 2m - 6$

Quotient: $m^2 + 2m - 6$ Remainder: 0

72. $\dfrac{w - 3}{3 - w} = -1$

Quotient: -1 Remainder: 0

73.
$$\begin{array}{r}
x + 1 \\
x - 1 \overline{\smash{\big)}\ x^2 + 0x - 5} \\
\underline{x^2 - x} \\
x - 5 \\
\underline{x - 1} \\
-4
\end{array}$$

$\dfrac{x^2 - 5}{x - 1} = x + 1 + \dfrac{-4}{x - 1}$

74.
$$\begin{array}{r}
x \\
x + 3 \overline{\smash{\big)}\ x^2 + 3x + 2} \\
\underline{x^2 + 3x} \\
0x + 2
\end{array}$$

$\dfrac{x^2 + 3x + 2}{x + 3} = x + \dfrac{2}{x + 3}$

75.
$$\begin{array}{r}
3 \\
x - 2 \overline{\smash{\big)}\ 3x + 0} \\
\underline{3x - 6} \\
6
\end{array}$$

$\dfrac{3x}{x - 2} = 3 + \dfrac{6}{x - 2}$

76.
$$\begin{array}{r}
4 \\
x - 5 \overline{\smash{\big)}\ 4x + 0} \\
\underline{4x - 20} \\
20
\end{array}$$

$\dfrac{4x}{x - 5} = 4 + \dfrac{20}{x - 5}$

77. When $x^3 - 2x^2 + 3x + 22$ is divided by $x + 2$ the quotient is $x^2 - 4x + 11$ and the remainder is 0. So the first polynomial is a factor of the second.

78. When $x^3 + x - 10$ is divided by $x - 2$, the quotient is $x^2 + 2x + 5$ and the remainder is 0. So the first polynomial is a factor of the second.

79. If $x^3 - x - 120$ is divided by $x - 5$ the quotient is $x^2 + 5x + 24$ and remainder is 0. So the first polynomial is a factor of the second.

80. If $x^3 + 2x + 15$ is divided by $x + 3$, the quotient is $x^2 - 3x + 11$ and the remainder is -18. So the first polynomial is not a factor of the second.

81. When $x^3 + x^2 - 3$ is divided by $x - 1$ the quotient is $x^2 + 2x + 2$ and the remainder is -1. So the first polynomial is not a factor of the second.

82. When $x^3 + 1$ is divided by $x - 1$ the quotient is $x^2 + x + 1$ and the remainder is 2. The first polynomial is not a factor of the second.

83. When $x^4 + x^3 + 5x^2 + 2x + 6$ is divided by $x^2 + 2$ the quotient is $x^2 + x + 3$ and the remainder is 0. So the first polynomial is a factor of the second.

84. When $x^4 - 1$ is divided by $x^2 + 1$ the quotient is $x^2 - 1$ and the remainder is 0. So the first polynomial is a factor of the second.

85. $3x - 6 = 3(x - 2)$

86. $7x^2 - x = x(7x - 1)$

87. $4a - 20 = -4(-a + 5)$

88. $w^2 - w = -w(-w + 1)$

89. $3w - w^2 = -w(-3 + w) = -w(w - 3)$

90. $3x - 6 = (-3)(2 - x)$

91. $y^2 - 81 = (y - 9)(y + 9)$

92. $r^2t^2 - 9v^2 = (rt)^2 - (3v)^2$
$\qquad = (rt - 3v)(rt + 3v)$

93. $4x^2 + 28x + 49$
$\qquad = (2x)^2 + 2 \cdot 2x \cdot 7 + 7^2$
$\qquad = (2x + 7)^2$

94. $y^2 - 20y + 100 = y^2 - 2 \cdot 10y + 10^2$
$\qquad = (y - 10)^2$

95. $t^2 - 18t + 81$
$\qquad = t^2 - 2 \cdot 9t + 9^2 = (t - 9)^2$

96. $4w^2 + 4ws + s^2 = (2w)^2 + 2 \cdot 2ws + s^2$
$\qquad = (2w + s)^2$

97. $t^3 - 125 = (t - 5)(t^2 + 5t + 25)$

98. $8y^3 + 1 = (2y)^3 + 1^3$
$\qquad = (2y + 1)(4y^2 - 2y + 1)$

99. Two numbers with a product of -30 and a sum of -7 are -10 and 3.
$x^2 - 7x - 30 = (x - 10)(x + 3)$

100. We need two numbers with a product of -32 and a sum of 4. The numbers are 8 and -4.
$y^2 + 4y - 32 = (y + 8)(y - 4)$

101. Two numbers with a product of -28 and a sum of -3 are -7 and 4.
$w^2 - 3w - 28 = (w - 7)(w + 4)$

102. Two integers with a product of 6 and a sum of -5 are -2 and -3.
$6t^2 - 5t + 1 = 6t^2 - 2t - 3t + 1$
$= 2t(3t - 1) - 1(3t - 1) = (2t - 1)(3t - 1)$

103. Two numbers with a product of -14 and a sum of 5 are -2 and 7.
$2m^2 + 5m - 7 = 2m^2 - 2m + 7m - 7$
$\qquad = 2m(m - 1) + 7(m - 1)$
$\qquad = (2m + 7)(m - 1)$

104. Two integers with a product of 72 and a sum of -17 are -8 and -9.
$12x^2 - 17x + 6 = 12x^2 - 8x - 9x + 6$

$\qquad = 4x(3x - 2) - 3(3x - 2)$
$\qquad = (4x - 3)(3x - 2)$

105. $m^7 - 3m^4 - 10m = m(m^6 - 3m^3 - 10)$
$\qquad = m(m^3 - 5)(m^3 + 2)$

106. $6w^5 - 7w^3 - 5w = w(6w^4 - 7w^2 - 5)$
$\qquad = w(3w^2 - 5)(2w^2 + 1)$

107. $5x^3 + 40 = 5(x^3 + 8)$
$\qquad = 5(x + 2)(x^2 - 2x + 4)$

108. $w^3 - 6w^2 + 9w = w(w^2 - 6w + 9)$
$\qquad = w(w - 3)^2$

109. Two numbers with a product of 18 and a sum of 9 are 6 and 3.
$9x^2 + 9x + 2 = 9x^2 + 3x + 6x + 2$
$\qquad = 3x(3x + 1) + 2(3x + 1)$
$\qquad = (3x + 2)(3x + 1)$

110. $ax^3 + a = a(x^3 + 1) = a(x^3 + 1^3)$
$\qquad = a(x + 1)(x^2 - x + 1)$

111. $x^3 + x^2 - x - 1$
$\qquad = x^2(x + 1) - 1(x + 1)$
$\qquad = (x^2 - 1)(x + 1)$
$\qquad = (x - 1)(x + 1)(x + 1)$
$\qquad = (x - 1)(x + 1)^2$

112. $16x^2 - 4x - 2 = 2(8x^2 - 2x - 1)$
$\qquad = 2(4x + 1)(2x - 1)$

113. $-x^2y + 16y = -y(x^2 - 16)$
$\qquad = -y(x - 4)(x + 4)$

114. $-5m^2 + 5 = -5(m^2 - 1)$
$\qquad = -5(m - 1)(m + 1)$

115. $-a^3b^2 + 2a^2b^2 - ab^2$
$\qquad = -ab^2(a^2 - 2a + 1)$
$\qquad = -ab^2(a - 1)^2$

116. $-2w^2 - 16w - 32 = -2(w^2 + 8w + 16)$
$\qquad = -2(w + 4)^2$

117. $x^3 - x^2 + 9x - 9$
$\qquad = x^2(x - 1) + 9(x - 1)$
$\qquad = (x - 1)(x^2 + 9)$

118. $w^4 + 2w^2 - 3 = (w^2 + 3)(w^2 - 1)$
$\qquad = (w^2 + 3)(w - 1)(w + 1)$

119. $x^4 - x^2 - 12 = (x^2 - 4)(x^2 + 3)$
$\qquad = (x - 2)(x + 2)(x^2 + 3)$

120. $8x^3 - 1 = (2x)^3 - 1^3$
$\qquad = (2x - 1)(4x^2 + 2x + 1)$

121. $a^6 - a^3 = a^3(a^3 - 1)$
$\qquad = a^3(a - 1)(a^2 + a + 1)$

122. $a^2 - ab + 2a - 2b$
$\quad = a(a-b) + 2(a-b)$
$\quad = (a+2)(a-b)$

123. $-8m^2 - 24m - 18$
$\quad = -2(4m^2 + 12m + 9)$
$\quad = -2(2m+3)^2$

124. $-3x^2 - 9x + 30 = -3(x^2 + 3x - 10)$
$\quad = -3(x+5)(x-2)$

125. Let $y = 2x - 3$:
$(2x-3)^2 - 16 = y^2 - 16$
$\quad = (y-4)(y+4)$
$\quad = (2x-3-4)(2x-3+4)$
$\quad = (2x-7)(2x+1)$

126. Let $a = m - 6$:
$(m-6)^2 - (m-6) - 12$
$\quad = a^2 - a - 12 = (a-4)(a+3)$
$\quad = (m-6-4)(m-6+3)$
$\quad = (m-10)(m-3)$

127. $x^6 + 7x^3 - 8 = (x^3+8)(x^3-1)$
$= (x+2)(x^2-2x+4)(x-1)(x^2+x+1)$

128. $32a^5 - 2a = 2a(16a^4 - 1)$
$\quad = 2a(4a^2-1)(4a^2+1)$
$\quad = 2a(2a-1)(2a+1)(4a^2+1)$

129. Let $y = a^2 - 9$:
$(a^2-9)^2 - 5(a^2-9) + 6$
$\quad = y^2 - 5y + 6$
$\quad = (y-2)(y-3)$
$\quad = (a^2-9-2)(a^2-9-3)$
$\quad = (a^2-11)(a^2-12)$

130. $x^3 - 9x + x^2 - 9$
$\quad = x(x^2-9) + 1(x^2-9)$
$\quad = (x+1)(x^2-9)$
$\quad = (x+1)(x-3)(x+3)$

131. $x^{2k} - 49 = (x^k - 7)(x^k + 7)$

132. $x^{6k} - 1 = (x^{3k} - 1)(x^{3k} + 1) =$
$(x^k - 1)(x^{2k} + x^k + 1)(x^k + 1)(x^{2k} - x^k + 1)$

133. $m^{2a} - 2m^a - 3 = (m^a - 3)(m^a + 1)$

134. $2y^{2n} - 7y^n + 6 = (2y^n - 3)(y^n - 2)$

135. $9z^{2k} - 12z^k + 4 = (3z^k - 2)^2$

136. $25z^{6m} + 20z^{3m} + 4 = (5z^{3m} + 2)^2$

137. $y^{2a} - by^a + cy^a - bc$
$= y^a(y^a - b) + c(y^a - b) = (y^a - b)(y^a + c)$

138. $x^3y^b - xy^b + 2x^3 - 2x$
$\quad = xy^b(x^2 - 1) + 2x(x^2 - 1)$
$\quad = (xy^b + 2x)(x^2 - 1)$
$\quad = x(y^b + 2)(x-1)(x+1)$

139. $\quad x^3 - 5x^2 = 0$
$\quad\quad x^2(x - 5) = 0$
$\quad x^2 = 0 \ \text{ or } \ x - 5 = 0$
$\quad x = 0 \ \text{ or } \quad x = 5$
Solution set: $\{0, 5\}$

140. $\quad 2m^2 + 10m + 12 = 0$
$\quad\quad 2(m^2 + 5m + 6) = 0$
$\quad\quad 2(m+2)(m+3) = 0$
$\quad m + 2 = 0 \ \text{ or } \ m + 3 = 0$
$\quad\quad m = -2 \ \text{or} \quad m = -3$
The solution set is $\{-3, -2\}$.

141. $\quad (a-2)(a-3) = 6$
$\quad\quad a^2 - 5a + 6 = 6$
$\quad\quad a^2 - 5a = 0$
$\quad\quad a(a-5) = 0$
$\quad a = 0 \ \text{ or } \ a - 5 = 0$
$\quad a = 0 \ \text{ or } \quad a = 5$
Solution set: $\{0, 5\}$

142. $\quad (w-2)(w+3) = 50$
$\quad\quad w^2 + w - 6 = 50$
$\quad\quad w^2 + w - 56 = 0$
$\quad\quad (w+8)(w-7) = 0$
$\quad w + 8 = 0 \ \text{ or } \ w - 7 = 0$
$\quad\quad w = -8 \ \text{ or } \quad w = 7$
The solution set is $\{-8, 7\}$.

143. $\quad\quad 2m^2 - 9m - 5 = 0$
$\quad\quad (2m+1)(m-5) = 0$
$\quad 2m + 1 = 0 \ \text{ or } \ m - 5 = 0$
$\quad\quad m = -1/2 \ \text{ or } \ m = 5$
Solution set: $\{-1/2, 5\}$

144. $\quad m^3 + 4m^2 - 9m - 36 = 0$
$\quad\quad m^2(m+4) - 9(m+4) = 0$
$\quad\quad\quad (m^2 - 9)(m+4) = 0$
$\quad\quad (m-3)(m+3)(m+4) = 0$
$m - 3 = 0 \text{ or } m + 3 = 0 \text{ or } m + 4 = 0$
$\quad m = 3 \text{ or } \quad m = -3 \text{ or } \quad m = -4$
The solution set is $\{-4, -3, 3\}$.

145. $\quad w^3 + 5w^2 - w - 5 = 0$
$\quad\quad w^2(w+5) - 1(w+5) = 0$
$\quad\quad\quad (w^2 - 1)(w+5) = 0$
$\quad\quad (w-1)(w+1)(w+5) = 0$
$w - 1 = 0 \text{ or } w + 1 = 0 \text{ or } w + 5 = 0$
$\quad w = 1 \ \text{ or } \ w = -1 \ \text{ or } \ w = -5$
Solution set: $\{-5, -1, 1\}$

146. $\quad 12x^2 + 5x - 3 = 0$
$\quad\quad (4x+3)(3x-1) = 0$

$4x + 3 = 0$ or $3x - 1 = 0$

$4x = -3$ or $3x = 1$

$x = -\frac{3}{4}$ or $x = \frac{1}{3}$

The solution set is $\left\{-\frac{3}{4}, \frac{1}{3}\right\}$.

147. $\qquad | x^2 - 5 | = 4$

$x^2 - 5 = 4$ or $x^2 - 5 = -4$

$x^2 - 9 = 0$ or $x^2 - 1 = 0$

$(x - 3)(x + 3) = 0$ or $(x - 1)(x + 1) = 0$

$x = 3$ or $x = -3$ or $x = 1$ or $x = -1$

Solution set: $\{-3, -1, 1, 3\}$

148. $\qquad | x^2 - 3x - 7 | = 3$

$x^2 - 3x - 7 = 3$ or $x^2 - 3x - 7 = -3$

$x^2 - 3x - 10 = 0$ or $x^2 - 3x - 4 = 0$

$(x - 5)(x + 2) = 0$ or $(x - 4)(x + 1) = 0$

$x - 5 = 0$ or $x + 2 = 0$ or $x - 4 = 0$

$\qquad\qquad\qquad\qquad$ or $x + 1 = 0$

$x = 5$ or $x = -2$ or $x = 4$ or $x = -1$

The solution set is $\{-2, -1, 4, 5\}$.

149. Let $x =$ the distance from the bottom of the ladder and the cactus and $x + 2 =$ the distance from the top of the ladder to the ground. Since the ladder is the hypotenuse of a right triangle, we can write

$x^2 + (x + 2)^2 = 10^2$

$x^2 + x^2 + 4x + 4 = 100$

$2x^2 + 4x - 96 = 0$

$x^2 + 2x - 48 = 0$

$(x + 8)(x - 6) = 0$

$x + 8 = 0$ or $x - 6 = 0$

$x = -8$ or $x = 6$

The ladder should be placed 6 feet from the cactus.

150. Let $x =$ the first integer, $x + 1 =$ the second integer, and $x + 2 =$ the third integer. Since the sum of their squares is 50, we can write the following equation.

$x^2 + (x + 1)^2 + (x + 2)^2 = 50$

$x^2 + x^2 + 2x + 1 + x^2 + 4x + 4 = 50$

$3x^2 + 6x + 5 = 50$

$3x^2 + 6x - 45 = 0$

$x^2 + 2x - 15 = 0$

$(x + 5)(x - 3) = 0$

$x + 5 = 0$ or $x - 3 = 0$

$x = -5$ or $x = 3$

$x + 1 = -4 \qquad x + 1 = 4$

$x + 2 = -3 \qquad x + 2 = 5$

The three consecutive integers are -5, -4, and -3, or 3, 4, and 5.

151. $A = 9a^2 + 6a + 1 = (3a + 1)^2$
So the side of the square is $3a + 1$ and its perimeter is $4(3a + 1)$ or $12a + 4$ km.

152. The side of the original square is x ft. The new square has sides of $x + 6$ ft and area $(x + 6)^2$ or $x^2 + 12x + 36$ ft². The difference is $12x + 36$ ft² for the daffodils.

153. a) $L = 64.3(1.0033)^{20} \approx 68.7$ yr
b) From Exercise 95 Section 5.2, a 20-yr old white male is expected to live 75.1 yr. The White male is expected to live 6.5 years longer.

154. $L = 72.9(1.002)^{20} \approx 75.9$ yr

155. a) The interest rate is approximately 15%.

b) $500{,}000 = R \cdot \dfrac{(1 + 0.07)^{20} - 1}{0.07}$

$R = 500{,}000 \div \dfrac{(1 + 0.07)^{20} - 1}{0.07}$

$\approx \$12{,}196.46$

156. $R = 16{,}222 \div \dfrac{(1 + 0.08)^{18} - 1}{0.08}$

$\approx \$433.16$

CHAPTER 5 TEST

1. $3^{-2} = \frac{1}{3^2} = \frac{1}{9}$

2. $\frac{1}{6^{-2}} = 6^2 = 36$

3. $\left(\frac{1}{2}\right)^{-3} = 2^3 = 8$

4. $3 \cdot 4x^4 x^3 = 12x^7$

5. $\frac{8y^9}{2y^{-3}} = 4y^{9-(-3)} = 4y^{12}$

6. $(4a^2 b)^3 = 4^3 (a^2)^3 b^3 = 64a^6 b^3$

7. $\left(\frac{x^2}{3}\right)^{-3} = \left(\frac{3}{x^2}\right)^3 = \frac{27}{x^6}$

8. $\dfrac{(2^{-1})^{-3}(a^2)^{-3} b^{-3}}{4a^{-9}} = \dfrac{2^3 a^{-6} b^{-3}}{4a^{-9}} = \dfrac{8a^3}{4b^3}$

$\qquad\qquad\qquad\qquad\qquad = \dfrac{2a^3}{b^3}$

9. $3.24 \times 10^9 = 3{,}240{,}000{,}000$

10. $8.673 \times 10^{-4} = 0.0008673$

11. $\dfrac{(8 \times 10^4)(6 \times 10^{-4})}{2 \times 10^6} = 24 \times 10^{-6}$

$\qquad = 2.4 \times 10^1 \times 10^{-6} = 2.4 \times 10^{-5}$

12. $\dfrac{(6 \times 10^{-5})^2 (5 \times 10^2)}{(3 \times 10^4)^2 (1 \times 10^{-2})}$

$= \dfrac{36 \times 10^{-10} \cdot 5 \times 10^2}{9 \times 10^8 \cdot 1 \times 10^{-2}}$

$$= 20 \times 10^{-14}$$
$$= 2 \times 10^{-13}$$

13. Add like terms to get $3x^3 + 3x^2 - 2x + 3$.

14. $(x^2 - 6x - 7) - (3x^2 + 2x - 4)$
$$= x^2 - 6x - 7 - 3x^2 - 2x + 4$$
$$= -2x^2 - 8x - 3$$

15. $(x^2 - 3x + 7)(x) - (x^2 - 3x + 7)(2)$
$$= x^3 - 3x^2 + 7x - 2x^2 + 6x - 14$$
$$= x^3 - 5x^2 + 13x - 14$$

16.
$$\begin{array}{r} x^2 + 4x - 5 \\ x+3 \overline{)\, x^3 + 7x^2 + 7x - 15} \\ \underline{x^3 + 3x^2} \\ 4x^2 + 7x \\ \underline{4x^2 + 12x} \\ -5x - 15 \\ \underline{-5x - 15} \\ 0 \end{array}$$

Quotient is $x^2 + 4x - 5$.

17. $(x - 2)^3 = (x - 2)^2(x - 2)$
$$= (x^2 - 4x + 4)(x - 2)$$
$$= (x^2 - 4x + 4)(x) - (x^2 - 4x + 4)(2)$$
$$= x^3 - 4x^2 + 4x - 2x^2 + 8x - 8$$
$$= x^3 - 6x^2 + 12x - 8$$

18. $\dfrac{x-3}{3-x} = \dfrac{(-1)(3-x)}{3-x} = -1$

19. $(x - 7)(2x + 3) = 2x^2 - 14x + 3x - 21$
$$= 2x^2 - 11x - 21$$

20. $(x - 6)^2 = x^2 - 2 \cdot 6x + 36$
$$= x^2 - 12x + 36$$

21. $(2x + 5)^2 = 4x^2 + 20x + 25$

22. $(3y^2 - 5)(3y^2 + 5) = 9y^4 - 25$

23.
$$\begin{array}{r} 5 \\ x+3 \overline{)\, 5x + 0} \\ \underline{5x + 15} \\ -15 \end{array}$$
$$\dfrac{5x}{x+3} = 5 + \dfrac{-15}{x+3}$$

24.
$$\begin{array}{r} x + 5 \\ x-2 \overline{)\, x^2 + 3x - 6} \\ \underline{x^2 - 2x} \\ 5x - 6 \\ \underline{5x - 10} \\ 4 \end{array}$$
$$\dfrac{x^2 + 3x - 6}{x - 2} = x + 5 + \dfrac{4}{x - 2}$$

25. Two numbers with a product of -24 and a sum of -2 are -6 and 4.

$$a^2 - 2a - 24 = (a - 6)(a + 4)$$

26. $4x^2 + 28x + 49$
$$= (2x)^2 + 2 \cdot 2x \cdot 7 + 7^2 = (2x + 7)^2$$

27. $3m^3 - 24 = 3(m^3 - 8)$
$$= 3(m - 2)(m^2 + 2m + 4)$$

28. $2x^2 y - 32y = 2y(x^2 - 16)$
$$= 2y(x - 4)(x + 4)$$

29. $2xa + 3a - 10x - 15$
$$= a(2x + 3) - 5(2x + 3)$$
$$= (a - 5)(2x + 3)$$

30. $x^4 + 3x^2 - 4 = (x^2 - 1)(x^2 + 4)$
$$= (x - 1)(x + 1)(x^2 + 4)$$

31. $2m^2 + 7m - 15 = 0$
$$(2m - 3)(m + 5) = 0$$
$$2m - 3 = 0 \text{ or } m + 5 = 0$$
$$m = \tfrac{3}{2} \text{ or } \quad m = -5$$
Solution set: $\left\{ -5, \tfrac{3}{2} \right\}$

32.
$$x^3 - 4x = 0$$
$$x(x^2 - 4) = 0$$
$$x(x - 2)(x + 2) = 0$$
$$x = 0 \text{ or } x - 2 = 0 \text{ or } x + 2 = 0$$
$$x = 0 \text{ or } \quad x = 2 \text{ or } \quad x = -2$$
Solution set: $\{-2, 0, 2\}$

33.
$$|x^2 + x - 9| = 3$$
$$x^2 + x - 9 = 3 \text{ or } x^2 + x - 9 = -3$$
$$x^2 + x - 12 = 0 \text{ or } x^2 + x - 6 = 0$$
$$(x + 4)(x - 3) = 0 \text{ or } (x + 3)(x - 2) = 0$$
$$x = -4 \text{ or } x = 3 \text{ or } x = -3 \text{ or } x = 2$$
Solution set: $\{-4, -3, 2, 3\}$

34. Let x = the height and $x + 2$ = the width. Using the Pythagorean theorem we can write
$$x^2 + (x + 2)^2 = 10^2$$
$$x^2 + x^2 + 4x + 4 = 100$$
$$2x^2 + 4x - 96 = 0$$
$$x^2 + 2x - 48 = 0$$
$$(x + 8)(x - 6) = 0$$
$$x = -8 \text{ or } \quad x = 6$$
$$x + 2 = -6 \text{ or } x + 2 = 8$$
The width is 8 inches and the height is 6 inches.

35. $d = (1.8 \times 10^{28})(1.032)^{-1950} \approx 38.0$
$$d = (1.8 \times 10^{28})(1.032)^{-1990} \approx 10.8$$
$$d = (1.8 \times 10^{28})(1.032)^{-2000} \approx 7.9$$

Making Connections

Chapters 1 - 5

1. $4^2 = 4 \cdot 4 = 16$

2. $4(-2) = -8$

3. $4^{-2} = \frac{1}{4^2} = \frac{1}{16}$

4. $2^3 \cdot 4^{-1} = 8 \cdot \frac{1}{4} = 2$

5. $2^{-1} + 2^{-1} = \frac{1}{2} + \frac{1}{2} = 1$

6. $2^{-1} \cdot 3^{-1} = \frac{1}{2} \cdot \frac{1}{3} = \frac{1}{6}$

7. $3^{-1} - 2^{-2} = \frac{1}{3} - \frac{1}{4} = \frac{4}{12} - \frac{3}{12} = \frac{1}{12}$

8. $3^2 - 4(5)(-2) = 9 - (-40) = 49$

9. $2^7 - 2^6 = 128 - 64 = 64$

10. $0.08(32) + 0.08(68) = 0.08(32 + 68)$
$$= 0.08(100) = 8$$

11. $3 - 2\,|\,5 - 7 \cdot 3\,| = 3 - 2\,|-16\,|$
$$= 3 - 2 \cdot 16 = 3 - 32 = -29$$

12. $5^{-1} + 6^{-1} = \frac{1}{5} + \frac{1}{6} = \frac{6}{30} + \frac{5}{30} = \frac{11}{30}$

13. $0.05a - 0.04(a - 50) = 4$
$$0.05a - 0.04a + 2 = 4$$
$$0.01a = 2$$
$$a = 200$$

Solution set: $\{200\}$

14. $15b - 27 = 0$
$$15b = 27$$
$$b = \frac{27}{15} = \frac{9}{5}$$

Solution set: $\left\{\frac{9}{5}\right\}$

15. $2c^2 + 15c - 27 = 0$
$$(2c - 3)(c + 9) = 0$$
$$2c - 3 = 0 \text{ or } c + 9 = 0$$
$$c = \frac{3}{2} \quad \text{or} \quad c = -9$$

Solution set: $\left\{-9, \frac{3}{2}\right\}$

16. $2t^2 + 15t = 0$
$$t(2t + 15) = 0$$
$$t = 0 \text{ or } 2t + 15 = 0$$
$$t = 0 \quad \text{or} \quad t = -\frac{15}{2}$$

Solution set: $\left\{-\frac{15}{2}, 0\right\}$

17. $|\,15v - 27\,| = 3$
$$15v - 27 = 3 \text{ or } 15v - 27 = -3$$
$$15v = 30 \text{ or } \quad 15v = 24$$
$$v = 2 \text{ or } \quad v = \frac{8}{5}$$

Solution set: $\left\{2, \frac{8}{5}\right\}$

18. $|\,15v - 27\,| = 0$
$$15v - 27 = 0$$
$$15v = 27$$
$$v = \frac{27}{15} = \frac{9}{5}$$

Solution set: $\left\{\frac{9}{5}\right\}$

19. Absolute value of any quantity is greater than or equal to 0. So the solution set is $\emptyset$.

20. $|\,x^2 + x - 4\,| = 2$
$$x^2 + x - 4 = 2 \text{ or } x^2 + x - 4 = -2$$
$$x^2 + x - 6 = 0 \text{ or } x^2 + x - 2 = 0$$
$$(x + 3)(x - 2) = 0 \text{ or } (x + 2)(x - 1) = 0$$
$$x = -3 \text{ or } x = 2 \text{ or } x = -2 \text{ or } x = 1$$

Solution set: $\{-3, -2, 1, 2\}$

21. $(2x - 1)(x + 5) = 0$
$$2x - 1 = 0 \text{ or } \quad x + 5 = 0$$
$$x = \frac{1}{2} \quad \text{or} \quad x = -5$$

Solution set: $\left\{-5, \frac{1}{2}\right\}$

22. $|\,3x - 1\,| + 6 = 9$
$$|\,3x - 1\,| = 3$$
$$3x - 1 = 3 \text{ or } \quad 3x - 1 = -3$$
$$3x = 4 \quad \text{or} \quad 3x = -2$$
$$x = \frac{4}{3} \quad \text{or} \quad x = -\frac{2}{3}$$

Solution set: $\left\{-\frac{2}{3}, \frac{4}{3}\right\}$

23. $(1.5 \times 10^{-4})w = 7 \times 10^6 + 5 \times 10^5$
$$w = \frac{7 \times 10^6 + 5 \times 10^5}{1.5 \times 10^{-4}}$$
$$= 5 \times 10^{10}$$

24. $y - 5 \times 10^3 = \dfrac{6 \times 10^{12}}{3 \times 10^7}$
$$y = \frac{6 \times 10^{12}}{3 \times 10^7} + 5 \times 10^3$$
$$y = 2.05 \times 10^5$$

25. a) If $E = \$100,000$, then
$$D = 0.75(100,000) + 5000$$
$$= \$80,000$$
$\$100,000 - \$80,000 = \$20,000$
So the tax is \$20,000.

b) If $E = \$10,000$, then
$$D = 0.75(10,000) + 5000 = 12,500$$
So Uncle Sam pays the person \$2500.

c) If $D = E$, then $E = 0.75E + 5000$ or $0.25E = 5000$, or $E = 20,000$.
So the lines intersect at an earned income of \$20,000.

d) At the intersection the earned income is equal to the disposable income, which means that if you earn \$20,000 then you pay no tax.

6.1 WARM-UPS

1. True, because a number is a monomial.
2. True, because it is a ratio of two binomials.
3. False, because the domain is any number except 2.
4. True, because 9 and $-\frac{1}{2}$ both give a denominator of 0.
5. False, because the numerator may be zero in a rational expression.
6. False, because 5 is not a factor of the numerator.
7. False, we would multiply the numerator and denominator by $x + 1$.
8. True, because we can multiply the numerator and denominator by -1.
9. True, because it is a correctly reduced rational expression.
10. False, it reduces to $x + y$.

6.1 EXERCISES

1. A rational expression is a ratio of two polynomials with the denominator not zero.
2. The domain of a rational expression is all real numbers except those that cause the denominator to be zero.
3. The basic principle of rational numbers says that $(ab)/(ac) = b/c$ provided a and c are not 0.
4. To reduce a rational expression, factor the numerator and denominator completely and then divide out the common factors.
5. We build up the denominator by multiplying the numerator and denominator by the same expression.
6. Average cost is total cost divide by the number of items.
7. If $x = 1$, then $x - 1 = 0$. So the domain is $\{x \mid x \neq 1\}$.
8. If $x = -5$, then $x + 5 = 0$. So the domain is $\{x \mid x \neq -5\}$.
9. If $z = 0$ then $7z = 0$. So the domain is $\{z \mid z \neq 0\}$.
10. If $z = 0$, then $4z = 0$. So the domain is $\{z \mid z \neq 0\}$.

11. If $y = -2$, then $y^2 - 4 = 0$. So the domain is $\{y \mid y \neq -2 \text{ and } y \neq 2\}$.
12. If $x = 3$ or $x = -3$, then $x^2 - 9 = 0$. So the domain is $\{x \mid x \neq -3 \text{ and } x \neq 3\}$.
13. To find the domain solve
$$a^2 + 5a + 6 = 0$$
$$(a + 2)(a + 3) = 0$$
$$a = -2 \text{ or } a = -3$$
The domain is $\{a \mid a \neq -2 \text{ and } a \neq -3\}$.
14. To find the domain solve the following equation.
$$2b^2 - 7b - 4 = 0$$
$$(2b + 1)(b - 4) = 0$$
$$2b + 1 = 0 \text{ or } b - 4 = 0$$
$$2b = -1 \text{ or } \quad b = 4$$
$$b = -\frac{1}{2} \text{ or } b = 4$$
The domain is $\left\{b \mid b \neq -\frac{1}{2} \text{ and } b \neq 4\right\}$.
15. To find the domain solve
$$x^2 + 4x = 0$$
$$x(x + 4) = 0$$
$$x = 0 \text{ or } x = -4$$
The domain is $\{x \mid x \neq -4 \text{ and } x \neq 0\}$.
16. To find the domain solve the equation
$$3x^2 + 9x = 0$$
$$3x(x + 3) = 0$$
$$3x = 0 \text{ or } x + 3 = 0$$
$$x = 0 \text{ or } \quad x = -3$$
The domain is $\{x \mid x \neq -3 \text{ and } x \neq 0\}$.
17. Solve the equation
$$x^3 + x^2 - 6x = 0$$
$$x(x + 3)(x - 2) = 0$$
$$x = 0 \text{ or } x = -3 \text{ or } x = 2$$
So the domain is $\{x \mid x \neq -3 \text{ and } x \neq 0 \text{ and } x \neq 2\}$.
18. Solve the equation
$$2x^5 - 2x = 0$$
$$2x(x^4 - 1) = 0$$
$$2x(x - 1)(x + 1)(x^2 + 1) = 0$$
$$x = 0 \text{ or } x = 1 \text{ or } x = -1 \text{ or } x^2 = -1$$
So the domain is
$$\{x \mid x \neq -1 \text{ and } x \neq 0 \text{ and } x \neq 1\}.$$
19. $\frac{6}{57} = \frac{3 \cdot 2}{3 \cdot 19} = \frac{2}{19}$

20. $\frac{14}{91} = \frac{2 \cdot 7}{7 \cdot 13} = \frac{2}{13}$

21. $\dfrac{42}{210} = \dfrac{42 \cdot 1}{42 \cdot 5} = \dfrac{1}{5}$

22. $\dfrac{242}{154} = \dfrac{2 \cdot 11^2}{2 \cdot 7 \cdot 11} = \dfrac{11}{7}$

23. $\dfrac{2x+2}{4} = \dfrac{2(x+1)}{2 \cdot 2} = \dfrac{x+1}{2}$

24. $\dfrac{3a+3}{3} = \dfrac{3(a+1)}{3} = a+1$

25. $\dfrac{3x-6y}{10y-5x} = \dfrac{3(x-2y)}{-5(x-2y)} = -\dfrac{3}{5}$

26. $\dfrac{5b-10a}{2a-b} = \dfrac{5(b-2a)}{-1(b-2a)} = -5$

27. $\dfrac{ab^2}{a^3b} = \dfrac{b}{a^2}$

28. $\dfrac{36y^3z^8}{54y^2z^9} = \dfrac{2y}{3z}$

29. $\dfrac{-2w^2x^3y}{6wx^5y^2} = \dfrac{-w}{3x^2y}$

30. $\dfrac{6a^3b^{12}c^5}{-8ab^4c^9} = \dfrac{-3a^2b^8}{4c^4}$

31. $\dfrac{a^3b^2}{a^3+a^4} = \dfrac{a^3 \cdot b^2}{a^3(1+a)} = \dfrac{b^2}{1+a}$

32. $\dfrac{b^8-ab^5}{ab^5} = \dfrac{b^5(b^3-a)}{ab^5} = \dfrac{b^3-a}{a}$

33. $\dfrac{a-b}{2b-2a} = \dfrac{a-b}{-2(a-b)} = -\dfrac{1}{2}$

34. $\dfrac{2m-2n}{4n-4m} = \dfrac{2(m-n)}{-4(m-n)} = -\dfrac{2}{4} = -\dfrac{1}{2}$

35. $\dfrac{3x+6}{3x} = \dfrac{3(x+2)}{3x} = \dfrac{x+2}{x}$

36. $\dfrac{7x-14}{7x} = \dfrac{7(x-2)}{7x} = \dfrac{x-2}{x}$

37. $\dfrac{a^3-b^3}{a-b} = \dfrac{(a-b)(a^2+ab+b^2)}{a-b}$
$= a^2+ab+b^2$

38. $\dfrac{27x^3+y^3}{6x+2y} = \dfrac{(3x+y)(9x^2-3xy+y^2)}{2(3x+y)}$
$= \dfrac{9x^2-3xy+y^2}{2}$

39. $\dfrac{4x^2-4}{4x^2+4} = \dfrac{4(x^2-1)}{4(x^2+1)} = \dfrac{x^2-1}{x^2+1}$

40. $\dfrac{2a^2-2b^2}{2a^2+2b^2} = \dfrac{2(a^2-b^2)}{2(a^2+b^2)} = \dfrac{a^2-b^2}{a^2+b^2}$

41. $\dfrac{2(x+3)(x-2)}{4(x-3)(x+3)} = \dfrac{x-2}{2x-6}$

42. $\dfrac{2x^2+10x+12}{2x^2-8} = \dfrac{2(x+2)(x+3)}{2(x-2)(x+2)}$
$= \dfrac{x+3}{x-2}$

43. $\dfrac{x^3+7x^2-4x}{x^3-16x} = \dfrac{x(x^2+7x-4)}{x(x-4)(x+4)}$
$= \dfrac{x^2+7x-4}{x^2-16}$

44. $\dfrac{2(x-2)(x+2)(x^2+4)}{4(x-2)}$
$= \dfrac{(x+2)(x^2+4)}{2}$

45. $\dfrac{ab+3a-by-3y}{a^2-y^2} = \dfrac{(a-y)(b+3)}{(a-y)(a+y)}$
$= \dfrac{b+3}{a+y}$

46. $\dfrac{2x^2-5x-3}{2x^2+11x+5} = \dfrac{(2x+1)(x-3)}{(2x+1)(x+5)}$
$= \dfrac{x-3}{x+5}$

47. $\dfrac{1}{5} = \dfrac{1 \cdot 10}{5 \cdot 10} = \dfrac{10}{50}$

48. $\dfrac{2}{3} = \dfrac{2 \cdot 3}{3 \cdot 3} = \dfrac{6}{9}$

49. $\dfrac{1}{x} = \dfrac{1 \cdot 3x}{x \cdot 3x} = \dfrac{3x}{3x^2}$

50. $\dfrac{3}{ab^2} = \dfrac{3 \cdot a^2b^3}{ab^2 \cdot a^2b^3} = \dfrac{3a^2b^3}{a^3b^5}$

51. $\dfrac{5}{x-1} = \dfrac{5(x-1)}{(x-1)(x-1)} = \dfrac{5x-5}{x^2-2x+1}$

52. $\dfrac{x}{x-3} = \dfrac{x(x+3)}{(x-3)(x+3)} = \dfrac{x^2+3x}{x^2-9}$

53. $\dfrac{1}{2x+2} = \dfrac{1(-3)}{(2x+2)(-3)} = \dfrac{-3}{-6x-6}$

54. $\dfrac{-2}{-3x+4} = \dfrac{-2(-5)}{(-3x+4)(-5)} = \dfrac{10}{15x-20}$

55. $5 = \dfrac{5 \cdot a}{1 \cdot a} = \dfrac{5a}{a}$

56. $3 = \dfrac{3(a+1)}{a+1} = \dfrac{3a+3}{a+1}$

221

57. $\dfrac{x+2}{x+3} = \dfrac{(x+2)(x-1)}{(x+3)(x-1)} = \dfrac{x^2+x-2}{x^2+2x-3}$

58. $\dfrac{x}{x-5} = \dfrac{x(x+4)}{(x-5)(x+4)} = \dfrac{x^2+4x}{x^2-x-20}$

59. $\dfrac{7}{x-1} = \dfrac{7(-1)}{(x-1)(-1)} = \dfrac{-7}{1-x}$

60. $\dfrac{1}{a-b} = \dfrac{1(-2)}{(a-b)(-2)} = \dfrac{-2}{2b-2a}$

61. $\dfrac{3}{x+2} = \dfrac{3(x^2-2x+4)}{(x+2)(x^2-2x+4)}$
$\qquad = \dfrac{3x^2-6x+12}{x^3+8}$

62. $\dfrac{x}{x-2} = \dfrac{x(x^2+2x+4)}{(x-2)(x^2+2x+4)}$
$\qquad = \dfrac{x^3+2x^2+4x}{x^3-8}$

63. $\dfrac{x+2}{3x-1} = \dfrac{(x+2)(2x+5)}{(3x-1)(2x+5)}$
$\qquad = \dfrac{2x^2+9x+10}{6x^2+13x-5}$

64. $\dfrac{a}{2a+1} = \dfrac{a(2a-9)}{(2a+1)(2a-9)}$
$\qquad = \dfrac{2a^2-9a}{4a^2-16a-9}$

65. $R(3) = \dfrac{3\cdot3-5}{3+4} = \dfrac{4}{7}$

66. $T(-9) = \dfrac{5-(-9)}{-9-5} = \dfrac{14}{-14} = -1$

67. $H(-2) = \dfrac{(-2)^2-5}{3(-2)-4} = \dfrac{-1}{-10} = \dfrac{1}{10}$

68. $G(5) = \dfrac{3-5(5)}{2(5)+7} = \dfrac{-22}{17} = -\dfrac{22}{17}$

69. $W(-2) = \dfrac{4(-2)^3-1}{(-2)^2-(-2)-6} = \dfrac{-33}{0}$

$W(-2)$ is undefined.

70. $N(3) = \dfrac{3+3}{3^3-2(3)^2-2(3)-3} = \dfrac{6}{0}$

$N(3)$ is undefined.

71. $\dfrac{1}{3} = \dfrac{1\cdot7}{3\cdot7} = \dfrac{7}{21}$

72. $4 = \dfrac{4\cdot3}{3} = \dfrac{12}{3}$

73. $5 = \dfrac{5\cdot2}{1\cdot2} = \dfrac{10}{2}$

74. $\dfrac{3}{4} = \dfrac{3\cdot4}{4\cdot4} = \dfrac{12}{16}$

75. $\dfrac{3}{a} = \dfrac{3a}{a\cdot a} = \dfrac{3a}{a^2}$

76. $\dfrac{5}{y} = \dfrac{5\cdot2}{y\cdot2} = \dfrac{10}{2y}$

77. $\dfrac{2}{a-b} = \dfrac{2(-1)}{(a-b)(-1)} = \dfrac{-2}{b-a}$

78. $\dfrac{3}{x-4} = \dfrac{3(-1)}{(x-4)(-1)} = \dfrac{-3}{4-x}$

79. $\dfrac{2}{x-1} = \dfrac{2(x+1)}{(x-1)(x+1)} = \dfrac{2x+2}{x^2-1}$

80. $\dfrac{5}{x+3} = \dfrac{5(x-3)}{(x+3)(x-3)} = \dfrac{5x-15}{x^2-9}$

81. $\dfrac{2}{w-3} = \dfrac{2(-1)}{(w-3)(-1)} = \dfrac{-2}{3-w}$

82. $\dfrac{-2}{5-x} = \dfrac{-2(-1)}{(5-x)(-1)} = \dfrac{2}{x-5}$

83. $\dfrac{2x+4}{6} = \dfrac{2(x+2)}{2\cdot3} = \dfrac{x+2}{3}$

84. $\dfrac{2x-3}{4x-6} = \dfrac{1(2x-3)}{2(2x-3)} = \dfrac{1}{2}$

85. $\dfrac{x+4}{x^2-16} = \dfrac{x+4}{(x-4)(x+4)} = \dfrac{1}{x-4}$

86. $\dfrac{2x+2}{2x} = \dfrac{2(x+1)}{2x} = \dfrac{x+1}{x}$

87. $\dfrac{3a+3}{3a} = \dfrac{3(a+1)}{3a} = \dfrac{a+1}{a}$

88. $\dfrac{x-3}{x^2-9} = \dfrac{1(x-3)}{(x-3)(x+3)} = \dfrac{1}{x+3}$

89. $\dfrac{1}{x-1} = \dfrac{1(x^2+x+1)}{(x-1)(x^2+x+1)}$
$\qquad = \dfrac{x^2+x+1}{x^3-1}$

90. $\dfrac{x^2+2x+4}{x+2} = \dfrac{(x^2+2x+4)(x-2)}{(x+2)(x-2)}$
$\qquad = \dfrac{x^3-8}{x^2-4}$

91. $\dfrac{x^{2a}-4}{x^a+2} = \dfrac{(x^a-2)(x^a+2)}{x^a+2} = x^a-2$

92. $\dfrac{x^{2b}+3x^b-18}{x^{2b}-36} = \dfrac{(x^b+6)(x^b-3)}{(x^b-6)(x^b+6)}$
$\qquad = \dfrac{x^b-3}{x^b-6}$

93. $\dfrac{x^a+m+wx^a+wm}{x^{2a}-m^2}$
$\qquad = \dfrac{(x^a+m)(1+w)}{(x^a-m)(x^a+m)}$
$\qquad = \dfrac{1+w}{x^a-m}$

94. $\dfrac{x^{3a}-8}{x^{2a}+2x^a+4}$
$\qquad = \dfrac{(x^a-2)(x^{2a}+2x^a+4)}{x^{2a}+2x^a+4}$
$\qquad = x^a-2$

95. $\dfrac{x^{3b+1}-x}{x^{2b+1}-x} = \dfrac{x(x^b-1)(x^{2b}+x^b+1)}{x(x^b-1)(x^b+1)}$
$\qquad = \dfrac{x^{2b}+x^b+1}{x^b+1}$

96. $\dfrac{2x^{2a+1}+3x^{a+1}+x}{4x^{2a+1}-x}$
$\qquad = \dfrac{x(2x^{2a}+3x^a+1)}{x(4x^{2a}-1)}$
$\qquad = \dfrac{x(2x^a+1)(x^a+1)}{x(2x^a-1)(2x^a+1)}$
$\qquad = \dfrac{x^a+1}{2x^a-1}$

97. Since $D = RT$, his rate is $\dfrac{500}{2x}$ or $\dfrac{250}{x}$ mph.

98. Marsha files $\dfrac{48}{2x+2}$ or $\dfrac{24}{x+1}$ suits/day.

99. a) Average cost per invitation is
$A(n) = \dfrac{0.50n + 45}{n}$ dollars.

b) $A(200) = \dfrac{0.50(200) + 45}{200} = \$0.725$

$A(300) = \dfrac{0.50(300) + 45}{300} = \$0.65$

It costs 7.5 cents less per invitation to print 300 rather than 200 invitations.

c) As the number of invitations increases, the average cost per invitation decreases.

d) As the number of invitations increases, the total cost of the invitations increases.

100. If $n =$ the number of people, then the average cost per person is

$A(n) = \dfrac{50,000 + 300n}{n}$.

$A(200) = \dfrac{50,000 + 300(200)}{200} = 550$

$A(100) = \dfrac{50,000 + 300(100)}{100} = 800$

The average cost per person is $250 lower when 200 people go.

101. a) $p(n) = \dfrac{0.053n^2 - 0.64n + 6.71}{3.43n + 87.24}$

b) $p(0) = \dfrac{0.053(0)^2 - 0.64(0) + 6.71}{3.43(0) + 87.24}$

$= 7.7\%$

$p(30) = \dfrac{0.053(30)^2 - 0.64(30) + 6.71}{3.43(30) + 87.24}$

$= 18.5\%$

$p(50) = \dfrac{0.053(50)^2 - 0.64(50) + 6.71}{3.43(50) + 87.24}$

$= 41.4\%$

102. a) $p(n) = \dfrac{25.2n + 1069}{41.7n + 1429}$

b) $p(20) = \dfrac{25.2(20) + 1069}{41.7(20) + 1429} = 69.5\%$

In 2010 bachelor's degrees will be 69.5% of all degrees awarded.

103. The value of $R(x)$ gets closer and closer to $1/2$.

104. The value of $H(x)$ gets closer and closer to $7/3$.

6.2 WARM-UPS

1. False, because we can multiply any two fractions.

2. False, $\dfrac{2}{7} \cdot \dfrac{3}{7} = \dfrac{6}{49}$.

3. True.

4. False, $a \div b = a \cdot \dfrac{1}{b}$.

5. True, because the expressions are correctly multiplied.

6. True, $\dfrac{1}{2} \cdot \dfrac{1}{3} = \dfrac{1}{6}$.

7. True, $\dfrac{1}{3} \div \dfrac{1}{2} = \dfrac{1}{3} \cdot \dfrac{2}{1} = \dfrac{2}{3}$.

8. True, $\dfrac{w - z}{z - w} = -1$.

9. True, $\dfrac{x}{3} \div 2 = \dfrac{x}{3} \cdot \dfrac{1}{2} = \dfrac{x}{6}$.

10. False, $\dfrac{a}{b} \div \dfrac{b}{a} = \dfrac{a}{b} \cdot \dfrac{a}{b} = \dfrac{a^2}{b^2}$.

6.2 EXERCISES

1. To multiply rational numbers, multiply the numerators and the denominators.

2. To multiply rational expressions, multiply the numerators and the denominators.

3. The expressions $a - b$ and $b - a$ are opposites.

4. To divide rational numbers, invert the divisor and multiply.

5. $\dfrac{12}{42} \cdot \dfrac{35}{22} = \dfrac{2 \cdot 2 \cdot 3}{2 \cdot 3 \cdot 7} \cdot \dfrac{5 \cdot 7}{2 \cdot 11} = \dfrac{5}{11}$

6. $\dfrac{3}{8} \cdot \dfrac{20}{21} = \dfrac{3}{2^3} \cdot \dfrac{2^2 \cdot 5}{3 \cdot 7} = \dfrac{5}{14}$

7. $\dfrac{3a}{2 \cdot 5b} \cdot \dfrac{5b^2}{2 \cdot 3} = \dfrac{ab}{4}$

8. $\dfrac{3x}{7y} \cdot \dfrac{14y^2}{9x} = \dfrac{3x}{7y} \cdot \dfrac{2 \cdot 7y^2}{3 \cdot 3x} = \dfrac{2y}{3}$

9. $\dfrac{3(x - 1)}{2 \cdot 3} \cdot \dfrac{x}{x(x - 1)} = \dfrac{1}{2}$

10. $\dfrac{-2(x + 2)}{2} \cdot \dfrac{2 \cdot 3}{3(x + 2)} = -2$

11. $\dfrac{5(2x + 1)}{5(x^2 + 1)} \cdot \dfrac{(2x - 1)(x + 1)}{(2x - 1)(2x + 1)} = \dfrac{x + 1}{x^2 + 1}$

12. $\dfrac{x(x^2 + 1)}{5} \cdot \dfrac{5(x - 1)}{x(x - 1)(x + 1)} = \dfrac{x^2 + 1}{x + 1}$

13. $\dfrac{(a + b)(x + w)}{(x - w)(x + w)} \cdot \dfrac{x - w}{(a - b)(a + b)} = \dfrac{1}{a - b}$

14. $\dfrac{3(a - y)}{(3 - b)(a - y)} \cdot \dfrac{(b - 3)(b + 3)}{6(b + 3)} = \dfrac{-3}{6}$

$= -\dfrac{1}{2}$

15. $\dfrac{a^2-2a+4}{(a+2)(a^2-2a+4)}\cdot\dfrac{(a+2)^3}{2(a+2)}$
$$=\dfrac{a+2}{2}$$

16. $\dfrac{w^3-1}{(w-1)^2}\cdot\dfrac{w^2-1}{w^2+w+1}$
$$=\dfrac{(w-1)(w^2+w+1)}{(w-1)^2}\cdot\dfrac{(w-1)(w+1)}{w^2+w+1}$$
$$=w+1$$

17. $\dfrac{x-9}{4\cdot3y}\cdot\dfrac{4\cdot2y}{-1(x-9)}=\dfrac{2}{-3}=-\dfrac{2}{3}$

18. $\dfrac{19x^2}{12y-1}\cdot\dfrac{-1(12y-1)}{3x}=-\dfrac{19x}{3}$

19. $(a^2-4)\cdot\dfrac{7}{2-a}$
$$=(a-2)(a+2)\cdot\dfrac{7}{-1(a-2)}$$
$$=-7(a+2)=-7a-14$$

20. $\dfrac{2x(5-2x)}{(2x-5)(2x-5)}\cdot x^2(2x-5)=-2x^3$

21. $\dfrac{15}{17}\div\dfrac{10}{17}=\dfrac{3\cdot5}{17}\cdot\dfrac{17}{2\cdot5}=\dfrac{3}{2}$

22. $\dfrac{3}{4}\div\dfrac{1}{8}=\dfrac{3}{4}\cdot8=\dfrac{3}{4}\cdot2\cdot4=6$

23. $\dfrac{36x}{5y}\div\dfrac{20x}{35y}=\dfrac{2^23^2x}{5y}\cdot\dfrac{5\cdot7y}{2^25x}=\dfrac{3^27}{5}$
$$=\dfrac{63}{5}$$

24. $\dfrac{18a^3b^4}{c^9}\cdot\dfrac{7c^2}{12ab^6}=\dfrac{2\cdot3\cdot3a^3b^4\cdot7c^2}{2^2\cdot3ab^6c^9}$
$$=\dfrac{21a^2}{2b^2c^7}$$

25. $\dfrac{2^3\cdot3a^5b^2}{5c^3}\cdot\dfrac{1}{2^2a^5bc^5}=\dfrac{6b}{5c^8}$

26. $\dfrac{2^2\cdot3\cdot5x^9y^2}{z}\cdot\dfrac{1}{2^4\cdot3x^4y^3}=\dfrac{5x^5}{4yz}$

27. $(w+1)\div\dfrac{w^2-1}{w}=(w+1)\cdot\dfrac{w}{w^2-1}$
$$=(w+1)\cdot\dfrac{w}{(w-1)(w+1)}=\dfrac{w}{w-1}$$

28. $(a-3)\cdot\dfrac{4}{(3-a)(3+a)}=\dfrac{-4}{a+3}$

29. $\dfrac{x-y}{5}\div\dfrac{x^2-2xy+y^2}{10}$
$$=\dfrac{x-y}{5}\cdot\dfrac{2\cdot5}{(x-y)^2}$$
$$=\dfrac{2}{x-y}$$

30. $\dfrac{(x+3)^2}{18}\cdot\dfrac{2\cdot18}{(x+3)^2}=2$

31. $\dfrac{2(2x-1)}{x(x-5)}\cdot\dfrac{(x-5)(x+5)}{(2x-1)(x+5)}=\dfrac{2}{x}$

32. $\dfrac{(2x+3)(x-4)}{2(3+2x)}\cdot\dfrac{2}{(x-4)(x+4)}$
$$=\dfrac{1}{x+4}$$

33. $\dfrac{x-y}{3}\cdot\dfrac{6}{1}=2x-2y$

34. $\dfrac{2a-b}{2\cdot5}\cdot\dfrac{5}{1}=\dfrac{2a-b}{2}$

35. $\dfrac{(x-5)(x+5)}{3}\cdot\dfrac{2\cdot3}{x-5}=2x+10$

36. $\dfrac{\frac{3x^2+3}{5}}{\frac{3x+3}{5}}=\dfrac{3x^2+3}{5}\cdot\dfrac{5}{3x+3}$
$$=\dfrac{3(x^2+1)\cdot5}{5\cdot3(x+1)}=\dfrac{x^2+1}{x+1}$$

37. $\dfrac{a-b}{2}\cdot\dfrac{1}{3}=\dfrac{a-b}{6}$

38. $\dfrac{\frac{10}{a+b}}{5}=\dfrac{10}{a+b}\cdot\dfrac{1}{5}=\dfrac{2\cdot5}{a+b}\cdot\dfrac{1}{5}$
$$=\dfrac{2}{a+b}$$

39. $(a-b)(a+b)\cdot\dfrac{3}{a+b}=3a-3b$

40. $\dfrac{x^2+5x+6}{\frac{x+2}{x+3}}=(x^2+5x+6)\cdot\dfrac{x+3}{x+2}$
$$=(x+2)(x+3)\cdot\dfrac{x+3}{x+2}=(x+3)^2$$
$$=x^2+6x+9$$

41. $\dfrac{5x}{2}\cdot\dfrac{1}{3}=\dfrac{5x}{6}$

42. $\dfrac{x}{a}\div2=\dfrac{x}{a}\cdot\dfrac{1}{2}=\dfrac{x}{2a}$

43. $\dfrac{3}{4}\cdot\dfrac{4}{1}=3$

44. $\dfrac{1}{4}\div\dfrac{1}{2}=\dfrac{1}{4}\cdot2=\dfrac{2}{4}=\dfrac{1}{2}$

45. $\dfrac{1}{2}\cdot\dfrac{1}{6}=\dfrac{1}{12}$

46. $\dfrac{1}{2}\cdot\dfrac{b}{a}=\dfrac{b}{2a}$

47. $\dfrac{1}{2}\cdot\dfrac{4x}{3}=\dfrac{2x}{3}$

48. $\dfrac{1}{3}\cdot\dfrac{6x}{y}=\dfrac{2x}{y}$

49. $\dfrac{a-b}{b-a}=-1$

50. $(a-b)\div(-1)=(a-b)\cdot(-1)=b-a$

51. $\dfrac{x-y}{3}\cdot\dfrac{2\cdot3}{y-x}=-2$

52. $\dfrac{5x-5y}{x}\cdot\dfrac{1}{x-y}=\dfrac{5(x-y)}{x}\cdot\dfrac{1}{x-y}=\dfrac{5}{x}$

53. $\dfrac{2(a+b)}{a}\cdot\dfrac{1}{2}=\dfrac{a+b}{a}$

54. $\dfrac{x-y}{y-x}\cdot\dfrac{1}{2}=(-1)\cdot\dfrac{1}{2}=-\dfrac{1}{2}$

55. $(a+b)\cdot2=2a+2b$

56. $\dfrac{x+3}{\frac{1}{3}}=(x+3)\cdot3=3x+9$

57. $\dfrac{3x}{5}\cdot\dfrac{1}{y}=\dfrac{3x}{5y}$

58. $\dfrac{\frac{b^2-4a}{2}}{a}=\dfrac{b^2-4a}{2}\cdot\dfrac{1}{a}=\dfrac{b^2-4a}{2a}$

59. $\dfrac{3a}{5b}\cdot\dfrac{1}{2}=\dfrac{3a}{10b}$

60. $\dfrac{\frac{6x}{a}}{x} = \dfrac{6x}{a} \cdot \dfrac{1}{x} = \dfrac{6}{a}$

61. $\dfrac{(3x-2)(x+5)}{x} \cdot \dfrac{x^3}{(3x-2)(3x+2)}$

$\qquad \cdot \dfrac{7(x-5)}{(x-5)(x+5)}$

$\qquad = \dfrac{7x^2}{3x+2}$

62. $\dfrac{x^2+5x+6}{x} \cdot \dfrac{x^2}{3x+6} \cdot \dfrac{9}{x^2-4}$

$\qquad = \dfrac{(x+2)(x+3)}{x} \cdot \dfrac{x^2}{3(x+2)} \cdot \dfrac{3\cdot 3}{(x-2)(x+2)}$

$\qquad = \dfrac{(x+3)3x}{(x-2)(x+2)} = \dfrac{3x^2+9x}{x^2-4}$

63. $\dfrac{(a^2b^3c)^2}{(-2ab^2c)^3} \cdot \dfrac{(a^3b^2c)^3}{(abc)^4} = \dfrac{a^4b^6c^2 a^9b^6c^3}{-8a^3b^6c^3 a^4b^4c^4}$

$\qquad = -\dfrac{a^6b^2}{8c^2}$

64. $\dfrac{(-wy^2)^3}{3w^2y} \cdot \dfrac{(2wy)^2}{4wy^3} = \dfrac{-w^3y^6}{3w^2y} \cdot \dfrac{4w^2y^2}{4wy^3}$

$\qquad = -\dfrac{w^5y^8}{3w^3y^4}$

$\qquad = -\dfrac{w^2y^4}{3}$

65. $\dfrac{(2mn)^3}{6mn^2} \cdot \dfrac{(m^2n)^4}{2m^2n^3} = \dfrac{8m^3n^3 m^8n^4}{12m^3n^5}$

$\qquad = \dfrac{2m^8n^2}{3}$

66. $\dfrac{(rt)^3}{rt^4} \div \dfrac{(rt^2)^3}{r^2t^3} = \dfrac{r^3t^3}{rt^4} \cdot \dfrac{r^2t^3}{r^3t^6}$

$\qquad = \dfrac{r^5t^6}{r^4t^{10}} = \dfrac{r}{t^4}$

67. $\dfrac{(2x-3)(x+5)}{4(x-5)(x+5)} \cdot \dfrac{(2x+1)(x-5)}{(2x-1)(2x+1)}$

$\qquad = \dfrac{2x-3}{8x-4}$

68. $\dfrac{x^3+1}{x^2-1} \cdot \dfrac{3x-3}{x^3-x^2+x}$

$\qquad = \dfrac{(x+1)(x^2-x+1)}{(x-1)(x+1)} \cdot \dfrac{3(x-1)}{x(x^2-x+1)}$

$\qquad = \dfrac{3}{x}$

69. We can factor $k^2 - 2km + m^2$ as $(k-m)^2$ or $(m-k)^2$.

$\qquad \dfrac{(k+m)^2}{(m-k)^2} \cdot \dfrac{(m-k)(m+3)}{(m+3)(m+k)} = \dfrac{k+m}{m-k}$

70. $\dfrac{a^2+2ab+b^2}{ac+bc-ad-bd} \div \dfrac{ac+ad-bc-bd}{c^2-d^2}$

$\qquad = \dfrac{(a+b)^2}{(c-d)(a+b)} \cdot \dfrac{(c-d)(c+d)}{(a-b)(c+d)}$

$\qquad = \dfrac{a+b}{a-b}$

71. $\dfrac{x^a}{y^2} \cdot \dfrac{y^{b+2}}{x^{2a}} = \dfrac{y^b}{x^a}$

72. $\dfrac{x^{3a+1}}{y^{2b-3}} \cdot \dfrac{y^{3b+4}}{x^{2a-1}} = x^{a+2}y^{b+7}$

73. $\dfrac{x^{2a}+x^a-6}{x^{2a}+6x^a+9} \div \dfrac{x^{2a}-4}{x^{2a}+2x^a-3}$

$\qquad = \dfrac{(x^a+3)(x^a-2)}{(x^a+3)^2} \cdot \dfrac{(x^a+3)(x^a-1)}{(x^a-2)(x^a+2)}$

$\qquad = \dfrac{x^a-1}{x^a+2}$

74. $\dfrac{w^{2b}+2w^b-8}{w^{2b}+3w^b-4} \div \dfrac{w^{2b}-w^b-2}{w^{2b}-1}$

$\qquad = \dfrac{(w^b+4)(w^b-2)}{(w^b+4)(w^b-1)} \cdot \dfrac{(w^b-1)(w^b+1)}{(w^b+1)(w^b-2)}$

$\qquad = 1$

75. $\dfrac{m^kv^k+3v^k-2m^k-6}{m^{2k}-9}$

$\qquad \cdot \dfrac{m^{2k}-2m^k-3}{v^km^k-2m^k+2v^k-4}$

$\qquad = \dfrac{(m^k+3)(v^k-2)}{(m^k-3)(m^k+3)} \cdot \dfrac{(m^k-3)(m^k+1)}{(v^k-2)(m^k+2)}$

$\qquad = \dfrac{m^k+1}{m^k+2}$

76. $\dfrac{m^{3k}-1}{m^{3k}+1} \cdot \dfrac{m^{2k+1}-m^{k+1}+m}{m^{3k}+m^{2k}+m^k}$

$\qquad = \dfrac{(m^k-1)(m^{2k}+m^k+1)}{(m^k+1)(m^{2k}-m^k+1)}$

$\qquad \cdot \dfrac{m(m^{2k}-m^k+1)}{m^k(m^{2k}+m^k+1)}$

$\qquad = \dfrac{(m^k-1)}{(m^k+1)m^{k-1}} = \dfrac{m^k-1}{m^{2k-1}+m^{k-1}}$

77. $\dfrac{1}{50} \div \dfrac{7}{25} = \dfrac{1}{50} \cdot \dfrac{25}{7} = \dfrac{1}{14} \approx 7.1\%$

78. $\dfrac{3}{25} \div \dfrac{2}{9} = \dfrac{3}{25} \cdot \dfrac{9}{2} = \dfrac{27}{50} \approx 54\%$

79. Her rate is $\dfrac{100}{x}$ miles/hour. Since $D = RT$, in $\frac{3}{4}$ hr she traveled $\dfrac{100}{x} \cdot \dfrac{3}{4}$ or $\dfrac{75}{x}$ miles.

80. Before lunch her time was $\dfrac{200}{x}$ hr. Since $R = \dfrac{D}{T}$, her speed after lunch was $250 \div \dfrac{200}{x}$ or $\dfrac{5x}{4}$ mph.

81. Because $x \div \dfrac{y}{z} = x \cdot \dfrac{z}{y} = \dfrac{xz}{y}$, only (e) is not equivalent to the given expression.

82. Because $\dfrac{x-1}{x^2-1}$ reduces to $\dfrac{1}{x+1}$ equation (b) is not an identity.

6.3 WARM-UPS

1. False, the LCM is 30.
2. False, the LCM is $24a^2b^3$.
3. True, because $x - 1$ is a factor of $x^2 - 1$.
4. False, the LCD is $x(x + 1)$.
5. False, $\frac{1}{2} + \frac{2}{3} = \frac{7}{6}$.
6. False, $5 + \frac{1}{x} = \frac{5x}{x} + \frac{1}{x} = \frac{5x+1}{x}$ for any nonzero x.
7. True, because the expressions are added correctly.
8. True, because the expressions are subtracted correctly.
9. True, because $\frac{8}{12} + \frac{9}{12} = \frac{17}{12}$.
10. False, he uses x reams per day

6.3 EXERCISES

1. The sum of a/b and c/b is $(a + c)/b$.
2. The LCD is the least common multiple of the denominators.
3. The least common multiple of some numbers is the smallest number that is a multiple of all of the numbers.
4. To find the LCM for some polynomials, first factor completely, then use the LCM of the coefficients and every other factor with the highest exponent that occurs on that factor in any of the polynomials.
5. To add rational expressions with different denominators, you must build-up the expressions to equivalent expressions with the same denominator.
6. You do not need identical denominators for division and multiplication.
7. $\frac{3x}{2} + \frac{5x}{2} = \frac{8x}{2} = 4x$
8. $\frac{5x^2}{3} + \frac{4x^2}{3} = \frac{9x^2}{3} = 3x^2$
9. $\frac{x-3}{2x} - \frac{3x-5}{2x} = \frac{x-3-3x+5}{2x}$
$= \frac{-2x+2}{2x} = \frac{2(-x+1)}{2x} = \frac{-x+1}{x}$
10. $\frac{9-4y}{3y} - \frac{6-y}{3y} = \frac{9-4y-6+y}{3y}$
$= \frac{3-3y}{3y} = \frac{3(1-y)}{3y} = \frac{1-y}{y}$
11. $\frac{3x-4}{2x-4} + \frac{2x-6}{2x-4} = \frac{5x-10}{2x-4} = \frac{5(x-2)}{2(x-2)}$
$= \frac{5}{2}$

12. $\frac{a^3}{a+b} + \frac{b^3}{a+b} = \frac{a^3+b^3}{a+b}$
$= \frac{(a+b)(a^2-ab+b^2)}{a+b}$
$= a^2 - ab + b^2$
13. $\frac{x^2+4x-6}{x^2-9} - \frac{x^2+2x-12}{x^2-9} = \frac{2x+6}{x^2-9}$
$= \frac{2(x+3)}{(x-3)(x+3)} = \frac{2}{x-3}$
14. $\frac{x^2+3x-3}{x-4} - \frac{x^2+4x-7}{x-4}$
$= \frac{x^2+3x-3-(x^2+4x-7)}{x-4}$
$= \frac{3x-3-4x+7}{x-4} = \frac{-x+4}{x-4}$
$= \frac{-1(x-4)}{x-4} = -1$
15. Since $24 = 2^3 \cdot 3$ and $20 = 2^2 \cdot 5$, the LCM $= 2^3 \cdot 3 \cdot 5 = 120$.
16. Since $12 = 2^2 \cdot 3$, $18 = 2 \cdot 3^2$, and $22 = 2 \cdot 11$, the LCM $= 2^2 \cdot 3^2 \cdot 11 = 396$
17. The LCM for 10 and 15 is 30. So the LCM is $30x^3y$.
18. The LCM for 12 and 18 is 36. So the LCM is $36a^3b^5$
19. The highest power of a is 3, the highest power of b is 5, and the highest power of c is 2. So the LCM $= a^3b^5c^2$.
20. In x^2yz, xy^2z^3, and xy^6 the highest power of x is 2, for y it is 6, and for z it is 3. So the LCM $= x^2y^6z^3$.
21. Since the three polynomials have no common factors, the LCM is the product of the polynomials: $x(x + 2)(x - 2)$
22. Since the three polynomials have no common factors, the LCM is the product of the polynomials: LCM $= y(y - 5)(y + 2)$
23. $4a + 8 = 4(a + 2)$, $6a + 12 = 6(a + 2)$ LCM $= 12(a + 2) = 12a + 24$
24. $4a - 6 = 2(2a - 3)$,
$2a^2 - 3a = a(2a - 3)$
LCM $= 2a(2a - 3) = 4a^2 - 6a$
25. $x^2 - 1 = (x - 1)(x + 1)$
$x^2 + 2x + 1 = (x + 1)^2$
LCM $= (x - 1)(x + 1)^2$
26. $y^2 - 2y - 15 = (y - 5)(y + 3)$
$y^2 + 6y + 9 = (y + 3)^2$
LCM $= (y - 5)(y + 3)^2$
27. $x^2 - 4x = x(x - 4)$
$x^2 - 16 = (x - 4)(x + 4)$

$x^2 + 6x + 8 = (x + 4)(x + 2)$

$\text{LCM} = x(x - 4)(x + 4)(x + 2)$

28. $z^2 - 25 = (z - 5)(z + 5)$

$5z - 25 = 5(z - 5)$

$5z + 25 = 5(z + 5)$

$\text{LCM} = 5(z - 5)(z + 5) = 5z^2 - 125$

29. $\dfrac{1 \cdot 5}{28 \cdot 5} + \dfrac{3 \cdot 4}{35 \cdot 4} = \dfrac{5}{140} + \dfrac{12}{140} = \dfrac{17}{140}$

30. $\dfrac{7}{48} - \dfrac{5}{36} = \dfrac{7 \cdot 3}{48 \cdot 3} - \dfrac{5 \cdot 4}{36 \cdot 4}$

$\qquad = \dfrac{21}{144} - \dfrac{20}{144} = \dfrac{1}{144}$

31. $\dfrac{7 \cdot 5}{24 \cdot 5} - \dfrac{4 \cdot 8}{15 \cdot 8} = \dfrac{35}{120} - \dfrac{32}{120} = \dfrac{3}{120}$

$\qquad\qquad\qquad\qquad\qquad = \dfrac{1}{40}$

32. $\dfrac{7}{52} + \dfrac{3}{40} = \dfrac{7 \cdot 10}{52 \cdot 10} + \dfrac{3 \cdot 13}{40 \cdot 13}$

$\qquad = \dfrac{70}{520} + \dfrac{39}{520} = \dfrac{109}{520}$

33. $\dfrac{3}{wz^2} + \dfrac{5}{w^2 z} = \dfrac{3 \cdot w}{wz^2 \cdot w} + \dfrac{5 \cdot z}{w^2 z \cdot z}$

$\qquad = \dfrac{3w}{w^2 z^2} + \dfrac{5z}{w^2 z^2} = \dfrac{3w + 5z}{w^2 z^2}$

34. $\dfrac{2 \cdot b}{a^2 b \cdot b} - \dfrac{3 \cdot a}{ab^2 \cdot a} = \dfrac{2b}{a^2 b^2} - \dfrac{3a}{a^2 b^2}$

$\qquad\qquad = \dfrac{2b - 3a}{a^2 b^2}$

35. $\dfrac{2x - 3}{8} - \dfrac{x - 2}{6}$

$\qquad = \dfrac{(2x - 3)3}{8 \cdot 3} - \dfrac{(x - 2)4}{6 \cdot 4}$

$\qquad = \dfrac{6x - 9}{24} - \dfrac{4x - 8}{24} = \dfrac{2x - 1}{24}$

36. $\dfrac{a - 5}{10} + \dfrac{3 - 2a}{15}$

$\qquad = \dfrac{(a - 5)3}{10 \cdot 3} + \dfrac{(3 - 2a)2}{15 \cdot 2}$

$\qquad = \dfrac{3a - 15}{30} + \dfrac{6 - 4a}{30} = \dfrac{-a - 9}{30}$

37. $\dfrac{x \cdot 5}{2a \cdot 5} + \dfrac{3x \cdot 2}{5a \cdot 2} = \dfrac{5x}{10a} + \dfrac{6x}{10a} = \dfrac{11x}{10a}$

38. $\dfrac{x}{6y} - \dfrac{3x}{8y} = \dfrac{x \cdot 4}{6y \cdot 4} - \dfrac{3x \cdot 3}{8y \cdot 3}$

$\qquad\qquad = \dfrac{4x}{24y} - \dfrac{9x}{24y} = -\dfrac{5x}{24y}$

39. $\dfrac{9}{4y} - x = \dfrac{9}{4y} - \dfrac{x \cdot 4y}{4y} = \dfrac{9}{4y} - \dfrac{4xy}{4y}$

$\qquad\qquad = \dfrac{9 - 4xy}{4y}$

40. $\dfrac{b^2}{4a} - c = \dfrac{b^2}{4a} - \dfrac{c \cdot 4a}{4a} = \dfrac{b^2 - 4ac}{4a}$

41. $\dfrac{5}{a + 2} - \dfrac{7}{a} = \dfrac{5 \cdot a}{(a + 2)a} - \dfrac{7(a + 2)}{a(a + 2)}$

$\qquad = \dfrac{5a}{a(a + 2)} - \dfrac{7a + 14}{a(a + 2)}$

$\qquad = \dfrac{5a - (7a + 14)}{a(a + 2)} = \dfrac{-2a - 14}{a(a + 2)}$

42. $\dfrac{2 \cdot x}{(x + 1)x} - \dfrac{3(x + 1)}{x(x + 1)}$

$\qquad = \dfrac{2x}{x(x + 1)} - \dfrac{3x + 3}{x(x + 1)}$

$\qquad = \dfrac{-x - 3}{x(x + 1)}$

43. $\dfrac{1}{a - b} + \dfrac{2}{a + b}$

$\qquad = \dfrac{1(a + b)}{(a - b)(a + b)} + \dfrac{2(a - b)}{(a + b)(a - b)}$

$\qquad = \dfrac{a + b}{(a - b)(a + b)} + \dfrac{2a - 2b}{(a - b)(a + b)}$

$\qquad = \dfrac{3a - b}{(a - b)(a + b)}$

44. $\dfrac{5(x - 2)}{(x + 2)(x - 2)} + \dfrac{3(x + 2)}{(x - 2)(x + 2)}$

$\qquad = \dfrac{5x - 10}{(x + 2)(x - 2)} + \dfrac{3x + 6}{(x + 2)(x - 2)}$

$\qquad = \dfrac{8x - 4}{(x + 2)(x - 2)}$

45. $\dfrac{x}{(x + 3)(x - 3)} + \dfrac{3(x + 3)}{(x - 3)(x + 3)}$

$\qquad = \dfrac{4x + 9}{(x + 3)(x - 3)}$

46. $\dfrac{x}{x^2 - 25} + \dfrac{5}{x - 5}$

$\qquad = \dfrac{x}{(x - 5)(x + 5)} + \dfrac{5(x + 5)}{(x - 5)(x + 5)}$

$\qquad = \dfrac{x}{(x - 5)(x + 5)} + \dfrac{5x + 25}{(x - 5)(x + 5)}$

$\qquad = \dfrac{6x + 25}{(x - 5)(x + 5)}$

47. $\dfrac{1}{a - b} + \dfrac{1(-1)}{(b - a)(-1)} = \dfrac{1}{a - b} + \dfrac{-1}{a - b}$

$\qquad\qquad = \dfrac{0}{a - b} = 0$

48. $\dfrac{3}{x - 5} + \dfrac{7}{5 - x} = \dfrac{3}{x - 5} + \dfrac{7(-1)}{(5 - x)(-1)}$

$\qquad = \dfrac{3}{x - 5} + \dfrac{-7}{x - 5} = \dfrac{-4}{x - 5}$

49. $\dfrac{5}{2(x - 2)} - \dfrac{3(-2)}{(2 - x)(-2)}$

$\qquad = \dfrac{5}{2x - 4} - \dfrac{-6}{2x - 4} = \dfrac{11}{2x - 4}$

50. $\dfrac{4}{3x-9} - \dfrac{7}{3-x}$

$\quad = \dfrac{4}{3x-9} - \dfrac{7(-3)}{(3-x)(-3)}$

$\quad = \dfrac{4}{3x-9} - \dfrac{-21}{3x-9} = \dfrac{25}{3x-9}$

51. $\dfrac{5(x+3)}{(x+2)(x-1)(x+3)}$

$\qquad\qquad - \dfrac{6(x+2)}{(x+3)(x-1)(x+2)}$

$\quad = \dfrac{5x+15}{(x-1)(x+2)(x+3)}$

$\qquad\qquad - \dfrac{6x+12}{(x-1)(x+2)(x+3)}$

$\quad = \dfrac{-x+3}{(x-1)(x+2)(x+3)}$

52. $\dfrac{2}{x^2-4} - \dfrac{5}{x^2-3x-10}$

$\quad = \dfrac{2}{(x-2)(x+2)} - \dfrac{5}{(x-5)(x+2)}$

$\quad = \dfrac{2(x-5)}{(x-2)(x+2)(x-5)}$

$\qquad\qquad - \dfrac{5(x-2)}{(x-5)(x+2)(x-2)}$

$\quad = \dfrac{2x-10}{(x-2)(x+2)(x-5)}$

$\qquad\qquad - \dfrac{5x-10}{(x-2)(x+2)(x-5)}$

$\quad = \dfrac{2x-10-(5x-10)}{(x-2)(x+2)(x-5)}$

$\quad = \dfrac{2x-10-5x+10}{(x-2)(x+2)(x-5)}$

$\quad = \dfrac{-3x}{(x-2)(x+2)(x-5)}$

53. $\dfrac{x(x+1)}{(x-3)(x+3)(x+1)}$

$\qquad\qquad + \dfrac{6(x-3)}{(x+3)(x+1)(x-3)}$

$\quad = \dfrac{x^2+x}{(x+1)(x+3)(x-3)}$

$\qquad\qquad + \dfrac{6x-18}{(x+1)(x+3)(x-3)}$

$\quad = \dfrac{x^2+7x-18}{(x+1)(x+3)(x-3)}$

54. $\dfrac{2x-1}{x^2-x-12} + \dfrac{x+5}{x^2+5x+6}$

$\quad = \dfrac{2x-1}{(x-4)(x+3)} + \dfrac{x+5}{(x+2)(x+3)}$

$\quad = \dfrac{(2x-1)(x+2)}{(x-4)(x+3)(x+2)}$

$\qquad\qquad + \dfrac{(x+5)(x-4)}{(x+2)(x+3)(x-4)}$

$\quad = \dfrac{2x^2+3x-2}{(x+2)(x+3)(x-4)}$

$\qquad\qquad + \dfrac{x^2+x-20}{(x+2)(x+3)(x-4)}$

$\quad = \dfrac{3x^2+4x-22}{(x+2)(x+3)(x-4)}$

55. $\dfrac{1(x-1)(x+2)}{x(x-1)(x+2)} + \dfrac{2x(x+2)}{(x-1)x(x+2)}$

$\qquad\qquad - \dfrac{3x(x-1)}{(x+2)x(x-1)}$

$\quad = \dfrac{x^2+x-2}{x(x-1)(x+2)} + \dfrac{2x^2+4x}{x(x-1)(x+2)}$

$\qquad\qquad - \dfrac{3x^2-3x}{x(x-1)(x+2)}$

$\quad = \dfrac{8x-2}{x(x-1)(x+2)}$

56. $\dfrac{2}{a} - \dfrac{3}{a+1} + \dfrac{5}{a-1}$

$\quad = \dfrac{2(a-1)(a+1)}{a(a-1)(a+1)} - \dfrac{3a(a-1)}{(a+1)a(a-1)}$

$\qquad\qquad + \dfrac{5a(a+1)}{(a-1)a(a+1)}$

$\quad = \dfrac{2a^2-2}{a(a+1)(a-1)} - \dfrac{3a^2-3a}{a(a+1)(a-1)}$

$\qquad\qquad + \dfrac{5a^2+5a}{a(a+1)(a-1)}$

$\quad = \dfrac{2a^2-2-(3a^2-3a)+5a^2+5a}{a(a+1)(a-1)}$

$\quad = \dfrac{4a^2+8a-2}{a(a+1)(a-1)}$

57. $\dfrac{1}{3} + \dfrac{1}{4} = \dfrac{1\cdot 4+1\cdot 3}{12} = \dfrac{7}{12}$

58. $\dfrac{3}{5} + \dfrac{1}{4} = \dfrac{3\cdot 4+1\cdot 5}{5\cdot 4} = \dfrac{17}{20}$

59. $\dfrac{1}{8} - \dfrac{3}{5} = \dfrac{1\cdot 5-8\cdot 3}{40} = -\dfrac{19}{40}$

60. $\dfrac{a}{2} + \dfrac{5}{3} = \dfrac{3a+2\cdot 5}{2\cdot 3} = \dfrac{3a+10}{6}$

61. $\dfrac{x}{3} + \dfrac{x}{2} = \dfrac{x\cdot 2+x\cdot 3}{6} = \dfrac{5x}{6}$

62. $\dfrac{y}{4} - \dfrac{y}{3} = \dfrac{y\cdot 3-y\cdot 4}{3\cdot 4} = -\dfrac{y}{12}$

63. $\dfrac{a}{b} - \dfrac{2}{3} = \dfrac{3\cdot a-2\cdot b}{3b} = \dfrac{3a-2b}{3b}$

64. $\dfrac{3}{x} + \dfrac{1}{9} = \dfrac{3\cdot 9+1\cdot x}{x\cdot 9} = \dfrac{x+27}{9x}$

65. $a + \dfrac{2}{3} = \dfrac{a\cdot 3+1\cdot 2}{3\cdot 1} = \dfrac{3a+2}{3}$

66. $\dfrac{m}{3} + y = \dfrac{m\cdot 1+3\cdot y}{3\cdot 1} = \dfrac{m+3y}{3}$

67. $\dfrac{3}{a} + 1 = \dfrac{a\cdot 1+3\cdot 1}{a\cdot 1} = \dfrac{a+3}{a}$

68. $\dfrac{1}{x} + 1 = \dfrac{1\cdot 1+1\cdot x}{x\cdot 1} = \dfrac{x+1}{x}$

69. $\dfrac{3+x}{x} - 1 = \dfrac{3+x-x}{x} = \dfrac{3}{x}$

70. $\dfrac{a+2}{a} + 3 = \dfrac{(a+2)1+3a}{a\cdot 1} = \dfrac{4a+2}{a}$

71. $\dfrac{2}{3} + \dfrac{1}{4x} = \dfrac{2\cdot 4x+1\cdot 3}{12x} = \dfrac{8x+3}{12x}$

72. $\dfrac{1}{5} + \dfrac{1}{5x} = \dfrac{1\cdot 5x+1\cdot 5}{25x}$

$\qquad\qquad = \dfrac{5x+5}{25x} = \dfrac{x+1}{5x}$

73. $\dfrac{w^2-3w+6}{w-5} + \dfrac{9-w^2}{w-5} = \dfrac{-3w+15}{w-5}$

$\qquad\qquad = \dfrac{-3(w-5)}{w-5} = -3$

74. $\dfrac{2z^2 - 3z + 6}{z^2 - 1} - \dfrac{z^2 - 5z + 9}{z^2 - 1}$

$= \dfrac{z^2 + 2z - 3}{z^2 - 1} = \dfrac{(z+3)(z-1)}{(z-1)(z+1)}$

$\qquad\qquad\qquad = \dfrac{z+3}{z+1}$

75. $\dfrac{1}{x+2} - \dfrac{2}{x+3} = \dfrac{1(x+3) - 2(x+2)}{(x+2)(x+3)}$

$\qquad\qquad = \dfrac{-x-1}{(x+2)(x+3)}$

76. $\dfrac{2}{a+3} - \dfrac{3}{a+1} = \dfrac{2(a+1) - 3(a+3)}{(a+3)(a+1)}$

$\qquad\qquad = \dfrac{-a-7}{(a+3)(a+1)}$

77. $\dfrac{1}{a^3 - 1} - \dfrac{1}{a^3 + 1} = \dfrac{a^3 + 1 - (a^3 - 1)}{(a^3 - 1)(a^3 + 1)}$

$\qquad\qquad\qquad = \dfrac{2}{(a^3 - 1)(a^3 + 1)}$

78. $\dfrac{1}{x^3 - 8} + \dfrac{1}{x^3 + 8}$

$\qquad = \dfrac{1(x^3 + 8) + 1(x^3 - 8)}{(x^3 + 8)(x^3 - 8)}$

$\qquad = \dfrac{2x^3}{(x^3 + 8)(x^3 - 8)}$

79. $\dfrac{a^8 b^{12}}{a^3 b^{12}} \cdot \dfrac{a^3 b^3}{a^8 b^2} = \dfrac{a^{11} b^{15}}{a^{11} b^{14}} = b$

80. $\dfrac{a^2 b^2}{(a+b)^2} \cdot \dfrac{(a+b)^3}{a^3 b^3} = \dfrac{a+b}{ab}$

81. $\dfrac{x^2 - 3x}{(x-1)(x^2 + x + 1)}$

$\qquad\qquad + \dfrac{4(x^2 + x + 1)}{(x-1)(x^2 + x + 1)}$

$= \dfrac{x^2 - 3x}{(x-1)(x^2 + x + 1)}$

$\qquad\qquad + \dfrac{4x^2 + 4x + 4}{(x-1)(x^2 + x + 1)}$

$= \dfrac{5x^2 + x + 4}{(x-1)(x^2 + x + 1)}$

82. $\dfrac{4a}{(a+1)^2} - \dfrac{3(a+1)}{(a+1)(a+1)}$

$\qquad = \dfrac{4a}{(a+1)^2} - \dfrac{3a+3}{(a+1)^2} = \dfrac{a-3}{(a+1)^2}$

83. $\dfrac{x^2 + 25}{(x-5)(x+5)} \cdot \dfrac{(x+5)^2}{x(x+5)} = \dfrac{x^2 + 25}{x(x-5)}$

84. $\dfrac{(a+2)(a-1)}{(a-1)(a^2 + a + 1)} \cdot \dfrac{a^2 + a + 1}{(a-2)(a+2)}$

$\qquad\qquad = \dfrac{1}{a-2}$

85. $\dfrac{(w^2 - 3)}{3(w+3)(w^2 - 3w + 9)}$

$\qquad - \dfrac{1(w^2 - 3w + 9)}{3(w+3)(w^2 - 3w + 9)}$

$\qquad\qquad - \dfrac{3(w-4)(w+3)}{3(w+3)(w^2 - 3w + 9)}$

$= \dfrac{w^2 - 3 - w^2 + 3w - 9 - 3(w^2 - w - 12)}{3(w+3)(w^2 - 3w + 9)}$

$= \dfrac{-w^2 + 2w + 8}{(w+3)(w^2 - 3w + 9)}$

86. $\dfrac{a-3}{a^3 + 8} - \dfrac{2}{a+2} - \dfrac{a-3}{a^2 - 2a + 4}$

$= \dfrac{a-3}{(a+2)(a^2 - 2a + 4)} - \dfrac{2}{a+2}$

$\qquad\qquad - \dfrac{a-3}{a^2 - 2a + 4}$

$= \dfrac{a-3}{(a+2)(a^2 - 2a + 4)} - \dfrac{2(a^2 - 2a + 4)}{(a+2)(a^2 - 2a + 4)}$

$\qquad\qquad - \dfrac{(a-3)(a+2)}{(a^2 - 2a + 4)(a+2)}$

$= \dfrac{a-3}{(a+2)(a^2 - 2a + 4)} - \dfrac{2a^2 - 4a + 8}{(a+2)(a^2 - 2a + 4)}$

$\qquad\qquad - \dfrac{a^2 - a - 6}{(a^2 - 2a + 4)(a+2)}$

$= \dfrac{a - 3 - 2a^2 + 4a - 8 - a^2 + a + 6}{(a+2)(a^2 - 2a + 4)}$

$= \dfrac{-3a^2 + 6a - 5}{a^3 + 8}$

87. $\dfrac{(a-3)^2}{(a-2)(a^2 + 2a + 4)} \cdot \dfrac{(a-2)(a+2)}{(a-3)(a+2)}$

$\qquad\qquad = \dfrac{a-3}{a^2 + 2a + 4}$

88. $\dfrac{1}{z^2 + 4} \cdot \dfrac{(z-2)(z+2)(z^2 + 4)}{(z-2)(z^2 + 2z + 4)}$

$\qquad\qquad = \dfrac{z+2}{z^2 + 2z + 4}$

89. $\dfrac{(w^2 + 3)(w+2)}{(w-2)(w^2 + 2w + 4)(w+2)}$

$\qquad - \dfrac{2w(w^2 + 2w + 4)}{(w-2)(w+2)(w^2 + 2w + 4)}$

$= \dfrac{w^3 + 3w + 2w^2 + 6 - (2w^3 + 4w^2 + 8w)}{(w-2)(w+2)(w^2 + 2w + 4)}$

$= \dfrac{-w^3 - 2w^2 - 5w + 6}{(w-2)(w+2)(w^2 + 2w + 4)}$

90. $\dfrac{x+5}{(x+3)(x^2 - 3x + 9)} - \dfrac{x-1}{(x-3)(x+3)}$

$= \dfrac{(x+5)(x-3)}{(x+3)(x^2 - 3x + 9)(x-3)}$

$\qquad - \dfrac{(x-1)(x^2 - 3x + 9)}{(x-3)(x+3)(x^2 - 3x + 9)}$

$= \dfrac{x^2 + 2x - 15}{(x+3)(x^2 - 3x + 9)(x-3)}$

$\qquad - \dfrac{x^3 - 4x^2 + 12x - 9}{(x-3)(x+3)(x^2 - 3x + 9)}$

$= \dfrac{-x^3 + 5x^2 - 10x - 6}{(x^2 - 9)(x^2 - 3x + 9)}$

91. $\dfrac{x+1}{(x-1)(x^2+x+1)(x+1)}$

$\qquad - \dfrac{x^2+x+1}{(x-1)(x+1)(x^2+x+1)}$

$\qquad + \dfrac{(x+1)(x^2+x+1)}{(x-1)(x+1)(x^2+x+1)}$

$= \dfrac{x+1-x^2-x-1+x^3+x^2+x+x^2+x+1}{(x-1)(x+1)(x^2+x+1)}$

$= \dfrac{x^3+x^2+2x+1}{(x-1)(x+1)(x^2+x+1)}$

92. $\dfrac{x-4}{x^3-1}+\dfrac{x-2}{x^2-1}$

$= \dfrac{x-4}{(x-1)(x^2+x+1)}+\dfrac{x-2}{(x-1)(x+1)}$

$= \dfrac{(x-4)(x+1)}{(x-1)(x^2+x+1)(x+1)}$

$\qquad + \dfrac{(x-2)(x^2+x+1)}{(x-1)(x+1)(x^2+x+1)}$

$= \dfrac{x^2-3x-4}{(x^3-1)(x+1)}+\dfrac{x^3-x^2-x-2}{(x^3-1)(x+1)}$

$= \dfrac{x^3-4x-6}{(x^3-1)(x+1)}$

93. Joe processes $\dfrac{1}{x}$ claims/hr while Ellen processes $\dfrac{1}{x+1}$ claims/hr. Together they process
$\dfrac{1}{x}+\dfrac{1}{x+1}$ or $\dfrac{2x+1}{x(x+1)}$ claims/hr. In 8 hours
they process $\dfrac{8(2x+1)}{x(x+1)}$ or $\dfrac{16x+8}{x^2+x}$ claims.

94. Bill's rate is $\dfrac{1}{x}$ bund/min while Julio's rate
is $\dfrac{1}{x-6}$ bund/min. Their rate together is
$\dfrac{1}{x}+\dfrac{1}{x-6}$ or $\dfrac{2x-6}{x(x-6)}$ bund/min. In 10 hr or
600
min they attach $\dfrac{600(2x-6)}{x(x-6)}$ or $\dfrac{1200x-3600}{x^2-6x}$
bundles.

95. George's rate is $\dfrac{1}{20}$ mag/min while
Theresa's rate is $\dfrac{1}{x}$ mag/min. Their rate
together is $\dfrac{1}{x}+\dfrac{1}{20}$ or $\dfrac{x+20}{20x}$ mag/min. In 60
min they will sell

$60\cdot\dfrac{x+20}{20x}$ or $\dfrac{3x+60}{x}$ magazines.

96. Harry's rate is $\dfrac{1}{6}$ house/day while Judy's
rate is $\dfrac{1}{x}$ house/day. Rate together is $\dfrac{1}{x}+\dfrac{1}{6}$ or
$\dfrac{x+6}{6x}$ house/day. In 2 days they will paint
$2\cdot\dfrac{x+6}{6x}$ or $\dfrac{x+6}{3x}$ of the house.

97. Let x be Joan's original speed and $x+5$ be
her increased speed. Since $F=\dfrac{D}{R}$, her total
travel time is $\dfrac{100}{x}+\dfrac{200}{x+5}$ or $\dfrac{300x+500}{x^2+5x}$
hours.

98. Let x be his original speed and $2x$ be his
speed after he doubled the speed. Since
$T=\dfrac{D}{R}$, his total time is $\dfrac{3}{x}+\dfrac{1}{2x}$ or $\dfrac{7}{2x}$ hours.

6.4 WARM-UPS

1. False, the LCM is $6x^2$.
2. True, since $2b-2a=-2(a-b)$.
3. True.
4. True, because $\dfrac{1}{2}+\dfrac{1}{3}=\dfrac{5}{6}$ and $1+\dfrac{1}{2}=\dfrac{3}{2}$.
5. False, because $2^{-1}+3^{-1}=\dfrac{1}{2}+\dfrac{1}{3}=\dfrac{5}{6}$
and $(2+3)^{-1}=\dfrac{1}{5}$.
6. False, because the left side is the reciprocal
of $\dfrac{5}{6}$ and the right side is 5.
7. False, because $2+3^{-1}=\dfrac{7}{3}$ and $5^{-1}=\dfrac{1}{5}$.
8. False, because $x+2^{-1}=x+\dfrac{1}{2}=\dfrac{2x+1}{2}$
for any value of x.
9. True, because ab is the LCD.
10. True, because multiplying by a^5b^2 will
eliminate all negative exponents.

6.4 EXERCISES

1. A complex fraction is a fraction that
contains fractions in the numerator,
denominator, or both.
2. One method is to perform the operations in
the numerator and then in the denominator, and
then divide the results. The other method is to
multiply the numerator and denominator by the
LCD for all of the fractions.
3. $\dfrac{\left(\frac{1}{2}-\frac{1}{3}\right)60}{\left(\frac{1}{4}-\frac{1}{5}\right)60}=\dfrac{30-20}{15-12}=\dfrac{10}{3}$

230

4. $\dfrac{\frac{1}{3}+\frac{1}{4}}{\frac{1}{5}+\frac{1}{6}}=\dfrac{\left(\frac{1}{3}+\frac{1}{4}\right)60}{\left(\frac{1}{5}+\frac{1}{6}\right)60}=\dfrac{20+15}{12+10}=\dfrac{35}{22}$

5. $\dfrac{24\cdot\frac{2}{3}+24\cdot\frac{5}{6}-24\cdot\frac{1}{2}}{24\cdot\frac{1}{8}-24\cdot\frac{1}{3}+24\cdot\frac{1}{12}}=\dfrac{16+20-12}{3-8+2}$

$$=-8$$

6. $\dfrac{\frac{2}{5}-\frac{x}{9}-\frac{1}{3}}{\frac{1}{3}+\frac{x}{5}+\frac{2}{15}}=\dfrac{\frac{2}{5}\cdot45-\frac{x}{9}\cdot45-\frac{1}{3}\cdot45}{\frac{1}{3}\cdot45+\frac{x}{5}\cdot45+\frac{2}{15}\cdot45}$

$$=\dfrac{18-5x-15}{15+9x+6}=\dfrac{3-5x}{9x+21}$$

7. $\dfrac{ab\left(\frac{a+b}{b}\right)}{ab\left(\frac{a-b}{ab}\right)}=\dfrac{a^2+ab}{a-b}$

8. $\dfrac{\frac{m-n}{m^2}}{\frac{m-3}{mn^3}}=\dfrac{\left(\frac{m-n}{m^2}\right)m^2n^3}{\left(\frac{m-3}{mn^3}\right)m^2n^3}=\dfrac{(m-n)n^3}{(m-3)m}$

$$=\dfrac{mn^3-n^4}{m^2-3m}$$

9. $\dfrac{ab\cdot a+ab\cdot\frac{3}{b}}{ab\cdot\frac{b}{a}+ab\cdot\frac{1}{b}}=\dfrac{a^2b+3a}{a+b^2}$

10. $\dfrac{m-\frac{2}{n}}{\frac{1}{m}-\frac{3}{n}}=\dfrac{\left(m-\frac{2}{n}\right)mn}{\left(\frac{1}{m}-\frac{3}{n}\right)mn}=\dfrac{m^2n-2m}{n-3m}$

11. $\dfrac{xy\left(\frac{x-3y}{xy}\right)}{xy\cdot\frac{1}{x}+xy\cdot\frac{1}{y}}=\dfrac{x-3y}{x+y}$

12. $\dfrac{\frac{2}{w}+\frac{3}{t}}{\frac{w-t}{4wt}}=\dfrac{\left(\frac{2}{w}+\frac{3}{t}\right)4wt}{\left(\frac{w-t}{4wt}\right)4wt}=\dfrac{8t+12w}{w-t}$

13. $\dfrac{18m\cdot3-18m\cdot\frac{m-2}{6}}{18m\cdot\frac{4}{9}+18m\cdot\frac{2}{m}}$

$=\dfrac{54m-3m^2+6m}{8m+36}=\dfrac{60m-3m^2}{8m+36}$

14. $\dfrac{6-\frac{2-z}{z}}{\frac{1}{3z}-\frac{1}{6}}=\dfrac{\left(6-\frac{2-z}{z}\right)6z}{\left(\frac{1}{3z}-\frac{1}{6}\right)6z}$

$=\dfrac{36z-(2-z)6}{2-z}=\dfrac{36z-12+6z}{2-z}$

$=\dfrac{42z-12}{2-z}$

15. $\dfrac{a^3b^3\left(\frac{a^2-b^2}{a^2b^3}\right)}{a^3b^3\left(\frac{a+b}{a^3b}\right)}=\dfrac{a(a^2-b^2)}{b^2(a+b)}$

$=\dfrac{a(a-b)(a+b)}{b^2(a+b)}=\dfrac{a^2-ab}{b^2}$

16. $\dfrac{\frac{4x^2-1}{x^2y}}{\frac{4x-2}{xy^2}}=\dfrac{\left(\frac{4x^2-1}{x^2y}\right)x^2y^2}{\left(\frac{4x-2}{xy^2}\right)x^2y^2}=\dfrac{(4x^2-1)y}{(4x-2)x}$

$=\dfrac{(2x-1)(2x+1)y}{2(2x-1)x}=\dfrac{2xy+y}{2x}$

17. $\dfrac{\frac{1}{x^2y^2}+\frac{1}{xy^3}}{\frac{1}{x^3y}-\frac{1}{xy}}=\dfrac{\left(\frac{1}{x^2y^2}+\frac{1}{xy^3}\right)x^3y^3}{\left(\frac{1}{x^3y}-\frac{1}{xy}\right)x^3y^3}$

$=\dfrac{xy+x^2}{y^2-x^2y^2}$

18. $\dfrac{\frac{1}{2a^3b}-\frac{1}{ab^4}}{\frac{1}{6a^2b^2}+\frac{1}{3a^4b}}=\dfrac{\left(\frac{1}{2a^3b}-\frac{1}{ab^4}\right)6a^4b^4}{\left(\frac{1}{6a^2b^2}+\frac{1}{3a^4b}\right)6a^4b^4}$

$=\dfrac{3ab^3-6a^3}{a^2b^2+2b^3}$

19. $\dfrac{(x+4)x+(x+4)\cdot\frac{4}{x+4}}{(x+4)x-(x+4)\cdot\frac{4x+4}{x+4}}$

$=\dfrac{x^2+4x+4}{x^2+4x-4x-4}=\dfrac{(x+2)^2}{(x-2)(x+2)}$

$$=\dfrac{x+2}{x-2}$$

20. $\dfrac{x-\frac{x+6}{x+2}}{x-\frac{4x+15}{x+2}}=\dfrac{\left(x-\frac{x+6}{x+2}\right)(x+2)}{\left(x-\frac{4x+15}{x+2}\right)(x+2)}$

$=\dfrac{x(x+2)-(x+6)}{x(x+2)-(4x+15)}=\dfrac{x^2+2x-x-6}{x^2+2x-4x-15}$

$=\dfrac{x^2+x-6}{x^2-2x-15}=\dfrac{(x+3)(x-2)}{(x-5)(x+3)}=\dfrac{x-2}{x-5}$

21.
$$\frac{(y-1)(y+1)\left(1-\frac{1}{y-1}\right)}{(y-1)(y+1)\left(3+\frac{1}{y+1}\right)}$$

$$=\frac{y^2-1-(y+1)}{3(y^2-1)+y-1}=\frac{y^2-y-2}{3y^2+y-4}$$

$$=\frac{y^2-y-2}{(y-1)(3y+4)}$$

22.
$$\frac{2-\frac{3}{a-2}}{4-\frac{1}{a+2}}=\frac{\left(2-\frac{3}{a-2}\right)(a-2)(a+2)}{\left(4-\frac{1}{a+2}\right)(a-2)(a+2)}$$

$$=\frac{2(a-2)(a+2)-3(a+2)}{4(a-2)(a+2)-1(a-2)}$$

$$=\frac{2a^2-8-3a-6}{4a^2-16-a+2}$$

$$=\frac{2a^2-3a-14}{4a^2-a-14}$$

23.
$$\frac{(x-3)\cdot\frac{2}{3-x}-(x-3)4}{(x-3)\cdot\frac{1}{x-3}-(x-3)1}$$

$$=\frac{-2-4x+12}{1-x+3}=\frac{-4x+10}{-x+4}=\frac{4x-10}{x-4}$$

24.
$$\frac{\frac{x}{x-5}-2}{\frac{2x}{5-x}-1}=\frac{\left(\frac{x}{x-5}-2\right)(x-5)}{\left(\frac{2x}{5-x}-1\right)(x-5)}$$

$$=\frac{x-2(x-5)}{2x(-1)-1(x-5)}=\frac{x-2x+10}{-2x-x+5}$$

$$=\frac{-x+10}{-3x+5}=\frac{x-10}{3x-5}$$

25.
$$\frac{w(w-1)\left(\frac{w+2}{w-1}-\frac{w-3}{w}\right)}{w(w-1)\left(\frac{w+4}{w}+\frac{w-2}{w-1}\right)}$$

$$=\frac{w^2+2w-(w-1)(w-3)}{(w-1)(w+4)+w^2-2w}$$

$$=\frac{w^2+2w-w^2+4w-3}{w^2+3w-4+w^2-2w}$$

$$=\frac{6w-3}{2w^2+w-4}$$

26.
$$\frac{\frac{x-1}{x+2}-\frac{x-2}{x+3}}{\frac{x-3}{x+3}+\frac{x+1}{x+2}}$$

$$=\frac{\left(\frac{x-1}{x+2}-\frac{x-2}{x+3}\right)(x+2)(x+3)}{\left(\frac{x-3}{x+3}+\frac{x+1}{x+2}\right)(x+2)(x+3)}$$

$$=\frac{(x-1)(x+3)-(x-2)(x+2)}{(x-3)(x+2)+(x+1)(x+3)}$$

$$=\frac{x^2+2x-3-[x^2-4]}{x^2-x-6+x^2+4x+3}=\frac{2x+1}{2x^2+3x-3}$$

27.
$$\frac{(a-b)(a+b)\left(\frac{1}{a-b}-\frac{3}{a+b}\right)}{(a-b)(a+b)\left(\frac{2}{b-a}+\frac{4}{a+b}\right)}$$

$$=\frac{a+b-3(a-b)}{-2(a+b)+4(a-b)}=\frac{-2a+4b}{2a-6b}$$

$$=\frac{2(2b-a)}{2(a-3b)}=\frac{2b-a}{a-3b}$$

28.
$$\frac{\frac{3}{2+x}-\frac{4}{2-x}}{\frac{1}{x+2}-\frac{3}{x-2}}$$

$$=\frac{\left(\frac{3}{2+x}-\frac{4}{2-x}\right)(x+2)(x-2)}{\left(\frac{1}{x+2}-\frac{3}{x-2}\right)(x+2)(x-2)}$$

$$=\frac{3(x-2)-4(x+2)(-1)}{1(x-2)-3(x+2)}$$

$$=\frac{3x-6+4x+8}{x-2-3x-6}$$

$$=\frac{7x+2}{-2x-8}$$

29.
$$\frac{(a-1)3-(a-1)\cdot\frac{4}{a-1}}{(a-1)5-(a-1)\cdot\frac{3}{1-a}}$$

$$=\frac{3a-3-4}{5a-5+3}=\frac{3a-7}{5a-2}$$

30.
$$\frac{\frac{x}{3}-\frac{x-1}{9-x}}{\frac{x}{6}-\frac{2-x}{x-9}}=\frac{\left(\frac{x}{3}-\frac{x-1}{9-x}\right)6(x-9)}{\left(\frac{x}{6}-\frac{2-x}{x-9}\right)6(x-9)}$$

$$=\frac{2x(x-9)-(x-1)(6)(-1)}{x(x-9)-(2-x)6}=\frac{2x^2-18x+6x-6}{x^2-9x-12+6x}$$

$$=\frac{2x^2-12x-6}{x^2-3x-12}$$

31.
$$\frac{m(m-3)(m-2)\left(\frac{2}{m-3}+\frac{4}{m}\right)}{m(m-3)(m-2)\left(\frac{3}{m-2}+\frac{1}{m}\right)}$$

$$=\frac{2m(m-2)+4(m-3)(m-2)}{3m(m-3)+(m-3)(m-2)}$$

$$=\frac{2m^2-4m+4m^2-20m+24}{3m^2-9m+m^2-5m+6}$$

$$=\frac{6m^2-24m+24}{4m^2-14m+6}=\frac{3m^2-12m+24}{2m^2-7m+3}$$

$$=\frac{3m^2-12m+12}{(m-3)(2m-1)}$$

32.
$$\frac{\frac{1}{y+2}-\frac{4}{3y}}{\frac{3}{y}-\frac{2}{y+3}}$$

$$=\frac{\left(\frac{1}{y+2}-\frac{4}{3y}\right)3y(y+2)(y+3)}{\left(\frac{3}{y}-\frac{2}{y+3}\right)3y(y+2)(y+3)}$$

$$=\frac{3y(y+3)-4(y+2)(y+3)}{9(y+2)(y+3)-6y(y+2)}$$

$$= \frac{3y^2 + 9y - 4y^2 - 20y - 24}{9y^2 + 45y + 54 - 6y^2 - 12y}$$

$$= \frac{-y^2 - 11y - 24}{3y^2 + 33y + 54}$$

33.

$$\frac{(x-1)(x+1)(x^2+x+1)\left(\frac{3}{x^2-1} - \frac{x-2}{x^3-1}\right)}{(x-1)(x+1)(x^2+x+1)\left(\frac{3}{x^2+x+1} + \frac{x-3}{x^3-1}\right)}$$

$$= \frac{3x^2 + 3x + 3 - (x+1)(x-2)}{3x^2 - 3 + (x+1)(x-3)}$$

$$= \frac{3x^2 + 3x + 3 - x^2 + x + 2}{3x^2 - 3 + x^2 - 2x - 3}$$

$$= \frac{2x^2 + 4x + 5}{4x^2 - 2x - 6}$$

34.
$$\frac{\frac{2}{a^3+8} - \frac{3}{a^2-2a+4}}{\frac{4}{a^2-4} + \frac{a-3}{a^3+8}}$$

$$= \frac{\left(\frac{2}{a^3+8} - \frac{3}{a^2-2a+4}\right)(a+2)(a-2)(a^2-2a+4)}{\left(\frac{4}{a^2-4} + \frac{a-3}{a^3+8}\right)(a+2)(a-2)(a^2-2a+4)}$$

$$= \frac{2(a-2) - 3(a+2)(a-2)}{4(a^2-2a+4) + (a-3)(a-2)}$$

$$= \frac{2a - 4 - 3a^2 + 12}{4a^2 - 8a + 16 + a^2 - 5a + 6}$$

$$= \frac{-3a^2 + 2a + 8}{5a^2 - 13a + 22}$$

35. $\dfrac{wyz(w^{-1} + y^{-1})}{wyz(z^{-1} + y^{-1})} = \dfrac{yz + wz}{wy + wz}$

36. $\dfrac{a^{-1} - b^{-1}}{a^{-1} + b^{-1}} = \dfrac{(a^{-1} - b^{-1})ab}{(a^{-1} + b^{-1})ab} = \dfrac{b-a}{b+a}$

37. $\dfrac{x^2(1 - x^{-1})}{x^2(1 - x^{-2})} = \dfrac{x^2 - x}{x^2 - 1} = \dfrac{x(x-1)}{(x-1)(x+1)}$

$$= \frac{x}{x+1}$$

38. $\dfrac{4 - a^{-2}}{2 - a^{-1}} = \dfrac{a^2(4 - a^{-2})}{a^2(2 - a^{-1})} = \dfrac{4a^2 - 1}{2a^2 - a}$

$$= \frac{(2a-1)(2a+1)}{a(2a-1)}$$

$$= \frac{2a+1}{a}$$

39. $\dfrac{a^2b^2(a^{-2} + b^{-2})}{a^2b^2(a^{-1}b)} = \dfrac{a^2 + b^2}{ab^3}$

40. $\dfrac{m^{-3} + n^{-3}}{mn^{-2}} = \dfrac{(m^{-3} + n^{-3})m^3n^3}{(mn^{-2})m^3n^3}$

$$= \frac{n^3 + m^3}{m^4 n}$$

41. $\dfrac{a(1 - a^{-1})}{a} = \dfrac{a-1}{a}$

42. $m^{-1} - a^{-1} = \dfrac{ma(m^{-1} - a^{-1})}{ma} = \dfrac{a-m}{am}$

43. $\dfrac{x^2(x^{-1} + x^{-2})}{x^2(x + x^{-2})} = \dfrac{x+1}{x^3+1}$

$$= \frac{x+1}{(x+1)(x^2 - x + 1)}$$

$$= \frac{1}{x^2 - x + 1}$$

44. $\dfrac{x - x^{-2}}{1 - x^{-2}} = \dfrac{(x - x^{-2})x^2}{(1 - x^{-2})x^2} = \dfrac{x^3 - 1}{x^2 - 1}$

$$= \frac{(x-1)(x^2 + x + 1)}{(x-1)(x+1)}$$

$$= \frac{x^2 + x + 1}{x+1}$$

45. $\dfrac{m^2(2m^{-1} - 3m^{-2})}{m^2(m^{-2})} = 2m - 3$

46. $\dfrac{4x^{-3} - 6x^{-5}}{2x^{-5}} = \dfrac{x^5(4x^{-3} - 6x^{-5})}{x^5(2x^{-5})}$

$$= \frac{4x^2 - 6}{2} = 2x^2 - 3$$

47. $\dfrac{ab(a^{-1} - b^{-1})}{ab(a - b)} = \dfrac{b - a}{-ab(b-a)} = -\dfrac{1}{ab}$

48. $\dfrac{a^2 - b^2}{a^{-2} - b^{-2}} = \dfrac{(a^2 - b^2)a^2b^2}{(a^{-2} - b^{-2})a^2b^2}$

$$= \frac{(a^2 - b^2)a^2b^2}{b^2 - a^2}$$

$$= (-1)a^2b^2 = -a^2b^2$$

49. $\dfrac{x^3 - y^3}{x^{-3} - y^{-3}} = \dfrac{(x^3 - y^3)x^3y^3}{(x^{-3} - y^{-3})x^3y^3}$

$$= \frac{(x^3 - y^3)x^3y^3}{y^3 - x^3}$$

$$= (-1)x^3y^3 = -x^3y^3$$

50. $\dfrac{a^2b^2(a-b)^2}{a^2b^2(a^{-2} - b^{-2})} = \dfrac{a^2b^2(a-b)^2}{b^2 - a^2}$

$$= \frac{a^2b^2(a-b)^2}{(b-a)(b+a)} = \frac{-a^2b^2(a-b)}{a+b}$$

$$= \frac{a^2b^3 - a^3b^2}{a+b}$$

51. $\dfrac{x^3(1 - 8x^{-3})}{x^3(x^{-1} + 2x^{-2} + 4x^{-3})}$

$$= \frac{x^3 - 8}{x^2 + 2x + 4}$$

$$= \frac{(x-2)(x^2 + 2x + 4)}{x^2 + 2x + 4}$$

$$= x - 2$$

52. $\dfrac{a + 27a^{-2}}{1 - 3a^{-1} + 9a^{-2}} = \dfrac{(a + 27a^{-2})a^2}{(1 - 3a^{-1} + 9a^{-2})a^2}$

$$= \frac{a^3 + 27}{a^2 - 3a + 9}$$

$$= \frac{(a+3)(a^2 - 3a + 9)}{a^2 - 3a + 9} = a + 3$$

53. $(x^{-1} + y^{-1})^{-1} = \dfrac{1}{x^{-1} + y^{-1}}$

$= \dfrac{xy \cdot 1}{xy(x^{-1} + y^{-1})} = \dfrac{xy}{x + y}$

54. $(a^{-1} - b^{-1})^{-2} = \dfrac{1}{(a^{-1} - b^{-1})^2}$

$= \dfrac{1}{a^{-2} - 2a^{-1}b^{-1} + b^{-2}}$

$= \dfrac{1a^2b^2}{(a^{-2} - 2a^{-1}b^{-1} + b^{-2})a^2b^2}$

$= \dfrac{a^2b^2}{b^2 - 2ab + a^2}$

55. $\dfrac{\frac{5}{3} - \frac{4}{5}}{\frac{1}{3} - \frac{5}{6}} \approx -1.7333 \text{ or } -26/15$

56. $\dfrac{\frac{1}{12} + \frac{1}{2} - \frac{3}{4}}{\frac{3}{5} + \frac{5}{6}} \approx -0.1163 \text{ or } -5/43$

57. $\dfrac{4^{-1} - 9^{-1}}{2^{-1} + 3^{-1}} \approx 0.1667 \text{ or } 1/6$

58. $\dfrac{2^{-1} + 3^{-1} - 6^{-1}}{3^{-1} - 5^{-1} + 4^{-1}} \approx 1.7391 \text{ or } 40/23$

59. If x = the number of students at Central, then $\frac{1}{2}x$ = the number at Northside and $\frac{2}{3}x$ = the number at Southside. To find the percentage of black students among the city's elementary students we divide the number of black students by the total number of students:

$\dfrac{\frac{1}{3} \cdot \frac{1}{2}x + \frac{3}{4} \cdot x + \frac{1}{6} \cdot \frac{2}{3}x}{\frac{1}{2}x + x + \frac{2}{3}x} = \dfrac{\frac{1}{6}x + \frac{3}{4}x + \frac{1}{9}x}{\frac{1}{2}x + x + \frac{2}{3}x}$

$= \dfrac{36\left(\frac{1}{6}x + \frac{3}{4}x + \frac{1}{9}x\right)}{36\left(\frac{1}{2}x + x + \frac{2}{3}x\right)} = \dfrac{6x + 27x + 4x}{18x + 36x + 24x}$

$= \dfrac{37x}{78x} = \dfrac{37}{78} = 47.4\%$

60. Let x = the number of employees in development, x = the number in manufacturing, and $2x$ = the number in sales. The number of women in development is $\frac{x}{5}$, the number in manufacturing is $\frac{x}{3}$, and the number in sales is $\frac{2x}{2}$ or x.

$\dfrac{\frac{x}{5} + \frac{x}{3} + x}{x + x + 2x} = \dfrac{\left(\frac{x}{5} + \frac{x}{3} + x\right)15}{(x + x + 2x)15}$

$= \dfrac{3x + 5x + 15x}{60x} = \dfrac{23x}{60x} = \dfrac{23}{60} \approx 38.3\%$

So 38.3% of the employees are women.

$\dfrac{\frac{x}{5} + \frac{x}{3} + x}{x} = \dfrac{x \cdot 15}{\left(\frac{x}{5} + \frac{x}{3} + x\right)15} = \dfrac{15x}{23x} = \dfrac{15}{23}$

$\approx 65.2\%$

So 65.2% of the women are in sales.

61. Let x = the distance and $\frac{x}{45}$ = the time from Clarksville to Leesville. We can also say that x = the distance and $\frac{x}{55}$ = the time for the return trip. To find the average speed for any trip we divide the total distance by the total time. In this case the total distance is $2x$ and the total time is $\frac{x}{45} + \frac{x}{55}$.

$\dfrac{2x}{\frac{x}{45} + \frac{x}{55}} = \dfrac{2x \cdot 5 \cdot 9 \cdot 11}{\left(\frac{x}{45} + \frac{x}{55}\right)5 \cdot 9 \cdot 11} = \dfrac{990x}{11x + 9x}$

$= \dfrac{990x}{20x} = \dfrac{99}{2} = 49.5$

Her average speed for the trip is 49.5 mph.

62. Let a = the amount in cents spent on each fill up. She got $\frac{a}{99.9}$ gal, $\frac{a}{109.9}$ gal, and $\frac{a}{119.9}$ gal. Average price per gallon is the total amount paid divided by the total number of gallons.

$\dfrac{3a}{\frac{a}{99.9} + \frac{a}{109.9} + \frac{a}{119.9}} = \dfrac{3}{\frac{1}{99.9} + \frac{1}{119.9} + \frac{1}{119.9}}$

≈ 109.3 cents per gallon

64. a) $5/8, 11/18$

b) The denominator is larger than the numerator in the first fraction.

65. The complex fraction simplifies to $\dfrac{2x + 1}{3x + 2}$. The complex fraction is undefined for $x = 0, -1, -1/2, -2/3$.

6.5 WARM-UPS

1. True, because that will eliminate all denominators.

2. False, we should multiply each side by $6x$.

3. False, extraneous roots are real numbers that are not roots to the equation.

4. True, $x^2 - 4$ is the LCD.

5. False, $-\frac{1}{2}$ cannot be a solution because it causes $2x + 1$ to be 0.

6. True, because the equation is equivalent to $2x = 15$.

7. False, because the extremes-means property is only applied to equations of the type $\frac{a}{b} = \frac{c}{d}$.

8. False, because $x^2 = x$ has two solutions, 0 and 1.

9. False, the solution set is $\left\{\frac{3}{2}, -\frac{4}{3}\right\}$.

10. True, because of the extremes-means property.

6.5 EXERCISES

1. The first step is to multiply each side of the equation by the LCD.

2. A solution to the equation can cause 0 to appear in a denominator.

3. A proportion is an equation expressing equality of two rational expressions.

4. In $a/b = c/d$ the means are b and c.

5. In $a/b = c/d$ the extremes are a and d.

6. The extremes-means property says that if $a/b = c/d$ then $bc = ad$.

7.
$$24x\left(\frac{1}{x} + \frac{1}{6}\right) = 24x\left(\frac{1}{8}\right)$$
$$24 + 4x = 3x$$
$$x = -24$$
Solution set: $\{-24\}$

8.
$$\frac{3}{x} + \frac{1}{5} = \frac{1}{2}$$
$$10x\left(\frac{3}{x} + \frac{1}{5}\right) = 10x \cdot \frac{1}{2}$$
$$30 + 2x = 5x$$
$$30 = 3x$$
$$10 = x$$
The solution set is $\{10\}$.

9.
$$30x\left(\frac{2}{3x} + \frac{1}{15x}\right) = 30x\left(\frac{1}{2}\right)$$
$$20 + 2 = 15x$$
$$22 = 15x$$
$$\frac{22}{15} = x$$
Solution set: $\left\{\frac{22}{15}\right\}$

10.
$$\frac{5}{6x} - \frac{1}{8x} = \frac{17}{24}$$
$$24x\left(\frac{5}{6x} - \frac{1}{8x}\right) = 24x \cdot \frac{17}{24}$$
$$20 - 3 = 17x$$
$$17 = 17x$$

$$1 = x$$
The solution set is $\{1\}$.

11.
$$x(x-2)\left(\frac{3}{x-2} + \frac{5}{x}\right) = x(x-2)\left(\frac{10}{x}\right)$$
$$3x + 5x - 10 = 10x - 20$$
$$8x - 10 = 10x - 20$$
$$10 = 2x$$
$$5 = x$$
Solution set: $\{5\}$

12.
$$\frac{5}{x-1} + \frac{1}{2x} = \frac{1}{x}$$
$$2x(x-1)\left(\frac{5}{x-1} + \frac{1}{2x}\right) = 2x(x-1)\frac{1}{x}$$
$$10x + x - 1 = 2x - 2$$
$$11x - 1 = 2x - 2$$
$$9x = -1$$
$$x = -\frac{1}{9}$$
The solution set is $\left\{-\frac{1}{9}\right\}$.

13.
$$x(x-2)\left(\frac{x}{x-2} + \frac{3}{x}\right) = x(x-2)2$$
$$x^2 + 3x - 6 = 2x^2 - 4x$$
$$-x^2 + 7x - 6 = 0$$
$$x^2 - 7x + 6 = 0$$
$$(x-6)(x-1) = 0$$
$$x - 6 = 0 \quad \text{or} \quad x - 1 = 0$$
$$x = 6 \quad \text{or} \quad x = 1$$
Solution set: $\{1, 6\}$

14.
$$\frac{x}{x-5} + \frac{5}{x} = \frac{11}{6}$$
$$6x(x-5)\left(\frac{x}{x-5} + \frac{5}{x}\right) = 6x(x-5)\frac{11}{6}$$
$$6x^2 + 30x - 150 = 11x^2 - 55x$$
$$-5x^2 + 85x - 150 = 0$$
$$x^2 - 17x + 30 = 0$$
$$(x-15)(x-2) = 0$$
$$x - 15 = 0 \text{ or } x - 2 = 0$$
$$x = 15 \text{ or } \quad x = 2$$
The solution set is $\{2, 15\}$.

15.
$$x(x+5)\left(\frac{100}{x}\right) = x(x+5)\left(\frac{150}{x+5} - 1\right)$$
$$100x + 500 = 150x - x(x+5)$$
$$100x + 500 = 150x - x^2 - 5x$$
$$x^2 - 45x + 500 = 0$$
$$(x-25)(x-20) = 0$$
$$x = 25 \text{ or } x = 20$$
Solution set: $\{20, 25\}$

16.
$$\frac{30}{x} = \frac{50}{x+10} + \frac{1}{2}$$
$$2x(x+10)\frac{30}{x} = 2x(x+10)\left(\frac{50}{x+10} + \frac{1}{2}\right)$$
$$60x + 600 = 100x + x^2 + 10x$$
$$-x^2 - 50x + 600 = 0$$
$$x^2 + 50x - 600 = 0$$
$$(x+60)(x-10) = 0$$
$$x + 60 = 0 \text{ or } x - 10 = 0$$
$$x = -60 \text{ or } x = 10$$
The solution set is $\{-60, 10\}$.

17. $(x-1)\left(\frac{3x-5}{x-1}\right) = (x-1)\left(2 - \frac{2x}{x-1}\right)$
$$3x - 5 = 2x - 2 - 2x$$
$$3x - 5 = -2$$
$$3x = 3$$
$$x = 1$$
Since replacing x by 1 gives 0 in the denominator, 1 is an extraneous root. The solution set is $\emptyset$.

18. $\frac{x-3}{x+2} = 3 - \frac{1-2x}{x+2}$
$$(x+2)\left(\frac{x-3}{x+2}\right) = (x+2)\left(3 - \frac{1-2x}{x+2}\right)$$
$$x - 3 = 3(x+2) - (1-2x)$$
$$x - 3 = 3x + 6 - 1 + 2x$$
$$x - 3 = 5x + 5$$
$$-8 = 4x$$
$$-2 = x$$
Since $x + 2$ is in the denominator -2 is an extraneous root. The solution set is $\emptyset$.

19. $x + 1 + \frac{2x-5}{x-5} = \frac{x}{x-5}$
$$(x-5)\left(x + 1 + \frac{2x-5}{x-5}\right) = (x-5)\frac{x}{x-5}$$
$$x^2 - 4x - 5 + 2x - 5 = x$$
$$x^2 - 3x - 10 = 0$$
$$(x-5)(x+2) = 0$$
$$x = 5 \text{ or } x = -2$$
Since $x - 5$ is in the denominator, 5 is an extraneous root. The solution set is $\{-2\}$

20. $\frac{x-3}{2} - \frac{1}{x-3} = \frac{8-3x}{x-3}$
$$2(x-3)\left(\frac{x-3}{2} - \frac{1}{x-3}\right) = 2(x-3)\frac{8-3x}{x-3}$$
$$x^2 - 6x + 9 - 2 = 16 - 6x$$
$$x^2 - 9 = 0$$
$$(x-3)(x+3) = 0$$
$$x = 3 \text{ or } x = -3$$
Since $x - 3$ is in the denominator, 3 is an extraneous root. The solution set is $\{-3\}$.

21. $\frac{2}{x+2} + \frac{x}{x-3} + \frac{1}{x^2-x-6} = 0$
Multiply each side by $(x+2)(x-3)$.
$$(x-3)2 + (x+2)x + 1 = 0$$
$$2x - 6 + x^2 + 2x + 1 = 0$$
$$x^2 + 4x - 5 = 0$$
$$(x+5)(x-1) = 0$$
$$x = -5 \text{ or } x = 1$$
The solution set is $\{-5, 1\}$.

22. $\frac{x-4}{x^2+2x-15} = 2 - \frac{2}{x-3}$
Multiply each side by $(x-3)(x+5)$.
$$x - 4 = 2(x-3)(x+5) - 2(x+5)$$
$$x - 4 = 2x^2 + 4x - 30 - 2x - 10$$
$$0 = 2x^2 + x - 36$$
$$0 = (2x+9)(x-4)$$
$$2x + 9 = 0 \text{ or } x - 4 = 0$$
$$x = -\frac{9}{2} \text{ or } x = 4$$
The solution set is $\{-\frac{9}{2}, 4\}$

23. $\frac{2}{x} = \frac{3}{4}$
$$3x = 8$$
$$x = \frac{8}{3}$$
Solution set: $\left\{\frac{8}{3}\right\}$

24. $\frac{5}{x} = \frac{7}{9}$
$$7x = 45$$
$$x = \frac{45}{7}$$
The solution set is $\left\{\frac{45}{7}\right\}$.

25. $\frac{a}{3} = \frac{-1}{4}$
$$4a = -3$$
$$a = -\frac{3}{4}$$
Solution set: $\left\{-\frac{3}{4}\right\}$

26. $\frac{b}{5} = \frac{-3}{7}$
$$7b = -15$$
$$b = -\frac{15}{7}$$
The solution set is $\left\{-\frac{15}{7}\right\}$.

27. $\frac{-5}{7} = \frac{2}{x}$
$$-5x = 14$$
$$x = -\frac{14}{5}$$
Solution set: $\left\{-\frac{14}{5}\right\}$

28. $-\frac{3}{8} = \frac{5}{x}$

$-3x = 40$

$x = -\frac{40}{3}$

The solution set is $\left\{-\frac{40}{3}\right\}$.

29. $\frac{10}{x} = \frac{20}{x+20}$

$10x + 200 = 20x$

$-10x = -200$

$x = 20$

Solution set: $\{20\}$

30. $\frac{x}{5} = \frac{x+2}{3}$

$3x = 5x + 10$

$-2x = 10$

$x = -5$

The solution set is $\{-5\}$.

31. $\frac{2}{x+1} = \frac{x-1}{4}$

$x^2 - 1 = 8$

$x^2 - 9 = 0$

$(x-3)(x+3) = 0$

$x = 3 \quad \text{or} \quad x = -3$

Solution set: $\{-3, 3\}$

32. $\frac{3}{x-2} = \frac{x+2}{7}$

$x^2 - 4 = 21$

$x^2 - 25 = 0$

$(x-5)(x+5) = 0$

$x - 5 = 0 \quad \text{or} \quad x + 5 = 0$

$x = 5 \quad \text{or} \quad x = -5$

The solution set is $\{-5, 5\}$.

33. $\frac{x}{6} = \frac{5}{x-1}$

$x^2 - x = 30$

$x^2 - x - 30 = 0$

$(x-6)(x+5) = 0$

$x = 6 \quad \text{or} \quad x = -5$

Solution set: $\{-5, 6\}$

34. $\frac{x+5}{2} = \frac{3}{x}$

$x^2 + 5x = 6$

$x^2 + 5x - 6 = 0$

$(x+6)(x-1) = 0$

$x + 6 = 0 \quad \text{or} \quad x - 1 = 0$

$x = -6 \quad \text{or} \quad x = 1$

The solution set is $\{-6, 1\}$.

35. $\frac{x}{x-3} = \frac{x+2}{x}$

$x^2 = (x+2)(x-3)$

$x^2 = x^2 - x - 6$

$x = -6$

Solution set: $\{-6\}$

36. $\frac{x+1}{x-5} = \frac{x+2}{x-4}$

$(x+1)(x-4) = (x-5)(x+2)$

$x^2 - 3x - 4 = x^2 - 3x - 10$

$-3x - 4 = -3x - 10$

$-4 = -10$

The solution set is $\emptyset$.

37. $\frac{x-2}{x-3} = \frac{x+5}{x+2}$

$(x-2)(x+2) = (x-3)(x+5)$

$x^2 - 4 = x^2 + 2x - 15$

$-2x = -11$

$x = \frac{11}{2}$

Solution set: $\left\{\frac{11}{2}\right\}$

38. $\frac{x}{x+5} = \frac{x}{x-2}$

$x^2 - 2x = x^2 + 5x$

$-2x = 5x$

$-7x = 0$

$x = 0$

The solution set is $\{0\}$.

39. $\frac{a}{9} = \frac{4}{a}$

$a^2 = 36$

$a^2 - 36 = 0$

$(a-6)(a+6) = 0$

$a = 6 \quad \text{or} \quad a = -6$

Solution set: $\{-6, 6\}$

40. $\frac{y}{3} = \frac{27}{y}$

$y^2 = 81$

$y^2 - 81 = 0$

$(y-9)(y+9) = 0$

$y - 9 = 0 \text{ or } y + 9 = 0$

$y = 9 \text{ or } \quad y = -9$

The solution set is $\{-9, 9\}$.

41. $4(x-2)\left(\frac{1}{2(x-2)}+\frac{1}{x-2}\right)$
$= 4(x-2)\cdot\frac{1}{4}$
$2+4=x-2$
$8=x$
Solution set: $\{8\}$

42. $\frac{7}{3x-9}-\frac{1}{x-3}=\frac{4}{9}$

$\frac{7}{3(x-3)}-\frac{1}{x-3}=\frac{4}{9}$
$9(x-3)\left(\frac{7}{3(x-3)}-\frac{1}{x-3}\right)=9(x-3)\frac{4}{9}$

$3(7)-9=4(x-3)$
$12=4x-12$
$24=4x$
$6=x$
The solution set is $\{6\}$.

43. $\frac{x-2}{4}=\frac{x-2}{x}$
$x^2-2x=4x-8$
$x^2-6x+8=0$
$(x-2)(x-4)=0$
$x=2$ or $x=4$
Solution set: $\{2, 4\}$

44. $\frac{y+5}{2}=\frac{y+5}{y}$
$2y\left(\frac{y+5}{2}\right)=2y\left(\frac{y+5}{y}\right)$
$y^2+5y=2y+10$
$y^2+3y-10=0$
$(y+5)(y-2)=0$
$y+5=0$ or $y-2=0$
$y=-5$ or $y=2$
Solution set: $\{-5, 2\}$

45. $2(x+2)(x-1)\left(\frac{5}{2(x+2)}-\frac{1}{x-1}\right)$
$= 2(x+2)(x-1)\left(\frac{3}{x+2}\right)$
$5x-5-2(x+2)= 6(x-1)$
$5x-5-2x-4=6x-6$
$3x-9=6x-6$
$-3x=3$
$x=-1$
Solution set: $\{-1\}$

46. $\frac{5}{2w+6}-\frac{1}{w-1}=\frac{1}{w+3}$
$\frac{5}{2(w+3)}-\frac{1}{w-1}=\frac{1}{w+3}$

$2(w+3)(w-1)\left(\frac{5}{2(w+3)}-\frac{1}{w-1}\right)$
$= 2(w+3)(w-1)\frac{1}{w+3}$
$5(w-1)-2(w+3)=2(w-1)$
$5w-5-2w-6=2w-2$
$3w-11=2w-2$
$w=9$
The solution set is $\{9\}$.

47. $\frac{5}{x-3}=\frac{x}{x-3}$
$5x-15=x^2-3x$
$-x^2+8x-15=0$
$x^2-8x+15=0$
$(x-3)(x-5)=0$
$x=3$ or $x=5$
Since replacing x by 3 causes 0 to appear in a denominator, 3 is an extraneous root. The solution set is $\{5\}$.

48. $\frac{6}{a+2}=\frac{a}{a+2}$
$6a+12=a^2+2a$
$-a^2+4a+12=0$
$a^2-4a-12=0$
$(a-6)(a+2)=0$
$a-6=0$ or $a+2=0$
$a=6$ or $a=-2$
Since the value of $a+2$ is 0 if a is replaced by -2, -2 is not a solution to the equation. The solution set is $\{6\}$.

49. $\frac{w}{6}=\frac{3}{2w}$
$2w^2=18$
$w^2=9$
$w^2-9=0$
$(w-3)(w+3)=0$
$w=3$ or $w=-3$
Solution set: $\{-3, 3\}$

50. $\frac{2m}{5}=\frac{10}{m}$
$2m^2=50$
$m^2=25$
$m^2-25=0$
$(m-5)(m+5)=0$
$m-5=0$ or $m+5=0$
$m=5$ or $m=-5$

The solution set is $\{-5, 5\}$.

51. $6(2x-1)(x+2)\left(\dfrac{5}{2(2x-1)} - \dfrac{-1}{2x-1}\right)$

$\qquad = 6(2x-1)(x+2)\left(\dfrac{7}{3(x+2)}\right)$

$15(x+2) + 6(x+2) = 14(2x-1)$
$15x + 30 + 6x + 12 = 28x - 14$
$\qquad 21x + 42 = 28x - 14$
$\qquad\qquad -7x = -56$
$\qquad\qquad\quad x = 8$

Solution set: $\{8\}$

52. $\dfrac{5}{x+1} - \dfrac{1}{1-x} = \dfrac{1}{x^2-1}$

$(x-1)(x+1)\left(\dfrac{5}{x+1} - \dfrac{1}{1-x}\right)$

$\qquad = (x-1)(x+1)\dfrac{1}{x^2-1}$

$5(x-1) - (x+1)(-1) = 1$
$\qquad 5x - 5 + x + 1 = 1$
$\qquad\qquad\quad 6x = 5$
$\qquad\qquad\quad\ x = \dfrac{5}{6}$

The solution set is $\left\{\dfrac{5}{6}\right\}$.

53. $\qquad \dfrac{5}{x} = \dfrac{2}{5}$

$\qquad 2x = 25$

$\qquad\ x = \dfrac{25}{2}$

Solution set: $\left\{\dfrac{25}{2}\right\}$

54. $\qquad \dfrac{-3}{2x} = \dfrac{1}{-5}$

$\qquad 2x = 15$

$\qquad\ x = \dfrac{15}{2}$

The solution set is $\left\{\dfrac{15}{2}\right\}$.

55. $(x-3)(x+3)\left(\dfrac{5}{x^2-9} + \dfrac{2}{x+3}\right)$

$\qquad = (x-3)(x+3)\left(\dfrac{1}{x-3}\right)$

$\qquad 5 + 2x - 6 = x + 3$
$\qquad\qquad\quad x = 4$

Solution set: $\{4\}$

56. $\dfrac{1}{x-2} - \dfrac{2}{x+3} = \dfrac{11}{x^2+x-6}$

$(x-2)(x+3)\left(\dfrac{1}{x-2} - \dfrac{2}{x+3}\right)$

$\qquad = (x-2)(x+3)\dfrac{11}{x^2+x-6}$

$x + 3 - 2(x-2) = 11$
$x + 3 - 2x + 4 = 11$

$\qquad -x + 7 = 11$
$\qquad\quad -x = 4$
$\qquad\qquad x = -4$

The solution set is $\{-4\}$.

57. $(x-1)(x^2+x+1)\left(\dfrac{9}{x^3-1} - \dfrac{1}{x-1}\right)$

$\qquad = (x-1)(x^2+x+1)\left(\dfrac{2}{x^2+x+1}\right)$

$9 - (x^2+x+1) = 2(x-1)$
$\ 9 - x^2 - x - 1 = 2x - 2$
$\quad -x^2 - 3x + 10 = 0$
$\qquad x^2 + 3x - 10 = 0$
$\qquad (x+5)(x-2) = 0$
$\qquad x = -5 \ \text{ or } \ x = 2$

Solution set: $\{-5, 2\}$

58. $\dfrac{x+4}{x^3+8} + \dfrac{x+2}{x^2-2x+4} = \dfrac{11}{2x+4}$

$\dfrac{x+4}{(x+2)(x^2-2x+4)} + \dfrac{x+2}{x^2-2x+4}$

$\qquad = \dfrac{11}{2(x+2)}$

Multiplying each rational expression by the
LCD $2(x+2)(x^2-2x+4)$ gives us the
following equation.

$2(x+4) + 2(x+2)(x+2) = 11(x^2-2x+4)$
$2x + 8 + 2x^2 + 8x + 8 = 11x^2 - 22x + 44$
$\qquad 2x^2 + 10x + 16 = 11x^2 - 22x + 44$
$\qquad -9x^2 + 32x - 28 = 0$
$\qquad\ 9x^2 - 32x + 28 = 0$
$\qquad (9x-14)(x-2) = 0$
$\qquad 9x - 14 = 0 \ \text{ or } \ x - 2 = 0$
$\qquad\quad x = \dfrac{14}{9} \ \text{ or } \quad x = 2$

The solution set is $\left\{\dfrac{14}{9}, 2\right\}$.

59. $\dfrac{300{,}000}{250{,}000} = \dfrac{200{,}000}{a}$

$\qquad 300{,}000a = 200{,}000 \cdot 250{,}000$

$\qquad\qquad a = \dfrac{200{,}000 \cdot 250{,}000}{300{,}000}$

$\qquad\qquad a = \$166{,}666.67$

60. $\dfrac{400{,}000}{300{,}000} = \dfrac{d}{150{,}000}$

$\qquad 300{,}000d = 400{,}000 \cdot 150{,}000$

$\qquad\qquad d = \dfrac{400{,}000 \cdot 150{,}000}{300{,}000}$

$\qquad\qquad d = \$200{,}000$

61.
$$\frac{2}{23} = \frac{12}{p}$$
$$2p = 12 \cdot 23$$
$$p = \frac{12 \cdot 23}{2} = 138$$

62. In the sample of 24, there were 21 tapes not rewound.
$$\frac{21}{24} = \frac{n}{872}$$
$$24n = 21 \cdot 872$$
$$n = \frac{21 \cdot 872}{24} = 763$$

63. Let w = the width and $w + 22$ = the length.
$$\frac{7}{6} = \frac{w + 22}{w}$$
$$7w = 6w + 132$$
$$w = 132$$
$$w + 22 = 154$$
The width is 132 cm and the length is 154 cm.

64. Let c = the number of cars and $c - 142$ = the number of pickups.
$$\frac{2}{3} = \frac{c - 142}{c}$$
$$2c = 3c - 426$$
$$426 = c$$
$$c - 142 = 284$$
The dealer sold 426 cars and 284 pickups.

65.
$$1,000,000 = \frac{4,000,000p}{100 - p}$$
$$100,000,000 - 1,000,000p = 4,000,000p$$
$$100,000,000 = 5,000,000p$$
$$p = 20$$
For $1 million, 20% of the pollution can be cleaned up. For $100 million, 96% of the pollution can be cleaned up.

66. $2,000,000 = \dfrac{1,000,000 + 2,000,000p}{100 - p}$

$200,000,000 - 2,000,000p$
$$= 1,000,000 + 2,000,000p$$
$$199,000,000 = 4,000,000p$$
$$p = 49.75$$
For $2 million she can expect 49.75% of the votes. From the graph we see that for $4 million, she can expect approximately 66% of the vote.

67. a) Let s = the amount invested in stocks and $s - 20,000$ = the amount invested in bonds. For a wealth-building portfolio, the ratio of stocks to bonds should be 65 to 30:

$$\frac{65}{30} = \frac{s}{s - 20,000}$$
$$65s - 1,300,000 = 30s$$
$$35s = 1,300,000$$
$$s = \$37,142.86$$
$$s - 20,000 = \$17,142.86$$
She invested $17,142.86 in bonds.

b) Since the stock investment is 65% of her bonus, b, we have $0.65b = 37,142.86$ or $b = 37,142.86/0.30 = \$57,142.86$.

68. a) $N = (1 + 1/5)465 - 1 = 557$

b) $255 = (1 + 1/C)224 - 1$
$$256 = (1 + 1/C)224$$
$$256 = 224 + \frac{224}{C}$$
$$32 = \frac{224}{C}$$
$$32C = 224$$
$$C = 7$$

70. a) 0, 1 **b)** 1 **c)** -1

6.6 WARM-UPS

6.6 EXERCISES

1. $(x - 2)\left(\dfrac{y - 3}{x - 2}\right) = (x - 2)(5)$
$$y - 3 = 5x - 10$$
$$y = 5x - 7$$

2. $\dfrac{y - 4}{x - 7} = -6$

$(x - 7)\left(\dfrac{y - 4}{x - 7}\right) = (x - 7)(-6)$
$$y - 4 = -6x + 42$$
$$y = -6x + 46$$

3. $(x-6)\left(\dfrac{y+1}{x-6}\right) = -\dfrac{1}{3}(x-6)$

$\qquad y+1 = -\dfrac{1}{3}x + 2$

$\qquad\quad y = -\dfrac{1}{3}x + 1$

4. $\dfrac{y+7}{x-2} = \dfrac{-2}{3}$

$(x-2)\left(\dfrac{y+7}{x-2}\right) = (x-2)\left(\dfrac{-2}{3}\right)$

$\qquad\quad y+7 = -\dfrac{2}{3}x + \dfrac{4}{3}$

$\qquad\qquad y = -\dfrac{2}{3}x + \dfrac{4}{3} - 7$

$\qquad\qquad y = -\dfrac{2}{3}x - \dfrac{17}{3}$

5. $(x-b)\left(\dfrac{y-a}{x-b}\right) = m(x-b)$

$\qquad y-a = mx - mb$

$\qquad\quad y = mx - bm + a$

6. $\dfrac{y-h}{x-k} = a$

$(x-k)\left(\dfrac{y-h}{x-k}\right) = (x-k)a$

$\qquad y-h = ax - ak$

$\qquad\quad y = ax - ak + h$

7. $(x+5)\left(\dfrac{y-2}{x+5}\right) = -\dfrac{7}{3}(x+5)$

$\qquad y-2 = -\dfrac{7}{3}x - \dfrac{35}{3}$

$\qquad\quad y = -\dfrac{7}{3}x - \dfrac{35}{3} + \dfrac{6}{3}$

$\qquad\quad y = -\dfrac{7}{3}x - \dfrac{29}{3}$

8. $\dfrac{y-3}{x+1} = -\dfrac{9}{4}$

$(x+1)\left(\dfrac{y-3}{x+1}\right) = (x+1)\left(-\dfrac{9}{4}\right)$

$\qquad y-3 = -\dfrac{9}{4}x - \dfrac{9}{4}$

$\qquad\quad y = -\dfrac{9}{4}x - \dfrac{9}{4} + 3$

$\qquad\quad y = -\dfrac{9}{4}x + \dfrac{3}{4}$

9. $f \cdot M = f \cdot \dfrac{F}{f}$

$\qquad fM = F$

$\qquad\ f = \dfrac{F}{M}$

10. $P = \dfrac{A}{1+rt}$

$(1+rt)P = (1+rt)\dfrac{A}{1+rt}$

$P(1+rt) = A$

$\qquad A = P(1+rt)$

11. $4 \cdot A = 4 \cdot \dfrac{\pi}{4} \cdot D^2$

$\qquad 4A = \pi D^2$

$\qquad D^2 = \dfrac{4A}{\pi}$

12. $V = \pi r^2 h$

$\dfrac{V}{\pi h} = \dfrac{\pi r^2 h}{\pi h}$

$\dfrac{V}{\pi h} = r^2$

$\quad r^2 = \dfrac{V}{\pi h}$

13. $Fr^2 = km_1 m_2$

$\quad m_1 = \dfrac{Fr^2}{km_2}$

14. $F = \dfrac{mv^2}{r}$

$r \cdot F = r \cdot \dfrac{mv^2}{r}$

$\quad rF = mv^2$

$\dfrac{rF}{m} = \dfrac{mv^2}{m}$

$\dfrac{rF}{m} = v^2$

$\quad v^2 = \dfrac{rF}{m}$

15. $pqf\left(\dfrac{1}{p} + \dfrac{1}{q}\right) = pqf \cdot \dfrac{1}{f}$

$\qquad qf + pf = pq$

$\qquad qf - pq = -pf$

$\qquad q(f - p) = -pf$

$\qquad\qquad q = \dfrac{-pf}{f - p}$

$\qquad\qquad q = \dfrac{pf}{p - f}$

16. $\dfrac{1}{R} = \dfrac{1}{R_1} + \dfrac{1}{R_2}$

$RR_1R_2 \cdot \dfrac{1}{R} = RR_1R_2 \cdot \dfrac{1}{R_1} + RR_1R_2 \cdot \dfrac{1}{R_2}$

$\qquad R_1R_2 = RR_2 + RR_1$

$R_1R_2 - RR_1 = RR_2$

$R_1(R_2 - R) = RR_2$

$\qquad\quad R_1 = \dfrac{RR_2}{R_2 - R}$

17. $a^2\left(e^2\right) = a^2\left(1 - \dfrac{b^2}{a^2}\right)$

$\qquad a^2 e^2 = a^2 - b^2$

$a^2 e^2 - a^2 = -b^2$

$a^2(e^2 - 1) = -b^2$

$\qquad\quad a^2 = \dfrac{-b^2}{e^2 - 1} = \dfrac{b^2}{1 - e^2}$

18.
$$e^2 = 1 - \frac{b^2}{a^2}$$
$$a^2 \cdot e^2 = a^2\left(1 - \frac{b^2}{a^2}\right)$$
$$a^2 e^2 = a^2 - b^2$$
$$b^2 + a^2 e^2 = a^2$$
$$b^2 = a^2 - a^2 e^2$$

19.
$$T_1 T_2 \left(\frac{P_1 V_1}{T_1}\right) = T_1 T_2 \left(\frac{P_2 V_2}{T_2}\right)$$
$$T_2 P_1 V_1 = T_1 P_2 V_2$$
$$\frac{T_2 P_1 V_1}{P_2 V_2} = \frac{T_1 P_2 V_2}{P_2 V_2}$$
$$T_1 = \frac{P_1 V_1 T_2}{P_2 V_2}$$

20.
$$\frac{P_1 V_1}{T_1} = \frac{P_2 V_2}{T_2}$$
$$T_1 T_2 \cdot \frac{P_1 V_1}{T_1} = T_1 T_2 \cdot \frac{P_2 V_2}{T_2}$$
$$T_2 P_1 V_1 = T_1 P_2 V_2$$
$$\frac{T_2 P_1 V_1}{T_1 V_2} = \frac{T_1 P_2 V_2}{T_1 T_2}$$
$$\frac{P_1 V_1 T_2}{T_1 V_2} = P_2$$

21.
$$3V = 3 \cdot \frac{4}{3}\pi r^2 h$$
$$3V = 4\pi r^2 h$$
$$\frac{3V}{4\pi r^2} = \frac{4\pi r^2 h}{4\pi r^2}$$
$$h = \frac{3V}{4\pi r^2}$$

22.
$$h = \frac{S - 2\pi r^2}{2\pi r}$$
$$2\pi r \cdot h = 2\pi r \cdot \frac{S - 2\pi r^2}{2\pi r}$$
$$2\pi r h = S - 2\pi r^2$$
$$2\pi r h + 2\pi r^2 = S$$
$$S = 2\pi r h + 2\pi r^2$$

23.
$$10 = \frac{5}{f}$$
$$10f = 5$$
$$f = \frac{1}{2}$$

24.
$$P = \frac{A}{1 + rt}$$
$$500 = \frac{550}{1 + r(2)}$$

$$500(1 + 2r) = 550$$
$$500 + 1000r = 550$$
$$1000r = 50$$
$$r = \frac{50}{1000} = 0.05$$

25.
$$6\pi = \frac{\pi}{4}D^2$$
$$\frac{4}{\pi} \cdot 6\pi = \frac{4}{\pi} \cdot \frac{\pi}{4}D^2$$
$$24 = D^2$$

26.
$$V = \pi r^2 h$$
$$12\pi = \pi(3)^2 h$$
$$12\pi = 9\pi h$$
$$\frac{12\pi}{9\pi} = h$$
$$h = \frac{12\pi}{9\pi} = \frac{12}{9} = \frac{4}{3}$$

27.
$$32 = k\frac{6 \cdot 8}{4^2}$$
$$32 = 3k$$
$$k = \frac{32}{3}$$

28.
$$F = \frac{mv^2}{r}$$
$$10 = \frac{8(6)^2}{r}$$
$$10r = 8 \cdot 36$$
$$r = \frac{8 \cdot 36}{10} = \frac{144}{5}$$

29.
$$\frac{1}{p} + \frac{1}{1.7} = \frac{1}{2.3}$$
$$\frac{1}{p} = -0.15345$$
$$p = \frac{1}{-0.15345} = -6.517$$

30.
$$\frac{1}{R} = \frac{1}{R_1} + \frac{1}{R_2}$$
$$\frac{1}{1.29} = \frac{1}{0.045} + \frac{1}{R_2}$$
$$\frac{1}{R_2} = \frac{1}{1.29} - \frac{1}{0.045} = -21.447$$
$$R_2 \approx -0.046$$

31.
$$(0.62)^2 = 1 - \frac{(3.5)^2}{a^2}$$
$$-0.6156 = -\frac{12.25}{a^2}$$
$$a^2 = \frac{12.25}{0.6156} = 19.899$$

32.
$$e^2 = 1 - \frac{b^2}{a^2}$$
$$(2.4)^2 = 1 - \frac{b^2}{(3.61)^2}$$
$$(2.4)^2 - 1 = -\frac{b^2}{(3.61)^2}$$
$$4.76 = -\frac{b^2}{(3.61)^2}$$
$$-(3.61)^2(4.76) = b^2$$
$$-62.033 \approx b^2$$

33.
$$25.6 = \frac{4}{3}\pi r^2(3.2)$$
$$25.6 = 13.404r^2$$
$$r^2 = \frac{25.6}{13.404} = 1.910$$

34.
$$h = \frac{S - 2\pi r^2}{2\pi r}$$
$$3.6 = \frac{S - 2\pi(2.45)^2}{2\pi(2.45)}$$
$$3.6 = \frac{S - 37.7148}{15.3938}$$
$$3.6(15.3938) = S - 37.7148$$
$$3.6(15.3938) + 37.7148 = S$$
$$93.133 \approx S$$

35. Let $x =$ her walking speed and $x + 10 =$ her riding speed. Since $T = D/R$, her time to school is $7/(x+10)$ and her time to the post office is $2/x$. Since the times are equal, we can write
$$\frac{2}{x} = \frac{7}{x + 10}$$
$$7x = 2x + 20$$
$$5x = 20$$
$$x = 4$$
She walks 4 mph.

36. Let $x =$ Beverly's speed and $x - 10 =$ Susan's speed. Since $T = D/R$, Beverly's time is $\frac{600}{x}$ hours and Susan's time is $\frac{500}{x-10}$ hours. We can write an equation expressing the fact that their times are equal.
$$\frac{600}{x} = \frac{500}{x - 10}$$
$$600x - 6000 = 500x$$
$$100x = 6000$$
$$x = 60$$
Beverly drives 60 miles per hour.

37. Let $x =$ the speed of each. Since $T = D/R$, Patrick's time is $\frac{40}{x}$ and Guy's time is $\frac{60}{x}$. Since Guy's time is $\frac{1}{5}$ hr longer than Patrick's we can write the equation
$$\frac{60}{x} - \frac{1}{5} = \frac{40}{x}$$
$$5x\left(\frac{60}{x} - \frac{1}{5}\right) = 5x \cdot \frac{40}{x}$$
$$300 - x = 200$$
$$100 = x$$
They are both driving 100 mph. Patrick takes $\frac{40}{100} = \frac{2}{5}$ hr $= 24$ minutes to get to work and Guy takes 12 minutes longer or 36 minutes.

38. Let $x =$ David's speed and $x + 10 =$ Keith's speed. Since $T = D/R$, David's time is $\frac{80}{x}$ hours and Keith's time is $\frac{100}{x+10}$ hours. We can write an equation expressing the fact that Keith's time is $\frac{1}{6}$ of an hour (10 minutes) less than David's.
$$\frac{80}{x} = \frac{100}{x + 10} + \frac{1}{6}$$
$$6x(x + 10)\left(\frac{80}{x}\right) = 6x(x + 10)\left(\frac{100}{x + 10} + \frac{1}{6}\right)$$
$$480(x + 10) = 600x + x(x + 10)$$
$$480x + 4800 = 600x + x^2 + 10x$$
$$-x^2 - 130x + 4800 = 0$$
$$x^2 + 130x - 4800 = 0$$
$$(x - 30)(x + 160) = 0$$
$$x - 30 = 0 \text{ or } x + 160 = 0$$
$$x = 30 \text{ or } \qquad x = -160$$
David's speed is 30 miles per hour.

39. Let $x =$ his walking speed and $x + 6 =$ his running speed. His time walking was $\frac{1}{x}$ hours and his time running was $\frac{5}{x+6}$ hours. Since his total time was 3/4 of an hour, we can write the equation
$$\frac{1}{x} + \frac{5}{x + 6} = \frac{3}{4}$$
$$4x(x + 6)\left(\frac{1}{x} + \frac{5}{x + 6}\right) = 4x(x + 6)\frac{3}{4}$$
$$4x + 24 + 20x = 3x^2 + 18x$$
$$-3x^2 + 6x + 24 = 0$$
$$x^2 - 2x - 8 = 0$$
$$(x - 4)(x + 2) = 0$$
$$x = 4 \text{ or } x = -2$$
Disregard the negative solution. Use $x = 4$ to find that his running speed was 10 mph.

40. Let $x =$ Norma's speed and $x + 15 =$ Marietta's speed. Norma's time is $\frac{12}{x}$ hours and Marietta's time is $\frac{36}{x+15}$ hours. Since their times are equal, we can write the following equation.

$$\frac{12}{x} = \frac{36}{x+15}$$
$$36x = 12x + 180$$
$$24x = 180$$
$$x = \frac{180}{24} = \frac{15}{2} = 7.5$$

Norma's speed is 7.5 miles per hour.

41. Let $x =$ the number of hours for the smaller pump to drain the pool working alone. In one hour of operation, the larger pump drains $\frac{1}{3}$ of the pool, the smaller pump drains $\frac{1}{x}$ of the pool, and together $\frac{1}{2}$ of the pool is emptied.

$$\frac{1}{3} + \frac{1}{x} = \frac{1}{2}$$
$$6x\left(\frac{1}{3} + \frac{1}{x}\right) = 6x\left(\frac{1}{2}\right)$$
$$2x + 6 = 3x$$
$$6 = x$$

The smaller pump would take 6 hours to drain the pool by itself.

42. Let $x =$ the time to do the job working together. Lourdes does $\frac{1}{8}$ of the job per hour and Rafael does $\frac{1}{15}$ of the job per hour. Since they complete $\frac{1}{x}$ of the job per hour when working together, we can write the following equation.

$$\frac{1}{8} + \frac{1}{15} = \frac{1}{x}$$
$$120x\left(\frac{1}{8} + \frac{1}{15}\right) = 120x \cdot \frac{1}{x}$$
$$15x + 8x = 120$$
$$23x = 120$$
$$x = \frac{120}{23}$$

It will take them $\frac{120}{23}$ hours working together.

43. Let $x =$ the number of minutes to fill the tub with the drain left open. In one minute, the faucet fills $\frac{1}{10}$ of the tub, the drain takes $\frac{1}{12}$ of the tub, but the tub is $\frac{1}{x}$ full.

$$\frac{1}{10} - \frac{1}{12} = \frac{1}{x}$$
$$60x\left(\frac{1}{10} - \frac{1}{12}\right) = 60x \cdot \frac{1}{x}$$
$$6x - 5x = 60$$
$$x = 60$$

The tub is filled in 60 minutes.

44. Let $x =$ the time it takes to empty the cookie jar. In one hour, he can empty $\frac{1}{1.5}$ of the cookie jar, while his mother fills $\frac{1}{2}$ of the cookie jar, and this amounts to $\frac{1}{x}$ of the jar being eaten.

$$\frac{1}{1.5} - \frac{1}{2} = \frac{1}{x}$$
$$6x\left(\frac{1}{1.5} - \frac{1}{2}\right) = 6x \cdot \frac{1}{x}$$
$$4x - 3x = 6$$
$$x = 6$$

In 6 hours the cookie jar will be empty.

45. Let $x =$ their time working together. Since Gina takes 90 minutes and Hilda works twice as fast, Hilda can do the job alone in 45 minutes. Hilda does $\frac{1}{45}$ of the job per minute and Gina does $\frac{1}{90}$ or the job per minute. Since together they do $\frac{1}{x}$ of the job per minute, we can write the following equation.

$$\frac{1}{45} + \frac{1}{90} = \frac{1}{x}$$
$$90x\left(\frac{1}{45} + \frac{1}{90}\right) = 90x \cdot \frac{1}{x}$$
$$2x + x = 90$$
$$3x = 90$$
$$x = 30$$

It will take them 30 minutes working together.

46. Let $x =$ Betsy's time alone. Julie does $\frac{1}{12}$ of the fence per hour and Betsy does $\frac{1}{x}$ of the fence per hour. Since together they do $\frac{1}{5}$ of the fence per hour, we can write the following equation.

$$\frac{1}{12} + \frac{1}{x} = \frac{1}{5}$$
$$60x\left(\frac{1}{12} + \frac{1}{x}\right) = 60x \cdot \frac{1}{5}$$
$$5x + 60 = 12x$$
$$60 = 7x$$
$$\frac{60}{7} = x$$

Betsy could paint the fence in $\frac{60}{7}$ hours working alone.

47. Let $x =$ the number of pounds of apples and $x + 2 =$ the number of pounds of oranges. The apples sell for $\frac{8.80}{x}$ dollars per pound and the oranges sell for $\frac{5.28}{x+2}$. The apples cost twice as much per pound is expressed as

$$\frac{8.80}{x} = 2\left(\frac{5.28}{x+2}\right)$$
$$\frac{8.80}{x} = \frac{10.56}{x+2}$$
$$8.80x + 17.60 = 10.56x$$
$$17.60 = 1.76x$$
$$10 = x$$

She bought 10 pounds of apples and 12 pounds of oranges.

48. Let x = the price per pound of rabbit meat and $3x$ = the price per pound of raccoon meat. The number of pounds of rabbit meat sold was $\frac{72}{x}$ and the number of pounds of raccoon meat sold was $\frac{72}{3x}$. Since he sold a total of 160 pounds of meat, we can write the following equation.

$$\frac{72}{x} + \frac{72}{3x} = 160$$
$$3x\left(\frac{72}{x} + \frac{72}{3x}\right) = 3x \cdot 160$$
$$216 + 72 = 480x$$
$$288 = 480x$$
$$0.60 = x$$
$$1.80 = 3x$$

Rabbit meat is $0.60 per pound and raccoon is $1.80 per pound.

49.
$$\frac{1}{2} = \frac{1}{3} + \frac{1}{R_2}$$
$$6R_2\left(\frac{1}{2}\right) = 6R_2\left(\frac{1}{3} + \frac{1}{R_2}\right)$$
$$3R_2 = 2R_2 + 6$$
$$R_2 = 6 \text{ ohms}$$

50.
$$R_1 = R_2 + 1$$
$$\frac{1}{1.2} = \frac{1}{R_2+1} + \frac{1}{R_2}$$
$$1.2R_2(R_2+1)\frac{1}{1.2}$$
$$= 1.2R_2(R_2+1)\left(\frac{1}{R_2+1} + \frac{1}{R_2}\right)$$

$$R_2^2 + R_2 = 1.2R_2 + 1.2R_2 + 1.2$$
$$R_2^2 - 1.4R_2 - 1.2 = 0$$
$$10R_2^2 - 14R_2 - 12 = 0$$
$$5R_2^2 - 7R_2 - 6 = 0$$
$$(5R_2 + 3)(R_2 - 2) = 0$$
$$R_2 = -\frac{3}{5} \quad \text{or} \quad R_2 = 2$$

Since resistance is not negative, we have $R_2 = 2$ ohms and $R_1 = 3$ ohms.

51. a) Let x = the number in the original group. Their cost is $\frac{24,000}{x}$ per person. For 40 more people, the cost is $\frac{24,000}{x+40}$. We have

$$\frac{24,000}{x} = \frac{24,000}{x+40} + 100$$
$$x(x+40)\frac{24,000}{x} = x(x+40)\left(\frac{24,000}{x+40} + 100\right)$$
$$24,000x + 960,000$$
$$= 24,000x + 100x^2 + 4000x$$
$$100x^2 + 4000x - 960,000 = 0$$
$$x^2 + 40x - 9600 = 0$$
$$(x-80)(x+120) = 0$$
$$x = 80 \quad \text{or} \quad x = -120$$

There are 80 people in the initial group.

b) $C(n) = \frac{24,000}{n}$ where n is the number of people sharing the cost and $C(n)$ is the cost per person in dollars.

52. Let x = the original number scheduled for the trip. The originally the cost was $\frac{1500}{x}$ per person. When 5 failed to show the cost was $\frac{1500}{x-5}$.

$$\frac{1500}{x-5} - 25 = \frac{1500}{x}$$
$$x(x-5)\left(\frac{1500}{x-5} - 25\right) = x(x-5)\frac{1500}{x}$$
$$1500x - 25x^2 + 125x = 1500x - 7500$$
$$-25x^2 + 125x + 7500 = 0$$
$$x^2 - 5x - 300 = 0$$
$$(x-20)(x+15) = 0$$
$$x = 20 \quad \text{or} \quad x = -15$$

There were originally 20 people scheduled for the trip.

53. Let x = the number of days for both dogs to eat a 50 pound bag together. Muffy eats at a rate of $\frac{25}{28}$ pounds per day, Missy eats at the rate of $\frac{25}{23}$ pounds per day, and together they eat at a rate of $\frac{50}{x}$ pounds per day.

$$\frac{25}{28} + \frac{25}{23} = \frac{50}{x}$$
$$1.9798 = \frac{50}{x}$$
$$x = \frac{50}{1.9798} \approx 25.255$$

It would take 25.255 days for them to eat 50 pounds of dog food together.

54. Let x = the time for the rats and mice to finish the box working together. The rats eat

245

$\frac{1}{13.6}$ of the box per minute and the mice eat $\frac{1}{34.7}$ of the box per minute. Since they eat $\frac{1}{x}$ of the box per minute when working together, we can write the following equation.

$$\frac{1}{x} = \frac{1}{13.6} + \frac{1}{34.7}$$
$$\frac{1}{x} = 0.102347855$$
$$x = 9.7706$$

They can finish the box in 9.7706 minutes when working together.

Enriching Your Mathematical Word Power
Chapter 6
1. b   2. d   3. b   4. d   5. b
6. a   7. a   8. d   9. a   10. b
11. d   12. a   13. c   14. d

CHAPTER 6   REVIEW

1. If $x = 1$, then $3x - 3 = 0$. So the domain is $\{x \mid x \neq 1\}$.

2. If $x = \pm 5$, then $x^2 - 25 = 0$. So the domain is $\{x \mid x \neq -5 \text{ and } x \neq 5\}$.

3. Solve $x^2 - x - 2 = 0$
$$(x - 2)(x + 1) = 0$$
$$x - 2 = 0 \text{ or } x + 1 = 0$$
$$x = 2 \text{ or } \quad x = -1$$
The domain is $\{x \mid x \neq -1 \text{ and } x \neq 2\}$.

4. Solve $x^3 - x^2 = 0$
$$x^2(x - 1) = 0$$
$$x^2 = 0 \text{ or } x - 1 = 0$$
$$x = 0 \text{ or } \quad x = 1$$
The domain is $\{x \mid x \neq 0 \text{ and } x \neq 1\}$.

5. $\dfrac{a^3 bc^3}{a^5 b^2 c} = \dfrac{c^2}{a^2 b}$

6. $\dfrac{x^4 - 1}{3x^2 - 3} = \dfrac{(x^2 - 1)(x^2 + 1)}{3(x^2 - 1)} = \dfrac{x^2 + 1}{3}$

7. $\dfrac{2 \cdot 2 \cdot 17 x^3}{3 \cdot 17 xy} = \dfrac{4x^2}{3y}$

8. $\dfrac{5x^2 - 15x + 10}{5x - 10} = \dfrac{5(x - 2)(x - 1)}{5(x - 2)}$
$$= x - 1$$

9. $\dfrac{a^3 b^2 b(a - b)}{b^3 a(-a)(a - b)} = -a$

10. $\dfrac{x^3 - 1}{3x} \cdot \dfrac{6x^2}{x - 1}$
$$= \dfrac{(x - 1)(x^2 + x + 1)}{3x} \cdot \dfrac{3x \cdot 2x}{x - 1}$$
$$= (x^2 + x + 1)2x = 2x^3 + 2x^2 + 2x$$

11. $\dfrac{w - 4}{3w} \cdot \dfrac{3 \cdot 3w}{2(w - 4)} = \dfrac{3}{2}$

12. $\dfrac{x^3 - xy^2}{y} \div \dfrac{x^3 + 2x^2 y + xy^2}{3y}$

$$= \dfrac{x(x - y)(x + y)}{y} \cdot \dfrac{3y}{x(x + y)^2}$$
$$= \dfrac{3(x - y)}{x + y} = \dfrac{3x - 3y}{x + y}$$

13. Since $6x = 2 \cdot 3x$, $3x - 6 = 3(x - 2)$, and $x^2 - 2x = x(x - 2)$, the LCM $= 6x(x - 2)$.

14. Since $x^3 - 8 = (x - 2)(x^2 + 2x + 4)$, $x^2 - 4 = (x - 2)(x + 2)$, and $2x + 8 = 2(x + 4)$, the LCM is $2(x - 2)(x + 2)(x + 4)(x^2 + 2x + 4)$ or $2(x + 2)(x + 4)(x^3 - 8)$.

15. Since $6ab^3 = 2 \cdot 3b^3$ and $4a^5 b^2 = 2 \cdot 2a^5 b^2$, the LCM $= 2 \cdot 2 \cdot 3a^5 b^3 = 12a^5 b^3$.

16. Since $4x^2 - 9 = (2x - 3)(2x + 3)$ and $4x^2 + 12x + 9 = (2x + 3)^2$, the LCM is $(2x - 3)(2x + 3)^2$.

17. $\dfrac{3(x + 3)}{2(x - 3)(x + 3)} + \dfrac{1 \cdot 2}{(x - 3)(x + 3)2}$

$$= \dfrac{3x + 9}{2(x - 3)(x + 3)} + \dfrac{2}{2(x - 3)(x + 3)}$$

$$= \dfrac{3x + 11}{2(x - 3)(x + 3)}$$

18. $\dfrac{3}{x - 3} - \dfrac{5}{x + 4}$

$$= \dfrac{3(x + 4)}{(x - 3)(x + 4)} - \dfrac{5(x - 3)}{(x + 4)(x - 3)}$$

$$= \dfrac{3x + 12}{(x - 3)(x + 4)} - \dfrac{5x - 15}{(x - 3)(x + 4)}$$

$$= \dfrac{3x + 12 - 5x + 15}{(x - 3)(x + 4)} = \dfrac{-2x + 27}{(x - 3)(x + 4)}$$

19. $\dfrac{w \cdot a}{ab^2 \cdot a} - \dfrac{5 \cdot b}{a^2 b \cdot b} = \dfrac{aw - 5b}{a^2 b^2}$

20. $\dfrac{x}{x-1} + \dfrac{3x}{x^2 - 1}$

$= \dfrac{x(x+1)}{(x-1)(x+1)} + \dfrac{3x}{(x+1)(x-1)}$

$= \dfrac{x^2 + x + 3x}{(x-1)(x+1)} = \dfrac{x^2 + 4x}{(x-1)(x+1)}$

21. $\dfrac{30x\left(\frac{3}{2x} - \frac{4}{5x}\right)}{30x\left(\frac{1}{3} - \frac{2}{x}\right)} = \dfrac{45 - 24}{10x - 60} = \dfrac{21}{10x - 60}$

22. $\dfrac{\frac{5}{x-2} - \frac{4}{4 - x^2}}{\frac{3}{x+2} - \frac{1}{2-x}} = \dfrac{\frac{5}{x-2} - \frac{4}{(2-x)(2+x)}}{\frac{3}{x+2} - \frac{1}{2-x}}$

$= \dfrac{\left(\frac{5}{x-2} - \frac{4}{(2-x)(2+x)}\right)(x-2)(x+2)}{\left(\frac{3}{x+2} - \frac{1}{2-x}\right)(x-2)(x+2)}$

$= \dfrac{5(x+2) - 4(-1)}{3(x-2) - 1(-1)(x+2)}$

$= \dfrac{5x + 10 + 4}{3x - 6 + x + 2}$

$= \dfrac{5x + 14}{4x - 4}$

23. $\dfrac{(y-2)\left(\frac{1}{y-2} - 3\right)}{(y-2)\left(\frac{5}{y-2} + 4\right)} = \dfrac{1 - 3(y-2)}{5 + 4(y-2)}$

$= \dfrac{7 - 3y}{4y - 3}$

24. $\dfrac{\frac{a}{b^2} - \frac{b}{a^3}}{\frac{a}{b} + \frac{b}{a^2}} = \dfrac{\left(\frac{a}{b^2} - \frac{b}{a^3}\right)a^3 b^2}{\left(\frac{a}{b} + \frac{b}{a^2}\right)a^3 b^2} = \dfrac{a^4 - b^3}{a^4 b + ab^3}$

25. $\dfrac{a^2 b^3 (a^{-2} - b^{-3})}{a^2 b^3 (a^{-1} b^{-2})} = \dfrac{b^3 - a^2}{ab}$

26. $p^{-1} + pq^{-2} = \dfrac{(p^{-1} + pq^{-2})pq^2}{pq^2}$

$= \dfrac{q^2 + p^2}{pq^2}$

27. $\dfrac{-3}{8} = \dfrac{2}{x}$

$-3x = 16$

$x = -\dfrac{16}{3}$

Solution set: $\left\{-\dfrac{16}{3}\right\}$

28. $\dfrac{2}{x} + \dfrac{5}{2x} = 1$

$2x\left(\dfrac{2}{x} + \dfrac{5}{2x}\right) = 2x \cdot 1$

$4 + 5 = 2x$

$9 = 2x$

$\dfrac{9}{2} = x$

The solution set is $\left\{\dfrac{9}{2}\right\}$.

29. $(a-5)(a+5)\left(\dfrac{15}{a^2 - 25} + \dfrac{1}{a-5}\right)$

$= (a-5)(a+5)\left(\dfrac{6}{a+5}\right)$

$15 + a + 5 = 6a - 30$

$-5a = -50$

$a = 10$

Solution set: $\{10\}$

30. $2 + \dfrac{3}{x-5} = \dfrac{x-1}{x-5}$

$(x-5)\left(2 + \dfrac{3}{x-5}\right) = (x-5)\dfrac{x-1}{x-5}$

$2x - 10 + 3 = x - 1$

$x = 6$

The solution set is $\{6\}$.

31. $m\left(\dfrac{y-b}{m}\right) = mx$

$y - b = mx$

$y = mx + b$

32. $\dfrac{2A}{h} = b_1 + b_2$

$2A = h(b_1 + b_2)$

$A = \dfrac{h}{2}(b_1 + b_2)$

33. $r \cdot F = r\left(\dfrac{mv^2}{r}\right)$

$rF = mv^2$

$m = \dfrac{Fr}{v^2}$

34. $P = \dfrac{A}{1 + rt}$

$P(1 + rt) = A$

$P + Prt = A$

$Prt = A - P$

$r = \dfrac{A - P}{Pt}$

35.
$$3 \cdot A = 3 \cdot \tfrac{2}{3}\pi rh$$
$$3A = 2\pi rh$$
$$\frac{3A}{2\pi h} = \frac{2\pi rh}{2\pi h}$$
$$r = \frac{3A}{2\pi h}$$

36.
$$\frac{a}{w^2} = \frac{2}{b}$$
$$ab = 2w^2$$
$$b = \frac{2w^2}{a}$$

37.
$$(x-7)\left(\frac{y+3}{x-7}\right) = (x-7)2$$
$$y + 3 = 2x - 14$$
$$y = 2x - 17$$

38.
$$\frac{y-5}{x+4} = \frac{-1}{2}$$
$$y - 5 = -\tfrac{1}{2}(x+4)$$
$$y - 5 = -\tfrac{1}{2}x - 2$$
$$y = -\tfrac{1}{2}x + 3$$

39. $\dfrac{1}{x} + \dfrac{1}{3x} = \dfrac{3}{3x} + \dfrac{1}{3x} = \dfrac{4}{3x}$

40.
$$\frac{1}{y} + \frac{3}{2y} = 5$$
$$2y\left(\frac{1}{y} + \frac{3}{2y}\right) = 2y \cdot 5$$
$$2 + 3 = 10y$$
$$5 = 10y$$
$$\tfrac{1}{2} = y$$
The solution set is $\left\{\tfrac{1}{2}\right\}$.

41. $\dfrac{5}{3xy} + \dfrac{7}{6x} = \dfrac{5 \cdot 2}{3xy \cdot 2} + \dfrac{7 \cdot y}{6x \cdot y}$
$$= \frac{10 + 7y}{6xy}$$

42. $\dfrac{2}{x-2} - \dfrac{3}{x} = \dfrac{2(x)}{(x-2)(x)} - \dfrac{3(x-2)}{x(x-2)}$

$$= \frac{2x}{x(x-2)} - \frac{3x-6}{x(x-2)} = \frac{2x - 3x + 6}{x(x-2)}$$

$$= \frac{-x+6}{x(x-2)}$$

43. $\dfrac{5}{a-5} - \dfrac{3}{-1(a+5)} = \dfrac{5}{a-5} + \dfrac{3}{a+5}$
$$= \frac{5(a+5)}{(a-5)(a+5)} + \frac{3(a-5)}{(a+5)(a-5)}$$
$$= \frac{8a+10}{(a-5)(a+5)}$$

44.
$$\frac{2}{x-2} - \frac{3}{x} = \frac{-1}{5x}$$
$$5x(x-2)\left(\frac{2}{x-2} - \frac{3}{x}\right) = 5x(x-2)\left(\frac{-1}{5x}\right)$$
$$10x - 15(x-2) = -x + 2$$
$$10x - 15x + 30 = -x + 2$$
$$-5x + 30 = -x + 2$$
$$-4x = -28$$
$$x = 7$$
The solution set is $\{7\}$.

45. $15(x-2)(x+2)\left(\dfrac{1}{x-2} - \dfrac{1}{x+2}\right)$

$$= 15(x-2)(x+2)\left(\tfrac{1}{15}\right)$$
$$15x + 30 - 15(x-2) = x^2 - 4$$
$$60 = x^2 - 4$$
$$x^2 - 64 = 0$$
$$(x-8)(x+8) = 0$$
$$x = 8 \quad \text{or} \quad x = -8$$
Solution set: $\{-8, 8\}$

46. $\dfrac{2}{x-3} \cdot \dfrac{6x-18}{30} = \dfrac{2}{x-3} \cdot \dfrac{6(x-3)}{6 \cdot 5} = \dfrac{2}{5}$

47. $\dfrac{-3}{x+2} \cdot \dfrac{5(x+2)}{2 \cdot 5} = -\dfrac{3}{2}$

48.
$$\frac{x}{10} = \frac{10}{x}$$
$$x^2 = 100$$
$$x^2 - 100 = 0$$
$$(x-10)(x+10) = 0$$
$$x - 10 = 0 \text{ or } x + 10 = 0$$
$$x = 10 \text{ or } \qquad x = -10$$
The solution set is $\{-10, 10\}$.

49.
$$\frac{x}{-3} = \frac{-27}{x}$$
$$x^2 = 81$$
$$x^2 - 81 = 0$$
$$(x-9)(x+9) = 0$$
$$x = 9 \text{ or } x = -9$$
Solution set: $\{-9, 9\}$

50. $\dfrac{x^2-4}{x} \div \dfrac{x^3-8}{x}$
$$= \frac{(x-2)(x+2)}{x} \cdot \frac{x}{(x-2)(x^2+2x+4)}$$
$$= \frac{x+2}{x^2+2x+4}$$

51. $\dfrac{(w+3)(x+m)}{(w-3)(w+3)} \cdot \dfrac{w-3}{(x-m)(x+m)}$

$$= \dfrac{1}{x-m}$$

52. $\dfrac{-5}{7} = \dfrac{3}{x}$

$$-5x = 21$$

$$x = -\dfrac{21}{5}$$

The solution set is $\left\{-\dfrac{21}{5}\right\}$.

53. $\dfrac{5(a+1)}{(a-5)(a+5)(a+1)}$

$$+ \dfrac{3(a+5)}{(a-5)(a+1)(a+5)}$$

$$= \dfrac{8a+20}{(a-5)(a+5)(a+1)}$$

54. $\dfrac{3}{w^2-1} + \dfrac{2}{2w+2}$

$$= \dfrac{3}{(w-1)(w+1)} + \dfrac{2}{2(w+1)}$$

$$= \dfrac{3}{(w-1)(w+1)} + \dfrac{1(w-1)}{(w+1)(w-1)}$$

$$= \dfrac{w+2}{(w+1)(w-1)}$$

55. $\dfrac{-7(a+2)}{2(a-3)(a+3)(a+2)}$

$$- \dfrac{4 \cdot 2(a-3)}{(a+2)(a+3)2(a-3)}$$

$$= \dfrac{-7a-14-(8a-24)}{2(a+2)(a+3)(a-3)}$$

$$= \dfrac{-15a+10}{2(a+2)(a+3)(a-3)}$$

56. $\dfrac{-5}{3a^2-12} - \dfrac{1}{a^2-3a+2}$

$$= \dfrac{-5}{3(a-2)(a+2)} - \dfrac{1}{(a-2)(a-1)}$$

$$= \dfrac{-5(a-1)}{3(a-2)(a+2)(a-1)}$$

$$- \dfrac{1 \cdot 3(a+2)}{(a-2)(a-1)3(a+2)}$$

$$= \dfrac{-5a+5-3a-6}{3(a-2)(a+2)(a-1)}$$

$$= \dfrac{-8a-1}{3(a-2)(a+2)(a-1)}$$

57. $(a-1)(a+1)\left(\dfrac{7}{a^2-1} + \dfrac{2}{1-a}\right)$

$$= (a-1)(a+1)\left(\dfrac{1}{a+1}\right)$$

$$7 - 2(a+1) = a-1$$

$$-2a+5 = a-1$$

$$-3a = -6$$

$$a = 2$$

Solution set: $\{2\}$

58. $2 + \dfrac{4}{x-1} = \dfrac{3x+1}{x-1}$

$$(x-1)\left(2 + \dfrac{4}{x-1}\right) = (x-1)\dfrac{3x+1}{x-1}$$

$$2x - 2 + 4 = 3x+1$$

$$2 = x+1$$

$$1 = x$$

Since the denominator $x-1$ has a value of 0 if $x = 1$, the solution set is $\emptyset$.

59. $(x-2)(x-3)\left(\dfrac{2x}{x-3} + \dfrac{3}{x-2}\right)$

$$= (x-2)(x-3)\dfrac{6}{(x-2)(x-3)}$$

$$2x(x-2) + 3(x-3) = 6$$

$$2x^2 - x - 15 = 0$$

$$(2x+5)(x-3) = 0$$

$$2x+5 = 0 \text{ or } x-3 = 0$$

$$x = -\dfrac{5}{2} \text{ or } x = 3$$

Since 3 is an extraneous root, the solution set is $\left\{-\dfrac{5}{2}\right\}$.

60. $\dfrac{a-3}{a+3} \div \dfrac{9-a^2}{3}$

$$= \dfrac{a-3}{a+3} \cdot \dfrac{3}{(3-a)(3+a)}$$

$$= \dfrac{-3}{(a+3)(a+3)} = \dfrac{-3}{(a+3)^2}$$

61. $\dfrac{x-2}{2 \cdot 3} \cdot \dfrac{2}{2-x} = -\dfrac{1}{3}$

62. $\dfrac{x}{x+4} - \dfrac{2}{x+1} = \dfrac{-2}{(x+1)(x+4)}$

$$(x+1)(x+4)\left(\dfrac{x}{x+4} - \dfrac{2}{x+1}\right)$$

$$= (x+1)(x+4)\dfrac{-2}{(x+1)(x+4)}$$

$$x(x+1) - 2(x+4) = -2$$

$$x^2 + x - 2x - 8 = -2$$

$$x^2 - x - 6 = 0$$

$$(x-3)(x+2) = 0$$

$$x-3 = 0 \text{ or } x+2 = 0$$

$$x = 3 \text{ or } x = -2$$

The solution set is $\{-2, 3\}$.

63. $\dfrac{x-3}{(x+2)(x+1)} \cdot \dfrac{(x-2)(x+2)}{3(x-3)}$

$\qquad = \dfrac{x-2}{3x+3}$

64. $\dfrac{x^2-1}{x^2+2x+1} \cdot \dfrac{x^3+1}{2x-2}$

$\quad = \dfrac{(x-1)(x+1)}{(x+1)(x+1)} \cdot \dfrac{(x+1)(x^2-x+1)}{2(x-1)}$

$\quad = \dfrac{x^2-x+1}{2}$

65. $\dfrac{a+4}{(a-2)(a^2+2a+4)} - \dfrac{-3}{a-2}$

$= \dfrac{a+4}{(a-2)(a^2+2a+4)}$

$\qquad - \dfrac{-3(a^2+2a+4)}{(a-2)(a^2+2a+4)}$

$= \dfrac{a+4+3a^2+6a+12}{a^3-8} = \dfrac{3a^2+7a+16}{a^3-8}$

66. $\dfrac{x+2}{5} = \dfrac{3}{x}$

$\qquad x^2+2x = 15$

$x^2+2x-15 = 0$

$(x+5)(x-3) = 0$

$x+5 = 0 \ \text{or} \ x-3 = 0$

$\quad x = -5 \ \text{or} \quad x = 3$

The solution set is $\{-5, 3\}$.

67. $\dfrac{x(x-3)(x+3)}{(1-x)(1+x)} \cdot \dfrac{x-1}{x(x+3)^2}$

$\qquad = \dfrac{3-x}{(x+1)(x+3)}$

68. $\dfrac{x+3}{2x+3} = \dfrac{x-3}{x-1}$

$\quad (x+3)(x-1) = (2x+3)(x-3)$

$\quad x^2+2x-3 = 2x^2-3x-9$

$\quad -x^2+5x+6 = 0$

$\quad x^2-5x-6 = 0$

$\quad (x-6)(x+1) = 0$

$\quad x-6 = 0 \ \text{or} \ x+1 = 0$

$\qquad x = 6 \ \text{or} \qquad x = -1$

The solution set is $\{-1, 6\}$.

69. $\dfrac{(a+w)(a+3)}{(a+2)(a+4)} \cdot \dfrac{(a+2)(a-w)}{(a-w)(a+3)}$

$\qquad = \dfrac{a+w}{a+4}$

70. $\dfrac{3}{4-2y} + \dfrac{6}{y^2-4} + \dfrac{3}{2+y}$

$= \dfrac{3}{-2(y-2)} + \dfrac{6}{(y-2)(y+2)} + \dfrac{3}{y+2}$

$= \dfrac{-3(y+2)}{2(y-2)(y+2)} + \dfrac{2\cdot 6}{2(y-2)(y+2)}$

$\qquad\qquad + \dfrac{3\cdot 2(y-2)}{2(y+2)(y-2)}$

$= \dfrac{-3y-6+12+6y-12}{2(y-2)(y+2)}$

$= \dfrac{3y-6}{2(y-2)(y+2)}$

$= \dfrac{3(y-2)}{2(y-2)(y+2)} = \dfrac{3}{2y+4}$

71. $5x(x+2)\left(\dfrac{5}{x} - \dfrac{4}{x+2}\right)$

$\qquad = 5x(x+2)\left(\dfrac{1}{5} + \dfrac{1}{5x}\right)$

$25x+50-20x = x^2+2x+x+2$

$\qquad 5x+50 = x^2+3x+2$

$-x^2+2x+48 = 0$

$\quad x^2-2x-48 = 0$

$\quad (x-8)(x+6) = 0$

$\qquad x = 8 \ \text{or} \ x = -6$

Solution set: $\{-6, 8\}$

72. $\dfrac{1}{x} + \dfrac{1}{x-5} = \dfrac{2x+1}{x^2-25} + \dfrac{9}{x^2+5x}$

$\dfrac{1}{x} + \dfrac{1}{x-5} = \dfrac{2x+1}{(x-5)(x+5)} + \dfrac{9}{x(x+5)}$

$x(x-5)(x+5)\left(\dfrac{1}{x} + \dfrac{1}{x-5}\right)$

$\quad = x(x-5)(x+5)\left(\dfrac{2x+1}{(x-5)(x+5)} + \dfrac{9}{x(x+5)}\right)$

$(x-5)(x+5) + x(x+5)$

$\qquad = x(2x+1) + 9(x-5)$

$x^2-25+x^2+5x = 2x^2+x+9x-45$

$\quad 2x^2+5x-25 = 2x^2+10x-45$

$\qquad 5x-25 = 10x-45$

$\qquad\qquad -5x = -20$

$\qquad\qquad\quad x = 4$

The solution set is $\{4\}$.

73. $\dfrac{6}{x} = \dfrac{6\cdot 3}{x\cdot 3} = \dfrac{18}{3x}$

74. $\dfrac{8}{4a} = \dfrac{4\cdot 2}{4a} = \dfrac{2}{a}$

75. $\dfrac{3}{a-b} = \dfrac{3(-1)}{(a-b)(-1)} = \dfrac{-3}{b-a}$

76. $\frac{-2}{a-x} = \frac{-2(-1)}{(a-x)(-1)} = \frac{2}{x-a}$

77. $4 = 4 \cdot \frac{x}{x} = \frac{4x}{x}$

78. $5a = \frac{5a \cdot b}{b} = \frac{5ab}{b}$

79. $5x \div \frac{1}{2} = 5x \cdot 2 = 10x$

80. $3a \div \frac{1}{a} = 3a \cdot a = 3a^2$

81. $4a \div \frac{1}{3} = 4a \cdot 3 = 12a$

82. $14x \div \frac{1}{2x} = 14x \cdot 2x = 28x^2$

83. $\frac{a-3}{a^2-9} = \frac{1(a-3)}{(a-3)(a+3)} = \frac{1}{a+3}$

84. $\frac{1}{x-2} = \frac{1(x+2)}{(x-2)(x+2)} = \frac{x+2}{x^2-4}$

85. $\frac{1}{2} - \frac{1}{5} = \frac{5}{10} - \frac{2}{10} = \frac{3}{10}$

86. $\frac{1}{4} - \frac{1}{5} = \frac{1 \cdot 5 - 1 \cdot 4}{4 \cdot 5} = \frac{1}{20}$

87. $\frac{a}{3} + \frac{a}{2} = \frac{2a}{6} + \frac{3a}{6} = \frac{5a}{6}$

88. $\frac{x}{5} + \frac{x}{3} = \frac{3x + 5x}{3 \cdot 5} = \frac{8x}{15}$

89. $\frac{1}{a} - \frac{1}{b} = \frac{b}{ab} - \frac{a}{ab} = \frac{b-a}{ab}$

90. $\frac{3}{w} - \frac{2}{b} = \frac{3b - 2w}{bw}$

91. $\frac{a}{3} - 1 = \frac{a}{3} - \frac{3}{3} = \frac{a-3}{3}$

92. $\frac{x}{y} - 1 = \frac{x}{y} - \frac{y}{y} = \frac{x-y}{y}$

93. $2 + \frac{1}{a} = \frac{2a}{a} + \frac{1}{a} = \frac{2a+1}{a}$

94. $3 - \frac{1}{x} = \frac{3x}{x} - \frac{1}{x} = \frac{3x-1}{x}$

95. $\frac{a}{5} - 1 = \frac{a}{5} - \frac{5}{5} = \frac{a-5}{5}$

96. $\frac{y^2-1}{y} = \frac{y^2}{y} - \frac{1}{y} = y - \frac{1}{y}$

97. $(x-1)(-1) = 1 - x$

98. $(a-3) \div (3-a) = \frac{a-3}{3-a} = \frac{-1(3-a)}{3-a}$
$= -1$

99. $(m-2) \div (2-m) = \frac{-1(2-m)}{2-m}$
$= -1$

100. $(x-2) \div (2x-4) = \frac{x-2}{2(x-2)} = \frac{1}{2}$

101. $\frac{\frac{b}{3a}}{2} = \frac{b}{3a} \cdot \frac{1}{2} = \frac{b}{6a}$

102. $\frac{a-3}{\frac{1}{2}} = (a-3) \cdot 2 = 2a - 6$

103. $\frac{a-6}{5} \cdot \frac{2 \cdot 5}{6-a} = -2$

104. $\frac{3}{w-2} + \frac{2}{2-w}$
$= \frac{3}{w-2} + \frac{2(-1)}{(2-w)(-1)}$
$= \frac{3}{w-2} + \frac{-2}{w-2} = \frac{1}{w-2}$

105. $\frac{2}{x^a-2} + \frac{1}{x^a+3}$

$= \frac{2(x^a+3)}{(x^a-2)(x^a+3)} + \frac{1(x^a-2)}{(x^a+3)(x^a-2)}$

$= \frac{3x^a+4}{(x^a-2)(x^a+3)}$

106. $\frac{x^k+1}{x^{k+1}-x} - \frac{x^{k-1}}{x^k-1}$
$= \frac{x^k+1}{x(x^k-1)} - \frac{x^{k-1}}{x^k-1}$
$= \frac{x^k+1}{x(x^k-1)} - \frac{x^{k-1} \cdot x}{(x^k-1)x}$
$= \frac{x^k+1}{x(x^k-1)} - \frac{x^k}{(x^k-1)x} = \frac{1}{x(x^k-1)}$

107. $\frac{x^{2k}-9}{3x^{k+3}+9x^3} \cdot \frac{6x^{k+5}}{x^{k+2}-3x^2}$
$= \frac{(x^k-3)(x^k+3)}{3x^3(x^k+3)} \cdot \frac{6x^{k+5}}{x^2(x^k-3)}$
$= 2x^k$

108. $\frac{y^{2a}-y^a-12}{y^{2a}-4y^a} \div \frac{y^{3a}+3y^{2a}}{y^{6a}}$
$= \frac{(y^a-4)(y^a+3)}{y^a(y^a-4)} \cdot \frac{y^{6a}}{y^{2a}(y^a+3)} = y^{3a}$

109. Let x = the number of reported female AIDs cases and $x + 373,486$ = the number of reported male AIDs cases.
$$\frac{5.98}{1} = \frac{x+373,486}{x}$$
$$5.98x = x + 373,486$$
$$4.98x = 373,486$$
$$x \approx 74,997$$
$$x + 373,486 = 448,483$$
There were 448,483 reported male AIDs cases.

251

110. a) Let $x =$ the number of AIDs cases reported in children and $x + 68,041 =$ the number of AIDs cases reported in females.
$$\frac{10.8}{1} = \frac{x + 68,041}{x}$$
$$10.8x = x + 68,041$$
$$9.8x = 68,041$$
$$x \approx 6943$$
There were 6,943 AIDs cases reported in children.

b) The number of female cases was $6943 + 68,041$ or $74,984$, and the number of male cases was $448,483$. So the total number of male, female and children cases was $530,410$.

111. If $x =$ the time east of Louisville, then we also have $x =$ the time west of Louisville. His speed east of Louisville was $\frac{310}{x}$ and his speed west of Louisville was $\frac{360}{x}$. We can write an equation expressing the fact that his speed west of Louisville was 10 mph greater than east of Louisville:
$$\frac{360}{x} - 10 = \frac{310}{x}$$
$$x\left(\frac{360}{x} - 10\right) = x\left(\frac{310}{x}\right)$$
$$360 - 10x = 310$$
$$-10x = -50$$
$$x = 5$$
His journey took a total of 10 hours.

112. Let $x =$ the speed in the gulf and $x + 5 =$ the speed in the river. The time in the gulf is $\frac{84}{x}$ hours and the time in the river is $\frac{144}{x+5}$ hours. Since the times are equal, we can write the following equation.
$$\frac{84}{x} = \frac{144}{x + 5}$$
$$144x = 84x + 420$$
$$60x = 420$$
$$x = 7$$
The speed in the gulf is 7 miles per hour.

113. Let $x =$ the time for all three to make the quilt working together. Debbie makes $\frac{1}{2000}$ of the quilt per hour, Pat makes $\frac{1}{1000}$ of the quilt per hour, and Cheryl makes $\frac{1}{1000}$ of the quilt per hour. Working together, $\frac{1}{x}$ of the quilt gets done per hour:

$$\frac{1}{1000} + \frac{1}{1000} + \frac{1}{2000} = \frac{1}{x}$$
$$2000x\left(\frac{1}{1000} + \frac{1}{1000} + \frac{1}{2000}\right) = 2000x \cdot \frac{1}{x}$$
$$2x + 2x + x = 2000$$
$$5x = 2000$$
$$x = 400$$
It will take them 400 hours to make the quilt together.

114. Let $x =$ the time for the two pumps to get the blood out working together. One pump does $\frac{1}{30}$ of the job per minute and the other does $\frac{1}{20}$ of the job per minute. Since together they get $\frac{1}{x}$ of the blood out per minute, we can write the following equation.
$$\frac{1}{30} + \frac{1}{20} = \frac{1}{x}$$
$$60x\left(\frac{1}{30} + \frac{1}{20}\right) = 60x \cdot \frac{1}{x}$$
$$2x + 3x = 60$$
$$5x = 60$$
$$x = 12$$
All of the blood will be removed in 12 minutes.

CHAPTER 6   TEST

1. The solution to $4 - 3x = 0$ is $\{4/3\}$. So the domain of the rational expression is $\{x \mid x \neq \frac{4}{3}\}$.

2. The solution to $x^2 - 9 = 0$ is $\{-3, 3\}$. So the domain of the rational expression is $\{x \mid x \neq 3 \text{ and } x \neq -3\}$.

3. There is no solution to $x^2 + 9 = 0$ in the real numbers. So the domain is the set of all real numbers, $(-\infty, \infty)$.

4. $\dfrac{12a^9b^8}{(2a^2b^3)^3} = \dfrac{12a^9b^8}{8a^6b^9} = \dfrac{3a^3}{2b}$

5. $\dfrac{(y - x)(y + x)}{2(x - y)^2} = \dfrac{-1(y + x)}{2(x - y)} = \dfrac{-x - y}{2x - 2y}$

6. $\dfrac{5}{12} - \dfrac{4}{9} = \dfrac{15}{36} - \dfrac{16}{36} = -\dfrac{1}{36}$

7. $\dfrac{3}{y} + 7y = \dfrac{3}{y} + \dfrac{7y^2}{y} = \dfrac{7y^2 + 3}{y}$

8. $\dfrac{4}{a - 9} - \dfrac{1(-1)}{(9 - a)(-1)} = \dfrac{5}{a - 9}$

9. $\dfrac{1}{6ab^2} + \dfrac{1}{8a^2b} = \dfrac{1 \cdot 4a}{6ab^2 \cdot 4a} + \dfrac{1 \cdot 3b}{8a^2b \cdot 3b}$

$= \dfrac{4a}{24a^2b^2} + \dfrac{3b}{24a^2b^2} = \dfrac{4a + 3b}{24a^2b^2}$

10. $\dfrac{3a^3b}{2 \cdot 2 \cdot 5ab} \cdot \dfrac{2a^2b}{3 \cdot 3ab^3} = \dfrac{a^3}{30b^2}$

11. $\dfrac{a-b}{7} \cdot \dfrac{3 \cdot 7}{(b-a)(b+a)} = -\dfrac{3}{a+b}$

12. $\dfrac{x-3}{x-1} \cdot \dfrac{1}{(x-3)(x+1)} = \dfrac{1}{x^2-1}$

13. $\dfrac{2}{(x-2)(x+2)} - \dfrac{6}{(x-5)(x+2)}$

$= \dfrac{2(x-5)}{(x-2)(x+2)(x-5)}$

$\qquad - \dfrac{6(x-2)}{(x-5)(x+2)(x-2)}$

$= \dfrac{2x-10-(6x-12)}{(x+2)(x-2)(x-5)}$

$= \dfrac{-4x+2}{(x+2)(x-2)(x-5)}$

14. $\dfrac{(m-1)(m^2+m+1)}{(m-1)^2} \cdot \dfrac{(m-1)(m+1)}{3(m^2+m+1)}$

$\qquad = \dfrac{m+1}{3}$

15. $\qquad \dfrac{3}{x} = \dfrac{7}{4}$

$\qquad 7x = 12$

$\qquad x = \dfrac{12}{7}$

Solution set: $\left\{ \dfrac{12}{7} \right\}$

16. $4x(x-2)\left(\dfrac{x}{x-2} - \dfrac{5}{x} \right) = 4x(x-2)\left(\dfrac{3}{4} \right)$

$\qquad 4x^2 - 5(4x-8) = 3x^2 - 6x$

$\qquad x^2 - 14x + 40 = 0$

$\qquad (x-4)(x-10) = 0$

$\qquad x = 4 \quad \text{or} \quad x = 10$

Solution set: $\{4, 10\}$

17. $\qquad \dfrac{3m}{2} = \dfrac{6}{m}$

$\qquad 3m^2 = 12$

$\qquad m^2 = 4$

$\qquad m^2 - 4 = 0$

$\qquad (m-4)(m+4) = 0$

$\qquad m = 2 \quad \text{or} \quad m = -2$

Solution set: $\{-2, 2\}$

18. $\qquad W = \dfrac{a^2}{t}$

$\qquad tW = a^2$

$\qquad t = \dfrac{a^2}{W}$

19. $2ab\left(\dfrac{1}{a} + \dfrac{1}{b} \right) = 2ab \cdot \dfrac{1}{2}$

$\qquad 2b + 2a = ab$

$\qquad 2b - ab = -2a$

$\qquad b(2-a) = -2a$

$\qquad b = \dfrac{-2a}{2-a}$

$\qquad b = \dfrac{2a}{a-2}$

20. $\dfrac{12x\left(\dfrac{1}{x} + \dfrac{1}{3x} \right)}{12x\left(\dfrac{3}{4x} - \dfrac{1}{2} \right)} = \dfrac{12+4}{9-6x} = \dfrac{16}{9-6x}$

21. $\dfrac{m^2w^2(m^{-2} - w^{-2})}{m^2w^2(m^{-2}w^{-1} + m^{-1}w^{-2})}$

$= \dfrac{w^2 - m^2}{w + m} = \dfrac{(w-m)(w+m)}{w+m} = w - m$

22. $\dfrac{a^2b^3}{2 \cdot 2a} \cdot \dfrac{2 \cdot 3a^2}{ab^3} = \dfrac{3a^2}{2}$

23. Let $x =$ the number of minutes to fill the leaky pool. In one minute, the hose is supposed to fill $\frac{1}{6}$ of the pool, the leak removes $\frac{1}{8}$ of the pool, but together $\frac{1}{x}$ of the pool actually gets filled.

$$\dfrac{1}{6} - \dfrac{1}{8} = \dfrac{1}{x}$$

$$24x\left(\dfrac{1}{6} - \dfrac{1}{8} \right) = 24x \cdot \dfrac{1}{x}$$

$$4x - 3x = 24$$

$$x = 24$$

The leaky pool will be filled in 24 minutes.

24. Let $x =$ the number of miles hiked in one day. Milton's time is $\frac{x}{4}$ and Bonnie's time is $\frac{x}{3}$ hours. Since Milton's time is 2.5 hours less than Bonnie's, we can write the equation

$$\dfrac{x}{4} + \dfrac{5}{2} = \dfrac{x}{3}$$

$$12\left(\dfrac{x}{4} + \dfrac{5}{2} \right) = 12 \cdot \dfrac{x}{3}$$

$$3x + 30 = 4x$$

$$30 = x$$

They hiked 30 miles that day.

25. Let $x =$ the number of sailors in the original group and $x + 3 =$ the number in the larger group. The cost is $\dfrac{72{,}000}{x}$ dollars per person for x people and $\dfrac{72{,}000}{x+3}$ dollars per person for $x + 3$ people.

$$\dfrac{72{,}000}{x} = \dfrac{72{,}000}{x+3} + 2000$$

$$x(x+3)\frac{72{,}000}{x} = x(x+3)\left(\frac{72{,}000}{x+3} + 2000\right)$$

$$72{,}000x + 216{,}000$$
$$= 72{,}000x + 2000x^2 + 6000x$$
$$2000x^2 + 6000x - 216{,}000 = 0$$
$$x^2 + 3x - 108 = 0$$
$$(x-9)(x+12) = 0$$
$$x = 9 \quad \text{or} \quad x = -12$$

There are 9 sailors in the original group.

Making Connections

Chapters 1 - 6

1. $\frac{3}{x} = \frac{4}{5}$
$$4x = 15$$
$$x = \frac{15}{4}$$
Solution set: $\left\{\frac{15}{4}\right\}$

2. $\frac{2}{x} = \frac{x}{8}$
$$x^2 = 16$$
$$x^2 - 16 = 0$$
$$(x-4)(x+4) = 0$$
$$x = 4 \text{ or } x = -4$$
Solution set: $\{-4, 4\}$

3. $\frac{x}{3} = \frac{4}{5}$
$$5x = 12$$
$$x = \frac{12}{5}$$
Solution set: $\left\{\frac{12}{5}\right\}$

4. $\frac{3}{x} = \frac{x+3}{6}$
$$x^2 + 3x = 18$$
$$x^2 + 3x - 18 = 0$$
$$(x+6)(x-3) = 0$$
$$x = -6 \text{ or } x = 3$$
Solution set: $\{-6, 3\}$

5. $\frac{1}{x} = 4$
$$4x = 1$$
$$x = \frac{1}{4}$$
Solution set: $\left\{\frac{1}{4}\right\}$

6. $\frac{2}{3}x = 4$
$$2x = 12$$
$$x = 6$$
Solution set: $\{6\}$

7. $2x + 3 = 4$
$$2x = 1$$
$$x = \frac{1}{2}$$
Solution set: $\left\{\frac{1}{2}\right\}$

8. $2x + 3 = 4x$
$$3 = 2x$$
$$\frac{3}{2} = x$$
Solution set: $\left\{\frac{3}{2}\right\}$

9. $\frac{2a}{3} = \frac{6}{a}$
$$2a^2 = 18$$
$$a^2 = 9$$
$$a^2 - 9 = 0$$
$$(a-3)(a+3) = 0$$
$$a = 3 \text{ or } a = -3$$
Solution set: $\{-3, 3\}$

10. $2x(x+1)\left(\frac{12}{x} - \frac{14}{x+1}\right) = 2x(x+1) \cdot \frac{1}{2}$
$$24x + 24 - 28x = x^2 + x$$
$$-x^2 - 5x + 24 = 0$$
$$x^2 + 5x - 24 = 0$$
$$(x+8)(x-3) = 0$$
$$x = -8 \text{ or } x = 3$$
Solution set: $\{-8, 3\}$

11. $|6x - 3| = 1$
$$6x - 3 = 1 \text{ or } 6x - 3 = -1$$
$$6x = 4 \text{ or } \quad 6x = 2$$
$$x = \frac{2}{3} \text{ or } \quad x = \frac{1}{3}$$

Solution set: $\left\{\frac{1}{3}, \frac{2}{3}\right\}$

12. $\frac{x}{2x+9} = \frac{3}{x}$
$$x^2 = 6x + 27$$
$$x^2 - 6x - 27 = 0$$
$$(x-9)(x+3) = 0$$
$$x = 9 \text{ or } x = -3$$
Solution set: $\{-3, 9\}$

13. $4(6x - 3)(2x + 9) = 0$
$$6x - 3 = 0 \text{ or } 2x + 9 = 0$$
$$6x = 3 \text{ or } \quad 2x = -9$$
$$x = \frac{1}{2} \text{ or } \quad x = -\frac{9}{2}$$
Solution set: $\left\{-\frac{9}{2}, \frac{1}{2}\right\}$

14. $5(x+2)\left(\frac{x-1}{x+2} - \frac{1}{5(x+2)}\right)$
$$= 5(x+2) \cdot 1$$
$$5x - 5 - 1 = 5x + 10$$
$$-6 = 10$$

Solution set: $\emptyset$

15. $\quad Ax + By = C$
$$By = C - Ax$$
$$y = \frac{C - Ax}{B}$$

16. $\quad \frac{y-3}{x+5} = -\frac{1}{3}$
$$y - 3 = -\frac{1}{3}(x+5)$$
$$y - 3 = -\frac{1}{3}x - \frac{5}{3}$$
$$y = -\frac{1}{3}x - \frac{5}{3} + \frac{9}{3}$$
$$y = -\frac{1}{3}x + \frac{4}{3}$$

17. $\quad Ay = By + C$
$$Ay - By = C$$
$$y(A - B) = C$$
$$y = \frac{C}{A - B}$$

18. $\quad \frac{A}{y} = \frac{y}{A}$
$$y^2 = A^2$$
$$y^2 - A^2 = 0$$
$$(y - A)(y + A) = 0$$
$$y - A = 0 \quad \text{or} \quad y + A = 0$$
$$y = A \quad \text{or} \quad y = -A$$

19. $\quad 2y\left(\frac{A}{y} - \frac{1}{2}\right) = 2y \cdot \frac{B}{y}$
$$2A - y = 2B$$
$$2A - 2B = y$$
$$y = 2A - 2B$$

20. $\quad 2Cy\left(\frac{A}{y} - \frac{1}{2}\right) = 2Cy \cdot \frac{B}{C}$
$$2AC - Cy = 2yB$$
$$2AC = Cy + 2yB$$
$$2AC = y(C + 2B)$$
$$\frac{2AC}{C + 2B} = y$$
$$y = \frac{2AC}{2B + C}$$

21. $\quad 3x - 4y = 6$
$$-4y = -3x + 6$$
$$y = \frac{-3x + 6}{-4}$$
$$y = \frac{3}{4}x - \frac{3}{2}$$

22. $\quad y^2 - 2y - Ay + 2A = 0$
$$y(y - 2) - A(y - 2) = 0$$
$$(y - A)(y - 2) = 0$$
$$y - A = 0 \quad \text{or} \quad y - 2 = 0$$
$$y = A \quad \text{or} \quad y = 2$$

23. $\quad A = \frac{1}{2}B(C + y)$
$$2A = B(C + y)$$
$$2A = BC + By$$
$$2A - BC = By$$
$$\frac{2A - BC}{B} = y$$
$$y = \frac{2A - BC}{B}$$

24. $\quad y^2 + Cy = BC + By$
$$y^2 + Cy - BC - By = 0$$
$$y(y + C) - B(y + C) = 0$$
$$(y - B)(y + C) = 0$$
$$y - B = 0 \quad \text{or} \quad y + C = 0$$
$$y = B \quad \text{or} \quad y = -C$$

25. $3x^5 \cdot 4x^8 = 12x^{13}$

26. $3x^2(x^3 + 5x^6) = 3x^5 + 15x^8$

27. $(5x^6)^2 = 25x^{12}$

28. $(3a^3b^2)^3 = 27a^9b^6$

29. $\frac{12a^9b^4}{-3a^3b^{-2}} = -4a^6b^6$

30. $\left(\frac{x^{-2}}{2}\right)^5 = \frac{x^{-10}}{2^5} = \frac{1}{32x^{10}}$

31. $\left(\frac{2x^{-4}}{3y^5}\right)^{-3} = \frac{2^{-3}x^{12}}{3^{-3}y^{-15}} = \frac{27x^{12}y^{15}}{8}$

32. $(-2a^{-1}b^3c)^{-2} = 2^{-2}a^2b^{-6}c^{-2} = \frac{a^2}{4b^6c^2}$

33. $\frac{a^{-1} + b^3}{a^{-2} + b^{-1}} = \frac{a^2b(a^{-1} + b^3)}{a^2b(a^{-2} + b^{-1})}$
$$= \frac{ab + a^2b^4}{b + a^2}$$

34. $\frac{(a + b)^{-1}}{(a + b)^{-2}} = a + b$

35. a) $B = 655 + 9.56(292/2.2)$
$$+ 1.85(86 \cdot 2.54) - 4.68(30)$$
$$= 2188 \text{ calories}$$

b) The graph shows the energy requirement increasing as the weight increases.

c) $B = 655 + 9.56W + 1.85(86 \cdot 2.54)$
$$- 4.68(30)$$
$$B = 9.56W + 918.7$$

d) $B = 655 + 9.56(292/2.2)$
$$+ 1.85(86 \cdot 2.54) - 4.68(A)$$
$$B = 2328 - 4.68A$$

7.1 WARM-UPS

1. True, because $4^{-1/2} = \frac{1}{4^{1/2}} = \frac{1}{2}$.
2. False, because $16^{1/2} = 4$.
3. True, because $(3^{2/3})^3 = 3^{6/3} = 3^2 = 9$.
4. False, because $8^{-2/3} = \frac{1}{2^2} = \frac{1}{4}$.
5. True, $2^{1/2} \cdot 2^{1/2} = 2^{1/2+1/2} = 2^1 = 2$.
6. True, because the square root of $\frac{1}{4}$ is $\frac{1}{2}$.
7. True, $\frac{3^1}{3^{1/2}} = 3^{1-1/2} = 3^{1/2}$
8. False, because $(2^9)^{1/2} = 2^{9/2}$.
9. False, because $3^{1/3}6^{1/3} = (3 \cdot 6)^{1/3} = 18^{1/3}$.
10. False, because $2^{3/4} \cdot 2^{1/4} = 2^{4/4} = 2^1 = 2$.

7.1 EXERCISES

1. If $a^n = b$ then a is an nth root of b.
2. If $a^n = b$ then a is an even root of b provided n is even and a is an odd root of b provided n is odd.
3. The principal root is the positive even root of a positive number.
4. The nth root of b is written as $b^{1/n}$.
5. The nth root of 0 is 0.
6. The expression $a^{-m/n}$ represents the reciprocal of the nth root of the mth power of a.
7. Because $10^2 = 100$, $100^{1/2} = 10$.
8. Because $13^2 = 169$, $169^{1/2} = 13$.
9. Because $3^4 = 81$, $81^{1/4} = 3$.
10. Because $2^6 = 64$, $64^{1/6} = 2$.
11. $-9^{1/2} = -(9^{1/2}) = -3$
12. $-4^{1/2} = -(4^{1/2}) = -2$
13. $\left(\frac{1}{64}\right)^{1/6} = \frac{1}{2}$
14. $\left(-\frac{1}{8}\right)^{1/3} = -\frac{1}{2}$
15. Square root of a negative number is not real.
16. The fourth root of a negative number is not real.
17. The cube root of 1000 is 10, because $10^3 = 1000$.
18. $27^{1/3} = 3$

19. $(-64)^{1/3} = -4$, because $(-4)^3 = -64$.
20. Since $(-2)^5 = -32$, $(-32)^{1/5} = -2$.
21. $-1^{1/5} = -1$
22. $-125^{1/3} = -5$
23. Take the fifth root and then cube it: $32^{3/5} = 2^3 = 8$.
24. Take the square root of 25 and then cube it: $25^{3/2} = 5^3 = 125$
25. $(-27)^{2/3} = (-3)^2 = 9$
26. Take the fifth root and then cube it: $(-32)^{3/5} = (-2)^3 = -8$
27. Take the square root of 25, cube it, and then take the opposite: $-25^{3/2} = -5^3 = -125$
28. $-100^{3/2} = -10^3 = -1000$
29. The expression is not a real number because it is an even root of a negative number.
30. The expression is not a real number because the sixth root of -64 is not real.
31. Take the square root and then find the reciprocal: $4^{-1/2} = \frac{1}{2}$.
32. Take the square root of 9 and then find the reciprocal of the result: $9^{-1/2} = 3^{-1} = \frac{1}{3}$
33. $8^{-4/3} = \frac{1}{8^{4/3}} = \frac{1}{2^4} = \frac{1}{16}$

34. $4^{-3/2} = \frac{1}{4^{3/2}} = \frac{1}{2^3} = \frac{1}{8}$

35. Take the fifth root, cube it, and then find the reciprocal: $(-32)^{-3/5} = \frac{1}{(-2)^3} = -\frac{1}{8}$.

36. Take the cube root, raise to the fourth power, then find the reciprocal: $(-27)^{-4/3} = \frac{1}{(-3)^4} = \frac{1}{81}$.

37. The square root of -9 is not real.
38. The expression is not real because the square root of a negative number is not real.
39. $3^{1/3} \cdot 3^{1/4} = 3^{\frac{1}{3}+\frac{1}{4}} = 3^{7/12}$
40. $2^{1/2} \cdot 2^{1/3} = 2^{\frac{1}{2}+\frac{1}{3}} = 2^{5/6}$
41. $3^{1/3} \cdot 3^{-1/3} = 3^0 = 1$
42. $5^{1/4} \cdot 5^{-1/4} = 5^0 = 1$
43. $\frac{8^{1/3}}{8^{2/3}} = 8^{1/3-2/3} = 8^{-1/3} = \frac{1}{8^{1/3}} = \frac{1}{2}$
44. $\frac{27^{-2/3}}{27^{-1/3}} = 27^{-\frac{2}{3}-(-\frac{1}{3})} = 27^{-1/3}$
$$= 3^{-1} = \frac{1}{3}$$
45. $4^{3/4} \div 4^{1/4} = 4^{3/4-1/4} = 4^{1/2} = 2$

256

46. $9^{1/4} \div 9^{3/4} = 9^{\frac{1}{4}-\frac{3}{4}} = 9^{-1/2}$
$= 3^{-1} = \frac{1}{3}$

47. $18^{1/2} \cdot 2^{1/2} = 36^{1/2} = 6$

48. $8^{1/2} \cdot 2^{1/2} = (8 \cdot 2)^{1/2} = 16^{1/2} = 4$

49. $(2^6)^{1/3} = 2^{6/3} = 2^2 = 4$

50. $(3^{10})^{1/5} = 3^{10/5} = 3^2 = 9$

51. $(3^8)^{1/2} = 3^{8/2} = 3^4 = 81$

52. $(3^{-6})^{1/3} = 3^{-6/3} = 3^{-2} = \frac{1}{3^2} = \frac{1}{9}$

53. $(2^{-4})^{1/2} = 2^{-2} = \frac{1}{4}$

54. $(5^4)^{1/2} = 5^{4/2} = 5^2 = 25$

55. $\left(\frac{3^4}{2^6}\right)^{1/2} = \frac{3^2}{2^3} = \frac{9}{8}$

56. $\left(\frac{5^4}{3^6}\right)^{1/2} = \frac{5^2}{3^3} = \frac{25}{27}$

57. $(x^4)^{1/4} = |x|$

58. $(y^6)^{1/6} = |y|$

59. $(a^8)^{1/2} = a^4$

60. $(b^{10})^{1/2} = |b^5|$

61. $(y^3)^{1/3} = y$

62. $(w^9)^{1/3} = w^{9/3} = w^3$

63. $(9x^6y^2)^{1/2} = |3x^3y|$

64. $(16a^8b^4)^{1/4} = |2a^2b|$

65. $\left(\frac{81x^{12}}{y^{20}}\right)^{1/4} = \left|\frac{3x^3}{y^5}\right|$

66. $\left(\frac{144a^8}{9y^{18}}\right)^{1/2} = \frac{12a^4}{3y^9} = \frac{4a^4}{|y^9|}$

67. $x^{1/2}x^{1/4} = x^{2/4+1/4} = x^{3/4}$

68. $y^{1/3}y^{1/3} = y^{2/3}$

69. $(x^{1/2}y)(x^{-3/4}y^{1/2}) = x^{-1/4}y^{3/2} = \frac{y^{3/2}}{x^{1/4}}$

70. $(a^{1/2}b^{-1/3})(ab) = a^{\frac{1}{2}+1}b^{-\frac{1}{3}+1} = a^{3/2}b^{2/3}$

71. $\frac{w^{1/3}}{w^3} = w^{\frac{1}{3}-3} = w^{-8/3} = \frac{1}{w^{8/3}}$

72. $\frac{a^{1/2}}{a^2} = a^{1/2-4/2} = a^{-3/2} = \frac{1}{a^{3/2}}$

73. $\frac{x^{1/2}y}{x} = x^{\frac{1}{2}-1}y = x^{-1/2}y = \frac{y}{x^{1/2}}$

74. $\frac{x^{1/3}y^{-1/2}}{xy^{-1}} = x^{\frac{1}{3}-1}y^{-\frac{1}{2}-(-1)}$
$= x^{-2/3}y^{1/2} = \frac{y^{1/2}}{x^{2/3}}$

75. $(144x^{16})^{1/2} = 12x^8$

76. $(125a^8)^{1/3} = 5a^{8/3}$

77. $(4x^{-1/2}yz^{1/2})^{-1/2}$

$= 4^{-1/2}x^{1/4}y^{-1/2}z^{-1/4}$
$= \frac{x^{1/4}}{2y^{1/2}z^{1/4}}$

78. $(9x^8y^{-10}z^{12})^{1/2} = 9^{1/2}x^4y^{-5}z^6 = \frac{3x^4z^6}{y^5}$

79. $\left(\frac{a^{-1/2}}{b^{-1/4}}\right)^{-4} = \frac{a^{4/2}}{b^{4/4}} = \frac{a^2}{b}$

80. $\left(\frac{2a^{1/2}}{b^{1/3}}\right)^6 = \frac{2^6a^{6/2}}{b^{6/3}} = \frac{64a^3}{b^2}$

81. $(9^2)^{1/2} = 9$

82. $(4^{16})^{1/2} = 4^{16/2} = 4^8$

83. $-16^{-3/4} = -\frac{1}{2^3} = -\frac{1}{8}$

84. $-25^{-3/2} = -\frac{1}{5^3} = -\frac{1}{125}$

85. $125^{-4/3} = \frac{1}{5^4} = \frac{1}{625}$

86. $27^{-2/3} = \frac{1}{3^2} = \frac{1}{9}$

87. $2^{1/2} \cdot 2^{-1/4} = 2^{2/4-1/4} = 2^{1/4}$

88. $9^{-1} \cdot 9^{1/2} = 9^{-1+\frac{1}{2}} = 9^{-1/2} = 3^{-1} = \frac{1}{3}$

89. $3^{0.26}3^{0.74} = 3^{0.26+0.74} = 3^1 = 3$

90. $2^{1.5} \cdot 2^{0.5} = 2^{1.5+0.5} = 2^2 = 4$

91. $3^{1/4} \cdot 27^{1/4} = (3 \cdot 27)^{1/4} = 81^{1/4} = 3$

92. $3^{2/3}9^{2/3} = (3 \cdot 9)^{2/3} = 27^{2/3} = 3^2 = 9$

93. $\left(-\frac{8}{27}\right)^{2/3} = \frac{(-8)^{2/3}}{27^{2/3}} = \frac{4}{9}$

94. $\left(-\frac{8}{27}\right)^{-1/3} = \left(-\frac{27}{8}\right)^{1/3} = -\frac{27^{1/3}}{8^{1/3}}$
$= -\frac{3}{2}$

95. Not a real number, because the fourth root of $-1/16$ is not real.

96. $\left(\frac{9}{16}\right)^{-1/2} = \frac{4}{3}$

97. $(9x^9)^{1/2} = 3x^{9/2}$

98. $(-27x^9)^{1/3} = -3x^3$

99. $(3a^{-2/3})^{-3} = 3^{-3}a^2 = \frac{a^2}{27}$

100. $(5x^{-1/2})^{-2} = 5^{-2}x^1 = \frac{x}{25}$

101. $(a^{1/2}b)^{1/2}(ab^{1/2}) = a^{1/4}b^{1/2}a^1b^{1/2}$
$= a^{5/4}b$

102. $(m^{1/4}n^{1/2})^2(m^2n^3)^{1/2} = m^{1/2}n \cdot mn^{3/2}$
$= m^{3/2}n^{5/2}$

103. $(km^{1/2})^3(k^3m^5)^{1/2} = k^3m^{3/2}k^{3/2}m^{5/2}$
$= k^{9/2}m^4$

104. $(tv^{1/3})^2(t^2v^{-3})^{-1/2} = t^2v^{2/3}t^{-1}v^{3/2}$
$= t^{2-1}v^{\frac{2}{3}+\frac{3}{2}} = tv^{13/6}$

105. $2^{1/3} \approx 2^{0.33333333} \approx 1.2599$

106. $5^{1/2} \approx 2.2361$

257

107. $-2^{1/2} = -(2^{0.5}) \approx -1.4142$

108. $(-3)^{1/3} \approx -1.4422$

109. $1024^{1/10} = 2$

110. $7776^{0.2} = 6$

111. $8^{0.33} = 1.9862$

112. $289^{0.5} = 17$

113. $\left(\dfrac{64}{15,625}\right)^{-1/6} = 2.5$

114. $\left(\dfrac{32}{243}\right)^{-3/5} = \left(\dfrac{32}{243}\right)^{-0.6} = 3.375$

115. $a^{m/2} \cdot a^{m/4} = a^{m/2+m/4} = a^{3m/4}$

116. $b^{n/2} \cdot b^{-n/3} = b^{n/2-n/3} = b^{n/6}$

117. $\dfrac{a^{-m/5}}{a^{-m/3}} = a^{-m/5+m/3} = a^{2m/15}$

118. $\dfrac{b^{-n/4}}{b^{-n/3}} = b^{-n/4+n/3} = b^{n/12}$

119. $\left(a^{-1/m}b^{-1/n}\right)^{-mn} = a^n b^m$

120. $\left(a^{-m/2}b^{-n/3}\right)^{-6} = a^{3m}b^{2n}$

121. $\left(\dfrac{a^{-3m}b^{-6n}}{a^{9m}}\right)^{-1/3} = \dfrac{a^m b^{2n}}{a^{-3m}} = a^{4m}b^{2n}$

122. $\left(\dfrac{a^{-3/m}b^{6/n}}{a^{-6/m}b^{9/n}}\right)^{-1/3} = \dfrac{a^{1/m}b^{-2/n}}{a^{2/m}b^{-3/n}}$
$= \dfrac{b^{1/n}}{a^{1/m}}$

123. $D = (12^2 + 4^2 + 3^2)^{1/2}$
$= (144 + 16 + 9)^{1/2}$
$= 169^{1/2} = 13$ inches

124. Use $V = 32\pi/3$ in $r = (0.75V/\pi)^{1/3}$.
$r = \left(\dfrac{0.75\left(\frac{32\pi}{3}\right)}{\pi}\right)^{1/3} = \left(\dfrac{8\pi}{\pi}\right)^{1/3} = 2$ meters

125. $S = (13.0368 + 7.84(18.42)^{1/3}$
$\qquad - 0.8(21.45))^2$
$S = 274.96$ m^2

126. a) $R = (1.881)^{2/3} = 1.52$ AU
b) From the graph it appears that Saturn takes about 27 years to orbit the sun.

127. $r = \left(\dfrac{31,895.06}{10,000}\right)^{1/3} - 1 = 0.472$
$\qquad\qquad\qquad\qquad = 47.2\%$

128. $r = \left(\dfrac{21,830.95}{10,000}\right)^{1/5} - 1 = 0.169$
$\qquad\qquad\qquad\qquad = 16.9\%$

129. $r = \left(\dfrac{141,600,000,000}{450,000}\right)^{1/213} - 1$
$\qquad\qquad = 0.061 = 6.1\%$

130. $r = \left(\frac{32.5}{19.9}\right)^{1/30} - 1 = 0.0165 = 1.65\%$

7.2 WARM-UPS

1. True, because of the definition of the fractional exponent $1/2$.
2. False, $3^{1/3} = \sqrt[3]{3}$.
3. True, $2^{2/3} = \sqrt[3]{2^2} = \sqrt[3]{4}$.
4. False, $\sqrt{81} = 9$.
5. True, $\sqrt{417^2} = (417^2)^{1/2} = 417$.
6. False, $\sqrt[3]{a^{27}} = (a^{27})^{1/3} = a^9$.
7. True, because $\dfrac{1 \cdot \sqrt{2}}{\sqrt{2} \cdot \sqrt{2}} = \dfrac{\sqrt{2}}{2}$.
8. False, $\dfrac{\sqrt{10}}{\sqrt{2}} = \sqrt{5}$.
9. True, $\sqrt{2^{-4}} = (2^{-4})^{1/2} = 2^{-2} = \frac{1}{4}$.
10. True, because $\sqrt{2} \cdot \sqrt{3} = \sqrt{6}$.

7.2 EXERCISES

1. The expression $\sqrt[n]{a}$ is called a radical.
2. The expressions $\sqrt[n]{a}$ and $a^{1/n}$ both represent the nth root of a.
3. The product rule for radicals says that $\sqrt[n]{a} \cdot \sqrt[n]{b} = \sqrt[n]{ab}$.
4. The product rule can be used to factor out a perfect square from the radicand as in $\sqrt{18} = \sqrt{9}\sqrt{2} = 3\sqrt{2}$.
5. The quotient rule for radicals says that $\sqrt[n]{a}/\sqrt[n]{b} = \sqrt[n]{a/b}$.
6. Simplified form for a radical expression has no perfect nth powers as factors of the radicand, no fractions inside the radical, and no radicals in the denominator.
7. $\sqrt{27} = 27^{1/2}$
8. $\sqrt[3]{-27} = (-27)^{1/3}$
9. The square root of x^5 is written $x^{5/2}$.
10. The square root of a^3 is written $a^{3/2}$.
11. The cube root of a^{12} is written $a^{12/3}$.
12. The cube root of w^{-27} is written $w^{-27/3}$.
13. The opposite of the cube root of 5: $-\sqrt[3]{5}$.
14. The opposite of the square root of 7 is written as $-\sqrt{7}$.
15. The fifth root of 2^2 is written $\sqrt[5]{2^2}$.
16. The cube root of 3^2 is written $\sqrt[3]{3^2}$.
17. The cube root of x^{-2} is written $\sqrt[3]{x^{-2}}$.
18. The fifth root of x^{-2} is written $\sqrt[5]{x^{-2}}$.
19. Since $11^2 = 121$, $\sqrt{121} = 11$.

20. Since $8^2 = 64$, $\sqrt{64} = 8$.

21. Since $(-10)^3 = -1000$, $\sqrt[3]{-1000} = -10$.

22. Since $(-1)^5 = -1$, $\sqrt[5]{-1} = -1$.

23. The expression is not a real number since it is an even root of a negative number.

24. Since $2^4 = 16$, $\sqrt[4]{16} = 2$.

25. $\sqrt{a^{16}} = a^{16/2} = a^8$

26. $\sqrt{b^{36}} = b^{36/2} = b^{18}$

27. $\sqrt{4^{16}} = 4^{16/2} = 4^8$

28. $\sqrt{w^4} = w^{4/2} = w^2$

29. $\sqrt[5]{w^{30}} = w^{30/5} = w^6$

30. $\sqrt[5]{a^{20}} = a^{20/5} = a^4$

31. $\sqrt{9w} = \sqrt{9}\sqrt{w} = 3\sqrt{w}$

32. $\sqrt{36m} = \sqrt{36}\sqrt{m} = 6\sqrt{m}$

33. $\sqrt{20} = \sqrt{4}\sqrt{5} = 2\sqrt{5}$

34. $\sqrt{50} = \sqrt{25 \cdot}\sqrt{2} = 5\sqrt{2}$

35. $\sqrt{45w} = \sqrt{9}\sqrt{5w} = 3\sqrt{5w}$

36. $\sqrt{48t} = \sqrt{16 \cdot}\sqrt{3t} = 4\sqrt{3t}$

37. $\sqrt{288} = \sqrt{144}\sqrt{2} = 12\sqrt{2}$

38. $\sqrt{242} = \sqrt{121 \cdot}\sqrt{2} = 11\sqrt{2}$

39. $\sqrt[3]{54} = \sqrt[3]{27} \cdot \sqrt[3]{2} = 3\sqrt[3]{2}$

40. $\sqrt[3]{-48} = \sqrt[3]{-8} \cdot \sqrt[3]{6} = -2\sqrt[3]{6}$

41. $\sqrt[4]{32a} = \sqrt[4]{16} \cdot \sqrt[4]{2a} = 2\sqrt[4]{2a}$

42. $\sqrt[4]{80xy} = \sqrt[4]{16} \cdot \sqrt[4]{5xy} = 2\sqrt[4]{5xy}$

43. $\sqrt{\dfrac{9}{100}} = \dfrac{\sqrt{9}}{\sqrt{100}} = \dfrac{3}{10}$

44. $\sqrt{\dfrac{25}{4}} = \dfrac{\sqrt{25}}{\sqrt{4}} = \dfrac{5}{2}$

45. $\sqrt{\dfrac{50}{9}} = \dfrac{\sqrt{50}}{\sqrt{9}} = \dfrac{\sqrt{25}\sqrt{2}}{3} = \dfrac{5\sqrt{2}}{3}$

46. $\sqrt{\dfrac{18}{25}} = \dfrac{\sqrt{18}}{\sqrt{25}} = \dfrac{\sqrt{9}\sqrt{2}}{5} = \dfrac{3\sqrt{2}}{5}$

47. $\sqrt[3]{-\dfrac{125}{8}} = \dfrac{\sqrt[3]{-125}}{\sqrt[3]{8}} = \dfrac{-5}{2} = -\dfrac{5}{2}$

48. $\sqrt[4]{\dfrac{16}{81}} = \dfrac{\sqrt[4]{16}}{\sqrt[4]{81}} = \dfrac{2}{3}$

49. $\sqrt[3]{\dfrac{16x}{27}} = \dfrac{\sqrt[3]{16x}}{\sqrt[3]{27}} = \dfrac{\sqrt[3]{8} \cdot \sqrt[3]{2x}}{3}$
$= \dfrac{2 \cdot \sqrt[3]{2x}}{3}$

50. $\sqrt[3]{\dfrac{-81a}{1000}} = \dfrac{\sqrt[3]{-81a}}{\sqrt[3]{1000}} = \dfrac{\sqrt[3]{-27} \cdot \sqrt[3]{3a}}{10}$
$= -\dfrac{3\sqrt[3]{3a}}{10}$

51. $\dfrac{2}{\sqrt{5}} = \dfrac{2\sqrt{5}}{\sqrt{5}\sqrt{5}} = \dfrac{2\sqrt{5}}{5}$

52. $\dfrac{5}{\sqrt{3}} = \dfrac{5\sqrt{3}}{\sqrt{3}\sqrt{3}} = \dfrac{5\sqrt{3}}{3}$

53. $\dfrac{\sqrt{3}}{\sqrt{7}} = \dfrac{\sqrt{3}\sqrt{7}}{\sqrt{7}\sqrt{7}} = \dfrac{\sqrt{21}}{\sqrt{49}} = \dfrac{\sqrt{21}}{7}$

54. $\dfrac{\sqrt{6}}{\sqrt{5}} = \dfrac{\sqrt{6}\sqrt{5}}{\sqrt{5}\sqrt{5}} = \dfrac{\sqrt{30}}{\sqrt{25}} = \dfrac{\sqrt{30}}{5}$

55. $\dfrac{1}{\sqrt[3]{4}} = \dfrac{1 \cdot \sqrt[3]{2}}{\sqrt[3]{4} \cdot \sqrt[3]{2}} = \dfrac{\sqrt[3]{2}}{\sqrt[3]{8}} = \dfrac{\sqrt[3]{2}}{2}$

56. $\dfrac{7}{\sqrt[3]{3}} = \dfrac{7 \cdot \sqrt[3]{9}}{\sqrt[3]{3} \cdot \sqrt[3]{9}} = \dfrac{7\sqrt[3]{9}}{\sqrt[3]{27}} = \dfrac{7\sqrt[3]{9}}{3}$

57. $\dfrac{\sqrt[3]{6}}{\sqrt[3]{5}} = \dfrac{\sqrt[3]{6} \cdot \sqrt[3]{25}}{\sqrt[3]{5} \cdot \sqrt[3]{25}} = \dfrac{\sqrt[3]{150}}{\sqrt[3]{125}} = \dfrac{\sqrt[3]{150}}{5}$

58. $\dfrac{\sqrt[4]{2}}{\sqrt[4]{27}} = \dfrac{\sqrt[4]{2} \cdot \sqrt[4]{3}}{\sqrt[4]{27} \cdot \sqrt[4]{3}} = \dfrac{\sqrt[4]{6}}{\sqrt[4]{81}} = \dfrac{\sqrt[4]{6}}{3}$

59. $\dfrac{\sqrt{5}}{\sqrt{12}} = \dfrac{\sqrt{5}\sqrt{3}}{\sqrt{12}\sqrt{3}} = \dfrac{\sqrt{15}}{\sqrt{36}} = \dfrac{\sqrt{15}}{6}$

60. $\dfrac{\sqrt{7}}{\sqrt{18}} = \dfrac{\sqrt{7}\sqrt{2}}{\sqrt{18}\sqrt{2}} = \dfrac{\sqrt{14}}{\sqrt{36}} = \dfrac{\sqrt{14}}{6}$

61. $\dfrac{\sqrt{3}}{\sqrt{12}} = \dfrac{\sqrt{3}}{\sqrt{4}\sqrt{3}} = \dfrac{1}{\sqrt{4}} = \dfrac{1}{2}$

62. $\dfrac{\sqrt{2}}{\sqrt{18}} = \dfrac{\sqrt{2}}{\sqrt{9}\sqrt{2}} = \dfrac{1}{\sqrt{9}} = \dfrac{1}{3}$

63. $\sqrt{\dfrac{1}{2}} = \dfrac{1}{\sqrt{2}} = \dfrac{1 \cdot \sqrt{2}}{\sqrt{2}\sqrt{2}} = \dfrac{\sqrt{2}}{2}$

64. $\sqrt{\dfrac{3}{8}} = \dfrac{\sqrt{3}}{\sqrt{8}} = \dfrac{\sqrt{3} \cdot \sqrt{2}}{\sqrt{8} \cdot \sqrt{2}} = \dfrac{\sqrt{6}}{4}$

65. $\sqrt[3]{\dfrac{7}{4}} = \dfrac{\sqrt[3]{7} \cdot \sqrt[3]{2}}{\sqrt[3]{4} \cdot \sqrt[3]{2}} = \dfrac{\sqrt[3]{14}}{2}$

66. $\sqrt[4]{\dfrac{1}{5}} = \dfrac{\sqrt[4]{1} \cdot \sqrt[4]{125}}{\sqrt[4]{5} \cdot \sqrt[4]{125}} = \dfrac{\sqrt[4]{125}}{5}$

67. $\sqrt{12x^8} = \sqrt{4x^8}\sqrt{3} = 2x^4\sqrt{3}$

68. $\sqrt{72x^{10}} = \sqrt{36x^{10}}\sqrt{2} = 6x^5\sqrt{2}$

69. $\sqrt{60a^9b^3} = \sqrt{4a^8b^2}\sqrt{15ab}$
$= 2a^4b\sqrt{15ab}$

70. $\sqrt{63w^{15}z^7} = \sqrt{9w^{14}z^6}\sqrt{7wz}$
$= 3w^7z^3\sqrt{7wz}$

71. $\sqrt{\dfrac{x}{y}} = \dfrac{\sqrt{x}\sqrt{y}}{\sqrt{y}\sqrt{y}} = \dfrac{\sqrt{xy}}{y}$

72. $\sqrt{\dfrac{x^2}{a}} = \dfrac{\sqrt{x^2}\sqrt{a}}{\sqrt{a}\sqrt{a}} = \dfrac{x\sqrt{a}}{a}$

73. $\dfrac{\sqrt{a^3}}{\sqrt{b^7}} = \dfrac{\sqrt{a^2}\sqrt{a}}{\sqrt{b^6}\sqrt{b}} = \dfrac{a\sqrt{a}\sqrt{b}}{b^3\sqrt{b}\sqrt{b}} = \dfrac{a\sqrt{ab}}{b^4}$

74. $\dfrac{\sqrt{w^5}}{\sqrt{y^8}} = \dfrac{\sqrt{w^4}\sqrt{w}}{\sqrt{y^8}} = \dfrac{w^2\sqrt{w}}{y^4}$

75. $\sqrt[3]{16x^{13}} = \sqrt[3]{8x^{12}} \cdot \sqrt[3]{2x} = 2x^4\sqrt[3]{2x}$

76. $\sqrt[3]{24x^{17}} = \sqrt[3]{8x^{15}} \cdot \sqrt[3]{3x^2} = 2x^5\sqrt[3]{3x^2}$

77. $\sqrt[4]{x^9y^6} = \sqrt[4]{x^8y^4}\sqrt[4]{xy^2} = x^2y\sqrt[4]{xy^2}$

78. $\sqrt[4]{w^{14}y^7} = \sqrt[4]{w^{12}y^4} \cdot \sqrt[4]{w^2y^3}$
$= w^3y\sqrt[4]{w^2y^3}$

79. $\sqrt[5]{64x^{22}} = \sqrt[5]{32x^{20}} \cdot \sqrt[5]{2x^2} = 2x^4\sqrt[5]{2x^2}$

80. $\sqrt[5]{x^{12}y^5z^3} = \sqrt[5]{x^{10}y^5} \cdot \sqrt[5]{x^2z^3}$
$= x^2y\sqrt[5]{x^2z^3}$

81. $\sqrt[3]{\dfrac{a}{b}} = \dfrac{\sqrt[3]{a}}{\sqrt[3]{b}} = \dfrac{\sqrt[3]{a} \cdot \sqrt[3]{b^2}}{\sqrt[3]{b} \cdot \sqrt[3]{b^2}} = \dfrac{\sqrt[3]{ab^2}}{\sqrt[3]{b^3}}$
$= \dfrac{\sqrt[3]{ab^2}}{b}$

82. $\sqrt[3]{\dfrac{a}{w^2}} = \dfrac{\sqrt[3]{a}}{\sqrt[3]{w^2}} = \dfrac{\sqrt[3]{a} \cdot \sqrt[3]{w}}{\sqrt[3]{w^2} \cdot \sqrt[3]{w}} = \dfrac{\sqrt[3]{aw}}{w}$

83. $\sqrt[4]{3^{12}} = 3^{12/4} = 3^3 = 27$

84. $\sqrt[3]{2^{-9}} = 2^{-9/3} = 2^{-3} = \dfrac{1}{8}$

85. $\sqrt{10^{-2}} = 10^{-2/2} = 10^{-1} = \dfrac{1}{10}$

86. Not a real number, because an even root of a negative number is not real.

87. $\sqrt{\dfrac{8x}{49}} = \dfrac{\sqrt{8x}}{\sqrt{49}} = \dfrac{\sqrt{4}\sqrt{2x}}{7} = \dfrac{2\sqrt{2x}}{7}$

88. $\sqrt{\dfrac{12b}{121}} = \dfrac{\sqrt{12b}}{\sqrt{121}} = \dfrac{\sqrt{4}\sqrt{3b}}{11} = \dfrac{2\sqrt{3b}}{11}$

89. $\sqrt[4]{\dfrac{32a}{81}} = \dfrac{\sqrt[4]{32a}}{\sqrt[4]{81}} = \dfrac{\sqrt[4]{16} \cdot \sqrt[4]{2a}}{3}$
$= \dfrac{2\sqrt[4]{2a}}{3}$

90. $\sqrt[4]{\dfrac{162y}{625}} = \dfrac{\sqrt[4]{162y}}{\sqrt[4]{625}} = \dfrac{\sqrt[4]{81} \cdot \sqrt[4]{2y}}{5}$
$= \dfrac{3\sqrt[4]{2y}}{5}$

91. $\sqrt[3]{-27x^9y^8} = \sqrt[3]{-27x^9y^6} \cdot \sqrt[3]{y^2}$
$= -3x^3y^2\sqrt[3]{y^2}$

92. $\sqrt[4]{32y^8z^{11}} = \sqrt[4]{16y^8z^8} \cdot \sqrt[4]{2z^3}$
$= 2y^2z^2\sqrt[4]{2z^3}$

93. $\dfrac{\sqrt{ab^3}}{\sqrt{a^3b^2}} = \dfrac{\sqrt{ab^3}\sqrt{a}}{\sqrt{a^3b^2}\sqrt{a}} = \dfrac{\sqrt{a^2b^3}}{\sqrt{a^4b^2}}$
$= \dfrac{\sqrt{a^2b^2}\sqrt{b}}{a^2b} = \dfrac{ab\sqrt{b}}{a^2b} = \dfrac{\sqrt{b}}{a}$

94. $\dfrac{\sqrt{m^3n^5}}{\sqrt{m^5n}} = \dfrac{\sqrt{m^2n^4}\sqrt{mn}}{\sqrt{m^4}\sqrt{mn}} = \dfrac{mn^2}{m^2} = \dfrac{n^2}{m}$

95. $\dfrac{\sqrt[3]{a^2b}}{\sqrt[3]{4ab^2} \cdot \sqrt[3]{3ab^5}} = \dfrac{\sqrt[3]{a^2b}}{\sqrt[3]{12a^2b^7}}$

$= \dfrac{\sqrt[3]{a^2b} \cdot \sqrt[3]{18ab^2}}{\sqrt[3]{12a^2b^7} \cdot \sqrt[3]{18ab^2}} = \dfrac{\sqrt[3]{18a^3b^3}}{\sqrt[3]{216a^3b^9}}$
$= \dfrac{ab \cdot \sqrt[3]{18}}{6ab^3} = \dfrac{\sqrt[3]{18}}{6b^2}$

96. $\dfrac{\sqrt[3]{5xy^2}}{\sqrt[3]{18x^2y}} = \dfrac{\sqrt[3]{5xy^2} \cdot \sqrt[3]{12xy^2}}{\sqrt[3]{18x^2y} \cdot \sqrt[3]{12xy^2}}$
$= \dfrac{\sqrt[3]{60x^2y^4}}{\sqrt[3]{216x^3y^3}} = \dfrac{\sqrt[3]{y^3} \cdot \sqrt[3]{60x^2y}}{6xy}$
$= \dfrac{y \cdot \sqrt[3]{60x^2y}}{6xy} = \dfrac{\sqrt[3]{60x^2y}}{6x}$

97. $\dfrac{5}{\sqrt{3}} = 2.887$

98. $\sqrt{\dfrac{2}{27}} = 0.272$

99. $\sqrt[3]{\dfrac{1}{3}} = 0.693$

100. $\sqrt[3]{56} = 3.826$

101. $\dfrac{\sqrt[3]{9}}{\sqrt[4]{4}} = 1.310$

102. $\dfrac{\sqrt[4]{25}}{\sqrt{5}} = 1$

103. $\dfrac{\sqrt[6]{16}}{\sqrt[3]{4}} = 1$

104. $\sqrt[5]{2.48832} = 1.2$

105.
$w = 91.4 - \dfrac{(10.5+6.7\sqrt{20}-0.45\cdot20)(457-5\cdot25)}{110}$
$w = -4°F$
If the air temp is 25°F and wind is 30 mph, then
$w = -10°F$

106. In Minneapolis $w = -18°F$ and in Chicago $w = -15°F$. So a person in Minneapolis feels colder.

107. a) $t = \sqrt{\dfrac{h}{16}} = \dfrac{\sqrt{h}}{4}$

b) $t = \dfrac{\sqrt{40}}{4} = \dfrac{2\sqrt{10}}{4} = \dfrac{\sqrt{10}}{2}$ sec

c) From the graph it appears that if a diver takes 2.5 seconds then the height is 100 feet.

108. $t = \sqrt{\dfrac{17,000}{16}} \approx 32.6$ sec

109. $M = 1.3\sqrt{20} \approx 5.8$ knots

110. $21.22 + 1.25\sqrt{320.13} - 9.8\sqrt[3]{21.44}$
≈ 16.36
No, these dimensions do not satisfy the inequality.
$1.25\sqrt{S} = 16.296 + 9.8\sqrt[3]{21.44} - 21.22$

$$S = \left(\frac{16.296 + 9.8\sqrt[3]{21.44} - 21.22}{1.25} \right)^2$$
$$= 318.29$$

$320.13 - 318.29 = 1.84 \text{ m}^2$

To satisfy the inequality, remove 1.84 m² of sail.

111. $V = \sqrt{\dfrac{841 \cdot 8700}{2.81 \cdot 200}} \approx 114.1 \text{ ft/sec}$

$114.1 \frac{\text{ft}}{\text{sec}} \cdot \frac{1 \text{ mi}}{5280 \text{ ft}} \cdot \frac{3600 \text{ sec}}{1 \text{ hr}} = 77.8 \text{ mph}$

112. a) $V = \sqrt{1.496(7{,}000)} = 102.3 \text{ ft/sec}$

b) $\qquad 115 = \sqrt{1.496L}$
$\qquad\quad 115^2 = 1.496L$
$\qquad\qquad L = \dfrac{115^2}{1.496} = 8840 \text{ lbs}$

7.3 WARM-UPS

1. False, because $\sqrt{3} + \sqrt{3} = 2\sqrt{3}$.

2. True, because
$\sqrt{8} + \sqrt{2} = 2\sqrt{2} + \sqrt{2} = 3\sqrt{2}$.

3. False, because $2\sqrt{3} \cdot 3\sqrt{3} = 6 \cdot 3 = 18$.

4. False, because $\sqrt[3]{2} \cdot \sqrt[3]{2} = \sqrt[3]{4}$.

5. True, because $\sqrt{5} \cdot \sqrt{2} = \sqrt{10}$.

6. False, because $2\sqrt{5} + 3\sqrt{5} = 5\sqrt{5}$.

7. True, because $\sqrt{2}\sqrt{3} = \sqrt{6}$ and
$\sqrt{2}\sqrt{2} = 2$.

8. False, because $\sqrt{12} = \sqrt{4}\sqrt{3} = 2\sqrt{3}$.

9. False, because $(\sqrt{2} + \sqrt{3})^2$
$\qquad = 2 + 2\sqrt{2}\sqrt{3} + 3 = 5 + 2\sqrt{6}$.

10. True,
$(\sqrt{3} - \sqrt{2})(\sqrt{3} + \sqrt{2}) = 3 - 2 = 1$.

7.3 EXERCISES

1. Like radicals are radicals with the same index and same radicand.

2. Like radicals are combined using the distributive property just like we combine like terms.

3. In the product rule the radicals must have the same index, but do not have to have the same radicand.

4. To multiply radicals of different indices, we convert them to equivalent radicals with the same index.

5. $1\sqrt{3} - 2\sqrt{3} = -1\sqrt{3} = -\sqrt{3}$

6. $\sqrt{5} - 3\sqrt{5} = 1\sqrt{5} - 3\sqrt{5} = -2\sqrt{5}$

7. $5\sqrt{7x} + 4\sqrt{7x} = (5+4)\sqrt{7x} = 9\sqrt{7x}$

8. $3\sqrt{6a} + 7\sqrt{6a} = 10\sqrt{6a}$

9. $2 \cdot \sqrt[3]{2} + 3 \cdot \sqrt[3]{2} = (2+3)\sqrt[3]{2} = 5\sqrt[3]{2}$

10. $\sqrt[3]{4} + 4\sqrt[3]{4} = 5\sqrt[3]{4}$

11. $\sqrt{3} + 3\sqrt{3} - \sqrt{5} - \sqrt{5} = 4\sqrt{3} - 2\sqrt{5}$

12. $\sqrt{2} - 5\sqrt{3} - 7\sqrt{2} + 9\sqrt{3}$
$\qquad = \sqrt{2} - 7\sqrt{2} + 9\sqrt{3} - 5\sqrt{3}$
$\qquad = -6\sqrt{2} + 4\sqrt{3}$

13. $\sqrt[3]{2} - \sqrt[3]{2} + \sqrt[3]{x} + 4\sqrt[3]{x} = 5\sqrt[3]{x}$

14. $\sqrt[3]{5y} - 4\sqrt[3]{5y} + \sqrt[3]{x} + \sqrt[3]{x}$
$\qquad = -3\sqrt[3]{5y} + 2\sqrt[3]{x}$

15. $\sqrt[3]{x} + \sqrt[3]{x} - \sqrt{2x} = 2\sqrt[3]{x} - \sqrt{2x}$

16. $\sqrt[3]{ab} + \sqrt{a} + 5\sqrt{a} + \sqrt[3]{ab}$
$\qquad = 2\sqrt[3]{ab} + 6\sqrt{a}$

17. $\sqrt{8} + \sqrt{28} = \sqrt{4}\sqrt{2} + \sqrt{4}\sqrt{7}$
$\qquad = 2\sqrt{2} + 2\sqrt{7}$

18. $\sqrt{12} + \sqrt{24} = \sqrt{4}\sqrt{3} + \sqrt{4}\sqrt{6}$
$\qquad = 2\sqrt{3} + 2\sqrt{6}$

19. $\sqrt{2} - \sqrt{8} = \sqrt{2} - 2\sqrt{2} = -\sqrt{2}$

20. $\sqrt{20} - \sqrt{125} = \sqrt{4}\sqrt{5} - \sqrt{25}\sqrt{5}$
$\qquad = 2\sqrt{5} - 5\sqrt{5} = -3\sqrt{5}$

21. $\dfrac{\sqrt{2}}{2} + \sqrt{2} = \dfrac{\sqrt{2}}{2} + \dfrac{2\sqrt{2}}{2} = \dfrac{3\sqrt{2}}{2}$

22. $\dfrac{\sqrt{3}}{3} - \sqrt{3} = \dfrac{\sqrt{3}}{3} - \dfrac{3\sqrt{3}}{3} = -\dfrac{2\sqrt{3}}{3}$

23. $\sqrt{80} + \sqrt{\dfrac{1}{5}} = \sqrt{16}\sqrt{5} + \dfrac{1\sqrt{5}}{\sqrt{5}\sqrt{5}}$
$= 4\sqrt{5} + \dfrac{\sqrt{5}}{5} = \dfrac{20\sqrt{5}}{5} + \dfrac{\sqrt{5}}{5} = \dfrac{21\sqrt{5}}{5}$

24. $\sqrt{32} + \sqrt{\dfrac{1}{2}} = \sqrt{16}\sqrt{2} + \dfrac{1\sqrt{2}\sqrt{2}}{\sqrt{2}\sqrt{2}}$
$= 4\sqrt{2} + \dfrac{\sqrt{2}}{2} = \dfrac{8\sqrt{2}}{2} + \dfrac{\sqrt{2}}{2} = \dfrac{9\sqrt{2}}{2}$

25. $\sqrt{45x^3} - \sqrt{18x^2} + \sqrt{50x^2} - \sqrt{20x^3}$
$\qquad = 3x\sqrt{5x} - 3x\sqrt{2} + 5x\sqrt{2} - 2x\sqrt{5x}$
$\qquad = x\sqrt{5x} + 2x\sqrt{2}$

26. $\sqrt{12x^5} - \sqrt{18x} - \sqrt{300x^5} + \sqrt{98x}$
$= \sqrt{4x^4}\sqrt{3x} - \sqrt{9}\sqrt{2x} - \sqrt{100x^4}\sqrt{3x}$
$\qquad\qquad + \sqrt{49}\sqrt{2x}$
$= 2x^2 \cdot \sqrt{3x} - 3\sqrt{2x} - 10x^2 \cdot \sqrt{3x} + 7\sqrt{2x}$

$= 4\sqrt{2x} - 8x^2\sqrt{3x}$

27. $\sqrt[3]{24} + \sqrt[3]{81} = \sqrt[3]{8} \cdot \sqrt[3]{3} + \sqrt[3]{27} \cdot \sqrt[3]{3}$
$\qquad = 2 \cdot \sqrt[3]{3} + 3 \cdot \sqrt[3]{3} = 5\sqrt[3]{3}$

28. $\sqrt[3]{24} + \sqrt[3]{375} = \sqrt[3]{8} \cdot \sqrt[3]{3} + \sqrt[3]{125} \cdot \sqrt[3]{3}$
$= 2 \cdot \sqrt[3]{3} + 5 \cdot \sqrt[3]{3} = 7\sqrt[3]{3}$

29. $\sqrt[4]{16 \cdot 3} - \sqrt[4]{81 \cdot 3} = 2 \cdot \sqrt[4]{3} - 3 \cdot \sqrt[4]{3}$
$= -\sqrt[4]{3}$

30. $\sqrt[5]{64} + \sqrt[5]{2} = \sqrt[5]{32} \cdot \sqrt[5]{2} + \sqrt[5]{2}$
$= 2 \cdot \sqrt[5]{2} + \sqrt[5]{2} = 3\sqrt[5]{2}$

31. $\sqrt[3]{54t^4y^3} - \sqrt[3]{16t^4y^3}$
$= \sqrt[3]{27t^3y^3} \cdot \sqrt[3]{2t} - \sqrt[3]{8t^3y^3} \cdot \sqrt[3]{2t}$
$= 3ty \cdot \sqrt[3]{2t} - 2ty \cdot \sqrt[3]{2t} = ty\sqrt[3]{2t}$

32. $\sqrt[3]{2000w^2z^5} - \sqrt[3]{16w^2z^5}$
$= \sqrt[3]{1000z^3} \cdot \sqrt[3]{2w^2z^2} - \sqrt[3]{8z^3} \cdot \sqrt[3]{2w^2z^2}$
$= 10z \cdot \sqrt[3]{2w^2z^2} - 2z \cdot \sqrt[3]{2w^2z^2} = 8z\sqrt[3]{2w^2z^2}$

33. $\sqrt{3}\sqrt{5} = \sqrt{15}$

34. $\sqrt{5} \cdot \sqrt{7} = \sqrt{35}$

35. $(2\sqrt{5})(3\sqrt{10}) = 6\sqrt{50} = 6\sqrt{25}\sqrt{2}$
$= 6 \cdot 5\sqrt{2} = 30\sqrt{2}$

36. $3\sqrt{2}(-4\sqrt{10}) = -12\sqrt{20} = -12 \cdot 2\sqrt{5}$
$= -24\sqrt{5}$

37. $(2\sqrt{7a})(3\sqrt{2a}) = 6\sqrt{14a^2} = 6\sqrt{a^2}\sqrt{14}$
$= 6a\sqrt{14}$

38. $(2\sqrt{5c})(5\sqrt{5}) = 10\sqrt{25c} = 10 \cdot 5\sqrt{c}$
$= 50\sqrt{c}$

39. $(\sqrt[4]{9})(\sqrt[4]{27}) = \sqrt[4]{243} = \sqrt[4]{81} \cdot \sqrt[4]{3}$
$= 3\sqrt[4]{3}$

40. $(\sqrt[3]{5})(\sqrt[3]{100}) = \sqrt[3]{500} = \sqrt[3]{125} \cdot \sqrt[3]{4}$
$= 5\sqrt[3]{4}$

41. $(2\sqrt{3})^2 = 4 \cdot 3 = 12$

42. $(-4\sqrt{2})^2 = (-4)^2(\sqrt{2})^2 = 16 \cdot 2 = 32$

43. $\sqrt[3]{\dfrac{4x^2}{3}} \cdot \sqrt[3]{\dfrac{2x^2}{3}} = \sqrt[3]{\dfrac{8x^4}{9}}$

$= \sqrt[3]{8x^3} \cdot \sqrt[3]{\dfrac{x}{9}} = 2x \cdot \dfrac{\sqrt[3]{x} \cdot \sqrt[3]{3}}{\sqrt[3]{9} \cdot \sqrt[3]{3}} = \dfrac{2x\sqrt[3]{3x}}{3}$

44. $\sqrt[4]{\dfrac{4x^2}{5}} \cdot \sqrt[4]{\dfrac{4x^3}{25}} = \sqrt[4]{\dfrac{16x^5}{125}}$

$= \sqrt[4]{16x^4} \cdot \sqrt[4]{\dfrac{x}{125}} = 2x \cdot \dfrac{\sqrt[4]{x} \cdot \sqrt[4]{5}}{\sqrt[4]{125} \cdot \sqrt[4]{5}}$

$= \dfrac{2x\sqrt[4]{5x}}{5}$

45. $2\sqrt{3}(\sqrt{6} + 3\sqrt{3}) = 2\sqrt{18} + 18$
$= 2\sqrt{9}\sqrt{2} + 18 = 6\sqrt{2} + 18$

46. $2\sqrt{5}(\sqrt{3} + 3\sqrt{5}) = 2\sqrt{15} + 30$

47. $\sqrt{5}(\sqrt{10} - 2) = \sqrt{50} - 2\sqrt{5}$
$= \sqrt{25}\sqrt{2} - 2\sqrt{5} = 5\sqrt{2} - 2\sqrt{5}$

48. $\sqrt{6}(\sqrt{15} - 1) = \sqrt{90} - \sqrt{6}$

$= \sqrt{9}\sqrt{10} - \sqrt{6} = 3\sqrt{10} - \sqrt{6}$

49. $\sqrt[3]{3t}(\sqrt[3]{9t} - \sqrt[3]{t^2}) = \sqrt[3]{27t^2} - \sqrt[3]{3t^3}$
$= 3\sqrt[3]{t^2} - t\sqrt[3]{3}$

50. $\sqrt[3]{2}(\sqrt[3]{12x} - \sqrt[3]{2x}) = \sqrt[3]{24x} - \sqrt[3]{4x}$
$= 2\sqrt[3]{3x} - \sqrt[3]{4x}$

51. $(\sqrt{3} + 2)(\sqrt{3} - 5)$
$= 3 + 2\sqrt{3} - 5\sqrt{3} - 10 = -7 - 3\sqrt{3}$

52. $(\sqrt{5} + 2)(\sqrt{5} - 6)$
$= 5 + 2\sqrt{5} - 6\sqrt{5} - 12$
$= -7 - 4\sqrt{5}$

53. $(\sqrt{11} - 3)(\sqrt{11} + 3) = 11 - 9 = 2$

54. $(\sqrt{2} + 5)(\sqrt{2} + 5)$
$= 2 + 5\sqrt{2} + 5\sqrt{2} + 25$
$= 27 + 10\sqrt{2}$

55. $(2\sqrt{5} - 7)(2\sqrt{5} + 4)$
$= 20 - 14\sqrt{5} + 8\sqrt{5} - 28$
$= -8 - 6\sqrt{5}$

56. $(2\sqrt{6} - 3)(2\sqrt{6} + 4)$
$= 24 - 6\sqrt{6} + 8\sqrt{6} - 12$
$= 12 + 2\sqrt{6}$

57. $(2\sqrt{3} - \sqrt{6})(\sqrt{3} + 2\sqrt{6})$
$= 6 - \sqrt{18} + 4\sqrt{18} - 12$
$= -6 - 3\sqrt{2} + 4 \cdot 3\sqrt{2} = -6 + 9\sqrt{2}$

58. $(3\sqrt{3} - \sqrt{2})(\sqrt{2} + \sqrt{3})$
$= 3\sqrt{6} - 2 + 9 - \sqrt{6} = 2\sqrt{6} + 7$

59. $\sqrt[3]{3} \cdot \sqrt{3} = 3^{1/3}3^{1/2} = 3^{5/6} = \sqrt[6]{3^5}$

60. $\sqrt{3} \cdot \sqrt[4]{3} = 3^{1/2}3^{1/4} = 3^{3/4} = \sqrt[4]{27}$

61. $\sqrt[3]{5} \cdot \sqrt[4]{5} = 5^{1/3}5^{1/4} = 5^{7/12} = \sqrt[12]{5^7}$

62. $\sqrt[3]{2} \cdot \sqrt[5]{2} = 2^{1/3}2^{1/5} = 2^{8/15} = \sqrt[15]{2^8}$

63. $\sqrt[3]{2} \cdot \sqrt{5} = 2^{1/3}5^{1/2} = 2^{2/6}5^{3/6}$
$= \sqrt[6]{2^25^3} = \sqrt[6]{500}$

64. $\sqrt{6} \cdot \sqrt[3]{2} = 6^{1/2}2^{1/3} = 6^{3/6}2^{2/6}$
$= \sqrt[6]{6^32^2} = \sqrt[6]{864}$

65. $\sqrt[3]{2} \cdot \sqrt[4]{3} = 2^{1/3}3^{1/4} = 2^{4/12}3^{3/12}$
$= \sqrt[12]{2^43^3} = \sqrt[12]{432}$

66. $\sqrt[3]{3} \cdot \sqrt[4]{2} = 3^{1/3}2^{1/4} = 3^{4/12}2^{3/12}$
$= \sqrt[12]{3^42^3} = \sqrt[12]{648}$

67. $(\sqrt{3} - 2)(\sqrt{3} + 2) = 3 - 4 = -1$

68. $(7 - \sqrt{3})(7 + \sqrt{3}) = 49 - 3 = 46$

69. $(\sqrt{5} + \sqrt{2})(\sqrt{5} - \sqrt{2}) = 5 - 2 = 3$

70. $(\sqrt{6} - \sqrt{5})(\sqrt{6} + \sqrt{5}) = 6 - 5 = 1$

71. $(2\sqrt{5} + 1)(2\sqrt{5} - 1) = 4 \cdot 5 - 1 = 19$

72. $(3\sqrt{2} - 4)(3\sqrt{2} + 4) = 9 \cdot 2 - 16$
$= 18 - 16 = 2$

73. $(3\sqrt{2} + \sqrt{5})(3\sqrt{2} - \sqrt{5}) = 9 \cdot 2 - 5$
$= 13$

74. $(2\sqrt{3} - \sqrt{7})(2\sqrt{3} + \sqrt{7}) = 4 \cdot 3 - 7$
$\qquad = 5$

75. $(5 - 3\sqrt{x})(5 + 3\sqrt{x}) = 25 - 9x$

76. $(4\sqrt{y} + 3\sqrt{z})(4\sqrt{y} - 3\sqrt{z}) = 16y - 9z$

77. $\sqrt{300} + \sqrt{3} = 10\sqrt{3} + \sqrt{3} = 11\sqrt{3}$

78. $\sqrt{50} + \sqrt{2} = 5\sqrt{2} + 1\sqrt{2} = 6\sqrt{2}$

79. $2\sqrt{5} \cdot 5\sqrt{6} = 10\sqrt{30}$

80. $3\sqrt{6} \cdot 5\sqrt{10} = 15\sqrt{60} = 15\sqrt{4}\sqrt{15}$
$\qquad = 15 \cdot 2\sqrt{15} = 30\sqrt{15}$

81. $(3 + 2\sqrt{7})(\sqrt{7} - 2)$
$\qquad = 3\sqrt{7} - 6 + 2 \cdot 7 - 4\sqrt{7}$
$\qquad = 8 - \sqrt{7}$

82. $(2 + \sqrt{7})(\sqrt{7} - 2)$
$\qquad = 2\sqrt{7} + 7 - 4 - 2\sqrt{7} = 3$

83. $4\sqrt{w} \cdot 4\sqrt{w} = 16(\sqrt{w})^2 = 16w$

84. $3\sqrt{m} \cdot 5\sqrt{m} = 3 \cdot 5\sqrt{m^2} = 15m$

85. $\sqrt{3x^3} \cdot \sqrt{6x^2} = \sqrt{18x^5} = \sqrt{9x^4} \cdot \sqrt{2x}$
$\qquad = 3x^2\sqrt{2x}$

86. $\sqrt{2t^5} \cdot \sqrt{10t^4} = \sqrt{20t^9} = \sqrt{4t^8}\sqrt{5t}$
$\qquad = 2t^4\sqrt{5t}$

87. $\dfrac{1}{\sqrt{2}} - \dfrac{1}{\sqrt{8}} + \dfrac{1}{\sqrt{18}}$
$= \dfrac{\sqrt{2}}{2} - \dfrac{\sqrt{8}}{8} + \dfrac{\sqrt{2}}{6}$
$= \dfrac{\sqrt{2}}{2} - \dfrac{2\sqrt{2}}{8} + \dfrac{\sqrt{2}}{6} = \sqrt{2}\left(\dfrac{1}{2} - \dfrac{1}{4} + \dfrac{1}{6}\right)$
$= \dfrac{5\sqrt{2}}{12}$

88. $\dfrac{1}{\sqrt{3}} + \dfrac{1}{\sqrt{3}} - \sqrt{3} = \dfrac{\sqrt{3}}{3} + \dfrac{\sqrt{3}}{3} - \dfrac{3\sqrt{3}}{3}$
$\qquad = \dfrac{-\sqrt{3}}{3}$

89. $(2\sqrt{5} + \sqrt{2})(3\sqrt{5} - \sqrt{2})$
$= 30 + 3\sqrt{10} - 2\sqrt{10} - 2 = 28 + \sqrt{10}$

90. $(3\sqrt{2} - \sqrt{3})(2\sqrt{2} + 3\sqrt{3})$
$\qquad = 12 - 2\sqrt{6} + 9\sqrt{6} - 9 = 3 + 7\sqrt{6}$

91. $\dfrac{\sqrt{2}}{3} + \dfrac{\sqrt{2}}{5} = \dfrac{5\sqrt{2}}{5 \cdot 3} + \dfrac{3\sqrt{2}}{3 \cdot 5} = \dfrac{8\sqrt{2}}{15}$

92. $\dfrac{\sqrt{2}}{4} + \dfrac{\sqrt{3}}{5} = \dfrac{5\sqrt{2}}{4 \cdot 5} + \dfrac{4\sqrt{3}}{5 \cdot 4}$
$\qquad = \dfrac{5\sqrt{2} + 4\sqrt{3}}{20}$

93. $(5 + 2\sqrt{2})(5 - 2\sqrt{2}) = 25 - 4 \cdot 2 = 17$

94. $(3 - 2\sqrt{7})(3 + 2\sqrt{7}) = 9 - 4 \cdot 7$
$\qquad = 9 - 28 = -19$

95. $(3 + \sqrt{x})^2 = 9 + 2 \cdot 3\sqrt{x} + x$
$\qquad = 9 + 6\sqrt{x} + x$

96. $(1 - \sqrt{x})^2 = 1 - 2\sqrt{x} + x$

97. $(5\sqrt{x} - 3)^2 = 25x - 2 \cdot 3 \cdot 5\sqrt{x} + 9$
$\qquad = 25x - 30\sqrt{x} + 9$

98. $(3\sqrt{a} + 2)^2 = 9a + 2 \cdot 3\sqrt{a} \cdot 2 + 2^2$
$\qquad = 9a + 12\sqrt{a} + 4$

99. $(1 + \sqrt{x+2})^2 = 1 + 2\sqrt{x+2} + x + 2$
$\qquad = x + 3 + 2\sqrt{x+2}$

100. $(\sqrt{x-1} + 1)^2 = x - 1 + 2\sqrt{x-1} + 1$
$\qquad = x + 2\sqrt{x-1}$

101. $\sqrt{4w} - \sqrt{9w} = 2\sqrt{w} - 3\sqrt{w}$
$\qquad = -\sqrt{w}$

102. $10\sqrt{m} - \sqrt{16m} = 10\sqrt{m} - 4\sqrt{m}$
$\qquad = 6\sqrt{m}$

103. $2\sqrt{a^3} + 3\sqrt{a^3} - 2a\sqrt{4a}$
$\qquad = 2a\sqrt{a} + 3a\sqrt{a} - 4a\sqrt{a} = a\sqrt{a}$

104. $5\sqrt{w^2y} - 7\sqrt{w^2y} + 6\sqrt{w^2y} = 4\sqrt{w^2y}$
$\qquad = 4w\sqrt{y}$

105. $\sqrt{25 \cdot 2a} + \sqrt{9 \cdot 2a} - \sqrt{2a}$
$\qquad = 5\sqrt{2a} + 3\sqrt{2a} - \sqrt{2a} = 7\sqrt{2a}$

106. $\sqrt{200z} + \sqrt{128z} - \sqrt{8z}$
$\qquad = 10\sqrt{2z} + 8\sqrt{2z} - 2\sqrt{2z} = 16\sqrt{2z}$

107. $\sqrt{x^5} + 2x\sqrt{x^3}$
$\qquad = \sqrt{x^4}\sqrt{x} + 2x\sqrt{x^2}\sqrt{x}$
$\qquad = x^2 \cdot \sqrt{x} + 2x^2 \cdot \sqrt{x} = 3x^2\sqrt{x}$

108. $\sqrt{8x^3} + \sqrt{50x^3} - x\sqrt{2x}$
$\qquad = \sqrt{4x^2}\sqrt{2x} + \sqrt{25x^2}\sqrt{2x} - x\sqrt{2x}$
$\qquad = 2x\sqrt{2x} + 5x\sqrt{2x} - x\sqrt{2x} = 6x\sqrt{2x}$

109. $(\sqrt{a} + a^3)(\sqrt{a} - a^3) = (\sqrt{a})^2 - (a^3)^2$
$\qquad = a - a^6$

110. $(\sqrt{wz} - 2y^4)(\sqrt{wz} + 2y^4) = wz - 4y^8$

111. $\sqrt[3]{-16x^4} + 5x\sqrt[3]{54x}$
$= -2x \cdot \sqrt[3]{2x} + 5x \cdot 3 \cdot \sqrt[3]{2x} = 13x\sqrt[3]{2x}$

112. $\sqrt[3]{3x^5y^7} - \sqrt[3]{24x^5y^7}$
$\qquad = xy^2 \cdot \sqrt[3]{3x^2y} - 2xy^2 \cdot \sqrt[3]{3x^2y}$
$\qquad = -xy^2\sqrt[3]{3x^2y}$

113. $\sqrt[3]{\dfrac{y^7}{4x}} = \dfrac{y^2\sqrt[3]{y}}{\sqrt[3]{4x}} = \dfrac{y^2\sqrt[3]{y} \cdot \sqrt[3]{2x^2}}{\sqrt[3]{4x} \cdot \sqrt[3]{2x^2}}$
$\qquad = \dfrac{y^2\sqrt[3]{2x^2y}}{\sqrt[3]{8x^3}} = \dfrac{y^2\sqrt[3]{2x^2y}}{2x}$

114. $\sqrt[4]{\dfrac{16}{9z^3}} = \dfrac{2 \cdot \sqrt[4]{9z}}{\sqrt[4]{9z^3} \cdot \sqrt[4]{9z}} = \dfrac{2 \cdot \sqrt[4]{9z}}{\sqrt[4]{81z^4}}$
$\qquad = \dfrac{2\sqrt[4]{9z}}{3z}$

115. $\sqrt[3]{\dfrac{x}{5}} \cdot \sqrt[3]{\dfrac{x^5}{5}} = \sqrt[3]{\dfrac{x^6}{25}} = \dfrac{x^2 \cdot \sqrt[3]{5}}{\sqrt[3]{25} \cdot \sqrt[3]{5}}$

$\qquad = \dfrac{x^2 \sqrt[3]{5}}{5}$

116. $\sqrt[4]{a^3}\left(\sqrt[4]{a} - \sqrt[4]{a^5}\right) = \sqrt[4]{a^4} - \sqrt[4]{a^8}$

$\qquad = a - a^2$

117. $\sqrt[3]{2x} \cdot \sqrt{2x} = (2x)^{1/3}(2x)^{1/2} = (2x)^{5/6}$

$\qquad = \sqrt[6]{32x^5}$

118. $\sqrt[3]{2m} \cdot \sqrt[4]{2n} = (2m)^{1/3}(2n)^{1/4}$

$\qquad = (2m)^{4/12}(2n)^{3/12} = \sqrt[12]{2^4 m^4 2^3 n^3}$

$\qquad = \sqrt[12]{128 m^4 n^3}$

119. $A = \sqrt{6} \cdot \sqrt{3} = \sqrt{18} = 3\sqrt{2}$ ft^2

120. $V = (\sqrt{3})^3 = \sqrt{27} = 3\sqrt{3}$ m^3

121. $A = \frac{1}{2}\sqrt{6}(\sqrt{3} + \sqrt{12})$

$\qquad = \frac{1}{2}\sqrt{6}(\sqrt{3} + 2\sqrt{3})$

$\qquad = \frac{1}{2}\sqrt{6} \cdot 3\sqrt{3} = \dfrac{3\sqrt{18}}{2}$

$\qquad = \dfrac{9\sqrt{2}}{2}$ ft^2

122. $A = \frac{1}{2}\sqrt{30}\sqrt{6} = \frac{1}{2}\sqrt{5}\sqrt{6}\sqrt{6} = \frac{6}{2}\sqrt{5}$

$\qquad = 3\sqrt{5}$ m^2

123. No because $\sqrt{9} + \sqrt{16} = 3 + 4 = 7$ and $\sqrt{25} = 5$.

124. The identities are (a) and (d) because product and quotient rules are correctly applied in those cases.

7.4 WARM-UPS

1. True, because $\sqrt{3}\sqrt{2} = \sqrt{6}$.

2. True, because

$\dfrac{2}{\sqrt{2}} = \dfrac{2\sqrt{2}}{\sqrt{2}\sqrt{2}} = \dfrac{2\sqrt{2}}{2} = \sqrt{2}$.

3. False, because $\dfrac{4-\sqrt{10}}{2} = 2 - \dfrac{\sqrt{10}}{2}$.

4. True, because $\dfrac{1}{\sqrt{3}} = \dfrac{1 \cdot \sqrt{3}}{\sqrt{3}\sqrt{3}} = \dfrac{\sqrt{3}}{3}$.

5. False, because $\dfrac{8\sqrt{7}}{2\sqrt{7}} = 4$.

6. True, because
$(2 - \sqrt{3})(2 + \sqrt{3}) = 4 - 3 = 1$.

7. False, because $\dfrac{\sqrt{12}}{3} = \dfrac{2\sqrt{3}}{3}$.

8. True, because
$\sqrt{20}\sqrt{5} = \dfrac{\sqrt{4}\sqrt{5}}{\sqrt{5}} = \sqrt{4} = 2$.

9. True, because $(2\sqrt{4})^2 = 4 \cdot 4 = 16$.

10. True, because
$(3\sqrt{5})^3 = 3^3 \cdot \sqrt{5^3} = 27\sqrt{125}$.

7.4 EXERCISES

1. $\sqrt{15} \div \sqrt{5} = \sqrt{\dfrac{15}{5}} = \sqrt{3}$

2. $\sqrt{14} \div \sqrt{7} = \sqrt{\dfrac{14}{7}} = \sqrt{2}$

3. $\sqrt{3} \div \sqrt{5} = \dfrac{\sqrt{3}}{\sqrt{5}} = \dfrac{\sqrt{3}\sqrt{5}}{\sqrt{5}\sqrt{5}} = \dfrac{\sqrt{15}}{5}$

4. $\sqrt{5} \div \sqrt{7} = \dfrac{\sqrt{5}}{\sqrt{7}} = \dfrac{\sqrt{5}\sqrt{7}}{\sqrt{7}\sqrt{7}} = \dfrac{\sqrt{35}}{7}$

5. $\dfrac{3\sqrt{3}}{5\sqrt{6}} = \dfrac{3}{5\sqrt{2}} = \dfrac{3\sqrt{2}}{5\sqrt{2}\sqrt{2}} = \dfrac{3\sqrt{2}}{10}$

6. $(2\sqrt{2}) \div (4\sqrt{10}) = \dfrac{2\sqrt{2}}{4\sqrt{10}} = \dfrac{\sqrt{2}\sqrt{10}}{2\sqrt{10}\sqrt{10}}$

$\qquad = \dfrac{\sqrt{20}}{20} = \dfrac{\sqrt{4}\sqrt{5}}{20} = \dfrac{2\sqrt{5}}{20} = \dfrac{\sqrt{5}}{10}$

7. $\dfrac{2\sqrt{3}}{3\sqrt{6}} = \dfrac{2}{3\sqrt{2}} = \dfrac{2\sqrt{2}}{3\sqrt{2}\sqrt{2}} = \dfrac{2\sqrt{2}}{3 \cdot 2}$

$\qquad = \dfrac{\sqrt{2}}{3}$

8. $\dfrac{5\sqrt{12}}{4\sqrt{6}} = \dfrac{5\sqrt{2}}{4}$

9. $\dfrac{\sqrt[3]{20}}{\sqrt[3]{2}} = \sqrt[3]{\dfrac{20}{2}} = \sqrt[3]{10}$

10. $\dfrac{\sqrt[4]{48}}{\sqrt[4]{3}} = \dfrac{\sqrt[4]{16} \cdot \sqrt[4]{3}}{\sqrt[4]{3}} = 2$

11. $\dfrac{\sqrt[3]{8x^7}}{\sqrt[3]{2x}} = \sqrt[3]{4x^6} = x^2\sqrt[3]{4}$

12. $\sqrt[4]{4a^{10}} \div \sqrt[4]{2a^2} = \dfrac{\sqrt[4]{a^8}\sqrt[4]{4a^2}}{\sqrt[4]{2a^2}} = a^2\sqrt[4]{2}$

13. $\dfrac{6 + \sqrt{9 \cdot 5}}{3} = \dfrac{6 + 3\sqrt{5}}{3} = 2 + \sqrt{5}$

14. $\dfrac{10 + \sqrt{50}}{5} = \dfrac{10 + 5\sqrt{2}}{5} = 2 + \sqrt{2}$

15. $\dfrac{-2 + \sqrt{4 \cdot 3}}{-2} = \dfrac{-2 + 2\sqrt{3}}{-2} = 1 - \sqrt{3}$

16. $\dfrac{-6 + \sqrt{72}}{-6} = \dfrac{-6 + 6\sqrt{2}}{-6} = 1 - \sqrt{2}$

17. $\dfrac{1 + \sqrt{2}}{\sqrt{3} - 1} = \dfrac{(1 + \sqrt{2})(\sqrt{3} + 1)}{(\sqrt{3} - 1)(\sqrt{3} + 1)}$

$\qquad = \dfrac{1 + \sqrt{6} + \sqrt{2} + \sqrt{3}}{2}$

18. $\dfrac{2 - \sqrt{3}}{\sqrt{2} + \sqrt{6}} = \dfrac{(2 - \sqrt{3})(\sqrt{2} - \sqrt{6})}{(\sqrt{2} + \sqrt{6})(\sqrt{2} - \sqrt{6})}$

$\quad = \dfrac{2\sqrt{2} - \sqrt{6} - 2\sqrt{6} + \sqrt{18}}{2 - 6}$

$\quad = \dfrac{2\sqrt{2} - 3\sqrt{6} + 3\sqrt{2}}{-4}$

$$= \frac{5\sqrt{2}-3\sqrt{6}}{-4} = \frac{(5\sqrt{2}-3\sqrt{6})(-1)}{(-4)(-1)}$$
$$= \frac{3\sqrt{6}-5\sqrt{2}}{4}$$

19. $\dfrac{\sqrt{2}}{\sqrt{6}+\sqrt{3}} = \dfrac{\sqrt{2}(\sqrt{6}-\sqrt{3})}{(\sqrt{6}+\sqrt{3})(\sqrt{6}-\sqrt{3})}$
$$= \frac{\sqrt{12}-\sqrt{6}}{6-3} = \frac{2\sqrt{3}-\sqrt{6}}{3}$$

20. $\dfrac{5}{\sqrt{7}-\sqrt{5}} = \dfrac{5(\sqrt{7}+\sqrt{5})}{(\sqrt{7}-\sqrt{5})(\sqrt{7}+\sqrt{5})}$
$$= \frac{5\sqrt{7}+5\sqrt{5}}{7-5} = \frac{5\sqrt{7}+5\sqrt{5}}{2}$$

21. $\dfrac{2\sqrt{3}(3\sqrt{2}+\sqrt{5})}{(3\sqrt{2}-\sqrt{5})(3\sqrt{2}+\sqrt{5})}$
$$= \frac{6\sqrt{6}+2\sqrt{15}}{18-5} = \frac{6\sqrt{6}+2\sqrt{15}}{13}$$

22. $\dfrac{3\sqrt{5}}{5\sqrt{2}+\sqrt{6}}$
$$= \frac{3\sqrt{5}(5\sqrt{2}-\sqrt{6})}{(5\sqrt{2}+\sqrt{6})(5\sqrt{2}-\sqrt{6})}$$
$$= \frac{15\sqrt{10}-3\sqrt{30}}{50-6} = \frac{15\sqrt{10}-3\sqrt{30}}{44}$$

23. $\dfrac{(1+3\sqrt{2})(2\sqrt{6}-3\sqrt{10})}{(2\sqrt{6}+3\sqrt{10})(2\sqrt{6}-3\sqrt{10})}$
$$= \frac{2\sqrt{6}+6\sqrt{12}-3\sqrt{10}-9\sqrt{20}}{24-90}$$
$$= \frac{2\sqrt{6}+12\sqrt{3}-3\sqrt{10}-18\sqrt{5}}{-66}$$
$$= \frac{18\sqrt{5}+3\sqrt{10}-2\sqrt{6}-12\sqrt{3}}{66}$$

24. $\dfrac{3\sqrt{3}+1}{4-5\sqrt{3}} = \dfrac{(3\sqrt{3}+1)(4+5\sqrt{3})}{(4-5\sqrt{3})(4+5\sqrt{3})}$
$$= \frac{12\sqrt{3}+4+45+5\sqrt{3}}{16-75} = -\frac{17\sqrt{3}+49}{59}$$

25. $(2\sqrt{2})^5 = 2^5 \cdot \sqrt{2^5} = 32\sqrt{16}\sqrt{2}$
$$= 128\sqrt{2}$$

26. $(3\sqrt{3})^4 = 3^4\sqrt{3}\sqrt{3}\sqrt{3}\sqrt{3} = 3^4 \cdot 3 \cdot 3$
$$= 729$$

27. $(\sqrt{x})^5 = \sqrt{x^5} = \sqrt{x^4}\sqrt{x} = x^2\sqrt{x}$

28. $(2\sqrt{y})^3 = 8\sqrt{y^3} = 8\sqrt{y^2}\sqrt{y} = 8y\sqrt{y}$

29. $(-3\sqrt{x^3})^3 = -27\sqrt{x^9} = -27\sqrt{x^8}\sqrt{x}$
$$= -27x^4\sqrt{x}$$

30. $(-2\sqrt{x^3})^4 = 16\sqrt{x^{12}} = 16x^6$

31. $(2x\sqrt[3]{x^2})^3 = 8x^3\sqrt[3]{x^6} = 8x^3 \cdot x^2 = 8x^5$

32. $(2y\sqrt[3]{4y})^3 = 8y^3 \cdot 4y = 32y^4$

33. $(-2\sqrt[3]{5})^2 = (-2)^2 \cdot \sqrt[3]{5^2} = 4\sqrt[3]{25}$

34. $(-3\sqrt[3]{4})^2 = 9\sqrt[3]{16} = 9\sqrt[3]{8}\sqrt[3]{2}$

$$= 9 \cdot 2\sqrt[3]{2} = 18\sqrt[3]{2}$$

35. $(\sqrt[3]{x^2})^6 = (x^2)^{6/3} = (x^2)^2 = x^4$

36. $(2\sqrt[4]{y^3})^3 = 8\sqrt[4]{y^9} = 8\sqrt[4]{y^8}\sqrt[4]{y}$
$$= 8y^2\sqrt[4]{y}$$

37. $\dfrac{\sqrt{3}}{\sqrt{2}} + \dfrac{2}{\sqrt{2}} = \dfrac{\sqrt{3}\sqrt{2}}{\sqrt{2}\sqrt{2}} + \dfrac{2\sqrt{2}}{\sqrt{2}\sqrt{2}}$
$$= \frac{\sqrt{6}}{2} + \frac{2\sqrt{2}}{2} = \frac{\sqrt{6}+2\sqrt{2}}{2}$$

38. $\dfrac{2}{\sqrt{7}} + \dfrac{5}{\sqrt{7}} = \dfrac{7}{\sqrt{7}} = \dfrac{7\sqrt{7}}{\sqrt{7}\sqrt{7}} = \dfrac{7\sqrt{7}}{7}$
$$= \sqrt{7}$$

39. $\dfrac{\sqrt{3}}{\sqrt{2}} + \dfrac{3\sqrt{6}}{2} = \dfrac{\sqrt{3}\sqrt{2}}{\sqrt{2}\sqrt{2}} + \dfrac{3\sqrt{6}}{2}$
$$= \frac{\sqrt{6}}{2} + \frac{3\sqrt{6}}{2} = \frac{4\sqrt{6}}{2} = 2\sqrt{6}$$

40. $\dfrac{\sqrt{3}}{2\sqrt{2}} + \dfrac{\sqrt{5}}{3\sqrt{2}}$
$$= \frac{\sqrt{3}\cdot 3\sqrt{2}}{2\sqrt{2}\cdot 3\sqrt{2}} + \frac{\sqrt{5}\cdot 2\sqrt{2}}{3\sqrt{2}\cdot 2\sqrt{2}}$$
$$= \frac{3\sqrt{6}}{12} + \frac{2\sqrt{10}}{12} = \frac{3\sqrt{6}+2\sqrt{10}}{12}$$

41. $\dfrac{\sqrt{6}}{2} \cdot \dfrac{1}{\sqrt{3}} = \dfrac{\sqrt{2}\sqrt{3}}{2\sqrt{3}} = \dfrac{\sqrt{2}}{2}$

42. $\dfrac{\sqrt{6}}{\sqrt{7}} \cdot \dfrac{\sqrt{14}}{\sqrt{3}} = \dfrac{\sqrt{2}\sqrt{3}}{\sqrt{7}} \cdot \dfrac{\sqrt{2}\sqrt{7}}{\sqrt{3}} = 2$

43. $\dfrac{2\sqrt{w}}{3\sqrt{w}} = \dfrac{2}{3}$

44. $2 \div 3\sqrt{a} = \dfrac{2\sqrt{a}}{3\sqrt{a}\sqrt{a}} = \dfrac{2\sqrt{a}}{3a}$

45. $\dfrac{8-\sqrt{16\cdot 2}}{20} = \dfrac{8-4\sqrt{2}}{20} = \dfrac{4(2-\sqrt{2})}{4\cdot 5}$
$$= \frac{2-\sqrt{2}}{5}$$

46. $\dfrac{4-\sqrt{28}}{6} = \dfrac{4-2\sqrt{7}}{6} = \dfrac{2(2-\sqrt{7})}{2\cdot 3}$
$$= \frac{2-\sqrt{7}}{3}$$

47. $\dfrac{5+5\sqrt{3}}{10} = \dfrac{5(1+\sqrt{3})}{5\cdot 2} = \dfrac{1+\sqrt{3}}{2}$

48. $\dfrac{3+\sqrt{18}}{6} = \dfrac{3+3\sqrt{2}}{6} = \dfrac{3(1+\sqrt{2})}{3\cdot 2}$
$$= \frac{1+\sqrt{2}}{2}$$

49. $\sqrt{a}(\sqrt{a}-3) = a-3\sqrt{a}$

50. $3\sqrt{m}(2\sqrt{m}-6) = 6m-18\sqrt{m}$

51. $4\sqrt{a}(a+\sqrt{a}) = 4a\sqrt{a}+4a$

52. $\sqrt{3ab}(\sqrt{3a}+\sqrt{3}) = \sqrt{9a^2b}+\sqrt{9ab}$
$$= 3a\sqrt{b}+3\sqrt{ab}$$

53. $(2\sqrt{3m})^2 = 4 \cdot 3m = 12m$

54. $(-3\sqrt{4y})^2 = 9 \cdot 4y = 36y$

55. $\left(-2\sqrt{xy^2z}\right)^2 = (-2)^2 xy^2z = 4xy^2z$

56. $(5a\sqrt{ab})^2 = 25a^2ab = 25a^3b$

57. $\sqrt[3]{m}\left(\sqrt[3]{m^2} - \sqrt[3]{m^5}\right) = \sqrt[3]{m^3} - \sqrt[3]{m^6}$
$$= m - m^2$$

58. $\sqrt[4]{w}(\sqrt[4]{w^3} - \sqrt[4]{w^7}) = \sqrt[4]{w^4} - \sqrt[4]{w^8}$
$$= w - w^2$$

59. $\sqrt[3]{8x^4} + \sqrt[3]{27x^4}$
$$= \sqrt[3]{8x^3} \cdot \sqrt[3]{x} + \sqrt[3]{27x^3} \cdot \sqrt[3]{x}$$
$$= 2x \cdot \sqrt[3]{x} + 3x \cdot \sqrt[3]{x} = 5x\sqrt[3]{x}$$

60. $\sqrt[3]{16a^4} + a \cdot \sqrt[3]{2a}$
$$= \sqrt[3]{8a^3} \cdot \sqrt[3]{2a} + a \cdot \sqrt[3]{2a}$$
$$= 2a\sqrt[3]{2a} + a\sqrt[3]{2a} = 3a\sqrt[3]{2a}$$

61. $\left(2m\sqrt[4]{2m^2}\right)^3 = 8m^3\sqrt[4]{8m^6}$
$$= 8m^3\sqrt[4]{m^4}\sqrt[4]{8m^2}$$
$$= 8m^3 \cdot m \cdot \sqrt[4]{8m^2} = 8m^4\sqrt[4]{8m^2}$$

62. $\left(-2t\sqrt[6]{2t^2}\right)^5 = -32t^5\sqrt[6]{32t^{10}}$
$$= -32t^5 \cdot t \cdot \sqrt[6]{32t^4} = -32t^6\sqrt[6]{32t^4}$$

63. $\dfrac{4}{2+\sqrt{8}} = \dfrac{4(2-\sqrt{8})}{(2+\sqrt{8})(2-\sqrt{8})}$
$$= \frac{8 - 8\sqrt{2}}{-4} = 2\sqrt{2} - 2$$

64. $\dfrac{6}{3-\sqrt{18}} = \dfrac{6(3+\sqrt{18})}{(3-\sqrt{18})(3+\sqrt{18})}$
$$= \frac{18 + 18\sqrt{2}}{-9} = -2 - 2\sqrt{2}$$

65.
$$\frac{5(\sqrt{2}+1)}{(\sqrt{2}-1)(\sqrt{2}+1)} + \frac{3(\sqrt{2}-1)}{(\sqrt{2}+1)(\sqrt{2}-1)}$$
$$= \frac{5\sqrt{2}+5}{2-1} + \frac{3\sqrt{2}-3}{2-1} = 2 + 8\sqrt{2}$$

66. $\dfrac{\sqrt{3}}{\sqrt{6}-1} - \dfrac{\sqrt{3}}{\sqrt{6}+1}$
$$= \frac{\sqrt{3}(\sqrt{6}+1)}{(\sqrt{6}-1)(\sqrt{6}+1)} - \frac{\sqrt{3}(\sqrt{6}-1)}{(\sqrt{6}+1)(\sqrt{6}-1)}$$
$$= \frac{\sqrt{18}+\sqrt{3}}{6-1} - \frac{\sqrt{18}-\sqrt{3}}{6-1}$$
$$= \frac{\sqrt{18}+\sqrt{3}-\sqrt{18}+\sqrt{3}}{5}$$
$$= \frac{2\sqrt{3}}{5}$$

67. $\dfrac{1}{\sqrt{2}} + \dfrac{1}{\sqrt{3}} = \dfrac{\sqrt{2}}{2} + \dfrac{\sqrt{3}}{3}$

$$= \frac{3\sqrt{2}}{3 \cdot 2} + \frac{2\sqrt{3}}{2 \cdot 3} = \frac{3\sqrt{2}+2\sqrt{3}}{6}$$

68. $\dfrac{4}{2\sqrt{3}} + \dfrac{1}{\sqrt{5}} = \dfrac{4\sqrt{5}}{2\sqrt{3}\sqrt{5}} + \dfrac{1 \cdot 2\sqrt{3}}{\sqrt{5} \cdot 2\sqrt{3}}$

$$= \frac{4\sqrt{5}}{2\sqrt{15}} + \frac{2\sqrt{3}}{2\sqrt{15}} = \frac{4\sqrt{5}+2\sqrt{3}}{2\sqrt{15}}$$
$$= \frac{(4\sqrt{5}+2\sqrt{3})(\sqrt{15})}{2\sqrt{15}\sqrt{15}} = \frac{4\sqrt{75}+2\sqrt{45}}{30}$$
$$= \frac{20\sqrt{3}+6\sqrt{5}}{30} = \frac{10\sqrt{3}+3\sqrt{5}}{15}$$

69. $\dfrac{3}{\sqrt{2}-1} + \dfrac{4}{\sqrt{2}+1}$

$$= \frac{3(\sqrt{2}+1)}{(\sqrt{2}-1)(\sqrt{2}+1)} + \frac{4(\sqrt{2}-1)}{(\sqrt{2}+1)(\sqrt{2}-1)}$$
$$= \frac{3\sqrt{2}+3}{1} + \frac{4\sqrt{2}-4}{1} = 7\sqrt{2} - 1$$

70. $\dfrac{3}{\sqrt{5}-\sqrt{3}} - \dfrac{2}{\sqrt{5}+\sqrt{3}}$

$$= \frac{3(\sqrt{5}+\sqrt{3})}{(\sqrt{5}-\sqrt{3})(\sqrt{5}+\sqrt{3})}$$
$$\qquad - \frac{2(\sqrt{5}-\sqrt{3})}{(\sqrt{5}+\sqrt{3})(\sqrt{5}-\sqrt{3})}$$
$$= \frac{3\sqrt{5}+3\sqrt{3}}{5-3} - \frac{2\sqrt{5}-2\sqrt{3}}{5-3} = \frac{\sqrt{5}+5\sqrt{3}}{2}$$

71. $\dfrac{\sqrt{x}(\sqrt{x}-2)}{(\sqrt{x}+2)(\sqrt{x}-2)}$
$$\qquad + \frac{3\sqrt{x}(\sqrt{x}+2)}{(\sqrt{x}-2)(\sqrt{x}+2)}$$
$$= \frac{x-2\sqrt{x}}{x-4} + \frac{3x+6\sqrt{x}}{x-4} = \frac{4x+4\sqrt{x}}{x-4}$$

72. $\dfrac{\sqrt{5}}{3-\sqrt{y}} - \dfrac{\sqrt{5y}}{3+\sqrt{y}}$

$$= \frac{\sqrt{5}(3+\sqrt{y})}{(3-\sqrt{y})(3+\sqrt{y})} - \frac{\sqrt{5y}(3-\sqrt{y})}{(3+\sqrt{y})(3-\sqrt{y})}$$
$$= \frac{3\sqrt{5}+\sqrt{5y}}{9-y} - \frac{3\sqrt{5y}-y\sqrt{5}}{9-y}$$
$$= \frac{3\sqrt{5}+y\sqrt{5}-2\sqrt{5y}}{9-y}$$

73. $\dfrac{1(1-\sqrt{x})}{\sqrt{x}(1-\sqrt{x})} + \dfrac{1\sqrt{x}}{(1-\sqrt{x})\sqrt{x}}$

$$= \frac{1-\sqrt{x}}{\sqrt{x}-x} + \frac{\sqrt{x}}{\sqrt{x}-x} = \frac{1}{\sqrt{x}-x}$$
$$= \frac{1(\sqrt{x}+x)}{(\sqrt{x}-x)(\sqrt{x}+x)} = \frac{x+\sqrt{x}}{x-x^2}$$

74. $\dfrac{\sqrt{x}}{\sqrt{x}-3}+\dfrac{5}{\sqrt{x}}$

$=\dfrac{\sqrt{x}(\sqrt{x}+3)}{(\sqrt{x}-3)\sqrt{x}+3)}+\dfrac{5\sqrt{x}}{\sqrt{x}\sqrt{x}}$

$=\dfrac{x+3\sqrt{x}}{x-9}+\dfrac{5\sqrt{x}}{x}$

$=\dfrac{(x+3\sqrt{x})x}{(x-9)x}+\dfrac{5\sqrt{x}(x-9)}{x(x-9)}$

$=\dfrac{x^2+3x\sqrt{x}+5x\sqrt{x}-45\sqrt{x}}{x^2-9x}$

$=\dfrac{x^2+8x\sqrt{x}-45\sqrt{x}}{x^2-9x}$

75. $\dfrac{\sqrt{2}}{\sqrt{3}}=\dfrac{\sqrt{2}\sqrt{3}}{\sqrt{3}\sqrt{3}}=\dfrac{\sqrt{6}}{3}$

76. $\sqrt{2}=\dfrac{\sqrt{2}\cdot\sqrt{2}}{\sqrt{2}}=\dfrac{2}{\sqrt{2}}$

77. $\dfrac{1}{\sqrt{2}-1}=\dfrac{1(\sqrt{2}+1)}{(\sqrt{2}-1)(\sqrt{2}+1)}$

$=\dfrac{\sqrt{2}+1}{1}$

78. $\dfrac{\sqrt{6}}{\sqrt{6}+2}=\dfrac{\sqrt{6}(\sqrt{6}-2)}{(\sqrt{6}+2)(\sqrt{6}-2)}$

$=\dfrac{6-2\sqrt{6}}{6-4}=\dfrac{6-2\sqrt{6}}{2}$

79. $\dfrac{1}{\sqrt{x}-1}=\dfrac{1(\sqrt{x}+1)}{(\sqrt{x}-1)(\sqrt{x}+1)}$

$=\dfrac{\sqrt{x}+1}{x-1}$

80. $\dfrac{5}{3-\sqrt{x}}=\dfrac{5(3+\sqrt{x})}{(3-\sqrt{x})(3+\sqrt{x})}$

$=\dfrac{15+5\sqrt{x}}{9-x}$

81. $\dfrac{3}{\sqrt{2}+x}=\dfrac{3(\sqrt{2}-x)}{(\sqrt{2}+x)(\sqrt{2}-x)}$

$=\dfrac{3\sqrt{2}-3x}{2-x^2}$

82. $\dfrac{4}{2\sqrt{3}+a}=\dfrac{4(2\sqrt{3}-a)}{(2\sqrt{3}+a)(2\sqrt{3}-a)}$

$=\dfrac{8\sqrt{3}-4a}{12-a^2}$

83. $\sqrt{3}+\sqrt{5}=3.968$

84. $\sqrt{5}+\sqrt{7}=4.882$

85. $2\sqrt{3}+5\sqrt{3}=12.124$

86. $7\sqrt{3}=12.124$

87. $(2\sqrt{3})(3\sqrt{2})=14.697$

88. $6\sqrt{6}=14.697$

89. $\sqrt{5}(\sqrt{5}+\sqrt{3})=8.873$

90. $5+\sqrt{15}=8.873$

91. $\dfrac{-1+\sqrt{6}}{2}=0.725$

92. $\dfrac{-1-\sqrt{6}}{2}=-1.725$

93. $\dfrac{4-\sqrt{10}}{-2}=-0.419$

94. $\dfrac{4+\sqrt{10}}{-2}=-3.581$

95. a) x^3-2

b) $(x+\sqrt[3]{5})(x^2-\sqrt[3]{5}\,x+\sqrt[3]{25})$

c) 3

d) $\left(\sqrt[3]{a}+\sqrt[3]{b}\right)\left(\sqrt[3]{a^2}-\sqrt[3]{ab}+\sqrt[3]{b^2}\right)$
$\left(\sqrt[3]{a}-\sqrt[3]{b}\right)\left(\sqrt[3]{a^2}+\sqrt[3]{ab}+\sqrt[3]{b^2}\right)$

96. Expression (b) is not equivalent to the others.

7.5 WARM-UPS

1. False, because $x^2=4$ is equivalent to the compound equation $x=2$ or $x=-2$.

2. True, because the square of any real number is nonnegative.

3. False, 0 is a solution.

4. False, because -2 is not a solution to $x^3=8$.

5. True, because if x is positive the left side of the equation is negative and the right side is positive.

6. False, we should square each side.

7. False, extraneous roots are found but they do not satisfy the equation.

8. True, because we get $x=49$, and 49 does not satisfy $\sqrt{x}=-7$.

9. True, because both square roots of 6 satisfy $x^2-6=0$.

10. True, we get extraneous roots only by raising each side to an even power.

7.5 EXERCISES

1. The odd root property says that if n is an odd positive integer then $x^n=k$ is equivalent to $x=\sqrt[n]{k}$ for any real number k.

2. The even root property says that if n is a positive even integer then $x^n=k$ is equivalent for $x=\pm\sqrt[n]{k}$ for $k>0$, $x=0$ for $k=0$, and has no solution for $k<0$.

3. An extraneous solution is a solution that appears when solving an equation, but does not satisfy the original equation.

4. Raising each side to an even power can produce an extraneous root because the even powers of both negative and positive numbers are positive. For example if $\sqrt{x} = -2$, then squaring each side produces an extraneous root.

5. $x^3 = -1000$
$$x = \sqrt[3]{-1000} = -10$$
Solution set: $\{-10\}$

6. $y^3 = 125$
$$y = \sqrt[3]{125} = 5$$
The solution set is $\{5\}$.

7. $32m^5 - 1 = 0$
$$32m^5 = 1$$
$$m^5 = \frac{1}{32}$$
$$m = \sqrt[5]{\frac{1}{32}} = \frac{1}{2}$$
Solution set: $\left\{\frac{1}{2}\right\}$

8. $243a^5 + 1 = 0$
$$243a^5 = -1$$
$$a^5 = -\frac{1}{243}$$
$$a = \sqrt[5]{-\frac{1}{243}} = -\frac{1}{3}$$
The solution set is $\left\{-\frac{1}{3}\right\}$.

9. $(y - 3)^3 = -8$
$$y - 3 = \sqrt[3]{-8}$$
$$y - 3 = -2$$
$$y = 1$$
Solution set: $\{1\}$

10. $(x - 1)^3 = -1$
$$x - 1 = \sqrt[3]{-1}$$
$$x - 1 = -1$$
$$x = 0$$
The solution set is $\{0\}$.

11. $\frac{1}{2}x^3 + 4 = 0$
$$\frac{1}{2}x^3 = -4$$
$$x^3 = -8$$
$$x = \sqrt[3]{-8} = -2$$
Solution set: $\{-2\}$

12. $3(x - 9)^7 = 0$
$$(x - 9)^7 = 0$$
$$x - 9 = 0$$
$$x = 9$$

The solution set is $\{9\}$.

13. $x^2 = 25$
$$x = \pm 5$$
Solution set: $\{-5, 5\}$

14. $x^2 = 36$
$$x = \pm\sqrt{36} = \pm 6$$
The solution set is $\{-6, 6\}$.

15. $x^2 - 20 = 0$
$$x^2 = 20$$
$$x = \pm\sqrt{20} = \pm 2\sqrt{5}$$
Solution set: $\{-2\sqrt{5}, 2\sqrt{5}\}$

16. $a^2 = 40$
$$a = \pm\sqrt{40} = \pm 2\sqrt{10}$$
The solution set is $\{-2\sqrt{10}, 2\sqrt{10}\}$

17. $x^2 = -9$
Since an even root of a negative number is not a real number, the solution set is $\emptyset$.

18. $w^2 + 49 = 0$
$$w^2 = -49$$
Since an even root of a negative number is not a real number, the solution set is $\emptyset$.

19. $(x - 3)^2 = 16$
$$x - 3 = \pm 4$$
$$x = 3 \pm 4$$
$$x = 3 + 4 \quad \text{or} \quad x = 3 - 4$$
$$x = 7 \quad\quad \text{or} \quad x = -1$$
Solution set: $\{-1, 7\}$

20. $(a - 2)^2 = 25$
$$a - 2 = \pm 5$$
$$a = 2 \pm 5$$
$$a = 2 + 5 \quad \text{or} \quad a = 2 - 5$$
$$a = 7 \quad\quad \text{or} \quad a = -3$$
The solution set is $\{-3, 7\}$.

21. $(x + 1)^2 = 8$
$$x + 1 = \pm\sqrt{8}$$
$$x = -1 \pm 2\sqrt{2}$$
Solution set: $\{-1 - 2\sqrt{2}, -1 + 2\sqrt{2}\}$

22. $(w + 3)^2 = 12$
$$w + 3 = \pm\sqrt{12} = \pm 2\sqrt{3}$$
$$w = -3 \pm 2\sqrt{3}$$
The solution set is $\{-3 - 2\sqrt{3}, -3 + 2\sqrt{3}\}$.

23. $\frac{1}{2}x^2 = 5$
$$x^2 = 10$$
$$x = \pm\sqrt{10}$$
Solution set: $\{-\sqrt{10}, \sqrt{10}\}$

24. $\frac{1}{3}x^2 = 6$

$\qquad x^2 = 18$

$\qquad x = \pm\sqrt{18} = \pm 3\sqrt{2}$

25. $(y-3)^4 = 0$

$\qquad y - 3 = \sqrt[4]{0} = 0$

$\qquad y = 3$

Solution set: $\{3\}$

26. $(2x-3)^6 = 0$

$\qquad 2x - 3 = 0$

$\qquad 2x = 3$

$\qquad x = \frac{3}{2}$

The solution set is $\left\{\frac{3}{2}\right\}$.

27. $\qquad 2x^6 = 128$

$\qquad x^6 = 64$

$\qquad x = \pm\sqrt[6]{64}$

$\qquad x = \pm 2$

Solution set: $\{-2, 2\}$

28. $\qquad 3y^4 = 48$

$\qquad y^4 = 16$

$\qquad y = \pm\sqrt[4]{16} = \pm 2$

The solution set is $\{-2, 2\}$.

29. $\qquad \sqrt{x-3} = 7$

$\qquad (\sqrt{x-3})^2 = 7^2$

$\qquad x - 3 = 49$

$\qquad x = 52$

Check 52 in the original equation.

Solution set: $\{52\}$

30. $\qquad \sqrt{a-1} = 6$

$\qquad (\sqrt{a-1})^2 = 6^2$

$\qquad a - 1 = 36$

$\qquad a = 37$

Check 37 in the original equation.

Solution set: $\{37\}$

31. $\qquad 2\sqrt{w+4} = 5$

$\qquad (2\sqrt{w+4})^2 = 5^2$

$\qquad 4(w+4) = 25$

$\qquad 4w + 16 = 25$

$\qquad 4w = 9$

$\qquad w = \frac{9}{4}$

Check $\frac{9}{4}$ in the original equation.

Solution set: $\left\{\frac{9}{4}\right\}$

32. $\qquad 3\sqrt{w+1} = 6$

$\qquad \sqrt{w+1} = 2$

$\qquad (\sqrt{w+1})^2 = 2^2$

$\qquad w + 1 = 4$

$\qquad w = 3$

The solution set is $\{3\}$.

33. $\qquad \sqrt[3]{2x+3} = \sqrt[3]{x+12}$

$\qquad (\sqrt[3]{2x+3})^3 = (\sqrt[3]{x+12})^3$

$\qquad 2x + 3 = x + 12$

$\qquad x = 9$

Check 9 in the original equation.

Solution set: $\{9\}$

34. $\qquad \sqrt[3]{a+3} = \sqrt[3]{2a-7}$

$\qquad (\sqrt[3]{a+3})^3 = (\sqrt[3]{2a-7})^3$

$\qquad a + 3 = 2a - 7$

$\qquad 10 = a$

The solution set is $\{10\}$.

35. $\qquad \sqrt{2t+4} = \sqrt{t-1}$

$\qquad (\sqrt{2t+4})^2 = (\sqrt{t-1})^2$

$\qquad 2t + 4 = t - 1$

$\qquad t = -5$

Check: $\sqrt{2(-5)+4} = \sqrt{-5-1}$

Since each side of the equation is the square root of a negative number, the solution set is $\emptyset$.

36. $\qquad \sqrt{w-3} = \sqrt{4w+15}$

$\qquad (\sqrt{w-3})^2 = (\sqrt{4w+15})^2$

$\qquad w - 3 = 4w + 15$

$\qquad -18 = 3w$

$\qquad -6 = w$

Check: $\sqrt{-6-3} = \sqrt{4(-6)+15}$

Since each side of the equation is the square root of a negative number, the solution set is $\emptyset$.

37. $\qquad \sqrt{4x^2+x-3} = 2x$

$\qquad (\sqrt{4x^2+x-3})^2 = (2x)^2$

$\qquad 4x^2 + x - 3 = 4x^2$

$\qquad x - 3 = 0$

$\qquad x = 3$

Check 3 in the original equation.

Solution set: $\{3\}$

38. $\qquad \sqrt{x^2-5x+2} = x$

$\qquad (\sqrt{x^2-5x+2})^2 = x^2$

$\qquad x^2 - 5x + 2 = x^2$

$\qquad -5x + 2 = 0$

$\qquad x = \frac{2}{5}$

The solution set is $\left\{\frac{2}{5}\right\}$.

39.
$$\sqrt{x^2 + 2x - 6} = 3$$
$$\left(\sqrt{x^2 + 2x - 6}\right)^2 = 3^2$$
$$x^2 + 2x - 6 = 9$$
$$x^2 + 2x - 15 = 0$$
$$(x + 5)(x - 3) = 0$$
$$x + 5 = 0 \text{ or } x - 3 = 0$$
$$x = -5 \text{ or } x = 3$$

Check 3 and -5 in the original equation.
Solution set: $\{-5, 3\}$

40.
$$\sqrt{x^2 - x - 4} = 4$$
$$\left(\sqrt{x^2 - x - 4}\right)^2 = 4^2$$
$$x^2 - x - 4 = 16$$
$$x^2 - x - 20 = 0$$
$$(x - 5)(x + 4) = 0$$
$$x - 5 = 0 \text{ or } x + 4 = 0$$
$$x = 5 \text{ or } x = -4$$

The solution set is $\{-4, 5\}$.

41.
$$\sqrt{2x^2 - 1} = x$$
$$\left(\sqrt{2x^2 - 1}\right)^2 = x^2$$
$$2x^2 - 1 = x^2$$
$$x^2 = 1$$
$$x = \pm 1$$

Checking in the original we find that if $x = -1$ we get $\sqrt{1} = -1$, which is incorrect. So the solution set is $\{1\}$.

42.
$$\sqrt{2x^2 - 3x - 10} = x$$
$$\left(\sqrt{2x^2 - 3x - 10}\right)^2 = x^2$$
$$2x^2 - 3x - 10 = x^2$$
$$x^2 - 3x - 10 = 0$$
$$(x - 5)(x + 2) = 0$$
$$x - 5 = 0 \text{ or } x + 2 = 0$$
$$x = 5 \text{ or } x = -2$$

If we check -2 in the original equation we get -2 on the right hand side and a radical on the left hand side. So -2 is not a solution to the equation. The solution set is $\{5\}$.

43.
$$\sqrt{2x^2 + 5x + 6} = x$$
$$\left(\sqrt{2x^2 + 5x + 6}\right)^2 = x^2$$
$$2x^2 + 5x + 6 = x^2$$
$$x^2 + 5x + 6 = 0$$
$$(x + 2)(x + 3) = 0$$
$$x = -2 \text{ or } x = -3$$

If we use $x = -2$ in the original equation we get $\sqrt{4} = -2$, and if $x = -3$ in the original we get $\sqrt{9} = -3$. Since both of these equations are incorrect, the solution set is $\emptyset$.

44.
$$\left(\sqrt{5x^2 - 9}\right)^2 = (2x)^2$$
$$5x^2 - 9 = 4x^2$$
$$x^2 = 9$$
$$x = \pm 3$$

If we use -3 in the original equation we get $\sqrt{36} = -6$. Since this equation is incorrect, -3 is not a solution to the equation. The solution set is $\{3\}$.

45.
$$\sqrt{x + 3} - \sqrt{x - 2} = 1$$
$$\sqrt{x + 3} = 1 + \sqrt{x - 2}$$
$$\left(\sqrt{x + 3}\right)^2 = \left(1 + \sqrt{x - 2}\right)^2$$
$$x + 3 = 1 + 2\sqrt{x - 2} + x - 2$$
$$4 = 2\sqrt{x - 2}$$
$$2 = \sqrt{x - 2}$$
$$2^2 = \left(\sqrt{x - 2}\right)^2$$
$$4 = x - 2$$
$$6 = x$$

Check 6 in the original equation. The solution set is $\{6\}$.

46.
$$\sqrt{2x + 1} - \sqrt{x} = 1$$
$$\sqrt{2x + 1} = 1 - \sqrt{x}$$
$$\left(\sqrt{2x + 1}\right)^2 = (1 - \sqrt{x})^2$$
$$2x + 1 = 1 - 2\sqrt{x} + x$$
$$x = -2\sqrt{x}$$
$$x^2 = (-2\sqrt{x})^2$$
$$x^2 = 4x$$
$$x^2 - 4x = 0$$
$$x(x - 4) = 0$$
$$x = 0 \text{ or } x - 4 = 0$$
$$x = 4$$

The solution set is $\{0, 4\}$.

47.
$$\sqrt{2x + 2} - \sqrt{x - 3} = 2$$
$$\sqrt{2x + 2} = 2 + \sqrt{x - 3}$$
$$(\sqrt{2x + 2})^2 = \left(2 + \sqrt{x - 3}\right)^2$$
$$2x + 2 = 4 + 4\sqrt{x - 3} + x - 3$$
$$x + 1 = 4\sqrt{x - 3}$$
$$(x + 1)^2 = \left(4\sqrt{x - 3}\right)^2$$
$$x^2 + 2x + 1 = 16(x - 3)$$

$$x^2 - 14x + 49 = 0$$
$$(x-7)^2 = 0$$
$$x = 7$$

Check 7 in the original equation.
Solution set: {7}

48. $\sqrt{3x} - \sqrt{x-2} = 4$
$$\sqrt{3x} = 4 + \sqrt{x-2}$$
$$\left(\sqrt{3x}\right)^2 = \left(4 + \sqrt{x-2}\right)^2$$
$$3x = 16 + 8\sqrt{x-2} + x - 2$$
$$2x - 14 = 8\sqrt{x-2}$$
$$x - 7 = 4\sqrt{x-2}$$
$$(x-7)^2 = \left(4\sqrt{x-2}\right)^2$$
$$x^2 - 14x + 49 = 16(x-2)$$
$$x^2 - 30x + 81 = 0$$
$$(x-27)(x-3) = 0$$
$$x - 27 = 0 \text{ or } x - 3 = 0$$
$$x = 27 \text{ or } \quad x = 3$$

Since 3 does not satisfy the original equation, the solution set is {27}.

49. $\sqrt{4-x} - \sqrt{x+6} = 2$
$$\sqrt{4-x} = 2 + \sqrt{x+6}$$
$$\left(\sqrt{4-x}\right)^2 = \left(2 + \sqrt{x+6}\right)^2$$
$$4 - x = 4 + 4\sqrt{x+6} + x + 6$$
$$-6 - 2x = 4\sqrt{x+6}$$
$$-3 - x = 2\sqrt{x+6}$$
$$(-3-x)^2 = \left(2\sqrt{x+6}\right)^2$$
$$9 + 6x + x^2 = 4(x+6)$$
$$x^2 + 2x - 15 = 0$$
$$(x+5)(x-3) = 0$$
$$x = -5 \text{ or } x = 3$$

If $x = 3$ in the original equation we get
$1 - 3 = 2$, which is incorrect. If $x = -5$ we
get $3 - 1 = 2$. So the solution set is $\{-5\}$.

50. $\sqrt{6-x} - \sqrt{x-2} = 2$
$$\sqrt{6-x} = 2 + \sqrt{x-2}$$
$$\left(\sqrt{6-x}\right)^2 = (2 + \sqrt{x-2})^2$$
$$6 - x = 4 + 4\sqrt{x-2} + x - 2$$
$$4 - 2x = 4\sqrt{x-2}$$
$$2 - x = 2\sqrt{x-2}$$
$$(2-x)^2 = (2\sqrt{x-2})^2$$
$$4 - 4x + x^2 = 4(x-2)$$
$$x^2 - 8x + 12 = 0$$
$$(x-6)(x-2) = 0$$
$$x - 6 = 0 \text{ or } x - 2 = 0$$

$$x = 6 \text{ or } \quad x = 2$$
Since 6 does not satisfy the original equation,
the solution set is {2}.

51. $\left(x^{2/3}\right)^3 = 3^3$
$$x^2 = 27$$
$$x = \pm\sqrt{27} = \pm 3\sqrt{3}$$
Solution set: $\{-3\sqrt{3}, 3\sqrt{3}\}$

52. $a^{2/3} = 2$
$$\left(a^{2/3}\right)^3 = 2^3$$
$$a^2 = 8$$
$$a = \pm\sqrt{8} = \pm 2\sqrt{2}$$
The solution set is $\{-2\sqrt{2}, 2\sqrt{2}\}$.

53. $\left(y^{-2/3}\right)^{-3} = (9)^{-3}$
$$y^2 = \frac{1}{729}$$
$$y = \pm\sqrt{\frac{1}{729}} = \pm\frac{1}{27}$$
Solution set: $\left\{-\frac{1}{27}, \frac{1}{27}\right\}$

54. $\left(w^{-2/3}\right)^{-3} = (4)^{-3}$
$$w^2 = \frac{1}{64}$$
$$w = \pm\sqrt{\frac{1}{64}} = \pm\frac{1}{8}$$
Solution set: $\left\{-\frac{1}{8}, \frac{1}{8}\right\}$

55. $\left(w^{1/3}\right)^3 = 8^3$
$$w = 512$$
Solution set: {512}

56. $a^{1/3} = 27$
$$\left(a^{1/3}\right)^3 = (27)^3$$
$$a = 19,683$$
The solution set is {19,683}.

57. $\left(t^{-1/2}\right)^{-2} = (9)^{-2}$
$$t = \frac{1}{81}$$
Solution set: $\left\{\frac{1}{81}\right\}$

58. $w^{-1/4} = \frac{1}{2}$
$$\left(w^{-1/4}\right)^{-4} = \left(\frac{1}{2}\right)^{-4}$$
$$w = 2^4 = 16$$
The solution set is {16}.

59. $\left((3a-1)^{-2/5}\right)^{-5} = 1^{-5}$
$$(3a-1)^2 = 1$$
$$3a - 1 = \pm 1$$
$$3a - 1 = 1 \quad \text{or } 3a - 1 = -1$$

271

$$3a = 2 \quad \text{or} \quad 3a = 0$$
$$a = \tfrac{2}{3} \quad \text{or} \quad a = 0$$
Solution set: $\left\{0, \tfrac{2}{3}\right\}$

60. $(r-1)^{-2/3} = 1$
$$\left((r-1)^{-2/3}\right)^{-3} = 1^{-3}$$
$$(r-1)^2 = 1$$
$$r - 1 = \pm 1$$
$$r = 1 \pm 1$$
$$r = 1 - 1 \quad \text{or} \quad r = 1 + 1$$
$$r = 0 \quad \text{or} \quad r = 2$$
The solution set is $\{0, 2\}$.

61. $\left((t-1)^{-2/3}\right)^{-3} = 2^{-3}$
$$(t-1)^2 = \tfrac{1}{8}$$
$$t - 1 = \pm\sqrt{\tfrac{1}{8}} = \pm\frac{\sqrt{2}}{4}$$
$$t = 1 \pm \frac{\sqrt{2}}{4} = \frac{4}{4} \pm \frac{\sqrt{2}}{4} = \frac{4 \pm \sqrt{2}}{4}$$
Solution set: $\left\{\dfrac{4 - \sqrt{2}}{4}, \dfrac{4 + \sqrt{2}}{4}\right\}$

62. $(w+3)^{-1/3} = \tfrac{1}{3}$
$$\left((w+3)^{-1/3}\right)^{-3} = \left(\tfrac{1}{3}\right)^{-3}$$
$$w + 3 = 3^3$$
$$w = 24$$
The solution set is $\{24\}$.

63. $(x-3)^{2/3} = -4$
$$\left((x-3)^{2/3}\right)^3 = (-4)^3$$
$$(x-3)^2 = -64$$
Because the square of any real number is nonnegative, the solution set is $\emptyset$.

64. $(x+2)^{3/2} = -1$
$$\left((x+2)^{3/2}\right)^2 = (-1)^2$$
$$(x+2)^3 = 1$$
$$x + 2 = 1$$
$$x = -1$$
Because -1 does not check in the original equation, it is an extraneous root and the solution set is $\emptyset$.

65. $\sqrt{(6-4)^2 + (5-2)^2} = \sqrt{4+9} = \sqrt{13}$

66. $\sqrt{(7-5)^2 + (3-1)^2} = \sqrt{4+4} = \sqrt{8}$
$$= 2\sqrt{2}$$

67. $\sqrt{(3-1)^2 + (5-(-3))^2} = \sqrt{4+64}$
$$= \sqrt{68} = 2\sqrt{17}$$

68. $\sqrt{(6-3)^2 + (2-(-5))^2} = \sqrt{9+49}$
$$= \sqrt{58}$$

69. $\sqrt{(4-(-3))^2 + (-2-(-6))^2}$
$$= \sqrt{49+16} = \sqrt{65}$$

70. $\sqrt{(-2-1)^2 + (3-(-4))^2} = \sqrt{9+49}$
$$= \sqrt{58}$$

71. $\quad 2x^2 + 3 = 7$
$$2x^2 = 4$$
$$x^2 = 2$$
$$x = \pm\sqrt{2}$$
Solution set: $\{-\sqrt{2}, \sqrt{2}\}$

72. $3x^2 - 5 = 16$
$$3x^2 = 21$$
$$x^2 = 7$$
$$x = \pm\sqrt{7}$$
The solution set is $\{-\sqrt{7}, \sqrt{7}\}$.

73. $\quad \sqrt[3]{2w+3} = \sqrt[3]{w-2}$
$$\left(\sqrt[3]{2w+3}\right)^3 = \left(\sqrt[3]{w-2}\right)^3$$
$$2w + 3 = w - 2$$
$$w = -5$$
Solution set: $\{-5\}$

74. $\quad \sqrt[3]{2-w} = \sqrt[3]{2w-28}$
$$\left(\sqrt[3]{2-w}\right)^3 = \left(\sqrt[3]{2w-28}\right)^3$$
$$2 - w = 2w - 28$$
$$30 = 3w$$
$$10 = w$$
The solution set is $\{10\}$.

75. $\quad 9x^2 - 1 = 0$
$$x^2 = \tfrac{1}{9}$$
$$x = \pm\sqrt{\tfrac{1}{9}} = \pm\tfrac{1}{3}$$
Solution set: $\left\{-\tfrac{1}{3}, \tfrac{1}{3}\right\}$

76. $\quad 4x^2 - 1 = 0$
$$4x^2 = 1$$
$$x^2 = \tfrac{1}{4}$$
$$x = \pm\sqrt{\tfrac{1}{4}} = \pm\tfrac{1}{2}$$
The solution set is $\left\{-\tfrac{1}{2}, \tfrac{1}{2}\right\}$.

77. $\left((w+1)^{2/3}\right)^3 = (-3)^3$
$$(w+1)^2 = -27$$
This equation has no solution by the even root property. The solution set is $\emptyset$.

78. $(x-2)^{3/4} = 2$

$\left((x-2)^{3/4}\right)^4 = 2^4$

$(x-2)^3 = 16$

$x-2 = \sqrt[3]{16} = 2 \cdot \sqrt[3]{2}$

$x = 2 + 2 \cdot \sqrt[3]{2}$

The solution set is $\left\{2 + 2\sqrt[3]{2}\right\}$.

79. $\left((a+1)^{1/3}\right)^3 = (-2)^3$

$a+1 = -8$

$a = -9$

Solution set: $\{-9\}$

80. $(a-1)^{1/3} = -3$

$\left((a-1)^{1/3}\right)^3 = (-3)^3$

$a-1 = -27$

$a = -26$

The solution set is $\{-26\}$.

81. $(4y-5)^7 = 0$

$4y - 5 = \sqrt[7]{0} = 0$

$4y = 5$

$y = \frac{5}{4}$

Solution set: $\left\{\frac{5}{4}\right\}$

82. $(5x)^9 = 0$

$5x = 0$

$x = 0$

The solution set is $\{0\}$.

83. $\sqrt{x^2 + 5x} = 6$

$\left(\sqrt{x^2 + 5x}\right)^2 = 6^2$

$x^2 + 5x = 36$

$x^2 + 5x - 36 = 0$

$(x+9)(x-4) = 0$

$x = -9$ or $x = 4$

Solution set: $\{-9, 4\}$

84. $\sqrt{x^2 - 8x} = -3$

$\left(\sqrt{x^2 - 8x}\right)^2 = (-3)^2$

$x^2 - 8x = 9$

$x^2 - 8x - 9 = 0$

$(x-9)(x+1) = 0$

$x - 9 = 0$ or $x + 1 = 0$

$x = 9$ or $x = -1$

Because of the -3 on the right hand side of the original equation, neither number satisfies the original equation. The solution set is the empty set $\emptyset$.

85. $\sqrt{4x^2} = x + 2$

$\left(\sqrt{4x^2}\right)^2 = (x+2)^2$

$4x^2 = x^2 + 4x + 4$

$3x^2 - 4x - 4 = 0$

$(3x+2)(x-2) = 0$

$3x + 2 = 0$ or $x - 2 = 0$

$x = -\frac{2}{3}$ or $x = 2$

Solution set: $\left\{-\frac{2}{3}, 2\right\}$

86. $\sqrt{9x^2} = x + 6$

$\left(\sqrt{9x^2}\right)^2 = (x+6)^2$

$9x^2 = x^2 + 12x + 36$

$8x^2 - 12x - 36 = 0$

$2x^2 - 3x - 9 = 0$

$(2x+3)(x-3) = 0$

$2x + 3 = 0$ or $x - 3 = 0$

$x = -\frac{3}{2}$ or $x = 3$

The solution set is $\left\{-\frac{3}{2}, 3\right\}$.

87. $(t+2)^4 = 32$

$t + 2 = \pm\sqrt[4]{32} = \pm 2 \cdot \sqrt[4]{2}$

$t = -2 \pm 2 \cdot \sqrt[4]{2}$

Solution set: $\left\{-2 - 2\sqrt[4]{2}, -2 + 2\sqrt[4]{2}\right\}$

88. $(w+1)^4 = 48$

$w + 1 = \pm\sqrt[4]{48} = \pm 2 \cdot \sqrt[4]{3}$

$w = -1 \pm 2 \cdot \sqrt[4]{3}$

The solution set is $\left\{-1 - 2\sqrt[4]{3}, -1 + 2\sqrt[4]{3}\right\}$.

89. $\sqrt{x^2 - 3x} = x$

$\left(\sqrt{x^2 - 3x}\right)^2 = x^2$

$x^2 - 3x = x^2$

$-3x = 0$

$x = 0$

Solution set: $\{0\}$

90. $\sqrt[4]{4x^4 - 48} = -x$

$\left(\sqrt[4]{4x^4 - 48}\right)^4 = (-x)^4$

$4x^4 - 48 = x^4$

$3x^4 = 48$

$x^4 = 16$

$x = \pm\sqrt[4]{16} = \pm 2$

If $x = 2$, the original equation becomes $2 = -2$. So 2 is not a solution to the original equation. The solution set is $\{-2\}$.

91.
$$x^{-3} = 8$$
$$\left(x^{-3}\right)^{-1} = 8^{-1}$$
$$x^3 = \frac{1}{8}$$
$$x = \sqrt[3]{\frac{1}{8}} = \frac{1}{2}$$
Solution set: $\left\{\frac{1}{2}\right\}$

92.
$$x^{-2} = 4$$
$$(x^{-2})^{-1} = 4^{-1}$$
$$x^2 = \frac{1}{4}$$
$$x = \pm\sqrt{\frac{1}{4}} = \pm\frac{1}{2}$$

93.
$$a^{-2} = 3$$
$$\left(a^{-2}\right)^{-1} = 3^{-1}$$
$$a^2 = \frac{1}{3}$$
$$a = \pm\sqrt{\frac{1}{3}} = \pm\frac{\sqrt{3}}{3}$$
Solution set: $\left\{-\frac{\sqrt{3}}{3}, \frac{\sqrt{3}}{3}\right\}$

94.
$$w^{-2} = 18$$
$$\left(w^{-2}\right)^{-1} = 18^{-1}$$
$$w^2 = \frac{1}{18}$$
$$w = \pm\sqrt{\frac{1}{18}} = \pm\frac{1\sqrt{2}}{\sqrt{18}\sqrt{2}} = \pm\frac{\sqrt{2}}{6}$$
The solution set is $\left\{-\frac{\sqrt{2}}{6}, \frac{\sqrt{2}}{6}\right\}$.

95. Let x = the length of a side. Two sides and the diagonal of a square form a right triangle. By the Pythagorean theorem we can write the equation
$$x^2 + x^2 = 8^2$$
$$2x^2 = 64$$
$$x^2 = 32$$
$$x = \pm\sqrt{32} = \pm 4\sqrt{2}$$
The length of the side is not a negative number. So the side is $4\sqrt{2}$ feet in length.

96. Since the area of the square is 40 m² and $A = s^2$, the length of each side is $\sqrt{40}$ m. Let x = the length of the diagonal of the square. We can use the Pythagorean theorem to write the following equation.
$$x^2 = (\sqrt{40})^2 + (\sqrt{40})^2$$
$$x^2 = 40 + 40$$
$$x^2 = 80$$
$$x = \pm\sqrt{80} = \pm 4\sqrt{5}$$
The length of the diagonal is $4\sqrt{5}$ meters.

97. Let s = the length of the side of the square. Since $A = s^2$ for a square, we can write the equation
$$s^2 = 50$$
$$s = \pm\sqrt{50} = \pm 5\sqrt{2}$$
Since the side of a square is not negative, the length of the side is $5\sqrt{2}$ feet.

98. Let s = the length of a side of the cube. Since $V = s^3$ for a cube, we can write the equation
$$s^3 = 80$$
$$s = \pm\sqrt[3]{80} = \pm 2 \cdot \sqrt[3]{10}$$
Since the length of a side is not negative, the side has length $2\sqrt[3]{10}$ feet.

99. Let d = the length of a diagonal of the rectangle whose sides are 30 and 40 feet. By the Pythagorean theorem we can write the equation
$$d^2 = 30^2 + 40^2$$
$$d^2 = 2500$$
$$d = \pm\sqrt{2500} = \pm 50$$
Since the diagonal is not negative, the length of the diagonal is 50 feet.

100. Let x = the length of the diagonal. Since the diagonal is the hypotenuse of a right triangle, we can write the following equation.
$$x^2 = 5^2 + 12^2$$
$$x^2 = 169$$
$$x = \pm\sqrt{169} = \pm 13$$
The length of the diagonal is 13 meters.

101. a) $C = 4(23,245)^{-1/3}(13.5) \approx 1.89$

b)
$$C = 4d^{-1/3}b$$
$$d^{-1/3} = \frac{C}{4b}$$
$$(d^{-1/3})^{-3} = \left(\frac{C}{4b}\right)^{-3}$$
$$d = \frac{64b^3}{C^3}$$

c) The capsize screening value is less than 2 when $d > 19,683$ pounds.

102. a) $S = 16(810)(23,245)^{-2/3} \approx 15.9$

b)
$$S = 16Ad^{-2/3}$$
$$d^{-2/3} = \frac{S}{16A}$$
$$(d^{-2/3})^{-3} = \left(\frac{S}{16A}\right)^{-3}$$
$$d^2 = \left(\frac{16A}{S}\right)^3$$
$$d = \left(\frac{16A}{S}\right)^{3/2}$$

103. If the volume of the cube is 2, each side of the cube has length $\sqrt[3]{2}$, because $V = s^3$. Let d = the length of the diagonal of a side. The diagonal of a side is the diagonal of a square with sides of length $\sqrt[3]{2}$. By the Pythagorean theorem we can write the equation

$$d^2 = \left(\sqrt[3]{2}\right)^2 + \left(\sqrt[3]{2}\right)^2$$
$$d^2 = \sqrt[3]{4} + \sqrt[3]{4}$$
$$d^2 = 2 \cdot \sqrt[3]{4} = \sqrt[3]{8} \cdot \sqrt[3]{4} = \sqrt[3]{32}$$
$$d = \left(\sqrt[3]{32}\right)^{1/2} = \left(32^{1/3}\right)^{1/2} = 32^{1/6}$$

The length of the diagonal is $\sqrt[6]{32}$ meters.

104. Let s = the length of the side of the cube. The diagonal of the side is the hypotenuse of a right triangle. By the Pythagorean theorem, we can write the following equation.

$$s^2 + s^2 = 2^2$$
$$2s^2 = 4$$
$$s^2 = 2$$
$$s = \pm\sqrt{2}$$

Since $V = s^3$ for a cube,
$V = (\sqrt{2})^3 = \sqrt{8} = 2\sqrt{2}$ cubic feet.

105. Let x = the third side to the triangle whose given sides are 3 and 5. By the Pythagorean theorem we can find x:

$$x^2 + 3^2 = 5^2$$
$$x^2 = 16$$
$$x = 4$$

Since $x = 4$, the base of length 12 is divided into 2 parts, one of length 4 and the other of length 8. The side marked a is the hypotenuse of a right triangle with legs 3 and 8:

$$a^2 = 3^2 + 8^2$$
$$a^2 = 73$$
$$a = \sqrt{73} \text{ km}$$

106. Let x = the length of the horizontal leg in the triangle whose hypotenuse is 5 and whose vertical leg is marked 3.

$$x^2 + 3^2 = 5^2$$
$$x^2 = 16$$
$$x = 4$$

Now draw a vertical line from the right hand endpoint of the upper base to the lower base. The length of this vertical line is 3 and it is a leg of a right triangle whose hypotenuse is b. By subtracting 6 and 4 from 12 we get the length 2

for the horizontal leg of this right triangle.

$$b^2 = 3^2 + 2^2$$
$$b^2 = 13$$
$$b = \sqrt{13}$$

The length of the side marked b is $\sqrt{13}$ km.

107.
$$r = \left(\frac{S}{P}\right)^{1/n} - 1$$
$$1 + r = \left(\frac{S}{P}\right)^{1/n}$$
$$\frac{S}{P} = (1+r)^n$$
$$S = P(1+r)^n$$

Solve for P:
$$P = \frac{S}{(1+r)^n}$$
$$P = S(1+r)^{-n}$$

108.
$$12 = 6V^{2/3}$$
$$V^{2/3} = 2$$
$$(V^{2/3})^3 = 2^3$$
$$V^2 = 8$$
$$V = \pm\sqrt{8}$$

The volume is $2\sqrt{2}$ ft^3.

109.
$$\frac{11.86^2}{5.2^3} = \frac{29.46^2}{R^3}$$
$$11.86^2 R^3 = 5.2^3 \cdot 29.46^2$$
$$R^3 = \frac{5.2^3 \cdot 29.46^2}{11.86^2}$$
$$R = \sqrt[3]{\frac{5.2^3 \cdot 29.46^2}{11.86^2}} \approx 9.5 \text{ AU}$$

110.
$$\frac{11.86^2}{5.2^3} = \frac{T^2}{(0.723)^3}$$
$$11.86^2(0.723)^3 = 5.2^3 \cdot T^2$$
$$T^2 = \frac{11.86^2(0.723)^3}{5.2^3}$$
$$T = \sqrt{\frac{11.86^2(0.723)^3}{5.2^3}} \approx 0.61 \text{ yr}$$

111.
$$x^2 = 3.24$$
$$x = \pm\sqrt{3.24} = \pm 1.8$$

Solution set: $\{-1.8, 1.8\}$

112.
$$(x+4)^3 = 7.51$$
$$x + 4 = \sqrt[3]{7.51}$$
$$x = -4 + \sqrt[3]{7.51} \approx -2.042$$

The solution set is $\{-2.042\}$.

113.
$$\sqrt{x-2} = 1.73$$
$$x - 2 = (1.73)^2$$
$$x = 2 + (1.73)^2 \approx 4.993$$

Solution set: $\{4.993\}$

114. $\sqrt[3]{x-5} = 3.7$

$$\left(\sqrt[3]{x-5}\right)^3 = (3.7)^3$$
$$x - 5 = (3.7)^3$$
$$x = 5 + (3.7)^3 = 55.653$$

The solution set is $\{55.653\}$.

115. $x^{2/3} = 8.86$

$$\left(x^{2/3}\right)^3 = (8.86)^3$$
$$x^2 = 695.506$$
$$x = \pm\sqrt{695.506} \approx \pm 26.372$$

Solution set: $\{-26.372, 26.372\}$

116. $(x-1)^{-3/4} = 7.065$

$$\left((x-1)^{-3/4}\right)^{-4} = (7.065)^{-4}$$
$$(x-1)^3 = 7.065^{-4}$$
$$x - 1 = \sqrt[3]{7.065^{-4}}$$
$$x = 1 + 7.065^{-4/3}$$
$$x = 1.074$$

The solution set is $\{1.074\}$.

7.6 WARM-UPS

1. True, because every real number is a complex number.

2. False, because $2 - \sqrt{-6} = 2 - i\sqrt{6}$.

3. False, $\sqrt{-9} = 3i$.

4. True, $(\pm 3i)^2 = -9$.

5. True, because we subtract complex numbers just like we subtract binomials.

6. True, because $i^4 = i^2 \cdot i^2 = (-1)(-1) = 1$.

7. True, because
$(2-i)(2+i) = 4 - i^2 = 4 - (-1) = 5$.

8. False, $i^3 = i^2 \cdot i = -1 \cdot i = -i$.

9. True, $i^{48} = (i^4)^{12} = 1^{12} = 1$.

10. False, $x^2 = 0$ has only one solution.

7.6 EXERCISES

1. A complex number is a number of the form $a + bi$ where a and b are real numbers.

2. An imaginary number is a complex number in which $b \neq 0$.

3. The union of the real numbers and the imaginary numbers is the set of complex numbers.

4. Addition, subtraction, and multiplication of complex numbers is done as if the complex numbers were binomials with i being a variable.

When i^2 occurs we replace it with -1.

5. The conjugate of $a + bi$ is $a - bi$.

6. To divide complex numbers write the quotient as a fraction and multiply the numerator and denominator by the conjugate of the denominator.

7. $(2 + 3i) + (-4 + 5i) = -2 + 8i$

8. $(-1 + 6i) + (5 - 4i) = 4 + 2i$

9. $(2 - 3i) - (6 - 7i) = 2 - 3i - 6 + 7i$
$$= -4 + 4i$$

10. $(2 - 3i) - (6 - 2i) = 2 - 3i - 6 + 2i$
$$= -4 - i$$

11. $(-1 + i) + (-1 - i) = -2$

12. $(-5 + i) + (-5 - i) = -10$

13. $(-2 - 3i) - (6 - i) = -2 - 3i - 6 + i$
$$= -8 - 2i$$

14. $(-6 + 4i) - (2 - i) = -6 + 4i - 2 + i$
$$= -8 + 5i$$

15. $3(2 + 5i) = 3 \cdot 2 + 3 \cdot 5i = 6 + 15i$

16. $4(1 - 3i) = 4 - 12i$

17. $2i(i - 5) = 2i^2 - 10i = 2(-1) - 10i$
$$= -2 - 10i$$

18. $3i(2 - 6i) = 6i - 18i^2 = 6i - 18(-1)$
$$= 18 + 6i$$

19. $-4i(3 - i) = -12i + 4i^2$
$$= -12i + 4(-1) = -4 - 12i$$

20. $-5i(2 + 3i) = -10i - 15i^2 = 15 - 10i$

21. $(2 + 3i)(4 + 6i) = 8 + 24i + 18i^2$
$$= 8 + 24i + 18(-1) = -10 + 24i$$

22. $(2 + i)(3 + 4i) = 6 + 11i + 4i^2$
$$= 6 + 11i + 4(-1) = 2 + 11i$$

23. $(-1 + i)(2 - i) = -2 + 3i - i^2$
$$= -2 + 3i - (-1) = -1 + 3i$$

24. $(3 - 2i)(2 - 5i) = 6 - 19i + 10i^2$
$$= 6 - 19i - 10 = -4 - 19i$$

25. $(-1 - 2i)(2 + i) = -2 - 5i - 2i^2$
$$= -2 - 5i - 2(-1) = -5i$$

26. $(1 - 3i)(1 + 3i) = 1 - 9i^2 = 1 + 9 = 10$

27. $(5 - 2i)(5 + 2i) = 25 - 4i^2$
$$= 25 - 4(-1) = 29$$

28. $(4 + 3i)(4 + 3i) = 16 + 24i + 9i^2$
$$= 16 + 24i - 9 = 7 + 24i$$

29. $(1 - i)(1 + i) = 1 - i^2 = 1 - (-1) = 2$

30. $(2 + 6i)(2 - 6i) = 4 - 36i^2 = 4 + 36$
$$= 40$$

31. $(4 + 2i)(4 - 2i) = 16 - 4i^2$
$$= 16 - 4(-1) = 20$$

32. $(4 - i)(4 + i) = 16 - i^2 = 16 - (-1)$
$$= 17$$

33. $(3i)^2 = 9i^2 = 9(-1) = -9$

34. $(5i)^2 = 25i^2 = 25(-1) = -25$

35. $(-5i)^2 = (-5)^2 i^2 = 25(-1) = -25$

36. $(-9i)^2 = (-9)^2 i^2 = 81(-1) = -81$

37. $(2i)^4 = 2^4 i^4 = 16(1) = 16$

38. $(-2i)^3 = (-2)^3 i^3 = -8(-i) = 8i$

39. $i^9 = (i^4)^2 \cdot i = 1^2 \cdot i = i$

40. $i^{12} = (i^4)^3 = 1^3 = 1$

41. $(3 + 5i)(3 - 5i) = 9 - 25i^2 = 9 + 25$
$$= 34$$

42. $(3 + i)(3 - i) = 9 - i^2 = 9 - (-1) = 10$

43. $(1 - 2i)(1 + 2i) = 1 - 4i^2 = 1 - 4(-1)$
$$= 5$$

44. $(4 - 6i)(4 + 6i) = 16 - 36i^2$
$$= 16 - 36(-1) = 52$$

45. $(-2 + i)(-2 - i) = 4 - i^2 = 4 - (-1)$
$$= 5$$

46. $(-3 - 2i)(-3 + 2i) = 9 - 4i^2 = 9 + 4$
$$= 13$$

47. $(2 - i\sqrt{3})(2 + i\sqrt{3}) = 4 - 3i^2$
$$= 4 - 3(-1) = 7$$

48. $(\sqrt{5} - 4i)(\sqrt{5} + 4i) = 5 - 16i^2 = 5 + 16$
$$= 21$$

49. $\dfrac{3}{4 + i} = \dfrac{3(4 - i)}{(4 + i)(4 - i)} = \dfrac{12 - 3i}{16 - i^2}$
$$= \dfrac{12 - 3i}{17} = \dfrac{12}{17} - \dfrac{3}{17}i$$

50. $\dfrac{6}{7 - 2i} = \dfrac{6(7 + 2i)}{(7 - 2i)(7 + 2i)} = \dfrac{42 + 12i}{49 - 4i^2}$
$$= \dfrac{42 + 12i}{53} = \dfrac{42}{53} + \dfrac{12}{53}i$$

51. $\dfrac{2 + i}{3 - 2i} = \dfrac{(2 + i)(3 + 2i)}{(3 - 2i)(3 + 2i)}$
$$= \dfrac{6 + 7i + 2i^2}{9 - 4i^2} = \dfrac{4 + 7i}{13} = \dfrac{4}{13} + \dfrac{7}{13}i$$

52. $\dfrac{3 + 5i}{2 - i} = \dfrac{(3 + 5i)(2 + i)}{(2 - i)(2 + i)}$
$$= \dfrac{6 + 13i + 5i^2}{4 - i^2} = \dfrac{6 + 13i - 5}{4 - (-1)}$$
$$= \dfrac{1 + 13i}{5} = \dfrac{1}{5} + \dfrac{13}{5}i$$

53. $\dfrac{4 + 3i}{i} = \dfrac{(4 + 3i)(-i)}{(i)(-i)} = \dfrac{-4i - 3i^2}{-i^2}$
$$= \dfrac{-4i + 3}{1} = 3 - 4i$$

54. $\dfrac{5 - 6i}{3i} = \dfrac{(5 - 6i)(-3i)}{3i(-3i)} = \dfrac{-15i + 18i^2}{-9i^2}$

$$= \dfrac{-15i - 18}{-9(-1)} = \dfrac{-18 - 15i}{9} = -2 - \dfrac{5}{3}i$$

55. $\dfrac{2 + 6i}{2} = \dfrac{2}{2} + \dfrac{6i}{2} = 1 + 3i$

56. $\dfrac{9 - 3i}{-6} = \dfrac{-3(-3 + i)}{-3 \cdot 2} = \dfrac{-3 + i}{2}$
$$= -\dfrac{3}{2} + \dfrac{1}{2}i$$

57. $2 + \sqrt{-4} = 2 + i\sqrt{4} = 2 + 2i$

58. $3 + \sqrt{-9} = 3 + i\sqrt{9} = 3 + 3i$

59. $2\sqrt{-9} + 5 = 2i\sqrt{9} + 5 = 2i \cdot 3 + 5$
$$= 5 + 6i$$

60. $3\sqrt{-16} + 2 = 3i\sqrt{16} + 2 = 2 + 12i$

61. $7 - \sqrt{-6} = 7 - i\sqrt{6}$

62. $\sqrt{-5} + 3 = 3 + i\sqrt{5}$

63. $\sqrt{-8} + \sqrt{-18} = i\sqrt{4}\sqrt{2} + i\sqrt{9}\sqrt{2}$
$$= 2i\sqrt{2} + 3i\sqrt{2} = 5i\sqrt{2}$$

64. $2\sqrt{-20} - \sqrt{-45} = 2i\sqrt{20} - i\sqrt{45}$
$$= 2i \cdot 2\sqrt{5} - i \cdot 3\sqrt{5}$$
$$= 4i\sqrt{5} - 3i\sqrt{5} = i\sqrt{5}$$

65. $\dfrac{2 + \sqrt{-12}}{2} = \dfrac{2 + i\sqrt{4}\sqrt{3}}{2} = 1 + i\sqrt{3}$

66. $\dfrac{-6 - \sqrt{-18}}{3} = \dfrac{-6 - i\sqrt{18}}{3}$
$$= \dfrac{-6 - 3i\sqrt{2}}{3} = -2 - i\sqrt{2}$$

67. $\dfrac{-4 - \sqrt{-24}}{4} = \dfrac{-4 - i\sqrt{4}\sqrt{6}}{4}$
$$= \dfrac{-4}{4} - \dfrac{2i\sqrt{6}}{4} = -1 - \dfrac{1}{2}i\sqrt{6}$$

68. $\dfrac{8 + \sqrt{-20}}{-4} = \dfrac{8 + i\sqrt{20}}{-4} = \dfrac{8 + 2i\sqrt{5}}{-4}$
$$= \dfrac{8}{-4} + \dfrac{2}{-4}i\sqrt{5} = -2 - \dfrac{1}{2}i\sqrt{5}$$

69. $x^2 = -36$
$$x = \pm\sqrt{-36} = \pm 6i$$
Solution set: $\{\pm 6i\}$

70. $x^2 + 4 = 0$
$$x^2 = -4$$
$$x = \pm\sqrt{-4} = \pm 2i$$
The solution set is $\{\pm 2i\}$.

71. $x^2 = -12$
$$x = \pm\sqrt{-12} = \pm i\sqrt{4}\sqrt{3} = \pm 2i\sqrt{3}$$
Solution set: $\{\pm 2i\sqrt{3}\}$

72. $x^2 = -25$
$$x = \pm\sqrt{-25} = \pm 5i$$
The solution set is $\{\pm 5i\}$.

73. $2x^2 + 5 = 0$
$$x^2 = -\tfrac{5}{2}$$
$$x = \pm\sqrt{-\tfrac{5}{2}} = \pm\frac{i\sqrt{5}}{\sqrt{2}} = \pm\frac{i\sqrt{10}}{2}$$
Solution set: $\left\{\pm\dfrac{i\sqrt{10}}{2}\right\}$

74. $3x^2 + 4 = 0$
$$x^2 = -\tfrac{4}{3}$$
$$x = \pm\sqrt{-\tfrac{4}{3}} = \pm i\frac{2}{\sqrt{3}} = \pm i\frac{2\sqrt{3}}{3}$$
The solution set is $\left\{\pm i\dfrac{2\sqrt{3}}{3}\right\}$.

75. $3x^2 + 6 = 0$
$$x^2 = -2$$
$$x = \pm\sqrt{-2} = \pm i\sqrt{2}$$
Solution set: $\{\pm i\sqrt{2}\}$

76. $x^2 + 1 = 0$
$$x^2 = -1$$
$$x = \pm\sqrt{-1} = i$$
Solution set: $\{\pm i\}$

77. $(2 - 3i)(3 + 4i) = 6 - i - 12i^2$
$$= 6 - i - 12(-1) = 18 - i$$

78. $(2 - 3i)(2 + 3i) = 4 - 9i^2$
$$= 4 - 9(-1) = 13$$

79. $(2 - 3i) + (3 + 4i) = 5 + i$

80. $(3 - 5i) - (2 - 7i) = 1 + 2i$

81. $\dfrac{2 - 3i}{3 + 4i} = \dfrac{(2 - 3i)(3 - 4i)}{(3 + 4i)(3 - 4i)}$
$$= \frac{6 - 17i + 12i^2}{9 - 16i^2} = \frac{6 - 17i + 12(-1)}{9 - 16(-1)}$$
$$= \frac{-6 - 17i}{25} = -\frac{6}{25} - \frac{17}{25}i$$

82. $\dfrac{-3i}{3 - 6i} = \dfrac{(-3i)(3 + 6i)}{(3 - 6i)(3 + 6i)} = \dfrac{-9i - 18i^2}{9 - 36i^2}$
$$= \frac{18 - 9i}{45} = \frac{18}{45} - \frac{9}{45}i = \frac{2}{5} - \frac{1}{5}i$$

83. $i(2 - 3i) = 2i - 3i^2 = 2i + 3 = 3 + 2i$

84. $-3i(4i - 1) = -12i^2 + 3i = 12 + 3i$

85. $(-3i)^2 = 9i^2 = -9$

86. $(-2i)^6 = 64i^6 = -64$

87. $\sqrt{-12} + \sqrt{-3} = 2i\sqrt{3} + i\sqrt{3} = 3i\sqrt{3}$

88. $\sqrt{-49} - \sqrt{-25} = 7i - 5i = 2i$

89. $(2 - 3i)^2 = 4 - 12i + 9i^2 = -5 - 12i$

90. $(5 + 3i)^2 = 25 + 30i + 9i^2 = 16 + 30i$

91. $\dfrac{-4 + \sqrt{-32}}{2} = \dfrac{-4 + 4i\sqrt{2}}{2}$
$$= -2 + 2i\sqrt{2}$$

92. $\dfrac{-2 - \sqrt{-27}}{-6} = \dfrac{-2 - 3i\sqrt{3}}{-6}$
$$= \frac{-2}{-6} - \frac{3i\sqrt{3}}{-6} = \frac{1}{3} + \frac{1}{2}i\sqrt{3}$$

Enriching Your Mathematical Word Power
1. d   2. b   3. b   4. b   5. d
6. b   7. c   8. a   9. d   10. c
11. a   12. c   13. d   14. b

CHAPTER 7 REVIEW

1. $(-27)^{-2/3} = \dfrac{1}{(-3)^2} = \dfrac{1}{9}$

2. $-25^{3/2} = -5^3 = -125$

3. $(2^6)^{1/3} = 2^{6/3} = 2^2 = 4$

4. $(5^2)^{1/2} = 5^{2/2} = 5^1 = 5$

5. $100^{-3/2} = \dfrac{1}{10^3} = \dfrac{1}{1000}$

6. $1000^{-2/3} = \dfrac{1}{10^2} = \dfrac{1}{100}$

7. $\dfrac{3x^{-1/2}}{3^{-2}x^{-1}} = 3^3 x^{-1/2 + 1} = 27x^{1/2}$

8. $\dfrac{(x^2 y^{-3} z)^{1/2}}{x^{1/2} y z^{-1/2}} = \dfrac{x y^{-3/2} z^{1/2}}{x^{1/2} y z^{-1/2}} = x^{1/2} y^{-5/2} z$
$$= \frac{x^{1/2} z}{y^{5/2}}$$

9. $a^{3/2} b^3 a^2 b^{2/4} = a^{7/2} b^{7/2}$

10. $(t^{-1/2})^{-2}(t^{-2}v^2) = t^{2/2} t^{-2} v^2 = t t^{-2} v^2$
$$= t^{-1} v^2 = \frac{v^2}{t}$$

11. $x^{1/2 + 1/4} y^{1/4 + 1} = x^{3/4} y^{5/4}$

12. $(a^{1/3} b^{1/6})^2 (a^{1/3} b^{2/3}) = a^{2/3} b^{1/3} a^{1/3} b^{2/3}$
$$= a^{3/3} b^{3/3} = ab$$

13. $\sqrt{72x^5} = \sqrt{36x^4}\sqrt{2x} = 6x^2\sqrt{2x}$

14. $\sqrt{90y^9 z^4} = \sqrt{9y^8 z^4}\sqrt{10y} = 3y^4 z^2\sqrt{10y}$

15. $\sqrt[3]{72x^5} = \sqrt[3]{8x^3}\cdot\sqrt[3]{9x^2} = 2x\sqrt[3]{9x^2}$

16. $\sqrt[3]{81a^8 b^9} = \sqrt[3]{27a^6 b^9}\sqrt[3]{3a^2}$
$$= 3a^2 b^3\sqrt[3]{3a^2}$$

17. $\sqrt{2^6} = 2^3 = 8$

18. $\sqrt{2^7} = \sqrt{2^6}\sqrt{2} = 2^3\cdot\sqrt{2} = 8\sqrt{2}$

19. $\sqrt{\dfrac{2}{5}} = \dfrac{\sqrt{2}\sqrt{5}}{\sqrt{5}\sqrt{5}} = \dfrac{\sqrt{10}}{5}$

20. $\sqrt{\dfrac{1}{6}} = \dfrac{1\sqrt{6}}{\sqrt{6}\sqrt{6}} = \dfrac{\sqrt{6}}{6}$

21. $\sqrt[3]{\dfrac{2}{3}} = \dfrac{\sqrt[3]{2}\cdot\sqrt[3]{9}}{\sqrt[3]{3}\cdot\sqrt[3]{9}} = \dfrac{\sqrt[3]{18}}{\sqrt[3]{27}} = \dfrac{\sqrt[3]{18}}{3}$

22. $\sqrt[3]{\dfrac{1}{9}} = \dfrac{1\cdot\sqrt[3]{3}}{\sqrt[3]{9}\cdot\sqrt[3]{3}} = \dfrac{\sqrt[3]{3}}{\sqrt[3]{27}} = \dfrac{\sqrt[3]{3}}{3}$

23. $\dfrac{2}{\sqrt{3x}} = \dfrac{2\sqrt{3x}}{\sqrt{3x}\sqrt{3x}} = \dfrac{2\sqrt{3x}}{3x}$

24. $\dfrac{3}{\sqrt{2y}} = \dfrac{3\sqrt{2y}}{\sqrt{2y}\sqrt{2y}} = \dfrac{3\sqrt{2y}}{2y}$

25. $\dfrac{\sqrt{10y^3}}{\sqrt{6}} = \dfrac{\sqrt{2}\sqrt{5y}\sqrt{y^2}}{\sqrt{2}\sqrt{3}} = \dfrac{y\sqrt{5y}}{\sqrt{3}}$

$\qquad = \dfrac{y\sqrt{5y}\sqrt{3}}{\sqrt{3}\sqrt{3}} = \dfrac{y\sqrt{15y}}{3}$

26. $\dfrac{\sqrt{5x^5}}{\sqrt{8}} = \dfrac{\sqrt{5x}\sqrt{x^4}\sqrt{2}}{\sqrt{8}\sqrt{2}} = \dfrac{x^2\sqrt{10x}}{\sqrt{16}}$

$\qquad = \dfrac{x^2\sqrt{10x}}{4}$

27. $\dfrac{3}{\sqrt[3]{2a}} = \dfrac{3\sqrt[3]{4a^2}}{\sqrt[3]{2a}\sqrt[3]{4a^2}} = \dfrac{3\sqrt[3]{4a^2}}{2a}$

28. $\dfrac{a}{\sqrt[3]{a^2}} = \dfrac{a\sqrt[3]{a}}{\sqrt[3]{a^2}\sqrt[3]{a}} = \dfrac{a\sqrt[3]{a}}{\sqrt[3]{a^3}} = \sqrt[3]{a}$

29. $\dfrac{5}{\sqrt[4]{3x^2}} = \dfrac{5\sqrt[4]{27x^2}}{\sqrt[4]{3x^2}\cdot\sqrt[4]{27x^2}}$

$\qquad = \dfrac{5\sqrt[4]{27x^2}}{\sqrt[4]{81x^4}} = \dfrac{5\sqrt[4]{27x^2}}{3x}$

30. $\dfrac{b}{\sqrt[4]{a^2b^3}} = \dfrac{b\sqrt[4]{a^2b}}{\sqrt[4]{a^2b^3}\cdot\sqrt[4]{a^2b}} = \dfrac{b\sqrt[4]{a^2b}}{\sqrt[4]{a^4b^4}}$

$\qquad = \dfrac{b\sqrt[4]{a^2b}}{ab} = \dfrac{\sqrt[4]{a^2b}}{a}$

31. $\sqrt[4]{48x^5y^{12}} = \sqrt[4]{16x^4y^{12}}\sqrt[4]{3x} = 2xy^3\sqrt[4]{3x}$

32. $\sqrt[5]{32x^{10}y^{12}} = \sqrt[5]{32x^{10}y^{10}}\cdot\sqrt[5]{y^2}$

$\qquad = 5x^2y^2\sqrt[5]{y^2}$

33. $\sqrt{13}\sqrt{13} = 13$

34. $\sqrt[3]{14}\cdot\sqrt[3]{14}\cdot\sqrt[3]{14} = \sqrt[3]{14^3} = 14$

35. $\sqrt{27} + \sqrt{45} - \sqrt{75}$

$\quad = 3\sqrt{3} + 3\sqrt{5} - 5\sqrt{3} = 3\sqrt{5} - 2\sqrt{3}$

36. $\sqrt{12} - \sqrt{50} + \sqrt{72}$

$\quad = 2\sqrt{3} - 5\sqrt{2} + 6\sqrt{2} = 2\sqrt{3} + \sqrt{2}$

37. $\sqrt{\dfrac{1}{3}} + \sqrt{27} = \dfrac{\sqrt{3}}{3} + 3\sqrt{3}$

$\qquad = \dfrac{\sqrt{3}}{3} + \dfrac{9\sqrt{3}}{3} = \dfrac{10\sqrt{3}}{3}$

38. $\sqrt{\dfrac{1}{2}} - \sqrt{\dfrac{1}{8}} = \dfrac{1\sqrt{2}}{\sqrt{2}\sqrt{2}} - \dfrac{1\sqrt{8}}{\sqrt{8}\sqrt{8}}$

$\quad = \dfrac{\sqrt{2}}{2} - \dfrac{2\sqrt{2}}{8} = \dfrac{2\sqrt{2}}{4} - \dfrac{\sqrt{2}}{4} = \dfrac{\sqrt{2}}{4}$

39. $3\sqrt{2}(5\sqrt{2} - 7\sqrt{3}) = 15\cdot 2 - 21\sqrt{6}$

$\qquad = 30 - 21\sqrt{6}$

40. $-2\sqrt{a}(\sqrt{a} - \sqrt{ab^6}) = -2a + 2\sqrt{a^2b^6}$

$\qquad = -2a + 2ab^3$

41. $(2 - \sqrt{3})(3 + \sqrt{2})$

$\qquad = 6 - 3\sqrt{3} + 2\sqrt{2} - \sqrt{6}$

42. $(2\sqrt{x} - \sqrt{y})(\sqrt{x} + \sqrt{y})$

$\quad = 2x - \sqrt{xy} + 2\sqrt{xy} - y = 2x + \sqrt{xy} - y$

43. $\sqrt[3]{40} - \sqrt[3]{5} = \sqrt[3]{8}\cdot\sqrt[3]{5} - \sqrt[3]{5}$

$\qquad = 2\sqrt[3]{5} - \sqrt[3]{5} = \sqrt[3]{5}$

44. $\sqrt[3]{54x^4} + x\sqrt[3]{16x}$

$\quad = \sqrt[3]{27x^3}\cdot\sqrt[3]{2x} + x\sqrt[3]{8}\cdot\sqrt[3]{2x}$

$\quad = 3x\cdot\sqrt[3]{2x} + 2x\cdot\sqrt[3]{2x} = 5x\sqrt[3]{2x}$

45. $5 \div \sqrt{2} = \dfrac{5}{\sqrt{2}} = \dfrac{5\sqrt{2}}{\sqrt{2}\sqrt{2}} = \dfrac{5\sqrt{2}}{2}$

46. $10\sqrt{6} \div (2\sqrt{2}) = \dfrac{10\sqrt{6}}{2\sqrt{2}} = 5\sqrt{\dfrac{6}{2}}$

$\qquad = 5\sqrt{3}$

47. $(\sqrt{3})^4 = 3^{4/2} = 3^2 = 9$

48. $(-2\sqrt{x})^9 = (-2)^9\sqrt{x^9} = -512x^4\sqrt{x}$

49. $\dfrac{2 - 2\sqrt{2}}{2} = \dfrac{2(1 - \sqrt{2})}{2} = 1 - \sqrt{2}$

50. $\dfrac{-3 - \sqrt{18}}{-6} = \dfrac{-3 - 3\sqrt{2}}{-6}$

$\qquad = \dfrac{-3(1 + \sqrt{2})}{-3\cdot 2} = \dfrac{1 + \sqrt{2}}{2}$

51. $\dfrac{\sqrt{6}(1 + \sqrt{3})}{(1 - \sqrt{3})(1 + \sqrt{3})} = \dfrac{\sqrt{6} + \sqrt{18}}{1 - 3}$

$\qquad = \dfrac{\sqrt{6} + 3\sqrt{2}}{-2} = \dfrac{-\sqrt{6} - 3\sqrt{2}}{2}$

52. $\dfrac{\sqrt{15}}{2 + \sqrt{5}} = \dfrac{\sqrt{15}(2 - \sqrt{5})}{(2 + \sqrt{5})(2 - \sqrt{5})}$

$\qquad = \dfrac{2\sqrt{15} - \sqrt{75}}{4 - 5}$

$\qquad = \dfrac{2\sqrt{15} - 5\sqrt{3}}{-1} = -2\sqrt{15} + 5\sqrt{3}$

53. $\dfrac{2\sqrt{3}}{3\sqrt{6} - 2\sqrt{3}}$

$\quad = \dfrac{2\sqrt{3}(3\sqrt{6} + 2\sqrt{3})}{(3\sqrt{6} - 2\sqrt{3})(3\sqrt{6} + 2\sqrt{3})}$

$\quad = \dfrac{6\sqrt{18} + 12}{54 - 12} = \dfrac{6\cdot 3\sqrt{2} + 12}{42} = \dfrac{6\cdot 3\sqrt{2} + 6\cdot 2}{6\cdot 7}$

$\quad = \dfrac{3\sqrt{2} + 2}{7}$

54. $\dfrac{-\sqrt{xy}}{3\sqrt{x} + \sqrt{xy}}$

$\quad = \dfrac{-\sqrt{xy}(3\sqrt{x} - \sqrt{xy})}{(3\sqrt{x} + \sqrt{xy})(3\sqrt{x} - \sqrt{xy})}$

$\quad = \dfrac{-3x\sqrt{y} + xy}{9x - xy} = \dfrac{-3\sqrt{y} + y}{9 - y}$

55. $\left(2w\sqrt[3]{2w^2}\right)^6 = 2^6 w^6 \sqrt[3]{2^6 w^{12}}$
$$= 2^6 2^2 w^6 w^4 = 256 w^{10}$$

56. $\left(m\sqrt[4]{m^3}\right)^8 = m^8 \sqrt[4]{m^{24}} = m^8 m^6$
$$= m^{14}$$

57. $\quad x^2 = 16$
$$x = \pm 4$$
Solution set: $\{-4, 4\}$

58. $\quad w^2 = 100$
$$w = \pm\sqrt{100} = \pm 10$$
The solution set is $\{-10, 10\}$.

59. $\quad (a-5)^2 = 4$
$$a - 5 = \pm 2$$
$$a = 5 \pm 2$$
$$a = 5 + 2 \quad \text{or} \quad a = 5 - 2$$
$$a = 7 \quad \text{or} \quad a = 3$$
Solution set: $\{3, 7\}$

60. $\quad (m-7)^2 = 25$
$$m - 7 = \pm 5$$
$$m = 7 \pm 5$$
$$m = 7 + 5 \quad \text{or} \quad m = 7 - 5$$
$$= 12 \quad \text{or} \quad m = 2$$
The solution set is $\{2, 12\}$

61. $\quad (a+1)^2 = 5$
$$a + 1 = \pm\sqrt{5}$$
$$a = -1 \pm\sqrt{5}$$
Solution set: $\{-1-\sqrt{5}, -1+\sqrt{5}\}$

62. $\quad (x+5)^2 = 3$
$$x + 5 = \pm\sqrt{3}$$
$$x = -5 \pm\sqrt{3}$$
The solution set is $\{-5-\sqrt{3}, -5+\sqrt{3}\}$

63. $\quad (m+1)^2 = -8$
Since the square root of -8 is not a real number, the solution set is $\emptyset$.

64. $\quad (w+4)^2 = 16$
$$w + 4 = \pm 4$$
$$w = -4 \pm 4$$
$$w = -4 + 4 \quad \text{or} \quad w = -4 - 4$$
$$w = 0 \quad \text{or} \quad w = -8$$
The solution set is $\{-8, 0\}$.

65. $\quad \sqrt{m-1} = 3$
$$(\sqrt{m-1})^2 = 3^2$$
$$m - 1 = 9$$
$$m = 10$$
Solution set: $\{10\}$

66. $\quad 3\sqrt{x+5} = 12$

67. $\quad \sqrt{x+5} = 4$
$$\left(\sqrt{x+5}\right)^2 = 4^2$$
$$x + 5 = 16$$
$$x = 11$$
The solution set is $\{11\}$.

67. $\quad \sqrt[3]{2x+9} = 3$
$$(\sqrt[3]{2x+9})^3 = 3^3$$
$$2x + 9 = 27$$
$$2x = 18$$
$$x = 9$$
Solution set: $\{9\}$

68. $\quad \sqrt[4]{2x-1} = 2$
$$\left(\sqrt[4]{2x-1}\right)^4 = 2^4$$
$$2x - 1 = 16$$
$$2x = 17$$
$$x = \frac{17}{2}$$
The solution set is $\left\{\frac{17}{2}\right\}$.

69. $\quad w^{2/3} = 4$
$$(w^{2/3})^3 = 4^3$$
$$w^2 = 64$$
$$w = \pm 8$$
Solution set: $\{-8, 8\}$

70. $\quad m^{-4/3} = 16$
$$\left(m^{-4/3}\right)^{-3} = 16^{-3}$$
$$m^4 = \frac{1}{16^3}$$
$$m = \pm\sqrt[4]{\frac{1}{16^3}} = \pm\frac{1}{\sqrt[4]{16^3}}$$
$$= \pm\frac{1}{2^3} = \pm\frac{1}{8}$$
The solution set is $\left\{-\frac{1}{8}, \frac{1}{8}\right\}$.

71. $\quad (m+1)^{1/3} = 5$
$$((m+1)^{1/3})^3 = 5^3$$
$$m + 1 = 125$$
$$m = 124$$
Solution set: $\{124\}$

72. $\quad (w-3)^{-2/3} = 4$
$$((w-3)^{-2/3})^{-3} = 4^{-3}$$
$$(w-3)^2 = \frac{1}{4^3}$$
$$w - 3 = \pm\sqrt{\frac{1}{4^3}} = \pm\frac{1}{2^3} = \pm\frac{1}{8}$$
$$w = 3 \pm\frac{1}{8}$$
$$w = 3 + \frac{1}{8} = \frac{25}{8} \quad \text{or} \quad w = 3 - \frac{1}{8} = \frac{23}{8}$$
The solution set is $\left\{\frac{23}{8}, \frac{25}{8}\right\}$.

73.
$$\sqrt{x-3} = \sqrt{x+2} - 1$$
$$\left(\sqrt{x-3}\right)^2 = \left(\sqrt{x+2}-1\right)^2$$
$$x-3 = x+2 - 2\sqrt{x+2} + 1$$
$$-6 = -2\sqrt{x+2}$$
$$3 = \sqrt{x+2}$$
$$3^2 = (\sqrt{x+2})^2$$
$$9 = x+2$$
$$7 = x$$
Solution set: $\{7\}$

74.
$$\sqrt{x^2+3x+6} = 4$$
$$\left(\sqrt{x^2+3x+6}\right)^2 = 4^2$$
$$x^2 + 3x + 6 = 16$$
$$x^2 + 3x - 10 = 0$$
$$(x+5)(x-2) = 0$$
$$x+5 = 0 \text{ or } x-2 = 0$$
$$x = -5 \text{ or } \quad x = 2$$
The solution set is $\{-5, 2\}$.

75.
$$\sqrt{5x - x^2} = \sqrt{6}$$
$$\left(\sqrt{5x-x^2}\right)^2 = \left(\sqrt{6}\right)^2$$
$$5x - x^2 = 6$$
$$-x^2 + 5x - 6 = 0$$
$$x^2 - 5x + 6 = 0$$
$$(x-2)(x-3) = 0$$
$$x = 2 \text{ or } x = 3$$
Solution set: $\{2, 3\}$

76.
$$\sqrt{x+4} - 2\sqrt{x-1} = -1$$
$$\sqrt{x+4} = 2\sqrt{x-1} - 1$$
$$\left(\sqrt{x+4}\right)^2 = \left(2\sqrt{x-1}-1\right)^2$$
$$x+4 = 4(x-1) - 4\sqrt{x-1} + 1$$
$$x+4 = 4x - 4 - 4\sqrt{x-1} + 1$$
$$-3x + 7 = -4\sqrt{x-1}$$
$$(-3x+7)^2 = (-4\sqrt{x-1})^2$$
$$9x^2 - 42x + 49 = 16(x-1)$$
$$9x^2 - 58x + 65 = 0$$
$$(9x-13)(x-5) = 0$$
$$9x - 13 = 0 \text{ or } x - 5 = 0$$
$$x = \tfrac{13}{9} \text{ or } \quad x = 5$$
The solution $\frac{13}{9}$ does not satisfy the original equation. The solution set is $\{5\}$.

77.
$$\sqrt{x+7} - 2\sqrt{x} = -2$$
$$\sqrt{x+7} = 2\sqrt{x} - 2$$
$$\left(\sqrt{x+7}\right)^2 = \left(2\sqrt{x}-2\right)^2$$
$$x+7 = 4x - 8\sqrt{x} + 4$$

$$8\sqrt{x} = 3x - 3$$
$$\left(8\sqrt{x}\right)^2 = \left(3x-3\right)^2$$
$$64x = 9x^2 - 18x + 9$$
$$0 = 9x^2 - 82x + 9$$
$$0 = (9x-1)(x-9)$$
$$x = \tfrac{1}{9} \text{ or } x = 9$$
Since $\sqrt{\tfrac{1}{9}+7} - 2\sqrt{\tfrac{1}{9}} = \tfrac{8}{3} - \tfrac{2}{3} = 2$, $1/9$ is an extraneous root. The solution set is $\{9\}$.

78.
$$\sqrt{x} - \sqrt{x-1} = 1$$
$$\sqrt{x} = 1 + \sqrt{x-1}$$
$$(\sqrt{x})^2 = (1+\sqrt{x-1})^2$$
$$x = 1 + 2\sqrt{x-1} + x - 1$$
$$0 = 2\sqrt{x-1}$$
$$0 = \sqrt{x-1}$$
$$0 = x - 1$$
$$1 = x$$
The solution set is $\{1\}$.

79.
$$2\sqrt{x} - \sqrt{x-3} = 3$$
$$2\sqrt{x} = \sqrt{x-3} + 3$$
$$\left(2\sqrt{x}\right)^2 = \left(\sqrt{x-3}+3\right)^2$$
$$4x = x - 3 + 6\sqrt{x-3} + 9$$
$$3x - 6 = 6\sqrt{x-3}$$
$$x - 2 = 2\sqrt{x-3}$$
$$(x-2)^2 = (2\sqrt{x-3})^2$$
$$x^2 - 4x + 4 = 4(x-3)$$
$$x^2 - 8x + 16 = 0$$
$$(x-4)^2 = 0$$
$$x = 4$$
Solution set: $\{4\}$

80.
$$1 + \sqrt{x+7} = \sqrt{2x+7}$$
$$(1+\sqrt{x+7})^2 = (\sqrt{2x+7})^2$$
$$1 + 2\sqrt{x+7} + x + 7 = 2x + 7$$
$$2\sqrt{x+7} = x - 1$$
$$(2\sqrt{x+7})^2 = (x-1)^2$$
$$4(x+7) = x^2 - 2x + 1$$
$$-x^2 + 6x + 27 = 0$$
$$x^2 - 6x - 27 = 0$$
$$(x-9)(x+3) = 0$$
$$x - 9 = 0 \text{ or } x + 3 = 0$$
$$x = 9 \text{ or } \quad x = -3$$
The solution -3 does not satisfy the original equation. The solution set is $\{9\}$.

81. $(2-3i)(-5+5i) = -10 + 25i - 15i^2$
$$= -10 + 25i + 15 = 5 + 25i$$

281

82. $(2+i)(5-2i) = 10 + i - 2i^2$
$$= 10 + i + 2 = 12 + i$$

83. $(2+i) + (5-4i) = 7 - 3i$

84. $(2+i) + (3-6i) = 5 - 5i$

85. $(1-i) - (2-3i) = 1 - i - 2 + 3i$
$$= -1 + 2i$$

86. $(3-2i) - (1-i) = 3 - 2i - 1 + i$
$$= 2 - i$$

87. $\dfrac{6+3i}{3} = \dfrac{6}{3} + \dfrac{3i}{3} = 2 + i$

88. $\dfrac{8+12i}{4} = \dfrac{8}{4} + \dfrac{12}{4}i = 2 + 3i$

89. $\dfrac{4-\sqrt{-12}}{2} = \dfrac{4 - 2i\sqrt{3}}{2} = 2 - i\sqrt{3}$

90. $\dfrac{6+\sqrt{-18}}{3} = \dfrac{6 + i\sqrt{18}}{3} = \dfrac{6 + 3i\sqrt{2}}{3}$
$$= 2 + i\sqrt{2}$$

91. $\dfrac{(2-3i)(4-i)}{(4+i)(4-i)} = \dfrac{5-14i}{17} = \dfrac{5}{17} - \dfrac{14}{17}i$

92. $\dfrac{3+i}{2-3i} = \dfrac{(3+i)(2+3i)}{(2-3i)(2+3i)}$
$$= \dfrac{6+11i+3i^2}{4-9i^2} = \dfrac{6+11i-3}{4+9} = \dfrac{3+11i}{13}$$
$$= \dfrac{3}{13} + \dfrac{11}{13}i$$

93. $x^2 + 100 = 0$
$$x^2 = -100$$
$$x = \pm\sqrt{-100} = \pm 10i$$
The solution set is $\{\pm 10i\}$.

94. $25a^2 + 3 = 0$
$$25a^2 = -3$$
$$a^2 = -\dfrac{3}{25}$$
$$a = \pm\sqrt{-\dfrac{3}{25}} = \pm\dfrac{i\sqrt{3}}{5}$$
The solution set is $\left\{\pm\dfrac{i\sqrt{3}}{5}\right\}$.

95. $2b^2 + 9 = 0$
$$2b^2 = -9$$
$$b^2 = -\dfrac{9}{2}$$
$$b = \sqrt{-\dfrac{9}{2}} = \pm\dfrac{3i}{\sqrt{2}} = \pm\dfrac{3i\sqrt{2}}{2}$$
The solution set is $\left\{\pm\dfrac{3i\sqrt{2}}{2}\right\}$.

96. $3y^2 + 6 = 0$
$$3y^2 = -8$$
$$y^2 = -\dfrac{8}{3}$$
$$y = \sqrt{-\dfrac{8}{3}} = \pm\dfrac{2i\sqrt{2}}{\sqrt{3}} = \pm\dfrac{2i\sqrt{6}}{3}$$
The solution set is $\left\{\pm\dfrac{2i\sqrt{6}}{3}\right\}$.

97. False, because $2^3 \cdot 3^2 = 8 \cdot 9 = 72$.

98. True, because $16^{1/4} = 2$ and $4^{1/2} = 2$.

99. True, because $(\sqrt{2})^3 = \sqrt{8} = 2\sqrt{2}$.

100. False, because $3^3 = 27$ or $\sqrt[3]{27} = 3$.

101. True, because
$8^{200}8^{200} = (8 \cdot 8)^{200} = 64^{200}$.

102. True, because
$\sqrt{295} \cdot \sqrt{295} = \sqrt{295^2} = 295$.

103. False, because $4^{1/2} = \sqrt{4} = 2$.

104. True, because $\sqrt{a^2}$ represents a nonnegative number whose square is a^2 and $|a|$ is nonnegative and $(|a|)^2 = a^2$.

105. False, because $5^2 \cdot 5^2 = 5^4 = 625$.

106. True, because
$$\sqrt{6} \div \sqrt{2} = \dfrac{\sqrt{6}}{\sqrt{2}} = \dfrac{\sqrt{2}\sqrt{3}}{\sqrt{2}} = \sqrt{3}.$$

107. False, $\sqrt{w^{10}} = |w^5|$.

108. False, because $\sqrt{a^{16}} = a^{16/2} = a^8$.

109. False, $\sqrt{x^6} = |x^3|$.

110. True, $\sqrt[3]{4}$ is a number that we cube to get 4 and $(\sqrt[6]{16})^3 = 16^{3/6} = 16^{1/2} = 4$.

111. True, $\sqrt{x^8} = x^{8/2} = x^4$.

112. True, because $\sqrt[9]{2^6} = 2^{6/9} = 2^{2/3}$.

113. False, $\sqrt{16} = 4$.

114. True, because $2^{1/2} \cdot 2^{1/4} = 2^{\frac{1}{2}+\frac{1}{4}} = 2^{3/4}$.

115. True, $2^{600} = (2^2)^{300} = 4^{300}$.

116. False, because
$\sqrt{2} \cdot \sqrt[4]{2} = 2^{1/2} \cdot 2^{1/4} = 2^{3/4}$.

117. False, $\dfrac{2+\sqrt{6}}{2} = 1 + \dfrac{\sqrt{6}}{2}$.

118. True, $\dfrac{4+2\sqrt{3}}{2} = \dfrac{2(2+\sqrt{3})}{2} = 2 + \sqrt{3}$.

119. False, $\sqrt{\dfrac{4}{6}} = \sqrt{\dfrac{2}{3}} = \dfrac{\sqrt{2}\sqrt{3}}{\sqrt{3}\sqrt{3}} = \dfrac{\sqrt{6}}{3}$.

120. True, $8^{200} \cdot 8^{200} = 8^{200+200} = 8^{400}$.

121. True, $81^{2/4} = 3^2 = 9 = \sqrt{81}$.

122. False, because $(-64)^{1/3} = -4$ but $(-64)^{2/6}$ is an even root of a negative number and it is not a real number.

123. True, because $(a^4b^2)^{1/2}$ is nonnegative and a^2b could be negative, absolute value symbols are necessary.

124. False, because is a is positive and b is negative, then the left side is positive and the right side is negative.

125. $\sqrt{(-4-2)^2 + (6-(-8))^2}$
$= \sqrt{36 + 196} = \sqrt{232} = \sqrt{4}\sqrt{58} = 2\sqrt{58}$

126. $\sqrt{(-3-5)^2 + (-5-(-7))^2}$
$= \sqrt{64+4} = \sqrt{68} = \sqrt{4}\sqrt{17} = 2\sqrt{17}$

127. To find the time for which $s = 12000$, solve the equation
$$16t^2 = 12000$$
$$t^2 = 750$$
$$t = \sqrt{750} = 5\sqrt{30}$$
The time is $5\sqrt{30}$ seconds.

128. Let $x =$ the distance from Anne to the tree. The rope forms the hypotenuse of a right triangle whose legs are length x and 60.
$$x^2 + 48^2 = 60^2$$
$$x^2 = 1296$$
$$x = \pm 36$$
Anne is standing 36 feet from the tree.

129. The guy wire of length 40 is the hypotenuse of a right triangle where one leg is length 30 and the other is length x. By the Pythagorean theorem we can write
$$x^2 + 30^2 = 40^2$$
$$x^2 = 700$$
$$x = \sqrt{700} = 10\sqrt{7}$$
The wire is attached to the ground $10\sqrt{7}$ feet from the base of the antenna.

130. Let $x =$ the length of the diagonal of the football field. The diagonal is the hypotenuse of a right triangle whose legs are 100 yards and $\frac{160}{3}$ yards.
$$x^2 = (100)^2 + \left(\frac{160}{3}\right)^2$$
$$x^2 = 10,000 + \frac{25600}{9}$$
$$x^2 = \frac{90,000}{9} + \frac{25,600}{9}$$
$$x^2 = \frac{116,600}{9}$$
$$x = \pm\sqrt{\frac{115,600}{9}} = \pm\frac{340}{3}$$
The length of the diagonal is $\frac{340}{3}$ or $113\frac{1}{3}$ yards.

131. Let $x =$ the length of the guy wire. The height of the antenna is 200 feet and the distance from the base of the antenna to the point on the ground where the guy wire is attached is 200 feet. The guy wire is the hypotenuse of a right triangle whose legs each have length 200. By the Pythagorean theorem we can write
$$x^2 = 200^2 + 200^2$$
$$x^2 = 80000$$
$$x = \sqrt{80000} = \sqrt{40000}\sqrt{2} = 200\sqrt{2}$$
The length of the guy wires should be $200\sqrt{2}$ feet.

132. Let $x =$ the height of the lamp post. The shadow is the side opposite 30° in the 30-60-90 right triangle. Since the length of the shadow is 8 feet, the length of the hypotenuse (from the tip of the shadow to the top of the lamp post) is 16 feet. Using the Pythagorean theorem, we can write the following equation.
$$x^2 + 8^2 = 16^2$$
$$x^2 = 192$$
$$x = \pm\sqrt{192} = \pm 8\sqrt{3}$$
The length of the shadow is $8\sqrt{3}$ feet.

133. If the volume is 40 ft^3, then each side is $\sqrt[3]{40}$ ft in length. The surface area of the six square sides is $6(\sqrt[3]{40})^2$ ft^2. Multiply by 1.1 to get $1.1 \cdot 6(\sqrt[3]{40})^2$ ft^2 as the amount of cardboard needed to make the box. Simplify:
$$6.6\left(2\sqrt[3]{5}\right)^2 = 26.4\sqrt[3]{25} \text{ ft}^2$$

134. The length of a side of the cubic box is $\sqrt[3]{32}$ ft. Find the diagonal of a side:
$$d^2 = (\sqrt[3]{32})^2 + (\sqrt[3]{32})^2 = 2(2\sqrt[3]{4})^2$$
$$= 2 \cdot 4\sqrt[3]{16} = 2 \cdot 4 \cdot 2\sqrt[3]{2} = 16\sqrt[3]{2}$$
$$d = \sqrt{16\sqrt[3]{2}} = 4\sqrt[6]{2} \text{ ft}$$
The length x that will fit diagonally in the box is the hypotenuse of a right triangle with legs $4\sqrt[6]{2}$ and $\sqrt[3]{32}$.
$$x^2 = (4\sqrt[6]{2})^2 + (\sqrt[3]{32})^2 = 16\sqrt[3]{2} + \sqrt[3]{32^2}$$
$$= 16\sqrt[3]{2} + \sqrt[3]{2^{10}} = 16\sqrt[3]{2} + 8\sqrt[3]{2} = 24\sqrt[3]{2}$$
$$x = \sqrt{24\sqrt[3]{2}} = \sqrt{24}\sqrt[6]{2} = 2\sqrt{6}\sqrt[6]{2}$$
$$= 2 \cdot 6^{3/6}2^{1/6} = 2\sqrt[6]{6^3 \cdot 2^1} = 2\sqrt[6]{432} \text{ ft}$$

135.
$$1035 = 700(1+r)^6$$
$$(1+r)^6 = \frac{1035}{700}$$
$$1+r = \left(\frac{1035}{700}\right)^{1/6}$$
$$r = \left(\frac{1035}{700}\right)^{1/6} - 1$$
$$r \approx 0.67 = 6.7\%$$

136. $248.7(1 + r)^8 = 270.1$

$$(1 + r)^8 = \frac{270.1}{248.7}$$

$$r = \left(\frac{270.1}{248.7}\right)^{1/8} - 1$$

$$r \approx 0.0104 = 1.04\%$$

137. $V = \sqrt{\dfrac{841L}{CS}} = \dfrac{\sqrt{841} \cdot \sqrt{L} \cdot \sqrt{CS}}{\sqrt{CS} \cdot \sqrt{CS}}$

$$V = \frac{29\sqrt{LCS}}{CS}$$

138. $Q = 3.32LH^{3/2}$

$Q = 3.32 \cdot 60 \cdot 5^{3/2}$

$Q \approx 2{,}227 \text{ ft}^3/\text{sec}$

$3{,}000 = 3.32 \cdot 70 \cdot H^{3/2}$

$H^{3/2} = \dfrac{3000}{3.32 \cdot 70}$

$H = \left(\dfrac{3000}{3.32 \cdot 70}\right)^{2/3} \approx 5.5 \text{ ft}$

CHAPTER 7   TEST

1. $8^{2/3} = 2^2 = 4$ **2.** $4^{-3/2} = \dfrac{1}{2^3} = \dfrac{1}{8}$

3. $\dfrac{\sqrt{21}}{\sqrt{7}} = \sqrt{\dfrac{21}{7}} = \sqrt{3}$

4. $2\sqrt{5} \cdot 3\sqrt{5} = 6 \cdot 5 = 30$

5. $\sqrt{20} + \sqrt{5} = 2\sqrt{5} + \sqrt{5} = 3\sqrt{5}$

6. $\sqrt{5} + \dfrac{1\sqrt{5}}{\sqrt{5}\sqrt{5}} = \sqrt{5} + \dfrac{\sqrt{5}}{5}$

$\qquad = \dfrac{5\sqrt{5}}{5} + \dfrac{\sqrt{5}}{5} = \dfrac{6\sqrt{5}}{5}$

7. $2^{1/2} \cdot 2^{1/2} = 2^1 = 2$

8. $\sqrt{72} = \sqrt{36}\sqrt{2} = 6\sqrt{2}$

9. $\sqrt{\dfrac{5}{12}} = \dfrac{\sqrt{5}\sqrt{3}}{\sqrt{12}\sqrt{3}} = \dfrac{\sqrt{15}}{\sqrt{36}} = \dfrac{\sqrt{15}}{6}$

10. $\dfrac{6 + 3\sqrt{2}}{6} = \dfrac{3(2 + \sqrt{2})}{3 \cdot 2} = \dfrac{2 + \sqrt{2}}{2}$

11. $(2\sqrt{3} + 1)(\sqrt{3} - 2)$

$\qquad = 6 + \sqrt{3} - 4\sqrt{3} - 2 = 4 - 3\sqrt{3}$

12. $\sqrt[4]{32a^5y^8} = \sqrt[4]{16a^4y^8} \cdot \sqrt[4]{2a}$

$\qquad = 2ay^2\sqrt[4]{2a}$

13. $\dfrac{1}{\sqrt[3]{2x^2}} = \dfrac{1 \cdot \sqrt[3]{4x}}{\sqrt[3]{2x^2} \cdot \sqrt[3]{4x}} = \dfrac{\sqrt[3]{4x}}{\sqrt[3]{8x^3}}$

$\qquad\qquad = \dfrac{\sqrt[3]{4x}}{2x}$

14. $\sqrt{\dfrac{8a^9}{b^3}} = \dfrac{2a^4\sqrt{2a}}{b\sqrt{b}} = \dfrac{2a^4\sqrt{2a}\sqrt{b}}{b\sqrt{b}\sqrt{b}}$

$\qquad\qquad = \dfrac{2a^4\sqrt{2ab}}{b^2}$

15. $\sqrt[3]{-27x^9} = -3x^{9/3} = -3x^3$

16. $\sqrt{20m^3} = \sqrt{4m^2}\sqrt{5m} = 2m\sqrt{5m}$

17. $x^{1/2}x^{1/4} = x^{1/2+1/4} = x^{3/4}$

18. $(9y^4x^{1/2})^{1/2} = 3y^2x^{1/4}$

19. $\sqrt[3]{40x^7} = \sqrt[3]{8x^6} \cdot \sqrt[3]{5x} = 2x^2\sqrt[3]{5x}$

20. $(4 + \sqrt{3})^2 = 16 + 8\sqrt{3} + 3 = 19 + 8\sqrt{3}$

21. $\dfrac{2}{5 - \sqrt{3}} = \dfrac{2(5 + \sqrt{3})}{(5 - \sqrt{3})(5 + \sqrt{3})}$

$\qquad = \dfrac{2(5 + \sqrt{3})}{25 - 3} = \dfrac{2(5 + \sqrt{3})}{22} = \dfrac{5 + \sqrt{3}}{11}$

22. $\dfrac{\sqrt{6}(4\sqrt{3} - \sqrt{2})}{(4\sqrt{3} + \sqrt{2})(4\sqrt{3} - \sqrt{2})}$

$\qquad = \dfrac{4\sqrt{18} - \sqrt{12}}{48 - 2} = \dfrac{12\sqrt{2} - 2\sqrt{3}}{46}$

$\qquad = \dfrac{6\sqrt{2} - \sqrt{3}}{23}$

23. $(3 - 2i)(4 + 5i) = 12 + 7i - 10i^2$

$\qquad\qquad\qquad = 22 + 7i$

24. $i^4 - i^5 = 1 - i^4 \cdot i = 1 - i$

25. $\dfrac{(3 - i)(1 - 2i)}{(1 + 2i)(1 - 2i)} = \dfrac{3 - 7i + 2i^2}{1 - 4i^2}$

$\qquad\qquad = \dfrac{1 - 7i}{5} = \dfrac{1}{5} - \dfrac{7}{5}i$

26. $\dfrac{-6 + \sqrt{-12}}{8} = \dfrac{-6 + 2i\sqrt{3}}{8}$

$\qquad = \dfrac{-3 + i\sqrt{3}}{4} = -\dfrac{3}{4} + \dfrac{1}{4}i\sqrt{3}$

27. $(x - 2)^2 = 49$

$\qquad\quad x - 2 = \pm 7$

$\qquad\qquad x = 2 \pm 7$

$\quad x = 2 + 7 \quad\text{or}\quad x = 2 - 7$

$\quad x = 9 \qquad\text{or}\qquad x = -5$

Solution set: $\{-5, 9\}$

28. $2\sqrt{x + 4} = 3$

$\qquad \left(2\sqrt{x + 4}\right)^2 = (3)^2$

$\qquad\quad 4(x + 4) = 9$

$\qquad\qquad\qquad 4x = -7, \qquad x = -\dfrac{7}{4}$

Solution set: $\left\{-\dfrac{7}{4}\right\}$

29. $w^{2/3} = 4$

$\qquad (w^{2/3})^3 = 4^3$

$\qquad\qquad w^2 = 64, \qquad w = \pm 8$

Solution set: $\{-8, 8\}$

30. $9y^2 + 16 = 0$

$\qquad\quad 9y^2 = -16$

$\qquad\quad y^2 = -\dfrac{16}{9}$

$\qquad\quad y = \pm\sqrt{-\dfrac{16}{9}} = \pm\dfrac{4}{3}$

The solution set is $\left\{\pm\dfrac{4}{3}i\right\}$.

31.
$$\sqrt{2x^2 + x - 12} = x$$
$$\left(\sqrt{2x^2 + x - 12}\right)^2 = x^2$$
$$2x^2 + x - 12 = x^2$$
$$x^2 + x - 12 = 0$$
$$(x + 4)(x - 3) = 0$$
$$x + 4 = 0 \quad \text{or} \quad x - 3 = 0$$
$$x = -4 \quad \text{or} \quad x = 3$$
Since -4 does not check in the original equation, the solution set is $\{3\}$.

32.
$$\sqrt{x - 1} + \sqrt{x + 4} = 5$$
$$\sqrt{x - 1} = 5 - \sqrt{x + 4}$$
$$\left(\sqrt{x - 1}\right)^2 = \left(5 - \sqrt{x + 4}\right)^2$$
$$x - 1 = 25 - 10\sqrt{x + 4} + x + 4$$
$$10\sqrt{x + 4} = 30$$
$$\left(\sqrt{x + 4}\right)^2 = (3)^2$$
$$x + 4 = 9$$
$$x = 5$$
Solution set: $\{5\}$

33.
$$\sqrt{(-1 - 1)^2 + (4 - 6)^2} = \sqrt{4 + 4}$$
$$= \sqrt{8} = 2\sqrt{2}$$

34. Let $x =$ the length of the side. Since the diagonal is the hypotenuse of a right triangle, we can write the equation
$$x^2 + x^2 = 3^2$$
$$2x^2 = 9$$
$$x^2 = \frac{9}{2}$$
$$x = \sqrt{\frac{9}{2}} = \frac{3\sqrt{2}}{\sqrt{2}\sqrt{2}} = \frac{3\sqrt{2}}{2}$$
The length of each side is $\frac{3\sqrt{2}}{2}$ feet.

35. Let $x =$ one number and $x + 11 =$ the other. Since their square roots differ by 1, we can write
$$\sqrt{x + 11} - \sqrt{x} = 1$$
$$\sqrt{x + 11} = \sqrt{x} + 1$$
$$\left(\sqrt{x + 11}\right)^2 = \left(\sqrt{x} + 1\right)^2$$
$$x + 11 = x + 2\sqrt{x} + 1$$
$$10 = 2\sqrt{x}$$
$$10^2 = (2\sqrt{x})^2$$
$$4x = 100$$
$$x = 25$$
$$x + 11 = 36$$
The numbers are 25 and 36.

36. If the perimeter is 20, the sum of the length and width is 10. Let $x =$ the length and $10 - x =$ the width. Use the Pythagorean theorem to write the equation
$$x^2 + (10 - x)^2 = \left(2\sqrt{13}\right)^2$$
$$x^2 + 100 - 20x + x^2 = 52$$
$$2x^2 - 20x + 48 = 0$$
$$x^2 - 10x + 24 = 0$$
$$(x - 4)(x - 6) = 0$$
$$x = 4 \quad \text{or} \quad x = 6$$
$$10 - x = 6 \quad \text{or} \quad 10 - x = 4$$
The length and width are 4 feet and 6 feet.

37. $R = (248.530)^{2/3} \approx 39.53$ AU
$$30.08 = T^{2/3}$$
$$T = 30.08^{3/2} = 164.97 \text{ years}$$

Making Connections

Chapters 1 - 7

1.
$$3x - 6 + 5 = 7 - 4x - 12$$
$$3x - 1 - -4x - 5$$
$$7x = -4$$
$$x = -\frac{4}{7}$$
Solution set: $\left\{-\frac{4}{7}\right\}$

2.
$$\left(\sqrt{6x + 7}\right)^2 = (4)^2$$
$$6x + 7 = 16$$
$$6x = 9$$
$$x = \frac{3}{2}$$
Solution set: $\left\{\frac{3}{2}\right\}$

3.
$$|2x + 5| > 1$$
$$2x + 5 > 1 \quad \text{or} \quad 2x + 5 < -1$$
$$2x > -4 \quad \text{or} \quad 2x < -6$$
$$x > -2 \quad \text{or} \quad x < -3$$
$$(-\infty, -3) \cup (-2, \infty)$$

4.
$$8x^3 - 27 = 0$$
$$x^3 = \frac{27}{8}$$
$$x = \sqrt[3]{\frac{27}{8}} = \frac{3}{2}$$
Solution set: $\left\{\frac{3}{2}\right\}$

5.
$$2x - 3 > 3x - 4$$
$$1 > x$$
$(-\infty, 1)$

6. $\sqrt{2x - 3} - \sqrt{3x + 4} = 0$
$$\left(\sqrt{2x - 3}\right)^2 = \left(\sqrt{3x + 4}\right)^2$$
$$2x - 3 = 3x + 4$$
$$-7 = x$$

Checking -7 gives us a square root of a negative number. So the solution set is $\emptyset$.

7. $6\left(\frac{w}{3} + \frac{w - 4}{2}\right) = 6\left(\frac{11}{2}\right)$
$$2w + 3w - 12 = 33$$
$$5w = 45$$
$$w = 9$$
Solution set: $\{9\}$

8. $2x + 14 - 4 = x - 10 + x$
$$2x + 10 = 2x - 10$$
$$10 = -10$$
Solution set: $\emptyset$

9. $(x + 7)^2 = 25$
$$x + 7 = \pm 5$$
$$x = -7 \pm 5$$
Solution set: $\{-12, -2\}$

10. $a^{-1/2} = 4$
$$\left(a^{-1/2}\right)^{-2} = (4)^{-2}$$
$$a = \frac{1}{16}$$
Solution set: $\left\{\frac{1}{16}\right\}$

11. $x - 3 > 2$ or $x < 2x + 6$
$$x > 5 \text{ or } -x < 6$$
$$x > 5 \text{ or } x > -6$$
$(-6, \infty)$

12. $a^{-2/3} = 16$
$$\left(a^{-2/3}\right)^{-3} = (16)^{-3}$$
$$a^2 = 2^{-12}$$
$$a = \pm\sqrt{2^{-12}} = \pm 2^{-6} = \pm\frac{1}{64}$$
Solution set: $\left\{-\frac{1}{64}, \frac{1}{64}\right\}$

13. $3x^2 - 1 = 0$

$$x^2 = \tfrac{1}{3}$$
$$x = \pm\sqrt{\frac{1}{3}} = \pm\frac{\sqrt{3}}{3}$$
Solution set: $\left\{-\frac{\sqrt{3}}{3}, \frac{\sqrt{3}}{3}\right\}$

14. $5 - 2x + 4 = 3x - 5x + 10 - 1$
$$-2x + 9 = -2x + 9$$
Solution set is all real numbers R.

15. $|3x - 4| < 5$
$$-5 < 3x - 4 < 5$$
$$-1 < 3x < 9$$
$$-\tfrac{1}{3} < x < 3$$
$\left(-\frac{1}{3}, 3\right)$

16. $3x - 1 = 0$
$$x = \tfrac{1}{3}$$
Solution set: $\left\{\frac{1}{3}\right\}$

17. $\left(\sqrt{y - 1}\right)^2 = 9^2$
$$y - 1 = 81$$
$$y = 82$$
Solution set: $\{82\}$

18. $|5x - 10 + 1| = 3$
$$|5x - 9| = 3$$
$$5x - 9 = 3 \text{ or } 5x - 9 = -3$$
$$5x = 12 \qquad 5x = 6$$
$$x = \tfrac{12}{5} \text{ or } \quad x = \tfrac{6}{5}$$
Solution set: $\left\{\frac{6}{5}, \frac{12}{5}\right\}$

19. $0.06x - 0.04x + 0.8 = 2.8$
$$0.02x = 2.0$$
$$x = 100$$
Solution set: $\{100\}$

20. $|3x - 1| > -2$
Since absolute value of any quantity is greater than or equal to zero, any real number satisfies this inequality. Solution set: R

21. $\dfrac{3\sqrt{2}}{x} = \dfrac{\sqrt{3}}{4\sqrt{5}}$
$$\sqrt{3}x = 12\sqrt{10}$$
$$x = \frac{12\sqrt{10}}{\sqrt{3}} = \frac{12\sqrt{10}\sqrt{3}}{\sqrt{3}\sqrt{3}} = 4\sqrt{30}$$

Solution set: $\{4\sqrt{30}\}$

22. $\dfrac{\sqrt{x}-4}{x} = \dfrac{1}{\sqrt{x}+5}$

$$x = (\sqrt{x}-4)(\sqrt{x}+5)$$
$$x = x + \sqrt{x} - 20$$
$$20 = \sqrt{x}$$
$$400 = x$$

Solution set: $\{400\}$

23. $\dfrac{3\sqrt{2}+4}{\sqrt{2}} = \dfrac{x\sqrt{18}}{3\sqrt{2}+2}$

$$6x = (3\sqrt{2}+4)(3\sqrt{2}+2)$$
$$6x = 18 + 18\sqrt{2} + 8$$
$$x = \frac{26+18\sqrt{2}}{6} = \frac{13+9\sqrt{2}}{3}$$

Solution set: $\left\{\dfrac{13+9\sqrt{2}}{3}\right\}$

24. $\dfrac{x}{2\sqrt{5}-\sqrt{2}} = \dfrac{2\sqrt{5}+\sqrt{2}}{x}$

$$x^2 = 20 - 2$$
$$x = \pm\sqrt{18} = \pm 3\sqrt{2}$$

Solution set: $\{-3\sqrt{2}, 3\sqrt{2}\,\}$

25. $\dfrac{\sqrt{2x}-5}{x} = \dfrac{-3}{\sqrt{2x}+5}$

$$-3x = 2x - 25$$
$$-5x = -25$$
$$x = 5$$

Solution sct: $\{5\}$

26. $\dfrac{\sqrt{6}+2}{x} = \dfrac{2}{\sqrt{6}+4}$

$$2x = (\sqrt{6}+2)(\sqrt{6}+4)$$
$$2x = 14 + 6\sqrt{6}$$
$$x = 7 + 3\sqrt{6}$$

Solution set: $\{7 + 3\sqrt{6}\,\}$

27. $\dfrac{x-1}{\sqrt{6}} = \dfrac{\sqrt{6}}{x}$

$$x^2 - x = 6$$
$$x^2 - x - 6 = 0$$
$$(x-3)(x+2) = 0$$
$$x = 3 \text{ or } x = -2$$

Solution set: $\{-2, 3\}$

28. $\dfrac{x+3}{\sqrt{10}} = \dfrac{\sqrt{10}}{x}$

$$x^2 + 3x = 10$$
$$x^2 + 3x - 10 = 0$$
$$(x+5)(x-2) = 0$$

$$x = -5 \text{ or } x = 2$$

Solution set: $\{-5, 2\}$

29. $6x(x-1)(\frac{1}{x} - \frac{1}{x-1}) = 6x(x-1)(-\frac{1}{6})$

$$6x - 6 - 6x = -x^2 + x$$
$$x^2 - x + 6 = 0$$
$$(x-3)(x+2) = 0$$
$$x - 3 = 0 \text{ or } x + 2 = 0$$
$$x = 3 \text{ or } \quad x = -2$$

Solution set: $\{-2, 3\}$

30. $3x(x-2)(\frac{1}{x^2-2x} + \frac{1}{x}) = 3x(x-2)\frac{2}{3}$

$$3 + 3x - 6 = 2x^2 - 4x$$
$$-2x^2 + 7x - 3 = 0$$
$$2x^2 - 7x + 3 = 0$$
$$(2x-1)(x-3) = 0$$
$$2x - 1 = 0 \text{ or } x - 3 = 0$$
$$x = \tfrac{1}{2} \text{ or } \quad x = 3$$

Solution set: $\left\{\tfrac{1}{2}, 3\right\}$

31. $\dfrac{-2 + \sqrt{2^2 - 4(1)(-15)}}{2(1)}$

$$= \frac{-2 + \sqrt{64}}{2} = 3$$

32. $\dfrac{-8 + \sqrt{8^2 - 4(1)(12)}}{2(1)}$

$$= \frac{-8 + \sqrt{16}}{2} = -2$$

33. $\dfrac{-5 + \sqrt{5^2 - 4(2)(-3)}}{2(2)}$

$$= \frac{-5 + \sqrt{49}}{4} = \tfrac{1}{2}$$

34. $\dfrac{-7 + \sqrt{7^2 - 4(6)(-3)}}{2(6)}$

$$= \frac{-7 + \sqrt{121}}{12} = \tfrac{1}{3}$$

35. $v = -94.8 + 21.4x - 0.761x^2$

$v = -94.8 + 21.4(11) - 0.761(11)^2$

$\quad = 48.5 \text{ cm}^3$

36. Moisture content of 14% will produce the maximum volume of popped corn. Maximum volume is about 56 cm^3.

8.1 WARM-UPS

1. False.
2. False, it is equivalent to $x - 3 = \pm 2\sqrt{3}$.
3. False, because some quadratic polynomials cannot be factored.
4. False, because one-half of 4/3 is 2/3 and 2/3 squared is 4/9.
5. True.
6. False, we must first divide each side of the equation by 2.
7. False, $x = 3/2$ or $x = -5/3$.
8. True, one-half of 3 is 3/2 and 3/2 squared is 9/4.
9. False, $x = \pm 2i\sqrt{2}$.
10. False, $(x - 3)^2 = 0$ is a quadratic equation with only one solution.

8.1 EXERCISES

1. In this section, quadratic equations are solved by factoring, the even root property, and completing the square.
2. If $b = 0$ in $ax^2 + bx + c = 0$, then the equation can be solved by the even-root property.
3. The last term is the square of one-half the coefficient of the middle term.
4. If the leading coefficient is not 1, then the first step is to divide each side by the leading coefficient.

5.
$$x^2 - x - 6 = 0$$
$$(x - 3)(x + 2) = 0$$
$$x - 3 = 0 \quad \text{or} \quad x + 2 = 0$$
$$x = 3 \quad \text{or} \quad x = -2$$
Solution set: $\{-2, 3\}$

6.
$$x^2 + 6x + 8 = 0$$
$$(x + 4)(x + 2) = 0$$
$$x + 4 = 0 \quad \text{or} \quad x + 2 = 0$$
$$x = -4 \quad \text{or} \quad x = -2$$
The solution set is $\{-4, -2\}$.

7.
$$a^2 + 2a - 15 = 0$$
$$(a + 5)(a - 3) = 0$$
$$a + 5 = 0 \quad \text{or} \quad a - 3 = 0$$
$$a = -5 \quad \text{or} \quad a = 3$$
Solution set: $\{-5, 3\}$

8.
$$w^2 - 2w = 15$$

$$w^2 - 2w - 15 = 0$$
$$(w - 5)(w + 3) = 0$$
$$w - 5 = 0 \quad \text{or} \quad w + 3 = 0$$
$$w = 5 \quad \text{or} \quad w = -3$$
The solution set is $\{-3, 5\}$.

9.
$$2x^2 - x - 3 = 0$$
$$(2x - 3)(x + 1) = 0$$
$$2x - 3 = 0 \quad \text{or} \quad x + 1 = 0$$
$$x = \tfrac{3}{2} \quad \text{or} \quad x = -1$$
Solution set: $\left\{-1, \tfrac{3}{2}\right\}$

10.
$$6x^2 - x - 15 = 0$$
$$(2x + 3)(3x - 5) = 0$$
$$2x + 3 = 0 \quad \text{or} \quad 3x - 5 = 0$$
$$x = -\tfrac{3}{2} \quad \text{or} \quad x = \tfrac{5}{3}$$
The solution set is $\left\{-\tfrac{3}{2}, \tfrac{5}{3}\right\}$.

11.
$$y^2 + 14y + 49 = 0$$
$$(y + 7)^2 = 0$$
$$y + 7 = 0$$
$$y = -7$$
Solution set: $\{-7\}$

12.
$$a^2 - 6a + 9 = 0$$
$$(a - 3)^2 = 0$$
$$a - 3 = 0$$
$$a = 3$$
The solution set is $\{3\}$.

13.
$$a^2 - 16 = 0$$
$$(a - 4)(a + 4) = 0$$
$$a - 4 = 0 \quad \text{or} \quad a + 4 = 0$$
$$a = 4 \quad \text{or} \quad a = -4$$
Solution set: $\{-4, 4\}$

14.
$$4w^2 - 25 = 0$$
$$(2w - 5)(2w + 5) = 0$$
$$2w - 5 = 0 \quad \text{or} \quad 2w + 5 = 0$$
$$w = \tfrac{5}{2} \quad \text{or} \quad w = -\tfrac{5}{2}$$
The solution set is $\left\{-\tfrac{5}{2}, \tfrac{5}{2}\right\}$.

15.
$$x^2 = 81$$
$$x = \pm\sqrt{81} = \pm 9$$
Solution set: $\{-9, 9\}$

16.
$$x^2 = \tfrac{9}{4}$$
$$x = \pm\sqrt{\tfrac{9}{4}} = \pm\tfrac{3}{2}$$
The solution set is $\left\{-\tfrac{3}{2}, \tfrac{3}{2}\right\}$.

288

17. $\quad x^2 = \frac{16}{9}$

$$x = \pm \sqrt{\frac{16}{9}} = \pm \frac{4}{3}$$

Solution set: $\left\{ -\frac{4}{3}, \frac{4}{3} \right\}$

18. $\quad a^2 = 32$

$$a = \pm \sqrt{32} = \pm 4\sqrt{2}$$

The solution set is $\left\{ -4\sqrt{2}, 4\sqrt{2} \right\}$.

19. $\quad (x - 3)^2 = 16$

$$x - 3 = \pm \sqrt{16}$$
$$x = 3 \pm 4$$
$$x = 3 + 4 \quad \text{or} \quad x = 3 - 4$$

Solution set: $\{-1, 7\}$

20. $\quad (x + 5)^2 = 4$

$$x + 5 = \pm 2$$
$$x = -5 \pm 2$$
$$x = -5 - 2 \quad \text{or} \quad x = -5 + 2$$
$$x = -7 \quad \text{or} \quad x = -3$$

The solution set is $\{-7, -3\}$.

21. $\quad (z + 1)^2 = 5$

$$z + 1 = \pm \sqrt{5}$$
$$z = -1 \pm \sqrt{5}$$

Solution set: $\{-1 - \sqrt{5}, -1 + \sqrt{5}\}$

22. $\quad (a - 2)^2 = 8$

$$a - 2 = \pm \sqrt{8} = \pm 2\sqrt{2}$$
$$a = 2 \pm 2\sqrt{2}$$

The solution set is $\left\{ 2 - 2\sqrt{2}, 2 + 2\sqrt{2} \right\}$

23. $\quad \left(w - \frac{3}{2} \right)^2 = \frac{7}{4}$

$$w - \frac{3}{2} = \pm \sqrt{\frac{7}{4}}$$
$$w = \frac{3}{2} \pm \frac{\sqrt{7}}{2} = \frac{3 \pm \sqrt{7}}{2}$$

Solution set: $\left\{ \frac{3 - \sqrt{7}}{2}, \frac{3 + \sqrt{7}}{2} \right\}$

24. $\quad \left(w + \frac{2}{3} \right)^2 = \frac{5}{9}$

$$w + \frac{2}{3} = \pm \sqrt{\frac{5}{9}} = \pm \frac{\sqrt{5}}{3}$$
$$w = -\frac{2}{3} \pm \frac{\sqrt{5}}{3}$$

The solution set is $\left\{ \frac{-2 - \sqrt{5}}{3}, \frac{-2 + \sqrt{5}}{3} \right\}$.

25. One-half of 2 is 1, and 1 squared is 1:
$x^2 + 2x + 1$

26. One-half of 14 is 7, and 7 squared is 49:
$m^2 + 14m + 49$

27. One-half of -3 is $-3/2$, and $-3/2$ squared is $9/4$: $x^2 - 3x + \frac{9}{4}$

28. One-half of -5 is $-5/2$, and $-5/2$ squared is $25/4$: $w^2 - 5w + \frac{25}{4}$

29. One-half of $1/4$ is $1/8$, and $1/8$ squared is $1/64$: $y^2 + \frac{1}{4}y + \frac{1}{64}$

30. One-half of $3/2$ is $3/4$, and $3/4$ squared is $9/16$: $z^2 + \frac{3}{2}z + \frac{9}{16}$

31. One-half of $2/3$ is $1/3$, and $1/3$ squared is $1/9$: $x^2 + \frac{2}{3}x + \frac{1}{9}$

32. One-half of $6/5$ is $3/5$, and $3/5$ squared is $9/25$: $p^2 + \frac{6}{5}p + \frac{9}{25}$

33. $x^2 + 8x + 16 = (x + 4)^2$

34. $x^2 - 10x + 25 = (x - 5)^2$

35. $y^2 - 5y + \frac{25}{4} = \left(y - \frac{5}{2} \right)^2$

36. $w^2 + w + \frac{1}{4} = \left(w + \frac{1}{2} \right)^2$

37. $z^2 - \frac{4}{7}z + \frac{4}{49} = \left(z - \frac{2}{7} \right)^2$

38. $m^2 - \frac{6}{5}m + \frac{9}{25} = \left(m - \frac{3}{5} \right)^2$

39. $t^2 + \frac{3}{5}t + \frac{9}{100} = \left(t + \frac{3}{10} \right)^2$

40. $h^2 + \frac{3}{2}h + \frac{9}{16} = \left(h + \frac{3}{4} \right)^2$

41. $\quad x^2 - 2x \quad = 15$

$$x^2 - 2x + 1 = 15 + 1$$
$$(x - 1)^2 = 16$$
$$x - 1 = \pm 4$$
$$x = 1 \pm 4$$
$$x = 5 \quad \text{or} \quad x = -3$$

Solution set: $\{-3, 5\}$

42. $\quad x^2 - 6x - 7 = 0$

$$x^2 - 6x \quad = 7$$
$$x^2 - 6x + 9 = 7 + 9$$
$$(x - 3)^2 = 16$$
$$x - 3 = \pm 4$$
$$x = 3 \pm 4$$
$$x = 3 - 4 = -1 \quad \text{or} \quad x = 3 + 4 = 7$$

The solution set is $\{-1, 7\}$.

43. $\quad x^2 + 8x \quad = 20$

$$x^2 + 8x + 16 = 20 + 16$$
$$(x + 4)^2 = 36$$
$$x + 4 = \pm 6$$
$$x = -4 \pm 6$$
$$x = 2 \quad \text{or} \quad x = -10$$

Solution set: $\{-10, 2\}$

44. $\quad x^2 + 10x \quad = -9$

$$x^2 + 10x + 25 = -9 + 25$$
$$(x + 5)^2 = 16$$

$$x + 5 = \pm\sqrt{16}$$
$$x = -5 \pm 4$$
$$x = -5 + 4 = -1 \text{ or } x = -5 - 4 = -9$$
The solution set is $\{-1, -9\}$.

45.
$$2x^2 - 4x = 70$$
$$x^2 - 2x = 35$$
$$x^2 - 2x + 1 = 35 + 1$$
$$(x - 1)^2 = 36$$
$$x - 1 = \pm 6$$
$$x = 1 \pm 6$$
$$x = 7 \text{ or } x = -5$$
Solution set: $\{-5, 7\}$

46.
$$3x^2 - 6x = 24$$
$$x^2 - 2x = 8$$
$$x^2 - 2x + 1 = 8 + 1$$
$$(x - 1)^2 = 9$$
$$x - 1 = \pm 3$$
$$x = 1 \pm 3$$
$$x = 1 + 3 = 4 \text{ or } x = 1 - 3 = -2$$
The solution set is $\{-2, 4\}$.

47.
$$w^2 - w = 20$$
$$w^2 - w + \tfrac{1}{4} = 20 + \tfrac{1}{4}$$
$$(w - \tfrac{1}{2})^2 = \tfrac{81}{4}$$
$$w - \tfrac{1}{2} = \pm \tfrac{9}{2}$$
$$w = \tfrac{1}{2} \pm \tfrac{9}{2}$$

$$x = \tfrac{10}{2} = 5 \text{ or } x = \tfrac{-8}{2} = -4$$
Solution set: $\{-4, 5\}$

48.
$$y^2 - 3y - 10 = 0$$
$$y^2 - 3y = 10$$
$$y^2 - 3y + \tfrac{9}{4} = 10 + \tfrac{9}{4}$$
$$(y - \tfrac{3}{2})^2 = \tfrac{49}{4}$$
$$y - \tfrac{3}{2} = \pm \tfrac{7}{2}$$
$$y = \tfrac{3}{2} \pm \tfrac{7}{2} = \tfrac{3 \pm 7}{2}$$
$$x = \tfrac{3+7}{2} = 5 \text{ or } x = \tfrac{3-7}{2} = -2$$
The solution set is $\{-2, 5\}$.

49.
$$q^2 + 5q = 14$$
$$q^2 + 5q + \tfrac{25}{4} = 14 + \tfrac{25}{4}$$
$$(q + \tfrac{5}{2})^2 = \tfrac{81}{4}$$
$$q + \tfrac{5}{2} = \pm \tfrac{9}{2}$$
$$q = -\tfrac{5}{2} \pm \tfrac{9}{2}$$
$$q = \tfrac{4}{2} = 2 \text{ or } q = \tfrac{-14}{2} = -7$$
Solution set: $\{-7, 2\}$

50.
$$z^2 + z = 2$$

$$z^2 + z + \tfrac{1}{4} = 2 + \tfrac{1}{4}$$
$$(z + \tfrac{1}{2})^2 = \tfrac{9}{4}$$
$$z + \tfrac{1}{2} = \pm \tfrac{3}{2}$$
$$z = -\tfrac{1}{2} \pm \tfrac{3}{2} = \tfrac{-1 \pm 3}{2}$$
$$z = \tfrac{-1+3}{2} = 1 \text{ or } z = \tfrac{-1-3}{2} = -2$$
The solution set is $\{-2, 1\}$.

51.
$$2h^2 - h = 3$$
$$h^2 - \tfrac{1}{2}h = \tfrac{3}{2}$$
$$h^2 - \tfrac{1}{2}h + \tfrac{1}{16} = \tfrac{3}{2} + \tfrac{1}{16}$$
$$(h - \tfrac{1}{4})^2 = \tfrac{25}{16}$$
$$h - \tfrac{1}{4} = \pm \tfrac{5}{4}$$
$$h = \tfrac{1}{4} \pm \tfrac{5}{4}$$
Solution set: $\left\{-1, \tfrac{3}{2}\right\}$

52.
$$2m^2 - m - 15 = 0$$
$$m^2 - \tfrac{1}{2}m = \tfrac{15}{2}$$
$$m^2 - \tfrac{1}{2}m + \tfrac{1}{16} = \tfrac{15}{2} + \tfrac{1}{16}$$
$$\left(m - \tfrac{1}{4}\right)^2 = \tfrac{121}{16}$$
$$m - \tfrac{1}{4} = \pm \tfrac{11}{4}$$
$$m = \tfrac{1}{4} \pm \tfrac{11}{4} = \tfrac{1 \pm 11}{4}$$
$$m = \tfrac{1+11}{4} = 3 \text{ or } m = \tfrac{1-11}{4} = -\tfrac{5}{2}$$
The solution set is $\left\{-\tfrac{5}{2}, 3\right\}$.

53.
$$x^2 + 4x = 6$$
$$x^2 + 4x + 4 = 6 + 4$$
$$(x + 2)^2 = 10$$
$$x + 2 = \pm \sqrt{10}$$
$$x = -2 \pm \sqrt{10}$$
Solution set: $\{-2 - \sqrt{10}, -2 + \sqrt{10}\}$

54.
$$x^2 + 6x - 8 = 0$$
$$x^2 + 6x = 8$$
$$x^2 + 6x + 9 = 8 + 9$$
$$(x + 3)^2 = 17$$
$$x + 3 = \pm \sqrt{17}$$
$$x = -3 \pm \sqrt{17}$$
The solution set is $\left\{-3 - \sqrt{17}, -3 + \sqrt{17}\right\}$.

55.
$$x^2 + 8x = 4$$
$$x^2 + 8x + 16 = 4 + 16$$
$$(x + 4)^2 = 20$$
$$x + 4 = \pm \sqrt{20}$$
$$x = -4 \pm 2\sqrt{5}$$
Solution set: $\{-4 - 2\sqrt{5}, -4 + 2\sqrt{5}\}$

56.
$$x^2 + 10x - 3 = 0$$
$$x^2 + 10x = 3$$
$$x^2 + 10x + 25 = 3 + 25$$
$$(x + 5)^2 = 28$$

$$x + 5 = \pm\sqrt{28} = \pm 2\sqrt{7}$$
$$x = -5 \pm 2\sqrt{7}$$

The solution set is $\left\{ -5 - 2\sqrt{7}, -5 + 2\sqrt{7} \right\}$.

57.
$$2x^2 + 3x = 4$$
$$x^2 + \tfrac{3}{2}x = 2$$
$$x^2 + \tfrac{3}{2}x + \tfrac{9}{16} = 2 + \tfrac{9}{16}$$
$$(x + \tfrac{3}{4})^2 = \tfrac{41}{16}$$
$$x + \tfrac{3}{4} = \pm \tfrac{\sqrt{41}}{4}$$
$$x = -\tfrac{3}{4} \pm \tfrac{\sqrt{41}}{4}$$

Solution set: $\left\{ \dfrac{-3-\sqrt{41}}{4}, \dfrac{-3+\sqrt{41}}{4} \right\}$

58.
$$2x^2 + 5x - 1 = 0$$
$$x^2 + \tfrac{5}{2}x - \tfrac{1}{2} = 0$$
$$x^2 + \tfrac{5}{2}x = \tfrac{1}{2}$$
$$x^2 + \tfrac{5}{2}x + \tfrac{25}{16} = \tfrac{1}{2} + \tfrac{25}{16}$$
$$(x + \tfrac{5}{4})^2 = \tfrac{33}{16}$$
$$x + \tfrac{5}{4} = \pm \tfrac{\sqrt{33}}{4}$$
$$x = -\tfrac{5}{4} \pm \tfrac{\sqrt{33}}{4} = \tfrac{-5 \pm \sqrt{33}}{4}$$

The solution set is $\left\{ \dfrac{-5-\sqrt{33}}{4}, \dfrac{-5+\sqrt{33}}{4} \right\}$.

59.
$$\sqrt{2x+1} = x - 1$$
$$(\sqrt{2x+1})^2 = (x-1)^2$$
$$2x + 1 = x^2 - 2x + 1$$
$$0 = x^2 - 4x$$
$$x(x - 4) = 0$$
$$x = 0 \text{ or } x = 4$$

Since 0 is an extraneous root, the solution set is $\{4\}$.

60.
$$\sqrt{2x-4} = x - 14$$
$$(\sqrt{2x-4})^2 = (x-14)$$
$$2x - 4 = x^2 - 28x + 196$$
$$0 = x^2 - 30x + 200$$
$$(x - 10)(x - 20) = 0$$
$$x = 10 \text{ or } x = 20$$

Since 10 is an extraneous root, the solution set is $\{20\}$.

61.
$$2w = \sqrt{w+1}$$
$$(2w)^2 = (\sqrt{w+1})^2$$
$$4w^2 = w + 1$$
$$4w^2 - w = 1$$
$$w^2 - \tfrac{1}{4}w = \tfrac{1}{4}$$
$$w^2 - \tfrac{1}{4}w + \tfrac{1}{64} = \tfrac{1}{4} + \tfrac{1}{64}$$
$$(w - \tfrac{1}{8})^2 = \tfrac{17}{64}$$

$$w - \tfrac{1}{8} = \pm \tfrac{\sqrt{17}}{8}$$
$$w = \tfrac{1}{8} \pm \tfrac{\sqrt{17}}{8}$$

The number $\dfrac{1-\sqrt{17}}{8}$ is a negative number. No negative number can be a solution to the original equation because the left side would be negative and the right side is a principal square root.

Solution set: $\left\{ \dfrac{1+\sqrt{17}}{8} \right\}$

62.
$$y - 1 = \frac{\sqrt{y+1}}{2}$$
$$(y-1)^2 = \left(\frac{\sqrt{y+1}}{2} \right)^2$$
$$y^2 - 2y + 1 = \frac{y+1}{4}$$
$$4y^2 - 8y + 4 = y + 1$$
$$4y^2 - 9y + 3 = 0$$
$$y^2 - \tfrac{9}{4}y = -\tfrac{3}{4}$$
$$y^2 - \tfrac{9}{4}y + \tfrac{81}{64} = -\tfrac{3}{4} + \tfrac{81}{64}$$
$$(y - \tfrac{9}{8})^2 = \tfrac{33}{64}$$
$$y - \tfrac{9}{8} = \pm \tfrac{\sqrt{33}}{8}$$
$$y = \tfrac{9}{8} \pm \tfrac{\sqrt{33}}{8} = \tfrac{9 \pm \sqrt{33}}{8}$$

Since $\dfrac{9-\sqrt{33}}{8} - 1 = -0.593$, the left hand side of the original equation is a negative number if $w = \dfrac{9-\sqrt{33}}{8}$. Since the right hand side is nonnegative, this number cannot be a solution to the equation. So the solution set is $\left\{ \dfrac{9+\sqrt{33}}{8} \right\}$.

63.
$$\frac{t}{t-2} = \frac{2t-3}{t}$$
$$t^2 = (t-2)(2t-3)$$
$$t^2 = 2t^2 - 7t + 6$$
$$-t^2 + 7t - 6 = 0$$
$$t^2 - 7t + 6 = 0$$
$$(t - 6)(t - 1) = 0$$
$$t = 6 \text{ or } t = 1$$

Solution set: $\{1, 6\}$

64.
$$\frac{z}{z+3} = \frac{3z}{5z-1}$$
$$5z^2 - z = 3z^2 + 9z$$
$$2z^2 - 10z = 0$$
$$2z(z - 5) = 0$$
$$2z = 0 \text{ or } z - 5 = 0$$
$$z = 0 \text{ or } z = 5$$

The solution set is $\{0, 5\}$.

65.
$$x^2\left(\frac{2}{x^2} + \frac{4}{x} + 1\right) = x^2(0)$$
$$2 + 4x + x^2 = 0$$
$$x^2 + 4x = -2$$
$$x^2 + 4x + 4 = -2 + 4$$
$$(x + 2)^2 = 2$$
$$x + 2 = \pm\sqrt{2}$$
$$x = -2 \pm \sqrt{2}$$
Solution set: $\{-2 - \sqrt{2}, -2 + \sqrt{2}\}$

66.
$$\frac{1}{x^2} + \frac{3}{x} + 1 = 0$$
$$x^2\left(\frac{1}{x^2} + \frac{3}{x} + 1\right) = x^2 \cdot 0$$
$$1 + 3x + x^2 = 0$$
$$x^2 + 3x = -1$$
$$x^2 + 3x + \frac{9}{4} = -1 + \frac{9}{4}$$
$$\left(x + \frac{3}{2}\right)^2 = \frac{5}{4}$$
$$x + \frac{3}{2} = \pm\frac{\sqrt{5}}{2}$$
$$x = -\frac{3}{2} \pm \frac{\sqrt{5}}{2} = \frac{-3 \pm \sqrt{5}}{2}$$
The solution set is $\left\{\frac{-3-\sqrt{5}}{2}, \frac{-3+\sqrt{5}}{2}\right\}$.

67. $x^2 + 2x + 5 = 0$
$$x^2 + 2x + 1 = -5 + 1$$
$$(x + 1)^2 = -4$$
$$x + 1 = \pm\sqrt{-4}$$
$$x = -1 \pm 2i$$
The solution set is $\{-1 - 2i, -1 + 2i\}$.

68. $x^2 + 4x + 5 = 0$
$$x^2 + 4x + 4 = -5 + 4$$
$$(x + 2)^2 = -1$$
$$x + 2 = \pm\sqrt{-1}$$
$$x = -2 \pm i$$
The solution set is $\{-2 - i, -2 + i\}$.

69. $x^2 + 12 = 0$
$$x^2 = -12$$
$$x = \pm\sqrt{-12}$$
$$x = \pm 2i\sqrt{3}$$
The solution set is $\{-2i\sqrt{3}, 2i\sqrt{3}\}$

70. $-3x^2 - 21 = 0$
$$x^2 = -7$$
$$x = \pm\sqrt{-7} = \pm i\sqrt{7}$$
The solution set is $\{-i\sqrt{7}, i\sqrt{7}\}$.

71. $5z^2 - 4z + 1 = 0$
$$z^2 - \frac{4}{5}z + \frac{4}{25} = -\frac{1}{5} + \frac{4}{25}$$
$$\left(z - \frac{2}{5}\right)^2 = \frac{-1}{25}$$
$$z - \frac{2}{5} = \pm\sqrt{\frac{-1}{25}}$$
$$z = \frac{2}{5} \pm \sqrt{\frac{-1}{25}}$$

$$z = \frac{2}{5} \pm \frac{i}{5} = \frac{2 \pm i}{5}$$
The solution set is $\left\{\frac{2 \pm i}{5}\right\}$.

72. $2w^2 - 3w + 2 = 0$
$$w^2 - \frac{3}{2}w + \frac{9}{16} = -1 + \frac{9}{16}$$
$$\left(w - \frac{3}{4}\right)^2 = -\frac{7}{16}$$
$$w - \frac{3}{4} = \pm\sqrt{-\frac{7}{16}}$$
$$w = \frac{3}{4} \pm \frac{i\sqrt{7}}{4} = \frac{3 \pm i\sqrt{7}}{4}$$
The solution set is $\left\{\frac{3 \pm i\sqrt{7}}{4}\right\}$.

73. $4x^2 = -25$
$$x^2 = -\frac{25}{4}$$
$$x = \pm\sqrt{-\frac{25}{4}} = \pm\frac{5}{2}i$$
Solution set: $\left\{-\frac{5}{2}i, \frac{5}{2}i\right\}$

74. $5w^2 = 3$
$$w^2 = \frac{3}{5}$$
$$w = \pm\sqrt{\frac{3}{5}} = \pm\frac{\sqrt{15}}{5}$$
The solution set is $\left\{-\frac{\sqrt{15}}{5}, \frac{\sqrt{15}}{5}\right\}$.

75. $\left(p + \frac{1}{2}\right)^2 = \frac{9}{4}$
$$p + \frac{1}{2} = \pm\frac{3}{2}$$
$$p = -\frac{1}{2} \pm \frac{3}{2}$$
The solution set is $\{-2, 1\}$

76. $\left(y - \frac{2}{3}\right)^2 = \frac{4}{9}$
$$y - \frac{2}{3} = \pm\frac{2}{3}$$
$$y = \frac{2}{3} \pm \frac{2}{3}$$
The solution set is $\left\{0, \frac{4}{3}\right\}$.

77. $5t^2 + 4t = 3$
$$t^2 + \frac{4}{5}t = \frac{3}{5}$$
$$t^2 + \frac{4}{5}t + \frac{4}{25} = \frac{3}{5} + \frac{4}{25}$$
$$\left(t + \frac{2}{5}\right)^2 = \frac{19}{25}$$
$$t + \frac{2}{5} = \pm\frac{\sqrt{19}}{5}$$
$$t = -\frac{2}{5} \pm \frac{\sqrt{19}}{5}$$
Solution set: $\left\{\frac{-2-\sqrt{19}}{5}, \frac{-2+\sqrt{19}}{5}\right\}$

78. $3v^2 + 4v - 1 = 0$
$$v^2 + \frac{4}{3}v - \frac{1}{3} = 0$$
$$v^2 + \frac{4}{3}v = \frac{1}{3}$$
$$v^2 + \frac{4}{3}v + \frac{4}{9} = \frac{1}{3} + \frac{4}{9}$$
$$\left(v + \frac{2}{3}\right)^2 = \frac{7}{9}$$
$$v + \frac{2}{3} = \pm\frac{\sqrt{7}}{3}$$

$$v = -\frac{2}{3} \pm \frac{\sqrt{7}}{3} = \frac{-2\pm\sqrt{7}}{3}$$

The solution set is $\left\{ \frac{-2-\sqrt{7}}{3}, \frac{-2+\sqrt{7}}{3} \right\}$.

79. $m^2 + 2m - 24 = 0$

$m^2 + 2m \quad = 24$

$m^2 + 2m + 1 = 24 + 1$

$(m+1)^2 = 25$

$m + 1 = \pm 5$

$m = -1 \pm 5$

$m = -1 - 5 = -6 \text{ or } m = -1 + 5 = 4$

The solution set is $\{-6, 4\}$.

80. $q^2 + 6q + 9 = 7 + 9$

$(q + 3)^2 = 16$

$q + 3 = \pm 4$

$q = -3 \pm 4$

The solution set is $\{-7, 1\}$.

81. $\left(a + \frac{2}{3}\right)^2 = -\frac{32}{9}$

$a + \frac{2}{3} = \pm i\sqrt{\frac{32}{9}}$

$a = -\frac{2}{3} \pm \frac{4i\sqrt{2}}{3} = \frac{-2 \pm 4i\sqrt{2}}{3}$

Solution set: $\left\{ \frac{-2 - 4i\sqrt{2}}{3}, \frac{-2 + 4i\sqrt{2}}{3} \right\}$

82. $\left(w + \frac{1}{2}\right)^2 = -6$

$w + \frac{1}{2} = \pm i\sqrt{6}$

$w = -\frac{1}{2} \pm \frac{2i\sqrt{6}}{2} = \frac{-1 \pm 2i\sqrt{6}}{2}$

The solution set is

$$\left\{ \frac{-1 - 2i\sqrt{6}}{2}, \frac{-1 + 2i\sqrt{6}}{2} \right\}.$$

83. $-x^2 + x = -6$

$x^2 - x = 6$

$x^2 - x + \frac{1}{4} = 6 + \frac{1}{4}$

$\left(x - \frac{1}{2}\right)^2 = \frac{25}{4}$

$x - \frac{1}{2} = \pm \frac{5}{2}$

$x = \frac{1}{2} \pm \frac{5}{2}$

Solution set: $\{-2, 3\}$

84. $-x^2 + x + 12 = 0$

$x^2 - x - 12 = 0$

$x^2 - x \quad = 12$

$x^2 - x + \frac{1}{4} = 12 + \frac{1}{4}$

$\left(x - \frac{1}{2}\right)^2 = \frac{49}{4}$

$x - \frac{1}{2} = \pm \frac{7}{2}$

$x = \frac{1}{2} \pm \frac{7}{2} = \frac{1 \pm 7}{2}$

The solution set is $\{-3, 4\}$.

85. $x^2 - 6x + 10 = 0$

$x^2 - 6x + 9 = -10 + 9$

$(x - 3)^2 = -1$

$x - 3 = \pm \sqrt{-1} = \pm i$

$x = 3 \pm i$

The solution set is $\{3 - i, 3 + i\}$.

86. $x^2 - 8x + 17 = 0$

$x^2 - 8x + 16 = -17 + 16$

$(x - 4)^2 = -1$

$x - 4 = \pm \sqrt{-1} = \pm i$

$x = 4 \pm i$

The solution set is $\{4 - i, 4 + i\}$.

87. $(2x - 5)^2 = (\sqrt{7x + 7})^2$

$4x^2 - 20x + 25 = 7x + 7$

$4x^2 - 27x + 18 = 0$

$(4x - 3)(x - 6) = 0$

$4x - 3 = 0 \text{ or } x - 6 = 0$

$x = \frac{3}{4} \text{ or } \quad x = 6$

Since 3/4 does not check, the solution set is $\{6\}$.

88. $(\sqrt{7x + 29})^2 = (x + 3)^2$

$7x + 29 = x^2 + 6x + 9$

$0 = x^2 - x - 20$

$(x - 5)(x + 4) = 0$

$x - 5 = 0 \text{ or } x + 4 = 0$

$x = 5 \text{ or } \quad x = -4$

Since -4 does not check, the solution set is $\{5\}$.

89. $4x(x - 1)\left(\frac{1}{x} + \frac{1}{x - 1}\right)$
$$= 4x(x - 1)\left(\frac{1}{4}\right)$$

$4x - 4 + 4x = x^2 - x$

$-x^2 + 9x - 4 = 0$

$x^2 - 9x + 4 = 0$

$x^2 - 9x + \frac{81}{4} = -4 + \frac{81}{4}$

$\left(x - \frac{9}{2}\right)^2 = \frac{65}{4}$

$x - \frac{9}{2} = \pm \frac{\sqrt{65}}{2}$

$x = \frac{9}{2} \pm \frac{\sqrt{65}}{2}$

Solution set: $\left\{ \frac{9 - \sqrt{65}}{2}, \frac{9 + \sqrt{65}}{2} \right\}$

90. $\frac{1}{x} - \frac{2}{1 - x} = \frac{1}{2}$

$2x(1 - x)\left(\frac{1}{x} - \frac{2}{1-x}\right) = 2x(1 - x)\frac{1}{2}$

$2 - 2x - 4x = x - x^2$

$x^2 - 7x \quad = -2$

$x^2 - 7x + \frac{49}{4} = -2 + \frac{49}{4}$

$\left(x - \frac{7}{2}\right)^2 = \frac{41}{4}$

$$x - \frac{7}{2} = \pm \frac{\sqrt{41}}{2}$$
$$x = \frac{7}{2} \pm \frac{\sqrt{41}}{2} = \frac{7 \pm \sqrt{41}}{2}$$

The solution set is $\left\{ \frac{7-\sqrt{41}}{2}, \frac{7+\sqrt{41}}{2} \right\}$.

91. $(2 + \sqrt{3})^2 - 4(2 + \sqrt{3}) + 1$
$= 4 + 4\sqrt{3} + 3 - 8 - 4\sqrt{3} + 1 = 0$
$(2 - \sqrt{3})^2 - 4(2 - \sqrt{3}) + 1$
$= 4 - 4\sqrt{3} + 3 - 8 + 4\sqrt{3} + 1 = 0$

92. $(1 + \sqrt{2})^2 - 2(1 + \sqrt{2}) - 1$
$= 1 + 2\sqrt{2} + 2 - 2 - 2\sqrt{2} - 1 = 0$
$(1 - \sqrt{2})^2 - 2(1 - \sqrt{2}) - 1$
$= 1 - 2\sqrt{2} + 2 - 2 + 2\sqrt{2} - 1 = 0$

93. $(i + 1)^2 - 2(i + 1) + 2$
$= -1 + 2i + 1 - 2i - 2 + 2 = 0$
$(1 - i)^2 - 2(1 - i) + 2$
$= 1 - 2i - 1 - 2 + 2i + 2 = 0$

94. $(2 + 3i)^2 - 4(2 + 3i) + 13$
$= 4 + 12i - 9 - 8 - 12i + 13 = 0$
$(2 - 3i)^2 - 4(2 - 3i) + 13$
$= 4 - 12i - 9 - 8 + 12i + 13 = 0$

95. $1211.1 \cdot 8700 = 2.81 A^2 \cdot 200$
$$A^2 = \frac{1211.1 \cdot 8700}{2.81 \cdot 200}$$
$$A = \sqrt{\frac{1211.1 \cdot 8700}{2.81 \cdot 200}} \approx 136.9 \text{ ft/sec}$$

96. $8 \cdot T^2 = \pi^2 \cdot 10$
$$T^2 = \frac{\pi^2 \cdot 10}{8}$$
$$T = \sqrt{\frac{\pi^2 \cdot 10}{8}} \approx 3.5 \text{ sec}$$

97.
$$17,568 = 1500x - 3x^2$$
$$3x^2 - 1500x = -17,568$$
$$x^2 - 500x = -5856$$
$$x^2 - 500x + 62500 = -5856 + 62500$$
$$(x - 250)^2 = 56644$$
$$x - 250 = \pm 238$$
$$x = 250 \pm 238$$
$$x = 12 \quad \text{or} \quad x = 488$$
Since x is less than 25, the answer is 12.

98. a) $-16t^2 + 36t = 18$
$$t^2 - \frac{9}{4}t = -\frac{9}{8}$$
$$t^2 - \frac{9}{4}t + \frac{81}{64} = -\frac{9}{8} + \frac{81}{64}$$
$$\left(t - \frac{9}{8}\right)^2 = \frac{9}{64}$$
$$t - \frac{9}{8} = \pm \frac{3}{8}$$
$$t = \frac{9}{8} \pm \frac{3}{8}$$
$$t = \frac{3}{2} \quad \text{or} \quad t = \frac{3}{4}$$
His height is 18 feet at 0.75 sec and 1.5 sec.

b) He was at his maximum height when t was approximately 1.125 sec.

c) From the graph we can see that he was in the air for approximately 2.25 sec.

99. Equation (c) is not quadratic because there is not x^2 term.

100. a) If $k = 4$ then $x^2 + 4x + 4 = (x + 2)^2$ and the equation has only one solution, -2.

b) The solutions are real if $k < 4$.

c) The solutions are imaginary if $k > 4$.

103. $\{4.56, 2.74\}$

104. $\{2.04, 0.58\}$

105. $\{3.53\}$

106. $\{-3.03, 3.68\}$

8.2 WARM-UPS

1. True.

2. False, before identifying a, b, and c, we must write the equation as
$3x^2 - 4x + 7 = 0$.

3. True, this is just the quadratic formula with $a = d$, $b = e$, and $c = f$.

4. False, the quadratic formula works to solve any quadratic equation.

5. True, because
$(-3)^2 - 4(2)(-4) = 9 + 32 = 41$.

6. True, if the discriminant is 0, then the quadratic equation has one real solution.

7. True.

8. True, because we can write the equation in the form $-1x^2 + 2x + 0 = 0$.

9. False, x and $6 - x$ have a sum of 6.

10. False, there can be one real solution, 2 real solutions, or 2 imaginary solutions.

8.2 EXERCISES

1. The quadratic formula can be used to solve any quadratic equation.

2. The even-root property is used when $b = 0$.

3. Factoring is used when the quadratic polynomial is simple enough to factor.

4. The quadratic formula can be use on any quadratic equation, but generally we use factoring or the even-root property when applicable.

5. The discriminant is $b^2 - 4ac$.

6. In the complex number system any quadratic equation has either one or two solutions.

7. $a = 1, b = 5, \ c = 6$
$$x = \frac{-5 \pm \sqrt{5^2 - 4(1)(6)}}{2(1)} = \frac{-5 \pm \sqrt{1}}{2}$$
$$= \frac{-5 \pm 1}{2} = \frac{-4}{2}, \frac{-6}{2}$$
Solution set: $\{-3, -2\}$

8. $a = 1, b = -7, \ c = 12$

$$x = \frac{-(-7) \pm \sqrt{(-7)^2 - 4(1)(12)}}{2(1)} = \frac{7 \pm \sqrt{1}}{2}$$
$$= \frac{7 \pm 1}{2} = \frac{8}{2}, \frac{6}{2}$$
Solution set: $\{3, 4\}$

9. $y^2 + y - 6 = 0$
$a = 1, b = 1, c = -6$
$$y = \frac{-1 \pm \sqrt{1^2 - 4(1)(-6)}}{2(1)} = \frac{-1 \pm \sqrt{25}}{2}$$
$$= \frac{-1 \pm 5}{2} = \frac{4}{2}, \frac{-6}{2}$$
Solution set: $\{-3, 2\}$

10. $m^2 + 2m - 8 = 0$
$a = 1, b = 2, \ c = -8$
$$m = \frac{-2 \pm \sqrt{2^2 - 4(1)(-8)}}{2(1)} = \frac{-2 \pm \sqrt{36}}{2}$$
$$= \frac{-2 \pm 6}{2} = \frac{4}{2}, \frac{-8}{2}$$
Solution set: $\{-4, 2\}$

11. $a = 6, b = -7, c = -3$
$$z = \frac{7 \pm \sqrt{(-7)^2 - 4(6)(-3)}}{2(6)} = \frac{7 \pm \sqrt{121}}{12}$$
$$= \frac{7 \pm 11}{12} = \frac{18}{12}, \frac{-4}{12}$$
Solution set: $\left\{-\frac{1}{3}, \frac{3}{2}\right\}$

12. $a = 8, b = 2, c = -1$
$$q = \frac{-2 \pm \sqrt{(2)^2 - 4(8)(-1)}}{2(8)} = \frac{-2 \pm \sqrt{36}}{16}$$
$$= \frac{-2 \pm 6}{16} = \frac{4}{16}, \frac{-8}{16}$$
Solution set: $\left\{-\frac{1}{2}, \frac{1}{4}\right\}$.

13. $a = 4, \ b = -4, \ c = 1$
$$x = \frac{4 \pm \sqrt{16 - 4(4)(1)}}{2(4)} = \frac{4 \pm 0}{8} = \frac{1}{2}$$
Solution set: $\left\{\frac{1}{2}\right\}$

14. $a = 4, b = -12, c = 9$
$$x = \frac{12 \pm \sqrt{(-12)^2 - 4(4)(9)}}{2(4)} = \frac{12 \pm \sqrt{0}}{8}$$
$$= \frac{12}{8} = \frac{3}{2}$$

Solution set: $\left\{\frac{3}{2}\right\}$.

15. $a = 9, b = -6, c = 1$
$$x = \frac{6 \pm \sqrt{36 - 4(9)(1)}}{2(9)} = \frac{6 \pm \sqrt{0}}{18} = \frac{1}{3}$$
Solution set: $\left\{\frac{1}{3}\right\}$

16. $a = 9, b = -24, c = 16$
$$x = \frac{24 \pm \sqrt{576 - 4(9)(16)}}{2(9)} = \frac{24 \pm \sqrt{0}}{18} = \frac{4}{3}$$
Solution set: $\left\{\frac{4}{3}\right\}$

17. $16x^2 + 24x + 9 = 0$
$a = 16, b = 24, c = 9$
$$x = \frac{-24 \pm \sqrt{576 - 4(16)(9)}}{2(16)} = \frac{-24 \pm \sqrt{0}}{32}$$
$$= -\frac{3}{4}$$
Solution set: $\left\{-\frac{3}{4}\right\}$

18. $25x^2 + 20x + 4 = 0$: $a = 25, b = 20,$
$c = 4$
$$x = \frac{-20 \pm \sqrt{400 - 4(25)(4)}}{2(25)} = \frac{-20 \pm \sqrt{0}}{50}$$
$$= -\frac{2}{5}$$
Solution set: $\left\{-\frac{2}{5}\right\}$

19. $a = 1, b = 8, c = 6$
$$v = \frac{-8 \pm \sqrt{8^2 - 4(1)(6)}}{2(1)} = \frac{-8 \pm \sqrt{40}}{2}$$
$$= \frac{-8 \pm 2\sqrt{10}}{2} = -4 \pm \sqrt{10}$$
Solution set: $\{-4 \pm \sqrt{10}\}$

20. $a = 1, b = 6, c = 4$
$$p = \frac{-6 \pm \sqrt{6^2 - 4(1)(4)}}{2(1)} = \frac{-6 \pm \sqrt{20}}{2}$$
$$= \frac{-6 \pm 2\sqrt{5}}{2} = -3 \pm \sqrt{5}$$
Solution set: $\{-3 \pm \sqrt{5}\}$

21. $x^2 + 5x - 1 = 0$: $a = 1, b = 5, c = -1$

$$x = \frac{-5 \pm \sqrt{5^2 - 4(1)(-1)}}{2(1)} = \frac{-5 \pm \sqrt{29}}{2}$$

Solution set: $\left\{\dfrac{-5 \pm \sqrt{29}}{2}\right\}$

22. $x^2 + 3x - 5 = 0$: $a = 1, b = 3, c = -5$

$$x = \frac{-3 \pm \sqrt{3^2 - 4(1)(-5)}}{2(1)} = \frac{-3 \pm \sqrt{29}}{2}$$

Solution set: $\left\{\dfrac{-3 \pm \sqrt{29}}{2}\right\}$

23. $a = 2, b = -6, c = 1$

$$t = \frac{6 \pm \sqrt{36 - 4(2)(1)}}{2(2)} = \frac{6 \pm \sqrt{28}}{4} = \frac{6 \pm 2\sqrt{7}}{4}$$

$$= \frac{2(3 \pm \sqrt{7})}{2(2)} = \frac{3 \pm \sqrt{7}}{2}$$

Solution set: $\left\{ \dfrac{3 \pm \sqrt{7}}{2} \right\}$

24. $a = 3, b = -8, c = 2$

$$z = \frac{8 \pm \sqrt{64 - 4(3)(2)}}{2(3)} = \frac{8 \pm \sqrt{40}}{6} = \frac{8 \pm 2\sqrt{10}}{6}$$

$$= \frac{2(4 \pm \sqrt{10})}{2(3)} = \frac{4 \pm \sqrt{10}}{3}$$

Solution set: $\left\{ \dfrac{4 \pm \sqrt{10}}{3} \right\}$

25. $2t^2 - 6t + 5 = 0$

$$t = \frac{6 \pm \sqrt{36 - 4(2)(5)}}{2(2)} = \frac{6 \pm \sqrt{-4}}{4} = \frac{6 \pm 2i}{4}$$

$$= \frac{3 \pm i}{2} \qquad \text{Solution set: } \left\{ \dfrac{3 \pm i}{2} \right\}$$

26. $2y^2 + 1 = 2y, \quad 2y^2 - 2y + 1 = 0$

$$y = \frac{2 \pm \sqrt{4 - 4(2)(1)}}{2(2)} = \frac{2 \pm \sqrt{-4}}{4} = \frac{2 \pm 2i}{4}$$

$$= \frac{1 \pm i}{2} \qquad \text{Solution set: } \left\{ \dfrac{1 \pm i}{2} \right\}$$

27. $-2x^2 + 3x - 6 = 0: a = -2, b = 3,$
$c = -6$

$$x = \frac{-3 \pm \sqrt{(3)^2 - 4(-2)(-6)}}{2(-2)} = \frac{-3 \pm \sqrt{-39}}{-4}$$

$$= \frac{-3 \pm i\sqrt{39}}{-4} = \frac{3 \pm i\sqrt{39}}{4}$$

Solution set: $\left\{ \dfrac{3 \pm i\sqrt{39}}{4} \right\}$

28. $-3x^2 - 2x - 5 = 0, \quad 3x^2 + 2x + 5 = 0$

$$x = \frac{-2 \pm \sqrt{4 - 4(3)(5)}}{2(3)} = \frac{-2 \pm \sqrt{-56}}{6}$$

$$= \frac{-2 \pm 2i\sqrt{14}}{6} = \frac{-1 \pm i\sqrt{14}}{3}$$

Solution set: $\left\{ \dfrac{-1 \pm i\sqrt{14}}{3} \right\}$

29. $\frac{1}{2}x^2 + 13 = 5x, \quad x^2 - 10x + 26 = 0$

$$x = \frac{10 \pm \sqrt{100 - 4(1)(26)}}{2(1)} = \frac{10 \pm \sqrt{-4}}{2}$$

$$= \frac{10 \pm 2i}{2} = 5 \pm i \quad \text{Solution set: } \{5 \pm i\}$$

30. $\frac{1}{4}x^2 + \frac{17}{4} = 2x, \quad x^2 - 8x + 17 = 0$

$$x = \frac{8 \pm \sqrt{64 - 4(1)(17)}}{2(1)} = \frac{8 \pm \sqrt{-4}}{2}$$

$$= \frac{8 \pm 2i}{2} = 4 \pm i \quad \text{Solution set: } \{4 \pm i\}$$

31. $x^2 - 6x + 2 = 0: a = 1, b = -6, c = 2$
$b^2 - 4ac = 36 - 4(1)(2) = 28$
So there are two real solutions to the equation.

32. $x^2 + 6x + 9 = 0: a = 1, b = 6, c = 9$
$b^2 - 4ac = 36 - 4(1)(9) = 0$
So there is one real solution to the equation.

33. $2x^2 - 5x + 6 = 0: a = 2, b = -5, c = 6$
$b^2 - 4ac = 25 - 4(2)(6) = -23$
So there are no real solutions to the equation.

34. $-x^2 + 3x - 4 = 0: a = -1, b = 3,$
$c = -4$
$b^2 - 4ac = 9 - 4(-1)(-4) = -7$
So there are no real solutions to the equation.

35. $4m^2 - 20m + 25 = 0: a = 4, b = -20,$
$c = 25$
$b^2 - 4ac = 400 - 4(4)(25) = 0$
So there is one real solution to the equation.

36. $v^2 - 3v - 5 = 0: a = 1, b = -3, c = -5$
$b^2 - 4ac = 9 - 4(1)(-5) = 29$
So there are two real solutions to the equation.

37. $a = 1, b = -\frac{1}{2}, c = \frac{1}{4}$
$b^2 - 4ac = \frac{1}{4} - 4(1)(\frac{1}{4}) = -\frac{3}{4}$
So there are no real solutions to the equation.

38. $a = \frac{1}{2}, b = -\frac{1}{3}, c = \frac{1}{4}$
$b^2 - 4ac = \frac{1}{9} - 4(\frac{1}{2})(\frac{1}{4}) = \frac{1}{9} - \frac{1}{2} = -\frac{7}{18}$
So there are no real solutions to the equation.

39. $a = -3, b = 5, c = 6$
$b^2 - 4ac = 25 - 4(-3)(6) = 97$
So there are two real solutions to the equation.

40. $9m^2 - 24m + 16 = 0: a = 9, b = -24,$
$c = 16$
$b^2 - 4ac = 576 - 4(9)(16) = 0$
So there is one real solution to the equation.

41. $16z^2 - 24z + 9 = 0: a = 16, b = -24,$
$c = 9$
$b^2 - 4ac = (-24)^2 - 4(16)(9) = 0$
So there is one real solution to the equation.

42. $x^2 - 7x + 12 = 0: a = 1, b = -7,$
$c = 12$
$b^2 - 4ac = 49 - 4(1)(12) = 1$
So there are two real solutions to the equation.

43. $5x^2 - 7 = 0$: $a = 5$, $b = 0$, $c = -7$

$b^2 - 4ac = 0 - 4(5)(-7) = 140$

So there are two real solutions to the equation.

44. $-6x^2 - 5$: $a = -6$, $b = 0$, $c = -5$

$b^2 - 4ac = 0 - 4(-6)(-5) = -120$

So there are no real solutions to the equation.

45. $x^2 - x = 0$: $a = 1$, $b = -1$, $c = 0$

$b^2 - 4ac = 1 - 4(1)(0) = 1$

So there are two real solutions to the equation.

46. $-3x^2 + 7x = 0$: $a = -3$, $b = 7$, $c = 0$

$b^2 - 4ac = 49 - 4(-3)(0) = 49$

So there are two real solutions to the equation.

47.
$$6\left(\tfrac{1}{3}x^2 + \tfrac{1}{2}x\right) = 6\left(\tfrac{1}{3}\right)$$
$$2x^2 + 3x = 2$$
$$2x^2 + 3x - 2 = 0$$
$$a = 2, b = 3, c = -2$$
$$x = \frac{-3 \pm \sqrt{9 - 4(2)(-2)}}{2(2)} = \frac{-3 \pm 5}{4}$$
$$= \frac{2}{4}, \frac{-8}{4}$$

Solution set: $\left\{-2, \tfrac{1}{2}\right\}$

48.
$$2\left(\tfrac{1}{2}x^2 + x\right) = 2 \cdot 1$$
$$x^2 + 2x = 2$$
$$x^2 + 2x - 2 = 0$$
$$a = 1, b = 2, c = -2$$
$$x = \frac{-2 \pm \sqrt{4 - 4(1)(-2)}}{2(1)} = \frac{-2 \pm \sqrt{12}}{2}$$
$$= \frac{-2 \pm 2\sqrt{3}}{2} = -1 \pm \sqrt{3}$$

Solution set: $\left\{-1 \pm \sqrt{3}\right\}$

49.
$$\frac{w}{w - 2} = \frac{w}{w - 3}$$
$$w^2 - 3w = w^2 - 2w$$
$$0 = w$$

Solution set: $\{0\}$

50.
$$\frac{y}{3y - 4} = \frac{2}{y + 4}$$
$$y^2 + 4y = 6y - 8$$
$$y^2 - 2y + 8 = 0$$
$$y^2 - 2y + 1 = -8 + 1$$
$$(y - 1)^2 = -7$$
$$y - 1 = \pm\sqrt{-7}$$
$$y = 1 \pm i\sqrt{7}$$

Solution set: $\{1 \pm i\sqrt{7}\}$

51.
$$\frac{9(3x - 5)^2}{4} = 1$$
$$(3x - 5)^2 = \frac{4}{9}$$
$$3x - 5 = \pm\frac{2}{3}$$
$$3x = 5 + \frac{2}{3} \quad \text{or} \quad 3x = 5 - \frac{2}{3}$$
$$3x = \frac{17}{3} \quad \text{or} \quad 3x = \frac{13}{3}$$
$$x = \frac{17}{9} \quad \text{or} \quad x = \frac{13}{9}$$

Solution set: $\left\{\frac{13}{9}, \frac{17}{9}\right\}$

52.
$$\frac{25(2x + 1)^2}{9} = 0$$
$$(2x + 1)^2 = 0$$
$$2x + 1 = 0$$
$$x = -\frac{1}{2}$$

Solution set: $\left\{-\frac{1}{2}\right\}$

53.
$$1 + \frac{20}{x^2} = \frac{8}{x}$$
$$x^2\left(1 + \frac{20}{x^2}\right) = x^2 \cdot \frac{8}{x}$$
$$x^2 - 8x + 20 = 0$$
$$x^2 - 8x + 16 = -20 + 16$$
$$(x - 4)^2 = -4$$
$$x - 4 = \pm 2i$$
$$x = 4 \pm 2i$$

Solution set: $\{4 \pm 2i\}$

54.
$$\frac{34}{x^2} = \frac{6}{x} - 1$$
$$x^2 \cdot \frac{34}{x^2} = x^2 \cdot \frac{6}{x} - x^2 \cdot 1$$
$$x^2 - 6x + 34 = 0$$
$$x^2 - 6x + 9 = -34 + 9$$
$$(x - 3)^2 = -25$$
$$x - 3 = \pm 5i$$
$$x = 3 \pm 5i$$

Solution set: $\{3 \pm 5i\}$

55.
$$(x - 8)(x + 4) = -42$$
$$x^2 - 4x + 10 = 0$$
$$x^2 - 4x + 4 = -10 + 4$$
$$(x - 2)^2 = -6$$
$$x - 2 = \pm i\sqrt{6}$$
$$x = 2 \pm i\sqrt{6}$$

Solution set: $\{2 \pm i\sqrt{6}\}$

56.
$$(x - 10)(x - 2) = -20$$
$$x^2 - 12x + 40 = 0$$
$$x^2 - 12x + 36 = -40 + 36$$
$$(x - 6)^2 = -4$$
$$x - 6 = \pm 2i$$
$$x = 6 \pm 2i$$

Solution set: $\{6 \pm 2i\}$

57.
$$y = \frac{3(2y+5)}{8(y-1)}$$
$$8y^2 - 8y = 6y + 15$$
$$8y^2 - 14y - 15 = 0$$
$$(4y+3)(2y-5) = 0$$
$$4y + 3 = 0 \quad \text{or} \quad 2y - 5 = 0$$
$$y = -\tfrac{3}{4} \text{ or } \quad\quad y = \tfrac{5}{2}$$
Solution set: $\left\{-\tfrac{3}{4}, \tfrac{5}{2}\right\}$

58.
$$z = \frac{7z-4}{12(z-1)}$$
$$12z^2 - 12z = 7z - 4$$
$$12z^2 - 19z + 4 = 0$$
$$(4z-1)(3z-4) = 0$$
$$4z - 1 = 0 \quad \text{or} \quad 3z - 4 = 0$$
$$z = \tfrac{1}{4} \text{ or } \quad\quad z = \tfrac{4}{3}$$
Solution set: $\left\{\tfrac{1}{4}, \tfrac{4}{3}\right\}$

59. $x = \dfrac{-3.2 \pm \sqrt{(3.2)^2 - 4(1)(-5.7)}}{2(1)}$

$= \dfrac{-3.2 \pm \sqrt{33.04}}{2} \qquad \{-4.474, 1.274\}$

60. $x = \dfrac{-7.15 \pm \sqrt{(7.15)^2 - 4(1)(3.24)}}{2(1)}$

$= \dfrac{-7.15 \pm \sqrt{38.1625}}{2} \qquad \{-6.664, -0.486\}$

61. $x = \dfrac{7.4 \pm \sqrt{(-7.4)^2 - 4(1)(13.69)}}{2(1)}$

$= \dfrac{7.4 \pm \sqrt{0}}{2(1)} = 3.7 \qquad \{3.7\}$

62. $x = \dfrac{-5.52 \pm \sqrt{(5.52)^2 - 4(1.44)(5.29)}}{2(1.44)}$

$= \dfrac{-5.52 \pm \sqrt{0}}{2.88} = -1.917 \qquad \{-1.917\}$

63. $x = \dfrac{-6.72 \pm \sqrt{(6.72)^2 - 4(1.85)(3.6)}}{2(1.85)}$

$= \dfrac{-6.72 \pm \sqrt{18.5184}}{3.7} \qquad \{-2.979, -0.653\}$

64.
$x = \dfrac{-4.35 \pm \sqrt{(4.35)^2 - 4(3.67)(-2.13)}}{2(3.67)}$

$= \dfrac{-4.35 \pm \sqrt{50.1909}}{7.34} \qquad \{-1.558, 0.373\}$

65. $x = \dfrac{-14379 \pm \sqrt{14379^2 - 4(3)(243)}}{2(3)}$

$= \dfrac{-14379 \pm 14378.8986}{6}$

Solution set: $\{-4792.983, -0.017\}$

66.
$x = \dfrac{-12{,}347 \pm \sqrt{(12{,}347)^2 - 4(1)(6{,}741)}}{2(1)}$

$= \dfrac{-12{,}347 \pm \sqrt{152421445}}{2}$

Solution set: $\{-12{,}346.454, -0.546\}$

67. $x = \dfrac{-0.00075 \pm \sqrt{0.00075^2 - 4 \cdot 1(-0.0062)}}{2(1)}$

$= \dfrac{-0.00075 \pm 0.1574819}{2} \qquad \{-0.079, 0.078\}$

68. $x = \dfrac{9.86 \pm \sqrt{(-9.86)^2 - 4(4.3)(-3.75)}}{2(4.3)}$

$= \dfrac{9.86 \pm \sqrt{161.7196}}{8.6} \qquad \{-0.332, 2.625\}$

69. Let $x =$ one number and $x + 1 =$ the other. Since their product is 16, we can write
$$x(x+1) = 16$$
$$x^2 + x = 16$$
$$x^2 + x - 16 = 0$$

$$x = \frac{-1 \pm \sqrt{1^2 - 4(1)(-16)}}{2(1)}$$
$$= \frac{-1 \pm \sqrt{65}}{2}$$

Since the numbers are positive, $x = \frac{-1+\sqrt{65}}{2}$

and $x + 1 = \frac{-1+\sqrt{65}}{2} + \frac{2}{2} = \frac{1+\sqrt{65}}{2}$.

The numbers are $\frac{1+\sqrt{65}}{2}$ and $\frac{-1+\sqrt{65}}{2}$.

70. Let $x =$ one of the numbers and $x - 2 =$ the other number. Since their product is 10, we can write the following equation.
$$x(x-2) = 10$$
$$x^2 - 2x = 10$$
$$x^2 - 2x - 10 = 0$$

$$x = \frac{2 \pm \sqrt{(-2)^2 - 4(1)(-10)}}{2(1)} = \frac{2 \pm \sqrt{44}}{2}$$
$$= \frac{2 \pm 2\sqrt{11}}{2} = 1 \pm \sqrt{11}$$

If $x = 1 + \sqrt{11}$, then $x - 2 = 1 + \sqrt{11} - 2$

$= -1 + \sqrt{11}$. Since $1 - \sqrt{11}$ is a negative number, we do not use it. The numbers are $1 + \sqrt{11}$ and $-1 + \sqrt{11}$.

71. Let $x =$ one of the numbers. If the numbers are to have a sum of 6, then $6 - x =$ the other number. Since their product is 4, we can write the equation

$$x(6 - x) = 4$$
$$-x^2 + 6x - 4 = 0$$
$$x^2 - 6x + 4 = 0$$

$$x = \frac{6 \pm \sqrt{36 - 4(1)(4)}}{2(1)} = \frac{6 \pm 2\sqrt{5}}{2}$$
$$= 3 \pm \sqrt{5}$$

If $x = 3 + \sqrt{5}$, then
$6 - x = 6 - (3 + \sqrt{5}) = 3 - \sqrt{5}$.
If $x = 3 - \sqrt{5}$, then
$6 - x = 6 - (3 - \sqrt{5}) = 3 + \sqrt{5}$.
So the numbers are $3 + \sqrt{5}$ and $3 - \sqrt{5}$.

72. Let $x =$ one of the numbers and $8 - x =$ the other number. Since their product is 2, we can write the following equation.

$$x(8 - x) = 2$$
$$8x - x^2 = 2$$
$$x^2 - 8x + 2 = 0$$
$$x = \frac{8 \pm \sqrt{64 - 4(1)(2)}}{2(1)} = \frac{8 \pm \sqrt{56}}{2}$$
$$= \frac{8 \pm 2\sqrt{14}}{2} = 4 \pm \sqrt{14}$$

If $x = 4 + \sqrt{14}$, then
$8 - x = 8 - (4 + \sqrt{14}) = 4 - \sqrt{14}$.
If $x = 4 - \sqrt{14}$, then
$8 - x = 8 - (4 - \sqrt{14}) = 4 + \sqrt{14}$.
The numbers are $4 - \sqrt{14}$ and $4 + \sqrt{14}$.
Their product is 2 and their sum is 8.

73. Let $x =$ the width and $x + 1 =$ the length. Since the diagonal is the hypotenuse of a right triangle, we can write

$$x^2 + (x + 1)^2 = (\sqrt{3})^2$$
$$x^2 + x^2 + 2x + 1 = 3$$
$$2x^2 + 2x - 2 = 0$$
$$x^2 + x - 1 = 0$$
$$x = \frac{-1 \pm \sqrt{1 - 4(1)(-1)}}{2(1)} = \frac{-1 \pm \sqrt{5}}{2}$$

Since the width of a rectangle is a positive number, we have width $= \frac{-1+\sqrt{5}}{2}$ feet and

length $= \frac{-1+\sqrt{5}}{2} + \frac{2}{2} = \frac{1+\sqrt{5}}{2}$ feet.

74. Let $x =$ the width and $x + 2 =$ the length. Since the diagonal is the hypotenuse of a right triangle, we can write the following equation.

$$x^2 + (x + 2)^2 = (\sqrt{6})^2$$
$$x^2 + x^2 + 4x + 4 = 6$$
$$2x^2 + 4x - 2 = 0$$
$$x^2 + 2x - 1 = 0$$

$$x = \frac{-2 \pm \sqrt{4 - 4(1)(-1)}}{2(1)} = \frac{-2 \pm 2\sqrt{2}}{2}$$
$$= -1 \pm \sqrt{2}$$

Since x must be positive, we can discard the solution $-1 - \sqrt{2}$. If $x = -1 + \sqrt{2}$, then $x + 2 = 1 + \sqrt{2}$. The width is $-1 + \sqrt{2}$ meters and the length is $1 + \sqrt{2}$ meters.

75. Let $x =$ the width, and $x + 4 =$ the length. Since the area is 10 square feet, we can write

$$x(x + 4) = 10$$
$$x^2 + 4x - 10 = 0$$
$$x = \frac{-4 \pm \sqrt{16 - 4(1)(-10)}}{2(1)} = \frac{-4 \pm 2\sqrt{14}}{2}$$
$$= -2 \pm \sqrt{14}$$

Since the width must be positive, the width is $-2 + \sqrt{14}$ feet, and the length is $-2 + \sqrt{14} + 4 = 2 + \sqrt{14}$ feet.

76. Let $x =$ the length of a side and $x + 2 =$ the length of the diagonal. Since the diagonal is the hypotenuse of a right triangle, we can write the following equation.

$$x^2 + x^2 = (x + 2)^2$$
$$2x^2 = x^2 + 4x + 4$$
$$x^2 - 4x - 4 = 0$$

$$x = \frac{4 \pm \sqrt{16 - 4(1)(-4)}}{2(1)} = \frac{4 \pm 4\sqrt{2}}{2}$$
$$= 2 \pm 2\sqrt{2}$$

Since the value of x must be positive, $2 - 2\sqrt{2}$ is discarded. So the length of the side of the square is $2 + 2\sqrt{2}$ meters.

77. The time it takes to reach the ground is found by solving the equation

$$-16t^2 + 16t + 96 = 0$$
$$t^2 - t - 6 = 0$$
$$(t - 3)(t + 2) = 0$$
$$t = 3 \quad \text{or} \quad t = -2$$

The pine cone reaches the earth 3 seconds after it is tossed.

78. We need to find t for which S is 0.
$$-16t^2 + 0 \cdot t + 96 = 0$$
$$-16t^2 = -96$$
$$t^2 = 6$$
$$t = \pm\sqrt{6}$$
It takes $\sqrt{6}$ seconds to reach the earth.

79. The time it takes to reach the river is found by solving the equation
$$-16t^2 - 30t + 1000 = 0$$
$$8t^2 + 15t - 500 = 0$$
$$t = \frac{-15 \pm \sqrt{15^2 - 4(8)(-500)}}{2(8)}$$
$$= \frac{-15 \pm \sqrt{16225}}{16} = \frac{-15 \pm 127.377}{16}$$
Since the time is positive, the time is $\frac{-15 + 127.377}{16}$, or 7.02 seconds.

80. a) We want the value of t for which S is 0.
$$-16t^2 + 150t + 5 = 0$$
$$16t^2 - 150t - 5 = 0$$
$$t = \frac{150 \pm \sqrt{(150)^2 - 4(16)(-5)}}{2(16)}$$
$$= \frac{150 \pm \sqrt{22,820}}{32}$$
Discard the negative value for t, $\frac{150 - \sqrt{22,820}}{32}$. It takes $\frac{150 + \sqrt{22,820}}{32}$, or 9.408 seconds for the ball return to earth.
b) The maximum height reached by the ball is 356.6 feet.

81. Let $x = $ the number originally purchased. She paid $\frac{200}{x}$ dollars for each melon. She sold them for $\frac{200}{x} + 1.50$ dollars each. When she sold $x - 30$ of them her revenue was $200:
$$(x - 30)(\frac{200}{x} + 1.50) = 200$$
$$200 - \frac{6000}{x} + 1.50x - 45 = 200$$
$$1.50x - 45 - \frac{6000}{x} = 0$$
$$1.50x^2 - 45x - 6000 = 0$$
$$x^2 - 30x - 4000 = 0$$
$$x = \frac{30 \pm \sqrt{900 - 4 \cdot 1(-4000)}}{2} = \frac{30 \pm 130}{2}$$
$$= 80 \text{ or } -50$$
She originally purchased 80 watermelons.

82. Let $x = $ the present membership. The cost is $\frac{200,000}{x}$ dollars each. If 5 more join, the cost is $\frac{200,000}{x} - 2000$. We have
$$(x + 5)(\frac{200,000}{x} - 2000) = 200,000$$
$$200,000 + \frac{1,000,000}{x} - 2000x - 10,000$$
$$= 200,000$$
$$-2000x - 10,000 + \frac{1,000,000}{x} = 0$$
$$-2000x^2 - 10,000x + 1,000,000 = 0$$
$$x^2 + 5x - 500 = 0$$
$$(x - 20)(x + 25) = 0$$
$$x - 20 = 0 \quad \text{or } x + 25 = 0$$
$$x = 20 \text{ or } \quad x = -25$$
There are presently 20 members.

83. If x is the width of the border, then
$$(30 - 2x)(40 - 2x) = 704$$
$$1200 - 140x + 4x^2 = 704$$
$$4x^2 - 140x + 496 = 0$$
$$x^2 - 35x + 124 = 0$$
$$x = \frac{35 \pm \sqrt{35^2 - 4 \cdot 1 \cdot 124}}{2} = \frac{35 \pm \sqrt{729}}{2}$$
$$= \frac{35 \pm 27}{2} = 31 \text{ or } 4$$
The width of the border is 4 inches.

89. {0.652, 5.678}

90. {−22.975, 21.642}

91. ∅

92. ∅

93. ∅

94. ∅

8.3 WARM-UPS

1. True, because if $w = x^2$ the equation becomes $w^2 - 5w + 6 = 0$.

2. False, the equation cannot be solved by substitution.

3. False, we can use factoring.

4. True, because $(x^{1/6})^2 = x^{2/6} = x^{1/3}$.

5. False, we should let $w = \sqrt{x}$.

6. False, because $(2^{1/2})^2 = 2^{2/2} = 2^1 = 2$.

7. False, his rate is $1/x$ of the fence per hour.

8. True, because $R = D/T$.

9. False, against a 5 mph current it will go 5 mph.

10. False, the dimensions of the bottom will be $11 - 2x$ by $14 - 2x$.

8.3 EXERCISES

1. If the coefficients are integers and the discriminant is a perfect square, then the quadratic polynomial can be factored.

2. The number k is a solution to a quadratic equation if and only if $x - k$ is a factor of the quadratic polynomial.

3. If the solutions are a and b, then the quadratic equation $(x - a)(x - b) = 0$ has those solutions.

4. An equation of quadratic form is one that can be converted to a quadratic equation by making a substitution.

5. $b^2 - 4ac = (-1)^2 - 4(2)4 = -31$
Polynomial is prime.

6. $b^2 - 4ac = (3)^2 - 4(2)(-5) = 49$
$2x^2 + 3x - 5 = (2x + 5)(x - 1)$

7. $b^2 - 4ac = 6^2 - 4(2)(-5) = 76$
Polynomial is prime.

8. $b^2 - 4ac = 5^2 - 4(3)(-1) = 37$
Polynomial is prime.

9. $b^2 - 4ac = 19^2 - 4(6)(-36) = 1225$
Since $\sqrt{1225} = 35$, the polynomial is not prime.
$6x^2 + 19x - 36 = (3x - 4)(2x + 9)$

10. $b^2 - 4ac = 6^2 - 4(8)(-27) = 900$
Since $\sqrt{900} = 30$, the polynomial is not prime.
$8x^2 + 6x - 27 = (2x - 3)(4x + 9)$

11. $b^2 - 4ac = 25 - 4(4)(-12) = 217$
Polynomial is prime.

12. $b^2 - 4ac = (-27)^2 - 4 \cdot 4 \cdot 45 = 9$
$4x^2 - 27x + 45 = (4x - 15)(x - 3)$

13. $b^2 - 4ac = (-18)^2 - 4 \cdot 8(-45) = 1764$
Since $\sqrt{1764} = 42$, the polynomial is not prime.
$8x^2 - 18x - 45 = (4x - 15)(2x + 3)$

14. $b^2 - 4ac = 9^2 - 4 \cdot 6(-16) = 465$
Polynomial is prime.

15. $(x - 3)(x + 7) = 0$
$x^2 + 4x - 21 = 0$

16. $(x + 8)(x - 2) = 0$
$x^2 + 6x - 16 = 0$

17. $(x - 4)(x - 1) = 0$
$x^2 - 5x + 4 = 0$

18. $(x - 3)(x - 2) = 0$
$x^2 - 5x + 6 = 0$

19. $(x - \sqrt{5})(x + \sqrt{5}) = 0$
$x^2 - 5 = 0$

20. $(x - \sqrt{7})(x + \sqrt{7}) = 0$
$x^2 - 7 = 0$

21. $(x - 4i)(x + 4i) = 0$
$x^2 + 16 = 0$

22. $(x - 3i)(x + 3i) = 0$
$x^2 + 9 = 0$

23. $(x - i\sqrt{2})(x + i\sqrt{2}) = 0$
$x^2 + 2 = 0$

24. $(x - 3i\sqrt{2})(x + 3i\sqrt{2}) = 0$
$x^2 + 18 = 0$

25. $(2x - 1)(3x - 1) = 0$
$6x^2 - 5x + 1 = 0$

26. $(5x + 1)(2x + 1) = 0$
$10x^2 + 7x + 1 = 0$

27. Let $w = 2a - 1$.
$$w^2 + 2w - 8 = 0$$
$$(w + 4)(w - 2) = 0$$
$$w + 4 = 0 \quad \text{or} \quad w - 2 = 0$$
$$w = -4 \quad \text{or} \quad w = 2$$
$$2a - 1 = -4 \quad \text{or} \quad 2a - 1 = 2$$
$$2a = -3 \quad \text{or} \quad 2a = 3$$
$$a = -\tfrac{3}{2} \quad \text{or} \quad a = \tfrac{3}{2}$$

Solution set: $\left\{ -\tfrac{3}{2}, \tfrac{3}{2} \right\}$

28. Let $w = 3a + 2$ in
$(3a + 2)^2 - 3(3a + 2) = 10$.
$$w^2 - 3w = 10$$
$$w^2 - 3w - 10 = 0$$
$$(w - 5)(w + 2) = 0$$
$$w - 5 = 0 \quad \text{or} \quad w + 2 = 0$$
$$w = 5 \quad \text{or} \quad w = -2$$
$$3a + 2 = 5 \quad \text{or} \quad 3a + 2 = -2$$
$$3a = 3 \quad \text{or} \quad 3a = -4$$
$$a = 1 \quad \text{or} \quad a = -\tfrac{4}{3}$$
The solution set is $\left\{ -\tfrac{4}{3}, 1 \right\}$.

29. Let $y = w - 1$.
$$y^2 + 5y + 5 = 0$$
$$y = \frac{-5 \pm \sqrt{25 - 4(1)(5)}}{2(1)} = \frac{-5 \pm \sqrt{5}}{2}$$
$$w - 1 = \frac{-5 \pm \sqrt{5}}{2}$$

$w = \dfrac{-5 \pm \sqrt{5}}{2} + 1 = \dfrac{-5 \pm \sqrt{5}}{2} + \dfrac{2}{2} = \dfrac{-3 \pm \sqrt{5}}{2}$

Solution set: $\left\{ \dfrac{-3 \pm \sqrt{5}}{2} \right\}$

30. Let $w = 2x - 1$ in the equation
$(2x - 1)^2 - 4(2x - 1) + 2 = 0$.

$$w^2 - 4w + 2 = 0$$
$$w = \dfrac{4 \pm \sqrt{16 - 4(1)(2)}}{2(1)} = \dfrac{4 \pm \sqrt{8}}{2} = 2 \pm \sqrt{2}$$

$$2x - 1 = 2 \pm \sqrt{2}$$
$$2x = 3 \pm \sqrt{2}$$
$$x = \dfrac{3 \pm \sqrt{2}}{2}$$

The solution set is $\left\{ \dfrac{3 \pm \sqrt{2}}{2} \right\}$.

31. Let $w = x^2$ and $w^2 = x^4$.
$$w^2 - 14w + 45 = 0$$
$$(w - 5)(w - 9) = 0$$
$$w - 5 = 0 \text{ or } w - 9 = 0$$
$$w = 5 \quad \text{or} \quad w = 9$$
$$x^2 = 5 \quad \text{or} \quad x^2 = 9$$
$$x = \pm\sqrt{5} \text{ or } x = \pm 3$$
Solution set: $\{ \pm\sqrt{5}, \pm 3 \}$

32. Let $w = x^2$ and $w^2 = x^4$ in $x^4 + 2x^2 = 15$.
$$w^2 + 2w = 15$$
$$w^2 + 2w - 15 = 0$$
$$(w + 5)(w - 3) = 0$$
$$w + 5 = 0 \text{ or } w - 3 = 0$$
$$w = -5 \text{ or } w = 3$$
$$x^2 = -5 \text{ or } x^2 = 3$$
$$x = \pm\sqrt{3}$$
Since $x^2 = -5$ has no real solution, the solution set is $\{ \pm\sqrt{3} \}$.

33. Let $w = x^3$, and $w^2 = x^6$.
$$w^2 + 7w = 8$$
$$w^2 + 7w - 8 = 0$$
$$(w - 1)(w + 8) = 0$$
$$w - 1 = 0 \text{ or } w + 8 = 0$$
$$w = 1 \text{ or } w = -8$$
$$x^3 = 1 \text{ or } x^3 = -8$$
$$x = 1 \text{ or } x = -2$$
Solution set: $\{-2, 1\}$

34. Let $w = a^3$ and $w^2 = a^6$ in $a^6 + 6a^3 = 16$.
$$w^2 + 6w = 16$$
$$w^2 + 6w - 16 = 0$$
$$(w + 8)(w - 2) = 0$$
$$w + 8 = 0 \text{ or } w - 2 = 0$$
$$w = -8 \text{ or } w = 2$$
$$a^3 = -8 \text{ or } a^3 = 2$$
$$a = -2 \text{ or } a = \sqrt[3]{2}$$
The solution set is $\left\{ -2, \sqrt[3]{2} \right\}$.

35. Let $w = x^2 + 2x$.
$$w^2 - 7w + 12 = 0$$
$$(w - 3)(w - 4) = 0$$
$$w - 3 = 0 \quad \text{or} \quad w - 4 = 0$$
$$w = 3 \quad \text{or} \quad w = 4$$
$$x^2 + 2x = 3 \quad \text{or} \quad x^2 + 2x = 4$$
$$x^2 + 2x - 3 = 0 \quad \text{or} \quad x^2 + 2x - 4 = 0$$
$$(x + 3)(x - 1) = 0 \text{ or}$$
$$x = \dfrac{-2 \pm \sqrt{4 - 4(1)(-4)}}{2}$$
$$x = -3 \text{ or } x = 1 \quad \text{or} \quad x = \dfrac{-2 \pm 2\sqrt{5}}{2}$$
Solution set: $\{-1 \pm \sqrt{5}, -3, 1\}$

36. Let $w = x^2 + 3x$ in the original equation.
$$w^2 + w - 20 = 0$$
$$(w + 5)(w - 4) = 0$$
$$w + 5 = 0 \quad \text{or} \quad w - 4 = 0$$
$$w = -5 \quad \text{or} \quad w = 4$$
$$x^2 + 3x = -5 \quad \text{or} \quad x^2 + 3x = 4$$
$$x^2 + 3x + 5 = 0 \text{ or } x^2 + 3x - 4 = 0$$
$$(x + 4)(x - 1) = 0$$
$$x = -4 \text{ or } x = 1$$

For $x^2 + 3x + 5 = 0$, $b^2 - 4ac = 9 - 4(1)(5)$ $= -11$. So this equation has no real solutions. The solution set is $\{-4, 1\}$.

37. Let $w = y^2 + y$.
$$(y^2 + y)^2 - 8(y^2 + y) + 12 = 0$$
$$w^2 - 8w + 12 = 0$$
$$(w - 6)(w - 2) = 0$$
$$w = 6 \quad \text{or} \quad w = 2$$
$$y^2 + y = 6 \quad \text{or} \quad y^2 + y = 2$$
$$y^2 + y - 6 = 0 \text{ or } y^2 + y - 2 = 0$$
$$(y + 3)(y - 2) = 0 \text{ or } (y + 2)(y - 1) = 0$$
$$y = -3 \text{ or } y = 2 \text{ or } y = -2 \text{ or } y = 1$$
Solution set: $\{-3, -2, 1, 2\}$

38. Let $t = w^2 - 2w$:
$$(w^2 - 2w)^2 + 24 = 11(w^2 - 2w)$$
$$t^2 + 24 = 11t$$
$$t^2 - 11t + 24 = 0$$
$$(t - 8)(t - 3) = 0$$
$$t = 8 \quad \text{or} \quad t = 3$$
$$w^2 - 2w = 8 \quad \text{or} \quad w^2 - 2w = 3$$
$$w^2 - 2w - 8 = 0 \quad \text{or} \quad w^2 - 2w - 3 = 0$$
$$(w - 4)(w + 2) = 0 \text{ or } (w - 3)(w + 1) = 0$$
$$w = 4 \text{ or } w = -2 \text{ or } w = 3 \text{ or } w = -1$$
Solution set: $\{-2, -1, 3, 4\}$

39. Let $w = x^{1/4}$ and $w^2 = x^{1/2}$.
$$w^2 - 5w + 6 = 0$$
$$(w - 3)(w - 2) = 0$$
$$w - 3 = 0 \quad \text{or} \quad w - 2 = 0$$
$$w = 3 \quad \text{or} \quad w = 2$$
$$x^{1/4} = 3 \quad \text{or} \quad x^{1/4} = 2$$
$$(x^{1/4})^4 = 3^4 \quad \text{or} \quad (x^{1/4})^4 = 2^4$$
$$x = 81 \quad \text{or} \quad x = 16$$
Solution set: $\{16, 81\}$

40. Let $w = \sqrt{x}$ and $w^2 = x$ in
$2x - 5\sqrt{x} + 2 = 0$.
$$2w^2 - 5w + 2 = 0$$
$$(2w - 1)(w - 2) = 0$$
$$2w - 1 = 0 \text{ or } w - 2 = 0$$
$$2w = 1 \text{ or } \quad w = 2$$
$$w = \tfrac{1}{2} \text{ or } \quad w = 2$$
$$\sqrt{x} = \tfrac{1}{2} \quad \text{or} \quad \sqrt{x} = 2$$
$$x = \tfrac{1}{4} \quad \text{or} \quad x = 4$$
The solution set is $\left\{\tfrac{1}{4}, 4\right\}$.

41. Let $w = x^{1/2}$ and $w^2 = x$.
$$2w^2 - 5w - 3 = 0$$
$$(2w + 1)(w - 3) = 0$$
$$2w + 1 = 0 \quad \text{or} \quad w - 3 = 0$$
$$w = -\tfrac{1}{2} \text{ or } \quad w = 3$$
$$x^{1/2} = -\tfrac{1}{2} \text{ or } \quad x^{1/2} = 3$$
$$x = \tfrac{1}{4} \quad \text{or} \quad x = 9$$
The solution $1/4$ does not check in the original equation. So the solution set is $\{9\}$.

42. Let $w = x^{1/4}$ and $w^2 = x^{1/2}$ in the equation.
$$w + 2 = w^2$$
$$-w^2 + w + 2 = 0$$
$$w^2 - w - 2 = 0$$
$$(w - 2)(w + 1) = 0$$
$$w - 2 = 0 \text{ or } w + 1 = 0$$

$$w = 2 \quad \text{or} \quad w = -1$$
$$x^{1/4} = 2 \quad \text{or} \quad x^{1/4} = -1$$
$$x = 16$$
Since $x^{1/4} = -1$ has no real solution, the solution set is $\{16\}$.

43. Let $t = x^{-1}$:
$$x^{-2} + x^{-1} - 6 = 0$$
$$t^2 + t - 6 = 0$$
$$(t + 3)(t - 2) = 0$$
$$t = -3 \quad \text{or} \quad t = 2$$
$$x^{-1} = -3 \quad \text{or} \quad x^{-1} = 2$$
$$x = -\tfrac{1}{3} \quad \text{or} \quad x = \tfrac{1}{2}$$
Solution set: $\left\{-\tfrac{1}{3}, \tfrac{1}{2}\right\}$

44.
$$x^{-2} - 2x^{-1} = 8$$
$$x^{-2} - 2x^{-1} - 8 = 0$$
$$(x^{-1} - 4)(x^{-1} + 2) = 0$$
$$x^{-1} = 4 \text{ or } x^{-1} = -2$$
$$x = \tfrac{1}{4} \text{ or } \quad x = -\tfrac{1}{2}$$

Solution set: $\left\{-\tfrac{1}{2}, \tfrac{1}{4}\right\}$

45. Let $w = x^{1/6}$ and $w^2 = x^{1/3}$.
$$w - w^2 + 2 = 0$$
$$w^2 - w - 2 = 0$$
$$(w - 2)(w + 1) = 0$$
$$w = 2 \quad \text{or} \quad w = -1$$
$$x^{1/6} = 2 \quad \text{or} \quad x^{1/6} = -1$$
$$(x^{1/6})^6 = 2^6 \quad \text{or } (x^{1/6})^6 = (-1)^6$$
$$x = 64 \quad \text{or} \quad x = 1$$
The original equation is not satisfied for $x = 1$. So the solution set is $\{64\}$.

46. Let $w = x^{1/3}$ and $w^2 = x^{2/3}$.
$$w^2 - w - 20 = 0$$
$$(w - 5)(w + 4) = 0$$
$$w - 5 = 0 \quad \text{or} \quad w + 4 = 0$$
$$w = 5 \quad \text{or} \quad w = -4$$
$$x^{1/3} = 5 \quad \text{or} \quad x^{1/3} = -4$$
$$x = 125 \text{ or } \quad x = -64$$
The solution set is $\{-64, 125\}$.

47. Let $w = \dfrac{1}{y - 1}$.
$$w^2 + w = 6$$
$$w^2 + w - 6 = 0$$
$$(w + 3)(w - 2) = 0$$
$$w = -3 \quad \text{or} \quad w = 2$$

$$\frac{1}{y-1} = -3 \quad \text{or} \quad \frac{1}{y-1} = 2$$

$$-3y + 3 = 1 \quad \text{or} \quad 2y - 2 = 1$$

$$-3y = -2 \quad \text{or} \quad 2y = 3$$

$$y = \frac{2}{3} \quad \text{or} \quad y = \frac{3}{2}$$

Solution set: $\left\{\frac{2}{3}, \frac{3}{2}\right\}$

48. Let $x = \dfrac{1}{w+1}$ in the original equation.

$$x^2 - 2x - 24 = 0$$

$$(x - 6)(x + 4) = 0$$

$$x - 6 = 0 \quad \text{or} \quad x + 4 = 0$$

$$x = 6 \quad \text{or} \quad x = -4$$

$$\frac{1}{w+1} = 6 \quad \text{or} \quad \frac{1}{w+1} = -4$$

$$1 = 6w + 6 \quad \text{or} \quad 1 = -4w - 4$$

$$-5 = 6w \quad \text{or} \quad 5 = -4w$$

$$-\frac{5}{6} = w \quad \text{or} \quad -\frac{5}{4} = w$$

The solution set is $\left\{-\frac{5}{6}, -\frac{5}{4}\right\}$.

49. Let $w = \sqrt{2x^2 - 3}$ and $w^2 = 2x^2 - 3$.

$$w^2 - 6w + 8 = 0$$

$$(w - 4)(w - 2) = 0$$

$$w = 4 \quad \text{or} \quad w = 2$$

$$\sqrt{2x^2 - 3} = 4 \quad \text{or} \quad \sqrt{2x^2 - 3} = 2$$

Square each side:

$$2x^2 - 3 = 16 \quad \text{or} \quad 2x^2 - 3 = 4$$

$$2x^2 = 19 \quad \text{or} \quad 2x^2 = 7$$

$$x^2 = \frac{19}{2} \quad \text{or} \quad x^2 = \frac{7}{2}$$

$$x = \pm\sqrt{\frac{19}{2}} \quad \text{or} \quad x = \pm\sqrt{\frac{7}{2}}$$

$$x = \pm\frac{\sqrt{38}}{2} \quad \text{or} \quad x = \pm\frac{\sqrt{14}}{2}$$

Solution set: $\left\{\pm\frac{\sqrt{14}}{2}, \pm\frac{\sqrt{38}}{2}\right\}$

50. Let $w = \sqrt{x^2 + x}$ and $w^2 = x^2 + x$.

$$w^2 + w - 2 = 0$$

$$(w + 2)(w - 1) = 0$$

$$w + 2 = 0 \quad \text{or} \quad w - 1 = 0$$

$$w = -2 \quad \text{or} \quad w = 1$$

$$\sqrt{x^2 + x} = -2 \quad \text{or} \quad \sqrt{x^2 + x} = 1$$

No solution

$$x^2 + x = 1$$

$$x^2 + x - 1 = 0$$

$$x = \frac{-1 \pm \sqrt{1 - 4(1)(-1)}}{2(1)}$$

$$= \frac{-1 \pm \sqrt{5}}{2}$$

Since $\sqrt{x^2 + x} = -2$ has no solution, the solution set to the equation is $\left\{\dfrac{-1 \pm \sqrt{5}}{2}\right\}$.

51. Let $t = x^{-1}$ in $x^{-2} - 2x^{-1} - 1 = 0$

$$t^2 - 2t - 1 = 0$$

$$t = \frac{2 \pm \sqrt{4 - 4(1)(-1)}}{2} = \frac{2 \pm 2\sqrt{2}}{2}$$

$$= 1 \pm \sqrt{2}$$

$$x = \frac{1}{1 + \sqrt{2}} \quad \text{or} \quad x = \frac{1}{1 - \sqrt{2}}$$

$$x = \frac{1(1 - \sqrt{2})}{(1 + \sqrt{2})(1 - \sqrt{2})} \quad \text{or}$$

$$x = \frac{1(1 + \sqrt{2})}{(1 - \sqrt{2})(1 + \sqrt{2})}$$

$$x = \frac{1 - \sqrt{2}}{-1} \quad \text{or} \quad x = \frac{1 + \sqrt{2}}{-1}$$

$$x = -1 + \sqrt{2} \quad \text{or} \quad x = -1 - \sqrt{2}$$

Solution set: $\{-1 + \sqrt{2}, -1 - \sqrt{2}\}$

52. Let $t = x^{-1}$ in $x^{-2} - 6x^{-1} + 6 = 0$:

$$t^2 - 6t + 6 = 0$$

$$t = \frac{6 \pm \sqrt{36 - 4(1)(6)}}{2} = \frac{6 \pm 2\sqrt{3}}{2}$$

$$= 3 \pm \sqrt{3}$$

$$x = \frac{1}{3 + \sqrt{3}} \quad \text{or} \quad x = \frac{1}{3 - \sqrt{3}}$$

$$x = \frac{1(3 - \sqrt{3})}{(3 + \sqrt{3})(3 - \sqrt{3})} \quad \text{or}$$

$$x = \frac{1(3 + \sqrt{3})}{(3 - \sqrt{3})(3 + \sqrt{3})}$$

$$x = \frac{3 - \sqrt{3}}{6} \quad \text{or} \quad x = \frac{3 + \sqrt{3}}{6}$$

Solution set: $\left\{\dfrac{3 - \sqrt{3}}{6}, \dfrac{3 + \sqrt{3}}{6}\right\}$

53. Let $x =$ Gary's travel time and $x + 1 =$ Harry's travel time. Since $R = D/T$, Gary's speed is $300/x$ and Harry's speed is $300/(x + 1)$. Since Gary travels 10 mph faster, we can write the following equation.

$$\frac{300}{x} = \frac{300}{x + 1} + 10$$

$$x(x + 1)\left(\frac{300}{x}\right) = x(x + 1)\left(\frac{300}{x + 1} + 10\right)$$

$$300x + 300 = 300x + 10x^2 + 10x$$

$$0 = 10x^2 + 10x - 300$$

$$0 = x^2 + x - 30$$

$$0 = (x + 6)(x - 5)$$

$$x + 6 = 0 \quad \text{or} \quad x - 5 = 0$$
$$x = -6 \quad \text{or} \quad x = 5$$
Gary travels 5 hours and they arrive at 2 P.M.

54. Let $x =$ the speed of the boat in still water. The speed upstream is $x - 4$ miles per hour and the speed downstream is $x + 4$ miles per hour. Since $T = D/R$, her time upstream is $5/(x - 4)$ hours and her time downstream is $5/(x + 4)$ hours. Since her time upstream is $1/3$ of an hour larger than her time downstream, we can write the following equation.

$$\frac{5}{x - 4} = \frac{5}{x + 4} + \frac{1}{3}$$
$$3(x - 4)(x + 4)\frac{5}{x - 4}$$
$$= 3(x - 4)(x + 4)\left(\frac{5}{x + 4} + \frac{1}{3}\right)$$
$$15(x + 4) = 15(x - 4) + (x - 4)(x + 4)$$
$$15x + 60 = 15x - 60 + x^2 - 16$$
$$136 = x^2$$
$$x = \pm\sqrt{136} = \pm 2\sqrt{34}$$

The speed of the boat in still water is $2\sqrt{34}$ or approximately 11.662 miles per hour.

55. Let $x =$ her speed before lunch and $x - 4 =$ her speed after lunch. Since $T = D/R$, her time before lunch was $60/x$ and her time after lunch was $46/(x - 4)$. Since she put in one hour more after lunch, we can write the following equation.

$$\frac{46}{x - 4} - 1 = \frac{60}{x}$$
$$x(x - 4)\left(\frac{46}{x - 4} - 1\right) = x(x - 4)\left(\frac{60}{x}\right)$$
$$46x - x^2 + 4x = 60x - 240$$
$$-x^2 - 10x + 240 = 0$$
$$x^2 + 10x - 240 = 0$$

$$x = \frac{-10 \pm \sqrt{100 - 4(1)(-240)}}{2(1)}$$
$$= \frac{-10 \pm \sqrt{1060}}{2} = \frac{-10 \pm 2\sqrt{265}}{2}$$
$$= -5 \pm \sqrt{265}$$

Since $-5 - \sqrt{265}$ is a negative number, we disregard that answer. Her speed before lunch was $-5 + \sqrt{265} \approx 11.3$ mph, and her speed after lunch was 4 mph slower: $-9 + \sqrt{265} \approx 7.3$ mph.

56. Let $x =$ Kim's speed and $x + 10 =$ Bryan's speed. Kim's time is $3/x$ hours and Bryan's time is $3/(x + 10)$ hours. Since Kim's time is $1/4$ hour longer than Brian's, we can write the following equation.

$$\frac{3}{x} = \frac{3}{x + 10} + \frac{1}{4}$$
$$4x(x + 10)\frac{3}{x} = 4x(x + 10)\left(\frac{3}{x + 10} + \frac{1}{4}\right)$$
$$12x + 120 = 12x + x^2 + 10x$$
$$-x^2 - 10x + 120 = 0$$
$$x^2 + 10x - 120 = 0$$

$$x = \frac{-10 \pm \sqrt{100 - 4(1)(-120)}}{2(1)}$$
$$= \frac{-10 \pm \sqrt{580}}{2} = \frac{-10 \pm 2\sqrt{145}}{2}$$
$$= -5 \pm \sqrt{145}$$

If $x = -5 + \sqrt{145}$, then
$$x + 10 = -5 + \sqrt{145} + 10$$
$$= 5 + \sqrt{145}.$$ So Kim's speed is $-5 + \sqrt{145}$ or approximately 7.042 mph and Bryan's speed is $5 + \sqrt{145}$ or approximately 17.042 mph.

57. Let $x =$ Andrew's time and $x + 3 =$ John's time. Andrew's rate is $1/x$ job/hr and John's rate is $1/(x + 3)$ job/hr. In 8 hours Andrew does $8/x$ job and John does $8/(x + 3)$ job.

$$\frac{8}{x} + \frac{8}{x + 3} = 1$$

$$x(x + 3)\left(\frac{8}{x} + \frac{8}{x + 3}\right) = x(x + 3)1$$
$$8x + 24 + 8x = x^2 + 3x$$
$$0 = x^2 - 13x - 24$$

$$x = \frac{13 \pm \sqrt{169 - 4(1)(-24)}}{2(1)} = \frac{13 \pm \sqrt{265}}{2}$$

Since $\frac{13 - \sqrt{265}}{2}$ is a negative number, we disregard that solution. Andrew's time is $\frac{13 + \sqrt{265}}{2} \approx 14.6$ hours and John's time is 3 hours more :
$$3 + \frac{13 + \sqrt{265}}{2} = \frac{19 + \sqrt{265}}{2} \approx 17.6 \text{ hours}$$

58. Let $x =$ Brent's time alone and $x - 1 =$ Calvin's time alone. Brent's rate is $1/x$ job/hr and Calvin's rate is $1/(x-1)$ job/hr. In 3/4 hr Brent does $\frac{3}{4} \cdot \frac{1}{x}$ or $\frac{3}{4x}$ job while Calvin does $\frac{3}{4} \cdot \frac{1}{x-1}$ or $\frac{3}{4(x-1)}$ job. Together they complete the job in 3/4 hr.

$$\frac{3}{4x} + \frac{3}{4(x-1)} = 1$$
$$4x(x-1)\left(\frac{3}{4x} + \frac{3}{4(x-1)}\right) = 4x(x-1)1$$
$$3x - 3 + 3x = 4x^2 - 4x$$
$$-4x^2 + 10x - 3 = 0$$
$$4x^2 - 10x + 3 = 0$$
$$x = \frac{10 \pm \sqrt{100 - 4(4)(3)}}{2(4)} = \frac{10 \pm \sqrt{52}}{8}$$
$$= \frac{10 \pm 2\sqrt{13}}{8} = \frac{5 \pm \sqrt{13}}{4}$$

If $x = \frac{5+\sqrt{13}}{4}$, then
$$x - 1 = \frac{5+\sqrt{13}}{4} - \frac{4}{4} = \frac{1+\sqrt{13}}{4}.$$

Brent's time alone is $\frac{5+\sqrt{13}}{4}$ or approximately 2.151 hours. Calvin's time alone is $\frac{1+\sqrt{13}}{4}$ or approximately 1.151 hours.

59. Let $x =$ the amount of increase. The new length and width will be $30 + x$ and $20 + x$. Since the new area is to be 1000, we can write the following equation.
$$(20 + x)(30 + x) = 1000$$
$$x^2 + 50x - 400 = 0$$

$$x = \frac{-50 \pm \sqrt{2500 - 4(1)(-400)}}{2(1)}$$

$$= \frac{-50 \pm \sqrt{4100}}{2} = \frac{-50 \pm 10\sqrt{41}}{2}$$
$$= -25 \pm 5\sqrt{41}$$

Disregard the negative solution.
Use $x = -25 + 5\sqrt{41}$ to get
$30 + x = 5 + 5\sqrt{41} \approx 37.02$ feet, and
$20 + x = -5 + 5\sqrt{41} \approx 27.02$ feet.

60. Let $x =$ the length of the side of the square. After squares are cut from each of the corners, the dimensions of the base will be $11 - 2x$ and $14 - 2x$. Since the base is 80 square inches, we can write the following equation.
$$(11 - 2x)(14 - 2x) = 80$$
$$154 - 28x - 22x + 4x^2 = 80$$
$$4x^2 - 50x + 74 = 0$$
$$2x^2 - 25x + 37 = 0$$

$$x = \frac{25 \pm \sqrt{625 - 4(2)(37)}}{2(2)} = \frac{25 \pm \sqrt{329}}{4}$$

Since $\frac{25+\sqrt{329}}{4}$ is too large, the value of x is $\frac{25-\sqrt{329}}{4}$ or approximately 1.715 inches.

61. Let $x =$ the number of hours for A to empty the pool and $x + 2 =$ the number of hours for B to empty the pool. A's rate is $\frac{1}{x}$ pool/hr and B's rate is $\frac{1}{x+2}$ pool/hr. A works for 9 hrs and does $\frac{9}{x}$ of the pool while B works for 6 hours and does $\frac{6}{x+2}$ of the pool. Since the pool is half full we have the following equation.
$$\frac{9}{x} + \frac{6}{x+2} = \frac{1}{2}$$
$$2x(x+2)\left(\frac{9}{x} + \frac{6}{x+2}\right) = 2x(x+2)\frac{1}{2}$$
$$18x + 36 + 12x = x^2 + 2x$$
$$-x^2 + 28x + 36 = 0$$
$$x^2 - 28x - 36 = 0$$
$$x = \frac{28 \pm \sqrt{28^2 - 4(1)(-36)}}{2} = \frac{28 \pm \sqrt{928}}{2}$$
$$= \frac{28 \pm 4\sqrt{58}}{2} = 14 \pm 2\sqrt{58} = -1.2 \text{ or } 29.2$$

A would take 29.2 hours working alone.

62. Let $x =$ Cicely's time alone and $x + 3 =$ Eva's time alone. At 5 P.M. Cicely has done $\frac{8}{x}$ of the payroll and Eva has done $\frac{6}{x+3}$ of the payroll. Since it is $\frac{9}{10}$ done at that time we have the following equation.
$$\frac{8}{x} + \frac{6}{x+3} = \frac{9}{10}$$
$$10(x)(x+3)\left(\frac{8}{x} + \frac{6}{x+3}\right) = 10x(x+3)\frac{9}{10}$$
$$80x + 240 + 60x = 9x^2 + 27x$$
$$0 = 9x^2 - 113x - 240$$
$$x = \frac{113 \pm \sqrt{113^2 - 4(9)(-240)}}{18} \approx 14.41 \text{ or}$$
-1.85

Rate together is $\frac{1}{14.41} + \frac{1}{17.41}$, or 0.1268 payroll/hr. So together they take $\frac{1}{0.1268}$ or 7.88 hrs to complete the payroll. So they will finish the last tenth of the payroll in 0.788 h, or 47 min.

63.
$$\frac{10}{W} = \frac{W}{10 - W}$$
$$100 - 10W = W^2$$
$$W^2 + 10W - 100 = 0$$

$$W = \frac{-10 \pm \sqrt{10^2 - 4(1)(-100)}}{2}$$
$$= \frac{-10 \pm 10\sqrt{5}}{2}$$
$$W = -5 \pm 5\sqrt{5} \approx -16.2 \text{ or } 6.2$$

So the width is 6.2 meters.

66. $\{1, 2\}$

67. $\{-10, -4, 4, 10\}$

68. $\{-4.25, -3.49, 0.49, 1.25\}$

69. $\{4.27\}$

8.4 WARM-UPS

1. False, solution set is $(-\infty, -2) \cup (2, \infty)$.

2. False, we do not multiply each side by a variable.

3. False, that is not how we solve a quadratic inequality.

4. False, we can solve any quadratic inequality.

5. True, that is why we make the sign graph.

6. True, because inequalities change direction when multiplied by a negative number and we do not know if the variable is positive or negative.

7. True, because the solution is based on rules for multiplying or dividing signed numbers.

8. True, multiply each side by 2.

9. True, subtract 1 from each side.

10. False, because 4 causes the denominator to be 0 and so it cannot be in the solution set.

8.4 EXERCISES

1. A quadratic inequality has the form $ax^2 + bx + c > 0$. In place of $>$ we can also use $<$, $\leq$, or $\geq$.

2. A sign graph shows signs of the factors for all possible values of x.

3. A rational inequality is an inequality involving a rational expression.

4. Multiplying each side by a positive number does not change the direction of the inequality, but multiplying by a negative number does. So if we multiply by a variable it is difficulty to know which way the inequality goes.

5. $(x + 3)(x - 2) < 0$

```
x + 3 - - - - 0 + + + + + + +
x - 2 - - - - - - - - 0 + + + +
        -3          2
```

The product is negative only if the factors have opposite signs. That happens when x is chosen between -3 and 2.

$(-3, 2)$

6. $x^2 - 3x - 4 \geq 0$
$(x - 4)(x + 1) \geq 0$

```
x - 4 - - - - - - 0 + + + + +
x + 1 - - 0 + + + + + + + + +
        -1          4
```

The product is positive only if the factors have the same sign. That happens if x is chosen to the left of -1 or to the right of 4. The product is 0 if x is either -1 or 4.

$(-\infty, -1] \cup [4, \infty)$

7. $y^2 - 4 > 0$
$(y - 2)(y + 2) > 0$

```
y + 2 - - - - 0 + + + + + + +
y - 2 - - - - - - - 0 + + + +
        -2          2
```

The product is positive if both factors are positive or both are negative.

$(-\infty, -2) \cup (2, \infty)$

8. $z^2 < 16$
$z^2 - 16 < 0$
$(z - 4)(z + 4) < 0$

```
z + 4 - - - 0 + + + + + + + +
z - 4 - - - - - - - 0 + + + +
        -4          4
```

The product is negative only if the factors have opposite signs. That happens if x is chosen between -4 and 4. At ± 4 the product is 0.

$(-4, 4)$

9. $2u^2 + 5u - 12 \geq 0$

    $(2u - 3)(u + 4) \geq 0$

$2u - 3 - - - - - - - 0 + + +$
$u + 4 - - - 0 + + + + + + +$
        -4 $3/2$

The product is positive only if the factors have the same sign. That happens if u is chosen to the left of -4 or to the right of $3/2$. The product is 0 if u is either -4 or $3/2$.
$(-\infty, -4] \cup [\frac{3}{2}, \infty)$

10. $2v^2 + 7v - 4 < 0$

    $(2v - 1)(v + 4) < 0$

$v + 4 - - - - 0 + + + + + + + +$
$2v - 1 - - - - - - - - - - 0 + + +$
        -4 $1/2$

The product is negative only if the value of v is between -4 and $1/2$. The solution set and its graph follow:
$(-4, \frac{1}{2})$

11. $4x^2 - 8x \geq 0$

    $4x(x - 2) \geq 0$

$4x - - - 0 + + + + + + + +$
$x - 2 - - - - - - - - 0 + + + +$
      0 2

The product is greater than zero when the signs are the same.
$(-\infty, 0] \cup [2, \infty)$

12. $x(x + 1) > 0$

$x + 1 - - - - 0 + + + + + + +$
$x \quad\quad - - - - - - - - - 0 + + +$
        -1 0

The product is positive only if the factors have the same sign.
$(-\infty, -1) \cup (0, \infty)$

13. $5x(1 - 2x) < 0$

$5x \quad\quad - - 0 + + + + + + + +$
$1 - 2x + + + + + + 0 - - - -$
        0 $1/2$

The product is negative only if the factors have opposite signs.
$(-\infty, 0) \cup (\frac{1}{2}, \infty)$

14. $3x - x^2 > 0$

        $x(3 - x) > 0$

$x \quad\quad - - 0 + + + + + + + + +$
$3 - x + + + + + + + 0 - - - -$
      0 3

The product is positive only if the factors have the same sign.
$(0, 3)$

15. $x^2 + 6x + 9 \geq 0$

    $(x + 3)(x + 3) \geq 0$

$x + 3 - - - - - 0 + + + +$
$x + 3 - - - - - 0 + + + +$
         -3

The product is positive only if the factors have the same sign. That happens for every value of x except -3, in which case the product is 0. The solution set is the set of all real numbers, $(-\infty, \infty)$.

16. $x^2 + 25 < 10x$

    $x^2 - 10x + 25 < 0$

        $(x - 5)^2 < 0$

$x - 5 - - - - - - 0+ + + +$
$x - 5 - - - - - - 0+ + + +$
$$\overline{}$$
$ 5$

The product is negative only if the factors have opposite signs. That cannot happen in this case. The solution set is the empty set $\emptyset$.

17. $\quad \dfrac{x}{x-3} > 0$

$x \quad - - - - 0+ + + + + + +$
$x - 3 - - - - - - 0+ + + +$
$$\overline{}$$
$ 0 3$

he quotient is positive only if the numerator and denominator have the same sign.
$(-\infty, 0) \cup (3, \infty)$

18. $\quad \dfrac{a}{a+2} > 0$

$a + 2 - - - - 0+ + + + + + + +$
$a \quad - - - - - - - - - - 0+ + +$
$$\overline{}$$
$ -2 0$

The quotient is positive only if the numerator and denominator have the same sign.
$(-\infty, -2) \cup (0, \infty)$

19. $\quad \dfrac{x+2}{x} \leq 0$

$x + 2 - - - - 0+ + + + + + +$
$x \quad - - - - - - - 0+ + + +$
$$\overline{}$$
$ -2 0$

The quotient is negative only if the numerator and denominator have opposite signs. Since the denominator must not be 0, we do not include 0 in the solution set.
$[-2, 0)$

20. $\quad \dfrac{w-6}{w} \leq 0$

$w - - - - 0+ + + + + + +$
$w - 6 - - - - - - 0+ + + +$
$$\overline{}$$
$ 0 6$

The quotient is negative only if the numerator and denominator have opposite signs. Since the denominator must not be 0, we do not include 0 in the solution set.
$(0, 6]$

21. $\quad \dfrac{t-3}{t+6} > 0$

$t + 6 - - - 0+ + + + + + +$
$t - 3 - - - - - - - 0+ + +$
$$\overline{}$$
$ -6 3$

The quotient is positive only if the numerator and denominator have the same sign.
$(-\infty, -6) \cup (3, \infty)$

22. $\quad \dfrac{x-2}{2x+5} < 0$

$2x + 5 - - - 0+ + + + + + + +$
$x - 2 - - - - - - - 0+ + + +$
$$\overline{}$$
$ -5/2 2$

The quotient is negative only if the numerator and denominator have opposite signs.
$\left(-\dfrac{5}{2}, 2\right)$

23. $\quad \dfrac{x}{x+2} + 1 > 0$
$ \dfrac{x}{x+2} + \dfrac{x+2}{x+2} > 0$
$ \dfrac{2x+2}{x+2} > 0$

$x + 2 - - - - 0+ + + + + + +$
$2x + 2 - - - - - - 0+ + + +$
$$\overline{}$$
$ -2 -1$

The quotient is positive only if the numerator and denominator have the same sign.
$(-\infty, -2) \cup (-1, \infty)$

24. $\quad \dfrac{x+3}{x} \leq -2$
$ \dfrac{x+3}{x} + 2 \leq 0$

$$\frac{x+3}{x} + \frac{2x}{x} \leq 0$$
$$\frac{3x+3}{x} \leq 0$$

$3x+3 \quad - \; - \; 0 + + + + + + + +$
$x \qquad\quad - \; - \; - \; - \; - \; - \; - \; - \; 0 + + + +$
$\qquad\qquad\qquad -1 \qquad\qquad\quad 0$

The quotient is negative only if the numerator and denominator have opposite signs. The quotient is zero only if the numerator is zero.
$[-1, 0)$

25.
$$\frac{2}{x-5} > \frac{1}{x+4}$$
$$\frac{2}{x-5} - \frac{1}{x+4} > 0$$
$$\frac{2(x+4)}{(x-5)(x+4)} - \frac{1(x-5)}{(x+4)(x-5)} > 0$$
$$\frac{x+13}{(x-5)(x+4)} > 0$$

$x+4 \quad - \; - \; - \; - \; 0 + + + + + + +$
$x+13 \quad - \; 0 + + + + + + + + +$
$x-5 \quad - \; - \; - \; - \; - \; - \; - \; 0 + + +$
$\qquad\qquad -13 \qquad -4 \qquad\quad 5$

This quotient will be positive only if an even number of the factors have negative values.
$(-13, -4) \cup (5, \infty)$

26.
$$\frac{3}{x+2} - \frac{2}{x-1} > 0$$
$$\frac{3(x-1)}{(x+2)(x-1)} - \frac{2(x+2)}{(x-1)(x+2)} > 0$$
$$\frac{x-7}{(x+2)(x-1)} > 0$$

$x-1 \quad - \; - \; - \; - \; 0 + + + + + + + +$
$x+2 \quad - \; - \; 0 + + + + + + + + + +$
$x-7 \quad - \; - \; - \; - \; - \; - \; - \; 0 + + + +$
$\qquad\qquad -2 \qquad\quad 1 \qquad\qquad 7$

This quotient will be positive only if an even number of the factors have negative values.
$(-2, 1) \cup (7, \infty)$

27. $\dfrac{m(m-1)}{(m-5)(m-1)} + \dfrac{3(m-5)}{(m-1)(m-5)} > 0$

$$\frac{m^2+2m-15}{(m-1)(m-5)} > 0$$
$$\frac{(m+5)(m-3)}{(m-1)(m-5)} > 0$$

$m-3 \quad - \; - \; - \; - \; - \; - \; - \; 0 + + + + +$
$m-1 \quad - \; - \; - \; - \; 0 + + + + + + + + +$
$m+5 \quad - \; - \; 0 + + + + + + + + + + +$
$m-5 \quad - \; - \; - \; - \; - \; - \; - \; - \; - \; - \; - \; 0 + +$
$\qquad\qquad -5 \qquad\quad 1 \qquad\quad 3 \qquad\quad 5$

This quotient is positive only if there is an even number of factors with negative signs.
$(-\infty, -5) \cup (1, 3) \cup (5, \infty)$

28.
$$\frac{p}{p-16} + \frac{2}{p-6} \leq 0$$
$$\frac{p(p-6)}{(p-16)(p-6)} + \frac{2(p-16)}{(p-6)(p-16)} \leq 0$$
$$\frac{p^2-4p-32}{(p-16)(p-6)} \leq 0$$
$$\frac{(p-8)(p+4)}{(p-16)(p-6)} \leq 0$$

$p-8 \quad - \; - \; - \; - \; - \; - \; 0 + + + + +$
$p-6 \quad - \; - \; - \; 0 + + + + + + + + +$
$p+4 \quad - \; 0 + + + + + + + + + + +$
$p-16 \quad - \; - \; - \; - \; - \; - \; - \; - \; 0 + + + +$
$\qquad\qquad -4 \qquad\quad 6 \qquad\quad 8 \qquad\quad 16$

The quotient is negative only if an odd number of factors have negative signs. Note that 6 and 16 cause the denominator to have a value of 0, and so they are excluded from the solution set.
$[-4, 6) \cup [8, 16)$

29.
$$\frac{x}{x-3} + \frac{8}{x-6} \leq 0$$
$$\frac{x(x-6)}{(x-3)(x-6)} + \frac{8(x-3)}{(x-6)(x-3)} \leq 0$$
$$\frac{x^2+2x-24}{(x-3)(x-6)} \leq 0$$
$$\frac{(x+6)(x-4)}{(x-3)(x-6)} \leq 0$$

$x-4 \quad - \; - \; - \; - \; - \; - \; - \; 0 + + + + +$
$x-3 \quad - \; - \; - \; - \; 0 + + + + + + + +$
$x+6 \quad - \; - \; 0 + + + + + + + + + + +$
$x-6 \quad - \; - \; - \; - \; - \; - \; - \; - \; - \; 0 + +$
$\qquad\qquad -6 \qquad\quad 3 \qquad\quad 4 \qquad\quad 6$

The quotient is negative only if an odd number of factors have negative signs. Note that 3 and 6 cause the denominator to have a value of 0, and so they are excluded from the solution set.
$[-6, 3) \cup [4, 6)$

30.
$$\frac{x}{x+20} > \frac{2}{x+8}$$
$$\frac{x}{x+20} - \frac{2}{x+8} > 0$$
$$\frac{x(x+8)}{(x+20)(x+8)} - \frac{2(x+20)}{(x+8)(x+20)} > 0$$
$$\frac{x^2 + 6x - 40}{(x+20)(x+8)} > 0$$
$$\frac{(x+10)(x-4)}{(x+8)(x+20)} > 0$$

$x+8 \ - - - - - - - 0 + + + + +$
$x+10 \ - - - - 0 + + + + + + +$
$x+20 \ - - 0 + + + + + + + + +$
$x-4 \ - - - - - - - - - - 0 + + +$
$\qquad -20 \quad -10 \quad -8 \qquad 4$

This quotient is positive only if there is an even number of factors with negative signs.
$(-\infty, -20) \cup (-10, -8) \cup (4, \infty)$

31. To solve $x^2 - 2x - 4 > 0$, first solve $x^2 - 2x - 4 = 0$:
$$x = \frac{2 \pm \sqrt{4 - 4(1)(-4)}}{2(1)} = \frac{2 \pm 2\sqrt{5}}{2}$$
$$= 1 \pm \sqrt{5}$$
The two solutions to the equation divide the number line into three regions. Choose one number in each region, say -10, 0, and 10. Now evaluate $x^2 - 2x - 4$ for the numbers -10, 0, and 10.
$$(-10)^2 - 2(-10) - 4 = 116$$
$$0^2 - 2(0) - 4 = -4$$
$$10^2 - 2(10) - 4 = 76$$
The signs of these answers indicate the solution to the inequality.
$(-\infty, 1 - \sqrt{5}) \cup (1 + \sqrt{5}, \infty)$

32. To solve $x^2 - 2x - 5 \leq 0$ we first solve $x^2 - 2x - 5 = 0$:
$$x = \frac{2 \pm \sqrt{4 - 4(1)(-5)}}{2(1)} = \frac{2 \pm 2\sqrt{6}}{2} = 1 \pm \sqrt{6}$$

The two solutions to the equation divide the number line into three regions. Choose one number in each region, say -10, 0, and 10. Now evaluate $x^2 - 2x - 5$ for the numbers -10, 0, and 10.
$$(-10)^2 - 2(-10) - 5 = 115$$
$$0^2 - 2(0) - 5 = -5$$
$$10^2 - 2(10) - 5 = 75$$
The signs of these answers indicate the solution to the inequality.
$[1 - \sqrt{6}, 1 + \sqrt{6}]$

33. To solve $2x^2 - 6x + 3 \geq 0$, we first solve $2x^2 - 6x + 3 = 0$.
$$x = \frac{6 \pm \sqrt{36 - 4(2)(3)}}{2(2)} = \frac{3 \pm \sqrt{3}}{2}$$
The two solutions to the equation divide the number line into three regions. Choose a test point in each region, say -10, 2, and 10. Evaluate the polynomial $2x^2 - 6x + 3$ at each of these points.
$$2(-10)^2 - 6(-10) + 3 = 263$$
$$2(2)^2 - 6(2) + 3 = -1$$
$$2(10)^2 - 6(10) + 3 = 143$$
The signs of these answers indicate the regions that satisfy the inequality.
$(-\infty, \frac{3-\sqrt{3}}{2}] \cup [\frac{3+\sqrt{3}}{2}, \infty)$

34. To solve $2x^2 - 8x + 3 < 0$, we first solve $2x^2 - 8x + 3 = 0$.
$$x = \frac{8 \pm \sqrt{64 - 4(2)(3)}}{2(2)} = \frac{8 \pm \sqrt{40}}{4}$$
$$= \frac{4 \pm \sqrt{10}}{2}$$
The two solutions to the equation divide the number line into three regions. Choose a test

point in each region, say -10, 2, and 10.
Evaluate the polynomial $2x^2 - 8x + 3$ at each of these points.

$$2(-10)^2 - 8(-10) + 3 = 283$$
$$2(2)^2 - 8(2) + 3 = -5$$
$$2(10)^2 - 8(10) + 3 = 123$$

The signs of these answers indicate the regions that satisfy the inequality.
$$\left(\frac{4-\sqrt{10}}{2}, \frac{4+\sqrt{10}}{2} \right)$$

35. To solve $y^2 - 3y - 9 \le 0$ we first solve $y^2 - 3y - 9 = 0$:

$$y = \frac{3 \pm \sqrt{9 - 4(1)(-9)}}{2} = \frac{3 \pm 3\sqrt{5}}{2}$$

Pick test points -10, 4, and 10, and evaluate $y^2 - 3y - 9$ for these numbers.

$$(-10)^2 - 3(-10) - 9 = 121$$
$$4^2 - 3(4) - 9 = -5$$
$$10^2 - 3(10) - 9 = 61$$

The signs of these answers indicate which regions satisfy the original inequality.
$$\left[\frac{3-3\sqrt{5}}{2}, \frac{3+3\sqrt{5}}{2} \right]$$

36. To solve $z^2 - 5z - 7 < 0$, we first solve $z^2 - 5z - 7 = 0$.

$$z = \frac{5 \pm \sqrt{25 - 4(1)(-7)}}{2(1)} = \frac{5 \pm \sqrt{53}}{2}$$

The two solutions to the equation divide the number line into three regions. Choose a test point in each region, say -10, 2, and 10. Evaluate the polynomial $z^2 - 5z - 7$ at each of these points.

$$(-10)^2 - 5(-10) - 7 = 143$$
$$(2)^2 - 5(2) - 7 = -13$$
$$(10)^2 - 5(10) - 7 = 43$$

The signs of these answers indicate the regions that satisfy the inequality.
$$\left(\frac{5-\sqrt{53}}{2}, \frac{5+\sqrt{53}}{2} \right)$$

37. $x^2 - 9 \le 0$

$$(x - 3)(x + 3) \le 0$$

The product is negative only if the factors have opposite signs. That happens if x is chosen between -3 and 3. At ± 3 the product is 0. The solution set is $[-3, 3]$.

38. $x^2 \ge 36$
$$x^2 - 36 \ge 0$$
$$(x - 6)(x + 6) \ge 0$$

The product is positive if both factors are positive or both are negative. The solution set is $(-\infty, -6] \cup [6, \infty)$.

39. $16 - x^2 > 0$
$$-1(16 - x^2) > -1(0)$$
$$x^2 - 16 < 0$$
$$(x - 4)(x + 4) < 0$$

The product is negative only if the value of x is between -4 and 4. The solution set is $(-4, 4)$.

40. $9 - x^2 < 0$
$$x^2 - 9 > 0$$
$$(x - 3)(x + 3) > 0$$

The product is positive only if the factors have the same sign. The solution set is $(-\infty, -3) \cup (3, \infty)$.

41. $x^2 - 4x \ge 0$
$$x(x - 4) \ge 0$$

312

The product is positive only if the factors have the same sign. The solution set is $(-\infty, 0] \cup [4, \infty)$.

42. $\quad 4x^2 - 9 > 0$
$\quad\quad (2x - 3)(2x + 3) > 0$

$2x + 3 - \;-\;0+ + + + + + + + + +$
$\underline{2x - 3 - \;-\;-\;-\;-\;-\;0+ + + + +}$
$\quad\quad -3/2 \quad\quad\quad 3/2$

The product is positive only if the factors have the same sign. The solution set is $(-\infty, -\frac{3}{2}) \cup (\frac{3}{2}, \infty)$.

43. $\quad\quad 6w^2 - 15 < w$
$\quad\quad\quad 6w^2 - w - 15 < 0$
$\quad\quad\quad (2w + 3)(3w - 5) < 0$

$2w + 3 - \;-\;-\;0+ + + + + + + + +$
$\underline{3w - 5 - \;-\;-\;-\;-\;-\;-\;-\;0+ + +}$
$\quad\quad\quad -3/2 \quad\quad\quad\quad 5/3$

The product is negative only if the factors have opposite signs. The solution set is $(-\frac{3}{2}, \frac{5}{3})$.

44. $\quad 6(y^2 - 2) + y < 0$
$\quad\quad 6y^2 - 12 + y < 0$
$\quad\quad 6y^2 + y - 12 < 0$
$\quad\quad (2y + 3)(3y - 4) < 0$

$2y + 3 - \;-\;0+ + + + + + + + + +$
$\underline{3y - 4 - \;-\;-\;-\;-\;-\;-\;-\;0+ + +}$
$\quad\quad -3/2 \quad\quad\quad\quad 4/3$

The product is negative only if the factors have opposite signs. The solution set is $(-\frac{3}{2}, \frac{4}{3})$.

45. $\quad\quad\quad z^2 \geq 4z + 12$
$\quad\quad\quad z^2 - 4z - 12 \geq 0$
$\quad\quad\quad (z - 6)(z + 2) \geq 0$

$z + 2 - \;-\;-\;-\;0+ + + + + + + + +$
$\underline{z - 6 - \;-\;-\;-\;-\;-\;-\;-\;0+ + + +}$
$\quad\quad -2 \quad\quad\quad\quad 6$

The product is positive only if the factors have the same sign. The solution set is $(-\infty, -2] \cup [6, \infty)$.

46. $\quad t^2 - 6t + 9 < 0$
$\quad\quad (t - 3)(t - 3) < 0$

$t - 3 - \;-\;-\;-\;-\;-\;-\;-\;0+ + + +$
$\underline{t - 3 - \;-\;-\;-\;-\;-\;-\;-\;0+ + + +}$
$\quad\quad\quad\quad\quad\quad 3$

The product is negative only if the factors have opposite signs, but that is impossible. The solution set is $\emptyset$.

47. $\quad q^2 + 8q + 16 > 10q + 31$
$\quad\quad q^2 - 2q - 15 > 0$
$\quad\quad (q + 3)(q - 5) > 0$

$q + 3 - \;-\;-\;-\;0+ + + + + + + + +$
$\underline{q - 5 - \;-\;-\;-\;-\;-\;-\;-\;0+ + + +}$
$\quad\quad -3 \quad\quad\quad\quad 5$

The product is positive only if the factors have the same sign. The solution set is $(-\infty, -3) \cup (5, \infty)$.

48. $\quad 2p^2 + 2p - 4 < p^2 + 4p + 4$
$\quad\quad p^2 - 2p - 8 < 0$
$\quad\quad (p - 4)(p + 2) < 0$

$p + 2 - \;-\;-\;-\;0+ + + + + + + + +$
$\underline{p - 4 - \;-\;-\;-\;-\;-\;-\;-\;0+ + + +}$
$\quad\quad -2 \quad\quad\quad\quad 4$

The product is negative only if the factors have opposite signs. The solution set is $(-2, 4)$.

49. $\quad\quad \frac{1}{2}x^2 \geq 4 - x$
$\quad\quad\quad x^2 \geq 8 - 2x$
$\quad\quad x^2 + 2x - 8 \geq 0$
$\quad\quad (x + 4)(x - 2) \geq 0$

$x + 4 - \;-\;-\;0+ + + + + + + + + +$
$\underline{x - 2 - \;-\;-\;-\;-\;-\;-\;0+ + + +}$
$\quad\quad -4 \quad\quad\quad\quad 2$

The product is positive only if the factors have the same sign. The solution set is $(-\infty, -4] \cup [2, \infty)$.

50. $\quad\quad \frac{1}{2}x^2 - x - 12 \leq 0$
$\quad\quad\quad x^2 - 2x - 24 \leq 0$
$\quad\quad (x - 6)(x + 4) \leq 0$

$x + 4 - \;-\;-\;-\;0+ + + + + + + + +$
$\underline{x - 6 - \;-\;-\;-\;-\;-\;-\;-\;0+ + + +}$
$\quad\quad -4 \quad\quad\quad\quad 6$

The product is negative only if the factors have opposite signs. The solution set is $[-4, 6]$.

51. $\frac{x-4}{x+3} \leq 0$

$$x+3 \;-\;-\;-\;-\;0+\;+\;+\;+\;+\;+\;+\;+$$
$$x-4 \;-\;-\;-\;-\;-\;-\;-\;-\;0+\;+\;+\;+$$
$$\overline{\qquad\qquad -3 \qquad\qquad 4 \qquad\quad}$$

The quotient is negative if the factors have opposite signs. The solution set is $(-3, 4]$.

52. $\frac{2x-1}{x+5} \geq 0$

$$x+5 \;-\;-\;-\;-\;0+\;+\;+\;+\;+\;+\;+\;+$$
$$2x-1 \;-\;-\;-\;-\;-\;-\;-\;0+\;+\;+\;+$$
$$\overline{\qquad\qquad -5 \qquad\qquad 1/2 \qquad\quad}$$

The quotient is positive if the factors have the same sign. The solution set is $(-\infty, -5) \cup [\frac{1}{2}, \infty)$.

53. $(x-2)(x+1)(x-5) \geq 0$

$$x-2 \;-\;-\;-\;-\;0+\;+\;+\;+\;+\;+\;+\;+$$
$$x+1 \;-\;-\;0+\;+\;+\;+\;+\;+\;+\;+\;+\;+$$
$$x-5 \;-\;-\;-\;-\;-\;-\;-\;-\;0+\;+\;+\;+$$
$$\overline{\quad -1 \qquad 2 \qquad\qquad 5 \qquad\quad}$$

The product of these three factors is positive only if an even number of the factors have negative signs. This happens between -1 and 2, and also above 5 where no factors have negative signs. The solution set is $[-1, 2] \cup [5, \infty)$.

54. $(x-1)(x+2)(2x-5) < 0$

$$x-1 \;-\;-\;-\;-\;-\;0+\;+\;+\;+\;+\;+\;+$$
$$x+2 \;-\;-\;0+\;+\;+\;+\;+\;+\;+\;+\;+\;+$$
$$2x-5 \;-\;-\;-\;-\;-\;-\;-\;-\;0+\;+\;+\;+$$
$$\overline{\quad -2 \qquad 1 \qquad\quad 2.5 \qquad\quad}$$

The product of these three factors is negative only if an odd number of them have negative signs. This happens to the left of -2 and also between 1 and 2.5. The solution set is $(-\infty, -2) \cup (1, 2.5)$.

55.
$$x^2(x+3) - 1(x+3) < 0$$
$$(x^2 - 1)(x+3) < 0$$
$$(x-1)(x+1)(x+3) < 0$$

$$x+1 \;-\;-\;-\;-\;-\;0+\;+\;+\;+\;+\;+\;+$$
$$x+3 \;-\;-\;0+\;+\;+\;+\;+\;+\;+\;+\;+\;+$$
$$x-1 \;-\;-\;-\;-\;-\;-\;-\;-\;0+\;+\;+$$
$$\overline{\quad -3 \qquad -1 \qquad\quad 1 \qquad\quad}$$

The product of these three factors is negative only if an odd number of them have negative signs. This happens to the left of -3 and also between -1 and 1. The solution set is $(-\infty, -3) \cup (-1, 1)$.

56.
$$x^3 + 5x^2 - 4x - 20 \geq 0$$
$$x^2(x+5) - 4(x+5) \geq 0$$
$$(x^2 - 4)(x+5) \geq 0$$
$$(x-2)(x+2)(x+5) \geq 0$$

$$x+2 \;-\;-\;-\;-\;-\;0+\;+\;+\;+\;+\;+\;+$$
$$x+5 \;-\;-\;0+\;+\;+\;+\;+\;+\;+\;+\;+\;+$$
$$x-2 \;-\;-\;-\;-\;-\;-\;-\;-\;-\;-\;0+\;+$$
$$\overline{\quad -5 \qquad -2 \qquad\qquad 2 \qquad\quad}$$

The product of these three factors is positive only if an even number of the factors have negative signs. This happens between -5 and -2, and also above 2 where no factors have negative signs. The solution set is $[-5, -2] \cup [2, \infty)$.

57. To solve $0.23x^2 + 6.5x + 4.3 < 0$, we first solve $0.23x^2 + 6.5x + 4.3 = 0$.
$$x = \frac{-6.5 \pm \sqrt{(6.5)^2 - 4(0.23)(4.3)}}{2(0.23)}$$

$x = -27.58$ or $x = -0.68$
Test the numbers -30, -1, and 0.
$$0.23(-30)^2 + 6.5(-30) + 4.3 = 16.3$$
$$0.23(-1)^2 + 6.5(-1) + 4.3 = -1.97$$
$$0.23(0)^2 + 6.5(0) + 4.3 = 4.3$$

According to the signs of the values of the polynomial at the test points, the value of the polynomial is negative between the two solutions to the equation. The solution set is $(-27.58, -0.68)$.

58. To solve $0.65x^2 + 3.2x + 5.1 > 0$, we first solve $0.65x^2 + 3.2x + 5.1 = 0$.
$$x = \frac{-3.2 \pm \sqrt{(3.2)^2 - 4(0.65)(5.1)}}{2(0.65)}$$

Because $(3.2)^2 - 4(0.65)(5.1)$ is negative there are no real solutions to the equation. So test any real number. Test the number 0.
$$0.65(0)^2 + 3.2(0) + 5.1 > 0$$
So the inequality is satisfied for any real number and the solution is $(-\infty, \infty)$.

59.

$$\frac{x}{x-2} + \frac{1}{x+3} > 0$$

$$\frac{x(x+3)}{(x-2)(x+3)} + \frac{1(x-2)}{(x+3)(x-2)} > 0$$

$$\frac{x^2+4x-2}{(x+3)(x-2)} > 0$$

Solve $x^2+4x-2 = 0$:

$$x = \frac{-4 \pm \sqrt{16-4(1)(-2)}}{2} = \frac{-4 \pm 2\sqrt{6}}{2}$$

$$= -2 \pm \sqrt{6} = -4.4, 0.4$$

The numbers -4.4, -3, 0.4, and 2 divide the number line into 5 regions. Pick a number in each region and test it in the original inequality. We get the solution set $(-\infty, -2-\sqrt{6}) \cup (-3, -2+\sqrt{6}) \cup (2, \infty)$.

60.

$$\frac{x}{3-x} > \frac{2}{x+5}$$

$$\frac{x}{3-x} - \frac{2}{x+5} > 0$$

$$\frac{x(x+5)}{(3-x)(x+5)} - \frac{2(3-x)}{(x+5)(3-x)} > 0$$

$$\frac{x^2+7x-6}{(3-x)(x+5)} > 0$$

Solve $x^2+7x-6 = 0$:

$$x = \frac{-7 \pm \sqrt{49-4(1)(-6)}}{2} = \frac{-7 \pm \sqrt{73}}{2}$$

$$\frac{-7-\sqrt{73}}{2} \approx -7.77$$

$$\frac{-7+\sqrt{73}}{2} \approx 0.772$$

The numbers -7.77, -5, 0.772, and 3 divide the number line into 5 regions. Pick a number in each region and test it in the original inequality. We get the solution set $\left(\frac{-7-\sqrt{73}}{2}, -5\right) \cup \left(\frac{-7+\sqrt{73}}{2}, 3\right)$.

61. To solve $x^2+5x-50 > 0$, we first solve $x^2+5x-50 = 0$:

$$(x+10)(x-5) = 0$$

$$x = -10 \text{ or } x = 5$$

Test a point in each region of the number line, to find that the profit is positive if $x < -10$ or if $x > 5$. He cannot sell negative mobile homes so he must sell more than 5 to have a positive profit. He should sell 6, 7, 8, etc.

62. Since profit is revenue minus cost, we can write

$$P = 50x - x^2 - (2x+40) = -x^2 + 48x - 40$$

We must solve the inequality $-x^2 + 48x - 40 > 0$. First solve the equation $-x^2 + 48x - 40 = 0$

$$x = \frac{-48 \pm \sqrt{(48)^2 - 4(-1)(-40)}}{2(-1)}$$

$$= \frac{-48 \pm \sqrt{2144}}{-2} = 47.15, \ 0.84$$

Test a point in each region, say 0, 1, 50.

$$-(0)^2 + 48(0) - 40 = -40$$

$$-(1)^2 + 48(1) - 40 = 7$$

$$-(50)^2 + 48(50) - 40 = -140$$

The profit is positive for values of x between 0.84 and 47.15. So her profit is positive if the number of fruit cakes is 1, 2, 3, ..., 47.

63. We must solve the inequality

$$-16t^2 + 96t + 6 > 86$$

$$-16t^2 + 96t - 80 > 0$$

$$t^2 - 6t + 5 < 0$$

Solve the equation $t^2 - 6t + 5 = 0$.

$$(t-5)(t-1) = 0$$

$$t = 5 \text{ or } t = 1$$

Using a test point we find that the inequality is satisfied for t between 1 and 5 seconds. So the arrow is more than 86 feet high for 4 seconds.

64. We must solve the inequality

$$-16t^2 + 30t + 5 < 15$$

$$-16t^2 + 30t - 10 < 0$$

$$8t^2 - 15t + 5 > 0$$

First solve $8t^2 - 15t + 5 = 0$.

$$t = \frac{15 \pm \sqrt{225 - 4(8)(5)}}{2(8)} = \frac{15 \pm \sqrt{65}}{16}$$

$$t = 0.43 \text{ or } t = 1.44$$

By testing a point in each region of the number line, we determine that the inequality is satisfied to the left of 0.43 or to the right of 1.44. So the shot is under 15 feet high when $t < 0.43$ seconds or $t > 1.44$ seconds.

65. a) From the graph it appears that the maximum height is 900 feet.

b) The projectile was above 864 feet for approximately 3 seconds.

c) $S = -16t^2 + \dfrac{240\sqrt{2}}{\sqrt{2}}t + 0$

Solve

$$-16t^2 + \frac{240\sqrt{2}}{\sqrt{2}}t > 864$$

$-16t^2 + 240t - 864 > 0$
$t^2 - 15t + 54 < 0$

Solve the equation

$(t - 6)(t - 9) = 0$
$t = 6$ or $t = 9$

Evaluate $t^2 - 15t + 54$ at the test points 0, 7, and 10.

$0^2 - 15(0) + 54 = 54$
$7^2 - 15(7) + 54 = -2$
$10^2 - 15(10) + 54 = 4$

So the inequality is satisfied for t in the interval $(6, 9)$. The projectile was above 864 ft for 3 sec.

66. $S = -16t^2 + \dfrac{644}{\sqrt{2}}t + 100$

Solve

$-16t^2 + \dfrac{644}{\sqrt{2}}t + 100 > 800$

$-16t^2 + \dfrac{644}{\sqrt{2}}t - 700 > 0$

$t^2 - 28.461t + 43.75 < 0$

Solve the equation

$t^2 - 28.461t + 43.75 < 0$

$t = \dfrac{28.461 \pm \sqrt{28.461^2 - 4(1)(43.75)}}{2}$

$= 26.83, 1.63$

So the inequality is satisfied for t in the interval $(1.63, 26.83)$. The projectile was above 800 ft for 25.2 sec.

67. a) (h, k)
b) $(-\infty, h) \cup (k, \infty)$
c) $(-k, -h)$
d) $(-\infty, -k] \cup [-h, \infty)$
e) $(-\infty, h] \cup (k, \infty)$
f) $(-k, -h]$

68. a) $(-\infty, -b/(2a)) \cup (-b/(2a), \infty)$
b) $\emptyset$
c) $(-\infty, \infty)$
d) $\emptyset$
e) $\left(-\infty, \dfrac{-b-\sqrt{b^2-4ac}}{2a}\right) \cup \left(\dfrac{-b+\sqrt{b^2-4ac}}{2a}, \infty\right)$
f) $\left(\dfrac{-b-\sqrt{b^2-4ac}}{2a}, \dfrac{-b+\sqrt{b^2-4ac}}{2a}\right)$

69. c
70. d
71 b
72 a

Enriching Your Mathematical Word Power
1. b   2. a   3. d   4. c   5. b
6. c   7. a   8. c   9. a   10. c

CHAPTER 8   REVIEW

1. $x^2 - 2x - 15 = 0$
$(x - 5)(x + 3) = 0$
$x - 5 = 0$ or $x + 3 = 0$
$x = 5$ or $x = -3$
Solution set: $\{-3, 5\}$

2. $x^2 - 2x - 24 = 0$
$(x - 6)(x + 4) = 0$
$x - 6 = 0$ or $x + 4 = 0$
$x = 6$ or $x = -4$
The solution set is $\{-4, 6\}$.

3. $2x^2 + x - 15 = 0$
$(2x - 5)(x + 3) = 0$
$2x - 5 = 0$ or $x + 3 = 0$
$x = \frac{5}{2}$ or $x = -3$
Solution set: $\left\{-3, \frac{5}{2}\right\}$

4. $2x^2 + 7x = 4$
$2x^2 + 7x - 4 = 0$
$(2x - 1)(x + 4) = 0$
$2x - 1 = 0$ or $x + 4 = 0$
$x = \frac{1}{2}$ or $x = -4$
The solution set is $\left\{-4, \frac{1}{2}\right\}$.

5. $w^2 - 25 = 0$
$(w - 5)(w + 5) = 0$
$w - 5 = 0$ or $w + 5 = 0$
$w = 5$ or $w = -5$
Solution set: $\{-5, 5\}$

6. $a^2 - 121 = 0$
$(a - 11)(a + 11) = 0$
$a - 11 = 0$ or $a + 11 = 0$
$a = 11$ or $a = -11$
The solution set is $\{-11, 11\}$

7. $4x^2 - 12x + 9 = 0$
$(2x - 3)^2 = 0$
$2x - 3 = 0$
$x = \frac{3}{2}$
Solution set: $\left\{\frac{3}{2}\right\}$

8. $x^2 - 12x + 36 = 0$
$(x - 6)^2 = 0$
$x - 6 = 0$
$x = 6$
The solution set is $\{6\}$.

9. $x^2 = 12$
$x = \pm\sqrt{12} = \pm 2\sqrt{3}$
Solution set: $\{\pm 2\sqrt{3}\}$

10. $x^2 = 20$
$x = \pm\sqrt{20} = \pm 2\sqrt{5}$
The solution set is $\{\pm 2\sqrt{5}\}$.

11. $(x - 1)^2 = 9$
$x - 1 = \pm 3$
$x = 1 \pm 3$
Solution set: $\{-2, 4\}$

12. $(x + 4)^2 = 4$
$x + 4 = \pm 2$
$x = -4 \pm 2$
The solution set is $\{-6, -2\}$.

13. $(x - 2)^2 = \frac{3}{4}$
$x - 2 = \pm\sqrt{\frac{3}{4}}$
$x = 2 \pm \frac{\sqrt{3}}{2} = \frac{4}{2} \pm \frac{\sqrt{3}}{2}$

Solution set: $\left\{\frac{4 \pm \sqrt{3}}{2}\right\}$

14. $(x - 3)^2 = \frac{1}{4}$
$x - 3 = \pm\sqrt{\frac{1}{4}} = \pm\frac{1}{2}$
$x = 3 \pm \frac{1}{2}$
$x = 3 + \frac{1}{2} = \frac{7}{2}$ or $x = 3 - \frac{1}{2} = \frac{5}{2}$

The solution set is $\left\{\frac{5}{2}, \frac{7}{2}\right\}$.

15. $4x^2 = 9$
$x^2 = \frac{9}{4}$
$x = \pm\sqrt{\frac{9}{4}} = \pm\frac{3}{2}$

Solution set: $\left\{\pm\frac{3}{2}\right\}$

16. $2x^2 = 3$
$x^2 = \frac{3}{2}$
$x = \pm\sqrt{\frac{3}{2}} = \pm\frac{\sqrt{6}}{2}$
The solution set is $\left\{\pm\frac{\sqrt{6}}{2}\right\}$.

17. $x^2 - 6x = -8$
$x^2 - 6x + 9 = -8 + 9$
$(x - 3)^2 = 1$
$x - 3 = \pm 1$
$x = 3 \pm 1$
Solution set: $\{2, 4\}$

18. $x^2 + 4x + 3 = 0$
$x^2 + 4x = -3$
$x^2 + 4x + 4 = -3 + 4$
$(x + 2)^2 = 1$
$x + 2 = \pm 1$
$x = -2 \pm 1$
$x = -2 + 1 = -1$ or $x = -2 - 1 = -3$
The solution set is $\{-3, -1\}$.

19. $x^2 - 5x = -6$
$x^2 - 5x + \frac{25}{4} = -\frac{24}{4} + \frac{25}{4}$
$(x - \frac{5}{2})^2 = \frac{1}{4}$
$x - \frac{5}{2} = \pm\frac{1}{2}$
$x = \frac{5}{2} \pm \frac{1}{2} \quad \left(\frac{6}{2} \text{ or } \frac{4}{2}\right)$

Solution set: $\{2, 3\}$

20. $x^2 - x - 6 = 0$
$x^2 - x = 6$
$x^2 - x + \frac{1}{4} = 6 + \frac{1}{4}$
$(x - \frac{1}{2})^2 = \frac{25}{4}$
$x - \frac{1}{2} = \pm\frac{5}{2}$
$x = \frac{1}{2} \pm \frac{5}{2}$
$x = \frac{1}{2} + \frac{5}{2} = 3$ or $x = \frac{1}{2} - \frac{5}{2} = -2$
The solution set is $\{-2, 3\}$.

21. $2x^2 - 7x = -3$
$x^2 - \frac{7}{2}x = -\frac{3}{2}$
$x^2 - \frac{7}{2}x + \frac{49}{16} = -\frac{24}{16} + \frac{49}{16}$
$(x - \frac{7}{4})^2 = \frac{25}{16}$
$x - \frac{7}{4} = \pm\frac{5}{4}$
$x = \frac{7}{4} \pm \frac{5}{4} \quad \left(\frac{12}{4} \text{ or } \frac{2}{4}\right)$
Solution set: $\left\{\frac{1}{2}, 3\right\}$

22. $2x^2 - x = 6$
$x^2 - \frac{1}{2}x = 3$
$x^2 - \frac{1}{2}x + \frac{1}{16} = 3 + \frac{1}{16}$
$(x - \frac{1}{4})^2 = \frac{49}{16}$
$x - \frac{1}{4} = \pm\frac{7}{4}$
$x = \frac{1}{4} \pm \frac{7}{4}$
$x = \frac{1}{4} + \frac{7}{4} = 2$ or $x = \frac{1}{4} - \frac{7}{4} = -\frac{3}{2}$
The solution set is $\left\{-\frac{3}{2}, 2\right\}$.

23.
$$x^2 + 4x = -1$$
$$x^2 + 4x + 4 = -1 + 4$$
$$(x + 2)^2 = 3$$
$$x + 2 = \pm \sqrt{3}$$
$$x = -2 \pm \sqrt{3}$$
Solution set: $\{-2 \pm \sqrt{3}\}$

24.
$$x^2 + 2x - 2 = 0$$
$$x^2 + 2x = 2$$
$$x^2 + 2x + 1 = 2 + 1$$
$$(x + 1)^2 = 3$$
$$x + 1 = \pm \sqrt{3}$$
$$x = -1 \pm \sqrt{3}$$
The solution set is $\{-1 \pm \sqrt{3}\}$.

25.
$$x^2 - 3x - 10 = 0$$
$$x = \frac{3 \pm \sqrt{9 - 4(1)(-10)}}{2(1)} = \frac{3 \pm \sqrt{49}}{2}$$
$$= \frac{3 \pm 7}{2}$$
Solution set: $\{-2, 5\}$

26. $x^2 - 5x - 6 = 0$
$$x = \frac{5 \pm \sqrt{25 - 4(1)(-6)}}{2(1)} = \frac{5 \pm \sqrt{49}}{2}$$
$$= \frac{5 \pm 7}{2}$$
The solution set is $\{-1, 6\}$.

27.
$$6x^2 - 7x - 3 = 0$$
$$x = \frac{7 \pm \sqrt{49 - 4(6)(-3)}}{2(6)} = \frac{7 \pm \sqrt{121}}{12}$$
$$= \frac{7 \pm 11}{12}$$
Solution set: $\left\{-\frac{1}{3}, \frac{3}{2}\right\}$

28.
$$6x^2 = x + 2$$
$$6x^2 - x - 2 = 0$$
$$x = \frac{1 \pm \sqrt{1 - 4(6)(-2)}}{2(6)} = \frac{1 \pm \sqrt{49}}{12}$$
$$= \frac{1 \pm 7}{12}$$
The solution set is $\left\{-\frac{1}{2}, \frac{2}{3}\right\}$.

29.
$$x^2 + 4x + 2 = 0$$
$$x = \frac{-4 \pm \sqrt{16 - 4(1)(2)}}{2(1)} = \frac{-4 \pm 2\sqrt{2}}{2}$$
$$= -2 \pm \sqrt{2}$$
Solution set: $\{-2 \pm \sqrt{2}\}$

30.
$$x^2 + 6x = 2$$
$$x^2 + 6x - 2 = 0$$
$$x = \frac{-6 \pm \sqrt{36 - 4(1)(-2)}}{2(1)} = \frac{-6 \pm 2\sqrt{11}}{2}$$
$$= -3 \pm \sqrt{11}$$

The solution set is $\left\{-3 \pm \sqrt{11}\right\}$.

31.
$$3x^2 - 5x + 1 = 0$$
$$x = \frac{5 \pm \sqrt{25 - 4(3)(1)}}{2(3)} = \frac{5 \pm \sqrt{13}}{6}$$
Solution set: $\left\{\frac{5 \pm \sqrt{13}}{6}\right\}$

32.
$$2x^2 + 3x - 1 = 0$$
$$x = \frac{-3 \pm \sqrt{9 - 4(2)(-1)}}{2(2)} = \frac{-3 \pm \sqrt{17}}{4}$$
The solution set is $\left\{\frac{-3 \pm \sqrt{17}}{4}\right\}$.

33. $b^2 - 4ac = (-20)^2 - 4(25)(4) = 0$
One real solution.

34. $16x^2 - 8x + 1 = 0$
$b^2 - 4ac = (-8)^2 - 4(16)(1) = 0$
One real solution

35. $b^2 - 4ac = (-3)^2 - 4(1)(7) = -19$
No real solutions

36. $b^2 - 4ac = (-1)^2 - 4(3)(8) = -95$
No real solutions

37. $2x^2 - 5x + 1 = 0$
$b^2 - 4ac = (-5)^2 - 4(2)(1) = 17$
Two real solutions

38. $b^2 - 4ac = (6)^2 - 4(-3)(-2) = 12$
Two real solutions

39.
$$2x^2 - 4x + 3 = 0$$
$$x = \frac{4 \pm \sqrt{16 - 4(2)(3)}}{2(2)} = \frac{4 \pm \sqrt{-8}}{4}$$
$$= \frac{4 \pm 2i\sqrt{2}}{4} = \frac{3 \pm i\sqrt{2}}{2}$$
Solution set: $\left\{\frac{2 \pm i\sqrt{2}}{2}\right\}$

40. $2x^2 - 6x + 5 = 0$
$$x = \frac{6 \pm \sqrt{36 - 4(2)(5)}}{2(2)} = \frac{6 \pm \sqrt{-4}}{4}$$
$$= \frac{6 \pm i\sqrt{4}}{4} = \frac{6 \pm 2i}{4} = \frac{3 \pm i}{2}$$
The solution set is $\left\{\frac{3 \pm i}{2}\right\}$.

41. $2x^2 - 3x + 3 = 0$
$$x = \frac{3 \pm \sqrt{9 - 4(2)(3)}}{2(2)} = \frac{3 \pm \sqrt{-15}}{4}$$
$$= \frac{3 \pm i\sqrt{15}}{4}$$
Solution set: $\left\{\frac{3 \pm i\sqrt{15}}{4}\right\}$

42. $x^2 + x + 1 = 0$
$$x = \frac{-1 \pm \sqrt{1 - 4(1)(1)}}{2(1)} = \frac{-1 \pm \sqrt{-3}}{2}$$

$$= \frac{-1 \pm i\sqrt{3}}{2}$$

The solution set is $\left\{ \dfrac{-1 \pm i\sqrt{3}}{2} \right\}$.

43. $3x^2 + 2x + 2 = 0$

$$x = \frac{-2 \pm \sqrt{4 - 4(3)(2)}}{2(3)} = \frac{-2 \pm \sqrt{-20}}{6}$$

$$= \frac{-2 \pm 2i\sqrt{5}}{6} = \frac{-1 \pm i\sqrt{5}}{3}$$

Solution set: $\left\{ \dfrac{-1 \pm i\sqrt{5}}{3} \right\}$

44. $x^2 + 2 = 2x$

$x^2 - 2x + 2 = 0$

$$x = \frac{2 \pm \sqrt{4 - 4(1)(2)}}{2(1)} = \frac{2 \pm \sqrt{-4}}{2}$$

$$= \frac{2 \pm 2i}{2} = 1 \pm i$$

The solution set is $\{1 \pm i\}$.

45. $x^2 + 6x + 16 = 0$

$$x = \frac{-6 \pm \sqrt{36 - 4(1)(16)}}{2(1)} = \frac{-6 \pm \sqrt{-28}}{2}$$

$$= \frac{-6 \pm 2i\sqrt{7}}{2} = -3 \pm i\sqrt{7}$$

Solution set: $\{-3 \pm i\sqrt{7}\}$

46. $\frac{1}{2}x^2 - 5x + 13 = 0$

$$x = \frac{5 \pm \sqrt{25 - 4\left(\frac{1}{2}\right)(13)}}{2\left(\frac{1}{2}\right)} = \frac{5 \pm \sqrt{-1}}{1}$$

$$= 5 \pm i$$

The solution set is $\{5 \pm i\}$.

47. $b^2 - 4ac = (-10)^2 - 4(8)(-3) = 196$
Since 196 is a perfect square, the polynomial is not prime.
$8x^2 - 10x - 3 = (4x + 1)(2x - 3)$

48. $b^2 - 4ac = (9)^2 - 4(18)(-2) = 225$
Since 225 is a perfect square, the polynomial is not prime.
$18x^2 + 9x - 2 = (6x - 1)(3x + 2)$

49. $b^2 - 4ac = (-5)^2 - 4(4)(2) = -7$
Since -7 is a not a perfect square, the polynomial is prime.

50. $b^2 - 4ac = (-7)^2 - 4(6)(-4) = 145$
Since 145 is not a perfect square, the polynomial is prime.

51. $b^2 - 4ac = (10)^2 - 4(8)(-25) = 900$
Since 900 is a perfect square, the polynomial is not prime.
$8y^2 + 10y - 25 = (4y - 5)(2y + 5)$

52. $b^2 - 4ac = (-15)^2 - 4(25)(-18) = 2025$

Since 2025 is a perfect square, the polynomial is not prime.
$25z^2 - 15z - 18 = (5z + 3)(5z - 6)$

53. $(x + 3)(x + 6) = 0$
$x^2 + 9x + 18 = 0$

54. $(x - 4)(x + 9) = 0$
$x^2 + 5x - 36 = 0$

55. $(x + 5\sqrt{2})(x - 5\sqrt{2}) = 0$
$x^2 - 50 = 0$

56. $(x + 2i\sqrt{3})(x - 2i\sqrt{3}) = 0$
$x^2 + 12 = 0$

57. $x^6 + 7x^3 - 8 = 0$
$(x^3 + 8)(x^3 - 1) = 0$
$x^3 + 8 = 0$ or $x^3 - 1 = 0$
$x^3 = -8$ or $x^3 = 1$
$x = -2$ or $x = 1$
Solution set: $\{-2, 1\}$

58. $8x^6 + 63x^3 - 8 = 0$
$(8x^3 - 1)(x^3 + 8) = 0$
$8x^3 - 1 = 0$ or $x^3 + 8 = 0$
$x^3 = \frac{1}{8}$ or $x^3 = -8$
$x = \frac{1}{2}$ or $x = -2$
The solution set is $\left\{-2, \frac{1}{2}\right\}$.

59. $x^4 - 13x^2 + 36 = 0$
$(x^2 - 4)(x^2 - 9) = 0$
$x^2 - 4 = 0$ or $x^2 - 9 = 0$
$x^2 = 4$ or $x^2 = 9$
$x = \pm 2$ or $x = \pm 3$
Solution set: $\{\pm 2, \pm 3\}$

60. $x^4 + 7x^2 + 12 = 0$
$(x^2 + 3)(x^2 + 4) = 0$
$x^2 + 3 = 0$ or $x^2 + 4 = 0$
$x^2 = -3$ or $x^2 = -4$
There is no real solution to either of these equations. The solution set is $\emptyset$.

61. Let $w = x^2 + 3x$.
$w^2 - 28w + 180 = 0$
$(w - 10)(w - 18) = 0$
$w = 10$ or $w = 18$
$x^2 + 3x = 10$ or $x^2 + 3x = 18$
$x^2 + 3x - 10 = 0$ or $x^2 + 3x - 18 = 0$
$(x + 5)(x - 2) = 0$ or $(x + 6)(x - 3) = 0$
$x = -5$ or $x = 2$ or $x = -6$ or $x = 3$
Solution set: $\{-6, -5, 2, 3\}$

62. $(x^2 + 1)^2 - 8(x^2 + 1) + 15 = 0$
Let $w = x^2 + 1$.

319

$$w^2 - 8w + 15 = 0$$
$$(w - 3)(w - 5) = 0$$
$$w - 3 = 0 \text{ or } w - 5 = 0$$
$$w = 3 \text{ or } w = 5$$
$$x^2 + 1 = 3 \text{ or } x^2 + 1 = 5$$
$$x^2 = 2 \text{ or } x^2 = 4$$
$$x = \pm\sqrt{2} \text{ or } x = \pm 2$$

The solution set is $\left\{ \pm\sqrt{2}, \pm 2 \right\}$.

63. Let $w = \sqrt{x^2 - 6x}$ and $w^2 = x^2 - 6x$.
$$w^2 + 6w - 40 = 0$$
$$(w + 10)(w - 4) = 0$$
$$w = -10 \quad \text{or} \quad w = 4$$
$$\sqrt{x^2 - 6x} = -10 \quad \text{or} \quad \sqrt{x^2 - 6x} = 4$$
No real solution here. $\qquad x^2 - 6x = 16$
$$x^2 - 6x - 16 = 0$$
$$(x - 8)(x + 2) = 0$$
$$x = 8 \text{ or } x = -2$$

Solution set: $\{-2, 8\}$

64. $x^2 - 3x - 3\sqrt{x^2 - 3x} + 2 = 0$
Let $w = \sqrt{x^2 - 3x}$ and $w^2 = x^2 - 3x$.
$$w^2 - 3w + 2 = 0$$
$$(w - 2)(w - 1) = 0$$
$$w - 2 = 0 \text{ or } w - 1 = 0$$
$$w = 2 \text{ or } w = 1$$
$$\sqrt{x^2 - 3x} = 2 \text{ or } \sqrt{x^2 - 3x} = 1$$
$$x^2 - 3x = 4 \text{ or } x^2 - 3x = 1$$
$$x^2 - 3x - 4 = 0 \text{ or } x^2 - 3x - 1 = 0$$
$$(x - 4)(x + 1) = 0 \text{ or } x = \frac{3 \pm \sqrt{9 - 4(1)(-1)}}{2(1)}$$
$$x = 4 \text{ or } x = -1 \text{ or } \quad x = \frac{3 \pm \sqrt{13}}{2}$$

The solution set is $\left\{ -1, 4, \frac{3 \pm \sqrt{13}}{2} \right\}$.

65. Let $w = t^{-1}$ and $w^2 = t^{-2}$.
$$w^2 + 5w - 36 = 0$$
$$(w + 9)(w - 4) = 0$$
$$w = -9 \quad \text{or} \quad w = 4$$
$$t^{-1} = -9 \quad \text{or} \quad t^{-1} = 4$$
$$t = -\tfrac{1}{9} \quad \text{or} \quad t = \tfrac{1}{4}$$

Solution set: $\left\{ -\tfrac{1}{9}, \tfrac{1}{4} \right\}$

66. $a^{-2} + a^{-1} - 6 = 0$
Let $w = a^{-1}$ and $w^2 = a^{-2}$.
$$w^2 + w - 6 = 0$$

$$(w + 3)(w - 2) = 0$$
$$w + 3 = 0 \text{ or } w - 2 = 0$$
$$w = -3 \text{ or } w = 2$$
$$a^{-1} = -3 \text{ or } a^{-1} = 2$$
$$a = -\tfrac{1}{3} \text{ or } a = \tfrac{1}{2}$$

The solution set is $\left\{ -\tfrac{1}{3}, \tfrac{1}{2} \right\}$.

67. Let $y = \sqrt{w}$ and $y^2 = w$.
$$y^2 - 13y + 36 = 0$$
$$(y - 9)(y - 4) = 0$$
$$y = 9 \quad \text{or} \quad y = 4$$
$$\sqrt{w} = 9 \quad \text{or} \quad \sqrt{w} = 4$$
$$w = 81 \quad \text{or} \quad w = 16$$

Solution set: $\{16, 81\}$

68. $4a - 5\sqrt{a} + 1 = 0$
Let $w = \sqrt{a}$ and $w^2 = a$.
$$4w^2 - 5w + 1 = 0$$
$$(4w - 1)(w - 1) = 0$$
$$4w - 1 = 0 \text{ or } w - 1 = 0$$
$$w = \tfrac{1}{4} \text{ or } w = 1$$
$$\sqrt{a} = \tfrac{1}{4} \text{ or } \sqrt{a} = 1$$
$$a = \tfrac{1}{16} \text{ or } a = 1$$

The solution set is $\left\{ \tfrac{1}{16}, 1 \right\}$.

69.
$$a^2 + a > 6$$
$$a^2 + a - 6 > 0$$
$$(a + 3)(a - 2) > 0$$

```
a + 3  - - - 0 + + + + + + + + + +
a - 2  - - - - - - - - - 0 + + + +
            -3           2
```

The inequality is satisfied if both factors are the same sign.
$$(-\infty, -3) \cup (2, \infty)$$

```
  ←——)+++++(——→
  -4 -3 -2 -1 0 1  2 3
```

70.
$$x^2 - 5x + 6 > 0$$
$$(x - 2)(x - 3) > 0$$

```
x - 2  - - - 0 + + + + + + + + + +
x - 3  - - - - - - - - - 0 + + + +
           2            3
```

The inequality is satisfied if both factors are the same sign.
$$(-\infty, 2) \cup (3, \infty)$$

```
  ←——+)(——+→
   0 1 2 3 4 5
```

71. $x^2 - x - 20 \leq 0$

$\quad (x-5)(x+4) \leq 0$

$x + 4 \;-\;-\;-\;0+\;+\;+\;+\;+\;+\;+\;+\;+$
$x - 5 \;-\;-\;-\;-\;-\;-\;-\;-\;0+\;+\;+\;+$
$\qquad\qquad -4 \qquad\qquad\quad 5$

The inequality is satisfied if the factors have opposite signs, or if one of the factors is zero.
$[-4, 5]$

72. $\quad a^2 + 2a \leq 15$

$\quad a^2 + 2a - 15 \leq 0$

$\quad (a+5)(a-3) \leq 0$

$a + 5 \;-\;-\;-\;0+\;+\;+\;+\;+\;+\;+\;+\;+$
$a - 3 \;-\;-\;-\;-\;-\;-\;-\;-\;0+\;+\;+$
$\qquad\quad -5 \qquad\qquad\qquad 3$

The inequality is satisfied if the factors have opposite signs, or if one of the factors is zero.
$[-5, 3]$

73. $\qquad w^2 - w < 0$

$\qquad w(w-1) < 0$

$w \;-\;-\;-\;0+\;+\;+\;+\;+\;+\;+\;+\;+\;+$
$w - 1 \;-\;-\;-\;-\;-\;-\;-\;-\;-\;0+\;+\;+$
$\qquad\quad 0 \qquad\qquad\qquad 1$

The inequality is satisfied if the factors have opposite signs.
$(0, 1)$

74. $\qquad x - x^2 \leq 0$

$\qquad x(1-x) \leq 0$

$x \;-\;-\;-\;0+\;+\;+\;+\;+\;+\;+\;+$
$1 - x \;+\;+\;+\;+\;+\;+\;+\;+\;0\;-\;-\;-\;-$
$\qquad\quad 0 \qquad\qquad\qquad 1$

The inequality is satisfied if the factors have opposite signs.
$(-\infty, 0] \cup [1, \infty)$

75. $\quad \dfrac{x-4}{x+2} \geq 0$

$x + 2 \;-\;-\;-\;0+\;+\;+\;+\;+\;+\;+\;+\;+$
$x - 4 \;-\;-\;-\;-\;-\;-\;-\;-\;0+\;+\;+\;+$
$\qquad\qquad -2 \qquad\qquad 4$

The inequality is satisfied if the factors have the same sign, or if the numerator is equal to zero.
$(-\infty, -2) \cup [4, \infty)$

76. $\quad \dfrac{x-3}{x+5} < 0$

$x + 5 \;-\;-\;-\;0+\;+\;+\;+\;+\;+\;+\;+\;+$
$x - 3 \;-\;-\;-\;-\;-\;-\;-\;-\;-\;0+\;+\;+$
$\qquad\quad -5 \qquad\qquad\qquad 3$

The inequality is satisfied if the factors have opposite signs.
$(-5, 3)$

77. $\quad \dfrac{x-2}{x+3} - 1 < 0$

$\quad \dfrac{x-2}{x+3} - \dfrac{x+3}{x+3} < 0$

$\qquad\quad \dfrac{-5}{x+3} < 0$

Since the numerator is definitely negative, the inequality is satisfied only if the denominator is positive:

$$x + 3 > 0$$
$$x > -3$$

$(-3, \infty)$

78. $\qquad \dfrac{x-3}{x+4} > 2$

$\qquad \dfrac{x-3}{x+4} - 2 > 0$

$\quad \dfrac{x-3}{x+4} - \dfrac{2(x+4)}{x+4} > 0$

$\qquad \dfrac{-x-11}{x+4} > 0$

$x + 4 \;-\;-\;-\;-\;-\;-\;-\;-\;-\;0+\;+\;+$
$-x - 11 \;+\;+\;+\;0\;-\;-\;-\;-\;-\;-\;-\;-$
$\qquad\qquad -11 \qquad\qquad -4$

The inequality is satisfied if the factors have the same sign.

321

$(-11, -4)$

79.
$$\frac{3}{x+2} - \frac{1}{x+1} > 0$$
$$\frac{3(x+1)}{(x+2)(x+1)} - \frac{1(x+2)}{(x+1)(x+2)} > 0$$
$$\frac{2x+1}{(x+2)(x+1)} > 0$$

$$x+1 \; - \; - \; - \; -0+ + + + + + + + +$$
$$x+2 \; - \; -0+ + + + + + + + + + +$$
$$2x+1 \; - \; - \; - \; - \; - \; - \; - \; - \; -0+ + +$$
$$-2 \qquad -1 \qquad\quad -1/2$$

The inequality is satisfied when an even number of the factors have negative signs.
$(-2, -1) \cup (-\frac{1}{2}, \infty)$

80.
$$\frac{1}{x+1} < \frac{1}{x-1}$$
$$\frac{1}{x+1} - \frac{1}{x-1} < 0$$
$$\frac{1(x-1)}{(x+1)(x-1)} - \frac{1(x+1)}{(x-1)(x+1)} < 0$$
$$\frac{-2}{(x+1)(x-1)} < 0$$
$$\frac{2}{(x+1)(x-1)} > 0$$

$$x+1 \; - \; - \; -0+ + + + + + + + + +$$
$$x-1 \; - \; - \; - \; - \; - \; - \; - \; - \; - \; -0+ + +$$
$$-1 \qquad\qquad\qquad 1$$

The inequality is satisfied if the factors have the same sign.
$(-\infty, -1) \cup (1, \infty)$

81. $144x^2 - 120x + 25 = 0$
$$(12x - 5)^2 = 0$$
$$12x - 5 = 0$$
$$x = \tfrac{5}{12}$$
Solution set: $\left\{ \tfrac{5}{12} \right\}$

82. $\qquad 49x^2 + 9 = 42x$
$$49x^2 - 42x + 9 = 0$$
$$(7x - 3)^2 = 0$$
$$7x - 3 = 0$$
$$x = \tfrac{3}{7}$$

Solution set: $\left\{ \tfrac{3}{7} \right\}$

83. $(2x + 3)^2 + 7 = 12$
$$(2x + 3)^2 = 5$$
$$2x + 3 = \pm \sqrt{5}$$
$$x = \frac{-3 \pm \sqrt{5}}{2}$$
Solution set: $\left\{ \frac{-3 \pm \sqrt{5}}{2} \right\}$

84. $\qquad 6x = -\dfrac{19x + 25}{x + 1}$
$$6x^2 + 6x = -19x - 25$$
$$6x^2 + 25x + 25 = 0$$
$$(3x + 5)(2x + 5) = 0$$
$$3x + 5 = 0 \quad\text{or}\quad 2x + 5 = 0$$
$$x = -\tfrac{5}{3} \quad\text{or}\quad x = -\tfrac{5}{2}$$
Solution set: $\left\{ -\tfrac{5}{3}, -\tfrac{5}{2} \right\}$

85. $9x^2 \left(1 + \dfrac{20}{9x^2}\right) = 9x^2 \cdot \dfrac{8}{3x}$
$$9x^2 + 20 = 24x$$
$$9x^2 - 24x + 20 = 0$$
$$x = \frac{24 \pm \sqrt{(-24)^2 - 4(9)(20)}}{2(9)} = \frac{24 \pm 12i}{18}$$
$$= \frac{4 \pm 2i}{3}$$
Solution set: $\left\{ \dfrac{4 \pm 2i}{3} \right\}$

86. $\qquad \dfrac{x-1}{x+2} = \dfrac{2x-3}{x+4}$
$$x^2 + 3x - 4 = 2x^2 + x - 6$$
$$0 = x^2 - 2x - 2$$
$$x = \frac{2 \pm \sqrt{(-2)^2 - 4(1)(-2)}}{2(1)} = \frac{2 \pm \sqrt{12}}{2}$$
$$= 1 \pm \sqrt{3}$$
Solution set: $\left\{ 1 \pm \sqrt{3} \right\}$

87. $\qquad \sqrt{3x^2 + 7x - 30} = x$
$$3x^2 + 7x - 30 = x^2$$
$$2x^2 + 7x - 30 = 0$$
$$(2x - 5)(x + 6) = 0$$
$$2x - 5 = 0 \quad\text{or}\quad x + 6 = 0$$
$$x = \tfrac{5}{2} \quad\text{or}\quad x = -6$$
Since -6 does not check, solution set is $\left\{ \tfrac{5}{2} \right\}$.

88. $\qquad\qquad \dfrac{x^4}{3} = x^2 + 6$
$$x^4 = 3x^2 + 18$$
$$x^4 - 3x^2 - 18 = 0$$
$$(x^2 - 6)(x^2 + 3) = 0$$
$$x^2 - 6 = 0 \quad\text{or}\quad x^2 + 3 = 0$$
$$x^2 = 6 \quad\text{or}\quad x^2 = -3$$
$$x = \pm \sqrt{6} \quad\text{or}\quad x = \pm i\sqrt{3}$$
Solution set: $\left\{ \pm \sqrt{6}, \pm i\sqrt{3} \right\}$

89. $2(2x+1)^2 + 5(2x+1) = 3$
$$2y^2 + 5y - 3 = 0$$
$$(2y-1)(y+3) = 0$$
$$2y - 1 = 0 \text{ or } y + 3 = 0$$
$$y = \tfrac{1}{2} \text{ or } \quad y = -3$$
$$2x + 1 = \tfrac{1}{2} \text{ or } 2x + 1 = -3$$
$$x = -\tfrac{1}{4} \text{ or } \quad x = -2$$
Solution set: $\left\{-2, -\tfrac{1}{4}\right\}$

90. $(w^2 - 1)^2 + 2(w^2 - 1) = 15$
$$y^2 + 2y - 15 = 0$$
$$(y+5)(y-3) = 0$$
$$y = -5 \text{ or } \quad y = 3$$
$$w^2 - 1 = -5 \text{ or } w^2 - 1 = 3$$
$$w^2 = -4 \text{ or } \quad w^2 = 4$$
$$w = \pm 2i \text{ or } \quad w = \pm 2$$
Solution set: $\{\pm 2i, \pm 2\}$

91. $x^{1/2} - 15x^{1/4} + 50 = 0 \quad$ Let $y = x^{1/4}$
$$y^2 - 15y + 50 = 0$$
$$(y-5)(y-10) = 0$$
$$y = 5 \quad \text{or} \quad y = 10$$
$$x^{1/4} = 5 \text{ or } x^{1/4} = 10$$
$$x = 5^4 \text{ or } \quad x = 10^4$$
$$x = 625 \text{ or } \quad x = 10{,}000$$
Solution set: $\{625, 10{,}000\}$

92. $x^{-2} - 9x^{-1} + 18 = 0$
$$(x^{-1} - 3)(x^{-1} - 6) = 0$$
$$x^{-1} - 3 = 0 \text{ or } x^{-1} - 6 = 0$$
$$x^{-1} = 3 \text{ or } \quad x^{-1} = 6$$
$$x = \tfrac{1}{3} \text{ or } \quad x = \tfrac{1}{6}$$
Solution set: $\left\{\tfrac{1}{6}, \tfrac{1}{3}\right\}$

93. If $x =$ one of the numbers, then $x + 4 =$ the other number. Since their product is 4, we can write the equation
$$x(x+4) = 4$$
$$x^2 + 4x = 4$$
$$x^2 + 4x + 4 = 4 + 4$$
$$(x+2)^2 = 8$$
$$x + 2 = \pm 2\sqrt{2}$$
$$x = -2 \pm 2\sqrt{2}$$
Disregard $-2 - 2\sqrt{2}$ since it is not positive. If $x = -2 + 2\sqrt{2}$ then $x + 4 = 2 + 2\sqrt{2}$. The two numbers are $-2 + 2\sqrt{2} \approx 0.83$ and $2 + 2\sqrt{2} \approx 4.83$.

94. Let $x =$ one number and $x + 1 =$ the other number. Since their product is 1, we can write the following equation.

$$x(x+1) = 1$$
$$x^2 + x - 1 = 0$$
$$x = \frac{-1 \pm \sqrt{1 - 4(1)(-1)}}{2(1)} = \frac{-1 \pm \sqrt{5}}{2}$$
$$x + 1 = \frac{-1 + \sqrt{5}}{2} + \frac{2}{2} = \frac{1 + \sqrt{5}}{2}$$
Since the numbers are positive we use
$$\frac{-1 + \sqrt{5}}{2} \approx 0.62 \text{ and } \frac{1 + \sqrt{5}}{2} \approx 1.62.$$

95. Let $x =$ the height and $x + 4 =$ the width. The diagonal 19 is the hypotenuse of a right triangle with legs x and $x + 4$. By the Pythagorean theorem we can write
$$x^2 + (x+4)^2 = 19^2$$
$$x^2 + x^2 + 8x + 16 = 361$$
$$2x^2 + 8x - 345 = 0$$
$$x = \frac{-8 \pm \sqrt{64 - 4(2)(-345)}}{2(2)}$$
$$= \frac{-8 \pm \sqrt{2824}}{4} = \frac{-8 \pm 2\sqrt{706}}{4}$$
$$= \frac{-4 \pm \sqrt{706}}{2}$$
Since the height must be positive, we have
$$x = \frac{-4 + \sqrt{706}}{2} \text{ and}$$

$$x + 4 = \frac{8}{2} + \frac{-4 + \sqrt{706}}{2} = \frac{4 + \sqrt{706}}{2}.$$

So the width is $\frac{4 + \sqrt{706}}{2} \approx 15.3$ inches and the

height is $\frac{-4 + \sqrt{706}}{2} \approx 11.3$ inches.

96. Let $x =$ the length of the diagonal of the square. Use the Pythagorean theorem to write the following equation.
$$x^2 = 20^2 + 20^2$$
$$x^2 = 800$$
$$x = \pm 20\sqrt{2}$$
The length of the diagonal is $20\sqrt{2} \approx 28.284$ feet.

97. Let $x =$ the width of the border. The dimensions of the printed area will be $8 - 2x$ by $10 - 2x$. Since the printed area is to be 24 square inches, we can write the equation
$$(8 - 2x)(10 - 2x) = 24$$
$$80 - 36x + 4x^2 = 24$$
$$4x^2 - 36x + 56 = 0$$
$$x^2 - 9x + 14 = 0$$

$$(x-7)(x-2) = 0$$
$$x = 7 \quad \text{or} \quad x = 2$$
Since 7 inches is too wide for a border on an 8 by 10 piece of paper, the border must be 2 inches wide.

98. Let $x =$ the time for Winston alone and $x + 1 =$ the time for Willie alone. Winston does $1/x$ of the lawn per hour and Willie does $1/(x + 1)$ of the lawn per hour. In 2 hours Winston does $2/x$ lawn and Willie does $2/(x + 1)$ lawn.
$$\frac{2}{x} + \frac{2}{x+1} = 1$$
$$x(x+1)\left(\frac{2}{x} + \frac{2}{x+1}\right) = x(x+1)1$$
$$2x + 2 + 2x = x^2 + x$$
$$-x^2 + 3x + 2 = 0$$
$$x^2 - 3x - 2 = 0$$
$$x = \frac{3 \pm \sqrt{9 - 4(1)(-2)}}{2(1)} = \frac{3 \pm \sqrt{17}}{2}$$

Since x must be positive, Winston's time alone is $\frac{3+\sqrt{17}}{2} \approx 3.562$ hours.

99. Let $x =$ width and $x + 4 =$ the length.
$$x(x + 4) = 45$$
$$x^2 + 4x - 45 = 0$$
$$(x + 9)(x - 5) = 0$$
$$x + 9 = 0 \text{ or } x - 5 = 0$$
$$x = -9 \text{ or } \quad x = 5$$
$$x + 4 = 9$$
The table is 5 ft wide and 9 feet long.

100. Since $2L + W = 60$, $W = 60 - 2L$. Since the area is 352, $LW = 352$.
$$L(60 - 2L) = 352$$
$$-2L^2 + 60L - 352 = 0$$
$$L^2 - 30L + 176 = 0$$
$$(L - 22)(L - 8) = 0$$
$$L = 22 \quad \text{or} \quad L = 8$$
$$W = 60 - 2L \quad W = 60 - 2L$$
$$= 16 \qquad\qquad = 44$$
Since L is greater than W, $L = 22$ yd and $W = 16$ yd.

101.
$$12 = -16t^2 + 32t$$
$$16t^2 - 32t + 12 = 0$$
$$4t^2 - 8t + 3 = 0$$

$$t = \frac{8 \pm \sqrt{64 - 4(4)(3)}}{2(4)} = \frac{8 \pm \sqrt{16}}{8}$$

$$= 1 \pm \tfrac{1}{2} = 1.5 \text{ or } 0.5$$
His height was 12 ft for $t = 0.5$ sec and $t = 1.5$ sec.

102.
$$-16t^2 + 32t = 0$$
$$-16t(t - 2) = 0$$
$$t = 0 \text{ or } t = 2$$
He was in the air for 2 seconds.
$$-16t^2 + 32t > 14$$
$$-16t^2 + 32t - 14 > 0$$
$$8t^2 - 16t + 7 < 0$$
Solve $8t^2 - 16t + 7 = 0$:

$$t = \frac{16 \pm \sqrt{16^2 - 4(8)(7)}}{2(8)} = \frac{16 \pm 4\sqrt{2}}{16}$$
$$= 1 \pm \tfrac{1}{4}\sqrt{2}$$

He was more than 14 feet in the air for t in the interval $(1 - 0.25\sqrt{2}, 1 + 0.25\sqrt{2})$, or for $0.5\sqrt{2}$ sec, or 0.707 sec.

CHAPTER 8   TEST

1. $(-3)^2 - 4(2)(2) = 9 - 16 = -7$
The equation has no real solutions.
2. $(5)^2 - 4(-3)(-1) = 25 - 12 = 13$
The equation has 2 real solutions.
3. $(-4)^2 - 4(4)(1) = 16 - 16 = 0$
The equation has 1 real solution.
4. $2x^2 + 5x - 3 = 0$
$$x = \frac{-5 \pm \sqrt{25 - 4(2)(-3)}}{2(2)} = \frac{-5 \pm \sqrt{49}}{4}$$
$$= \frac{-5 \pm 7}{4} \quad \left(\frac{2}{4} \text{ or } \frac{-12}{4}\right)$$
Solution set: $\left\{-3, \frac{1}{2}\right\}$

5. $x^2 + 6x + 6 = 0$
$$x = \frac{-6 \pm \sqrt{36 - 4(1)(6)}}{2} = \frac{-6 \pm \sqrt{12}}{2}$$
$$= \frac{-6 \pm 2\sqrt{3}}{2} = -3 \pm \sqrt{3}$$
Solution set: $\{-3 \pm \sqrt{3}\}$

6. $x^2 + 10x + 25 = 0$
$$(x + 5)^2 = 0$$
$$x + 5 = 0$$
$$x = -5$$
Solution set: $\{-5\}$

7. $2x^2 + x = 6$
$$x^2 + \tfrac{1}{2}x = 3$$
$$x^2 + \tfrac{1}{2}x + \tfrac{1}{16} = 3 + \tfrac{1}{16}$$

$$(x + \tfrac{1}{4})^2 = \tfrac{49}{16}$$
$$x + \tfrac{1}{4} = \pm \tfrac{7}{4}$$
$$x = -\tfrac{1}{4} \pm \tfrac{7}{4} \quad \left(\tfrac{6}{4} \text{ or } \tfrac{-8}{4}\right)$$

Solution set: $\left\{-2, \tfrac{3}{2}\right\}$

8.
$$x(x + 1) = 12$$
$$x^2 + x - 12 = 0$$
$$(x + 4)(x - 3) = 0$$
$$x = -4 \quad \text{or} \quad x = 3$$
Solution set: $\{-4, 3\}$

9.
$$a^4 - 5a^2 + 4 = 0$$
$$(a^2 - 4)(a^2 - 1) = 0$$
$$a^2 - 4 = 0 \quad \text{or} \quad a^2 - 1 = 0$$
$$a^2 = 4 \quad \text{or} \quad a^2 = 1$$
$$a = \pm 2 \quad \text{or} \quad a = \pm 1$$
Solution set: $\{\pm 1, \pm 2\}$

10. Let $w = \sqrt{x - 2}$ and $w^2 = x - 2$.
$$w^2 - 8w + 15 = 0$$
$$(w - 3)(w - 5) = 0$$
$$w = 3 \quad \text{or} \quad w = 5$$
$$\sqrt{x - 2} = 3 \quad \text{or} \quad \sqrt{x - 2} = 5$$
$$x - 2 = 9 \quad \text{or} \quad x - 2 = 25$$
$$x = 11 \quad \text{or} \quad x = 27$$
Solution set: $\{11, 27\}$

11.
$$x^2 + 36 = 0$$
$$x^2 = -36$$
$$x = \pm \sqrt{-36} = \pm 6i$$
Solution set: $\{\pm 6i\}$

12. $x^2 + 6x + 10 = 0$
$$x = \frac{-6 \pm \sqrt{36 - 4(1)(10)}}{2(1)} = \frac{-6 \pm \sqrt{-4}}{2}$$
$$= \frac{-6 \pm 2i}{2} = -3 \pm i$$
Solution set: $\{-3 \pm i\}$

13. $3x^2 - x + 1 = 0$
$$x = \frac{1 \pm \sqrt{1 - 4(3)(1)}}{2(3)} = \frac{1 \pm \sqrt{-11}}{6}$$

Solution set: $\left\{\dfrac{1 \pm i\sqrt{11}}{6}\right\}$

14. $(x + 4)(x - 6) = 0$
$$x^2 - 2x - 24 = 0$$
15. $(x - 5i)(x + 5i) = 0$
$$x^2 + 25 = 0$$
16. $w^2 + 3w - 18 < 0$
$$(w + 6)(w - 3) < 0$$

$w + 6 - - - - 0 + + + + + + + + +$
$w - 3 - - - - - - - - - 0 + + + +$
$\qquad\qquad -6 \qquad\qquad 3$

The inequality is satisfied when the factors have opposite signs.

$(-6, 3)$

17.
$$\frac{2}{x - 2} - \frac{3}{x + 1} < 0$$
$$\frac{2(x + 1)}{(x - 2)(x + 1)} - \frac{3(x - 2)}{(x + 1)(x - 2)} < 0$$
$$\frac{-x + 8}{(x - 2)(x + 1)} < 0$$

$x - 2 - - - - 0 + + + + + + + + +$
$x + 1 - - 0 + + + + + + + + + + +$
$-x + 8 + + + + + + + + + + 0 - - -$
$\qquad -1 \qquad 2 \qquad\qquad 8$

This quotient will be negative only if an odd number of factors are negative.

$(-1, 2) \cup (8, \infty)$

18. Let $x =$ the width and $x + 2 =$ the length. Since the area is 16 square feet, we can write the equation
$$x(x + 2) = 16$$
$$x^2 + 2x - 16 = 0$$
$$x = \frac{-2 \pm \sqrt{4 - 4(1)(-16)}}{2} = \frac{-2 \pm \sqrt{68}}{2}$$
$$= \frac{-2 \pm 2\sqrt{17}}{2} = -1 \pm \sqrt{17}$$
Since the width must be positive, we have $x = -1 + \sqrt{17}$ and $x + 2 = 1 + \sqrt{17}$. The width is $-1 + \sqrt{17}$ feet and the length is $1 + \sqrt{17}$ feet.

19. Let $x =$ time for the new computer and $x + 1 =$ time for the old computer. New computer's rate is $\frac{1}{x}$ payroll/hr and old computer's rate is $\frac{1}{x + 1}$ payroll/hr. In 3 hrs new computer does $\frac{3}{x}$ payroll and old computer does $\frac{3}{x + 1}$ payroll.
$$\frac{3}{x} + \frac{3}{x + 1} = 1$$

325

$$x(x+1)\left(\tfrac{3}{x}+\tfrac{3}{x+1}\right)=x(x+1)1$$
$$3x+3+3x=x^2+x$$
$$0=x^2-5x-3$$
$$x=\frac{5\pm\sqrt{5^2-4(1)(-3)}}{2}=\frac{5\pm\sqrt{37}}{2}$$
$$\approx 5.5 \text{ or } -0.5$$

It takes the new computer 5.5 hrs to do the payroll by itself.

Making Connections

Chapters 1 - 8

1. $2x-15=0$
$$2x=15$$
$$x=\tfrac{15}{2}$$
Solution set: $\left\{\tfrac{15}{2}\right\}$

2. $2x^2-15=0$
$$2x^2=15$$
$$x^2=\tfrac{15}{2}$$
$$x=\pm\sqrt{\tfrac{15}{2}}=\pm\frac{\sqrt{15}\sqrt{2}}{\sqrt{2}\sqrt{2}}=\pm\frac{\sqrt{30}}{2}$$
Solution set: $\left\{\pm\frac{\sqrt{30}}{2}\right\}$

3. $2x^2+x-15=0$
$$(2x-5)(x+3)=0$$
$$2x-5=0 \text{ or } x+3=0$$
$$x=\tfrac{5}{2} \text{ or } \quad x=-3$$
Solution set: $\left\{-3,\tfrac{5}{2}\right\}$

4. $2x^2+4x-15=0$
$$x=\frac{-4\pm\sqrt{16-4(2)(-15)}}{2(2)}=\frac{-4\pm\sqrt{136}}{4}$$
$$=\frac{-4\pm2\sqrt{34}}{4}=\frac{-2\pm\sqrt{34}}{2}$$
Solution set: $\left\{\frac{-2\pm\sqrt{34}}{2}\right\}$

5. $|4x+11|=3$
$$4x+11=3 \text{ or } 4x+11=-3$$
$$4x=-8 \text{ or } \quad 4x=-14$$
$$x=-2 \text{ or } \quad x=-\tfrac{7}{2}$$
Solution set: $\left\{-\tfrac{7}{2},-2\right\}$

6. $|4x^2+11x|=3$
$$4x^2+11x=3 \text{ or } \quad 4x^2+11x=-3$$
$$4x^2+11x-3=0 \text{ or } 4x^2+11x+3=0$$
$$(4x-1)(x+3)=0 \text{ or } \quad x=\frac{-11\pm\sqrt{73}}{8}$$
$$4x-1=0 \text{ or } x+3=0$$
$$x=\tfrac{1}{4} \text{ or } \quad x=-3$$
Solution set: $\left\{-3,\tfrac{1}{4},\frac{-11\pm\sqrt{73}}{8}\right\}$

7. $\sqrt{x}=x-6$
$$(\sqrt{x})^2=(x-6)^2$$
$$x=x^2-12x+36$$
$$0=x^2-13x+36$$
$$0=(x-4)(x-9)$$
$$x-4=0 \text{ or } x-9=0$$
$$x=4 \text{ or } \quad x=9$$
Since $\sqrt{4}=4-6$ is incorrect and $\sqrt{9}=9-6$ is correct, the solution set is $\{9\}$.

8. $\left((2x-5)^{2/3}\right)^3=4^3$
$$(2x-5)^2=64$$
$$2x-5=\pm8$$
$$2x=5\pm8$$
$$x=\frac{5\pm8}{2}$$
Solution set: $\left\{-\tfrac{3}{2},\tfrac{13}{2}\right\}$

9. $1-2x<5-x$
$$-x<4$$
$$x>-4$$
$(-4,\infty)$

10. $(1-2x)(5-x)\le0$

$$1-2x \ + \ + \ +0 \ - \ - \ - \ - \ - \ - \ - \ -$$
$$5-x \ + \ + \ + \ + \ + \ + \ + \ +0 \ - \ - \ - \ -$$
$$\overline{1/25}$$

The inequality is satisfied when the factors have opposite signs. The solution set is $[\tfrac{1}{2},5]$.

11. $\frac{1-2x}{5-x}\le0$ Same as last exercise, but 5 is excluded from the solution set because of the denominator $5-x$. The solution set is $[\tfrac{1}{2},5)$.

12. $|5-x|<3$
$$-3<5-x<3$$
$$-8<-x<-2$$
$$8>x>2$$
The solution set is $(2,8)$.

13. $3x-1<5$ and $-3\le x$
$$x<2 \text{ and } \quad x\ge-3$$
The solution set is $[-3,2)$.

14. $x-3<1$ or $2x\ge8$
$$x<4 \text{ or } x\ge4$$
The solution set is $(-\infty,\infty)$.

15.
$$2x - 3y = 9$$
$$-3y = -2x + 9$$
$$y = \frac{-2x + 9}{-3}$$
$$y = \frac{2}{3}x - 3$$

16.
$$\frac{y - 3}{x + 2} = -\frac{1}{2}$$
$$y - 3 = -\frac{1}{2}(x + 2)$$
$$y - 3 = -\frac{1}{2}x - 1$$
$$y = -\frac{1}{2}x + 2$$

17.
$$3y^2 + cy + d = 0$$
$$y = \frac{-c \pm \sqrt{c^2 - 4(3)(d)}}{2(3)}$$

$$y = \frac{-c \pm \sqrt{c^2 - 12d}}{6}$$

18.
$$my^2 - ny - w = 0$$
$$y = \frac{-(-n) \pm \sqrt{(-n)^2 - 4(m)(-w)}}{2m}$$

$$y = \frac{n \pm \sqrt{n^2 + 4mw}}{2m}$$

19.
$$30\left(\frac{1}{3}x - \frac{2}{5}y\right) = 30\left(\frac{5}{6}\right)$$

$$10x - 12y = 25$$

$$-12y = -10x + 25$$

$$y = \frac{-10}{-12}x + \frac{25}{-12}$$

$$y = \frac{5}{6}x - \frac{25}{12}$$

20.
$$y - 3 = -\frac{2}{3}(x - 4)$$

$$y - 3 = -\frac{2}{3}x + \frac{8}{3}$$

$$y = -\frac{2}{3}x + \frac{8}{3} + \frac{9}{3}$$

$$y = -\frac{2}{3}x + \frac{17}{3}$$

21. $m = \frac{3 - 7}{2 - 5} = \frac{-4}{-3} = \frac{4}{3}$

22. $m = \frac{5 - (-6)}{-3 - 4} = -\frac{11}{7}$

23. $m = \frac{0.8 - 0.4}{0.3 - 0.5} = \frac{0.4}{-0.2} = -2$

24. $m = \dfrac{\frac{3}{5} - \left(-\frac{4}{3}\right)}{\frac{1}{2} - \frac{1}{3}} = \dfrac{\frac{29}{15}}{\frac{1}{6}} = \frac{29}{15} \cdot \frac{6}{1} = \frac{58}{5}$

25. At \$20 per ticket,
$$n = 48{,}000 - 400(20) = 40{,}000.$$

At \$25 per ticket
$$n = 48{,}000 - 400(25) = 38{,}000$$

If 35,000 tickets are sold, then the price is \$32.50 per ticket.

26. If $p = \$20$, then
$$R = 20(48{,}000 - 400 \cdot 20)$$
$$= \$800{,}000$$

If $p = \$25$, then $R = 25(48{,}000 - 400 \cdot 25)$
$$= \$950{,}000$$

$$1{,}280{,}000 = p(48{,}000 - 400p)$$
$$1{,}280{,}000 = 48{,}000p - 400p^2$$
$$400p^2 - 48{,}000p + 1{,}280{,}000 = 0$$
$$p^2 - 120p + 3{,}200 = 0$$
$$(p - 80)(p - 40) = 0$$
$$p = 80 \quad \text{or} \quad p = 40$$

A revenue of \$1.28 million occurs at a price of \$40 and at a price of \$80.

The price that determines the maximum revenue is \$60 per ticket.

9.1 WARM-UPS

1. True, because $(f - g)(x) = f(x) - g(x)$
$= x - 2 - (x + 3) = -5$.

2. True, because $(f/g)(2) = f(2)/g(2)$
$= (2 + 4)/(3 \cdot 2) = 6/6 = 1$

3. False, because if $f(x) = 3x$ and
$g(x) = x + 1$, then $f(g(x)) = 3(x + 1)$
$= 3x + 3$ and $g(f(x)) = 3x + 1$.

4. False, because $(f \circ g)(x) = f(x + 2)$
$= (x + 2)^2 = x^2 + 4x + 4$.

5. False, because if $f(x) = 3x$ and
$g(x) = x + 1$, then
$(f \circ g)(x) = f(x + 1) = 3x + 3$
and $(f \cdot g)(x) = 3x(x + 1) = 3x^2 + 3x$.

6. False, because $g[f(x)] = \sqrt{x} - 9$ and
$f[g(x)] = \sqrt{x - 9}$ which are not equal for all
values of x.

7. True, because
$(f \circ g)(x) = f(\frac{x}{3}) = 3 \cdot \frac{x}{3} = x$.

8. True, because b determines a and a
determines c so b determines the value of c.

9. True, $F(x) = \sqrt{x - 5}$ is a composition of
$g(x) = x - 5$ and $h(x) = \sqrt{x}$.

10. True, because $(g \circ h)(x) = g[h(x)]$
$= g[x - 1] = (x - 1)^2 = F(x)$.

9.1 EXERCISES

1. The basic operations of functions are
addition, subtraction, multiplication, and
division.

2. We perform the operation with functions by
adding, subtracting, multiplying, or dividing the
expressions that define the functions.

3. In the composition of functions the second
function is evaluated on the result of the first
function.

4. Since each operation is a function, the order
of operations determines the order in which the
functions are composed.

5. $(f + g)(x) = f(x) + g(x)$
$$= 4x - 3 + x^2 - 2x$$
$$= x^2 + 2x - 3$$

6. $(f - g)(x) = f(x) - g(x)$
$$= 4x - 3 - (x^2 - 2x)$$
$$= -x^2 + 6x - 3$$

7. $(f \cdot g)(x) = f(x) \cdot g(x)$
$$= (4x - 3)(x^2 - 2x)$$
$$= 4x^3 - 11x^2 + 6x$$

8. $(f/g)(x) = f(x)/g(x)$
$$= \frac{4x - 3}{x^2 - 2x}$$

9. Use $x = 3$ in the formula of Exercise 1:
$(f + g)(3) = 3^2 + 2(3) - 3 = 12$

10. $(f + g)(2) = f(2) + g(2)$
$$= 4(2) - 3 + 2^2 - 2 \cdot 2$$
$$= 5$$

11. $(f - g)(-3) = f(-3) - g(-3)$
$$= 4(-3) - 3 - [(-3)^2 - 2(-3)]$$
$$= -12 - 3 - [9 + 6]$$
$$= -30$$

12. $(f - g)(-2) = f(-2) - g(-2)$
$$= 4(-2) - 3 - [(-2)^2 - 2(-2)]$$
$$= -8 - 3 - [4 + 4]$$
$$= -8 - 3 - 8$$
$$= -19$$

13. Use $x = -1$ in the formula of Exercise 3:
$(f \cdot g)(-1) = 4(-1)^3 - 11(-1)^2 + 6(-1)$
$$= -4 - 11 - 6$$
$$= -21$$

14. $(f \cdot g)(-2) = f(-2) \cdot g(-2)$
$$= [4(-2) - 3] \cdot [(-2)^2 - 2(-2)]$$
$$= [-11] \cdot [8]$$
$$= -88$$

15. $(f/g)(4) = \frac{f(4)}{g(4)} = \frac{4(4) - 3}{4^2 - 2(4)} = \frac{13}{8}$

16. $(f/g)(-2) = f(-2)/g(-2)$
$$= \frac{4(-2) - 3}{(-2)^2 - 2(-2)} = \frac{-11}{8} = -\frac{11}{8}$$

17. Since $a = 2x - 6$, and $y = 3a - 2$ we
have
$$y = 3(2x - 6) - 2$$
$$y = 6x - 18 - 2$$
$$y = 6x - 20$$

18. Since $c = -3x + 4$ and $y = 2c + 3$ we
have
$$y = 2(-3x + 4) + 3$$
$$y = -6x + 8 + 3$$
$$y = -6x + 11$$

19. Let $d = (x+1)/2$ in $y = 2d + 1$.
$$y = 2\left(\frac{x+1}{2}\right) + 1$$
$$y = x + 1 + 1$$
$$y = x + 2$$

20. Let $d = (2-x)/3$ in $y = -3d + 2$.
$$y = -3\left(\frac{2-x}{3}\right) + 2$$
$$y = -1(2-x) + 2$$
$$y = x$$

21. Let $m = x + 1$ in $y = m^2 - 1$.
$$y = (x+1)^2 - 1$$
$$y = x^2 + 2x + 1 - 1$$
$$y = x^2 + 2x$$

22. Let $n = x + 2$ in $y = n^2 - 3n + 1$.
$$y = (x+2)^2 - 3(x+2) + 1$$
$$y = x^2 + 4x + 4 - 3x - 6 + 1$$
$$y = x^2 + x - 1$$

23.
$$y = \frac{\frac{2x+3}{1-x} - 3}{\frac{2x+3}{1-x} + 2}$$
$$y = \frac{\left(\frac{2x+3}{1-x} - 3\right)(1-x)}{\left(\frac{2x+3}{1-x} + 2\right)(1-x)}$$
$$y = \frac{2x + 3 - 3(1-x)}{2x + 3 + 2(1-x)}$$
$$y = \frac{2x + 3 - 3 + 3x}{2x + 3 + 2 - 2x} = \frac{5x}{5}$$
$$y = x$$

24. Use $w = \frac{5x+2}{x-1}$ in $y = \frac{w+2}{w-5}$.
$$y = \frac{\frac{5x+2}{x-1} + 2}{\frac{5x+2}{x-1} - 5}$$
$$y = \frac{\left(\frac{5x+2}{x-1} + 2\right)(x-1)}{\left(\frac{5x+2}{x-1} - 5\right)(x-1)}$$
$$y = \frac{5x + 2 + 2(x-1)}{5x + 2 - 5(x-1)}$$
$$y = \frac{7x}{7}$$
$$y = x$$

25. $(g \circ f)(1) = g[f(1)] = g(-1)$
$$= (-1)^2 + 3(-1) = -2$$

26. $(f \circ g)(-2) = f[g(-2)] = f[-2]$
$$= 2(-2) - 3 = -7$$

27. $(f \circ g)(1) = f[g(1)] = f[4]$
$$= 2(4) - 3 = 5$$

28. $(g \circ f)(-2) = g[f(-2)] = g[-7]$
$$= (-7)^2 + 3(-7) = 28$$

29. $(f \circ f)(4) = f[f(4)] = f[5]$
$$= 2(5) - 3 = 7$$

30. $(h \circ h)(3) = h[h(3)] = h[3] = \frac{3+3}{2} = 3$

31. $(h \circ f)(5) = h[f(5)] = h[7] = \frac{7+3}{2} = 5$

32. $(f \circ h)(0) = f[h(0)] = f[3/2] = 2 \cdot \frac{3}{2} - 3$
$$= 0$$

33. $(f \circ h)(5) = f[h(5)] = f[4] = 2(4) - 3$
$$= 5$$

34. $(h \circ f)(0) = h[f(0)] = h[-3] = \frac{-3+3}{2}$
$$= 0$$

35. $(g \circ h)(-1) = g[h(-1)] = g[1] = 4$

36. $(h \circ g)(-1) = h[g(-1)] = h[-2]$
$$= \frac{-2+3}{2} = \frac{1}{2}$$

37. $(f \circ g)(2.36) = f[g(2.36)] = f[12.6496]$
$$= 22.2992$$

38. $(h \circ f)(23.761) = h[f(23.761)]$
$$= h[44.522] = \frac{44.522+3}{2} = 23.761$$

39. $(g \circ f)(x) = g[f(x)] = g[2x - 3]$
$$= (2x-3)^2 + 3(2x-3)$$
$$= 4x^2 - 12x + 9 + 6x - 9$$
$$= 4x^2 - 6x$$

40. $(g \circ h)(x) = g[h(x)] = g\left(\frac{x+3}{2}\right)$
$$= \left(\frac{x+3}{2}\right)^2 + 3\left(\frac{x+3}{2}\right)$$
$$= \frac{x^2 + 6x + 9}{4} + \frac{3x+9}{2}$$
$$= \frac{x^2 + 6x + 9}{4} + \frac{6x+18}{4}$$
$$= \frac{x^2 + 12x + 27}{4}$$

41. $f[g(x)] = f[x^2 + 3x] = 2(x^2 + 3x) - 3$
$$= 2x^2 + 6x - 3$$

42. $(h \circ g)(x) = h[g(x)] = h[x^2 + 3x]$
$$= \frac{x^2 + 3x + 3}{2}$$

43. $(h \circ f)(x) = h[f(x)] = h[2x - 3]$
$$= \frac{2x - 3 + 3}{2} = x$$

44. $(f \circ h)(x) = f[h(x)] = f[\frac{x+3}{2}]$
$$= 2\left(\frac{x+3}{2}\right) - 3 = x + 3 - 3 = x$$

45. $(f \circ f)(x) = f[f(x)] = f[2x - 3]$
$$= 2(2x - 3) - 3 = 4x - 9$$

46. $(g \circ g)(x) = g(g(x)) = g(x^2 + 3x)$
$$= (x^2 + 3x)^2 + 3(x^2 + 3x)$$
$$= x^4 + 6x^3 + 9x^2 + 3x^2 + 9x$$
$$= x^4 + 6x^3 + 12x^2 + 9x$$

47. $(h \circ h)(x) = h[h(x)] = h[\frac{x+3}{2}]$

$= \frac{\frac{x+3}{2} + 3}{2} = \frac{(\frac{x+3}{2} + 3)2}{2 \cdot 2}$

$= \frac{x+3+6}{4} = \frac{x+9}{4}$

48. $(f \circ f \circ f)(x) = f(f(f(x)))$
$= f(f(2x-3) = f(4x-9)$
$= 2(4x-9) - 3$
$= 8x - 21$

49. $F(x) = \sqrt{x-3} = \sqrt{h(x)} = f[h(x)]$
Therefore, $F = f \circ h$.

50. $N(x) = \sqrt{x} - 3 = f(x) - 3 = h[f(x)]$
$= (h \circ f)(x)$
Therefore, $N = h \circ f$.

51. $G(x) = x^2 - 6x + 9 = (x-3)^2$
$= [h(x)]^2 = g[h(x)]$
Therefore $G = g \circ h$.

52. $P(x) = x = \sqrt{x^2} = \sqrt{g(x)}$
$= f[g(x)] = (f \circ g)(x)$
Therefore, $P = f \circ g$ for $x \geq 0$. We also have
$P = g \circ f$ for $x \geq 0$.

53. $H(x) = x^2 - 3 = g(x) - 3 = h[g(x)]$
Therefore $H = h \circ g$.

54. $M(x) = x^{1/4} = (x^{1/2})^{1/2} = \sqrt{\sqrt{x}}$
$= \sqrt{f(x)} = f[f(x)] = (f \circ f)(x)$
Therefore, $M = f \circ f$.

55. $J(x) = x - 6 = x - 3 - 3$
$= h(x) - 3 = h[h(x)]$
Therefore, $J = h \circ h$.

56. $R(x) = \sqrt{x^2 - 3} = \sqrt{g(x) - 3}$
$= \sqrt{h[g(x)]} = f(h[g(x)])$
Therefore, $R = f \circ h \circ g$.

57. $K(x) = x^4 = (x^2)^2 = [g(x)]^2 = g[g(x)]$
Therefore, $K = g \circ g$.

58. $Q(x) = \sqrt{x^2 - 6x + 9} = \sqrt{(x-3)^2}$
$= \sqrt{(h(x))^2} = \sqrt{g[h(x)]} = f(g[h(x)])$
Therefore, $Q = f \circ g \circ h$.

59. $f[g(x)] = f\left(\frac{x-5}{3}\right) = 3\left(\frac{x-5}{3}\right) + 5$
$= x$
$g[f(x)] = g(3x + 5) = \frac{3x + 5 - 5}{3} = x$

60. $f[g(x)] = f\left(\frac{x+7}{3}\right)$
$= 3\left(\frac{x+7}{3}\right) - 7 = x$
$g[f(x)] = g(3x - 7) = \frac{3x - 7 + 7}{3} = x$

61. $f[g(x)] = f\left(\sqrt[3]{x+9}\right)$
$= \left(\sqrt[3]{x+9}\right)^3 - 9 = x + 9 - 9 = x$
$g[f(x)] = g[x^3 - 9] = \sqrt[3]{x^3 - 9 + 9}$
$= \sqrt[3]{x^3} = x$

62. $f[g(x)] = f\left(\sqrt[3]{x-1}\right)$
$= \left(\sqrt[3]{x-1}\right)^3 + 1 = x - 1 + 1 = x$
$g[f(x)] = g(x^3 + 1) = \sqrt[3]{x^3 + 1 - 1} = \sqrt[3]{x^3}$
$= x$

63. $f[g(x)] = f\left(\frac{x+1}{1-x}\right) = \frac{\frac{x+1}{1-x} - 1}{\frac{x+1}{1-x} + 1}$

$= \frac{\left(\frac{x+1}{1-x} - 1\right)(1-x)}{\left(\frac{x+1}{1-x} + 1\right)(1-x)} = \frac{x+1-(1-x)}{x+1+1-x} = \frac{2x}{2}$

$= x$

$g[f(x)] = g\left(\frac{x-1}{x+1}\right) = \frac{\frac{x-1}{x+1} + 1}{1 - \frac{x-1}{x+1}}$

$= \frac{\left(\frac{x-1}{x+1} + 1\right)(x+1)}{\left(1 - \frac{x-1}{x+1}\right)(x+1)} = \frac{x-1+x+1}{x+1-(x-1)}$

$= \frac{2x}{2} = x$

64. $f[g(x)] = f\left(\frac{3x+1}{x-1}\right) = \frac{\frac{3x+1}{x-1} + 1}{\frac{3x+1}{x-1} - 3}$

$= \frac{\left(\frac{3x+1}{x-1} + 1\right)(x-1)}{\left(\frac{3x+1}{x-1} - 3\right)(x-1)} = \frac{3x+1+1(x-1)}{3x+1-3(x-1)}$

$= \frac{4x}{4} = x$

$g[f(x)] = g\left(\frac{x+1}{x-3}\right) = \frac{3 \cdot \frac{x+1}{x-3} + 1}{\frac{x+1}{x-3} - 1}$

$= \frac{3x+3+1(x-3)}{x+1-1(x-3)} = \frac{4x}{4} = x$

65. $f[g(x)] = f\left(\frac{1}{x}\right) = \frac{1}{\frac{1}{x}} = x$

$g[f(x)] = g\left(\frac{1}{x}\right) = \frac{1}{\frac{1}{x}} = x$

66. $f[g(x)] = f[\left(\frac{x}{2}\right)^{1/3}] = 2 \cdot \left(\left(\frac{x}{2}\right)^{1/3}\right)^3$
$= 2 \cdot \frac{x}{2} = x$
$g[f(x)] = g[2x^3] = \left(\frac{2x^3}{2}\right)^{1/3} = (x^3)^{1/3} = x$

67. Let $s = $ the length of a side of the square.
$15^2 = s^2 + s^2$
$2s^2 = 225$
$s^2 = \frac{225}{2}$

$$s = \sqrt{\frac{225}{2}}$$

Since $A = s^2$, we have $A = \frac{225}{2} = 112.5$ in.^{2}
In general if d is the diagonal of a square and s is the length of a side, we have $d^2 = s^2 + s^2$ or $s^2 = \frac{d^2}{2}$. Since $A = s^2$, we have $A = \frac{d^2}{2}$.

68. For a square, $P = 4s$. Since $A = s^2$, we have $s = \sqrt{A}$ or $P = 4\sqrt{A}$.

69. $P(x) = R(x) - C(x)$
$= x^2 - 10x + 30 - (2x^2 - 30x + 200)$
$= -x^2 + 20x - 170$

70. The area of a circle of radius x is πx^2. So the area of a semicircle of radius x is $\frac{\pi x^2}{2}$. The area of a circle with diameter x (radius $x/2$) is $\frac{\pi x^2}{4}$. So the area of a semicircle with diameter x is $\frac{\pi x^2}{8}$. Since the sides of the square are $2x$, the area of the square is $4x^2$. The area of the sign is the area of the square plus the area of the first semicircle, minus the area of the second semicircle.

$A = 4x^2 + \frac{\pi x^2}{2} - \frac{\pi x^2}{8}$
$A = \frac{32x^2}{8} + \frac{4\pi x^2}{8} - \frac{\pi x^2}{8} = \frac{32x^2 + 3\pi x^2}{8}$
$A = \frac{(32 + 3\pi)x^2}{8}$

71. Substitute $F = 0.25I$ into $J = 0.10F$.
$J = 0.10(0.25I)$
$J = 0.025I$

72. If the area of the square is M, then $A = s^2 = M$. So $s = \sqrt{M}$. The radius of a circle inscribed in a square is one-half the length of a side of the square. So the radius of the circle is $\frac{\sqrt{M}}{2}$. The area of the circle is

$A = \pi\left(\frac{\sqrt{M}}{2}\right)^2 = \pi\frac{M}{4}$

73. a) $x = (30.25/100)^3 \approx 0.0277$
$D = (24665/2240)/0.0277 \approx 397.8$
b) $x = (L/100)^3$
$D = (25000/2240)/x$
$D = (25000/2240)/(L/100)^3$
$D = \frac{25000}{2240} \cdot \frac{100^3}{L^3}$
$D = \frac{1.116 \times 10^7}{L^3}$

c) From the graph it appears that the displacement-length ratio decreases as the length increases.

74. a) $y = (24665/64)^{2/3} \approx 52.958$
$S = 846/y \approx 15.97$
b) $y = (d/64)^{2/3} = d^{2/3}/16$
$S = 900/y$
$S = 900/(d^{2/3}/16) = 900 \cdot \frac{16}{d^{2/3}}$
$S = 14,400d^{-2/3}$
c) From the formula in part (b) we see that for a fixed sail area S decreases as the displacement increases.

75. The domain of $f(x) = \sqrt{x-4}$ is $[0, \infty)$. The domain of $g(x) = \sqrt{x}$ is $[0, \infty)$.
$(g \circ f)(x) = g(\sqrt{x-4}) = \sqrt{\sqrt{x-4}}$
So that $\sqrt{x-4} \geq 0$ we must have $x \geq 16$. So the domain of $g \circ f$ is $[16, \infty)$.

76. The domain of $f(x) = \sqrt{x-4}$ is $[4, \infty)$. The domain of $g(x) = \sqrt{x-8}$ is $[8, \infty)$.
$(f + g)(x) = \sqrt{x-4} + \sqrt{x-8}$
So that both $x - 4 \geq 0$ and $x - 8 \geq 0$ we must have $x \geq 4$ and $x \geq 8$. So the domain of $f + g$ is $[8, \infty)$

77. The graph of $y = x + \sqrt{x}$ appears only for $x \geq 0$. So the domain is $[0, \infty)$. The graph starts at $(0, 0)$ and goes up from there. So the range is $[0, \infty)$.

78. Any value for x is allowed in the function $y = |x| + |x - 3|$. So the domain is $(-\infty, \infty)$. From the graph we see that the y-coordinates are greater than or equal to 3. So the range is $[3, \infty)$.

9.2 WARM-UPS

1. False, because the inverse function is obtained by interchanging the coordinates in every ordered pair.
2. False, because the points $(0, 3)$ and $(1, 3)$ both satisfy $f(x) = 3$.
3. False, because the inverse of multiplication by 2 is division by 2. If $g(x) = 2x$, then $g^{-1}(x) = x/2$.
4. True, because if we interchange the coordinates in a function that is not one-to-one, we do not obtain a function.

5. True, because in an inverse function the domain and range of the function are reversed.

6. False, because it is not one-to-one. Both (2, 16) and (−2, 16) satisfy $f(x) = x^4$.

7. True, because taking the opposite of a number twice gives back the original number.

8. True, because the inverse function interchanges the coordinates in all of the ordered pairs of the function.

9. True, the inverse of $k(x) = 3x - 6$ is $k^{-1}(x) = (x + 6)/3 = (1/3)x + 2$.

10. False, because $f^{-1}(x) = (x + 4)/3$.

9.2 EXERCISES

1. The inverse of a function is a function with the same ordered pairs except that the coordinates are reversed.

2. The domain of f^{-1} is the range of f.

3. The range of f^{-1} is the domain of f.

4. The −1 in f^{-1} is not treated as an exponent. It is simply a notation for the inverse of the function f.

5. A function is one-to-one if no two ordered pairs have the same second coordinate with different first coordinates.

6. The horizontal line test says that if a horizontal line can be drawn to cross the graph of a function more than once, then the function is not one-to-one.

7. The switch and solve strategy is used to find a formula for an inverse function.

8. The graphs of f and f^{-1} are symmetric with respect to the line $y = x$.

9. The function is not one-to-one because of the pairs (−2, 2) and (2, 2). Therefore, the function is not invertible.

10. This function is one-to-one. The inverse is {(1, 1), (8, 2), (27, 3)}. It is obtained by interchanging the coordinates in each ordered pair.

11. The function is one-to-one. The inverse is {(4, 16), (3, 9), (0, 0)}.
It is obtained by interchanging the coordinates in each ordered pair.

12. The function is not one-to-one because of the pairs (−3, 81) and (3, 81). Therefore, the function is not invertible.

13. The function is not one-to-one because of the pairs (5, 0) and (6, 0). Therefore, it is not invertible.

14. This function is one-to-one and therefore invertible. Its inverse, {(−3, 3), (2, −2), (−1, 1)}, is obtained by interchanging the coordinates in each ordered pair.

15. This function is one-to-one. Its inverse is obtained by interchanging the coordinates in each ordered pair: {(0, 0), (2, 2), (9, 9)}.

16. The function is not one-to-one because of the pairs (9, 1) and (2, 1). Therefore, the function is not invertible.

17. This function is not one-to-one because we can draw a horizontal line that crosses the graph twice.

18. This function is not one-to-one because we can draw a horizontal line that crosses the graph more than once.

19. This function is one-to-one because we cannot draw a horizontal line that crosses the graph more than once.

20. This function is one-to-one because we cannot draw a horizontal line that crosses the graph more than once.

21. Since $(f \circ g)(x) = f(g(x)) = f(0.5x) = 2(0.5x) = x$ and $(g \circ f)(x) = g(f(x)) = g(2x) = 0.5(2x) = x$, the functions are inverses of each other.

22. Since $(f \circ g)(x) = f(g(x)) = f(0.33x) = 3(0.33x) = 0.99x$, the functions are not inverses of each other.

23. $(f \circ g)(x) = f(g(x)) = f(\frac{1}{2}x + 5)$
$= 2(\frac{1}{2}x + 5) - 10 = x + 10 - 10 = x$
$(g \circ f)(x) = g(f(x)) = g(2x - 10)$
$= \frac{1}{2}(2x - 10) + 5 = x - 5 + 5 = x$
Therefore, the functions are inverses of each other.

24. $(f \circ g)(x) = f(g(x)) = f\left(\frac{x-7}{3}\right)$
$$= 3\left(\frac{x-7}{3}\right) + 7 = x - 7 + 7 = x$$
$(g \circ f)(x) = g(f(x)) = g(3x + 7) = \frac{3x + 7 - 7}{3}$
$$= \frac{3x}{3} = x$$

Therefore, the functions are inverses of each other.

25. $(f \circ g)(x) = f(g(x)) = f(-x) = -(-x)$
$$= x$$
$(g \circ f)(x) = g(f(x)) = g(-x) = -(-x) = x$

Therefore, the functions are inverses of each other.

26. $(f \circ g)(x) = f(g(x)) = f\left(\frac{1}{x}\right) = \frac{1}{\frac{1}{x}} = x$

$(g \circ f)(x) = g(f(x)) = g(\frac{1}{x}) = \frac{1}{\frac{1}{x}} = x$

Therefore, the functions are inverses of each other.

27. $(g \circ f)(x) = g(f(x)) = g(x^4) = (x^4)^{1/4}$
$$= |x|$$
For example, $g(f(-2)) = g(16) = 2$. So the functions are not inverses of each other.

28. $(f \circ g)(x) = f(g(x)) = f(|x/2|)$
$= |2 \cdot |x/2|| = |x|$
For example,
$(f \circ g)(-2) = f(g(-2)) = f(1) = 2$.
So the functions are not inverses of each other.

29. $y = 5x$, $x = 5y$, $y = \frac{1}{5}x$
So $f^{-1}(x) = \frac{x}{5}$.

30. $y = -3x$, $x = -3y$, $y = -\frac{1}{3}x$
So $h^{-1}(x) = -\frac{1}{3}x$.

31. $y = x - 9$, $x = y - 9$, $y = x + 9$
So $g^{-1}(x) = x + 9$.

32. $y = x + 7$, $x = y + 7$, $y = x - 7$
So $j^{-1}(x) = x - 7$.

33. $y = 5x - 9$, $x = 5y - 9$, $5y = x + 9$,
$y = \frac{x+9}{5}$
So $k^{-1}(x) = \frac{x+9}{5}$.

34. $y = 2x - 8$, $x = 2y - 8$, $2y = x + 8$,
$y = \frac{x+8}{2}$
So $r^{-1}(x) = \frac{x+8}{2}$.

35. $y = \frac{2}{x}$, $x = \frac{2}{y}$, $xy = 2$, $y = \frac{2}{x}$
So $m^{-1}(x) = \frac{2}{x}$.

36. $y = \frac{-1}{x}$, $x = \frac{-1}{y}$, $xy = -1$, $y = \frac{-1}{x}$

So $s^{-1}(x) = -\frac{1}{x}$.

37. $y = \sqrt[3]{x-4}$, $x = \sqrt[3]{y-4}$, $x^3 = y - 4$,
$y = x^3 + 4$ So $f^{-1}(x) = x^3 + 4$.

38. $y = \sqrt[3]{x+2}$, $x = \sqrt[3]{y+2}$, $x^3 = y + 2$,
$y = x^3 - 2$ So $f^{-1}(x) = x^3 - 2$.

39. $y = \frac{3}{x-4}$, $x = \frac{3}{y-4}$, $x(y-4) = 3$,
$y - 4 = \frac{3}{x}$
$y = \frac{3}{x} + 4$ So $f^{-1}(x) = \frac{3}{x} + 4$.

40. $y = \frac{2}{x+1}$, $x = \frac{2}{y+1}$, $x(y+1) = 2$,
$y + 1 = \frac{2}{x}$
$y = \frac{2}{x} - 1$ So $f^{-1}(x) = \frac{2}{x} - 1$.

41. $f(x) = \sqrt[3]{3x+7}$
$\qquad y = \sqrt[3]{3x+7}$
$\qquad x = \sqrt[3]{3y+7}$
$\qquad x^3 = 3y + 7$
$\qquad x^3 - 7 = 3y$
$\qquad \frac{x^3 - 7}{3} = y$
$\qquad f^{-1}(x) = \frac{x^3 - 7}{3}$

42. $f(x) = \sqrt[3]{7-5x}$
$\qquad y = \sqrt[3]{7-5x}$
$\qquad x = \sqrt[3]{7-5y}$
$\qquad x^3 = (\sqrt[3]{7-5y})^3$
$\qquad x^3 = 7 - 5y$
$\qquad 5y = -x^3 + 7$
$\qquad y = \frac{-x^3 + 7}{5}$
$\qquad f^{-1}(x) = \frac{-x^3 + 7}{5}$

43. $f(x) = \frac{x+1}{x-2}$
$\qquad y = \frac{x+1}{x-2}$
$\qquad x = \frac{y+1}{y-2}$
$\qquad x(y-2) = y + 1$
$\qquad xy - 2x = y + 1$
$\qquad xy - y = 2x + 1$
$\qquad y(x-1) = 2x + 1$
$\qquad y = \frac{2x+1}{x-1}$
$\qquad f^{-1}(x) = \frac{2x+1}{x-1}$

44. $f(x) = \frac{1-x}{x+3}$
$\qquad y = \frac{1-x}{x+3}$
$\qquad x = \frac{1-y}{y+3}$

$$x(y+3) = 1 - y$$
$$xy + 3x = 1 - y$$
$$xy + y = 1 - 3x$$
$$y(x+1) = 1 - 3x$$
$$y = \frac{1-3x}{x+1}$$

$$f^{-1}(x) = \frac{1-3x}{x+1}$$

45. $f(x) = \frac{x+1}{3x-4}$

$$y = \frac{x+1}{3x-4}$$
$$x = \frac{y+1}{3y-4}$$
$$x(3y-4) = y+1$$
$$3xy - 4x = y + 1$$
$$3xy - y = 1 + 4x$$
$$y(3x-1) = 1 + 4x$$
$$y = \frac{1+4x}{3x-1}$$
$$f^{-1}(x) = \frac{1+4x}{3x-1}$$

46. $f(x) = \frac{3x+5}{2x-3}$

$$y = \frac{3x+5}{2x-3}$$
$$x = \frac{3y+5}{2y-3}$$
$$x(2y-3) = 3y+5$$
$$2xy - 3x = 3y + 5$$
$$2xy - 3y = 5 + 3x$$
$$y(2x-3) = 5 + 3x$$
$$y = \frac{5+3x}{2x-3}$$
$$f^{-1}(x) = \frac{3x+5}{2x-3}$$

47. The function $p(x) = \sqrt[4]{x}$ finds the fourth root. The inverse must be the fourth power. Since the domain and range of p are both the set of nonnegative real numbers, $p^{-1}(x) = x^4$ for $x \geq 0$.

48. The function $v(x) = \sqrt[6]{x}$ finds the sixth root. The inverse must be the sixth power. Since the domain and range of v are both the set of nonnegative real numbers, $v^{-1}(x) = x^6$ for $x \geq 0$.

49. $y = (x-2)^2$, $x = (y-2)^2$,
$y - 2 = \pm \sqrt{x}$
$y = 2 \pm \sqrt{x}$.   Since $x \geq 2$ in the function, we must have $y \geq 2$ in the inverse function. So $y = 2 - \sqrt{x}$ is not the inverse and $f^{-1}(x) = 2 + \sqrt{x}$.

50. $y = (x+5)^2$, $x = (y+5)^2$,
$y + 5 = \pm \sqrt{x}$
$y = -5 \pm \sqrt{x}$.   Since $x \geq -5$ in the function, $y \geq -5$ in the inverse function. So $y = -5 - \sqrt{x}$ is not the inverse and $f^{-1}(x) = -5 + \sqrt{x}$.

51. $y = x^2 + 3$, $x = y^2 + 3$, $y^2 = x - 3$,
$y = \pm \sqrt{x-3}$. Since $x \geq 0$ in the function, $y \geq 0$ in the inverse function. So $f^{-1}(x) = \sqrt{x-3}$.

52. $y = x^2 - 5$, $x = y^2 - 5$, $y^2 = x + 5$,
$y = \pm \sqrt{x+5}$. Since $x \geq 0$ in the function, $y \geq 0$ in the inverse function. So $f^{-1}(x) = \sqrt{x+5}$.

53. $f(x) = \sqrt{x+2}$
$$y = \sqrt{x+2}$$
$$x = \sqrt{y+2}$$
$$x^2 = y + 2$$
$$x^2 - 2 = y$$
Since $y \geq 0$ in the function, $x \geq 0$ in the inverse.
So $f^{-1}(x) = x^2 - 2$ for $x \geq 0$.

54. $f(x) = \sqrt{x-4}$
$$y = \sqrt{x-4}$$
$$x = \sqrt{y-4}$$
$$x^2 = y - 4$$
$$x^2 + 4 = y$$
Since $y \geq 0$ in the function, $x \geq 0$ in the inverse function. So $f^{-1}(x) = x^2 + 4$ for $x \geq 0$.

55. The inverse of $f(x) = 2x + 3$ is a function that subtracts 3 and then divides by 2, $f^{-1}(x) = \frac{x-3}{2} = \frac{1}{2}x - \frac{3}{2}$. Use y-intercepts and slopes to graph each straight line.

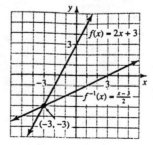

56. The graph of $f(x) = -3x + 2$ is a line with y-intercept $(0, 2)$ and slope -3. The inverse function is
$$f^{-1}(x) = \frac{x-2}{-3} = -\frac{1}{3}x + \frac{2}{3}.$$
The function f^{-1} is a straight line with y-intercept $(0, 2/3)$ and slope $-1/3$.

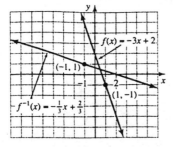

57. The graph of $f(x) = x^2 - 1$ for $x \geq 0$ contains the points $(0, -1)$, $(1, 0)$, and $(2, 3)$. For the inverse function we add 1 and then take the square root, $f^{-1}(x) = \sqrt{x+1}$. The function f^{-1} contains $(-1, 0)$, $(0, 1)$, and $(3, 2)$.

58. The graph of $f(x) = x^2 + 3$ for $x \geq 0$ includes the points $(0, 3)$, $(1, 4)$, and $(2, 7)$. Its graph is half of a parabola. The inverse of squaring and adding 3 is subtracting 3 and then taking the square root, $f^{-1}(x) = \sqrt{x-3}$. The graph of f^{-1} includes the points $(3, 0)$, $(4, 1)$, and $(7, 2)$.

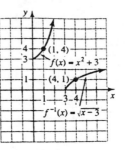

59. The graph of f is a line through $(0, 0)$ with slope 5, and the graph of $f^{-1}(x) = x/5$ is a straight line through $(0, 0)$ with slope $1/5$.

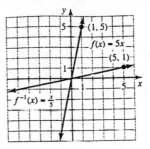

60. The graph of $f(x) = x/4$ is a line through $(0, 0)$ with slope $1/4$. The graph of $f^{-1}(x) = 4x$ is a line through $(0, 0)$ with slope 4.

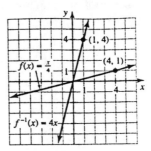

61. The inverse of cubing is the cube root. So $f^{-1}(x) = \sqrt[3]{x}$. The graph of f contains the points $(0, 0)$, $(1, 1)$, $(-1, -1)$, $(2, 8)$, and

335

$(-2, -8)$. The graph of f^{-1} contains the points $(0, 0)$, $(1, 1)$, $(-1, -1)$, $(8, 2)$, and $(-8, -2)$.

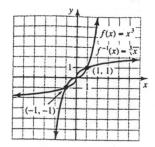

62. The graph of $f(x) = 2x^3$ includes the points $(-1, -2)$, $(0, 0)$, and $(1, 2)$. The function f consists of cubing x and then multiplying by 2. The inverse must be dividing by 2 and then taking the cube root. So $f^{-1}(x) = \sqrt[3]{x/2}$. The graph of f^{-1} includes the points $(-2, -1)$, $(0, 0)$, and $(2, 1)$.

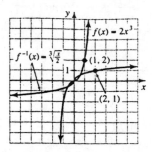

63. The inverse of subtracting 2 and then taking a square root is squaring and then adding 2. So $f^{-1}(x) = x^2 + 2$ for $x \geq 0$. The graph of f contains $(2, 0)$, $(3, 1)$, and $(6, 2)$. The graph of f^{-1} contains $(0, 2)$, $(1, 3)$, and $(2, 6)$.

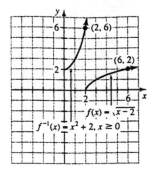

64. The graph of $f(x) = \sqrt{x + 3}$ includes the points $(-3, 0)$, $(-2, 1)$ and $(1, 2)$. The function f consists of adding 3 and then taking the square root. The inverse function must consist of squaring and then subtracting 3. So $f^{-1}(x) = x^2 - 3$. Since the range of f is the nonnegative real numbers, the domain of f^{-1} is the nonnegative real numbers. The graph of f^{-1} includes the points $(0, -3)$, $(1, -2)$, and $(2, 1)$.

65. $(f^{-1} \circ f)(x) = f^{-1}(f(x)) = f^{-1}(x^3 - 1)$
$\quad\quad = \sqrt[3]{x^3 - 1 + 1} = x$

66. $(f^{-1} \circ f)(x) = f^{-1}(f(x)) = f^{-1}(2x^3 + 1)$
$= \sqrt[3]{\dfrac{2x^3 + 1 - 1}{2}} = \sqrt[3]{\dfrac{2x^3}{2}} = \sqrt[3]{x^3} = x$

67. $(f^{-1} \circ f)(x) = f^{-1}(f(x)) = f^{-1}(\tfrac{1}{2}x - 3)$
$\quad\quad = 2(\tfrac{1}{2}x - 3) + 6 = x - 6 + 6 = x$

68. $(f^{-1} \circ f)(x) = f^{-1}(f(x)) = f^{-1}(3x - 9)$
$= \tfrac{1}{3}(3x - 9) + 3 = x - 3 + 3 = x$

69. $(f^{-1} \circ f)(x) = f^{-1}(f(x)) = f^{-1}(\tfrac{1}{x} + 2)$
$\quad\quad = \dfrac{1}{\frac{1}{x} + 2 - 2} = \dfrac{1}{\frac{1}{x}} = x$

70. $(f^{-1} \circ f)(x) = f^{-1}(f(x)) = f^{-1}(4 - \tfrac{1}{x})$
$= \dfrac{1}{4 - \left(4 - \frac{1}{x}\right)} = \dfrac{1}{4 - 4 + \frac{1}{x}} = \dfrac{1}{\frac{1}{x}} = x$

71. $(f^{-1} \circ f)(x) = f^{-1}(f(x)) = f^{-1}(\tfrac{x+1}{x-2})$

$= \dfrac{2(\frac{x+1}{x-2}) + 1}{\frac{x+1}{x-2} - 1} = \dfrac{\left(\frac{2x+2}{x-2} + 1\right)(x - 2)}{\left(\frac{x+1}{x-2} - 1\right)(x - 2)}$

$= \dfrac{2x + 2 + x - 2}{x + 1 - x + 2} = \dfrac{3x}{3} = x$

72. $(f^{-1} \circ f)(x) = f^{-1}(f(x)) = f^{-1}\left(\frac{3x-2}{x+2}\right)$

$$= \frac{2\left(\frac{3x-2}{x+2}\right) + 2}{3 - \left(\frac{3x-2}{x+2}\right)} = \frac{\left(2\left(\frac{3x-2}{x+2}\right) + 2\right)(x+2)}{\left(3 - \left(\frac{3x-2}{x+2}\right)\right)(x+2)}$$

$$= \frac{2(3x-2) + 2(x+2)}{3(x+2) - (3x-2)} = \frac{6x - 4 + 2x + 4}{3x + 6 - 3x + 2}$$

$$= \frac{8x}{8} = x$$

73. a) $S = \sqrt{30 \cdot 50 \cdot 0.75} \approx 33.5$ mph
b) From the graph you can see that the drag factor decreases when a road gets wet because the skid marks for a given speed will be longer.
c)
$$S = \sqrt{30L \cdot 1}$$
$$S^2 = 30L$$
$$L = \frac{S^2}{30}$$

74. $h(x) = \pi x^2$, In $h^{-1}(x)$, x represents the area of the circle. $h^{-1}(x) = \sqrt{\frac{x}{\pi}}$

75. $T(x) = x + 0.09x + 125$ or
$T(x) = 1.09x + 125$
$T^{-1}(x) = \frac{x - 125}{1.09}$

76. $C(x) = \frac{x^2}{9} \cdot 18 + 50$, or $C(x) = 2x^2 + 50$
$y = 2x^2 + 50$, $x = 2y^2 + 50$, $2y^2 = x - 50$
$y^2 = \frac{x - 50}{2}$, $y = \sqrt{\frac{x - 50}{2}}$

$C^{-1}(x) = = \sqrt{\frac{x - 50}{2}}$

77. Only the odd powers of x are one-to-one functions. So $f(x) = x^n$ is invertible if n is an odd positive integer.
78. These functions cannot be inverse functions, because if f and g are inverse functions then the range of f must equal the domain of g.
79. The functions f and g are not inverses of each other because the function
$y_2 = \sqrt{y_1} = \sqrt{x^2}$ is the absolute value function and not the identity function.
80. The functions y_1 and y_2 are inverse functions because the graph of the composition function is the same as $y = x$.

9.3 WARM-UPS

1. True, because direct variation means that a is a constant multiple of b.
2. False, because a inversely proportional to b means $a = k/b$.
3. False, because jointly proportional means $a = kbc$ for some constant k.
4. True, a is a constant multiple of the square root of c.
5. False, b is directly proportional to a means that $b = ka$.
6. True, because a is a multiple of b and b is divided by c.
7. False, a is jointly proportional to c and the square of b means that $a = kcb^2$.
8. False, $a = kc/\sqrt{b}$ is correct.
9. False, b is directly proportional to a and inversely proportional to the square of c means that $b = ka/c^2$.
10. True, b is equal to a constant divided by the square of c.

9.3 EXERCISES

1. If y varies directly as x, then $y = kx$ for some constant k.
2. The constant of proportionality in $y = kx$ is k.
3. If y is inversely proportional to x, then $y = k/x^2$.
4. In direct variation $y = kx$ while in inverse variation $y = k/x$.
5. If y is jointly proportional to x and z, then $y = kxz$ for some constant k.
6. Varies directly is the same as directly proportional.
7. If a varies directly as m, then a is equal to a constant multiple of m, $a = km$.
8. If w varies directly with P, then w is equal to a constant multiple of P, $w = kP$.
9. If d varies inversely as e, then d is equal to a constant divided by e, $d = k/e$.
10. If y varies inversely with x, then y is equal to a constant divided by x, $y = k/x$.
11. If I varies jointly as r and t, then I is a constant multiple of the product of r and t, $I = krt$.

12. If q varies jointly as w and v, then q is a constant multiple of the product of w and v, $q = kwv$.

13. If m is directly proportional to the square of p, then m is a constant multiple of the square of p, $m = kp^2$.

14. If g is directly proportional to the cube of r, then g is a constant multiple of r cubed, $g = kr^3$.

15. If B is directly proportional to the cube root of w, then B is a constant multiple of the cube root of w, $B = k\sqrt[3]{w}$.

16. If F is directly proportional to the square of m, then F is equal to a constant multiple of m squared, $F = km^2$.

17. If t is inversely proportional to the square of x, then t is equal to a constant divided by the square of x, $t = \dfrac{k}{x^2}$.

18. If y is inversely proportional to the square root of z, then y is equal to a constant divided by the square root of z, $y = \dfrac{k}{\sqrt{z}}$.

19. If v varies directly as m and inversely as n, then v is equal to a constant multiple of m divided by n, $v = \dfrac{km}{n}$.

20. If b varies directly as the square of n and inversely as the square root of v, then b is equal to a constant multiple of n^2 divided by $\sqrt{v}$, $b = \dfrac{kn^2}{\sqrt{v}}$.

21. If y varies directly as x, then $y = kx$. If $y = 6$ when $x = 4$, then $6 = k \cdot 4$, or $k = \frac{6}{4} = \frac{3}{2}$. Therefore, $y = kx$ can be written as $y = \frac{3}{2}x$.

22. If m varies directly as w, then $m = kw$. If $m = 1/3$ when $w = 1/4$, then $\frac{1}{3} = k\frac{1}{4}$, or $k = \frac{4}{3}$. So $m = kw$ can be written as $m = \frac{4}{3}w$.

23. If A varies inversely as B, then $A = \frac{k}{B}$. If $A = 10$ when $B = 3$, then $10 = \frac{k}{3}$ or $k = 30$. Therefore, $A = \frac{k}{B}$ can be written as $A = \frac{30}{B}$.

24. If c varies inversely as d, then $c = k/d$. If $c = 0.31$ when $d = 2$, then $0.31 = k/2$, or $k = 0.62$. So $c = k/d$ can be written as $c = \dfrac{0.62}{d}$.

25. If m varies inversely as the square root of p, then $m = \dfrac{k}{\sqrt{p}}$. If $m = 12$ when $p = 9$, then $12 = \dfrac{k}{\sqrt{9}}$ or $k = 12\sqrt{9} = 36$. Therefore, $m = \dfrac{k}{\sqrt{p}}$ can be written as $m = \dfrac{36}{\sqrt{p}}$.

26. If s varies inversely as the square root of v, then $s = \dfrac{k}{\sqrt{v}}$. If $s = 6$ when $v = 3/2$, then $6 = \dfrac{k}{\sqrt{\frac{3}{2}}}$, or $k = 6\sqrt{\frac{3}{2}} = 6\frac{\sqrt{6}}{2} = 3\sqrt{6}$.

So $s = \dfrac{k}{\sqrt{v}}$ can be written as $s = \dfrac{3\sqrt{6}}{\sqrt{v}}$.

27. If A varies jointly as t and u, then $A = ktu$. If $A = 6$ when $t = 5$ and $u = 3$, then $6 = k(5)(3)$ or $k = \frac{2}{5}$. Therefore, $A = \frac{2}{5}tu$.

28. If N varies jointly as the square of p and the cube of q, then $N = kp^2q^3$. If $N = 72$ when $p = 3$ and $q = 2$, then $72 = k(3)^2(2)^3$, or $72 = 72k$, or $k = 1$. So $N = kp^2q^3$ can be written as $N = p^2q^3$.

29. If y varies directly as x and inversely as z, then $y = \dfrac{kx}{z}$. If $y = 2.37$ when $x = \pi$ and $z = \sqrt{2}$, then $2.37 = \dfrac{k\pi}{\sqrt{2}}$ or $k = 2.37\dfrac{\sqrt{2}}{\pi} = 1.067$. So, $y = \dfrac{1.067x}{z}$.

30. If a varies directly as the square root of m and inversely as the square of n, then $a = \dfrac{k\sqrt{m}}{n^2}$. If $a = 5.47$ when $m = 3$ and $n = 1.625$, then $5.47 = \dfrac{k\sqrt{3}}{(1.625)^2}$, or $k = \dfrac{5.47(1.625)^2}{\sqrt{3}} = 8.339$.

So $a = \dfrac{k\sqrt{m}}{n^2}$ can be written as $a = \dfrac{8.339\sqrt{m}}{n^2}$.

31. If y varies directly as x, then $y = kx$. Since $y = 7$ when $x = 5$, we have $7 = k(5)$ or $k = \frac{7}{5}$. So, $y = kx$ can be written as $y = \frac{7}{5}x$. To find y when $x = -3$, we get $y = \frac{7}{5}(-3) = -\frac{21}{5}$.

32. If n varies directly as p, then $n = kp$. If $n = 0.6$ when $p = 0.2$, then $0.6 = k(0.2)$, or

$k = 3$. So the formula is $n = 3p$. Now if $p = \sqrt{2}$, then $n = 3\sqrt{2}$.

33. If w varies inversely as z, then $w = \frac{k}{z}$. Since $w = 6$ when $z = 2$, we have $6 = \frac{k}{2}$ or $k = 12$. Therefore, $w = \frac{12}{z}$. Now when $z = -8$, we get $w = \frac{12}{-8} = -\frac{3}{2}$.

34. If p varies inversely as q, then $p = \frac{k}{q}$. If $p = 5$ when $q = \sqrt{3}$, then $5 = \frac{k}{\sqrt{3}}$, or $k = 5\sqrt{3}$. So the formula is $p = \frac{5\sqrt{3}}{q}$. Now if $q = 5$, then $p = \frac{5\sqrt{3}}{5} = \sqrt{3}$.

35. If A varies jointly as F and T, then $A = kFT$. Since $A = 6$ when $F = 3\sqrt{2}$ and $T = 4$, we have $6 = k3\sqrt{2}(4)$ or $k = \frac{\sqrt{2}}{4}$. Therefore, $A = \frac{\sqrt{2}}{4}FT$. When $F = 2\sqrt{2}$ and $T = \frac{1}{2}$, we get $A = \frac{\sqrt{2}}{4}(2\sqrt{2})(\frac{1}{2}) = \frac{1}{2}$.

36. If j varies jointly as the square of r and the cube of v, then $j = kr^2v^3$. If $j = -3$ when $r = 2\sqrt{3}$ and $v = \frac{1}{2}$, then $-3 = k(2\sqrt{3})^2(\frac{1}{2})^3$, or $-3 = \frac{3}{2}k$, or $k = -2$. So the formula is $j = -2r^2v^3$. Now if $r = 3\sqrt{5}$ and $v = 2$, we get $j = -2(3\sqrt{5})^2(2^3) = -2(45)(8) = -720$.

37. If D varies directly with t and inversely with the square of s, then $D = \frac{kt}{s^2}$. Since $D = 12.35$ when $t = 2.8$ and $s = 2.48$, we get
$$12.35 = \frac{k2.8}{(2.48)^2} \text{ or } k = \frac{12.35(2.48)^2}{2.8}$$
$$= 27.128.$$
When $t = 5.63$ and $s = 6.81$, we get
$$D = \frac{(27.128)(5.63)}{(6.81)^2} = 3.293.$$

38. If M varies jointly with x and the square of v, then $M = kxv^2$. If $M = 39.5$ when $x = \sqrt{10}$ and $v = 3.87$, then
$$39.5 = k(\sqrt{10})(3.87)^2, \text{ or }$$
$$k = \frac{39.5}{\sqrt{10}(3.87)^2} = 0.834. \text{ So the formula is}$$
$M = 0.834xv^2$. Now if $x = \sqrt{30}$ and $v = 7.21$, then
$$M = 0.834(\sqrt{30})(7.21)^2 = 237.469.$$

39. Inverse variation, y varies inversely as x.

40. Inverse variation, y varies inversely as x.

41. Direct variation, y varies directly as x.

42. Direct variation, y varies directly as x.

43. Combined variation, y varies directly as x and inversely as w.

44. Combined variation, y varies directly as the square of t and inversely as the square root of x.

45. Joint variation, y varies jointly as x and z.

46. Joint variation, y varies jointly as q and v.

47. The cost c varies directly with the size of the lawn s means that $c = ks$. Since $c = \$280$ when $s = 4000$, we get $280 = k(4000)$ or $k = 0.07$. The formula is now written as $c = 0.07s$. For a 6000 square foot lawn, the cost is
$$c = 0.07(6000) = \$420.$$

48. If the weight is directly proportional to its length then $W = kL$. If a length of 4 feet corresponds to a weight of 30 pounds, then $30 = k(4)$, or $k = 7.5$. The formula is $W = 7.5L$. If the length is 5 feet, then
$$W = 7.5(5) = 37.5 \text{ pounds.}$$

49. The volume v is inversely proportional to the weight w means that $v = k/w$. Since the volume is 6 when the weight is 30, we have $6 = k/30$ or $k = 180$. Therefore, $v = 180/w$. If the weight is 20 kg, then
$$v = 180/20 = 9 \text{ cm}^3.$$

50. Since the price is inversely proportional to the number sold, $P = \frac{k}{n}$. If the price is $80 when 900 are sold, then $80 = \frac{k}{900}$, or $k = 72,000$. So the formula is $P = \frac{72,000}{n}$. Now if $n = 1000$, then
$$P = \frac{72,000}{1,000} = \$72 \text{ each.}$$

51. The price is jointly proportional to the radius and length means that $P = kRL$. Since a 12 foot culvert with a 6 inch radius costs $324, we have $324 = k(6)(12)$ or $k = 4.5$. Therefore, the formula is $P = 4.5RL$. The price of a 10 foot culvert with an 8 inch radius is $P = 4.5(8)(10) = \$360$.

52. Since the cost varies jointly as the diameter and the length, we can write $C = kDL$. If $C = \$6.80$, when $D = 1$ inch and $L = 20$ feet, then $6.80 = k(1)(20)$, or $k = 0.34$. So the formula is written as $C = 0.34DL$. Now if

$L = 10$ feet and $D = 3/4$ inch, we can write $C = 0.34(\frac{3}{4})(10) = \$2.55$.

53. The price varies jointly as the length and the square of the diameter means that $P = kLD^2$. Since an 18 foot rod with a diameter of 2 inches has a price of \$12.60, we get $12.60 = k(18)(2)^2$ or $k = 0.175$. Now the formula is written $P = 0.175LD^2$. The cost of a 12 foot rod with a 3 inch diameter is $P = 0.175(12)(3)^2 = \$18.90$.

54. Since the weight varies jointly with the height and the square of the radius, we can write $W = khr^2$. If $W = 16$ ounces when $h = 4$ inches and $r = 1.5$ inches, then $16 = k(4)(1.5)^2$, or $k = \frac{16}{4(1.5)^2} = \frac{16}{9}$. So the formula is $W = \frac{16}{9}hr^2$. Now if $h = 5$ inches and $r = 3$ inches, then
$$W = \frac{16}{9}(5)(3)^2 = 80 \text{ ounces.}$$

55. a) The distance varies directly as the square of the time means that $d = kt^2$. If an object falls 0.16 feet in 0.1 seconds, then $0.16 = k(0.1)^2$ or $k = 16$. So the formula is $d = 16t^2$.

b) In 0.5 seconds the object falls $d = 16(0.5)^2 = 4$ feet.

c) $16t^2 = 100$
$$t^2 = 6.25$$
$$t = \pm 2.5$$
It takes 2.5 seconds to reach the ground.

56. Since the cost varies directly with the square of the diameter, we have $C = kD^2$. If $C = \$0.45$ when $D = 9$ inches, then $0.45 = k(9)^2$, or $k = \frac{0.45}{9^2} = \frac{1}{180}$. So $C = \frac{1}{180}D^2$. Now if $D = 12$ inches, then $C = \frac{1}{180}(12)^2 = \$0.80$.

57. The force is inversely proportional to the length means that $F = k/L$. If a force of 2000 pounds is needed at 2 feet, then $2000 = k/2$ or $k = 4000$. The formula is now written as $F = 4000/L$. At 10 feet the force would be $F = 4000/10 = 400$ pounds.

58. Since the resistance varies directly with the length and inversely as the square of the diameter, $R = \frac{kL}{D^2}$. If $R = 2$ ohms when $L = 20$ feet and $D = 0.1$ in., then $2 = \frac{k(20)}{(0.1)^2}$,

or $k = \frac{2(0.1)^2}{20} = 0.001$. So the formula is $R = \frac{0.001L}{D^2}$. Now if $L = 30$ feet and $D = 0.2$ in., then $R = \frac{0.001(30)}{(0.2)^2} = 0.75$ ohm.

59. Since $t = \frac{kc}{n}$ and $t = 8$ when $n = 3$ and $c = 6$, we have $8 = \frac{k6}{3}$, or $k = 4$. So $t = \frac{4c}{n}$. Now if $c = 9$ and $n = 5$, $t = \frac{4\cdot9}{5} = 7.2$ days.

60. Since $V = \frac{kT}{P}$ and $V = 10$ when $T = 20$ and $P = 40$, we have $10 = \frac{k20}{40}$, or $k = 20$. So $V = \frac{20T}{P}$. Now if $T = 30$ and $P = 25$, then $V = \frac{20\cdot30}{25} = 24$ cm^3.

61. a) $G = \frac{kNd}{c}$
$$54 = \frac{k\cdot52\cdot27}{26}$$
$$54 = k\cdot54$$
$$1 = k$$
So $G = \frac{Nd}{c}$.

b) $G = \frac{42\cdot26}{13} = 84$

c) $\quad G = \frac{Nd}{c}$
$$cG = Nd$$
$$c = \frac{Nd}{G}$$
$c = \frac{44\cdot27}{52} \approx 23 \qquad c = \frac{44\cdot27}{59} \approx 20$
$c = \frac{44\cdot27}{70} \approx 17 \qquad c = \frac{44\cdot27}{79} \approx 15$
$c = \frac{44\cdot27}{91} \approx 13$

d) The gear ratio decreases as the number of teeth on the cog increases.

62. The function y_1 is increasing and y_2 is decreasing.

63. The curves cross at $(1, 1)$. The function y_1 is increasing and y_2 is decreasing. The function y_1 represents direct variation and y_2 represents inverse variation.

9.4 WARM-UPS

1. True, when dividing by $x - 5$ we use 5 for synthetic division.

2. True, when dividing by $x + 7$, or $x - (-7)$, -7 is used in synthetic division.

3. False, because the remainder of synthetic division is 2 and not 0.

4. True, because 2 is a solution to $x^3 - 8 = 0$ implies that $x - 2$ is a factor of $x^3 - 8$ and so the remainder is 0.

5. True, because of the factor theorem.

6. True, because of the factor theorem. If c is a solution to $P(x) = 0$, then $x - c$ is a factor of $P(x)$.

7. True, because $1^{35} - 3(1)^{24} + 2(1)^{18} = 0$ and so by the factor theorem $x - 1$ is a factor of the polynomial.

8. True, because $(-1)^3 - 3(-1)^2 + (-1) + 5 = 0$ and so by the factor theorem $x + 1$ is a factor of the polynomial.

9. True, because $1^3 - 5(1) + 4 = 0$ implies that $x - 1$ is a factor and so the remainder is 0.

10. True, because of the factor theorem.

9.4 EXERCISES

1. A zero of the function f is a number a such that $f(a) = 0$.

2. A root of a function is the same as a zero.

3. Two statements are equivalent means that they are either both true or both false.

4. To divide by $x - c$ quickly, use synthetic division.

5. If the remainder is zero when $P(x)$ is divided by $x - c$, then $P(c) = 0$.

6. The number c is a zero of a polynomial if the remainder in synthetic division is zero or if directly evaluating the polynomial at $x = c$ gives a value of zero.

7.

$$\begin{array}{r|rrrr} 1 & 1 & -1 & 1 & -1 \\ & & 1 & 0 & 1 \\ \hline & 1 & 0 & 1 & 0 \end{array}$$

Since the remainder is 0, 1 is a zero of the polynomial function.

8.

$$\begin{array}{r|rrrr} -2 & -2 & -5 & 3 & 10 \\ & & 4 & 2 & -10 \\ \hline & -2 & -1 & 5 & 0 \end{array}$$

Since the remainder is 0, -2 is a zero of the polynomial function.

9.

$$\begin{array}{r|rrrrr} -3 & -1 & -3 & -2 & 0 & 18 \\ & & 3 & 0 & 6 & -18 \\ \hline & -1 & 0 & -2 & 6 & 0 \end{array}$$

Since the remainder is 0, -3 is a zero of the function.

10.

$$\begin{array}{r|rrrrr} 4 & 1 & 0 & -1 & -8 & -16 \\ & & 4 & 16 & 60 & 208 \\ \hline & 1 & 4 & 15 & 52 & 192 \end{array}$$

Since the remainder is not 0, 4 is not a zero of the function.

11.

$$\begin{array}{r|rrrr} 2 & 2 & -4 & -5 & 9 \\ & & 4 & 0 & 10 \\ \hline & 2 & 0 & -5 & 19 \end{array}$$

Since the remainder is 19 and not 0, 2 is not a zero of the function.

12.

$$\begin{array}{r|rrrr} -3 & 1 & 5 & 2 & 1 \\ & & -3 & -6 & 12 \\ \hline & 1 & 2 & -4 & 13 \end{array}$$

Since the remainder is 13 and not 0, -3 is not a zero of the function.

13.

$$\begin{array}{r|rrrr} -3 & 1 & 5 & 2 & -12 \\ & & -3 & -6 & 12 \\ \hline & 1 & 2 & -4 & 0 \end{array}$$

Since the remainder is 0, -3 is a solution to the equation.

14.

$$\begin{array}{r|rrr} -5 & 1 & -3 & -40 \\ & & -5 & 40 \\ \hline & 1 & -8 & 0 \end{array}$$

Since the remainder is 0, -5 is a solution to the equation.

15.

$$\begin{array}{r|rrrrr} -2 & 1 & 3 & -5 & -10 & 5 \\ & & -2 & -2 & 14 & -8 \\ \hline & 1 & 1 & -7 & 4 & -3 \end{array}$$

Since the remainder is -3 and not 0, -2 is not a solution to the equation.

16.

$$\begin{array}{r|rrrr} -3 & -1 & -4 & 1 & 12 \\ & & 3 & 3 & -12 \\ \hline & -1 & -1 & 4 & 0 \end{array}$$

Since the remainder is 0, -3 is a solution to the equation.

17.

$$\begin{array}{r|rrrrr} 4 & -2 & 0 & 30 & 5 & 12 \\ & & -8 & -32 & -8 & -12 \\ \hline & -2 & -8 & -2 & -3 & 0 \end{array}$$

Since the remainder is 0, 4 is a solution to the equation.

18. 6 | 1 1 −40 0 −72
$$\ \underline{6\ \ 42\ \ 12\ \ 72}$$
   1 7   2 12   0

Since the remainder is 0, 6 is a solution to the equation.

19. 3 | 0.8 −0.3 −6.3
$$\ \underline{2.4\ \ 6.3}$$
   0.8 2.1 0

Since the remainder is not 0, 3 is not a solution to the equation.

20. 5 | 6.2 −28.2 −41.7
$$\ \underline{31.0\ \ 14.0}$$
   6.2 2.8 −27.7

Since the remainder is not 0, 5 is not a solution to the equation.

21. 3 | 1 0 −6 −9
$$\ \underline{3\ \ 9\ \ 9}$$
   1 3 3 0

Since the remainder is 0, $x - 3$ is a factor. The other factor is the quotient.
$$x^3 - 6x - 9 = (x - 3)(x^2 + 3x + 3)$$

22. −2 | 1 0 −6 −4
$$\ \underline{-2\ \ 4\ \ 4}$$
   1 −2 −2 0

Since the remainder is 0, $x + 2$ is a factor. The other factor is the quotient $x^2 - 2x - 2$.
$$x^3 - 6x - 4 = (x + 2)(x^2 - 2x - 2)$$

23. −5 | 1 9 23 15
$$\ \underline{-5\ -20\ -15}$$
   1 4 3   0

Since the remainder is 0, $x + 5$ is a factor of the polynomial. The quotient is the other factor.
$$x^3 + 9x^2 + 23x + 15 = (x + 5)(x^2 + 4x + 3)$$
$$= (x + 5)(x + 3)(x + 1)$$

24. 3 | 1 0 −9 1 −7
$$\ \underline{3\ \ 9\ \ 0\ \ 3}$$
   1 3 0 1 −4

Since the remainder is −4 and not 0, $x - 3$ is not a factor of the polynomial.

25. 2 | 1 −8 4 −6
$$\ \underline{2\ -12\ \ 16}$$
   1 −6 8 10

Since the remainder is 10 and not 0, $x - 2$ is not a factor of the polynomial.

26. −5 | 1 0 0 125
$$\ \underline{-5\ \ 25\ -125}$$
    1 −5 25   0

Since the remainder is 0, $x + 5$ is a factor of the polynomial. The quotient is the other factor.
$$x^3 + 125 = (x + 5)(x^2 - 5x + 25)$$

27. −1 | 1 1 0 −8 −8
$$\ \underline{-1\ \ 0\ \ 0\ \ 8}$$
    1 0 0 −8 0

Since the remainder is 0, $x + 1$ is a factor. The other factor is the quotient.
$$x^4 + x^3 - 8x - 8 = (x + 1)(x^3 - 8)$$
$$= (x + 1)(x - 2)(x^2 + 2x + 4)$$

28. 2 | 1 −6 12 −8
$$\ \underline{2\ -8\ \ 8}$$
   1 −4 4 0

Since the remainder is 0, $x - 2$ is a factor of the polynomial. The quotient is the other factor.
$$x^3 - 6x^2 + 12x - 8 = (x - 2)(x^2 - 4x + 4)$$
$$= (x - 2)(x - 2)(x - 2)$$
$$= (x - 2)^3$$

29. 0.5 | 2 −3 −11 6
$$\ \underline{1\ -1\ -6}$$
    2 −2 −12 0

Since the remainder is 0, $x - 0.5$ is a factor.
$$2x^3 - 3x^2 - 11x + 6$$
$$= (x - 0.5)(2x^2 - 2x - 12)$$
$$= (x - 0.5)(2)(x^2 - x - 6)$$
$$= (x - 0.5)(2)(x - 3)(x + 2)$$
$$= (2x - 1)(x - 3)(x + 2)$$

30. $\frac{1}{3}$ | 3 −10 −27 10
$$\phantom{\frac{1}{3}}\ \underline{1\ -3\ -10}$$
    3 −9 −30   0

Since the remainder is 0, $x - \frac{1}{3}$ is a factor of the polynomial.
$$3x^3 - 10x^2 - 27x + 10$$
$$= \left(x - \tfrac{1}{3}\right)(3x^2 - 9x - 30)$$
$$= \left(x - \tfrac{1}{3}\right)3(x^2 - 3x - 10)$$

342

$$= (3x - 1)(x^2 - 3x - 10)$$
$$= (3x - 1)(x - 5)(x + 2)$$

31. Try integers between -5 and 5 with synthetic division until we find a solution. Try 1 first.

$$
\begin{array}{r|rrrr}
1 & 1 & 0 & -13 & 12 \\
  &   & 1 & 1 & -12 \\
\hline
  & 1 & 1 & -12 & 0
\end{array}
$$

$$x^3 - 13x + 12 = 0$$
$$(x - 1)(x^2 + x - 12) = 0$$
$$(x - 1)(x + 4)(x - 3) = 0$$
$$x - 1 = 0 \text{ or } x + 4 = 0 \text{ or } x - 3 = 0$$
$$x = 1 \quad \text{or} \quad x = -4 \quad \text{or} \quad x = 3$$

The solution set is $\{-4, 1, 3\}$.

32. Try integers between -5 and 5 with synthetic division until we find a solution. Try 2 first.

$$
\begin{array}{r|rrrr}
2 & 1 & 2 & -5 & -6 \\
  &   & 2 & 8 & 6 \\
\hline
  & 1 & 4 & 3 & 0
\end{array}
$$

$$x^3 + 2x^2 - 5x - 6 = 0$$
$$(x - 2)(x^2 + 4x + 3) = 0$$
$$(x - 2)(x + 1)(x + 3) = 0$$
$$x - 2 = 0 \text{ or } x + 1 = 0 \text{ or } x + 3 = 0$$
$$x = 2 \quad \text{or} \quad x = -1 \quad \text{or} \quad x = -3$$

The solution set is $\{-3, -1, 2\}$.

33. Try integers between -5 and 5 with synthetic division to find a solution. Try 2 first.

$$
\begin{array}{r|rrrr}
2 & 2 & -9 & 7 & 6 \\
  &   & 4 & -10 & -6 \\
\hline
  & 2 & -5 & -3 & 0
\end{array}
$$

$$2x^3 - 9x^2 + 7x + 6 = 0$$
$$(x - 2)(2x^2 - 5x - 3) = 0$$
$$(x - 2)(2x + 1)(x - 3) = 0$$
$$x - 2 = 0 \text{ or } 2x + 1 = 0 \text{ or } x - 3 = 0$$
$$x = 2 \quad \text{or} \quad x = -1/2 \text{ or } x = 3$$

The solution set is $\left\{-\frac{1}{2}, 2, 3\right\}$.

34. Try integers between -5 and 5 with synthetic division to find a solution. Try -2 first.

$$
\begin{array}{r|rrrr}
-2 & 6 & 13 & 0 & -4 \\
   &   & -12 & -2 & 4 \\
\hline
   & 6 & 1 & -2 & 0
\end{array}
$$

$$6x^3 + 13x^2 - 4 = 0$$
$$(x + 2)(6x^2 + x - 2) = 0$$
$$(x + 2)(2x - 1)(3x + 2) = 0$$
$$x + 2 = 0 \text{ or } 2x - 1 = 0 \text{ or } 3x + 2 = 0$$
$$x = -2 \quad \text{or} \quad x = 1/2 \text{ or } \quad x = -2/3$$

The solution set is $\left\{-\frac{2}{3}, -2, \frac{1}{2}\right\}$.

35. The only integral solution between -5 and 5 is -4:

$$
\begin{array}{r|rrrr}
-4 & 2 & -3 & -50 & -24 \\
   &   & -8 & 44 & 24 \\
\hline
   & 2 & -11 & -6 & 0
\end{array}
$$

$$2x^3 - 3x^2 - 50x - 24 = 0$$
$$(x + 4)(2x^2 - 11x - 6) = 0$$
$$(x + 4)(2x + 1)(x - 6) = 0$$
$$x + 4 = 0 \text{ or } 2x + 1 = 0 \text{ or } x - 6 = 0$$
$$x = -4 \quad \text{or} \quad x = -1/2 \text{ or } x = 6$$

The solution set is $\left\{-4, -\frac{1}{2}, 6\right\}$.

36. Try integers between -5 and 5. Try -2 first.

$$
\begin{array}{r|rrrr}
-2 & 1 & -7 & 2 & 40 \\
   &   & -2 & 18 & -40 \\
\hline
   & 1 & -9 & 20 & 0
\end{array}
$$

$$x^3 - 7x^2 + 2x + 40 = 0$$
$$(x + 2)(x^2 - 9x + 20) = 0$$
$$(x + 2)(x - 4)(x - 5) = 0$$
$$x + 2 = 0 \text{ or } x - 4 = 0 \text{ or } x - 5 = 0$$
$$x = -2 \text{ or } \quad x = 4 \quad \text{or} \quad x = 5$$

The solution set is $\{-2, 4, 5\}$.

37. Check to see if 1 is a solution.

$$
\begin{array}{r|rrrr}
1 & 1 & 5 & 3 & -9 \\
  &   & 1 & 6 & 9 \\
\hline
  & 1 & 6 & 9 & 0
\end{array}
$$

$$x^3 + 5x^2 + 3x - 9 = 0$$
$$(x - 1)(x^2 + 6x + 9) = 0$$
$$(x - 1)(x + 3)^2 = 0$$
$$x - 1 = 0 \text{ or } x + 3 = 0$$
$$x = 1 \text{ or } \quad x = -3$$

The solution set is $\{-3, 1\}$.

38. Check to see it -2 is a solution.

$$\begin{array}{r|rrrr} -2 & 1 & 6 & 12 & 8 \\ & & -2 & -8 & -8 \\ \hline & 1 & 4 & 4 & 0 \end{array}$$

$$(x+2)(x^2+4x+4)=0$$
$$(x+2)(x+2)(x+2)=0$$
$$x+2=0$$
$$x=-2$$

The solution set is $\{-2\}$.

39. Check to see if 2 is a solution.

$$\begin{array}{r|rrrrr} 2 & 1 & -4 & 3 & 4 & -4 \\ & & 2 & -4 & -2 & 4 \\ \hline & 1 & -2 & -1 & 2 & 0 \end{array}$$

$$x^4-4x^3+3x^2+4x-4=0$$
$$(x-2)(x^3-2x^2-x+2)=0$$
$$(x-2)(x^2[x-2]-1[x-2])=0$$
$$(x-2)(x^2-1)(x-2)=0$$
$$(x-2)(x-1)(x+1)(x-2)=0$$
$$x-2=0 \text{ or } x-1=0 \text{ or } x+1=0$$
$$x=2 \text{ or } \quad x=1 \text{ or } \quad x=-1$$

The solution set is $\{-1,1,2\}$.

40. Check to see if -3 is a solution.

$$\begin{array}{r|rrrrr} -3 & 1 & 1 & -7 & -1 & 6 \\ & & -3 & 6 & 3 & -6 \\ \hline & 1 & -2 & -1 & 2 & 0 \end{array}$$

$$(x+3)(x^3-2x^2-x+2)=0$$

Now factor by grouping.

$$(x+3)(x^2[x-2]-1[x-2])=0$$
$$(x+3)(x^2-1)(x-2)=0$$
$$(x+3)(x-1)(x+1)(x-2)=0$$
$$x+3=0 \text{ or } x-1=0 \text{ or } x+1=0 \text{ or}$$
$$x-2=0$$
$$x=-3 \text{ or } x=1 \text{ or } x=-1 \text{ or } x=2$$

The solution set is $\{-3,-1,1,2\}$.

41. a) $f(x)=x+2$
b) $f(x)=x^2-25$
c) $f(x)=(x-1)(x+3)(x-4)$
d) Yes, the degree is the same as the number of zeros.

42. a) $\{-2,1,3\}$ **b)** $\left\{-\frac{1}{3},\frac{1}{2},\frac{3}{2}\right\}$

43. a) $\{-2,1,5\}$ **b)** $\left\{-\frac{3}{2},\frac{3}{2},\frac{5}{2}\right\}$

Enriching Your Mathematical Word Power
Chapter 9
1. a   **2.** b   **3.** d   **4.** d   **5.** a
6. b   **7.** d   **8.** c   **9.** d   **10.** b

CHAPTER 9 REVIEW

1. $f(-3)=3(-3)+5=-4$

2. $h(-4)=\dfrac{-4-5}{3}=-3$

3. $(h\circ f)(\sqrt{2})=h(f(\sqrt{2}))=h(3\sqrt{2}+5)$
$$=\dfrac{3\sqrt{2}+5-5}{3}=\dfrac{3\sqrt{2}}{3}=\sqrt{2}$$

4. $(f\circ h)(\pi)=f[h(\pi)]=f[\dfrac{\pi-5}{3}]$
$$=3[\dfrac{\pi-5}{3}]+5=\pi-5+5=\pi$$

5. $(g\circ f)(2)=g(f(2))=g(11)=11^2-2(11)$
$$=99$$

6. $(g\circ f)(x)=g[f(x)]=g[3x+5]$
$$=(3x+5)^2-2(3x+5)$$
$$=9x^2+30x+25-6x-10$$
$$=9x^2+24x+15$$

7. $(f+g)(3)=f(3)+g(3)$
$$=3\cdot 3+5+3^2-2\cdot 3=17$$

8. $(f-g)(x)=f(x)-g(x)$
$$=3x+5-(x^2-2x)$$
$$=3x+5-x^2+2x=-x^2+5x+5$$

9. $(f\cdot g)(x)=f(x)\cdot g(x)=(3x+5)(x^2-2x)$
$$=3x^3+5x^2-6x^2-10x=3x^3-x^2-10x$$

10. $(f/g)(1)=\dfrac{f(1)}{g(1)}=\dfrac{3(1)+5}{(1)^2-2(1)}=\dfrac{8}{-1}$
$$=-8$$

11. $(f\circ f)(0)=f(f(0))=f(5)=3\cdot 5+5$
$$=20$$

12. $(f\circ f)(x)=f[f(x)]=f(3x+5)$
$$=3(3x+5)+5$$
$$=9x+15+5=9x+20$$

13. $F(x)=|x+2|=|g(x)|=f(g(x))$
$$=(f\circ g)(x)$$

Therefore, F is the same function as f composite g, and we write $F=f\circ g$.

14. $G(x)=|x|+2=f(x)+2=g[f(x)]$
$$=(g\circ f)(x)$$

Therefore, G is the same function as g composite f, and we write $G=g\circ f$.

15. $H(x)=x^2+2=h(x)+2=g(h(x))$
$$=(g\circ h)(x)$$

Therefore, H is the same function as g composite h, and we write $H=g\circ h$.

16. $K(x) = x^2 + 4x + 4 = (x+2)^2 = [g(x)]^2$
$= h[g(x)] = (h \circ g)(x)$
Therefore, K is the same function as h composite g, and we write $K = h \circ g$.

17. $I(x) = x + 4 = x + 2 + 2 = g(x) + 2$
$= g(g(x)) = (g \circ g)(x)$
Therefore, I is the same function as g composite g, and we write $I = g \circ g$.

18. $J(x) = x^4 + 2 = (x^2)^2 + 2 = [h(x)]^2 + 2$
$= h[h(x)] + 2 = g(h[h(x)]) = (g \circ h \circ h)(x)$
Therefore, J is the same function as g composite h composite h, and we write $J = g \circ h \circ h$.

19. This function is not invertible, because it is not one-to-one. The ordered pairs have different first coordinates and the same second coordinate.

20. The function is one-to-one and so it is invertible. The inverse is $\{(1, 1), (3, 3)\}$.

21. The function $f(x) = 8x$ is invertible. The inverse of multiplication by 8 is division by 8 and $f^{-1}(x) = x/8$.

22. The function $i(x) = -\frac{x}{3}$ is one-to-one and so it is invertible. The inverse of dividing by 3 and then taking the opposite is taking the opposite and then multiplying by 3, $i^{-1}(x) = -3x$.

23. The function $g(x) = 13x - 6$ is one-to-one and so it is invertible. The inverse of multiplying by 13 and subtracting 6 is adding 6 and then dividing by 13, $g^{-1}(x) = \frac{x+6}{13}$.

24. The function $h(x) = \sqrt[3]{x-6}$ is invertible. The inverse of subtracting 6 and then taking the cube root is cubing and then adding 6. Therefore, $h^{-1}(x) = x^3 + 6$.

25. $j(x) = \frac{x+1}{x-1}$
$y = \frac{x+1}{x-1}$
$x = \frac{y+1}{y-1}$
$x(y - 1) = y + 1$
$xy - x = y + 1$
$xy - y = x + 1$
$y(x - 1) = x + 1$
$y = \frac{x+1}{x-1}$
$j^{-1}(x) = \frac{x+1}{x-1}$

26. The ordered pairs $(1, 8)$ and $(-1, 8)$ both satisfy $k(x) = |x| + 7$. So the function is not one-to-one and so the function $k(x) = |x| + 7$ is not invertible.

27. The function $m(x) = (x - 1)^2$ is not invertible because it is not one-to-one. The ordered pairs $(2, 1)$ and $(0, 1)$ are both in the function.

28. $n(x) = \frac{3}{x}$
$y = \frac{3}{x}$
$x = \frac{3}{y}$
$xy = 3$
$y = \frac{3}{x}$
$n^{-1}(x) = \frac{3}{x}$

29. The function $f(x) = 3x - 1$ is inverted by adding 1 and then dividing by 3:
$$f^{-1}(x) = \frac{x+1}{3} = \frac{1}{3}x + \frac{1}{3}$$
Use slope and y-intercept to graph both functions on the same coordinate system.

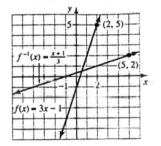

30. Find the inverse of $f(x) = 2 - x^2$ for $x \geq 0$.
$$f(x) = 2 - x^2$$
$$y = 2 - x^2$$
$$x = 2 - y^2$$
$$y^2 = 2 - x$$
$$y = \sqrt{2 - x}$$
$$f^{-1}(x) = \sqrt{2 - x}$$

The graph of f includes the points $(0, 2)$, $(1, 1)$, and $(2, -2)$. While the graph of f^{-1} includes the points $(2, 0)$, $(1, 1)$, and $(-2, 2)$.

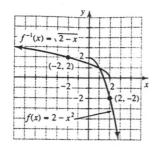

31. The function $f(x) = x^3/2$ is inverted by multiplying by 2 and then taking the cube root:
$$f^{-1}(x) = \sqrt[3]{2x}$$
The graph of f includes the points $(0, 0)$, $(1, 1/2)$, $(-1, -1/2)$, $(2, 4)$, and $(-2, 4)$. The graph of f^{-1} includes the points $(0, 0)$, $(1/2, 1)$, $(-1/2, -1)$, $(4, 2)$, and $(-4, -2)$. Plot these points and graph both functions on the same coordinate system.

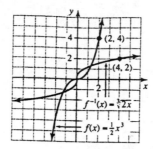

32. The inverse of the function $f(x) = -\frac{1}{4}x$ is $f^{-1}(x) = -4x$. The graph of f is a line with y-intercept $(0, 0)$ and slope $-1/4$. The graph of f^{-1} is a line with y-intercept $(0, 0)$ and slope -4.

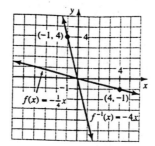

33. If y varies directly as m, then $y = km$. If $y = -3$ when $m = 1/4$, then
$$-3 = k \cdot \tfrac{1}{4}$$
or
$$-12 = k.$$
Since $y = -12m$, when $m = -2$ we get
$$y = -12(-2) = 24.$$

34. If a varies inversely as b, then $a = k/b$. If $a = 6$ when $b = -3$, then $6 = \frac{k}{-3}$, or $k = -18$. So the formula is $a = \frac{-18}{b}$. Now if $b = 4$, then $a = \frac{-18}{4} = -\frac{9}{2}$.

35. If c varies directly as m and inversely as n, then $c = km/n$. If $c = 20$ when $m = 10$ and $n = 4$, then
$$20 = \frac{k(10)}{4}$$
or
$$8 = k.$$
Since $c = 8m/n$, when $m = 6$ and $n = -3$, we get
$$c = \frac{8(6)}{-3} = -16.$$

36. If V varies jointly as h and the square of r, then $V = khr^2$. If $V = 32$ when $h = 6$ and $r = 3$, then $32 = k(6)(3)^2$, or $32 = 54k$, or $k = \frac{32}{54} = \frac{16}{27}$.
So the formula is $V = \frac{16}{27}hr^2$. Now if $h = 3$ and $r = 4$, then $V = \frac{16}{27}(3)(4)^2 = \frac{256}{9}$.

37. Use synthetic division to check the possible solutions. Try 2 first.
$$
\begin{array}{r|rrrr}
2 & 1 & -4 & -11 & 30 \\
  &   & 2 & -4 & -30 \\
\hline
  & 1 & -2 & -15 & 0
\end{array}
$$
$$x^3 - 4x^2 - 11x + 30 = (x - 2)(x^2 - 2x - 15)$$
$$= (x - 2)(x - 5)(x + 3)$$
There is one solution for each factor. The solution set is $\{-3, 2, 5\}$.

38. Use synthetic division to check the possible solutions. Try 2 first.
$$
\begin{array}{r|rrrr}
2 & 1 & -2 & -6 & 12 \\
  &   & 2 & 0 & -12 \\
\hline
  & 1 & 0 & -6 & 0
\end{array}
$$
$$x^3 - 2x^2 - 6x + 12 = 0$$
$$(x - 2)(x^2 - 6) = 0$$
$$x - 2 = 0 \text{ or } x^2 - 6 = 0$$

$$x = 2 \text{ or } \quad x^2 = 6$$
$$x = \pm\sqrt{6}$$

There are 3 solutions to the polynomial. The solution set is $\{-\sqrt{6}, \sqrt{6}, 2\}$.

39. Use synthetic division to check the possible solutions. Try -2 first.

$$\begin{array}{r|rrrr} -2 & 1 & -5 & -2 & 24 \\ & & -2 & 14 & -24 \\ \hline & 1 & -7 & 12 & 0 \end{array}$$

$$x^3 - 5x^2 - 2x + 24 = (x + 2)(x^2 - 7x + 12)$$
$$= (x + 2)(x - 3)(x - 4)$$

There is one solution for each factor of the polynomial. The solution set is $\{-2, 3, 4\}$.

40. Use synthetic division to check the possible solutions. Try -2 first.

$$\begin{array}{r|rrrr} -2 & 1 & 7 & 4 & -12 \\ & & -2 & -10 & 12 \\ \hline & 1 & 5 & -6 & 0 \end{array}$$

$$x^3 + 7x^2 + 4x - 12 = (x + 2)(x^2 + 5x - 6)$$
$$= (x + 2)(x + 6)(x - 1)$$

There is one solution for each factor of the polynomial. The solution set is $\{-6, -2, 1\}$.

41. Use synthetic division to check for possible factors.

$$\begin{array}{r|rrrr} 3 & 1 & 4 & -11 & -30 \\ & & 3 & 21 & 30 \\ \hline & 1 & 7 & 10 & 0 \end{array}$$

$$x^3 + 4x^2 - 11x - 30 = (x - 3)(x^2 + 7x + 10)$$
$$= (x - 3)(x + 2)(x + 5)$$

42. Use synthetic division to check for possible factors.

$$\begin{array}{r|rrrr} -4 & 1 & 1 & -10 & 8 \\ & & -4 & 12 & -8 \\ \hline & 1 & -3 & 2 & 0 \end{array}$$

$$x^3 + x^2 - 10x + 8 = (x + 4)(x^2 - 3x + 2)$$
$$= (x + 4)(x - 2)(x - 1)$$

43. Use synthetic division to check for possible factors.

$$\begin{array}{r|rrrr} -2 & 1 & 0 & -5 & -6 \\ & & -2 & 4 & 2 \\ \hline & 1 & -2 & -1 & -4 \end{array}$$

Since the remainder is not 0, $x + 2$ is not a factor of the polynomial.

44. Use synthetic division to check for possible factors.

$$\begin{array}{r|rrrr} 1 & 2 & -5 & 2 & -9 \\ & & 2 & -3 & -1 \\ \hline & 2 & -3 & -1 & -10 \end{array}$$

Since the remainder is not 0, $x - 1$ is not a factor of the polynomial.

45. If the distance varies directly with the square of the time, then $d = kt^2$. If the ball travels 144 feet in 3 seconds, then $144 = k3^2$, or $k = 16$ and $d = 16t^2$. So in 4 seconds the ball falls $d = 16 \cdot 4^2 = 256$ feet.

46. If the grade g varies directly with the number of hours studying s and inversely with the number of hours spent partying p, then $g = \frac{ks}{p}$. If $g = 90$ when $s = 10$ and $p = 2$, then $90 = \frac{k10}{2}$, or $90 = 5k$, or $k = 18$. So the formula is written $g = \frac{18s}{p}$. Now if $s = 4$ and $p = 6$, then $g = \frac{18(4)}{6} = 12$.

47. The area of the circle is $A = \pi r^2$. Let $s = $ the length of the side of the square. Since the square is inscribed in the circle, the length of the diagonal of the square is the same as the diameter of the circle $2r$. Since the diagonal of the square is the hypotenuse of a right triangle whose sides are s and s, we can write the following equation.

$$s^2 + s^2 = (2r)^2$$
$$2s^2 = 4r^2$$
$$s^2 = 2r^2$$

Since the area of the square is s^2, we have $B = s^2$, or $B = 2r^2$. Since $r^2 = \frac{A}{\pi}$, we can write $B = 2 \cdot \frac{A}{\pi}$, or $B = \frac{2A}{\pi}$.

48. The area of a square of side s is s^2. The radius of the semicircle is $s/2$. The area of a circle with radius $s/2$ is $\pi\left(\frac{s}{2}\right)^2 = \frac{\pi s^2}{4}$. So the area of a semicircle with radius $\frac{s}{2}$ is

$$\frac{1}{2} \cdot \frac{\pi s^2}{4} = \frac{\pi s^2}{8}.$$

The total area of the window is expressed by the following function.

$$A = s^2 + \frac{\pi s^2}{8}$$
$$A = \frac{8s^2}{8} + \frac{\pi s^2}{8}$$

$$A = \frac{8s^2 + \pi s^2}{8}$$
$$A = \frac{(8 + \pi)s^2}{8}$$

49. Substitute $k = 5w - 6$ into the equation $a = 3k + 2$:
$$a = 3(5w - 6) + 2$$
$$a = 15w - 18 + 2$$
$$a = 15w - 16$$

50. Since $V = 10\pi r^2$ and $A = \pi r^2$ we have $V = 10A$.

51. $A = s^2$, $s = \sqrt{A}$

52. $A = \pi r^2$ expresses the area as a function of the side.
$$\frac{A}{\pi} = r^2$$
$$\sqrt{\frac{A}{\pi}} = r$$

The formula $r = \sqrt{\frac{A}{\pi}}$ expresses the radius as a function of the area.
$$A = \pi r^2$$
$$A = \pi \left(\frac{d}{2}\right)^2$$

The formula $A = \frac{\pi d^2}{4}$ expresses the area as a function of the diameter.

CHAPTER 9 TEST

1. $f(-3) = -2(-3) + 5 = 6 + 5 = 11$

2. $(g \circ f)(-3) = g(f(-3)) = g(11) = 11^2 + 4$
$$= 125$$

3. Because $f(-3) = 11$, $f^{-1}(11) = -3$.

4. Because f consists of multiplying by -2 and adding 5, f^{-1} consists of subtracting 5 and dividing by -2:

$$f^{-1}(x) = \frac{x - 5}{-2} \text{ or } f^{-1}(x) = -\frac{1}{2}x + \frac{5}{2}$$

5. $(g + f)(x) = g(x) + f(x)$
$$= x^2 + 4 + (-2x + 5)$$
$$= x^2 - 2x + 9.$$

6. $(f \cdot g)(1) = f(1) \cdot g(1) = 3 \cdot 5 = 15$

7. Because f^{-1} is the inverse of f we have $(f^{-1} \circ f)(1776) = 1776$

8. $(f/g)(2) = f(2)/g(2) = 1/8$

9. $(f \circ g)(x) = f(g(x)) = f(x^2 + 4)$
$$= -2(x^2 + 4) + 5 = -2x^2 - 8 + 5$$
$$= -2x^2 - 3$$

10. $(g \circ f)(x) = g(f(x)) = g(-2x + 5)$
$$= (-2x + 5)^2 + 4 = 4x^2 - 20x + 29$$

11. $f(g(x)) = f(x^2) = x^2 - 7 = H(x)$
So $H = f \circ g$.

12. $g(f(x)) = g(x - 7) = (x - 7)^2$
$$= x^2 - 14x + 49$$
So $W = g \circ f$.

13. The function is not invertible because it is not one-to-one.

14. The function is invertible and its inverse is $f^{-1}(x) = (x - 9)^3$.

15.
$$f(x) = \frac{2x + 1}{x - 1}$$
$$y = \frac{2x + 1}{x - 1}$$
$$x = \frac{2y + 1}{y - 1}$$
$$x(y - 1) = 2y + 1$$
$$xy - x = 2y + 1$$
$$xy - 2y = x + 1$$
$$y(x - 2) = x + 1$$
$$y = \frac{x + 1}{x - 2}$$
$$f^{-1}(x) = \frac{x + 1}{x - 2}$$

16. Since the volume varies directly as the cube of the radius, we have $V = kr^3$. If $V = 36\pi$ when $r = 3$, we have $36\pi = k3^3$ or $k = 4\pi/3$. To find the volume of a sphere with a radius of 2, use $r = 2$ and $k = 4\pi/3$ in the formula $V = kr^3$:

$$V = \frac{4\pi}{3}(2)^3 = \frac{32\pi}{3} \text{ cubic feet}$$

17. If y varies directly as x and inversely as the square root of z, then $y = kx/\sqrt{z}$. If $y = 12$ when $x = 7$ and $z = 9$, we have

$$12 = \frac{k(7)}{\sqrt{9}} \text{ or } k = \frac{36}{7}.$$

18. If the cost varies jointly as the length and width, then $C = kLW$.

$$2256 = k(6)(8)$$
$$k = 47$$

So $C = 47LW$. So the cost of a 9 by 12 rug is

$$C = 47(9)(12) = \$5076.$$

19.

$$-1 \quad \begin{array}{rrrrr} 2 & -5 & 3 & 6 & -4 \\ & -2 & 7 & -10 & 4 \\ \hline 2 & -7 & 10 & -4 & 0 \end{array}$$

Because the remainder is 0, $x + 1$ is a factor of the polynomial.

20. Use synthetic division to check each integer from 1 to 10 to see if it is a solution. If the remainder is not 0, try a different number. We will try 3 first.

$$3 \quad \begin{array}{rrrr} 1 & -12 & 47 & -60 \\ & 3 & -27 & 60 \\ \hline 1 & -9 & 20 & 0 \end{array}$$

$$x^3 - 12x^2 + 47x - 60 = 0$$
$$(x - 3)(x^2 - 9x + 20) = 0$$
$$(x - 3)(x - 4)(x - 5) = 0$$
$$x - 3 = 0 \text{ or } x - 4 = 0 \text{ or } x - 5 = 0$$
$$x = 3 \text{ or } \quad x = 4 \text{ or } \quad x = 5$$

The solution set to the equation is $\{3, 4, 5\}$.

Making Connections

Chapters 1 - 9

1. $125^{-2/3} = 5^{-2} = \frac{1}{25}$

2. $\left(\frac{8}{27}\right)^{-1/3} = \left(\frac{27}{8}\right)^{1/3} = \frac{3}{2}$

3. $\sqrt{18} - \sqrt{8} = 3\sqrt{2} - 2\sqrt{2} = \sqrt{2}$

4. $x^5 \cdot x^3 = x^{5+3} = x^8$

5. $16^{1/4} = 2$, because $2^4 = 16$.

6. $\frac{x^{12}}{x^3} = x^{12-3} = x^9$

7. $\quad x^2 = 9$
$$x = \pm\sqrt{9} = \pm 3$$

The solution set is $\{\pm 3\}$.

8. $x^2 = 8, x = \pm\sqrt{8} = \pm 2\sqrt{2}$

The solution set is $\{\pm 2\sqrt{2}\}$.

9. $\quad x^2 - x = 0$
$$x(x - 1) = 0$$
$$x = 0 \text{ or } x - 1 = 0$$

The solution set is $\{0, 1\}$.

10. $x^2 - 4x - 6 = 0$

$$x = \frac{4 \pm \sqrt{(-4)^2 - 4(1)(-6)}}{2(1)}$$
$$= \frac{4 \pm \sqrt{40}}{2} = \frac{4 \pm 2\sqrt{10}}{2} = 2 \pm \sqrt{10}$$

The solution set is $\{2 \pm \sqrt{10}\}$.

11. $\quad x^{1/4} = 3$
$$(x^{1/4})^4 = 3^4$$
$$x = 81$$

Since we raised each side to an even power we must check. Since the fourth root of 81 is 3, the solution set is $\{81\}$.

12. If we raise each side to the sixth power, we will get $x = 64$. However, the sixth root of 64 is 2 and not -2. So 64 does not check. The solution set is $\emptyset$.

13. $\quad |x| = 8$
$$x = 8 \text{ or } x = -8$$

The solution set is $\{\pm 8\}$.

14. $\quad |5x - 4| = 21$
$$5x - 4 = 21 \text{ or } 5x - 4 = -21$$
$$5x = 25 \quad \text{ or } \quad 5x = -17$$
$$x = 5 \quad \text{ or } \quad x = -\frac{17}{5}$$

The solution set is $\{-\frac{17}{5}, 5\}$.

15. $\quad x^3 = 8$
$$(x^3)^{1/3} = 8^{1/3}$$
$$x = 2$$

The solution set is $\{2\}$.

16. $(3x - 2)^3 = 27$
$$3x - 2 = 3$$
$$3x = 5$$
$$x = \frac{5}{3}$$

The solution set is $\{\frac{5}{3}\}$.

17.
$$\sqrt{2x - 3} = 9$$
$$(\sqrt{2x - 3})^2 = 9^2$$
$$2x - 3 = 81$$
$$2x = 84$$
$$x = 42$$

The solution set is $\{42\}$.

18.
$$\sqrt{x - 2} = x - 8$$
$$x - 2 = (x - 8)^2$$
$$x - 2 = x^2 - 16x + 64$$
$$x^2 - 17x + 66 = 0$$
$$(x - 6)(x - 11) = 0$$
$$x = 6 \text{ or } x = 11$$

Only 11 satisfies the original equation. The solution set is $\{11\}$.

19. The graph of the set of points that satisfy the equation $y = 5$ is a horizontal straight line with y-intercept $(0, 5)$.

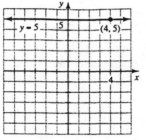

20. The graph of the set of points that satisfy $y = 2x - 5$ is a straight line with y-intercept $(0, -5)$ and slope 2.

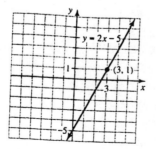

21. The graph of the set of points that satisfy $x = 5$ is a vertical line with x-intercept $(5, 0)$.

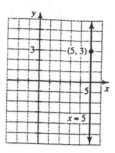

22. The graph of $3y = x$ is the same as the graph of $y = (1/3)x$, a straight line with y-intercept $(0, 0)$ and slope $1/3$.

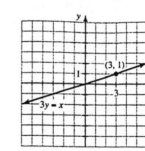

23. The graph of $y = 5x^2$ is a parabola going through $(0, 0)$, $(1, 5)$, and $(-1, 5)$.

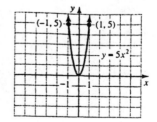

24. The graph of $y = -2x^2$ is a parabola going through $(0, 0)$, $(1, -2)$, and $(-1, -2)$.

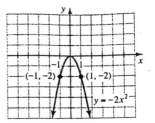

25. Because $2^2 = 4$, and $2^3 = 8$, we have $(2, 4)$ and $(3, 8)$. Because $2^1 = 2$ and $2^4 = 16$, we have $(1, 2)$ and $(4, 16)$.

26. Because $4^{1/2} = 2$ and $4^{-1} = 1/4$, we have $(1/2, 2)$ and $(-1, 1/4)$. Because $4^2 = 16$ and $4^0 = 1$, we have $(2, 16)$ and $(0, 1)$.

27. In $\sqrt{x}$ we must have $x \geq 0$. So the domain is $[0, \infty)$.

28. In $\sqrt{6 - 2x}$ we must have $6 - 2x \geq 0$ or $6 \geq 2x$, or $3 \geq x$, or $x \leq 3$. So the domain is $(-\infty, 3]$.

29. Because there are no real solutions to $x^2 + 1 = 0$, we can use any real number for x in this expression. The domain is $(-\infty, \infty)$

30. Solve $x^2 - 10x + 9 = 0$ by factoring.

$$(x - 9)(x - 1) = 0$$
$$x - 9 = 0 \text{ or } x - 1 = 0$$
$$x = 9 \text{ or } \qquad x = 1$$

So the domain is all real numbers except 1 and 9, which is written in interval notation as $(-\infty, 1) \cup (1, 9) \cup (9, \infty)$

31. a) $C = 0.12x + 3000$

b) Find the equation of the line through

$(0, 0.15)$ and $(100,000, 0.25)$

$$m = \frac{0.25 - 0.15}{100,000 - 0} = 0.000001$$
P-intercept is $(0, 0.15)$

$$P = 0.000001x + 0.15$$
$$P = 1 \times 10^{-6}x + 0.15$$

32. a) $T = \frac{C}{x} + P$

$$T = \frac{3000 + 0.12x}{x} + 0.000001x + 0.15$$
$$T = \frac{3000}{x} + 0.000001x + 0.27$$

If $x = 20,000$, then $T = \$0.44$
If $x = 30,000$, then $T = \$0.40$
If $x = 90,000$, then $T = \$0.39$

b)

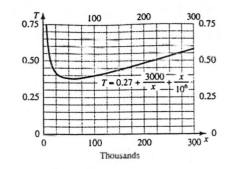

c) $\frac{3000}{x} + 0.000001x + 0.27 = 0.38$
$$\frac{3000}{x} + 0.000001x = 0.11$$
$$3000 + 0.000001x^2 = 0.11x$$
$$0.000001x^2 - 0.11x + 3000 = 0$$

$$x = \frac{0.11 \pm \sqrt{0.11^2 - 4(0.000001)(3000)}}{2(0.000001)}$$
$$= 50,000 \text{ or } 60,000$$

The car will be replaced at 60,000 miles.

d) The total cost is less than or equal to $0.38 per mile for mileage in the interval $[50,000, 60,000]$

10.1 WARM-UPS

1. False, because $f(-1/2) = 4^{-1/2} = 1/2$.

2. True, because $(1/3)^{-1} = 3$.

3. False, because the variable is not in the exponent.

4. True, because $(1/2)^x = (2^{-1})^x = 2^{-x}$.

5. True, because it is a one-to-one function.

6. False, the equation $(1/3)^x = 0$ has on solution.

7. True, because $e^0 = 1$.

8. False, because the domain of the exponential function $f(x) = 2^x$ is the set of all real numbers.

9. True, because $2^{-x} = 1/(2^x)$.

10. False, at the end of 3 years the investment is worth $500(1.005)^{36}$ dollars

10.1 EXERCISES

1. An exponential function has the form $f(x) = a^x$ where $a > 0$ and $a \neq 1$.

2. The domain of an exponential function is all real numbers.

3. The two most popular bases are e and 10.

4. The one-to-one property says that if $a^m = a^n$, then $m = n$.

5. The compound interest formula is $A = P(1 + i)^n$.

6. When money is compounded continuously we use the formula $A = Pe^{rt}$

7. $f(2) = 4^2 = 16$

8. $f(-1) = 4^{-1} = 1/4$

9. $f(1/2) = 4^{1/2} = 2$

10. $f(-3/2) = 4^{-3/2} = 2^{-3} = 1/8$

11. $g(-2) = (1/3)^{-2+1} = (1/3)^{-1} = 3$

12. $g(1) = (1/3)^{1+1} = 1/9$

13. $g(0) = (1/3)^{0+1} = (1/3)^1 = \frac{1}{3}$

14. $g(-3) = (1/3)^{-2} = 9$

15. $h(0) = -2^0 = -1$

16. $h(3) = -2^3 = -8$

17. $h(-2) = -2^{-2} = -1/4$

18. $h(-4) = -2^{-4} = -1/16$

19. $h(0) = 10^0 = 1$

20. $h(-1) = 10^{-1} = 0.1$

21. $h(2) = 10^2 = 100$

22. $h(3.4) = 10^{3.4} = 2511.886$

23. $j(1) = e^1 = 2.718$

24. $j(3.5) = e^{3.5} = 33.115$

25. $j(-2) = e^{-2} = 0.135$

26. $j(0) = e^0 = 1$

27. The graph of $f(x) = 4^x$ includes the points $(0, 1)$, $(1, 4)$, $(2, 16)$, and $(-1, 1/4)$.

28. The graph of $f(x) = 5^x$ includes the points $(0, 1)$, $(1, 5)$, $(2, 25)$, and $(-1, 1/5)$.

29. The graph of $h(x) = \left(\frac{1}{3}\right)^x$ includes the points $(0, 1)$, $(1, 1/3)$, $(2, 1/9)$, $(-1, 3)$, and $(-2, 9)$.

30. The graph of $i(x) = \left(\frac{1}{5}\right)^x$ includes the points $(0, 1)$, $(1, 1/5)$, $(2, 1/25)$, $(-1, 5)$, and $(-2, 25)$.

31. The graph of $y = 10^x$ includes the points $(0, 1)$, $(1, 10)$, and $(-1, 1/10)$.

35. The graph of $f(x) = -2^x$ includes the points $(0, -1)$, $(1, -2)$, $(2, -4)$, $(-1, -1/2)$, and $(-2, -1/4)$.

32. The graph of $y = (0.1)^x$ includes the points $(0, 1)$, $(1, 0.1)$, and $(-1, 10)$.

36. The graph of $k(x) = -2^{x-2}$ includes the points $(0, -1/4)$, $(2, -1)$, $(3, -2)$, and $(4, -4)$.

33. The graph of $y = 10^{x+2}$ includes the points $(0, 100)$, $(-1, 10)$, $(-2, 1)$, and $(-3, 1/10)$.

37. The graph of $g(x) = 2^{-x}$ includes the points $(0, 1)$, $(-1, 2)$, $(-2, 4)$, and $(1, 1/2)$.

34. The graph of $y = 3^{2x+1}$ includes the points $(0, 3)$, $(-1, 1/3)$, and $(1, 27)$.

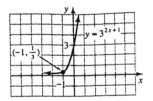

38. The graph of $A(x) = 10^{1-x}$ includes the points $(0, 10)$, $(1, 1)$, and $(2, 0.1)$.

39. The graph of $f(x) = -e^x$ includes the points $(0, -1)$, $(1, -2.7)$, $(2, -7.4)$, $(-1, -0.4)$.

40. The graph of $g(x) = e^{-x}$ includes the points $(0, 1)$, $(1, 0.4)$, $(-1, 2.7)$, $(-2, 7.4)$.

41. The graph of $H(x) = 10^{|x|}$ includes the points $(0, 1)$, $(1, 10)$, and $(-1, 10)$.

42. The graph of $s(x) = 2^{(x^2)}$ includes the points $(0, 1)$, $(1, 2)$, $(-1, 2)$, $(2, 16)$, and $(-2, 16)$.

43. The graph of $P = 5000(1.05)^t$ includes the points $(0, 5000)$, $(20, 13266)$, and $(-10, 3070)$.

44. The graph of $d = 800 \cdot 10^{-4t}$ includes the points $(-1/4, 8000)$, $(0, 800)$, and $(1, 0.08)$.

45.
$$2^x = 64$$
$$2^x = 2^6$$
$$x = 6 \quad \text{By the one-to-one property}$$
The solution set is $\{6\}$.

46.
$$3^x = 9$$
$$3^x = 3^2$$
$$x = 2 \quad \text{By the one-to-one property}$$

47.
$$10^x = 0.001$$
$$10^x = 10^{-3}$$
$$x = -3$$
The solution set is $\{-3\}$.

48.
$$10^{2x} = 0.1$$
$$10^{2x} = 10^{-1}$$
$$2x = -1$$
$$x = -\frac{1}{2}$$
The solution set is $\left\{-\frac{1}{2}\right\}$.

49.
$$2^x = \frac{1}{4}$$
$$2^x = 2^{-2}$$
$$x = -2$$
The solution set is $\{-2\}$.

50. $3^x = \frac{1}{9}$

$3^x = 3^{-2}$

$x = -2$ By the one-to-one property

The solution set is $\{-2\}$.

51. $\left(\frac{2}{3}\right)^{x-1} = \frac{9}{4}$

$\left(\frac{2}{3}\right)^{x-1} = \left(\frac{2}{3}\right)^{-2}$

$x - 1 = -2$

$x = -1$

The solution set is $\{-1\}$.

52. $\left(\frac{1}{4}\right)^{3x} = 16$

$\left(\frac{1}{4}\right)^{3x} = \left(\frac{1}{4}\right)^{-2}$

$3x = -2$

$x = -\frac{2}{3}$

The solution set is $\left\{-\frac{2}{3}\right\}$.

53. $5^{-x} = 25$

$5^{-x} = 5^2$

$-x = 2$ By the one-to-one property

$x = -2$

The solution set is $\{-2\}$.

54. $10^{-x} = 0.01$

$10^{-x} = 10^{-2}$

$-x = -2$

$x = 2$

The solution set is $\{2\}$.

55. $-2^{1-x} = -8$

$-2^{1-x} = -2^3$

$2^{1-x} = 2^3$

$1 - x = 3$

$x = -2$

The solution set is $\{-2\}$.

56. $-3^{2-x} = -81$

$-3^{2-x} = -3^4$

$2 - x = 4$

$-2 = x$

The solution set is $\{-2\}$.

57. $10^{|x|} = 1000$

$10^{|x|} = 10^3$

$|x| = 3$

$x = 3$ or $x = -3$

The solution set is $\{-3, 3\}$.

58. $3^{|2x-5|} = 81$

$3^{|2x-5|} = 3^4$

$|2x - 5| = 4$

$2x - 5 = 4$ or $2x - 5 = -4$

$x = \frac{9}{2}$ or $x = \frac{1}{2}$

The solution set is $\left\{\frac{1}{2}, \frac{9}{2}\right\}$.

59. If $f(x) = 2^x$ and $f(x) = 4 = 2^2$, then we must have $x = 2$ by the one-to-one property of exponential functions.

60. If $f(x) = 1/4$, then $2^x = \frac{1}{4}$. Since $2^{-2} = \frac{1}{4}$, we must have $x = -2$.

61. Note that $4^{2/3} = (2^2)^{2/3} = 2^{4/3}$. So if $2^x = 2^{4/3}$, then $x = \frac{4}{3}$.

62. If $f(x) = 1$, then $2^x = 1$. Since $2^0 = 1$, we must have $x = 0$.

63. Note that $9 = 3^2 = (1/3)^{-2}$. So if $(1/3)^x = (1/3)^{-2}$, then $x = -2$.

64. If $g(x) = 1/9$, then $(1/3)^x = 1/9$. Since $(1/3)^2 = 1/9$, we must have $x = 2$.

65. Note that $1 = (1/3)^0$. So if $(1/3)^x = (1/3)^0$, then $x = 0$.

66. If $g(x) = \sqrt{3}$, then $(1/3)^x = \sqrt{3}$. Since $(1/3)^{-1/2} = 3^{1/2} = \sqrt{3}$, we must have $x = -1/2$.

67. Note that $16 = 4^2$. So if $h(x) = 4^{2x-1} = 4^2$, then

$2x - 1 = 2$

$2x = 3$

$x = \frac{3}{2}$.

68. If $h(x) = 1/2$, then $4^{2x-1} = 1/2$. Since $4^{-1/2} = 1/2$, we must have $2x - 1 = -\frac{1}{2}$.

$2x = -\frac{1}{2} + 1$

$2x = \frac{1}{2}$

$x = \frac{1}{4}$

69. Since $1 = 4^0$, $h(x) = 4^{2x-1} = 4^0$ implies that $2x - 1 = 0$ or $x = \frac{1}{2}$.

70. If $h(x) = \sqrt{2}$, then $4^{2x-1} = \sqrt{2}$. Since $4^{1/4} = (2^2)^{1/4} = 2^{2/4} = 2^{1/2} = \sqrt{2}$, we must have $2x - 1 = \frac{1}{4}$.

$2x = \frac{1}{4} + 1$

$2x = \frac{5}{4}$

$x = \frac{5}{8}$

71. Compounded quarterly for 10 years means that interest will be paid 40 times at 1.25%.

$S = 6000\left(1 + \frac{0.05}{4}\right)^{40} = 6000(1.0125)^{40}$

$= \$9861.72$

72. Ten percent compounded quarterly for 7 years means that interest will be paid 28 times at 2.5% each time.

$S = 400\left(1 + \frac{0.10}{4}\right)^{28} \approx \$798.60$

73. a) $\$10,000(1 + 0.276)^{10} \approx \$114,421.26$
b) From the graph it appears that the $10,000 was worth $75,000approximately 8 years after 1988 or around 1996.

74. $\$10,000(1 + 0.265)^{10} \approx \$104,931.35$

75. When the book is new, $t = 0$, and the value is $V = 45 \cdot 2^{-0.9(0)} = \$45$. When $t = 2$, the value is $V = 45 \cdot 2^{-0.9(2)} \approx \$12.92$.

76. Use $t = 10$, $t = 20$, and $t = 30$ in the formula $N = 10^{0.1t+2}$.
If $t = 10$, $N = 10^{0.1(10)+2} = 10^3 = 1,000$
If $t = 20$, $N = 10^{0.1(20)+2} = 10^4 = 10,000$
If $t = 30$, $N = 10^{0.1(30)+2} = 10^5 = 100,000$

77. A deposit of $500 for 3 years at 7% compounded continuously amounts to
$S = 500 \cdot e^{0.07(3)} \approx \$616.84$.

78. A deposit of $7000 for 4 years at 8% compounded continuously amounts to
$S = 7000 \cdot e^{0.08(4)} = 7000 \cdot e^{0.32} \approx \$9639.89$.

79. A deposit of $80,000 at 7.5% compounded continuously for 1 year amounts to
$S = 80,000 \cdot e^{0.075(1)} \approx \$86,230.73$. The interest earned is
$\$86,230.73 - \$80,000 = \$6230.73$.

80. Divide 215 by 365 to convert 215 days to 0.589 years. A deposit of $7500 compounded continuously for 5.589 years at 6.75% amounts to $S = 7500 \cdot e^{.0675(5.589)} = 7500 \cdot e^{0.37726}$
$\approx \$10,937.13$.

81. The amount at time $t = 0$ is
$A = 300 \cdot e^{-0.06(0)} = 300$ grams. The amount present after 20 years, $t = 20$, is
$A = 300 \cdot e^{-0.06(20)} \approx 90.4$ grams.
One-half of the substance decays in about 12 years.

82. The population in 1980 is found using $t = 0$ in the formula $P = 20 \cdot e^{0.1t}$.
$P = 20 \cdot e^{0.1(0)} = 20$ million
The population in the year 2000 is found by using $t = 20$ in the formula.
$P = 20 \cdot e^{0.1(20)} \approx 147.8$ million

83. 2.66666667, 0.0516, 2.8×10^{-5}

84. $(0, 1)$

85. The graph of $y = 3^{x-k}$ lies k units to the right of $y = 3^x$ when $k > 0$ and $|k|$ units to the left of $y = 3^x$ when $k < 0$.

10.2 WARM-UPS

1. True, because 3 is the exponent of a that produces 2.
2. False, because $b = 8^a$ is equivalent to $\log_8(b) = a$.
3. True, because the inverse of the base a exponential function is the base a logarithm function.
4. True, because the inverse of the base e exponential function is the base e logarithm function.
5. False, the domain is $(0, \infty)$.
6. False, $\log_{25}(5) = 1/2$.
7. False, $\log(-10)$ is undefined because -10 is not in the domain of the base 10 logarithm function.
8. False, $\log(0)$ is undefined.
9. True, because $\log_5(125) = 3$ and $5^3 = 125$.
10. True, because $(1/2)^{-5} = 2^5 = 32$.

10.2 EXERCISES

1. If $f(x) = 2^x$ then $f^{-1}(x) = \log_2(x)$.
2. The expression $\log_a(x)$ is the exponent of a the produces x. So $a^{\log_a(x)} = x$.
3. The common logarithm uses the base 10 and the natural logarithm uses base e.
4. The domain of $f(x) = \log_a(x)$ is $(0, \infty)$.
5. The one-to-one property for logarithmic functions says that if $\log_a(m) = \log_a(n)$ then $m = n$.
6. The graphs of $f(x) = a^x$ and $f^{-1}(x) = \log_a(x)$ are symmetric about the line $y = x$.
7. $\log_2(8) = 3$ is equivalent to $2^3 = 8$.
8. $\log_{10}(10) = 1$ is equivalent to $10^1 = 10$.
9. $10^2 = 100$ is equivalent to $\log(100) = 2$.
10. $5^3 = 125$ is equivalent to $\log_5(125) = 3$.
11. $y = \log_5(x)$ is equivalent to $5^y = x$.
12. $m = \log_b(N)$ is equivalent to $b^m = N$.
13. $2^a = b$ is equivalent to $\log_2(b) = a$.
14. $a^3 = c$ is equivalent to $\log_a(c) = 3$.

15. $\log_3(x) = 10$ is equivalent to $3^{10} = x$.
16. $\log_c(t) = 4$ is equivalent to $c^4 = t$.
17. $e^3 = x$ is equivalent to $\ln(x) = 3$.
18. $m = e^x$ is equivalent to $\ln(m) = x$.
19. Because $2^2 = 4$, $\log_2(4) = 2$.
20. Because $2^0 = 1$, $\log_2(1) = 0$.
21. Because $2^4 = 16$, $\log_2(16) = 4$.
22. Because $4^2 = 16$, $\log_4(16) = 2$.
23. Because $2^6 = 64$, $\log_2(64) = 6$.
24. Because $8^2 = 64$, $\log_8(64) = 2$.
25. Because $4^3 = 64$, $\log_4(64) = 3$.
26. Because $64^1 = 64$, $\log_{64}(64) = 1$.
27. Because $2^{-2} = \frac{1}{4}$, $\log_2(1/4) = -2$.
28. Because $2^{-3} = \frac{1}{8}$, $\log_2(1/8) = -3$.
29. Because $10^2 = 100$, $\log(100) = 2$.
30. Because $10^0 = 1$, $\log(10) = 0$.
31. Because $10^{-2} = 0.01$, $\log(0.01) = -2$.
32. Because $10^4 = 10,000$, $\log(10,000) = 4$.
33. Because $(1/3)^1 = 1/3$, $\log_{1/3}(1/3) = 1$.
34. Because $(1/3)^2 = 1/9$, $\log_{1/3}(1/9) = 2$.
35. Because $(1/3)^{-3} = 27$, $\log_{1/3}(27) = -3$.
36. Because $(1/3)^0 = 1$, $\log_{1/3}(1) = 0$.
37. Because $e^3 = e^3$, $\ln(e^3) = 3$.
38. Because $e^0 = 1$, $\ln(1) = 0$.
39. Because $e^2 = e^2$, $\ln(e^2) = 2$.
40. Because $e^{-1} = 1/e$, $\ln(1/e) = -1$.
41. Use a calculator with a base 10 logarithm key to find $\log(5) \approx 0.6990$.
42. Use a calculator with a base 10 logarithm key to find $\log(0.03) \approx -1.5229$.
43. Use a calculator with a natural logarithm key to find $\ln(6.238) \approx 1.8307$.
44. Use a calculator with a natural logarithm key to find $\ln(0.23) \approx -1.4697$.
45. The graph of $f(x) = \log_3(x)$ includes the points (3, 1), (1, 0), and (1/3, −1). All graphs of logarithm functions have similar shapes.

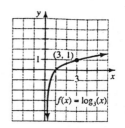

46. The graph of $g(x) = \log_{10}(x)$ includes the points (1, 0), (10, 1), and (0.1, −1).

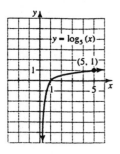

47. The graph of $y = \log_4(x)$ includes the points (4, 1), (1, 0), and (1/4, −1).

48. The graph of $y = \log_5(x)$ includes the points (1, 0), (5, 1), and (1/5, −1).

49. The graph of $y = \log_{1/4}(x)$ includes the points $(1, 0)$, $(4, -1)$, and $(1/4, 1)$.

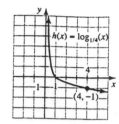

50. The graph of $h(x) = \log_{1/3}(x)$ includes the points $(1, 0)$, $(3, -1)$, and $(1/3, 1)$.

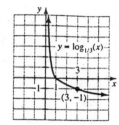

51. The graph of $h(x) = \log_{1/5}(x)$ includes the points $(1, 0)$, $(5, -1)$, and $(1/5, 1)$.

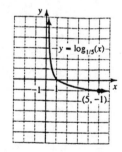

52. The graph of $h(x) = \log_{1/6}(x)$ includes the points $(1, 0)$, $(6, -1)$, and $(1/6, 1)$.

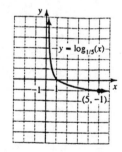

53. The inverse of $f(x) = 6^x$ is $f^{-1}(x) = \log_6(x)$.

54. The inverse of $f(x) = 4^x$ is $f^{-1}(x) = \log_4(x)$.

55. The inverse of $f(x) = \ln(x)$ is $f^{-1}(x) = e^x$.

56. The inverse of $f(x) = \log(x)$ is $f^{-1}(x) = 10^x$.

57. If $f(x) = \log_{1/2}(x)$ then $f^{-1}(x) = \left(\frac{1}{2}\right)^x$.

58. If $f(x) = \log_{1/4}(x)$ then $f^{-1}(x) = \left(\frac{1}{4}\right)^x$.

59. $x = (1/2)^{-2} = 2^2 = 4$
The solution set is $\{4\}$.

60. $\quad x = 3^2$
$\quad\quad x = 9$
The solution set is $\{9\}$.

61. $\quad 5 = 25^x$
$\quad\quad x = \log_{25}(5) = 1/2$
The solution set is $\left\{\frac{1}{2}\right\}$.

62. $\quad 0.1 = 10^x$
$\quad\quad x = \log(0.1)$
$\quad\quad x = -1$
The solution set is $\{-1\}$.

63. $\quad \log(x) = -3$
$\quad\quad x = 10^{-3} = 0.001$
The solution set is $\{0.001\}$.

64. $\quad \log(x) = 5$
$\quad\quad x = 10^5$
$\quad\quad x = 100{,}000$
The solution set is $\{100{,}000\}$.

65. $\quad \log_x(36) = 2$
$\quad\quad x^2 = 36$
$\quad\quad x = \pm 6$
Omit -6 because the base of any logarithm function is positive. The solution set is $\{6\}$.

66. $\quad \log_x(100) = 2$
$\quad\quad x^2 = 100$
$\quad\quad x = \pm 10$
Omit -10 because the base of any logarithm function is positive. The solution set is $\{10\}$.

67. $\quad \log_x(5) = -1$
$\quad\quad x^{-1} = 5$
$\quad\quad (x^{-1})^{-1} = 5^{-1}$
$\quad\quad x = \frac{1}{5}$
The solution set is $\left\{\frac{1}{5}\right\}$.

358

68. $\log_x(16) = -2$

$\quad x^{-2} = 16$

$\quad x^2 = \frac{1}{16}$

$\quad x = \pm \frac{1}{4}$

Omit $-1/4$ because the base of any logarithm function is positive. The solution set is $\{1/4\}$.

69. $\quad \log(x^2) = \log(9)$

$\quad\quad x^2 = 9$

$\quad\quad x = \pm 3$

Both 3 and -3 check in the original equation. The solution set is $\{\pm 3\}$.

70. $\quad \ln(2x - 3) = \ln(x + 1)$

$\quad\quad 2x - 3 = x + 1$

$\quad\quad x - 3 = 1$

$\quad\quad x = 4$

The solution set is $\{4\}$.

71. $\quad 3 = 10^x$

$\quad\quad x = \log(3) \approx 0.4771$

The solution set is $\{0.4771\}$.

72. $\quad 10^x = 0.03$

$\quad\quad x = \log(0.03)$

$\quad\quad x \approx -1.5229$

The solution set is $\{-1.5229\}$.

73. $\quad 10^x = \frac{1}{2}$

$\quad\quad x = \log(1/2) = \log(0.5) \approx -0.3010$

The solution set is $\{-0.3010\}$.

74. $\quad 75 = 10^x$

$\quad\quad x = \log(75)$

$\quad\quad x \approx 1.8751$

The solution set is $\{1.8751\}$.

75. $\quad e^x = 7.2$

$\quad\quad x = \ln(7.2) \approx 1.9741$

The solution set is $\{1.9741\}$.

76. $\quad e^{3x} = 0.4$

$\quad\quad 3x = \ln(0.4)$

$\quad\quad x = \frac{\ln(0.4)}{3} \approx -0.3054$

The solution set is $\{-0.3054\}$.

77. Use the continuous compounding formula.

$\quad 10,000 = 5000 \cdot e^{0.12t}$

$\quad\quad 2 = e^{0.12t}$

$\quad 0.12t = \ln(2)$

$\quad\quad t = \frac{\ln(2)}{0.12} \approx 5.776$ years

78. Use the continuous compounding formula.

$\quad 10,000 = 5,000 \cdot e^{0.06t}$

$\quad\quad 2 = e^{0.06t}$

$\quad 0.06t = \ln(2)$

$\quad\quad t = \frac{\ln(2)}{0.06}$

$\quad\quad t \approx 11.552$ years

79. To earn $1000 in interest, the principal must increase from $6000 to $7000 in t years.

$\quad 7000 = 6000 \cdot e^{0.08t}$

$\quad\quad 7/6 = e^{0.08t}$

$\quad 0.08t = \ln(7/6)$

$\quad\quad t = \frac{\ln(7/6)}{0.08} \approx 1.9269$ years

80. To earn $1000 interest, the principal must increase from $1,000,000 to $1,001,000 in t years.

$\quad 1,001,000 = 1,000,000 \cdot e^{0.09t}$

$\quad\quad 1.001 = e^{0.09t}$

$\quad 0.09t = \ln(1.001)$

$\quad\quad t = \frac{\ln(1.001)}{0.09} \approx 0.011105559$ yr

$\quad\quad t \approx 4.054$ days

81. a) $r = \frac{1}{13}\ln\left(\frac{231,800}{10,000}\right) \approx 1.04776$

$\quad\quad\quad \approx 104.8\%$

b) In 2002,

$A = 10,000e^{7(1.04776)} \approx \$15,320,208.$

82. $r = \frac{1}{18}\ln\left(\frac{563,000}{10,000}\right) \approx 0.2239 = 22.39\%$

83. $\text{pH} = -\log_{10}(10^{-4.1}) = -(-4.1) = 4.1$

84. $\text{pH} = -\log_{10}(10^{-1}) = -(-1) = 1$

85. $\text{pH} = -\log(1.58 \times 10^{-7}) \approx 6.8$

86. $\text{pH} = -\log(1.995 \times 10^{-7}) \approx 6.7$

87. $L = 10 \cdot \log(0.001 \times 10^{12}) = 90$ db

88. $\quad t = -5 \cdot \ln\left(\frac{1000 - 100}{999 \cdot 100}\right) \approx 23.5$

$\quad\quad t = -5 \cdot \ln\left(\frac{1000 - 200}{999 \cdot 200}\right) \approx 27.6$

$\quad\quad t = -5 \cdot \ln\left(\frac{1000 - 998}{999 \cdot 998}\right) \approx 65.6$

$\quad\quad t = -5 \cdot \ln\left(\frac{1000 - 999}{999 \cdot 999}\right) \approx 69.1$

89. $f^{-1}(x) = 2^{x-5} + 3$

Domain $(-\infty, \infty)$, Range $(3, \infty)$

90. $f^{-1}(x) = \ln(x - 2) - 4$

Domain $(2, \infty)$, range $(-\infty, \infty)$

91. $y = \ln(e^x) = x$ for $-\infty < x < \infty$

$y = e^{\ln(x)} = x$ for $0 < x < \infty$

92. $y = 6e^{0.016(100)} \approx 29.7$ billion

$y = 6e^{0.016(200)} \approx 147.2$ billion

10.3 WARM-UPS

1. True, because
$$\log_2(x^2/8) = \log_2(x^2) - \log_2(8)$$
$$= \log_2(x^2) - 3.$$
2. False, because
$\log(100) = 2$ and $\log(10) = 1$, and
$2 \div 1 \neq 2 - 1$.
3. True,
$\ln(\sqrt{2}) = \ln(2^{1/2}) = \frac{1}{2} \cdot \ln(2) = \frac{\ln(2)}{2}$.
4. True, because $\log_3(17)$ is the exponent that
we place on 3 to obtain 17.
5. False, because $\log_2(1/8) = -3$ and
$\log_2(8) = 3$.
6. True, because $\ln(8) = \ln(2^3) = 3 \cdot \ln(2)$.
7. False, because $\ln(1) = 0$.
8. False, because $\log(100) = 2$ and
$\log(10) = 1$.
9. False, because $\log_2(8) = 3$, $\log_2(2) = 1$, and
$\log_2(4) = 2$.
10. True, because
$\ln(2) + \ln(3) - \ln(7) = \ln(6) - \ln(7) = \ln(6/7)$.

10.3 EXERCISES

1. The product rule for logarithms says that
$\log_a(MN) = \log_a(M) + \log_a(N)$.
2. The quotient rule for logarithms says that
$\log_a(M/N) = \log_a(M) - \log_a(N)$.
3. The power rule for logarithms says that
$\log_a(M^N) = N \cdot \log_a(M)$.
4. Since $\log_a(a^M)$ is the exponent that is used
on a to obtain a^M, we have $\log_a(a^M) = M$.
5. Since $\log_a(M)$ is the exponent that you
would use on a to obtain M, using $\log_a(M)$ as
the exponent produces M: $a^{\log_a(M)} = M$.
6. We have $\log_a(1) = 0$ because $a^0 = 1$.
7. $\log(3) + \log(7) = \log(3 \cdot 7) = \log(21)$
8. $\ln(5) + \ln(4) = \ln(5 \cdot 4) = \ln(20)$
9. $\log_3(\sqrt{5}) + \log_3(\sqrt{x}) = \log_3(\sqrt{5x})$
10. $\ln(\sqrt{x}) + \ln(\sqrt{y}) = \ln(\sqrt{xy})$
11. $\log(x^2) + \log(x^3) = \log(x^2 \cdot x^3) = \log(x^5)$
12. $\ln(a^3) + \ln(a^5) = \ln(a^3 \cdot a^5) = \ln(a^8)$
13. $\ln(2) + \ln(3) + \ln(5) = \ln(2 \cdot 3 \cdot 5)$
$$= \ln(30)$$
14. $\log_2(x) + \log_2(y) + \log_2(z) = \log_2(xyz)$

15. $\log(x) + \log(x + 3) = \log(x^2 + 3x)$
16. $\ln(x - 1) + \ln(x + 1) = \ln(x^2 - 1)$
17. $\log_2(x - 3) + \log_2(x + 2)$
$$= \log_2(x^2 - x - 6)$$
18. $\log_3(x - 5) + \log_3(x - 4)$
$$= \log_3(x^2 - 9x + 20)$$
19. $\log(8) - \log(2) = \log(8/2) = \log(4)$
20. $\ln(3) - \ln(6) = \ln\left(\frac{3}{6}\right) = \ln\left(\frac{1}{2}\right)$
21. $\log_2(x^6) - \log_2(x^2) = \log_2\left(\frac{x^6}{x^2}\right)$
$$= \log_2(x^4)$$
22. $\ln(w^9) - \ln(w^3) = \ln\left(\frac{w^9}{w^3}\right) = \ln(w^6)$
23. $\log(\sqrt{10}) - \log(\sqrt{2}) = \log\left(\frac{\sqrt{10}}{\sqrt{2}}\right)$
$$= \log(\sqrt{5})$$
24. $\log_3(\sqrt{6}) - \log_3(\sqrt{3}) = \log_3\left(\frac{\sqrt{6}}{\sqrt{3}}\right)$
$$= \log_3\left(\sqrt{2}\right)$$
25. $\ln(4h - 8) - \ln(4) = \ln\left(\frac{4h - 8}{4}\right)$
$$= \ln(h - 2)$$
26. $\log\left(\frac{3x - 6}{3}\right) = \log(x - 2)$
27. $\log_2\left(\frac{w^2 - 4}{w + 2}\right) = \log_2\left(\frac{(w - 2)(w + 2)}{w + 2}\right)$
$$= \log_2(w - 2)$$
28. $\log_3\left(\frac{k^2 - 9}{k - 3}\right) = \log_3(k + 3)$
29. $\ln\left(\frac{x^2 + x - 6}{x + 3}\right) = \ln\left(\frac{(x + 3)(x - 2)}{x + 3}\right)$
$$= \ln(x - 2)$$
30. $\ln\left(\frac{t^2 - t - 12}{t - 4}\right) = \ln\left(\frac{(t - 4)(t + 3)}{t - 4}\right)$
$$= \ln(t + 3)$$
31. $\log(27) = \log(3^3) = 3\log(3)$
32. $\log(1/9) = \log(1) - \log(3^2)$
$$= 0 - 2 \cdot \log(3) = -2\log(3)$$
33. $\log(\sqrt{3}) = \log(3^{1/2}) = \frac{1}{2}\log(3)$
34. $\log(\sqrt[4]{3}) = \log(3^{1/4}) = \frac{1}{4}\log(3)$
35. $\log(3^x) = x\log(3)$
36. $\log(3^{-99}) = -99\log(3)$
37. $\log_2(2^{10}) = 10$
38. $\ln(e^9) = 9$
39. $5^{\log_5(19)} = 19$
40. $10^{\log(2.3)} = 2.3$
41. $\log(10^8) = 8$
42. $\log_4(4^5) = 5$

43. $e^{\ln(4.3)} = 4.3$

44. $3^{\log_3(5.5)} = 5.5$

45. $\log(15) = \log(3 \cdot 5) = \log(3) + \log(5)$

46. $\log(9) = \log(3^2) = 2\log(3)$

47. $\log(5/3) = \log(5) - \log(3)$

48. $\log(3/5) = \log(3) - \log(5)$

49. $\log(25) = \log(5^2) = 2\log(5)$

50. $\log(1) - \log(27) = 0 - \log(3^3)$
$$= -3\log(3)$$

51. $\log(75) = \log(5^2 \cdot 3) = 2\log(5) + \log(3)$

52. $\log(0.6) = \log(3/5) = \log(3) - \log(5)$

53. $\log\left(\frac{1}{3}\right) = \log(1) - \log(3)$
$$= 0 - \log(3) = -\log(3)$$

54. $\log(45) = \log(3^2 \cdot 5) = \log(3^2) + \log(5)$
$$= 2\log(3) + \log(5)$$

55. $\log(0.2) = \log(1/5) = \log(1) - \log(5)$
$$= 0 - \log(5) = -\log(5)$$

56. $\log(9/25) = \log(9) - \log(25)$
$$= \log(3^2) - \log(5^2)$$
$$= 2\log(3) - 2\log(5)$$

57. $\log(xyz) = \log(x) + \log(y) + \log(z)$

58. $\log(3y) = \log(3) + \log(y)$

59. $\log_2(8x) = \log_2(8) + \log_2(x)$
$$= 3 + \log_2(x)$$

60. $\log_2(16y) = \log_2(2^4 \cdot y)$
$$= \log_2(2^4) + \log_2(y)$$
$$= 4 + \log_2(y)$$

61. $\ln(x/y) = \ln(x) - \ln(y)$

62. $\ln(z/3) = \ln(z) - \ln(3)$

63. $\log(10x^2) = \log(10) + \log(x^2)$
$$= 1 + 2\log(x)$$

64. $\log(100\sqrt{x}) = \log(100) + \log(x^{1/2})$
$$= 2 + \frac{1}{2}\log(x)$$

65. $\log_5\left[\frac{(x-3)^2}{\sqrt{w}}\right]$
$$= \log_5\left[(x-3)^2\right] - \log_5(\sqrt{w})$$
$$= 2\log_5(x-3) - \frac{1}{2}\log_5(w)$$

66. $\log_3\left(\frac{(y+6)^3}{y-5}\right)$
$$= \log_3\left((y+6)^3\right) - \log_3(y-5)$$
$$= 3\log_3(y+6) - \log_3(y-5)$$

67. $\ln\left[\frac{yz\sqrt{x}}{w}\right] = \ln[yz\sqrt{x}] - \ln(w)$
$$= \ln(y) + \ln(z) + \ln(\sqrt{x}) - \ln(w)$$
$$= \ln(y) + \ln(z) + \frac{1}{2}\ln(x) - \ln(w)$$

68. $\ln\left(\frac{(x-1)\sqrt{w}}{x^3}\right)$
$$= \ln(x-1) + \ln(\sqrt{w}) - \ln(x^3)$$
$$= \ln(x-1) + \frac{1}{2}\ln(w) - 3\ln(x)$$

69. $\log(x) + \log(x-1) = \log(x^2 - x)$

70. $\log_2(x-2) + \log_2(5) = \log_2(5x - 10)$

71. $\ln(3x-6) - \ln(x-2) = \ln\left(\frac{3x-6}{x-2}\right)$
$$= \ln(3)$$

72. $\log_3\left(\frac{x^2-1}{x-1}\right) = \log_3(x+1)$

73. $\ln(x) - \ln(w) + \ln(z) = \ln(xz) - \ln(w)$
$$= \ln\left(\frac{xz}{w}\right)$$

74. $\ln(x) - \ln(3) - \ln(7)$
$$= \ln(x) - [\ln(3) + \ln(7)]$$
$$= \ln(x) - \ln(3 \cdot 7) = \ln(x) - \ln(21)$$
$$= \ln\left(\frac{x}{21}\right)$$

75. $3 \cdot \ln(y) + 2 \cdot \ln(x) - \ln(w)$
$$= \ln(y^3) + \ln(x^2) - \ln(w)$$
$$= \ln(x^2 y^3) - \ln(w) = \ln\left(\frac{x^2 y^3}{w}\right)$$

76. $5 \cdot \ln(r) + 3 \cdot \ln(t) - 4 \cdot \ln(s)$
$$= \ln(r^5) + \ln(t^3) - \ln(s^4)$$
$$= \ln(r^5 t^3) - \ln(s^4)$$
$$= \ln\left(\frac{r^5 t^3}{s^4}\right)$$

77. $\frac{1}{2} \cdot \log(x-3) - \frac{2}{3} \cdot \log(x+1)$
$$= \log\left((x-3)^{1/2}\right) - \log\left((x+1)^{2/3}\right)$$
$$= \log\left(\frac{(x-3)^{1/2}}{(x+1)^{2/3}}\right)$$

78. $\frac{1}{2}\log(y-4) + \frac{1}{2}\log(y+4)$
$$= \log[(y-4)^{1/2}] + \log[(y+4)^{1/2}]$$
$$= \log(\sqrt{y-4}) + \log(\sqrt{y+4})$$
$$= \log(\sqrt{y-4}\sqrt{y+4})$$
$$= \log(\sqrt{(y-4)(y+4)})$$
$$= \log(\sqrt{y^2 - 16})$$

79. $\frac{2}{3} \cdot \log_2(x-1) - \frac{1}{4} \cdot \log_2(x+2)$
$$= \log_2\left((x-1)^{2/3}\right) - \log_2\left((x+2)^{1/4}\right)$$
$$= \log_2\left(\frac{(x-1)^{2/3}}{(x+2)^{1/4}}\right)$$

80. $\frac{1}{2}\log_3(y+3) + 6 \cdot \log_3(y)$
$$= \log_3(\sqrt{y+3}) + \log_3(y^6)$$
$$= \log_3(y^6\sqrt{y+3})$$

81. False, because
$$\log(56) = \log(7 \cdot 8) = \log(7) + \log(8).$$

361

82. False, because $\log(5/9) = \log(5) - \log(9)$.

83. True, because $\log_2(4^2) = \log_2(16) = 4$ and $(\log_2(4))^2 = (2)^2 = 4$.

84. False, because $\ln(4^2) = 2 \cdot \ln(4)$.

85. True, because $\ln(25) = \ln(5^2) = 2 \cdot \ln(5)$.

86. True, because $\ln(3e) = \ln(3) + \ln(e)$
$$= \ln(3) + 1 = 1 + \ln(3).$$

87. False, because $\log_2(64) = 6$ and $\log_2(8) = 3$.

88. True, because $\dfrac{\log_2(16)}{\log_2(4)} = \dfrac{4}{2} = 2 = \log_2 4$.

89. True, because $\log(1/3) = \log(1) - \log(3)$
$$= 0 - \log(3) = -\log(3).$$

90. True,
$$\log_2(8 \cdot 2^{59}) = \log_2(2^3 2^{59}) = \log_2(2^{62}) = 62.$$

91. True,
$$\log_2(16^5) = 5 \cdot \log_2(16) = 5 \cdot 4 = 20.$$

92. True, because
$$\log_2(5/2) = \log_2(5) - \log_2(2) = \log_2(5) - 1.$$

93. True, $\log(10^3) = 3 \cdot \log(10) = 3 \cdot 1 = 3$.

94. True, because $\log_3(3^7) = 7$.

95. False, because $\log(100 + 3) = \log(103)$ and
$$2 + \log(3) = \log(100) + \log(3) = \log(300).$$

96. True, because
$$\frac{\log_7(32)}{\log_7(8)} = \frac{\log_7(2^5)}{\log_7(2^3)} = \frac{5 \cdot \log_7 2}{3 \cdot \log_7 2} = \frac{5}{3}.$$

97. $r = \dfrac{\ln(A) - \ln(P)}{t} = \dfrac{1}{t} \cdot \ln(A/P)$
$$= \ln\big((A/P)^{1/t}\big)$$
If $A = 27P$ when $t = 8$, then
$$r = \ln\big((27P/P)^{1/8}\big) = \ln\big(17^{1/8}\big) \approx 0.412$$
$$= 41.2\%.$$

98. $-\frac{2}{3}\log_2\left(\frac{2}{3}\right) - \frac{1}{3}\log_2\left(\frac{1}{3}\right)$
$$= \log_2\big((2/3)^{-2/3}\big) + \log_2\big((1/3)^{-1/3}\big)$$
$$= \log_2\big((2/3)^{-2/3} \cdot (1/3)^{-1/3}\big)$$
$$= \log_2\left(\sqrt[3]{(2/3)^{-2} \cdot (1/3)^{-1}}\right)$$
$$= \log_2\left(\sqrt[3]{\frac{9}{4} \cdot \frac{3}{1}}\right) = \log_2\left(\sqrt[3]{\frac{27 \cdot 2}{4 \cdot 2}}\right)$$
$$= \log_2\left(\frac{3\sqrt[3]{2}}{2}\right)$$

99. Only (b) is an identity, because it is the only one that is a correct application of a property of logarithms.

100. Only (c) cannot be obtained from $\log(5^{2/3})$ using the properties of logarithms.

101. The graphs are the same because $\ln(\sqrt{x}) = \ln(x^{1/2}) = \frac{1}{2}\ln(x)$.

102. Because $\log(10x) = 1 + \log(x)$, $\log(100x) = 2 + \log(x)$, and $\log(1000x) = 3 + \log(x)$, the graphs lie 1, 2, and 3 units above $y = \log(x)$.

103. The graph is a straight line because $\log(e^x) = x\log(e) \approx 0.434x$. The slope is $\log(e)$ or approximately 0.434.

10.4 WARM-UPS

1. True, because $\log(x - 2) + \log(x + 2) = \log[(x - 2)(x + 2)] = \log(x^2 - 4)$.

2. True, because of the one-to-one property of logarithms.

3. True, because of the one-to-one property of exponential functions.

4. False, because the bases are different and the one-to-one property does not apply.

5. True, because $\log_2(x^2 - 3x + 5) = 3$ is equivalent to $x^2 - 3x + 5 = 2^3 = 8$.

6. True, $a^x = y$ is equivalent to $\log_a(y) = x$.

7. True, if $5^x = 23$, then $\ln(5^x) = \ln(23)$, or $x \cdot \ln(5) = \ln(23)$.

8. False, because $\log_3(5) = \dfrac{\ln(5)}{\ln(3)}$.

9. True, $\log_6(2) = \dfrac{\ln(2)}{\ln(6)}$ and $\log_6(2) = \dfrac{\log(2)}{\log(6)}$.

10. False, $\log(5) \approx 0.699$ and $\ln(5) \approx 1.609$.

10.4 EXERCISES

1. Equivalent to $\log_a(x) = y$ is $a^y = x$.

2. According to the base change formula, $\log_a(x) = \ln(x)/\ln(a)$.

3. $\log_2(x + 1) = 3$
$$x + 1 = 2^3$$
$$x + 1 = 8$$
$$x = 7$$
The solution set is $\{7\}$.

362

4. $\log_3(x^2) = 4$

$\quad\quad x^2 = 3^4$

$\quad\quad x^2 = 81$

$\quad\quad\; x = \pm 9$

The solution set is $\{\pm 9\}$.

5. $\log(x) + \log(5) = 1$

$\quad\quad \log(5x) = 1$

$\quad\quad\quad\; 5x = 10^1$

$\quad\quad\quad\;\; x = 2$

The solution set is $\{2\}$.

6. $\ln(x) + \ln(3) = 0$

$\quad\quad \ln(3x) = 0$

$\quad\quad\quad 3x = e^0$

$\quad\quad\quad 3x = 1$

$\quad\quad\quad\; x = \frac{1}{3}$

The solution set is $\left\{\frac{1}{3}\right\}$.

7. $\log_2(x-1) + \log_2(x+1) = 3$

$\quad\quad \log_2[(x-1)(x+1)] = 3$

$\quad\quad\quad \log_2(x^2 - 1) = 3$

$\quad\quad\quad\quad\quad x^2 - 1 = 2^3$

$\quad\quad\quad\quad\quad\quad x^2 = 9$

$\quad\quad\quad\quad\quad\quad\; x = \pm 3$

If $x = -3$ in the original equation, $\log_2(-3-1)$ is undefined. The solution set is $\{3\}$.

8. $\log_3(x-4) + \log_3(x+4) = 2$

$\quad\quad \log_3[(x-4)(x+4)] = 2$

$\quad\quad\quad \log_3[x^2 - 16] = 2$

$\quad\quad\quad\quad\; x^2 - 16 = 3^2$

$\quad\quad\quad\quad\quad\quad x^2 = 25$

$\quad\quad\quad\quad\quad\quad\; x = \pm 5$

If $x = -5$ in the original equation, $\log_3(-5-4)$ is undefined. The solution set is $\{5\}$.

9. $\log_2(x-1) - \log_2(x+2) = 2$

$\quad\quad \log_2\left(\frac{x-1}{x+2}\right) = 2$

$\quad\quad\quad\; \frac{x-1}{x+2} = 2^2$

$\quad\quad\quad\; x - 1 = 4(x+2)$

$\quad\quad\quad\; x - 1 = 4x + 8$

$\quad\quad\quad\quad\; -9 = 3x$

$\quad\quad\quad\quad\; -3 = x$

If $x = -3$ in the original equation, we get the logarithm of a negative number, which is undefined. The solution set is $\emptyset$.

10. $\log_4(8x) - \log_4(x-1) = 2$

$\log_4\left(\frac{8x}{x-1}\right) = 2$

$\quad\quad \frac{8x}{x-1} = 4^2$

$\quad\quad\quad 8x = 16x - 16$

$\quad\quad\; -8x = -16$

$\quad\quad\quad\; x = 2$

The solution set is $\{2\}$.

11. $\log_2(x-4) + \log_2(x+2) = 4$

$\quad\quad \log_2(x^2 - 2x - 8) = 4$

$\quad\quad\quad x^2 - 2x - 8 = 2^4$

$\quad\quad\quad x^2 - 2x - 8 = 16$

$\quad\quad\quad x^2 - 2x - 24 = 0$

$\quad\quad\quad (x-6)(x+4) = 0$

$\quad\; x - 6 = 0 \;\; \text{or} \;\; x + 4 = 0$

$\quad\quad\quad x = 6 \;\;\; \text{or} \quad\quad\; x = -4$

If $x = -4$ in the original equation, we get $\log_2(-8)$, which is undefined. The solution set is $\{6\}$.

12. $\log_6(x+6) + \log_6(x-3) = 2$

$\quad\quad \log_6[(x+6)(x-3)] = 2$

$\quad\quad \log_6[x^2 + 3x - 18] = 2$

$\quad\quad\quad\; x^2 + 3x - 18 = 6^2$

$\quad\quad\quad\; x^2 + 3x - 54 = 0$

$\quad\quad\quad\; (x+9)(x-6) = 0$

$x + 9 = 0 \;\; \text{or} \;\; x - 6 = 0$

$\quad\; x = -9 \;\; \text{or} \quad\quad x = 6$

If $x = -9$ in the original equation we get $\log_6(-9+6)$, which is undefined. The solution set is $\{6\}$.

13. $\ln(x) + \ln(x+5)$

$\quad\quad = \ln(x+1) + \ln(x+3)$

$\quad \ln(x^2 + 5x) = \ln(x^2 + 4x + 3)$

$\quad\quad x^2 + 5x = x^2 + 4x + 3$

$\quad\quad\quad\quad\; x = 3$

The solution set is $\{3\}$.

14. $\log(x) + \log(x+5) = 2 \cdot \log(x+2)$

$\quad\quad \log(x^2 + 5x) = \log[(x+2)^2]$

$\quad\quad\quad x^2 + 5x = x^2 + 4x + 4$

$\quad\quad\quad\quad\quad x = 4$

The solution set is $\{4\}$.

15. $\log(x+3) + \log(x+4)$

$\quad\quad = \log(x^3 + 13x^2) - \log(x)$

$\log(x^2 + 7x + 12) = \log(x^2 + 13x)$

$\quad\quad x^2 + 7x + 12 = x^2 + 13x$

$\quad\quad\quad\quad\quad 12 = 6x$

$\quad\quad\quad\quad\quad\; 2 = x$

The solution set is $\{2\}$.

16. $\log(x^2 - 1) - \log(x - 1) = \log(6)$

$$\log\left(\frac{x^2 - 1}{x - 1}\right) = \log(6)$$
$$\frac{x^2 - 1}{x - 1} = 6$$
$$x^2 - 1 = 6x - 6$$
$$x^2 - 6x + 5 = 0$$
$$(x - 5)(x - 1) = 0$$
$$x - 5 = 0 \text{ or } x - 1 = 0$$
$$x = 5 \text{ or } \quad x = 1$$

If $x = 1$ in the original equation, we get $\log(1 - 1)$, which is undefined. The solution set is $\{5\}$.

17. $2 \cdot \log(x) = \log(20 - x)$

$$\log(x^2) = \log(20 - x)$$
$$x^2 = 20 - x$$
$$x^2 + x - 20 = 0$$
$$(x - 4)(x + 5) = 0$$
$$x - 4 = 0 \text{ or } x + 5 = 0$$
$$x = 4 \text{ or } \quad x = -5$$

If $x = -5$ in the original equation we get a logarithm of a negative number, which is undefined. The solution set is $\{4\}$.

18. $2 \cdot \log(x) + \log(3) = \log(2 - 5x)$

$$\log(x^2) + \log(3) = \log(2 - 5x)$$
$$\log(3x^2) = \log(2 - 5x)$$
$$3x^2 = 2 - 5x$$
$$3x^2 + 5x - 2 = 0$$
$$(3x - 1)(x + 2) = 0$$
$$3x - 1 = 0 \text{ or } x + 2 = 0$$
$$x = \tfrac{1}{3} \text{ or } \quad x = -2$$

If $x = -2$ in the original equation, we get $\log(-2)$, which is undefined. The solution set is $\{\tfrac{1}{3}\}$.

19. $3^x = 7$

$$x = \log_3(7)$$

The solution set is $\{\log_3(7)\}$.

20. $2^{x-1} = 5$

$$x - 1 = \log_2(5)$$
$$x = 1 + \log_2(5)$$

The solution set is $\{1 + \log_2(5)\}$.

21. $2^{3x+4} = 4^{x-1}$

$$2^{3x+4} = (2^2)^{x-1}$$
$$2^{3x+4} = (2)^{2x-2}$$
$$3x + 4 = 2x - 2$$
$$x = -6$$

The solution set is $\{-6\}$.

22. $9^{2x-1} = 27^{1/2}$

$$(3^2)^{2x-1} = (3^3)^{1/2}$$
$$3^{4x-2} = 3^{3/2}$$
$$4x - 2 = \tfrac{3}{2}$$
$$4x = \tfrac{7}{2}$$
$$x = \tfrac{7}{8}$$

The solution set is $\{\tfrac{7}{8}\}$.

23. $(1/3)^x = 3^{1+x}$

$$(3^{-1})^x = 3^{1+x}$$
$$3^{-x} = 3^{1+x}$$
$$-x = 1 + x$$
$$-2x = 1$$
$$x = -1/2$$

The solution set is $\{-\tfrac{1}{2}\}$.

24. $4^{3x} = (1/2)^{1-x}$

$$(2^2)^{3x} = (2^{-1})^{1-x}$$
$$2^{6x} = 2^{-1+x}$$
$$6x = -1 + x$$
$$5x = -1$$
$$x = -\tfrac{1}{5}$$

The solution set is $\{-\tfrac{1}{5}\}$.

25. $2^x = 3^{x+5}$

$$\ln(2^x) = \ln(3^{x+5})$$
$$x \cdot \ln(2) = (x + 5)\ln(3)$$
$$x \cdot \ln(2) = x \cdot \ln(3) + 5 \cdot \ln(3)$$
$$x \cdot \ln(2) - x \cdot \ln(3) = 5 \cdot \ln(3)$$
$$x(\ln(2) - \ln(3)) = 5 \cdot \ln(3)$$
$$x = \frac{5 \cdot \ln(3)}{\ln(2) - \ln(3)}$$

This is the exact solution.
Use a calculator to find an approximate solution: $\dfrac{5\ln(3)}{\ln(2) - \ln(3)} \approx -13.548$.

26. $e^x = 10^x$

$$\ln(e^x) = \ln(10^x)$$
$$x = x \cdot \ln(10)$$
$$x - x \cdot \ln(10) = 0$$
$$x(1 - \ln(10)) = 0$$
$$x = 0$$

27. $5^{x+2} = 10^{x-4}$

$$\log(5^{x+2}) = \log(10^{x-4})$$
$$(x + 2)\log(5) = x - 4$$
$$x \cdot \log(5) + 2 \cdot \log(5) = x - 4$$
$$x \cdot \log(5) - x = -4 - 2 \cdot \log(5)$$
$$x[\log(5) - 1] = -4 - 2 \cdot \log(5)$$

$$x = \frac{-4 - 2 \cdot \log(5)}{\log(5) - 1}$$
$$= \frac{4 + 2\log(5)}{1 - \log(5)}$$
$$\approx 17.932$$

28.
$$3^{2x} = 6^{x+1}$$
$$2x \cdot \ln(3) = (x + 1)\ln(6)$$
$$2x \cdot \ln(3) = x \cdot \ln(6) + \ln(6)$$
$$2x \cdot \ln(3) - x \cdot \ln(6) = \ln(6)$$
$$x[2 \cdot \ln(3) - \ln(6)] = \ln(6)$$
$$x = \frac{\ln(6)}{\ln(9) - \ln(6)} \approx 4.419$$

29.
$$8^x = 9^{x-1}$$
$$\ln(8^x) = \ln(9^{x-1})$$
$$x \cdot \ln(8) = (x - 1)\ln(9)$$
$$x \cdot \ln(8) = x \cdot \ln(9) - \ln(9)$$
$$x \cdot \ln(8) - x \cdot \ln(9) = -\ln(9)$$
$$x[\ln(8) - \ln(9)] = -\ln(9)$$
$$x = \frac{-\ln(9)}{\ln(8) - \ln(9)} = \frac{\ln(9)}{\ln(9) - \ln(8)}$$
$$\approx 18.655$$

30.
$$5^{x+1} = 8^{x-1}$$
$$(x + 1)\ln(5) = (x - 1)\ln(8)$$
$$x \cdot \ln(5) + \ln(5) = x \cdot \ln(8) - \ln(8)$$
$$x \cdot \ln(5) - x \cdot \ln(8) = -\ln(5) - \ln(8)$$
$$x[\ln(5) - \ln(8)] = -\ln(5) - \ln(8)$$
$$x = \frac{-\ln(5) - \ln(8)}{\ln(5) - \ln(8)} = \frac{\ln(5) + \ln(8)}{\ln(8) - \ln(5)}$$
$$\approx 7.849$$

31. $\log_2(3) = \frac{\ln(3)}{\ln(2)} \approx 1.5850$

32. $\log_3(5) = \frac{\ln(5)}{\ln(3)} \approx 1.4650$

33. $\log_3(1/2) = \frac{\ln(0.5)}{\ln(3)} \approx -0.6309$

34. $\log_5(2.56) = \frac{\ln(2.56)}{\ln(5)} \approx 0.5841$

35. $\log_{1/2}(4.6) = \frac{\ln(4.6)}{\ln(0.5)} \approx -2.2016$

36. $\log_{1/3}(3.5) = \frac{\ln(3.5)}{\ln(1/3)} \approx -1.1403$

37. $\log_{0.1}(0.03) = \frac{\ln(0.03)}{\ln(0.1)} \approx 1.5229$

38. $\log_{0.2}(1.06) = \frac{\ln(1.06)}{\ln(0.2)} \approx -0.0362$

39. $x \cdot \ln(2) = \ln(7)$
$$x = \frac{\ln(7)}{\ln(2)}$$

This is the exact solution.

Use a calculator to find the approximate value of x, $x \approx 2.807$.

40. $x \cdot \log(3) = \log(5)$
$$x = \frac{\log(5)}{\log(3)}$$

This is the exact solution. Use a calculator to find the approximate value of x, $x \approx 1.465$.

41. $3x - x \cdot \ln(2) = 1$
$$x(3 - \ln(2)) = 1$$
$$x = \frac{1}{3 - \ln(2)}$$

Exact solution.
Use a calculator to find an approximate value for x: $\frac{1}{3 - \ln(2)} \approx 0.433$.

42. $2x + x \cdot \log(5) = \log(7)$
$$x(2 + \log(5)) = \log(7)$$
$$x = \frac{\log(7)}{2 + \log(5)} \approx 0.313$$

43. $3^x = 5$
$$x = \log_3(5) = \frac{\ln(5)}{\ln(3)}$$

This is the exact solution.
Use a calculator to find an approximate value for x that satisfies the equation,
$\frac{\ln(5)}{\ln(3)} \approx 1.465$.

44. $2^x = \frac{1}{3}$
$$x = \log_2\left(\frac{1}{3}\right) = \log_2(3^{-1})$$
$$x = -\log_2(3)$$
$$x = -\frac{\ln(3)}{\ln(2)} \approx -1.585$$

45.
$$2^{x-1} = 9$$
$$\ln(2^{x-1}) = \ln(9)$$
$$(x - 1)\ln(2) = \ln(9)$$
$$x - 1 = \frac{\ln(9)}{\ln(2)}$$
$$x = 1 + \frac{\ln(9)}{\ln(2)} \quad \text{Exact solution}$$

Use a calculator to find an approximate value for x: $1 + \frac{\ln(9)}{\ln(2)} \approx 4.170$.

46.
$$10^{x-2} = 6$$
$$x - 2 = \log(6)$$
$$x = 2 + \log(6) \approx 2.778$$

47. $3^x = 20$
$$x = \log_3(20) \approx 2.727$$

48.
$$2^x = 128$$
$$2^x = 2^7$$
$$x = 7$$

49.
$$\log_3(x) + \log_3(5) = 1$$
$$\log_3(5x) = 1$$
$$5x = 3^1$$
$$x = \tfrac{3}{5}$$

50. $\log(x) - \log(3) = \log(6)$
$$\log\left(\tfrac{x}{3}\right) = \log(6)$$
$$\tfrac{x}{3} = 6$$
$$x = 18$$

51.
$$8^x = 2^{x+1}$$
$$(2^3)^x = 2^{x+1}$$
$$2^{3x} = 2^{x+1}$$
$$3x = x + 1$$
$$2x = 1$$
$$x = \tfrac{1}{2}$$

52.
$$2^x = 5^{x+1}$$
$$x \cdot \ln(2) = (x+1)\ln(5)$$
$$x \cdot \ln(2) = x \cdot \ln(5) + \ln(5)$$
$$x \cdot \ln(2) - x \cdot \ln(5) = \ln(5)$$
$$x[\ln(2) - \ln(5)] = \ln(5)$$
$$x = \frac{\ln(5)}{\ln(2) - \ln(5)}$$
$$\approx -1.756$$

53. Use the formula $S = P(1 + i)^n$.
$$1500 = 1000(1 + 0.01)^n$$
$$1.5 = (1.01)^n$$
$$n = \log_{1.01}(1.5) = \frac{\ln(1.5)}{\ln(1.01)}$$
$$\approx 40.749$$
It takes approximately 41 months.

54. Use the formula $S = P(1 + i)^n$.
$$100 = 25(1 + 0.08)^n$$
$$4 = (1.08)^n$$
$$n = \log_{1.08}(4) = \frac{\ln(4)}{\ln(1.08)}$$
$$\approx 18.01$$
It takes approximately 18 years.

55. $y = 114.308e^{(0.265 \cdot 15.8)} \approx 7524 \text{ ft}^3/\text{sec}$

56.
$$50,500 = 114.308e^{0.265x}$$
$$e^{0.265x} = 50,500/114.308$$
$$0.265x = \ln(50,500/114.308)$$
$$x = \frac{\ln(50,500/114.308)}{0.265}$$
$$\approx 22.98 \text{ ft}$$

57.
$$40 = 28e^{0.05t}$$
$$\tfrac{10}{7} = e^{0.05t}$$
$$0.05t = \ln(10/7)$$

$$t = \frac{\ln(10/7)}{0.05} \approx 7.133$$
There will be 40 million people above the poverty level in approximately 7.1 years.

58.
$$40 = 20e^{0.07t}$$
$$2 = e^{0.07t}$$
$$0.07t = \ln(2)$$
$$t = \frac{\ln(2)}{0.07} \approx 9.9$$
There will be 40 million people below the poverty level in approximately 9.9 years.

59.
$$28e^{0.05t} = 20e^{0.07t}$$
$$\ln(28e^{0.05t}) = \ln(20e^{0.07t})$$
$$\ln(28) + \ln(e^{0.05t}) = \ln(20) + \ln(e^{0.07t})$$
$$\ln(28) + 0.05t = \ln(20) + 0.07t$$
$$-0.02t = \ln(20) - \ln(28)$$
$$t = \frac{\ln(20) - \ln(28)}{-0.02}$$
$$\approx 16.824$$
The number of people above the poverty level will equal the number below the poverty level in approximately 16.8 years.

60.
$$100e^{-0.01t} = 40e^{0.09t}$$
$$\frac{100e^{-0.01t}}{e^{0.09t}} = 40$$
$$100e^{-0.10t} = 40$$
$$e^{-0.10t} = 0.40$$
$$-0.10t = \ln(0.40)$$
$$t = \frac{\ln(0.40)}{-0.10} \approx 9.1629$$
The number of workers will equal the number of retired people in approximately 9.2 years.

61.
$$\text{pH} = -\log(\text{H}^+)$$
$$3.7 = -\log(\text{H}^+)$$
$$-3.7 = \log(\text{H}^+)$$
$$\text{H}^+ = 10^{-3.7} \approx 2.0 \times 10^{-4}$$

62.
$$\text{pH} = -\log(\text{H}^+)$$
$$7.4 = -\log(\text{H}^+)$$
$$-7.4 = \log(\text{H}^+)$$
$$\text{H}^+ = 10^{-7.4} \approx 4.0 \times 10^{-8}$$

63. $d = 0.9183$

64. $d = -[0.05 \cdot \log_2(0.05) + 0.1 \cdot \log_2(0.1)$
$$+ 0.2 \cdot \log_2(0.2) + 0.15 \cdot \log_2(0.15)$$
$$+ 0.23 \cdot \log_2(0.23) + 0.27 \cdot \log_2(0.27)]$$
$$\approx 2.42$$

65. 2.2894

66. a) Consider the graph of $y = \log_2(x)$. The y coordinates are negative for $0 < x < 1$ and positive for $x > 1$. So $\log_2(0.45)$ is negative.
b) positive
c) negative
d) positive
67. $(2.71, 6.54)$
68. $y = 1000e^{0.06x}$,
$y = 1200(1 + 0.05/12)^{12x}$, 18.0 years
69. $(1.03, 0.04), (4.73, 2.24)$

Enriching Your Mathematical Word Power
Chapter 10
1. a   2. d   3. b   4. d   5. d
6. b   7. a   8. b   9. b   10. c

CHAPTER 10 REVIEW

1. $f(-2) = 5^{-2} = \frac{1}{5^2} = \frac{1}{25}$
2. $f(0) = 5^0 = 1$
3. $f(3) = 5^3 = 125$
4. $f(4) = 5^4 = 625$
5. $g(1) = 10^{1-1} = 10^0 = 1$
6. $g(-1) = 10^{-1-1} = 10^{-2} = \frac{1}{100}$
7. $g(0) = 10^{0-1} = 10^{-1} = \frac{1}{10}$
8. $g(3) = 10^{3-1} = 10^2 = 100$
9. $h(-1) = (1/4)^{-1} = 4$
10. $h(2) = \left(\frac{1}{4}\right)^2 = \frac{1}{16}$
11. $h(1/2) = (1/4)^{1/2} = \sqrt{\frac{1}{4}} = \frac{1}{2}$
12. $h(-1/2) = \left(\frac{1}{4}\right)^{-1/2} = 4^{1/2} = 2$
13. If $f(x) = 25$, then $5^x = 25$, $x = 2$.
14. If $f(x) = -1/125$, then $5^x = -1/125$.
$$5^x = -\frac{1}{125}$$
There is no solution to this equation since no power of 5 is negative.
15. If $g(x) = 1000$, then $10^{x-1} = 1000$.
$$10^{x-1} = 10^3$$
$$x - 1 = 3$$
$$x = 4$$
16. If $g(x) = 0.001$, then $10^{x-1} = 0.001$.
$$10^{x-1} = \frac{1}{1000}$$
$$10^{x-1} = 10^{-3}$$
$$x - 1 = -3$$
$$x = -2$$
17. If $h(x) = 32$, then $(1/4)^x = 32$.

$$(2^{-2})^x = 2^5$$
$$2^{-2x} = 2^5$$
$$-2x = 5$$
$$x = -\frac{5}{2}$$
18. If $h(x) = 8$, then $(1/4)^x = 8$.
$$(2^{-2})^x = 2^3$$
$$2^{-2x} = 2^3$$
$$-2x = 3$$
$$x = -\frac{3}{2}$$
19. If $h(x) = 1/16$, then $(1/4)^x = 1/16$, or $(1/4)^x = (1/4)^2$, $x = 2$.
20. If $h(x) = 1$, then $(1/4)^x = 1$, or $x = 0$.
21. $f(1.34) = 5^{1.34} \approx 8.6421$
22. $f(-3.6) = 5^{-3.6} \approx 0.00305$
23. $g(3.25) = 10^{3.25-1} = 10^{2.25} \approx 177.828$
24. $g(4.87) = 10^{4.87-1} = 10^{3.87} \approx 7413.102$
25. $h(2.82) = (1/4)^{2.82} = (0.25)^{2.82}$
$$\approx 0.02005$$
26. $h(\pi) = (1/4)^\pi = (0.25)^{3.14159}$
$$\approx 0.01284$$
27. $h(\sqrt{2}) = (1/4)^{\sqrt{2}} = (0.25)^{1.414} \approx 0.1408$
28. $h(1/3) = (1/4)^{1/3} \approx 0.6300$
29. The graph of $f(x) = 5^x$ includes the points $(0, 1), (1, 5)$, and $(-1, 1/5)$.

30. The graph of $g(x) = e^x$ includes the points $(0, 1), (1, 2.718), (-1, 0.368)$.

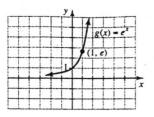

31. The graph of $y = \left(1/5\right)^{x}$ includes the points $(1, 1/5)$, $(0, 1)$ and $(-1, 5)$.

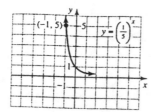

32. The graph of $y = e^{-x}$ includes the points $(0, 1)$, $(1, 0.368)$, and $(-1, 2.718)$.

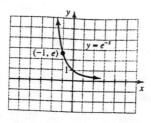

33. The graph of $y = 3^{-x}$ includes the points $(0, 1)$, $(1, 1/3)$, and $(-1, 3)$.

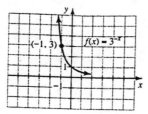

34. The graph of $f(x) = -3^{x-1}$ includes the points $(0, -1/3)$, $(1, -1)$, and $(2, -3)$.

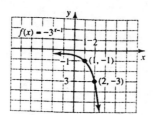

35. The graph of $y = 1 + 2^{x}$ includes the points $(0, 2)$, $(1, 3)$, $(2, 5)$, and $(-1, 1.5)$.

36. The graph of $y = 1 - 2^{x}$ includes the points $(0, 0)$, $(1, -1)$, $(2, -3)$, and $(-1, 1/2)$.

37. $\log(n) = m$

38. $\log_a(b) = 5$

39. $k^{h} = t$

40. $v^{u} = 5$

41. $f(1/8) = \log_2(1/8) = -3$, because $2^{-3} = 1/8$.

42. $f(64) = \log_2(64) = 6$, because $2^{6} = 64$.

43. $g(0.1) = \log(0.1) = -1$, because $10^{-1} = 0.1$.

44. $g(1) = \log(1) = 0$, because $10^{0} = 1$.

45. $g(100) = \log(100) = 2$, because $10^{2} = 100$.

46. $h(1/8) = \log_{1/2}(1/8) = 3$, because $\left(\frac{1}{2}\right)^{3} = \frac{1}{8}$.

47. $h(1) = \log_{1/2}(1) = 0$, because $(1/2)^{0} = 1$.

48. $h(4) = \log_{1/2}(4) = -2$, because $(1/2)^{-2} = 4$.

49. If $f(x) = 8$, then $\log_2(x) = 8$, $x = 2^{8} = 256$.

50. If $g(x) = 3$, then $\log(x) = 3$, or $x = 10^{3} = 1000$.

51. $f(77) = \log_2(77) = \dfrac{\ln(77)}{\ln(2)} \approx 6.267$

368

52. $g(88.4) = \log(88.4) \approx 1.946$

53. $h(33.9) = \log_{1/2}(33.9) = \dfrac{\ln(33.9)}{\ln(0.5)}$
≈ -5.083

54. $h(0.05) = \log_{1/2}(0.05) = \dfrac{\ln(0.05)}{\ln(0.5)}$
≈ 4.322

55. If $f(x) = 2.475$, then $\log_2(x) \approx 2.475$.
$x = 2^{2.475} \approx 5.560$

56. If $g(x) = 1.426$, then $\log(x) = 1.426$.
$x = 10^{1.426} \approx 26.669$

57. The inverse of the function $f(x) = 10^x$ is
the base 10 logarithm function,
$f^{-1}(x) = \log(x)$.
The graph of $f(x)$ includes the points $(1, 10)$,
$(0, 1)$, and $(-1, 0.1)$. The graph of $f^{-1}(x)$
includes the points $(10, 1)$, $(1, 0)$, and
$(0.1, -1)$.

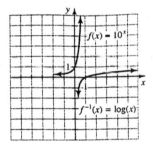

58. The inverse of the function $f(x) = \log_8(x)$
is $f^{-1}(x) = 8^x$. The graph of f includes the
points $(8, 1)$, $(2, 1/3)$, $(1, 0)$, and $(1/8, -1)$.
The graph of f^{-1} includes the points $(1, 8)$,
$(1/3, 2)$, $(0, 1)$, and $(-1, 1/8)$.

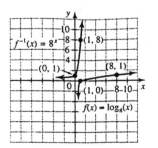

59. The inverse of the function $f(x) = e^x$ is
$f^{-1}(x) = \ln(x)$. The graph of $f(x)$ includes the
points $(1, e)$, $(0, 1)$, and $(-1, 1/e)$. The graph
of $f^{-1}(x)$ includes the points $(e, 1)$, $(1, 0)$, and
$(1/e, -1)$.

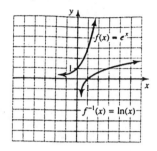

60. The inverse of $f(x) = \log_3(x)$ is
$f^{-1}(x) = 3^x$. The graph of f includes the
points $(3, 1)$, $(1, 0)$, $(9, 2)$, and $(1/3, -1)$. The
graph of f^{-1} includes the points $(1, 3)$, $(0, 1)$,
$(2, 9)$, and $(-1, 1/3)$.

61. $\log(x^2 y) = \log(x^2) + \log(y)$
$\qquad\qquad = 2\log(x) + \log(y)$

62. $\log_3(x^2 + 2x) = \log_3[x(x+2)]$
$\qquad\qquad\quad = \log_3(x) + \log_3(x+2)$

63. $\ln(16) = \ln(2^4) = 4\ln(2)$

64. $\log(y/\sqrt{x}) = \log(y) - \log(\sqrt{x})$
$\qquad\quad = \log(y) - \log[x^{1/2}]$
$\qquad\quad = \log(y) - \tfrac{1}{2}\log(x)$

65. $\log_5(1/x) = \log_5(1) - \log_5(x)$
$\qquad\quad = -\log_5(x)$

66. $\ln(xy/z) = \ln(xy) - \ln(z)$
$\qquad\quad = \ln(x) + \ln(y) - \ln(z)$

67. $\frac{1}{2} \cdot \log(x+2) - 2 \cdot \log(x-1)$
$$= \log\big((x+2)^{1/2}\big) - \log\big((x-1)^2\big)$$
$$= \log\left(\frac{\sqrt{x+2}}{(x-1)^2}\right)$$

68. $3 \cdot \ln(x) + 2 \cdot \ln(y) - \frac{1}{3} \cdot \ln(z)$
$$= \ln(x^3) + \ln(y^2) - \ln(\sqrt[3]{z})$$
$$= \ln\left(\frac{x^3 y^2}{\sqrt[3]{z}}\right)$$

69. $\quad \log_2(x) = 8$
$$x = 2^8 = 256$$
The solution set is $\{256\}$.

70. $\quad \log_3(x) = 0.5$
$$x = 3^{0.5} = 3^{1/2} = \sqrt{3}$$
The solution set is $\left\{\sqrt{3}\right\}$.

71. $\quad \log_2(8) = x$
$$3 = x$$
The solution set is $\{3\}$.

72. $\quad 3^x = 8$
$$x = \log_3(8)$$
The solution set is $\{\log_3(8)\}$.

73. $\quad x^3 = 8$
$$x = \sqrt[3]{8} = 2$$
The solution set is $\{2\}$.

74. $\quad 3^2 = x$
$$9 = x$$
The solution set is $\{9\}$.

75. $\quad \log_x(27) = 3$
$$x^3 = 27$$
$$x = \sqrt[3]{27} = 3$$
The solution set is $\{3\}$.

76. $\quad \log_x(9) = -1/3$
$$9 = x^{-1/3}$$
$$(9)^{-3} = (x^{-1/3})^{-3}$$
$$\frac{1}{729} = x$$
The solution set is $\left\{\frac{1}{729}\right\}$.

77. $\quad x \cdot \ln(3) - x = \ln(7)$
$$x[\ln(3) - 1] = \ln(7)$$
$$x = \frac{\ln(7)}{\ln(3) - 1}$$
The solution set is $\left\{\frac{\ln(7)}{\ln(3) - 1}\right\}$.

78. $\quad x \cdot \log(8) = x \cdot \log(4) + \log(9)$
$$\log(8^x) = \log(4^x) + \log(9)$$
$$\log(8^x) = \log(9 \cdot 4^x)$$
$$8^x = 9 \cdot 4^x$$

$$\frac{8^x}{4^x} = 9$$
$$\left(\frac{8}{4}\right)^x = 9$$
$$2^x = 9$$
$$x = \log_2(9) = \frac{\log(9)}{\log(2)}$$

The solution set is $\left\{\frac{\log(9)}{\log(2)}\right\}$.

79. $\qquad 3^x = 5^{x-1}$
$$\ln(3^x) = \ln(5^{x-1})$$
$$x \cdot \ln(3) = (x-1)\ln(5)$$
$$x \cdot \ln(3) = x \cdot \ln(5) - \ln(5)$$
$$x \cdot \ln(3) - x \cdot \ln(5) = -\ln(5)$$
$$x[\ln(3) - \ln(5)] = -\ln(5)$$

$$x = \frac{-\ln(5)}{\ln(3) - \ln(5)} = \frac{\ln(5)}{\ln(5) - \ln(3)}$$

The solution set is $\left\{\frac{\ln(5)}{\ln(5) - \ln(3)}\right\}$.

80. $\qquad 5^{(2x^2)} = 5^{3-5x}$
$$2x^2 = 3 - 5x$$
$$2x^2 + 5x - 3 = 0$$
$$(2x - 1)(x + 3) = 0$$
$$2x - 1 = 0 \ \text{ or } \ x + 3 = 0$$
$$x = \tfrac{1}{2} \ \text{ or } \qquad x = -3$$

The solution set is $\left\{-3, \frac{1}{2}\right\}$.

81. $\qquad 4^{2x} = 2^{x+1}$
$$(2^2)^{2x} = 2^{x+1}$$
$$2^{4x} = 2^{x+1}$$
$$4x = x + 1$$
$$3x = 1$$
$$x = \tfrac{1}{3}$$
The solution set is $\left\{\frac{1}{3}\right\}$.

82. $\qquad \log(12) = \log(x) + \log(7 - x)$
$$\log(12) = \log(7x - x^2)$$
$$12 = 7x - x^2$$
$$x^2 - 7x + 12 = 0$$
$$(x - 3)(x - 4) = 0$$
$$x - 3 = 0 \ \text{ or } \ x - 4 = 0$$
$$x = 3 \ \text{ or } \qquad x = 4$$
The solution set is $\{3, 4\}$.

83. $\ln(x + 2) - \ln(x - 10) = \ln(2)$
$$\ln\left(\frac{x + 2}{x - 10}\right) = \ln(2)$$
$$\frac{x + 2}{x - 10} = 2$$
$$x + 2 = 2(x - 10)$$
$$x + 2 = 2x - 20$$
$$22 = x$$

The solution set is $\{22\}$.

84. $2 \cdot \ln(x + 3) = 3 \cdot \ln(4)$
$$\ln[(x + 3)^2] = \ln(4^3)$$
$$(x + 3)^2 = 64$$
$$x + 3 = \pm 8$$
$$x = -3 \pm 8$$

$x = -3 + 8 = 5$ or $x = -3 - 8 = -11$
If $x = -11$ in the original equation we get $\ln(-11 + 3)$, which is undefined. The solution set is $\{5\}$.

85. $\log(x) - \log(x - 2) = 2$
$$\log\left(\frac{x}{x - 2}\right) = 2$$
$$\frac{x}{x - 2} = 10^2$$
$$x = 100(x - 2)$$
$$x = 100x - 200$$
$$-99x = -200$$
$$x = \frac{-200}{-99} = \frac{200}{99}$$

The solution set is $\left\{\frac{200}{99}\right\}$.

86. $\log_2(x) = \log_2(x + 16) - 1$
$$\log_2(x) - \log_2(x + 16) = -1$$
$$\log_2\left(\frac{x}{x + 16}\right) = -1$$
$$\frac{x}{x + 16} = 2^{-1}$$
$$\frac{x}{x + 16} = \frac{1}{2}$$
$$2x = x + 16$$
$$x = 16$$

The solution set is $\{16\}$.

87. $6^x = 12$
$$x = \log_6(12) = \frac{\ln(12)}{\ln(6)} \approx 1.3869$$

The solution set is $\{1.3869\}$.

88. $5^x = 8^{3x+2}$
$$x \cdot \ln(5) = (3x + 2)\ln(8)$$
$$x \cdot \ln(5) = 3x \cdot \ln(8) + 2 \cdot \ln(8)$$
$$x \cdot \ln(5) - 3x \cdot \ln(8) = 2 \cdot \ln(8)$$
$$x[\ln(5) - 3 \cdot \ln(8)] = 2 \cdot \ln(8)$$
$$x = \frac{2 \cdot \ln(8)}{\ln(5) - 3 \cdot \ln(8)} \approx -0.8985$$

The solution set is $\{-0.8985\}$.

89. $3^{x+1} = 5$
$$x + 1 = \log_3(5)$$
$$x = -1 + \log_3(5) = -1 + \frac{\ln(5)}{\ln(3)}$$
$$\approx 0.4650$$

The solution set is $\{0.4650\}$.

90. $\log_3(x) = 2.634$
$$x = 3^{2.634} \approx 18.0608$$

The solution set is $\{18.0608\}$.

91. Use the formula $S = P(1 + i)^n$ with $i = 11.5\% = 0.115$, $n = 15$, and $P = \$10,000$.
$$S = 10,000(1.115)^{15} \approx \$51,182.68$$

92. Use the formula $S = P(1 + i)^n$ with $P = 1$, $S = 2$, $i = 0.065$. Find n.
$$2 = 1(1 + 0.065)^n$$
$$2 = (1.065)^n$$
$$\ln(2) = n \cdot \ln(1.065)$$
$$n = \frac{\ln(2)}{\ln(1.065)} \approx 11.007 \text{ years}$$

93. Use the formula $A = A_0 e^{-0.0003t}$ with $A_0 = 218$ and $t = 1000$.
$$A = 218e^{-0.0003(1000)} = 218e^{-0.3}$$
$$\approx 161.5 \text{ grams}$$

94. a) To find the population in 2000, use $t = 0$.
$$P = 517 + 10 \cdot \ln(8 \cdot 0 + 1)$$
$$= 517 + 10 \cdot \ln(1) = 517$$

The deer population in 2000 is 517.

b) Use $P = 600$ and solve for t.
$$600 = 517 + 10 \cdot \ln(8t + 1)$$
$$83 = 10 \cdot \ln(8t + 1)$$
$$8.3 = \ln(8t + 1)$$
$$e^{8.3} = 8t + 1$$
$$e^{8.3} - 1 = 8t$$
$$t = \frac{e^{8.3} - 1}{8} \approx 502.85$$

In about 503 years, in the year 2503 there will be 600 deer.

c) From the graph, the population appears to be growing faster between 2000 and 2005.

d) $\dfrac{554 - 517}{2005 - 2000} = 7.4 \text{ deer/year}$

$\dfrac{561 - 554}{2010 - 2005} = 1.4 \text{ deer/year}$

The solution set is $\{-0.8985\}$.

95. The amount in Melissa's account is given by the formula $S = 1000(1.05)^t$ for any number of years t. The amount in Frank's account is given by the formula $S = 900e^{0.07t}$ for any number of years t. To find when they have the same amount, we set the two expressions equal and solve for t.

$$1000(1.05)^t = 900e^{0.07t}$$
$$\ln\left(1000(1.05)^t\right) = \ln\left(900e^{0.07t}\right)$$
$$\ln(1000) + t \cdot \ln(1.05) = \ln(900) + \ln(e^{0.07t})$$
$$\ln(1000) + t \cdot \ln(1.05) = \ln(900) + 0.07t$$
$$t \cdot \ln(1.05) - 0.07t = \ln(900) - \ln(1000)$$
$$t[\ln(1.05) - 0.07] = \ln(900) - \ln(1000)$$
$$t = \frac{\ln(900) - \ln(1000)}{\ln(1.05) - 0.07} \approx 4.9675$$

The amounts will be equal in approximately 5 years.

96. a) To find the value of imports in 2000, let $t = 0$ in the import formula.
$$I = 15 \cdot \log(16 \cdot 0 + 33) = 15 \cdot \log(33)$$
$$\approx \$22.8 \text{ million}$$
To find the value of exports, let $t = 0$ in the export formula.
$$E = 30 \cdot \log(0 + 3) = 30 \cdot \log(3)$$
$$\approx \$14.3 \text{ million}$$
b) From the graph it appears that imports will equal exports in approximately 2010.
c) To find the number of years until the imports equal the exports, set the two formulas equal and solve for t.
$$30 \cdot \log(t + 3) = 15 \cdot \log(16t + 33)$$
$$2 \cdot \log(t + 3) = \log(16t + 33)$$
$$\log[(t + 3)^2] = \log(16t + 33)$$
$$t^2 + 6t + 9 = 16t + 33$$
$$t^2 - 10t - 24 = 0$$
$$(t - 12)(t + 2) = 0$$
$$t - 12 = 0 \text{ or } t + 2 = 0$$
$$t = 12 \text{ or } t = -2$$

The value of imports will equal the value of exports in 12 years, or in the year 2012.

97. $114.308e^{0.265(20.6-6.87)} \approx 4347.5 \text{ ft}^3/\text{sec}$

98.
$$y = 114.308e^{0.265(h-6.87)}$$
$$y/114.308 = e^{0.265(h-6.87)}$$
$$\ln(y/114.308) = 0.265(h - 6.87)$$
$$h - 6.87 = \frac{\ln(y/114.308)}{0.265}$$
$$h = \frac{\ln(y/114.308)}{0.265} + 6.87$$

If $y = 10,000$, then $h = 23.74$ feet

CHAPTER 10 TEST

1. $f(2) = 5^2 = 25$
2. $f(-1) = 5^{-1} = \frac{1}{5}$
3. $f(0) = 5^0 = 1$
4. $g(125) = \log_5(125) = 3$, because $5^3 = 125$.
5. $g(1) = \log_5(1) = 0$, because $5^0 = 1$.
6. $g(1/5) = \log_5(1/5) = -1$, because $5^{-1} = 1/5$.
7. The graph of $y = 2^x$ includes the points $(0, 1)$, $(1, 2)$, $(2, 4)$, and $(-1, 1/2)$.

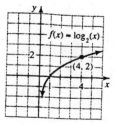

8. The graph of $f(x) = \log_2(x)$ includes the points $(1, 0)$, $(2, 1)$, $(4, 2)$, and $(1/2, -1)$.

9. The graph of $y = \left(\frac{1}{3}\right)^x$ includes the points $(1, 1/3)$, $(0, 1)$, and $(-1, 3)$.

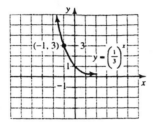

10. The graph of $g(x) = \log_{1/3}(x)$ includes the points $(1, 0)$, $(3, -1)$, and $(1/3, 1)$.

11. $\log_a(MN) = \log_a(M) + \log_a(N) = 6 + 4$
$$= 10$$

12. $\log_a(M^2/N) = 2 \cdot \log_a(M) - \log_a(N)$
$$= 2 \cdot 6 - 4 = 8$$

13. $\dfrac{\log_a(M)}{\log_a(N)} = \dfrac{6}{4} = \dfrac{3}{2}$

14. $\log_a(a^3 M^2) = 3 \cdot \log_a(a) + 2 \cdot \log_a(M)$
$$= 3 \cdot 1 + 2 \cdot 6 = 15$$

15. $\log_a(1/N) = \log_a(1) - \log_a(N)$
$$= 0 - 4 = -4$$

16. $\quad 3^x = 12$
$$x = \log_3(12)$$
The solution set is $\{\log_3(12)\}$.

17. $\log_3(x) = 1/2$
$$x = 3^{1/2} = \sqrt{3}$$
The solution set is $\{\sqrt{3}\}$.

18. $\qquad 5^x = 8^{x-1}$
$$\ln(5^x) = \ln(8^{x-1})$$
$$x \cdot \ln(5) = (x-1)\ln(8)$$

$$x \cdot \ln(5) = x \cdot \ln(8) - \ln(8)$$
$$x \cdot \ln(5) - x \cdot \ln(8) = -\ln(8)$$
$$x[\ln(5) - \ln(8)] = -\ln(8)$$
$$x = \frac{-\ln(8)}{\ln(5) - \ln(8)} = \frac{\ln(8)}{-\ln(5) + \ln(8)}$$
The solution set is $\left\{\dfrac{\ln(8)}{\ln(8) - \ln(5)}\right\}$.

19. $\log(x) + \log(x + 15) = 2$
$$\log(x^2 + 15x) = 2$$
$$x^2 + 15x = 10^2$$
$$x^2 + 15x - 100 = 0$$
$$(x + 20)(x - 5) = 0$$
$$x + 20 = 0 \quad \text{or} \quad x - 5 = 0$$
$$x = -20 \quad \text{or} \quad x = 5$$
If $x = -20$ in the original equation, we get a logarithm of a negative number, which is undefined. So the solution set is $\{5\}$.

20. $\qquad 2 \cdot \ln(x) = \ln(3) + \ln(6 - x)$
$$\ln(x^2) = \ln(18 - 3x)$$
$$x^2 = 18 - 3x$$
$$x^2 + 3x - 18 = 0$$
$$(x + 6)(x - 3) = 0$$
$$x + 6 = 0 \quad \text{or} \quad x - 3 = 0$$
$$x = -6 \quad \text{or} \quad x = 3$$
If $x = -6$ in the original equation, we get a logarithm of a negative number, which is undefined. So the solution set is $\{3\}$.

21. $\quad 20^x = 5$
$$x = \log_{20}(5) = \frac{\ln(5)}{\ln(20)} \approx 0.5372$$
The solution set is $\{0.5372\}$.

22. $\quad \log_3(x) = 2.75$
$$x = 3^{2.75} \approx 20.5156$$
The solution set is $\{20.5156\}$

23. To find the number present initially, let $t = 0$ in the formula:
$$N = 10e^{0.4(0)} = 10e^0 = 10 \cdot 1 = 10$$
To find the number present after 24 hours, let $t = 24$ in the formula:
$$N = 10e^{0.4(24)} = 10e^{9.6} \approx 147{,}648$$

24. To find how long it takes for the population to double, we must find the value of t for which $e^{0.4t} = 2$. Solve for t.
$$0.4t = \ln(2)$$
$$t = \frac{\ln(2)}{0.4} \approx 1.733$$
The bacteria population doubles in 1.733 hours.

Making Connections

Chapters 1 - 10

1. $(x-3)^2 = 8$

$$x - 3 = \pm\sqrt{8}$$
$$x = 3 \pm 2\sqrt{2}$$

The solution set is $\left\{3 \pm 2\sqrt{2}\right\}$.

2. $\log_2(x-3) = 8$

$$x - 3 = 2^8$$
$$x = 256 + 3 = 259$$

The solution set is $\{259\}$.

3.
$$2^{x-3} = 8$$
$$2^{x-3} = 2^3$$
$$x - 3 = 3$$
$$x = 6$$

The solution set is $\{6\}$.

4. $2x - 3 = 8$

$$2x = 11$$
$$x = \frac{11}{2}$$

The solution set is $\left\{\frac{11}{2}\right\}$.

5. $|x-3| = 8$

$$x - 3 = 8 \quad \text{or} \quad x - 3 = -8$$
$$x = 11 \quad \text{or} \quad x = -5$$

The solution set is $\{-5, 11\}$

6.
$$\sqrt{x-3} = 8$$
$$(\sqrt{x-3})^2 = 8^2$$
$$x - 3 = 64$$
$$x = 67$$

The solution set is $\{67\}$.

7. $\log_2(x-3) + \log_2(x) = \log_2(18)$

$$\log_2(x^2 - 3x) = \log_2(18)$$
$$x^2 - 3x = 18$$
$$x^2 - 3x - 18 = 0$$
$$(x-6)(x+3) = 0$$
$$x - 6 = 0 \quad \text{or} \quad x + 3 = 0$$
$$x = 6 \quad \text{or} \quad x = -3$$

If $x = -3$ in the original equation, then we get a logarithm of a negative number, which is undefined. The solution set is $\{6\}$.

8. $2 \cdot \log_2(x-3) = \log_2(5-x)$

$$\log_2[(x-3)^2] = \log_2(5-x)$$
$$(x-3)^2 = 5 - x$$
$$x^2 - 6x + 9 = 5 - x$$
$$x^2 - 5x + 4 = 0$$
$$(x-4)(x-1) = 0$$
$$x - 4 = 0 \quad \text{or} \quad x - 1 = 0$$
$$x = 4 \quad \text{or} \quad x = 1$$

If $x = 1$ in the original equation, we get a logarithm of a negative number. The solution set is $\{4\}$.

9. $60\left(\frac{1}{2}x - \frac{2}{3}\right) = 60\left(\frac{3}{4}x + \frac{1}{5}\right)$

$$30x - 40 = 45x + 12$$
$$-52 = 15x$$
$$-\frac{52}{15} = x$$

The solution set is $\left\{-\frac{52}{15}\right\}$.

10. To solve $3x^2 - 6x + 2 = 0$ use the quadratic formula.

$$x = \frac{6 \pm \sqrt{(-6)^2 - 4(3)(2)}}{2(3)} = \frac{6 \pm \sqrt{12}}{6}$$
$$= \frac{6 \pm 2\sqrt{3}}{6} = \frac{3 \pm \sqrt{3}}{3}$$

The solution set is $\left\{\frac{3 \pm \sqrt{3}}{3}\right\}$.

11. The inverse of dividing by 3 is multiplying by 3. So $f^{-1}(x) = 3x$.

12. The inverse of the base 3 logarithm function is the base 3 exponential function, $g^{-1}(x) = 3^x$.

13. The inverse of multiplying by 2 and then subtracting 4 is adding 4 and then dividing by 2,

$$f^{-1}(x) = \frac{x+4}{2}.$$

14. The inverse of the square root function is the squaring function. To keep the domain of one function equal to the range of the inverse function we must restrict the squaring function to the nonnegative numbers:

$$h^{-1}(x) = x^2 \text{ for } x \geq 0$$

15. The reciprocal function is its own inverse, $j^{-1}(x) = \frac{1}{x}$.

16. The inverse of the base 5 exponential function is the base 5 logarithm function, $k^{-1}(x) = \log_5(x)$

17. We will find the inverse for m by using the technique of interchanging x and y and then solving for y.

$$m(x) = e^{x-1}$$
$$y = e^{x-1}$$
$$x = e^{y-1}$$
$$y - 1 = \ln(x)$$
$$y = 1 + \ln(x)$$
$$m^{-1}(x) = 1 + \ln(x)$$

18. The inverse of the natural logarithm function is the base e exponential function, $n^{-1}(x) = e^x$.

19. The graph of $y = 2x$ is a straight line with slope 2 and y-intercept $(0, 0)$. Start at the origin and rise 2 and go 1 to the right to find a second point on the line.

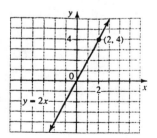

20. The graph of $y = 2^x$ includes the points $(0, 1)$, $(1, 2)$, $(2, 2)$, and $(-1, 1/2)$.

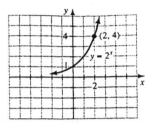

21. The graph of $y = x^2$ is a parabola through $(0, 0)$, $(1, 1)$, $(2, 4)$, $(-1, 1)$, and $(-2, 4)$.

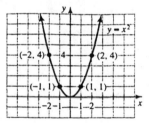

22. The graph of $y = \log_2(x)$ includes the points $(1, 0)$, $(2, 1)$, $(1/2, -1)$ and $(4, 2)$.

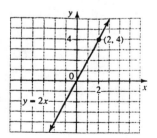

23. The graph of $y = \frac{1}{2}x - 4$ is a straight line with slope 1/2 and y-intercept $(0, -4)$. Start at $(0, -4)$, rise 1 and go 2 to the right to locate a second point on the line.

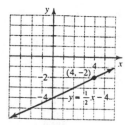

24. The graph of $y = |2 - x|$ is a v-shaped graph through $(-2, 4)$, $(-1, 3)$, $(0, 2)$, $(1, 1)$, $(2, 0)$, $(3, 1)$, $(4, 2)$, and $(5, 3)$.

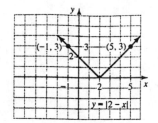

25. The graph of $y = 2 - x^2$ is a parabola with a vertex at $(0, 2)$. It also includes the points $(1, 1)$, $(-1, 1)$, $(2, -2)$, and $(-2, -2)$.

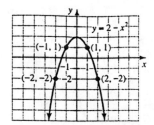

26. Note that e^2 is not a variable. The value of e^2 is approximately 7.389. The graph of $y = e^2$ is a straight line with 0 slope and y-intercept $(0, 7.389)$.

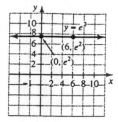

27. a) The graph of $n = 1.53t + 113.82$ is a straight line through $(0, 113.82)$ and $(10, 129.12)$. The graph of $n = 114.0e^{t/80}$ is an exponential curve through $(0, 114.0)$, $(5, 121.35)$, $(10, 129.18)$, and $(15, 137.51)$.

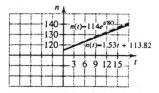

b) If $t = 11$, $n = 1.53(11) + 113.82 = 130.7$ million

If $t = 11$, $n = 114.0e^{11/80} = 130.8$ million

28. a) Use $D = RT$ to get $2d_1 = v(0.270)$ or $d_1 = 0.135v$.

b) Using $D = RT$ we get $2d_2 = v(0.432)$ or $d_2 = 0.216v$.

c) Using the Pythagorean theorem we get $(d_2)^2 = (d_1)^2 + 250^2$. Use $d_1 = 0.135v$ and $d_2 = 0.216v$ to get

$$(0.216v)^2 = (0.135v)^2 + 250^2$$
$$0.028431v^2 = 250^2$$
$$v^2 = 2198304.667$$
$$v = 1482.668091$$

$d_1 = 0.135v = 200.2$ meters

376

11.1 WARM-UPS

1. True, because any equation of the form $y = ax^2 + bx + c$ has a graph that is a parabola.
2. False, because absolute value has a v-shaped graph.
3. False, because $-4 \neq \sqrt{5(3) + 1}$.
4. True, because $y = \sqrt{x}$ lies entirely in the first quadrant, and $y = -x - 2$ has no points in the first quadrant.
5. False, because we can also use addition.
6. True.
7. True, because a 30-60-90 triangle is half of an equilateral triangle.
8. True, because for any rectangular solid we have $V = LWH$.
9. True, because the surface area consists of 6 rectangles, of which two have area LW, two have area WH, and two have area LH.
10. True, because the area of a triangle is $(bh)/2$.

11.1 EXERCISES

1. If the graph of an equation is not a straight line then it is called nonlinear.
2. With a graph we can see the approximate value of the solutions and the number of solutions.
3. Graphing is not an accurate method for solving a system and the graphs might be difficult to draw.
4. We generally use substitution and addition to solve nonlinear systems.
5. The graph of $y = x^2$ is a parabola and the graph of $x + y = 6$ is a straight line.

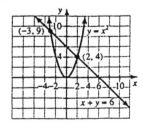

To solve the system, substitute $y = x^2$ into $x + y = 6$.

$$x + x^2 = 6$$
$$x^2 + x - 6 = 0$$
$$(x + 3)(x - 2) = 0$$
$$x = -3 \text{ or } x = 2$$

If $x = -3$, $y = (-3)^2 = 9$, and if $x = 2$, $y = 2^2 = 4$. The solution set to the system is $\{(2, 4), (-3, 9)\}$.

6. The graph of $y = x^2 - 1$ is a parabola, and the graph of $x + y = 11$ is a line.

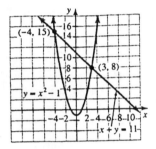

To solve the system, substitute $y = x^2 - 1$ into $x + y = 11$.

$$x + x^2 - 1 = 11$$
$$x^2 + x - 12 = 0$$
$$(x + 4)(x - 3) = 0$$

$x + 4 = 0$ or $x - 3 = 0$
$x = -4$ or $x = 3$
$y = (-4)^2 - 1$ $y = (3)^2 - 1$
$y = 15$ $y = 8$

The solution set to the system is $\{(-4, 15), (3, 8)\}$.

7. The graph of $y = |x|$ is v-shaped, and the graph of $2y - x = 6$ is a straight line. To solve the system, substitute $x = 2y - 6$ into $y = |x|$.

$$y = |2y - 6|$$
$y = 2y - 6 \text{ or } y = -(2y - 6)$
$6 = y$ or $y = -2y + 6$
$3y = 6$
$y = 2$

Use $y = 6$ in $x = 2y - 6$ to get $x = 6$. Use $y = 2$ in $x = 2y - 6$ to get $x = -2$. The graphs intersect at the points $(-2, 2)$ and $(6, 6)$.

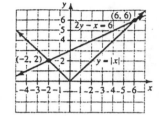

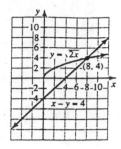

The solution set is $\{(-2, 2), (6, 6)\}$.

8. For $y = |x|$ draw a v-shaped graph through $(0, 0)$, $(1, 1)$, and $(-1, 1)$. Write $3y = x + 6$ as $y = (1/3)x + 2$ and draw a line with y-intercept $(0, 2)$ and slope $1/3$.

Substitute $y = \sqrt{2x}$ into $y = x - 4$.
$$\sqrt{2x} = x - 4$$
$$(\sqrt{2x})^2 = (x - 4)^2$$
$$2x = x^2 - 8x + 16$$
$$0 = x^2 - 10x + 16$$
$$0 = (x - 8)(x - 2)$$
$$x = 8 \quad \text{or} \quad x = 2$$
$$y = \sqrt{2(8)} \quad \text{or} \quad y = \sqrt{2(2)}$$
$$= 4 \quad \text{or} \quad = 2$$

Since we squared both sides, we must check. The pair $(8, 4)$ satisfies both equations, but $(2, 2)$ does not. The solution set to the system is $\{(8, 4)\}$.

10. The graph of $y = \sqrt{x}$ includes the points $(0, 0)$, $(1, 1)$, and $(4, 2)$. The graph of $x - y = 6$ (or $y = x - 6$) is a straight line with y-intercept $(0, -6)$ and slope 1.

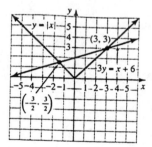

Substitute $x = 3y - 6$ into $y = |x|$.
$$y = |3y - 6|$$
$$y = 3y - 6 \quad \text{or} \quad y = -(3y - 6)$$
$$-2y = -6 \quad \text{or} \quad y = -3y + 6$$
$$y = 3 \quad \text{or} \quad 4y = 6$$
$$y = 3 \quad \text{or} \quad y = \frac{3}{2}$$
$$x = 3(3) - 6 \quad x = 3\left(\frac{3}{2}\right) - 6$$
$$x = 3 \quad x = -\frac{3}{2}$$

The solution set is $\left\{ \left(-\frac{3}{2}, \frac{3}{2}\right), (3, 3) \right\}$.

9. The graph of $y = \sqrt{2x}$ includes the points $(0, 0)$, $(2, 2)$, and $(4.5, 3)$. The graph of $x - y = 4$ is a straight line with slope 1 and y-intercept $(0, -4)$.

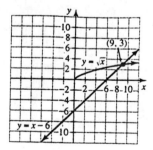

Substitute $y = x - 6$ into $y = \sqrt{x}$ to get $x - 6 = \sqrt{x}$.
$$(x - 6)^2 = (\sqrt{x})^2$$
$$x^2 - 12x + 36 = x$$
$$x^2 - 13x + 36 = 0$$
$$(x - 9)(x - 4) = 0$$
$$x - 9 = 0 \quad \text{or} \quad x - 4 = 0$$

378

$x = 9$ or $\qquad x = 4$
$y = 9 - 6$
$y = 3$
Note that $x = 4$ does not satisfy $x - 6 = \sqrt{x}$.
The solution set is $\{(9, 3)\}$.

11. The graph of $4x - 9y = 9$ is a straight line. The equation $xy = 1$ can be written as $y = 1/x$. Substitute $y = 1/x$ into $4x - 9y = 9$.

$$4x - 9\left(\tfrac{1}{x}\right) = 9$$
$$4x^2 - 9 = 9x$$
$$4x^2 - 9x - 9 = 0$$
$$(4x + 3)(x - 3) = 0$$
$$x = -\tfrac{3}{4} \qquad \text{or} \qquad x = 3$$
$$y = \tfrac{1}{-3/4} = -\tfrac{4}{3} \qquad \qquad y = \tfrac{1}{3}$$

The solution set is $\left\{\left(-\tfrac{3}{4}, -\tfrac{4}{3}\right), \left(3, \tfrac{1}{3}\right)\right\}$.

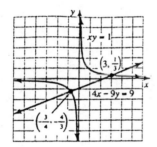

12. The graph of $2x + 2y = 3$ has intercepts at $(0, 1.5)$, and $(1.5, 0)$. The graph of $xy = -1$ (or $y = -1/x$) includes the points $(1, -1)$, $(2, -1/2)$, $(1/2, -2)$, $(-1, 1)$, and $(-2, 1/2)$.

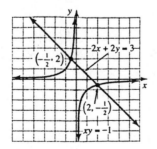

Write $xy = -1$ as $2xy = -2$, and substitute $2x = 3 - 2y$ into that equation.

$$(3 - 2y)y = -2$$
$$3y - 2y^2 = -2$$
$$-2y^2 + 3y + 2 = 0$$
$$2y^2 - 3y - 2 = 0$$
$$(2y + 1)(y - 2) = 0$$
$$2y + 1 = 0 \quad \text{or} \qquad y - 2 = 0$$
$$y = -\tfrac{1}{2} \quad \text{or} \qquad y = 2$$

Use $x = \dfrac{3 - 2y}{2}$ to find x.

If $y = -\tfrac{1}{2}$, then $x = \dfrac{3 - 2\left(-\tfrac{1}{2}\right)}{2} = \dfrac{3+1}{2} = 2$.

If $y = 2$, then $x = \dfrac{3 - 2(2)}{2} = \dfrac{3 - 4}{2} = -\tfrac{1}{2}$.

The solution set is $\left\{\left(-\tfrac{1}{2}, 2\right), \left(2, -\tfrac{1}{2}\right)\right\}$.

13. The graph of $y = x^2$ is a parabola opening upward, and the graph of $y = -x^2 + 1$ is a parabola opening downward.

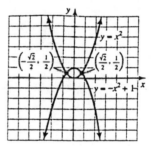

Substitute $y = x^2$ into $y = -x^2 + 1$.

$$x^2 = -x^2 + 1$$
$$2x^2 = 1$$
$$x^2 = \tfrac{1}{2}$$
$$x = \pm \sqrt{\tfrac{1}{2}} = \pm \tfrac{\sqrt{2}}{2}$$

Since $y = x^2$, $y = \tfrac{1}{2}$ for either value of x. The solution set is $\left\{\left(\tfrac{\sqrt{2}}{2}, \tfrac{1}{2}\right), \left(-\tfrac{\sqrt{2}}{2}, \tfrac{1}{2}\right)\right\}$.

14. The graph of $y = x^2$ is a parabola through $(0, 0)$, $(1, 1)$, and $(-1, 2)$. The graph of $y = \sqrt{x}$ includes the points $(0, 0)$, $(1, 1)$, and $(4, 2)$.

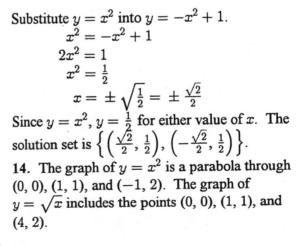

379

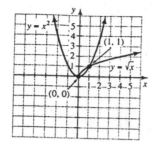

Substitute $y = x^2$ into $y = \sqrt{x}$.

$$x^2 = \sqrt{x}$$
$$(x^2)^2 = (\sqrt{x})^2$$
$$x^4 = x$$
$$x^4 - x = 0$$
$$x(x^3 - 1) = 0$$

$x = 0$ or $x^3 - 1 = 0$
$x = 0$ or $x^3 = 1$
$x = 0$ or $x = 1$
$y = 0^2$ $y = 1^2$
$y = 0$ $y = 1$

The solution set is $\{(0, 0), (1, 1)\}$.

15. Write $y = x^2 - 5$ as $x^2 = y + 5$ and substitute into $x^2 + y^2 = 25$

$$y + 5 + y^2 = 25$$
$$y^2 + y - 20 = 0$$
$$(y + 5)(y - 4) = 0$$
$$y = -5 \quad \text{or} \quad y = 4$$

Use $y = -5$ in $x^2 = y + 5$ to get $x^2 = 0$ or $x = 0$. Use $y = 4$ in $x^2 = y + 5$ to get $x^2 = 9$ or $x = \pm 3$. The solution set to the system is $\{(0, -5), (3, 4), (-3, 4)\}$.

16. Substitute $y = x + 1$ into $x^2 + y^2 = 25$.

$$x^2 + (x + 1)^2 = 25$$
$$x^2 + x^2 + 2x + 1 = 25$$
$$2x^2 + 2x - 24 = 0$$
$$x^2 + x - 12 = 0$$
$$(x + 4)(x - 3) = 0$$

$x + 4 = 0$ or $x - 3 = 0$
$x = -4$ or $x = 3$
$y = -4 + 1$ $y = 3 + 1$
$y = -3$ $y = 4$

The solution set is $\{(-4, -3), (3, 4)\}$.

17. Substitute $y = x + 1$ into $xy - 3x = 8$.

$$x(x + 1) - 3x = 8$$
$$x^2 + x - 3x = 8$$
$$x^2 - 2x - 8 = 0$$
$$(x - 4)(x + 2) = 0$$

$x = 4$ or $x = -2$
$y = 5$ $y = -1$

The solution set is $\{(4, 5), (-2, -1)\}$.

18. Write $x - y = 2$ as $y = x - 2$ and substitute into $xy + 2x = 9$.

$$x(x - 2) + 2x = 9$$
$$x^2 - 2x + 2x = 9$$
$$x^2 = 9$$
$$x = \pm 3$$

If $x = 3$, then $y = 3 - 2 = 1$. If $x = -3$, then $y = -3 - 2 = -5$. The solution set is $\{(3, 1), (-3, -5)\}$.

19. Write $xy - x = 8$ as $xy = x + 8$, and substitute for xy in $xy + 3x = -4$.

$$x + 8 + 3x = -4$$
$$4x = -12$$
$$x = -3$$

Use $x = -3$ in $xy = x + 8$.

$$-3y = -3 + 8$$
$$-3y = 5$$
$$y = -5/3$$

The solution set is $\left\{\left(-3, -\frac{5}{3}\right)\right\}$.

20. Write $xy + 5x = -7$ as $xy = -5x - 7$ and substitute this equation into $2xy - 3x = -1$.

$$2(-5x - 7) - 3x = -1$$
$$-10x - 14 - 3x = -1$$
$$-13x - 14 = -1$$
$$-13x = 13$$
$$x = -1$$

Use $x = -1$ in $xy = -5x - 7$ to find y.

$$-1y = -5(-1) - 7$$
$$-y = -2$$
$$y = 2$$

The solution set is $\{(-1, 2)\}$.

21. If we just add the equations as they are given, then y is eliminated.

$$\frac{1}{x} - \frac{1}{y} = 5$$
$$\frac{2}{x} + \frac{1}{y} = -3$$
$$\overline{\quad\frac{3}{x}\quad\quad = 2}$$
$$3 = 2x$$

$$3/2 = x$$

Use $x = 3/2$ in $\frac{1}{x} - \frac{1}{y} = 5$.

$$\frac{1}{3/2} - \frac{1}{y} = 5$$

$$\frac{2}{3} - \frac{1}{y} = 5$$
$$2y - 3 = 15y$$
$$-3 = 13y$$
$$-3/13 = y$$

The solution set is $\left\{ \left(\frac{3}{2}, -\frac{3}{13} \right) \right\}$.

22. Multiply the second equation by 3 and add the result to the first equation.

$$\frac{2}{x} - \frac{3}{y} = \frac{1}{2}$$
$$\frac{9}{x} + \frac{3}{y} = \frac{3}{2}$$
$$\frac{11}{x} \quad\quad = \frac{4}{2}$$
$$4x = 22$$
$$x = \frac{11}{2}$$

Use $x = 11/2$ in the first equation to find y.

$$\frac{2}{11/2} - \frac{3}{y} = \frac{1}{2}$$
$$\frac{4}{11} - \frac{3}{y} = \frac{1}{2}$$
$$22y\left(\frac{4}{11} - \frac{3}{y} \right) = 22y \cdot \frac{1}{2}$$
$$8y - 66 = 11y$$
$$-66 = 3y$$
$$-22 = y$$

The solution set is $\left\{ \left(\frac{11}{2}, -22 \right) \right\}$.

23. Substitute $y = 20/x^2$ into $xy + 2 = 6x$.

$$x \cdot \frac{20}{x^2} + 2 = 6x$$
$$\frac{20}{x} + 2 = 6x$$
$$20 + 2x = 6x^2$$
$$0 = 6x^2 - 2x - 20$$
$$3x^2 - x - 10 = 0$$
$$(3x + 5)(x - 2) = 0$$
$$x = -5/3 \quad \text{or} \quad x = 2$$

Use $y = 20/x^2$ to get

$$y = 36/5 \quad\quad y = 5.$$

The solution set is $\left\{ \left(-\frac{5}{3}, \frac{36}{5} \right), (2, 5) \right\}$.

24. Substitute $x = 3/y^2$ into $xy + 1 = 6x$.

$$\frac{3}{y^2} \cdot y + 1 = 6 \cdot \frac{3}{y^2}$$
$$\frac{3}{y} + 1 = \frac{18}{y^2}$$
$$y^2\left(\frac{3}{y} + 1 \right) = y^2 \cdot \frac{18}{y^2}$$
$$3y + y^2 = 18$$
$$y^2 + 3y - 18 = 0$$
$$(y + 6)(y - 3) = 0$$

$$y + 6 = 0 \quad \text{or} \quad y - 3 = 0$$
$$y = -6 \quad \text{or} \quad y = 3$$
$$x = \frac{3}{(-6)^2} \quad\quad x = \frac{3}{3^2}$$
$$x = \frac{1}{12} \quad\quad x = \frac{1}{3}$$

The solution set is $\left\{ \left(\frac{1}{12}, -6 \right), \left(\frac{1}{3}, 3 \right) \right\}$.

25. If we add the equations we get $2x^2 = 10$.

$$x^2 = 5$$
$$x = \pm \sqrt{5}$$

Use $x = \sqrt{5}$ in $y^2 = 8 - x^2$, to get $y = \pm \sqrt{3}$. Use $x = -\sqrt{5}$ in $y^2 = 8 - x^2$, to get $y = \pm \sqrt{3}$.

The solution set contains four points,
$$\left\{ (\sqrt{5}, \sqrt{3}), (\sqrt{5}, -\sqrt{3}), (-\sqrt{5}, \sqrt{3}), (-\sqrt{5}, -\sqrt{3}) \right\}$$

26. Write $x^2 + 2y^2 = 8$ as $x^2 = 8 - 2y^2$ and substitute this equation into $2x^2 - y^2 = 1$.

$$2(8 - 2y^2) - y^2 = 1$$
$$16 - 4y^2 - y^2 = 1$$
$$-5y^2 = -15$$
$$y^2 = 3$$
$$y = \pm \sqrt{3}$$

If $y = \sqrt{3}$, then $x^2 = 8 - 2(\sqrt{3})^2 = 2$, or $x = \pm \sqrt{2}$.

If $y = -\sqrt{3}$, then $x^2 = 8 - 2(-\sqrt{3})^2 = 2$, or $x = \pm \sqrt{2}$. The solution set is
$$\left\{ (\sqrt{2}, \sqrt{3}), (\sqrt{2}, -\sqrt{3}), (-\sqrt{2}, \sqrt{3}), (-\sqrt{2}, -\sqrt{3}) \right\}$$

27. Substitute $y = 7 - x$ in
$x^2 + xy - y^2 = -11$.

$$x^2 + x(7 - x) - (7 - x)^2 = -11$$
$$x^2 + 7x - x^2 - 49 + 14x - x^2 = -11$$
$$-x^2 + 21x - 38 = 0$$
$$x^2 - 21x + 38 = 0$$
$$(x - 2)(x - 19) = 0$$
$$x = 2 \quad \text{or} \quad x = 19$$

Since $y = 7 - x$

$$y = 5 \quad\quad\quad y = -12$$

The solution set is $\{(2, 5), (19, -12)\}$.

28. Substitute $y = 2x - 5$ into
$x^2 + xy + y^2 = 3$.

$$x^2 + x(2x - 5) + (2x - 5)^2 = 3$$
$$x^2 + 2x^2 - 5x + 4x^2 - 20x + 25 = 3$$
$$7x^2 - 25x + 22 = 0$$
$$(7x - 11)(x - 2) = 0$$
$$7x - 11 = 0 \quad \text{or} \quad x - 2 = 0$$
$$x = \frac{11}{7} \quad \text{or} \quad x = 2$$

If $x = \frac{11}{7}$, then $y = 2\left(\frac{11}{7} \right) - 5 = -\frac{13}{7}$.

If $x = 2$, then $y = 2(2) - 5 = -1$.
The solution set is $\left\{ \left(\frac{11}{7}, -\frac{13}{7}\right), (2, -1) \right\}$.

29. If $x^2 = y$, then $x^4 = y^2$. Substitute for x^4 in the equation $3y - 2 = x^4$.

$$3y - 2 = y^2$$
$$0 = y^2 - 3y + 2$$
$$0 = (y - 1)(y - 2)$$
$$y = 1 \quad \text{or} \quad y = 2$$

Use $y = 1$ in $x^2 = y$ to get $x^2 = 1$, or $x = \pm 1$. Use $y = 2$ in $x^2 = y$ to get $x^2 = 2$, or $x = \pm\sqrt{2}$.
The solution set is
$$\left\{ (\sqrt{2}, 2), (-\sqrt{2}, 2), (1, 1), (-1, 1) \right\}.$$

30. Substitute $y = 7x^2$ into $y - 3 = 2x^4$.

$$7x^2 - 3 = 2x^4$$
$$-2x^4 + 7x^2 - 3 = 0$$
$$2x^4 - 7x^2 + 3 = 0$$
$$(2x^2 - 1)(x^2 - 3) = 0$$

$2x^2 - 1 = 0$ or	$x^2 - 3 = 0$
$x^2 = \frac{1}{2}$ or	$x^2 = 3$
$x = \pm\sqrt{\frac{1}{2}} = \pm\frac{\sqrt{2}}{2}$ or	$x = \pm\sqrt{3}$
$y = 7x^2$	$y = 7x^2$
$y = 7\left(\frac{1}{2}\right) = \frac{7}{2}$	$y = 7 \cdot 3$
	$= 21$

The solution set is
$$\left\{ \left(\frac{\sqrt{2}}{2}, \frac{7}{2}\right), \left(-\frac{\sqrt{2}}{2}, \frac{7}{2}\right), \left(\sqrt{3}, 21\right), \left(-\sqrt{3}, 21\right) \right\}$$

31. Eliminate y by substitution.

$$\log_2(x - 1) = 3 - \log_2(x + 1)$$
$$\log_2(x - 1) + \log_2(x + 1) = 3$$
$$\log_2[x^2 - 1] = 3$$
$$x^2 - 1 = 8$$
$$x^2 = 9$$
$$x = \pm 3$$

If $x = -3$, we get a logarithm of a negative number. If $x = 3$, then $y = \log_2(3 - 1) = 1$. The solution set is $\{(3, 1)\}$.

32. Substitute $y = \log_3(x - 4)$ into $y = 2 - \log_3(x + 4)$.

$$\log_3(x - 4) = 2 - \log_3(x + 4)$$
$$\log_3(x - 4) + \log_3(x + 4) = 2$$
$$\log_3(x^2 - 16) = 2$$
$$x^2 - 16 = 3^2$$
$$x^2 = 25$$
$$x = \pm 5$$

If $x = -5$, then $\log_3(-5 - 4)$ is undefined. If $x = 5$, then $y = \log_3(5 - 4) = \log_3(1) = 0$. The solution set to the system is $\{(5, 0)\}$.

33. Use substitution to eliminate y.

$$\log_2(x - 1) = 2 + \log_2(x + 2)$$
$$\log_2(x - 1) - \log_2(x + 2) = 2$$
$$\log_2\left(\frac{x - 1}{x + 2}\right) = 2$$
$$\frac{x - 1}{x + 2} = 4$$
$$x - 1 = 4x + 8$$
$$-9 = 3x$$
$$-3 = x$$

If $x = -3$ in either of the original equations, we get a logarithm of a negative number. So the solution set is the empty set, $\emptyset$.

34. Use substitution to eliminate y.

$$\log_4(8x) = 2 + \log_4(x - 1)$$
$$\log_4(8x) - \log_4(x - 1) = 2$$
$$\log_4\left(\frac{8x}{x - 1}\right) = 2$$
$$\frac{8x}{x - 1} = 4^2$$
$$8x = 16(x - 1)$$
$$-8x = -16$$
$$x = 2$$

If $x = 2$, then $y = \log_4(8 \cdot 2) = \log_4(16) = 2$. The solution set is $\{(2, 2)\}$.

35. Use substitution to eliminate y.

$$2^{3x+4} = 4^{x-1}$$
$$2^{3x+4} = (2^2)^{x-1}$$
$$2^{3x+4} = 2^{2x-2}$$
$$3x + 4 = 2x - 2$$
$$x = -6$$

If $x = -6$, then $y = 4^{-6-1} = 4^{-7}$. So the solution set is $\left\{ \left(-6, 4^{-7}\right) \right\}$.

36. Use substitution to eliminate y.

$$4^{3x} = (1/2)^{1-x}$$
$$(2^2)^{3x} = (2^{-1})^{1-x}$$
$$2^{6x} = 2^{-1+x}$$
$$6x = -1 + x$$
$$5x = -1$$
$$x = -\frac{1}{5}$$

If $x = -1/5$, then $y = 4^{3(-1/5)} = 4^{-3/5}$. The solution set is $\left\{ \left(-\frac{1}{5}, 4^{-3/5}\right) \right\}$.

37. Let $x =$ the length of one leg and $y =$ the length of the other. We write one equation for the area: $3 = \frac{1}{2}xy$. We write the other

382

equation from the Pythagorean theorem:
$x^2 + y^2 = 15$.
Substitute $y = 6/x$ into $x^2 + y^2 = 15$.

$$x^2 + \left(\frac{6}{x}\right)^2 = 15$$
$$x^2 + \frac{36}{x^2} = 15$$
$$x^4 + 36 = 15x^2$$
$$x^4 - 15x^2 + 36 = 0$$
$$(x^2 - 3)(x^2 - 12) = 0$$
$$x = \sqrt{3} \quad \text{or} \quad x = \sqrt{12} = 2\sqrt{3}$$

If $x = \sqrt{3}$, then $y = 6/\sqrt{3} = 2\sqrt{3}$. If $x = 2\sqrt{3}$, then $y = 6/(2\sqrt{3}) = \sqrt{3}$. So the lengths of the legs are $\sqrt{3}$ feet and $2\sqrt{3}$ feet.

38. Let $x =$ the length of the screen and $y =$ the width of the screen. Since the diagonal is 5 inches we can write $x^2 + y^2 = 25$. Since the area is 12 square inches, we have $xy = 12$. Substitute $y = 12/x$ into $x^2 + y^2 = 25$.

$$x^2 + \left(\frac{12}{x}\right)^2 = 25$$
$$x^2 + \frac{144}{x^2} = 25$$
$$x^2\left(x^2 + \frac{144}{x^2}\right) = x^2(25)$$
$$x^4 + 144 = 25x^2$$
$$x^4 - 25x^2 + 144 = 0$$
$$(x^2 - 9)(x^2 - 16) = 0$$
$$x^2 - 9 = 0 \quad \text{or} \quad x^2 - 16 = 0$$
$$x^2 = 9 \quad \text{or} \quad x^2 = 16$$
$$x = \pm 3 \quad \text{or} \quad x = \pm 4$$

The value of x must be positive. If $x = 3$, $y = 12/3 = 4$. If $x = 4$, then $y = 12/4 = 3$. The screen is 3 inches by 4 inches.

39. Let $x =$ the height of each triangle, and $y =$ the length of the base of each triangle. Since the 7 triangles are to have a total area of 3,500, the area of each must be 500: $\frac{1}{2}xy = 500$. The ratio of the height to base must be 1 to 4 is expressed as $\frac{x}{y} = \frac{1}{4}$. These two equations can be written as $xy = 1000$ and $y = 4x$. Use substitution.

$$x(4x) = 1000$$
$$x^2 = 250$$
$$x = \sqrt{250} = 5\sqrt{10}$$

Since $y = 4x$, $y = 20\sqrt{10}$. So the height is $5\sqrt{10}$ inches and the base is $20\sqrt{10}$ inches.

40. Let $x =$ the length of the side opposite the 30° angle. Since the side opposite 30 is half the length of the hypotenuse, $2x =$ the length of the hypotenuse. Let $y =$ the length of the side opposite the 60° angle. Using the Pythagorean theorem, we can write $(2x)^2 = x^2 + y^2$. Since the perimeter is 6 feet, $x + 2x + y = 6$. We must solve the following system.

$$4x^2 = x^2 + y^2$$
$$3x + y = 6$$
$$3x^2 = y^2$$
$$y = 6 - 3x$$

Substitute $y = 6 - 3x$ into $3x^2 = y^2$.

$$3x^2 = (6 - 3x)^2$$
$$3x^2 = 36 - 36x + 9x^2$$
$$-6x^2 + 36x - 36 = 0$$
$$x^2 - 6x + 6 = 0$$
$$x = \frac{6 \pm \sqrt{36 - 4(1)(6)}}{2(1)} = \frac{6 \pm \sqrt{12}}{2}$$
$$= 3 \pm \sqrt{3}$$

If $x = 3 + \sqrt{3}$, then $y = 6 - 3(3 + \sqrt{3}) = -3 - 3\sqrt{3}$, which is negative and it is discarded. If $x = 3 - \sqrt{3}$, then $y = 6 - 3(3 - \sqrt{3}) = -3 + 3\sqrt{3}$, and $2x = 6 - 2\sqrt{3}$. The three sides have lengths $3 - \sqrt{3}$ feet, $6 - 2\sqrt{3}$ feet and $-3 + 3\sqrt{3}$ feet.

41. Let $x =$ the number of hours for pump A to fill the tank alone, and $y =$ the number of hours for pump B to fill the tank alone.

$$\frac{1}{x} + \frac{1}{y} = \frac{1}{6}$$
$$\frac{1}{y} - \frac{1}{x} = \frac{1}{12}$$

Adding these two equations eliminates x.

$$\frac{2}{y} = \frac{1}{6} + \frac{1}{12}$$
$$\frac{2}{y} = \frac{1}{4}$$
$$y = 8$$

Use $y = 8$ in the first equation.

$$\frac{1}{x} + \frac{1}{8} = \frac{1}{6}$$
$$\frac{1}{x} = \frac{1}{24}$$
$$x = 24$$

It would take pump A 24 hours to fill the tank alone and pump B 8 hours to fill the tank alone.

42. Let $x =$ the number of hours it takes her mother to clean the house by herself without interference. Let $y =$ the number of hours it takes Roxanne to mess up (or clean up) the house by herself. Roxanne does $1/y$ of the job per hour and her mother does $1/x$ of the job per hour. When they are working together, they clean 1/6 of the house per hour, but when Roxanne is working against her mother only 1/9 of the house gets cleaned per hour.

$$\frac{1}{x} + \frac{1}{y} = \frac{1}{6}$$
$$\frac{1}{x} - \frac{1}{y} = \frac{1}{9}$$
$$\frac{2}{x} = \frac{5}{18}$$
$$5x = 36$$
$$x = \frac{36}{5}$$

Her mother can clean the house by herself in 36/5 hours, or 7 hours 12 minutes

43. Let $x =$ the time for Jan to do the job alone. Let $y =$ the time for Beth to do the job alone. Since they do the job together in 24 minutes we have the equation
$$\frac{1}{x} + \frac{1}{y} = \frac{1}{24}.$$
In 50 minutes the job was completed, but not by working together. This implies that the total of their times alone is 100, $x + y = 100$. Substitute $y = 100 - x$ into the first equation.
$$\frac{1}{x} + \frac{1}{100-x} = \frac{1}{24}$$
$$24(100 - x) + 24x = x(100 - x)$$
$$2400 - 24x + 24x = 100x - x^2$$
$$x^2 - 100x + 2400 = 0$$
$$(x - 40)(x - 60) = 0$$
$$x = 40 \quad \text{or} \quad x = 60$$
Since $y = 100 - x$
$$y = 60 \qquad y = 40$$
Since Jan is the faster worker, it would take her 40 minutes to complete the catfish by herself.

44. Let $x =$ the original length and $y =$ the original width. If the width is increased by 2 feet, the new area is 30 square feet more than the original area, xy. So $x(y + 2) = 30 + xy$. If the width is increased by 1 foot and the length by 3 feet, then the new area is 54 square feet more than the original area, xy. So $(x + 3)(y + 1) = 54 + xy$. Simplify the first equation.
$$xy + 2x = 30 + xy$$
$$2x = 30$$
$$x = 15$$

Use $x = 15$ in $(x + 3)(y + 1) = 54 + xy$.
$$18(y + 1) = 54 + 15y$$
$$18y + 18 = 54 + 15y$$
$$3y = 36$$
$$y = 12$$
The original patio is 12 feet by 15 feet.

45. Let $x =$ the length and $y =$ the width. The area is 72 is expressed as $xy = 72$. The perimeter is 34 is expressed as $2x + 2y = 34$ or $x + y = 17$. Substitute $y = 17 - x$ into $xy = 72$.
$$x(17 - x) = 72$$
$$-x^2 + 17x - 72 = 0$$
$$x^2 - 17x + 72 = 0$$
$$(x - 9)(x - 8) = 0$$
$$x = 9 \quad \text{or} \quad x = 8$$
$$y = 8 \qquad\qquad y = 9$$
The rectangular area is 8 feet by 9 feet.

46. Let $x =$ one number and $y =$ the other. Since their sum is 8, $x + y = 8$. Since their product is 10, $xy = 10$. Substitute $y = 8 - x$ into $xy = 10$.
$$x(8 - x) = 10$$
$$8x - x^2 = 10$$
$$-x^2 + 8x - 10 = 0$$
$$x^2 - 8x + 10 = 0$$
$$x = \frac{8 \pm \sqrt{64 - 4(1)(10)}}{2} = \frac{8 \pm \sqrt{24}}{2}$$
$$= 4 \pm \sqrt{6}$$
If $x = 4 - \sqrt{6}$, the
$y = 8 - (4 - \sqrt{6}) = 4 + \sqrt{6}$.
If $x = 4 + \sqrt{6}$, then
$y = 8 - (4 + \sqrt{6}) = 4 - \sqrt{6}$.
The two numbers are $4 - \sqrt{6}$ and $4 + \sqrt{6}$.

47. Let x and y represent the numbers.
$$x + y = 8$$
$$xy = 20$$
Substitute $y = 8 - x$ into $xy = 20$.
$$x(8 - x) = 20$$
$$-x^2 + 8x - 20 = 0$$
$$x^2 - 8x + 20 = 0$$
$$x = \frac{8 \pm \sqrt{64 - 4(1)(20)}}{2} = \frac{8 \pm \sqrt{-16}}{2}$$
$$= 4 \pm 2i$$
If $x = 4 + 2i$, then $y = 8 - (4 + 2i) = 4 - 2i$.
If $x = 4 - 2i$, then $y = 8 - (4 - 2i) = 4 + 2i$.
So the numbers are $4 - 2i$ and $4 + 2i$.

48. Let $x =$ one number and $y =$ the other number.

$$x + y = -6$$
$$xy = 10$$

Substitute $y = -x - 6$ into $xy = 10$.

$$x(-x - 6) = 10$$
$$-x^2 - 6x - 10 = 0$$
$$x^2 + 6x + 10 = 0$$
$$x = \frac{-6 \pm \sqrt{36 - 4(1)(10)}}{2} = \frac{-6 \pm \sqrt{-4}}{2}$$
$$= \frac{-6 \pm 2i}{2} = -3 \pm i$$

If $x = -3 - i$, then
$y = -(-3 - i) - 6 = -3 + i$.
If $x = -3 + i$, then
$y = -(-3 + i) - 6 = -3 - i$.
The two complex numbers are $-3 + i$ and $-3 - i$.

49. Let $x =$ the length of the side of the square, and $y =$ the height of the triangle. The total height of 10 feet means that $x + y = 10$. The total area is 72 means that $x^2 + 0.5xy = 72$. Substitute $y = 10 - x$ into the second equation.

$$x^2 + 0.5x(10 - x) = 72$$
$$x^2 + 5x - 0.5x^2 = 72$$
$$0.5x^2 + 5x - 72 = 0$$
$$x^2 + 10x - 144 = 0$$
$$(x - 8)(x + 18) = 0$$
$$x = 8 \text{ or } \qquad x = -18$$
$$y = 2$$

The side of the square is 8 feet and the height of the triangle is 2 feet.

50. Let $x =$ the length and $y =$ the height. Since the box is 2 inches wide and contains 120 cubic inches, we have $2xy = 120$. Write another equation expressing the fact that the total area of the six sides is 184 square inches.

$$2xy + 2(2x) + 2(2y) = 184$$
$$2xy + 4x + 4y = 184$$
$$xy + 2x + 2y = 92$$

From the equation $2xy = 120$, we get $xy = 60$ and $y = 60/x$. Use substitution.

$$60 + 2x + 2\left(\frac{60}{x}\right) = 92$$
$$2x + \frac{120}{x} = 32$$
$$x\left(2x + \frac{120}{x}\right) = x(32)$$
$$2x^2 + 120 = 32x$$

$$x^2 - 16x + 60 = 0$$
$$(x - 6)(x - 10) = 0$$
$$x - 6 = 0 \text{ or } \qquad x - 10 = 0$$
$$x = 6 \text{ or } \qquad x = 10$$

If $x = 6$, then $y = 60/6 = 10$. If $x = 10$, then $y = 60/10 = 6$. The dimensions of the box should by 6 inches by 10 inches by 2 inches.

51. a) $(1.71, 1.55)$, $(-2.98, -3.95)$
b) $(1, 1)$, $(0.40, 0.16)$
c) $(1.17, 1.62)$, $(-1.17, -1.62)$

11.2 WARM-UPS

1. False, because if the focus is $(2, 3)$ and the directrix is $y = 1$, then the vertex is $(2, 2)$.
2. True, because the focus is 1 unit above the vertex which is $(0, 1)$.
3. True, because in $y = a(x - h)^2 + k$, the vertex is (h, k).
4. False, because $y = 6x + 3x + 2$ is equivalent to $y = 9x + 2$, which is a straight line.
5. False, because $y = -2x^2 + 2x + 9$ opens downward.
6. True, the vertex is $(0, 0)$ and so is the y-intercept.
7. True, because it opens upward from $(2, 3)$ and it cannot intersect the x-axis.
8. False, because the y-intercept is $(0, 0)$.
9. True, because $(3, 5)$ is 1 unit from $x = 2$ and $(1, 5)$ has the same y-coordinate and is 1 unit on the other side of $x = 2$.
10. True, because it opens upward from its vertex $(5, 0)$.

11.2 EXERCISES

1. A parabola is the set of all points in a plane that are equidistant from a given line and a fixed point not on the line.
2. The vertex is the midpoint of the line segment joining the focus and directrix, perpendicular to the directrix.
3. A parabola can be written in the forms $y = ax^2 + bx + c$ or $y = a(x - h)^2 + k$.
4. The distance from the focus to the directrix is $|2p|$ where $a = 1/(4p)$.

5. We use completing the square to convert $y = ax^2 + bx + c$ into $y = a(x - h)^2 + k$.

6. To convert $y = a(x - h)^2 + k$ into the form $y = ax^2 + bx + c$ square the binomial, multiply by a, then add the like terms.

7. The vertex is $(0, 0)$. Since $2 = 1/(4p)$, $p = 1/8$. So the focus is $(0, 1/8)$ and the directrix is $y = -1/8$.

8. The vertex is $(0, 0)$. Since $1/2 = 1/(4p)$, $4p = 2$, or $p = 1/2$. So the focus is $(0, 1/2)$ and the directrix is $y = -1/2$.

9. The vertex is $(0, 0)$. Since $-1/4 = 1/(4p)$, $4p = -4$, or $p = -1$. So the focus is $(0, -1)$ and the directrix is $y = 1$.

10. The vertex is $(0, 0)$. Since $-1/12 = 1/(4p)$, $4p = -12$, or $p = -3$. So the focus is $(0, -3)$ and the directrix is $y = 3$.

11. The vertex is $(3, 2)$. Since $1/2 = 1/(4p)$, $p = 1/2$. So the focus is $(3, 2.5)$ and the directrix is $y = 1.5$.

12. The vertex is $(-2, -5)$. Since $1/4 = 1/(4p)$, $p = 1$. So the focus is $(-2, -4)$ and the directrix is $y = -6$.

13. The vertex is $(-1, 6)$. Since $-1 = 1/(4p)$, $p = -1/4$. So the focus is $(-1, 5.75)$ and the directrix is $y = 6.25$.

14. The vertex is $(4, 1)$. Since $-3 = 1/(4p)$, $p = -1/12$. So the focus is $(4, 11/12)$ and the directrix is $y = 13/12$.

15. Since the distance between the focus and directrix is 4, $p = 2$ and $a = \frac{1}{4p} = \frac{1}{4(2)} = \frac{1}{8}$.

Since the vertex is half way between the focus and directrix, the vertex is $(0, 0)$. Use the form $y = a(x - h)^2 + k$ to get the equation.
$$y = \tfrac{1}{8}(x - 0)^2 + 0$$
$$y = \tfrac{1}{8}x^2$$

16. Since the distance between the focus and directrix is 6 and the focus is below the directrix, $p = -3$ and $a = \frac{1}{4p} = \frac{1}{4(-3)} = -\frac{1}{12}$.

Since the vertex is half way between the focus and directrix, the vertex is $(0, 0)$. Use the form $y = a(x - h)^2 + k$ to get the equation.
$$y = -\tfrac{1}{12}(x - 0)^2 + 0$$
$$y = -\tfrac{1}{12}x^2$$

17. Since the distance between the focus and directrix is 1 and the focus is below the directrix,
$p = -\tfrac{1}{2}$ and $a = \frac{1}{4p} = \frac{1}{4(-\frac{1}{2})} = -\tfrac{1}{2}$. Since the vertex is half way between the focus and directrix, the vertex is $(0, 0)$. Use the form $y = a(x - h)^2 + k$ to get the equation.
$$y = -\tfrac{1}{2}(x - 0)^2 + 0$$
$$y = -\tfrac{1}{2}x^2$$

18. Since the distance between the focus and directrix is $\tfrac{1}{4}$ and the parabola opens upward, $p = \tfrac{1}{8}$ and $a = \frac{1}{4p} = \frac{1}{4(\frac{1}{8})} = 2$. Since the vertex is half way between the focus and directrix, the vertex is $(0, 0)$. Use the form $y = a(x - h)^2 + k$ to get the equation.
$$y = 2(x - 0)^2 + 0$$
$$y = 2x^2$$

19. Since the distance between the focus and directrix is 1 and the parabola opens upward, $p = \tfrac{1}{2}$ and $a = \frac{1}{4p} = \frac{1}{4(\frac{1}{2})} = \tfrac{1}{2}$. Since the vertex is half way between the focus and directrix, the vertex is $\left(3, \tfrac{3}{2}\right)$. Use the form $y = a(x - h)^2 + k$ to get the equation.
$$y = \tfrac{1}{2}(x - 3)^2 + \tfrac{3}{2}$$
$$y = \tfrac{1}{2}x^2 - 3x + \tfrac{9}{2} + \tfrac{3}{2}$$
$$y = \tfrac{1}{2}x^2 - 3x + 6$$

20. Since the distance between the focus and directrix is 1 and the parabola opens upward, $p = \tfrac{1}{2}$ and $a = \frac{1}{4p} = \frac{1}{4(\frac{1}{2})} = \tfrac{1}{2}$. Since the vertex is half way between the focus and directrix, the vertex is $\left(-4, \tfrac{9}{2}\right)$. Use the form $y = a(x - h)^2 + k$ to get the equation.
$$y = \tfrac{1}{2}(x + 4)^2 + \tfrac{9}{2}$$
$$y = \tfrac{1}{2}x^2 + 4x + 8 + \tfrac{9}{2}$$
$$y = \tfrac{1}{2}x^2 + 4x + \tfrac{25}{2}$$

21. Since the distance between the focus and directrix is 4 and the parabola opens downward, $p = -2$ and $a = \frac{1}{4p} = \frac{1}{4(-2)} = -\tfrac{1}{8}$. Since the vertex is half way between the focus and directrix, the vertex is $(1, 0)$. Use the form $y = a(x - h)^2 + k$ to get the equation.

$$y = -\tfrac{1}{8}(x-1)^2 + 0$$
$$y = -\tfrac{1}{8}x^2 + \tfrac{1}{4}x - \tfrac{1}{8}$$

22. Since the distance between the focus and directrix is 4 and the parabola opens downward, $p = -2$ and $a = \tfrac{1}{4p} = \tfrac{1}{4(-2)} = -\tfrac{1}{8}$. Since the vertex is half way between the focus and directrix, the vertex is $(2, -1)$. Use the form $y = a(x-h)^2 + k$ to get the equation.
$$y = -\tfrac{1}{8}(x-2)^2 - 1$$
$$y = -\tfrac{1}{8}x^2 + \tfrac{1}{2}x - \tfrac{3}{2}$$

23. Since the distance between the focus and directrix is $\tfrac{1}{2}$ and the parabola opens upward, $p = \tfrac{1}{4}$ and $a = \tfrac{1}{4p} = \tfrac{1}{4(0.25)} = 1$. Since the vertex is half way between the focus and directrix, the vertex is $(-3, 1)$. Use the form $y = a(x-h)^2 + k$ to get the equation.
$$y = 1(x+3)^2 + 1$$
$$y = x^2 + 6x + 10$$

24. Since the distance between the focus and directrix is $\tfrac{1}{4}$ and the parabola opens upward, $p = \tfrac{1}{8}$ and $a = \tfrac{1}{4p} = \tfrac{1}{4\left(\tfrac{1}{8}\right)} = 2$. Since the vertex is half way between the focus and directrix, the vertex is $(5, 2)$. Use the form $y = a(x-h)^2 + k$ to get the equation.
$$y = 2(x-5)^2 + 2$$
$$y = 2x^2 - 20x + 52$$

25.
$$y = x^2 - 6x + 1$$
$$y = x^2 - 6x + 9 - 9 + 1$$
$$y = (x-3)^2 - 8$$
The vertex is $(3, -8)$. Because $a = 1$, the parabola opens upward, and $p = 1/4$. The focus is $(3, -7.75)$ and the directrix is $y = -8.25$.

26.
$$y = x^2 + 4x - 7$$
$$y = x^2 + 4x + 4 - 4 - 7$$
$$y = (x+2)^2 - 11$$
The vertex is $(-2, -11)$. Since $a = 1$, $p = 1/4$ and the focus is $(-2, -10.75)$. The directrix is $y = -11.25$.

27.
$$y = 2x^2 + 12x + 5$$
$$y = 2(x^2 + 6x) + 5$$
$$y = 2(x^2 + 6x + 9) + 5 - 18$$
$$y = 2(x+3)^2 - 13$$
The vertex is $(-3, -13)$ and the parabola opens upward. Because $a = 2$, $p = 1/8 = 0.125$

The focus is $(-3, -12.875)$ and the directrix is $y = -13.125$.

28.
$$y = 3x^2 + 6x - 7$$
$$y = 3(x^2 + 2x) - 7$$
$$y = 3(x^2 + 2x + 1) - 7 - 3$$
$$y = 3(x+1)^2 - 10$$
The vertex is $(-1, -10)$ and the parabola opens upward. Because $a = 3$, $p = 1/12$. The focus is $(-1, -9\tfrac{11}{12})$ and the directrix is $y = -10\tfrac{1}{12}$.

29.
$$y = -2x^2 + 16x + 1$$
$$y = -2(x^2 - 8x) + 1$$
$$y = -2(x^2 - 8x + 16) + 1 + 32$$
$$y = -2(x-4)^2 + 33$$
The vertex is $(4, 33)$ and the parabola opens downward. Because $a = -2$, $p = -1/8 = -0.125$. The focus is $(4, 32\tfrac{7}{8})$ and the directrix is $y = 33\tfrac{1}{8}$.

30.
$$y = -3x^2 - 6x + 7$$
$$y = -3(x^2 + 2x) + 7$$
$$y = -3(x^2 + 2x + 1) + 7 + 3$$
$$y = -3(x+1)^2 + 10$$
The vertex is $(-1, 10)$ and the parabola opens downward. Because $a = -3$, $p = -1/12$. The focus is $(-1, 9\tfrac{11}{12})$ and the directrix is $y = 10\tfrac{1}{12}$.

31.
$$y = 5x^2 + 40x$$
$$y = 5(x^2 + 8x)$$
$$y = 5(x^2 + 8x + 16) - 80$$
$$y = 5(x+4)^2 - 80$$
The vertex is $(-4, -80)$ and the parabola opens upward. Because $a = 5$, $p = 1/20$. The focus is $(-4, -79\tfrac{19}{20})$ and the directrix is $y = -80\tfrac{1}{20}$.

32.
$$y = -2x^2 + 10x$$
$$y = -2(x^2 - 5x)$$
$$y = -2(x^2 - 5x + \tfrac{25}{4}) + \tfrac{25}{2}$$
$$y = -2(x - \tfrac{5}{2})^2 + \tfrac{25}{2}$$
The vertex is $\left(\tfrac{5}{2}, \tfrac{25}{2}\right)$ and the parabola opens downward. Because $a = -2$, $p = -1/8$. The focus is $(\tfrac{5}{2}, \tfrac{99}{8})$ and the directrix is $y = \tfrac{101}{8}$.

33. The x-coordinate of the vertex is $x = \tfrac{-b}{2a}$.
$$x = \tfrac{-(-4)}{2(1)} = 2$$
$$y = 2^2 - 4(2) + 1 = -3$$

The vertex is $(2, -3)$ and the parabola opens upward. Because $a = 1$, $p = 1/4$. The focus is $(2, -2\frac{3}{4})$ and the directrix is $y = -3\frac{1}{4}$.

34. The x-coordinate of the vertex is $x = \frac{-b}{2a}$.
$$x = \frac{-(-6)}{2(1)} = 3$$
$$y = (3)^2 - 6(3) - 7 = -16$$
The vertex is $(3, -16)$ and the parabola opens upward. Because $a = 1$, $p = 1/4$. The focus is $(3, -15\frac{3}{4})$ and the directrix is $y = -16\frac{1}{4}$.

35. The x-coordinate of the vertex is $x = \frac{-b}{2a}$.
$$x = \frac{-(2)}{2(-1)} = 1$$
$$y = -1^2 + 2(1) - 3 = -2$$
The vertex is $(1, -2)$ and the parabola opens downward. Because $a = -1$, $p = -1/4$. The focus is $(1, -2\frac{1}{4})$ and the directrix is $y = -1\frac{3}{4}$.

36. The x-coordinate of the vertex is $x = \frac{-b}{2a}$.
$$x = \frac{-4}{2(-1)} = 2$$
$$y = -(2)^2 + 4(2) + 9 = 13$$
The vertex is $(2, 13)$ and the parabola opens downward. Because $a = -1$, $p = -1/4$. The focus is $(2, 12\frac{3}{4})$ and the directrix is $y = 13\frac{1}{4}$.

37. The x-coordinate of the vertex is $x = \frac{-b}{2a}$.
$$x = \frac{-(-6)}{2(3)} = 1$$
$$y = 3(1^2) - 6(1) + 1 = -2$$
The vertex is $(1, -2)$ and the parabola opens upward. Because $a = 3$, $p = 1/12$. The focus is $(1, -1\frac{11}{12})$ and the directrix is $y = -2\frac{1}{12}$.

38. The x-coordinate of the vertex is $x = \frac{-b}{2a}$.
$$x = \frac{-(4)}{2(2)} = -1$$
$$y = 2(-1)^2 + 4(-1) - 3 = -5$$
The vertex is $(-1, -5)$ and the parabola opens upward. Because $a = 2$, $p = 1/8$. The focus is $(-1, -4\frac{7}{8})$ and the directrix is $y = -5\frac{1}{8}$.

39. The x-coordinate of the vertex is $x = \frac{-b}{2a}$.
$$x = \frac{-(-3)}{2(-1)} = -\frac{3}{2}$$
$$y = -(-\frac{3}{2})^2 - 3(-\frac{3}{2}) + 2 = \frac{17}{4}$$
The vertex is $(-\frac{3}{2}, \frac{17}{4})$ and the parabola opens downward. Because $a = -1$, $p = -1/4$. The focus is $(-\frac{3}{2}, 4)$ and the directrix is $y = \frac{9}{2}$.

40. The x-coordinate of the vertex is $x = \frac{-b}{2a}$.
$$x = \frac{-(3)}{2(-1)} = \frac{3}{2}$$

$$y = -(\tfrac{3}{2})^2 + 3 \cdot \tfrac{3}{2} - 1$$
$$= -\frac{9}{4} + \frac{18}{4} - \frac{4}{4} = \frac{5}{4}$$
The vertex is $(\frac{3}{2}, \frac{5}{4})$ and the parabola opens downward. Because $a = -1$; $p = -1/4$. The focus is $(\frac{3}{2}, 1)$ and the directrix is $y = \frac{3}{2}$.

41. The x-coordinate of the vertex is $x = \frac{-b}{2a}$.
$$x = \frac{-(0)}{2(3)} = 0$$
$$y = 3(0)^2 + 5 = 5$$
The vertex is $(0, 5)$ and the parabola opens upward. Because $a = 3$, $p = 1/12$. The focus is $(0, 5\frac{1}{12})$ and the directrix is $y = 4\frac{11}{12}$.

42. The x-coordinate of the vertex is $x = \frac{-b}{2a}$.
$$x = \frac{-(0)}{2(-2)} = 0$$
$$y = -2(0)^2 - 6 = -6$$
The vertex is $(0, -6)$ and the parabola opens downward. Because $a = -2$, $p = -1/8$. The focus is $(0, -6\frac{1}{8})$ and the directrix is $y = -5\frac{7}{8}$.

43. Since $a = 1$, the parabola opens upward. The x-coordinate of the vertex is $x = \frac{-(-3)}{2(1)} = \frac{3}{2}$. The vertex is $(\frac{3}{2}, -\frac{1}{4})$. The axis of symmetry is the vertical line $x = \frac{3}{2}$. The y-intercept is $(0, 2)$. The x-intercepts are found by solving $x^2 - 3x + 2 = 0$. They are $(1, 0)$ and $(2, 0)$.

44. Since $a = 1$, the parabola opens upward. The x-coordinate of the vertex is $x = \frac{-(6)}{2(1)} = -3$. The vertex is $(-3, -1)$. The axis of symmetry is the vertical line $x = -3$. The y-intercept is $(0, 8)$. The x-intercepts are found by solving $x^2 + 6x + 8 = 0$. They are $(-4, 0)$ and $(-2, 0)$.

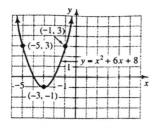

45. Since $a = -1$, the parabola opens downward. The x-coordinate of the vertex is $x = \frac{-(-2)}{2(-1)} = -1$. The vertex is $(-1, 9)$. The axis of symmetry is the vertical line $x = -1$. The y-intercept is $(0, 8)$. The x-intercepts are found by solving $-x^2 - 2x + 8 = 0$. They are $(-4, 0)$ and $(2, 0)$.

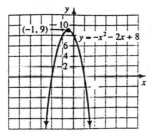

46. Since $a = -1$, the parabola opens downward. The x-coordinate of the vertex is $x = \frac{-(-2)}{2(-1)} = -1$. The vertex is $(-1, 16)$. The axis of symmetry is the vertical line $x = -1$. The y-intercept is $(0, 15)$. The x-intercepts are found by solving $-x^2 - 2x + 15 = 0$. They are $(-5, 0)$ and $(3, 0)$.

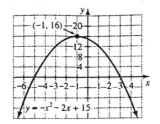

47. Since $a = 1$, the parabola opens upward. The vertex is $(-2, 1)$. The axis of symmetry is the vertical line $x = -2$. The y-intercept is $(0, 5)$. Since the graph opens upward from $(-2, 1)$, there are no x-intercepts.

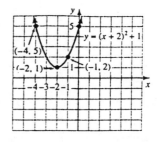

48. Since $a = -2$, the parabola opens downward. The vertex is $(-1, 3)$. The y-intercept is $(0, 1)$. The x-intercepts are found by solving $-2(x + 1)^2 + 3 = 0$.
$$(x + 1)^2 = \frac{3}{2}$$
$$x + 1 = \pm\sqrt{\frac{3}{2}}$$
$$x = -1 \pm \sqrt{\frac{3}{2}} = -1 \pm \frac{\sqrt{6}}{2}$$
The x-intercepts are
$$\left(-1 + \frac{\sqrt{6}}{2}, 0\right) \text{ and } \left(-1 - \frac{\sqrt{6}}{2}, 0\right).$$

49. We can write $y = x^2 + 2x + 1$ as $y = (x + 1)^2$. The vertex is $(-1, 0)$. The axis of symmetry is $x = -1$. The y-intercept is

$(0, 1)$. Since the parabola opens upward from $(-1, 0)$, the only x-intercept is $(-1, 0)$.

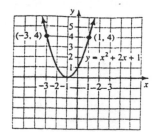

50. We can write $y = x^2 - 6x + 9$ as $y = (x - 3)^2$. The vertex is $(3, 0)$. The parabola opens upward. The y-intercept is $(0, 9)$. The x-intercept is at the vertex, $(3, 0)$.

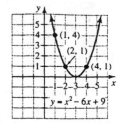

51. Since $a = -4$, the parabola opens downward. The x-coordinate of the vertex is $x = \frac{-(4)}{2(-4)} = \frac{1}{2}$. The vertex is $(\frac{1}{2}, 0)$. The axis of symmetry is the vertical line $x = \frac{1}{2}$. The intercepts are $(0, -1)$ and $(\frac{1}{2}, 0)$. Since the parabola opens downward from the x-axis, the only x-intercept is at the vertex.

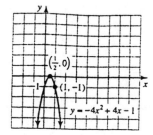

52. Rewrite $y = -4x^2 + 12x - 9$ as $y = -(2x - 3)^2$. The vertex is $(3/2, 0)$. The parabola opens downward. The x-intercept is $(3/2, 0)$. The y-intercept is $(0, -9)$. The axis of symmetry is the vertical line $x = 3/2$.

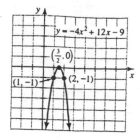

53. Since $a = 1$, the parabola opens upward. The x-coordinate of the vertex is $x = \frac{-(-5)}{2(1)} = \frac{5}{2}$. The vertex is $(\frac{5}{2}, -\frac{25}{4})$. The axis of symmetry is the vertical line $x = \frac{5}{2}$. The y-intercept is $(0, 0)$. The x-intercepts are found by solving $x^2 - 5x = 0$. They are $(0, 0)$ and $(5, 0)$.

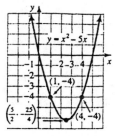

54. Since $a = 3$, the parabola opens upward. The x-coordinate of the vertex is $x = \frac{-(-9)}{2(3)} = \frac{3}{2}$. The vertex is $(\frac{3}{2}, -\frac{27}{4})$. The axis of symmetry is the vertical line $x = \frac{3}{2}$. The y-intercept is $(0, 0)$. The x-intercepts are found by solving $3x^2 - 9x = 0$. They are $(0, 0)$ and $(3, 0)$.

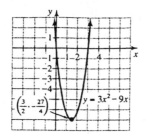

57. Since $a = 1$, the parabola opens upward. The x-coordinate of the vertex is $x = \frac{-(-2)}{2(1)} = 1$. The vertex is $(1, -2)$. The axis of symmetry is the vertical line $x = 1$. The y-intercept is $(0, -1)$. The x-intercepts are found by solving $x^2 - 2x - 1 = 0$. They are $(1 + \sqrt{2}, 0)$ and $(1 - \sqrt{2}, 0)$.

55. Since $a = 3$, the parabola opens upward. The x-coordinate of the vertex is $x = \frac{-(0)}{2(3)} = 0$. The vertex is $(0, 5)$. The axis of symmetry is the vertical line $x = 0$. The y-intercept is $(0, 5)$. Since the graph opens upward from $(0, 5)$ there are no x-intercepts.

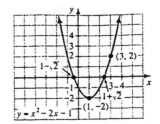

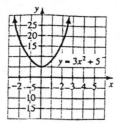

56. Since $a = -2$, the parabola opens downward. The x-coordinate of the vertex is $x = \frac{-(0)}{2(-2)} = 0$. The vertex is $(0, 3)$. The axis of symmetry is the vertical line $x = 0$. The y-intercept is $(0, 3)$. To find the x-intercepts, solve $-2x^2 + 3 = 0$. We get $x = \pm\sqrt{\frac{3}{2}} = \pm\frac{\sqrt{6}}{2}$.

The x-intercepts are $\left(-\frac{\sqrt{6}}{2}, 0\right)$ and $\left(\frac{\sqrt{6}}{2}, 0\right)$.

58. Since $a = 1$, the parabola opens upward. The x-coordinate of the vertex is $x = \frac{-(-4)}{2(1)} = 2$. The vertex is $(2, -3)$. The axis of symmetry is the vertical line $x = 2$. The y-intercept is $(0, 1)$. The x-intercept is found by solving $x^2 - 4x + 1 = 0$. The x-intercepts are $(2 - \sqrt{3}, 0)$ and $(2 + \sqrt{3}, 0)$.

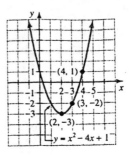

59. The vertex $y = (x - 5)^2$ is $(5, 0)$. Since $a = 1$, the parabola opens upward. The axis of symmetry is the vertical line $x = 5$. The y-intercept is $(0, 25)$. Since the parabola opens upward from $(5, 0)$, the x-intercept is $(5, 0)$.

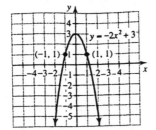

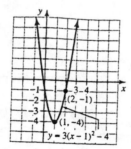

60. Since $a = 3$, the parabola opens upward. The vertex is $(1, -4)$ and the axis of symmetry is $x = 1$. The y-intercept is $(0, -1)$. The x-intercepts are found by solving $3(x - 1)^2 - 4 = 0$.
The x-intercepts are
$(1 + \frac{2\sqrt{3}}{3}, 0)$ and $(1 - \frac{2\sqrt{3}}{3}, 0)$.

61. Two numbers that have a sum of 8 are expressed as x and $8 - x$. If y is their product, then $y = x(8 - x) = -x^2 + 8x$. The maximum value for y is obtained when $x = \frac{-8}{2(-1)} = 4$. If $x = 4$ then $8 - x = 4$ also. The numbers 4 and 4 have the largest product among numbers that have a sum of 8.

62. Let x and $-6 - x$ represent two numbers that have a sum of -6. If y is their product, then $y = x(-6 - x) = -x^2 - 6x$. The maximum value of y is obtained when $x = \frac{-(-6)}{2(-1)} = -3$. If $x = -3$, then $y = -(-3)^2 - 6(-3) = 9$. So the maximum possible product is 9.

63. Let $x =$ the length and $y =$ the width. We have $2x + 2y = 160$, or $x + y = 80$. So

$A = xy$ or $A = x(80 - x) = -x^2 + 80x$. So A is maximized if $x = \frac{-80}{2(-1)} = 40$. If $x = 40$, then $y = 40$. The maximum area is obtained when the rectangle is 40 ft by 40 ft.

64. Let $x =$ the length and $y =$ the width. Since the gate is part of the perimeter, we have $2x + 2y = 104$, or $x + y = 52$. So $A = xy$, or $A = x(52 - x) = -x^2 + 52x$. The maximum value of A occurs when $x = \frac{-52}{2(-1)} = 26$. If $x = 26$, then $y = 26$. So the maximum area occurs if the garden is 26 ft by 26 ft.

65. Since the sum of the lengths of the legs is 6 feet, we can use x and $6 - x$ to represent the lengths of the legs. By the Pythagorean theorem, the square of the hypotenuse, c^2, is the sum of the squares of the legs.
$$c^2 = x^2 + (6 - x)^2 = 2x^2 - 12x + 36$$
The minimum value for c^2 occurs when $x = \frac{-(-12)}{2(2)} = 3$. If $x = 3$, then $6 - x = 3$ also. So the minimum value for c^2 occurs when each leg is 3 feet.

66. Maximum R occurs for $p = \frac{-7500}{2(-250)} = 15$. Maximum revenue occurs if the tickets are \$15 each.

67. The maximum value for s in the formula $s = -16t^2 + 128t + 6$ is attained when
$$t = \frac{-128}{2(-16)} = 4.$$
If $t = 4$, then
$s = -16(4)^2 + 128(4) + 6 = 262$.
So the maximum height reached by the ball is 262 feet and it will not hit the roof.

68. The maximum value for $s = -16t^2 + 150t + 5$ is obtained when $t = \frac{-(150)}{2(-16)} = \frac{75}{16}$. The maximum value for s is $s = -16\left(\frac{75}{16}\right)^2 + 150\left(\frac{75}{16}\right) + 5 = 356.5625$ feet. It takes 75/16 or 4.6875 seconds for the ball to reach its maximum height.

69. The minimum value of C in the formula $C = 0.009x^2 - 1.8x + 100$ is attained when
$$x = \frac{-(-1.8)}{2(0.009)} = 100.$$
The cost per hour will be at a minimum when they produce 100 balls per hour.

70. The maximum value for $P = -25x^2 + 300x$ is obtained when

$x = \frac{-(300)}{2(-25)} = 6$ clerks. The maximum value of P is $P = -25(6)^2 + 300(6) = \$900$.

71. The distance from the vertex to the focus is 15. So $p = 15$ and $a = 1/(4 \cdot 15) = 1/60$. the equation of the parabola is $y = \frac{1}{60}x^2$.

72. The equation of the parabola is of the form $y = ax^2$. Since (500, 200) is a point on the parabola, $200 = a \cdot 500^2$, or $a = 0.0008$. So the equation is $y = 0.0008x^2$. Use $a = 1/(4p)$ to get $p = 312.5$. So the antenna is 312.5 ft above the vertex.

73. The graph of $y = -x^2 + 3$ is a parabola opening downward, and the graph of $y = x^2 + 1$ is a parabola opening upward. To find the points of intersection, eliminate y by substitution.

$$x^2 + 1 = -x^2 + 3$$
$$2x^2 = 2$$
$$x^2 = 1$$
$$x = \pm 1$$

If $x = \pm 1$, then $y = 2$ (since $y = x^2 + 1$). The solution set for the system is $\{(-1, 2), (1, 2)\}$.

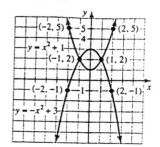

74. The graph of $y = x^2 - 3$ is a parabola opening upward. The graph of $y = -x^2 + 5$ is a parabola opening downward.

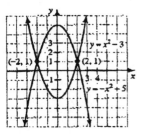

Use substitution to eliminate y.
$$x^2 - 3 = -x^2 + 5$$
$$2x^2 = 8$$
$$x^2 = 4$$
$$x = \pm 2$$
If $x = 2$, then $y = (2)^2 - 3 = 1$. If $x = -2$, then $y = (-2)^2 - 3 = 1$. The solution set to the system is $\{(2, 1), (-2, 1)\}$.

75. The graph of $y = x^2 - 2$ is a parabola opening upward, and the graph of $y = 2x - 3$ is a straight line.

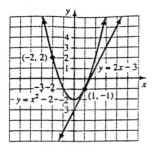

We eliminate y by substitution.
$$x^2 - 2 = 2x - 3$$
$$x^2 - 2x + 1 = 0$$
$$(x - 1)^2 = 0$$
$$x = 1$$
If $x = 1$, then $y = -1$ (because $y = 2x - 3$). The solution set for the system is $\{(1, -1)\}$.

76. The graph of $y = x^2 + x - 6$ is a parabola opening upward. The graph of $y = 7x - 15$ is a line with y-intercept $(0, -15)$ and slope 7.

393

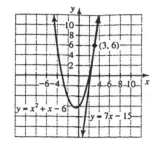

The solution set for the system is
$\left\{\left(\frac{3}{2}, \frac{11}{4}\right), (-4, 0)\right\}$.

78. The graph of $y = x^2 + 2x - 8$ is a parabola opening upward. The graph of $y = -x^2 - x + 12$ is a parabola opening downward.

Use substitution to eliminate y.
$$x^2 + x - 6 = 7x - 15$$
$$x^2 - 6x + 9 = 0$$
$$(x - 3)^2 = 0$$
$$x - 3 = 0$$
$$x = 3$$

If $x = 3$, then $y = 7(3) - 15 = 6$. The solution set is $\{(3, 6)\}$.

77. The graph of $y = x^2 + 3x - 4$ is a parabola opening upward, and the graph of $y = -x^2 - 2x + 8$ is a parabola opening downward.

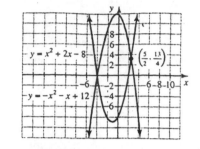

Use substitution to eliminate y.
$$x^2 + 2x - 8 = -x^2 - x + 12$$
$$2x^2 + 3x - 20 = 0$$
$$(2x - 5)(x + 4) = 0$$
$$2x - 5 = 0 \quad \text{or} \quad x + 4 = 0$$
$$x = \frac{5}{2} \quad \text{or} \quad x = -4$$

If $x = \frac{5}{2}$, then $y = \left(\frac{5}{2}\right)^2 + 2\left(\frac{5}{2}\right) - 8 = \frac{13}{4}$. If $x = -4$, then $y = (-4)^2 + 2(-4) - 8 = 0$.
The solution set to the system is
$\left\{\left(\frac{5}{2}, \frac{13}{4}\right), (-4, 0)\right\}$.

79. The graph of $y = x^2 + 3x - 4$ is a parabola opening upward. The graph of $y = 2x + 2$ is a straight line with slope 2 and y-intercept $(0, 2)$.

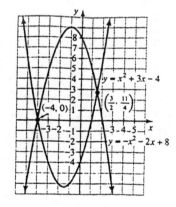

Eliminate y by substitution.
$$x^2 + 3x - 4 = -x^2 - 2x + 8$$
$$2x^2 + 5x - 12 = 0$$
$$(2x - 3)(x + 4) = 0$$
$$x = 3/2 \quad \text{or} \quad x = -4$$

If $x = 3/2$, then
$$y = (3/2)^2 + 3(3/2) - 4 = 11/4.$$
If $x = -4$, then
$$y = (-4)^2 + 3(-4) - 4 = 0.$$

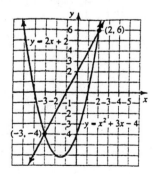

Use substitution to eliminate y.

$$x^2 + 3x - 4 = 2x + 2$$
$$x^2 + x - 6 = 0$$
$$(x+3)(x-2) = 0$$
$$x = -3 \quad \text{or} \quad x = 2$$

Since $y = 2x + 2$

$$y = -4 \qquad y = 6$$

The solution set for the system is $\{(-3, -4), (2, 6)\}$.

80. The graph of $y = x^2 + 5x + 6$ is a parabola opening upward. The graph of $y = x + 11$ is a line with slope 1 and y-intercept $(0, 11)$.

Use substitution to eliminate y.

$$x^2 + 5x + 6 = x + 11$$
$$x^2 + 4x - 5 = 0$$
$$(x+5)(x-1) = 0$$
$$x + 5 = 0 \quad \text{or} \quad x - 1 = 0$$
$$x = -5 \quad \text{or} \quad x = 1$$

If $x = -5$, then $y = -5 + 11 = 6$. If $x = 1$, then $y = 1 + 11 = 12$. The solution set is $\{(-5, 6), (1, 12)\}$.

81. Since vertex is $(0, 4)$, the equation is $y = a(x - 0)^2 + 4$, or $y = ax^2 + 4$. Since $(2, 0)$ is on the parabola, $0 = a \cdot 2^2 + 4$, or $a = -1$. So the equation is $y = -x^2 + 4$.

82. The vertex is $(0, 0)$. So $y = a(x - 0)^2 + 0$, or $y = ax^2$. Since $(3, 3)$ is on the parabola, $3 = a \cdot 3^2$, or $a = \frac{1}{3}$. The equation is $y = \frac{1}{3}x^2$.

83. The vertex is $(2, 2)$. So $y = a(x - 2)^2 + 2$. Since $(0, 0)$ is on the parabola, $0 = a(0 - 2)^2 + 2$, or $a = -\frac{1}{2}$. The equation is $y = -\frac{1}{2}(x - 2)^2 + 2$, or

$$y = -\tfrac{1}{2}x^2 + 2x.$$

84. The vertex is $(2, 0)$. So $y = a(x - 2)^2 + 0$, or $y = a(x - 2)^2$. Since $(0, -3)$ is on the parabola, $-3 = a(0 - 2)^2$, or $a = -\frac{3}{4}$. So the equation is $y = -\frac{3}{4}(x - 2)^2$, or $y = -\frac{3}{4}x^2 + 3x - 3$.

86. a) Opens to the right for $a > 0$ and to the left for $a < 0$. b) Axis of symmetry is $y = h$.

87. The graphs have identical shapes.

88.
$$x^2 = 6x - 9$$
$$x^2 - 6x + 9 = 0$$
$$(x - 3)^2 = 0$$
$$x = 3$$
$$y = 3^2 = 9$$

So the line intersects the curve at $(3, 9)$.

11.3 WARM-UPS

1. False, the radius of a circle is a positive real number.

2. False, the coordinates of the center do not satisfy the equation of the circle, only points on the circle satisfy the equation.

3. True, the center is $(0, 0)$.

4. False, the equation of the circle centered at the origin with radius 9 is $x^2 + y^2 = 81$.

5. False, because $(x - 2)^2 + (y - 3)^2 = 4$ has radius 2.

6. False, because $(x - 3)^2 + (y + 5)^2 = 9$ is a circle of radius 3 centered at $(3, -5)$

7. True, because the distance from $(-3, -1)$ to $(0, 0)$ is the radius.

8. False, the center is $(3, 4)$.

9. True, because there is only an x^2 term and no x-term.

10. False, because if we complete the square for x then the right side will no longer be 4.

11.3 EXERCISES

1. A circle is the set of all points in a plane that lie at a fixed distance from a fixed point.

2. The equation $(x - h)^2 + (y - k)^2 = r^2$ is the standard equation of a circle with center (h, k) and radius r (for $r > 0$).

3. Use $h = 0$, $k = 3$, and $r = 5$ in the standard equation $(x - h)^2 + (y - k)^2 = r^2$ to get the equation $x^2 + (y - 3)^2 = 25$.

4. Use $h = 2$, $k = 0$, and $r = 3$ in the standard equation $(x - h)^2 + (y - k)^2 = r^2$ to get the equation $(x - 2)^2 + y^2 = 9$.

5. Use $h = 1$, $k = -2$, and $r = 9$ in the standard equation $(x - h)^2 + (y - k)^2 = r^2$ to get the equation $(x - 1)^2 + (y + 2)^2 = 81$.

6. Use $h = -3$, $k = 5$, and $r = 4$ in the standard equation $(x - h)^2 + (y - k)^2 = r^2$ to get the equation $(x + 3)^2 + (y - 5)^2 = 16$.

7. Use $h = 0$, $k = 0$, and $r = \sqrt{3}$ in the standard equation $(x - h)^2 + (y - k)^2 = r^2$ to get the equation $x^2 + y^2 = 3$.

8. Use $h = 0$, $k = 0$, and $r = \sqrt{2}$ in the standard equation $(x - h)^2 + (y - k)^2 = r^2$ to get the equation $x^2 + y^2 = 2$.

9. Use $h = -6$, $k = -3$, and $r = 1/2$ in the standard equation $(x - h)^2 + (y - k)^2 = r^2$ to get the equation $(x + 6)^2 + (y + 3)^2 = \frac{1}{4}$.

10. Use $h = -3$, $k = -5$, and $r = 1/4$ in the standard equation $(x - h)^2 + (y - k)^2 = r^2$ to get the equation $(x + 3)^2 + (y + 5)^2 = \frac{1}{16}$.

11. Use $h = 1/2$, $k = 1/3$, and $r = 0.1$ in the standard equation $(x - h)^2 + (y - k)^2 = r^2$ to get the equation $(x - \frac{1}{2})^2 + (y - \frac{1}{3})^2 = 0.01$.

12. Use $h = -1/2$, $k = 3$, and $r = 0.2$ in the standard equation $(x - h)^2 + (y - k)^2 = r^2$ to get the equation $(x + \frac{1}{2})^2 + (y - 3)^2 = 0.04$.

13. Compare $(x - 3)^2 + (y - 5)^2 = 2$ with $(x - h)^2 + (y - k)^2 = r^2$ *(where the center is (h, k) and radius is r)*, to get a center at $(3, 5)$ and radius $\sqrt{2}$.

14. Compare $(x + 3)^2 + (y - 7)^2 = 6$ with $(x - h)^2 + (y - k)^2 = r^2$ *(where the center is (h, k) and radius is r)*, to get a center at $(-3, 7)$ and radius $\sqrt{6}$.

15. Compare $x^2 + (y - \frac{1}{2})^2 = \frac{1}{2}$ with $(x - h)^2 + (y - k)^2 = r^2$ *(where the center is (h, k) and radius is r)*, to get a center at $(0, \frac{1}{2})$ and radius $\frac{\sqrt{2}}{2}$.

16. Divide each side of $5x^2 + 5y^2 = 5$ by 5 to get $x^2 + y^2 = 1$. Compare $x^2 + y^2 = 1$ with $(x - h)^2 + (y - k)^2 = r^2$ *(where the center is*

(h, k) and radius is r), to get a center at $(0, 0)$ and radius 1.

17. Divide each side by 4 to get $x^2 + y^2 = \frac{9}{4}$. Compare with $(x - h)^2 + (y - k)^2 = r^2$ *(where the center is (h, k) and radius is r)*, to get a center at $(0, 0)$ and radius $\sqrt{\frac{9}{4}} = \frac{3}{2}$.

18. Divide each side of $9x^2 + 9y^2 = 49$ by 9 to get $x^2 + y^2 = \frac{49}{9}$. Compare with $(x - h)^2 + (y - k)^2 = r^2$ *(where the center is (h, k) and radius is r)*, to get a center at $(0, 0)$ and radius $\sqrt{\frac{49}{9}} = \frac{7}{3}$.

19. Rewrite the equation as $(x - 2)^2 + y^2 = 3$. Compare with $(x - h)^2 + (y - k)^2 = r^2$ *(where the center is (h, k) and radius is r)*, to get a center at $(2, 0)$ and radius $\sqrt{3}$.

20. Rewrite the equation as $x^2 + (y + 1)^2 = 9$. Compare with $(x - h)^2 + (y - k)^2 = r^2$ *(where the center is (h, k) and radius is r)*, to get a center at $(0, -1)$ and radius 3.

21. The graph of $x^2 + y^2 = 9$ is a circle with radius 3, centered at $(0, 0)$.

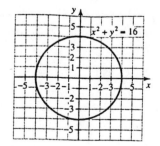

22. The graph of $x^2 + y^2 = 16$ is a circle with radius 4, centered at $(0, 0)$.

23. The graph of $x^2 + (y-3)^2 = 9$ is a circle with radius 3, centered at $(0, 3)$.

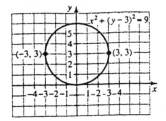

24. The graph of $(x-4)^2 + y^2 = 16$ is a circle with radius 4, centered at $(4, 0)$.

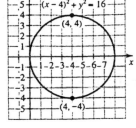

25. The graph of $(x+1)^2 + (y-1)^2 = 2$ is a circle with radius $\sqrt{2}$, centered at $(-1, 1)$.

26. The graph of $(x-2)^2 + (y+2)^2 = 8$ is a circle with radius $\sqrt{8} = 2\sqrt{2}$, centered at $(2, -2)$.

27. The graph of $(x-4)^2 + (y+3)^2 = 16$ is a circle of radius 4, centered at $(4, -3)$.

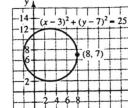

28. The graph of $(x-3)^2 + (y-7)^2 = 25$ is a circle with radius 5, centered at $(3, 7)$.

29. The graph of $(x-\frac{1}{2})^2 + (y+\frac{1}{2})^2 = \frac{1}{4}$ is a circle of radius $1/2$, centered at $(1/2, -1/2)$.

397

$$(x-5)^2 + (y-4)^2 = 9$$

This circle has radius 3 and center (5, 4).

36.
$$x^2 + y^2 = 8x - 10y$$
$$x^2 - 8x + \quad y^2 + 10y \quad = 0$$
$$x^2 - 8x + 16 + y^2 + 10y + 25 = 0 + 16 + 25$$
$$(x-4)^2 + (y+5)^2 = 41$$

This circle has radius $\sqrt{41}$ and center (4, −5).

37.
$$x^2 - x + \quad y^2 + y \quad = 0$$
$$x^2 - x + \tfrac{1}{4} + y^2 + y + \tfrac{1}{4} = \tfrac{1}{4} + \tfrac{1}{4}$$

$$(x-\tfrac{1}{2})^2 + (y+\tfrac{1}{2})^2 = \tfrac{1}{2}$$

Center is (1/2, −1/2) and radius is $\sqrt{\tfrac{1}{2}} = \tfrac{\sqrt{2}}{2}$.

38.
$$x^2 - 3x + \quad y^2 = 0$$
$$x^2 - 3x + \tfrac{9}{4} + y^2 = 0 + \tfrac{9}{4}$$
$$(x-\tfrac{3}{2})^2 + y^2 = \tfrac{9}{4}$$

This circle has radius 3/2 and center (3/2, 0).

39.
$$x^2 - 3x + \quad y^2 - y \quad = 1$$
$$x^2 - 3x + \tfrac{9}{4} + y^2 - y + \tfrac{1}{4} = 1 + \tfrac{9}{4} + \tfrac{1}{4}$$

$$(x-\tfrac{3}{2})^2 + (y-\tfrac{1}{2})^2 = \tfrac{7}{2}$$

Center is (3/2, 1/2) and radius $\sqrt{\tfrac{7}{2}} = \tfrac{\sqrt{14}}{2}$.

40.
$$x^2 - 5x + \quad y^2 + 3y \quad = 2$$
$$x^2 - 5x + \tfrac{25}{4} + y^2 + 3y + \tfrac{9}{4} = 2 + \tfrac{25}{4} + \tfrac{9}{4}$$
$$(x-\tfrac{5}{2})^2 + (y+\tfrac{3}{2})^2 = \tfrac{21}{2}$$

Center is (5/2, −3/2) and radius is $\sqrt{\tfrac{21}{2}} = \tfrac{\sqrt{42}}{2}$.

41.
$$x^2 - \tfrac{2}{3}x + \quad y^2 + \tfrac{3}{2}y \quad = 0$$

$$x^2 - \tfrac{2}{3}x + \tfrac{1}{9} + y^2 + \tfrac{3}{2}y + \tfrac{9}{16} = 0 + \tfrac{1}{9} + \tfrac{9}{16}$$

$$(x-\tfrac{1}{3})^2 + (y+\tfrac{3}{4})^2 = \tfrac{97}{144}$$

Center is (1/3, −3/4) and radius is $\sqrt{\tfrac{97}{144}} = \tfrac{\sqrt{97}}{12}$.

42.
$$x^2 + \tfrac{1}{3}x + \quad y^2 - \tfrac{2}{3}y \quad = \tfrac{1}{9}$$

$$x^2 + \tfrac{1}{3}x + \tfrac{1}{36} + y^2 - \tfrac{2}{3}y + \tfrac{1}{9} = \tfrac{1}{9} + \tfrac{1}{36} + \tfrac{1}{9}$$

$$(x+\tfrac{1}{6})^2 + (y-\tfrac{1}{3})^2 = \tfrac{1}{4}$$

Circle has center $(-\tfrac{1}{6}, \tfrac{1}{3})$ and radius $\tfrac{1}{2}$.

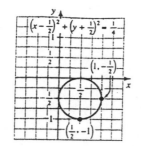

30. The graph of $(x + \tfrac{1}{3})^2 + y^2 = \tfrac{1}{9}$ is a circle with radius 1/3, centered at (−1/3, 0).

31.
$$x^2 + 4x + \quad y^2 + 6y \quad = 0$$
$$x^2 + 4x + 4 + y^2 + 6y + 9 = 0 + 4 + 9$$
$$(x+2)^2 + (y+3)^2 = 13$$

This circle has radius $\sqrt{13}$ and center (−2, −3).

32.
$$x^2 - 10x + \quad y^2 + 8y \quad = 0$$
$$x^2 - 10x + 25 + y^2 + 8y + 16 = 0 + 25 + 16$$
$$(x-5)^2 + (y+4)^2 = 41$$

This circle has radius $\sqrt{41}$ and center (5, −4).

33.
$$x^2 - 2x + \quad y^2 - 4y - 3 = 0$$
$$x^2 - 2x + 1 + y^2 - 4y + 4 = 3 + 1 + 4$$
$$(x-1)^2 + (y-2)^2 = 8$$

This circle has radius $\sqrt{8} = 2\sqrt{2}$ and center (1, 2).

34.
$$x^2 - 6x + \quad y^2 - 2y + 9 = 0$$
$$x^2 - 6x + 9 + y^2 - 2y + 1 = -9 + 9 + 1$$
$$(x-3)^2 + (y-1)^2 = 1$$

This circle has radius 1 and center (3, 1).

35.
$$x^2 - 10x + y^2 - 8y = -32$$
$$x^2 - 10x + 25 + y^2 - 8y + 16$$
$$= -32 + 25 + 16$$

398

43. The graph of $x^2 + y^2 = 10$ is a circle centered at $(0, 0)$ with radius $\sqrt{10}$. The graph of $y = 3x$ is a straight line through $(0, 0)$ with slope 3. Use substitution to eliminate y.
$$x^2 + (3x)^2 = 10$$
$$10x^2 = 10$$
$$x^2 = 1$$
$$x = 1 \quad \text{or} \quad x = -1$$
$$y = 3 \quad \text{or} \quad y = -3 \text{ Since } y = 3x$$
The solution set is $\{(1, 3), (-1, -3)\}$.

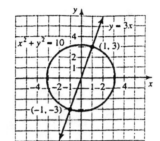

44. The graph of $x^2 + y^2 = 4$ is a circle of radius 2 centered at the origin. The graph of $y = x - 2$ is a line with y-intercept $(0, -2)$ and slope 1.

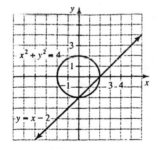

Use substitution to solve the system.
$$x^2 + (x - 2)^2 = 4$$
$$x^2 + x^2 - 4x + 4 = 4$$
$$2x^2 - 4x = 0$$
$$2x(x - 2) = 0$$
$$2x = 0 \quad \text{or} \quad x - 2 = 0$$
$$x = 0 \quad \text{or} \quad x = 2$$

If $x = 0$, then $y = 0 - 2 = -2$. If $x = 2$, then $y = 2 - 2 = 0$. The solution set to the system is $\{(0, -2), (2, 0)\}$.

45. The graph of $x^2 + y^2 = 9$ is a circle centered at $(0, 0)$ with radius 3. The graph of $y = x^2 - 3$ is a parabola opening upward.

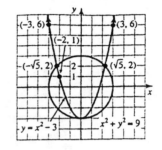

Use $x^2 = y + 3$ to eliminate x.
$$y + 3 + y^2 = 9$$
$$y^2 + y - 6 = 0$$
$$(y + 3)(y - 2) = 0$$
$$y = -3 \quad \text{or} \quad y = 2$$
If $y = -3$, then $x^2 = -3 + 3 = 0$ or $x = 0$. If $y = 2$, then $x^2 = 2 + 3 = 5$ or $x = \pm\sqrt{5}$. The solution set is $\{(0, -3), (\sqrt{5}, 2), (-\sqrt{5}, 2)\}$.

46. The graph of $x^2 + y^2 = 4$ is a circle of radius 2 centered at the origin. The graph of $y = x^2 - 2$ is a parabola opening upward.

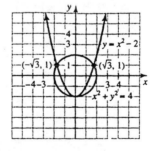

Substitute $x^2 = y + 2$ into $x^2 + y^2 = 4$.
$$y + 2 + y^2 = 4$$
$$y^2 + y - 2 = 0$$
$$(y + 2)(y - 1) = 0$$
$$y + 2 = 0 \quad \text{or} \quad y - 1 = 0$$

$y = -2$ or $y = 1$

If $y = -2$, then $x^2 = -2 + 2 = 0$, or $x = 0$.
If $y = 1$, then $x^2 = 1 + 2 = 3$, or $x = \pm\sqrt{3}$.
The solution set is
$\{(0, -2), (-\sqrt{3}, 1), (\sqrt{3}, 1)\}$

47. The graph of $(x - 2)^2 + (y + 3)^2 = 4$ is a circle centered at $(2, -3)$ with radius 2. The graph of $y = x - 3$ is a line through $(0, -3)$ with slope 1.

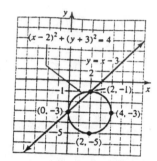

Use substitution to eliminate y.
$$(x - 2)^2 + (x - 3 + 3)^2 = 4$$
$$x^2 - 4x + 4 + x^2 = 4$$
$$2x^2 - 4x = 0$$
$$x^2 - 2x = 0$$
$$x(x - 2) = 0$$
$$x = 0 \quad \text{or} \quad x = 2$$
Since $y = x - 3$
$$y = -3 \qquad\qquad y = -1$$
The solution set is $\{(0, -3), (2, -1)\}$.

48. The graph of $(x + 1)^2 + (y - 4)^2 = 17$ is a circle centered at $(-1, 4)$ with radius $\sqrt{17}$.
The graph of $y = x + 2$ is a line with y-intercept $(0, 2)$ and slope 1.

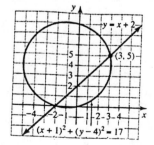

Use substitution to eliminate y.
$$(x + 1)^2 + (x + 2 - 4)^2 = 17$$
$$(x + 1)^2 + (x - 2)^2 = 17$$
$$x^2 + 2x + 1 + x^2 - 4x + 4 = 17$$
$$2x^2 - 2x - 12 = 0$$
$$x^2 - x - 6 = 0$$
$$(x - 3)(x + 2) = 0$$
$$x - 3 = 0 \quad \text{or} \quad x + 2 = 0$$
$$x = 3 \quad \text{or} \qquad x = -2$$
If $x = 3$, then $y = 3 + 2 = 5$. If $x = -2$, then $y = -2 + 2 = 0$. Solution set is $\{(3, 5), (-2, 0)\}$.

49. To find the y-intercepts, use $x = 0$ in the equation of the circle.
$$(0 - 1)^2 + (y - 2)^2 = 4$$
$$1 + y^2 - 4y + 4 = 4$$
$$y^2 - 4y + 1 = 0$$

$$y = \frac{4 \pm \sqrt{16 - 4(1)(1)}}{2(1)} = \frac{4 \pm 2\sqrt{3}}{2}$$
$$= 2 \pm \sqrt{3}$$
The y-intercepts are $(0, 2 + \sqrt{3})$ and $(0, 2 - \sqrt{3})$.

50. To find the x-intercepts, use $y = 0$ in the equation of the circle.
$$x^2 + (0 - 3)^2 = 25$$
$$x^2 + 9 = 25$$
$$x^2 = 16$$
$$x = \pm 4$$
The x-intercepts are $(-4, 0)$ and $(4, 0)$.

51. The radius is the distance from $(2, -5)$ to $(0, 0)$.
$$r = \sqrt{(2 - 0)^2 + (-5 - 0)^2} = \sqrt{4 + 25}$$
$$= \sqrt{29}$$

52. The radius is the distance from $(-2, 3)$ to $(3, -1)$.
$$r = \sqrt{(-2 - 3)^2 + (3 - (-1))^2} = \sqrt{25 + 16}$$
$$= \sqrt{41}$$

53. The radius is the distance from $(2, 3)$ to $(-2, -1)$.
$$r = \sqrt{(-2 - 2)^2 + (-1 - 3)^2} = \sqrt{16 + 16}$$
$$= \sqrt{32}$$
The equation of a circle centered at $(2, 3)$ with radius $\sqrt{32}$ is $(x - 2)^2 + (y - 3)^2 = 32$.

54. The radius is the distance from $(3, 4)$ to $(0, 0)$.

$$r = \sqrt{(3-0)^2 + (4-0)^2} = \sqrt{9+16} = \sqrt{25}$$
$$= 5$$

The equation of a circle centered at (3, 4) with radius 5 is $(x-3)^2 + (y-4)^2 = 25$.

55. Substitute $y^2 = 9 - x^2$ into $(x-5)^2 + y^2 = 9$ to eliminate y.

$$(x-5)^2 + 9 - x^2 = 9$$
$$x^2 - 10x + 25 + 9 - x^2 = 9$$
$$-10x = -25$$
$$x = 5/2$$

Use $x = 5/2$ in $y^2 = 9 - x^2$ to find y.

$$y^2 = 9 - \left(\tfrac{5}{2}\right)^2 = \tfrac{11}{4}$$
$$y = \pm\sqrt{\tfrac{11}{4}} = \pm\tfrac{\sqrt{11}}{2}$$

The circles intersect at $\left(\tfrac{5}{2}, -\tfrac{\sqrt{11}}{2}\right)$ and $\left(\tfrac{5}{2}, \tfrac{\sqrt{11}}{2}\right)$.

56. The distance between (2, −3) and (6, 7) is
$$d = \sqrt{(2-6)^2 + (-3-7)^2} = \sqrt{16+100}$$
$$= \sqrt{116}.$$

Since $\sqrt{116}$ is smaller than 12, the donkey can reach the turnips.

57. From the equation of the bore we see that the radius is $\sqrt{83.72}$. The volume is given by $V = \pi r^2 h = \pi \cdot 83.72 \cdot 2874 = 755{,}903 \text{ mm}^3$.

58. The new cross sectional area is $0.943 \cdot \pi \cdot 83.72 = 248.02 \text{ mm}^2$. Solve $\pi R^2 = 248.0223$ to find that the new radius is $R = 8.89$ mm. So the equation of the bore is $x^2 + y^2 = 8.885^2$, or $x^2 + y^2 = 78.95$. The volume of air is the cross sectional area times the length.

$248.0223 \text{ mm}^2 \cdot 0.943 \cdot 2874 \text{ mm} = 672{,}186$ mm^3.

59. Since both x^2 and y^2 are nonnegative for real values of x and y, the only way their sum could be zero is to choose both x and y equal to zero. So the graph consists of (0, 0) only.

60. The equation $x^2 - y^2 = 0$ is equivalent to $(x-y)(x+y) = 0$.

$$x^2 - y^2 = 0$$
$$(x-y)(x+y) = 0$$
$$x - y = 0 \quad \text{or} \quad x + y = 0$$
$$y = x \quad \text{or} \quad y = -x$$

The graph of $x^2 - y^2 = 0$ consists of two lines. The line $y = x$ together with the line $y = -x$.

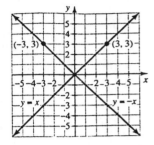

61. If we square both sides of $y = \sqrt{1-x^2}$ we get $x^2 + y^2 = 1$, which is a circle with center (0, 0) and radius 1. In the equation $y = \sqrt{1-x^2}$, y must be nonnegative. So the graph of $y = \sqrt{1-x^2}$ is the top half of the graph of $x^2 + y^2 = 1$.

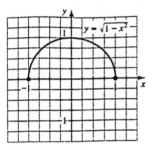

62. If we square both sides of $y = -\sqrt{1-x^2}$ we get $x^2 + y^2 = 1$, which is a circle centered at (0, 0) with radius 1. In $y = -\sqrt{1-x^2}$, y must be nonpositive. So the graph of $y = -\sqrt{1-x^2}$ is the bottom half of the graph of $x^2 + y^2 = 1$.

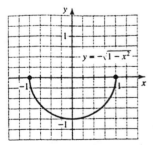

63. B and D can be any real numbers, but A must equal C. So that the radius is positive, we must also have

$$\frac{E}{A} + \left(\frac{B}{2A}\right)^2 + \left(\frac{D}{2A}\right)^2 > 0, \text{ or}$$
$$4AE + B^2 + D^2 > 0.$$

64. If the distance from A is 2, then the ship is somewhere on a circle of radius 2 centered at the origin. The ship is on the circle $x^2 + y^2 = 4$. If the distance from B is 5, then the ship is somewhere on a circle of radius 5 centered at $(0, 6)$. The ship is on the circle $x^2 + (y - 6)^2 = 25$. Since the ship is at a point that satisfies the equation for each circle, we need to find the intersection of the two circles. Substitute $x^2 = 4 - y^2$ into the other equation.

$$4 - y^2 + (y - 6)^2 = 25$$
$$4 - y^2 + y^2 - 12y + 36 = 25$$
$$-12y = -15$$
$$y = \frac{15}{12} = \frac{5}{4}$$

If $y = \frac{5}{4}$, then $x^2 = 4 - \frac{25}{16} = \frac{39}{16}$, or $x = \pm\frac{\sqrt{39}}{4}$. So the possible coordinates for the ship are $\left(-\frac{\sqrt{39}}{4}, \frac{5}{4}\right)$ and $\left(\frac{\sqrt{39}}{4}, \frac{5}{4}\right)$.

65. $y = \pm\sqrt{4 - x^2}$

66.
$$(y + 2)^2 = 1 - (x - 1)^2$$
$$y + 2 = \pm\sqrt{1 - (x - 1)^2}$$
$$y = -2 \pm\sqrt{1 - (x - 1)^2}$$

67. $y = \pm\sqrt{x}$

68.
$$(y + 2)^2 = x + 1$$
$$y + 2 = \pm\sqrt{x + 1}$$
$$y = -2 \pm\sqrt{x + 1}$$

69.
$$x = (y + 1)^2$$
$$y + 1 = \pm\sqrt{x}$$
$$y = -1 \pm\sqrt{x}$$

70.
$$x = (2y + 1)^2$$
$$2y + 1 = \pm\sqrt{x}$$
$$y = \frac{-1 \pm\sqrt{x}}{2}$$

11.4 WARM-UPS

1. False, the x-intercepts are $(-6, 0)$ and $(6, 0)$.
2. False, because both x^2 and y^2 must appear in the equation for an ellipse.

3. True, because if the foci coincide then every point on the ellipse will be a fixed distance from one fixed point.
4. True, because if we divide each side of the equation by 2, then it fits the standard equation for an ellipse.
5. True, because if we use $x = 0$ in the equation, we get $y = \pm\sqrt{3}$.
6. False, because both x^2 and y^2 must appear in the equation of a hyperbola.
7. False, because in this hyperbola there are no y-intercepts.
8. True, because it has y-intercepts at $(0, -3)$ and $(0, 3)$.
9. True, because if we divide each side of the equation by 4, then it fits the standard form for the equation of a hyperbola.
10. True, the asymptotes are the extended diagonals of the fundamental rectangle.

11.4 EXERCISES

1. An ellipse is the set of all points in a plane such that the sum of their distances from two fixed points is constant.
2. Attach a string to two thumb tacks and use a pencil to take up the slack as shown in the text.
3. The center of an ellipse is the point that is midway between the focii.
4. The equation of an ellipse centered at the origin is $\frac{x^2}{a^2} + \frac{y^2}{b^2} = 1$.
5. The equation of an ellipse centered at (h, k) is $\frac{(x - h)^2}{a^2} + \frac{(y - k)^2}{b^2} = 1$.

6. A hyperbola is the set of all points in a plane such that the difference of their distances from two fixed points is constant.

7. The asymptotes of a hyperbola are the extended diagonals of the fundamental rectangle.

8. The equation of a hyperbola centered at the origin and opening left and right is of the form $\frac{x^2}{a^2} - \frac{y^2}{b^2} = 1$.

9. The graph of $\frac{x^2}{9} + \frac{y^2}{4} = 1$ is an ellipse with x-intercepts $(-3, 0)$ and $(3, 0)$, and y-intercepts $(0, 2)$ and $(0, -2)$.

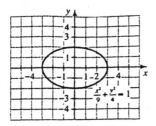

10. The graph of $\frac{x^2}{9} + \frac{y^2}{16} = 1$ is an ellipse with x-intercepts $(-3, 0)$ and $(3, 0)$, and y-intercepts $(0, 4)$ and $(0, -4)$.

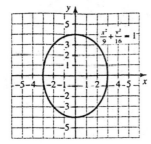

11. The graph of $\frac{x^2}{9} + y^2 = 1$ is an ellipse with x-intercepts $(-3, 0)$ and $(3, 0)$, and y-intercepts $(0, -1)$ and $(0, 1)$.

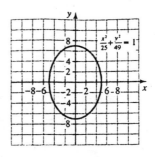

12. The graph of $x^2 + \frac{y^2}{4} = 1$ is an ellipse with x-intercepts $(-1, 0)$ and $(1, 0)$, and y-intercepts $(0, 2)$ and $(0, -2)$.

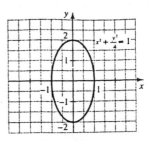

13. The graph of $\frac{x^2}{36} + \frac{y^2}{25} = 1$ is an ellipse with x-intercepts $(-6, 0)$ and $(6, 0)$, and y-intercepts $(0, -5)$ and $(0, 5)$.

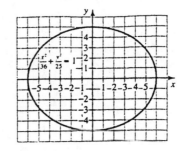

14. The graph of $\frac{x^2}{25} + \frac{y^2}{49} = 1$ is an ellipse with x-intercepts $(-5, 0)$ and $(5, 0)$, and y-intercepts $(0, 7)$ and $(0, -7)$.

403

15. The graph of $\frac{x^2}{24} + \frac{y^2}{5} = 1$ is an ellipse with x-intercepts $(-\sqrt{24}, 0)$ and $(\sqrt{24}, 0)$, and y-intercepts $(0, -\sqrt{5})$ and $(0, \sqrt{5})$.

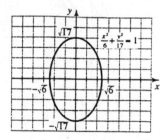

16. The graph of $\frac{x^2}{6} + \frac{y^2}{17} = 1$ is an ellipse with x-intercepts $(-\sqrt{6}, 0)$ and $(\sqrt{6}, 0)$, and y-intercepts $(0, \sqrt{17})$ and $(0, -\sqrt{17})$.

17. The graph $9x^2 + 16y^2 = 144$ is an ellipse with x-intercepts $(-4, 0)$ and $(4, 0)$, and y-intercepts $(0, -3)$ and $(0, 3)$.

18. The graph $9x^2 + 25y^2 = 225$ is an ellipse with x-intercepts $(-5, 0)$ and $(5, 0)$, and y-intercepts $(0, -3)$ and $(0, 3)$.

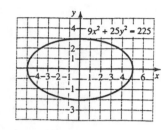

19. The graph of $25x^2 + y^2 = 25$ is an ellipse with x-intercepts $(-1, 0)$ and $(1, 0)$, and y-intercepts $(0, -5)$ and $(0, 5)$.

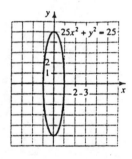

20. The graph $x^2 + 16y^2 = 16$ is an ellipse with x-intercepts $(-4, 0)$ and $(4, 0)$, and y-intercepts $(0, -1)$ and $(0, 1)$.

21. The graph of $4x^2 + 9y^2 = 1$ is an ellipse with x-intercepts $(1/2, 0)$ and $(-1/2, 0)$, and y-intercepts $(0, 1/3)$ and $(0, -1/3)$.

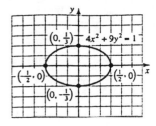

24. The graph of $\dfrac{(x+5)^2}{49} + \dfrac{(y-2)^2}{25} = 1$ is an ellipse centered at $(-5, 2)$. The 49 in the denominator indicates that the ellipse passes through points that are 7 units to the right and 7 units to the left of the center: $(-12, 2)$ and $(2, 2)$. The 25 in the denominator indicates that the ellipse passes through points that are 5 units above and 5 units below the center: $(-5, 7)$ and $(-5, -3)$.

22. The graph $25x^2 + 16y^2 = 1$ is an ellipse with x-intercepts $(-\frac{1}{5}, 0)$ and $(\frac{1}{5}, 0)$, and y-intercepts $(0, -\frac{1}{4})$ and $(0, \frac{1}{4})$.

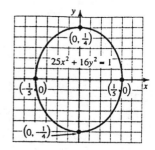

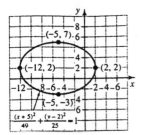

23. The graph of $\dfrac{(x-3)^2}{4} + \dfrac{(y-1)^2}{9} = 1$ is an ellipse centered at $(3, 1)$. The 4 in the denominator indicates that the ellipse passes through points that are 2 units to the right and 2 units to the left of the center: $(5, 1)$ and $(1, 1)$. The 9 in the denominator indicates that the ellipse passes through points that are 3 units above and 3 units below the center: $(3, 4)$ and $(3, -2)$.

25. The graph of $\dfrac{(x+1)^2}{16} + \dfrac{(y-2)^2}{25} = 1$ is an ellipse centered at $(-1, 2)$. The 16 in the denominator indicates that the ellipse passes through points that are 4 units to the right and 4 units to the left of the center: $(3, 2)$ and $(-5, 2)$. The 25 in the denominator indicates that the ellipse passes through points that are 5 units above and 5 units below the center: $(-1, 7)$ and $(-1, -3)$.

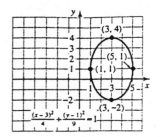

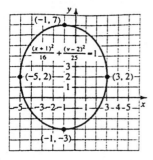

26. The graph of $\dfrac{(x-3)^2}{36} + \dfrac{(y+4)^2}{64} = 1$ is an ellipse centered at $(3, -4)$. The 36 in the denominator indicates that the ellipse passes through points that are 6 units to the right and 6 units to the left of the center: $(-3, -4)$ and $(9, -4)$. The 64 in the denominator indicates that the ellipse passes through points that are 8 units above and 8 units below the center: $(3, 4)$ and $(3, -12)$.

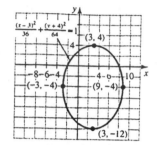

27. The graph of $(x-2)^2 + \dfrac{(y+1)^2}{36} = 1$ is an ellipse centered at $(2, -1)$. The 1 in the denominator indicates that the ellipse passes through points that are 1 unit to the right and 1 unit to the left of the center: $(3, -1)$ and $(1, -1)$. The 36 in the denominator indicates that the ellipse passes through points that are 6 units above and 6 units below the center: $(2, 5)$ and $(2, -7)$.

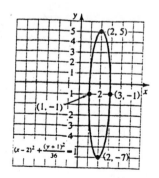

28. The graph of $\dfrac{(x+3)^2}{9} + \dfrac{(y+1)^2}{1} = 1$ is an ellipse centered at $(-3, -1)$. The 9 in the denominator indicates that the ellipse passes through points that are 3 units to the right and 3 units to the left of the center: $(-6, -1)$ and $(0, -1)$. The 1 in the denominator indicates that the ellipse passes through points that are 1 unit above and 1 unit below the center: $(-3, 0)$ and $(-3, -2)$.

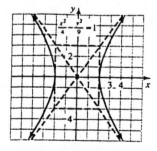

29. The graph of $\dfrac{x^2}{4} - \dfrac{y^2}{9} = 1$ is a hyperbola centered at $(0, 0)$ with x-intercepts at $(-2, 0)$ and $(2, 0)$. There are no y-intercepts. Use 9 to determine the size of the fundamental rectangle. The fundamental rectangle passes through $(0, 3)$ and $(0, -3)$. extend the diagonals of the rectangle to determine the asymptotes. The hyperbola opens to the left and right. The equations of the asymptotes are $y = \pm \frac{3}{2}x$.

30. The graph of $\dfrac{x^2}{16} - \dfrac{y^2}{9} = 1$ is a hyperbola centered at $(0, 0)$ with x-intercepts at $(-4, 0)$ and $(4, 0)$. There are no y-intercepts. Use 9 to determine the size of the fundamental rectangle. The fundamental rectangle passes through $(0, 3)$

406

and (0, −3). extend the diagonals of the rectangle to determine the asymptotes. The hyperbola opens to the left and right. The equations of the asymptotes are $y = \pm \frac{3}{4}x$.

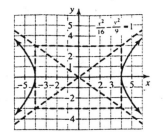

31. The graph of $\frac{y^2}{4} - \frac{x^2}{25} = 1$ is a hyperbola with y-intercepts (0, −2) and (0, 2). The fundamental rectangle passes through the y-intercepts, (−5, 0), and (5, 0). The extended diagonals determine the asymptotes.

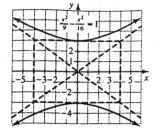

33. The graph of $\frac{x^2}{25} - y^2 = 1$ is a hyperbola with x-intercepts (−5, 0) and (5, 0). The fundamental rectangle passes through the intercepts, (0, −1), and (0, 1). The extended diagonals determine the asymptotes. The equations of the asymptotes are $y = \pm \frac{1}{5}x$.

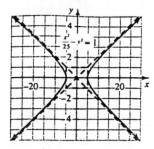

32. The graph of $\frac{y^2}{9} - \frac{x^2}{16} = 1$ is a hyperbola centered at (0, 0) with y-intercepts at (0, −3) and (0, 3). There are no x-intercepts. Use 16 to determine the size of the fundamental rectangle. The fundamental rectangle passes through (4, 0) and (−4, 0). extend the diagonals of the rectangle to determine the asymptotes. The hyperbola opens up and down. The equations of the asymptotes are $y = \pm \frac{3}{4}x$.

34. The graph of $\frac{x^2}{1} - \frac{y^2}{9} = 1$ is a hyperbola centered at (0, 0) with x-intercepts at (−1, 0) and (1, 0). There are no y-intercepts. Use 9 to determine the size of the fundamental rectangle. The fundamental rectangle passes through (0, 3) and (0, −3). extend the diagonals of the rectangle to determine the asymptotes. The hyperbola opens to the left and right. The equations of the asymptotes are $y = \pm 3x$.

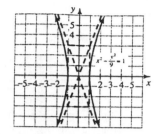

37. Divide each side of $9x^2 - 16y^2 = 144$ by 144 to get $\frac{x^2}{16} - \frac{y^2}{9} = 1$. The graph is a hyperbola with x-intercepts at $(-4, 0)$ and $(4, 0)$. The fundamental rectangle passes through the y-intercepts, $(0, -3)$, and $(0, 3)$. The extended diagonals determine the asymptotes. The equations of the asymptotes are $y = \pm \frac{3}{4}x$.

35. The graph of $x^2 - \frac{y^2}{25} = 1$ is a hyperbola with x-intercepts $(-1, 0)$ and $(1, 0)$. Plot $(0, 5)$ and $(0, -5)$ for the fundamental rectangle and extend the diagonals. The equations of the asymptotes are $y = \pm 5x$.

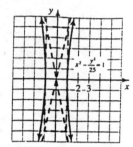

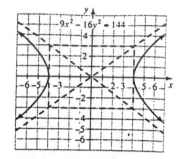

38. Divide each side of $9x^2 - 25y^2 = 225$ by 225 to get $\frac{x^2}{25} - \frac{y^2}{9} = 1$. The graph is a hyperbola with x-intercepts at $(-5, 0)$ and $(5, 0)$. The fundamental rectangle passes through the y-intercepts, $(0, 3)$, and $(0, -3)$. The extended diagonals determine the asymptotes, $y = \pm \frac{3}{5}x$.

36. The graph of $\frac{x^2}{9} - \frac{y^2}{1} = 1$ is a hyperbola centered at $(0, 0)$ with x-intercepts at $(-3, 0)$ and $(3, 0)$. There are no y-intercepts. Use 1 to determine the size of the fundamental rectangle. The fundamental rectangle passes through $(0, 1)$ and $(0, -1)$. extend the diagonals of the rectangle to determine the asymptotes. The hyperbola opens to the left and right. The equations of the asymptotes are $y = \pm \frac{1}{3}x$.

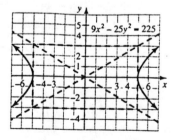

39. The graph of $x^2 - y^2 = 1$ is a hyperbola with x-intercepts $(-1, 0)$ and $(1, 0)$. The fundamental rectangle passes through the y-intercepts, $(0, -1)$, and $(0, 1)$. The extended diagonals determine the asymptotes, $y = \pm x$.

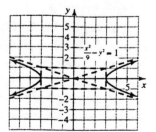

$$x^2 + 4x^2 = 8$$
$$5x^2 = 8$$
$$x^2 = \tfrac{8}{5}$$
$$x = \pm\sqrt{\tfrac{8}{5}} = \pm\tfrac{2\sqrt{10}}{5}$$

Use $x^2 = 8/5$ in the second equation.

$$\tfrac{8}{5} - \tfrac{y^2}{9} = 1$$
$$-\tfrac{y^2}{9} = -\tfrac{3}{5}$$
$$y^2 = \tfrac{27}{5}$$
$$y = \pm\sqrt{\tfrac{27}{5}} = \pm\tfrac{3\sqrt{15}}{5}$$

The graphs intersect at $\left(\tfrac{2\sqrt{10}}{5}, \tfrac{3\sqrt{15}}{5}\right)$, $\left(\tfrac{2\sqrt{10}}{5}, -\tfrac{3\sqrt{15}}{5}\right)$, $\left(-\tfrac{2\sqrt{10}}{5}, \tfrac{3\sqrt{15}}{5}\right)$, and $\left(-\tfrac{2\sqrt{10}}{5}, -\tfrac{3\sqrt{15}}{5}\right)$.

42. First graph the hyperbola and the ellipse.

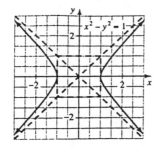

40. The graph of $y^2 - x^2 = 1$ is a hyperbola with y-intercepts $(0, -1)$ and $(0, 1)$. The fundamental rectangle passes through the x-intercepts, $(-1, 0)$, and $(1, 0)$. The extended diagonals determine the asymptotes, $y = \pm x$.

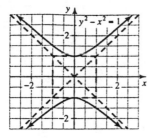

41. First graph the hyperbola and the ellipse.

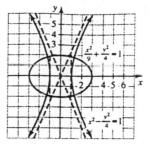

If we add the equations the variable y will be eliminated and we get the following equation.
$$\tfrac{x^2}{9} + x^2 = 2$$

Now multiply both sides by 9:
$$x^2 + 9x^2 = 18$$
$$10x^2 = 18$$
$$x^2 = \tfrac{9}{5}$$
$$x = \pm\sqrt{\tfrac{9}{5}} = \pm\tfrac{3\sqrt{5}}{5}$$

Use $x^2 = 9/5$ in the first equation.
$$\tfrac{9}{5} - \tfrac{y^2}{4} = 1$$
$$-\tfrac{y^2}{4} = -\tfrac{4}{5}$$
$$y^2 = \tfrac{16}{5}$$
$$y = \pm\sqrt{\tfrac{16}{5}} = \pm\tfrac{4\sqrt{5}}{5}$$

If we add the equations the variable y will be eliminated and we get the following equation.
$$\tfrac{x^2}{4} + x^2 = 2$$
Now multiply both sides by 4:

The graphs intersect at $\left(\frac{3\sqrt{5}}{5}, \frac{4\sqrt{5}}{5}\right)$, $\left(\frac{3\sqrt{5}}{5}, -\frac{4\sqrt{5}}{5}\right)$, $\left(-\frac{3\sqrt{5}}{5}, \frac{4\sqrt{5}}{5}\right)$, and $\left(-\frac{3\sqrt{5}}{5}, -\frac{4\sqrt{5}}{5}\right)$.

43. The graphs are an ellipse and a circle.

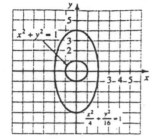

From the graph we can see that there are no points of intersection. If we eliminate y by substituting $y^2 = 1 - x^2$ into the first equation, we get the following equation.
$$\frac{x^2}{4} + \frac{1 - x^2}{16} = 1$$
Now multiply both sides by 16:
$$4x^2 + 1 - x^2 = 16$$
$$3x^2 = 15$$
$$x^2 = 5$$
From $y^2 = 1 - x^2$, we get $y^2 = -4$, which has no real solution. There are no points of intersection.

44. The graphs are an ellipse and a circle.

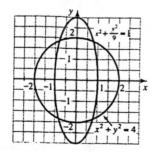

From the graph we can see that there are four points of intersection. If we eliminate y by

substituting $y^2 = 4 - x^2$ into the first equation, we get the following equation.
$$x^2 + \frac{4 - x^2}{9} = 1$$
Multiply both sides by 9:
$$9x^2 + 4 - x^2 = 9$$
$$8x^2 = 5$$
$$x^2 = \frac{5}{8}$$
$$x = \pm\sqrt{\frac{5}{8}} = \pm\frac{\sqrt{10}}{4}$$
From $y^2 = 4 - x^2$, we get $y^2 = 4 - \frac{5}{8} = \frac{27}{8}$, or $y = \pm\sqrt{\frac{27}{8}} = \pm\frac{3\sqrt{6}}{4}$. The solution set to the system is $\left\{\left(\frac{\sqrt{10}}{4}, \frac{3\sqrt{6}}{4}\right), \left(\frac{\sqrt{10}}{4}, -\frac{3\sqrt{6}}{4}\right), \left(-\frac{\sqrt{10}}{4}, \frac{3\sqrt{6}}{4}\right), \left(-\frac{\sqrt{10}}{4}, -\frac{3\sqrt{6}}{4}\right)\right\}$.

45. The graphs are a circle and a hyperbola.

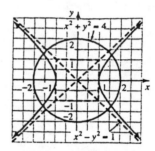

It appears that there are 4 points of intersection. To find them, add the equations to get the following equation.

$$2x^2 = 5$$
$$x^2 = \frac{5}{2}$$
$$x = \pm\sqrt{\frac{5}{2}} = \pm\frac{\sqrt{10}}{2}$$

From $y^2 = 4 - x^2$, we get $y^2 = 4 - \frac{5}{2} = \frac{3}{2}$, or $y = \pm\sqrt{\frac{3}{2}} = \pm\frac{\sqrt{6}}{2}$.

The graphs intersect at $\left(\frac{\sqrt{10}}{2}, \frac{\sqrt{6}}{2}\right)$, $\left(\frac{\sqrt{10}}{2}, -\frac{\sqrt{6}}{2}\right)$, $\left(-\frac{\sqrt{10}}{2}, \frac{\sqrt{6}}{2}\right)$, and $\left(-\frac{\sqrt{10}}{2}, -\frac{\sqrt{6}}{2}\right)$.

46. The graphs are a circle and a hyperbola.

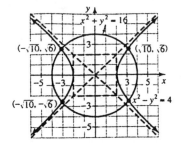

It appears that there are 4 points of intersection. To find them, add the equations to get the following equation.

$$2x^2 = 20$$
$$x^2 = 10$$
$$x = \pm\sqrt{10}$$

From $y^2 = 16 - x^2$, we get $y^2 = 16 - 10 = 6$, or $y = \pm\sqrt{6}$. The graphs intersect at $\left(\sqrt{10}, \sqrt{6}\right)$, $\left(\sqrt{10}, -\sqrt{6}\right)$, $\left(-\sqrt{10}, \sqrt{6}\right)$, and $\left(-\sqrt{10}, -\sqrt{6}\right)$.

47. The graphs are an ellipse and a circle.

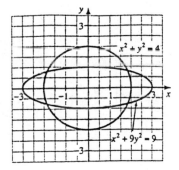

The graphs appear to intersect at 4 points. To find the points, substitute $y^2 = 4 - x^2$ into the first equation.

$$x^2 + 9(4 - x^2) = 9$$
$$-8x^2 + 36 = 9$$
$$-8x^2 = -27$$
$$x^2 = \frac{27}{8}$$
$$x = \pm\sqrt{\frac{27}{8}} = \pm\frac{3\sqrt{6}}{4}$$

Use $x^2 = 27/8$ in $y^2 = 4 - x^2$.

$$y^2 = 4 - \frac{27}{8} = \frac{5}{8}$$
$$y = \pm\sqrt{\frac{5}{8}} = \pm\frac{\sqrt{10}}{4}$$

The graphs intersect at $\left(\frac{3\sqrt{6}}{4}, \frac{\sqrt{10}}{4}\right)$, $\left(\frac{3\sqrt{6}}{4}, -\frac{\sqrt{10}}{4}\right)$, $\left(-\frac{3\sqrt{6}}{4}, \frac{\sqrt{10}}{4}\right)$, and $\left(-\frac{3\sqrt{6}}{4}, -\frac{\sqrt{10}}{4}\right)$.

48. The graphs are an ellipse and a circle.

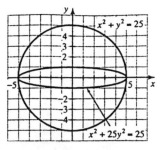

The graphs appear to intersect at 2 points. To find the points, substitute $y^2 = 25 - x^2$ into the second equation.

$$x^2 + 25(25 - x^2) = 25$$
$$-24x^2 + 625 = 25$$
$$-24x^2 = -600$$
$$x^2 = 25$$
$$x = \pm 5$$

Use $x^2 = 25$ in $y^2 = 25 - x^2$ to get $y^2 = 25 - 25 = 0$, or $y = 0$. The solution set to the system is $\{(5, 0), (-5, 0)\}$.

49. Graph the parabola and the ellipse.

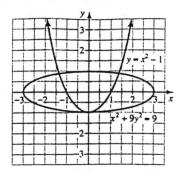

411

The graphs appear to intersect at 3 points. To find them, substitute $x^2 = y + 1$ into the first equation.

$$y + 1 + 9y^2 = 9$$
$$9y^2 + y - 8 = 0$$
$$(9y - 8)(y + 1) = 0$$
$$y = \tfrac{8}{9} \quad \text{or} \quad y = -1$$

If $y = -1$, the $x^2 = -1 + 1 = 0$ or $x = 0$. If $y = 8/9$, then

$$x^2 = \tfrac{8}{9} + 1 = \tfrac{17}{9} \quad \text{or} \quad x = \pm \tfrac{\sqrt{17}}{3}.$$

The three points of intersection are $\left(\tfrac{\sqrt{17}}{3}, \tfrac{8}{9} \right)$, $\left(-\tfrac{\sqrt{17}}{3}, \tfrac{8}{9} \right)$, and $(0, -1)$.

50. Graph the parabola and the ellipse.

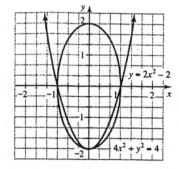

The graphs appear to intersect at 3 points. Substitute $x^2 = \tfrac{1}{2}y + 1$ into the first equation.

$$4\left(\tfrac{1}{2}y + 1 \right) + y^2 = 4$$
$$y^2 + 2y = 0$$
$$y(y + 2) = 0$$
$$y = 0 \text{ or } y = -2$$

If $y = 0$, then $x^2 = \tfrac{1}{2}(0) + 1$, or $x^2 = 1$, or $x = \pm 1$. If $y = -2$, then $x^2 = \tfrac{1}{2}(-2) + 1 = 0$, or $x = 0$. The solution set to the system is $\{(-1, 0), (1, 0), (0, -2)\}$.

51. Graph the hyperbola and the line.

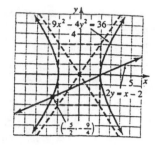

To find the points of intersection, substitute $x = 2y + 2$ into the first equation.

$$9(2y + 2)^2 - 4y^2 = 36$$
$$9(4y^2 + 8y + 4) - 4y^2 = 36$$
$$36y^2 + 72y + 36 - 4y^2 = 36$$
$$32y^2 + 72y = 0$$
$$4y^2 + 9y = 0$$
$$y(4y + 9) = 0$$
$$y = 0 \quad \text{or} \quad y = -9/4$$

If $y = 0$, then $x = 2(0) + 2 = 2$. If $y = -9/4$, then $x = 2(-9/4) + 2 = -5/2$. The two points of intersection are $(2, 0)$ and $(-5/2, -9/4)$.

52. Graph the hyperbola and the line.

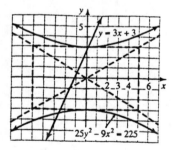

Substitute $y = 3x + 3$ into the first equation.

$$25(3x + 3)^2 - 9x^2 = 225$$
$$25(9x^2 + 18x + 9) - 9x^2 = 225$$
$$225x^2 + 450x + 225 - 9x^2 = 225$$
$$216x^2 + 450x = 0$$
$$x(216x + 450) = 0$$
$$x = 0 \text{ or } 216x + 450 = 0$$
$$x = 0 \quad \text{or} \qquad x = -\tfrac{25}{12}$$

If $x = 0$, then $y = 3(0) + 3 = 3$. If $x = -\frac{25}{12}$, then $y = 3\left(-\frac{25}{12}\right) + 3 = -\frac{13}{4}$. The solution set to the system is $\left\{(0, 3), \left(-\frac{25}{12}, -\frac{13}{4}\right)\right\}$.

53. a) From the graph it appears that the boat is approximately at (2.5, 1.5)

b) Substitute $x^2 = 1 + 3y^2$ into $4y^2 - x^2 = 1$.
$$4y^2 - (1 + 3y^2) = 1$$
$$y^2 = 2$$
$$y = \pm\sqrt{2}$$
$$x^2 = 1 + 3(\pm\sqrt{2})^2 = 1 \pm 3(2) = 1 \pm 6$$
$$= 7 \text{ or } -5$$
If $x^2 = 7$, then $x = \pm\sqrt{7}$. If $x^2 = -5$, there is no real solution. Since the boat is in the first quadrant, the boat is at $(\sqrt{7}, \sqrt{2})$.

54. If $x = 40$, then $\frac{40^2}{400} - \frac{y^2}{100} = 1$, or $y = \pm 10\sqrt{3}$. So the width of carpet is $2 \cdot 10 \cdot \sqrt{3}$ or $20\sqrt{3}$ miles. Since altitude is $\frac{1}{5}$ of width, the altitude is $\frac{1}{5} \cdot 20\sqrt{3}$, or $4\sqrt{3}$, or 6.9 miles.

11.5 WARM-UPS

1. False, because $x^2 + y = 4$ is the equation of a parabola.
2. True, because if we divide each side by 9 we get the standard form for an ellipse.
3. True, because it can be written as $y^2 - x^2 = 1$.
4. True, because $2(0)^2 - 0 < 3$ is correct.
5. False, because $0 > 0^2 - 3(0) + 2$ is incorrect.
6. False, because the origin is on the parabola $x^2 = y$.
7. False, because (0, 0) does not satisfy the inequality.
8. True, because $x^2 + y^2 = 4$ is a circle of radius 2 centered at (0, 0), and the points inside this circle satisfy the inequality.
9. True, because both $0^2 - 4^2 < 1$ and $4 > 0^2 - 2(0) + 3$ are correct.
10. True, because both $0^2 + 0^2 < 1$ and $0 < 0^2 + 1$ are correct.

11.5 EXERCISES

1. Graph the parabola $y = x^2$. Since (0, 4) satisfies $y > x^2$, shade the region containing (0, 4).

2. First graph the parabola $y = x^2 + 1$. Use a solid curve because of the $\leq$ symbol. Since (0, 0) satisfies $y \leq x^2 + 1$, we shade the region containing (0, 0).

3. First graph the parabola $y = x^2 - x$. Since (5, 0) satisfies $y < x^2 - x$, we shade the region containing (5, 0).

4. First graph the parabola $y = x^2 + x$. Since (0, 5) satisfies $y > x^2 + x$, we shade the region containing (0, 5).

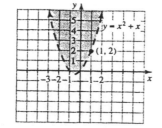 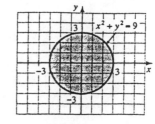

5. First graph the parabola $y = x^2 - x - 2$. Since $(0, 5)$ satisfies $y > x^2 - x - 2$, shade the region containing $(0, 5)$.

8. First graph the circle $x^2 + y^2 = 16$ using a dashed curve. Since $(0, 0)$ does not satisfy $x^2 + y^2 > 16$, shade the outside of the circle.

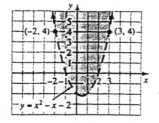 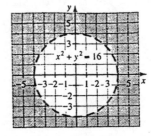

6. First graph the parabola $y = x^2 + x - 6$, using a dashed curve. Since $(5, 0)$ satisfies $y < x^2 + x - 6$, shade the region containing $(5, 0)$.

9. First graph the ellipse $x^2 + 4y^2 = 4$ using a dashed curve. Since $(0, 0)$ does not satisfy the inequality $x^2 + 4y^2 > 4$, we shade the region outside the ellipse.

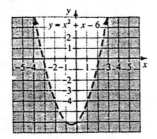

10. First graph the ellipse $4x^2 + y^2 = 4$ using a solid curve. Since $(0, 0)$ satisfies the inequality $4x^2 + y^2 \leq 4$, we shade the region inside the ellipse.

7. First graph the circle $x^2 + y^2 = 9$ using a solid curve. Since $(0, 0)$ satisfies $x^2 + y^2 \leq 9$, shade the inside of the circle.

414

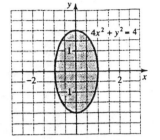

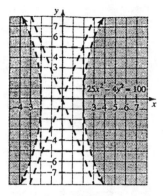

11. First divide both sides of the inequality by 36.

$$\frac{x^2}{9} - \frac{y^2}{4} < 1$$

Now graph the hyperbola $\frac{x^2}{9} - \frac{y^2}{4} = 1$.
Testing a point in each of the three regions, we find that only points in the region containing the origin satisfy $4x^2 - 9y^2 < 36$.

13. First graph the circle centered at (2, 3) with radius 2, using a dashed curve. Since (2, 3) satisfies $(x - 2)^2 + (y - 3)^2 < 4$, shade the region inside the circle.

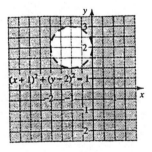

14. First graph the circle centered at $(-1, 2)$ with radius 1, using a dashed curve. Since $(-1, 2)$ does not satisfy $(x + 1)^2 + (y - 2)^2 > 1$, shade the region outside the circle.

12. Divide both sides of the inequality by 100.

$$\frac{x^2}{4} - \frac{y^2}{25} > 1$$

Now graph the hyperbola $\frac{x^2}{4} - \frac{y^2}{25} = 1$.
Testing a point in each of the three regions, we find that only points in the regions not containing the origin satisfy $25x^2 - 4y^2 > 100$.

415

15. First graph the circle centered at (0, 0) with radius 1. Since (0, 0) does not satisfy $x^2 + y^2 > 1$, shade the region outside the circle.

16. First graph the circle centered at (0, 0) with radius 5. Since (0, 0) satisfies $x^2 + y^2 < 25$, shade the region inside the circle.

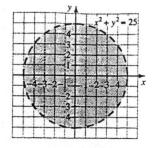

17. Graph the hyperbola $4x^2 - y^2 = 4$, using a dashed curve. After testing a point in each of the three regions, we see that only points in the region containing (0, 0) fail to satisfy $4x^2 - y^2 > 4$.

18. Graph the hyperbola $x^2 - 9y^2 = 9$, using a solid curve. After testing a point in each of the

three regions, we see that only points in the region containing (0, 0) satisfy $x^2 - 9y^2 \leq 9$.

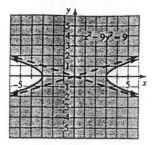

19. Graph the hyperbola $y^2 - x^2 = 1$. After testing a point in each of the three regions, we see that only points in the region containing (0, 0) satisfy $y^2 - x^2 \leq 1$.

20. Graph the hyperbola $x^2 - y^2 = 1$. After testing a point in each of the three regions, we see that only points in the region containing (0, 0) fail to satisfy $x^2 - y^2 > 1$.

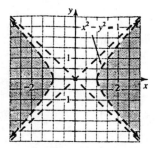

21. The graph of $y = x$ is a line with slope 1 and y-intercept $(0, 0)$. Since $(5, -5)$ satisfies $x > y$, we shade the region below the line.

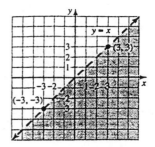

22. The graph of $x = 2y - 1$ is a line with y-intercept $(0, 1/2)$ and x-intercept $(-1, 0)$. Since $(0, 5)$ satisfies $x < 2y - 1$, we shade the region containing $(0, 5)$.

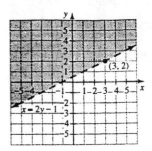

23. Graph the circle $x^2 + y^2 = 9$ and the line $y = x$. The graph of $x^2 + y^2 < 9$ is the region inside the circle. the graph of $y > x$ is the region above the line. The intersection of these two regions is shown as follows.

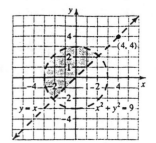

We could have used test points to determine which of the 4 regions determined by the circle and the line satisfies both inequalities.

24. Graph the circle $x^2 + y^2 = 1$ and the line $y = x$. The graph of $x^2 + y^2 > 1$ is the region outside the circle. the graph of $x > y$ is the region below the line. The intersection of these two regions is shown as follows.

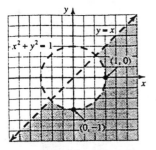

We could determine what region to shade by using test points. Only points in the shaded region satisfy both inequalities.

25. The graph of $x^2 - y^2 = 1$ is a hyperbola. The graph of $x^2 + y^2 = 4$ is a circle of radius 2. Points that satisfy $x^2 + y^2 < 4$ are inside the circle. The hyperbola divides the plane into 3 regions. Points in the 2 regions not containing $(0, 0)$ are the points that satisfy $x^2 - y^2 > 1$. The intersection of these regions is shown in the following graph.

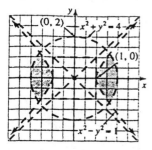

26. The graph of $y^2 - x^2 = 1$ is a hyperbola. The graph of $x^2 + y^2 = 9$ is a circle of radius 3. Points that satisfy $x^2 + y^2 > 9$ are outside the circle. The hyperbola divides the plane into

3 regions. Points in the region containing (0, 0) are the points that satisfy $y^2 - x^2 < 1$. The intersection of these regions is shown in the following graph.

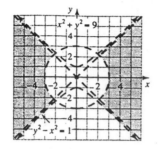

27. The graph of $y = x^2 + x$ is a parabola opening upward, with x-intercepts at $(0, 0)$ and $(-1, 0)$. The graph of $y > x^2 + x$ is the region inside this parabola. The graph of $y = 5$ is a horizontal line through $(0, 5)$. The graph of $y < 5$ is the region below this horizontal line. The points that satisfy both inequalities are the points inside the parabola and below $y = 5$, as shown in the following graph.

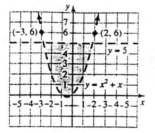

28. The graph of $y = x^2 + x - 6$ is a parabola opening upward, with x-intercepts at $(-3, 0)$ and $(2, 0)$. The graph of $y > x^2 + x - 6$ is the region inside this parabola. The graph of $y = x + 3$ is a line with y-intercept $(0, 3)$ and slope 1. The graph of $y < x + 3$ is the region below this line. The points that satisfy both inequalities are the points inside the parabola and below $y = x + 3$, as shown in the following graph.

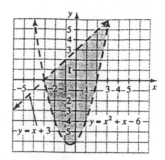

29. The graph of $y = x + 2$ is a line with y-intercept $(0, 2)$ and slope 1. The graph of $y \geq x + 2$ is the region above and including the line. The graph of $y = 2 - x$ is a line with y-intercept $(0, 2)$ and slope -1. The graph of $y \leq 2 - x$ is the region below and including this line. The region above the first line and below the second is shown in the following graph. We could have tested a point in each of the 4 regions determined by the two lines. We would find that only points in the region shown satisfy both inequalities.

30. The graph of $y = 2x - 3$ is a line with y-intercept $(0, -3)$ and slope 2. The graph of $y \geq 2x - 3$ is the region above and including the line. The graph of $y = 3 - 2x$ is a line with y-intercept $(0, 3)$ and slope -2. The graph of $y \leq 3 - 2x$ is the region below and including this line. The region above the first line and below the second is shown in the following graph. We could have tested a point in each of the 4 regions determined by the two lines. We would find that only points in the region shown satisfy both inequalities.

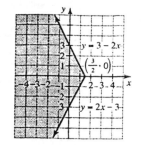

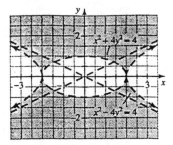

31. The graph of $4x^2 - y^2 = 4$ is a hyperbola opening to the left and right. Points that satisfy $4x^2 - y^2 < 4$ are in the region between the two branches of the hyperbola. The graph of $x^2 + 4y^2 = 4$ is an ellipse passing through $(0, 1)$, $(0, -1)$, $(2, 0)$, and $(-2, 0)$. Points that satisfy $x^2 + 4y^2 > 4$ are outside the ellipse. Points that satisfy both inequalities are outside the ellipse and between the two branches of the hyperbola.

33. The graph of $x - y = 0$ is the same as the line $y = x$ (through $(0, 0)$ with slope 1). Points that satisfy $x - y < 0$ are above the line $y = x$. The graph of $y + x^2 = 1$ is the same as the parabola $y = -x^2 + 1$, which opens downward. Points that satisfy $y + x^2 < 1$ are below the parabola. The points that satisfy both inequalities, below the parabola and above the line, are shown in the following graph.

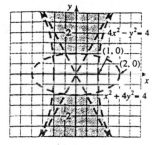

32. The graph of $x^2 - 4y^2 = 4$ is a hyperbola opening to the left and right. Points that satisfy $x^2 - 4y^2 < 4$ are in the region between the two branches of the hyperbola. The graph of $x^2 + 4y^2 = 4$ is an ellipse passing through $(0, 1)$, $(0, -1)$, $(2, 0)$, and $(-2, 0)$. Points that satisfy $x^2 + 4y^2 > 4$ are outside the ellipse. Points that satisfy both inequalities are outside the ellipse and between the two branches of the hyperbola.

34. The graph of $x + y = 2$ is the same as the line $y = -x + 2$. Points that satisfy $x + y < 2$ are below the line $y = -x + 2$. The graph of $y + 1 = x^2$ (or $y = x^2 - 1$) is a parabola that opens upward. Points that satisfy $y + 1 > x^2$ are inside the parabola. The points that satisfy both inequalities, inside the parabola and below the line, are shown in the following graph.

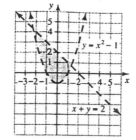

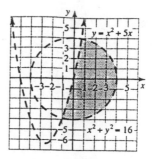

35. The graph of $y = 5x - x^2$ is a parabola opening downward. Points that satisfy $y < 5x - x^2$ are the points below the parabola. The graph of $x^2 + y^2 = 9$ is a circle of radius 3. Points that satisfy $x^2 + y^2 < 9$ are inside the circle. Points that satisfy both inequalities are the points inside the circle and below the parabola.

37. Points that satisfy $y \geq 3$ are above or on the horizontal line $y = 3$. Points that satisfy $x \leq 1$ are on or to the left of the vertical line $x = 1$. Points that satisfy both inequalities are shown in the following graph. The points graphed are the points with x-coordinate less than or equal to 1, and y-coordinate greater than or equal to 3.

36. The graph of $y = x^2 + 4x$ is a parabola opening upward. Points that satisfy $y < x^2 + 4x$ are the points outside the parabola. The graph of $x^2 + y^2 = 16$ is a circle of radius 4. Points that satisfy $x^2 + y^2 < 16$ are inside the circle. Points that satisfy both inequalities are the points inside the circle and outside the parabola.

38. Points that satisfy $y < 2$ are below the horizontal line $y = 2$. Points that satisfy $x > -3$ are to the right of the vertical line $x = -3$. Points that satisfy both inequalities are shown in the following graph. The points graphed are the points with x-coordinate greater than -3, and y-coordinate less than 2.

39. The graph of $4y^2 - 9x^2 = 36$ is a hyperbola opening up and down. Points that satisfy $4y^2 - 9x^2 < 36$ are the points between the two branches of the hyperbola. The graph of $x^2 + y^2 = 16$ is a circle of radius 4. Points that satisfy $x^2 + y^2 < 16$ are inside the circle. The points that satisfy both inequalities are indicated as follows.

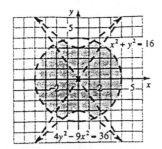

40. The graph of $25y^2 - 16x^2 = 400$ is a hyperbola opening up and down. Points that satisfy $25y^2 - 16x^2 < 400$ are the points between the two branches of the hyperbola. The graph of $x^2 + y^2 = 4$ is a circle of radius 2 centered at the origin. Points that satisfy $x^2 + y^2 > 4$ are outside the circle. The points that satisfy both inequalities are those points that are between the branches of the hyperbola and outside the circle, indicated as follows.

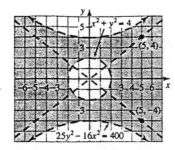

41. The graph of $y = x^2$ is a parabola opening upward. Points that satisfy $y < x^2$ are below this parabola. The graph of $x^2 + y^2 = 1$ is a circle of radius 1. Points that satisfy $x^2 + y^2 < 1$ are inside the circle. The graph of

the system of inequalities consists of points that are below the parabola and inside the circle.

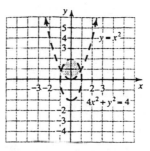

42. The graph of $y = x^2$ is a parabola opening upward. Points that satisfy $y > x^2$ are inside this parabola. The graph of $4x^2 + y^2 = 4$ is an ellipse with intercepts $(1, 0)$, $(-1, 0)$, $(0, 2)$, and $(0, -2)$. Points that satisfy $4x^2 + y^2 < 4$ are inside the ellipse. The graph of the system of inequalities consists of points that are inside the parabola and inside the ellipse.

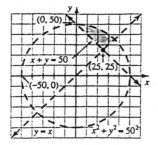

43. Let $x =$ the number of paces he walked to the east and $y =$ the number of paces he walked to the north. So $x + y \geq 50$, $x^2 + y^2 \leq 50^2$, and $y > x$. The graph of this system follows.

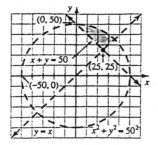

421

45. No solution

Enriching Your Mathematical Word Power
Chapter 11
1. c   2. a   3. d   4. a   5. c
6. d   7. b   8. d   9. c   10. a

CHAPTER 11   REVIEW

1. The graph of $y = x^2$ is a parabola and the graph of $y = -2x + 15$ is a straight line.

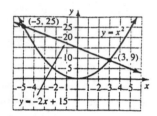

Use substitution to eliminate y.
$$x^2 = -2x + 15$$
$$x^2 + 2x - 15 = 0$$
$$(x + 5)(x - 3) = 0$$
$$x = -5 \text{ or } x = 3$$
$$y = 25 \qquad y = 9 \text{ Since } y = x^2$$
The solution set is $\{(3, 9), (-5, 25)\}$.

2. The graph of $y = \sqrt{x}$ includes the points $(0, 0)$, $(1, 1)$, and $(4, 2)$. The graph of $y = \frac{1}{3}x$ is a line with slope $1/3$ through the origin.

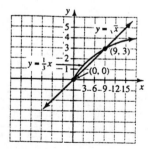

To solve the system, substitute $y = \frac{1}{3}x$ into $y = \sqrt{x}$.

$$\tfrac{1}{3}x = \sqrt{x}$$
$$\left(\tfrac{1}{3}x\right)^2 = (\sqrt{x})^2$$
$$\tfrac{1}{9}x^2 = x$$
$$x^2 - 9x = 0$$
$$x(x - 9) = 0$$
$$x = 0 \text{ or } x - 9 = 0$$
$$x = 0 \qquad\qquad x = 9$$
$$y = 0 \qquad\qquad y = 3 \text{ Since } y = \sqrt{x}$$

The solution set is $\{(0, 0), (9, 3)\}$.

3. First graph $y = 3x$ and $y = 1/x$.

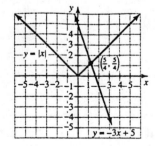

Use substitution to eliminate y.
$$3x = \tfrac{1}{x}$$
$$3x^2 = 1$$
$$x^2 = \tfrac{1}{3}$$
$$x = \pm\sqrt{\tfrac{1}{3}} = \pm\tfrac{\sqrt{3}}{3}$$
If $x = \tfrac{\sqrt{3}}{3}$, then $y = \sqrt{3}$. If $x = -\tfrac{\sqrt{3}}{3}$, then $y = -\sqrt{3}$. The solution set is

$$\left\{ \left(\tfrac{\sqrt{3}}{3}, \sqrt{3}\right), \left(-\tfrac{\sqrt{3}}{3}, -\sqrt{3}\right) \right\}.$$

4. The graph of $y = |x|$ includes the points $(0, 0)$, $(1, 1)$, and $(-1, 1)$. The graph of $y = -3x + 5$ has y-intercept $(0, 5)$ and slope -3.

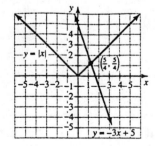

To solve the system, substitute $y = |x|$ into $y = -3x + 5$.

$$|x| = -3x + 5$$
$$x = -3x + 5 \quad \text{or} \quad x = -(-3x + 5)$$
$$4x = 5 \quad \text{or} \quad -2x = -5$$
$$x = \tfrac{5}{4} \quad \text{or} \quad x = \tfrac{5}{2}$$

Note that 5/2 does not satisfy $|x| = -3x + 5$. If $x = 5/4$, then $y = |5/4| = 5/4$. The solution set is $\left\{\left(\tfrac{5}{4}, \tfrac{5}{4}\right)\right\}$.

5. The second equation can be written as $x^2 = 3y$. Substitute this equation into the first equation.

$$3y + y^2 = 4$$
$$y^2 + 3y - 4 = 0$$
$$(y + 4)(y - 1) = 0$$
$$y = -4 \quad \text{or} \quad y = 1$$

If $y = -4$, then $x^2 = 3(-4)$ has no solution. If $y = 1$, then $x^2 = 3(1)$ gives us $x = \pm\sqrt{3}$. The solution set is $\{(\sqrt{3}, 1), (-\sqrt{3}, 1)\}$.

6. Substitute $x = y^2$ into $12y^2 - 4x^2 = 9$.

$$12x - 4x^2 = 9$$
$$-4x^2 + 12x - 9 = 0$$
$$4x^2 - 12x + 9 = 0$$
$$(2x - 3)^2 = 0$$
$$2x - 3 = 0$$
$$x = \tfrac{3}{2}$$

Use $x = 3/2$ in $y^2 = x$ to get $y^2 = 3/2$, or $y = \pm\sqrt{\tfrac{3}{2}} = \pm\tfrac{\sqrt{6}}{2}$.

The solution set is $\left\{\left(\tfrac{3}{2}, -\tfrac{\sqrt{6}}{2}\right), \left(\tfrac{3}{2}, \tfrac{\sqrt{6}}{2}\right)\right\}$.

7. Use substitution to eliminate y.

$$x^2 + (x + 2)^2 = 34$$
$$x^2 + x^2 + 4x + 4 = 34$$
$$2x^2 + 4x - 30 = 0$$
$$x^2 + 2x - 15 = 0$$
$$(x + 5)(x - 3) = 0$$
$$x = -5 \quad \text{or} \quad x = 3$$
$$y = -3 \quad \quad y = 5 \quad \text{Since } y = x + 2$$

The solution set is $\{(-5, -3), (3, 5)\}$.

8. Substitute $y = 2x + 1$ into $xy - y = 5$.

$$x(2x + 1) - (2x + 1) = 5$$
$$2x^2 + x - 2x - 1 = 5$$
$$2x^2 - x - 6 = 0$$
$$(2x + 3)(x - 2) = 0$$
$$2x + 3 = 0 \quad \text{or} \quad x - 2 = 0$$

$$x = -\tfrac{3}{2} \quad \text{or} \quad x = 2$$
$$y = 2\left(-\tfrac{3}{2}\right) + 1 \quad y = 2(2) + 1$$
$$y = -2 \quad \quad y = 5$$

The solution set is $\left\{\left(-\tfrac{3}{2}, -2\right), (2, 5)\right\}$.

9. Use substitution to eliminate y.

$$\log(x - 3) = 1 - \log(x)$$
$$\log(x - 3) + \log(x) = 1$$
$$\log(x^2 - 3x) = 1$$
$$x^2 - 3x = 10$$
$$x^2 - 3x - 10 = 0$$
$$(x - 5)(x + 2) = 0$$
$$x = 5 \quad \text{or} \quad x = -2$$

If $x = 5$, then $y = \log(5 - 3) = \log(2)$. If $x = -2$, we get a logarithm of a negative number. So the solution set is $\{(5, \log(2))\}$.

10. Use substitution to eliminate y.

$$(1/2)^x = 2^{x-1}$$
$$(2^{-1})^x = 2^{x-1}$$
$$2^{-x} = 2^{x-1}$$
$$-x = x - 1$$
$$-2x = -1$$
$$x = \tfrac{1}{2}$$

If $x = 1/2$, then $y = (1/2)^{1/2} = \sqrt{\tfrac{1}{2}} = \tfrac{\sqrt{2}}{2}$.

The solution set is $\left\{\left(\tfrac{1}{2}, \tfrac{\sqrt{2}}{2}\right)\right\}$.

11. Use substitution to eliminate x.

$$y^2 = 2(12 - y)$$
$$y^2 = 24 - 2y$$
$$y^2 + 2y - 24 = 0$$
$$(y + 6)(y - 4) = 0$$
$$y = -6 \quad \text{or} \quad y = 4$$

If $y = -6$, then $-6 = x^2$ has no solution. If $y = 4$, then $x^2 = 4$ and $x = \pm 2$. The solution set is $\{(2, 4), (-2, 4)\}$.

12. Add the equations to get $2x^2 = 2$. Divide each side by 2 to get $x^2 = 1$ or $x = \pm 1$. If $x = \pm 1$, then

$$x^2 + 2y^2 = 7$$
$$1 + 2y^2 = 7$$
$$2y^2 = 6$$
$$y^2 = 3$$
$$y = \pm\sqrt{3}$$

The solution set is
$$\{(1, \sqrt{3}), (1, -\sqrt{3}), (-1, \sqrt{3}), (-1, -\sqrt{3})\}.$$

13. The y-intercept is $(0, -18)$. To find the x-intercepts, solve $x^2 + 3x - 18 = 0$.
$$(x + 6)(x - 3) = 0$$
$$x = -6 \text{ or } x = 3$$
The x-intercepts are $(-6, 0)$ and $(3, 0)$. Use $x = -b/(2a)$ to find the x-coordinate of the vertex. The vertex is $(-\frac{3}{2}, -\frac{81}{4})$ and the axis of symmetry is $x = -3/2$. Since $a = 1$, $p = 1/4$. The focus is $(-\frac{3}{2}, -20)$ and the directrix is $y = -\frac{41}{2}$.

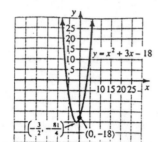

14. The y-intercept for $y = x - x^2$ is $(0, 0)$. To find the x-intercepts, solve $x - x^2 = 0$.
$$x(1 - x) = 0$$
$$x = 0 \text{ or } x = 1$$
The x-intercepts are $(0, 0)$ and $(1, 0)$. Use $x = -b/(2a)$ to find the x-coordinate of the vertex. The vertex is $(\frac{1}{2}, \frac{1}{4})$ and the axis of symmetry is $x = 1/2$. Since $a = -1$, $p = -1/4$. The focus is $(\frac{1}{2}, 0)$ and the directrix is $y = \frac{1}{2}$.

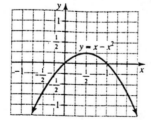

15. The y-intercept is $(0, 2)$. To find the x-intercepts, solve $x^2 + 3x + 2 = 0$.
$$(x + 2)(x + 1) = 0$$

$$x = -2 \text{ or } x = -1$$
The x-intercepts are $(-2, 0)$ and $(-1, 0)$. Use $x = -b/(2a)$ to find the x-coordinate of the vertex. The vertex is $(-\frac{3}{2}, -\frac{1}{4})$ and the axis of symmetry is $x = -3/2$. Since $a = 1$, $p = 1/4$. The focus is $(-\frac{3}{2}, 0)$ and the directrix is $y = -\frac{1}{2}$.

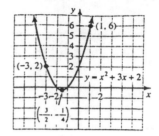

16. The y-intercept for $y = -x^2 - 3x + 4$ is $(0, 4)$. To find the x-intercepts, solve $-x^2 - 3x + 4 = 0$.
$$x^2 + 3x - 4 = 0$$
$$(x + 4)(x - 1) = 0$$
$$x = -4 \text{ or } x = 1$$
The x-intercepts are $(-4, 0)$ and $(1, 0)$. Use $x = -b/(2a)$ to find the x-coordinate of the vertex. The vertex is $(-\frac{3}{2}, \frac{25}{4})$ and the axis of symmetry is $x = -3/2$. The parabola opens downward. Since $a = -1$, $p = -1/4$. The focus is $(-\frac{3}{2}, 6)$ and the directrix is $y = \frac{13}{2}$.

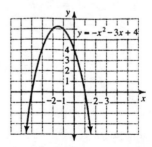

17. The y-intercept is $(0, 1)$. To find the x-intercepts solve
$$-\frac{1}{2}(x - 2)^2 + 3 = 0$$
$$(x - 2)^2 = 6$$
$$x - 2 = \pm\sqrt{6}$$

$$x = 2 \pm \sqrt{6}$$

The x-intercepts are $(2 \pm \sqrt{6}, 0)$. The vertex is $(2, 3)$ and the parabola opens down. The axis of symmetry is $x = 2$. Since $a = -1/2$, $p = -1/2$. The focus is $(2, 2\frac{1}{2})$ and the directrix is $y = 3\frac{1}{2}$.

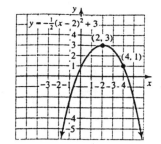

18. The y-intercept is $(0, -7/4)$. To find the x-intercepts solve
$$\frac{1}{4}(x + 1)^2 - 2 = 0$$
$$(x + 1)^2 = 8$$
$$x + 1 = \pm \sqrt{8}$$
$$x = -1 \pm 2\sqrt{2}$$
The x-intercepts are $(-1 \pm 2\sqrt{2}, 0)$. The vertex is $(-1, -2)$ and the parabola opens up. The axis of symmetry is $x = -1$. Since $a = 1/4$, $p = 1$. The focus is $(-1, -1)$ and the directrix is $y = -3$.

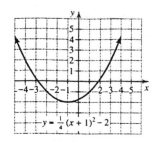

19.
$$y = 2(x^2 - 4x) + 1$$
$$y = 2(x^2 - 4x + 4 - 4) + 1$$
$$y = 2(x^2 - 4x + 4) - 8 + 1$$
$$y = 2(x - 2)^2 - 7$$
Vertex $(2, -7)$

20.
$$y = -2(x^2 + 3x) - 1$$
$$y = -2(x^2 + 3x + \tfrac{9}{4} - \tfrac{9}{4}) - 1$$
$$y = -2(x^2 + 3x + \tfrac{9}{4}) + \tfrac{9}{2} - 1$$
$$y = -2(x + \tfrac{3}{2})^2 + \tfrac{7}{2}$$
Vertex $(-\tfrac{3}{2}, \tfrac{7}{2})$

21.
$$y = -\tfrac{1}{2}(x^2 + 2x) + \tfrac{1}{2}$$
$$y = -\tfrac{1}{2}(x^2 + 2x + 1 - 1) + \tfrac{1}{2}$$
$$y = -\tfrac{1}{2}(x + 1)^2 + \tfrac{1}{2} + \tfrac{1}{2}$$
$$y = -\tfrac{1}{2}(x + 1)^2 + 1$$
Vertex $(-1, 1)$

22.
$$y = \tfrac{1}{4}(x^2 + 4x) - 9$$
$$y = \tfrac{1}{4}(x^2 + 4x + 4 - 4) - 9$$
$$y = \tfrac{1}{4}(x^2 + 4x + 4) - 1 - 9$$
$$y = \tfrac{1}{4}(x + 2)^2 - 10$$
Vertex $(-2, -10)$

23. Two numbers that have a sum of 6 are x and $6 - x$. If we let y be their product, then $y = x(6 - x) = -x^2 + 6x$. The maximum value for y is attained when
$$x = \frac{-b}{(2a)} = \frac{-6}{2(-1)} = 3.$$
If $x = 3$, then $6 - x = 3$ also. Two number that have the largest product among numbers with a sum of 6 are 3 and 3.

24. Two numbers that have a difference of 10 can be represented as x and $x + 10$. If we let y be their product, then
$$y = x(x + 10) = x^2 + 10x.$$
The minimum value for y occurs when
$$x = \frac{-b}{2a} = \frac{-10}{2(1)} = -5.$$
If $x = -5$, then $x + 10 = 5$. So the numbers that have the smallest product are 5 and -5.

25. Since the perimeter is 90 feet, the length and width have a sum of 45 feet. Let $x = $ the length and $45 - x = $ the width. If y is the area, then $y = x(45 - x) = -x^2 + 45x$. The maximum value for y is attained when
$$x = \frac{-b}{2a} = \frac{-45}{2(-1)} = 22.5.$$
If $x = 22.5$, then $45 - x = 22.5$ also. A square 22.5 feet by 22.5 feet will be the rectangular shape with the maximum area for the amount of fencing available.

26. Including the 6-foot gate, the perimeter of the area is 96 feet. Since the sum of the length and width is half of the perimeter, 48 feet, we

can let $x =$ the width and $48 - x =$ the length. Since area is length times width, we have $A = x(48 - x) = -x^2 + 48x$. The maximum value for A is attained when

$$x = \frac{-b}{2a} = \frac{-48}{2(-1)} = 24.$$

If $x = 24$, then $48 - x = 24$ also. So the maximum area is enclosed when a square 24 feet on each side is formed.

27. The graph of $x^2 + y^2 = 100$ is a circle centered at $(0, 0)$ with radius 10.

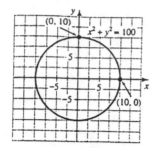

28. The graph of $x^2 + y^2 = 20$ is a circle centered at $(0, 0)$ with radius $\sqrt{20} = 2\sqrt{5}$.

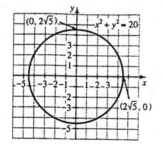

29. The graph of $(x - 2)^2 + (y + 3)^2 = 81$ is a circle centered at $(2, -3)$ with radius 9.

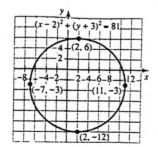

30. To find the center and radius we must write the standard equation of the circle.

$$x^2 + 2x \quad + y^2 = 8$$
$$x^2 + 2x + 1 + y^2 = 8 + 1$$
$$(x + 1)^2 + y^2 = 9$$

The circle has center at $(-1, 0)$ and radius 3.

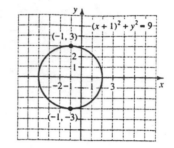

31.
$$9y^2 + 9x^2 = 4$$
$$x^2 + y^2 = \tfrac{4}{9}$$

The graph is a circle with center $(0, 0)$ and radius $2/3$.

32.
$$x^2 + 4x \quad + y^2 - 6y \quad = 3$$
$$x^2 + 4x + 4 + y^2 - 6y + 9 = 3 + 4 + 9$$
$$(x + 2)^2 + (y - 3)^2 = 16$$

The circle has center $(-2, 3)$ and radius 4.

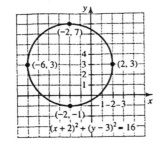

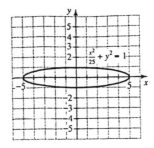

33. The equation of a circle with center (h, k) and radius r is $(x - h)^2 + (y - k)^2 = r^2$. The equation of a circle with center $(0, 3)$ and radius 6 is $x^2 + (y - 3)^2 = 36$.

34. The equation of a circle with center $(0, 0)$ and radius $\sqrt{6}$ is $x^2 + y^2 = 6$.

35. The equation of a circle with center $(2, -7)$ and radius 5 is $(x - 2)^2 + (y + 7)^2 = 25$.

36. The equation of a circle with center $(1/2, -3)$ and radius $1/2$ is $\left(x - \frac{1}{2}\right)^2 + (y + 3)^2 = \frac{1}{4}$.

37. The graph of $\frac{x^2}{36} + \frac{y^2}{49} = 1$ is an ellipse with x-intercepts at $(-6, 0)$ and $(6, 0)$, y-intercepts at $(0, -7)$ and $(0, 7)$, and centered at the origin.

39. The graph of $25x^2 + 4y^2 = 100$ is an ellipse with x-intercepts $(-2, 0)$ and $(2, 0)$, y-intercepts $(0, -5)$ and $(0, 5)$, and centered at the origin.

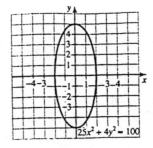

40. The graph of $6x^2 + 4y^2 = 24$ is an ellipse with x-intercepts $(-2, 0)$ and $(2, 0)$, y-intercepts $(0, -\sqrt{6})$ and $(0, \sqrt{6})$, and centered at the origin.

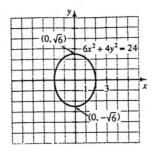

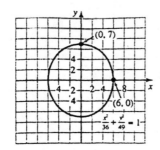

38. The graph of $\frac{x^2}{25} + y^2 = 1$ is an ellipse with x-intercepts at $(-5, 0)$ and $(5, 0)$, y-intercepts at $(0, -1)$ and $(0, 1)$, and centered at the origin.

41. The graph of $\frac{x^2}{49} - \frac{y^2}{36} = 1$ is a hyperbola with x-intercepts $(-7, 0)$ and $(7, 0)$. The fundamental rectangle passes through the x-

427

intercepts and the points $(0, -6)$ and $(0, 6)$. Extend the diagonals of the fundamental rectangle to get the asymptotes and draw a hyperbola opening to the left and right.

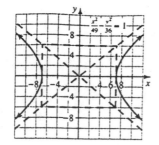

42. The graph of $\frac{y^2}{25} - \frac{x^2}{49} = 1$ is a hyperbola with y-intercepts $(0, -5)$ and $(0, 5)$. The fundamental rectangle passes through the y-intercepts and the points $(-7, 0)$ and $(7, 0)$. Extend the diagonals of the fundamental rectangle to get the asymptotes and draw a hyperbola opening up and down.

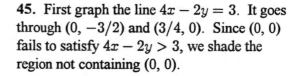

43. Write $4x^2 - 25y^2 = 100$ as $\frac{x^2}{25} - \frac{y^2}{4} = 1$. The graph has x-intercepts at $(-5, 0)$ and $(5, 0)$. The fundamental rectangle passes through the x-intercepts and the points $(0, -2)$ and $(0, 2)$. Extend the diagonals of the rectangle to get the asymptotes and draw a hyperbola opening to the left and right.

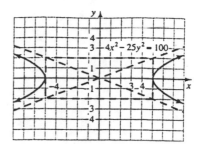

44. Write $6y^2 - 16x^2 = 96$ as $\frac{y^2}{16} - \frac{x^2}{6} = 1$. The graph has y-intercepts at $(0, -4)$ and $(0, 4)$. The fundamental rectangle passes through the y-intercepts and the points $(\sqrt{6}, 0)$ and $(-\sqrt{6}, 0)$. Extend the diagonals of the rectangle to get the asymptotes and draw a hyperbola opening up and down.

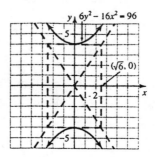

45. First graph the line $4x - 2y = 3$. It goes through $(0, -3/2)$ and $(3/4, 0)$. Since $(0, 0)$ fails to satisfy $4x - 2y > 3$, we shade the region not containing $(0, 0)$.

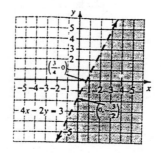

428

46. First graph the parabola $y = x^2 - 3x$. The parabola opens upward and has x-intercepts at $(0, 0)$ and $(3, 0)$. Test $(0, 5)$ in the inequality $y < x^2 - 3x$. Since $(0, 5)$ does not satisfy $y < x^2 - 3x$, points in the region not containing $(0, 5)$ satisfy the inequality. Shade the region below the parabola.

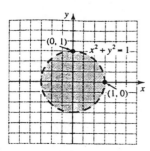

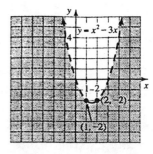

47. Write $y^2 < x^2 - 1$ as $x^2 - y^2 > 1$. Graph the hyperbola $x^2 - y^2 = 1$ and test a point in each of the three regions: $(-5, 0)$, $(0, 0)$, and $(5, 0)$. Since $(-5, 0)$ and $(5, 0)$ satisfy the inequality, we shade the regions containing those points.

49. Write $4x^2 + 9y^2 > 36$ as $\frac{x^2}{9} + \frac{y^2}{4} > 1$. First graph the ellipse $\frac{x^2}{9} + \frac{y^2}{4} = 1$ through $(-3, 0)$, $(3, 0)$, $(0, -2)$, and $(0, 2)$. Since $(0, 0)$ fails to satisfy the inequality, we shade the region outside of the ellipse.

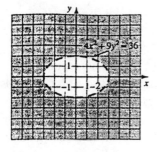

50. Rewrite $x^2 + y > 2x - 1$ as $y > -x^2 + 2x - 1$. The graph of $y = -x^2 + 2x - 1$ is a parabola opening downward, with vertex at $(1, 0)$. Since $(0, 0)$ satisfies $y > -x^2 + 2x - 1$, we shade the region containing $(0, 0)$ to indicate the solution set to the inequality.

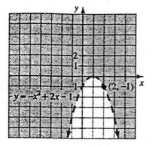

48. Write $y^2 < 1 - x^2$ as $x^2 + y^2 < 1$. The graph of $x^2 + y^2 = 1$ is a circle of radius 1 centered at $(0, 0)$. Since $(0, 0)$ satisfies $x^2 + y^2 < 1$, we shade the region containing $(0, 0)$.

429

51. The graph of $y < 3x - x^2$ is the region below the parabola $y = 3x - x^2$. The graph of $x^2 + y^2 < 9$ is the region inside the circle $x^2 + y^2 = 9$. Points that are inside the circle and below the parabola are shown in the following graph.

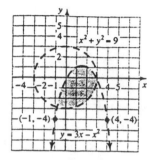

52. The graph of $x^2 - y^2 = 1$ is a hyperbola with x-intercepts at $(1, 0)$ and $(-1, 0)$. Points in the region containing $(0, 0)$ satisfy $x^2 - y^2 < 1$. The graph of $y = 1$ is a horizontal line through $(0, 1)$. Points that satisfy $y < 1$ lie below this line. The points in the solution set to the system are the points that are in between the two branches of the hyperbola and also below the horizontal line.

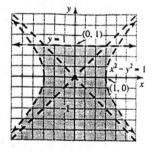

53. The set of points that satisfy $4x^2 + 9y^2 > 36$ is the set of points outside the ellipse $4x^2 + 9y^2 = 36$. The set of points that satisfy $x^2 + y^2 < 9$ is the set of points inside the circle $x^2 + y^2 = 9$. The solution set to the system consists of points that are outside the ellipse and inside the circle, as shown in the following graph.

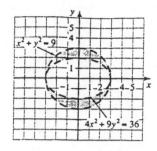

54. The graph of $y^2 - x^2 = 4$ is a hyperbola with y-intercepts at $(0, 2)$ and $(0, -2)$. Points in the region containing $(0, 0)$ do not satisfy $y^2 - x^2 > 4$, while points in the other two regions do. The graph of $y^2 + 16x^2 = 16$ is an ellipse passing through $(1, 0)$, $(-1, 0)$, $(0, 4)$, and $(0, -4)$. Since $(0,0)$ satisfies $y^2 + 16x^2 < 16$, all points inside the ellipse satisfy $y^2 + 16x^2 < 16$. The points $(0, 3)$ and $(0, -3)$ satisfy both inequalities of the system. Shade the regions containing these points.

55. The equation $x^2 = y^2 + 1$ is the equation of a hyperbola because it could be written as $x^2 - y^2 = 1$.

56. The equation $x = y + 1$ is the equation of a straight line, because it could be written as $y = x - 1$, the slope-intercept form of the equation of a line.

57. The equation $x^2 = 1 - y^2$ is the equation of a circle because it could be written as $x^2 + y^2 = 1$.

58. The equation $x^2 = y + 1$ could be written as $y = x^2 - 1$. This is the equation of a parabola opening upward.

59. The equation $x^2 + x = 1 - y^2$ is the equation of a circle because we could write $x^2 + x + y^2 = 1$, and then complete the square to get the standard equation for a circle.

60. The equation $(x - 3)^2 + (y + 2)^2 = 7$ is the equation of a circle with center $(3, -2)$ and radius $\sqrt{7}$.

61. The equation $x^2 + 4x = 6y - y^2$ is the equation of a circle because we could write it as $x^2 + 4x + y^2 - 6y = 0$, and then complete the squares for both x and y to get the standard equation of a circle.

62. The equation $4x + 6y = 1$ is the equation of a straight line written in standard form.

63. The equation is the equation of a hyperbola in standard form.

64. The equation $x^2 + \frac{y^2}{3} = 1$ is the equation of an ellipse with intercepts at $(0, -\sqrt{3})$, $(0, \sqrt{3})$, $(-1, 0)$, and $(1, 0)$.

65. The equation $4y^2 - x^2 = 8$ is the equation of a hyperbola because we could divide by 8 to get the standard equation $\frac{y^2}{2} - \frac{x^2}{8} = 1$.

66. The equation $9x^2 + y = 9$ could be written as $y = -9x^2 + 9$. This is the equation of a parabola opening downward.

67. Write $x^2 = 4 - y^2$ as $x^2 + y^2 = 4$ to see that it is the equation of a circle of radius 2 centered at the origin.

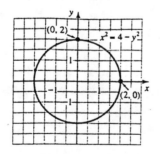

68. Write $x^2 = 4y^2 + 4$ as $\frac{x^2}{4} - y^2 = 1$. This is the equation of a hyperbola with x-intercepts

at $(-2, 0)$ and $(2, 0)$. The fundamental rectangle goes through the x-intercepts and also the points $(0, 1)$ and $(0, -1)$.

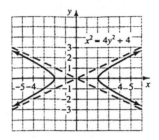

69. Write $x^2 = 4y + 4$ as $y = \frac{1}{4}x^2 - 1$ to see that it is the equation of a parabola opening upward with vertex at $(0, -1)$.

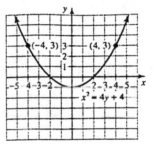

70. The graph of $x = 4y + 4$ is a straight line through $(0, -1)$ and $(4, 0)$.

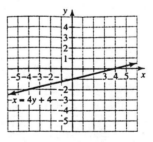

71. Write $x^2 = 4 - 4y^2$ as $\frac{x^2}{4} + y^2 = 1$ to see that it is the equation of an ellipse centered at

431

(0, 0) and passing through $(0, -1)$, $(0, 1)$, $(-2, 0)$, and $(2, 0)$.

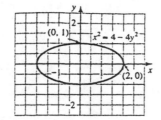

72. Write $x^2 = 4y - y^2$ as follows.
$$x^2 + y^2 - 4y = 0$$
$$x^2 + y^2 - 4y + 4 = 0 + 4$$
$$x^2 + (y - 2)^2 = 4$$
The graph of $x^2 + (y - 2)^2 = 4$ is a circle centered at $(0, 2)$ with radius 2.

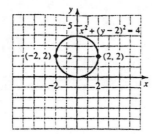

73. Write $x^2 = 4 - (y - 4)^2$ as $x^2 + (y - 4)^2 = 4$ to see that it is the equation of a circle of radius 2 centered at $(0, 4)$.

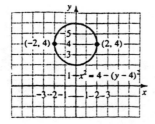

74. The graph of $(x - 2)^2 + (y - 4)^2 = 4$ is a circle centered at $(2, 4)$ with radius 2.

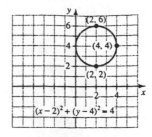

75. The radius of the circle is the distance between $(0, 0)$ and $(3, 4)$.
$$r = \sqrt{(3 - 0)^2 + (4 - 0)^2} = \sqrt{9 + 16}$$
$$= \sqrt{25} = 5$$
The equation of the circle centered at $(0, 0)$ with radius 5 is $x^2 + y^2 = 25$.

76. The radius of the circle is the distance between $(2, -3)$ and $(-1, 4)$.
$$r = \sqrt{(2 - (-1))^2 + (-3 - 4)^2}$$
$$= \sqrt{9 + 49} = \sqrt{58}$$
The equation of the circle centered at $(2, -3)$ with radius $\sqrt{58}$ is $(x - 2)^2 + (y + 3)^2 = 58$.

77. Use the center $(-1, 5)$ and radius 6 in the form $(x - h)^2 + (y - k)^2 = r^2$ to get the equation $(x + 1)^2 + (y - 5)^2 = 36$.

78. The radius of the circle is the distance from $(0, -3)$ to $(0, 0)$. The radius is 3. The equation of the circle is $x^2 + (y + 3)^2 = 9$.

79. The vertex is half way between the focus and directrix at $(1, 3)$. Since the distance from $(1, 3)$ to $(1, 4)$ is 1, we have $p = 1$, and $a = 1/4$. So the equation is
$$y = \tfrac{1}{4}(x - 1)^2 + 3.$$

80. The vertex is $(-2, 3)$. Because the parabola opens down, $p = -2$ and $a = -1/8$. The equation is
$$y = -\tfrac{1}{8}(x + 2)^2 + 3.$$

81. Since the vertex is below the focus, $p = 1/4$ and $a = 1$. The equation is
$$y = 1(x - 0)^2 + 0 \text{ or } y = x^2.$$

82. Since the vertex is above the focus, $p = -1/2$ and $a = -1/2$. The equation is $y = -\frac{1}{2}(x - 1)^2 + 2$.

83. Since the vertex is (0, 0) the parabola has equation $y = ax^2$. Since (3, 2) is on the parabola, $2 = a \cdot 3^2$, or $a = 2/9$. The equaiton is $y = \frac{2}{9}x^2$.

84. Since the vertex is (1, 3), we have $y = a(x - 1)^2 + 3$. Since the parabola goes through (0, 0) we have $0 = a(0 - 1)^2 + 3$, or $a = -3$. The equation is $y = -3(x - 1)^2 + 3$.

85. Substitute $y = -x + 1$ into $x^2 + y^2 = 25$ to eliminate y.
$$x^2 + (-x + 1)^2 = 25$$
$$x^2 + x^2 - 2x + 1 = 25$$
$$2x^2 - 2x - 24 = 0$$
$$x^2 - x - 12 = 0$$
$$(x - 4)(x + 3) = 0$$
$$x = 4 \quad \text{or} \quad x = -3$$
$$y = -3 \qquad y = 4 \quad \text{Since } y = -x + 1$$

The solution set is $\{(4, -3), (-3, 4)\}$

86. Add the equations to eliminate y.
$$x^2 - y^2 = 1$$
$$\underline{x^2 + y^2 = 7}$$
$$2x^2 \qquad = 8$$
$$x^2 = 4$$
$$x = \pm 2$$
If $x = 2$, then $4 + y^2 = 7$, or $y^2 = 3$, or $y = \pm \sqrt{3}$.
If $x = -2$, then $4 + y^2 = 7$, or $y = \pm \sqrt{3}$.
The solution set to the system is
$\{(2, \sqrt{3}), (2, -\sqrt{3}), (-2, \sqrt{3}), (-2, -\sqrt{3})\}$.

87. If we add the two equations to eliminate y, we get the equation $5x^2 = 25$. Solving this equation gives $x^2 = 5$ or $x = \pm \sqrt{5}$. Use $x^2 = 5$ in the first equation.
$$4(5) + y^2 = 4$$
$$y^2 = -16$$

There are no real numbers that satisfy the system of equations. The solution set is $\emptyset$.

88. Use substitution to eliminate y.
$$x^2 + x = -x^2 + 3x + 12$$
$$2x^2 - 2x - 12 = 0$$
$$x^2 - x - 6 = 0$$
$$(x - 3)(x + 2) = 0$$
$$x - 3 = 0 \quad \text{or} \quad x + 2 = 0$$
$$x = 3 \quad \text{or} \quad x = -2$$

If $x = 3$, then $y = 3^2 + 3 = 12$. If $x = -2$, then $y = (-2)^2 + (-2) = 2$. The solution set to the system is $\{(3, 12), (-2, 2)\}$.

89. Let $x =$ the length and $y =$ the width. We can write the following 2 equations.
$$2x + 2y = 16$$
$$xy = 12$$

The first equation can be written as $y = 8 - x$. Substitute $y = 8 - x$ into the second equation.
$$x(8 - x) = 12$$
$$-x^2 + 8x - 12 = 0$$
$$x^2 - 8x + 12 = 0$$
$$(x - 6)(x - 2) = 0$$
$$x = 6 \quad \text{or} \quad x = 2$$
$$y = 2 \qquad y = 6 \quad \text{Since } y = 8 - x$$
So the length is 6 feet and the width is 2 feet.

90. Let $x =$ the larger radius and $y =$ the smaller radius.
$$\pi x^2 - \pi y^2 = 10\pi$$
$$x - y = 2$$

$$x^2 - y^2 = 10$$
$$x = y + 2$$

$$(y + 2)^2 - y^2 = 10$$
$$y^2 + 4y + 4 - y^2 = 10$$
$$4y = 6$$
$$y = \frac{3}{2}$$

If $y = 3/2$ and $x = y + 2$, then $x = 7/2$. So the radius of the larger circle is 7/2 inches and the radius of the smaller circle is 3/2 inches.

CHAPTER 11 TEST

1. The graph of $x^2 + y^2 = 25$ is a circle of radius 5 centered at (0, 0).

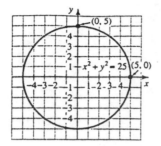

2. The graph of $\frac{x^2}{16} - \frac{y^2}{25} = 1$ is a hyperbola centered at the origin. the x-intercepts are $(-4, 0)$ and $(4, 0)$. The fundamental rectangle passes through the x-intercepts, $(0, -5)$, and $(0, 5)$. Extend the diagonals of the fundamental rectangle to obtain the asymptotes. The hyperbola opens to the left and right.

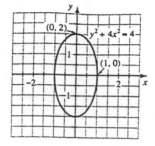

4. The graph of $y = x^2 + 4x + 4$ is a parabola opening upward with y-intercept (0, 4). We can write this equation as $y = (x + 2)^2$. In this form we see that the vertex is $(-2, 0)$.

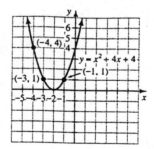

5. Write $y^2 - 4x^2 = 4$ as $\frac{y^2}{4} - x^2 = 1$. The graph is a hyperbola with y-intercepts at $(0, -2)$ and $(0, 2)$. The fundamental rectangle passes through the y-intercepts, $(-1, 0)$, and $(1, 0)$. Extend the diagonals to get the asymptotes. The hyperbola opens up and down.

3. The graph of $y^2 + 4x^2 = 4$ is an ellipse with x-intercepts at $(-1, 0)$ and $(1, 0)$. Its y-intercepts are $(0, -2)$ and $(0, 2)$.

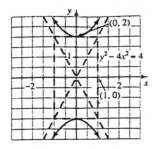

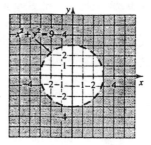

6. The graph of $y = -x^2 - 2x + 3$ is a parabola opening downward. The vertex is at $(-1, 4)$. The y-intercept is $(0, 3)$. The x-intercepts are $(-3, 0)$ and $(1, 0)$.

9. The graph of $y = x^2 - 9$ is a parabola opening upward. Its vertex is $(0, -9)$. To find its x-intercepts solve $x^2 - 9 = 0$. The x-intercepts are $(-3, 0)$ and $(3, 0)$. The graph of $y > x^2 - 9$ is the region containing the origin because $(0, 0)$ satisfies the inequality.

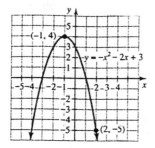

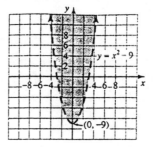

7. First graph the hyperbola $\frac{x^2}{9} - \frac{y^2}{9} = 1$. Since $(0, 0)$ satisfies the inequality, the region containing $(0, 0)$ is shaded.

10. The graph of $x^2 + y^2 < 9$ is the region inside the circle $x^2 + y^2 = 9$. To find the graph of $x^2 - y^2 > 1$ first graph the hyperbola $x^2 - y^2 = 1$. By testing points, we can see that the two regions not containing the origin satisfy $x^2 - y^2 > 1$. The points in these two regions that are also inside the circle are the points that satisfy both inequalities of the system.

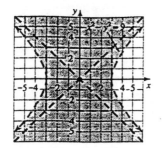

8. First graph the circle $x^2 + y^2 = 9$, centered at $(0, 0)$ with radius 3. Since $(0, 0)$ fails to satisfy $x^2 + y^2 > 9$, we shade the region outside the circle.

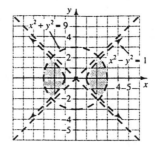

435

11. The graph of $y = -x^2 + x$ is a parabola opening downward. Points below this parabola satisfy $y < -x^2 + x$. The graph of $y = x - 4$ is a line through $(0, -4)$ with slope 1. Points below this line satisfy $y < x - 4$. The solution set to the system of inequalities consists of points below the parabola and below the line.

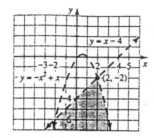

12. Use substitution to eliminate y.
$$x^2 - 2x - 8 = 7 - 4x$$
$$x^2 + 2x - 15 = 0$$
$$(x + 5)(x - 3) = 0$$
$$x = -5 \quad \text{or} \quad x = 3$$
$$y = 27 \qquad y = -5 \quad \text{Since } y = 7 - 4x$$
The solution set is $\{(-5, 27), (3, -5)\}$.

13. Substitute $x^2 = y$ into $x^2 + y^2 = 12$.
$$y + y^2 = 12$$
$$y^2 + y - 12 = 0$$
$$(y + 4)(y - 3) = 0$$
$$y = -4 \quad \text{or} \quad y = 3$$
If $y = -4$, the $x^2 = -4$ has no solution. If $y = 3$, then $x^2 = 3$ or $x = \pm\sqrt{3}$. The solution set is $\{(\sqrt{3}, 3), (-\sqrt{3}, 3)\}$.

14. Complete the square to get the equation into the standard form.
$$x^2 + 2x + \quad y^2 + 10y \quad = 10$$
$$x^2 + 2x + 1 + y^2 + 10y + 25 = 10 + 1 + 25$$
$$(x + 1)^2 + (y + 5)^2 = 36$$
The center is $(-1, -5)$ and the radius is 6.

15. The x-coordinate of the vertex is
$$x = \frac{-b}{2a} = \frac{-1}{2(1)} = -\frac{1}{2}.$$

Use $x = -1/2$ in $y = x^2 + x + 3$, to get the vertex $\left(-\frac{1}{2}, \frac{11}{4}\right)$. Since $a = 1$, we have $p = 1/4$. The focus is $\left(-\frac{1}{2}, 3\right)$ and the directrix is $y = \frac{5}{2}$. The axis of symmetry is $x = -\frac{1}{2}$ and the parabola opens up.

16.
$$y = \tfrac{1}{2}x^2 - 3x - \tfrac{1}{2}$$
$$y = \tfrac{1}{2}(x^2 - 6x) - \tfrac{1}{2}$$
$$y = \tfrac{1}{2}(x^2 - 6x + 9 - 9) - \tfrac{1}{2}$$
$$y = \tfrac{1}{2}(x^2 - 6x + 9) - \tfrac{9}{2} - \tfrac{1}{2}$$
$$y = \tfrac{1}{2}(x - 3)^2 - 5$$

17. The maximum value of s in the formula $s = -16t^2 + 64t + 20$ occurs when $t = \dfrac{-64}{2(-16)} = 2$. The maximum height is $s = -16(2)^2 + 64(2) + 20 = 84$ feet.

18. The radius of the circle is the distance between $(-1, 3)$ and $(2, 5)$.
$$r = \sqrt{(-1 - 2)^2 + (3 - 5)^2} = \sqrt{9 + 4}$$
$$= \sqrt{13}$$

The equation of the circle with center $(-1, 3)$ and radius $\sqrt{13}$ is $(x + 1)^2 + (y - 3)^2 = 13$.

19. Let $x =$ the length and $y =$ the width. We can write the following two equations.

$$2x + 2y = 42$$
$$xy = 108$$

If we solve $2x + 2y = 42$ for y, we get $y = 21 - x$.

$$x(21 - x) = 108$$
$$-x^2 + 21x - 108 = 0$$
$$x^2 - 21x + 108 = 0$$
$$(x - 9)(x - 12) = 0$$
$$x = 9 \quad \text{or} \quad x = 12$$
$$y = 12 \qquad y = 9 \quad \text{Since } y = 21 - x$$

The length is 12 feet and the width is 9 feet.

Making Connections

Chapters 1 - 11

1. The graph of $y = 9x - x^2$ is a parabola that opens downward. Solve $9x - x^2 = 0$ to find the x-intercepts.

$$x(9 - x) = 0$$
$$x = 0 \quad \text{or} \quad x = 9$$

The x-intercepts are $(0, 0)$ and $(9, 0)$.

The x-coordinate of the vertex is
$$x = \frac{-(9)}{2(-1)} = \frac{9}{2}.$$
The vertex is $(9/2, 81/4)$.

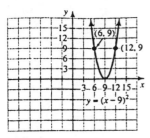

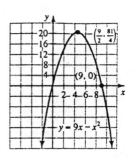

2. The graph of $y = 9x$ is a line through $(0, 0)$ with slope 9.

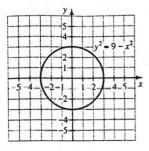

4. Write $y^2 = 9 - x^2$ as $x^2 + y^2 = 9$ to see that it is the equation of a circle of radius 3 centered at the origin.

5. The graph of $y = 9x^2$ is a parabola opening upward with vertex at $(0, 0)$.

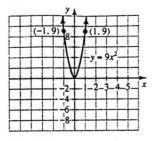

3. The graph of $y = (x - 9)^2$ is a parabola opening upward, with vertex at $(9, 0)$.

437

6. The graph of $y = |9x|$ is v-shaped. It contains the points $(0, 0)$, $(-1, 9)$, and $(1, 9)$.

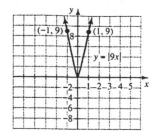

7. Write $4x^2 + 9y^2 = 36$ as $\frac{x^2}{9} + \frac{y^2}{4} = 1$ to see that it is the equation of an ellipse through $(-3, 0)$, $(3, 0)$, $(0, 2)$, and $(0, -2)$.

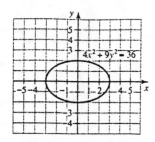

8. Write $4x^2 - 9y^2 = 36$ as $\frac{x^2}{9} - \frac{y^2}{4} = 1$ to see that it is the equation of a hyperbola with x-intercepts $(-3, 0)$ and $(3, 0)$. The fundamental rectangle goes through the x-intercepts, $(0, -2)$, and $(0, 2)$. Extend the diagonals of the rectangle to get the asymptotes.

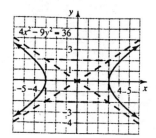

9. The graph of $y = 9 - x$ is a line through $(0, 9)$ with slope -1.

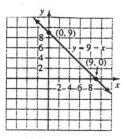

10. The graph of $y = 9^x$ goes through $(0, 1)$, $(1, 9)$, and $(-1, 1/9)$.

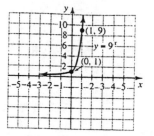

11. $(x + 2y)^2 = x^2 + 2(x)(2y) + (2y)^2$
$= x^2 + 4xy + 4y^2$

12. $(x + y)(x^2 + 2xy + y^2)$
$= x(x^2 + 2xy + y^2) + y(x^2 + 2xy + y^2)$
$= x^3 + 2x^2y + xy^2 + x^2y + 2xy^2 + y^3$
$= x^3 + 3x^2y + 3xy^2 + y^3$

13. $(a + b)^3 = (a + b)(a^2 + 2ab + b^2)$
$= a(a^2 + 2ab + b^2) + b(a^2 + 2ab + b^2)$
$= a^3 + 2a^2b = ab^2 + a^2b + 2ab^2 + b^3$
$= a^3 + 3a^2b + 3ab^2 + b^3$

14. $(a - 3b)^2 = a^2 - 2(a)(3b) + (3b)^2$
$= a^2 - 6ab + 9b^2$

15. $(2a + 1)(3a - 5) = 6a^2 + 3a - 10a - 5$
$= 6a^2 - 7a - 5$

16. $(x - y)(x^2 + xy + y^2)$
$= x(x^2 + xy + y^2) - y(x^2 + xy + y^2)$
$= x^3 + x^2y + xy^2 - x^2y - xy^2 - y^3$
$= x^3 - y^3$

17. Multiply the second equation by -2 and add the result to the first equation.
$$2x - 3y = -4$$
$$\underline{-2x - 4y = -10}$$
$$-7y = -14$$
$$y = 2$$
Use $y = 2$ in $x + 2y = 5$ to find x.
$$x + 2(2) = 5$$
$$x = 1$$
The solution set is $\{(1, 2)\}$.

18. Substitute $y = 7 - x$ into $x^2 + y^2 = 25$.
$$x^2 + (7 - x)^2 = 25$$
$$x^2 + 49 - 14x + x^2 = 25$$
$$2x^2 - 14x + 24 = 0$$
$$x^2 - 7x + 12 = 0$$
$$(x - 3)(x - 4) = 0$$
$$x = 3 \quad \text{or} \quad x = 4$$
$$y = 4 \qquad y = 3 \text{ Since } y = 7 - x$$

The solution set is $\{(3, 4), (4, 3)\}$.

19. Adding the first and second equations to eliminate z, we get $3x - 3y = 9$. Adding the second and third equations to eliminate z, we get $2x - y = 4$. Divide $3x - 3y = 9$ by -3 and add the result to $2x - y = 4$.
$$-x + y = -3$$
$$\underline{2x - y = 4}$$
$$x = 1$$
Use $x = 1$ in $-x + y = -3$.
$$-1 + y = -3$$
$$y = -2$$
Use $x = 1$ and $y = -2$ in $x + y + z = 2$.
$$1 + (-2) + z = 2$$
$$z = 3$$
The solution set is $\{(1, -2, 3)\}$.

20. Substitute $y = x^2$ into $y - 2x = 3$.
$$x^2 - 2x = 3$$
$$x^2 - 2x - 3 = 0$$

$$(x - 3)(x + 1) = 0$$
$$x = 3 \quad \text{or} \quad x = -1$$
$$y = 9 \qquad y = 1 \text{ Since } y = x^2$$

The solution set is $\{(-1, 1), (3, 9)\}$.

21. $ax + b = 0$
$$ax = -b$$
$$x = -\frac{b}{a}$$

22. Use the quadratic formula with $a = w$, $b = d$, and $c = m$.
$$x = \frac{-d \pm \sqrt{d^2 - 4wm}}{2w}$$

23. $A = \frac{1}{2}h(B + b)$
$$2A = h(B + b)$$
$$2A = hB + hb$$
$$2A - bh = hB$$
$$B = \frac{2A - bh}{h}$$

24. $\frac{1}{x} + \frac{1}{y} = \frac{1}{2}$
$$2xy\left(\frac{1}{x} + \frac{1}{y}\right) = 2xy\left(\frac{1}{2}\right)$$
$$2y + 2x = xy$$
$$2y = xy - 2x$$
$$2y = x(y - 2)$$
$$x = \frac{2y}{y - 2}$$

25. $L = m + mxt$
$$L = m(1 + xt)$$
$$m = \frac{L}{1 + xt}$$

26. $y = 3a\sqrt{t}$
$$(y)^2 = (3a\sqrt{t})^2$$
$$y^2 = 9a^2t$$
$$\frac{y^2}{9a^2} = t$$
$$t = \frac{y^2}{9a^2}$$

27. First find the slope.
$$m = \frac{-3 - 1}{2 - (-4)} = \frac{-4}{6} = -\frac{2}{3}$$
Use point-slope form with $(2, -3)$.
$$y - (-3) = -\frac{2}{3}(x - 2)$$

$$y + 3 = -\tfrac{2}{3}x + \tfrac{4}{3}$$

$$y = -\tfrac{2}{3}x - \tfrac{5}{3}$$

28. Write $2x - 4y = 5$ as $y = \tfrac{1}{2}x - \tfrac{5}{4}$. The slope of any line perpendicular to this line is -2. The line through $(0, 0)$ with slope -2 is $y = -2x$.

29. The radius is the distance between $(2, 5)$ and $(-1, -1)$.
$$r = \sqrt{(-1 - 2)^2 + (-1 - 5)^2} = \sqrt{9 + 36}$$
$$= \sqrt{45}$$
The equation of circle with center $(2, 5)$ and radius $\sqrt{45}$ is $(x - 2)^2 + (y - 5)^2 = 45$.

30. Use completing the square to get the equation into standard form for a circle.
$$x^2 + 3x + y^2 - 6y = 0$$
$$x^2 + 3x + \tfrac{9}{4} + y^2 - 6y + 9 = 0 + \tfrac{9}{4} + 9$$
$$(x + \tfrac{3}{2})^2 + (y - 3)^2 = \tfrac{45}{4}$$
The center is $(-\tfrac{3}{2}, 3)$ and radius is $\sqrt{\tfrac{45}{4}}$, or $\tfrac{3\sqrt{5}}{2}$.

31. $2i(3 + 5i) = 6i + 10i^2 = -10 + 6i$

32. $i^6 = i^4 \cdot i^2 = 1(-1) = -1$

33. $(2i - 3) + (6 - 7i) = 3 - 5i$

34. $(3 + i\sqrt{2})^2 = 9 + 6i\sqrt{2} + 2i^2$
$= 7 + 6i\sqrt{2}$

35. $(2 - 3i)(5 - 6i) = 10 - 15i - 12i + 18i^2$
$$= -8 - 27i$$

36. $(3 - i) + (-6 + 4i) = -3 + 3i$

37. $(5 - 2i)(5 + 2i) = 25 - 4i^2 = 29$

38. $\dfrac{2 - 3i}{2i} = \dfrac{(2 - 3i)(-i)}{2i(-i)} = \dfrac{-2i + 3i^2}{2(1)}$
$$= -\tfrac{3}{2} - i$$

39. $\dfrac{(4 + 5i)(1 + i)}{(1 - i)(1 + i)} = \dfrac{4 + 9i + 5i^2}{2}$
$$= \dfrac{-1 + 9i}{2} = -\tfrac{1}{2} + \tfrac{9}{2}i$$

40. $\dfrac{4 - \sqrt{-8}}{2} = \dfrac{4 - 2i\sqrt{2}}{2} = 2 - i\sqrt{2}$

41. a) $m = \dfrac{250 - 200}{0.30 - 0.40} = \dfrac{50}{-0.1} = -500$
$$q - 250 = -500(x - 0.30)$$
$$q - 250 = -500x + 150$$
$$q = -500x + 400$$

b) $R = qx = (-500x + 400)x$
$$R = -500x^2 + 400x$$

c) The graph is a parabola through $(0, 0)$, $(0.80, 0)$, $(0.40, 80)$.

d) The maximum revenue occurs at the vertex of the parabola.
$$x = \dfrac{-400}{2(-500)} = 0.40$$
The maximum revenue occurs when bananas are $0.40 per pound.

e) To find the maximum revenue use the formula for revenue with $x = 0.40$.
$$R = -500(0.40)^2 + 400(0.40) = 80$$
The maximum revenue is $80 when the bananas are $0.40 per pound.

12.1 WARM-UPS

1. True, because the formula $a_n = 2n$ will produce even numbers when n is a positive integer.

2. True, because the formula $a_n = 2n - 1$ will produce odd numbers when n is a positive integer.

3. True, by the definition of sequence.

4. False, because the domain of a finite sequence is the set of positive integers less than or equal to some fixed positive integer.

5. False, because if $n = 1$, $a_1 = (-1)^2 \cdot 1^2 = 1$.

6. False, because the independent variable is n.

7. True.

8. False, because the 6th term is $a_6 = (-1)^7 2^6 = -64$.

9. True.

10. True, because the sequence is $a_n = 2^n$ and $a_{10} = 2^{10} = 1024$.

12.1 EXERCISES

1. A sequence is a list of numbers.

2. Each number in the sequence is called a term of the sequence.

3. A finite sequence is a function whose domain is the set of positive integers less than or equal to some fixed positive integer.

4. An infinite sequence is a function whose domain is the set of all positive integers.

5. The terms of the sequence a_n are found by squaring the integers from 1 through 8, because of the formula $a_n = n^2$. So the terms are 1, 4, 9, 16, 25, 36, 49, and 64.

6. The terms of the sequence a_n are found by taking the opposite of the squares of the integers from 1 through 4, because of the formula $a_n = -n^2$. So the terms are -1, -4, -9, and -16.

7. $b_1 = \frac{(-1)^1}{1} = -1$, $b_2 = \frac{(-1)^2}{2} = \frac{1}{2}$,
$b_3 = \frac{(-1)^3}{3} = -\frac{1}{3}$, $b_4 = \frac{(-1)^4}{4} = \frac{1}{4}$,
$b_5 = \frac{(-1)^5}{5} = -\frac{1}{5}$, etc.
The 10 terms of the sequence are
$-1, \frac{1}{2}, -\frac{1}{3}, \frac{1}{4}, -\frac{1}{5}, \frac{1}{6}, -\frac{1}{7}, \frac{1}{8}, -\frac{1}{9}$, and $\frac{1}{10}$.

8. $b_1 = \frac{(-1)^{1+1}}{1} = 1$, $b_2 = \frac{(-1)^{2+1}}{2} = -\frac{1}{2}$,
$b_3 = \frac{(-1)^{3+1}}{3} = \frac{1}{3}$, $b_4 = \frac{(-1)^{4+1}}{4} = -\frac{1}{4}$,
$b_5 = \frac{(-1)^{5+1}}{5} = \frac{1}{5}$, etc.
The 6 terms are $1, -\frac{1}{2}, \frac{1}{3}, -\frac{1}{4}, \frac{1}{5}$, and $-\frac{1}{6}$.

9. $c_1 = (-2)^{1-1} = 1$, $c_2 = (-2)^{2-1} = -2$,
$c_3 = (-2)^{3-1} = 4$, $c_4 = (-2)^{4-1} = -8$,
$c_5 = (-2)^{5-1} = 16$
The five terms of the sequence are $1, -2, 4, -8$, and 16.

10. $c_1 = (-3)^{1-2} = -\frac{1}{3}$, $c_2 = (-3)^{2-2} = 1$,
$c_3 = (-3)^{3-2} = -3$, $c_4 = (-3)^{4-2} = 9$,
$c_5 = (-3)^{5-2} = -27$
The five terms of the sequence are $-\frac{1}{3}, 1, -3$, 9, and -27.

11. $a_1 = 2^{-1} = \frac{1}{2}$, $a_2 = 2^{-2} = \frac{1}{4}$,
$a_3 = 2^{-3} = \frac{1}{8}$, $a_4 = 2^{-4} = \frac{1}{16}$, etc.
The six terms of the sequence are $\frac{1}{2}, \frac{1}{4}, \frac{1}{8}, \frac{1}{16}, \frac{1}{32}$, and $\frac{1}{64}$.

12. $a_1 = 2^{-1+2} = 2$, $a_2 = 2^{-2+2} = 1$,
$a_3 = 2^{-3+2} = \frac{1}{2}$, $a_4 = 2^{-4+2} = \frac{1}{4}$, etc.
The 5 terms of the sequence are 2, 1, $\frac{1}{2}, \frac{1}{4}$, and $\frac{1}{8}$.

13. $b_1 = 2(1) - 3 = -1$, $b_2 = 2(2) - 3 = 1$,
$b_3 = 2(3) - 3 = 3$, $b_4 = 2(4) - 3 = 5$,
$b_5 = 2(5) - 3 = 7$, $b_6 = 2(6) - 3 = 9$,
$b_7 = 2(7) - 3 = 11$
The seven terms of the sequence are $-1, 1, 3, 5, 7, 9$, and 11.

14. $b_1 = 2(1) + 6 = 8$, $b_2 = 2(2) + 6 = 10$,
$b_3 = 2(3) + 6 = 12$, $b_4 = 2(4) + 6 = 14$,
$b_5 = 2(5) + 6 = 16$, $b_6 = 2(6) + 6 = 18$,
$b_7 = 2(7) + 6 = 20$
The seven terms of the sequence are 8, 10, 12, 14, 16, 18, and 20.

15. $c_1 = 1^{-1/2} = 1$, $c_2 = 2^{-1/2} = \frac{1}{\sqrt{2}}$,
$c_3 = 3^{-1/2} = \frac{1}{\sqrt{3}} = \frac{\sqrt{3}}{3}$, $c_4 = 4^{-1/2} = \frac{1}{2}$,

$c_5 = 5^{-1/2} = \frac{1}{\sqrt{5}} = \frac{\sqrt{5}}{5}$

The five terms are 1, $\frac{\sqrt{2}}{2}$, $\frac{\sqrt{3}}{3}$, $\frac{1}{2}$, and $\frac{\sqrt{5}}{5}$.

16. $c_1 = 1^{1/2}2^{-1} = \frac{1}{2}$,

$c_2 = 2^{1/2}2^{-2} = \frac{\sqrt{2}}{4}$

$c_3 = 3^{1/2}2^{-3} = \frac{\sqrt{3}}{8}$,

$c_4 = 4^{1/2}2^{-4} = \frac{1}{8}$,

The four terms are $\frac{1}{2}$, $\frac{\sqrt{2}}{4}$, $\frac{\sqrt{3}}{8}$, and $\frac{1}{8}$.

17. $a_1 = \frac{1}{1^2+1} = \frac{1}{2}$, $a_2 = \frac{1}{2^2+2} = \frac{1}{6}$,

$a_3 = \frac{1}{3^2+3} = \frac{1}{12}$, $a_4 = \frac{1}{4^2+4} = \frac{1}{20}$

The first four terms are $\frac{1}{2}$, $\frac{1}{6}$, $\frac{1}{12}$, and $\frac{1}{20}$.

18. $b_1 = \frac{1}{(1+1)(1+2)} = \frac{1}{6}$,

$b_2 = \frac{1}{(2+1)(2+2)} = \frac{1}{12}$,

$b_3 = \frac{1}{(3+1)(3+2)} = \frac{1}{20}$,

$b_4 = \frac{1}{(4+1)(4+2)} = \frac{1}{30}$

The first four terms are $\frac{1}{6}$, $\frac{1}{12}$, $\frac{1}{20}$, and $\frac{1}{30}$.

19. $b_1 = \frac{1}{2(1)-5} = -\frac{1}{3}$, $b_2 = \frac{1}{2(2)-5} = -1$,

$b_3 = \frac{1}{2(3)-5} = 1$, $b_4 = \frac{1}{2(4)-5} = \frac{1}{3}$

The first four terms are $-\frac{1}{3}$, -1, 1, and $\frac{1}{3}$.

20. $a_1 = \frac{4}{2(1)+5} = \frac{4}{7}$, $a_2 = \frac{4}{2(2)+5} = \frac{4}{9}$,

$a_3 = \frac{4}{2(3)+5} = \frac{4}{11}$, $a_4 = \frac{4}{2(4)+5} = \frac{4}{13}$

The first four terms are $\frac{4}{7}$, $\frac{4}{9}$, $\frac{4}{11}$, and $\frac{4}{13}$.

21. $c_1 = (-1)^1(1-2)^2 = -1$,

$c_2 = (-1)^2(2-2)^2 = 0$,

$c_3 = (-1)^3(3-2)^2 = -1$,

$c_4 = (-1)^4(4-2)^2 = 4$

The first four terms are -1, 0, -1, and 4.

22. $c_1 = (-1)^1(2(1)-1)^2 = -1$,

$c_2 = (-1)^2(2(2)-1)^2 = 9$,

$c_3 = (-1)^3(2(3)-1)^2 = -25$,

$c_4 = (-1)^4(2(4)-1)^2 = 49$

The first four terms are -1, 9, -25, and 49.

23. $a_1 = \frac{(-1)^{2(1)}}{1^2} = 1$, $a_2 = \frac{(-1)^{2(2)}}{2^2} = \frac{1}{4}$,

$a_3 = \frac{(-1)^{2(3)}}{3^2} = \frac{1}{9}$, $a_4 = \frac{(-1)^{2(4)}}{4^2} = \frac{1}{16}$

The first four terms are 1, $\frac{1}{4}$, $\frac{1}{9}$, and $\frac{1}{16}$.

24. $a_1 = (-1)^{2\cdot1+1}2^{1-1} = -1$

$a_2 = (-1)^{2\cdot2+1}2^{2-1} = -2$

$a_3 = (-1)^{2\cdot3+1}2^{3-1} = -4$

$a_4 = (-1)^{2\cdot4+1}2^{4-1} = -8$

The first four terms are -1, -2, -4, and -8.

25. This sequence is a sequence of odd integers starting at 1. Even integers are represented by $2n$ and odd integers are all one less than an even integer. Try the formula $a_n = 2n - 1$. To see that it is correct, find a_1 through a_5.

26. This sequence is a sequence of odd integers starting at 5. Even integers are represented by 2n and odd integers are all one more than an even integer. Try the formula $a_n = 2n + 1$. This formula would produce odd integers starting at 3. To get odd integers starting at 5 (when $n = 1$) we can use $a_n = 2n + 3$.

27. A sequence of alternating ones and negative ones is obtained by using a power of -1. Since we want a_1 to be positive when $n = 1$, we use the $n + 1$ power on -1. A formula for the general term is $a_n = (-1)^{n+1}$.

28. A sequence of alternating ones and negative ones is obtained by using a power of -1. Since we want a_1 to be negative when $n = 1$, we use the n power on -1. A formula for the general term is $a_n = (-1)^n$.

29. This sequence is a sequence of even integers starting at 0. Even integers can be generated by $2n$, but to make the first one 0 (when $n = 1$), we use the formula $a_n = 2n - 2$.

30. This sequence is a sequence of even integers starting at 4. Even integers can be generated by $2n$, but to make the first one 4 (when $n = 1$), we use the formula $a_n = 2n + 2$.

31. This sequence is a sequence consisting of the positive integral multiples of 3. Try the formula $a_n = 3n$ to see that it generates the appropriate numbers.

32. This sequence is a sequence consisting of the positive integral multiples of 4. Try the formula $a_n = 4n$ to see that it generates the appropriate numbers.

33. Each term in this sequence is one larger than the corresponding term in the sequence of Exercise 31. Try the formula $a_n = 3n + 1$ to see that it generates the given sequence.

34. Each term in this sequence is one unit smaller than the corresponding term in the sequence of Exercise 32. Try the formula $a_n = 4n - 1$ to see that it generates the given sequence.

35. To get the alternating signs on the terms of the sequence, we use a power of -1. Next we observe that the numbers 1, 2, 4, 8, 16 are powers of 2. The formula $a_n = (-1)^n 2^{n-1}$ will produce the given sequence. Remember that n always starts at 1, so in this case we use $n - 1$ as the power of 2 to get $2^0 = 1$.

36. To get the alternating signs on the terms of the sequence, we use a power of -1. Next we observe that the numbers 1, 3, 9, 27 are powers of 3. The formula $a_n = (-1)^{n-1} 3^{n-1}$ or $a_n = (-3)^{n-1}$ will produce the given sequence. Remember that n always starts at 1, so in this case we use $n - 1$ as the power of -3 to get $(-3)^0 = 1$.

37. Notice that the numbers 0, 1, 4, 9, 16, ... are the squares of the nonnegative integers: 0^2, $1^2, 2^2, 3^2, 4^2,....$. We would use n^2 to generate squares, but since n starts at 1, we use $a_n = (n - 1)^2$ to get the given sequence.

38. Notice that the numbers 0, 1, 8, 27, 64,... are the cubes of the nonnegative integers: 0^3, 1^3, 2^3, 3^3, 4^3. We would use n^3 to generate cubes, but since n starts at 1, we use $a_n = (n - 1)^3$ to get the given sequence.

39. After the first penalty the ball is on the 4-yard line. After the second penalty the ball is on the 2-yard line. After the third penalty the ball is on the 1-yard line, and so on. The sequence of five terms is $4, 2, 1, \frac{1}{2}, \frac{1}{4}$.

40. After the first week she has $\frac{2}{3} \cdot 9 = 6$ acres left. After the second week she had $\frac{2}{3} \cdot 6 = 4$ acre left. The number of acres remaining at the end of each week is given by the following sequence.
$$6, 4, \frac{8}{3}, \frac{16}{9}, \frac{32}{27}, \frac{64}{81}, \frac{128}{243} \cdots$$
After 6 weeks he has only $64/81$ of an acre healthy.

41. To find the amount of increase, we take 5% of $32,535 to get $1627 increase. We could just multiply $32,535 by 1.05 to obtain the new

price. In either case the price the next year is $34,162. To find the price for the next year we multiply the last year's price by 1.05: $1.05(\$34,161.75) = \$35,870$. Repeating this process gives us the prices $34,162, $35,870, $37,663, $39,546, $41,524, and $43,600 as the price of the truck through 2005.

42. In 2000 the car sells for $21,455 + $1000 or $22,455. The price each year for 2000 through 2005 will be $22,455, $23,455, $24,455, $25,455, $26,455, $27,455.

43. Of the $1 million, 80% is respent in the community. So $800,000 is respent. Of the $800,000 we have 80% respent in the community. So $640,000 is respent in the community, and so on. The first four terms of the sequence are $1,000,000, $800,000, $640,000, $512,000.

44. $1,000,000, $500,000, $250,000, $125,000

45. Possible vertical repeats are 27 in., 13.5 in., 9 in., 6.75 in., and 5.4 in.

46. Calculate $262 \cdot 2^{n/12}$ for $n = 1$ through 11 to get 278, 294, 312, 330, 350, 371, 393, 416, 441, 467, and 495 Hz.

47. If we put the word great in front of the word grandparents 35 times, then we have 2^{37} of this type of relative. Use a calculator to find that $2^{37} = 137,438,953,500$. This is certainly larger than the present population of the earth.

48. On the first you deposit 1 cent. On the second you deposit 2 cents. On the third you deposit 4 cents, and note that $4 = 2^{3-1}$. On the fourth you deposit 8 cents, and note that $8 = 2^{4-1}$. Continuing this pattern, we find that on the thirtieth you deposit $2^{30-1} = 2^{29} = 536870912$ cents, or $5,368,709.12.
$$1 + 2 = 3 = 2^2 - 1$$
$$1 + 2 + 4 = 7 = 2^3 - 1$$
$$1 + 2 + 4 + 8 = 15 = 2^4 - 1$$
$$1 + 2 + 4 + 8 + 16 + .. + 2^{29} = 2^{30} - 1$$
$$= \$10,737,418.23$$

51. a) Use a calculator to find

$$a_{100} = (0.999)^{100} = 0.9048,$$
$$a_{1000} = (0.999)^{1000} = 0.3677,$$

and $\quad a_{10000} = (0.999)^{10000} = 0.00004517.$

b) a_n approaches zero as n gets larger and larger.

12.2 WARM-UPS

1. True, because of the definition of series.

2. False, the sum of a series can be any real number.

3. False, there are 9 terms in 2^3 through 10^3.

4. False, because the terms in the first series are opposites of the terms in the second series.

5. False, the ninth term is $\frac{(-1)^9}{(9+1)(9+2)} = -\frac{1}{110}$.

6. True, because the terms are -2 and 4 and the sum is 2.

7. True, because of the distributive property.

8. True, because the notation indicates to add the number 4 five times.

9. True, because $2i + 7i = 9i$.

10. False, because in the series on the left side the 1 is added in three times and in the series on the right side the 1 is only added in once.

12.2 EXERCISES

1. Summation notation provides a way of writing a sum without writing out all of the terms.

2. The index of summation is the variable used in summation notation.

3. A series is the indicated sum of the terms of a sequence.

4. A finite series is the indicated sum of the terms of a finite sequence.

5. $\displaystyle\sum_{i=1}^{4} i^2 = 1^2 + 2^2 + 3^2 + 4^2$

$$= 1 + 4 + 9 + 16 = 30$$

6. $\displaystyle\sum_{j=0}^{3}(j+1)^2 = (0+1)^2 + (1+1)^2$

$$+ (2+1)^2 + (3+1)^2$$
$$= 1 + 4 + 9 + 16 = 30$$

7. $\displaystyle\sum_{j=0}^{5}(2j-1) = (2 \cdot 0 - 1) + (2 \cdot 1 - 1)$

$$+ (2 \cdot 2 - 1) + (2 \cdot 3 - 1)$$
$$+ (2 \cdot 4 - 1) + (2 \cdot 5 - 1)$$
$$= -1 + 1 + 3 + 5 + 7 + 9 = 24$$

8. $\displaystyle\sum_{i=1}^{6}(2i-3) = (2 \cdot 1 - 3) + (2 \cdot 2 - 3)$

$$+ (2 \cdot 3 - 3) + (2 \cdot 4 - 3)$$
$$+ (2 \cdot 5 - 3) + (2 \cdot 6 - 3)$$
$$= -1 + 1 + 3 + 5 + 7 + 9 = 24$$

9. $\displaystyle\sum_{i=1}^{5} 2^{-i} = 2^{-1} + 2^{-2} + 2^{-3} + 2^{-4} + 2^{-5}$

$$= \tfrac{1}{2} + \tfrac{1}{4} + \tfrac{1}{8} + \tfrac{1}{16} + \tfrac{1}{32} = \tfrac{31}{32}$$

10. $\displaystyle\sum_{i=1}^{5}(-2)^{-i} = (-2)^{-1} + (-2)^{-2} + (-2)^{-3}$

$$+ (-2)^{-4} + (-2)^{-5}$$
$$= -\tfrac{1}{2} + \tfrac{1}{4} - \tfrac{1}{8} + \tfrac{1}{16} - \tfrac{1}{32} = -\tfrac{11}{32}$$

11. $\displaystyle\sum_{i=1}^{10} 5i^0 = 5(1)^0 + 5(2)^0 + 5(3)^0 + 5(4)^0$

$$+ 5(5)^0 + 5(6)^0 + 5(7)^0$$
$$+ 5(8)^0 + 5(9)^0 + 5(10)^0$$
$$= 5 + 5 + 5 + 5 + 5 + 5 + 5 + 5 + 5 + 5$$
$$= 50$$

12. $\displaystyle\sum_{j=1}^{20} 3 = 20(3) = 60$

13. $\displaystyle\sum_{i=1}^{3}(i-3)(i+1) = (1-3)((1+1)$

$$+ (2-3)(2+1) + (3-3)(3+1)$$
$$= -4 + (-3) + 0 = -7$$

14. $\displaystyle\sum_{i=0}^{5} i(i-1)(i-2)(i-3)$

$$= 0(-1)(-2)(-3) + 1(0)(-1)(-2)$$
$$+ 2(1)(0)(-1) + 3(2)(1)(0)$$
$$+ 4(3)(2)(1) + 5(4)(3)(2)$$
$$= 24 + 120 = 144$$

15. $\displaystyle\sum_{j=1}^{10}(-1)^j$

$$= (-1)^1 + (-1)^2 + \ldots + (-1)^{10}$$
$$= -1 + 1 - 1 + 1 - 1 + 1 - 1$$
$$+ 1 - 1 + 1$$
$$= 0$$

16. $\displaystyle\sum_{j=1}^{11}(-1)^j = (-1)^1 + (-1)^2 + \ldots + (-1)^{11}$

$$= -1 + 1 - 1 + 1 - 1 + 1 - 1$$
$$+ 1 - 1 + 1 - 1$$
$$= -1$$

17. The sum of the first six positive integers is written as $\sum\limits_{i=1}^{6} i$. There are other ways to indicate this series in summation notation but this is the simplest.

18. The sum of the first five positive even integers is written as $\sum\limits_{i=1}^{5} 2i$. There are other ways to indicate this series in summation notation but this is the simplest.

19. To get the signs of the terms to alternate from positive to negative we use a power of -1. To get odd integers we use the formula $2i - 1$. So this series is written $\sum\limits_{i=1}^{6} (-1)^i (2i - 1)$.

20. To get the signs of the terms to alternate from positive to negative we use a power of -1. To get odd integers we use the formula $2i - 1$. So this series is written $\sum\limits_{i=1}^{5} (-1)^{i+1} (2i - 1)$.

21. This series consists of the squares of the first six positive integers. It is written in summation notation as $\sum\limits_{i=1}^{6} i^2$.

22. This series consists of the cubes of the first five positive integers. It is written in summation notation as $\sum\limits_{i=1}^{5} i^3$.

23. This series consists of the reciprocals of the positive integers. If the index i goes from 1 to 4, we must use $2 + i$ to get the numbers 3 through 6. So the series is written as $\sum\limits_{i=1}^{4} \frac{1}{2+i}$.

24. This series consists of the reciprocals of the positive integers. To get alternating signs use a power of -1. So the series is written as $\sum\limits_{i=1}^{6} \frac{(-1)^{i+1}}{i}$.

25. The terms of this series are logarithms of positive integers. If the index i goes from 1 to 3, we must use $i + 1$ to get the numbers 2 through 4. The series is written as $\sum\limits_{i=1}^{3} \ln(i + 1)$.

26. The terms of this series are the powers of e from the first through the fourth power. The series is written as $\sum\limits_{i=1}^{4} e^i$

27. Since the subscripts range from 1 through 4, we let i range from 1 through 4: $\sum\limits_{i=1}^{4} a_i$.

28. This is a series of 4 terms. Since the powers of a are 2 through 5, we let i range from 1 through 4 and use the exponent $i + 1$: $\sum\limits_{i=1}^{4} a^{i+1}$.

29. The subscripts on x range from 3 through 50, so i ranges from 1 through 48: $\sum\limits_{i=1}^{48} x_{i+2}$.

30. The subscripts on y range from 1 through 30, so i ranges from 1 through 30: $\sum\limits_{i=1}^{30} y_i$.

31. The subscripts on w range from 1 through n, so i ranges from 1 through n: $\sum\limits_{i=1}^{n} w_i$.

32. The subscripts on m range from 1 through k, so i ranges from 1 through k: $\sum\limits_{i=1}^{k} m_i$.

33. If $j = 0$ when $i = 1$, then $i = j + 1$ and j ranges from 0 through 4: $\sum\limits_{j=0}^{4} (j + 1)^2$

34. If $j = 0$ when $i = 1$, then $i = j + 1$ and j ranges from 0 through 5: $\sum\limits_{j=0}^{5} (j + 1)^3$

35. If $j = 1$ when $i = 0$, then $i = j - 1$ and j ranges from 1 through 13. If we substitute $i = j - 1$ into $2i - 1$ we get $2i - 1 = 2(j - 1) - 1 = 2j - 3$. So the series is written $\sum\limits_{j=1}^{13} (2j - 3)$.

36. If $j = 0$ when $i = 1$, then $i = j + 1$ and j ranges from 0 to 2. If we use $i = j + 1$ in the expression $3i + 2$ we get $3i + 2 = 3(j + 1) + 2 = 3j + 5$. So the series is written $\sum\limits_{j=0}^{2} (3j + 5)$.

37. If $j = 1$ when $i = 4$, then $i = j + 3$ and j ranges from 1 through 5. Substitute $j + 3$ for i to get $\sum_{j=1}^{5} \frac{1}{j+3}$.

38. If $j = 1$ when $i = 5$, then $i = j + 4$. So if i ranges from 5 through 10, j ranges from 1 through 6. If we us $i = j + 4$ in the expression 2^{-i} we get $2^{-i} = 2^{-(j+4)} = 2^{-j-4}$. So the series is written $\sum_{j=1}^{6} 2^{-j-4}$

39. If $j = 0$ when $i = 1$, then $i = j + 1$ and j ranges from 0 through 3. The exponent $2i + 3$ becomes $2(j+1) + 3 = 2j + 5$. The series is written as $\sum_{j=0}^{3} x^{2j+5}$.

40. If $i = 0$ when $j = 1$, then $i = j - 1$. So if i ranges from 0 through 2, j ranges from 1 through 3. If we us $i = j - 1$ in the expression x^{3-2i}, we get $x^{3-2i} = x^{3-2(j-1)} = x^{5-2j}$.

So the series is written as $\sum_{j=1}^{3} x^{5-2j}$.

41. If $j = 0$ when $i = 1$, then $i = j + 1$ and j ranges from 0 through n − 1. Replacing i by $j + 1$ gives us the series $\sum_{j=0}^{n-1} x^{j+1}$.

42. If $i = 0$ when $j = 1$, then $i = j - 1$. So if i ranges from 0 through n, j must range from 1 through $n + 1$. If we use $i = j - 1$ in the expression x^{-i}, we get $x^{-i} = x^{-(j-1)} = x^{-j+1}$.

So the series is written as $\sum_{j=1}^{n+1} x^{-j+1}$.

43. $\sum_{i=1}^{6} x^i = x + x^2 + x^3 + x^4 + x^5 + x^6$

44. $\sum_{i=1}^{5} (-1)^i x^{i-1} = (-1)^1 x^{1-1} + (-1)^2 x^{2-1}$
$+ (-1)^3 x^{3-1} + (-1)^4 x^{4-1}$
$+ (-1)^5 x^{5-1}$
$= -1 + x - x^2 + x^3 - x^4$

45. $\sum_{j=0}^{3} (-1)^j x_j$
$= (-1)^0 x_0 + (-1)^1 x_1 + (-1)^2 x_2 + (-1)^3 x_3$
$= x_0 - x_1 + x_2 - x_3$

46. $\sum_{j=1}^{5} \frac{1}{x_j} = \frac{1}{x_1} + \frac{1}{x_2} + \frac{1}{x_3} + \frac{1}{x_4} + \frac{1}{x_5}$

47. $\sum_{i=1}^{3} ix^i = 1x^1 + 2x^2 + 3x^3$
$= x + 2x^2 + 3x^3$

48. $\sum_{i=1}^{5} \frac{x}{i} = \frac{x}{1} + \frac{x}{2} + \frac{x}{3} + \frac{x}{4} + \frac{x}{5}$
$= x + \frac{x}{2} + \frac{x}{3} + \frac{x}{4} + \frac{x}{5}$

49. On the first jump he has moved $\frac{1}{2}$ yard. On the second jump he moves $\frac{1}{4}$ yard. On the third jump he moves $\frac{1}{8}$ yard, and so on. To express the reciprocals of the powers of 2, we use 2^{-i}. His total movement after nine jumps is expressed as the series $\sum_{i=1}^{9} 2^{-i}$.

50. Since the first $1000 receives interest for 5 years, at the end of 5 years it amounts to $1000(1 + 0.10)^5$. Since the second $1000 receives interest for 4 years, at the end of 4 years it amounts to $1000(1 + 0.10)^4$. The third $1000 deposit amounts to $1000(1 + 0.10)^3$. The fourth $1000 deposit amounts to $1000(1 + 0.10)^2$. The fifth deposit receives interest for only one year and it amounts to $1000(1 + 0.10)^1$. The total of all 5 deposits at the end of the fifth year will be $1000(1.1)^1 + 1000(1.1)^2 + 1000(1.1)^3$
$+ 1000(1.1)^4 + 1000(1.1)^5 = \sum_{i=1}^{5} 1000(1.1)^i$.

51. $\sum_{i=1}^{4} 1{,}000{,}000(0.8)^{i-1}$.

52. $\sum_{i=1}^{31} i$

53. A sequence is basically a list of numbers. A series is the indicated sum of the terms of a sequence.

54. Through trial an error you can determine that $n \geq 31$.

12.3 WARM-UPS

1. False, because the common difference is -2 $(1 - 3 = -2)$.

2. False, because the difference between consecutive terms is not constant.

3. False, because the difference between the consecutive terms is sometimes 2 and sometimes -2.

4. False, because the nth term is given by $a_n = a_1 + (n-1)d$.

5. False, because the second must be 7.5, making $d = 2.5$ and the fourth term 12.5.

6. False, because if the first is 6 and the third is 2, the second must be 4 in order to have a common difference.

7. True, because that is the definition of arithmetic sequence.

8. True, because the series is $5 + 7 + 9 + 11 + 13$ and the common difference is 2.

9. True, because of the formula for the sum of an arithmetic series.

10. False, because there are 11 even integers from 8 through 28 inclusive and the sum is $\frac{11}{2}(8 + 28)$.

12.3 EXERCISES

1. An arithmetic sequence is one in which each term after the first is obtained by adding a fixed amount to the previous term.

2. The nth term of an arithmetic sequence is $a_1 + (n-1)d$ where a_1 is the first term.

3. An arithmetic series is an indicated sum of an arithmetic sequence.

4. The formula for the sum of the first n terms of an arithmetic series is $\frac{n}{2}(a_1 + a_n)$.

5. The common difference is $d = 6$ and the first term is $a_1 = 0$. Use the formula $a_n = a_1 + (n-1)d$ to find that the nth term is $a_n = 0 + (n-1)6 = 6n - 6$.

6. The common difference is $d = 5$ and the first term is $a_1 = 0$. Use the formula $a_n = a_1 + (n-1)d$ to find that the nth term is $a_n = 0 + (n-1)5 = 5n - 5$.

7. The common difference is $d = 5$ and the first term is 7. The nth term is $a_n = 7 + (n-1)5 = 5n + 2$.

8. The common difference is $d = 11$ and the first term is $a_1 = 4$. Use the formula $a_n = a_1 + (n-1)d$ to find that the nth term is $a_n = 4 + (n-1)11 = 11n - 7$.

9. The common difference is $d = 2$ and the first term is $a_1 = -4$. Use the formula $a_n = a_1 + (n-1)d$ to find that the nth term is $a_n = -4 + (n-1)2 = 2n - 6$.

10. The common difference is $d = 3$ and the first term is $a_1 = -3$. Use the formula $a_n = a_1 + (n-1)d$ to find that the nth term is $a_n = -3 + (n-1)3 = 3n - 6$.

11. The common difference is $d = 1 - 5 = -4$ and the first term is $a_1 = 5$. The nth term is $a_n = 5 + (n-1)(-4) = -4n + 9$.

12. The common difference is $d = -3$ and the first term is $a_1 = 8$. Use the formula $a_n = a_1 + (n-1)d$ to find that the nth term is $a_n = 8 + (n-1)(-3) = -3n + 11$.

13. The common difference is $d = -9 - (-2) = -7$ and the first term is -2. The nth term is $a_n = -2 + (n-1)(-7) = -7n + 5$.

14. The common difference is $d = -7 - (-5) = -2$ and the first term is -5. The nth term is $a_n = -5 + (n-1)(-2) = -2n - 3$.

15. The common difference is $d = -2.5 - (-3) = 0.5$ and the first term is -3. The nth term is $a_n = -3 + (n-1)(0.5) = 0.5n - 3.5$.

16. The common difference is $d = -1.25 - (-2) = 0.75$ and the first term is -2. The nth term is $a_n = -2 + (n-1)(0.75) = 0.75n - 2.75$.

17. The common difference is $d = -6.5 - (-6) = -0.5$ and the first term is -6. The nth term is $a_n = -6 + (n-1)(-0.5) = -0.5n - 5.5$.

18. The common difference is $d = 0.5 - (1) = -0.5$ and the first term is 1. The nth term is $a_n = 1 + (n-1)(-0.5) = -0.5n + 1.5$.

19. $a_1 = 9 + (1 - 1)4 = 9,$
$a_2 = 9 + (2 - 1)4 = 13,$
$a_3 = 9 + (3 - 1)4 = 17,$
$a_4 = 9 + (4 - 1)4 = 21,$
$a_5 = 9 + (5 - 1)4 = 25$
The first five terms of the arithmetic sequence are 9, 13, 17, 21, and 25.

20. $a_1 = 13 + (1 - 1)(6) = 13,$
$a_2 = 13 + (2 - 1)(6) = 19,$
$a_3 = 13 + (3 - 1)(6) = 25,$
$a_4 = 13 + (4 - 1)(6) = 31,$
$a_5 = 13 + (5 - 1)(6) = 37$
The first five terms of the arithmetic sequence are 13, 19, 25, 31, and 37.

21. $a_1 = 7 + (1 - 1)(-2) = 7,$
$a_2 = 7 + (2 - 1)(-2) = 5,$
$a_3 = 7 + (3 - 1)(-2) = 3,$
$a_4 = 7 + (4 - 1)(-2) = 1,$
$a_5 = 7 + (5 - 1)(-2) = -1$
The first five terms of the arithmetic sequence are 7, 5, 3, 1, and -1.

22. $a_1 = 6 + (1 - 1)(-3) = 6,$
$a_2 = 6 + (2 - 1)(-3) = 3,$
$a_3 = 6 + (3 - 1)(-3) = 0,$
$a_4 = 6 + (4 - 1)(-3) = -3,$
$a_5 = 6 + (5 - 1)(-3) = -6$
The first five terms of the arithmetic sequence are 6, 3, 0, -3, and -6.

23. $a_1 = -4 + (1 - 1)3 = -4,$
$a_2 = -4 + (2 - 1)3 = -1,$
$a_3 = -4 + (3 - 1)3 = 2,$
$a_4 = -4 + (4 - 1)3 = 5,$
$a_5 = -4 + (5 - 1)3 = 8$
The first five terms of the arithmetic sequence are -4, -1, 2, 5, and 8.

24. $a_1 = -19 + (1 - 1)12 = -19,$
$a_2 = -19 + (2 - 1)12 = -7,$
$a_3 = -19 + (3 - 1)12 = 5,$
$a_4 = -19 + (4 - 1)12 = 17,$
$a_5 = -19 + (5 - 1)12 = 29$
The first five terms of the arithmetic sequence are -19, -7, 5, 17, and 29.

25. $a_1 = -2 + (1 - 1)(-3) = -2,$
$a_2 = -2 + (2 - 1)(-3) = -5,$
$a_3 = -2 + (3 - 1)(-3) = -8,$
$a_4 = -2 + (4 - 1)(-3) = -11,$

$a_5 = -2 + (5 - 1)(-3) = -14$
The first five terms of the arithmetic sequence are -2, -5, -8, -11, and -14.

26. $a_1 = -1 + (1 - 1)(-2) = -1,$
$a_2 = -1 + (2 - 1)(-2) = -3,$
$a_3 = -1 + (3 - 1)(-2) = -5,$
$a_4 = -1 + (4 - 1)(-2) = -7,$
$a_5 = -1 + (5 - 1)(-2) = -9$
The first five terms of the arithmetic sequence are -1, -3, -5, -7, and -9.

27. $a_1 = -4(1) - 3 = -7,$
$a_2 = -4(2) - 3 = -11,$
$a_3 = -4(3) - 3 = -15,$
$a_4 = -4(4) - 3 = -19,$
$a_5 = -4(5) - 3 = -23$
The first five terms of the arithmetic sequence are -7, -11, -15, -19, and -23.

28. $a_1 = -3(1) + 1 = -2,$
$a_2 = -3(2) + 1 = -5, a_3 = -3(3) + 1 = -8,$
$a_4 = -3(4) + 1 = -11,$
$a_5 = -3(5) + 1 = -14$
The first five terms of the arithmetic sequence are -2, -5, -8, -11, and -14.

29. $a_1 = 0.5(1) + 4 = 4.5,$
$a_2 = 0.5(2) + 4 = 5, a_3 = 0.5(3) + 4 = 5.5,$
$a_4 = 0.5(4) + 4 = 6, a_5 = 0.5(5) + 4 = 6.5$
The first five terms of the arithmetic sequence are 4.5, 5, 5.5, 6, and 6.5.

30. $a_1 = 0.3(1) + 1 = 1.3,$
$a_2 = 0.3(2) + 1 = 1.6, a_3 = 0.3(3) + 1 = 1.9,$
$a_4 = 0.3(4) + 1 = 2.2, a_5 = 0.3(5) + 1 = 2.5$
The first five terms of the arithmetic sequence are 1.3, 1.6, 1.9, 2.2, and 2.5.

31. $a_1 = 20(1) + 1000 = 1020,$
$a_2 = 20(2) + 1000 = 1040,$
$a_3 = 20(3) + 1000 = 1060,$
$a_4 = 20(4) + 1000 = 1080,$
$a_5 = 20(5) + 1000 = 1100$
The first five terms of the arithmetic sequence are 1020, 1040, 1060, 1080, and 1100.

32. $a_1 = -600(1) + 4000 = 3400,$
$a_2 = -600(2) + 4000 = 2800,$
$a_3 = -600(3) + 4000 = 2200,$
$a_4 = -600(4) + 4000 = 1600,$
$a_5 = -600(5) + 4000 = 1000$
The first five terms of the arithmetic sequence are 3400, 2800, 2200, 1600, and 1000.

33. Use $a_1 = 9$, $n = 8$, and $d = 6$ in the formula $a_n = a_1 + (n-1)d$.
$$a_8 = 9 + (8-1)6 = 51$$
34. Use $a_1 = -2$, $n = 12$, and $d = -3$ in the formula $a_n = a_1 + (n-1)d$.
$$a_{12} = -2 + (12-1)(-3) = -35$$
35. Use $a_1 = 6$, $a_{20} = 82$, and $n = 20$ in the formula $a_n = a_1 + (n-1)d$.
$$82 = 6 + (20-1)d$$
$$82 = 6 + 19d$$
$$76 = 19d$$
$$4 = d$$
36. Use $a_1 = -8$, $a_9 = -64$, and $n = 9$ in the formula $a_n = a_1 + (n-1)d$.
$$-64 = -8 + (9-1)d$$
$$-64 = -8 + 8d$$
$$-56 = 8d$$
$$-7 = d$$
37. Use $a_7 = 14$, $d = -2$, and $n = 7$ in the formula $a_n = a_1 + (n-1)d$.
$$14 = a_1 + (7-1)(-2)$$
$$14 = a_1 - 12$$
$$26 = a_1$$
38. Use $a_{12} = -7$, $d = 5$, and $n = 12$ in the formula $a_n = a_1 + (n-1)d$.
$$-7 = a_1 + (12-1)(5)$$
$$-7 = a_1 + 55$$
$$-62 = a_1$$
39. From the fact that the fifth term is 13 and the first term is -3, we can find the common difference.
$$13 = -3 + (5-1)d$$
$$13 = -3 + 4d$$
$$16 = 4d$$
$$4 = d$$
Use $a_1 = -3$, $n = 6$, and $d = 4$ in the formula $a_n = a_1 + (n-1)d$.
$$a_6 = -3 + (6-1)4 = 17$$

40. From the fact that the sixth term is -42 and the first term is 3, we can find the common difference.
$$-42 = 3 + (6-1)d$$
$$-42 = 3 + 5d$$
$$-45 = 5d$$
$$-9 = d$$
Use $a_1 = 3$, $n = 8$, and $d = -9$ in the formula $a_n = a_1 + (n-1)d$.
$$a_8 = 3 + (8-1)(-9) = -60$$
41. Use $a_1 = 1$, $a_{48} = 48$, and $n = 48$ in the formula $S_n = \frac{n}{2}(a_1 + a_n)$.
$$S_{48} = \frac{48}{2}(1 + 48) = 1176$$
42. Use $a_1 = 1$, $a_{12} = 12$, and $n = 12$ in the formula $S_n = \frac{n}{2}(a_1 + a_n)$.
$$S_{12} = \frac{12}{2}(1 + 12) = 78$$

43. To find n, use $a_1 = 8$, $d = 2$, and $a_n = 36$ in the formula $a_n = a_1 + (n-1)d$.
$$36 = 8 + (n-1)2$$
$$36 = 8 + 2n - 2$$
$$30 = 2n$$
$$15 = n$$
Use $a_1 = 8$, $a_{15} = 36$, and $n = 15$ in the formula $S_n = \frac{n}{2}(a_1 + a_n)$.
$$S_{15} = \frac{15}{2}(8 + 36) = 330$$

44. To find n, use $a_1 = 9$, $d = 3$, and $a_n = 72$ in the formula $a_n = a_1 + (n-1)d$.
$$72 = 9 + (n-1)3$$
$$72 = 9 + 3n - 3$$
$$66 = 3n$$
$$22 = n$$
Use $a_1 = 9$, $a_{22} = 72$, and $n = 22$ in the formula $S_n = \frac{n}{2}(a_1 + a_n)$.
$$S_{22} = \frac{22}{2}(9 + 72) = 891$$
45. To find n, use $a_1 = -1$, $d = -6$, and $a_n = -73$ in the formula $a_n = a_1 + (n-1)d$.
$$-73 = -1 + (n-1)(-6)$$
$$-78 = -1 - 6n + 6$$
$$-78 = -6n$$
$$13 = n$$
Use $a_1 = -1$, $a_{13} = -73$, and $n = 13$ in the formula $S_n = \frac{n}{2}(a_1 + a_n)$.
$$S_{13} = \frac{13}{2}(-1 + (-73)) = -481$$

46. To find n, use $a_1 = -7$, $d = -5$, and $a_n = -72$ in the formula $a_n = a_1 + (n-1)d$.
$$-72 = -7 + (n-1)(-5)$$
$$-72 = -7 - 5n + 5$$
$$-70 = -5n$$
$$14 = n$$
Use $a_1 = -7$, $a_{14} = -72$, and $n = 14$ in the formula $S_n = \frac{n}{2}(a_1 + a_n)$.
$$S_{14} = \frac{14}{2}(-7 + (-72)) = -553$$

47. To find n, use $a_1 = -6$, $d = 5$, and $a_n = 64$ in the formula $a_n = a_1 + (n-1)d$.
$$64 = -6 + (n-1)5$$
$$64 = -6 + 5n - 5$$
$$75 = 5n$$
$$15 = n$$
Use $a_1 = -6$, $a_{15} = 64$, and $n = 15$ in the formula $S_n = \frac{n}{2}(a_1 + a_n)$.
$$S_{15} = \frac{15}{2}(-6 + 64) = 435$$

48. To find n, use $a_1 = -9$, $d = 8$, and $a_n = 103$ in the formula $a_n = a_1 + (n-1)d$.
$$103 = -9 + (n-1)8$$
$$103 = -9 + 8n - 8$$
$$120 = 8n$$
$$15 = n$$
Use $a_1 = -9$, $a_{15} = 103$, and $n = 15$ in the formula $S_n = \frac{n}{2}(a_1 + a_n)$.
$$S_{15} = \frac{15}{2}(-9 + 103) = 705$$

49. To find n, use $a_1 = 20$, $d = -8$, and $a_n = -92$ in the formula $a_n = a_1 + (n-1)d$.
$$-92 = 20 + (n-1)(-8)$$
$$-92 = 20 - 8n + 8$$
$$-120 = -8n$$
$$15 = n$$
Use $a_1 = 20$, $a_{15} = -92$, and $n = 15$ in the formula $S_n = \frac{n}{2}(a_1 + a_n)$.
$$S_{15} = \frac{15}{2}(20 + (-92)) = -540$$

50. To find n, use $a_1 = 19$, $d = -18$, and $a_n = -125$ in the formula $a_n = a_1 + (n-1)d$.
$$-125 = 19 + (n-1)(-18)$$
$$-125 = 19 - 18n + 18$$
$$-162 = -18n$$
$$9 = n$$
Use $a_1 = 19$, $a_9 = -125$, and $n = 9$ in the formula $S_n = \frac{n}{2}(a_1 + a_n)$.

$$S_9 = \frac{9}{2}(19 + (-125)) = -477$$

51. $\displaystyle\sum_{i=1}^{12}(3i - 7) = -4 + (-1) + \ldots + 29$
Use $a_1 = -4$, $a_{12} = 29$, and $n = 12$ in the formula $S_n = \frac{n}{2}(a_1 + a_n)$.
$$S_{12} = \frac{12}{2}(-4 + 29) = 150$$

52. $\displaystyle\sum_{i=1}^{7}(-4i + 6) = 2 + (-2) + \ldots + (-22)$
Use $a_1 = 2$, $a_7 = -22$, and $n = 7$ in the formula $S_n = \frac{n}{2}(a_1 + a_n)$.
$$S_7 = \frac{7}{2}(2 + (-22)) = -70$$

53. $\displaystyle\sum_{i=1}^{11}(-5i + 2) = -3 + (-8) + \ldots + (-53)$
Use $a_1 = -3$, $a_{11} = -53$, and $n = 11$ in the formula $S_n = \frac{n}{2}(a_1 + a_n)$.
$$S_{11} = \frac{11}{2}(-3 + (-53)) = -308$$

54. $\displaystyle\sum_{i=1}^{19}(3i - 5) = -2 + (1) + \ldots + (52)$
Use $a_1 = -2$, $a_{19} = 52$, and $n = 19$ in the formula $S_n = \frac{n}{2}(a_1 + a_n)$.
$$S_{19} = \frac{19}{2}(-2 + (52)) = 475$$

55. Use $a_1 = \$22{,}000$, $n = 7$, and $d = \$500$ in the formula $a_n = a_1 + (n-1)d$.
$$a_7 = 22{,}000 + (7 - 1)500 = \$25{,}000$$

56. To find the total salary in the last exercise, we need to find
$\$22{,}000 + \$22{,}500 + \$23{,}000 + \ldots + \$25{,}000$.
Use $a_1 = \$22{,}000$, $n = 7$, and $d = \$500$ in the formula $S_n = \frac{n}{2}(a_1 + a_n)$.

$$S_7 = \frac{7}{2}(22{,}000 + 25{,}000) = \$164{,}500$$

57. The students read 5 pages the first day, 7 pages the second day, 9 pages the third day, and so on. To find the number they read on the 31st day, let $n = 31$, $d = 2$, and $a = 5$ in the formula $a_n = a_1 + (n-1)d$.
$$a_{31} = 5 + (31 - 1)2 = 65$$
To find the sum $5 + 7 + 9 + \ldots + 65$, use $n = 31$, $a_1 = 5$, and $a_{31} = 65$ in the formula $S_n = \frac{n}{2}(a_1 + a_n)$.
$$S_{31} = \frac{31}{2}(5 + 65) = 1085$$

58. The total amount of penalties for 10 days late is $500 + 600 + 700 + 800 + 900 + 1000 + 1100 + 1200 + 1300 + 1400$. To find the sum we can use $a_1 = 500$, $n = 10$, and $a_{10} = 1400$ in the formula $S_n = \frac{n}{2}(a_1 + a_n)$.
$$S_{10} = \frac{10}{2}(500 + 1400) = \$9,500$$
59. The only sequence that does not have a common difference is (b) and so it is not arithmetic.
60. Use a calculator and trial and error to find that $n = 14$.

12.4 WARM-UPS

1. False, because the ratio of two consecutive terms is not constant.
2. False, there is a common ratio of 2 between adjacent terms.
3. True, because the general form for a geometric sequence is $a_n = a_1 r^{n-1}$.
4. True, because if $n = 1$, then $3(2)^{-1+3} = 12$.
5. True, because $a_1 = 12$ and $a_2 = 6$ gives $r = 1/2$.
6. True, because of the definition of geometric series.
7. False, because we have a formula for the sum of a finite geometric series.
8. False, because $a_1 = 6$.
9. True, because this is the correct formula for the sum of all of the terms of an infinite geometric series with first term 10 and ratio 1/2.
10. False, because there is no sum for an infinite geometric series with a ratio of 2.

12.4 EXERCISES

1. A geometric sequence is one in which each term after the first is obtained by multiplying the preceding term by a constant.
2. The nth term of a geometric sequence is $a_1 r^{n-1}$ where a_1 is the first term and r is the common ratio.
3. A geometric series is an indicated sum of a geometric sequence.

4. The sum of the first n terms of a geometric series is given by $S_n = \frac{a_1(1 - r^n)}{1 - r}$.
5. The approximate value of r^n when n is large and $|r| < 1$ is 0.
6. The sum of an infinite geometric series is given by $S = \frac{a_1}{1 - r}$ provided $|r| < 1$.
7. Since the first term is 1/3 and the common ratio is 3, the nth term is $a_n = \frac{1}{3}(3)^{n-1}$.
8. Since the first term is 1/4 and the common ratio is 8, the nth term is $a_n = \frac{1}{4}(8)^{n-1}$.
9. Since the first term is 64 and the common ratio is 1/8, the nth term is $a_n = 64\left(\frac{1}{8}\right)^{n-1}$.
10. Since the first term is 100 and the common ratio is 1/10, the nth term is
$$a_n = 100\left(\frac{1}{10}\right)^{n-1}.$$
11. Since the first term is 8 and the common ratio is $-1/2$, the nth term is
$$a_n = 8\left(-\frac{1}{2}\right)^{n-1}.$$
12. Since the first term is -9 and the common ratio is $-1/3$, the nth term is
$$a_n = -9\left(-\frac{1}{3}\right)^{n-1}.$$
13. Since the first term is 2 and the common ratio is $-4/2 = -2$, the nth term is
$$a_n = 2(-2)^{n-1}.$$
14. Since the first term is $-1/2$ and the common ratio is -4, the nth term is
$$a_n = -\frac{1}{2}(-4)^{n-1}.$$
15. Since the first term is $-1/3$ and the common ratio is $(-1/4)/(-1/3) = 3/4$, the nth term is $a_n = -\frac{1}{3}\left(\frac{3}{4}\right)^{n-1}.$
16. Since the first term is $-1/4$ and the common ratio is $(-1/5)/(-1/4) = 4/5$, the nth term is $a_n = -\frac{1}{4}\left(\frac{4}{5}\right)^{n-1}.$

17. $a_1 = 2(1/3)^{1-1} = 2,$
$a_2 = 2(1/3)^{2-1} = 2/3,$
$a_3 = 2(1/3)^{3-1} = 2/9,$
$a_4 = 2(1/3)^{4-1} = 2/27,$
$a_5 = 2(1/3)^{5-1} = 2/81$
The first 5 terms are $2, \frac{2}{3}, \frac{2}{9}, \frac{2}{27},$ and $\frac{2}{81}.$

18. $a_1 = -5(1/2)^{1-1} = -5$,
$a_2 = -5(1/2)^{2-1} = -5/2$,
$a_3 = -5(1/2)^{3-1} = -5/4$,
$a_4 = -5(1/2)^{4-1} = -5/8$,
$a_5 = -5(1/2)^{5-1} = -5/16$
The first 5 terms are -5, $-\frac{5}{2}$, $-\frac{5}{4}$, $-\frac{5}{8}$, and $-\frac{5}{16}$.

19. $a_1 = (-2)^{1-1} = 1$,
$a_2 = (-2)^{2-1} = -2$, $\quad a_3 = (-2)^{3-1} = 4$,
$a_4 = (-2)^{4-1} = -8$, $\quad a_5 = (-2)^{5-1} = 16$
The first 5 terms are $1, -2, 4, -8$, and 16.

20. $a_1 = (-1/3)^{1-1} = 1$,
$a_2 = (-1/3)^{2-1} = -1/3$,
$a_3 = (-1/3)^{3-1} = 1/9$,
$a_4 = (-1/3)^{4-1} = -1/27$,
$a_5 = (-1/3)^{5-1} = 1/81$
The first 5 terms are 1, $-\frac{1}{3}$, $\frac{1}{9}$, $-\frac{1}{27}$, and $\frac{1}{81}$.

21. $a_1 = 2^{-1} = 1/2$,
$a_2 = 2^{-2} = 1/4$, $\quad a_3 = 2^{-3} = 1/8$,
$a_4 = 2^{-4} = 1/16$, $\quad a_5 = 2^{-5} = 1/32$
The first 5 terms are $\frac{1}{2}$, $\frac{1}{4}$, $\frac{1}{8}$, $\frac{1}{16}$, and $\frac{1}{32}$.

22. $a_1 = 3^{-1} = 1/3$,
$a_2 = 3^{-2} = 1/9$, $\quad a_3 = 3^{-3} = 1/27$,
$a_4 = 3^{-4} = 1/81$, $\quad a_5 = 3^{-5} = 1/243$
The first 5 terms are $\frac{1}{3}$, $\frac{1}{9}$, $\frac{1}{27}$, $\frac{1}{81}$, and $\frac{1}{243}$.

23. $a_1 = (0.78)^1 = 0.78$,
$a_2 = (0.78)^2 = 0.6084$,
$a_3 = (0.78)^3 = 0.4746$,
$a_4 = (0.78)^4 = 0.3702$, $a_5 = (0.78)^5 = 0.2887$
The first 5 terms are $0.78, 0.6084, 0.4746,$
$0.3702,$ and 0.2887.

24. $a_1 = (-0.23)^1 = -0.23$,
$a_2 = (-0.723)^2 = 0.0529$,
$a_3 = (-0.23)^3 = -0.0122$,
$a_4 = (-0.23)^4 = 0.0028$,
$a_5 = (-0.23)^5 = -0.0006$
The first 5 terms are $-0.23, 0.0529, -0.0122,$
$0.0028,$ and -0.0006.

25. Use $a_4 = 40$, $n = 4$, and $r = 2$ in the formula $a_n = a_1 r^{n-1}$.
$$40 = a_1(2)^{4-1}$$
$$40 = 8a_1$$
$$5 = a_1$$

26. Use $a_5 = 4$, $n = 5$, and $r = 1/2$ in the formula $a_n = a_1 r^{n-1}$.
$$4 = a_1(1/2)^{5-1}$$
$$4 = \tfrac{1}{16}a_1$$
$$64 = a_1$$

27. Use $a_4 = 2/9$, $n = 4$, and $a_1 = 6$ in the formula $a_n = a_1 r^{n-1}$.

$$\tfrac{2}{9} = 6r^{4-1}$$

$$\tfrac{1}{27} = r^3$$

$$\tfrac{1}{3} = r$$

28. Use $a_4 = -27$, $n = 4$, and $a_1 = 1$ in the formula $a_n = a_1 r^{n-1}$.
$$-27 = 1r^{4-1}$$
$$-27 = r^3$$
$$-3 = r$$

29. Use $r = 1/3$, $n = 4$, and $a_1 = -3$ in the formula $a_n = a_1 r^{n-1}$.
$$a_4 = -3\left(\tfrac{1}{3}\right)^{4-1} = -3\left(\tfrac{1}{27}\right) = -\tfrac{1}{9}$$

30. Use $r = -2/3$, $n = 5$, and $a_1 = -2/3$ in the formula $a_n = a_1 r^{n-1}$.
$$a_5 = -\tfrac{2}{3}\left(-\tfrac{2}{3}\right)^{5-1} = -\tfrac{2}{3}\left(\tfrac{16}{81}\right) = -\tfrac{32}{243}$$

31. Use $r = 1/2$, $a_1 = 1/2$, and $a_n = 1/512$ in the formula $a_n = a_1 r^{n-1}$ to find n.

$$\tfrac{1}{512} = \tfrac{1}{2}\left(\tfrac{1}{2}\right)^{n-1}$$

$$\tfrac{1}{2^9} = \left(\tfrac{1}{2}\right)^n$$

$$n = 9$$

Use $n = 9$, $a_1 = 1/2$, and $r = 1/2$ in the formula $S_n = \dfrac{a_1(1 - r^n)}{1 - r}$.

$$S_9 = \frac{\tfrac{1}{2}\left(1 - \left(\tfrac{1}{2}\right)^9\right)}{1 - \tfrac{1}{2}} = 1 - \tfrac{1}{512} = \tfrac{511}{512}$$

32. Use $r = 1/3$, $a_1 = 1$, and $a_n = 1/81$ in the formula $a_n = a_1 r^{n-1}$ to find n.

$$\frac{1}{81} = 1\left(\frac{1}{3}\right)^{n-1}$$

$$\left(\frac{1}{3}\right)^4 = \left(\frac{1}{3}\right)^{n-1}$$

$$n - 1 = 4$$
$$n = 5$$

Use $n = 5$, $a_1 = 1$, and $r = 1/3$ in the formula $S_n = \dfrac{a_1(1 - r^n)}{1 - r}$.

$$S_5 = \frac{1\left(1 - \left(\frac{1}{3}\right)^5\right)}{1 - \frac{1}{3}} = \frac{\frac{242}{243}}{\frac{2}{3}} = \frac{121}{81}$$

33. Use $n = 5$, $a_1 = 1/2$, and $r = -1/2$ in the formula $S_n = \dfrac{a_1(1 - r^n)}{1 - r}$.

$$S_5 = \frac{\frac{1}{2}\left(1 - \left(-\frac{1}{2}\right)^5\right)}{1 - \left(-\frac{1}{2}\right)} = \frac{\frac{1}{2}\left(\frac{33}{32}\right)}{\frac{3}{2}} = \frac{11}{32}$$

34. Use $n = 6$, $a_1 = 3$, and $r = -1/3$ in the formula $S_n = \dfrac{a_1(1 - r^n)}{1 - r}$.

$$S_6 = \frac{3\left(1 - \left(-\frac{1}{3}\right)^6\right)}{1 - \left(-\frac{1}{3}\right)} = \frac{3\left(\frac{728}{729}\right)}{\frac{4}{3}} = \frac{182}{81}$$

35. First determine the number of terms. Since $r = 2/3$, the nth term is $30\left(\frac{2}{3}\right)^{n-1}$. Solve

$$30\left(\frac{2}{3}\right)^{n-1} = \frac{1280}{729}$$
$$\left(\frac{2}{3}\right)^{n-1} = \frac{128}{2187} = \left(\frac{2}{3}\right)^7$$
$$n - 1 = 7$$
$$n = 8$$

Use $n = 8$, $a_1 = 30$, and $r = 2/3$ in the formula $S_n = \dfrac{a_1(1 - r^n)}{1 - r}$.

$$S_8 = \frac{30\left(1 - \left(\frac{2}{3}\right)^8\right)}{1 - \left(\frac{2}{3}\right)} = \frac{30\left(\frac{6305}{6561}\right)}{\frac{1}{3}}$$
$$= \frac{63050}{729} \approx 86.4883$$

36. First determine the number of terms. Since $r = -2/3$, the nth term is $9\left(-\frac{2}{3}\right)^{n-1}$. Solve

$$9\left(-\frac{2}{3}\right)^{n-1} = -\frac{128}{243}$$
$$\left(-\frac{2}{3}\right)^{n-1} = -\frac{128}{2187} = \left(-\frac{2}{3}\right)^7$$
$$n - 1 = 7$$
$$n = 8$$

Use $n = 8$, $a_1 = 9$, and $r = -2/3$ in the formula $S_n = \dfrac{a_1(1 - r^n)}{1 - r}$.

$$S_8 = \frac{9\left(1 - \left(-\frac{2}{3}\right)^8\right)}{1 - \left(-\frac{2}{3}\right)} = \frac{9\left(\frac{6305}{6561}\right)}{\frac{5}{3}}$$
$$= \frac{1261}{243} \approx 5.1893$$

37. $\displaystyle\sum_{i=1}^{10} 5(2)^{i-1} = S_{10} = \dfrac{5\left(1 - (2)^{10}\right)}{1 - (2)}$

$$= \frac{5(-1023)}{-1} = 5115$$

38. $\displaystyle\sum_{i=1}^{7} (10000)(0.1)^{i-1} = S_7$

$$= \frac{10000\left(1 - (0.1)^7\right)}{1 - 0.1} = \frac{10000(0.9999999)}{0.9}$$

$$= 11{,}111.11$$

39. $\displaystyle\sum_{i=1}^{6} (0.1)^i = S_6 = \dfrac{0.1\left(1 - (0.1)^6\right)}{1 - (0.1)}$

$$= \frac{0.1(0.999999)}{0.9} = 0.111111$$

40. $\displaystyle\sum_{i=1}^{5} (0.2)^i = S_5 = \dfrac{0.2\left(1 - (0.2)^5\right)}{1 - (0.2)}$

$$= 0.24992$$

41. $\displaystyle\sum_{i=1}^{6} 100(0.3)^i = S_6$

$$= \frac{100(0.3)\left(1 - (0.3)^6\right)}{1 - (0.3)}$$
$$= \frac{100(0.3)(1 - (0.3)^6)}{0.7} = 42.8259$$

42. $\displaystyle\sum_{i=1}^{7} 36(0.5)^i = S_7 = \dfrac{36(0.5)\left(1 - (0.5)^7\right)}{1 - (0.5)}$

$$= 35.71875$$

43. Use $a_1 = 1/8$ and $r = 1/2$ in the formula for the sum of an infinite geometric series $S = \dfrac{a_1}{1 - r}$.

$$S = \frac{\frac{1}{8}}{1 - \frac{1}{2}} = \frac{\frac{1}{8}}{\frac{1}{2}} = \frac{1}{4}$$

44. Use $a_1 = 1/9$ and $r = 1/3$ in the formula for the sum of an infinite geometric series $S = \dfrac{a_1}{1 - r}$.

$$S = \frac{\frac{1}{9}}{1 - \frac{1}{3}} = \frac{\frac{1}{9}}{\frac{2}{3}} = \frac{1}{6}$$

45. Use $a_1 = 3$ and $r = 2/3$ in $S = \dfrac{a_1}{1 - r}$.

$$S = \frac{3}{1 - \frac{2}{3}} = \frac{3}{\frac{1}{3}} = 9$$

46. Use $a_1 = 2$ and $r = 1/2$ in $S = \frac{a_1}{1-r}$.

$$S = \frac{2}{1-\frac{1}{2}} = \frac{2}{\frac{1}{2}} = 4$$

47. Use $a_1 = 4$ and $r = -1/2$ in $S = \frac{a_1}{1-r}$.

$$S = \frac{4}{1-\left(-\frac{1}{2}\right)} = \frac{4}{\frac{3}{2}} = \frac{8}{3}$$

48. Use $a_1 = 16$ and $r = -3/4$ in $S = \frac{a_1}{1-r}$.

$$S = \frac{16}{1-\left(-\frac{3}{4}\right)} = \frac{16}{\frac{7}{4}} = \frac{64}{7}$$

49. Use $a_1 = 0.3$ and $r = 0.3$ in $S = \frac{a_1}{1-r}$.

$$S = \frac{0.3}{1-0.3} = \frac{0.3}{0.7} = \frac{3}{7}$$

50. Use $a_1 = 0.2$ and $r = 0.2$ in $S = \frac{a_1}{1-r}$.

$$S = \frac{0.2}{1-0.2} = \frac{0.2}{0.8} = \frac{1}{4}$$

51. Use $a_1 = 3$ and $r = 0.5$ in $S = \frac{a_1}{1-r}$.

$$S = \frac{3}{1-0.5} = \frac{3}{0.5} = 6$$

52. Use $a_1 = 7$ and $r = 0.4$ in $S = \frac{a_1}{1-r}$.

$$S = \frac{7}{1-0.4} = \frac{7}{0.6} = \frac{35}{3}$$

53. Use $a_1 = 3$ and $r = 0.1$ in $S = \frac{a_1}{1-r}$.

$$S = \frac{0.3}{1-0.1} = \frac{0.3}{0.9} = \frac{1}{3}$$

54. Use $a_1 = 0.6$ and $r = 0.1$ in $S = \frac{a_1}{1-r}$.

$$S = \frac{0.6}{1-0.1} = \frac{0.6}{0.9} = \frac{2}{3}$$

55. Use $a_1 = 0.12$ and $r = 0.01$ in $S = \frac{a_1}{1-r}$.

$$S = \frac{0.12}{1-0.01} = \frac{0.12}{0.99} = \frac{12}{99} = \frac{4}{33}$$

56. Use $a_1 = 0.72$ and $r = 0.01$ in $S = \frac{a_1}{1-r}$.

$$S = \frac{0.72}{1-0.01} = \frac{0.72}{0.99} = \frac{72}{99} = \frac{8}{11}$$

57. We want the sum of the geometric series

$$2000(1.12)^{45} + 2000(1.12)^{44} + \ldots + 2000(1.12).$$

Note that the last deposit is made at the beginning of the 45th year and earns interest for only one year. Rewrite the series as
$2000(1.12) + 2000(1.12)^2 + \ldots + 2000(1.12)^{45}$
where the $a_1 = 2000(1.12)$, $n = 45$, and $r = 1.12$.

$$S_{45} = \frac{2000(1.12)\left(1 - (1.12)^{45}\right)}{1 - 1.12}$$

$$= \$3,042,435.27$$

58. We want the sum of the geometric series
$5000(1.1897)^{10} + 5000(1.1897)^9 + \ldots + 5000(1.1897)$
Note that the last deposit is made at the beginning of the 40th year and earns interest for only one year. Rewrite the series as
$5000(1.1897) + 5000(1.1897)^2 + \ldots + 5000(1.1897)^{10}.$
If $a_1 = 5000(1.1897)$, $n = 10$, and $r = 1.1897$, then

$$S_{10} = \frac{5000(1.1897)\left(1 - 1.1897^{10}\right)}{1 - 1.1897}$$

$$= \$146,763.44$$

59. We want the sum of the finite geometric series $1 + 2 + 4 + 8 + 16 + \ldots + 2^{30}$, which has 31 terms and a ratio of 2.

$$S_{31} = \frac{1(1 - 2^{31})}{1 - 2} = 2^{31} - 1$$

$$= 2,147,483,647 \text{ cents}$$

$$= \$21,474,836.47$$

60. We want the sum of the finite geometric series $1 + 2 + 4 + 8 + 16 + \ldots + 2^{42}$, which has 43 terms and a ratio of 2.

$$S_{43} = \frac{1(1 - 2^{43})}{1 - 2} = 2^{43} - 1$$

$$= 8.796 \times 10^{12}$$

61. Use $r = 0.80$, $a_1 = 1,000,000$ in $S = \frac{a_1}{1-r}$.

$$S = \frac{1,000,000}{1-0.80} = \$5,000,000$$

62. Use $r = 0.50$, $a_1 = 1,000,000$ in $S = \frac{a_1}{1-r}$.

$$S = \frac{1,000,000}{1-0.50} = \$2,000,000$$

63. Only sequence (d) is not geometric because it is the only one that does not have a constant ratio.

64. Use $a_1 = 4/10 = 0.4$ and $r = 1/10 = 0.1$ in the formula for the sum of an infinite geometric series $S = \dfrac{a_1}{1-r}$.
$$S = \frac{0.4}{1-0.1} = \frac{0.4}{0.9} = \frac{4}{9}$$

65. Use $a_1 = 24/100 = 0.24$ and $r = 1/100 = 0.01$ in the formula for $S = \dfrac{a_1}{1-r}$.
$$S = \frac{0.24}{1-0.01} = \frac{0.24}{0.99} = \frac{8}{33}$$

12.5 WARM-UPS

1. False, because there are 13 terms in a binomial to the 12th power.

2. False, because the 7th term has variable part a^6b^6.

3. False, because if $x = 1$ the equation is incorrect.

4. True, because the signs alternate in any expansion of a difference.

5. True, because we can obtain it from the 7th line.

6. True, because $1 + 4 + 6 + 4 + 1 = 2^4$.

7. True, because of the binomial theorem.

8. True, because $2^n = (1+1)^n$
$$= \sum_{i=0}^{n} \frac{n!}{(n-i)!i!} 1^{n-i} 1^i = \sum_{i=0}^{n} \frac{n!}{(n-i)!i!},$$
and the last sum is the sum of the coefficients in the nth row.

9. True, by definition of 0! and 1!.

10. True, because $\dfrac{7 \cdot 6 \cdot 5 \cdot 4 \cdot 3 \cdot 2 \cdot 1}{5 \cdot 4 \cdot 3 \cdot 2 \cdot 1 \cdot 2 \cdot 1} = 21$

12.5 EXERCISES

1. The sum obtained for a power of a binomial is called a binomial expansion.

2. Pascal's triangle gives the coefficients for $(a+b)^n$ for $n = 1, 2, 3$, and so on. Each row starts and ends with a 1. The other terms are obtained by adding the closest two terms in the preceding row.

3. The expression $n!$ is the product of the positive integers from 1 through n.

4. The binomial theorem gives the expansion of $(a+b)^n$.

5. $\dfrac{5!}{2!3!} = \dfrac{5 \cdot 4}{2} = 10$

6. $\dfrac{6!}{5!1!} = 6$

7. $\dfrac{8!}{5!3!} = \dfrac{8 \cdot 7 \cdot 6}{3 \cdot 2 \cdot 1} = 56$

8. $\dfrac{9!}{2!7!} = \dfrac{9 \cdot 8}{2} = 36$

9. The coefficients in the 5th row of Pascal's triangle are 1, 5, 10, 10, 5, 1. Use these coefficients with the pattern for the exponents.
$$(r+t)^5$$
$$= r^5 + 5r^4t + 10r^3t^2 + 10r^2t^3 + 5rt^4 + t^5$$

10. The coefficients in the 6th row of Pascal's triangle are 1, 6, 15, 20, 15, 6, 1. Use these coefficients with the pattern for the exponents.
$$(r+t)^6 = r^6 + 6r^5t + 15r^4t^2 + 20r^3t^3$$
$$+ 15r^2t^4 + 6rt^5 + t^6$$

11. The coefficients in the 3rd row are 1, 3, 3, 1. Use these coefficients with the pattern for the exponents, and alternate the signs.
$$(m-n)^3 = m^3 - 3m^2n + 3mn^2 - n^3$$

12. The coefficients in the 4th row are 1, 4, 6, 4, 1. Use these coefficients with the pattern for the exponents, and alternate the signs.
$$(m-n)^4$$
$$= m^4 - 4m^3n + 6m^2n^2 - 4mn^3 + n^4$$

13. Use the coefficients 1, 3, 3, 1 and let $y = 2a$ in the binomial theorem.
$$(x+2a)^3$$
$$= 1x^3(2a)^0 + 3x^2(2a)^1 + 3x(2a)^2 + (2a)^3$$
$$= x^3 + 6ax^2 + 12a^2x + 8a^3$$

14. Use the coefficients 1, 4, 6, 4, 1 and let $x = a$ and $y = 3b$ in the binomial theorem.
$$(a+3b)^4$$
$$= 1a^4(3b)^0 + 4a^3(3b)^1 + 6a^2(3b)^2$$
$$+ 4a(3b)^3 + (3b)^4$$
$$= a^4 + 12a^3b + 54a^2b^2 + 108ab^3 + 81b^4$$

15. Use the coefficients 1, 4, 6, 4, 1 in the binomial theorem.
$$(x^2 - 2)^4 = (x^2)^4 - 4(x^2)^3 2 + 6(x^2)^2 2^2$$
$$- 4x^2 2^3 + 1(x^2)^0 2^4$$
$$= x^8 - 8x^6 + 24x^4 - 32x^2 + 16$$

16. Use the coefficients 1, 5, 10, 10, 5, 1 in the binomial theorem.

$(x^2 - a^2)^5$

$= 1(x^2)^5 - 5(x^2)^4(a^2) + 10(x^2)^3(a^2)^2$
$\quad - 10(x^2)^2(a^2)^3 + 5(x^2)(a^2)^4 - 1(a^2)^5$

$= x^{10} - 5a^2x^8 + 10a^4x^6 - 10a^6x^4$
$\quad + 5a^8x^2 - a^{10}$

17. Use the coefficients from the 7th line 1, 7, 21, 35, 35, 21, 7, 1 and alternate the signs of the terms.

$(x - 1)^7 = x^7 - 7x^6 + 21x^5 - 35x^4 + 35x^3$
$\quad - 21x^2 + 7x - 1$

18. Use the coefficients 1, 6, 15, 20, 15, 6, 1 in the binomial theorem.

$(x + 1)^6$

$= 1x^6 + 6x^51 + 15x^41^2 + 20x^31^3 + 15x^21^4$
$\quad + 6x1^5 + 1 \cdot 1^6$

$= x^6 + 6x^5 + 15x^4 + 20x^3 + 15x^2 + 6x + 1$

19. Use the binomial theorem to write the first 4 terms of $(a - 3b)^{12}$.

$\frac{12!}{12!0!}a^{12}b^0 - \frac{12!}{11!1!}a^{11}b^1 + \frac{12!}{10!2!}a^{10}b^2$
$\quad - \frac{12!}{9!3!}a^9b^3$

$= a^{12} - 36a^{11}b + 594a^{10}b^2 - 5940a^9b^3$

20. Use the binomial theorem to write the first 4 terms of $(x - 2y)^{10}$.

$\frac{10!}{10!0!}x^{10}(2y)^0 - \frac{10!}{9!1!}x^9(2y)^1 + \frac{10!}{8!2!}x^8(2y)^2$
$\quad - \frac{10!}{7!3!}x^7(2y)^3$

$= x^{10} - 20x^9y + 180x^8y^2 - 960x^7y^3$

21. Use the binomial theorem to write the first 4 terms of $(x^2 + 5)^9$.

$\frac{9!}{9!0!}(x^2)^95^0 + \frac{9!}{8!1!}(x^2)^85^1 + \frac{9!}{7!2!}(x^2)^75^2$
$\quad + \frac{9!}{6!3!}(x^2)^65^3$

$= x^{18} + 45x^{16} + 900x^{14} + 10500x^{12}$

22. Use the binomial theorem to write the first 4 terms of $(x^2 + 1)^{20}$.

$\frac{20!}{20!0!}(x^2)^{20}1^0 + \frac{20!}{19!1!}(x^2)^{19}1^1 + \frac{20!}{18!2!}(x^2)^{18}1^2$
$\quad + \frac{20!}{17!3!}(x^2)^{17}1^3$

$= x^{40} + 20x^{38} + 190x^{36} + 1140x^{34}$

23. Use the binomial theorem to write the first 4 terms of $(x - 1)^{22}$.

$\frac{22!}{22!0!}x^{22}1^0 - \frac{22!}{21!1!}x^{21}1^1 + \frac{22!}{20!2!}x^{20}1^2$
$\quad - \frac{22!}{19!3!}x^{19}1^3$

$= x^{22} - 22x^{21} + 231x^{20} - 1540x^{19}$

24. Use the binomial theorem to write the first 4 terms of $(2x - 1)^8$.

$\frac{8!}{8!0!}(2x)^81^0 - \frac{8!}{7!1!}(2x)^71^1 + \frac{8!}{6!2!}(2x)^61^2$
$\quad - \frac{8!}{5!3!}(2x)^51^3$

$= (2x)^8 - 8(2x)^7 + 28(2x)^6 - 56(2x)^5$

$= 256x^8 - 1024x^7 + 1792x^6 - 1792x^5$

25. Use the binomial theorem to write the first 4 terms of $\left(\frac{x}{2} + \frac{y}{3}\right)^{10}$.

$\frac{10!}{10!0!}\left(\frac{x}{2}\right)^{10}\left(\frac{y}{3}\right)^0 + \frac{10!}{9!1!}\left(\frac{x}{2}\right)^9\left(\frac{y}{3}\right)^1$
$\quad + \frac{10!}{8!2!}\left(\frac{x}{2}\right)^8\left(\frac{y}{3}\right)^2 + \frac{10!}{7!3!}\left(\frac{x}{2}\right)^7\left(\frac{y}{3}\right)^3$

$= \frac{x^{10}}{1024} + \frac{5x^9y}{768} + \frac{5x^8y^2}{256} + \frac{5x^7y^3}{144}$

26. Use the binomial theorem to write the first 4 terms of $\left(\frac{a}{2} + \frac{b}{5}\right)^8$.

$\frac{8!}{8!0!}\left(\frac{a}{2}\right)^8\left(\frac{b}{5}\right)^0 + \frac{8!}{7!1!}\left(\frac{a}{2}\right)^7\left(\frac{b}{5}\right)^1$
$\quad + \frac{8!}{6!2!}\left(\frac{a}{2}\right)^6\left(\frac{b}{5}\right)^2 + \frac{8!}{5!3!}\left(\frac{a}{2}\right)^5\left(\frac{b}{5}\right)^3$

$= \frac{a^8}{256} + \frac{a^7b}{80} + \frac{7a^6b^2}{400} + \frac{7a^5b^3}{500}$

27. Use the formula for the kth term of $(x + y)^n$ with $k = 6$ and $n = 13$.

$\frac{13!}{(13-6+1)!(6-1)!}a^{13-6+1}w^{6-1}$

$\quad = \frac{13!}{8!5!}a^8w^5 = 1287a^8w^5$

28. Use the formula for the kth term of $(x + y)^n$ with $k = 7$ and $n = 12$.

$\frac{12!}{(12-7+1)!(7-1)!}m^{12-7+1}n^{7-1}$

$\quad = \frac{12!}{6!6!}m^6n^6 = 924m^6n^6$

29. Use the formula for the kth term with $k = 8$ and $n = 16$.

$\frac{16!}{(16-8+1)!(8-1)!}m^{16-8+1}(-n)^{8-1}$

$\quad = \frac{16!}{9!7!}m^9(-n)^7 = -11440m^9n^7$

30. Use the formula for the kth term with $k = 6$ and $n = 14$.

$\frac{14!}{(14-6+1)!(6-1)!}a^{14-6+1}(-b)^{6-1}$

$\quad = \frac{14!}{9!5!}a^9(-b)^5 = -2002a^9b^5$

31. Use the formula for the kth term with $k = 4$ and $n = 8$.

$$\frac{8!}{(8-4+1)!(4-1)!}x^{8-4+1}(2y)^{4-1}$$
$$= \frac{8!}{5!3!}x^5(2y)^3 = 56x^5 8y^3 = 448x^5 y^3$$

32. Use the formula for the kth term with $k = 4$ and $n = 7$.

$$\frac{7!}{(7-4+1)!(4-1)!}(3a)^{7-4+1}(b)^{4-1}$$
$$= \frac{7!}{4!3!}(3a)^4 b^3 = 2835a^4 b^3$$

33. Use the formula for the kth term with $k = 7$ and $n = 20$.

$$\frac{20!}{(20-7+1)!(7-1)!}(2a^2)^{20-7+1}b^{7-1}$$
$$= \frac{20!}{14!6!}(2a^2)^{14}b^6 = 635043840a^{28}b^6$$

34. Use the formula for the kth term with $k = 5$ and $n = 12$.

$$\frac{12!}{(12-5+1)!(5-1)!}(a^2)^{12-5+1}(-w^2)^{5-1}$$

$$= \frac{12!}{8!4!}(a^2)^8(-w^2)^4 = 495a^{16}w^8$$

35. Use $n = 8$, $x = a$, and $y = b$ in the binomial theorem with summation notation.

$$(a + m)^8 = \sum_{i=0}^{8} \frac{8!}{(8-i)!\,i!} a^{8-i}m^i$$

36. Use $n = 13$, $x = z$, and $y = w$ in the binomial theorem with summation notation.

$$(z + w)^{13} = \sum_{i=0}^{13} \frac{13!}{(13-i)!\,i!} z^{13-i}w^i$$

37. Use $n = 5$, $x = a$, and $y = -2x$ in the binomial theorem with summation notation.

$$(a + (-2x))^5 = \sum_{i=0}^{5} \frac{5!}{(5-i)!\,i!} a^{5-i}(-2x)^i$$
$$= \sum_{i=0}^{5} \frac{5!\,(-2)^i}{(5-i)!\,i!} a^{5-i}x^i$$

38. Use $n = 7$, $x = w$, and $y = -3m$ in the binomial theorem with summation notation.

$$(w + (-3m))^7 = \sum_{i=0}^{7} \frac{7!}{(7-i)!\,i!} w^{7-i}(-3m)^i$$
$$= \sum_{i=0}^{7} \frac{7!\,(-3)^i}{(7-i)!\,i!} w^{7-i}m^i$$

39. $(a + (b + c))^3$
$= a^3 + 3a^2(b + c) + 3a(b + c)^2 + (b + c)^3$
$= a^3 + 3a^2 b + 3a^2 c + 3ab^2 + 6abc + 3ac^2$
$+ b^3 + 3b^2 c + 3bc^2 + c^3$
$= a^3 + b^3 + c^3 + 3a^2 b + 3a^2 c + 3ab^2 + 3ac^2$
$+ 3b^2 c + 3bc^2 + 6abc$

40. Large factorials like 120! may not be possible on your calculator. In that case you cannot use the factorial key. The fourth term in $(x + y)^{120}$ is
$$\frac{120!}{117!3!}x^{117}y^3 = \frac{120 \cdot 119 \cdot 118}{3 \cdot 2 \cdot 1}x^{117}y^3$$

$$= 280{,}840x^{117}y^3$$

The fifth term of $(x - 2y)^{100}$ is

$$\frac{100!}{96!4!}x^{96}(-2y)^4 = 62{,}739{,}600x^{96}y^4$$

Enriching Your Mathematical Word Power
Chapter 12
1. a   2. d   3. c   4. b   5. a
6. c   7. d   8. b   9. d   10. a

CHAPTER 12 REVIEW

1. $a_1 = 1^3$, $a_2 = 2^3$, $a_3 = 3^3$, $a_4 = 4^3$,
$a_5 = 5^3$
The terms of the sequence are 1, 8, 27, 64, 125.

2. $b_1 = (1 - 1)^4 = 0$, $b_2 = (2 - 1)^4 = 1$,
$b_3 = (3 - 1)^4 = 16$, $b_4 = (4 - 1)^4 = 81$
The terms of the sequence are 0, 1, 16, and 81.

3. $c_1 = (-1)^1(2 \cdot 1 - 3) = 1$,
$c_2 = (-1)^2(2 \cdot 2 - 3) = 1$,
$c_3 = (-1)^3(2 \cdot 3 - 3) = -3$,
$c_4 = (-1)^4(2 \cdot 4 - 3) = 5$,
$c_5 = (-1)^5(2 \cdot 5 - 3) = -7$
$c_6 = (-1)^6(2 \cdot 6 - 3) = 9$
The terms of the sequence are 1, 1, -3, 5, -7, 9.

4. $d_1 = (-1)^{1-1}(3 - 1) = 2$
$d_2 = (-1)^{2-1}(3 - 2) = -1$
$d_3 = (-1)^{3-1}(3 - 3) = 0$
$d_4 = (-1)^{4-1}(3 - 4) = 1$
$d_5 = (-1)^{5-1}(3 - 5) = -2$
$d_6 = (-1)^{6-1}(3 - 6) = 3$
$d_7 = (-1)^{7-1}(3 - 7) = -4$
The terms of the sequence are 2, -1, 0, 1, -2, 3, and -4.

5. $a_1 = -\frac{1}{1} = -1$, $a_2 = -\frac{1}{2}$, $a_3 = -\frac{1}{3}$

The first three terms are $-1, -\frac{1}{2}, -\frac{1}{3}$.

6. $b_1 = \frac{(-1)^1}{1^2} = -1$, $b_2 = \frac{(-1)^2}{2^2} = \frac{1}{4}$

$b_3 = \frac{(-1)^3}{3^2} = -\frac{1}{9}$

The first three terms are $-1, \frac{1}{4}$, and $-\frac{1}{9}$.

7. $b_1 = \frac{(-1)^{2\cdot 1}}{2\cdot 1+1} = \frac{1}{3}$, $b_2 = \frac{(-1)^{2\cdot 2}}{2\cdot 2+1} = \frac{1}{5}$

$b_3 = \frac{(-1)^{2\cdot 3}}{2\cdot 3+1} = \frac{1}{7}$

The first three terms are $\frac{1}{3}, \frac{1}{5}$, and $\frac{1}{7}$.

8. $a_1 = \frac{-1}{(2\cdot 1-3)} = 1$, $a_2 = \frac{-1}{(2\cdot 2-3)} = -1$

$a_3 = \frac{-1}{(2\cdot 3-3)} = -\frac{1}{3}$

The first three terms are $1, -1$, and $-\frac{1}{3}$.

9. $c_1 = \log_2(2^{1+3}) = \log_2(2^4) = 4$
$c_2 = \log_2(2^{2+3}) = \log_2(2^5) = 5$
$c_3 = \log_2(2^{3+3}) = \log_2(2^6) = 6$
The first three terms are $4, 5$, and 6.

10. $c_1 = \ln(e^{2\cdot 1}) = 2$, $c_2 = \ln(e^{2\cdot 2}) = 4$
$c_3 = \ln(e^{2\cdot 3}) = 6$
The first three terms are $2, 4$, and 6.

11. $\displaystyle\sum_{i=1}^{3} i^3 = 1^3 + 2^3 + 3^3 = 36$

12. $\displaystyle\sum_{i=0}^{4} 6 = 6+6+6+6+6 = 30$

13. $\displaystyle\sum_{n=1}^{5} n(n-1)$
$= 1(1-1) + 2(2-1) + 3(3-1)$
$\qquad + 4(4-1) + 5(5-1)$
$= 0 + 2 + 6 + 12 + 20 = 40$

14. $\displaystyle\sum_{j=0}^{3} (-2)^j$
$= (-2)^0 + (-2)^1 + (-2)^2 + (-2)^3$
$= 1 - 2 + 4 - 8 = -5$

15. The terms in the series are reciprocals of even integers. Even integers are usually represent as $2i$, but to get 4 in the denominator when $i = 1$, we use $2(i + 1)$.

$$\sum_{i=1}^{\infty} \frac{1}{2(i+1)}$$

16. The terms in the series are reciprocals of integers. When $i = 1$, we want $i + 2 = 3$ in the denominator of the first term. So the series is written as follows.

$$\sum_{i=1}^{\infty} \frac{1}{i+2}$$

17. The terms in this series are the squares of integers. Squares are usually represented as i^2, but to get the first term 0 when $i = 1$, we use $(i - 1)^2$.

$$\sum_{i=1}^{\infty} (i-1)^2$$

18. To get alternating signs in the series, we use powers of -1. If $i = 1$, then $(-1)^i = -1$. To represent the positive integers we can use i.

$$\sum_{i=1}^{\infty} i(-1)^i$$

19. To get alternating signs for the terms, we use a power of -1. If we use $(-1)^i$, then $i = 1$ makes the first term negative. So we use $(-1)^{i+1}$.

$$\sum_{i=1}^{\infty} (-1)^{i+1} x_i$$

20. To get alternating signs we need $(-1)^i$. When $i = 1$, we want x^2. So we need x^{i+1}. The series is written as follows.

$$\sum_{i=1}^{\infty} (-1)^i x^{i+1}$$

21. $a_1 = 6 + (1-1)5 = 6$
Since the common difference is 5, the first four terms are 6, 11, 16, and 21.

22. $a_1 = -7 + (1-1)4 = -7$
Since the common difference is 4, the first four terms are $-7, -3, 1$, and 5.

23. $a_1 = -20 + (1-1)(-2) = -20$
Since the common difference is -2, the first four terms are $-20, -22, -24$, and -26.

24. $a_1 = 10 + (1-1)(-2.5) = 10$
Since the common difference is -2.5, the first four terms are 10, 7.5, 5, and 2.5.

458

25. $a_1 = 1000(1) + 2000 = 3000$
Since the common difference is 1000, the first four terms are 3000, 4000, 5000, and 6000.
26. $a_1 = -500(1) + 5000 = 4500$
Since the common difference is -500, the first four terms are 4500, 4000, 3500, and 3000.
27. Use $a_1 = 1/3$, $d = 1/3$, and the formula $a_n = a_1 + (n-1)d$.
$$a_n = \tfrac{1}{3} + (n-1)\tfrac{1}{3} = \tfrac{n}{3}$$

28. Use $a_1 = 10$, $d = -4$, and the formula $a_n = a_1 + (n-1)d$.
$$a_n = 10 + (n-1)(-4) = -4n + 14$$

29. Use $a_1 = 2$, $d = 2$, and the formula $a_n = a_1 + (n-1)d$.
$$a_n = 2 + (n-1)(2) = 2n$$
30. Use $a_1 = 20$, $d = -10$, and the formula $a_n = a_1 + (n-1)d$.
$$a_n = 20 + (n-1)(-10) = -10n + 30$$
31. Use $a_1 = 1$, $a_{24} = 24$, $n = 24$, and the formula $S_n = \tfrac{n}{2}(a_1 + a_n)$.
$$S_{24} = \tfrac{24}{2}(1 + 24) = 300$$
32. Use $a_1 = -5$, $d = 3$, $a_n = 34$, and the formula $a_n = a_1 + (n-1)d$ to find n.
$$34 = -5 + (n-1)3$$
$$34 = -8 + 3n$$
$$42 = 3n$$
$$14 = n$$
Use $a_1 = -5$, $a_{14} = 34$, $n = 14$, and the formula $S_n = \tfrac{n}{2}(a_1 + a_n)$.
$$S_{14} = \tfrac{14}{2}(-5 + 34) = 203$$
33. Use $a_1 = 1/6$, $d = 1/3$, $a_n = 11/2$, and the formula $a_n = a_1 + (n-1)d$ to find n.
$$\tfrac{11}{2} = \tfrac{1}{6} + (n-1)\tfrac{1}{3}$$
$$33 = 1 + (n-1)2$$
$$32 = 2n - 2$$
$$34 = 2n$$
$$17 = n$$
Now use $n = 17$, $a_1 = 1/6$, $a_{17} = 11/2$, and the formula $S_n = \tfrac{n}{2}(a_1 + a_n)$ to find the sum.
$$S_{17} = \tfrac{17}{2}\left(\tfrac{1}{6} + \tfrac{11}{2}\right) = \tfrac{17}{2}\left(\tfrac{34}{6}\right) = \tfrac{289}{6}$$
34. Use $a_1 = -3$, $d = -3$, $a_n = -36$, and the formula $a_n = a_1 + (n-1)d$ to find n.
$$-36 = -3 + (n-1)(-3)$$

$$-36 = -3n$$
$$12 = n$$
Now use $n = 12$, $a_1 = -3$, $a_{12} = -36$, and the formula $S_n = \tfrac{n}{2}(a_1 + a_n)$ to find the sum.
$$S_{12} = \tfrac{12}{2}(-3 + (-36)) = \tfrac{12}{2}(-39) = -234$$
35. Use $a_1 = -1$, $a_7 = 11$, $n = 7$, and the formula $S_n = \tfrac{n}{2}(a_1 + a_n)$ to find the sum.
$$S_7 = \tfrac{7}{2}(-1 + 11) = 35$$
36. Use $a_1 = 12$, $a_6 = 37$, $n = 6$, and the formula $S_n = \tfrac{n}{2}(a_1 + a_n)$ to find the sum.
$$S_6 = \tfrac{6}{2}(12 + 37) = 147$$
37. $a_1 = 3\left(\tfrac{1}{2}\right)^{1-1} = 3$, $a_2 = 3\left(\tfrac{1}{2}\right)^{2-1} = \tfrac{3}{2}$,

$$a_3 = 3\left(\tfrac{1}{2}\right)^{3-1} = \tfrac{3}{4}, \quad a_4 = 3\left(\tfrac{1}{2}\right)^{4-1} = \tfrac{3}{8}$$

The first four terms are 3, $\tfrac{3}{2}$, $\tfrac{3}{4}$, and $\tfrac{3}{8}$.

38. $a_1 = 6\left(-\tfrac{1}{3}\right)^1 = -2$, $a_2 = 6\left(-\tfrac{1}{3}\right)^2 = \tfrac{2}{3}$

$$a_3 = 6\left(-\tfrac{1}{3}\right)^3 = -\tfrac{2}{9}, \quad a_4 = 6\left(-\tfrac{1}{3}\right)^4 = \tfrac{2}{27}$$

The first four terms are -2, $\tfrac{2}{3}$, $-\tfrac{2}{9}$, and $\tfrac{2}{27}$.

39. $a_1 = 2^{1-1} = 1$, $a_2 = 2^{1-2} = \tfrac{1}{2}$

$$a_3 = 2^{1-3} = \tfrac{1}{4}, \quad a_4 = 2^{1-4} = \tfrac{1}{8}$$
The first four terms are 1, $\tfrac{1}{2}$, $\tfrac{1}{4}$, and $\tfrac{1}{8}$.
40. $a_1 = 5(10)^{1-1} = 5$
   $a_2 = 5(10)^{2-1} = 50$
   $a_3 = 5(10)^{3-1} = 500$
   $a_4 = 5(10)^{4-1} = 5,000$
The first 4 terms are 5, 50, 500, and 5,000.
41. $a_1 = 23(10)^{-2(1)} = 0.23$,
   $a_2 = 23(10)^{-2(2)} = 0.0023$,
   $a_3 = 23(10)^{-2(3)} = 0.000023$,
   $a_4 = 23(10)^{-2(4)} = 0.00000023$
The first four terms of the geometric sequence are 0.23, 0.0023, 0.000023, and 0.00000023.
42. $a_1 = 4(10)^{-1} = 0.4$
   $a_2 = 4(10)^{-2} = 0.04$
   $a_3 = 4(10)^{-3} = 0.004$
   $a_4 = 4(10)^{-4} = 0.0004$
The first 4 terms are 0.4, 0.04, 0.004, and 0.0004.

43. Use $a_1 = 1/2$, $r = 6$, and the formula $a_n = a_1 r^{n-1}$.
$$a_n = \tfrac{1}{2}(6)^{n-1}$$

44. Use $a_1 = -6$, $r = -1/3$, and the formula $a_n = a_1 r^{n-1}$.
$$a_n = -6\left(-\tfrac{1}{3}\right)^{n-1}$$

45. Use $a_1 = 7/10$, $r = 1/10$, and the formula $a_n = a_1 r^{n-1}$.
$$a_n = 0.7(0.1)^{n-1}$$

46. Use $a_1 = 2$, $r = x$, and the formula $a_n = a_1 r^{n-1}$.
$$a_n = 2(x)^{n-1} = 2x^{n-1}$$

47. Use $a_1 = 1/3$, $r = 1/3$, $n = 4$, and the formula $S_n = \dfrac{a_1(1 - r^n)}{1 - r}$.
$$S_4 = \frac{\tfrac{1}{3}\left(1 - \left(\tfrac{1}{3}\right)^4\right)}{1 - \tfrac{1}{3}} = \frac{\tfrac{1}{3}\left(\tfrac{80}{81}\right)}{\tfrac{2}{3}} = \frac{40}{81}$$

48. Use $a_1 = 2$, $r = 2$ and $a_n = 512$ in the formula for a_n, $a_n = a_1 r^{n-1}$.
$$512 = 2 \cdot 2^{n-1}$$
$$512 = 2^n$$
$$2^9 = 2^n$$
$$9 = n$$
Use $a_1 = 2$, $r = 2$, $n = 9$, and the formula $S_n = \dfrac{a_1(1 - r^n)}{1 - r}$.
$$S_9 = \frac{2\left(1 - (2)^9\right)}{1 - 2} = \frac{2(-511)}{-1} = 1022$$

49. Use $a_1 = 0.3$, $r = 0.1$, $n = 10$, and the formula $S_n = \dfrac{a_1(1 - r^n)}{1 - r}$.

$$S_{10} = \frac{0.3\left(1 - (0.1)^{10}\right)}{1 - 0.1} = \frac{0.3(0.9999999999)}{0.9}$$

$$= 0.3333333333$$
Your calculator may not give ten 3's after the decimal point, but doing this computation without a calculator does give ten 3's and this is the exact answer.

50. Use $a_1 = 0.1$, $r = 0.1$, $n = 5$, and the

formula $S_n = \dfrac{a_1(1 - r^n)}{1 - r}$.

$$S_5 = \frac{0.1\left(1 - (0.1)^5\right)}{1 - 0.1} = \frac{0.1(0.99999)}{0.9}$$
$$= 0.11111$$

51. Use $a_1 = 1/4$, $r = 1/3$, and the formula for the sum of an infinite geometric series $S = \dfrac{a_1}{1 - r}$.
$$S = \frac{\tfrac{1}{4}}{1 - \tfrac{1}{3}} = \frac{\tfrac{1}{4}}{\tfrac{2}{3}} = \frac{3}{8}$$

52. Use $a_1 = 12$, $r = -1/2$, and the formula for the sum of an infinite geometric series $S = \dfrac{a_1}{1 - r}$.
$$S = \frac{12}{1 - \left(-\tfrac{1}{2}\right)} = \frac{12}{\tfrac{3}{2}} = 8$$

53. Use $a_1 = 18$, $r = 2/3$, and the formula for the sum of an infinite geometric series $S = \dfrac{a_1}{1-r}$.
$$S = \frac{18}{1 - \tfrac{2}{3}} = \frac{18}{\tfrac{1}{3}} = 54$$

54. Use $a_1 = 0.9$, $r = 0.1$, and the formula for the sum of an infinite geometric series $S = \dfrac{a_1}{1 - r}$.
$$S = \frac{0.9}{1 - 0.1} = \frac{0.9}{0.9} = 1$$

55. The coefficients for the fifth power of a binomial are 1, 5, 10, 10, 5, and 1.
$$(m + n)^5 = m^5 + 5m^4 n + 10m^3 n^2$$
$$+ 10m^2 n^3 + 5mn^4 + n^5$$

56. The coefficients for the fourth power of a binomial are 1, 4, 6, 4, and 1.
$$(2m - y)^4 = (2m)^4 - 4(2m)^3 y + 6(2m)^2 y^2$$
$$- 4(2m)y^3 + y^4$$
$$= 16m^4 - 32m^3 y + 24m^2 y^2 - 8my^3 + y^4$$

57. The coefficients for the third power of a binomial are 1, 3, 3, and 1. Alternate the signs because it is a difference to a power.
$$(a^2 - 3b)^3 = 1(a^2)^3(3b)^0 - 3(a^2)^2(3b)^1$$
$$+ 3(a^2)^1(3b)^2 - 1(a^2)^0(3b)^3$$
$$= a^6 - 9a^4 b + 27a^2 b^2 - 27b^3$$

58. The coefficients for a fifth power of a binomial are 1, 5, 10, 10, 5, and 1.

$$\left(\frac{x}{2} + 2a\right)^5 = \left(\frac{x}{2}\right)^5 + 5\left(\frac{x}{2}\right)^4(2a)$$
$$+ 10\left(\frac{x}{2}\right)^3(2a)^2 + 10\left(\frac{x}{2}\right)^2(2a)^3$$
$$+ 5\left(\frac{x}{2}\right)(2a)^4 + (2a)^5$$
$$= \frac{x^5}{32} + \frac{5x^4 a}{8} + 5x^3 a^2 + 20x^2 a^3$$
$$+ 40xa^4 + 32a^5$$

59. Use $n = 12$ and $k = 5$ in the formula for the kth term.

$$\frac{12!}{(12-5+1)!(5-1)!}x^{12-5+1}y^{5-1} = \frac{12!}{8!4!}x^8 y^4$$
$$= 495x^8 y^4$$

60. Use $n = 9$ and $k = 5$ in the formula for the kth term.

$$\frac{9!}{(9-5+1)!(5-1)!}x^{9-5+1}(-2y)^{5-1}$$
$$= \frac{9!}{5!4!}x^5(-2y)^4 = 2016x^5 y^4$$

61. Use $n = 14$ and $k = 3$ in the formula for the kth term.

$$\frac{14!}{(14-3+1)!(3-1)!}(2a)^{14-3+1}(-b)^{3-1}$$
$$= \frac{14!}{12!2!}(2a)^{12}(-b)^2 = 372{,}736a^{12}b^2$$

62. Use $n = 10$ and $k = 4$ in the formula for the kth term.

$$\frac{10!}{(10-4+1)!(4-1)!}(a)^{10-4+1}(b)^{4-1}$$
$$= \frac{10!}{7!3!}(a)^7(b)^3 = 120a^7 b^3$$

63. Use the binomial theorem expressed in summation notation, with $n = 7$.

$$(a + w)^7 = \sum_{i=0}^{7} \frac{7!}{(7-i)!\,i!}\,a^{7-i}w^i$$

64. Use the binomial theorem expressed in summation notation, with $n = 9$.

$$(m - 3y)^9 = \sum_{i=0}^{9} \frac{9!}{(9-i)!\,i!}\,m^{9-i}(-3y)^i$$

$$= \sum_{i=0}^{9} \frac{9!(-3)^i}{(9-i)!\,i!}\,m^{9-i}y^i$$

65. The sequence has neither a constant difference nor a constant ratio. So it is neither arithmetic nor geometric.

66. The sequence has a constant ratio of $12/9 = 4/3$. So the series is a geometric sequence.

67. There is a constant difference of 3. So the sequence is an arithmetic sequence.

68. The sequence has a constant ratio of 2. The sequence is a geometric sequence.

69. There is a constant difference of 2. So the sequence is an arithmetic sequence.

70. The sequence has neither a constant ratio nor a constant difference. So the sequence is neither.

71. Use $a_1 = 6$, $n = 4$, $a_4 = 1/30$, and the formula $a_n = a_1 r^{n-1}$.

$$\frac{1}{30} = 6r^{4-1}$$
$$\frac{1}{180} = r^3$$
$$r = \sqrt[3]{\frac{1}{180}} = \frac{1}{\sqrt[3]{180}}$$

72. Use $a_1 = 6$, $a_4 = 36$, and $n = 4$ in the formula $a_n = a_1 + (n-1)d$.

$$36 = 6 + (4-1)d$$
$$36 = 6 + 3d$$
$$30 = 3d$$
$$10 = d$$

The common difference is 10.

73. $\displaystyle\sum_{i=1}^{5} \frac{(-1)^i}{i!} = \frac{(-1)^1}{1!} + \frac{(-1)^2}{2!} + \frac{(-1)^3}{3!}$

$$+ \frac{(-1)^4}{4!} + \frac{(-1)^5}{5!}$$
$$= -1 + \frac{1}{2} - \frac{1}{6} + \frac{1}{24} - \frac{1}{120}$$

74. Each row of Pascal's triangle starts and ends with a 1. The 0th row is 1 and the first row is 1 1, and the numbers in every row after the first are found by adding two numbers in the row above.

```
           1
          1 1
         1 2 1
        1 3 3 1
       1 4 6 4 1
      1 5 10 10 5 1
     1 6 15 20 15 6 1
    1 7 21 35 35 21 7 1
   1 8 28 56 70 56 28 8 1
```

75. This is the summation notation for the binomial expansion of $(a + b)^5$.

$$\frac{5!}{5!0!}a^5 b^0 + \frac{5!}{4!1!}a^4 b^1 + \frac{5!}{3!2!}a^3 b^2 + \frac{5!}{2!3!}a^2 b^3$$

$$+ \tfrac{5!}{1!4!}a^1b^4 + \tfrac{5!}{0!5!}a^0b^5$$

$$= a^5 + 5a^4b + 10a^3b^2 + 10a^2b^3$$
$$+ 5ab^4 + b^5$$

76. To find the terms of the series, let i vary from 0 through 8 in the formula.

$$\sum_{i=0}^{8} \tfrac{8!}{(8-i)!i!}x^{8-i}y^i = \tfrac{8!}{8!0!}x^8y^0 + \tfrac{8!}{7!1!}x^7y^1$$

$$+ \tfrac{8!}{6!2!}x^6y^2 + \tfrac{8!}{5!3!}x^5y^3 + \tfrac{8!}{4!4!}x^4y^4 + \tfrac{8!}{3!5!}x^3y^5$$

$$+ \tfrac{8!}{2!6!}x^2y^6 + \tfrac{8!}{1!7!}x^1y^7 + \tfrac{8!}{0!8!}x^0y^8$$

$$= x^8 + 8x^7y + 28x^6y^2 + 56x^5y^3 + 70x^4y^4$$

$$+ 56x^3y^5 + 28x^2y^6 + 8xy^7 + y^8$$

77. There are 26 terms because in the expansion of $(x+y)^n$ there are $n+1$ terms.

78. $\tfrac{12!}{8!4!} = \tfrac{12\cdot11\cdot10\cdot9\cdot8\cdot7\cdot6\cdot5\cdot4\cdot3\cdot2\cdot1}{8\cdot7\cdot6\cdot5\cdot4\cdot3\cdot2\cdot1\cdot4\cdot3\cdot2\cdot1}$

$$= \tfrac{12\cdot11\cdot10\cdot9}{4\cdot3\cdot2\cdot1} = 11\cdot5\cdot9 = 495$$

79. The first \$3000 earns interest for 16 years. The second \$3000 earns interest for 15 years, and so on. The last \$3000 earns interest for 1 year. The total in the account at the end of 16 years is the sum of the following series.

$$3000(1.1) + 3000(1.1)^2 + \dots + 3000(1.1)^{16}$$

This is a geometric series with $n = 16$, $a_1 = 3000(1.1)$ and $r = 1.1$.
$$S_{16} = \frac{3000(1.1)\big(1-(1.1)^{16}\big)}{1-1.1} = \$118,634.11$$

80. The first \$3000 earns interest for 8 years. The second \$3000 earns interest for 7 years, and so on. The last \$3000 earns interest for 1 year. The total in the account at the end of 8 years is the sum of the following series.

$$3000(1.1) + 3000(1.1)^2 + \dots + 3000(1.1)^8$$

This is a geometric series with $n = 8$, $a_1 = 3000(1.1)$ and $r = 1.1$.

$$S_8 = \frac{3000(1.1)\big(1-(1.1)^8\big)}{1-1.1} = \$37,738.43$$

This amount is about $1/3$ as much as the amount in the previous exercise.

81. We compute a new balance 16 times by multiplying by $1 + 0.10$ each time.
$$3000(1.10)^{16} = \$13,784.92$$

CHAPTER 12 TEST

1. $a_1 = -10 + (1-1)6 = -10$
$a_2 = -10 + (2-1)6 = -4$
$a_3 = -10 + (3-1)6 = 2$
$a_4 = -10 + (4-1)6 = 8$
The first four terms are $-10, -4, 2,$ and 8.

2. $a_1 = 5(0.1)^{1-1} = 5$
$a_2 = 5(0.1)^{2-1} = 0.5$
$a_3 = 5(0.1)^{3-1} = 0.05$
$a_4 = 5(0.1)^{4-1} = 0.005$
The first four terms are $5, 0.5, 0.05,$ and 0.005.

3. $a_1 = \tfrac{(-1)^1}{1!} = -1$, $a_2 = \tfrac{(-1)^2}{2!} = \tfrac{1}{2}$,

$a_3 = \tfrac{(-1)^3}{3!} = -\tfrac{1}{6}$, $a_4 = \tfrac{(-1)^4}{4!} = \tfrac{1}{24}$

The first four terms are $-1, \tfrac{1}{2}, -\tfrac{1}{6},$ and $\tfrac{1}{24}$.

4. $a_1 = \tfrac{2(1)-1}{(1)^2} = 1$, $a_2 = \tfrac{2(2)-1}{(2)^2} = \tfrac{3}{4}$,

$a_3 = \tfrac{2(3)-1}{(3)^2} = \tfrac{5}{9}$, $a_4 = \tfrac{2(4)-1}{(4)^2} = \tfrac{7}{16}$

The first four terms are $1, \tfrac{3}{4}, \tfrac{5}{9},$ and $\tfrac{7}{16}$.

5. The sequence is an arithmetic sequence with $a_1 = 7$ and $d = -3$. So the general term is
$a_n = 7 + (n-1)(-3) = 7 - 3n + 3$
$$= 10 - 3n.$$

6. This sequence is a geometric sequence with $a_1 = -25$, and $r = -1/5$. So the general term is $a_n = -25\left(-\tfrac{1}{5}\right)^{n-1}$.

7. This sequence is a sequence of even integers, which we can represent as $2n$. To get the signs to alternate, we use a power of -1. So the general term is $a_n = (-1)^{n-1}2n$.

8. This sequence is a sequence of squares of the positive integers. So the general term is $a_n = n^2$.

9. $\displaystyle\sum_{i=1}^{5}(2i+3) = 2(1)+3+2(2)+3$
$$+\,2(3)+3+2(4)+3+2(5)+3$$
$$= 5+7+9+11+13$$

10. $\displaystyle\sum_{i=1}^{6}5(2)^{i-1} = 5(2)^{1-1}+5(2)^{2-1}$
$$+\,5(2)^{3-1}+5(2)^{4-1}+5(2)^{5-1}+5(2)^{6-1}$$
$$= 5+10+20+40+80+160$$

11. $\displaystyle\sum_{i=0}^{4}\frac{4!}{(4-i)!i!}m^{4-i}q^{i} = \frac{4!}{4!0!}m^4q^0$

$$+\,\tfrac{4!}{3!1!}m^3q^1+\tfrac{4!}{2!2!}m^2q^2$$
$$+\,\tfrac{4!}{1!3!}m^1q^3+\tfrac{4!}{0!4!}m^0q^4$$
$$= m^4+4m^3q+6m^2q^2+4mq^3+q^4$$

12. Use $a_1 = 9$, $a_{20} = 66$, and $n = 20$ in the formula for the sum of an arithmetic series.
$S_{20} = \frac{20}{2}(9+66) = 10(75) = 750$

13. Use $a_1 = 10$, $n = 5$, and $r = 1/2$ in the formula for the sum of a finite geometric series.
$$S_5 = \frac{10\left(1-\left(\frac{1}{2}\right)^5\right)}{1-\frac{1}{2}} = \frac{10\left(\frac{31}{32}\right)}{\frac{1}{2}} = \frac{155}{8}$$

14. Use $a_1 = 0.35$ and $r = 0.93$ in the formula for the sum of an infinite geometric series.
$S = \frac{0.35}{1-0.93} = \frac{0.35}{0.07} = 5$

15. Use $a_1 = 2$, $a_{100} = 200$, and $n = 100$ in the formula for the sum of a finite arithmetic series.
$S_{100} = \frac{100}{2}(2+200) = 50(202) = 10{,}100$

16. Use $a_1 = 1/4$ and $r = 1/2$ in the formula for the sum of an infinite geometric series.
$S = \frac{1/4}{1-1/2} = \frac{1/4}{1/2} = \frac{1}{2}$

17. Use $a_1 = 2$, $r = 1/2$ and $a_n = 1/128$ to find n:
$$2\left(\tfrac{1}{2}\right)^{n-1} = \tfrac{1}{128}$$
$$\left(\tfrac{1}{2}\right)^{n-1} = \tfrac{1}{256} = \tfrac{1}{2^8}$$
$$n-1 = 8$$
$$n = 9$$
Use $a_1 = 2$, $n = 9$, and $r = 1/2$ to find the sum of the 9 terms.
$$S_9 = \frac{2(1-(1/2)^9)}{1-1/2} = \frac{511}{128} \approx 3.9922$$

18. Use $a_1 = 3$, $a_5 = 48$, $n = 5$ in the formula for the general term of a geometric sequence.
$$48 = 3r^{5-1}$$
$$16 = r^4$$
$$\pm 2 = r$$

19. Use $a_1 = 1$, $a_{12} = 122$, $n = 12$, and the formula for the general term of an arithmetic sequence.
$$122 = 1+(12-1)d$$
$$121 = 11d$$
$$11 = d$$

20. Use $n = 15$ and $k = 5$ in the formula for the kth term of a binomial expansion.
$$\frac{15!}{(15-5+1)!(5-1)!}r^{15-5+1}(-t)^{5-1}$$
$$= \frac{15!}{11!4!}r^{11}t^4 = 1365r^{11}t^4$$

21. Use $n = 8$ and $k = 4$ in the formula for the kth term of a binomial expansion.
$$\frac{8!}{(8-4+1)!(4-1)!}(a^2)^{8-4+1}(-2b)^{4-1}$$
$$= \frac{8!}{5!3!}a^{10}(-2)^3b^3 = -448a^{10}b^3$$

22. $800(1.10)^1 + 800(1.10)^2 + \ldots$
$$+\,800(1.10)^{25}$$
$$= \frac{800(1.10)(1-1.10^{25})}{1-1.10} = \$86{,}545.41$$

Making Connections

Chapters 1 - 12

1. $f(3) = 3^2 - 3 = 9 - 3 = 6$

2. $f(n) = n^2 - 3$

3. $f(x + h) = (x + h)^2 - 3$
$$= x^2 + 2xh + h^2 - 3$$

4. $f(x) - g(x) = x^2 - 3 - (2x - 1)$
$$= x^2 - 2x - 2$$

5. $g(f(3)) = g(6) = 2(6) - 1 = 11$

6. $(f \circ g)(2) = f(g(2)) = f(3) = 3^2 - 3 = 6$

7. $m(16) = \log_2(16) = 4$

8. $(h \circ m)(32) = h(m(32)) = h(5) = 2^5 = 32$

9. $h(-1) = 2^{-1} = 1/2$

10. $h^{-1}(8) = \log_2(8) = 3$

11. $m^{-1}(0) = 2^0 = 1$

12. $(m \circ h)(x) = m(h(x)) = m(2^x)$
$$= \log_2(2^x) = x$$
So $(m \circ h)(x) = x$.

13. If y varies directly as x, then $y = kx$. Since $y = -6$ when $x = 4$, we have $-6 = 4k$, or $k = -3/2$. When $x = 9$, we can use the original formula with $k = -3/2$.
$$y = -\tfrac{3}{2}(9) = -\tfrac{27}{2}$$

14. If a varies inversely as b, then $a = k/b$. If $a = 2$ when $b = -4$, we can find k.
$$2 = \frac{k}{-4}$$
$$-8 = k$$
To find a, use $k = -8$ and $b = 3$.
$$a = \tfrac{-8}{3} = -\tfrac{8}{3}$$

15. If y varies directly as w and inversely as t, then $y = (kw)/t$. Use $y = 16$, $w = 3$, and $t = -4$ to find k.
$$16 = \frac{k(3)}{-4}$$
$$-64 = 3k$$
$$\tfrac{-64}{3} = k$$
To find y, use $k = -64/3$, $w = 2$, and $t = 3$.
$$y = -\frac{64(2)}{3(3)} = -\frac{128}{9}$$

16. If y varies jointly as h and the square of r, then $y = khr^2$. Use $y = 12$, $h = 2$, and $r = 3$ to find k.
$$12 = k(2)(3)^2$$
$$12 = 18k$$
$$\tfrac{2}{3} = k$$
To find y, use $k = 2/3$, $h = 6$, and $r = 2$.

$$y = \tfrac{2}{3}(6)(2)^2 = 16$$

17. The graph of $x > 3$ is the region to the right of the vertical line $x = 3$. The graph of $x + y < 0$ is the region below the line $y = -x$. The region to the right of $x = 3$ and below $y = -x$ is shown in the following graph.

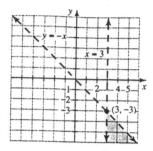

18. The inequality $|x - y| \geq 2$ is equivalent to the compound inequality $x - y \geq 2$ or $x - y \leq -2$. The graph of $x - y \geq 2$ is the region below the line $y = x - 2$. The graph of $x - y \leq -2$ is the region above the line $y = x + 2$. Since the word or is used, the graph of the compound inequality is the union of these two regions as shown in the following diagram.

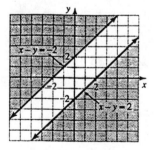

19. The graph of $y < -2x + 3$ is the region below the line $y = -2x + 3$. The graph of $y > 2^x$ is the region above the curve $y = 2^x$. Since the word and is used, the graph of the compound inequality is the intersection of these two regions, the points that lie above $y = 2^x$ and below $y = -2x + 3$. We could have used

a test point in each of the four regions to see
which region satisfies both inequalities.

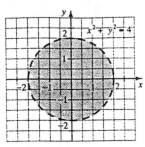

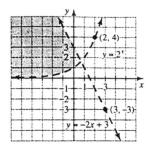

20. The inequality $|y + 2x| < 1$ is
equivalent to $-1 < y + 2x < 1$. This
inequality is also written as
$$y + 2x > -1 \quad \text{and} \quad y + 2x < 1$$
$$y > -2x - 1 \text{ and} \qquad y < -2x + 1$$
The graph of $y > -2x - 1$ is the region above
the line $y = -2x - 1$. The graph of
$y < -2x + 1$ is the region below the line
$y = -2x + 1$. The points that satisfy both
inequalities are the points that lie between these
two parallel lines.

22. The graph of $x^2 - y^2 = 1$ is a hyperbola
with x-intercepts $(-1, 0)$ and $(1, 0)$. The
fundamental rectangle passes through the x-
intercepts and $(0, 1)$ and $(0, -1)$. Extend the
diagonals for the asymptotes. The hyperbola
opens to the left and right. Test a point in each
region to see that only points in the region
containing the origin satisfy the inequality.

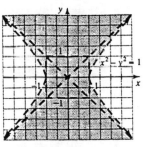

23. Graph the curve $y = \log_2(x)$ and shade the
region below the curve to show the graph of
$y < \log_2(x)$.

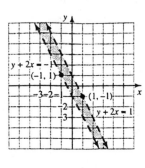

21. The graph of $x^2 + y^2 = 4$ is a circle of
radius 2 centered at the origin. Since $(0, 0)$
satisfies the inequality $x^2 + y^2 < 4$, we shade
the region inside the circle.

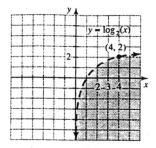

24. Write $x^2 + 2y < 4$ as $y < -\frac{1}{2}x^2 + 2$, to see that the boundary is a parabola opening downward with vertex at $(0, 2)$.

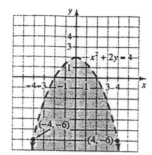

25. The graph of $\frac{x^2}{4} + \frac{y^2}{9} < 1$ is the region inside the ellipse $\frac{x^2}{4} + \frac{y^2}{9} = 1$. The graph of $y > x^2$ is the region above the parabola $y = x^2$. The points that satisfy the compound inequality are inside the ellipse and above the parabola as shown in the diagram.

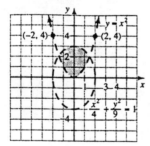

26. $\frac{a}{b} + \frac{b}{a} = \frac{a(a)}{b(a)} + \frac{b(b)}{a(b)} = \frac{a^2 + b^2}{ab}$

27. $1 - \frac{3}{y} = \frac{y}{y} - \frac{3}{y} = \frac{y - 3}{y}$

28. $\dfrac{x - 2}{x^2 - 9} - \dfrac{x - 4}{x^2 - 2x - 3}$

$= \dfrac{(x - 2)(x + 1)}{(x - 3)(x + 3)(x + 1)}$
$\quad - \dfrac{(x - 4)(x + 3)}{(x - 3)(x + 1)(x + 3)}$

$= \dfrac{x^2 - x - 2}{(x - 3)(x + 3)(x + 1)}$
$\quad - \dfrac{x^2 - x - 12}{(x - 3)(x + 3)(x + 1)}$

$= \dfrac{10}{(x - 3)(x + 3)(x + 1)}$

29. $\dfrac{(x - 4)(x + 4)}{2(x + 4)} \cdot \dfrac{4(x^2 + 4x + 16)}{x^3 - 16}$

$= \dfrac{2(x^3 - 64)}{x^3 - 16}$

30. $\dfrac{(a^2 b)^3}{(ab^2)^4} \cdot \dfrac{ab^3}{a^{-4} b^2} = \dfrac{a^6 b^3}{a^4 b^8} \cdot \dfrac{ab^3}{a^{-4} b^2}$

$= \dfrac{a^7 b^6}{b^{10}} = \dfrac{a^7}{b^4}$

31. $\dfrac{x^2 y}{(xy)^3} \div \dfrac{xy^2}{x^2 y^4} = \dfrac{x^2 y}{x^3 y^3} \cdot \dfrac{x^2 y^4}{xy^2}$

$= \dfrac{x^4 y^5}{x^4 y^5} = 1$

32. $8^{2/3} = (\sqrt[3]{8})^2 = 2^2 = 4$

33. $16^{-5/4} = \dfrac{1}{(\sqrt[4]{16})^5} = \dfrac{1}{(2)^5} = \dfrac{1}{32}$

34. $-4^{1/2} = -\sqrt{4} = -2$

35. $27^{-2/3} = \dfrac{1}{(\sqrt[3]{27})^2} = \dfrac{1}{3^2} = \dfrac{1}{9}$

36. $-2^{-3} = -\dfrac{1}{2^3} = -\dfrac{1}{8}$

37. $2^{-3/5} \cdot 2^{-7/5} = 2^{-10/5} = 2^{-2} = \dfrac{1}{2^2} = \dfrac{1}{4}$

38. $5^{-2/3} \div 5^{1/3} = 5^{-\frac{2}{3} - \frac{1}{3}} = 5^{-1} = \dfrac{1}{5}$

39. $(9^{1/2} + 4^{1/2})^2 = (3 + 2)^2 = 5^2 = 25$

40. a) Age 4 years 3 months is 4.25 years.
$h(4.25)$
$\quad = 79.041 + 6.39(4.25) - e^{3.261 - 0.993(4.25)}$
$\quad = 105.8$ cm

105.8 cm $\cdot \dfrac{1 \text{ in}}{2.54 \text{ cm}} = 41.7$ in.

c) Using a graphing calculator we get that a child who has a height of 80 cm has an age of 1.3 years

Notes on Collaborative Learning

The NCTM Standards

The *Curriculum and Evaluation Standards for School Mathematics*, published in 1989 by the National Council of Teachers of Mathematics (NCTM), recommends that students develop collaborative learning skills as well as the ability to analyze problem solutions. The recommendation is the use of group work to give the students a chance to practice collaborative learning skills in the context of mathematical problem solving. The NCTM also recommends the use of open-ended problems so that students get a feel for how to use mathematics in the world outside of the college environment.

About These Collaborative Activities

At the end of each chapter you will find a collaborative activity that incorporates the material presented in the chapter. These activities are designed to be catalysts for creating dialog among students and between students and their instructor. You will need to be actively participating with your students in the group learning process.

Some of the activities will stretch the students' abilities to formulate the mathematics. The students may need some help from you as the instructor. You may want to use something akin to the Socratic method in answering the students' questions; answer with a question that will point their thinking in the direction it should go.

Some of these activities incorporate different learning styles: visual, auditory, kinesthetic, and so on. Students will appreciate the opportunity to use a style that works more naturally for them.

Many of these activities present the mathematical problem in the context of a scenario used to catch the students attention and help them begin to think creatively. Do not be surprised if some of your students take the scenario further in their answers.

Thus the goal of these activities is to encourage students to think creatively, use other ways of learning from the standard paradigm, and find power in their own abilities to solve mathematical problems.

Implementing Collaborative Activities in the Classroom

Instructor notes that give tips and comments on how to use each activity are provided following these general notes. There is a range of types of activities; some requiring in-class time only and others requiring outside group work. You will want to structure the type and size of the groups in order to best fit the activity assigned. Also, be aware of the group interactions. Students may need help at first learning how to work effectively in groups.

Techniques for Forming Groups

Below is a list of some types of groups you may wish to use and a brief description of each.

- Proximity Pairing - Each student is "paired" with one or two students in his or her immediate vicinity.

• Number Off or Count Off - Students count off, out loud from 1 to n, where n is determined by dividing the number of students in the class by the number of students desired in each group.

• Structured Groups or Teams - Use this type of grouping after two or three weeks of class so that you have an opportunity to become acquainted with the students. Keep groups small, no more than four students per group. You may either mix abilities of students in the group or form groups with "matched" ability. In mixed ability grouping each group consists of an "A" student, a "B" student, a "C" student, and so on. Matched ability groups are formed to allow students with the same ability level to learn together.

Assigning Roles

Each group should have a moderator, a quality manager, a recorder, and a messenger. (These are merely suggested roles, and others might also be beneficial.) The moderator keeps the group on task, asks appropriate questions, and encourages everyone to participate. The quality manager makes sure the work and the finished activity is the best the group can produce. The recorder keeps track of ideas and solutions during the group interaction. The messenger interfaces with the instructor by asking questions, or with the rest of the class by reporting results. These roles may be switched or combined during the time that students are working together. Eventually the students will fall into a natural rhythm of working together with the four suggested roles as appropriate, but with flexibility.

Tips for Using Groups

The amount of instructor involvement in helping students work together will depend on the type of activity on which the students are working. For a short, in-class assignment, groups will need less structure. For longer assignments, students will need a structure to help them learn to work together.

Not only will the groups themselves need to work together effectively, but you will need to maintain the proper environment for effective group work. Here are some tips on how to do that:

• Explain the assignment to the whole class, before forming them into groups. This allows the groups to start work quickly.

• Encourage the groups to brainstorm together to solve the problem and not be afraid to ask questions when they are stuck.

• Keep moving about the classroom during an in-class group assignment. This makes you available to the students if they have questions and helps them keep on task.

• Observe progress in an unobtrusive way. You many need to ask leading questions if a group is stuck for some time on one part of the activity.

• Look for students that may be experiencing exceptional difficulty in understanding what is happening in the group.

• Communicate enthusiasm for group work and respect for the students' experience and abilities.

More Help
These are some brief tips on how to get started with collaborative learning in your classroom. For a more extensive discussion on how to use groups effectively, the issues that can come up when using collaborative learning, tips on grading and evaluation, and more collaborative learning activities, refer to the *Collaborative Learning Manual* by Aldrich, Cohen, and Hartsell (Addison-Wesley, 1995).

Notes on End of Chapter Collaborative Activities

Chapter 1: OOOP! Order of Operations Game
Goals: Since this will be assigned at the beginning of the semester, the mathematical content of the activity is very basic. This activity has as its main goal a way for students to "get their feet wet" with group work.

Time: In class time 20 to 30 minutes

Teaching Tips: Make sure each student in each group has an assigned role. You may either pick a problem from the book, put one on the chalkboard or overhead, or make up a template with the assigned problem written on it. Circulate around the room to answer any questions students may have. Because of the way the activity is structured, you should observe each group passing their paper around. If the paper isn't moving, this can clue you to a need for intervention.

Comments: Because of the way the activity is designed, it is easy to pick out groups that are not working well together. This will give you a chance to notice the students who tend to take over, students who hang back and don't participate, students who would rather talk, and any other special interactions.

Sample Problem:

Simplify: $5\{-2 + [4 - 2(5 - 3)^2] \div 4\}$

Original Expression: $5\{-2 + [4 - 2(5 - 3)^2] \div 4\}$

A: $5\{-2 + [4 - 2(2)^2] \div 4\}$

E: $5\{-2 + [4 - 2(4)] \div 4\}$

M: $5\{-2 + [4 - 8] \div 4\}$

A: $5\{-2 + [-4] \div 4\}$

M: $5\{-2 + (-1)\}$

A: $5\{-3\}$

M: -15

The answer should now be on the last line. Some Other Problems to Use:

1. $\frac{2}{3}[5 - (6 - 10)] \div \frac{1}{5} - \{21 \div 3 + [8 - 2 \cdot 5 + 1)]\}^2$
2. $(6 + 3)^2 - \{5 \div 4(7 - 5) - [4 + (-3)] \div 8\}^3$
3. $\frac{1}{2}[8 - 2(3 + 5)]^2$

Chapter 2: Every Day Algebra
Goals: The goal of this activity is to give students insight into how algebra is used in "every day life." It also provides a way for students to practice converting a "word problem" into algebra.

Time: In class time 20 to 30 minutes

Teaching Tips: Make sure each student in each group has an assigned role. It may not be obvious at first how to solve the problem, so encourage the students truly to brainstorm together in their groups: make a list of ideas on a procedure (write down all ideas even if they sound silly), look over the list for the best ideas, implement those ideas and see if they work. Give the students hints only if they are very stuck. They may find that working together gives them different insights and perspectives. You may also be surprised at the number of different correct ways the students can find to solve the problem. You may wish to have them explain their thought processes on the paper they hand in to you.

Comments: Watch for the students who think they know how to solve the problem immediately and won't listen to other students in their groups.

Answer Key:

1. Variable names may vary. C = wholesale cost, L = buying club price, M = store markup, P = store price before discount, S = store price after discount.

2. Want to find when the buying club price is equal or less than the store price.

(a) Buying Club price: $L = C + 0.08C = 1.08C$

(b) Store price: $P = C + MC = (1 + M)C$;

Discounted price: $S = P - 0.1P = 0.09P = 0.9(1 + M)C$

(c) Inequality: $L \leq S$, or $1.08C \leq 0.9(1 + M)C$

3. Since C is not zero, divide both sides of the inequality by C

(a) $1.08 \leq 0.9(1 + M)$, now divide both sides by $\;0.9$

(b) $1.2 \leq 1 + M$, now subtract 1 from each side

(c) $0.2 \leq M$

(d) The store must have a markup of 20% or more for it to be cheaper to buy through the buying club.

Chapter 3: Parallel and Perpendicular Explorations

Goals: This activity allows students to relate the graphs of parallel and perpendicular lines to their equations and analyze what makes lines parallel or perpendicular to each other.

Time: In-class time 30 to 45 minutes.

Teaching Tips: Circulate around the room during the activity to make sure the students in each pair are taking turns at graphing and performing the algebra to find the equations, slopes and points in the problems. This is a good activity in which to introduce the use of graphing calculators if you have enough class time. You may need to give some help or direction if they are not familiar with graphing calculators.

Comments: Students usually enjoy working in pairs on this activity and many times have a better understanding of the topic after completing it.

Answer Key:

Part I

1. G: Graphs the line through the given points.　A: $y = -\frac{1}{3}x + \frac{11}{3}$

2. G: Graphs a line parallel to the original line three units above.　A: $y = -\frac{1}{3}x + \frac{20}{3}$

3. G: Graphs a line parallel to the original but five units to the left.　A: $y = -\frac{1}{3}x + 2$

4. G, A: The lines have the same slope but different y-intercepts. Moving the same number of units from both points did not change the slope.

5. Any line of the form $y = -\frac{1}{3}x + b$

Part II

6. G: Graphs the line through the given points. A: $y = \frac{3}{4}x - \frac{5}{4}$

7. G: Graphs the line through the given points. A: $(6, -3)$, $y = -\frac{4}{3}x + 5$, various answers (i.e. The movements given describe the slope).

8. G: Graphs the line M parallel to Q. A: $y = -\frac{4}{3}x - \frac{10}{3}$

9. G, A: Line M is perpendicular to line T and parallel to line Q; the perpendicular lines have slopes that are negative reciprocals, the parallel lines have the same slope and different y-intercepts.

10. G, A: Would need to move right 3 units and down 4 or left 3 and up 4 to describe the correct slope. Various answers (line parallel to T and perpendicular to Q; with slope $\frac{3}{4}$)

Chapter 4: Types of Systems

Goals: Students will attempt to solve systems of equations of the three types (independent, inconsistent, and dependent) and relate these types of solutions to real-to-life situations. The extension asks the students to decide how to fix the inconsistent and dependent systems to make them solvable.

Time: In-class time 30 minutes; assign extension as a group homework assignment

Teaching Tips: Have students assign roles in their groups. Allow them a chance to brainstorm about how to set up the correct equations. Have the messenger in their group show you their equations before they attempt to solve them. You may wish to assign the extension as a homework assignment or have a discussion about what to do with the entire class. Give them some time to brainstorm possible ways to fix the inconsistent and dependent systems as a group before holding the class discussion.

Answer Key:

Part I   1. $2t + \frac{1}{6}k = 250$; $1t = 100$ 2. $k = 300$; $t = 100$

Part II   3. $\frac{1}{4}m + \frac{1}{2}l = 60$; $1m + 2l = 240$

4. Both equations become: $m + 2l = 240$ giving a dependent solution (they are the same line). There is not enough information to solve for this system. Karif can make any combination of medium and large kerchiefs that corresponds to points on the $m + 2l = 240$ line.

Part III   5. $2y + \frac{7}{2}w = 150$; $2y + \frac{7}{2}w = 200$

6. These lines are parallel. The system is inconsistent. One equation has no relation to the other, i.e. the number of cotton mantillas she makes does not depend on the number of lace ones and vice versa. Again, there is not enough information to find a unique solution. She can make any combination of the two sizes that corresponds to points on both lines.

Extension: The systems in Parts II and III are not uniquely solvable as explained above. There would need to be another limiting factor in each, say, for example, if Karif decided to put an appliqué on the large kerchiefs or if Maria decided to trim the cotton mantillas with a lace trim.

Chapter 5: Magic Tricks

Goals: The main goal of this activity is understanding the rules of multiplying polynomials and working with exponents. A scenario such as this one gives the students a setting in which to do some of the drill and practice needed to learn new rules or skills and to review ones they already know.

Time: In-class time 30 minutes

Teaching Tips: Pairing students rather than putting them into larger groups allows the shy students, who may have been "hanging back," to participate in the problem solving. The problem given in the activity focuses on the square of a binomial. Students can then come up with their own scenarios for some of the other standard forms, for example, the product of a sum and a difference. Encourage them to brainstorm together to come up with their own magic trick. Save the best ones for a quiz or test.

Answer Key:

Answers will vary depending on the number chosen at the beginning. Below is a sample solution.

Sadar: Pick a number. (Jim picks 5) Now add x. $(x + 5)$ Multiply everything by 2. $(2x + 10)$ Square the polynomial. $(4x^2 + 40x + 100)$ Subtract $4x^2$. $(40x + 100)$ Divide by 4. $(10x + 25)$ Subtract the x term. (25)

The coefficient of the x term will be twice the original number picked and the constant term will be the square of the original number picked.

Chapter 6: Beorg's Business

Goals: This activity provides a true-to-life example of where work problems are useful. The students are also given a chance to write a report, presenting their results in a professional manner.

Time: In-class time is about 30 minutes. Some out-of-class time may be required to finish and write the report.

Teaching Tips: Have the students assign roles in their groups so that each group member is involved in solving the problem. Remind students that a neatly presented report is part of the assignment. Help them schedule outside-of-class time to complete any work and to write their report. You may need to remind them that weekends are possible times for group meetings. Some students may find it hard to be part of a group. You will need to decide whether those students should work on the activity alone. You may wish to check to see that the answers are correct before the students write their reports.

Comments: This will be a good time to start putting the students into long-term groups. The groups can remain the same for several activities or the rest of the semester or quarter.

Chapter 7: Laws of Falling Bodies

Goals: This activity allows students to use formulas with radicals to solve problems. Not all of the information needed is supplied in the problem, so students will need to "do some digging" to find the formulas they need.

Time: In-class time 30 minutes. Some out-of-class time may be required to finish.

Teaching Tips: The scenario in this activity appeals to the problem-solving detective in each one of your students. Remind your students to assign roles. Below are some hints (formulas) the students will need to complete the activity. Some of this information is also available to them further on in the book. Allow the students some time to go home and think about what else they need to know to complete the activity before giving them these hints. Write each hint on a piece of paper (one per group) and have the Messenger in each group come up and get each hint in sequence from you. You may also wish to have the students present their results in a report.

Hints:

For Problem 1: Use the Pythagorean formula to determine the height of the building.

For Problem 2: For an object with initial velocity of v_0 feet per second at a height of s_0 feet, its altitude S after t seconds is given by $S = -16t^2 + v_0 t + s_0$ (from Chapter 6).

For Problem 2: The initial velocity, v_0, is 0 feet per second and the initial height, s_0, is the height of the building.

For Problem 3: Use the formula $D = RT$, where R is how fast the woman is walking and T is the time it takes her to travel D feet.

Answer Key:

1. 59.9 feet   2. 1.9 seconds

3. 5 feet/second; answers will vary as to whether Jaki's client could have "done it."

Chapter 8: Building a Room Addition

Goals: This activity provides a real life example of an application of the quadratic formula.

Time: In-class time 30 minutes.

Teaching Tips: Area is a common example of when a quadratic equation is useful. Have your students form groups of two to four students. If they have not been working much in groups, have them assign roles. How to solve the second part of the activity may not be immediately obvious to the students. Give them a chance to brainstorm in their groups before giving them hints. They will need to remember some basic geometry to complete it. (See sample solution below.)

Comments: This may be a good time to assess how well groups are working together. Have them complete a paragraph about how things are going in their groups to hand in with this activity. If there are problems, brainstorm with the class about how to solve them.

Answer Key:

1. Let $x =$ internal width of studio. Then we have $(x + 2)(2x + 4) = 400$. Solving for x and rounding to the nearest foot we get $x = 12$ feet and the length will be $2x$ or 24 feet.

2. In order to find out how far the patio extends past the house, divide the studio in half and notice that the diagonal of the square formed is the same as the radius of the semicircle. The radius of the semicircle is 19.8 feet; students may decide this is too close to the tree for the plan to work and remove the tree.

Chapter 9: Betting on Rockets

Goals: This activity gives a scenario for an application of graphing quadratic equations and finding the maxima.

Time: In-class time 15 to 20 minutes on the first day and 20-30 minutes on the second day; out-of-class time, individual homework assignment.

Teaching Tips: On the day the activity is assigned, have the students form groups of three and have each one pick one of the rocket trials. Have them complete Problems 1 and 2 as an individual homework assignment with the understanding that they may wish to ask for help from their group members. Allow them class time on the next class day to compare answers and discuss in their groups how they each solved their part of the activity.

Answer Key:

First Trial:

1. For Gretchen's rocket: $H = 0$, $t = 14$, $V = 224$ ft/sec,
For Rafael's rocket: $H = 0$, $t = 10$, $V = 160$ ft/sec

2. For Gretchen's rocket: The vertex is (7, 784), so Gretchen's rocket went 784 feet high.
For Rafael's rocket: The vertex is (5, 400) , so Rafael's rocket went 400 feet high.

Second Trial:

1. For Gretchen's rocket: $H = 0$, $t = 11.5$, $V = 184$ ft/sec
For Rafael's rocket: $H = 0$, $t = 12$, $V = 192$ ft/sec

2. For Gretchen's rocket: Vertex is (5.75, 529) , so Gretchen's rocket went 529 ft high.
For Rafael's rocket: The vertex is (6, 576) , so Rafael's rocket went 576 ft high.

Third Trial:

1. For Gretchen's rocket: $H = 0$, $t = 11.25$, $V = 180$ ft/sec
For Rafael's rocket: $H = 0$, $t = 11.3$, $V = 180.8$ ft/sec

2. For Gretchen's rocket:
The vertex is (5.625, 506.25), so Gretchen's rocket went 506.25 feet high. For Rafael's rocket: The vertex is (5.65, 510.76) , so Rafael's rocket went 510.76 feet high.
Rafael wins if the students don't round too soon on the third trial.

Chapter 10: In How Much Space Could We Live?

Goals: This activity provides a timely situation in which exponential and logarithmic functions allow students to analyze the outcome of population growth.

Time: In-class time 30 minutes to complete problem. If you wish, assign the activity as a group homework assignment and use class time for discussion.

Teaching Tips: After covering exponential growth, pair students by ability, mixing students with different abilities. Rather than having the students turn in written solutions, allow class time for the class as a whole to share their solutions and conclusions. You may wish to assign the work as a group homework assignment and then allow the class time for discussion.

Comments: This activity may elicit lively discussions.

Answer Key:

All answers are found assuming that rounded values are used in the succeeding computations. 1. 2.3% 2. The surface area computed is 1.1×10^{14} 3. 230.4 years 4. Answers will vary.

Chapter 11: Focus on Comets

Goals: This activity presents applications of conic sections that those who have looked at the night sky will appreciate.

Time: In-class time 15 to 20 minutes in class on the first day and 20 to 30 minutes on the second day; group homework assignment

Teaching Tips: Pairing students will be especially useful in this activity if you have graphing calculators or computer software available for the students to use. The solution may not be immediately obvious to some of your students. Allow them time outside of class to brainstorm in their groups and dig in their books in order to find what they need. Encourage them to sketch the situation in each problem so that they will know how to begin.

Comments: Students will appreciate the visual and kinesthetic aspects of this activity--- drawing the ellipse with a pencil and string. Some students will come away with a better understanding of the equations for conics.

Answer Key:

1. $\frac{x^2}{(17.8)^2} + \frac{y^2}{(4.58)^2} = 1$; See students' models on cardboard.

2. $p = 0.75$; $y = \frac{1}{4(0.75)}x^2 = \frac{1}{3}x^2$; Since the direction of the parabola is not determined by the information in the problem, students may come up with the equation for a parabola opening downward.

3. $\frac{x^2}{(1.5)^2} - \frac{y^2}{(2.6)^2} = 1$

Chapter 12: Lotteries are Series(ous)

Goals: Many students will identify with the concept of state lotteries and will appreciate the use of series to find out how good (or bad) a deal buying lottery tickets can be.

Time: In-class time---20 to 30 minutes

Teaching Tips: Have students assign roles in their groups if needed. Allow the students a chance to come up with the two series in the activity by themselves before giving them hints. Have students share their discussions of the results with the rest of the class.

Comments: State lotteries are becoming more and more prevalent. This activity will help students assess the benefits of buying the lottery tickets.

Answer Key:

1. $\sum_{n=1}^{260} 4 = 4(260) = \$1040.00$

2. 1.25% per quarter, 20 compounding periods,

$\frac{52}{4} \cdot \$4 = \$52$ per quarter deposited

3. $\sum_{n=1}^{20} 52(1 + 0.0125)^n = \$11187.94$

4. Answers will vary.

477

479

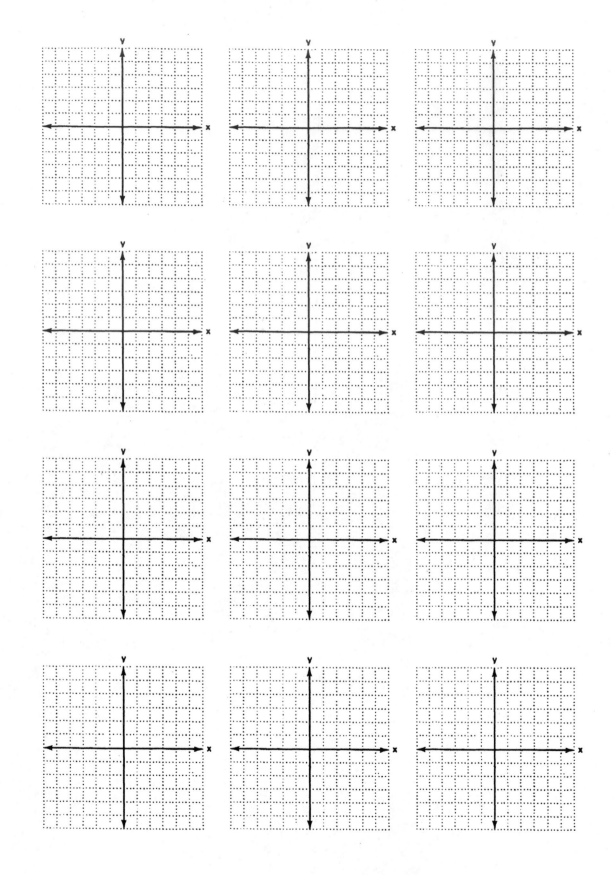

482